Praise for

DB2 10.1/10.5 for Linux, UNIX, and Windows Database Administration: Certification Study Guide

This book is far more than a typical certification and study guide. The authors go out of their way to ensure the various topics tested in the certification exam are not simply covered, but rather well understood by the reader. That is to say this book serves as an excellent guide to understanding DB2's various features and functionalities, and more importantly, under what circumstances they should be used.

Hamdi Roumani
DB2 Developer
IBM Toronto Software Lab

Mohan and Kent's updates have taken what was already a great book to a new level. In the book, you'll find all you need to know about most new features in V10.1/10.5. There is also additional information on V9.*x* functionality that will help new and experienced DBAs alike. I particularly enjoyed the sample questions, which are cleverly designed to make the reader think and have detailed explanations behind the correct and incorrect answers.

Colin A. Chapman
DB2 DBA Lead
IBM UK

This book is a terrific piece of work. I've worked with many DBAs over the years, and Mohan/Kent are the best—here, they have distilled years of DBA experience into a comprehensive tome that goes beyond passing certification exams. Whether you are a new DBA, an experienced DBA looking at DB2, or an experienced DBA needing to deepen or extend your skills, this book is for you.

Simon Woodcock
Data Warehouse Consultant
IBM Information Management

This book isn't just a valuable study guide, but also an excellent reference that you will likely refer to frequently. The command examples are very helpful, and the study flash cards are brilliant. You will not only find sample certification questions, but also answers to the questions with explanations. Mohan won the worldwide DB2's GOT TALENT contest in 2013, and Kent has appeared as a guest on The DB2Night Show™ talking about his early and successful experiences with IBM BLU and pureScale. It is absolutely refreshing to have such a helpful book authored by real people with abundant hands-on experience.

Scott Hayes
President and Founder, DBI Software
IBM DB2 GOLD Consultant and IBM Champion
Creator and Host of The DB2Night Show

Takes you from the basics all the way to the advanced concepts used to optimize real-world production systems. This guide will be useful to everyone from neophytes who are setting up their first system to longtime DB2 DBAs who are catching up on the latest and greatest tools and tricks. And the self-guided exams in each chapter make sure you've gotten it right before you touch production.

Andrew Buckler
IBM, Information Management Cloud Go-To-Market

I have had the extremely good fortune to work with Mohan over the past several years and have come to rely on his DB2 knowledge and expertise to design, implement, as well as keep many of our highly available, business critical systems operating at optimal performance. As you are no doubt aware, the range of material covered on certification exams is quite broad. This resource is designed to give the DB2 professional the information required in order to successfully obtain certification, or even to simply enhance their existing scope of DB2 knowledge.

Mohan and Kent have done an excellent job of distilling their many years of experience, both within the lab environment and within the live production environment of a large global consumer goods company, into a logical, well-organized reference. Each section contains the fundamentals, plus valuable insights from the authors, and is backed up with sample exam questions, as well as detailed answers, which I found very useful in reinforcing the material. I am confident that with this guide, your certification will not be far away!

Enjoy and best of luck on your certification!

Eric Sheley
Global IT Director
FTSE 100 Global Consumer Goods Company

DB2 10.1/10.5 for Linux, UNIX, and Windows Database Administration

Certification Study Guide

Mohankumar (Mohan) Saraswatipura and Robert (Kent) Collins

MC Press Online, LLC
Boise, ID 83703 USA

DB2 10.1/10.5 for Linux, UNIX, and Windows Database Administration: Certification Study Guide

Mohankumar (Mohan) Saraswatipura and Robert (Kent) Collins

First Edition

MC Press offers excellent discounts on this book when ordered in quantity for bulk purchases or special sales, which may include custom covers and content particular to your business, training goals, marketing focus, and branding interest.

MC Press Online, LLC

Corporate Offices: 3695 W. Quail Heights Court, Boise, ID 83703-3861 USA

Sales and Customer Service: (208) 629-7275 ext. 500;

service@mcpressonline.com

Permissions and Bulk/Special Orders: mcbooks@mcpressonline.com

www.mcpressonline.com • www.mc-store.com

ISBN: 978-1-58347-375-7 WB201507

About the Authors

Mohankumar (Mohan) Saraswatipura works as a database solutions architect at Kronsys, Inc., focusing on IBM DB2, Linux, UNIX, and Windows solutions. Prior to his current position, he worked as a database solutions architect at Reckitt Benckiser Group, plc (UK), focusing on IBM Smart Analytics System 5600, Siebel, SQL Server, and SAP HANA solutions. Mohan is an IBM Champion (2010-2015) and a DB2's Got Talent 2013 winner. He has written dozens of technical papers for IBM developerWorks and *IBM Data Magazine*. He is an IBM Certified DB2 Advanced Database Administrator, DB2 Application Developer, and DB2 Problem Determination Master. Mohan holds a Master's of Technology (M Tech) degree in computer science and an Executive MBA (IT). He lives in the Washington, D.C., area with his wife, Dr. Nirmala; they have one child.

Robert (Kent) Collins, founder of Shiloh Consulting, Inc., is currently a Database Solutions Architect with BNSF Railway. He is an IBM Champion (2010–2015) and a frequent speaker at the DB2Night Show and IDUG and IOD (IBM Insight) conferences. Kent has worked continually with DB2 from its introduction to the market in 1984, amassing a wealth of knowledge and experience. He graduated from the University of Texas at Dallas with majors in mathematics and computer science. He is an IBM Certified Solutions Expert and also holds certifications in DB2, AIX, Linux, .NET, Oracle, SQL Server, Windows, and z/OS. Kent is proficient in many programming languages and, as a Java Architect, specializes in Enterprise HA/Performance systems. He lives in Dallas with his wife, Vicki; together, they have three children and one grandchild.

Acknowledgments

Mohan and Kent want to express their gratitude to Hamdi Roumani, Colin A. Chapman, and Simon Woodcock for their dedication during the review process. Their review of the book and suggestions were invaluable in ensuring that the material is beneficial and understandable to the DB2 community.

We want to thank the following people for providing a great deal of assistance, either through contributions to the book, technical suggestions, or comments.

- Paul Zikopoulos (Vice President, Customer Success - IBM Analytics, IBM Toronto Lab, Canada), for reviewing the entire book and writing the foreword for the book.
- Scott Hayes (President and Founder, DBI Software), for reviewing the monitoring chapter from the expert standpoint and writing a testimonial.
- Andrew Bucker (IBM, IM Cloud Go-To-Market), for reviewing the entire book and writing a testimonial.
- Eric Sheley (Global IT Director, FTSE 100 Global Consumer Goods Company), for reviewing the book from the customer standpoint and writing a testimonial.

Thanks also to our DB2 marketing star, Susan Visser, for working tirelessly to get this book to the market and also for making book announcements via social media.

Finally, thanks to our MC Press Online editorial and production team, especially Cindy Bushong, Anne Grubb, and Katie Tipton, for their diligent work during the editing process.

Book Reviewers:

Hamdi Roumani

Hamdi has been a software developer within the DB2 data recovery services new development team for over five years. As such, he has been directly involved with many of the new functional pieces and improvements introduced through the DB2 V10.1 and V10.5 releases, which are covered in this book. His passions include best practices in software development and designing features that are easily consumable by end users.

Colin A. Chapman

Colin has worked for over 30 years as an IT professional in a broad range of technical roles. His experience covers mainframe operations, application design and development, systems programming, and database design and administration.

More recently, Colin has specialized in DB2 on the Linux, UNIX, and Windows platforms. He has a broad range of in-depth DB2 skills, particularly in areas such as large partitioned databases, clustering and high availability, cross-platform replication, performance, recovery, security, and complex problem diagnostics.

Simon Woodcock

Simon Woodcock has 30 years' experience working in IBM, bringing his systems design skills to bear for many clients in the UK and across Europe. More than half this time has been spent on databases, mainly on large data warehouses, starting with DB2 and extending through Netezza and most recently, Hadoop big data systems.

Contents

Foreword

I remember the days when folks would ask me why I work on database software—to some, a relatively boring, commodity product area. In today's era of computing, where greater business value is delivered through big data and analytics, that question has been well answered.

Polyglot. That's the best word I can think of to characterize the approach needed to be successful in today's analytics-driven data environments. These environments are made up of various data persistence technologies, such as NoSQL, Hadoop, and RDBMS, among others. To the pundits who decree "one size fits all," there's been a strong wake-up call. The point? The RDBMS isn't dead, and investing in credentialed skills in this area will not only prove to be a wise investment of your time, but will deliver economies of scale and downstream benefits into other projects—the ones you might be working on now … and the ones you don't know about, yet.

This book was thoughtfully designed not only to prepare you for a credentialed DB2 career but to give you a strong basis in the knowledge domain around database management, no matter what the vendor. Think about it: Regardless of the database, implementation of business rules, mapping logical to physical design, high availability, security, and other topics detailed in this book are ubiquitous across data landscapes. To me, although a key instrument to the end goal of DB2 10.5 certification, this book is so much more. I enjoyed reading the book, and I realized there is always more to learn about database technology and DB2. Today, I feel fully prepared to write the latest DB2 certification test, but even better prepared to have a positive influence on the data environments I participate in.

I've personally written 15 books on DB2, including those aimed at certification. It is with gratitude that I see this book as betterment over what I could ever deliver in this space. This book was written by two of the more "brainiac" database practitioners I've ever come across—folks who get more enjoyment out of finding even higher performance levels on a late Friday night than catching an episode of *Homeland*. I've watched these individuals at work, and the breadth of knowledge is beyond impressive.

Finally, as DB2 practitioners watching the world of IT evolve, we are faced with a shift, lift, rift, or cliff. Those who embrace the concepts in this book set themselves up for a foundation that is ignited by a shift and lift, ability to bring together the rift, and avoid the cliff. As I mentioned earlier, RDBMS technologies are not going away—if anything, they are permeating. What is the hottest thing in NoSQL? SQL! When you compose a query over Hadoop using IBM's BigSQL, that SQL API is near fully DB2-compliant (DB2 SQL is in this book). When you leverage IBM's data warehouse as a service (DWaaS) platform dashDB, it's BLU Acceleration technology that's part of that solution (technology that first debuted in DB2 and is covered in Chapter 10). If you are composing applications on IBM Bluemix and storing data in the SQLDB database as a service (DBaaS), you will be right at home with the DB2 skills you learn in this book. There's more … but for now, just remember that as your data demands stretch you from ground to cloud, NoSQL to SQL, and all parts in between, the skills you learn here will be invaluable.

Best of luck on your journey.

Paul Zikopoulos
Vice President, Customer Success – IBM Analytics
Big Data, Competitive, and Technical Sales

CHAPTER 1

IBM DB2 10.1 Certification

Recognized throughout the world, the *IBM® Professional Certification Program* offers a range of certification options for IT professionals. This chapter will introduce you to the various paths to obtain DB2® 10.1 Certification from IBM and will describe the testing software you will use when you take your DB2 10.1 certification exam.

DB2 10.1 Certification Roles

One of the biggest trends in the IT industry today is certification. Many application and software vendors now have certification programs in place that evaluate and validate an individual's proficiency with the vendor's latest product release. In fact, one reason IBM developed the *Professional Certification Program* was to provide a way for skilled technical professionals to demonstrate their knowledge and expertise with a particular version of an IBM product.

The *Professional Certification Program* from IBM consists of several distinct certification roles that are designed to guide you in your professional development.

You begin the certification process by selecting the role that is right for you and familiarizing yourself with the certification requirements for that role. To help get you started, the following subsections provide you with the prerequisites and requirements associated with each IBM DB2 10.1 and DB2 9.7 certification available.

DB2 10.1 Certification Tracks

IBM offers broadly three certification tracks for DB2 for Linux®, UNIX®, and Windows® (LUW) certification to cover expert areas such as database administration, application development, and solution development. Figure 1.1 shows the Database Administration track.

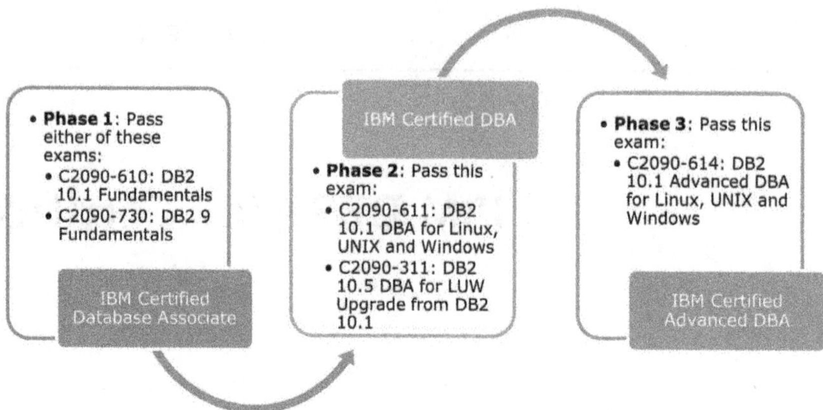

Figure 1.1: IBM DB2 10.1 Database Administrator Certification exam track

Track 1: Database Administration

IBM Certified Database Associate—DB2 10.1 Fundamentals

This certification is intended for entry-level DB2 users who are knowledgeable about the fundamental concepts of DB2 10.1 for Linux, UNIX, and Windows. In addition to having some hands-on experience with DB2 10.1, some formal training, or both, individuals seeking this certification should:

- ✓ Know what DB2 10.1 products are available and be familiar with the various ways DB2 10.1 is packaged
- ✓ Know which DB2 10.1 products must be installed to create a desired environment
- ✓ Know what features and functions are provided by the tools shipped with DB2 10.1
- ✓ Possess an in-depth knowledge of Structured Query Language (SQL), Data Definition Language (DDL), Data Manipulation Language (DML), and Data Control Language (DCL) statements that are available with DB2 10.1
- ✓ Know how to create, access, and manipulate basic DB2 objects, such as tables, views, and indexes, along with the new temporal table feature
- ✓ Have a basic understanding of the methods used to isolate transactions from each other in a multiuser environment
- ✓ Be familiar with the methods used to control how locking is performed

- ✓ Be familiar with the different types of constraints and know how each is used
- ✓ Possess a strong knowledge about the mechanisms DB2 10.1 uses to protect data and database objects against unauthorized access and/or modification, including row and column access control (RCAC) and trusted context
- ✓ Be familiar with how Extensible Markup Language (XML) data can be stored and manipulated

To acquire the **IBM Certified Database Associate – DB2 10.1 Fundamentals** certification, candidates must take and pass one exam: *DB2 10.1 Fundamentals* (C2090-610).

IBM Certified Database Administrator—DB2 10.1 for Linux, UNIX, and Windows

This certification is intended for experienced DB2 users who possess the knowledge and skills necessary to perform the day-to-day administration of DB2 10.1 instances and databases residing on Linux, UNIX, or Windows platforms. In addition to being knowledgeable about the fundamental concepts of DB2 10.1 and having significant hands-on experience as a DB2 database administrator (DBA), individuals seeking this certification should:

- ✓ Know how to create, configure, and manage DB2 10.1 instances and databases
- ✓ Know how to configure client/server connectivity
- ✓ Be able to obtain and modify the values of environment and registry variables
- ✓ Be able to obtain and modify DB2 database manager (instance) and database configuration parameter values
- ✓ Know how to use the IBM Data Studio GUI tools to manage instances and databases, create and access objects, and manage database changes and tasks
- ✓ Know how to create, access, modify, and manage the different DB2 10.1 objects
- ✓ Be able to create constraints on and between table objects
- ✓ Possess a strong knowledge about System Managed Space (SMS), Database Managed Space (DMS), and automatic storage table spaces, as well as database storage groups
- ✓ Know how to use autonomic features such as automatic maintenance, the self-tuning memory manager (STMM), and the Configuration Advisor
- ✓ Know how to manage XML data and modify it by using XPATH expressions
- ✓ Know how to use the DB2 administration views and table functions, along with event monitors to monitor the database
- ✓ Know how to capture and interpret snapshot monitor data
- ✓ Know how to capture and analyze DB2 Explain information
- ✓ Possess an in-depth knowledge of the Export, Import, Load, and Ingest utilities
- ✓ Know how to use the REORGCHK, REORG, REBIND, RUNSTATS, db2look, db2move, and db2pd commands

- ✓ Possess a strong knowledge about the mechanisms DB2 10.1 uses to protect data and database objects against unauthorized access or modification, including the label-based access control (LBAC) and RCAC mechanisms
- ✓ Have a basic understanding of the transaction logging mechanism and archival techniques
- ✓ Know how to perform database-level and table space–level backup, restore, and roll-forward recovery operations
- ✓ Known how to implement High Availability and Disaster Recovery (HADR), and understand multiple standby HADR implementation guidelines
- ✓ Be able to interpret information stored in the administration notification log
- ✓ Possess a basic knowledge of the pureScale operations

Candidates who have passed either the *DB2 10.1 Fundamentals* exam (C2090-610) or the *DB2 9 Fundamentals* exam (C2090-730) must take and pass the *DB2 10.1 for Linux, UNIX, and Windows Database Administration* exam (C2090-611) to acquire the **IBM Certified Database Administrator—DB2 10.1 for Linux, UNIX, and Windows** certification.

IBM Certified Database Administrator—DB2 10.5 DBA for LUW Upgrade from 10.1

This certification is intended for experienced DB2 users who possess the knowledge and skills necessary to perform the day-to-day administration of DB2 10.5 instances and databases residing on Linux, UNIX, or Windows platforms. In addition to being knowledgeable about DB2 10.1 database administration concepts and having significant hands-on experience as a DB2 DBA for 10.5, especially with BLU Acceleration, individuals seeking this certification should:

- ✓ Know how to design, create, and manage databases on DB2 10.5 BLU
- ✓ Know how to configure DB2 workload for analytics system
- ✓ Know how to use autonomic computing features in DB2 10.5 BLU Acceleration
- ✓ Know how to use IBM Data Studio 4.1 and Optim™ Query Workload Tuner tools
- ✓ Be able to understand DB2 10.5 BLU Acceleration's seven big ideas:
    1. It is simple—no indexes, multidimensional clustered (MDC) tables, materialized query tables (MQTs), range partitioning, or statistical views
    2. Extreme compression and computer-friendly encoding
    3. Deep hardware exploitation using single instruction, multiple data (SIMD) sets
    4. Core-friendly parallelism
    5. Column-organized store
    6. Scan-friendly memory caching
    7. Data skipping through a SYNOPSYS table
- ✓ Know how to implement table compression and backup compression
- ✓ Know how to use expression-based indexes and how to use RUNSTATS on the expression-based indexes

- ✓ Know how to use Oracle® compatibility features such as deep-nested object trees, extended row length, and three new index enhancements
- ✓ Know how to monitor a DB2 10.5 database instance and databases by using new monitoring elements
- ✓ Know how to use Explain to capture Column Table Queue (CTQ) operators in DB2 10.5 BLU
- ✓ Know how to use HADR monitoring enhancements
- ✓ Know how to use online REORG in a pureScale environment
- ✓ Know how to set up HADR in a pureScale cluster environment
- ✓ Know how to use the rolling fix pack upgrade, STMM Multi-Tenancy, and explicit hierarchical locking in a pureScale cluster
- ✓ Know how to install, activate, and configure DB2 Advanced Copy Services customized scripts for backup operations
- ✓ Know how to convert row-organized tables to column-organized tables by using the db2convert utility
- ✓ Know how LOAD command execution differs between row-organized tables and column-organized tables

To acquire the **IBM Certified Database Administrator—DB2 10.5 DBA for LUW Upgrade from 10.1**, candidates must hold the **IBM Certified Database Administrator—DB2 10.1 for Linux, UNIX, and Windows** certification, and they must take and pass the *DB2 10.5 DBA for LUW Upgrade from 10.1* exam (C2090-311).

IBM Certified Advanced Database Administrator—DB2 10.1 for Linux, UNIX, and Windows

This certification is intended for lead database administrators who possess extensive knowledge about DB2 and who have vast experience using DB2 10.1 on one or more of the following supported platforms: Linux, AIX, HP-UX, Sun Solaris, or Windows. In addition to being knowledgeable about the more complex concepts of DB2 and having significant experience as a DB2 10.1 database administrator, individuals seeking this certification should:

- ✓ Know how to design, create, and manage buffer pools
- ✓ Know how to design, create, and manage SMS, DMS, automatic storage table spaces and storage groups, as well as multi-temperature data
- ✓ Be able to create and manage MDC, range partitioning, range clustered, and insert time clustering (ITC) tables
- ✓ Be able to create constraints on and between table objects
- ✓ Be able to identify and modify the DB2 database manager and database configuration file parameter values that have the most impact on performance
- ✓ Possess a strong knowledge of query optimizations

- ✓ Be able to correctly analyze, isolate, and correct database performance problems
- ✓ Know how to manage a large number of users and connections, including connections to host systems
- ✓ Know when the creation of an index will improve database performance
- ✓ Be able to fully exploit intrapartition parallelism and interpartition parallelism
- ✓ Be able to design, configure, and manage Database Partition Feature (DPF) databases spanning multiple servers
- ✓ Know how to manage federated servers and distributed units of work
- ✓ Possess a strong knowledge about the external authentication mechanisms that DB2 10.1 uses to protect data and database objects against unauthorized access or modification
- ✓ Know how to implement data encryption by using LBAC and RCAC
- ✓ Know how to design, implement, and manage the DB2 audit feature
- ✓ Be able to understand and develop a logging strategy
- ✓ Know how to perform database-level and table space–level backup, restore, and roll-forward recovery operations
- ✓ Be able to use the advanced backup and recovery features
- ✓ Know how to implement a standby database by using log shipping, replication, failover, fault monitoring, and HADR with multiple standby features
- ✓ Know how to design, configure, and maintain the DB2 Workload Manager (WLM)
- ✓ Know how to manage pureScale systems

To acquire the **IBM Certified Advanced Database Administrator—DB2 10.1 for Linux, UNIX, and Windows** certification, candidates must hold the **IBM Certified Database Administrator—DB2 10.1 for Linux, UNIX, and Windows** certification, and they must take and pass the *DB2 10.1 for Linux, UNIX, and Windows Advanced Database Administration* exam (C2090-614).

Track 2: Database Application Development

IBM Certified Application Developer—DB2 9.7 for Linux, UNIX, and Windows

This certification is intended for intermediate- to advanced-level application developers who possess the knowledge and skills necessary to create applications that interact with DB2 9.7 databases. In addition to being knowledgeable about the fundamental concepts of DB2 and having strong skills in embedded SQL programming, ODBC/CLI programming, Java database connectivity (JDBC) programming, or Structured Query Language Interface (SQLJ) programming, individuals seeking this certification should:

- ✓ Be familiar with the naming conventions used to identify DB2 9.7 objects
- ✓ Possess an in-depth knowledge of the complex database objects available with DB2 9.7

- ✓ Possess an in-depth knowledge of the SQL, DDL, DML, and DCL statements available with DB2 9.7
- ✓ Know the difference between static and dynamic SQL
- ✓ Be able to execute queries across multiple tables and views
- ✓ Be able to query tables across multiple databases, including federated databases
- ✓ Know what authorities and privileges are needed to access data within an application
- ✓ Possess an in-depth knowledge of the SQL functions
- ✓ Know when to use embedded SQL, CLI/ODBC, JDBC, SQLJ, PHP, Perl, Python, .NET, and XML
- ✓ Be able to identify the types of cursors, as well as know when to use cursors in an application and what their scope will be
- ✓ Be able to work with MQTs
- ✓ Possess an in-depth knowledge of XML document encoding management
- ✓ Be able to identify the results of XML parsing and XML serialization
- ✓ Know how to validate XML schemas
- ✓ Be able to execute and identify the results of an XQuery expression
- ✓ Be familiar with the SQL and XML functions available with DB2
- ✓ Be able to establish a connection to a database within an embedded SQL, CLI/ODBC, JDBC, SQLJ, or .NET application
- ✓ Possess the ability to analyze the contents of an SQL Communications Area (SQLCA) data structure
- ✓ Possess the ability to obtain and analyze CLI/ODBC diagnostic information and.NET diagnostic information
- ✓ Possess the ability to obtain and analyze JDBC trace, SQL exception, and JDBC error log information
- ✓ Be able to create triggers and identify their results
- ✓ Know how to cast data types
- ✓ Know when to use compound SQL, parameter markers, and distributed units of work
- ✓ Know when and how to create user-defined functions (UDFs) and stored procedures
- ✓ Know when and how to use the trusted context

Candidates who have passed either the *DB2 V8.1 Family Fundamentals* exam (C2090-700) or the *DB2 9 Family Fundamentals* exam (C2090-730) must take and pass the *DB2 9.7 Application Development* exam (C2090-543) to acquire the **IBM Certified Application Developer—DB2 9.7 for Linux, UNIX, and Windows** certification, as Figure 1.2 shows.

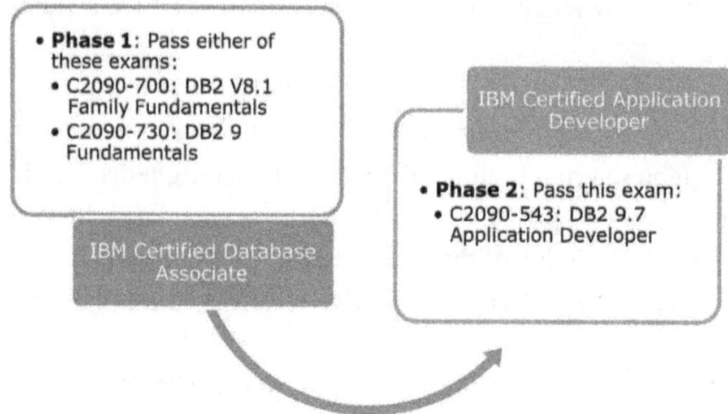

Figure 1.2: IBM DB2 9.7 Database Application Developer Certification exam track

Track 3: Database Solution Development

IBM Certified Solution Developer—DB2 9.7 SQL Procedure

This certification is intended for intermediate to advanced-level application and solution developers who possess the knowledge and skills necessary to create SQL procedures that interact with DB2 9.7 databases. In addition to being knowledgeable about the fundamental concepts of DB2 and having strong skills in DB2 functions, triggers, and SQL procedures, individuals seeking this certification should:

- ✓ Be familiar with the naming conventions used to identify DB2 9.7 objects
- ✓ Know what authorities and privileges are needed to access data within an application
- ✓ Possess an in-depth knowledge of the complex database objects available with DB2 9.7
- ✓ Possess an in-depth knowledge of the SQL, DDL, DML, and DCL statements available with DB2 9.7
- ✓ Know the difference between static and dynamic SQL
- ✓ Possess an in-depth knowledge of the available SQL functions
- ✓ Know how to design, create, test, and deploy SQL procedures, including nested procedures
- ✓ Know how to design, create, test, and deploy functions and triggers
- ✓ Know how to use DB2 advanced features such as declared global temporary tables, ADMIN_CMD procedure, global variables, modules, and arrays
- ✓ Know how to use DB2 development tools and explain tools

Candidates who have passed either the *DB2 V8.1 Family Fundamentals* exam (C2090-700) or the *DB2 9 Family Fundamentals* exam (C2090-730) must take and pass the *DB2 9.7 SQL Procedure Developer* exam (C2090-545) to acquire the **IBM Certified Solution Developer—DB2 9.7 SQL Procedure Developer** certification, as Figure 1.3 illustrates.

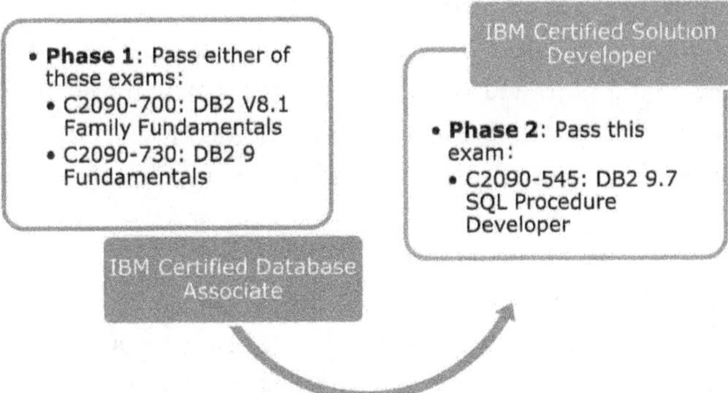

Figure 1.3: IBM DB2 9.7 Database Solution Developer Certification exam track

The Certification Process

A close examination of the IBM certification roles quickly reveals that, to obtain a particular DB2 10.1 certification, you must take and pass one or more exams that have been designed specifically for that certification role. (Each exam is a software-based test that is neither platform- nor product-specific.) Thus, once you have chosen the certification role you wish to pursue and have familiarized yourself with the requirements for that particular role, the next step is to prepare for and take the appropriate certification exam or exams. Figure 1.4 shows the complete certification process flow.

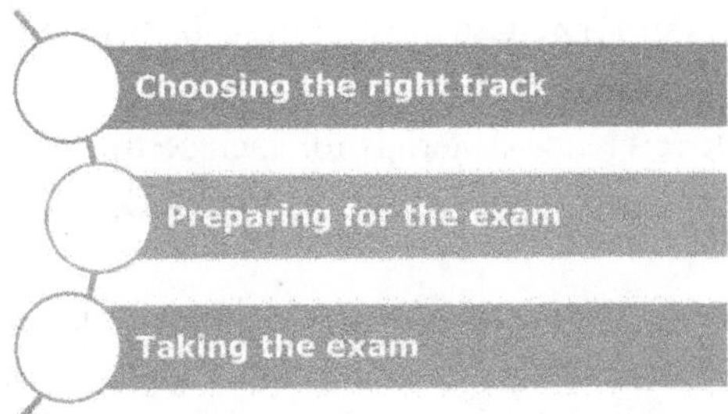

Figure 1.4: IBM DB2 Database Certification exam process

Choosing the Right Track

The *DB2 10.1 Fundamentals* examination is necessary for all the tracks. After completing the fundamentals exam, a core database administrator who does all the database maintenance and security audit activities will follow Track 1: Database Administration. Whereas Track 2: Database Application Development and Track 3: Database Solution Development will suit an application developer who works on any of the application development programming languages on DB2 data server.

Preparing for the Certification Exams

If you have experience using DB2 10.1 in the context of the certification role you have chosen, you might already possess the skills and knowledge needed to pass the exams required for that role. However, if your familiarity with DB2 10.1 is limited (and even if it is not), you can prepare for the certification exams by taking advantage of the following resources:

Formal Education

IBM Learning Services offers courses designed to help you prepare for DB2 10.1 certification. To find a listing of the courses recommended for each certification exam, use the Certification Navigator tool provided on the IBM Professional Certification Program website (*www.ibm.com/certify*), or go to IBM's Certification and Skills for Information Management website (*www-01.ibm.com/software/data/education*). For more information on course schedules, locations, and pricing, contact IBM Learning Services or visit its website at *www-304.ibm.com/services/learning*.

Publications

You can find all the information you need to pass any of the available certification exams in the documentation provided with DB2 10.1. A complete set of manuals comes with the product, and the manuals are accessible through the Knowledge Center once you have installed the DB2 10.1 software. DB2 10.1 documentation is also downloadable from IBM's website in both HTML and PDF formats.

Self-study books (such as this one) that focus on one or more DB2 10.1 certification exams or roles are available as well. You can purchase most of these books at your local bookstore or order them from many online book retailers.

To find a listing of possible reference materials for each certification exam, use the Certification Navigator tool provided at the IBM Professional Certification Program website (*www.ibm.com/certify*).

In addition to the DB2 product documentation, IBM often produces manuals known as *Redbooks* that cover advanced DB2 topics (as well as other topics). These manuals are available as downloadable PDF files on IBM's Redbook website (*www.redbooks.ibm.com*). Or if you prefer to have a bound hard copy, you can obtain one for a modest fee by following the appropriate links on the Redbook website. There is no charge for the downloadable PDF files.

To obtain a list of possible reference materials for each certification exam, use the Certification Navigator tool provided at the IBM Professional Certification Program website (*www.ibm.com/certify*). Ordering information is often included with the listing.

Practice Examinations

Sample questions and practice tests let you become familiar with the format and wording used on the actual certification exams. They can also help you decide whether you possess the knowledge needed to pass a particular exam. Sample questions, along with descriptive answers, are provided at the end of every chapter and in Chapter 11 of this book. You can find online assessment tests for each DB2 10.1 certification role by clicking the **click here** link at IBM's Information Management Certification website (*www.ibm.com/software/data/education/cert/assessment.html*). There is a $30 charge for each exam.

It is important to note that the certification exams are rigorous. Very specific answers are expected for most test questions. Because of this and because the range of material covered on a certification exam is usually broader than the knowledge base of many DB2 professionals, be sure to take advantage of exam preparation resources if you want to guarantee your success in obtaining the certifications you desire.

Valuable Free Education

The DB2Night Show webinars by DBI Software are one of the best resources for all new DB2 features. Please do not forget to register for sessions at *www.dbisoftware.com/db2nightshow*.

Arranging to Take a Certification Exam

When you are confident that you are ready to take a specific DB2 10.1 certification exam, your next step is to contact an IBM-authorized testing vendor. The DB2 certification exams are administered by Pearson VUE and, in rare cases, by IBM (for example, IBM administers the DB2 certifications free of charge at some of the larger database conferences, such as the International DB2 User's Group North American conference). However, before you contact either testing vendor, visit Pearson VUE's website (*www.pearsonvue.com/ibm*) and click the **Locate a test center** button to find a testing center that is convenient for you. Once you have located a testing center, you can then contact the vendor to arrange to take the certification exam. (You can also find contact information for the testing vendors on their respective websites; in some cases, you can schedule an exam online.)

You must make arrangements to take a certification exam at least 24 hours in advance. When you contact the testing vendor, be ready to provide the following information:

- Your name (as you want it to appear on your certificate)
- An identification number (if you have taken an IBM certification exam before, this is the number assigned to you at that time; if not, the testing vendor will supply one)
- A telephone number where you can be reached
- A fax number
- The mailing address where you want all certification correspondence, including your certification welcome package, to be sent
- Your billing address, if it is different from your mailing address
- Your email address
- The number that identifies the exam you wish to take (for example, C2090-611)

- The method of payment (credit card or check) you wish to use, along with any relevant payment information (such as credit card number and expiration date)
- Your company's name (if applicable)
- The testing center where you want to take the certification exam
- The date when you would like to take the certification test

Before you make arrangements to take a certification exam, have paper and pencil or pen handy so that you can write down the test applicant identification number the testing center will assign you. You will need this information when you arrive at the testing center to take the certification exam. You will receive an email confirmation containing the number of the certification exam you have been scheduled to take, along with corresponding date, time, and location information.

Remember: If you have already taken one or more of the certification exams offered, make the testing vendor aware of this and ask it to assign you the same applicant identification number that was previously used. This will allow the certification team at IBM to quickly recognize when you have met all the exam requirements for a particular certification role. (If you were assigned a unique applicant identification number each time you took an exam, go to the IBM Professional Certification Member website at *www.ibm.com/certify/members* and select **Member Services** to merge all your exam results under one ID.)

Each certification exam costs $200 (in the United States and in the United Kingdom). Scheduling procedures vary according to how you choose to pay for the test. If you pay by credit card, you can arrange to take the exam immediately, after providing the testing vendor with the appropriate information. However, if you pay by check, you must wait until the check has been received and payment has been confirmed before you can arrange to take the exam. (Pearson VUE recommends that if you pay by check, you write your registration ID on the front and contact the testing center seven business days after the check is mailed. At that time, Pearson VUE should have received and confirmed your payment, and you should be able to make arrangements to take the test.)

If, for some reason, you need to reschedule or cancel your testing appointment after it is made, you must do so at least 24 hours before your scheduled test time. Otherwise, you will still be charged the price of the exam.

Taking an IBM Certification Exam

On the day you are scheduled to take a certification exam, arrive at the testing center at least 15 minutes before the scheduled start time to sign in. As part of the sign-in process, you must provide the applicant identification number you were assigned when you arranged to take the exam and two forms of identification. One form of identification must feature a recent photograph, and the other must show your signature. Examples of valid forms of identification include a driver's license (photograph) and a credit card (signature).

After you are signed in, the exam administrator will instruct you to enter the testing area and select an available workstation. The exam administrator will then enter your name and identification number into the workstation you have chosen, provide you with a pencil and some paper, and tell you to begin the exam when you are ready. At that point, the title screen of the IBM Certification Exam testing software should appear on the computer monitor in front of you. Figure 1.5 illustrates what this screen looks like.

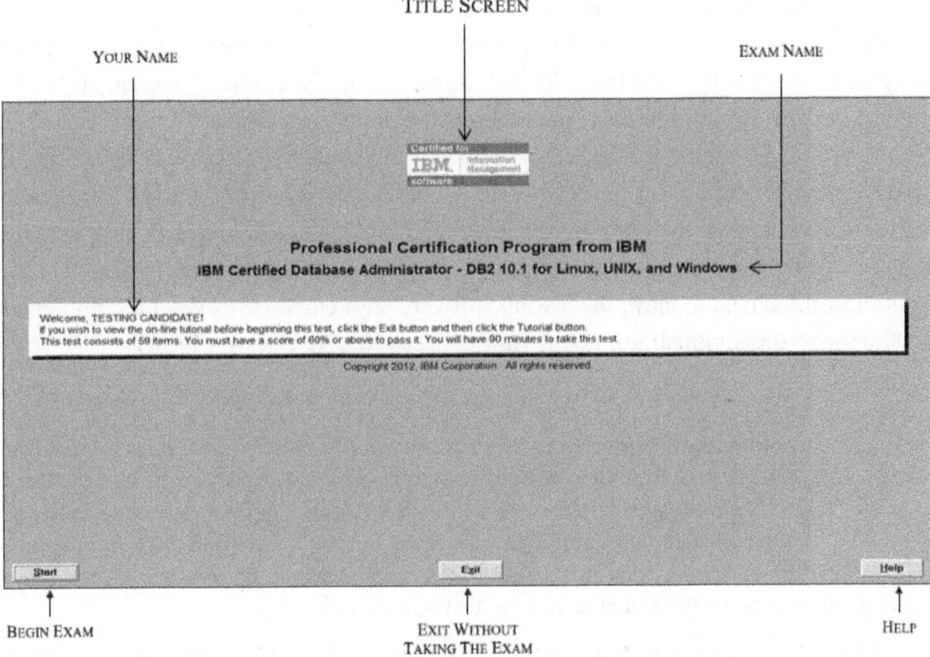

Figure 1.5: Title screen of the IBM Certification Exam testing software

The title screen of the IBM Certification Exam testing software consists of the IBM Certification Logo, the title "Professional Certification Program from IBM," the name of the exam that is about to be administered, and a welcome message containing your name and some basic information on how to get started. Before proceeding, be sure to do the following:

- Verify that the exam you are about to take is indeed the exam you expected to take. If the name of the exam on the title screen is different from the name of the exam you had planned to take, immediately bring this to the attention of the exam administrator.

- Verify that your name is spelled correctly. The way your name appears in the welcome message on the title screen reflects how it has been stored in the IBM Certification database. This is how all correspondence to you will be addressed and, more important, is how your name will appear on the certification credentials you will receive if you pass the exam.

In addition to displaying which exam is about to be administered, the title screen of the IBM Certification Exam testing software lets you know how many questions are on the exam, the score you must receive to pass it, and the time frame in which you must complete the exam. With one exception, each test contains between 50 and 70 questions and allots 90 minutes for completion. The *DB2 10.1 for Linux, UNIX, and Windows Database Administration* exam (C2090-611) contains 59 questions and allows 90 minutes for completion.

Although you must complete each certification exam within a predefined time limit, never rush through an exam just because the "clock is running." The time limits imposed are more than adequate for you to work through the exam at a relaxed, but steady, pace.

When you are ready, begin by clicking the **Start** button, located in the lower left corner of the screen. If instead you would like a quick refresher course on how to use the IBM Certification Exam testing software, click the **Help** button, located in the lower right corner of the screen. (If you panic and decide you are not ready to take the exam, click the **Exit** button, located at the center bottom of the screen to leave the testing software altogether. However, I recommend that you talk with the exam administrator about your concerns before clicking **Exit**.)

Remember: If you plan to take a quick refresher course on how to use the IBM Certification Exam testing software, make sure you do so before you click **Start** to begin the exam. Although help is available at any time, the clock does not start running until you click the **Start** button. By viewing help information before the clock is started, you avoid using what may prove to be valuable testing time reading documentation instead of answering test questions.

After you click **Start** on the title screen of the IBM Certification Exam testing software, the clock will start running, and the first exam question will be presented in a question panel that looks something like the one in Figure 1.6.

Aside from the question itself, one of the first things you may notice when you examine the question panel of the IBM Certification Exam testing software is the question number displayed in the top left corner of the screen. If you answer the questions in the order they are presented, this portion of the screen will act as a progress indicator because the current question number is displayed along with the total number of questions contained in the exam.

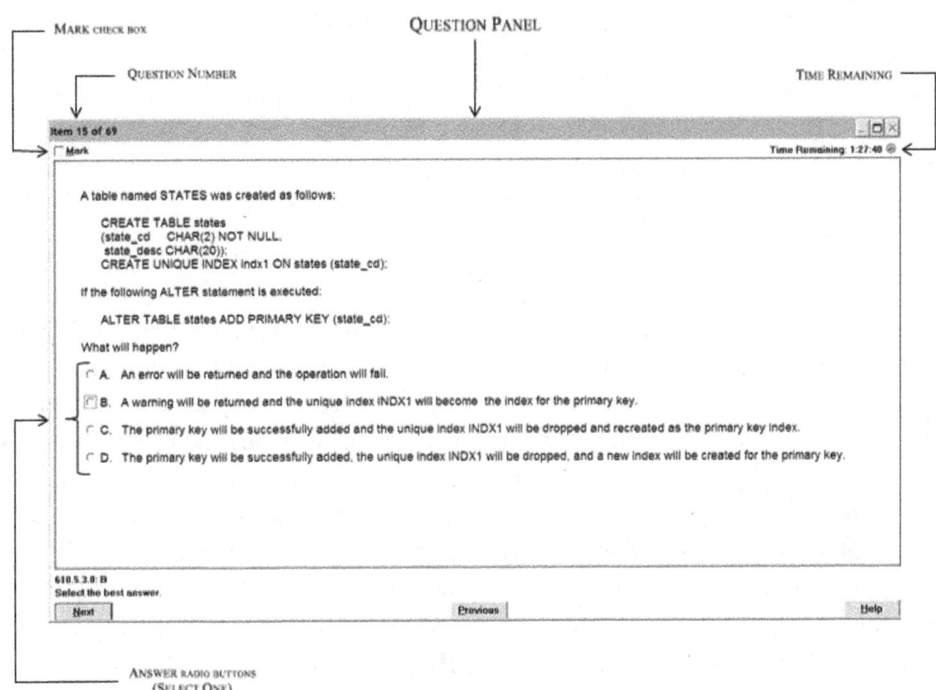

Figure 1.6: Typical question panel of the IBM Certification Exam testing software

Immediately below the question number, you will find a special check box called **Mark**. If you wish to skip the current question for now and come back to it later, or if you are uncertain about the answer you have chosen and would like to look at this question again after you have completed the rest of the exam, mark this check box (by placing the mouse pointer over it and pressing the left mouse button). After viewing every question once, you will be given the opportunity to review just the marked questions again. At that time, you can answer any unanswered questions remaining as well as re-evaluate any answers about which you have some concerns.

Another important feature on the question panel is the **Time Remaining** information displayed in the top right corner of the screen. As the title implies, this area of the question panel provides continuous feedback on the amount of time you have to finish and review the exam. To see more detailed information, such as the actual wall-clock time at which you began the exam and the time frame within which you are expected to complete the exam, you can view that information by clicking the clock icon located just to the right of the **Time Remaining** information. When you click this icon (by placing the mouse pointer over it and pressing the left mouse button), a dialog similar to the one in Figure 1.7 appears.

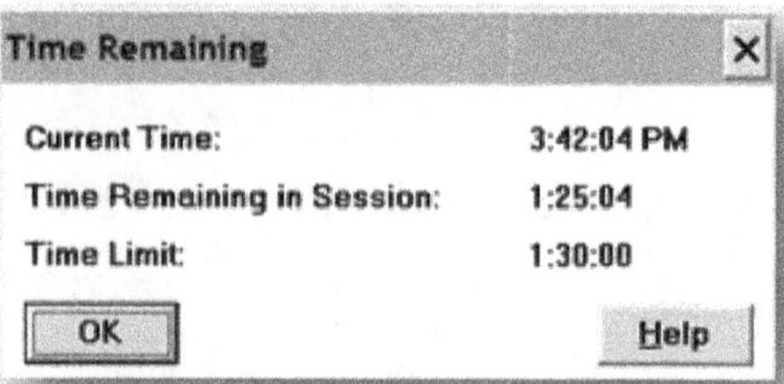

Figure 1.7: Time Remaining dialog

Obviously, the most important part of the question panel is the exam question itself, along with the corresponding list of possible answers provided. Take the time to read each question carefully. When you have located the correct answer in the list provided, mark it by clicking the radio-button positioned just to the left of the answer text (by placing the mouse pointer over the desired answer radio-button and pressing the left mouse button). Once you have selected an answer for that question (or marked it by clicking the **Mark** check box), you can move to the next question by clicking the **Next** button, located in the lower left corner of the screen (refer to Figure 1.6).

If at any time you wish to return to the previous question, you can do so by clicking the **Previous** button, located at the center bottom of the screen. To access help on how to use the IBM Certification Exam testing software, click the **Help** button in the lower right corner of the screen. It is important to note that although you can use the **Next** and **Previous** buttons to navigate through the questions, the navigation process itself is not cyclic in nature—that is, when you are on the first question, you cannot go to the last question by clicking **Previous** (in fact, the **Previous** button will not be displayed on the first question).

Likewise, when you are on the last question, you cannot go to the first question simply by clicking **Next**. However, there is a way to navigate quickly to a specific question from the item review panel, which we will look at shortly. Although typically only one answer in the list provided is the correct answer to the question at hand, there are times when multiple answers are valid. On those occasions, the answer radio-buttons will be replaced with answer check boxes, and the question will be worded in such a way that you will know how many answers are expected. Figure 1.8 illustrates an example of such a question.

To answer these types of questions, click the answer check box positioned just to the left of the text *for every correct answer found*. (Again, you do this by placing the mouse pointer over each desired answer check box and pressing the left mouse button.)

Sometimes, an illustration or the output from some diagnostic tool will accompany a question. You will be required to view that illustration or output (referred to as an exhibit) before you can successfully answer the question presented. On those occasions, a message instructing you to display the exhibit for the question will precede the actual test question, and a special button called **Exhibit** will be positioned at the bottom of the screen, between the **Previous** and **Help** buttons. Figure 1.9 shows an example of such a question.

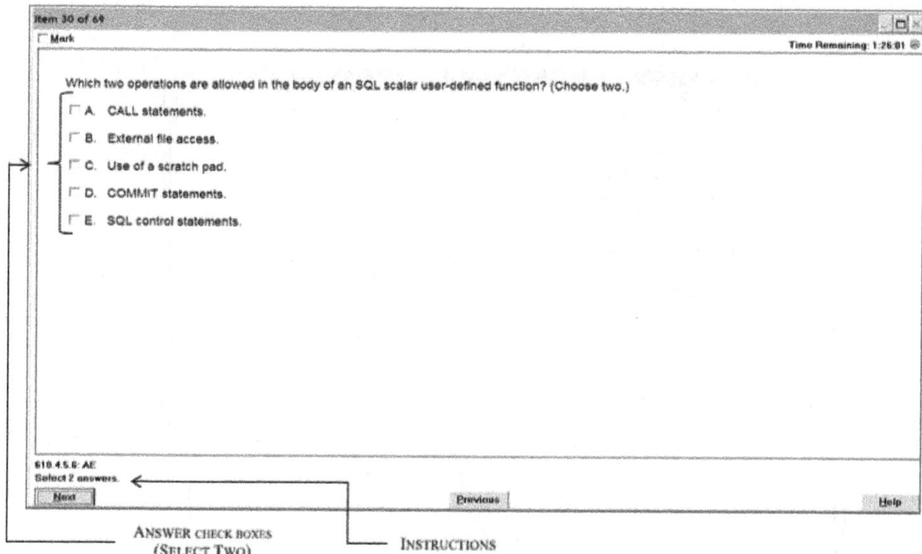

Figure 1.8: Question panel for questions expecting multiple answers

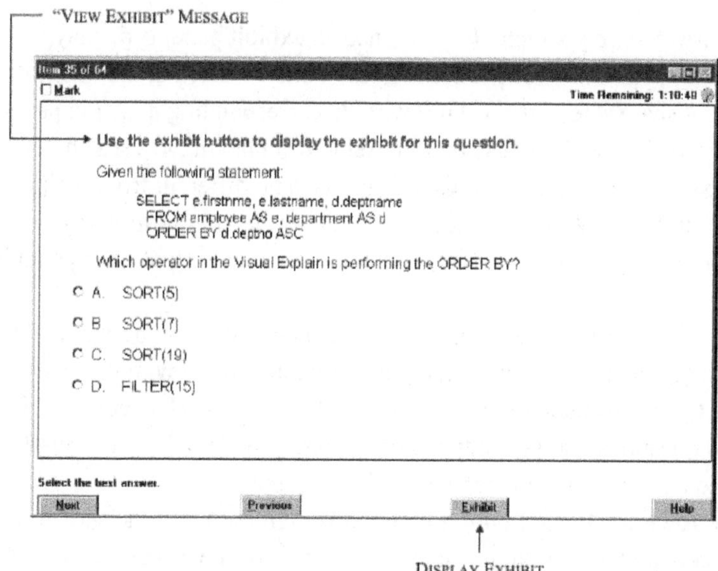

Figure 1.9: Question panel for questions that contain an exhibit

To view the exhibit associated with such a question, simply click the **Exhibit** button to display the corresponding exhibit panel. (You can see a sample exhibit panel in Figure 1.10 on the next page.)

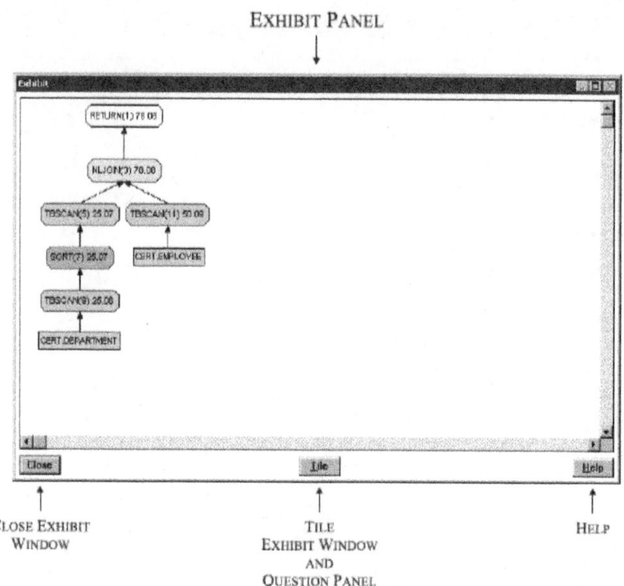

Figure 1.10: Sample exhibit panel

Exhibit panels are relatively simple. In fact, once an exhibit panel is displayed, you can do only two things with it: close it by clicking the **Close** button located at the bottom of the screen, or tile it (i.e., make it share screen real estate) with its corresponding question panel by clicking the **Tile** button, located beside the **Close** button. Aside from having to view the exhibit provided, the process used to answer questions that have exhibits is no different from the process used to answer questions that do not. When you have viewed every exam question (by clicking **Next** on every question panel), an item review panel, which looks something like the panel in Figure 1.11, will display.

As you can see in Figure 1.11, the item review panel contains a numerical listing of the questions that make up the certification exam you are taking, along with the answers you have provided for each. Questions that you marked (by clicking the **Mark** check box) are preceded by the letter "M," and questions that you skipped or did not provide the correct number of answers for are assigned the letter "I" to indicate they are incomplete.

By clicking the **Review Marked** button in the lower left corner of the screen (refer to Figure 1.11), you can quickly go back through just the questions that have been marked. When you review marked items in this manner, each time you click the **Next** button on a question panel, you go to the next marked question in the list until you eventually return to the item review panel.

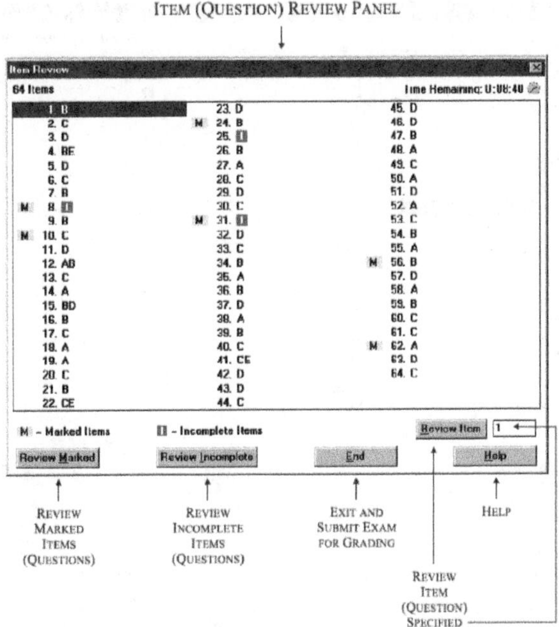

Figure 1.11: Item (question) review panel of the IBM Certification Exam testing software

Likewise, by clicking the **Review Incomplete** button, located next to the **Review Marked** button, you can go back through just the questions that have been identified as incomplete. (Navigation works the same as when you click **Review Marked.**) If, instead, you wish to review a specific question, you can do so by either highlighting that question's number or typing it in the entry field provided just to the right of the **Review Item** button (which is located above the **Help** button in the lower right corner of the screen) and clicking **Review Item.**

One of the first things you should do when the item review panel displays is to resolve any incomplete items. (When the exam is graded, each incomplete item is marked incorrect, and points are deducted from your final score.) Then, if time permits, go back and review the questions that you marked. It is important to note that when you finish reviewing a marked question, you unmark it (by placing the mouse pointer over the **Mark** check box and pressing the left mouse button) before going on to the next marked question or returning to the item review panel. Doing so will make it easier to keep track of which questions you have reviewed and which you have not.

As soon as you have resolved all incomplete items, the **Review Incomplete** button is automatically removed from the item review panel. Likewise, when no more marked questions remain, the **Review Marked** button also disappears from the item review panel. Thus, when every incomplete and marked item has been resolved, the item review panel will look similar to the one in Figure 1.12.

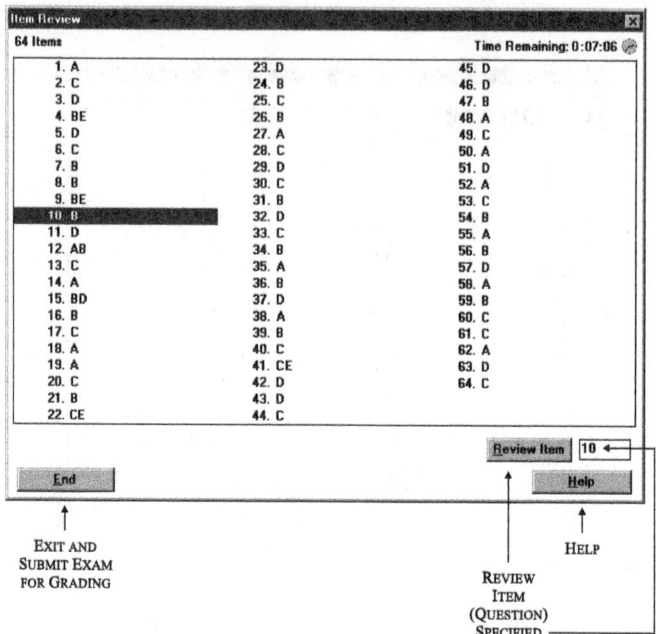

Figure 1.12: Item (question) review panel with all incomplete and marked items (questions) resolved

Keep in mind that even when the **Review Incomplete** and **Review Marked** buttons are no longer available, you can still go back to review a specific question by either highlighting that question's number or typing it in the entry field provided and clicking **Review Item** (refer to Figure 1.12).

As soon as you feel comfortable with the answers you have provided, you can end the exam and submit it for grading by clicking the **End** button, which you will find in the lower left corner of the item review panel. After you click this button (by placing the mouse pointer over it and pressing the left mouse button), a dialog similar to the one in Figure 1.13 will appear.

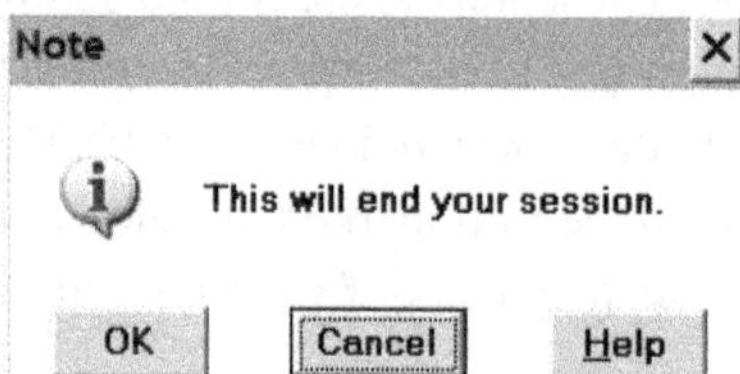

Figure 1.13: End exam session confirmation dialog

If you click **End** on the item review panel before resolving all incomplete items, a dialog similar to the one in Figure 1.14 will display instead.

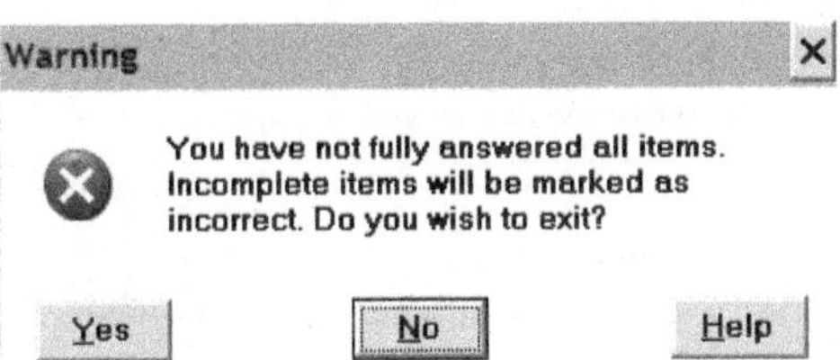

Figure 1.14: Ending exam with incomplete items warning dialog

Both of these dialogs give you the opportunity to confirm your decision to end the exam and submit it for grading or to reconsider and continue resolving or reviewing exam questions. If you wish to do the former, click **OK** or **Yes** when one of these dialogs is presented; if you wish to do the latter, click **Cancel** or **No**, which will return you to the item review panel. Keep in mind that if you click the **Yes** button when the dialog in Figure 1.14 displays, all incomplete items will be marked as incorrect, and this will have a negative impact on your final score.

Once you confirm that you do indeed wish to end the exam, the IBM Certification Exam testing software will evaluate your answers and produce a score report that indicates whether you passed the exam. This report will then appear on an exam results panel that looks something like the panel in Figure 1.15, and a corresponding hard copy (printout) will be generated.

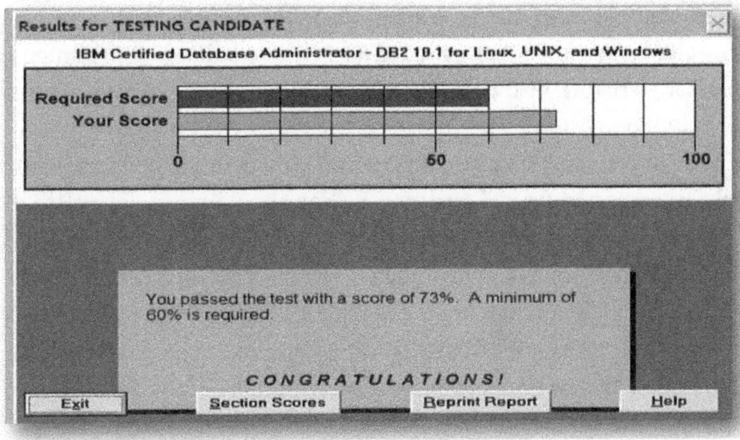

Figure 1.15: Exam results panel of the IBM Certification Exam testing software

If you click the **Section Scores** button in the exam results panel, you will get to see the scores for each section of the examination, as the Figure 1.16 shows.

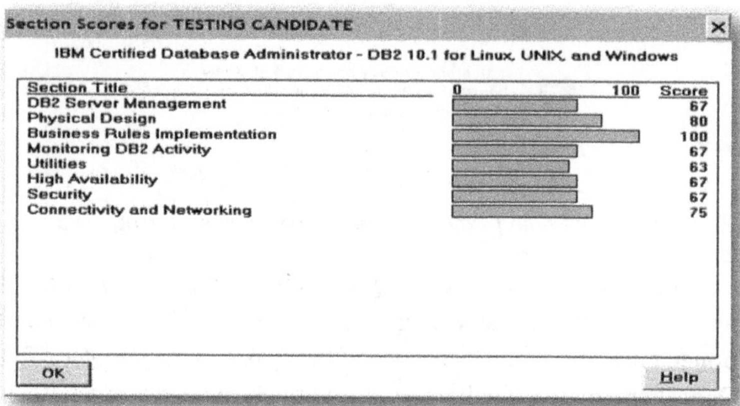

Figure 1.16: Exam section score result of the IBM Certification Exam testing software

Shortly after you take a certification exam (usually within five working days), the testing vendor sends your results, along with your demographic data (e.g., name, address, phone number) to the IBM Certification Group for processing. If you passed the exam, you will receive credit toward the certification role the exam was designed for, and if the exam you took completes the requirements that have been outlined for a particular certification role, you will receive an email (at the email address you provided during registration) containing a copy of the IBM Certification Agreement and a welcome package that includes a certificate suitable for framing (in the form of a PDF file), camera-ready artwork of the IBM certification logo, and guidelines for using the "IBM Certified" mark.

Upon receipt of the welcome package, you are officially certified and can begin using the IBM Professional Certification title and trademark. (You should receive the IBM Certification Agreement and welcome package within four to six weeks after IBM processes the exam results.) However, if you failed to pass the exam and you still wish to become certified, you must make arrangements to retake it (including paying the testing fee again). There are no restrictions on the number of times you can take a particular certification test, but you cannot take the same certification exam more than two times within a 30-day period.

CHAPTER 2

DB2 Server Management

This chapter will prepare you to configure and manage DB2 servers, instances, and databases. You will learn to use many of the DB2 autonomic computing features to improve system availability and performance. By the end of the chapter, you will also be able to install and configure IBM Data Studio to perform database administration activities, such as database maintenance job schedules and Visual Explain plan generation.

Exam Objectives

- ✓ Demonstrate the ability to create and manage DB2 instances
- ✓ Demonstrate the ability to view and modify DB2 system registry variables
- ✓ Demonstrate the ability to view and modify DB2 database manager configuration information
- ✓ Demonstrate the ability to view and modify database configuration information
- ✓ Demonstrate the ability to gain exclusive control of a database
- ✓ Demonstrate the ability to use automatic maintenance
- ✓ Demonstrate the ability to use the STMM
- ✓ Demonstrate the ability to use the Configuration Advisor
- ✓ Demonstrate the ability to use automatic storage features
- ✓ Demonstrate the ability to use data compression features
- ✓ Demonstrate the ability to throttle utilities
- ✓ Demonstrate the ability to schedule and manage jobs by using IBM Data Studio

Working with Instances

DB2 sees the world as a hierarchy of objects. *Workstations* or *servers* on which DB2 has been installed occupy the highest level of this hierarchy. When any edition of DB2 is installed on a workstation, program files for a background process known as the *DB2 database manager* are physically copied to a specific location on that workstation, and in most cases, an instance of the DB2 database manager is created.

Instances occupy the second level in the hierarchy and are responsible for managing system resources and databases that fall under their control. Although only one instance is created initially, several instances can coexist on a single server. Each instance behaves like a separate installation of DB2, even though all instances within a system share the same DB2 database manager program files (unless each instance is running a different version of DB2). And although multiple instances share the same binary code, each runs independently of the others and has its own environment, which can be modified by altering the contents of its associated configuration file.

Databases make up the third level in the hierarchy and are responsible for managing the storage, modification, and retrieval of data. Like instances, databases work independently of each other. Each database has its own environment that is controlled by a set of configuration parameters, as well as its own set of grantable authorities and privileges to govern how users interact with the data and database objects it controls. Figure 2.1 shows the hierarchical relationship between systems, instances, and databases.

Although most DB2 environments consist of one instance per server, at times it is advantageous to create multiple instances on the same physical server. Reasons for creating multiple instances include the following:

- To separate your development environment from your production environment
- To obtain optimum performance for special applications (for example, you may choose to create an instance for one or more applications, and then fine-tune each instance specifically for the applications it will service)
- To prevent database administrators from accessing sensitive data (for example, a company's payroll database could reside in its own instance, in which case owners of other databases in other instances on the same server would be unable to access payroll data)

Obviously, multiple instances will require additional system resources such as disk space, memory, and CPUs based on the workload you run on the databases created on the additional instance.

As you might imagine, DB2 provides several commands for creating and managing instances. Table 2.1 shows these commands, referred to as system commands because they are executed from the system command prompt rather than from the DB2 Command Line Processor (CLP).

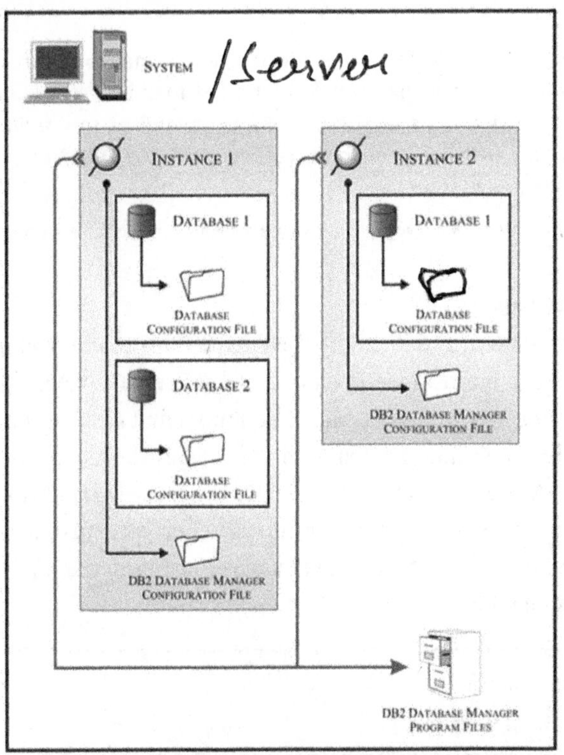

Figure 2.1: Hierarchical relationship between systems, instances, and databases

Table 2.1: DB2 instance management commands

Command	Purpose
db2icrt [InstanceName]	Create a new instance
db2idrop [InstanceName]	Delete (drop) an existing instance
db2ilist	List all instances that have been defined within one installation
db2ckupgrade [DatabaseName]	Verify that local databases are ready to be upgraded
db2iupgrade [InstanceName]	Upgrade an existing instance to a newer version of DB2
db2iupdt [InstanceName]	Update an existing instance to exploit new functionality that is provided when product fix packs are installed (also used to convert a 32-bit instance to a 64-bit instance)
db2start	Start the DB2 database manager background processes for the current instance
db2stop	Stop the DB2 database manager background processes for the current instance

Note: Although Table 2.1 presents the basic syntax for the instance management commands, the actual syntax supported may be more complex. To view the complete syntax for a specific DB2 command or to obtain more information about a particular command, refer to the IBM DB2 Version 10.1 Command Reference product documentation.

Attaching to an Instance

The default instance for a system is defined by the DB2INSTANCE environment variable, and often, this is the instance that all instance-level operations are performed against. If you need to perform an operation against a different instance, you must first change the value assigned to the DB2INSTANCE variable by executing the command "set DB2INSTANCE=[*InstanceName*]" (export DB2INSTANCE=[*InstanceName*] on Linux and UNIX), where *InstanceName* is the name assigned to the instance that you want to make the default instance, or you must *attach* to that instance.

Applications and users can attach to any instance by executing the ATTACH command. The basic syntax for this command is:

```
ATTACH TO [InstanceName]
USER [UserID] USING [Password]
```

where:

InstanceName	Identifies the name to assign to the instance to make an attachment (this instance must have a matching entry in the local node directory)
UserID	Identifies the user (by authorization ID) under whom the instance will attach
Password	Identifies the password that corresponds to the specified authorization ID

Thus, if you want to attach to an instance named db2inst1 by using the authentication ID db2admin and the password ibmdb2, you can do so by executing an ATTACH command:

```
ATTACH TO db2inst1 USER db2admin USING ibmdb2
```

Detaching from an Instance

Once you have made an attachment to an instance and all necessary tasks have been performed against that instance, you terminate the instance attachment if it is no longer needed. By terminating an instance attachment, you eliminate the potential to accidentally perform new operations against the wrong instance. The easiest way to terminate an attachment to an instance is by establishing an attachment to another one. That is because an application or user can attach to only one instance at a time—if an attachment is made to another instance, the current instance attachment is automatically terminated.

Applications and users can also detach from an instance by executing the DETACH command. The syntax for this command is:

```
DETACH
```

As you will notice, the DETACH command requires no additional parameters.

Starting and Stopping an Instance

The DB2 database manager background processes that are associated with a particular instance must be active and ready to process requests before any operation can be performed against the instance or a database under the instance's control. If they are not already running, you can start these background processes by executing the START DATABASE MANAGER command. The basic syntax for this command is:

```
START [DATABASE MANAGER | DB MANAGER | DBM]
```

or

```
db2start
```

Thus, to start the DB2 database manager background processes for the default instance, you execute a command that looks something like this:

```
START DATABASE MANAGER
```

If at any time you want to stop the DB2 database manager background processes, you can do so by executing the STOP DATABASE MANAGER command. The basic syntax for this command is:

```
STOP [DATABASE MANAGER | DB MANAGER | DBM]
<FORCE>
```

or

```
db2stop
```

Therefore, to stop the DB2 database manager background processes for the default instance, execute a command that looks something like this:

```
STOP DATABASE MANAGER
```

Note: On Linux, UNIX, and Windows operating systems, instances created using db2icrt are set to a manual start after the system reboot. You can enable instances to start automatically by using the following steps.

On the Windows platform, change the property of the DB2 services in the services panel to automatic. On UNIX and Linux platforms, run the command db2iauto -on <*InstanceName*>, where *InstanceName* is the name of the instance that needs auto-starting.

Quiescing an Instance

Because any number of users can be granted access to an instance or one or more databases under an instance's control, it can be difficult, if not impossible, to coordinate the work efforts of everyone who is using a specific instance at a given point in time. This can present a problem if a database administrator needs exclusive access to a particular instance for a short time (for example, to perform a maintenance operation). Therefore, individuals holding the proper authority can place an instance in a "restricted access" or "quiesced" state. When an instance is quiesced, all users are forced off the instance, all active transactions are immediately rolled back, and all databases under the instance's control are put into quiesced mode. You can place instances (and databases) in quiesced mode by executing the QUIESCE command. The basic syntax for this command is:

```
QUIESCE [INSTANCE [InstanceName ]
<USER [UserName] | GROUP [GroupName]>
[RESTRICTED ACCESS] [IMMEDIATE | DEFER <WITH TIMEOUT [Minutes]>]
<FORCE CONNECTIONS>
```

where:

InstanceName	Identifies the name to assign to the instance to place in quiesced mode
UserName	Identifies the name of a specific user who has permission to access the specified instance or database while it is in quiesced mode
GroupName	Identifies the name of a specific group of users that has permission to access the specified instance or database while it is in quiesced mode
Minutes	Specifies a time, in minutes, to wait for applications to commit their current transactions before quiescing the instance; if no value is specified, the default value is 10 minutes

Thus, to place an instance named db2inst1 into quiesced mode immediately, but allow a user named db2admin to continue to have access to it, you execute a QUIESCE command:

```
QUIESCE INSTANCE db2inst1 USER db2admin IMMEDIATE
```

Eventually, you will need to return the instance or database put into quiesced mode to a normal state. You can remove instances and databases from quiesced mode by executing the UNQUIESCE command. The basic syntax for this command is:

```
UNQUIESCE [INSTANCE [InstanceName] | DB]
```

where:

InstanceName	Identifies the name assigned to the instance that is to be taken out of quiesced mode

Therefore, if you want to take an instance named db2inst1 out of quiesced mode, you can do so by executing an UNQUIESCE command that looks like this:

```
UNQUIESCE INSTANCE db2inst1
```

You can also quiesce and unquiesce instances and databases by selecting the **Quiesce** or **Unquiesce** action from either the **Instances** menu or the **Databases** menu in IBM Data Studio. Figure 2.2 shows the Data Studio menu items that must be selected to activate the Quiesce instance dialog.

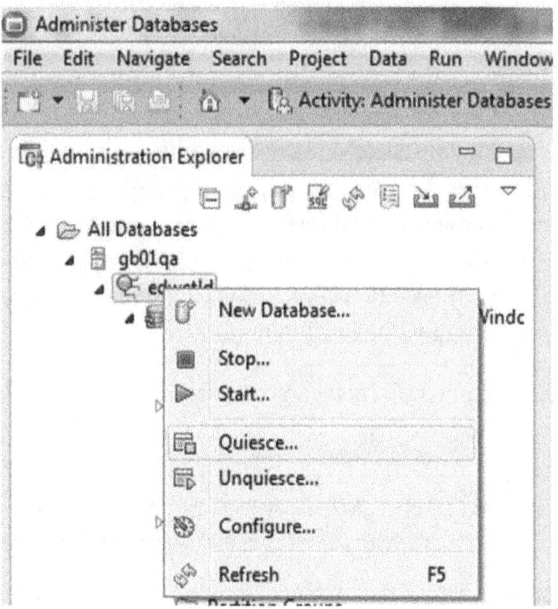

Figure 2.2: Invoking the Quiesce dialog from IBM Data Studio

It is important to note that only users with System Administrator (SYSADM) or System Control (SYSCTRL) authority are allowed to quiesce an instance. Once an instance is in a quiesced state, only users with System Administrator (SYSADM), System Control (SYSCTRL), or System Maintenance (SYSMAINT) authority; users who are members of a specified group (if a group name was specified when the instance was placed in quiesced mode); and users with a specified user name (if a user name was specified when the instance was placed in quiesced mode) can connect to the instance.

Similarly, only users with System Administrator (SYSADM) or Database Administrator (DBADM) authority are permitted to quiesce a database. After a database is in a quiesced state, only users with System Administrator (SYSADM), System Control (SYSCTRL), System Maintenance (SYSMAINT), or Database Administrator (DBADM) authority; users who are members of a specified group (if a group name was specified when the database was placed in quiesced mode); and users with a specified user name (if a user name was specified when the database was placed in quiesced mode) can connect to the database.

The basic syntax for QUIESCE and UNQUIESCE database are:

```
QUIESCE DATABASE [IMMEDIATE | DEFER <WITH TIMEOUT [Minutes]>]
<FORCE CONNECTIONS>
```

The database connection must be established before running the QUIESCE command on the database. There are no additional parameters necessary for running the UNQUIESCE command:

```
UNQUIESCE DATABASE
```

Upgrading Instances

To upgrade your DB2 server from DB2 9.5, DB2 9.7, or DB2 9.8 to DB2 10.1, you must upgrade the instance by using the db2iupgrade command. If the DB2 servers are running on a release before DB2 9.5, migrate the instance by using the db2imigr command to the latest DB2 9.5 fix pack, and then follow the DB2 10.1 upgrade procedure.

Table 2.2 lists the four major steps to follow during the upgrade process (these steps are specifically for UNIX systems).

Table 2.2: DB2 10.1 upgrade procedure

Step	Task	Detailed Information
1	Prerequisites	List the db2 instances and the installation locations by using the db2ls command. Understand the compatibilities between the operating system and DB2 10.1. Check the known issues for DB2 on your platform by using the links below: • AIX®: *www-01.ibm.com/support/docview.wss?uid=swg21165448* • HP-UX: *www-01.ibm.com/support/docview.wss?uid=swg21257602* • Solaris: *www-01.ibm.com/support/docview.wss?uid=swg21257606* • Linux: *www.ibm.com/software/data/db2/linux/validate* Download the DB2 10.1 product and the license from IBM Passport Advantage®. Run the db2prereqcheck command on the server to check whether the system meets DB2 10.1 prerequisites. Extract all the registry, instance, and database parameter current values: db2set –all db2cfexp cfexp backup LIST DB DIRECTORY LIST NODE DIRECTORY LIST DCS DIRECTORY GET DBM CFG SHOW DETAIL cp -p ~/sqllib/userprofile userprofile.bak cp -p ~/sqllib/db2nodes.cfg db2nodes.cfg.bak

Table 2.2: DB2 10.1 upgrade procedure (continued)		
Step	**Task**	**Detailed Information**
2	Preupgrade	Install the DB2 10.1 software on the server by using the db2setup silent installation procedure. You can make use of the install.rsp response file present in the samples directory to run through the silent installation. Perform the installation file validation by using the db2val command, which in turn does the following validations for you: ● Installation file sets ● Embedded run-time path for DB2 executables and libraries ● Accessibility to the installation path ● Accessibility to the /etc/services file Apply the DB2 license by using the db2licm command. Check the database upgrade by using the db2ckupgrade command. Increase the LOGSECOND database configuration parameter value to double the current. Update the database manager configuration parameter DIAGLEVEL to 4.
3	Upgrade	Upgrade the existing instance to the newer version; the commands are: db2 LIST APPLICATIONS db2 FORCE APPLICATIONS ALL db2 DEACTIVATE DATABASE <dbname> db2stop db2diag –A ipclean;ipcrm db2_kill exit As the root authority, run the db2iupgrade command to upgrade an instance from the old release to a new release: db2iupgrade –u <*FencedUser*> <*InstanceName*> where: ● *FencedUser* runs UDFs and stored procedures outside the address space used by the DB2 database. You can find the fenced user for the instance by using the db2pd command: db2pd -fmp | grep -i fenced Trusted Path: /db2home/db2inst1/sqllib/function/unfenced Fenced User: db2fence ● *InstanceName* is the instance you would like to upgrade. Start the DB2 database manager by using the db2start command. Perform the database upgrade by using the UPGRADE command: UPGRADE DATABASE <DatabaseName> where: DatabaseName is the name of the database you want to upgrade to the new release.
4	Postupgrade	Activate all the databases. Perform the RUNSTATS on all the tables, and rebind all packages. Update the DB2 database manager configuration parameter DIAGLEVEL to 3. Restart the instance by using the db2stop and db2start commands.

Dropping Instances

To drop your DB2 root instance, issue the db2idrop command; to drop nonroot instances, uninstall your DB2 database product. It is necessary to stop the instance before dropping it, and a good practice is to back up the $INSTHOME/sqllib directory before dropping the instance.

The instance drop command is:

```
db2idrop <InstanceName>
```

where:

InstanceName Identifies the name of the specific instance to upgrade; to list all the instances, use the db2ilist command on the server

A Word About the DB2 Administration Server (DAS)

The DB2 Administration Server (DAS) has been deprecated in DB2 9.7 and will receive no more enhancements. Furthermore, the DAS might be removed in the near future. The reason for discussing DAS here is simply for completeness of the topic.

The tools that used to come with DB2, such as the Control Center (a discontinued DB2 GUI tool), require a separate instance that operates independently of, yet concurrently with, all other instances that have been defined for a particular workstation. For this reason, a special instance, known as the *DB2 Administration Server (DAS)* instance, is also created as part of the DB2 installation process. In contrast to other instances, only one DAS instance can exist on a single workstation. The DB2 global-level profile registry variable DB2ADMINSERVER contains the name of the DAS instance that has been defined for a particular workstation.

Once created, the DAS instance runs continuously as a background process whenever the system it was created on is online; the DAS instance is usually activated automatically each time the workstation it resides on is started (or rebooted). Furthermore, the DAS instance must be running on every DB2 server that you wish to administer remotely. That is because, among other things, the DAS instance provides remote clients with the information needed to establish communications with other instances.

It is important to note that to administer a server from a remote client, a user must have System Administration (SYSADM) authority for the DAS instance used. Furthermore, once a remote instance and database have been registered on a client workstation, the user must hold the authorities and privileges needed to perform administrative tasks.

In addition to enabling remote administration of DB2 servers, the DAS instance assists the Control Center and the Configuration Assistant in the following:

- Providing job (task) management, including the ability to schedule and run user-defined shell scripts and batch files that contain both DB2 and operating system commands
- Scheduling jobs, viewing the results of completed jobs, and performing administrative tasks against jobs executed either remotely or locally (by using the Task Center)

Note: The Control Center tools and associated DB2 commands such as db2am, db2ca, db2cc, db2eva, db2hc, db2indbt, db2lc, and db2tc have been discontinued. In DB2 10.1 onward, it is advisable to use IBM Data Studio, which is discussed at the end of the chapter.

Configuring the DB2 System Environment

During normal operation, the DB2 database manager's behavior is controlled, in part, by a collection of values that defines the DB2 operating environment. Some of these values are operating system environment variables, and others are special DB2-specific system-level values known as *environment* or *registry* variables. Registry variables provide a way to centrally control the database environment. Four different registry profiles are available, and each controls the database environment at a different level. The registry profiles are as follows:

- **The DB2 global-level profile registry**—All machine-wide environment variable settings reside in this registry; one global-level profile registry exists on each DB2 workstation. To set an environment variable for all instances, use this profile registry.
- **The DB2 instance-level profile registry**—The environment variable settings for a particular instance are kept in this registry; this is where you set the majority of the DB2 environment variables. The values defined in this profile registry override any corresponding settings in the global-level profile registry.
- **The DB2 instance node-level profile registry**—This profile registry level contains variable settings that are specific to a partition (node) in a multi-partitioned database environment. The values defined in this profile registry override any corresponding settings in the global-level and instance-level profile registries.
- **The DB2 user-level profile registry**—This profile registry level contains variable settings that are specific to each user and takes higher precedence over other registry settings.

Table 2.3 shows the order in which DB2 resolves the registry settings and the environment variables when configuring the system.

Table 2.3: DB2 Registry location and precedence

Profile Registry	Precedence	Location on Windows platform	Location on Linux and UNIX platform	Authorization required on Windows platform	Authorization required on Linux and UNIX platform
Environment variables	1	Not applicable	For Bourne or korn shell: instance_home/sqllib/db2profile For C shell: instance_home/sqllib/db2cshrc	Not applicable	-rwxr-xr-x on db2profile or db2cshrc files, and part of the SYSADM group
User level	2	Lightweight Directory Access Protocol (LDAP) directory	Not applicable	Member of DB2 administrators group (DB2ADMNS)	Not applicable
Instance node level	3	\HKEY_LOCAL_MACHINE\SOFTWARE\IBM\DB2\PROFILES\instance_name\NODES\node_number	$INSTHOME/sqllib/nodes File Name: <nodenumber>.env	Member of DB2 administrators group (DB2ADMNS)	drwxrwxr-x on the nodes directory and -rw-rw-r— on the env file, and part of the SYSADM group
Instance level	4	\HKEY_LOCAL_MACHINE\SOFTWARE\IBM\DB2\PROFILES\instance_name	$INSTHOME/sqllib/profile.env	Member of DB2 administrators group (DB2ADMNS)	-rw-rw-r—on the file profile.env, and part of the SYSADM group
Global level	5	\HKEY_LOCAL_MACHINE\SOFTWARE\IBM\DB2\GLOBAL_PROFILE	For root installations: /var/db2/global.reg For nonroot installations: home_directory/sqllib/global.reg	Member of DB2 administrators group (DB2ADMNS)	For root installation, root authority is required; for nonroot installation, the user who installed the product can modify the global setting

You can use the db2greg command to view and alter the global registry settings, which then modifies the file /var/db2/global.reg in root installations and $HOME/sqllib/global.reg in nonroot installations.

The command output in a root installation looks like this:

```
db2greg -dump
V,DB2GPRF,DB2SYSTEM,gb01qa,/opt/ibm/db2/V10.1,
S,TSA,3.2.2.5,/opt/IBM/tsamp,-,-,0,0,-,1389969042,0
S,DB2,10.1.0.3,/opt/ibm/db2/V10.1,,,3,0,,1389969093,0
I,DB2,10.1.0.3,db2inst1,/home/db2inst1/sqllib,,1,0,/opt/ibm/db2/V10.1,,
V,DB2GPRF,DB2INSTDEF,db2inst1,/opt/ibm/db2/V10.1,
```

The global registry consists of three record types:

- **Service (S)**—This records product-level information, such as version and install path.
- **Instance (I)**—This records instance-level information, such as instance name, instance path, DB2 version, and the start-at-boot flag.
- **Variables (V)**—This records variables and the value settings.

You can edit the global registry setting by using the db2greg command; editing in root installation needs a root privilege.

A wide variety of registry variables are available, and they vary depending on the operating system being used. Chapter 22 of the *Database Administration Concepts and Configuration Reference* manual contains a complete listing.

So how do you determine which registry variables have been set and what they have been set to? Or more important, how do you assign values to one or more registry variables? One way is by executing the db2set system command. The syntax for this command is:

```
db2set [variable=[value]]
       [-g|-i instance [member-number]]
       [-all]
       [-null]
       [-r [instance] [member-number]]
       [-im|-immediate]
       [-info]
       [-n DAS Node [-u user [-p password]]]
       [-l|-lr]
       [-v]
       [-ul|-ur]
       [-?|-h]
```

where:

Variable	Identifies the registry variable whose value is to be displayed, set, or removed
Value	Identifies the value to assign to the specified registry variable; if no value is provided but a registry variable is specified, the specified registry variable is deleted
Instance	Identifies the instance profile with which to associate the specified registry variable
Member-number	Identifies the node number of the instance in cases regarding the use of a DPF database
DAS Node	Identifies the name of the node where the DAS instance resides (this is deprecated in DB2 9.7 and is no longer required to be created)
User	Identifies the authentication ID to use to attach to the DAS instance
Passwords	Identifies the password (for the authentication ID) to use to attach to the DB2 Administration Server instance

Table 2.4 describes all other options with this command.

Table 2.4: The db2set command options

Option	Meaning
-g	Indicates that a global profile variable is to be displayed, set, or removed
-gl	Indicates that a global profile variable stored in LDAP is to be displayed, set, or removed; this option is effective only if the registry variable DB2_ENABLE_LDAP has been set to YES
-i	Indicates that an instance profile variable is to be displayed, set, or removed
-all	Indicates that all occurrences of the registry variable, as defined in the following, are to be displayed: • The environment (denoted by [-e]) • The node-level registry (denoted by [-n]) • The instance-level registry (denoted by [-i]) • The global-level registry (denoted by [-g])
-null	Indicates that the value of the variable at the specified registry level is to be set to NULL
-r	Indicates that the profile registry for the given instance is to be reset
-n	Indicates that a remote DAS instance node name is specified
-u	Indicates that an authentication ID that will attach to the DAS instance is specified
-p	Indicates that a password for the specified authentication ID is provided
-l	Indicates that all instance profiles will be listed
-lr	Indicates that all registry variables supported will be listed
-v	Indicates that the db2set command is to be executed in verbose mode
-ul	Accesses the user profile variables (this parameter is supported only on Windows operating systems)

Table 2.4: The db2set command options (continued)	
Option	**Meaning**
-ur	Refreshes the user profile variables (this parameter is supported only on Windows operating systems)
-h | -?	Displays help information; when this option is specified, all other options are ignored, and only the help information is displayed

It is important to note that if you execute the db2set command without options, a list containing every registry variable that has been set for the current (default) instance, along with its value, will be returned.

Thus, if you want to determine which registry variables have been set for each profile, execute the db2set command:

```
db2set -all
```

And the resulting output might look something like this:

```
[i] DB2FCMCOMM=TCPIP4
[i] DB2_SKIPINSERTED=ON
[i] DB2_OBJECT_TABLE_ENTRIES=10000
[i] DB2_USE_ALTERNATE_PAGE_CLEANING=ON
[i] DB2_LOAD_COPY_NO_OVERRIDE=nonrecoverable
[i] DB2_INLIST_TO_NLJN=YES
[i] DB2_REDUCED_OPTIMIZATION=ON
[i] DB2_EVALUNCOMMITTED=ON
[i] DB2_EXTENDED_OPTIMIZATION=Y
[i] DB2_ANTIJOIN=Y
[i] DB2TCPCONNMGRS=16
[i] DB2_SKIPDELETED=ON
[i] DB2DBDFT=SAMPLE
[i] DB2COMM=TCPIP
[i] DB2_PARALLEL_IO=*:5
[i] DB2AUTOSTART=YES
[g] DB2SYSTEM=prodbcuapp001
[g] DB2INSTDEF=db2inst1
```

Alternatively, to see the current value of the DB2COMM registry variable for all DB2 instances, execute a db2set command that looks something like this:

```
db2set -l DB2COMM
```

And finally, if you want to assign a value to the DB2COMM registry variable for all DB2 instances on a server, you can do so by executing a db2set command that looks something like this:

```
db2set -g DB2COMM=[Protocol, ...]
```

where:

Protocol Identifies one or more communications protocols to start when the DB2 database manager for the instance is started; any combination of the following values is valid: NPIPE, TCPIP, and SSL

Thus, to set the DB2COMM instance-level registry variable such that the DB2 database manager will start the TCP/IP communication manager each time any instance is started, execute a db2set command that looks like this:

```
/home/db2inst1/sqllib/adm/db2set -g DB2COMM=TCPIP
```

You can unset the value assigned to any registry variable by providing just the variable name and the equal sign as input to the db2set command. Thus, if you want to disable the DB2COMM instance-level registry variable for an instance named db2inst1, you can do so by executing a db2set command that looks like this:

```
db2set -i DB2INST1 DB2COMM=
```

A Word About Aggregate Registry Variables

An aggregate registry variable is a group of several registry variables as a configuration that is identified by one registry variable name. Each registry variable that is part of the group has a predefined setting. The purpose of an aggregate registry variable is to ease registry configuration for broad operational objectives.

In DB2 10.1, the only valid aggregated registry variable is DB2_WORKLOAD, and the valid values for this variable are:

Value	Description
1C	1C application-specific workload setting
CM	Content Manager–specific workload setting
COGNOS_CS	Cognos® Content Server–specific workload setting
FILENET_CM	FileNet® Content Manager–specific workload setting
INFOR_ERP_LN	Infor ERP Baan–specific workload setting
MAXIMO	Maximo®-specific workload setting
MDM	Master Data Management–specific workload setting
SAP	SAP application–specific workload setting
TPM	Tivoli® Provisioning Manager–specific workload setting
WAS	WebSphere® Application Server–specific workload setting
WC	WebSphere Commerce–specific workload setting
WP	WebSphere Portal–specific workload setting

You can use an aggregate registry variable to explicitly define any registry variable that is implicitly configured, which in a way overrides the aggregated registry variable implicit value.

If you attempt to modify an explicitly set registry variable by using an aggregate registry variable, a warning is issued and the explicitly set value is kept. This warning tells you that the explicit value is maintained and will override the implicit value. For example, setting DB2_REDUCED_OPTIMIZATION to YES and then setting the DB2_WORKLOAD to SAP will generate a warning message something like the following:

```
db2set DB2_REDUCED_OPTIMIZATION=YES
db2set DB2_WORKLOAD=SAP
DBI1319W The variable "DB2_REDUCED_OPTIMIZATION" has been explicitly set and
will not be affected by the configuration of the aggregate variable "DB2_
WORKLOAD".
```

If the aggregate registry variable is used first, and then you specify an explicit registry variable, no warning is given. To identify the override settings, use the db2set -all command and check for [O] displayed next to its value, as follows:

```
[i] DB2_INLIST_TO_NLJN=YES [O]
[i] DB2_REDUCED_OPTIMIZATION=YES [O]
[i] DB2COMM=TCPIP [O]
```

And wherever the DB2_WORKLOAD setting value is active, you will see [DB2_WORKLOAD] appear next to its value something like this:

```
[i] DB2_ROWCOMPMODE_DEFAULT=STATIC [DB2_WORKLOAD]
[i] DB2_INDEX_PCTFREE_DEFAULT=0 [DB2_WORKLOAD]
[i] DB2_SKIP_VIEWRECREATE_SAP=TRUE [DB2_WORKLOAD]
```

Configuring DB2 Instances and Databases

Along with the comprehensive set of registry variables, DB2 uses an extensive array of configuration parameters to control how system resources are allocated and used on behalf of an instance and a database. The default values provided for many of these configuration parameters were produced with very simple systems in mind. The goal was for DB2 to run out of the box, on virtually any platform, not for DB2 to run optimally on the platform on which it is installed.

Thus, even though the default values for these configuration parameters are sufficient to meet most database needs, you can usually greatly improve overall system and application performance simply by changing the values of one or more configuration parameters. In fact, the values assigned to DB2 configuration parameters must always be modified or set to AUTOMATIC if your database environment contains one or more of the following:

- Large databases
- Databases that normally service large numbers of concurrent connections
- One or more special applications that have high performance requirements
- A special hardware configuration
- Unique query or transaction loads
- Unique query or transaction types

Chapter 5, "Monitoring DB2 Activity," discusses ways to measure transaction loads and performance to determine how to alter configuration parameter values. For now, let's examine the configuration parameters.

The DB2 Database Manager Instance Configuration

Whenever an instance is created, a corresponding DB2 database manager configuration file is also created and initialized as part of the instance creation process. Each DB2 database manager configuration file consists of about 96 different parameter values, and most control the amount of system resources that are allocated to a single DB2 database manager instance. Table 2.5 shows the parameters that make up a DB2 10.1 DB2 database manager configuration file.

Table 2.5: DB2 database manager instance configuration parameters				
Parameter	**Config Online**	**Performance Impact**	**Default and Value Range**	**Description**
agent_stack_sz	No	Low	Windows: 16 [8–1000] 4 KB pages Linux: 1024 [256–32768] 4 KB pages	Specifies the amount of memory (in 4 KB pages) that the operating system is to allocate for each DB2 agent thread stack.
agentpri	No	None	Windows: -1 (system) [0–6] Linux: -1 (system) [1–99] AIX: -1 (system) [41–125]	Specifies the execution priority that the operating system scheduler is to give, both to all agents and to other DB2 database manager instance processes and threads. This parameter is deprecated, and the recommendation is to use Workload Manager (WLM) dispatcher capability instead.
alt_diagpath	Yes	None	NULL [Any Valid Path]	Specifies a fully qualified alternate path for DB2 diagnostic information to use when the diagpath is unavailable.
alternate_auth_enc	No	Low	NOT_SPECIFIED [AES_CMP; AES_ONLY]	Specifies the alternate encryption algorithm to encrypt the user ID and password combination submitted to DB2 database server for authentication, especially when the authentication on the server is set to SERVER_ENCRYPT and no effect when it is set to DATA_ENCRYPT.
aslheapsz	No	High	15 [1–524288] 4 KB pages	Specifies the amount of memory (in 4 KB pages) to share between a local client application and a DB2 database manager agent. The application support layer heap represents a communication buffer between the local application and its associated agent. This buffer is allocated as shared memory by each DB2 database manager agent that is started.
audit_buf_sz	No	High	0 [0–65,000] 4 KB pages	Specifies the amount of memory (in 4 KB pages) to use to store audit records that are generated by the audit facility. If this parameter is set to 0, no audit buffer is used.

Table 2.5: DB2 database manager instance configuration parameters (continued)				
Parameter	**Config Online**	**Performance Impact**	**Default and Value Range**	**Description**
authentication	No	Low	SERVER [CLIENT, SERVER, SERVER_ ENCRYPT, KERBEROS, KRB_SERVER_ENCRYPT, DATA_ENCRYPT, DATA_ENCRYPT_CMP, GSSPLUGIN, GSS_ SERVER_ENCRYPT]	Specifies how and where user authentication takes place. If this parameter is set to CLIENT, authentication occurs at the client workstation; if this parameter is set to SERVER, the user ID and password are sent from the client workstation to the server workstation so that authentication can occur the server. The value SERVER_ ENCRYPT provides the same behavior as SERVER, except that any passwords sent over the network are encrypted. A value of DATA_ENCRYPT means the server accepts encrypted SERVER authentication schemes and user data is encrypted.
cf_diaglevel	No	None	2 [1–4] 0: No diagnostic data being captured 1: Severe errors only 2: All errors 3: All errors and warning messages 4: All error, warning and informational messages	Specifies the type of diagnostic errors that will be captured in the cfdiag*.log file in the pureScale® cluster caching facility (CF) servers.
cf_diagpath	No	None	$INSTHOME/sqllib/ db2dump/$m [Any Valid Path]	Specifies the fully qualified path for the diagnostic information file for the CF in the pureScale environment.
cf_mem_sz	No	High	AUTOMATIC [32768–4 294 967 295] 4 KB pages	Specifies the total amount of memory that the CF uses. The memory allocates when CF starts and de-allocates when it stops. When the parameter is set to AUTOMATIC, typically the system allocates 70 percent–90 percent of the available memory to CF.

Table 2.5: DB2 database manager instance configuration parameters (continued)				
Parameter	**Config Online**	**Performance Impact**	**Default and Value Range**	**Description**
cf_num_conns	Yes	High	AUTOMATIC [4–256]	Specifies the size of the CF connection pool. When this parameter is set to AUTOMATIC, the DB2 database manager creates an initial number of CF connections based on the number of worker threads, number of connections per worker threads, and number of member in the cluster.
cf_num_workers	No	High	AUTOMATIC [1–31]	Specifies the total number of worker threads on the CF. When this parameter is set to AUTOMATIC, the parameter value is configured to be one less than the number of available processors on the CF. To calculate the number of worker threads assigned to each cluster interconnect interface, divide the total number of CF worker threads by the number of communication adapter ports defined for the CF.
catalog_noauth	Yes	None	NO [YES, NO]	Specifies whether users without System Administrator (SYSADM) authority are allowed to catalog and uncatalog nodes, databases, or DCS and ODBC directories.
clnt_krb_plugin	No	None	NULL on Linux/UNIX and IBMkrb5 on Windows servers [Any valid string is acceptable]	Specifies the name of the default Kerberos plug-in library to use for client-side authentication and local authorization. This plug-in library is used when the client is authenticated using KERBEROS authentication.
clnt_pw_plugin	No	None	NULL [Any valid character string is acceptable]	Specifies the name of the User ID–Password plug-in library to use for client-side authentication and local authorization. This plug-in library is used when the client is authenticated using CLIENT, SERVER, SERVER_ENCRYPT, DATA_ENCRYPT, or DATA_ENCRYPT_CMP authentication.

Table 2.5: DB2 database manager instance configuration parameters (continued)

Parameter	Config Online	Performance Impact	Default and Value Range	Description
cluster_mgr	No	None	No default value [Set to TSA in pureScale and Tivoli System Automation (TSA)-enabled high-availability (HA) systems]	Specifies the cluster manager name for the database manager to communicate incremental cluster configuration changes.
comm_bandwidth	Yes	Medium	-1 [0.1–100,000] MB per second	Specifies the calculated value for the communications bandwidth (in MB per second) the DB2 optimizer is to use to estimate the cost of performing certain SQL operations between the database partition servers of a partitioned database system.
comm_exit_list	No	Low	NULL [Any valid string]	Specifies the list of communication buffer exit libraries that DB2 will use. A communication buffer exit library is a dynamically loaded library that vendor applications can use to gain access to and examine DB2 communication buffers used to communicate with client applications.
conn_elapse	Yes	Medium	10 [0–100] seconds	Specifies the number of seconds within to establish a TCP/IP connection between two nodes. If a connection is not established within the time specified by this parameter, other attempts are made up to the number of times specified by the max_connretries parameter; if all attempts made fail, an error is returned. This parameter is applicable when DB2 is running in pureScale and DPF system.
cpuspeed	Yes	High	-1 [10-10 –1] milliseconds	Specifies the speed of the CPU, in milliseconds per instruction, being used by the workstation or the server on which DB2 has been installed.
dft_account_str	Yes	None	NULL [Any valid character string]	Specifies the default charge-back accounting string to use when connecting to DRDA® servers.
dft_mon_bufpool	Yes	Medium	OFF [ON, OFF]	Specifies the default value of the snapshot monitor's buffer pool switch.

Table 2.5: DB2 database manager instance configuration parameters (continued)

Parameter	Config Online	Performance Impact	Default and Value Range	Description
dft_mon_lock	Yes	Medium	OFF [ON, OFF]	Specifies the default value of the snapshot monitor's lock switch.
dft_mon_sort	Yes	Medium	OFF [ON, OFF]	Specifies the default value of the snapshot monitor's sort switch.
dft_mon_stmt	Yes	Medium	OFF [ON, OFF]	Specifies the default value of the snapshot monitor's statement switch.
dft_mon_table	Yes	Medium	OFF [ON, OFF]	Specifies the default value of the snapshot monitor's table switch.
dft_mon_timestamp	Yes	Medium	OFF [ON, OFF]	Specifies the default value of the snapshot monitor's timestamp switch.
dft_mon_uow	Yes	Medium	OFF [ON, OFF]	Specifies the default value of the snapshot monitor's unit of work (UOW) switch.
dftdbpath	Yes	None	By default on UNIX, the home directory of the instance, and on Windows, the drive on which database system is installed [Any valid path]	Specifies the default drive (Windows) or directory path (UNIX) to use to store new databases. If no path is specified when a database is created, the database is created in the location identified by this parameter.
diaglevel	Yes	Low	3 [0–4] 0: Critical errors, event and administration notification messages 1: Severe, critical, event and administration notification messages 2: All errors, event and administration notification messages 3: All errors, warnings, event and administration notification messages 4: All errors, warnings, informational, event and administration messages	Specifies the type of diagnostic errors that will be recorded in the database administration notification log file and the DB2 diagnostics log file (db2diag.log).
diagpath	Yes	None	$INSTHOME/sqllib/db2dump [Any valid path]	Specifies the fully qualified path where DB2 diagnostic information is to be stored.
diagsize	No	Low	0 [2–free space on the file system] in MB	Specifies the maximum sizes of the diagnostic log and administration notification log files.

Table 2.5: DB2 database manager instance configuration parameters (continued)				
Parameter	**Config Online**	**Performance Impact**	**Default and Value Range**	**Description**
dir_cache	No	Medium	YES [YES, NO]	Specifies whether directory cache support is enabled. If this parameter is set to YES, then node, database, and DCS directory files are cached in memory. This reduces connect overhead by eliminating directory file I/O and minimizing the directory searches required to retrieve directory information.
discover	No	Medium	SEARCH [DISABLE, KNOWN, SEARCH]	Specifies the type of DB2 discovery requests that are supported. If this parameter is set to SEARCH, then search discovery, in which the DB2 client searches the network for DB2 databases, is supported. If this parameter is set to KNOWN, then known discovery, in which the discovery request is issued against the administration server specified by the user, is supported. If this parameter is set to DISABLE, the workstation will not respond to any type of discovery request.
discover_inst	Yes	Low	ENABLE [ENABLE, DISABLE]	Specifies whether this instance can be detected by DB2 discovery requests.
fcm_num_buffers	Yes	Medium	32-bit platforms: AUTOMATIC [895–65,300] buffers 64-bit platforms: AUTOMATIC [895–524,288] buffers	Specifies the number of 4 KB buffers to use for internal communications (messages) both among and within database servers. When set to AUTOMATIC, FCM monitors resource usage and incrementally releases resources if they are not used within 30 minutes. If the database manager cannot allocate the number of resources specified when an instance is started, it scales back the configuration values incrementally until it can start the instance.

Table 2.5: DB2 database manager instance configuration parameters (continued)				
Parameter	**Config Online**	**Performance Impact**	**Default and Value Range**	**Description**
fcm_num_ channels	Yes	Medium	32-bit platforms: AUTOMATIC [128–20,000] 64-bit platforms: AUTOMATIC [128–524,288]	Specifies the number of channels to use for internal communications (messages) both among and within database servers. An FCM channel represents a logical communication end point between EDUs running in the DB2 engine. When set to AUTOMATIC, FCM monitors channel usage, incrementally allocating and releasing resources as requirements change.
fcm_parallelism	No	High	1 [1–8]	Specifies the degree of parallelism to use for communication between the members within an instance. This parameter determines the number of sender and receiver fast communication manager channel pairs.
fed_noauth	Yes	None	NO [YES, NO]	Specifies whether to bypass authentication at the instance because authentication will happen at the data source. When fed_noauth is set to YES, authentication is set to SERVER or SERVER_ENCRYPT, and federated is set to YES, then authentication at the instance is bypassed.
federated	Yes	Medium	NO [YES, NO] Default: NO	Specifies whether federated database object support is enabled (i.e., whether applications can submit distributed requests for data being managed by DB2 Family and Oracle database management systems).
federated_async	Yes	Medium	0 [0–32 767, -1, ANY]	Specifies the maximum number of Asynchronous Table Queues (ATQs) in the access plan that the federated server supports. When -1 or ANY is specified, the optimizer determines the number of ATQs for the access plan.

Table 2.5: DB2 database manager instance configuration parameters (continued)				
Parameter	**Config Online**	**Performance Impact**	**Default and Value Range**	**Description**
fenced_pool	Yes	Medium	-1, [AUTOMATIC [-1, 0–64 000]]	Specifies the maximum number of fenced processes or threads that may reside at the database server. Once this limit is reached, no new fenced requests may be invoked.
group_plugin	No	None	NULL [Any valid character string]	Specifies the name of the group plug-in library to use for all group lookups.
health_mon	Yes	Low	ON [ON, OFF]	Specifies whether to monitor the health of the instance and database objects that have been configured in the Health Center. When turned on, the DB2 Health Monitor collects information from these objects and takes actions when an object is considered unhealthy. The monitor can be started and stopped dynamically by modifying the switch setting.
indexrec	Yes	Medium	RESTART [RESTART, RESTART_NO_REDO ACCESS, ACCESS_NO_ REDO]	Specifies when the DB2 database manager will attempt to rebuild invalid indexes and whether to redo any index build during roll-forward or HADR log replay on the standby database. This parameter is used only if the database configuration parameter indexrec is set to SYSTEM.
instance_memory	Yes	Medium	AUTOMATIC [0–68 719 476 736] 4 KB pages	Specifies the amount of memory to reserve for instance management, including memory areas that describe the database under the instance's control. The memory allocated by this parameter establishes the maximum number of databases that can be active at the same time and the maximum number of agents that can be active at any given time. If this parameter is set to AUTOMATIC, DB2 will calculate the amount of instance memory needed for the current configuration.

Table 2.5: DB2 database manager instance configuration parameters (continued)

Parameter	Config Online	Performance Impact	Default and Value Range	Description
intra_parallel	No	High	NO [SYSTEM, YES, NO]	Specifies whether the DB2 database manager instance can use intrapartition parallelism.
java_heap_sz	No	High	2048 [0–524 288] 4 KB pages	Specifies the maximum amount of memory (in pages) the Java interpreter is to use to service Java DB2 stored procedures and UDFs.
jdk_path	No	None	Default Java install path $INSTHOME/sqllib/java/jdk64 [Any valid character string]	Specifies the directory under which the Software Developer's Kit (SDK) for Java, to be used for running Java stored procedures and UDFs, is installed. CLASSPATH and other environment variables the Java interpreter uses are computed using the value of this parameter.
keepfenced	No	Medium	YES [YES, NO]	Specifies whether to keep a fenced process after a fenced call is completed. If this parameter is set to NO, a new fenced process is created and destroyed for each fenced invocation; if set to YES, a fenced process is reused for subsequent fenced calls.
local_gssplugin	No	None	NULL [Any valid character string]	Specifies the name of the default GSS API plug-in library to use for instance-level local authorization when the value of the authentication database manager configuration parameter is set to GSSPLUGIN or GSS_SERVER_ENCRYPT.
max_connections	Yes	Medium	-1 and AUTOMATIC [1–64,000]	Specifies the maximum number of client application connections that can be connected to the instance.
max_connretries	Yes	Medium	5 [0–100]	Specifies the maximum number of times to make an attempt to establish a network connection between the two members (i.e., pureScale and DPF systems).

Table 2.5: DB2 database manager instance configuration parameters (continued)				
Parameter	**Config Online**	**Performance Impact**	**Default and Value Range**	**Description**
max_coordagents	Yes	Medium	200, AUTOMATIC [-1, 0-64 000]	Specifies the maximum number of coordinating agents that can exist on a node at one time. Use this parameter to limit the number of coordinating agents or to control the workload in a database.
max_querydegree	Yes	High	ANY [1–32 767]	Specifies the maximum degree of intrapartition parallelism to use for any SQL statement executing on this instance of the DB2 database manager.
max_time_diff	No	Medium	60 [1–1 440] minutes	Specifies the maximum time difference, in minutes, to permit among the system clocks of the database partition servers listed in the db2nodes.cfg file.
mon_heap_sz	Yes	Low	AUTOMATIC [0–60 000] 4 KB pages	Specifies the amount of memory (in 4 KB pages) to allocate for database system monitor data.
nodetype	None	Informational	N/A	Is read-only. Provides information about the DB2 products that you have installed on your machine.
notifylevel	Yes	Low	3 [0–4]	Specifies the type of administration notification messages to write to the administration notification log. For Windows NT®, notifications are written to the Windows NT event log. For all other operating systems and node types, notifications are written to the notification file instance. nfy. DB2, the Health Monitor, the Capture and Apply programs, and user applications can write notifications.
num_initagents	No	Medium	0 [0–64 000]	Specifies the initial number of idle agents to create in the agent pool when the DB2 database manager is started.

Table 2.5: DB2 database manager instance configuration parameters (continued)

Parameter	Config Online	Performance Impact	Default and Value Range	Description
num_initfenced	No	Medium	0 [0–64 000]	Specifies the initial number of idle, nonthreaded, fenced processes to create in the fenced pool when the DB2 database manager is started. This parameter can reduce the initial startup time required for running nonthread safe C and COBOL routines.
num_poolagents	Yes	High	100, AUTOMATIC [-1, 0–64 000]	Specifies the size to allow the idle agent pool to grow.
numdb	No	Low	32 [1–256]	Specifies the maximum number of local databases that can be active—that is, that can have applications connected to them at one time.
release	None	Informational	N/A	Is read-only. Specifies the release level of the DB2 database manager configuration file.
resync_interval	No	None	180 [1–60 000] seconds	Specifies the time interval in seconds after which a Transaction Manager (TM), Resource Manager (RM), or Sync Point Manager (SPM) should retry to recover any outstanding in-doubt transactions found in the TM, RM, or SPM. Use this parameter value only when transactions are running in a distributed unit of work (DUOW) environment.
rqrioblk	No	High	32 767 [4096–65 535] bytes	Specifies the size in bytes of the buffer to use for communication between remote applications and their corresponding database agents on the database server.
sheapthres	No	High	0 [250–2 147 483 647] 4 KB pages	Specifies the instance-wide soft limit on the total amount of memory in 4 KB pages to make available for sorting operations.
spm_log_file_sz	No	Low	256 [4–1 000] 4 KB pages	Specifies the size in 4 KB pages of the SPM log file.
spm_log_path	No	Medium	NULL [Any valid character string]	Specifies the directory where SPM log files are to be written.

Table 2.5: DB2 database manager instance configuration parameters (continued)				
Parameter	**Config Online**	**Performance Impact**	**Default and Value Range**	**Description**
spm_max_resync	No	Low	20 [10–256]	Specifies the number of agents that can simultaneously perform resynchronization operations.
spm_name	No	None	Derived from TCP/ IP hostname [Any valid character string]	Specifies the name of the SPM instance that the DB2 database manager is to use.
srvcon_auth	No	None	NULL [CLIENT, SERVER, SERVER_ENCRYPT, DATA_ENCRYPT, DATA_ENCRYPT_CMP, KERBEROS, KRB_ SERVER_ENCRYPT, GSSPLUGIN, GSS_ SERVER_ENCRYPT]	Specifies how and where user authentication is to occur when handling incoming connections at the server. Use this parameter to override the current authentication type.
srvcon_gssplugin_ list	No	None	NULL [Any valid character string]	Specifies the GSS API plug-in libraries that the database server supports. If the authentication type is GSSPLUGIN and this parameter is NULL, an error is returned; if the authentication type is KERBEROS and this parameter is NULL, the DB2-supplied Kerberos module or library is used.
srv_plugin_mode	No	None	UNFENCED	Specifies whether to run plug-ins in fenced mode or unfenced mode. At this time, unfenced mode is the only supported mode.
srvcon_pw_plugin	No	None	NULL [Any valid character string]	Specifies the name of the default User ID–Password plug-in library to use for server-side authentication. By default, the DB2-supplied User ID–Password plug-in library will be used if no other library is specified.
ssl_svr_keydb	No	None	NULL [Any valid path; GSK_ MS_CERTIFICATE_STORE]	Specifies the key file to use for SSL setup at server-side. To avail the SSL support, it is mandatory to set the DB2COMM registry variable to SSL.
ssl_svr_stash	No	None	NULL [Any valid path]	Specifies a fully qualified file path of the stash file to use for SSL setup at server-side.
ssl_svr_label	No	None	NULL	Specifies a label of the personal certificate of the server in the key database.

Table 2.5: DB2 database manager instance configuration parameters (continued)				
Parameter	**Config Online**	**Performance Impact**	**Default and Value Range**	**Description**
ssl_svcename	No	None	NULL [Any valid string]	Specifies the name of the port that a database server will use to await communications from remote client nodes using SSL protocol. Set this parameter to the service name associated with the main connection port so that when the database server is started, it can determine on which port to listen for incoming connection requests.
ssl_cipherspecs	No	None	NULL [Multiple cipher specifications]	Specifies the cipher suites that the server allows for incoming connection requests when using SSL protocol.
ssl_versions	No	None	NULL [TLSV1, TLSV12]	Specifies SSL and Transport Layer Security (TLS) versions that the server supports for incoming connection requests.
ssl_clnt_keydb	No	None	NULL [Any valid path; GSK_ MS_CERTIFICATE_STORE]	Specifies the key file to use for SSL setup at the client-side.
ssl_clnt_stash	No	None	NULL [Any valid path]	Specifies a fully qualified file path of the stash file to use for SSL setup at the client-side.
start_stop_time	Yes	Low	10 [1–1 440] minutes	Specifies the time, in minutes, in which all nodes of a partitioned database must respond to DB2START, DB2STOP, and ADD DBPARTITIONNUM commands.
svcename	No	None	NULL [Any valid string]	Specifies the name of the TCP/IP port that a database server will use to await communications from remote client nodes. Set this parameter to the service name associated with the main connection port so that when the database server is started, it can determine on which port to listen for incoming connection requests.
sysadm_group	No	None	NULL [Any valid character string]	Specifies the group name that has System Administrator (SYSADM) authority for the DB2 database manager instance.

Table 2.5: DB2 database manager instance configuration parameters (continued)

Parameter	Config Online	Performance Impact	Default and Value Range	Description
sysctrl_group	No	None	NULL [Any valid character string]	Specifies the group name that has System Control (SYSCTRL) authority for the DB2 database manager instance.
sysmaint_group	No	None	NULL [Any valid character string]	Specifies the group name that has System Maintenance (SYSMAINT) authority for the DB2 database manager instance.
sysmon_group	No	None	NULL [Any valid character string]	Specifies the group name that has System Monitor (SYSMON) authority for the DB2 database manager instance.
tm_database	No	None	1ST_CONN [Any valid database name]	Specifies the name of the TM database for each DB2 database manager instance. The TM database is a special database that is used as a logger and coordinator and to perform recovery for in-doubt transactions.
tp_mon_name	No	None	CICS, MQ, ENCINA, CB, SF, TUXEDO, TOPEND, blank, or Any valid character string	Specifies the name of the transaction processing (TP) monitor product being used.
trust_allclnts	No	None	YES [YES, NO, DRDAONLY]	Specifies whether all clients are treated as trusted clients. If set to YES, the server assumes that a level of security is available at the client and the possibility that users can be validated at the client. If set to DRDAONLY, the server assumes that a level of security is available at the client only if the client is DB2 for OS/390 and z/OS, DB2 for VM and VSE, or DB2 for OS/400.
trust_clntauth	No	None	CLIENT [CLIENT, SERVER]	Specifies whether a trusted client is authenticated at the server or the client when the client provides a user ID and password combination for a connection.

Table 2.5: DB2 database manager instance configuration parameters (continued)				
Parameter	**Config Online**	**Performance Impact**	**Default and Value Range**	**Description**
util_impact_lim	Yes	High	10 [1–100] percentage	Specifies the percentage that the execution of a throttled utility will impact a database workload. For example, a value of 10 indicates that a throttled backup operation will not impact the current database workload by more than 10 percent.
wlm_dispatcher	Yes	Medium	NO [NO, YES]	Specifies the CPU scheduling capabilities at the service-class level in the DB2 database manager by using shares-based allocation of CPU resources or CPU limits, or both.
wlm_disp_concur	Yes	Low	COMPUTED [COMPUTED, Manually set value between 1–32 767] number of concurrent threads	Specifies how the DB2 WLM dispatcher sets the thread concurrency level.
wlm_disp_cpu_shares	Yes	Low	NO [NO, YES]	Specifies the controlling behavior of CPU shares by the DB2 WLM dispatcher. When both wlm_dispatcher and wlm_disp_cpu_shares are set to NO, no service class management will be activated. Setting wlm_dispatcher to YES and wlm_disp_cpu_shares to NO activates only CPU limiting capabilities in service class management; setting both parameters to YES enables both CPU limits and sharing capabilities.
wlm_disp_min_util	Yes	Low	5 [0–100] percentage	Specifies the minimum amount of CPU utilization that is necessary to include a service class in the DB2 WLM-managed sharing of CPU resources.
Adapted from Chapter 23 of *Database Administration Concepts and Configuration Reference Manual (DB2 10.1)*				

You can display the contents of the DB2 database manager configuration file for a particular instance by attaching to the instance and executing the GET DATABASE MANAGER CONFIGURATION command.

The syntax for this command is:

```
GET [DATABASE MANAGER | DB MANAGER | DBM]
[CONFIGURATION | CONFIG | CFG]
<SHOW DETAIL>
```

Thus, to view the contents of the DB2 database manager configuration file for the current instance, you execute a GET DATABASE MANAGER CONFIGURATION command:

```
GET DBM CFG
```

You can change the value assigned to a particular DB2 database manager configuration file parameter by attaching to the instance and executing the UPDATE DATABASE MANAGER CONFIGURATION command. The syntax for this command is:

```
UPDATE [DATABASE MANAGER | DB MANAGER | DBM]
[CONFIGURATION | CONFIG | CFG]
USING [[Parameter] [Value] |
       [Parameter] [Value] AUTOMATIC |
       [Parameter] AUTOMATIC |
       [Parameter] MANUAL ,...]
<IMMEDIATE | DEFERRED>
```

where:

Parameter	Identifies one or more DB2 database manager configuration parameters (by keyword) whose values are to be modified; (often, the keyword for a parameter is the same as the parameter name itself)
Value	Identifies the new value or values to assign to the specified DB2 database manager configuration parameters

If the AUTOMATIC keyword is specified as the value for a particular parameter, DB2 will automatically adjust the parameter value to reflect the current resource requirements. (Refer to Table 2.5 to identify the configuration parameters that you can set using the AUTOMATIC keyword.) If you specify a value along with the AUTOMATIC keyword, that value may influence the automatic calculations performed.

If you specify the DEFERRED clause with the UPDATE DATABASE MANAGER CONFIGURATION command, changes made to the DB2 database manager configuration file will not take effect until the instance is stopped and restarted. Specifying the IMMEDIATE clause instead, or specifying neither clause, will make all changes to the DB2 database manager configuration file take effect immediately—provided that the necessary resources are available. You can use GET DBM CFG SHOW DETAIL command with an instance attachment to see any pending database manager configuration parameter changes.

So if you want to configure the current instance such that the maximum number of application connections that can be executing concurrently at any given point in time is 200, execute an UPDATE DATABASE MANAGER CONFIGURATION command:

```
UPDATE DBM CFG USING MAX_COORDAGENTS 200
```

Or to specify the name of the TCP/IP port that the current instance is to use to receive communications from remote clients, you execute an UPDATE DATABASE MANAGER CONFIGURATION command that looks like this:

```
UPDATE DBM CFG USING SVCENAME db2c_db2inst1
```

The values assigned to all DB2 database manager configuration file parameters can be returned to their factory settings by attaching to the appropriate instance and executing the RESET DATABASE MANAGER CONFIGURATION command. The syntax for this command is:

```
RESET [DATABASE MANAGER | DB MANAGER | DBM]
[CONFIGURATION | CONFIG | CFG]
```

Thus, if you want to return the DB2 database manager configuration file parameters for the current instance to their system default settings, execute a RESET DATABASE MANAGER CONFIGURATION command:

```
RESET DBM CFG
```

You can also view or alter the contents of a DB2 database manager configuration file by using the configure dialog in the IBM Data Studio Administration Explorer. Figure 2.3 shows the IBM Data Studio menu item that you must select to open the database manager Configuration wizard.

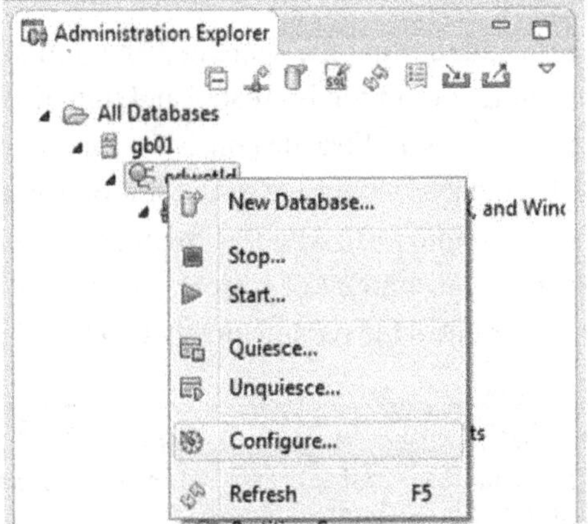

Figure 2.3: Invoking the Configure wizard from IBM Data Studio

Figure 2.4 displays how this wizard might look after it has been opened to view or modify the configuration parameters.

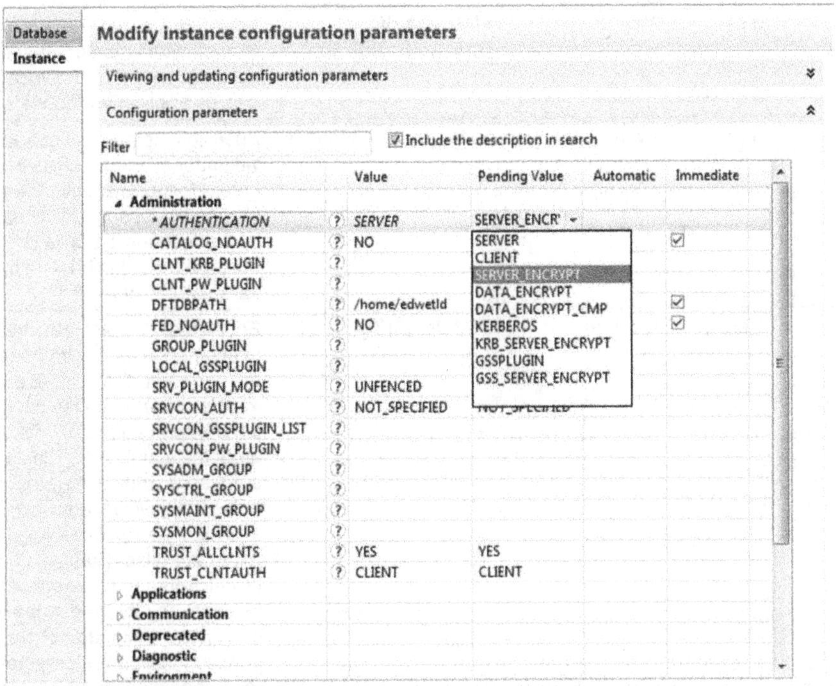

Figure 2.4: Altering the database manager configuration parameter via IBM Data Studio

The DB2 Database Configuration

Just as a DB2 database manager configuration file is created and initialized whenever a new instance is created, a database configuration file is created and initialized each time a new database is created. Each database configuration file consists of approximately 117 different parameters, and just as most DB2 database manager configuration parameters control the amount of system resources to allocate to a single DB2 database manager instance, many of the database configuration file parameters control the amount of system resources to allocate to a database during normal operation. Table 2.6 shows the parameters that make up a database configuration file.

Table 2.6: DB2 database configuration parameters

Parameter	Config Online	Performance Impact	Default and Value Range	Description
alt_collate	No	None	NULL [IDENTITY_16BIT]	Specifies the collating sequence to use for Unicode tables in a non-Unicode database.
applheapsz	Yes	Medium	AUTOMATIC [16–60 000] 4 KB pages	Specifies the total amount of application memory that the entire application can consume.
appl_memory	Yes	Medium	AUTOMATIC [128–4 294 967 295]	Specifies the maximum amount of application memory that DB2 database agents can allocate to service application requests.
archretrydelay	Yes	None	20 [0–65 535] seconds	Specifies the number of seconds to wait after a failed archive attempt before trying to archive the log file again. Subsequent retries will take effect only if the value of the numarchretry database configuration parameter is at least 1.
auto_maint	Yes	Medium	ON [ON, OFF]	Enables or disables automatic maintenance for the database. This is the parent of all the other automatic maintenance database configuration parameters (auto_db_backup, auto_tbl_maint, auto_runstats, auto_stats_prof, auto_stmt_stats, auto_stats_views, auto_prof_upd, and auto_reorg). Disabling this parameter also disables all of its children parameters, but their settings, as recorded in the database configuration file, do not change; enabling this parent parameter causes recorded values for its children parameters to take effect.
auto_db_backup	Yes	Medium	ON [ON, OFF]	Enables or disables automatic backup operations for the database.

Table 2.6: DB2 database configuration parameters (continued)

Parameter	Config Online	Performance Impact	Default and Value Range	Description
auto_tbl_maint	Yes	Medium	ON [ON, OFF]	Enables or disables automatic table maintenance operations for the database. This parameter is the parent of all table maintenance parameters (auto_runstats, auto_stats_prof, auto_prof_upd, and auto_reorg). Disabling this parameter also disables all of its children parameters, but their settings, as recorded in the database configuration file, do not change; enabling this parent parameter causes recorded values for its children parameters to take effect.
auto_runstats	Yes	Medium	ON [ON, OFF]	Enables or disables automatic table RUNSTATS operations for the database.
auto_stats_prof	Yes	Medium	ON [ON, OFF]	Enables or disables automatic statistical profile generation for the database.
auto_stmt_stats	Yes	Medium	ON [ON, OFF]	Enables or disables collection of real-time statistics.
auto_stats_views	Yes	Medium	ON [ON, OFF]	Enables or disables automatic statistics collection on statistical views.
auto_prof_upd	Yes	Medium	ON [ON, OFF]	Enables or disables automatic RUNSTATS profile updating for the database.
auto_reorg	Yes	Medium	ON [ON, OFF]	Enables or disables automatic table and index reorganization for the database.
auto_sampling	Yes	Medium	OFF [ON, OFF]	Controls whether automatic statistics collection uses sampling when collecting statistics for a large table. To enable automatic sampling, set auto_maint, auto_tbl_maint, auto_runstats and auto_sampling to ON.
auto_del_rec_obj	Yes	Medium	OFF [ON, OFF]	Specifies whether to delete database log files, backup images, and load copy images when their associated recovery history file entry is pruned.
autorestart	Yes	Low	ON [ON, OFF]	Specifies whether the database manager will automatically initiate crash recovery when a user connects to a database that previously terminated abnormally.

Table 2.6: DB2 database configuration parameters (continued)				
Parameter	**Config Online**	**Performance Impact**	**Default and Value Range**	**Description**
auto_reval	Yes	Medium	DEFERRED [IMMEDIATE, DISABLED, DEFERRED, DEFERRED_FORCE]	Controls the revalidation and invalidation semantics for all dependent objects.
avg_appls	Yes	High	AUTOMATIC [1–MAXAPPLS]	Specifies the average number of active applications that normally access the database. The SQL optimizer uses this parameter to help estimate how much buffer pool memory will be available for the chosen access plan at application run time.
blk_log_dsk_ful	Yes	None	NO [YES, NO]	Specifies whether applications should hang whenever the DB2 database manager encounters a log-full error. This configuration parameter can be set to prevent disk-full errors from being generated when DB2 cannot create a new log file in the active log location.
blocknonlogged	Yes	None	NO [YES, NO]	Specifies whether the database manager will allow tables to have the NOT LOGGED or NOT LOGGED INITIALLY attributes activated.
catalogcache_sz	Yes	Medium	-1 [MAXAPPLS*5, 8–524 288]	Specifies the amount of memory (in pages) to use to cache system catalog information.
chngpgs_thresh	No	High	60 [5–99]	Specifies the level (percentage) of changed pages at which the asynchronous page cleaners will be started, if they are not currently active.
connect_proc	Yes	None	NULL [<SCHEMA>.<PROCEDURE>]	Specifies a two-part connect procedure to execute every time an application connects to the database.
cur_commit	No	Medium	ON [ON, AVAILABLE, DISABLED]	Specifies the data scan behavior while using a cursor stability isolation level. Three registry variables (DB2_EVALUNCOMMITTED, DB2_SKIPDELETED, and DB2_SKIPINSERTED) are affected, and these registry variables are ignored when USE CURRENTLY COMMITTED or WAIT FOR OUTCOME are specified explicitly on the BIND or at statement prepare time.

Table 2.6: DB2 database configuration parameters (continued)				
Parameter	**Config Online**	**Performance Impact**	**Default and Value Range**	**Description**
database_ memory	Yes	Medium	AUTOMATIC [COMPUTED, 0–4 294 967 295] 4 KB pages	Specifies the minimum amount of shared memory to reserve for the database's shared memory region. If this parameter is set to AUTOMATIC, DB2 will calculate the amount of memory needed for the database and allocate it at database activation time.
dbheap	Yes	Medium	AUTOMATIC [32–524 288] 4 KB pages	Specifies the size, in pages, of the database heap, which is used to hold control information on all open cursors accessing the database. Both log buffers and catalog cache buffers are allocated from the database heap.
db_mem_thresh	Yes	Low	10 [0–100]	Specifies the maximum percentage of committed, but currently unused, database shared memory that the DB2 database manager will allow before starting to release committed pages of memory back to the operating system.
decflt_rounding	No	None	ROUND_HALF_EVEN [ROUND_CEILING, ROUND_FLOOR, ROUND_HALF_UP, ROUND_DOWN]	Specifies the rounding mode for floating point. This parameter affects decimal floating-point operations in the server and in LOAD.
dec_to_char_fmt	Yes	Medium	NEW [NEW, V95]	Controls the result of the CHAR scalar function and the CAST specification for converting decimal to character values.
dft_degree	Yes	Medium	1 [-1(ANY), 1–32 767]	Specifies the default value for the CURRENT DEGREE special register and the DEGREE bind option.
dft_extent_sz	Yes	Medium	32 [2–256] pages	Specifies the default extent size (in pages) to use when new table spaces are created if no extent size is specified.
dft_loadrec_ses	Yes	Medium	1 [1–30 000]	Specifies the default number of sessions to use during the recovery of a table load.
dft_mttb_types	No	None	SYSTEM [ALL, NONE, FEDERATED_TOOL, SYSTEM, USER, or a list of values]	Specifies the default value for the CURRENT MAINTAINED TABLE TYPES FOR OPTIMIZATION special register. The value of this register determines the types of refresh deferred MQTs to use during query optimization.

Table 2.6: DB2 database configuration parameters (continued)				
Parameter	**Config Online**	**Performance Impact**	**Default and Value Range**	**Description**
dft_prefetch_sz	Yes	Medium	AUTOMATIC [0–32 767] 4 KB pages	Specifies the default prefetch size (in pages) to use when new table spaces are created if no prefetch size is specified.
dft_queryopt	Yes	Medium	5 [0–9]	Specifies the default query optimization class to use when neither the SET CURRENT QUERY OPTIMIZATION statement nor the QUERYOPT option on the bind command is used. The query optimization class is used to direct the DB2 optimizer to use different degrees of optimization when compiling SQL queries and XQuery expressions.
dft_refresh_age	No	Medium	0 [0, 99999999999999 (ANY)] seconds	Specifies the default value to use for the refresh age of summary tables if the CURRENT REFRESH AGE special register has not been set. Use this parameter to determine whether summary tables are to be considered when optimizing the processing of dynamic SQL queries.
dft_schemas_dcc	Yes	Medium	No [Yes, No]	Controls the default setting for DATA CAPTURE CHANGES on newly created schemas for replication purposes. When set to YES, all newly created schemas by default will have the DATA CAPTURE CHANGES clause.
dft_sqlmathwarn	No	None	NO [Yes, No]	Specifies whether to handle arithmetic errors and retrieval conversion errors as errors or as warnings during SQL statement compilation.
discover_db	Yes	Medium	ENABLE [DISABLE, ENABLE]	Specifies whether to return information about the database when a DB2 Discovery request is received at the server.
dlchktime	Yes	Medium	10 000 [1 000–600 000]milliseconds	Specifies the frequency with which the DB2 database manager checks for deadlocks among all applications connected to the database.
enable_xmlchar	Yes	None	Yes [Yes, No]	Specifies whether XMLPARSE operations can be performed on non-BIT DATA CHAR (or CHAR-type) expressions in an SQL statement.

Table 2.6: DB2 database configuration parameters (continued)				
Parameter	**Config Online**	**Performance Impact**	**Default and Value Range**	**Description**
failarchpath	Yes	None	NULL [Any valid path]	Specifies a path to which DB2 will try to archive log files if they cannot be archived to either the primary or the secondary (if set) archive destinations because of a media problem.
hadr_local_host	No	No	NULL [Any valid string]	Specifies the local host for HADR TCP communication. Use either a host name or an IP address.
hadr_local_svc	No	None	NULL [Any valid string]	Specifies the TCP service name or port number for which the local HADR process accepts connections.
hadr_peer_ window	No	Low	0 [0–4 294 967 295] seconds	Specifies how long (in seconds) the HADR primary-standby database pair continues to behave as though still in peer state when there is a connection problem between primary and standby servers. This parameter has no effect if hadr_syncmode is set to ASYNC, SUPERASYNC.
hadr_remote_ host	No	None	NULL [Any valid string]	Specifies the TCP/IP host name or IP address of the remote HADR node.
hadr_remote_inst	No	None	NULL [Any valid string]	Specifies the instance name of the remote server. Administration tools, such as the Control Center, use this parameter to contact the remote server; HADR also checks whether a remote database requesting a connection belongs to the declared remote instance.
hadr_remote_svc	No	None	NULL [Any valid string]	Specifies the TCP service name or port number that the HADR node will use.
hadr_replay_ delay	Yes	None	0 [0–2147483647] seconds	Specifies the number of seconds that must pass from the time that a transaction is committed on the primary database to the time that the transaction is committed on the standby database.
hadr_spool_limit	Yes	None	0 [-1–2 147 483 647] 4 KB pages	Specifies the maximum amount of log data that is allowed to be spooled to disk on HADR standby.
hadr_syncmode	No	None	NEARSYNC [ASYNC, SUPERASYNC, SYNC]	Specifies the synchronization mode, which determines how primary log writes are synchronized with the standby when the systems are in peer state.

Table 2.6: DB2 database configuration parameters (continued)				
Parameter	**Config Online**	**Performance Impact**	**Default and Value Range**	**Description**
hadr_target_list	Yes	None	NULL [Any valid string]	Specifies up to three target host:port pairs that act as HADR standby databases in the HADR multiple-standby setup.
hadr_timeout	No	None	120 [1–4 294 967 295] seconds	Specifies the time (in seconds) that the HADR process waits before considering a communication attempt to have failed.
indexrec	Yes	Medium	SYSTEM [SYSTEM, RESTART, RESTART_NO_ REDO, ACCESS, ACCESS_NO_REDO]	Specifies when the DB2 database manager will attempt to rebuild invalid indexes and whether to redo any index build during roll-forward or HADR log replay on the standby database.
locklist	Yes	High	AUTOMATIC [4–134217728] 4 KB pages	Specifies the maximum amount of memory (in pages) to allocate and use to hold the lock list.
locktimeout	No	Medium	-1 [-1; 0–32 767] seconds	Specifies the number of seconds that an application will wait to obtain a lock. Setting it to -1 designates an indefinite wait time.
log_appl_info	No	Low	No [Yes, No]	Specifies to write the application log record at the start of each update transaction.
log_ddl_stmts	Yes	None	NO [YES, NO]	Specifies to write additional information regarding DDL statements to the transaction log. Setting this to YES causes a replication program to capture changes from the log and use the captured information to replicate the DDL operation.
logarchcompr1	Yes	None	OFF [OFF, ON]	Specifies whether to compress the log files written to the primary archive destination for logs.
logarchcompr2	Yes	None	OFF [OFF, ON]	Specifies whether to compress the log files written to the secondary archive destination for logs.
logarchmeth1	Yes	None	OFF, LOGRETAIN, USEREXIT, DISK, TSM, VENDOR	Specifies the media type of the primary destination for archived log files and whether to use archival logging.

Table 2.6: DB2 database configuration parameters (continued)				
Parameter	**Config Online**	**Performance Impact**	**Default and Value Range**	**Description**
logarchmeth2	Yes	None	OFF, LOGRETAIN, USEREXIT, DISK, TSM, VENDOR	Specifies the media type of the secondary destination for archived logs. Specifying this path will archive log files to both this destination and the destination specified by the logarchmeth1 database configuration parameter.
logarchopt1	Yes	None	NULL [Any valid string]	Specifies the options field for the primary destination for archived logs.
logarchopt2	Yes	None	NULL [Any valid string]	Specifies the options field for the secondary destination for archived logs.
logbufsz	No	High	256 [4–131 070] 4 KB pages	Specifies the amount of memory (in pages) to use to buffer log records before they are written to disk.
logfilsiz	No	Medium	1000 [4–1 048 572] 4 KB pages	Specifies the amount of disk storage space (in pages) to allocate to log files that are used for data recovery. This parameter defines the size of each primary and secondary log file used.
logindexrebuild	Yes	None	OFF [ON, OFF]	Specifies whether to log index creation, recreation, or reorganization operations so that indexes can be reconstructed during DB2 roll-forward recovery operations or HADR log replay procedures.
logprimary	No	Medium	3 [2–256]	Specifies the number of primary log files to use for database recovery.
logsecond	Yes	Medium	10 [-1, 0–254]	Specifies the number of secondary log files to use for database recovery.
max_log	Yes	None	0 [0–100]	Specifies whether there is a limit to the percentage of log space that a transaction can consume and, if so, stipulates what that limit is.
maxappls	Yes	Medium	AUTOMATIC [1–60 000]	Specifies the maximum number of concurrent applications, both local and remote, that can connect to the database at one time. Setting this parameter to AUTOMATIC causes DB2 to dynamically allocate the resources it needs to support new applications.
maxfilop	Yes	Medium	61 440 [64–61 440]	Specifies the maximum number of file handles that a database agent can have open at one time.

Table 2.6: DB2 database configuration parameters (continued)				
Parameter	**Config Online**	**Performance Impact**	**Default and Value Range**	**Description**
maxlocks	Yes	High	AUTOMATIC [1–100]	Specifies a percentage of the lock list held by an application that must be filled before the DB2 database manager performs lock escalation.
min_dec_div_3	No	High	NO [YES, NO]	Specifies whether the results of decimal division arithmetic operations are to always have a scale of at least 3.
mirrorlogpath	No	Low	NULL [Any valid path]	Specifies the location to store a second copy of active log files.
mon_act_metrics	Yes	Medium	BASE [NONE, BASE, EXTENDED]	Controls the collection of activity metrics on the entire database and affects activities submitted by connections associated with any DB2 workload definitions.
mon_deadlock	Yes	Medium	WITHOUT_HIST [NONE, WITHOUT_ HIST, HISTORY, HIST_AND_VALUES]	Controls the generation of deadlock events at the database level for the lock event monitor.
mon_locktimeout	Yes	Medium	NONE [NONE, WITHOUT_HIST, HISTORY, HIST_ AND_VALUES]	Controls the generation of lock timeout events at the database level for the lock event monitor and affects all DB2 workload definitions.
mon_lockwait	Yes	Medium	NONE [NONE, WITHOUT_HIST, HISTORY, HIST_ AND_VALUES]	Controls the generation of lock wait events at the database level for the lock event monitor.
mon_lw_thresh	Yes	Medium	5000000 [1000 ... MAX_INT] microseconds	Controls the amount of time spent in lock wait before generating an event for mon_lockwait.
mon_lck_msg_lvl	Yes	None	1 [0–3]	Controls the logging of messages to the administration notification log when lock timeout, deadlock, and lock escalation events occur: Level 0: No Notification Level 1: Notification of lock escalation Level 2: Notification of lock escalation and deadlock Level 3: Notification of lock escalation, deadlock, and lock timeout
mon_obj_metrics	Yes	Medium	EXTENDED [NONE, BASE, EXTENDED]	Controls the collection of data object metrics on an entire database.
mon_pkglist_sz	Yes	Low	32 [0–1024] number of entries	Controls the maximum number of entries that can appear in the package listing per unit of work as captured by the unit of work event monitor.

Table 2.6: DB2 database configuration parameters (continued)				
Parameter	**Config Online**	**Performance Impact**	**Default and Value Range**	**Description**
mon_req_metrics	Yes	Medium	BASE [NONE, BASE, EXTENDED]	Controls the collection of request metrics on the entire database and affects requests executing in any DB2 service classes.
mon_uow_data	Yes	Medium	NONE [NONE, BASE]	Controls the generation of unit of work events at the database level for the unit of work event monitor and affects units of work on the data server. It is a parent parameter to the mon_uow_execlist and mon_uow_pkglist configuration parameters.
mon_uow_execlist	Yes	Medium	OFF [OFF, ON]	Controls the generation of unit of work events with executable ID listing information.
mon_uow_pkglist	Yes	Medium	OFF [OFF, ON]	Controls the generation of unit of work events with package listing information.
multipage_alloc	None	None	Yes	Is informational only. Specifies whether to allocate new storage for SMS table spaces one page at a time or one extent at a time.
newlogpath	No	Low	NULL [Any valid path]	Specifies an alternate path to use for storing recovery log files.
num_db_backup	Yes	None	12 [1–32 767]	Specifies the number of database backup images to retain for a database. (After the specified number of backups is reached, old backups are marked as expired in the recovery history file.)
num_freqvalues	Yes	Low	10 [0–32 767]	Specifies the number of the most frequent values to collect when the WITH DISTRIBUTION option is specified with the RUNSTATS command.
num_iocleaners	No	High	AUTOMATIC [0–255]	Specifies the number of asynchronous page cleaners that the database is to use.
num_ioservers	No	High	AUTOMATIC [1–255]	Specifies the number of I/O servers to use on behalf of database agents to perform prefetch I/O and asynchronous I/O needed by utilities such as backup and restore.
num_log_span	Yes	None	0 [0–65 535]	Specifies the number of active log files that a single active transaction can span.

Table 2.6: DB2 database configuration parameters (continued)

Parameter	Config Online	Performance Impact	Default and Value Range	Description
num_quantiles	Yes	Low	20 [0–32 767]	Specifies the number of quantiles (values in a column that satisfy a RANGE predicate) to collect when the WITH DISTRIBUTION option is specified with the RUNSTATS command.
numarchretry	Yes	None	5 [0–65 535]	Specifies the number of times that the DB2 database manager is to try archiving a log file to the primary or secondary archive directory before attempting to archive log files to the failover directory.
overflowlogpath	Yes	Medium	NULL [Any valid path]	Specifies the location to store archived log files needed for roll-forward and rollback operations.
pckcachesz	Yes	High	AUTOMATIC [-1, 32–2 147 483 646]	Specifies the amount of application memory (in pages) to use to cache packages for static and dynamic SQL statements and XQuery expressions.
rec_his_retentn	No	None	366 [-1; 0–30 000] days	Specifies the number of days to retain historical information on backups in the recovery history file.
section_actuals	Yes	High	NONE [NONE, BASE]	Specifies collection of section actuals (runtime statistics that are measured during section execution) such that the statistics can be viewed when an event monitor is subsequently created.
self_tuning_mem	Yes	High	ON [ON, OFF]	Enables or disables the self-tuning memory manager for the database. When this parameter is set to ON, the memory tuner dynamically distributes available memory resources as required between all memory consumers that are enabled for self-tuning.
seqdetect	Yes	High	YES [YES, NO]	Specifies whether the DB2 database manager can monitor I/O and, if sequential page reading is occurring, can activate I/O prefetching on behalf of the database.
sheapthres_shr	Yes	High	AUTOMATIC [250–2 147 483 647]	Specifies the maximum amount of memory (in pages) to use at any one time to perform sort operations.

Table 2.6: DB2 database configuration parameters (continued)				
Parameter	**Config Online**	**Performance Impact**	**Default and Value Range**	**Description**
smtp_server	Yes	None	NULL [Any valid string]	Specifies a Simple Mail Transfer Protocol (STMP) server name to transmit email sent by the UTL_MAIL built-in module.
softmax	No	Medium	100 [1–100 * logprimary] percentage	Specifies the maximum percentage of log file space to consume before a soft checkpoint is recorded.
sortheap	Yes	High	AUTOMATIC [16–4 194 303]	Specifies the maximum number of private memory pages to use for private sorts or the maximum number of shared memory pages to use for shared sorts.
sql_ccflags	Yes	None	NULL [Any valid string]	Specifies the list of conditional compilation values for use in conditional compilation of selected SQL statements. After updating the value of sql_ccflags, it can be queried using SQL_CCFLAGS special register.
stat_heap_sz	Yes	Low	AUTOMATIC [1 096–524 288]	Specifies the maximum size of the heap space (in pages) to use when creating and collecting table statistics (using the RUNSTATS command).
stmt_conc	Yes	Medium	OFF [OFF, LITERALS]	Specifies the default statement concentrator behavior. Enabling this parameter modifies dynamic statements to allow increased sharing of package cache entries.
stmtheap	Yes	Medium	AUTOMATIC [128–524288]	Specifies the heap size (in pages) to use for precompiling and binding SQL statements.
system_period_adj	Yes	None	NO [NO, YES]	Specifies the action to take when a history row for a system-period temporal table is generated with an end timestamp that is less than the begin timestamp.
trackmod	No	Low	NO [NO, YES]	Specifies whether to track database modifications so that the BACKUP utility can detect which subsets of the database pages must be examined by an incremental backup and potentially included in the backup image.

Table 2.6: DB2 database configuration parameters (continued)				
Parameter	**Config Online**	**Performance Impact**	**Default and Value Range**	**Description**
tsm_mgmtclass	Yes	None	NULL [Any valid string]	Specifies how the server is to manage backup versions or archive copies of the objects being backed up. The TSM management class is assigned from the TSM administrator.
tsm_nodename	Yes	None	NULL [Any valid string]	Specifies the node name to use to override the default setting for the node name associated with the Tivoli Storage Manager (TSM) product. The node name is needed to allow you to restore a database that was backed up to TSM from another node.
tsm_owner	Yes	None	NULL [Any valid string]	Specifies the owner name to use to override the default setting for the owner associated with the TSM product. The owner name is needed to allow you to restore a database that was backed up to TSM from another node.
tsm_password	Yes	None	NULL [Any valid string]	Specifies the password to use to override the default setting for the password associated with the TSM product. The password is needed to allow you to restore a database that was backed up to TSM from another node.
util_heap_sz	Yes	Low	5000 [16–524 288] 4 KB pages	Specifies the maximum amount of shared memory that the Backup, Restore, and Load utilities can use simultaneously.
vendoropt	Yes	None	NULL [Any valid string]	Specifies additional parameters that DB2 might need to use to communicate with storage systems during backup, restore, or load copy operations.
wlm_collect_int	Yes	Low	0 [0, 5–32 767] minutes	Specifies a collect and reset interval, in minutes for WLM statistics. When this parameter is set to 0, no collection is performed.
Adapted from Chapter 23 of *Database Administration Concepts and Configuration Reference Manual (DB2 10.1)*				

To display the contents of the database configuration file for a particular database, execute the GET DATABASE CONFIGURATION command.

The syntax for this command is:

```
GET [DATABASE | DB] [CONFIGURATION | CONFIG | CFG]
FOR [DatabaseAlias]
<SHOW DETAIL>
```

where:

DatabaseAlias Identifies the alias to assign to the database for which to display configuration information

Thus, if you want to view the contents of the database configuration file for a database named SAMPLE, you can do so by executing a GET DATABASE CONFIGURATION command:

```
GET DB CFG FOR sample
```

The value assigned to a particular database configuration file parameter can be changed by executing the UPDATE DATABASE CONFIGURATION command. The syntax for this command is:

```
UPDATE [DATABASE | DB]
[CONFIGURATION | CONFIG | CFG]
FOR [DatabaseAlias]
USING [[Parameter] [Value] |
       [Parameter] [Value] AUTOMATIC |
       [Parameter] AUTOMATIC |
       [Parameter] MANUAL ,...]
<IMMEDIATE | DEFERRED>
```

where:

DatabaseAlias Identifies the alias assigned to the database for which to modify configuration information

Parameter Identifies one or more database configuration parameters (by keyword) whose values are to be modified (often, the keyword for a parameter is the same as the parameter name itself)

Value Identifies the new values to assign to the specified database configuration parameter

If the AUTOMATIC keyword is specified as the value for a particular parameter, DB2 will automatically adjust the parameter value to reflect the current resource requirements. (Refer to Table 2.6 to identify the configuration parameters that you can set using the AUTOMATIC keyword.) If you specify a value along with the AUTOMATIC keyword, that value may influence the automatic calculations performed.

If you specify the DEFERRED clause with the UPDATE DATABASE CONFIGURATION command, changes made to the database configuration file will not take effect until all connections to the corresponding database have been terminated and a new connection is established. Specifying the IMMEDIATE clause instead, or specifying neither clause, will make all changes to the database configuration file take effect immediately—provided the necessary resources are available. Applications running against a database at the time database configuration changes are made will see the change the next time an SQL statement is executed.

So if you want to configure a database named SAMPLE such that any application connected to the database will wait up to 10,000 seconds to acquire a lock before rolling back the current transaction, you execute an UPDATE DATABASE CONFIGURATION command:

```
UPDATE DB CFG FOR sample USING LOCKTIMEOUT 10000
```

Or to configure a database named SAMPLE to use archival logging and instruct it to store a second copy of the active log files in a directory named mirrorlogs that resides on the /data file system, you execute an UPDATE DATABASE CONFIGURATION command that looks like this:

```
UPDATE DB CFG FOR sample
USING LOGARCHMETH1 LOGRETAIN MIRRORLOGPATH /data/mirrorlogs
```

The values assigned to all database configuration file parameters can be returned to their system defaults by executing the RESET DATABASE CONFIGURATION command. The syntax for this command is:

```
RESET [DATABASE | DB]
[CONFIGURATION | CONFIG | CFG]
FOR [DatabaseAlias]
```

where:

DatabaseAlias Identifies the alias to assign to the database whose configuration information is to be modified

Therefore, if you want to return the database configuration file parameters for a database named SAMPLE to their system default settings (thereby losing any configuration changes made), you execute a RESET DATABASE CONFIGURATION command that looks like this:

```
RESET DB CFG FOR sample
```

You can also view or alter the contents of a database configuration file by using the IBM Data Studio Administration Explorer. To do so, right-click the database in the Administration Explorer menu, and then select the **Set Up and Configure** and **Configure** actions, as Figure 2.5 shows.

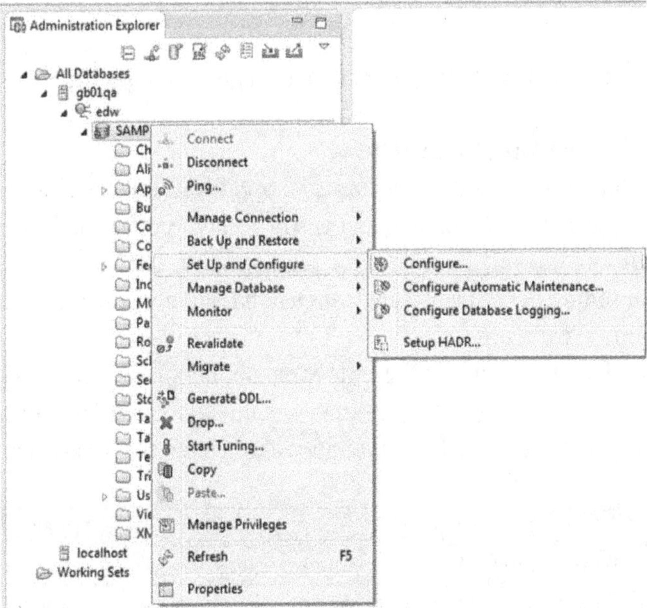

Figure 2.5: Using IBM Data Studio to invoke the database Set Up and Configure action

Figure 2.6 displays the "Modify database configuration parameters" wizard and shows how to update the parameter AVG_APPLS from 1 to 10.

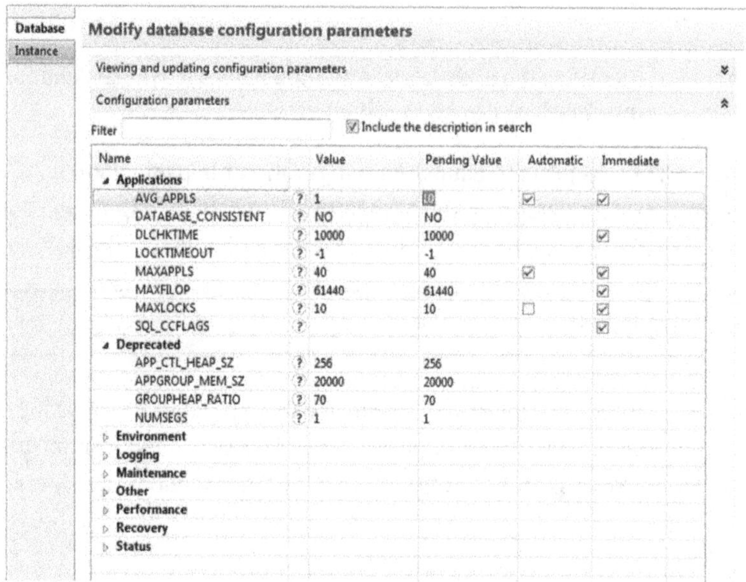

Figure 2.6: Using IBM Data Studio to update database configuration parameters

DB2 Autonomic Computing Features

Today's business challenges require that databases be optimized for the best possible performance. The database engine must be highly tunable and easily configured for the best performance, regardless of the DBA's skill level. To meet these requirements, DB2 comes with a rich set of automatic features for tuning the database environment adaptively and accurately by sensing and responding to situations that occur.

When you create a database, some of the following autonomic computing capabilities are enabled by default; however, others you must enable manually. Table 2.7 provides a summary of DB2 automatic features and associated commands to activate or deactivate the feature.

Table 2.7: DB2 autonomic computing features

Automatic Feature	Description	Parameter or Commands
Self-tuning memory (STMM)	STMM simplifies the task of setting up several memory configuration parameters during database startup and run time. STMM has an intelligent control mechanism to keep track of the characteristics of varying workloads, memory consumption by each memory parameter, and demand for numerous shared memory resources in the database. It dynamically adjusts the memory resource memory usage as needed.	Enable or disable this feature by setting the self_tuning_mem database configuration parameter to ON or OFF.

Table 2.7: DB2 autonomic computing features (continued)

Automatic Feature	Description	Parameter or Commands
Automatic storage	The automatic storage feature simplifies storage management for table spaces by using storage paths. While creating a new database, the database manager creates containers across the storage paths and extends them as and when required.	Create a database. Create storage groups (optional, by default DB2 creates IBMSTOGROUP storage group). Create table spaces by using the MANAGED BY AUTOMATIC STORAGE clause.
Data compression	Automatic data compression feature works both on tables and indexes to save storage cost for the organization. Recently, DB2 introduced adaptive compression to create page-level compression dictionaries, along with the earlier table-level compression dictionaries, to avoid regular data reorganization for optimal compression. Temporary tables are compressed automatically, and indexes for compressed tables are compressed automatically by default.	Use the COMPRESS YES clause during CREATE TABLE or ALTER TABLE and CREATE INDEX or ALTER INDEX commands.
Automatic database backup	Database backups are necessary to protect data in case hardware or software failures occur. The automatic database backup feature simplifies the database backup management task by providing an effective backup policy, which can easily be incorporated for regular and proper backups.	Enable or disable automatic backup maintenance by setting the AUTO_DB_BACKUP and AUTO_MAINT database configuration parameters to ON or OFF.
Automatic reorganization	The automatic reorganization process periodically evaluates tables and indexes to determine whether table and indexes are fragmented due to many data changes and require reorganization. It schedules automatic reorganization of the data and indexes when necessary based on the reorganization policy.	Enable or disable automatic reorganization maintenance by setting AUTO_MAINT, AUTO_TBL_MAINT, and AUTO_REORG database configuration parameters to ON or OFF.
Automatic statistics collection	Automatic statistics collection helps to improve database performance by keeping table statistics updated. The DB2 optimizer uses these statistics to determine the most cost-effective access plan for any given SQL statement. The database manager collects the statistics required for any workload synchronously or asynchronously by gathering runtime statistics when SQL statements are complied.	Enable or disable automatic statistics collection by setting the following set of database configuration parameters based on the kinds of statistics requirements: AUTO_MAINT AUTO_TBL_MAINT AUTO_RUNSTATS AUTO_STMT_STATS AUTO_STATS_PROF AUTO_PROD_UPD

Table 2.7: DB2 autonomic computing features (continued)		
Automatic Feature	**Description**	**Parameter or Commands**
Configuration Advisor	The Configuration Advisor is designed to capture specific information about the database environment and recommend or make changes to configuration parameters based on the information provided to achieve better performance in relatively less time.	When a new database is created, this tool automatically runs to determine and set the database configuration parameters and the size of the default buffer pool. Use the AUTOCONFIGURE command to invoke this tool on an existing database.
Utility throttling	Automatic maintenance activities consume resources when they are run, so their executing can affect database performance. To minimize system impact, you can regulate the resource usage of some automatic maintenance activities by using DB2's adaptive utility throttling system.	To set the instance-wide limit that all throttled utilities can cumulatively have on production workloads to 10 percent, assign the util_impact_lim configuration parameter the value 10.

Self-Tuning Memory Manager

System performance benefits when memory is adaptively tuned based on workload requirements. To achieve the greatest performance, it is necessary to adapt the memory configuration as the workload shifts. STMM simplifies the task of setting up several memory configuration parameters during database startup and run time. STMM's intelligent control mechanism keeps track of characteristics of varying workloads, memory consumption by each memory parameter, and demand for numerous shared memory resources in the database. It dynamically adjusts the resources' memory usage as needed.

STMM constantly monitors the system to make use of any operating system memory that is available only if the system is set to tune the total database memory consumption. It works iteratively to determine an optimal memory configuration for the following memory parameters and is pictorially represented in Figure 2.7:

- database_memory—Database shared memory size
- locklist—Maximum storage for lock list
- maxlocks—Maximum percent of lock list before escalation
- pckcachesz—Package cache size
- sheapthres_shr—Sort heap threshold for shared sorts
- sortheap—Maximum storage for sort heap

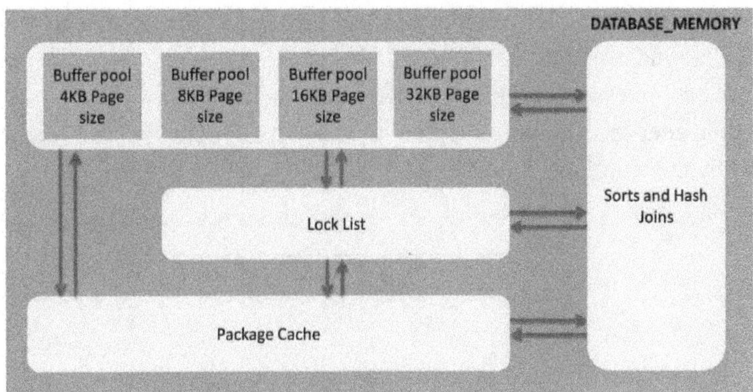

Figure 2.7: STMM memory structure

STMM works on the following database shared memory parameters:

- Buffer pools are controlled by the ALTER BUFFERPOOL and CREATE BUFFERPOOL statements. The database buffer pool is a chunk of memory used to cache a table's index and data pages as they are read from disk to be selected or updated.
- Package cache is controlled by the pckcachesz database configuration parameter. This parameter is allocated from the database shared memory and is used for buffering the sections for static SQL, dynamic SQL, and XQuery statements.
- Locking memory is controlled by the locklist and maxlocks database configuration parameters. The locklist parameter indicates the amount of storage allocated to the lock list. There is one locklist per database, which contains the locks held by all applications concurrently connected to the database. The maxlocks parameter defines a percentage of the lock list held by an application that must be filled before the database manager performs lock escalation.
- Sort memory is controlled by the sheapthres_shr and the sortheap database configuration parameters. The total size of the shared sort memory allocated is based on the value of the sheapthres_shr parameter during database activation. The sortheap parameter determines the maximum number of memory pages for use for each sort.
- Total database shared memory is controlled by the database_memory database configuration parameter. This parameter specifies the amount of shared memory that is reserved for the database shared memory region.

Figure 2.8 shows the STMM work flow, which is as follows:

- The tuner wakes up (1) and checks whether any memory parameter needs more memory (2).
- If the answer is yes, it examines the amount of free operating system memory—if DATABASE_MEMORY is set to automatic (5). If enough free physical memory is available at

the operating system level, it gives some of that memory to the needy heap (6). If memory is not available, it finds another memory heap that can donate memory to the needy heap (7).

- This process continues until no more memory can be moved.
- The tuner then goes to sleep until required to wake up (4). The wakeup frequency is determined by the workload characteristics (3).

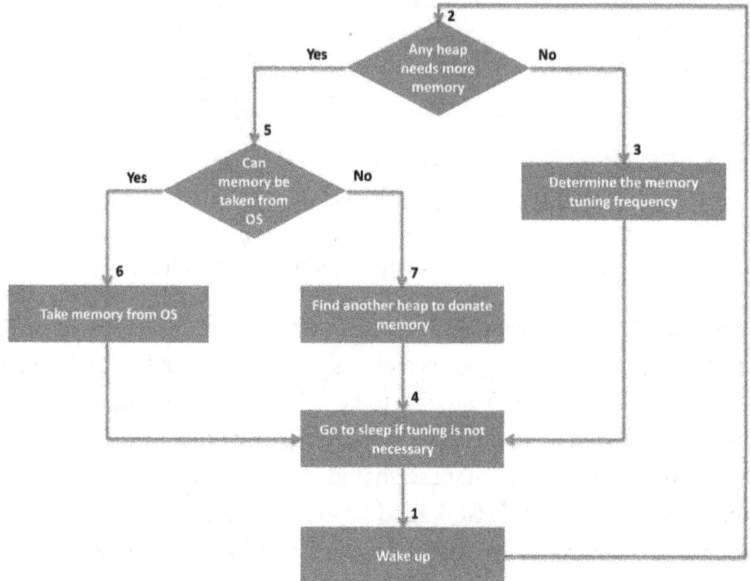

Figure 2.8: STMM work flow

STMM Modes of Operation

STMM works in four different modes, which you can use based on your application and business requirement:

- **Mode 1:** When DATABASE_MEMORY= AUTOMATIC
  In this case, the required memory is taken from and returned to the operating system when required. The total amount of memory that DB2 uses can grow over time and is limited only by the operating system's memory availability.
- **Mode 2:** When DATABASE_MEMORY= <NUMERIC VALUE> AUTOMATIC
  Here, memory tuning still occurs, but the total memory that the database uses starts from the NUMERIC value and can grow over time. It is only limited by the operating system's available memory.
- **Mode 3:** When DATABASE_MEMORY=<NUMERIC VALUE>
  DB2 will allocate this amount of memory during startup. This memory setting is static—it cannot take or give memory to the operating system on demand.

- **Mode 4:** When DATABASE_MEMORY=COMPUTED
  The database memory is computed based on the sum of the database memory heaps' initial values during the database startup. In this case, database_memory is not enabled for self-tuning.

Activating STMM

You can activate STMM by setting the self_tuning_mem database configuration parameter to ON using the command line processor or IBM Data Studio:

```
CONNECT TO sample
UPDATE DB CFG FOR sample USING SELF_TUNING_MEM ON
```

Alternatively, STMM can also be activated by changing the pending value for the self_tuning_mem configuration parameter through IBM Data Studio's Configure wizard and clicking the **Run** option.

Figure 2.9 shows the "Modify database configuration parameters" wizard and how to update self_tuning_mem from OFF to ON.

Database
Instance

Modify database configuration parameters

Viewing and updating configuration parameters

Configuration parameters

Filter ☑ Include the description in search

Name	Value	Pending Value	Automatic	Immediate
DB_MEM_THRESH	10	10		☑
DBHEAP	5389	5389	☑	☑
DFT_EXTENT_SZ	32	32		☑
DFT_PREFETCH_SZ	32	32	☑	☑
INDEXSORT	YES	YES		☑
LOCKLIST	13984	13984	☑	☑
LOGBUFSZ	2150	2150		
MULTIPAGE_ALLOC	YES	YES		
NUM_FREQVALUES	10	10		☑
NUM_IOCLEANERS	6	6	☑	
NUM_IOSERVERS	6	6	☑	
NUM_QUANTILES	20	20		☑
PCKCACHESZ	12288	12288	☑	☑
SELF_TUNING_MEM	OFF	ON		☑
SEQDETECT	YES	OFF		☑
SHEAPTHRES_SHR	67453	ON	☑	☑
SORTHEAP	13490		☑	☑
STAT_HEAP_SZ	4384	4384	☑	☑
STMTHEAP	8192	8192	☑	☑

Figure 2.9: Modifying the STMM parameter through IBM Data Studio

Figure 2.10 displays the deployment status for the self_tuning_mem database configuration update command.

Deployment status for the current command

Display in SQL Results view

✓ **Succeeded** CONNECT TO SAMPLE

✓ **Succeeded** UPDATE DB CFG USING SELF_TUNING_MEM ON

Figure 2.10: Deployment status for STMM parameter update

To activate other memory areas of STMM controlled by memory configuration parameters, set those parameters to AUTOMATIC by using the UPDATE DATABASE CONFIGURATION command or through IBM Data Studio:

```
UPDATE DB CFG FOR sample USING PCKCACHESZ AUTOMATIC
UPDATE DB CFG FOR sample USING LOCKLIST AUTOMATIC
UPDATE DB CFG FOR sample USING MAXLOCKS AUTOMATIC
UPDATE DB CFG FOR sample USING SORTHEAP AUTOMATIC
UPDATE DB CFG FOR sample USING SHEAPTHRES_SHR AUTOMATIC
UPDATE DB CFG FOR sample USING DATABASE_MEMORY AUTOMATIC
```

Finally, to activate self-tuning of buffer pools, set the buffer pool size to AUTOMATIC. You can do this by using the ALTER BUFFERPOOL statement for existing buffer pools or the CREATE BUFFERPOOL statement for new buffer pools:

```
ALTER BUFFERPOOL bp16k SIZE AUTOMATIC
CREATE BUFFERPOOL bp16k SIZE AUTOMATIC PAGESIZE 16 K
```

Executing the GET DB CFG SHOW DETAIL command displays the current STMM memory parameter settings:

```
CONNECT TO sample
GET DB CFG SHOW DETAIL
```

You can see STMM in three different states:

- OFF
- ON (Active)
- ON (Inactive)

If the parameter is ON (Active), the memory tuner is actively tuning the memory on the system. If the parameter is ON (Inactive), it means that, although the parameter is set ON, self-tuning is not occurring because fewer than two memory parameters are enabled for self-tuning. If the parameter is OFF, of course no memory tuning enabled.

You can also review the changes made by the self-tuning memory manager process recorded in memory tuning log files, which reside in the stmmlog subdirectory of the instance. The first file created is assigned the name stmm.0.log, the second is assigned the name stmm.1.log, and so on. Each memory tuning log file contains summaries of the resource demands for each memory consumer at the time a tuning operation was performed. You can determine tuning intervals by examining the timestamps for the entries made in the memory tuning log files.

Notes: Self-tuning redistributes memory between different memory parameters. When database_memory is set to a numeric value, only one other memory consumer must be set to AUTOMATIC for tuning to occur.

To enable the locklist configuration parameter for self-tuning, you must also enable maxlocks.

To enable the sheapthres_shr configuration parameter for self-tuning, you must enable sortheap as well.

Automatic tuning of sheapthres_shr or sortheap is allowed only when the database manager configuration parameter sheapthres is set to 0.

Self-tuning memory runs only on the HADR primary server. When self-tuning memory is activated on an HADR pair, it does not run on the secondary server. If the HADR TAKEOVER command is run on the current secondary machine, self-tuning memory operations also switch to the new primary machine.

Buffer pools that are set to AUTOMATIC will show NPAGES as -2 in the SYSCAT. BUFFERPOOLS catalog view. To determine the exact number of bytes consumed by any buffer pool, use SYSIBMADM.SNAPDB_MEMORY_POOL administrative view something like this:

```
SELECT SUBSTR (BPNAME,1,12) AS BPNAME, NPAGES, PAGESIZE
   FROM SYSCAT.BUFFERPOOLS

BPNAME       NPAGES      PAGESIZE
----------   ----------- -----------
IBMDEFAULTBP          -2        4096

  1 record(s) selected.

                                                     Continued
```

```
SELECT
   SUBSTR (DB_NAME, 1, 8) AS DBNAME,
   SUBSTR (POOL_ID,1,5) AS POOL_ID,
   POOL_CUR_SIZE,
   POOL_CONFIG_SIZE,
   POOL_WATERMARK
FROM SYSIBMADM.SNAPDB_MEMORY_POOL WHERE POOL_ID = 'BP'

DBNAME   POOL_ID POOL_CUR_SIZE        POOL_CONFIG_SIZE     POOL_WATERMARK
         (Bytes)                      (Bytes)              (Bytes)
-------- ------- -------------------- -------------------- --------------------
SAMPLE   BP                3972726784           3972726784           3972726784
SAMPLE   BP                    851968               851968               851968
SAMPLE   BP                    589824               589824               589824
SAMPLE   BP                    458752               458752               458752
SAMPLE   BP                    393216               393216               393216

  5 record(s) selected.
```

Wondering why we have five entries for the buffer pool in SYSIBMADM.SNAPDB_MEMORY_POOL administrative view when we have only one buffer pool in SYSCAT.BUFFERPOOLS system catalog view? The reason is very simple: DB2 creates four hidden system buffer pools, namely IBMSYSTEMBP4K, IBMSYSTEMBP8K, IBMSYSTEMBP16K, and IBMSYSTEMBP32K of page size 4 KB, 8 KB, 16 KB, and 32 KB, respectively, of 16 pages each for emergency circumstances. You can also check the actual size of AUTOMATIC buffer pool by using the GET SNAPSHOT FOR BUFFERPOOLS command:

```
GET SNAPSHOT FOR BUFFERPOOLS ON sample
```

When you enable self-tuning memory for partitioned databases, a single database partition is designated as the tuning partition, and all memory tuning decisions are based on the memory and workload characteristics of that database partition. After tuning decisions on that partition are made, the memory adjustments are distributed to the other database partitions to ensure that all database partitions maintain similar configurations.

Automatic Storage

The automatic storage feature was initially introduced in DB2 V8.2 FP9, with the intention to make storage management easier for database administrators. In DB2 9.7, rather than managing storage at the table space–level by using explicit container definitions, storage was managed at the database level, and in DB2 10.1, it is managed at the storage group level. In a way, the responsibility of creating, extending, and adding containers is completely taken over by the database manager from the database administrators.

By default, all databases that are created in DB2 10.1 use the automatic storage feature. However, if the database is created with AUTOMATIC STORAGE NO clause, you cannot create automatic storage-managed table spaces within it.

When you create a database in DB2 10.1, the default storage group IBMSTOGROUP is automatically created. You can establish one or more initial storage paths for it in the CREATE DATABASE command. As the database grows, the database manager creates containers across those storage paths, and then extends them or automatically creates new ones as needed.

You can use CREATE DATABASE command to create an automatic storage-enabled database on /stogroup1 and /stogroup2 file system paths:

```
CREATE DATABASE sample ON '/stogroup1', '/stogroup1'
```

To verify the storage status of the database created, use the db2pd or GET SNAPSHOT FOR DATABASE command:

```
db2pd -d sample -storagepaths

Database Member 0 -- Database SAMPLE -- Active -- Up 0 days 00:06:55 --
Date 2014-06-28-11.48.24.453060

Storage Group Configuration:
Address            SGID  Default  DataTag    Name
0x00007FFE05206B40 0     Yes      0          IBMSTOGROUP

Storage Group Statistics:
Address            SGID  State      Numpaths  NumDropPen
0x00007FFE05206B40 0     0x00000000 2         0

Storage Group Paths:
Address            SGID  PathID     PathState     PathName
0x00007FFE05206C60 0     0          InUse         /stogroup1
0x00007FFE05207040 0     1          InUse         /stogroup2
```

Continued

```
GET SNAPSHOT FOR DATABASE ON SAMPLE
...
...
Number of automatic storage paths              = 2
Automatic storage path                         = /stogroup1
      Node number                              = 0
      State                                    = In Use
      File system ID                           = 64781
      Storage path free space (bytes)          = 96227627008
      File system used space (bytes)           = 9394679808
      File system total space (bytes)          = 105689415680
Automatic storage path                         = /stogroup2
      Node number                              = 0
      State                                    = In Use
      File system ID                           = 64781
      Storage path free space (bytes)          = 96227627008
      File system used space (bytes)           = 9394679808
      File system total space (bytes)          = 105689415680
```

If the db2pd command's **Numpaths** and the database snapshot command's **Number of automatic storage paths** indicate a value 0, then the database in question is a non-automatic storage-enabled database. A nonzero value represents that a database is automatic storage-enabled. In the above example, **Numpaths** is listed with value 2 because the SAMPLE database is created on two storage paths.

The default storage group for the database SAMPLE is IBMSTOGROUP with its two associated storage paths. All the default table spaces—SYSCATSPACE, TEMPSPACE1, USERSPACE1, and SYSTOOLSPACE—are created in IBMSTOGROUP.

You can use the GET SNAPSHOT FOR TABLESPACES command to verify the current status of the table spaces created:

```
db2 "GET SNAPSHOT FOR TABLESPACES ON sample" | grep -i "automatic storage"
 Using automatic storage                      = Yes
 Using automatic storage                      = Yes
 Using automatic storage                      = Yes
 Using automatic storage                      = Yes
```

Now that you have specified the storage group paths in the CREATE DATABASE command, the DB2 database manager associates the database path with the first storage group path:

```
GET SNAPSHOT FOR TABLESPACES ON sample


            Tablespace Snapshot


First database connect timestamp                = 06/28/2014 11:41:29.540153
Last reset timestamp                            =
Snapshot timestamp                              = 06/28/2014 12:06:42.195041
Database name                                   = SAMPLE
Database path                                   = /stogroup1/db2inst1/NODE0000/
SQL00001/MEMBER0000/
Input database alias                            = SAMPLE
Number of accessed tablespaces                  = 4
```

The **Database path** is the path where the database manager keeps all the database configuration information, such as the database configuration parameter file (SQLDBCONF), log control files (SQLOGMIR.LFH, SQLOGCTL.LFH.1), on so on.

You can also use ADMIN_GET_STORAGE_PATHS table function to list automatic storage paths for each database storage group, including file system information for each storage group:

```
SELECT
      VARCHAR (STORAGE_GROUP_NAME, 30) AS STOGROUP,
      VARCHAR (DB_STORAGE_PATH, 40) AS STORAGE_PATH
   FROM TABLE (ADMIN_GET_STORAGE_PATHS ('',-1)) AS T

STOGROUP                       STORAGE_PATH
------------------------------ ----------------------------------------
IBMSTOGROUP                    /stogroup1
IBMSTOGROUP                    /stogroup2

  2 record(s) selected.
```

Note: This is just a foundation to the DB2 automatic storage capabilities. This topic, including multi-temperature data management, is discussed comprehensively in Chapter 3, "Physical Design."

Data Compression

Disk storage is often the most expensive component of a database solution. In general, organizations tend to keep multiple copies of the same information at multiple locations for better availability, such as storing data at the primary site, secondary site, and central storage locations. The DB2 compression features will help reduce storage space requirement dramatically, resulting in lower storage cost and improved I/O performance.

Several forms of the compression feature existed before DB2 9.1: value compression, MDC block indexes (not exactly a data compression technique, but it reduces the index storage space by creating indexes at block level instead of row level), and backup compression. In DB2 9.1, IBM introduced a game changing compression technology called *row compression*, which is based on the Lempel-Ziv (LZ) static dictionary-based compression algorithm. With static row compression, repeating patterns within a table are replaced by 12-bit symbols, and the corresponding real data values are stored in an in-memory static dictionary.

In DB2 9.5, IBM introduced the Automatic Dictionary Creation (ADC) process, wherein the database manager automatically builds a compression dictionary after a table reaches 2 MB in size. What does this mean to DBAs? No offline REORG or INSPECT command is required to be run on the system to build the in-memory compression dictionary.

In DB2 9.7, IBM introduced a stack of compression capabilities, including index compression, temporary table compression, inline large object compression, and XML object compression.

In DB2 10.1, IBM introduced yet another data compression technique called *adaptive compression*. Adaptive row compression relies on a compression dictionary built at page level and compresses patterns within the page that are not part of the static dictionary. That way, adaptive compression not only yields a significantly better performance ratio but also adapts to changing data characteristics.

Table 2.8 provides a summary of DB2 data compression capabilities and associated commands and table functions to verify the data compression ratios.

Table 2.8: History of DB2 data compression feature

Version	Compression Feature	Associated Activation and Verify Commands
Prior to DB2 9.1	Value compression MDC block indexes Backup compression	CREATE TABLE ... VALUE COMPRESSION ALTER TABLE ... ACTIVATE VALUE COMPRESSION CREATE TABLE ... ORGANIZE BY DIMENSIONS BACKUP DATABASE ... COMPRESS

Table 2.8: History of DB2 data compression feature (continued)		
Version	**Compression Feature**	**Associated Activation and Verify Commands**
DB2 9.1	Static row compression	CREATE TABLE ... COMPRESS YES ALTER TABLE ... COMPRESS YES REORG TABLE ... RESETDICTIONARY Use the following command to verify the storage savings: INSPECT ROWCOMPESTIMATE TABLE NAME <table> SCHEMA <schema> RESULTS KEEP inspect_out.txt db2inspf inspect_out.txt db2inspf_out.txt
DB2 9.5	Automatic Dictionary Creation (ADC)	Use table function SYSPROC.ADMIN_GET_TAB_COMPRESS_INFO to verify the compression ratio on a table.
DB2 9.7	• Index compression • Temporary table compression • Inline LOB compression • XML object compression	Use the table functions listed below to verify compression efficiency on a table and indexes, respectively: SYSPROC.ADMIN_GET_TAB_COMPRESS_INFO SYSPROC.ADMIN_GET_INDEX_COMPRESS_INFO
DB2 10.1	• Adaptive compression • Log archive compression	CREATE TABLE ... COMPRESS YES ALTER TABLE ... COMPRESS YES And use the following table function to verify the compression efficiency: SYSPROC.ADMIN_GET_TAB_COMPRESS_INFO Update database configuration parameters LOGARCHCOMPR1 and LOGARCHCOMPR2 to ON to enable log archive compressions both in first and second log archive methods.

Note: This is just a foundation for DB2 data compression capabilities, which are discussed extensively in the "Storage Optimization" section in Chapter 3, "Physical Design."

Automatic Database Maintenance

The database manager provides automatic maintenance capabilities for performing database backups, keeping up-to-date statistics, and reorganizing tables and indexes as necessary. Performing maintenance activities on your databases is essential in ensuring that they are optimized for performance and recoverability. You can use automatic maintenance to perform the following maintenance operations:

- Create a backup image of the database. Automatic database backup provides users with a solution to help ensure their database is being backed up both properly and regularly, without their having to worry about when to back up or having any knowledge of the BACKUP command syntax.

- Defragment data (table or index reorganization). This maintenance activity can increase the efficiency with which the DB2 database manager accesses tables. Automatic reorganization manages offline table and index reorganization without users having to worry about when and how to reorganize their data.
- Optimize data access (running RUNSTATS). The DB2 database manager updates the system catalog statistics on the data in a table, the data in a table's indexes, or the data in both a table and its indexes. The DB2 optimizer uses these statistics to determine which path to use to access data in response to a query. Automatic statistics collection attempts to improve database performance by maintaining up-to-date table statistics. The goal is to allow the DB2 optimizer to always choose an access plan based on accurate statistics.
- Conduct statistics profiling. Automatic statistics profiling advises when and how to collect table statistics by detecting outdated, missing, and incorrectly specified statistics and by generating statistical profiles based on query feedback.

In most cases, it is a hard way to determine whether and when to run database maintenance activities. However, the automatic maintenance feature manages it all for you, allowing you to tackle other critical business problems.

Configuring Automatic Maintenance Using CLP and IBM Data Studio

To activate automatic database maintenance capability, update the maintenance database configuration parameters, as follows:

```
UPDATE DB CFG FOR sample USING
      AUTO_MAINT ON
      AUTO_DB_BACKUP ON
      AUTO_TBL_MAINT ON
      AUTO_RUNSTATS ON
      AUTO_STMT_STATS ON
      AUTO_STATS_VIEWS ON
      AUTO_STATS_VIEWS ON
      AUTO_STATS_PROF ON
      AUTO_PROF_UPD ON
      AUTO_REORG ON
```

You can also use IBM Data Studio to configure automatic maintenance on your database. Figure 2.11 shows how to invoke the Configure Automatic Maintenance wizard in the IBM Data Studio Administration Explorer.

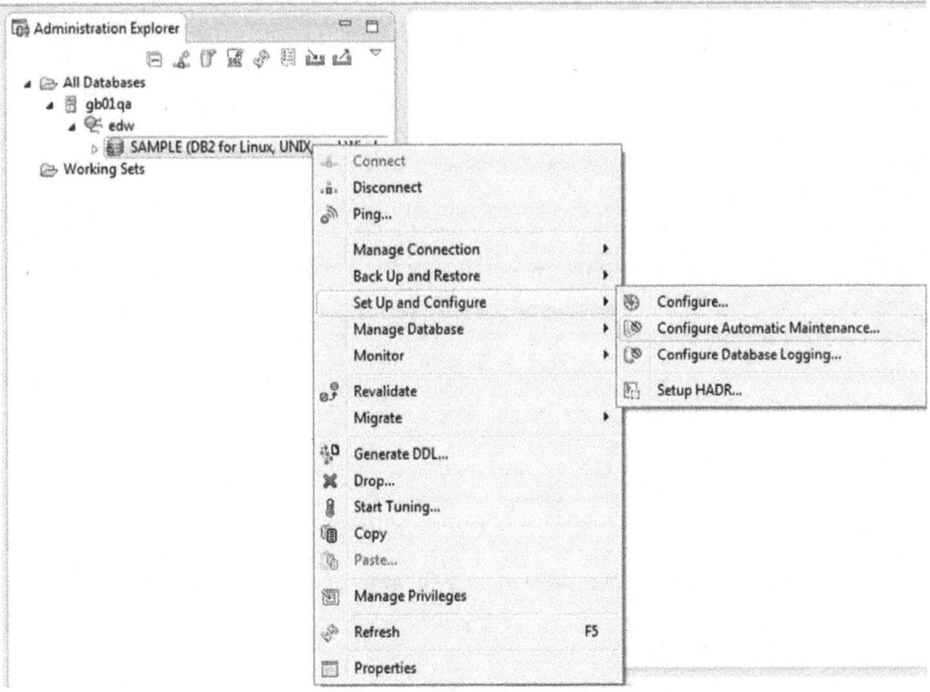

Figure 2.11: Automatic Maintenance wizard in IBM Data Studio

The first tab in the wizard, **Options**, lists database configuration parameters associated with automatic maintenance, along with a check box for each, as in Figure 2.12. These database configuration parameters allow you to enable or disable automatic maintenance features selectively or as a group. For example, if AUTO_MAINT is set to OFF (a cleared check box), which is the top root parameter for the maintenance, all other automatic maintenance parameters are considered to be ineffective, regardless of their actual value.

Similarly, if AUTO_TBL_MAINT is set to OFF, the AUTO_REORG, AUTOSTATS_PROF, AUTO_PROF_UPD, AUTO_RUNSTATS, and AUTO_STMT_STATS parameters are considered to have an effective value of OFF. If AUTO_TBL_MAINT is set to ON, the AUTO_REORG, AUTOSTATS_PROF, AUTO_PROF_UPD, AUTO_RUNSTATS, and AUTO_STMT_STATS parameters will have an effective value of their actual value. Select a parameter's check box to set the value to ON or clear it to set the value to OFF.

You can change the automatic maintenance option values as per business need, and click **Run** to update the database configuration parameter file. Figure 2.13 shows the deployment status for the recently updated options.

Configure Automatic Maintenance SAMPLE

Settings

Specify any additional settings to use. Click Run when you are done.

Preview Command | Run

Options

Online Maintenance Window

Offline Maintenance Window

Backup Policy

Reorg Policy

Runstats Policy

Select automatic maintenance options

Select the automatic maintenance options for the database.

The automatic maintenance options are displayed in a parent and child hierarchy. When a parent parameter is disabled, its child parameters are also disabled. However, the child parameter settings, as recorded in the database configuration file, do not change. When a parent parameter is enabled, the recorded values for its child parameters take effect.

Automatic maintenance options

- [ ] Automatic maintenance (AUTO_MAINT)
  - [x] Automatic database backup (AUTO_DB_BACKUP)
  - [x] Automatic table maintenance (AUTO_TBL_MAINT)
    - [ ] Automatic table and index reorganization (AUTO_REORG)
    - [ ] Automatic statistics profiling (AUTO_STATS_PROF)
      - [ ] Automatic profile updates (AUTO_PROF_UPD)
    - [x] Automatic runstats (AUTO_RUNSTATS)
      - [x] Automatic real-time statistics (AUTO_STMT_STATS)

Figure 2.12: Automatic Maintenance Options tab in IBM Data Studio

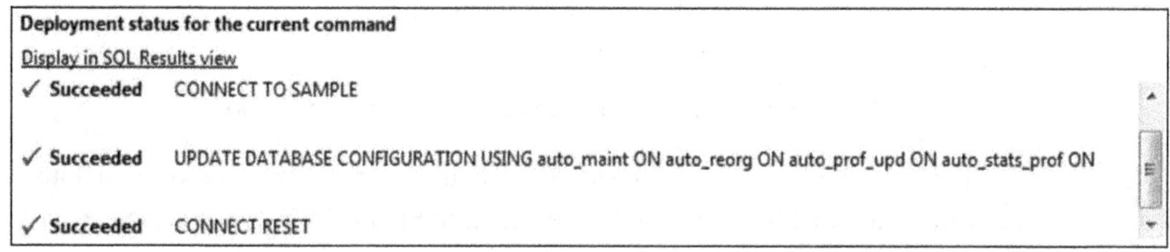
Deployment status for the current command
Display in SQL Results view
✓ Succeeded CONNECT TO SAMPLE
✓ Succeeded UPDATE DATABASE CONFIGURATION USING auto_maint ON auto_reorg ON auto_prof_upd ON auto_stats_prof ON
✓ Succeeded CONNECT RESET

Figure 2.13: Automatic Maintenance command deployment status

The second and third tabs in the configure maintenance wizard allow you to set up online and offline maintenance windows. The maintenance windows are periods of time you define to enable the DB2 database manager to perform automatic maintenance activities, instead of letting it run at any time, including business hours. The online maintenance window is the time period for maintenance operations that leaves the object of the maintenance accessible to the application and users. Likewise, the offline maintenance window is the time period for maintenance operations that keeps the object of the maintenance in an inaccessible mode from the application and users.

Figure 2.14 shows the online maintenance window options specifying the start time, the total duration that the maintenance activity can go up to, and the days of the week. You can also choose not to run any maintenance activities during business hours by selecting **Not during the specified time** in the drop-down menu section. Similar options within the **Offline Maintenance Window** tab allow offline maintenance activities to occur.

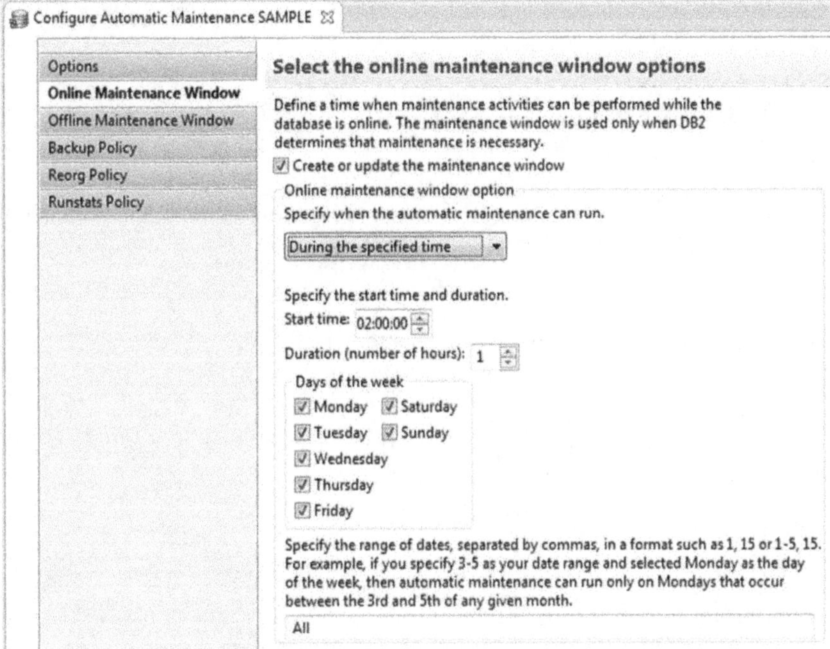

Figure 2.14: Online Maintenance Window options

To activate automatic backup maintenance on your database, follow these three simple steps:

Step 1: Update the AUTO_MAINT and AUTO_DB_BACKUP database configuration parameters by using the proper CLP command or the IBM Data Studio check box option, as in Figure 2.12.

Step 2: Define an online or offline maintenance window based on the business requirements, as Figure 2.14 shows.

Step 3: Define a backup policy to control the behavior of automatic backup such as backup criteria, backup location, and backup mode, as in Figure 2.15.

The backup criteria indicate how frequently to back up your database. An automatic backup will be scheduled when any of the following conditions are true:

- You have no backups available for the database.
- The time elapsed since the last backup is more than a specified number period such as day, week, and month.
- The active transaction log space consumed since the last backup (applicable only for archive logging-enabled databases) is more than the specified value.

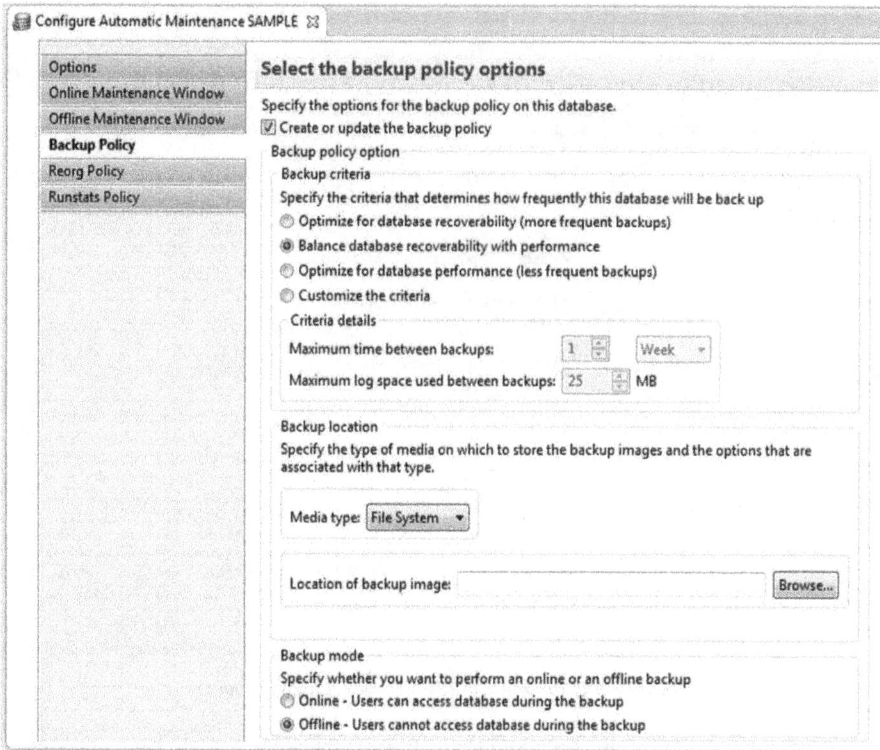

Figure 2.15: Backup Policy options

The backup location specifies where to copy the database backup image. You can change the location of your backup image to any of the following:

- File system
- Tape
- TSM
- XBSA (NetBackup Interfaces for VERITAS/Symantec)
- Vendor DLL media files

The backup mode specifies whether to perform automatic backup online or offline. If the database is enabled for roll-forward recovery, automatic database backup can be enabled for online or offline backup. Otherwise, only offline backup is available. Once you complete the policy selection, you can commit it by clicking **Run**.

You can also set the backup policy by using the SYSPROC.AUTOMAINT_SET_POLICY system stored procedure. You can find the sample XML file DB2AutoBackupPolicySample.xml at $INSTHOME/sqllib/samples/automaintcfg and modify it to work for your environment:

```
CALL SYSPROC.AUTOMAINT_SET_POLICY ( 'AUTO_BACKUP',
BLOB(
' <?xml version="1.0" encoding="UTF-8"?>
<DB2AutoBackupPolicy xmlns="http://www.ibm.com/xmlns/prod/db2/autonomic/
config">
        <BackupOptions mode="Online">
                <BackupTarget>
                        <DiskBackupTarget>
                                <PathName>/home/edw</PathName>
                        </DiskBackupTarget>
                </BackupTarget>
        </BackupOptions>
        <BackupCriteria numberOfFullBackups="1" timeSinceLastBackup="24"
logSpaceConsumedSinceLastBackup="2560"/>
</DB2AutoBackupPolicy> '
) )
```

Using the system procedure SYSPROC.AUTOMAINT_GET_POLICYFILE, you can extract the current policy from the system. When you run the following command, it extracts the XML file and stores it at $INSTHOME/sqllib/tmp in the UNIX environment:

```
CALL SYSPROC.AUTOMAINT_GET_POLICYFILE ('AUTO_BACKUP','AutoBackup.xml');

~/sqllib/tmp> more AutoBackup.xml
<?xml version="1.0" encoding="UTF-8"?>
<DB2AutoBackupPolicy
xmlns="http://www.ibm.com/xmlns/prod/db2/autonomic/config" >
                                                        Continued
```

```
<!--   Backup Options  -->
<BackupOptions mode="Online">
 <BackupTarget>
 <DiskBackupTarget>
   <PathName>/home/edw</PathName>
 </DiskBackupTarget>
 </BackupTarget>
</BackupOptions>

<!--  Frequency of automatic backups -->

<BackupCriteria numberOfFullBackups="1" timeSinceLastBackup="24" logSpace-
ConsumedSinceLastBackup="2560"/>

</DB2AutoBackupPolicy>
```

To activate automatic reorganization maintenance on your database, follow these three simple steps:

Step 1: Update the AUTO_MAINT, AUTO_TBL_MAINT, and AUTO_REORG database configuration parameters by using the proper CLP command or the IBM Data Studio check box option, as in Figure 2.12.

Step 2: Define an online or offline maintenance window based on the business requirements, as Figure 2.14 shows.

Step 3: Define a reorganization policy to control the behavior of automatic table and index reorganization such as table scope, size criteria, and reorganization options, as Figure 2.16 illustrates.

The **Table scope** section specifies the tables to consider for automatic data reorganization. Options are **All tables**, **Include system tables**, and **Selected tables**, which you base on a simple or custom filter predicate. The **Size criteria** section allows you to exclude tables on the basis of per-partition table size, and it is applicable only to the offline reorganization operation. The tables that exceed the specified size will not be considered for the offline table or index reorganization due to a larger offline maintenance window; however, these tables are still considered for an online table and index reorganization.

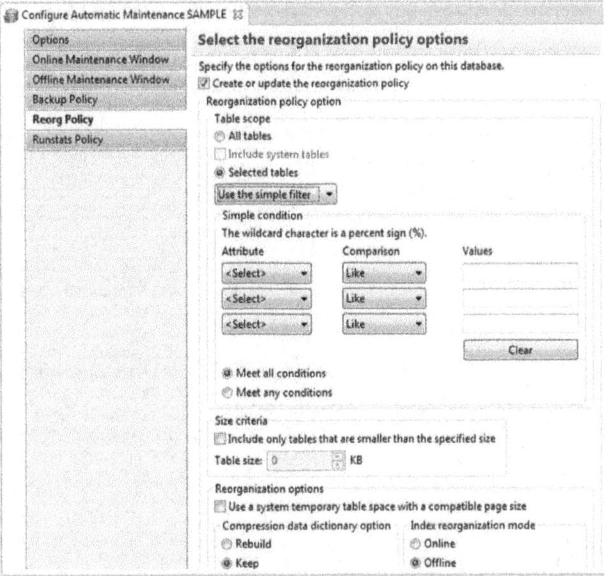

Figure 2.16: Data reorganization policy options

The reorganization options allow you to modify the behavior of data and index reorganization operation by specifying the following choices:

- Use a system temporary table space with a compatible page size. By default, the database manager stores a working copy of the table in the table spaces that contain the table when a table is being reorganized. The reorganization operation will fail if the table space does not have enough space to store the copy of table and the table space is not set to grow automatically, or if the underlying file system has run out of space. If this option is checked, reorganization will automatically choose a temporary table space of compatible page size for the reorganization operation to store a working copy of the table.
- Use the index reorganization mode to specify whether to reorganize indexes in the online or offline maintenance window. In online index reorganization mode, users will still be able to read and write to the index pages while the index is being reorganized, because that reorganization command, which is executed by automatic reorganization, will include the ALLOW WRITE ACCESS clause. For tables that do not support online index reorganization (MDC tables, and spatial indexes), automatic reorganization will perform the index reorganization in an offline maintenance window even if the online index reorganization mode is specified.
- Use a compression data dictionary to choose whether to rebuild the compression dictionary or whether to keep the existing compression dictionary for a table.

You can also set the reorganization policy by using the SYSPROC.AUTOMAINT_SET_POLICY system stored procedure. You can find the sample XML file DB2AutoReorgPolicySample.xml at $INSTHOME/sqllib/samples/automaintcfg and modify it to work for your environment:

```
CALL SYSPROC.AUTOMAINT_SET_POLICY ('AUTO_REORG',
BLOB
('<?xml version="1.0" encoding="UTF-8"?>
<DB2AutoReorgPolicy xmlns="http://www.ibm.com/xmlns/prod/db2/autonomic/
config">
<ReorgOptions dictionaryOption="Keep" indexReorgMode="Offline" useSystemTemp
TableSpace="true"/>
<ReorgTableScope >
<FilterClause />
</ReorgTableScope >
</DB2AutoReorgPolicy> ') )
```

To activate automatic RUNSTATS maintenance on your database, follow these three simple steps:

Step 1: Update the AUTO_MAINT and AUTO_TBL_MAINT database configuration parameters by using the proper CLP command or the IBM Data Studio check box option, as in Figure 2.12.

- To enable automatic background statistics collection, set the AUTO_RUNSTATS database configuration parameter to ON.
- To enable automatic real-time statistics collection, set the AUTO_STMT_STATS and AUTO_RUNSTATS database configuration parameters to ON.
- Likewise, to enable automatic statistics profile generation, set the AUTO_STATS_PROF and AUTO_PROF_UPD database configuration parameters to ON.

Step 2: Define an online or offline maintenance window based on the business requirements, as Figure 2.14 shows.

Step 3: Define a RUNSTATS policy to control the behavior of automatic table statistics collection such as the table scope, as Figure 2.17 illustrates.

The table scope section's **Runstats policy option** specifies the tables to consider for automatic RUNSTATS policy. Options are **All tables**, **Include system tables**, and **Selected tables**, which you base on a simple or custom filter predicate.

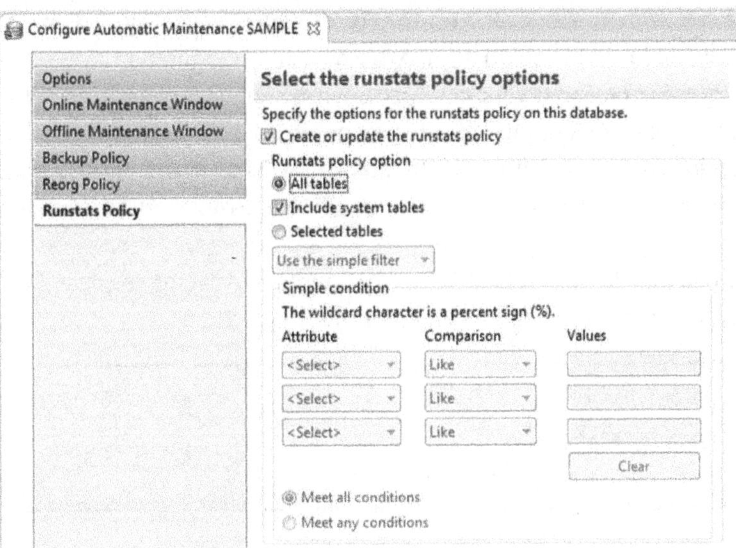

Figure 2.17: Runstats Policy options

You can also set the reorganization policy by using the SYSPROC.AUTOMAINT_SET_POLICY system stored procedure. You can find the sample XML file DB2AutoRunstatsPolicySample.xml $INSTHOME/sqllib/samples/automaintcfg and modify it to work for your environment:

```
CALL SYSPROC.AUTOMAINT_SET_POLICY ('AUTO_RUNSTATS',
BLOB(
' <?xml version="1.0" encoding="UTF-8"?>
<DB2AutoRunstatsPolicy
xmlns="http://www.ibm.com/xmlns/prod/db2/autonomic/config">
            <RunstatsTableScope>
                  <FilterCondition/>
            </RunstatsTableScope>
</DB2AutoRunstatsPolicy> '
))
```

The Configuration Advisor

With a broad range of database manager and database configuration parameters to choose from, including the buffer pool size (if it is not set to automatic), deciding where to start and what changes to make can be a difficult task. Fortunately, DB2 comes packaged with a tool to help you get started; that tool is the Configuration Advisor. The Configuration Advisor is designed to capture specific information about your database environment and recommend or make changes to configuration parameters based on the information provided.

The Configuration Advisor is automatically invoked whenever you create a database. You can change this behavior by assigning the value NO to the DB2_ENABLE_AUTOCONFIG_DEFAULT registry variable.

To obtain the functionality provided by the Configuration Advisor, execute the AUTOCONFIGURE command. The basic syntax for this command is:

```
AUTOCONFIGURE
USING [[Keyword] [Value] ,...]
APPLY [DB ONLY | DB AND DBM | NONE]
```

where:

Keyword — Identifies one or more special keywords that are recognized by the AUTOCONFIGURE command; the following values are valid for this parameter: mem_percent, workload_type, num_stmts, tpm, admin_priority, is_populated, num_local_apps, num_remote_apps, isolation, and bp_resizable

Value — Identifies the value to associate with the keyword provided; Table 2.8 lists the values that are valid for each keyword recognized by the AUTOCONFIGURE command

Table 2.8: AUTOCONFIGURE command keywords and values

Keyword	Valid Values / Default	Description
mem_percent	1–100 Default: 25	Percentage of available server memory (RAM) the DB2 database manager is to use when performing database operations.
workload_type	simple, complex, mixed Default: mixed	The type of workload that usually is run against the database. Valid values are as follows: simple—database is used primarily for transaction processing (for example, order entry and OLTP); complex—database is used primarily to resolve queries (for example, data warehousing), and mixed—database is used to resolve queries and to process transactions. Simple workloads tend to be I/O-intensive and mostly transactions, whereas complex workloads tend to be CPU-intensive and mostly queries.
num_stmts	1–1,000,000 Default: 10	Average number of SQL statements executed within a single transaction (i.e., between commits). Note: If unknown, choose a number greater than 10.

Table 2.8: AUTOCONFIGURE command keywords and values (continued)		
Keyword	**Valid Values / Default**	**Description**
tpm	1–200,000 Default: 60	Average number of transactions executed per minute (estimated). Note: The DB2 Performance Monitor can help you get a more accurate TPM measurement.
admin_priority	performance, recovery, both Default: both	Type of activity for which the database should be optimized. Valid values include the following: performance—database is optimized for transaction performance (slower backup/ recovery); recovery—database is optimized for backup and recovery (slower transaction performance); or both—database is optimized for both transaction performance and backup/ recovery (both are equally important).
is_populated	yes, no Default: yes	Indicates whether the database currently contains data. Valid values are as follows: yes—the database contains data, and no—the database does not contain data.
num_local_apps	0–5,000 Default: 0	Number of local applications that will be connected to the database at one time.
num_remote_apps	0–5,000 Default: 10	Number of remote applications that will be connected to the database at one time. Allocating memory to handle all connections needed (both local and remote) ensures that users never have to wait for an existing connection to be terminated before they can get connected. However, over-allocating memory for connections can result in wasted resources. The DB2 Performance Monitor can help you determine how many connections are actually acquired within a specified time frame.
isolation	RR, RS, CS, UR Default: RR	Isolation level used by most applications that access the database. Valid values include the following: RR—Repeatable Read (large number of locks acquired for long periods of time); RS—Read Stability (small number of locks acquired for long periods of time); CS—Cursor Stability (large number of locks acquired for short periods of time); and UR—Uncommitted Read (no locks acquired).
bp_resizeable	yes, no Default: yes	Indicates whether buffer pools are resizable. Valid values are: yes—buffer pools are resizable; and no—buffer pools are not resizable.

If you specify the APPLY DB ONLY clause with the AUTOCONFIGURE command, database configuration and buffer pool changes recommended by the Design Advisor will be applied to the appropriate database configuration file. If you specify the APPLY DB AND DBM clause, database configuration and buffer pool changes recommended will be applied to the database configuration file, and instance configuration changes recommended will be applied to the appropriate DB2 database manager configuration file. Specifying the APPLY NONE clause instead will display change recommendations but will not apply them.

Thus, to determine the best configuration to use for an OLTP database named SAMPLE that uses resizable buffer pools and is populated, and to review any configuration changes recommended before applying them to the appropriate database configuration file, execute an AUTOCONFIGURE command:

```
AUTOCONFIGURE USING workload_type complex
 is_populated yes
 bp_resizeable yes
APPLY NONE
```

Or, if you want to determine the best configuration to use if 60 percent of a system's memory will be available for the DB2 database manager to use when performing database operations, and the instance controls only one database (named SAMPLE), and you want to automatically update the appropriate configuration files to reflect any configuration changes recommended, you execute an AUTOCONFIGURE command that looks like this:

```
AUTOCONFIGURE USING mem_percent 60 APPLY DB AND DBM
```

However, if you want to determine the optimum configuration to use if 60 percent of a system's memory will be available for a DB2 database manager instance, and the instance controls two active databases that must use memory equally, you execute an AUTOCONFIGURE command that looks like this *for each database*:

```
AUTOCONFIGURE USING mem_percent 30 APPLY DB AND DBM APPLY NONE
```

Note: The AUTOCONFIGURE command (and the Configuration Advisor) will always recommend that a database be configured to take advantage of STMM. However, if you run the AUTOCONFIGURE command against a database that resides in an instance where the sheapthres database manager configuration parameter has been assigned a value other than zero, the sort memory heap database configuration parameter (sortheap) will not be configured for automatic tuning. Therefore, you must execute the command UPDATE DATABASE MANAGER CONFIGURATION USING SHEAPTHRES 0 before you execute the AUTOCONFIGURE command to enable sort memory tuning.

Adaptive Utility Throttling

The database maintenance activities consume resources when they are run, so their executing can affect database performance. To minimize system impact, you can regulate the resource usage of some automatic maintenance activities by using DB2's adaptive utility throttling system.

The adaptive utility throttling system allows maintenance utilities to be run concurrently with workloads during critical periods, while keeping their impact on the system within acceptable limits. The following maintenance operations can take advantage of utility throttling:

- Statistics collection
- Backup operations
- Rebalancing operations
- Asynchronous index cleanups

Setting an Impact Policy

To control utility throttling, you must establish an impact policy. The impact policy refers to the instance-wide limit that all throttled utilities can cumulatively have on the production workload; once such a policy is established, it is the system's responsibility to ensure that the policy is obeyed. To define the impact policy for all throttled utilities, you simply assign a value between 1 and 100 to the util_impact_lim DB2 database manager configuration parameter.

For example, to set the instance-wide limit that all throttled utilities can cumulatively have on production workloads to 10 percent (in other words, to ensure performance degradation from all throttled utilities will not impact the system workload by more than 10 percent), you assign the util_impact_lim configuration parameter the value 10 by executing an UPDATE DBM CFG command:

```
UPDATE DATABASE MANAGER CONFIGURATION USING UTIL_IMPACT_LIM 10
```

As you would expect, a throttled utility will usually take longer to complete than an unthrottled utility. If you find that a utility is running for an excessively long time, you can increase the value assigned to the util_impact_lim configuration parameter, or you can disable throttling altogether by setting the util_impact_lim configuration parameter to 100. If util_impact_lim is set to 100, no utility invocations will be throttled. In this case, the utilities can complete faster, but they most likely will have an undesirable impact on workload performance.

Executing a Utility in Throttled Mode

Defining an impact policy does not mean that all utility invocations will run throttled. In fact, by default, utilities run unthrottled even when an impact policy has been defined. To execute a utility in throttled mode, you must enable throttling either at the time the utility is invoked or after it has been started.

To enable throttling when a utility is invoked, you must specify the UTIL_IMPACT_PRIORITY option with the command that is used to execute the utility. Currently, the only commands that recognize the UTIL_IMPACT_PRIORITY clause are BACKUP DATABASE and RUNSTATS. Keep in mind that an impact policy must be defined via the util_impact_lim configuration parameter before the UTIL_IMPACT_PRIORITY clause will have any effect on these commands.

The UTIL_IMPACT_PRIORITY clause takes an optional relative priority argument (a value between 0 and 100 where 0 is OFF), which differentiates among the importance of throttled utilities. A throttled utility with a high priority will run more aggressively than one with a low priority.

Changing a Running Utility's Impact Priority

To change the impact priority (level of throttling) of a utility that is already running, execute the SET UTIL_IMPACT_PRIORITY command. With this command, you can

- Throttle a running utility that was started in unthrottled mode
- Unthrottle a running throttled utility (disable throttling)
- Reprioritize a running throttled utility (this capability is useful if multiple simultaneous throttled utilities are running and one is more important than the others)

The syntax for the SET UTIL_IMPACT_PRIORITY command is:

```
SET UTIL_IMPACT_PRIORITY FOR [UtilityID] TO [Priority]
```

where:

UtilityID	Identifies the running utility, by ID, whose priority is to be changed
Priority	Specifies an instance-level limit on the impact associated with running the specified utility (a value of 100 represents the highest priority; a value of 1 represents the lowest—setting Priority to 0 will force a throttled utility to continue running unthrottled; setting Priority to a nonzero value will force an unthrottled utility to continue running in throttled mode)

Thus, if you want to force an active unthrottled backup operation whose utility ID is 21 to continue running in throttled mode, execute the following command:

```
SET UTIL_IMPACT_PRIORITY FOR 21 TO 50
```

Once this statement is executed, the cumulative impact of the backup operation and other concurrently executing throttled utilities will be less than the percentage impact value assigned to the util_impact_lim configuration parameter. The value 50 defines the throttling importance of the backup operation with respect to other throttled utilities.

Running Utilities Information

If you want to find out which, if any, utilities are running against an instance and what their current impact priority is, you can do so by executing the LIST UTILITIES command. The syntax for this command is:

```
LIST UTILITIES <SHOW DETAIL>
```

So, say someone starts a backup operation for a database named SAMPLE, and you want to obtain detailed information about the operation. To do so, you execute a LIST UTILITIES command:

```
LIST UTILITIES SHOW DETAIL
```

Assuming the backup operation was started unthrottled, the information returned will look something like this:

```
ID                               = 21
Type                             = BACKUP
Database Name                    = SAMPLE
Member Number                    = 0
Description                      = online db
Start Time                       = 06/30/2014 07:58:16.160950
State                            = Executing
Invocation Type                  = User
Throttling:
   Priority                      = Unthrottled
Progress Monitoring:
   Estimated Percentage Complete = 7
      Total Work                 = 4570864623 bytes
      Completed Work             = 304095063 bytes
      Start Time                 = 06/30/2014 07:58:16.160962
```

To change the impact priority of this backup operation, you execute a SET UTIL_IMPACT_PRIORITY command and specify the utility ID 21:

```
SET UTIL_IMPACT_PRIORITY FOR 21 to 50
DB20000I The SET UTIL_IMPACT_PRIORITY command completed successfully.

LIST UTILITIES SHOW DETAIL

ID                               = 21
Type                             = BACKUP
Database Name                    = SAMPLE
Member Number                    = 0
Description                      = online db
Start Time                       = 06/30/2014 07:58:16.160950
State                            = Executing
Invocation Type                  = User
Throttling:
   Priority                      = 50
Progress Monitoring:
   Estimated Percentage Complete = 17
      Total Work                 = 4570864623 bytes
      Completed Work             = 788663821 bytes
      Start Time                 = 06/30/2014 07:58:16.160962
```

In the previous two command snippets, you may have noticed that the database backup was running earlier in unthrottled mode, but after we set the UTIL_IMPACT_PRIORITY to 50, it started running with priority 50.

Taking Control of a DB2 Server

Because any number of clients (maximum of 64,000 concurrent connections as per MAX_COORDAGENTS configuration) can access a server, and in turn any number of users can be granted the privileges needed to work with a particular database, it can be difficult, if not impossible, to coordinate the work efforts of everyone using a specific database at any given point in time. This situation can create a problem because, to perform routine maintenance operations, a database administrator will need all users to stop using a particular instance or database. If your organization is small, it may be possible to contact each database user and ask him or her to disconnect long enough to perform any necessary maintenance operations. But what if your organization consists of several hundred users? Or what if an employee went home early and inadvertently left an instance attachment or database connection open? How can you find out which users and applications are interacting with the instance or database you need exclusive access to?

Determining Who Is Using the Instance or Database

If you have System Administrator (SYSADMN), System Control (SYSCTRL), System Maintenance (SYSMAINT) or System Monitoring (SYSMON) authority for a DB2 database server, you can find out who is using an instance or a database on that server by executing the LIST APPLICATIONS command. The basic syntax for this command is:

```
LIST APPLICATIONS
<FOR [DATABASE | DB] [DatabaseAlias]>
<SHOW DETAIL>
```

where:

DatabaseAlias Identifies the alias assigned to the database for which to obtain application information

Thus, to determine which applications are currently connected to a database named SAMPLE (along with the authorization IDs associated with the users running those applications), you execute a LIST APPLICATIONS command:

```
LIST APPLICATIONS FOR DATABASE sample
```

And when this command is executed, you might see output that looks something like this:

```
         Application    Appl.                                    DB         # of
Auth Id  Name           Handle    Application Id                 Name       Agents
-------- -------------- --------- ------------------------------ ---------- ------
DB2INST1 db2jcc_applica 3499      10.121.20.13.53652.140630192713 SAMPLE         1
DB2INST1 db2jcc_applica 3498      10.121.20.13.53651.140630192712 SAMPLE         1
DB2INST1 db2bp          3500      *LOCAL.db2inst1.140630192934    SAMPLE         1
```

(Note: In this book, the format of SQL output such as the preceding example has, in some cases, been modified to fit the book page width; for example, output column headings may be split over multiple lines and extra spaces between columns removed.)

You can also discover which applications are attached to an instance or connected to a database within that instance by selecting the **Monitor** and **Application Connections** actions from the IBM Data Studio Administration Explorer. Figure 2.18 shows the Data Studio menu items that you must select to activate the Application Connections console.

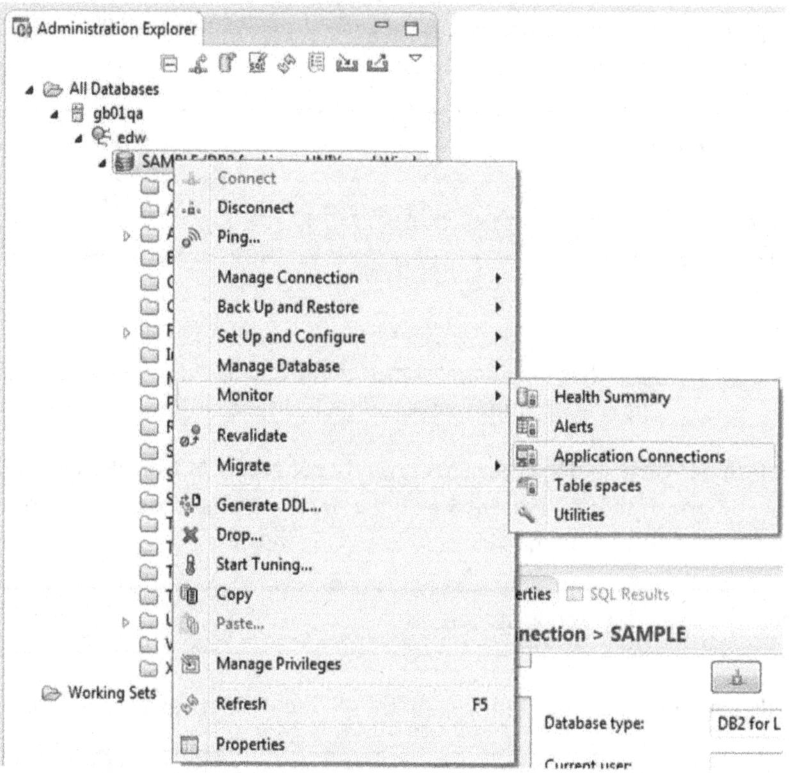

Figure 2.18: Application Connections monitor console activation

Figure 2.19 shows how the web console might look if an application is connected to a database within the specified instance.

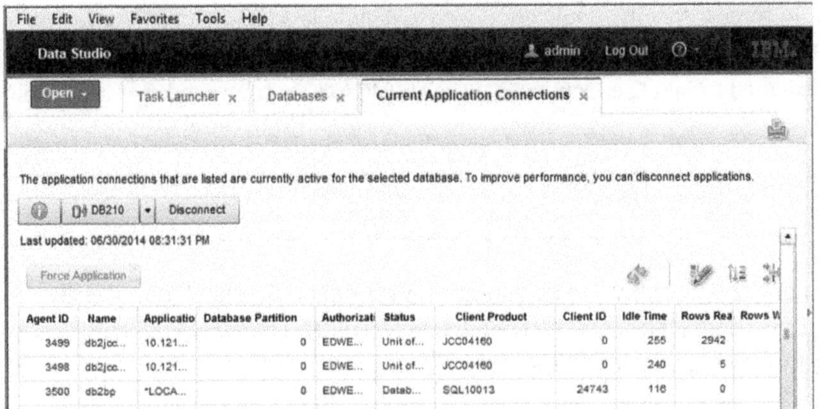

Agent ID	Name	Applicatio	Database Partition	Authorizati	Status	Client Product	Client ID	Idle Time	Rows Rea	Rows W
3499	db2jcc...	10.121...	0	EDWE...	Unit of...	JCC04160	0	255	2942	
3498	db2jcc...	10.121...	0	EDWE...	Unit of...	JCC04160	0	240	5	
3500	db2bp	*LOCA...	0	EDWE...	Datab...	SQL10013	24743	116	0	

Figure 2.19: IBM Data Studio Application Connections web console

Forcing Application Connections

Once you know which applications are using a particular instance or database, you can terminate one or more of those applications prematurely by executing the FORCE APPLICATION command (assuming you have SYSADMN, SYSCTRL, or SYSMAINT authority). The basic syntax for this command is:

```
FORCE APPLICATION ALL
```

or

```
FORCE APPLICATION ([ApplicationHandle], ...)
```

where:

ApplicationHandle Identifies the handle to associate with one or more applications whose instance attachments or database connections are to be terminated

Thus, if you want to force all users and applications connected to databases stored on a server named DB210 to terminate their database connections, you execute a FORCE APPLICATION command:

```
FORCE APPLICATION ALL
```

However, to force a specific application whose handle is 3500 (refer to the sample output for the LIST APPLICATIONS command to see where this value came from) to terminate its connection to a database named SAMPLE, execute a FORCE APPLICATION command that looks something like this:

```
FORCE APPLICATION (3500)
```

It is important to note that when an application's instance attachment or database connection is terminated by the FORCE APPLICATION command, any SQL operations that have been performed by the application but have not yet been committed are rolled back.

Note: To preserve database integrity, only applications that are idle or that are performing interruptible database operations can be terminated when the FORCE APPLICATION command is processed. In addition, the DB2 database manager for the instance cannot be stopped during a force operation; the DB2 database manager must remain active so that subsequent instance-level operations can be handled without having to restart the instance. Finally, because the FORCE APPLICATION command is run asynchronously, other applications or users can attach to the instance or connect to a database within the instance after this command has been executed. Multiple FORCE APPLICATION commands may be required to completely terminate all instance attachments and database connections.

If you are using the IBM Data Studio web console to see which users or applications are currently attached to an instance or connected to a database, you can terminate instance attachments and database connections by highlighting one or more entries in the list on the Applications Connections page and clicking **Force Application** (refer to Figure 2.19).

Working with IBM Data Studio

IBM Data Studio provides application developers and database administrators with a single integrated environment for creating, deploying, debugging, and administering data-centric applications. The product consists of the following components:

- The IBM Data Studio client, which is an Eclipse-centric tool that provides an integrated development environment for database and instance administration, routine and Java application development, and query-tuning tasks
- The IBM Data Studio web console, which is a web-based tool with health and availability monitoring, job creation, and database administration tasks

Using IBM Data Studio and the IBM Data Studio web console, you can perform various tasks, including:

- Connecting to instances and databases
- Generating DDL scripts
- Performing database administration tasks
- Performing database development tasks
- Scheduling database jobs
- Analyzing SQL queries

Connecting to Instances and Databases

To perform any tasks against an instance or a database, you must attach to the instance or connect to a database. To establish a connection to the instance or the database, follow these steps.

Step 1: Launch IBM Data Studio by clicking **Start** > **All Programs** > **IBM Data Studio** > **Data Studio 4.1.0.0 Client**, as in Figure 2.20.

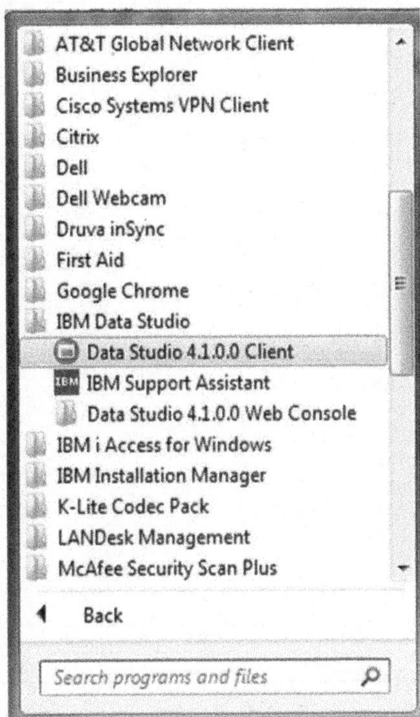

Figure 2.20: Launching IBM Data Studio Client

Step 2: Open the database administration perspective, as Figures 2.21 and 2.22 show.

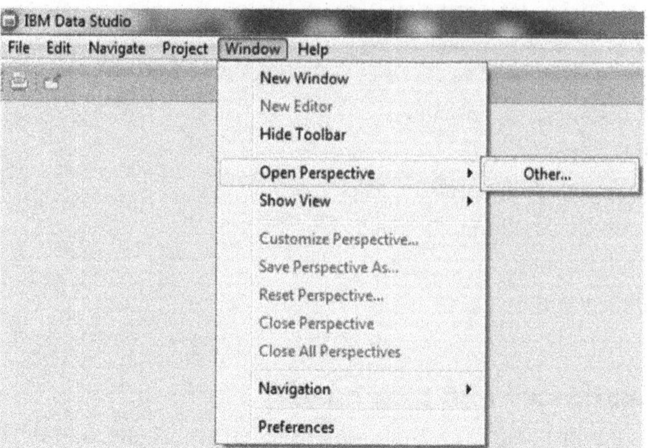

Figure 2.21: Opening the database perspectives

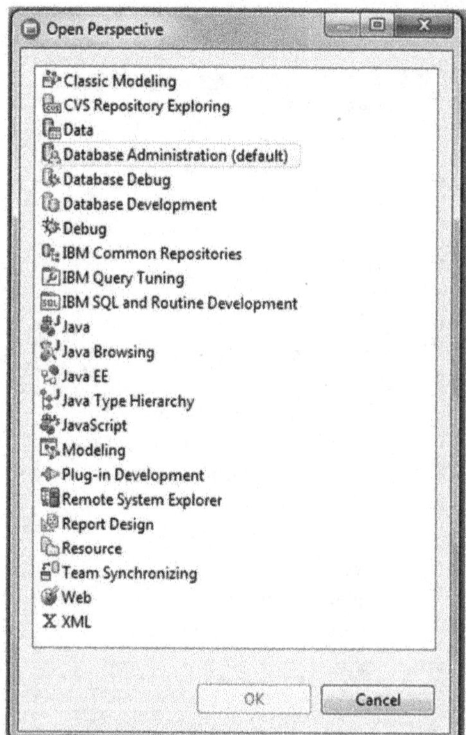

Figure 2.22: Data Studio perspectives

Step 3: Click the **New Connection to a database** icon in Administration Explorer within the Database Administration perspective, as Figure 2.23 illustrates.

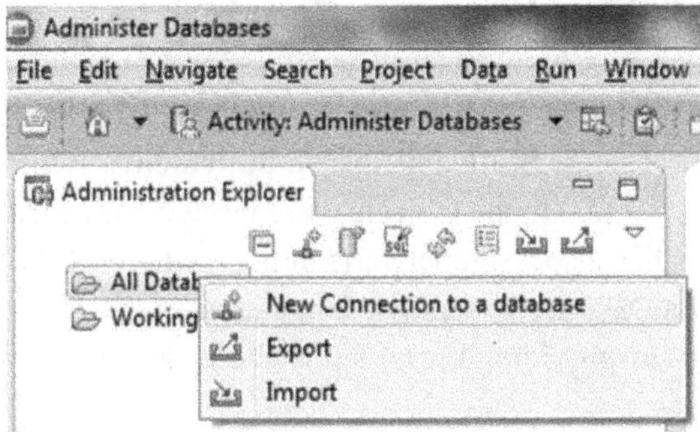

Figure 2.23: New Connection icon in Administration Explorer

Step 4: Select the required driver, the connection name, and any desired options to enable tracing while creating the new connection, as in Figure 2.24. Upon completing the connection parameters, click **Test Connection** to see whether the connection finishes successfully.

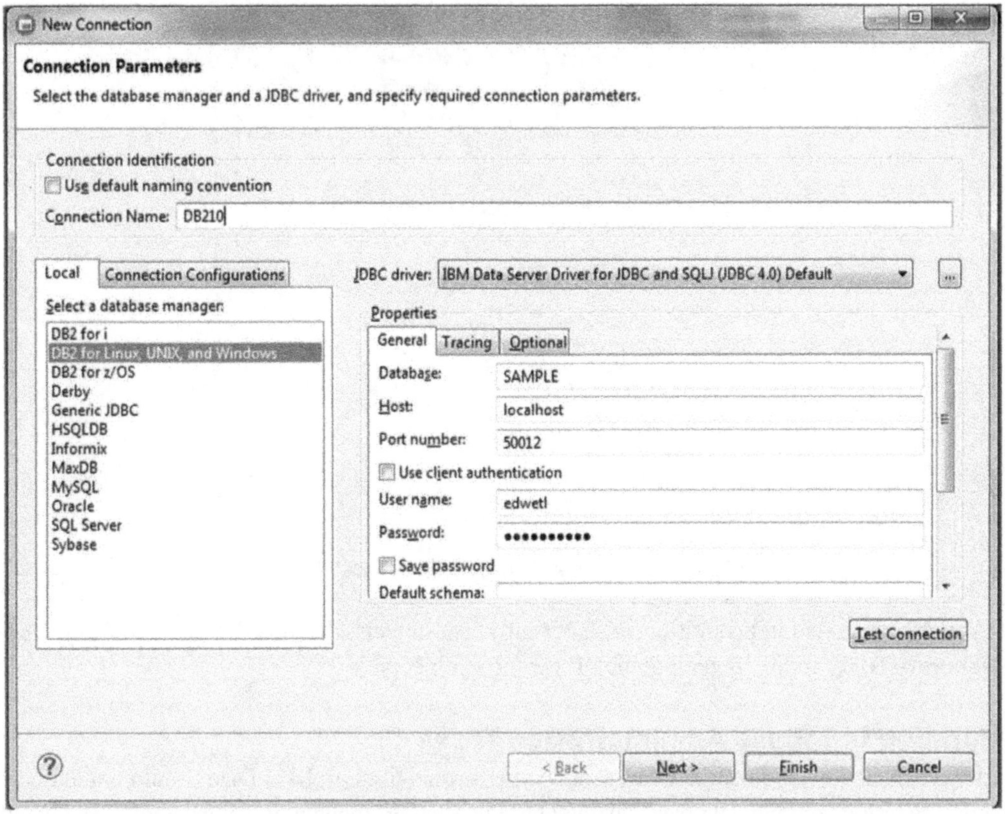

Figure 2.24: New connection parameters

Generating Data Definition Language Scripts

You can extract the DDL for the whole database or for a specific object by right-clicking the database and choosing the **Generate DDL** option, as in Figure 2.25. On the Options screen, select the model elements (such as **Create Statement**, **Drop Statements**, **Replace Clause**) that you want to include in the DDL script. On the Objects screen, select the model objects (for example, tables, alias, buffer pools, table spaces, global variables, stored procedures) to include in the DDL script. On the Save and Run DDL screen, specify a path to save the generated DDL script. You can also run the DDL script by providing the target database connection information.

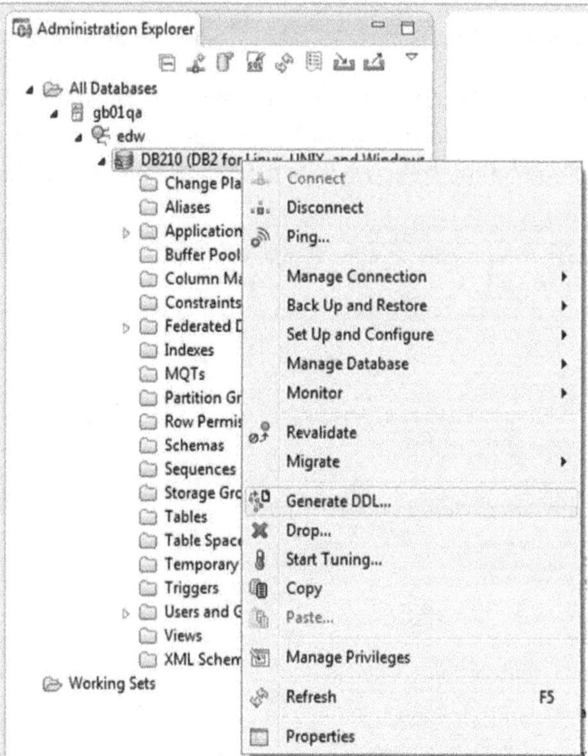

Figure 2.25: Generating DDL for the database

If you are interested in generating DDL for only few objects, right-click the objects and choose the **Generate DDL** option to generate DDL for those objects.

Performing Database Administration Tasks

A variety of database administrative tasks can be performed through IBM Data Studio, including managing security; copying data from one database to another; managing database jobs; and creating or modifying the objects, database backup, database restore, instance stop, and instance start.

To launch the database administration key task list, click the **Task Launcher** icon (see Figure 2.26), and invoke the key administrative tasks by clicking the respective task list, as Figure 2.27 shows.

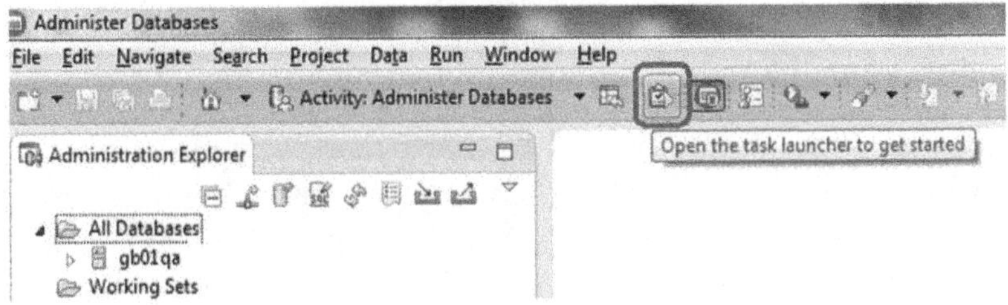

Figure 2.26: Open the Task Launcher in the Administration perspective

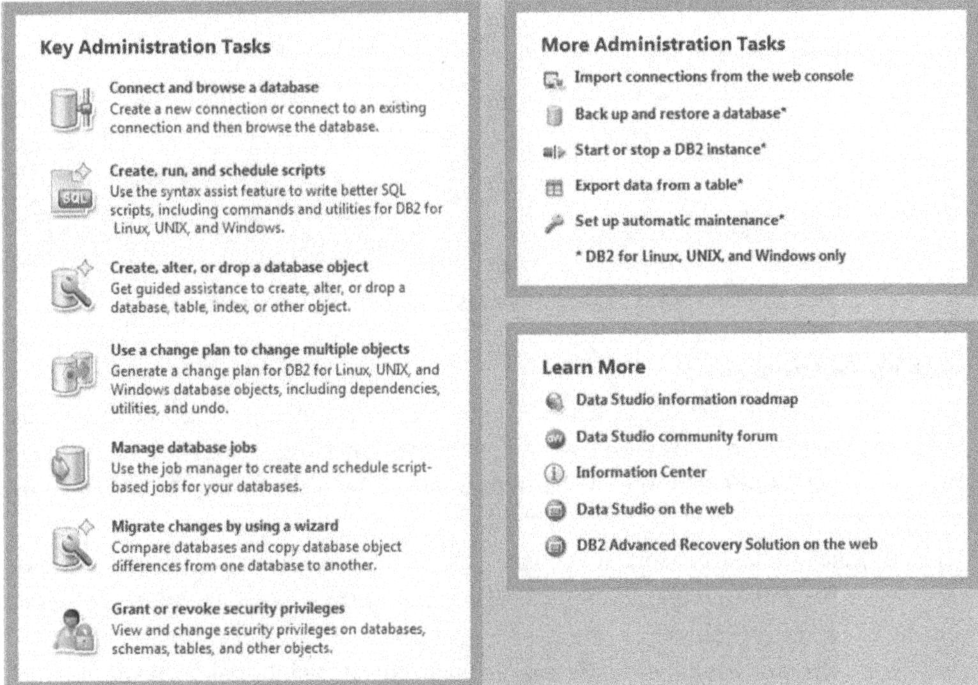

Figure 2.27: Key Administration Task list in the Task Launcher

Performing Database Development Tasks

You can perform database development tasks such as creating and running SQL statements, developing and debugging stored procedures and UDFs, and creating database applications in IBM Data Studio via the Task Launcher **Develop** tab, as Figure 2.28 illustrates.

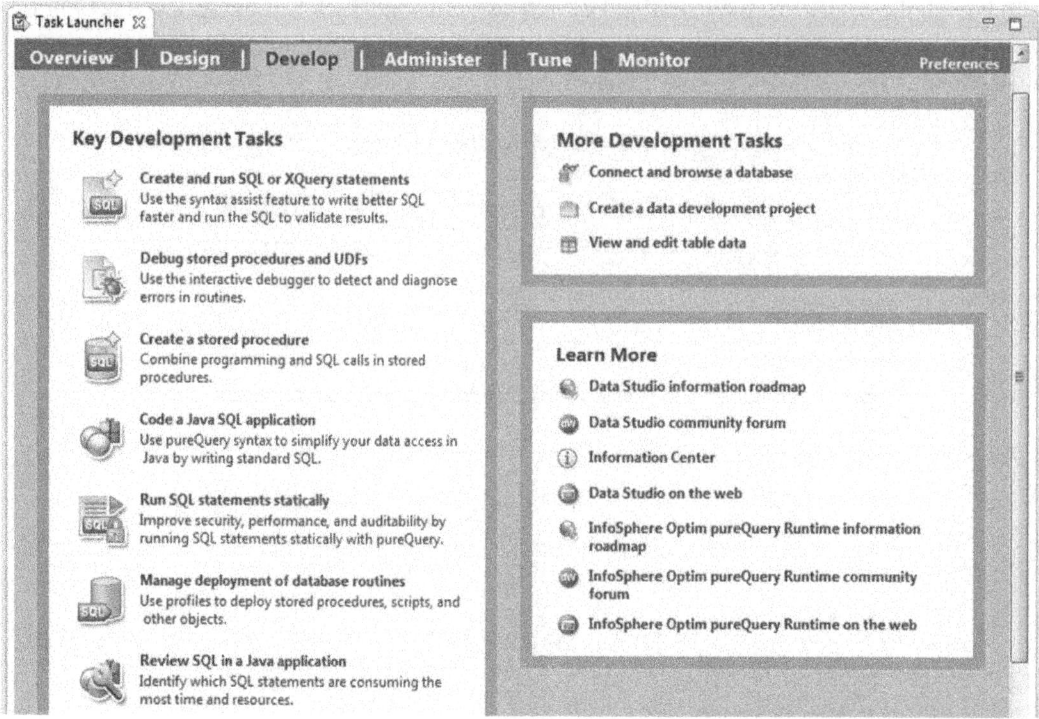

Figure 2.28: Performing development tasks via Task Launcher Develop tab

Scheduling Database Jobs

IBM Data Studio provides a web console to create, schedule, and manage database jobs. You can launch the IBM Data Studio web console (by default, http://localhost:11086/console) from **Start** > **All Programs** > **IBM Data Studio** > **IBM Data Studio 4.1.0.0 Web Console** > **Web Console**, as in Figure 2.29.

When you launch the web console, it will take you to the **Task Launcher** tab and an **Open** option to activate the **Job Manager**, multiple health monitoring and alerting utilities, and security management, as Figure 2.30 shows.

A close look at the **Job Manager** is necessary to understand the job scheduling capabilities within the IBM Data Studio web console. You can perform the following listed actions in the **Job Manager**:

- Add, edit, run, and delete jobs from the **Job List** tab
- Add, edit, delete schedules, and create job chains from the **Schedules** tab
- Add, edit, and delete notifications from the **Notifications** tab
- Edit the job history setting, view, cancel, run (rerun the earlier executed job), and delete a specific job history from the **History** tab

Figure 2.29: Launching the IBM Data Studio web console

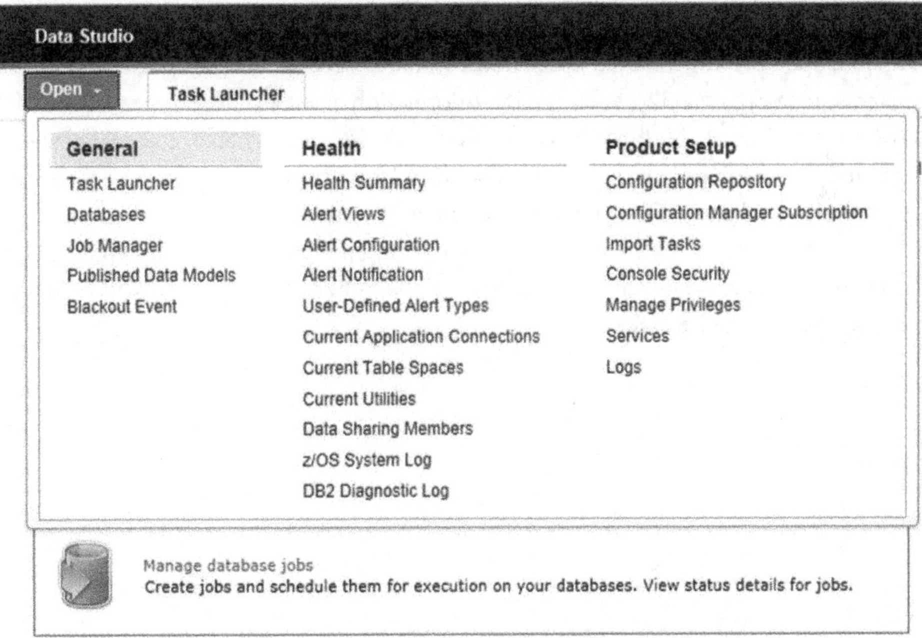

Figure 2.30: The IBM Data Studio web console Open options

You need to create a database connection before scheduling or managing any jobs in the IBM Data Studio web console. To create a connection, select **Databases** in the **General** section of the **Open** menu, and then click "Add a database connection" (see Figure 2.31). Once you have created the required database connections, you can start scheduling the jobs over them by using the IBM Data Studio web console job manager.

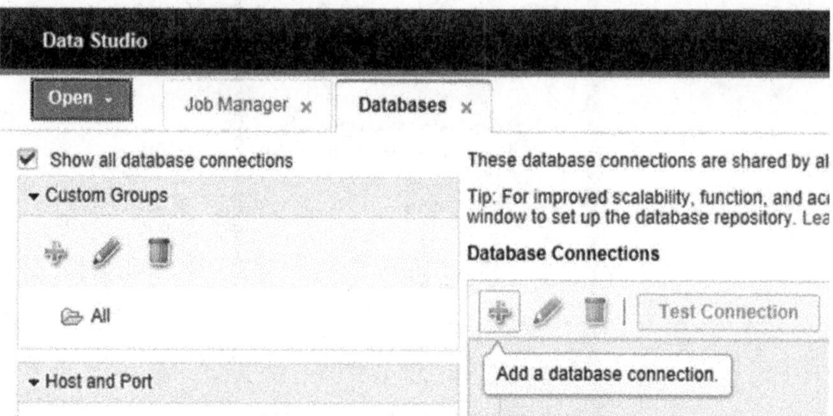

Figure 2.31: Adding a new database connection

Creating and Scheduling Jobs

To create a job, open the **Job List** tab in the **Job Manager** section, and click **Add Job**. On the resulting screen (see Figure 2.32), enter the job information, such as name; type (DB2 CLP Script, SQL Only Script, or Executable/Shell Script); job description; and whether to enable scheduling.

You can update the job properties, script, schedules (add or use the existing schedule), chain, and notification list in the **Job Components** section, as Figure 2.33 shows.

You have the flexibility to add a schedule to an existing job chain. However, you can use the **Schedule** tab to do this as well (see Figure 2.34). On the **Schedules** tab, click **Add Schedule** and choose the job to schedule from the list.

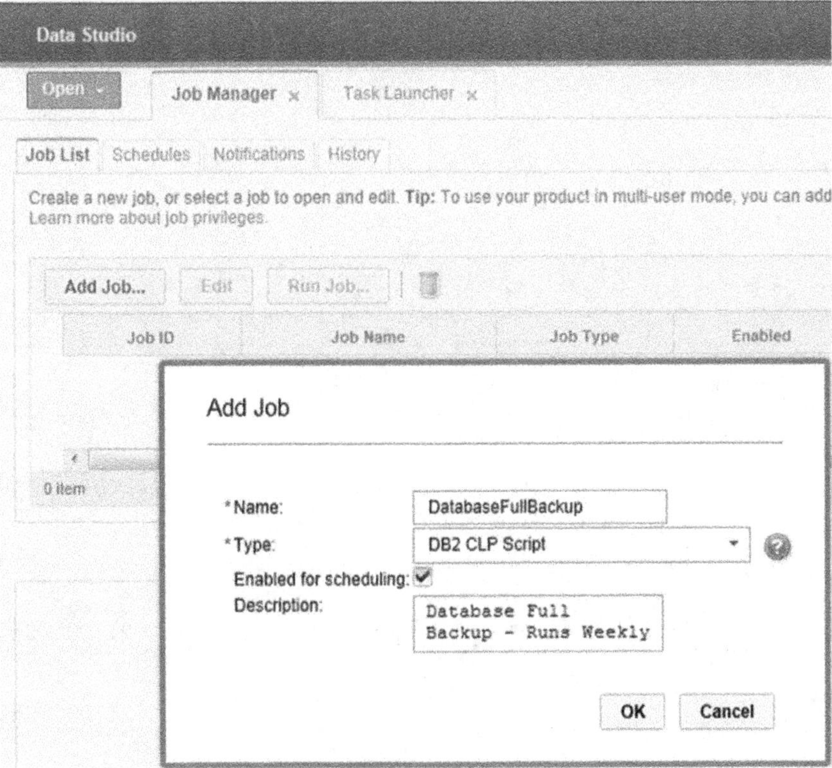

Figure 2.32: Adding a new job in the Job List

*DatabaseFullBackup ×

Save All | Run Job...

Job Components
- Properties
- Script
- Schedules
- Chain
- Notifications

Enter or paste the script that will be run on the database when you run the job.

DB2 statement termination characters: ;

☑ If the connection to a member of a DB2 pureScale environment fails, try to run the script on another member.

```
CONNECT TO sample;
BACKUP DATABASE sample ONLINE USE TSM UTIL_IMPACT_PRIORITY 10 INCLUDE LOGS WITHOUT PROMPTING;
TERMINATE;
```

Figure 2.33: Adding a script into the job in the job list

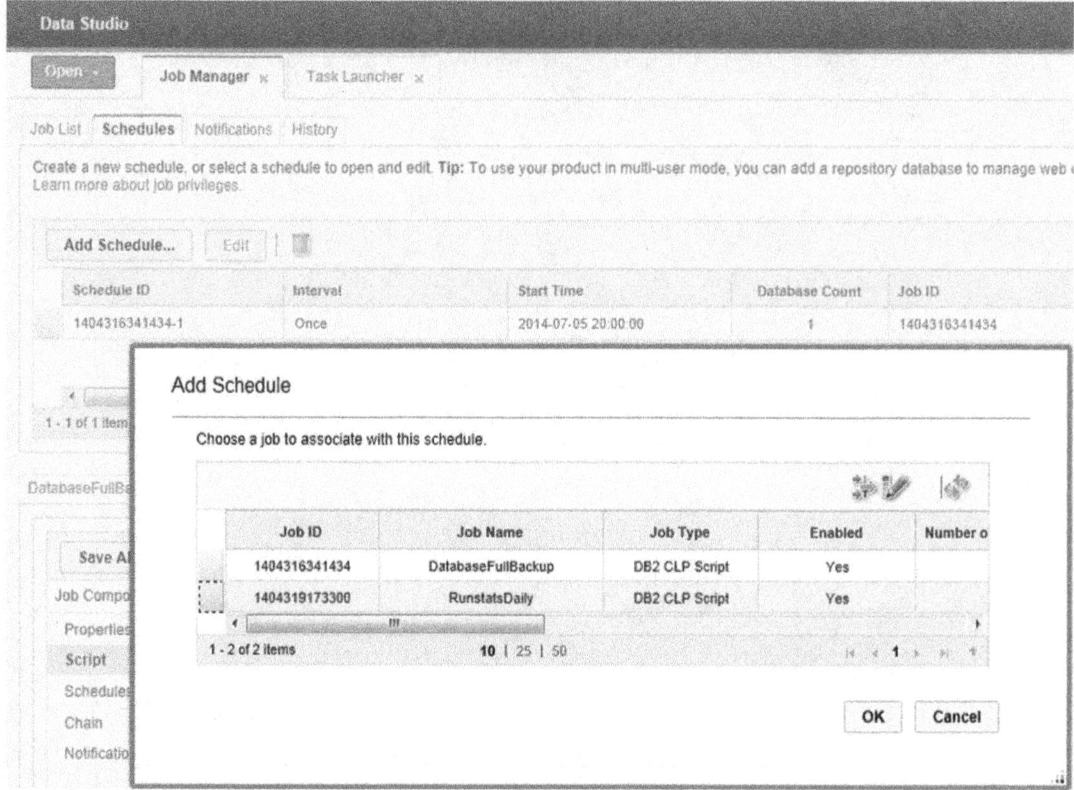

Figure 2.34: Adding a schedule

In the **Schedule Details** section, you can specify the initial date, initial time, repetition (Monthly, Weekly, Everyday, DailyInterval, Hourly, EveryMinute), and how long to keep this job running. Within the **Databases** section, you have the option to choose the databases on which to run the job. And finally, with **Timeout Settings**, you can specify an action (such as cancelling the job) to be performed if the script execution duration exceeds a timeout period, as in Figure 2.35.

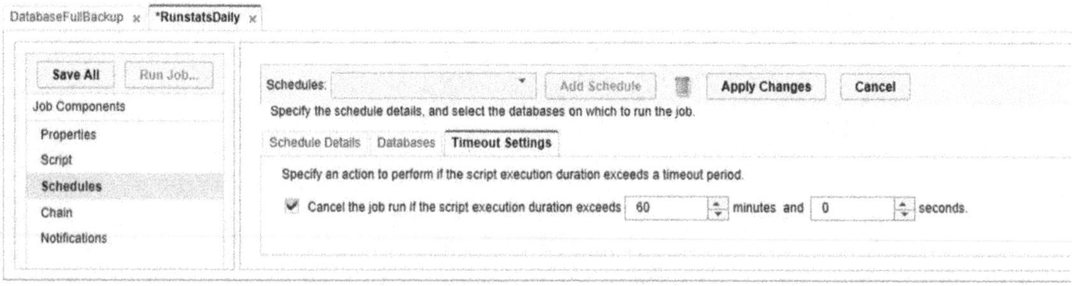

Figure 2.35: Schedule parameters

Scheduling Jobs in a Job Chain

A job chain executes one or more jobs (up to three) in sequence. The primary job initiates the job execution within the job chain and is followed by a dependent job and a closing job, as Figure 2.36 illustrates.

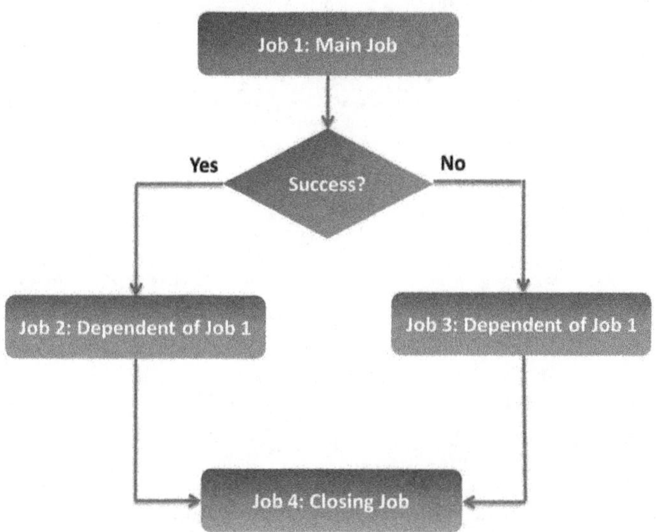

Figure 2.36: Job chains in scheduled jobs

To create a job chain, navigate to **Schedules** in the **Job Manager**, and click **Add Schedule**. This activates the Add Schedule window, wherein you can highlight the primary job and click **OK**, as Figure 2.37 shows. The **Job Manager** has four jobs with the following characteristics ready to go into a job chain:

1. RunstatsDaily (Job ID: 1404319173300—main job)
2. REORGDaily (Job ID: 1404334014453—dependent job)
3. DB2LookDaily (Job ID: 1404334590445—dependent job)
4. DatabaseFullBackup (Job ID: 1404316341434—closing job)

As Figure 2.37 shows, you highlight the RunstatsDaily job in the Add Schedule window, and click **OK**. Doing so will then display the Job Component properties page, where you can select **Chain** and key in dependent and closing job details (see Figure 2.38).

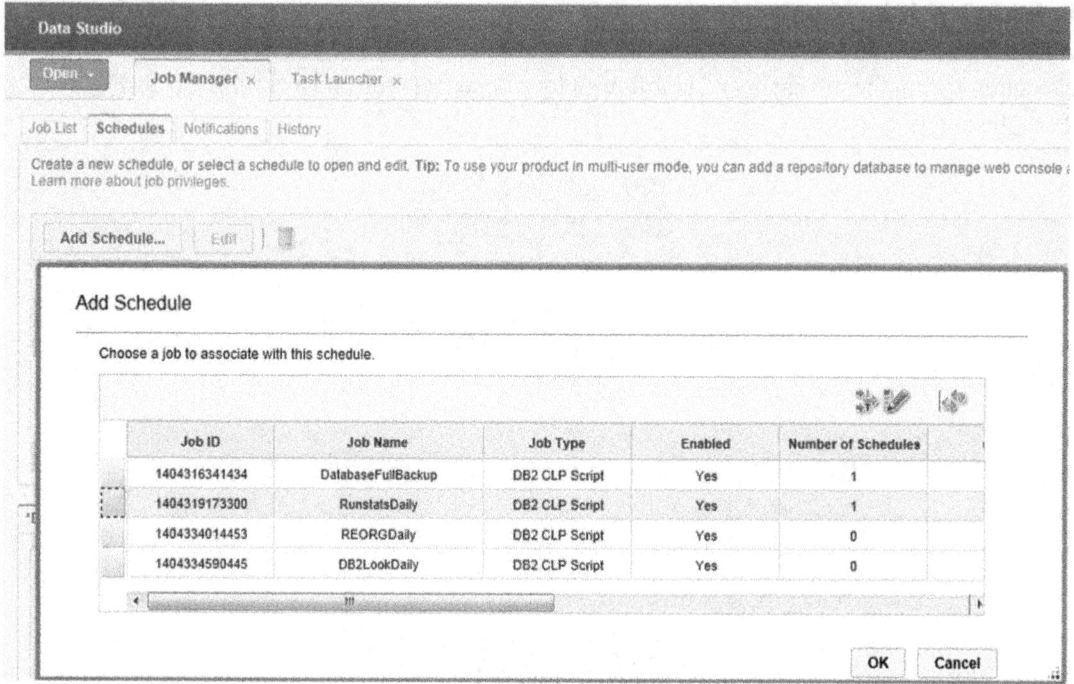

Figure 2.37: Job chain creation step 1—choosing the main job

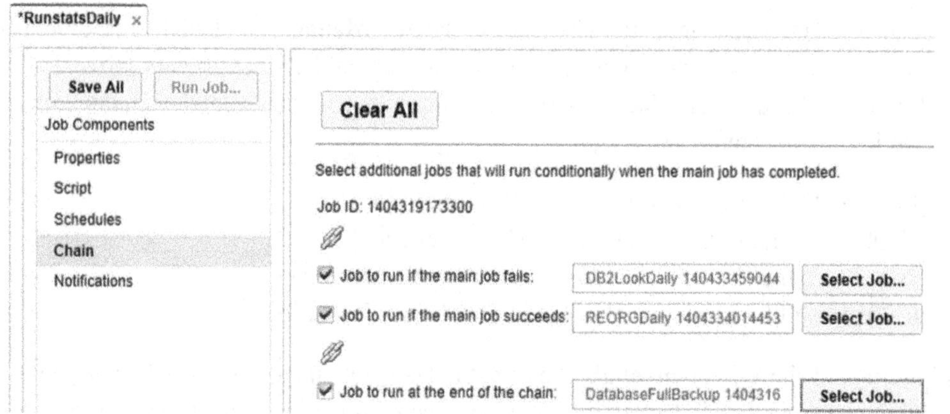

Figure 2.38: Job chain creation step 2—choosing the dependents

In this example, RunstatsDaily is the parent job; when it finishes successfully, it triggers the REORGDaily job or the DB2LookDaily job. However, DatabaseFullBackup is the closing job, so no success or failure condition is associated to it.

Once you schedule the job chain, you can check the status of the schedule and the type in the **Schedules** tab. Figure 2.39 shows that the recently scheduled job is a job chain, not just a job.

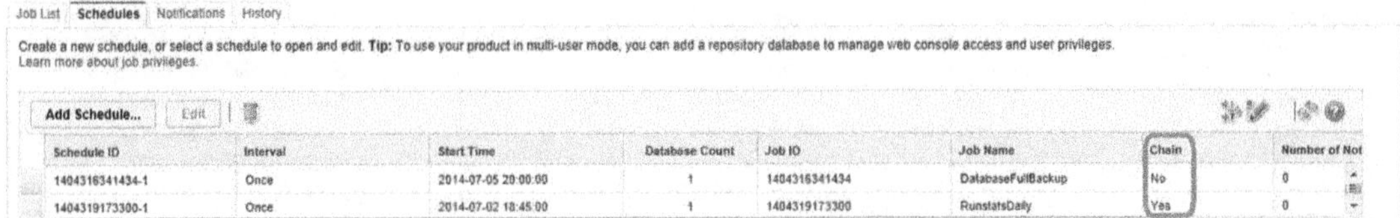

Figure 2.39: Job schedule status and the job chain flag

Setting Up Job Notifications

You can configure email notifications to be sent to one or more users depending on a success, failure, or warning status of the job. You can also choose to send a notification irrespective of the job execution status. To activate the notification, navigate to **Notifications** tab in the **Job Manager**, and key in the email recipients and the notification criteria (see Figure 2.40).

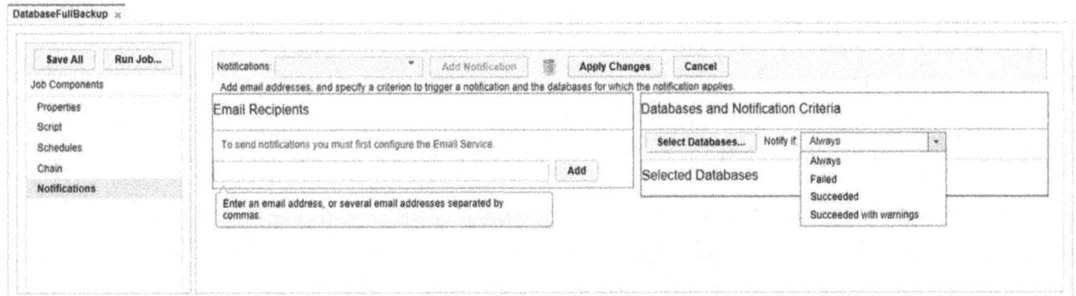

Figure 2.40: Job notification with criteria

Viewing the Job History

After the job is scheduled, you can open the **History** tab to view the job execution status through a progress bar, and see the complete job log by clicking **View Log in browser**. You can configure the job history retention period in the **Job History Settings**. Even though you scheduled the job chain, you will see job logs for each job instead of a consolidated job history log, as Figure 2.41 shows.

Analyzing SQL Queries

IBM Data Studio query tuning can generate a diagram of the current access plan for an SQL or XPATH statement to detect how the SQL compiler processes the statement. You can use this information to tune your SQL statement to improve performance.

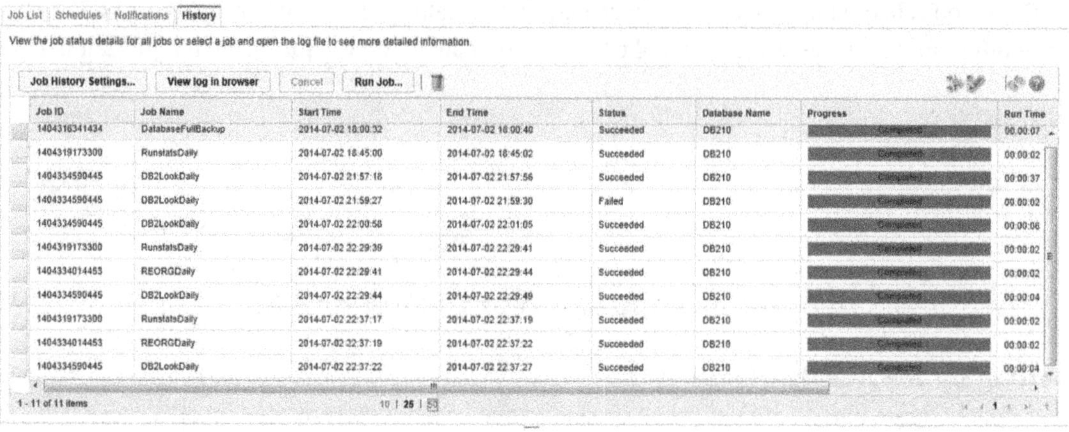

Job List | Schedules | Notifications | **History**

View the job status details for all jobs or select a job and open the log file to see more detailed information.

Job History Settings... | **View log in browser** | Cancel | **Run Job...**

Job ID	Job Name	Start Time	End Time	Status	Database Name	Progress	Run Time
1404316341434	DatabaseFullBackup	2014-07-02 18:00:32	2014-07-02 18:00:40	Succeeded	DB210	Completed	00:00:07
1404319173300	RunstatsDaily	2014-07-02 18:45:00	2014-07-02 18:45:02	Succeeded	DB210	Completed	00:00:02
1404334590445	DB2LookDaily	2014-07-02 21:57:18	2014-07-02 21:57:56	Succeeded	DB210	Completed	00:00:37
1404334590445	DB2LookDaily	2014-07-02 21:59:27	2014-07-02 21:59:30	Failed	DB210	Completed	00:00:02
1404334590445	DB2LookDaily	2014-07-02 22:00:58	2014-07-02 22:01:05	Succeeded	DB210	Completed	00:00:06
1404319173300	RunstatsDaily	2014-07-02 22:29:39	2014-07-02 22:29:41	Succeeded	DB210	Completed	00:00:02
1404334014453	REORGDaily	2014-07-02 22:29:41	2014-07-02 22:29:44	Succeeded	DB210	Completed	00:00:02
1404334590445	DB2LookDaily	2014-07-02 22:29:44	2014-07-02 22:29:49	Succeeded	DB210	Completed	00:00:04
1404319173300	RunstatsDaily	2014-07-02 22:37:17	2014-07-02 22:37:19	Succeeded	DB210	Completed	00:00:02
1404334014453	REORGDaily	2014-07-02 22:37:19	2014-07-02 22:37:22	Succeeded	DB210	Completed	00:00:02
1404334590445	DB2LookDaily	2014-07-02 22:37:22	2014-07-02 22:37:27	Succeeded	DB210	Completed	00:00:04

1 - 11 of 11 items　　10 | 25 | 50

Figure 2.41: Job history with the progress bar

The IBM Query Tuner Workflow Assistant (QTWA), which comes with IBM Data Studio, can perform these actions:

- Statistics Advisor recommendations
- SQL or XPATH query formatting
- Visual access plan generation
- Summary report generation

To generate hints for query revisions, index recommendations, and query optimization, you must activate the InfoSphere® Optim Query Workload Tuner (OQWT) for DB2 for Linux, UNIX, and Windows license by using the activation kit available at the IBM Passport Advantage site. By default, the IBM DB2 Advanced Enterprise Server Edition includes a license for the OQWT tool; otherwise, you will have to explicitly buy the license for the product by contacting an IBM sales representative.

To analyze the SQL or XPATH statements, activate the **Start Tuning** feature by right-clicking the database in Administration Explorer, as Figure 2.42 illustrates.

Doing so invokes the QTWA, which provides no-charge query-tuning features in the IBM Query Tuning perspective (see Figure 2.43).

You can follow these steps to tune an SQL statement in QTWA. First, capture the SQL statement that you want to tune. For example, if you want to tune `SELECT * FROM employee WHERE SALARY > 10000`, enter the SQL statement in the Input Text window of QTWA, and click **Invoke Advisors** and **Tools** (see Figure 2.44).

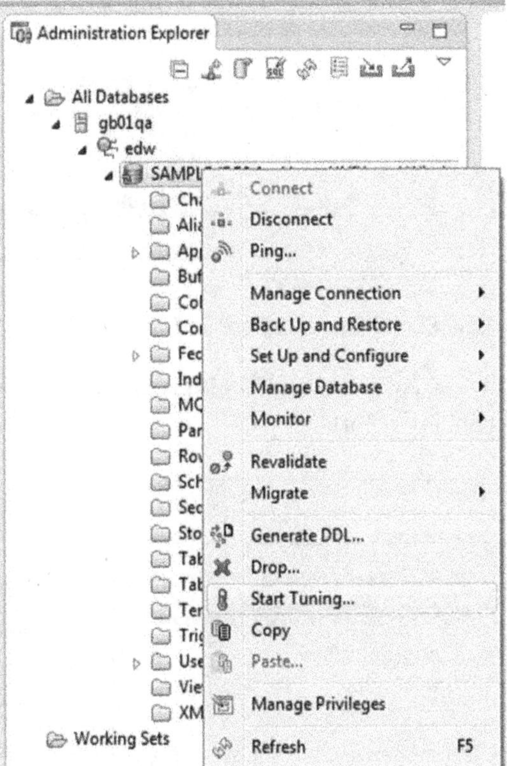

Figure 2.42: Activating the SQL/XPATH tuning in IBM Data Studio

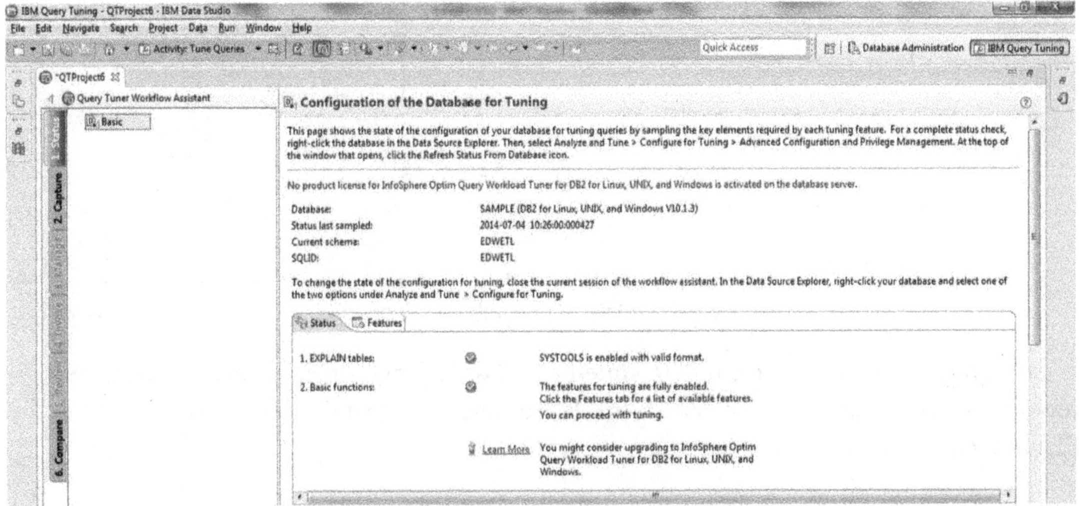

Figure 2.43: IBM Query Tuner Workflow Assistant

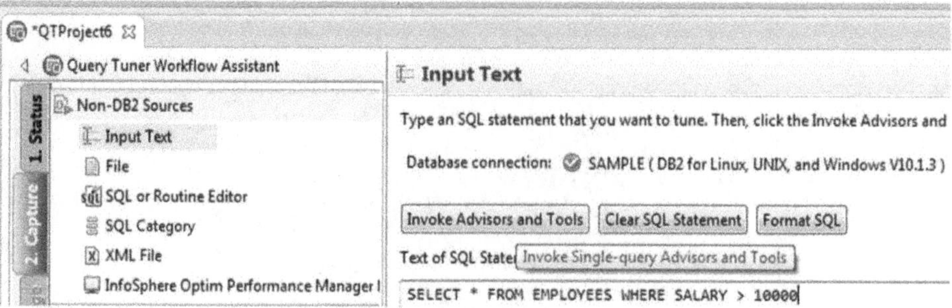

Figure 2.44: Using Advisor and Tools in QTWA

As Figure 2.45 shows, **Invoke Advisors and Tools** gives you analysis tool options to generate the recommendations and summary report.

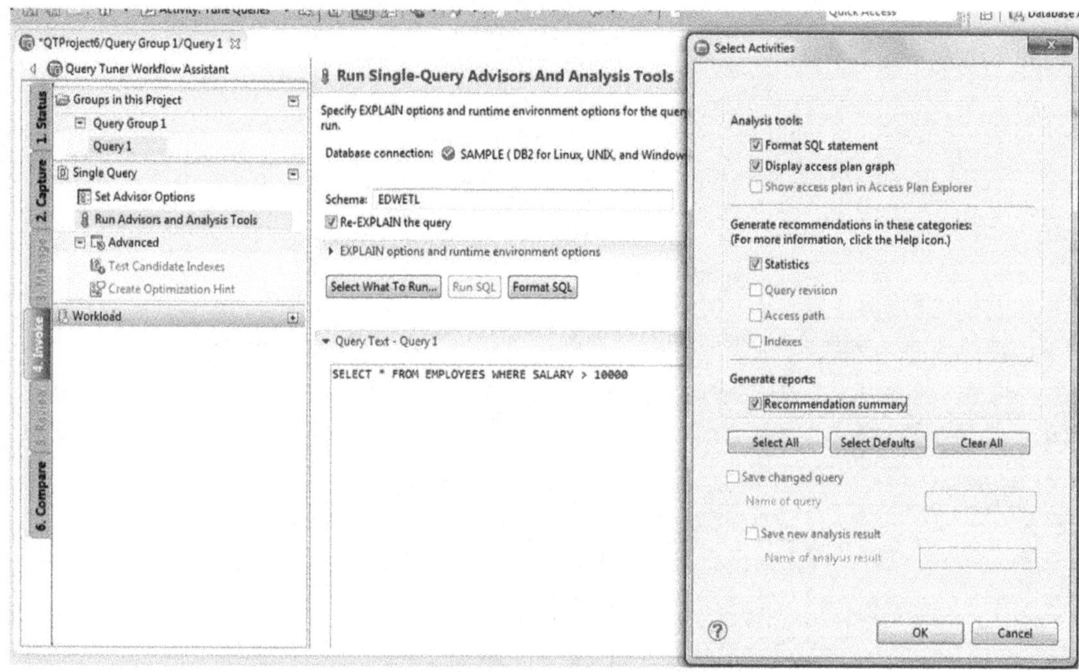

Figure 2.45: Analysis tool and report options

Next, run the tool with **Format SQL statement**, **Display access plan graph**, and **Statistics** recommendations along with a summary enabled to generate output that looks something like Figure 2.46.

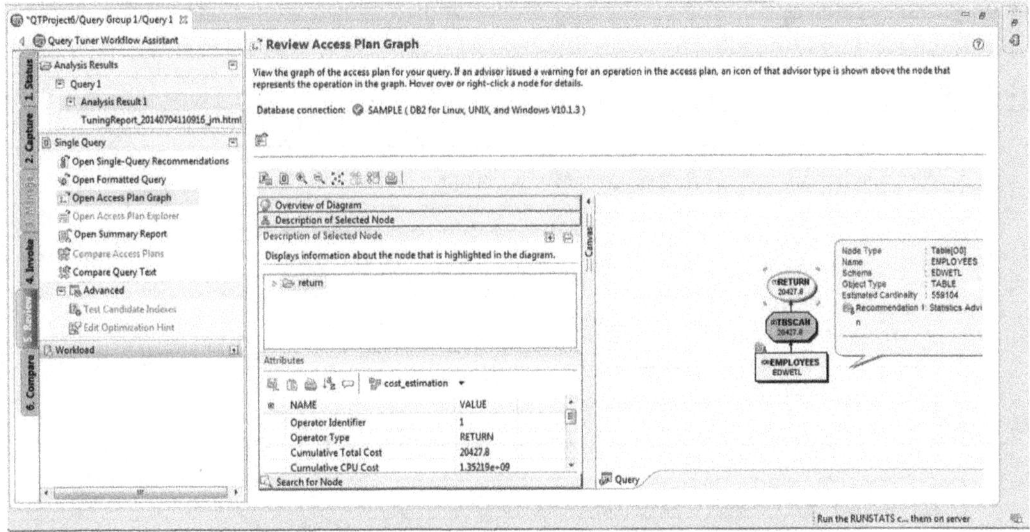

Figure 2.46: Analysis tool reviews and recommendations

And finally, select any of the options below to see the review comments and the recommendations from the advisor.

- **Open Formatted Query**—Formats the SQL statement in a more readable fashion
- **Open Access Plan Graph**—Provides pictorial representation of the access plan
- **Open Summary Report**—Provides recommendations actions, SQL in question, access plan, and database statistics information all in one report for versioning/recording perspective
- **Compare Query Text screens**—Provides an option to verify and compare an SQL Query Text between two different systems (production and nonproduction) or on the same system

Chapter Summary

The objective of this chapter was to familiarize you with

- The DB2 instance commands to create, list, update, and drop an instance
- The DB2 registry and operating system environment variables, along with the ways to set them up on the server
- The DB2 instance and database configuration parameter update commands
- The DB2 autonomic computing features and associated application or business benefits
- IBM Data Studio features as well as Query Tuner Workflow Assistant examples
- The job and job chain schedules using the IBM Data Studio web console

On completion of this chapter, you will be equipped with sufficient knowledge to answer the server management questions in the certification exam. It is also highly recommended that you complete the sample questions at the end of the chapter.

Practice Questions

Question 1

Which authority must a user have to quiesce an instance named `db2inst1`?

- ❍ A. SYSADM
- ❍ B. SECADM
- ❍ C. SYSMAINT
- ❍ D. SYSMON

Question 2

Which command will start a default instance named `db2inst1`?

- ❍ A. START db2inst1
- ❍ B. START DB MANAGER
- ❍ C. db2start -i db2inst1
- ❍ D. START DBMGR

Question 3

A DB2 server contains two instances named `TEST` and `PROD`. The instance named `TEST` is the default instance. Which command must you execute before an attempt is made to start the instance named `PROD`?

- ❍ A. db2set DB2_INSTANCE=prod
- ❍ B. UPDATE DBM CFG USING DB2INSTANCE prod
- ❍ C. set DB2INSTANCE=prod
- ❍ D. UPDATE DBM CFG USING DB2_INSTANCE prod

Question 4

Which command will assign the value `TCPIP` to the variable `DB2COMM` for all instances on a DB2 server?

- ❍ A. db2set DB2COMM=TCPIP
- ❍ B. db2set -g DB2COMM=TCPIP
- ❍ C. db2set -all DB2COMM=TCPIP
- ❍ D. set DB2COMM=TCPIP

Question 5

What will happen if you execute the following command?

```
db2set DB2COMM=
```

- ❍ A. The value assigned to the DB2COMM registry variable will be displayed.
- ❍ B. A list of communications protocols that are recognized by the server will be assigned to the DB2COMM registry variable.
- ❍ C. The value assigned to the global DB2COMM variable will be copied to the DB2COMM registry variable for the default instance.
- ❍ D. The DB2COMM registry-level variable for the default instance will be deleted or unset.

Question 6

Which command returns information about how memory has been allocated for a database named `SAMPLE`?

- ❍ A. GET DB CFG FOR sample SHOW DETAIL
- ❍ B. GET MEMORY USAGE FOR sample
- ❍ C. GET DBM CFG
- ❍ D. GET CFG DETAILS FOR sample

Question 7

Which DB2 database configuration parameter controls the maximum number of applications that can be connected to a database?

- ❍ A. MAXAPPLS
- ❍ B. AVG_APPLS
- ❍ C. NUM_INITAGENTS
- ❍ D. NUM_POOLAGENTS

Question 8

Which command disables roll-forward recovery for a database named SAMPLE and causes the database to create a duplicate copy of the transaction log files in a separate location?

- ❍ A. UPDATE DB CFG FOR sample USING LOGARCHMETH1 LOGRETAIN;
  UPDATE DB CFG FOR sample USING NEWLOGPATH D:\dup_logs;
- ❍ B. UPDATE DB CFG FOR sample USING LOGARCHMETH1 OFF;
  UPDATE DB CFG FOR sample USING MIRRORLOGPATH D:\dup_logs;
- ❍ C. UPDATE DB CFG FOR sample USING LOGARCHMETH1 LOGRETAIN;
  UPDATE DB CFG FOR sample USING LOGSECOND D:\dup_logs;
- ❍ D. UPDATE DB CFG FOR sample USING LOGARCHMETH1 OFF;
  UPDATE DB CFG FOR sample USING LOGARCHMETH2 DISK: D:\dup_logs;

Question 9

A database administrator successfully executes the following commands:

```
UPDATE DBM CFG USING SHEAPTHRES 37500
UPDATE DB CFG FOR sample USING SORTHEAP 2500
```

Assuming each sort operation performed against the SAMPLE database consumes 10 MB of memory, what is the maximum number of unrestricted sort operations that can run concurrently?

- ❍ A. 5
- ❍ B. 10
- ❍ C. 15
- ❍ D. 20

Question 10

Which database configuration parameter forces an application to wait indefinitely to obtain a lock on a table?

- ❍ A. LOCKLIST
- ❍ B. LOCKTIMEOUT
- ❍ C. DLCHKTIME
- ❍ D. MAXLOCKS

Question 11

A database administrator executes the following commands:

```
CONNECT TO sample;
UPDATE DB CFG FOR sample USING SORTHEAP 25;
UPDATE DB CFG FOR sample USING UTIL_HEAP_SZ 32;
COMMIT;
```

Assuming sufficient memory is available, when will the changes take place?

- ❍ A. The next time the instance is stopped and restarted.
- ❍ B. The next time the SAMPLE database is stopped and restarted.
- ❍ C. Immediately after the commands are executed.
- ❍ D. The changes will not take place because the database was not placed in quiesced mode first.

Question 12

A database administrator successfully changes the value of the SORTHEAP database configuration parameter while a running application is accessing the database. When will the application see the effects?

- ❍ A. When a new SQL statement is executed.
- ❍ B. When a new transaction is started.
- ❍ C. When a new database connection is established.
- ❍ D. When the application terminates and is restarted.

Question 13

Which command will recommend and make configuration changes for an instance named DB2INST1?

- ❍ A. AUTOCONFIGURE USING db2inst1 APPLY
- ❍ B. AUTOCONFIGURE USING mem_percent 60 APPLY db2inst1
- ❍ C. AUTOCONFIGURE USING mem_percent 60 APPLY DBM ONLY
- ❍ D. AUTOCONFIGURE USING mem_percent 60 APPLY DB AND DBM

Question 14

After running the AUTOCONFIGURE command, a database administrator noticed that the SORTHEAP database configuration parameter for a database named SAMPLE had not been set to AUTOMATIC, even though the SELF_TUNING_MEM configuration parameter had been set to ON.

To get the desired results, which command must be executed before the AUTOCONFIGURE command is run again?

- ❍ A. UPDATE DBM CFG USING SHEAPTHRES 0
- ❍ B. UPDATE DB CFG FOR sample USING SHEAPTHRES_SHR AUTOMATIC
- ❍ C. UPDATE DBM CFG USING SHEAPTHRES AUTOMATIC
- ❍ D. UPDATE DB CFG FOR sample USING SHEAPTHRES_SHR 0

Question 15

Consider the following information about a DB2 server:

- Instance name: db2inst1
- Port number: 60000
- Service name: db2c_db2inst1
- Host name: db2host
- Host TCP/IP address: 10.205.15.100
- Protocol: TCP/IP
- Database name: PROD_DB

Assuming the following entry has been made to the services file:

```
db2c_db2inst1          60000/tcp
```

which two of the following commands must you execute to correctly configure communications for the server?

- ❐ A. UPDATE DBM CFG USING SVCENAME db2c_db2inst1
- ❐ B. UPDATE DBM CFG USING SVCEPORT 60000
- ❐ C. db2set DB2COMM=TCPIP
- ❐ D. UPDATE DBM CFG USING NNAME db2host
- ❐ E. db2set DB2COMM=TCP/IP

Question 16

Which command will define an alternate diagnostic data directory path as /db2dump?

- ❍ A. UPDATE DBM CFG USING ALT_DIAGPATH /db2dump
- ❍ B. UPDATE DB CFG FOR sample UGING ALT_DIAGPATH /db2dump
- ❍ C. db2set ALT_DIAGPATH=/db2dump
- ❍ D. export ALT_DIAGPATH=/db2dump

Question 17

Which statement is true with respect to aggregated registry variable functionality?

- ❍ A. A registry variable that is explicitly set by an application can only be overwritten by an aggregated registry setting.
- ❍ B. An aggregated registry variable that is explicitly set by an application cannot be overwritten.
- ❍ C. A registry variable that is implicitly configured through an aggregated registry variable can also be explicitly configured.
- ❍ D. A registry variable that is implicitly configured through an aggregated registry variable takes precedence over an explicitly configured value.

Question 18

A `LIST APPLICATIONS` command returned the following output:

```
Auth Id  Application   Appl.      Application Id              DB         # of
         Name          Handle                                 Name       Agents
-------- ------------- ---------- --------------------------- ---------- ------
COGNOS  db2bp          45190      *LOCAL.db2inst1.140713204326 SAMPLE         1
COGNOS  db2bp          45234      *LOCAL.db2inst1.140713204352 SAMPLE         1
```

Which two of the following commands will terminate all the applications that are currently running? (Choose two.)

- ❒ A. FORCE APPLICATION (45190, 45234)
- ❒ B. FORCE APPLICATION (LOCAL.db2inst1.140713204326, LOCAL.db2inst1.140713204352)
- ❒ C. FORCE APPLICATION (db2bp, db2bp)
- ❒ D. FORCE APPLICATION ALL
- ❒ E. FORCE ALL APPLICATIONS

Question 19

The values of the automatic maintenance database configuration parameters for a database named SAMPLE are as follows:

```
Automatic maintenance                              (AUTO_MAINT) = OFF
  Automatic database backup                    (AUTO_DB_BACKUP) = OFF
  Automatic table maintenance                  (AUTO_TBL_MAINT) = OFF
    Automatic runstats                          (AUTO_RUNSTATS) = OFF
      Real-time statistics                    (AUTO_STMT_STATS) = OFF
      Statistical views                      (AUTO_STATS_VIEWS) = OFF
      Automatic sampling                        (AUTO_SAMPLING) = OFF
    Automatic statistics profiling            (AUTO_STATS_PROF) = OFF
      Statistics profile updates                (AUTO_PROF_UPD) = OFF
    Automatic reorganization                       (AUTO_REORG) = OFF
```

Which commands must you run to enable real-time statistics collection on the SAMPLE database?

❍ A. UPDATE DB CFG FOR sample USING AUTO_MAINT ON AUTO_STMT_STATS ON

❍ B. UPDATE DB CFG FOR sample USING AUTO_MAINT ON AUTO_TBL_MAINT ON AUTO_STMT_STATS ON

❍ C. UPDATE DB CFG FOR sample USING AUTO_MAINT ON AUTO_TBL_MAINT ON AUTO_RUNSTATS ON AUTO_STMT_STATS ON

❍ D. UPDATE DB CFG FOR sample USING AUTO_MAINT ON AUTO_STMT_STATS ON AUTO_STATS_VIEWS ON

Question 20

What is the significance of the following SELF_TUNING_MEM configuration current value setting?

```
Self tuning memory                    (SELF_TUNING_MEM) = ON (Inactive)
```

❍ A. The STMM is actively fine-tuning the instance memory, but not the database memory.

❍ B. The STMM is actively fine-tuning the operating system memory, but not the instance or database memory.

❍ C. The self-tuning memory is not happening because it is waiting on an instance restart.

❍ D. The self-tuning memory is not happening because fewer than two memory consumers are set to AUTOMATIC.

Question 21

Which command will activate automatic reorganization on the database SAMPLE?

- ❍ A. UPDATE DB CFG FOR sample USING AUTO_MAINT ON AUTO_TBL_MAINT ON AUTO_REORG ON
- ❍ B. UPDATE DB CFG FOR sample USING AUTO_MAINT OFF AUTO_TBL_MAINT ON AUTO_REORG ON
- ❍ C. UPDATE DB CFG FOR sample USING AUTO_MAINT ON AUTO_REORG ON
- ❍ D. UPDATE DB CFG FOR sample USING AUTO_MAINT ON AUTO_TBL_MAINT ON AUTO_STMT_STATS ON

Question 22

Which activity *cannot* be performed with automatic maintenance?

- ❍ A. Database-level backups
- ❍ B. Snapshot monitoring
- ❍ C. Statistics collection and statistics profiling
- ❍ D. Table and index reorganization

Question 23

A database administrator needs to create a new DB2 10.1 database and wants offline table and index reorganization operations to be performed automatically whenever the database's data becomes fragmented. Which of the following is the minimum set of steps required to meet this objective?

- ❍ A. Create the new database by using the CREATE DATABASE command; define an appropriate maintenance window.
- ❍ B. Create the new database by using the CREATE DATABASE command; assign the value ON to the AUTO_MAINT database configuration parameter; define an appropriate maintenance window.
- ❍ C. Create the new database by using the CREATE DATABASE command; assign the value ON to the AUTO_REORG database configuration parameter; define an appropriate maintenance window.
- ❍ D. Create the new database by using the CREATE DATABASE command; assign the value ON to the AUTO_MAINT database configuration parameter; assign the value ON to the AUTO_REORG database configuration parameter; define an appropriate maintenance window.

Question 24

A database administrator wants to ensure that backup operations performed against a database named SAMPLE will not impact a production workload by more than 20 percent. Which command can achieve this objective?

- ❍ A. UPDATE DBM CFG USING UTIL_IMPACT_LIM 80
- ❍ B. UPDATE DBM CFG USING UTIL_IMPACT_PRIORITY 80
- ❍ C. UPDATE DBM CFG USING UTIL_IMPACT_LIM 20
- ❍ D. UPDATE DBM CFG USING UTIL_IMPACT_PRIORITY 20

Question 25

A LIST UTILITIES SHOW DETAIL command returned the following output:

```
ID                            = 191
Type                          = BACKUP
Database Name                 = SAMPLE
Member Number                 = 0
Description                   = offline db
Start Time                    = 07/04/2014 17:36:23.914033
State                         = Executing
Invocation Type               = User
Throttling:
   Priority                   = 20
Progress Monitoring:
   Estimated Percentage Complete = 2
      Total Work              = 4570864892 bytes
      Completed Work          = 92542746 bytes
      Start Time              = 07/04/2014 17:36:23.914244
```

Which command will allow the backup operation to continue running unthrottled?

- ❍ A. SET UTIL_IMPACT_PRIORITY FOR 191 TO 0
- ❍ B. SET UTIL_IMPACT_LIM FOR 191 TO 0
- ❍ C. SET UTIL_IMPACT_PRIORITY FOR 191 TO 100
- ❍ D. SET UTIL_IMPACT_LIM FOR 191 TO 100

Question 26

Which memory consumer *cannot* be tuned automatically by the STMM as the database workload changes?

- ❍ A. Buffer pools
- ❍ B. Locking memory
- ❍ C. Utility memory
- ❍ D. Database shared memory

Question 27

Where are changes made by STMM recorded?

- ❍ A. In memory tuning log files
- ❍ B. In the DB2 diagnostics log file
- ❍ C. In the administration notification log
- ❍ D. In the IBM Data Studio HealthSnapshotLogger log

Question 28

Which statement describes the DB2 10.1 adaptive compression feature?

- ❍ A. The adaptive compression consists of both classic table-level and page-level compression.
- ❍ B. The adaptive compression consists of database-level compression, table space–level compression, and table-level compression.
- ❍ C. The adaptive compression consists of classic table-level, page-level, and table space–level compression.
- ❍ D. The adaptive compression consists of archive log compression.

Question 29

Which command will activate automatic database backup maintenance on the database `SAMPLE`?

❍ A. UPDATE DB CFG FOR sample USING AUTO_MAINT ON AUTO_DEL_REC_OBJ ON
❍ B. UPDATE DB CFG FOR sample USING AUTO_MAINT OFF AUTO_DB_BACKUP ON
❍ C. UPDATE DB CFG FOR sample USING AUTO_MAINT ON AUTO_DB_BACKUP ON
❍ D. UPDATE DB CFG FOR sample USING AUTO_MAINT ON AUTO_BACKUP ON

Question 30

Which statement regarding the `UPDATE DB CFG FOR sample USING DATABASE_MEMORY 5000 AUTOMATIC` command is true?

❍ A. The memory tuning stops at the 5000 pages threshold.
❍ B. The memory tuning starts from 100 pages and sends an alert when it reaches 5000 pages overtime.
❍ C. The memory tuner returns a warning message upon execution of the above command.
❍ D. The memory tuning starts from 5000 pages of initial memory allocation and can grow overtime.

Question 31

Which two of the following are valid STMM statuses? (Choose two.)

❒ A. ON (Active)
❒ B. ON (Superactive)
❒ C. OFF (Active)
❒ D. ON (Inactive)
❒ E. OFF (Superinactive)

Question 32

Which command will upgrade a database instance `DB2INST1` and the database `SAMPLE` from DB2 9.7 to DB2 10.1?

- ❍ A. db2imigr –u db2fence db2inst1
  UPGRADE DATABASE sample
- ❍ B. db2iupgrade –u db2fence db2inst1
  UPGRADE DATABASE sample
- ❍ C. UPGRADE INSTANCE db2inst1
  UPGRADE DATABASE sample
- ❍ D. db2iupdt db2inst1
  UPGRADE DATABASE sample

Question 33

Which of the following is a valid aggregated registry variable?

- ❍ A. DB2_ROWCOMPMODE_DEFAULT
- ❍ B. DB2_WORKLOAD
- ❍ C. DB2_SAS_SETTINGS
- ❍ D. DB2_SQLWORKSPACE_CACHE

Question 34

Which of the following is most likely a default storage group?

- ❍ A. IBMDEFAULTBP
- ❍ B. IBMSYSTEMBP32K
- ❍ C. IBMSTORAGEGROUP
- ❍ D. IBMSTOGROUP

Question 35

Which of the following will list all the automatic storage paths for each database storage group?

- ❍ A. ADMIN_GET_STORAGE_PATHS table function
- ❍ B. STO_PATH_FREE_SIZE monitor element
- ❍ C. ADMIN_GET_TAB_COMPRESS_INFO table function
- ❍ D. ADMIN_GET_DB_STORAGE_INFO table function

Question 36

Which compression feature is not available in DB2 10.1?

- ❍ A. Adaptive row compression
- ❍ B. Archive log compression
- ❍ C. Actionable compression
- ❍ D. XML object compression

Question 37

Which setting is necessary to automatically invoke the Configuration Advisor while creating a database?

- ❍ A. db2set DB2_ENABLE_AUTOCONFIG_DEFAULT=YES
- ❍ B. AUTOCONFIGURE USING workload_type simple is_populated yes bp_resizeable yes APPLY DB AND DBM
- ❍ C. db2set DB2_ATS_ENABLE=YES
- ❍ D. db2set DB2_ENABLE_SINGLE_NIS_GROUP=YES

Question 38

Which parameter do you set to automatic to activate the `locklist` configuration parameter for self-tuning?

❍ A. MAXLOCKS
❍ B. IBMDEFAULTBP
❍ C. SORTHEAP
❍ D. PCKCACHESZ

Question 39

Which statement is true regarding STMM in a DPF database?

❍ A. All memory-tuning decisions are based on the multiple partition workload and memory characteristics.
❍ B. All memory-tuning decisions are based on a single designated partition workload and memory characteristics.
❍ C. STMM is enabled on each server of the DPF system.
❍ D. STMM dynamically deallocates memory from one server and allocates it to another.

Question 40

Which statement is true regarding STMM in an HADR environment?

❍ A. STMM runs only on the standby server and replicates it back to the primary server to save the system resources on the primary machine.
❍ B. STMM runs only on the primary server and runs on the standby server only after executing a HADR TAKEOVER command.
❍ C. STMM runs on both primary and standby servers.
❍ D. STMM stops running after executing the HADR TAKEOVER command on the standby server.

Question 41

IBM Data Studio provides which two of the following functionalities?

❒ A. Environment for database administration
❒ B. Environment for UNIX operating system administration
❒ C. Environment for network management
❒ D. Environment for database storage LUN management
❒ E. Environment for database application development

Question 42

Which option is not part of the IBM Data Studio Task Launcher?

❍ A. Design
❍ B. Develop
❍ C. Deploy
❍ D. Administer

Question 43

Which functionality of IBM Data Studio will allow you to generate a Visual Explain plan?

❍ A. IBM Data Studio web console Task Launcher
❍ B. SQL and XQuery editor
❍ C. Query Tuner Workflow Assistant
❍ D. DB2 Command Line Processor Plus

Question 44

Which task *cannot* be performed through the IBM Data Studio web console?

❍ A. View alerts
❍ B. View application connections
❍ C. Manage database jobs
❍ D. Visual access plan generation

Question 45

Where will the IBM Data Studio web console allow you to schedule CLP or UNIX Shell-based script jobs?

- ❍ A. Task Manager
- ❍ B. Job Manager
- ❍ C. Blackout Event
- ❍ D. Current Utilities

Question 46

Using the IBM Data Studio web console, users must possess which access to run DB2 CLP scripts against a database running on a UNIX platform?

- ❍ A. Permission to log in to the server using SSH
- ❍ B. Permission to log in to the server using VNC
- ❍ C. Permission to log in to the server using telnet
- ❍ D. Permission to log in to the server using terminal services

Question 47

How many maximum jobs can actually be run within a job chain?

- ❍ A. 1
- ❍ B. 2
- ❍ C. 3
- ❍ D. 4

Question 48

Which command activates the log archive compression for the database SAMPLE?

- ❍ A. UPDATE DB CFG FOR sample USING LOGARCHCOMPR1 ON LOGARCHCOMPR2 ON
- ❍ B. UPDATE DB CFG FOR sample USING LOGARCHMETH1 DISK:/ db2transactionlogs
- ❍ C. UPDATE DB CFG FOR sample USING MIRRORLOGPATH /db2mirrorlogs
- ❍ D. UPDATE DB CFG FOR sample USING FAILARCHPATH /db2failarchpath

Question 49

Which REORG command helps to reclaim index space on the EMPLOYEE table without the need for full index reorganization?

- ❍ A. REORG INDEXES ALL FOR TABLE EMPLOYEE ALLOW WRITE ACCESS CLEANUP ALL RECLAIM EXTENTS
- ❍ B. REORG TABLE EMPLOYEE ALLOW READ ACCESS
- ❍ C. REORG TABLE EMPLOYEE RESETDICTIONARY
- ❍ D. REORG TABLE EMPLOYEE KEEPDICTIONARY

Question 50

Which DB2 command is deprecated in DB2 10.1?

- ❍ A. db2setup
- ❍ B. db2_install
- ❍ C. db2rfe
- ❍ D. db2rspgn

Answers

Question 1

The correct answer is **A**. Only users with System Administrator (SYSADM) authority or System Control (SYSCTRL) authority are allowed to quiesce an instance. Once an instance has been placed in a quiesced state, only users with System Administrator (SYSADM), System Control (SYSCTRL), or System Maintenance (SYSMAINT) authority; users who are members of a specified group (if a group name was specified when the instance was placed in quiesced mode); or users with a specified user name (if a user name was specified when the instance was placed in quiesced mode) are allowed to connect to the instance.

Question 2

The correct answer is **B**. If they are not already running, the DB2 database manager background processes that are associated with a particular instance can be started by executing the `START DATABASE MANAGER` command. The basic syntax for this command is:

```
START [DATABASE MANAGER | DB MANAGER | DBM]
```

or

```
db2start
```

Thus, to start the DB2 database manager background processes for the default instance (regardless of its name), you execute a command that looks like this:

```
START DB MANAGER
```

Question 3

The correct answer is **C**. The default instance for a system is defined by the `DB2INSTANCE` environment variable, and in many cases this is the instance that all instance-level operations are performed against. If you need to perform an operation against a different instance, you must first change the value assigned to the `DB2INSTANCE` variable (by executing the command `set DB2INSTANCE=[`*`InstanceName`*`]`, or executing the `export DB2INSTANCE=[`*`InstanceName`*`]` command on Linux and UNIX, where *InstanceName* is the name assigned to the instance that you want to make the default instance), or you must *attach* to that instance. Applications and users can attach to any instance by executing the `ATTACH` command.

Question 4

The correct answer is **B**. You use the `db2set` system command to determine which registry variables have been set and what they have been set to, or to assign values to one or more registry variables. The `-g` option indicates that a global profile variable is to be displayed, set, or removed (remember this command needs a root privilege on the UNIX server), so answer B is correct. The `-all` option specifies that all occurrences of the registry variable (environment, node, instance, and global) are to be displayed, so answer C is not valid, and answer A will only set the DB2COMM variable for the default instance.

Question 5

The correct answer is **D**. You can remove the value assigned to any registry variable by providing just the variable name and the equal sign as input to the db2set command. Thus, to disable the DB2COMM instance-level registry variable for an instance named TEST, you execute a db2set command that looks like this:

```
db2set -i TEST DB2COMM=
```

Question 6

The correct answer is **A**. The contents of the database configuration file for a particular database can be displayed by executing the GET DATABASE CONFIGURATION command. The syntax for this command is:

```
GET [DATABASE | DB] [CONFIGURATION | CONFIG | CFG]
FOR [DatabaseAlias]
<SHOW DETAIL>
```

where:

DatabaseAlias	Identifies the alias to assign to the database for which to display configuration information

Thus, to view the contents of the database configuration file for a database named SAMPLE, you execute a GET DATABASE CONFIGURATION command:

```
GET DB CFG FOR sample SHOW DETAIL
```

Question 7

The correct answer is **A**. The MAXAPPLS configuration parameter specifies the maximum number of concurrent applications that can be connected to a database. Setting MAXAPPLS to AUTOMATIC has the effect of allowing any number of connected applications to a database. To a certain extent, the maximum number of applications is also governed by the MAX_COORDAGENTS database manager configuration parameter. An application can connect to the database only if both a connection and coordinator agent are available.

The AVG_APPLS database parameter is used by the optimizer to determine buffer pool space available at run time for the access plan chosen for an SQL statement. NUM_INITAGENTS is a database manager configuration parameter that determines the initial number of idle agents that are created in the agent pool when the instance is started. NUM_POOLAGENTS is a database manager configuration parameter that sets the maximum size of the idle agent pool.

Question 8

The correct answer is **B**. You use the LOGARCHMETH1 database configuration parameter to specify the media type of the primary destination for archived log files and whether or not to use archival logging. If this parameter is set to OFF, circular logging is used and roll-forward recovery is not possible; if this parameter is set to LOGRETAIN, archival logging is used and roll-forward recovery is possible. The MIRRORLOGPATH database configuration parameter designates where to store a second copy of active log files.

NEWLOGPATH specifies an alternate path to use for storing recovery log files; LOGSECOND indicates the number of secondary log files that can be used for database recovery; and LOGARCHMETH2 specifies the media type of the secondary destination for archived logs.

Question 9

The correct answer is **C**. The SHEAPTHRESH DB2 database manager configuration parameter specifies the instance-wide soft limit on the total amount of memory (in pages) to make available for sorting operations; the SORTHEAP database configuration parameter indicates the maximum number of private memory pages to use for private sorts, or the maximum number of shared memory pages to use for shared sorts. Each sort operation consumes 10 MB—or 2,500 pages (10,000 KB / 4 KB page size = 2,500 4 KB pages). The total amount of memory available for sorts is 37,500 pages, and each sort operation can consume up to 2,500 pages of memory, so 37,500 / 2,500 = 15.

Question 10

The correct answer is **B**. You use the LOCKTIMEOUT database configuration parameter to specify the number of seconds that an application will wait to obtain a lock—if you assign this parameter the value -1, applications will wait indefinitely to obtain a needed lock. The LOCKLIST database configuration parameter specifies the maximum amount of memory (in pages) to allocate and use to hold the lock list; the DLCHKTIME configuration parameter indicates the frequency at which the DB2 database manager checks for deadlocks among all applications connected to the database; and the MAXLOCKS configuration parameter specifies a percentage of the lock list held by an application that must be filled before the DB2 database manager performs lock escalation.

Question 11

The correct answer is **C**. The value assigned to a particular database configuration file parameter can be changed by executing the UPDATE DATABASE CONFIGURATION command. The syntax for this command is:

```
UPDATE [DATABASE | DB]
       [CONFIGURATION | CONFIG | CFG]
FOR [DatabaseAlias]
USING [[Parameter] [Value] |
       [Parameter] [Value] AUTOMATIC |
       [Parameter] AUTOMATIC |
       [Parameter] MANUAL ,...]
<IMMEDIATE | DEFERRED>
```

where:

DatabaseAlias — Identifies the alias to assign to the database for which to modify configuration information

Parameter — Identifies one or more database configuration parameters (by keyword) whose values are to be modified (frequently, the keyword for a parameter is the same as the parameter name itself)

Value — Identifies the new values to assign to the specified database configuration parameters

If you specify the DEFERRED clause with the UPDATE DATABASE CONFIGURATION command, changes made to the database configuration file will not take effect until all connections to the corresponding database have been terminated and a new connection is established. If you specify the IMMEDIATE clause instead, or specify neither clause, all changes made to the database configuration file will take effect immediately—provided the necessary resources are available.

Question 12

The correct answer is **A**. If you specify the IMMEDIATE clause with the UPDATE DATABASE CONFIGURATION command, or specify neither clause, all changes made to the database configuration file will take effect immediately—provided the necessary resources are available. Applications running against a database at the time configuration changes are made will see the change the next time an SQL statement is executed.

Question 13

The correct answer is **D**. The AUTOCONFIGURE command is designed to capture specific information about your database environment and recommend and/or make changes to configuration parameters based upon the information provided. The basic syntax for this command is:

```
AUTOCONFIGURE
USING [ [Keyword] [Value] ,...]
APPLY [DB ONLY | DB AND DBM | NONE]
```

where:

Keyword — Specifies one or more special keywords that the AUTOCONFIGURE command will recognize; valid values include mem_percent, workload_type, num_stmts, tpm, admin_priority, is_populated, num_local_apps, num_remote_apps, isolation, and bp_resizable

Value — Identifies the value to associate with the keyword provided

If you specify the APPLY DB ONLY clause with the AUTOCONFIGURE command, database configuration and buffer pool changes recommended by the Design Advisor will be applied to the appropriate database configuration file; if you specify the APPLY DB AND DBM clause, recommended database configuration and buffer pool changes will be applied to the database configuration file, and recommended instance configuration changes will be applied to the appropriate DB2 database manager configuration file. If you specify the APPLY NONE clause instead, change recommendations will be displayed, but not applied.

Question 14

The correct answer is **A**. The AUTOCONFIGURE command (and the Design Advisor) will always recommend that a database be configured to take advantage of STMM. However, if you run the AUTOCONFIGURE command against a database in an instance where the SHEAPTHRES configuration parameter has been assigned a value other than zero, the SORTHEAP configuration parameter will not be configured for automatic tuning. Therefore, you must execute the command UPDATE DATABASE MANAGER CONFIGURATION USING SHEAPTHRES 0 before you execute the AUTOCONFIGURE command to enable sort memory tuning.

Question 15

The correct answers are **A** and **C**. If you choose to manually configure communications, the steps you must follow can vary according to the communications protocol you use. For example, to configure a server to use TCP/IP, you must perform the following steps:

1. Assign the value TCPIP to the DB2COMM registry variable.

   The value assigned to the DB2COMM registry variable determines which communications managers will be activated when the DB2 database manager for a particular instance is started. You assign the DB2COMM registry variable the value TCPIP by executing a db2set command:

   ```
   db2set DB2COMM=tcpip
   ```

2. Assign the name of the TCP/IP port that the database server will use to receive communications from remote clients to the svcename parameter of the DB2 database manager configuration file.

   The svcename parameter is set to the service name associated with the main connection port, so that when the database server is started, it can determine which port to listen on for incoming connection requests. To set this parameter, execute an UPDATE DATABASE MANAGER CONFIGURATION command:

   ```
   UPDATE DBM CFG USING SVCENAME db2c_db2inst1
   ```

3. Update the services file on the database server.

   The TCP/IP services file identifies the ports that server applications will listen on for client requests. If you specify a service name in the svcename parameter of the DB2 database manager configuration file, you must add the appropriate service name-to-port number/protocol mapping to the services file on the server. (If you specify a port number in the svcename parameter, you will not need to update the services file.)

   An entry in the services file for a DB2 database server might look something like this:

   ```
   db2c_db2inst1        50001/tcp
   ```

Question 16

The correct answer is **A**. ALT_DIAGPATH is a database manager configuration parameter that specifies a fully qualified alternate path for DB2 diagnostic information to use when the primary diagnostic data path DIAGPATH is unavailable. The other options—B, C, and D—are incorrect, as there is no database, DB2 registry, and environment variable for the alternate diagnostic log path.

Question 17

The correct answer is **C**. An aggregate registry variable is a group of several registry variables as a configuration that is identified by one registry variable name. Each registry variable that is part of the group has a predefined setting. The purpose of an aggregate registry variable is to ease registry configuration for broad operational objectives.

You can use an aggregate registry variable to explicitly define any registry variable that is implicitly configured, which in a way overrides the aggregated registry variable implicit value.

Option A is incorrect—an aggregated registry variable cannot override the registry variable. Option B is also incorrect—an aggregated registry variable can easily be overwritten by explicitly setting the value for a registry. Option D is incorrect as well—the explicit registry setting takes precedence over the implicit aggregated registry setting.

Question 18

The correct answers are **A** and **D**. You can terminate one or more running applications prematurely by executing the FORCE APPLICATION command (assuming you have SYSADMN or SYSCTRL authority). The basic syntax for this command is:

```
FORCE APPLICATION ALL
```

or

```
FORCE APPLICATION ( [ApplicationHandle], ... )
```

where:

ApplicationHandle Identifies the handle to associate with one or more applications whose instance attachments and/or database connections are to be terminated

Thus, to force all users and applications connected to databases stored on a server named DB_SERVER to terminate their database connections, execute a FORCE APPLICATION command:

```
FORCE APPLICATION ALL
```

However, if you want to force a specific application whose handle is 148 to terminate its processing, you execute a FORCE APPLICATION command that looks like this:

```
FORCE APPLICATION (148)
```

Question 19

The correct answer is **C**. With automatic statistics collection, the database manager determines whether statistics must be updated. Automatic statistics collection can occur synchronously at statement compilation time by using the real-time statistics feature, or by enabling the RUNSTATS command to simply run in the background for asynchronous collection. You can enable or disable automatic statistics collection by setting the following set of database configuration parameters:

- AUTO_MAINT
- AUTO_TBL_MAINT
- AUTO_RUNSTATS
- AUTO_STMT_STATS

In answers A, B, and D, one or the other parameter is not set to make it a complete workable automatic statistics collection.

Question 20

The correct answer is **D**. STMM works in three different states:

- OFF
- ON (Active)
- ON (Inactive)

If the parameter specifies ON (Active), the memory tuner is actively tuning the memory on the system. If the parameter indicates ON (Inactive), although the parameter is set to ON, self-tuning is not occurring because fewer than two memory parameters are enabled for self-tuning. If the parameter specifies OFF, then of course no memory tuning is enabled.

Option A is incorrect because STMM will not tune instance memory during the Inactive state. Option B is incorrect, as STMM does not tune operating system memory. Option C is incorrect because STMM parameters are all configurable online and no instance or database restart is necessary.

Question 21

The correct answer is **A**. You can enable or disable automatic reorganization maintenance by setting AUTO_MAINT, AUTO_TBL_MAINT, and AUTO_REORG database configuration parameters to ON or OFF. The other database configuration parameter options are incorrect in one way or the other.

Question 22

The correct answer is **B**. You can use automatic maintenance to perform the following maintenance operations:

- Create a backup image of the database. Automatic database backup provides users with a solution to help ensure their database is being backed up both properly and regularly, without their having to worry about when to back up or having any knowledge of the syntax for the BACKUP command.
- Defragment data (table or index reorganization). This maintenance activity can increase the efficiency with which the DB2 database manager accesses tables. Automatic reorganization manages offline table and index reorganization without users having to worry about when and how to reorganize their data.

- Optimize data access (running RUNSTATS). The DB2 database manager updates the system catalog statistics on the data in a table, the data in a table's indexes, or the data in both a table and its indexes. The DB2 optimizer uses these statistics to determine which path to use to access data in response to a query. Automatic statistics collection attempts to improve the performance of the database by maintaining up-to-date table statistics. The goal is to allow the DB2 optimizer to always choose an access plan based on accurate statistics.
- Conduct statistics profiling. Automatic statistics profiling advises when and how to collect table statistics by detecting outdated, missing, and incorrectly specified statistics and by generating statistical profiles based on query feedback.

Question 23

The correct answer is **C**. When a DB2 10.1 database is created, automatic RUNSTATS and real-time statistics collection maintenances are enabled by default. However, you will need to enable reorganization maintenance explicitly by executing the UPDATE DB CFG USING AUTO_REORG ON command on the newly created database. The default database configuration parameter settings are as follows:

```
Automatic maintenance                          (AUTO_MAINT) = ON
  Automatic database backup                (AUTO_DB_BACKUP) = OFF
  Automatic table maintenance              (AUTO_TBL_MAINT) = ON
    Automatic runstats                      (AUTO_RUNSTATS) = ON
      Real-time statistics                (AUTO_STMT_STATS) = ON
      Statistical views                  (AUTO_STATS_VIEWS) = OFF
      Automatic sampling                    (AUTO_SAMPLING) = OFF
    Automatic statistics profiling        (AUTO_STATS_PROF) = OFF
      Statistics profile updates            (AUTO_PROF_UPD) = OFF
    Automatic reorganization                   (AUTO_REORG) = OFF
```

Question 24

The correct answer is **C**. To control utility throttling, you must establish an impact policy. The impact policy refers to the instance-wide limit that all throttled utilities can cumulatively have on the production workload; once such a policy is established, it is the system's responsibility to ensure that the policy is obeyed. The impact policy for all throttling-enabled utilities running within an instance is controlled through the util_impact_lim DB2 database manager configuration parameter. This parameter is dynamic, so it can be changed without stopping and restarting the instance; it can even be set while throttling-enabled utilities are running. To define the impact policy for all throttled utilities, you simply assign a value between 1 and 100 to the util_impact_lim configuration parameter.

Thus, to set the instance-wide limit that all throttled utilities can cumulatively have on a production workload to 20 percent (or in other words, to ensure performance degradation from all throttled utilities will not impact the system workload by more than 20 percent), you assign the util_impact_lim configuration parameter the value 20 by executing an UPDATE DATABASE MANAGER CONFIGURATION command:

```
UPDATE DATABASE MANAGER CONFIGURATION USING UTIL_IMPACT_LIM 20
```

Question 25

The correct answer is **A**. To change the impact priority (level of throttling) of a utility that is already running, execute the `SET UTIL_IMPACT_PRIORITY` command. With this command, you can:

- Throttle a running utility that was started in unthrottled mode
- Unthrottle a running throttled utility (disable throttling)
- Reprioritize a running throttled utility (this is useful if multiple simultaneous throttled utilities are running and one is more important than the others)

The syntax for the `SET UTIL_IMPACT_PRIORITY` command is:

```
SET UTIL_IMPACT_PRIORITY FOR [UtilityID]
TO [Priority]
```

where:

UtilityID	Identifies the running utility, by ID, whose priority is to be changed (to obtain the ID assigned to a running utility, execute the `LIST UTILITIES` command)
Priority	Specifies an instance-level limit on the impact associated with running the specified utility; a value of 100 represents the highest priority; a value of 1 represents the lowest—setting `Priority` to 0 will force a throttled utility to continue running unthrottled; setting `Priority` to a nonzero value will force an unthrottled utility to continue running in throttled mode

Thus, if you want force a throttled backup operation that has been assigned a utility ID of 191 to continue running unthrottled, you execute a `SET UTIL_IMPACT_PRIORITY` command:

```
SET UTIL_IMPACT_PRIORITY FOR 191 TO 0
```

Question 26

The correct answer is **C**. When a database has been enabled for self-tuning, the memory tuner responds to significant changes in database workload characteristics, adjusting the values of memory configuration parameters and buffer pool sizes to optimize performance. You can enable the following memory consumers for self-tuning:

- Buffer pools (controlled by the `ALTER BUFFERPOOL` and `CREATE BUFFERPOOL` statements)
- Package cache (controlled by the `PCKCACHESZ` parameter)
- Locking memory (controlled by the `LOCKLIST` and `MAXLOCKS` parameters)
- Sort memory (controlled by the `SHEAPTHRES_SHR` and the `SORTHEAP` parameters)
- Database shared memory (controlled by the `DATABASE_MEMORY` parameter)

Question 27

The correct answer is **A**. Changes made by STMM are recorded in memory-tuning log files, which reside in the `stmmlog` subdirectory of the instance. (The first file created will be assigned the name `stmm.0.log`, the second will be assigned the name `stmm.1.log`, and so on.) Each memory-tuning log file contains summaries of the resource demands for each memory consumer at the time a tuning operation was performed. You can determine tuning intervals by examining the timestamps for the entries made in the memory-tuning log files.

Question 28

The correct answer is **A**. Adaptive compression uses two compression approaches. The first works at the table-level compression dictionary (classic row compression) to compress data based on repetition within a sampling of data from the table as a whole. The second works at the page-level dictionary to compress data based on data repetition within each page of data. The dictionaries map repeated byte patterns to much smaller symbols; these symbols then replace the longer byte patterns in the table. The table-level compression dictionary resides within the table object for which it is created and is used to compress data throughout the table. The page-level compression dictionary is stored with the data in the data page; it is used to compress only the data within that page.

Question 29

The correct answer is **C**. You can enable or disable automatic backup maintenance by setting the AUTO_MAINT and AUTO_DB_BACKUP database configuration parameters to ON or OFF. When you create a new database, by default, AUTO_MAINT will be set to ON. To activate automatic database backup maintenance, you must explicitly set AUTO_DB_BACKUP to ON and implement an online or offline maintenance policy to specify a backup maintenance window.

Question 30

The correct answer is **D**. STMM works in four different modes (as follows). You can use one based on the application and business requirement.

Mode 1: When DATABASE_MEMORY= AUTOMATIC

In this case, the required memory is taken from and returned to the operating system when required. The total amount of memory used by DB2 can grow over time and is limited only by the operating system's memory availability.

Mode 2: When DATABASE_MEMORY= <NUMERIC VALUE> AUTOMATIC

Here, memory tuning still occurs, but the total memory used by the database starts from the NUMERIC value and can grow over time. It is limited only by the operating system's available memory.

Mode 3: When DATABASE_MEMORY=<NUMERIC VALUE>

DB2 will allocate this amount of memory during startup, and this memory setting is static. It cannot take memory from or give memory to the operating system on demand.

Mode 4: When DATABASE_MEMORY=COMPUTED

Database memory is computed based on the sum of initial values of the database memory heaps during database startup. In this case, database_memory is not enabled for self-tuning.

Question 31

The correct answers are **A** and **D**. STMM works in three different states:

- OFF
- ON (Active)
- ON (Inactive)

If the parameter specifies ON (Active), the memory tuner is actively tuning the memory on the system. If the parameter indicates ON (Inactive), although the parameter is set to ON, self-tuning is not occurring because fewer than two memory parameters are enabled for self-tuning. If the parameter specifies OFF, no memory tuning is enabled.

Question 32

The correct answer is **B**. You use the instance upgrade command db2iupgrade to upgrade an instance from the DB2 9.7 code base to the DB2 10.1 code base. You use the db2iupdt command to perform fix pack upgrades within the version release. The instance migration command db2imigr is deprecated in DB2 10.1 and should not be used for upgrade purposes. There is no change to the database upgrade command, which you run after upgrading the instance. For more details, please refer back to the upgrading instances section in the beginning of this chapter.

Question 33

The correct answer is **B**. An aggregate registry variable is a group of several registry variables as a configuration that is identified by one registry variable name. Each registry variable that is part of the group has a predefined setting. The purpose of an aggregate registry variable is to ease registry configuration for broad operational objectives.

In DB2 10.1, the only valid aggregated registry variable is DB2_WORKLOAD.

Question 34

The correct answer is **D**. When you create a database in DB2 10.1, the default storage group IBMSTOGROUP is automatically created. You can establish one or more initial storage paths for it in the CREATE DATABASE command. As a database grows, the database manager creates containers across those storage paths and extends them or automatically creates new ones as needed.

Question 35

The correct answer is **A**. You can also use ADMIN_GET_STORAGE_PATHS table function to list automatic storage paths for each database storage group, including file system information for each storage group:

```
SELECT
      VARCHAR (STORAGE_GROUP_NAME, 30) AS STOGROUP,
      VARCHAR (DB_STORAGE_PATH, 40)AS STORAGE_PATH
   FROM TABLE (ADMIN_GET_STORAGE_PATHS ('',-1)) AS T

STOGROUP                        STORAGE_PATH
------------------------------- ----------------------------------------
IBMSTOGROUP                     /stogroup1
IBMSTOGROUP                     /stogroup2
```

Question 36

The correct answer is **C**. The compression features in DB2 10.1 are:

- Adaptive compression—a combination of classic row and page-level compression; you activate this by using the CREATE TABLE or ALTER TABLE command:

```
CREATE TABLE <SCHEMA>.<TABLE> COMPRESS YES
ALTER TABLE <SCHEMA>.<TABLE> COMPRESS YES
```

- Archive log compression—compresses transaction logs before archiving them on a storage server; you activate this feature by using the UPDATE DB CFG command:

```
UPDATE DB CFG USING LOGARCHCOMPR1 ON LOGARCHCOMPR2 ON
```

- XML object compression—introduced in DB2 9.7 and compresses XML data that resides within the XDA area; this feature activates implicitly when a table is created with the COMPRESS YES option or when a table is altered to use compression

The actionable compression is a DB2 10.5 BLU feature, which uses approximate Huffman encoding, prefix compression, and offset compression. Actionable compression provides many benefits, and one is that the data is not uncompressed when processing SQL filter predicates such as =, <, >, >=, <=, BETWEEN, joins, aggregations, and more. Rather, the decompression occurs only when the result set is returned to the user.

Question 37

The correct answer is **A**. The Configuration Advisor is automatically invoked whenever you create a database. To change this behavior, you assign the value NO to the DB2_ENABLE_AUTOCONFIG_DEFAULT registry variable. It is recommended that you check this registry variable setting before creating a database.

Question 38

The correct answer is **A**. Locking memory is controlled by the locklist and maxlocks database configuration parameters. The locklist parameter indicates the amount of storage that is allocated to the lock list. There is one `locklist` per database, and it contains the locks held by all applications concurrently connected to the database. The `maxlocks` parameter defines a percentage of the lock list held by an application that must be filled before the database manager performs lock escalation. To enable the `locklist` configuration parameter for self-tuning, `maxlocks` must also be enabled.

Question 39

The correct answer is **B**. When you enable self-tuning memory for partitioned databases, a single database partition is designated as the tuning partition, and all memory tuning decisions are based on the memory and workload characteristics of that database partition. After tuning decisions on that partition are made, the memory adjustments are distributed to the other database partitions to ensure that all database partitions maintain similar configurations.

Question 40

The correct answer is **B**. Self-tuning memory runs only on the HADR primary server. When self-tuning memory is activated on an HADR pair, it does not run on the secondary server, but runs only on the primary server. If you run the HADR `TAKEOVER` command on the current secondary machine, self-tuning memory operations also switch to the new primary machine.

Question 41

The correct answers are **A** and **E**. IBM Data Studio consists of the following components:

- The IBM Data Studio client, which is an Eclipse-centric tool that provides an integrated development environment for database and instance administration, routine and Java application development, and query-tuning tasks.
- The IBM Data Studio web console, which is a web-based tool with health and availability monitoring, job creation, and database administration tasks.

There are no capabilities built around managing the operating system, network, and storage within IBM Data Studio.

Question 42

The correct answer is **C**. The IBM Data Studio Task Launcher has the following options:

- Design. You can view the database object diagrams, data models, and relationships.
- Develop. You can develop stored procedures, UDFs, and so on.
- Administer. You can perform database administration tasks such as schedule scripts, create maintenance jobs, and so forth.
- Tune. You can generate Visual Explain plans and analyze the SQL statements.
- Monitor. You can perform database monitoring activities.

There is no functionality built around deploying any project or the code in a controlled way within IBM Data Studio.

Question 43

The correct answer is **C**. IBM Data Studio query tuning can generate a diagram of the current access plan for an SQL or XPATH statement to determine how the SQL compiler processes the statement. You can use this information to tune your SQL statement to improve performance.

The IBM Query Tuner Workflow Assistant, included with IBM Data Studio, can perform these actions:

- Statistics Advisor recommendations
- SQL or XPATH query formatting
- Visual access plan generation
- Summary report generation

Question 44

The correct answer is **D**. The IBM Data Studio web console will allow you to create and manage jobs, multiple health monitoring and alerting utilities, application connection information, and security management (see Figure 2.30).

To generate a visual access plan, you will have to use IBM Data Studio Task Launcher's Start Tuning wizard.

Question 45

The correct answer is **B**. You can perform the following actions in the Job Manager:

- Add, edit, run, and delete jobs from the Job List tab
- Add, edit, and delete schedules, and create job chains from the Schedules tab
- Add, edit, and delete notifications from the Notifications tab
- Edit the job history setting, view, cancel, run (rerun the earlier executed job), and delete a specific job history from the History tab

Question 46

The correct answer is **A**. User must have SSH (Secure Shell) access to the database server to run any CLP, shell scripts commands, or files through the IBM Data Studio web console.

Question 47

The correct answer is **C**. A job chain executes one or more jobs (up to three) in sequence. The primary job initiates the job execution within the job chain and is followed by a dependent job and a closing job (see Figure 2.36). It allows you to use four jobs within a job chain; however, it can run only three of them in a job chain execution.

Question 48

The correct answer is **A**. Set the update database configuration parameters LOGARCHCOMPR1 and LOGARCHCOMPR2 to ON to enable log archive compressions in both first and second log archive methods.

Question 49

The correct answer is **A**. DB2 10.1 introduced an enhancement to the REORG INDEX command to free up the unused extents from an index object back to the table space. These extents can exist anywhere within the index object. You can use the CLEANUP clause to clear pseudo-deleted keys and pseudo-empty pages from the index without having to run a complete INDEX REORG command.

Question 50

The correct answer is **B**. The command db2_install was used in earlier DB2 versions to install the product; however, this is now deprecated. The preferred way of installing the product from DB2 10.1 is to use the db2setup command along with a response file. You can use a sample response file to modify based on your need. The install image is in the location/db2/<platform>/samples directory. Then use the command to install the product on the system:

```
db2setup -l db210setup.log -t db210setup.trace -r db210setup.response
```

You can use the db2rspgn command in DB2 to generate a response file, if you want to create your own instead of modifying the sample response file.

You use the db2rfe command in nonroot installations to explicitly enable certain root installation features using the configuration file. The following features can be enabled by using this command.

- HA feature enablement:

  ```
  ENABLE_HA=NO [YES, NO]
  ```

- User data limits on UNIX platform:

  ```
  SET_ULIMIT=NO [YES, NO]
  ```

- Operating system authentication enablement:

  ```
  ENABLE_OS_AUTHENTICATION=NO [YES, NO]
  ```

- Service port reservation:

  ```
  RESERVE_REMOTE_CONNECTION=NO [YES, NO]
  ```

  ```
  SVCENAME
  SVCEPORT
  ```

- Text search service reservation:

  ```
  RESERVE_TEXT_SEARCH_CONNECTION=NO [YES, NO]
  SVCENAME_TEXT_SEARCH
  SVCEPORT_TEXT_SEARCH
  ```

CHAPTER 3

Physical Design

This chapter will prepare you to design physical database objects along with the choices and physical storage parameters required to generate a design in a data definition language. You will learn to use many of the new storage features, including storage groups and multi-temperature storage. You will also be presented information pertaining to the new Time Travel Query feature and its business use. At the end of the chapter, you will be able to understand the benefits of adaptive compression, an industry-leading compression solution.

Exam Objectives

- ✓ Demonstrate knowledge of system-managed (SMS), database-managed (DMS), and automatic storage table spaces
- ✓ Demonstrate the ability to create a DB2 database
- ✓ Demonstrate the ability to understand the relationship between pages, extents, table spaces, buffer pools, and storage groups
- ✓ Demonstrate the ability to create and alter storage groups and table spaces
- ✓ Demonstrate the ability to use the multi-temperature storage feature to optimize the use of various storage types based on the business need
- ✓ Demonstrate the ability to create range partitioned tables and range clustered tables (RCTs)
- ✓ Demonstrate the ability to create Time Travel Queries by using temporal tables
- ✓ Demonstrate the ability to work with XML data and construct XML indexes
- ✓ Demonstrate the ability to use classic (table-level) compression and adaptive (page-level) compression

Servers, Instances, and Databases

In Chapter 2, "DB2 Server Management," you learned that DB2 sees the world as a hierarchy of objects. Workstations (or servers) on which DB2 has been installed occupy the highest level of this hierarchy. Instances occupy the second level in the hierarchy and are responsible for managing system resources and databases that fall under their control. Databases make up the third level in the hierarchy and are accountable for managing the storage, modification, and retrieval of data. Each database has its own environment controlled by a set of configuration parameters, as well as its own set of grantable authorities and privileges to govern how users interact with the data and database objects it controls.

From a user's perspective, a database is a collection of tables (preferably related in some way) that store data. However, from a database administrator's viewpoint, a DB2 database is much more; a database is an entity composed of many physical and logical components. Some of these components help determine how data is organized while others control how and where data is physically stored.

DB2 Database Objects

A DB2 database is a collection of database objects that are related to each other. Table 3.1 provides information about the database objects available within DB2 and the default settings.

Table 3.1: DB2 database objects

Database Object	Description
Partition groups	A logical database object that allows the grouping of one or more database partitions in a group; by default DB2 creates three partition groups: IBMCATGROUP, IBMDEFAULTGROUP, and IBMTEMPGROUP
Storage groups	A logical database object that defines a set of storage paths where data can be stored; by default DB2 creates one storage group: IBMSTOGROUP
Buffer pools	A physical database object that defines working memory and cache for database pages; by default DB2 creates one buffer pool: IBMDEFAULTBP
Table spaces	A logical database object that associates tables, indexes, large, and long object data to the physical storage device (containers) where these objects are stored; by default DB2 creates three table spaces: SYSCATSPACE, TEMPSPACE1, and USERSPACE1
Schemas	A logical database object that provides the logical grouping of application database objects such as tables, indexes, and views based on business needs; by default DB2 creates SYSCAT, SYSCAT, SYSIBMADM, SYSPUBLIC, SYSSTAT, SQLJ, SYSFUN, SYSPROC, and SYSTOOLS schemas
Tables	A physical database object that consists of rows and columns facilitating insert, update, delete, and select operations on user data; by default DB2 10.1 creates 146 system tables in the SYSCATSPACE table space to store metadata information
Constraints	A database object that enforces certain restrictions or relationships between the tables based on the business need

Table 3.1: DB2 database objects (continued)	
Database Object	**Description**
Indexes	A database object with a set of pointers that are logically ordered by the values of one or more keys; by default DB2 10.1 creates 375 indexes on the metadata system tables
Sequences	A database object that enables automatic generation of unique values
Views	A logical database object that enables representing data without actually storing it; by default DB2 10.1 creates 276 views on the metadata tables
Usage lists	A database object that records each DML statement execution form of the query that references a particular table or index
XML	A data type that allows storing well-formed XML documents in a database table column
Triggers	A database object that defines a set of actions performed against insert, update, and delete operations on a specific table
Stored procedures	A database object that transforms the application business logic into a set of SQL statements
User defined functions	A database object that transforms the application business logic into a set of SQL statements and calls them like DB2 built-in functions
Packages	A database object that stores the compiled version of the SQL statements and access plans that the DB2 Optimizer uses while retrieving data from the database for a specific query request

Creating a DB2 Database

You can create a DB2 database by using the CREATE DATABASE command. In its simplest form, the syntax for the CREATE DATABASE command is:

```
CREATE [DATABASE | DB] [DatabaseName]
```

where:

DatabaseName Identifies a unique name to assign to the database once it is created

The only value you must provide when executing this command is a name to assign to the new database. This name

- Should always be less than or equal to 8 characters
- Can consist of only the characters a through z, A through Z, 0 through 9, @, #, $, and _ (underscore)
- Cannot begin with a number
- Cannot begin with the letter sequences "SYS," "DBM," or "IBM"
- Cannot be the same as the name already assigned to another database within the same instance

Of course, a more complex form of the CREATE DATABASE command that provides you with much more control over database parameters is available, and we will examine it shortly. But for now, let us look at what happens when you execute this form of the CREATE DATABASE command.

What Happens When a Database Is Created?

Regardless of how you initiate the process, whenever you create a new DB2 10.1 database, the following tasks are performed, in the following order:

1. All directories and subdirectories needed are created in the appropriate location.

   Information about every DB2 database you create is stored in a special hierarchical directory tree. Where to create this directory tree is determined by the information you provide with the CREATE DATABASE command—if you supply no location information, this directory tree is created in the location specified by the dftdbpath DB2 database manager configuration parameter associated with the instance under which the database is being created.

   The root directory of this hierarchical tree is assigned the name of the instance with which the database is associated. This directory will contain a subdirectory that shares a name corresponding to the partition's node. If the database is a partitioned database, this directory will be named NODE*xxxx*, where *xxxx* is the unique node number that has been assigned to the partition. If the database is a nonpartitioned one, this directory will be named NODE0000, considering that nobody has made any modifications to the db2nodes.cfg file on DB2 Enterprise Server Edition. The node directory, in turn, will contain one subdirectory for each created database, along with one subdirectory that includes the containers to hold the database's data.

   The name given to the subdirectory that holds the containers to house the database's data is the same as that specified for the database; the name of the subdirectory that contains the base files for the database will correspond to the database token that is assigned to the database during the creation process (the subdirectory for the first database created will be named SQL00001, the subdirectory for the second database will be named SQL00002, and so on). Figure 3.1 illustrates how this directory hierarchy typically looks in a nonpartitioned database environment.

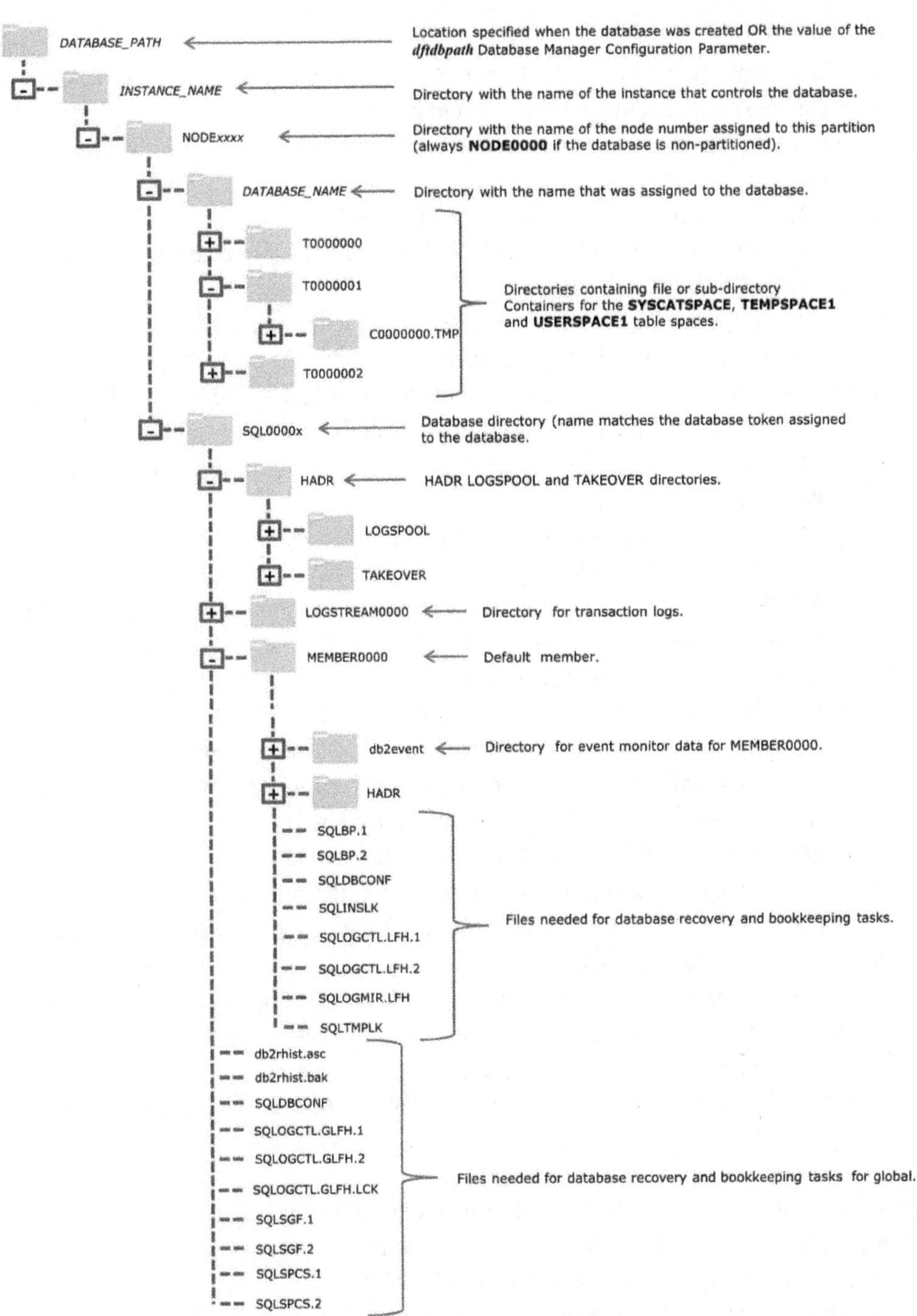
DATABASE_PATH
Location specified when the database was created OR the value of the dftdbpath Database Manager Configuration Parameter.
INSTANCE_NAME
Directory with the name of the instance that controls the database.
NODExxxx
Directory with the name of the node number assigned to this partition (always NODE0000 if the database is non-partitioned).
DATABASE_NAME
Directory with the name that was assigned to the database.
T0000000
T0000001
C0000000.TMP
T0000002
Directories containing file or sub-directory Containers for the SYSCATSPACE, TEMPSPACE1 and USERSPACE1 table spaces.
SQL0000x
Database directory (name matches the database token assigned to the database.
HADR
HADR LOGSPOOL and TAKEOVER directories.
LOGSPOOL
TAKEOVER
LOGSTREAM0000
Directory for transaction logs.
MEMBER0000
Default member.
db2event
Directory for event monitor data for MEMBER0000.
HADR
SQLBP.1
SQLBP.2
SQLDBCONF
SQLINSLK
SQLOGCTL.LFH.1
SQLOGCTL.LFH.2
SQLOGMIR.LFH
SQLTMPLK
Files needed for database recovery and bookkeeping tasks.
db2rhist.asc
db2rhist.bak
SQLDBCONF
SQLOGCTL.GLFH.1
SQLOGCTL.GLFH.2
SQLOGCTL.GLFH.LCK
SQLSGF.1
SQLSGF.2
SQLSPCS.1
SQLSPCS.2
Files needed for database recovery and bookkeeping tasks for global.

Figure 3.1: DB2 database hierarchy

2. Files needed for management, monitoring, and database recovery are created.

   After the subdirectory that shares the name of the database's token is created, the following files and directories are created in it:

   - SQLSGF.1: This file contains storage path information associated with automatic storage.
   - SQLSGF.2: This file is a backup copy of SQLSGF.1.
   - HADR: This directory has LOGSPOOL and TAKEOVER subdirectories that are used with the HADR TAKEOVER command.
   - LOGSTREAM0000: This directory contains transaction log files and stores transaction log records as SQL operations are performed against the database.
   - MEMBER0000: This is a member-specific directory that includes the following files:
     - SQLTMPLK: This file contains information about temporary table spaces.
     - db2event: This directory has event monitor information, and a detailed deadlocks event monitor is created by default.
     - SQLBP.1: This file contains buffer pool information.
     - SQLBP.2: This file is a backup copy of SQLBP.1.
     - SQLOGCTL.LFH.1: This file includes information about active transaction log files. Recovery operations use information stored in this file to determine how far back in the logs to begin the recovery process.
     - SQLOGCTL.LFH.2: This file is a mirror copy of SQLOGCTL.LFH.1.
     - SQLOGMIR.LFH: This file is a mirror copy of SQLOGCTL.LFH.1.
     - SQLINSLK: This file contains information that ensures that the database is assigned to only one instance of the DB2 database manager.
     - SQLDBCONF: This file has database configuration information.
   - db2rhist.lock and SQLOGCTL.GLFH.LCK: These files provide instancewide serialization for the recovery history file and logging recovery file, respectively.
   - db2rhist.asc: This file contains historical information about backup operations, restore operations, table load operations, table reorganization operations, table space alterations, and similar database changes (i.e., the recovery history file).
   - db2rhist.bak: This file is a backup copy of db2rhist.asc.
   - SQLOGCTL.LFH.1: This file contains information about active transaction log files. Recovery operations use information stored in this file to determine how far back in the logs to begin the recovery process.
   - SQLOGCTL.LFH.2: This file is a mirror copy of SQLOGCTL.LFH.1.
   - SQLSPCS.1: This file has table space information.
   - SQLSPCS.2: This file is a backup copy of SQLSPCS.1.
   - SQLDBCONF: This file contains database configuration information.

3. A buffer pool is created for the database.

   During the database creation process, a buffer pool is created and assigned the name IBMDEFAULTBP. On Linux, UNIX, and Windows platforms, this buffer pool is created with a 4 KB page size and automatic by default. The memory that this buffer pool uses (and for that matter, by any other buffer pools that may exist) is allocated when the first connection to the database is established and freed when all connections to the database have been terminated. The DB2 database manager also creates four hidden system buffer pools: IBMSYSTEMBP4K, IBMSYSTEMBP8K, IBMSYSTEMBP16K, and IBMSYSTEMBP32K. Usually, these buffer pools are used when the main buffer pool cannot be allocated because of insufficient memory or other similar conditions.

4. Two regular table spaces and one system temporary table space are created.

   Immediately after the creation of buffer pool IBMDEFAULTBP, three table spaces are created and associated with this buffer pool. These three table spaces are as follows:

   - A regular table space named SYSCATSPACE, which stores the system catalog tables and views associated with the database
   - A regular table space named USERSPACE1, which stores all user-defined objects (such as tables, indexes, and so on) along with user data, index data, and long value data
   - A system temporary table space named TEMPSPACE1, which is a temporary storage area for operations such as sorting data, reorganizing tables, and creating indexes

   Unless otherwise specified, SYSCATSPACE and USERSPACE1 are DMS file table spaces, and TEMPSPACE1 is an SMS table space. You can provide characteristics for each of these table spaces as input to the CREATE DATABASE command or in the Create Database wizard.

5. The system catalog tables and views are created.

   After the table space SYSCATSPACE is created, a special set of tables (known as the *system catalog tables*) are constructed within that table space. The DB2 database manager uses the system catalog tables to keep track of information such as database object definitions, database object dependencies, database object privileges, column data types, table constraints, and object relationships. A set of system catalog views is created along with the system catalog tables, and these views are typically used when you access data stored in the system catalog tables. You cannot modify the system catalog tables and views with DDL SQL statements (however, you can view their contents). Instead, the DB2 database manager will alter them whenever one of the following events occurs:

   - A database object (such as a table, view, or index) is created, altered, or dropped.
   - Authorizations or privileges are granted or revoked.

- Statistical information is collected for a table.
- Packages are bound to the database.

Usually, all characteristics of a database object are stored in one or more system catalog tables when the object is created. However, in some cases, such as when you define triggers and constraints, the SQL used to create the object is stored instead.

6. The database is cataloged in the system and local database directory (a system or local database directory is created first if it does not already exist).

   DB2 uses a set of special files to keep track of where databases are stored and to provide access to those databases. Because you use the information stored in these files the same way you use information contained in an office-building directory, they are referred to as *directory files*. Whenever you create a database, these directories are updated with the database's name and alias. If specified, a comment and code set values are also stored in these directories.

7. The database configuration file for the database is initialized.

   Some of the parameters in the database configuration file (such as code set, territory, and collating sequence) will be set by using values that you specified as input for the CREATE DATABASE command or in the Create Database wizard; others are assigned system default values.

8. Four schemas are created.

   After the creation of the system catalog tables and views, the following schemas are created: SYSIBM, SYSCAT, SYSSTAT, and SYSFUN. A special user named SYSIBM is made the owner of each schema.

9. A set of utility programs is bound to the database.

   Before some of the DB2 utilities can work with a database, you must create the packages needed to run those utilities by binding a set of predefined DB2 database manager bind files to the database (the bind files are listed in the utilities bind list file db2ubind.lst).

10. Authorities and privileges are granted to the appropriate users.

    To connect to and work with a particular database, a user must have the authorities and privileges required to use that database.

Therefore, whenever you create a new database, unless otherwise specified, the following authorities and privileges are granted:

- Database Administrator (DBADM) authority as well as CONNECT, CREATETAB, BINDADD, CREATE_NOT_FENCED, IMPLICIT_SCHEMA, and LOAD privileges are granted to the user who created the database.
- USE privilege on the table space USERSPACE1 is granted to the group PUBLIC.
- CONNECT, CREATETAB, BINDADD, and IMPLICIT_SCHEMA privileges are granted to the group PUBLIC.
- SELECT privilege on each system catalog table is granted to the group PUBLIC.
- EXECUTE privilege on all procedures in the SYSIBM schema is granted to the group PUBLIC.
- EXECUTE WITH GRANT privilege on all functions in the SYSFUN schema is granted to the group PUBLIC.
- BIND and EXECUTE privileges for each successfully bound utility are granted to the group PUBLIC.

11. Several autonomic features are enabled.

    To help make management easy, whenever you create a new database, the following features are enabled:

    - Automatic maintenance (table and index reorganization, data access optimization, and statistics profiling)
    - Self-tuning memory manager (package cache, locking memory, sort memory, database shared memory, and buffer pool memory)
    - Utility throttling

12. The Configuration Advisor is launched.

    The Configuration Advisor is a tool that helps you tune performance and balance memory requirements for a database by suggesting which configuration parameters to modify based on information you provide about the database. In DB2, the Configuration Advisor is automatically invoked whenever you create a database, unless the default behavior is changed by assigning the value NO to the DB2_ENABLE_AUTOCONFIG_DEFAULT registry variable.

A Complete CREATE DATABASE Command

When you execute the simplest form of the CREATE DATABASE command, the characteristics of the database, such as the storage and transaction logging method to use, are determined by several predefined defaults. To change any of the default characteristics, you must specify one or more options when executing the CREATE DATABASE command. The complete syntax for this command is:

```
CREATE [DATABASE | DB] [DatabaseName] <AT DBPARTITIONNUM>
```

or

```
CREATE [DATABASE | DB] [DatabaseName]
<AUTOMATIC STORAGE [YES | NO]>
<ON [StoragePath ,...] <DBPATH [DBPath]>>
<ALIAS [Alias]>
<USING CODESET [CodeSet] TERRITORY [Territory]>
<COLLATE USING [CollateType]>
<PAGESIZE [4096 | Pagesize <K>]>
<NUMSEGS [NumSegments]>
<DFT_EXTENT_SZ [DefaultExtSize]>
<RESTRICTIVE>
<CATALOG TABLESPACE [TS_Definition]>
<USER TABLESPACE [TS_Definition]>
<TEMPORARY TABLESPACE [TS_Definition]>
<WITH "[Description]">
<AUTOCONFIGURE <USING [Keyword] [Value] ,...>
<APPLY [DB ONLY | DB AND DBM | NONE>>
```

where:

DatabaseName Identifies the unique name to assign to the database to be created

StoragePath Identifies one or more storage paths defined to the default storage group IBMSTOGROUP to use to hold table space containers used by automatic storage if you specify AUTOMATIC STORAGE YES (the default); otherwise, identifies the location (drive or directory) to physically store the directory hierarchy and files associated with the database to be created

DBPath	Identifies the location (drive or directory) to physically store the directory hierarchy and metadata files associated with the database to be created if you specify AUTOMATIC STORAGE YES (the default); if you do not specify this parameter, and automatic storage is used, the metadata files will be stored in the first storage path indicated in the StoragePath parameter
Alias	Identifies the alias to assign to the database to be created
CodeSet	Identifies the code set to use for storing data in the database to be created (in a DB2 database, each single-byte character is represented internally as a unique number between 0 and 255—this number is referred to as the code point of the character; the assignments of code points to every character in a particular character set are called the *code page*, and the International Organization for Standardization term for a code page is *code set*)
Territory	Identifies the territory to use for storing data in the database to be created
CollateType	Specifies the collating sequence (i.e., the sequence in which to order characters for the purpose of sorting, merging, and making comparisons) for the database to be created to use; the following values are valid for this parameter: COMPATABILITY, IDENTITY, IDENTITY_16BIT, UCA400_NO, UCA400_LSK, UCA400_LTH, NLSCHAR, and SYSTEM
NumSegments	Specifies the number of directories to create and use to store files for the default SMS table space used by the database to be created (TEMPSPACE1)
DefaultExtSize	Specifies the default extent size to use whenever a table space is created; no extent size is specified during the creation process
Description	Specifies a comment to use to describe the database entry that will be made in the database directory for the database to be created; you must enclose the description in double quotation marks
Keyword	Identifies one or more keywords that the AUTOCONFIGURE command will recognize; valid values include mem_percent, workload_type, num_stmts, tpm, admin_priority, is_populated, num_local_apps, num_remote_apps, isolation, and bp_resizable
Value	Identifies the value to associate with the keyword specified
TS_Definition	Specifies the definition to use to create the table space that will hold the system catalog tables (SYSCATSPACE), user-defined objects (USERSPACE1), and temporary objects (TEMPSPACE1)

The syntax to define an SMS table space is:

```
MANAGED BY SYSTEM
USING ('[Container]' ,...)
<EXTENTSIZE [ExtentSize]>
<PREFETCHSIZE [PrefetchSize]>
<OVERHEAD [Overhead]>
<TRANSFERRATE [TransferRate]>
<NO FILE SYSTEM CACHING | FILE SYSTEM CACHING>
```

The syntax to define a DMS table space is:

```
MANAGED BY DATABASE
USING ([FILE | DEVICE] '[Container]' NumberOfPages ,...)
<EXTENTSIZE [ExtentSize]>
<PREFETCHSIZE [PrefetchSize]>
<OVERHEAD [Overhead]>
<TRANSFERRATE [TransferRate]>
<NO FILE SYSTEM CACHING | FILE SYSTEM CACHING>
<AUTORESIZE [NO | YES]>
<INCREASESIZE [Increment] <PERCENT | K | M | G>>
<MAXSIZE [NONE | MaxSize <K | M | G>]>
```

And the syntax to define an automatic storage table space is:

```
MANAGED BY AUTOMATIC STORAGE
<EXTENTSIZE [ExtentSize]>
<PREFETCHSIZE [PrefetchSize]>
<OVERHEAD [Overhead]>
<TRANSFERRATE [TransferRate]>
<NO FILE SYSTEM CACHING | FILE SYSTEM CACHING>
<AUTORESIZE [NO | YES]>
<INITIALSIZE [InitialSize] <K | M | G>>
<INCREASESIZE [Increment] <PERCENT | K | M | G>>
<MAXSIZE [NONE | MaxSize <K | M | G>]>
```

where:

Container	Identifies one or more containers to use to store data that will be assigned to the table space specified; for SMS table spaces, each container you specify must identify a valid directory; for DMS file containers, each container you indicate must identify a valid file; and for DMS device containers, each container you specify must identify an existing device
NumberOfPages	Specifies the number of pages that the table space container is to use
ExtentSize	Specifies the number of pages of data to write in a round-robin fashion to each table space container used
PrefetchSize	Specifies the number of pages of data to read from the specified table space when data prefetching is performed
Overhead	Identifies the I/O controller overhead and disk-seek latency time (in number of milliseconds) associated with the containers that belong to the specified table space
TransferRate	Identifies the time, in the number of milliseconds, that it takes to read one page of data from a table space container and store it in memory
InitialSize	Specifies the initial size for an autoresized DMS or an automatic storage table space
Increment	Specifies the amount by which to increase a table space that has been enabled for automatic resizing when the table space becomes full and a request for space is made
MaxSize	Specifies the maximum size to which a table space that has been enabled for automatic resizing can be increased

If you specify the RESTRICTIVE clause, the RESTRICT ACCESS database configuration parameter for the database being created will be set to YES, and no privileges will be granted to the group PUBLIC.

Suppose you want to create a DB2 database that has the following characteristics:

- Will be physically located on drive E:
- Will not use automatic storage
- Will be assigned the name SAMPLE
- Will recognize the United States/Canada code set (the code page, along with the territory, is used to convert alphanumeric data to binary data that is stored in the database)
- Will use a collating sequence that is based on the territory used (which in this case is United States/Canada)
- Will not automatically be accessible to the group PUBLIC

- Will store the system catalog in a DMS table space that uses the file SYSCATSPACE.DAT as its container (this file is stored on drive E: and is capable of holding up to 50,000 pages that are 4 KB in size.)

In this case, you execute a CREATE DATABASE command that looks similar to the following:

```
CREATE DATABASE sample
AUTOMATIC STORAGE NO
ON E:
USING CODESET 1252 TERRITORY US
COLLATE USING SYSTEM
PAGESIZE 4096
RESTRICTIVE
CATALOG TABLESPACE MANAGED BY DATABASE
USING (FILE 'E:\syscatspace.dat' 50000)
DB20000I  The CREATE DATABASE command completed successfully.
```

On a Windows platform, the database path must be a drive letter only like the one in the above example. If you want to specify a directory within the drive letter, you must set the registry variable DB2_CREATE_DB_ON_PATH to YES.

On a UNIX platform, you can execute the CREATE DATABASE command to create an AUTOMATIC STORAGE enabled database, something like this:

```
CREATE DATABASE sample ON /database DBPATH ON /home/db2inst1/
USING CODESET 1252 TERRITORY US
COLLATE USING SYSTEM
PAGESIZE 16 K
DFT_EXTENT_SZ 16 RESTRICTIVE
USER TABLESPACE MANAGED BY AUTOMATIC STORAGE PREFETCHSIZE 16
CATALOG TABLESPACE MANAGED BY AUTOMATIC STORAGE EXTENTSIZE 8 PREFETCHSIZE 8
TEMPORARY TABLESPACE MANAGED BY AUTOMATIC STORAGE PREFETCHSIZE 16;
DB20000I  The CREATE DATABASE command completed successfully.
```

The above example uses /database as the storage path defined to the default storage group IBMSTOGROUP and /home/db2inst1 as the database path to record the local database directory information.

Design Aspects of Databases

Consider the following areas of physical database design when transforming the physical data model into a physical database based on application requirements:

- Database partition groups (play an important role in database warehouse systems)
- Block-based buffer pools
- Table spaces
- Tables
- Indexes
- Range partitioned tables
- MDC tables (play a critical role in database warehouse systems)
- MQT (plays an important role in database warehouse systems)
- Multi-temperature management using storage groups

Listing Databases

When you create a database, information about the database such as the database name, alias, database release, type of database (local or remote), alternate server name for automatic client reroute, and mapping between the database and an instance are recorded automatically in the system and local database directories. If you want to list the system database directory information, execute the LIST DB DIRECTORY command:

```
LIST DB DIRECTORY

 System Database Directory

 Number of entries in the directory = 1

Database 1 entry:

 Database alias                       = SAMPLE
 Database name                        = SAMPLE
 Local database directory             = /home/db2inst1
 Database release level               = f.00
 Comment                              =
```

Continued

```
 Directory entry type                          = Indirect
 Catalog database partition number             = 0
 Alternate server hostname                     =
 Alternate server port number                  =
```

To list the local database directory information, issue this command:

```
LIST DB DIRECTORY ON /home/db2inst1

Database 1 entry:

 Database alias                                = SAMPLE
 Database name                                 = SAMPLE
 Database directory                            = SQL00001
 Database release level                        = f.00
 Comment                                       =
 Directory entry type                          = Home
 Catalog database partition number             = 0
 Database member number                        = 0
```

Dropping Databases

If a database is no longer necessary, you can delete the database from the system by using the DROP DATABASE command:

```
DROP DATABASE sample
DB20000I  The DROP DATABASE command completed successfully.
```

Enabling Automatic Storage for Your Database

You can convert an existing nonautomatic storage database to use automatic storage by using the CREATE STOGROUP command:

```
CREATE STOGROUP sg_sample ON '/database'
DB20000I  The SQL command completed successfully.
```

Upon creating a new storage group, you can check the usage by running the db2pd command:

```
db2pd -db sample -storagepaths

Database Member 0 -- Database SAMPLE -- Active -- Up 0 days 00:01:41 --
Date 2014-12-19-12.57.33.841142

Storage Group Configuration:
Address            SGID  Default  DataTag    Name
0x00007FFF01ECA500 0     Yes      0          SG_SAMPLE

Storage Group Statistics:
Address            SGID  State      Numpaths  NumDropPen
0x00007FFF01ECA500 0     0x00000000 1         0

Storage Group Paths:
Address            SGID  PathID    PathState    PathName
0x00007FFF01ECA620 0     0         NotInUse     /database
```

You can then convert available DMS table spaces to use automatic storage by using the ALTER TABLESPACE command:

```
ALTER TABLESPACE USERSPACE1 MANAGED BY AUTOMATIC STORAGE
DB20000I  The SQL command completed successfully.

db2pd -db sample -storagepaths

Database Member 0 -- Database SAMPLE -- Active -- Up 0 days 00:02:42 --
Date 2014-12-19-12.58.34.148698

Storage Group Configuration:
Address            SGID  Default  DataTag    Name
0x00007FFF01ECA500 0     Yes      0          SG_SAMPLE

                                                          Continued
```

```
Storage Group Statistics:
Address            SGID  State      Numpaths  NumDropPen
0x00007FFF01ECA500 0     0x00000000 1         0

Storage Group Paths:
Address            SGID  PathID     PathState    PathName
0x00007FFF01ECA620 0     0          InUse        /database
```

Buffer Pools

A buffer pool is an area in main memory that the database manager allocates for caching tables and index pages as they are read from disk during a processing of transaction. A buffer pool hit occurs when the necessary page is found in the buffer pool, and a miss happens when the necessary page is not found in the buffer pool and must be read from the external storage.

When a record in a table is first accessed, the database manager engages prefetcher processes to read data asynchronously from the storage device to the buffer pool and, in a few cases (such as reading binary object data), will engage agents to read data synchronously. Similarly, when records have been changed in the buffer pool, the database manager engages page-cleaner processes to write data asynchronously from the buffer pool to the disk and, in a few cases (such as writing binary object data), will engage agents to write data synchronously.

The pages in the buffer pool can be in one of the three states:

- **In Use** pages are currently being read or updated.
- **Dirty** pages contain data that has been altered but has not been written to disk yet.
- **Clean** pages contain data that has been changed and written to disk.

The key element of database tuning involves setting the configuration parameters that control the movement of data between the storage device and the buffer pool. What does this means to a database administrator? It is as simple as maximizing asynchronous I/O and minimizing the data extraction wait times.

Design Aspects of Buffer Pools

An important consideration in designing a buffer pool is the page size and the actual number of pages in addition to these attributes:

- Prefetching data into the buffer pool: The **List prefetch** algorithm efficiently reads a set of nonconsecutive data pages; the **Sequential prefetch** algorithm efficiently reads a set of consecutive data pages.

- Block-based buffer pools for improved sequential prefetching: This improves performance considerably when contiguous blocks of pages from disk are to be moved into contiguous portions of memory.

Creating a Buffer Pool

If you want to create a buffer pool having a page size of 16 KB and the total number of pages at 10,000, execute the CREATE BUFFERPOOL command, something like this:

```
CREATE BUFFERPOOL bpool_16k SIZE 10000 PAGESIZE 16K
DB20000I  The SQL command completed successfully.
```

To specify the number of pages that should exist in the block-based area to improve the sequential prefetching, you execute the following command:

```
CREATE BUFFERPOOL bpool_16k SIZE 10000 PAGESIZE 16K
NUMBLOCKPAGES 5000 BLOCKSIZE 128
DB20000I  The SQL command completed successfully.
```

Finally, if you want to create a buffer pool that is automatic, you can do so by executing this command:

```
CREATE BUFFERPOOL auto_bpool_16k PAGESIZE 16K
DB20000I  The SQL command completed successfully.
```

Listing Buffer Pools

To view the available buffer pool information, you can query the SYSCAT.BUFFERPOOLS catalog table:

```
SELECT SUBSTR (BPNAME, 1, 15) AS BPNAME, NPAGES, PAGESIZE,
       NUMBLOCKPAGES, BLOCKSIZE FROM SYSCAT.BUFFERPOOLS

BPNAME          NPAGES      PAGESIZE    NUMBLOCKPAGES BLOCKSIZE
--------------- ----------- ----------- ------------- -----------
IBMDEFAULTBP             -2       16384             0           0
```

Continued

```
BPOOL_16K              10000      16384        5000        128
AUTO_BPOOL_16K            -2      16384           0          0

  3 record(s) selected.
```

Altering Buffer Pools

You can modify the following attributes of a buffer pool by using the ALTER BUFFERPOOL command:

- SIZE. The number of pages allocated for the specific buffer pool
- NUMBLOCKPAGES. The block-based total area
- BLOCKSIZE. The block size within the block-based total area
- ESTORE. Enabling or disabling the extended storage
- DBPGNAME. The database partition group

If you want to change the block-based total area and the block size, you can do so by executing this command:

```
ALTER BUFFERPOOL bpool_16k NUMBLOCKPAGES 8000 BLOCKSIZE 256
SQL20149W  The buffer pool operation has been completed but will not take
effect until the next database restart.  SQLSTATE=01649
```

Dropping a Buffer Pool

You can drop a buffer pool only when there are no table spaces associated to the buffer pool. To drop a buffer pool, use the command DROP BUFFERPOOL, something like this:

```
DROP BUFFERPOOL bpool_16k
DB20000I  The SQL command completed successfully.
```

A Word About DB2 Storage Hierarchy

As you know, DB2 sees the world as a hierarchy of objects, and that is true for storage as well. In DB2, the hierarchy of storage units includes databases, table spaces, storage groups or storage paths, physical disks or devices, extents, and pages, as Figure 3.2 shows.

A database comprises a number of table spaces, and the size of the database is the sum of the table spaces it contains. If you want to find the database size and capacity, use the built-in procedure GET_DBSIZE_INFO:

```
CALL GET_DBSIZE_INFO (?, ?, ?, 0)

  Value of output parameters
  --------------------------
  Parameter Name  : SNAPSHOTTIMESTAMP
  Parameter Value : 2014-12-21-05.43.30.951747

  Parameter Name  : DATABASESIZE
  Parameter Value : 370027634688

  Parameter Name  : DATABASECAPACITY
  Parameter Value : 1278166970368

  Return Status = 0
```

The parameter DATABASESIZE shows the actual database size in bytes, and DATABASECAPACITY displays the maximum capacity a database can grow on the server in bytes.

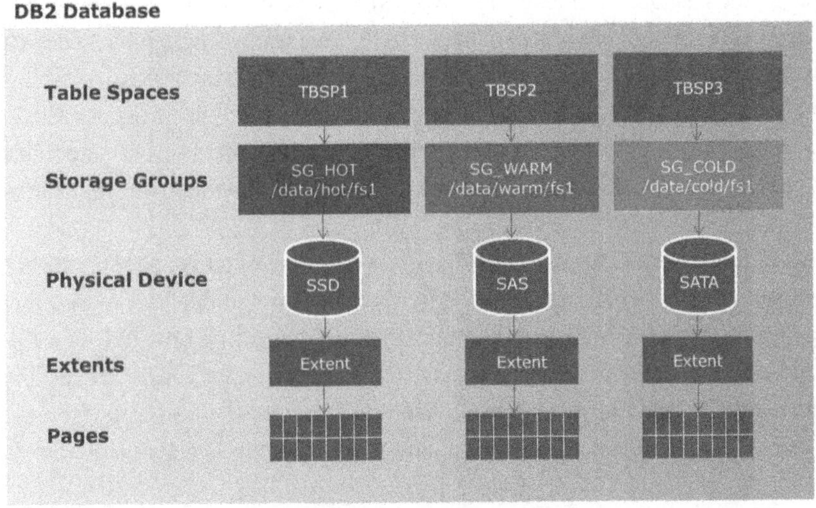

Figure 3.2: DB2 storage hierarchy

Table spaces are very important structures in DB2 and contain tables, indexes, large, and long objects. In earlier versions of DB2, table spaces comprised the number of containers that map to the physical disk. In DB2 10.1 onward, storage groups provide a layer of abstraction between table spaces and physical disk, allowing table spaces to be moved between the storage groups based on the business need (fast SSD drives for recent data, medium SAS drives for the previous month's data, and slow SATA drives for archive data). The next sections will cover table spaces and storage groups in more detail.

Containers are actual physical devices that store the data and have three categories of management: DMS, SMS, and automatic storage. Again, the next section will deal with these in greater detail.

An extent in DB2 contains a number of contiguous pages in the storage device. You configure an extent by using the DFT_EXTENT_SZ clause while creating the database or by using the EXTENTSIZE clause while creating the table space. Once specified, the extent size cannot be altered for the life of the database or the table space. DB2 I/O works with extents so that a set of contiguous pages are read from disk into buffer pool in a single I/O. A good rule of thumb is to have an extent size of 256 KB (i.e., 8 KB page size x 32 pages) for OLTP and 512 KB (16 KB page size x 32 pages) for data warehouse applications.

A page is the lowest level in the storage structure. DB2 supports 4 KB, 8 KB, 16 KB, and 32 KB page sizes within a database, allowing you to have multiple table spaces with different page sizes for different application workloads.

Table Spaces

Table spaces control where data is physically stored and provide a layer of indirection between database objects (such as tables, indexes, and MQTs) and one or more containers (i.e., directories, files, or raw devices) in which the object's data actually resides. A single table space can span many containers, but each container can belong to only one table space. When a table space spans multiple containers, data is written in a round-robin fashion (in groups of pages called extents) to each container assigned to that table space. This helps balance data across all containers that belong to a given table space. Figure 3.3 shows the relationship between pages, extents, and table space containers.

Three types of table spaces can exist: SMS table spaces, DMS table spaces and automatic storage table spaces. With SMS table spaces, only directory containers can be used for storage, and the operating system's file manager is responsible for controlling how that space is used. The SMS storage model consists of many files (each representing a table, index, or long data object) that reside within the file system space—the user decides the location of the files, the DB2 database manager assigns the files their names, and the file system is responsible for managing their growth.

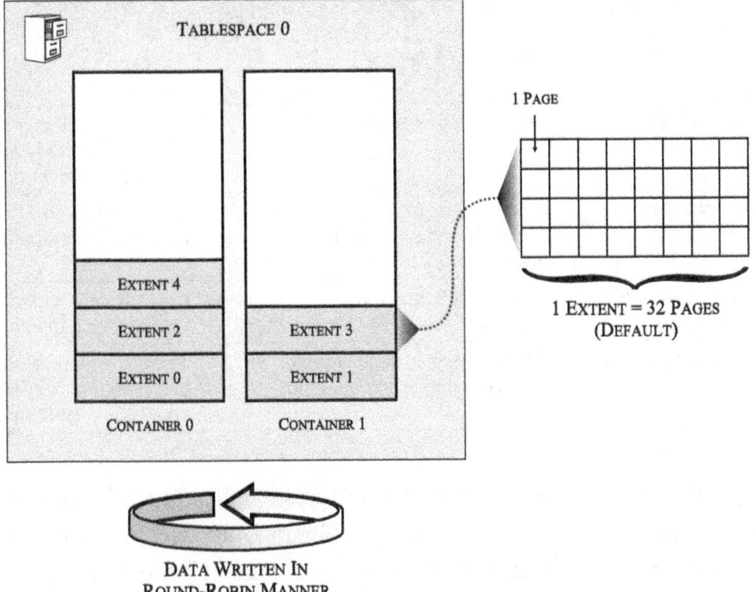

Figure 3.3: How data is written to table space containers

With DMS table spaces, only file and device containers can be used for storage, and the DB2 database manager is responsible for controlling how the space is used. With automatic storage table spaces, DB2 will select the optimal underlying table space based on the type of data it stores. Generally, it chooses SMS for temporary table spaces and DMS for regular and large table spaces. Table 3.2 shows other differences between SMS, DMS, and automatic table spaces.

Table 3.2: Differences between SMS, DMS, and automatic storage table spaces

SMS Table Space	DMS Table Space	Automatic Storage Space Table Space
Storage space is allocated and managed by the operating system's file manager.	Storage space is allocated, if so specified, and managed by the DB2 database manager.	Storage space is allocated and managed by the DB2 database manager.
Only directory containers can be used for storage; file and device containers cannot be used.	File or device containers can be used as storage; directory containers cannot be used.	DB2 chooses the type of container based on the type of data it stores.
No additional containers can be added to a table space (using the ALTER TABLESPACE SQL statement) once it has been created.	Additional containers can be added to a table space after it has been created. When new containers are added, existing data can automatically be rebalanced across the new set of containers to retain optimal I/O efficiency.	Additional containers are automatically created when a new storage path is added to the storage group and the existing container reached the maximum capacity.

Table 3.2: Differences between SMS, DMS, and automatic storage table spaces (continued)		
SMS Table Space	**DMS Table Space**	**Automatic Storage Space Table Space**
Storage space is allocated as it is needed.	Storage space is preallocated.	Storage space is managed at the storage group's level, and the storage grows on demand.
A container's size cannot be changed once a table space has been created.	A container's size can be increased or decreased after a table space has been created.	A container's size will be managed by the DB2 database manager.
Regular data and long data are stored in the same table space.	Regular data and long data can be split across multiple table spaces.	Regular data and long data can be split across multiple table spaces.
Table spaces are easier to create and manage.	Table access is slightly faster, so overall performance is better.	Table spaces are easier to create and manage like SMS and also show better performance like DMS.

Both SMS and DMS table spaces are classified according to the type of data they are intended to store. The three classifications are regular, large, and temporary. Regular data and index data reside in regular table spaces, whereas long field data and large object data can reside in large table spaces—but only if DMS table spaces are used. (The use of large table spaces is optional, given that large data can reside in regular table spaces as well.) Temporary table spaces are further classified as being either system or user—system temporary table spaces store internal temporary data generated when some types of operations are performed (for example, sorting data, reorganizing tables, creating indexes, and joining tables), whereas user temporary table spaces store declared global temporary tables, which in turn store application-specific data for a brief time.

If you enable a database for automatic storage, one other type of table space—an automatic storage table space—can exist. Although at first glance, automatic storage table spaces appear to be a third type of table space, they are really just an extension of SMS and DMS table spaces. You create regular and large table spaces as DMS table spaces with one or more file containers; you create system and user temporary table as SMS table spaces with one or more directory containers. Unlike when you define SMS and DMS table spaces, no container definitions are needed for automatic storage table spaces; the DB2 database manager assigns containers to automatic storage table spaces automatically.

Obtaining Information About Existing Table Spaces

As with other objects, whenever a table space object is created, information about that table space is recorded in the system catalog. As a result, you can obtain specific information about any table space in a database by querying the appropriate system catalog tables or system catalog views. You can also obtain information about all table spaces that have been created for a particular database by executing the LIST TABLESPACES command.

The syntax for this command is:

```
LIST TABLESPACES <SHOW DETAIL>
```

Executing this command without specifying the SHOW DETAIL option will display the following information for every table space that has been created for a database:

- The internal ID that was assigned to the table space when it was created
- The name that has been assigned to the table space
- Table space type (SMS table space or DMS table space)
- The type of data the table space is designed to hold (i.e., regular data, large data, or temporary data)
- The current state of the table space (Table 3.3 contains a list of the table space states)

Table 3.3: Table space states

Table Space State	Hexadecimal Value
Normal	0x0
Quiesced: SHARE	0x1
Quiesced: UPDATE	0x2
Quiesced: EXCLUSIVE	0x4
Load pending	0x8
Delete pending	0x10
Backup pending	0x20
Roll-forward recovery in progress	0x40
Roll-forward recovery pending	0x80
Restore pending	0x100
Disable pending	0x200
Reorganization in progress	0x400
Backup in progress	0x800
Storage must be defined	0x1000
Restore in progress	0x2000
Offline and not accessible	0x4000
Drop pending	0x8000
Storage may be defined	0x2000000
StorDef is in "Final" state	0x4000000
StorDef was changed before roll-forward recovery	0x8000000
DMS rebalance in progress	0x10000000

Table 3.3: Table space states (continued)	
Table Space State	**Hexadecimal Value**
Table space deletion in progress	0x20000000
Table space creation in progress	0x40000000
Load in progress*	0x20000
A single table space can be in more than one state at a given point in time. If this is the case, multiple table space state hexadecimal values will be ANDed together to keep track of the multiple states. You can use the Get Table Space State command (db2tbst) to obtain the table space state associated with any given hexadecimal value. **The Load utility will place a table space in the "Load in progress" state if the COPY NO option is specified when data is being loaded into a recoverable database. The table space remains in this state for the duration of the load operation and is returned to normal state when the load operation is completed. This state does not have a hexadecimal value.*	

Executing the LIST TABLESPACES command with the SHOW DETAIL option specified will display the following additional information about each table space:

- **Total number of pages the table space is designed to hold**. For DMS table spaces, this is the sum of all pages available from all containers associated with the table space. For SMS table spaces, this is the total amount of file space currently being used.
- **Number of usable pages in the table space where user data can be stored**. For DMS table spaces, this number is calculated by subtracting the number of pages required for overhead from the total number of pages available. For SMS table spaces, this number is equal to the total number of pages the table space is designed to hold.
- **Number of used pages in the table space that already contains data**. For SMS table spaces, this value is equal to the total number of pages the table space is designed to hold.
- **Number of free pages in the table space that are currently empty**. This information is applicable only for DMS table spaces.
- **High watermark**. This is the number of pages that mark the current "high watermark" or "end" of the table space's address space (i.e., the page number of the first free page following the last allocated extent of the table space). This information is applicable only to DMS table spaces.
- **Page size**. This is the page size, in bytes, that one page of data in the table space will occupy.
- **Extent size**. This is the number of pages contained in one extent of the table space.
- **Prefetch size**. This is the number of pages of data that will be read from the table space in advance of those pages currently being referenced by a query, in anticipation that they will be needed to resolve the query (prefetched).

- **Number of containers**. This is the number of containers used by the table space.
- **Minimum recovery time**. This is the earliest point in time that you can specify if a point-in-time roll-forward recovery operation is to be performed on the table space.
- **State change table space ID**. This is the ID of the table space that caused the table space being queried to be placed in the Load Pending or Delete Pending state. (This information will display only if the table space being queried has been placed in the Load Pending or Delete Pending state.)
- **State change object ID**. This is the ID of the object that caused the table space being queried to be placed in the Load Pending or Delete Pending state. (This information will display only if the table space being queried has been placed in the Load Pending or Delete Pending state.)
- **Number of quiescers**. This is the number of users or applications that have placed the table space in a quiesced (restricted access) state. (This information will display only if the table space being queried has been placed in the Quiesced:SHARE, Quiesced:UPDATE, or Quiesced:EXCLUSIVE state.)
- **Table space ID and object ID for each quiescer**. This is the ID of the table spaces and objects that caused the table space being queried to be placed in a quiesced state. (This information is displayed only if the number of users or applications that have placed the table space in a quiesced state is greater than zero.)

So if you want to obtain detailed information about all table spaces that have been created for a database named SAMPLE, you can do so by connecting to the database and executing a LIST TABLESPACES command:

```
LIST TABLESPACES SHOW DETAIL
```

And when this command is executed, the resulting output should look something like this:

```
          Tablespaces for Current Database

 Tablespace ID                  = 0
 Name                           = SYSCATSPACE
 Type                           = System managed space
 Contents                       = All permanent data. Regular table space.
 State                          = 0x0000
                                                              Continued
```

```
  Detailed explanation:
    Normal
Total pages                          = 6979
Useable pages                        = 6979
Used pages                           = 6979
Free pages                           = Not applicable
High water mark (pages)              = Not applicable
Page size (bytes)                    = 16384
Extent size (pages)                  = 16
Prefetch size (pages)                = 96
Number of containers                 = 1

Tablespace ID                        = 1
Name                                 = TEMPSPACE1
Type                                 = System managed space
Contents                             = System Temporary data
State                                = 0x0000
  Detailed explanation:
    Normal
Total pages                          = 1
Useable pages                        = 1
Used pages                           = 1
Free pages                           = Not applicable
High water mark (pages)              = Not applicable
Page size (bytes)                    = 16384
Extent size (pages)                  = 16
Prefetch size (pages)                = 96
Number of containers                 = 1

Tablespace ID                        = 2
Name                                 = USERSPACE1
Type                                 = Database managed space
Contents                             = All permanent data. Large table space.
State                                = 0x0004
```

Continued

```
  Detailed explanation:
    Quiesced: EXCLUSIVE
Total pages                              = 5000
Useable pages                            = 4976
Used pages                               = 80
Free pages                               = 4896
High water mark (pages)                  = 80
Page size (bytes)                        = 16384
Extent size (pages)                      = 16
Prefetch size (pages)                    = 16
Number of containers                     = 1
Number of quiescers                      = 1
  Quiescer 1:
    Tablespace ID                        = 2
    Object ID                            = 4

Tablespace ID                            = 3
Name                                     = SYSTOOLSPACE
Type                                     = Database managed space
Contents                                 = All permanent data. Large table space.
State                                    = 0x0000
  Detailed explanation:
    Normal
Total pages                              = 2048
Useable pages                            = 2044
Used pages                               = 88
Free pages                               = 1956
High water mark (pages)                  = 88
Page size (bytes)                        = 16384
Extent size (pages)                      = 4
Prefetch size (pages)                    = 24
  Number of containers                   = 1
```

You can also obtain detailed information about all table spaces that have been created for a particular database by using the MON_GET_TABLESPACE built-in table function. (Chapter 5, "Monitoring DB2 Activity," will cover these monitoring elements more closely.)

Obtaining Information About the Containers

Just as you can obtain information about the table spaces that have been created for a particular database, you can obtain information about the containers that physically hold table space data by executing the LIST TABLESPACE CONTAINERS command. The syntax for this command is:

```
LIST TABLESPACE CONTAINERS FOR [TablespaceID]
<SHOW DETAIL>
```

where:

TablespaceID Identifies the internal ID assigned to the table space for which to obtain container information

Executing this command without the SHOW DETAIL option specified will display the following information for every table space that has been created for a database:

- The internal ID that was assigned to the container when it was associated with the table space specified
- The name that was used to reference the container when it was assigned to the table space specified
- Indication that the container is a directory (path) container, a file container, or a device container

However, if you execute this command and specify the SHOW DETAIL option, you can obtain the following additional information about each table space container:

- **Total number of pages the table space container is designed to hold**. For SMS table spaces, this is the total amount of storage space that the container is currently using.
- **Number of usable pages in the table space container where user data can be stored.** For DMS table spaces, this number is calculated by subtracting the number of pages needed for overhead from the total number of pages available. For SMS table spaces, this value is equal to the total number of pages the table space container is designed to hold.
- **Accessibility**. This is indicates whether the container is accessible.

So to obtain detailed information about the containers that are associated with the table space whose internal ID is 2 (in a database named SAMPLE), you can execute a LIST TABLESPACE CONTAINERS command:

```
LIST TABLESPACE CONTAINERS FOR 2 SHOW DETAIL
```

And when this command is executed, you might see output that looks something like this:

```
            Tablespace Containers for Tablespace 2

  Container ID                          = 0
  Name                                  = /database/db2inst1/userspace1.dat
  Type                                  = File
  Total pages                           = 5000
  Useable pages                         = 4976
  Accessible                            = Yes
```

Note that if for some reason a particular table space container becomes inaccessible (Accessible = No), the table space associated with that container will automatically be placed in the Offline state. After you resolve the issue that made the container inaccessible, you can return the associated table space to the Normal state by executing the ALTER TABLESPACE SQL statement with the SWITCH ONLINE option specified. You can also obtain detailed information about containers that have been created for a particular table space by using the MON_GET_CONTAINER built-in table function. (Chapter 5, "Monitoring DB2 Activity," will discuss these monitoring elements.)

Both the LIST TABLESPACE and LIST TABLESPACE CONTAINERS commands are deprecated in DB2 9.7 and might be removed in the near future. So the recommendation is to use the DB2 built-in table functions instead.

Creating Table Spaces

Earlier, you saw that with the creation of a DB2 database, one buffer pool named IBMDEFAULTBP is created, and three table spaces are constructed and associated with this buffer pool as part of the database initialization process. These three table spaces are sufficient for small databases; however, large databases usually consist of many different buffer pool and table space objects.

You can create additional table spaces by executing the CREATE TABLESPACE SQL statement. The basic syntax for this statement is:

```
CREATE
<REGULAR | LARGE | SYSTEM TEMPORARY | USER TEMPORARY>
TABLESPACE [TablespaceName]
<PAGESIZE [PageSize] <K>>
MANAGED BY SYSTEM USING ('[Container]' ,...)
                                                    Continued
```

```
<EXTENTSIZE [ExtentPages | ExtentSize <K | M | G>]> <PREFETCHSIZE [AUTOMATIC
|
     PrefetchPages |
     PrefetchSize <K | M | G>]>
<BUFFERPOOL [BufferPoolName]>
<<NO> FILE SYSTEM CACHING>
<DROPPED TABLE RECOVERY <ON | OFF>>
```

or

```
CREATE
<REGULAR | LARGE | SYSTEM TEMPORARY | USER TEMPORARY>
TABLESPACE [TablespaceName]
<PAGESIZE [PageSize] <K>>
MANAGED BY DATABASE USING ([FILE | DEVICE] '[Container]'
   [ContainerPages | ContainerSize <K | M | G>] ,...)
<AUTORESIZE [YES | NO]>
<INCREASESIZE [IncSize <PERCENT | K | M | G>]>
<MAXSIZE [NONE | MaxSize <K | M | G>]>
<EXTENTSIZE [ExtentPages / ExtentSize <K | M | G>]> <PREFETCHSIZE [AUTOMATIC
|
     PrefetchPages |
     PrefetchSize <K | M | G>]>
<BUFFERPOOL [BufferPoolName]>
<<NO> FILE SYSTEM CACHING>
<DROPPED TABLE RECOVERY <ON | OFF>>
```

or

```
CREATE
<REGULAR | LARGE | SYSTEM TEMPORARY | USER TEMPORARY>
TABLESPACE [TablespaceName]
<PAGESIZE [PageSize] <K>>
MANAGED BY AUTOMATIC STORAGE
```

Continued

```
<AUTORESIZE [YES | NO]>
<INITIALSIZE [InitSize <K | M | G>]>
<INCREASESIZE [IncSize <PERCENT | K | M | G>]>
<MAXSIZE [NONE | MaxSize <K | M | G>]>
<EXTENTSIZE [ExtentPages | ExtentSize <K | M | G>]> <PREFETCHSIZE [AUTOMATIC
|
     PrefetchPages |
     PrefetchSize <K | M | G>]>
<BUFFERPOOL [BufferPoolName]>
<<NO> FILE SYSTEM CACHING>
<DROPPED TABLE RECOVERY <ON | OFF>>
```

where:

TablespaceName	Identifies the name to assign to the table space to be created
PageSize	Specifies the size of each page the table space being created will use; the following values are valid for this parameter: 4,096; 8,192; 16,384; or 32,768 bytes—if the suffix K (for kilobytes) is provided, you must set this parameter to 4, 8, 16, or 32; unless otherwise specified, pages used by table spaces are 4 KB in size
Container	Identifies, by name, one or more containers to use to store the data associated with the table space to be created
ContainerPages	Identifies the amount of storage, by the number of pages, to preallocate for the containers identified in the Container parameter
ContainerSize	Identifies the amount of storage to preallocate for the containers identified in the Container parameter; the value you specify for this parameter is treated as the total number of bytes, unless you also indicate the letter K (for kilobytes), M (for megabytes), or G (for gigabytes)—if you specify a ContainerSize value, it is converted to a ContainerPages value by using the PageSize value provided
InitSize	Identifies the amount of storage to preallocate for an autoresized DMS or automatic storage table space
IncSize	Identifies the amount by which to automatically increase a table space enabled for automatic resizing when the table space is full and a request for more space is made
MaxSize	Identifies the maximum size to which a table space enabled for automatic resizing can automatically be increased

ExtentPages	Identifies the number of pages of data to write to a single table space container before another container is used
ExtentSize	Identifies the amount of data to write to a single table space container before another container is used; the value you specify for this parameter is treated as the total number of bytes, unless you also indicate the letter K (for kilobytes), M (for megabytes), or G (for gigabytes)—if you specify an ExtentSize value, it is converted to an ExtentPages value by using the PageSize value provided
PrefetchPages	Identifies the number of pages of data to read from the table space when data prefetching is performed (prefetching allows data needed by a query to be read before it is referenced so that the query spends less time waiting for I/O)
PrefetchSize	Identifies the amount of data to read from the table space when data prefetching is performed; the value you specify for this parameter is treated as the total number of bytes, unless you also indicate the letter K (for kilobytes), M (for megabytes), or G (for gigabytes) is —if you specify a PrefetchSize value, it is converted to a PrefetchPages value by using the PageSize value provided
BufferPoolName	Identifies the name of the buffer pool that the table space to be created will use (the page size of the buffer pool you specify must match the page size of the table space to be created, or the CREATE TABLESPACE statement will fail)

If you execute the MANAGED BY SYSTEM version of this statement, the resulting table space will be an SMS table space. However, if you execute the MANAGED BY DATABASE version, the resulting table space will be a DMS table space. Furthermore, an SMS table space can include only directories as its storage containers; a DMS table space can have only fixed-size preallocated files or physical raw devices as its storage containers.

Thus, to create an SMS table space that has the name TS_SMALL_SMS, consists of pages that are 16 KB in size, uses the directory /database/ts_small as its storage container, and uses the buffer pool IBMDEFAULTBP, you execute a CREATE TABLESPACE SQL statement that looks something like this:

```
CREATE REGULAR TABLESPACE TS_SMALL_SMS
PAGESIZE 16 K MANAGED BY SYSTEM USING ('/database/ts_small')
EXTENTSIZE 32
PREFETCHSIZE 96
BUFFERPOOL IBMDEFAULTBP
DB20000I  The SQL command completed successfully.
```

However, if you want to create a large DMS table space that has the name TS_SMALL_DATA, consists of pages that are 16 KB in size, uses the file ts_small_data as its storage container, and uses the buffer pool IBMDEFAULTBP, execute a CREATE TABLESPACE SQL statement similar to the following:

```
CREATE LARGE TABLESPACE TS_SMALL_DATA PAGESIZE 16384
MANAGED BY DATABASE USING (FILE '/data/ts_small_data' 18240)
 EXTENTSIZE 32
 PREFETCHSIZE AUTOMATIC
 BUFFERPOOL IBMDEFAULTBP
 OVERHEAD 3.690000
 TRANSFERRATE 0.070000
 AUTORESIZE YES
 MAXSIZE NONE
 NO FILE SYSTEM CACHING
 DROPPED TABLE RECOVERY ON
DB20000I  The SQL command completed successfully.
```

And finally, to create an automatic storage table space that has the name TS_LARGE_DATA and uses the buffer pool IBMDEFAULTBP, you can execute this CREATE TABLESPACE SQL statement:

```
CREATE REGULAR TABLESPACE TS_LARGE_DATA MANAGED BY AUTOMATIC STORAGE
DB20000I  The SQL command completed successfully.
```

If a database is enabled for automatic storage, you can omit the MANAGED BY AUTOMATIC STORAGE clause completely—its absence implies automatic storage. No container definitions are provided in this case because the DB2 database manager assigns containers automatically. Although you can create a database by specifying the AUTOMATIC STORAGE NO clause, the AUTOMATIC STORAGE clause is deprecated and might be removed from a future release.

Altering Table Spaces

Because SMS table spaces rely on the operating system for physical storage space management, they rarely need to be modified after they have been successfully created. DMS table spaces, however, must be monitored closely to ensure that the fixed-size preallocated files or physical raw devices that they use for storage always have enough free space available to meet the database's needs. When the amount of free storage space available to a DMS table space becomes dangerously low (typically less than 10 percent), you can add more free space either by increasing the size of one or more of its containers or by adding one or more new containers to it.

To resize existing table space containers, make new containers available to an existing table space, and change an existing table space's properties, you can execute the ALTER TABLESPACE SQL statement. The basic syntax for this statement is:

```
ALTER TABLESPACE [TablespaceName]
[ADD | EXTEND | REDUCE | RESIZE]
   ([FILE | DEVICE] '[Container]'
   [ContainerPages | ContainerSize <K | M | G>] ,...)
```

or

```
ALTER TABLESPACE [TablespaceName]
[EXTEND | REDUCE | RESIZE]
   (ALL <CONTAINERS>
     [ContainerPages | ContainerSize <K | M | G>])
```

or

```
ALTER TABLESPACE [TablespaceName]
DROP ([FILE | DEVICE] '[Container]' ,...)
```

or

```
ALTER TABLESPACE [TablespaceName]
< PREFETCHSIZE AUTOMATIC |
  PREFETCHSIZE [PrefetchPages | PrefetchSize <K | M | G>]>
<BUFFERPOOL [BufferPoolName]>
<<NO> FILE SYSTEM CACHING>
<AUTORESIZE [NO | YES]>
<INCREASESIZE [IncSize <PERCENT | K | M | G>]>
<MAXSIZE [NONE | MaxSize <K | M | G>]>
<DROPPED TABLE RECOVERY [ON | OFF]>
<CONVERT TO LARGE>
```

where:

TablespaceName	Identifies the name to assign to the table space to be altered
Container	Identifies one or more containers to add to, resize, or remove from the table space specified
ContainerPages	Identifies the amount of storage, by the number of pages, to add to, remove from, or allocate for all containers or for the containers identified in the Container parameter
ContainerSize	Identifies the amount of storage to add to, remove from, or allocate for all containers or for the containers identified in the Container parameter; the value you specify for this parameter is treated as the total number of bytes, unless you also indicate the letter K (for kilobytes), M (for megabytes), or G (for gigabytes)—if you specify a ContainerSize value, it is converted to a ContainerPages value by using the PageSize value provided
PrefetchPages	Identifies the number of pages of data to read from the table space when data prefetching is performed
PrefetchSize	Identifies the amount of data to read from the table space when data prefetching is performed; the value you specify for this parameter is treated as the total number of bytes, unless you also indicate the letter K (for kilobytes), M (for megabytes), or G (for gigabytes)—if you specify a PrefetchSize value, it is converted to a PrefetchPages value by using the page size of the table space being altered
BufferPoolName	Identifies the name of the buffer pool that the table space to be altered will use (the page size of the buffer pool you specify must match the page size used by the table space to be altered)
IncSize	Identifies the amount by which to automatically increase a table space enabled for automatic resizing when the table space is full and a request for more space is made
MaxSize	Identifies the maximum size to which a table space enabled for automatic resizing can automatically be increased

Thus, if you want to use a fixed-size preallocated file named smalldata.1.tbs that is 5 GB in size and resides in the directory /database/data/ as a new storage container for an existing DMS table space named TS_SMALL_DATA, you can do so by executing an ALTER TABLESPACE SQL statement that looks like this:

```
ALTER TABLESPACE TS_SMALL_DATA
ADD (FILE '/database/data/smalldata.1.tbs' 10 G)
DB20000I  The SQL command completed successfully.
```

However, to expand the size of all containers associated with an existing DMS table space named TS_SMALL_DATA by 200 MB, execute this ALTER TABLESPACE SQL statement:

```
ALTER TABLESPACE TS_SMALL_DATA EXTEND (ALL CONTAINERS 200 M)
DB20000I  The SQL command completed successfully.
```

If you want to rename the table space, execute the RENAME TABLESPACE command (remember, SYSCATSPACE cannot be renamed):

```
RENAME TABLESPACE TS_SMALL_DATA TO TS_NEW_DATA
DB20000I  The SQL command completed successfully.
```

Other than the containers' size, you can change a table space's PREFETCHSIZE, OVERHEAD, and TRANSFERRATE, similar to the following:

```
ALTER TABLESPACE TS_SMALL_DATA PREFETCHSIZE 64 OVERHEAD 1 TRANSFERRATE 128
DB20000I  The SQL command completed successfully.
```

Adding Containers to Automatic Storage Table Spaces

As discussed earlier, if you enable a database for automatic storage, the container- and space-management characteristics of its table spaces are determined by the DB2 database manager. And although you can use the ALTER TABLESPACE command to add new containers to existing DMS table spaces, you cannot use the command to add new containers to automatic storage table spaces.

So how can you add new storage paths to the collection of paths that are used for automatic storage table spaces once you have created a database? To perform this operation, you must use the ALTER STOGROUP statement. The basic syntax for this statement is:

```
ALTER STOGROUP [StoGrpName]
ADD '[StoragePath]' ,...)
```

where:

StoGrpName	Identifies the storage group name to add a new storage path to its pool of storage paths that are used for automatic storage
StoragePath	Identifies one or more new storage paths (absolute path) to add to the collection of storage paths that are used for automatic storage table spaces

Thus, if you want to add the storage locations /database/path1 and /database/path2 to a database named SAMPLE that is configured for automatic storage and resides on a UNIX system, you can do so by executing an ALTER STOGROUP SQL statement:

```
ALTER STOGROUP IBMSTOGROUP ADD '/database/path1', '/database/path2'
DB20000I  The SQL command completed successfully.
```

To list the storage group attributes, use the table function ADMIN_GET_STORAGE_PATHS, something like this:

```
SELECT
      VARCHAR (STORAGE_GROUP_NAME, 20) AS STOGROUP,
      VARCHAR (DB_STORAGE_PATH, 30) AS STORAGE_PATH
   FROM TABLE (ADMIN_GET_STORAGE_PATHS ('',-1)) AS T

STOGROUP             STORAGE_PATH
-------------------- ------------------------------
IBMSTOGROUP          /database/sample/path
IBMSTOGROUP          /database/path2
IBMSTOGROUP          /database/path1

  3 record(s) selected.
```

Table Space Rebalance Operation

When you add a new storage path to an existing storage group, or when you remove an available storage path from an existing storage group by using the ALTER STOGROUP command, the DB2 database manager performs a rebalance operation. It does a forward rebalance when you add a storage path and a reverse rebalance when you remove a storage path.

If you want to monitor the rebalance operation, you can do so by using the MON_GET_REBALANCE_STATUS table function, something like this:

```
SELECT
      VARCHAR (TBSP_NAME, 15) AS TBSP_NAME,
      REBALANCER_MODE,
```

Continued

```
      REBALANCER_STATUS,
      REBALANCER_EXTENTS_REMAINING,
      REBALANCER_EXTENTS_PROCESSED,
      REBALANCER_START_TIME
   FROM TABLE (MON_GET_REBALANCE_STATUS (NULL,-2)) AS T

           REBALANCER_ REBALANCER_ REBALANCER_        REBALANCER_
TBSP_NAME  MODE        STATUS      EXTENTS_REMAINING EXTENTS_PROCESSED REBALANCER_START_TIME
---------- ----------- ----------- ----------------- ----------------- --------------------------
USERSPACE1 FWD_REBAL   ACTIVE      419               1022              2014-12-22-06.03.36.000000
```

Reclaimable Storage

Reclaimable storage, a feature introduced in DB2 9.7, consolidates in-use extents below the high watermark and returns unused extents in your table space to the operating system for reuse. In earlier versions of DB2, the only way to release the container storage to the operating system was to drop containers or to reduce the size of containers by eliminating unused extents above the high watermark. No direct mechanism was available to reduce the high watermark; however, the indirect mechanism was to perform an online/offline reorganization of tables and indexes based on the db2dart tool recommendations.

For automatic storage table spaces, you can use the ALTER TABLESPACE command with the REDUCE MAX clause to release all unused space and to also lower the high watermark. This eliminates the process of running db2dart, dropping and re-creating objects, and exporting and importing the data. The command looks something like this:

```
ALTER TABLESPACE USERSPACE1 REDUCE MAX
DB20000I  The SQL command completed successfully.
```

DMS table spaces require a two-step process to release unused extents:

Step 1: Reduce the high watermark by using the ALTER TABLESPACE command:

```
ALTER TABLESPACE TS_SMALL_DATA LOWER HIGH WATER MARK
DB20000I  The SQL command completed successfully.
```

Step 2: Reduce the container size by specifying the REDUCE, RESIZE, or DROP clause in the ALTER TABLESPACE command:

```
ALTER TABLESPACE TS_SMALL_DATA REDUCE (ALL CONTAINERS 10 M)
DB20000I  The SQL command completed successfully.
```

To view the table space attributes such as the high watermark, total number of pages allocated, number of pages used, and reclaimable status, use the MON_GET_TABLESPACE table function, similar to the following:

```
SELECT
      SUBSTR (TBSP_NAME, 1, 15) as TBSP_NAME,
      TBSP_TOTAL_PAGES, TBSP_USED_PAGES,
      TBSP_PAGE_TOP AS HIGH_WATER_MARK,
      RECLAIMABLE_SPACE_ENABLED
   FROM TABLE (MON_GET_TABLESPACE (NULL, -1)) AS TBSP

              TBSP_        TBSP_       HIGH_       RECLAIMABLE_
TBSP_NAME     TOTAL_PAGES  USED_PAGES  WATER_MARK  SPACE_ENABLED
------------- ------------ ----------  ----------  ------------
SYSCATSPACE          32768      26676       26676             1
TEMPSPACE1               1          1           0             0
USERSPACE1           16576         96       15936             1
TS_LARGE_DATA         8192         96          96             1
SYSTOOLSPACE          8192        152         152             1
TS_SMALL_DATA       523776         96      441888             1

  6 record(s) selected.
```

To view the extent movement operation, you can use this MON_GET_EXTENT_MOVEMENT_STATUS table function:

```
SELECT SUBST (TBSP_NAME, 1, 15) AS TBSP_NAME, LAST_EXTENT, NUM_EXTENTS_MOVED,
NUM_EXTENTS_LEFT, TOTAL_MOVE_TIME
   FROM TABLE (MON_GET_EXTENT_MOVEMENT_STATUS ('USERSPACE1',-1)) AS TBSP
```

Dropping Table Spaces

When you drop a table space, the DB2 database manager deletes all the data in that table space, deletes the container from the operation system, removes the catalog entries, and causes all objects defined in the table space to be either dropped or marked as invalid. Remember, you cannot drop a table space without dropping all related table spaces. For example, if you have table data in table space TS_SMALL_DATA and index data in TS_SMALL_INDEX, then you must drop both TS_SMALL_INDEX and TS_SMALL_DATA.

If you want to drop user table spaces, execute the DROP TABLESPACE command, something like this:

```
DROP TABLESPACE TS_SMALL_INDEX, TS_SMALL_DATA
DB20000I  The SQL command completed successfully.
```

To drop a user temporary table space, verify that no declared or created temporary tables are defined in the table space. And similarly, if you want to drop a system temporary table space, make sure you create another system temporary table space of a similar page size and drop the old one.

Converting DMS Table Spaces to Use Automatic Storage

To simplify storage management, you can convert an existing DMS table space to use automatic storage by performing the following steps:

Step 1: Identify the table space that you want to convert from DMS to automatic storage, and identify the storage group that you want the table space to use.

You can use the SNAP_GET_TBSP table function to find the candidate for the conversion by executing this command:

```
SELECT
      SUBSTR (TBSP_NAME, 1, 12) AS TBSP_NAME, TBSP_ID, TBSP_TYPE,
      TBSP_CONTENT_TYPE, TBSP_USING_AUTO_STORAGE
   FROM TABLE (SNAP_GET_TBSP ('')) AS T
   WHERE TBSP_USING_AUTO_STORAGE=0

TBSP_NAME    TBSP_ID    TBSP_TYPE  TBSP_CONTENT_TYPE TBSP_USING_AUTO_STORAGE
------------ ---------- ---------- ----------------- -----------------------
TS_DMS_DATA          11 DMS        LARGE                                   0

  1 record(s) selected.
```

To find the best suitable storage group in which to place the table space, use the ADMIN_GET_STORAGE_PATHS table function, similar to the following:

```
SELECT
      SUBSTR(STORAGE_GROUP_NAME,1,15)  AS STOGROUP,
      SUBSTR(DB_STORAGE_PATH,1,20)  AS STORAGE_PATH,
      SUBSTR(DB_STORAGE_PATH_STATE,1,10)  AS DB_STORAGE_PATH_STATE
   FROM TABLE (ADMIN_GET_STORAGE_PATHS ('',-1)) AS T

STOGROUP        STORAGE_PATH         DB_STORAGE_PATH_STATE
--------------- -------------------- ---------------------
IBMSTOGROUP     /data/data_fs        IN_USE
SG_HOT          /data/hot_fs1        IN_USE

  2 record(s) selected.
```

Step 2: Once you have the data ready, you can convert the table space to use automatic storage by executing this command:

```
ALTER TABLESPACE TS_DMS_DATA MANAGED BY
AUTOMATIC STORAGE USING STOGROUP SG_HOT
DB20000I  The SQL command completed successfully.
```

Step 3: Move the content from the old container to the new automatic storage path by executing the REBALANCE command:

```
ALTER TABLESPACE TS_DMS_DATA REBALANCE
DB20000I  The SQL command completed successfully.
```

Step 4: Monitor the progress of the rebalance operation by using this command:

```
SELECT
      VARCHAR (TBSP_NAME, 15) AS TBSP_NAME,
      REBALANCER_MODE,
```

Continued

```
        REBALANCER_STATUS,
        REBALANCER_EXTENTS_REMAINING,
        REBALANCER_EXTENTS_PROCESSED,
        REBALANCER_START_TIME
    FROM TABLE (MON_GET_REBALANCE_STATUS (NULL,-2)) AS T
```

Design Aspects of Table Spaces

A poor table space design can lead to a significant negative impact on database server performance. The design principles around the table spaces are as follows:

- **Extent size.** This is the amount of data to write to a single table space container before another container is used. A good rule of thumb is to have an extent size of 256 KB, and extent sizes 128 KB or 512 KB are also a wise choice based on application type.
- **Page size.** This is the size of each page the table space being created will use. Specify a 4 KB or an 8 KB page size to store static configuration or master data, and choose 16 KB or 32 KB to store dynamic transaction or fact data.
- **File system caching.** The NO FILE SYSTEM CACHING clause enables direct or concurrent I/O. As we all know, the DB2 database manager caches regular data in respective buffer pools before sending the data back to the client. It is advisable not to cache the data in the operating system file system cache. However, the temporary table spaces will use the file system cache irrespective of the command option.
- **Prefetch size.** This is the amount of data to read whenever a prefetch is triggered. Setting the prefetch size to be a multiple of the extent size causes multiple extents to be read in parallel. The recommendation is to set this parameter to AUTOMATIC.
- **Parallel I/O.** You can use DB2 registry variable DB2_PARALLEL_IO to explicitly specify a prefetch request for each container. For example, if a table space container exists on a RAID 5 4+1 array file system, then set DB2_PARALLEL_IO=*:5 to activate a prefetch for each physical disk.
- **AUTOMATIC.** It is recommended to set the number of prefetchers and the number of page-cleaners to AUTOMATIC.
- **TRUNCATE ... LOAD.** It is recommended to create TRUNCATE and LOAD tables in a separate table space to eliminate the conflict between BACKUP and TRUNCATE.
- **NOT LOGGED INITIALLY.** It is recommended to create NOT LOGGED INITIALLY tables in a separate table space.

Storage Groups

As you learned from previous sections, a storage group is a named set of storage paths where you can store data. Storage groups help in segregating different classes of storage available to the database system, such as Solid State Drives (SSD—very fast disks), Serial Attached SCSI (SAS—medium fast disks), and Serial ATA (SATA—slow disks). You can use storage groups only when you create automatic storage table spaces. A storage group can be associated with multiple table spaces; however, a table space can be associated with only one storage group. What does that mean? You cannot create a table space on multiple storage groups.

You can create a storage group by using the CREATE STOGROUP command. In its simplest form, the syntax for the CREATE STOGROUP command is:

```
CREATE STOGROUP [StogrpName] ON ['StoragePath']
OVERHEAD [DeviceOverHead]
DEVICE READ RATE [DeviceReadRate]
DATA TAG [DataTag]
SET AS DEFAULT
```

where:

StoGrpName	Identifies a unique name to assign to the storage group once it is created
StoragePath	Identifies storage paths to add for the named storage group
DeviceOverHead	Identifies I/O controller time and the disk seek and latency time in milliseconds; generally, you will obtain this information from the storage manufacturer (the default value is 6.725 milliseconds)
DeviceReadRate	Identifies the device specification for the read transfer date in MB/second; the default value is 100 MB/second
DataTag	Identifies the tag name for the DB2 Workload Manager (WLM) to use to determine the processing priority of the database activities; the default setting is NONE

If you want to create a storage group SG_HOT with an overhead rate of 0.8 and the device read date of 512 MB/second, execute the CREATE STOGROUP command, something like this:

```
CREATE STOGROUP SG_HOT ON '/data/hot_fs1' OVERHEAD 0.8
DEVICE READ RATE 512 DATA TAG 1
DB20000I  The SQL command completed successfully.
```

To create a table space Q4_2014 to store recent data by using the storage group SG_HOT, you can execute the CREATE TABLESPACE command, similar to the following:

```
CREATE TABLESPACE Q4_2014 MANAGED BY AUTOMATIC STORAGE
USING STOGROUP SG_HOT
INITIALSIZE 5M INCREASESIZE 5M
OVERHEAD INHERIT TRANSFERRATE INHERIT
DB20000I  The SQL command completed successfully.
```

As you can see from the above statement, the automatic storage table space inherits the overhead and transfer rate attributes from the storage group. Then, the DB2 database manager converts the device read rate into transfer rate by using this formula:

```
TRANSFERRATE = (1 / DEVICE READ RATE) * 1000/1024000 * PAGESIZE
```

Altering Storage Groups

You can use the ALTER STOGROUP command to change the following storage group settings:

- OVERHEAD
- DEVICE READ RATE
- DATA TAG
- Add or remove storage paths

To add a new storage path to an existing storage group, execute this command:

```
ALTER STOGROUP SG_HOT ADD '/data/hot_fs2'
DB20000I  The SQL command completed successfully.
```

You can use the ADMIN_GET_STORAGE_PATHS table function to verify the state of the newly added storage path, something like this:

```
SELECT
      SUBSTR(STORAGE_GROUP_NAME,1,15)  AS STOGROUP,
      SUBSTR(DB_STORAGE_PATH,1,20)  AS STORAGE_PATH,
      SUBSTR(DB_STORAGE_PATH_STATE,1,10)  AS DB_STORAGE_PATH_STATE
                                                            Continued
```

```
   FROM TABLE (ADMIN_GET_STORAGE_PATHS ('',-1)) AS T

STOGROUP        STORAGE_PATH         DB_STORAGE_PATH_STATE
--------------- -------------------- ---------------------
IBMSTOGROUP     /data/data_fs        IN_USE
SG_HOT          /data/hot_fs1        IN_USE
SG_HOT          /data_hot_fs2        NOT_IN_USE

  3 record(s) selected.
```

To use the newly added storage path, run the ALTER TABLESPACE with REBALANCE clause:

```
SELECT
      SUBSTR (TBSP_NAME, 1, 15) AS TBSP_NAME,
      SUBSTR (STORAGE_GROUP_NAME, 1, 15) AS STORAGE_GROUP_NAME
   FROM TABLE MON_GET_TABLESPACE ('',-2)) AS T

TBSP_NAME       STORAGE_GROUP_NAME
--------------- ------------------
SYSCATSPACE     IBMSTOGROUP
TEMPSPACE1      IBMSTOGROUP
USERSPACE1      IBMSTOGROUP
Q4_2014         SG_HOT
SYSTOOLSPACE    IBMSTOGROUP
SYSTOOLSTMPSPAC IBMSTOGROUP

  6 record(s) selected.

ALTER TABLESPACE Q4_2014 REBALANCE
DB20000I  The SQL command completed successfully.

SELECT
      SUBSTR (STORAGE_GROUP_NAME,1 , 15)  AS STOGROUP,
                                                    Continued
```

```
      SUBSTR (DB_STORAGE_PATH, 1, 20) AS STORAGE_PATH,
      SUBSTR (DB_STORAGE_PATH_STATE, 1, 10) AS DB_STORAGE_PATH_STATE
   FROM TABLE (ADMIN_GET_STORAGE_PATHS ('',-1)) AS T

STOGROUP         STORAGE_PATH          DB_STORAGE_PATH_STATE
---------------- -------------------- ---------------------
IBMSTOGROUP      /data/data_fs         IN_USE
SG_HOT           /data/hot_fs1         IN_USE
SG_HOT           /data_hot_fs2         IN_USE

  3 record(s) selected.
```

If you want to drop a storage path, you can do so by executing the following command:

```
ALTER STOGROUP SG_HOT DROP '/data/hot_fs2'
DB20000I  The SQL command completed successfully.
```

Renaming a Storage Group

You can use the RENAME STOGROUP command to rename an available storage group, as this sample command shows:

```
RENAME STOGROUP SG_HOT TO SG_SSD
DB20000I  The SQL command completed successfully.
```

Dropping a Storage Group

To drop an available storage group, execute the DROP STOGROUP command, something like this:

```
DROP STOGROUP SG_HOT
DB21034E  The command was processed as an SQL statement because it was not
a valid Command Line Processor command.  During SQL processing it returned:
SQL0478N  DROP, ALTER, TRANSFER OWNERSHIP or REVOKE on object type "STO-
GROUP" cannot be processed because there is an object "Q4_2014", of type
"TABLESPACE", which depends on it.  SQLSTATE=42893
```

Before you drop an available storage group, you will have to move associated table spaces to another storage group:

```
ALTER TABLESPACE Q4_2014 USING STOGROUP IBMSTOGROUP
DB20000I  The SQL command completed successfully.

DROP STOGROUP SG_HOT
DB20000I  The SQL command completed successfully.
```

Design Aspects of Storage Groups

A storage group contains storage paths of similar characteristics. Some critical storage attributes to consider regarding storage groups are:

- Storage capacity
- Latency
- Data transfer rate
- RAID level

A Word About Declared Temporary Tables and User Temporary Table Spaces

A declared temporary table is a special table that holds temporary data on behalf of a single application. As with base tables, you can create indexes on and collect statistics for declared temporary tables. Unlike base tables, whose descriptions and constraints are stored in the system catalog tables of the database to which they belong, declared temporary tables are not persistent and can be used only by the application that creates them—and only for the life of the application. When the application that creates a declared temporary table terminates, the rows of the table are deleted and the description of the table is dropped. (However, data stored in a temporary table can exist across transaction boundaries.)

Another significant difference focuses on where the data for each type of table is stored. Before an application can create and use a declared temporary table, a user must create at least one user temporary table space for the database that the application will be working with, and the appropriate users must possess the privileges needed to use that table space. (User temporary table spaces are not created by default when a user creates a database.) Base tables, however, are created in regular table spaces; if you specify no table space for the base table, its data will be stored in the table space USERSPACE1, which is created by default when you create the database.

Schemas

Whereas table spaces physically store objects in a database, schemas logically classify and group other objects in the database, regardless of where they are physically stored. And because schemas are objects themselves, they have privileges associated with them that allow the schema owner to control which users can create, alter, and drop objects within them.

Most objects in a database are named by using a two-part naming convention. The first (leftmost) part of the name is called the *schema name* or *qualifier*, and the second (rightmost) part is called the *object name*. Syntactically, these two parts are concatenated and delimited with a period (for example, HR.EMPLOYEE). When you first create an object that can be qualified by a schema name (such as a table, view, index, user-defined data type, UDF, nickname, package, or trigger), it is assigned to a particular schema based on the qualifier in its name. Figure 3.4 illustrates how a table named STAFF is assigned to the PAYROLL schema during the table creation process.

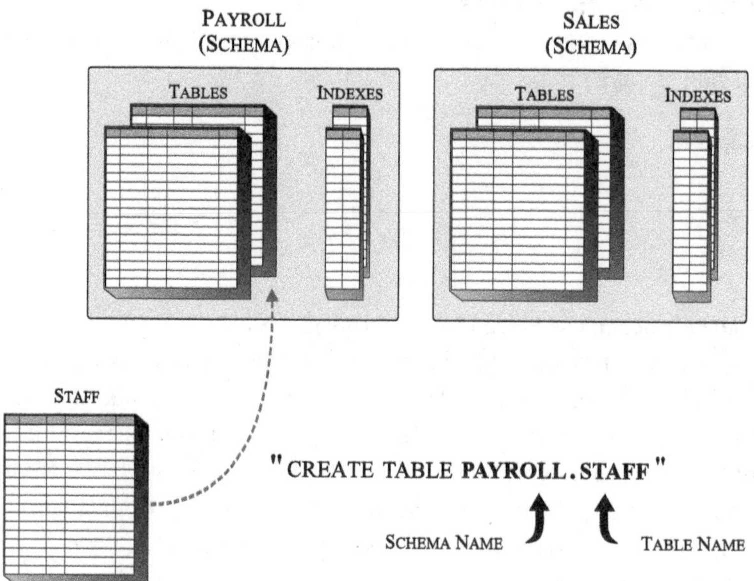

Figure 3.4: Assigning a table object to a schema

Some schema names are reserved and cannot be used. An example includes the names assigned to the four schemas that are automatically created when a database is created: SYSIBM, SYSCAT, SYSSTAT, and SYSFUN. If a user does not specify a schema/qualifier name when creating an object, that object will be assigned to the default schema, which is usually the user ID of the individual who is currently connected to the database and creating the object.

Schemas are implicitly created whenever a data object that has been assigned a qualifier that is different from existing schema names is created—provided the user creating the object holds IMPLICIT_SCHEMA authority. (Unless otherwise specified, when a new database is created, the group PUBLIC is given IMPLICIT_SCHEMA privilege. This privilege allows any user who can successfully connect to the database to implicitly create new schemas if they do not already exist.)

You can explicitly create schemas by executing the CREATE SCHEMA SQL statement. The basic syntax for this statement is:

```
CREATE SCHEMA [SchemaName]
<SQLStatement ,...>
```

or

```
CREATE SCHEMA
AUTHORIZATION [AuthorizationName]
<SQLStatement ,...>
```

or

```
CREATE SCHEMA [SchemaName]
AUTHORIZATION [AuthorizationName]
<SQLStatement ,...>
```

where:

SchemaName Identifies the name to assign to the schema to be created

AuthorizationName Identifies the user to whom to give ownership of the schema once it is created

SQLStatement Specifies one or more SQL statements to execute with the CREATE SCHEMA statement (only the following SQL statements are valid: CREATE TABLE, CREATE VIEW, CREATE INDEX, COMMENT ON, and GRANT)

If you specify a schema name but provide no authorization name, the authorization ID of the user who issued the CREATE SCHEMA statement is given ownership of the newly created schema. However, if you specify an authorization name but provide no schema name, the new schema is assigned the same name as the authorization name used.

So if you want to explicitly create a schema named PAYROLL and give ownership of the schema to the user DB2ADMIN, execute a CREATE SCHEMA SQL statement that looks something like this:

```
CREATE SCHEMA payroll AUTHORIZATION db2admin
DB20000I  The SQL command completed successfully.
```

But if you want to explicitly create a schema named INVENTORY, along with a table named PARTS inside the schema named INVENTORY, you can do so by executing a CREATE SCHEMA statement that is similar to the following:

```
CREATE SCHEMA inventory
DB20000I  The SQL command completed successfully.

SET CURRENT SCHEMA inventory
DB20000I  The SQL command completed successfully.

CREATE TABLE PARTS (partno       INTEGER NOT NULL,
                    description  VARCHAR(50),
                    quantity     SMALLINT)
DB20000I  The SQL command completed successfully.
```

Given that schemas can be implicitly created by creating an object and assigning it a new schema name, you may be wondering why anyone would want to explicitly create a schema by using the CREATE SCHEMA statement. The primary reason for explicitly creating a schema has to do with access control. An explicitly created schema has an owner, who is identified either by the authorization ID of the user who executed the CREATE SCHEMA statement or by the authorization ID of the user to whom ownership was passed when the schema was created. A schema owner has the privileges needed to create, alter, and drop any object stored in the schema, as well as to drop the schema itself; the schema owner also has the right to grant the privileges required to create, alter, and drop objects in the schema (CREATEIN, ALTERIN, and DROPIN privileges) to other users and groups. (We will examine schema privileges in Chapter 8, "Security.")

However, implicitly created schemas are considered to be owned by the user SYSIBM. Any user can create an object in an implicitly created schema, and each object in the schema is controlled by the user who created it. Furthermore, only users with SYSADM or DBADM authority are allowed to drop implicitly created schemas. Thus, for users other than system administrators and database administrators to have complete control over a schema, as well as all data objects stored in that schema, the schema must be created explicitly.

Before you drop a schema, you must be dropping all the objects in that schema or move them to another schema. To drop a schema, execute the DROP SCHEMA command:

```
DROP SCHEMA payroll RESTRICT
DB20000I  The SQL command completed successfully.
```

Range Clustering and Range Partitioning Tables

Earlier, you saw that table spaces control where data is physically stored and provide a layer of indirection between database objects (such as tables, indexes, and views) and one or more containers (i.e., directories, files, or raw devices) in which the object's data actually resides. Consequently, how database objects are assigned to table spaces when they are created determines how data is physically stored on disk. You can control the physical storage of table data even further by creating range clustered tables (RCTs) or by taking advantage of range partitioning tables.

Range Clustered Tables

An RCT is a table whose data is organized in ascending key sequence with a fixed size based on the specified range of key sequence values. RCTs are useful when data is tightly clustered across one or more columns in a table—the smallest and largest values in select columns define the range of possible values. Each possible key value in the defined range has a predetermined location in the physical table. Thus, the storage required for an RCT must be pre-allocated and available when you create the table, and it must be sufficient to store the number of rows found in the specified range multiplied by the row size.

RCTs can result in significant performance advantages during query processing because fewer I/O operations are required. Additionally, RCTs require less cache buffer allocation because no secondary objects exist to maintain; indexes are not required nor are they supported.

You create RCTs by specifying the ORGANIZE BY KEY SEQUENCE clause of the CREATE TABLE SQL statement when you create a table. The syntax for this optional clause is:

```
ORGANIZE BY KEY SEQUENCE
([ColumnName]
  <STARTING <FROM> [Start]>
  ENDING <AT> [End] ,...)
<ALLOW OVERFLOW | DISALLOW OVERFLOW>
<PCTFREE [PercentFree]>
```

where:

ColumnName	Identifies one or more columns, by name, whose values are to be used to determine the sequence of the RCT
Start	Specifies the low end of the range of values allowed (values less than the starting value indicated are allowed only if you specify the ALLOW OVERFLOW option)

End	Specifies the high end of the range of values allowed (values greater than the ending value indicated are allowed only if you specify the ALLOW OVERFLOW option)
PercentFree	Specifies the percentage of each page to leave as free space (the first row on each page is added without restriction; when additional rows are added to a page, a check is performed to ensure the specified percentage of the page remains free)

If you specify the DISALLOW OVERFLOW clause, key values will not be allowed to exceed the defined range. However, specifying the ALLOW OVERFLOW clause will allow key values to exceed the defined range, in which case overflow data will be placed in an overflow area, which is dynamically allocated. An RCT that overflows data that falls outside the predefined range will suffer from poor performance.

Thus, if you want to create an RCT named CUSTOMERS that has two columns named CUSTOMER_ID and CUSTOMER_NAME, where the CUSTOMER_ID column will become the unique key that determines how records are physically stored and where only unique values between 1 and 100 can be assigned to the CUSTOMER_ID column, execute a CREATE TABLE SQL statement that looks something like this:

```
CREATE TABLE customers
      (customer_id   INTEGER NOT NULL,
       customer_name VARCHAR (80))
ORGANIZE BY KEY SEQUENCE
(customer_id STARTING FROM 1 ENDING AT 100)DISALLOW OVERFLOW
DB20000I  The SQL command completed successfully.
```

Once this table is created and populated, if an application needs to access a row for the customer whose ID is 2, the DB2 database manager will look for the second row in the CUSTOMERS table by using a predetermined offset from the logical start of the table. If a row is updated such that the key column values are modified, the updated row is copied to the new location, and the old copy of the row is deleted, maintaining the clustering of data in the table.

Restrictions on RCTs

There are cases where you cannot use RCTs, and certain utilities that cannot operate on the RCTs. The restrictions are as follows:

- RCTs cannot be used in a pureScale environment.
- A partitioned table cannot be an RCT.

- Declared and created temporary tables cannot be RCTs.
- Automatic summary tables cannot be RCTs.
- The LOAD command is not supported.
- The REORG command is not supported.
- Multidimensional clustering and clustering indexes are not compatible with RCTs.
- Compression is not supported.
- Reverse scans on RCTs are not supported.
- The IMPORT command's REPLACE parameter is not supported.
- The WITH EMPTY TABLE clause is not supported on the ALTER TABLE ... ACTIVATE NOT LOGGED INITIALLY.

Range Partitioned Tables

Table partitioning (also referred to as *range partitioning*) is a data organization scheme in which table data is divided across multiple storage objects called *data partitions* or *ranges* based on values in one or more columns. Each data partition is stored separately, and the storage objects used can be in different table spaces, in the same table space, or a combination of the two. Table partitioning improves performance and eliminates the need to create a partitioned database by using the Data Partitioning Feature (DPF). Other advantages of using table partitioning include:

- **Easy roll-in and roll-out of data.** Rolling in partitioned table data allows a new range to be easily incorporated into a partitioned table as an additional data partition. Rolling out partitioned table data allows you to easily separate ranges of data from a partitioned table for subsequent purging or archiving. Data can be quickly rolled in and out by using the ATTACH PARTITION and DETACH PARTITION clauses of the ALTER TABLE statement.
- **Easier administration of large tables.** Table-level administration becomes more flexible because you can perform administrative tasks on individual data partitions. Such tasks include detaching and reattaching a data partition, backing up and restoring individual data partitions, and reorganizing individual indexes. In addition, time-consuming maintenance operations can be shortened by breaking them down into a series of smaller operations.

  For example, you can perform backup operations at the data-partition level when each data partition is placed in a separate table space. Thus, it is possible to back up one data partition of a partitioned table at a time.
- **Flexible index placement.** With table partitioning, you can place indexes in different table spaces, allowing for more granular control of index placement.
- **Better query processing.** In the process of resolving queries, one or more data partitions may be automatically eliminated based on the query predicates used. This functionality, known as *data partition elimination*, improves the performance of many decision-support queries because less data must be analyzed before a result data set can be returned.

Data from a given table is partitioned into multiple storage objects based on the specifications provided in the PARTITION BY clause of the CREATE TABLE statement. The syntax for this optional clause is:

```
PARTITION BY <RANGE>
  ([ColumnName] <NULLS LAST | NULLS FIRST> ,...)
  (STARTING <FROM>
       <(> [Start | MINVALUE | MAXVALUE] < ,...)>
       <INCLUSIVE | EXCLUSIVE>
    ENDING <AT>
       <(> [End | MINVALUE | MAXVALUE] < ,...)>
       <INCLUSIVE | EXCLUSIVE>
    EVERY <(>[Constant] <DurationLabel><)>
    )
```

or

```
PARTITION BY <RANGE>
  ([ColumnName] <NULLS LAST | NULLS FIRST> ,...)
  (<PARTITION [PartitionName]>
   STARTING <FROM>
       <(> [Start | MINVALUE | MAXVALUE] < ,...)>
       <INCLUSIVE | EXCLUSIVE>
    ENDING <AT>
       <(> [End | MINVALUE | MAXVALUE] < ,...)>
       <INCLUSIVE | EXCLUSIVE>
    <IN [TableSpaceName]>
  )
```

where:

ColumnName — Identifies one or more columns, by name, whose values are to be used to determine in which data partition to store a particular row (the group of columns you specify make up the partitioning key for the table)

PartitionName — Identifies the unique name to assign to the data partition to be created

Start — Specifies the low end of the range for each data partition

End	Specifies the high end of the range for each data partition
Constant	Specifies the width of each data-partition range when you use the automatically generated form of the syntax; data partitions will be created starting at the STARTING FROM value and will contain this number of values in the range—this form of the syntax is supported only if the partitioning key is made up of a single column that has been assigned a numeric, date, time, or timestamp data type
DurationLabel	Identifies the duration to associate with the Constant value specified if you have assigned the partitioning key column a date, time, or timestamp data type; the following values are valid for this parameter: YEAR, YEARS, MONTH, MONTHS, DAY, DAYS, HOUR, HOURS, MINUTE, MINUTES, SECOND, SECONDS, MICROSECOND, and MICROSECONDS
TableSpaceName	Identifies the table space in which to store each data partition

Thus, if you want to create a table named SALES that is partitioned such that each quarter's data is stored in a different data partition, and each partition resides in a different table space, execute a CREATE TABLE SQL statement that looks something like this:

```
CREATE TABLE sales
    (sales_date     DATE,
     sales_amt      NUMERIC (5, 2))
    IN tbsp0, tbsp1, tbsp2, tbsp3
    PARTITION BY RANGE (sales_date NULLS FIRST)
        (STARTING '1/1/2014' ENDING '12/31/2014' EVERY 3 MONTHS)
DB20000I  The SQL command completed successfully.
```

However, to create a table named DEPARTMENTS that is partitioned such that rows with numerical values that fall in the range of 0 to 9 are stored in one partition that resides in one table space, rows with numerical values that fall in the range of 10 to 19 are stored in another partition that resides in another table space, and so on, execute a CREATE TABLE SQL statement similar to the following:

```
CREATE TABLE departments
    (dept_no   INT
     desc      CHAR (3))
    PARTITION BY (dept_no NULLS FIRST)
        (STARTING  0 ENDING  9 IN tbsp0,
```

Continued

```
        STARTING 10 ENDING 19 IN tbsp1,
        STARTING 20 ENDING 29 IN tbsp2,
        STARTING 30 ENDING 39 IN tbsp3)
DB20000I  The SQL command completed successfully.
```

Note that when you create an index for a range partitioned table, the data for that index will be stored in the table space that holds the first partition's data, unless you specify otherwise. For example, suppose you execute the following CREATE INDEX SQL statement to create an index for the DEPARTMENTS table just created:

```
CREATE INDEX dept_idx ON departments (dept_no)
DB20000I  The SQL command completed successfully.
```

After this statement is executed, data for the index named DEPT_IDX will be stored in the table space named TBSP0. If you want the index data to be stored in the table space that holds the last partition's data (the table space named TBSP3), you must execute the following CREATE INDEX SQL statement instead:

```
CREATE INDEX dept_idx ON departments (dept_no) IN tbsp3
DB20000I  The SQL command completed successfully.
```

You can create partitioned indexes on partitioned tables for efficient ATTACH and DETACH PARTITION operations. It also helps in the reorganization of a specific data partition when necessary instead of reorganizing the entire table. You can use the CREATE TABLE command to specify separate table spaces for indexes for each data partition:

```
CREATE TABLE "STAGING"."SALES_ORDER_INCR_STG"(
      "INSTANCE_ID" INTEGER ,
      "COMPANY_ORDER" VARCHAR(10) ,
      "DOCUMENT_NO" INTEGER ,
      "ORDER_TYPE" VARCHAR(5) ,
      "LINE_NO" INTEGER ,
      "RECORD_LOAD_TIMESTAMP" TIMESTAMP WITH DEFAULT CURRENT TIMESTAMP)
```

Continued

```
COMPRESS YES
INDEX IN "TS_LARGE_INDEX" PARTITION BY RANGE ("INSTANCE_ID")
(PART "0" STARTING(0) ENDING(0) IN "TBSP0" INDEX IN "TBSP_IX0",
PART "101" STARTING(101) ENDING(101) IN "TBSP1" INDEX IN "TBSP_IX1",
PART "102" STARTING(102) ENDING(102) IN "TBSP2" INDEX IN "TBSP_IX2",
PART "112" STARTING(112) ENDING(112) IN "TBSP3" INDEX IN "TBSP_IX3",
PART "183" STARTING(183) ENDING(183) IN "TBSP4" INDEX IN "TBSP_IX4",
PART "191" STARTING(191) ENDING(191) IN "TBSP5" INDEX IN "TBSP_IX5",
PART "192" STARTING(192) ENDING(192) IN "TBSP6" INDEX IN "TBSP_IX6",
PART "400" STARTING(400) ENDING(400) IN "TBSP7" INDEX IN "TBSP_IX7")
DB20000I  The SQL command completed successfully.
```

Listing the Data Partitions

If you want to list the data partition attributes such as partition ID, partition name, table space ID, access mode, and the range, you can use the DESCRIBE DATA PARTITIONS command, something like this:

```
DESCRIBE DATA PARTITIONS FOR TABLE STAGING.SALES_ORDER_INCR_STG SHOW DETAIL

PartitionId Inclusive (y/n)                   Inclusive (y/n)
              Low Value                         High Value
----------- - ------------------------------ - --------------------------
          0 Y 0                               Y 0
          2 Y 102                             Y 102
          3 Y 112                             Y 112
          4 Y 183                             Y 183
          1 Y 191                             Y 191
          6 Y 192                             Y 192
          7 Y 400                             Y 400

  7 record(s) selected.

                                                              Continued
```

```
PartitionId PartitionName TableSpId PartObjId IndexTblSpId LongTblSpId AccessMode Status
----------- ------------- --------- --------- ------------ ----------- ---------- ------
          0 0                    15      1315           16          15          F
          2 102                  15      1317           16          15          F
          3 112                  15      1318           16          15          F
          4 183                  15      1319           16          15          F
          1 191                  15      1320           16          15          F
          6 192                  15      1321           16          15          F
          7 400                  15      1322           16          15          F

  7 record(s) selected.
```

The access mode F (full access) represents high data quality in the data partition. However, if there are any N's (no access), you will have to identify the data problem.

Detaching a Data Partition

Detaching a data partition from the base table consists of two phases: detaching the logical partitions and converting the detached partition into a standalone base table through an asynchronous index cleanup process.

You can use the ALTER TABLE ... DETACH PARTITION command to detach a data partition from the base table:

```
ALTER TABLE STAGING.SALES_ORDER_INCR_STG
     DETACH PARTITION "102" INTO STAGING.SALES_ORDER_INCR_STG_102
DB20000I  The SQL command completed successfully.
```

To view the asynchronous partition detach operation, execute the LIST UTILITIES SHOW DETAIL command, something like this:

```
LIST UTILITIES SHOW DETAIL

ID                               = 1924
Type                             = ASYNCHRONOUS PARTITION DETACH
Database Name                    = SAMPLE
Partition Number                 = 0
```

Continued

```
Description                         = Finalize detach for partition '2' of table
                                      'STAGING.SALES_ORDER_INCR_STG' and make table
                                      'STAGING.SALES_ORDER_INCR_STG_102' available
Start Time                          = 12/23/2014 16:44:48.020365
State                               = Executing
Invocation Type                     = Automatic
Progress Monitoring:
      Description                   = Performing detach operation and making the
                                      target table available; new compilations
                                      blocked

      Start Time                    = 12/23/2014 16:44:48.030252
```

Attaching a Data Partition

Attaching a data partition to a base table consists of two steps: attaching the partition to the base table and performing the data integrity checks, such as range validation and constraint checking.

To attach a data partition to the base table, use the ALTER TABLE ... ATTACH PART command:

```
ALTER TABLE STAGING.SALES_ORDER_INCR_STG ATTACH PART "102"
    STARTING (102) ENDING (102) FROM STAGING.SALES_ORDER_INCR_STG_102
SQL3601W  The statement caused one or more tables to automatically be placed
in the Set Integrity Pending state.  SQLSTATE=01586
```

You can query the system catalog table to identify the tables that are in Set Integrity Pending state by executing the following command:

```
SELECT SUBSTR (RTRIM (TABSCHEMA) ||'.'||RTRIM (TABNAME), 1, 50)
   FROM SYSCAT.TABLES WHERE STATUS = 'C'
```

To resolve the Set Integrity Pending state on a table, use this sample command:

```
SET INTEGRITY FOR STAGING.SALES_ORDER_INCR_STG IMMEDIATE CHECKED
DB20000I  The SQL command completed successfully.
```

Multi-temperature Storage

The amount of data stored in enterprise data warehouse environments is growing at an exponential rate. At the same time, the end-user experience expectations are getting higher and higher. The challenge here is to store enormous amount of data without impacting application query performance and storage costs.

With DB2 10.1, you can classify the data warehouse data according to its temperature—Hot, Warm, or Cold. The temperature of the data is decided based on these factors:

- How often the data is accessed
- How critical the performance of the queries that access the data is
- How old the data is

You can configure the database so that frequently accessed data is stored on fast storage such as SSD drives, infrequently accessed data is stored on slightly slower storage such as SAS drives, and rarely accessed data is stored on slow storage such as SATA drives, as in Figure 3.2. This feature reduces storage costs because not all data is required to be stored on fast, expensive drives. It also helps achieve better end-user experience due to the ability to store recent data on fast drives.

The following steps provide more information about how to implement multi-temperature data storage for the sales data in the current financial year:

Step 1: Create three storage groups: SG_HOT to store frequently access data, SG_WARM to store infrequently accessed data, and SG_COLD to store occasionally accessed data:

```
CREATE STOGROUP SG_HOT ON '/data/hot/fs1' OVERHEAD 0.825
DEVICE READ RATE 512 DATA TAG 1
DB20000I  The SQL command completed successfully.

CREATE STOGROUP SG_WARM ON '/data/warm/fs1' OVERHEAD 6.725
DEVICE READ RATE 100 DATA TAG 2
DB20000I  The SQL command completed successfully.

CREATE STOGROUP SG_COLD ON '/data/cold/fs1' OVERHEAD 7.525
DEVICE READ RATE 70 DATA TAG 3
DB20000I  The SQL command completed successfully.
```

Step 2: Create four table spaces to store quarter data and assign it to each respective storage group:

```
CREATE TABLESPACE TBSP3 USING STOGROUP SG_HOT
DB20000I  The SQL command completed successfully.

CREATE TABLESPACE TBSP2 USING STOGROUP SG_WARM
DB20000I  The SQL command completed successfully.

CREATE TABLESPACE TBSP1 USING STOGROUP SG_COLD
DB20000I  The SQL command completed successfully.

CREATE TABLESPACE TBSP0 USING STOGROUP SG_COLD
DB20000I  The SQL command completed successfully.
```

Step 3: Create a range partitioned table to store sales data based on the date:

```
CREATE TABLE SALES
    (SALES_DATE         DATE,
     SALES_AMOUNT       NUMERIC (5, 2))
    IN TBSP0, TBSP1, TBSP2, TBSP3
    PARTITION BY RANGE (SALES_DATE NULLS FIRST)
        (STARTING '1/1/2014' ENDING '12/31/2014' EVERY 3 MONTHS)
DB20000I  The SQL command completed successfully.
```

In the above example, 2014 Q1 data is stored in table space TBSP0, 2014 Q2 data in table space TBSP1, 2014 Q3 data in table space TBSP2, and 2014 Q4 data in table space TBSP3. You can also verify the storage allocation by executing the DESCRIBE DATA PARTITIONS command:

```
DESCRIBE DATA PARTITIONS FOR TABLE sales SHOW DETAIL

PartitionId PartitionName TableSpId PartObjId IndexTblSpId LongTblSpId AccessMode Status
----------- ------------- --------- --------- ------------ ----------- ---------- ------
          0 PART0                 5         4            5           5          F
          1 PART1                 7         4            7           7          F
                                                                            Continued
```

```
          2 PART2                    8         4          8          8         F
          3 PART3                    9         4          9          9         F

  4 record(s) selected.


PartitionId Inclusive (y/n)                  Inclusive (y/n)
            Low Value                        High Value
----------- - ---------------------------- - -------------------------
          0 Y '2014-01-01'                   N '2014-04-01'
          1 Y '2014-04-01'                   N '2014-07-01'
          2 Y '2014-07-01'                   N '2014-10-01'
          3 Y '2014-10-01'                   Y '2014-12-31'

  4 record(s) selected.
```

Step 4: Re-adjust the temperature. At some point, new data for 2015 Q1 will be loaded into the database, which will take the higher priority for performance reasons. You can then associate the table space TBSP2 with the storage group SG_COLD and table space TBSP3 with the storage group SG_WARM, keeping the new table space TBSP4 on the fastest storage group—SG_HOT. To move the table spaces online from one storage group to another, use the ALTER TABLESPACE command. The set of commands look something like this:

```
CREATE TABLESPACE TBSP4 USING STOGROUP SG_HOT
DB20000I  The SQL command completed successfully.

ALTER TABLE sales ADD PARTITION "PART4"
STARTING FROM ('2015-01-01') ENDING AT ('2015-04-01')
IN TBSP4 INDEX IN TBSP4
DB20000I  The SQL command completed successfully.

ALTER TABLESPACE TBSP2 USING STOGROUP SG_COLD
DB20000I  The SQL command completed successfully.

ALTER TABLESPACE TBSP3 USING STOGROUP SG_WARM
DB20000I  The SQL command completed successfully.
```

A Word About MDC, MQT, and ITC

Multidimensional clustering (MDC) provides an elegant method for clustering data in tables along multiple dimensions in a flexible, continuous, and automatic way. MDC allows a table to be physically clustered on more than one key, or dimension, simultaneously. Like any other table, an MDC table can have, among other things, views, MQTs, referential integrity, triggers, RID indexes, and replication defined upon it. In the case of query performance, range queries involving any combination of the specified dimensions of the clustered table will benefit, because they must access only those pages that have records with the specified dimension values.

When creating an MDC table, you can specify the dimensional key (or keys) along which to cluster the table's data. Each of the specified dimensions can be defined with one or more columns, the same as an index key. A dimension block index will be automatically created for each of the dimensions indicated, and the index will be used to quickly and efficiently access data along each of the specified dimensions. The dimension blocks' indexes point to extents instead of individual rows and are thus much smaller than regular indexes. You can use these dimension block indexes to very quickly access only those extents of the table that contain particular dimension values.

In addition, a block index will also be automatically created, containing all dimension key columns. The block index maintains the clustering of the data during insert and update activity as well as provides quick and efficient access to the data. A composite block index containing all dimension key columns is also created automatically. The composite block index maintains the clustering of data during insert and update activity. The composite block index is also used in query processing to access data in a table having particular dimension values.

You can create MDC tables by specifying the ORGANIZE BY DIMENSIONS clause of the CREATE TABLE SQL statement when you create a table. The syntax for this optional clause is:

```
ORGANIZE BY DIMENSIONS
( <(>[ColumnName] ,...<)> ,...)
```

where:

ColumnName Identifies one or more columns, by name, whose values are to be used to cluster the table's data; the use of parentheses within the column list specifies to treat a group of columns as a single dimension

Thus, if you want to create an MDC table named SALES so that its data is organized into extents based on unique combinations of values in the CUSTOMER, REGION, and YEAR columns, execute a CREATE TABLE SQL statement that looks something like this:

```
CREATE TABLE sales
    (CUSTOMER      VARCHAR (80),
     REGION        CHAR (5),
     YEAR          INTEGER,
     Volume        INTEGER,
     PERIOD        INTEGER,
     REC_LOAD_DT   TIMESTAMP   )
ORGANIZE BY DIMENSIONS (CUSTOMER, REGION, YEAR)
DB20000I  The SQL command completed successfully.
```

The above command creates three dimension block indexes and one composite index, as follows:

```
SELECT
      SUBSTR (INDSCHEMA, 1, 10) AS INDSCHEMA,
      SUBSTR (INDNAME, 1, 25) AS INDNAME, INDEXTYPE,
      SUBSTR (COLNAMES, 1, 30) AS COLNAMES
   FROM SYSCAT.INDEXES WHERE TABNAME='SALES'

INDSCHEMA  INDNAME                   INDEXTYPE COLNAMES
---------- ------------------------- --------- -----------------------
SYSIBM     SQL141229141543060        BLOK      +CUSTOMER+REGION+YEAR
SYSIBM     SQL141229141543170        DIM       +YEAR
SYSIBM     SQL141229141543200        DIM       +REGION
SYSIBM     SQL141229141543230        DIM       +CUSTOMER

  4 record(s) selected.
```

A materialized query table (MQT) is a table that is defined on a result of an SQL statement. You generally use MQTs to avoid repetitive calculations by storing precomputed aggregated results in the table. If the DB2 database manager determines that a portion of an SQL statement can be resolved by using an MQT, the database manager will rewrite the access plan to use the appropriate MQT on behalf of a regular base table. This process is very transparent to the application or to the end user.

Creating and maintaining an MQT is a two-step process. First, you create an MQT based on the business logic and need, and second, you refresh the MQT data. If you want to build an MQT to record the sum of SALES_AMOUNT for each SALES_DATE, execute the CREATE TABLE command, something like this:

```
CREATE TABLE sales_mqt AS
(SELECT SUM (SALES_AMOUNT) AS TOTAL_SUM, SALES_DATE
    FROM sales
    GROUP BY SALES_DATE)
    DATA INITIALLY DEFERRED REFRESH DEFERRED
DB20000I  The SQL command completed successfully.

REFRESH TABLE sales_mqt
DB20000I  The SQL command completed successfully.
```

When you have REFRESH DEFERRED MQTs available, try setting the DFT_REFRESH_AGE database configuration parameter to ANY.

If you run the following SQL statement on the database SAMPLE, the database manager will try using the available MQT to quickly return the data to the client. You can validate this by using an Explain plan:

```
SELECT SUM (SALES_AMOUNT), SALES_DATE
   FROM SALES GROUP BY SALES_DATE

Optimized Statement:
-------------------
SELECT
  Q1.TOTAL_SUM,
  Q1.SALES_DATE AS "SALES_DATE"
FROM
  MOHAN.SALES_MQT AS Q1

                                                  Continued
```

```
Access Plan:
-----------
        Total Cost:               6.77334
        Query Degree:             1

      Rows
     RETURN
     (   1)
      Cost
       I/O
       |
        2
     TBSCAN
     (   2)
     6.77334
        1
       |
        2
 TABLE: MOHAN
    SALES_MQT
       Q1
```

If no matching MQT is available, the DB2 optimizer will generate an Explain plan (of course an expensive one):

```
Optimized Statement:
-------------------
SELECT
  Q3.$C0,
  Q3.SALES_DATE AS "SALES_DATE"
FROM
  (SELECT
     SUM (Q2.SALES_AMOUNT),
     Q2.SALES_DATE
```

Continued

```
  FROM
    (SELECT
       Q1.SALES_DATE,
       Q1.SALES_AMOUNT
     FROM
       MOHAN.SALES AS Q1
    ) AS Q2
  GROUP BY
    Q2.SALES_DATE
 ) AS Q3

Access Plan:
-----------
        Total Cost:             27.0707
        Query Degree:           1

        Rows
       RETURN
       (   1)
        Cost
         I/O
         |
          2
       GRPBY
       (   2)
       27.0705
          4
         |
          2
       TBSCAN
       (   3)
       27.0704
          4
         |
```

Continued

```
       2
     SORT
     (   4)
     27.0701
       4
       |
       5
     TBSCAN
     (   5)
     27.0691
       4
       |
       5
DP-TABLE: MOHAN
      SALES
       Q1
```

Insert time clustering (ITC) tables provide an effective way of maintaining data clustering based on the insert time with easier space management. The characteristics of ITC tables are as follows:

- ITC table records are clustered based on their insert time.
- ITC tables have similar characteristics to MDC tables; they use block-based data allocation and a dimension block index. However, the data organization scheme is based on an implicitly created virtual dimension (record insert time) instead of an explicitly stated dimension columns.
- ITC tables are created by using the CREATE TABLE ... ORGANIZE BY INSERT TIME clause.
- ITC table's space reclamation can be done by executing the REORG TABLE ... RECLAIM EXTENTS command.

If you want to create ITC table SALES_ITC, you can do so by executing this command:

```
CREATE TABLE sales_itc
    (CUSTOMER             VARCHAR (80),
     REGION               CHAR (5),
```

Continued

```
    YEAR                INTEGER,
    Volume              INTEGER,
    PERIOD              INTEGER,
    REC_LOAD_DT         TIMESTAMP)
ORGANIZE BY INSERT TIME
DB20000I  The SQL command completed successfully.

CREATE INDEX ix1_sales_itc ON sales_itc (REGION, YEAR, PERIOD)
DB20000I  The SQL command completed successfully.
```

The above command creates one dimension block index and one regular index, as follows:

```
SELECT SUBSTR (INDSCHEMA, 1, 10) AS INDSCHEMA,
       SUBSTR (INDNAME, 1, 25) AS INDNAME, INDEXTYPE,
       SUBSTR (COLNAMES, 1, 30) AS COLNAMES
   FROM SYSCAT.INDEXES WHERE TABNAME='SALES_ITC'

INDSCHEMA  INDNAME                   INDEXTYPE COLNAMES
---------- ------------------------- --------- ----------------------
SYSIBM     SQL150109091701660        DIM       +SQL000000000000000
MOHAN      IX1_SALES_ITC             REG       +REGION+YEAR+PERIOD

  2 record(s) selected.
```

Time Travel Query Using Temporal Tables

Temporal data management is a method of managing and processing data in relationship with time. Nowadays, many businesses needs require the storage and maintenance of time-based data.

DB2 10.1 introduced a set of temporal data management capabilities to retrieve information from the present, future, and past. Three temporal table types are available:

- System-period temporal table
- Application-period temporal table
- Bitemporal table

System-Period Temporal Tables

A system-period temporal table is a table that maintains current versions of records in the base table and historical versions of records in a history table. Let us look at an example to understand the behavior of a system-period temporal table and the necessary steps to configure the base and history tables.

Step 1: Create a base temporal table to record employee promotions and salary increments:

```
CREATE TABLE employee_st (
        EMPID        INT PRIMARY KEY NOT NULL,
        FIRSTNAME    VARCHAR (10),
        LASTNAME     VARCHAR (10),
        DEPTNAME     VARCHAR (10),
        SALARY       DECIMAL (10, 2),
        BAND         VARCHAR (5),
        SYS_START    TIMESTAMP (12) GENERATED ALWAYS AS ROW BEGIN NOT NULL,
        SYS_END      TIMESTAMP (12) GENERATED ALWAYS AS ROW END NOT NULL,
        TXN_ID       TIMESTAMP (12) GENERATED ALWAYS AS TRANSACTION START ID
          IMPLICITLY HIDDEN,
        PERIOD SYSTEM_TIME (SYS_START, SYS_END))
DB20000I  The SQL command completed successfully.
```

As you can see, the system-period temporal table includes a SYSTEM_TIME period with columns that capture the begin and end time when the data in a record is current. It also uses SYSTEM_TIME period to preserve historical versions of each table record whenever an update or delete occurs. The TRANSACTION START ID column captures the time when execution started for a transaction that affects the records in the table. This is useful when you want to identify all the records in a table that were written or modified by a transaction.

Step 2: Create a history table and associate it with the base temporal table.

When a record is updated in or deleted from the base table, the DB2 database manager inserts a copy of the old record into the history table to enable data retrieval from a past point in time. It is mandatory to create a history table with the same column names, in the same order, and of similar data types. By default, when you drop the base temporal table, the DB2 database manager automatically drops any associated history table. To avoid losing historical data when dropping a base table, you can create history table with the RESTRICT ON DROP attribute.

If you want to create a history table for the EMPLOYEE_ST base table, you can do so by executing the CREATE TABLE command, something like this:

```
CREATE TABLE employee_st_history LIKE employee_st WITH RESTRICT ON DROP
DB20000I  The SQL command completed successfully.
```

To link the history table with the base table, execute the ALTER TABLE command:

```
ALTER TABLE employee_st ADD VERSIONING USE HISTORY TABLE employee_st_history
DB20000I  The SQL command completed successfully.
```

Step 3: Validate the temporal table type.

You can validate the temporal table type by querying the SYSCAT.TABLES system catalog view:

```
SELECT SUBSTR (TABNAME, 1, 15) AS TABNAME, TEMPORALTYPE FROM SYSCAT.TABLES
   WHERE TABNAME='EMPLOYEE_ST'

TABNAME         TEMPORALTYPE
--------------- ------------
EMPLOYEE_ST     S

  1 record(s) selected.
```

The return value S indicates it as a system-period temporal table.

Step 4: Insert data into the temporal table.

When inserting data into a system-period temporal table, the DB2 database manager automatically inserts a value into row begin, row end, and transaction start ID columns:

```
INSERT INTO employee_st (EMPID, FIRSTNAME, LASTNAME, DEPTNAME, SALARY, BAND)
   VALUES (001, 'COLIN','CHAPMAN','IS', 12000.00, 'A1')
DB20000I  The SQL command completed successfully.
```

Continued

```
INSERT INTO employee_st (EMPID, FIRSTNAME, LASTNAME, DEPTNAME, SALARY, BAND)
   VALUES (002, 'HAMDI','ROUMANI','IS', 12000.00, 'A1')
DB20000I  The SQL command completed successfully.

SELECT * FROM employee_st

EMPID       FIRSTNAME  LASTNAME   DEPTNAME   SALARY       BAND
----------- ---------- ---------- ---------- ------------ -----
          1 COLIN      CHAPMAN    IS             12000.00 A1
          2 HAMDI      ROUMANI    IS             12000.00 A1

SYS_START                      SYS_END
------------------------------ ------------------------------
2014-12-31-17.44.28.316318000000 9999-12-30-00.00.00.000000000000
2014-12-31-17.45.32.757548000000 9999-12-30-00.00.00.000000000000

  2 record(s) selected.

SELECT * FROM employee_st_history

EMPID       FIRSTNAME  LASTNAME   DEPTNAME   SALARY       BAND
----------- ---------- ---------- ---------- ------------ -----

SYS_START                      SYS_END
------------------------------ --------------------------

  0 record(s) selected.
```

The history table remains empty because no history records are generated by an INSERT command.

Step 5: Perform a DML operation on an existing record.

Updating a record in a system-period temporal table results in records that are added to its associated history table:

```
UPDATE employee_st SET (BAND, SALARY) = ('A2', 12800.00) WHERE EMPID=1
DB20000I  The SQL command completed successfully.
```

The update to EMPID 1 affects the system-period temporal table and its history table, as follows:

- The BAND and SALARY column values are updated to A2 and 12800.00 for EMPID 1.
- The DB2 database manager automatically updates SYS_START and TXN_ID columns.
- The original record is moved to the history table.

```
SELECT * FROM employee_st

EMPID       FIRSTNAME  LASTNAME   DEPTNAME   SALARY       BAND
----------- ---------- ---------- ---------- ------------ -----
          1 COLIN      CHAPMAN    IS             12800.00 A2
          2 HAMDI      ROUMANI    IS             12000.00 A1

SYS_START                        SYS_END
-------------------------------- --------------------------------
2014-12-31-17.49.19.315851000000 9999-12-30-00.00.00.000000000000
2014-12-31-17.45.32.757548000000 9999-12-30-00.00.00.000000000000

  2 record(s) selected.

SELECT * FROM employee_st_history

EMPID       FIRSTNAME  LASTNAME   DEPTNAME   SALARY       BAND
----------- ---------- ---------- ---------- ------------ -----
          1 COLIN      CHAPMAN    IS             12000.00 A1
```

Continued

```
SYS_START                      SYS_END
------------------------------ ------------------------------
2014-12-31-17.44.28.316318000000 2014-12-31-17.49.19.315851000000

  1 record(s) selected.
```

Execute a similar UPDATE command on the EMPLOYEE_ST for EMPID 2:

```
UPDATE employee_st SET (BAND, SALARY) = ('A2', 12790.00) WHERE EMPID=2
DB20000I  The SQL command completed successfully.

SELECT * FROM employee_st

EMPID       FIRSTNAME  LASTNAME   DEPTNAME   SALARY       BAND
----------- ---------- ---------- ---------- ------------ -----
          1 COLIN      CHAPMAN    IS             12800.00 A2
          2 HAMDI      ROUMANI    IS             12790.00 A2

SYS_START                      SYS_END
------------------------------ ------------------------------
2014-12-31-17.49.19.315851000000 9999-12-30-00.00.00.000000000000
2014-12-31-17.51.47.411996000000 9999-12-30-00.00.00.000000000000

  2 record(s) selected.

SELECT * FROM employee_st_history

EMPID       FIRSTNAME  LASTNAME   DEPTNAME   SALARY       BAND
----------- ---------- ---------- ---------- ------------ -----
          1 COLIN      CHAPMAN    IS             12000.00 A1
          2 HAMDI      ROUMANI    IS             12000.00 A1
```

Continued

```
SYS_START                        SYS_END
-------------------------------- --------------------------------
2014-12-31-17.45.32.757548000000 2014-12-31-17.51.47.411996000000
2014-12-31-17.44.28.316318000000 2014-12-31-17.49.19.315851000000

  2 record(s) selected.
```

If you want to delete a record from the base system-period temporal table, you can do so by using the DELETE command, something like this:

```
DELETE FROM employee_st WHERE EMPID=2
DB20000I  The SQL command completed successfully.

SELECT * FROM employee_st

EMPID       FIRSTNAME  LASTNAME   DEPTNAME   SALARY       BAND
----------- ---------- ---------- ---------- ------------ -----
          1 COLIN      CHAPMAN    IS             12800.00 A2

SYS_START                        SYS_END
-------------------------------- --------------------------------
2014-12-31-17.49.19.315851000000 9999-12-30-00.00.00.000000000000

  1 record(s) selected.

SELECT * FROM employee_st_history

EMPID       FIRSTNAME  LASTNAME   DEPTNAME   SALARY       BAND
----------- ---------- ---------- ---------- ------------ -----
          1 COLIN      CHAPMAN    IS             12000.00 A1
          2 HAMDI      ROUMANI    IS             12000.00 A1
          2 HAMDI      ROUMANI    IS             12790.00 A2
```

Continued

```
SYS_START                          SYS_END
--------------------------------   --------------------------------
2014-12-31-17.44.28.316318000000 2014-12-31-17.49.19.315851000000
2014-12-31-17.45.32.757548000000 2014-12-31-17.51.47.411996000000
2014-12-31-17.51.47.411996000000 2014-12-31-18.54.26.641540000000

  3 record(s) selected.
```

You can see, the DB2's temporal feature moved the deleted record from the base table to the history table and also updated the SYS_END column value to the timestamp of the delete operation.

Step 6: Query the system-period temporal table.

When you want to query the system-period temporal tables, you can use any of the following period specifications in the FROM clause of a SELECT statement:

- FOR SYSTEM_TIME AS OF <ts1>: Enables you to query data as of a certain point in time.
- FOR SYSTEM_TIME FROM <ts1> TO <ts2>: Enables you to query data from a certain time ts1 to a certain time ts2.
- FOR SYSTEM_TIME BETWEEN <ts1> AND <ts2>: Enables you to query data between a range of times.

You can use a simple SELECT statement to retrieve the records from the base table:

```
SELECT EMPID, SALARY, BAND, SYS_START, SYS_END FROM EMPLOYEE_ST

EMPID       SALARY   BAND  SYS_START                        SYS_END
----------- -------- ----- -------------------------------- --------------------------------
          1 12800.00    A2 2014-12-31-17.49.19.315851000000 9999-12-30-00.00.00.000000000000

  1 record(s) selected.
```

As the above example shows, a simple SELECT statement retrieves information only from the base temporal table. If you want to retrieve information from both the base and the history table automatically based on a timestamp, use the FOR SYSTEM_TIME clause:

```
SELECT EMPID, BAND, SYS_START, SYS_END
   FROM employee_st
   FOR SYSTEM_TIME BETWEEN '2014-12-31-17.44.28.316318000000'
                       AND '2014-12-31-18.54.26.641540000000'

EMPID       BAND  SYS_START                        SYS_END
----------- ----- -------------------------------- --------------------------------
          1 A1    2014-12-31-17.44.28.316318000000 2014-12-31-17.49.19.315851000000
          2 A1    2014-12-31-17.45.32.757548000000 2014-12-31-17.51.47.411996000000
          2 A2    2014-12-31-17.51.47.411996000000 2014-12-31-18.54.26.641540000000
          1 A2    2014-12-31-17.49.19.315851000000 9999-12-30-00.00.00.000000000000

  4 record(s) selected.
```

As you can see, the above query transparently extracted information from both the base table and the history table without explicitly creating any complex application logic in a procedure or a function.

Utilities, Tools, and File Type Modifiers

Like other base tables, the system-period temporal table supports several tools and utilities to manage data movement activities:

- Import
- Load
- ADMIN_MOVE_TABLE procedure
- Replication
- ADMIN_COPY_SCHEMA procedure
- QUIESCE table space
- Roll Forward

Before you begin working with the data movement utilities, it is essential to understand the file type modifiers for system-period temporal tables (see Table 3.4).

Table 3.4: File type modifiers for system-period temporal tables

File Type Modifier	Utility	Description
PERIODIGNORE	Import, Load	This modifier informs the utility that the data for SYSTEM_TIME period columns is present in the external file and should be ignored. This also enables automatic generation of the time period column values by the utility.
PERIODMISSING	Import, Load	This modifier informs the utility that the data for SYSTEM_TIME period columns is not present in the external file. This also enables automatic generation of the time period column values by the utility.
TRANSACTIONIDIGNORE	Import, Load	This modifier informs the utility that the data for the TRANSACTION START ID column is present in the external file and should be ignored. This also enables automatic generation of the transaction start ID column value by the utility.
TRANSACTIONIDMISSING	Import, Load	This modifier informs the utility that the data for the TRANSACTION START ID column is not present in the external file. This also enables automatic generation of the transaction start ID column value by the utility.
PERIODOVERRIDE	Load	This modifier informs the utility that the data for SYSTEM_TIME period columns is present in the external file and should be used.
TRANSACTIONOVERRIDE	Load	This modifier informs the utility that the data for the TRANSACTION START ID column is present in the external file and should be used.

Restrictions for System-Period Temporal Tables

There are a few rules and restrictions around the system-period temporal and history tables:

- The history table cannot be dropped explicitly by using the DROP TABLE command. If you try dropping it, you will receive an error that looks something like this:

```
DROP TABLE employee_st_history
DB21034E  The command was processed as an SQL statement because it was not
a valid Command Line Processor command.  During SQL processing it returned:
SQL0478N  DROP, ALTER, TRANSFER OWNERSHIP or REVOKE on object type "TABLE"
cannot be processed because there is an object "MOHAN.EMPLOYEE_ST", of type
"SYSTEM PERIOD TEMPORAL TABLE", which depends on it.  SQLSTATE=42893
```

- History table columns cannot be explicitly added, dropped, or altered.
- The history table must not have a constraint defined on it by any means.
- System-period temporal tables and history tables do not support label-based access control (LBAC).
- A system-period temporal table cannot be an MQT.

- The ALTER TABLE ACTIVATE NOT LOGGED INITIALLY statement is blocked both on base table and the history table.
- LOAD and IMPORT commands do not support REPLACE command options.
- System-period temporal tables do not support the TRUNCATE command.
- System-period temporal tables and history tables do not support the following set of commands:

```
ALTER TABLE DROP COLUMN
ALTER TABLE ALTER COLUMN
ALTER TABLE ADD GENERATED COLUMN
```

- For point-in-time recovery, if a table space containing a system-period temporal table is being rolled forward to a point in time, the table space that contains the associated history table must also be rolled forward to the same point in time.

Application-Period Temporal Tables

An application-period temporal table is a table that stores in-effect business data (for example, a product promotional offer of 25 percent discount for a month and 5 percent discount after the promotion expires). So you can use application-period temporal tables to manage data based on time criteria by defining the time periods when data is valid. Like a system-period temporal table, an application-period temporal table uses the BUSINESS_TIME period with columns that indicate the time period when the data in a row is valid.

Let us look at an example to understand the behavior of an application-period temporal table and the necessary steps to configure it.

Step 1: Create an application-period temporal table to capture the discount validity:

```
CREATE TABLE sellproduct_bt
       (ID                INT NOT NULL,
        NAME              VARCHAR (10),
        WEIGHT            INT,
        PRICE             DECIMAL (10, 2),
        DISCOUNT          DECIMAL (5, 2),
        SELLPRICE         DECIMAL (10, 2),
        BUSINESS_START    DATE NOT NULL,
        BUSINESS_END      DATE NOT NULL,
                                                    Continued
```

```
    PERIOD BUSINESS_TIME (BUSINESS_START, BUSINESS_END),
    PRIMARY KEY (ID, BUSINESS_TIME WITHOUT OVERLAPS))
DB20000I  The SQL command completed successfully.
```

When you define a BUSINESS_TIME period, the begin period is always inclusive and the end period is always exclusive. The DB2 database manager creates an implicit CHECK constraint named DB2_GENERATED_CHECK_CONSTRAINT_FOR_BUSINESS_TIME to ensure the value for the end of the validity period is greater than the value for the start of the validity period.

You can use the WITHOUT OVERLAPS clause to a primary key, to a UNIQUE constraint, or to a UNIQUE INDEX statement to eliminate overlapping business-time periods for the same key.

Step 2: Insert data into the application-period temporal table.

To enter data into an application-period temporal table, execute the INSERT command:

```
INSERT INTO SELLPRODUCT_BT VALUES
(01, 'LYSOL', 100, 124.00, 25, 93.00, '2015-01-01', '2015-02-01')
DB20000I  The SQL command completed successfully.

INSERT INTO SELLPRODUCT_BT VALUES
(01, 'LYSOL', 100, 124.00, 25, 117.8, '2015-02-01', '9999-12-30')
DB20000I  The SQL command completed successfully.

INSERT INTO SELLPRODUCT_BT VALUES
(02, 'FINISH', 220, 110.00, 25, 82.5, '2015-01-01', '2015-02-01')
DB20000I  The SQL command completed successfully.

INSERT INTO SELLPRODUCT_BT VALUES
(02, 'FINISH', 220, 110.00, 5, 104.5,  '2015-02-01', '9999-12-30')
DB20000I  The SQL command completed successfully.
```

If you try inserting an overlapping period, you will get an error something like this:

```
INSERT INTO SELLPRODUCT_BT VALUES
(02, 'FINISH', 220, 110.00, 10, 99.0, '2015-03-01', '9999-12-30')
SQL0803N  One or more values in the INSERT statement, UPDATE statement, or
foreign key update caused by a DELETE statement are not valid because the
primary key, unique constraint or unique index identified by "1" constrains
table "MOHAN.SELLPRODUCT_BT" from having duplicate values for the index key.
SQLSTATE=23505

SELECT * FROM SELLPRODUCT_BT

ID   NAME   WEIGHT  PRICE DISCOUNT SELLPRICE BUSINESS_START BUSINESS_END
---- ------ ------ ------ -------- --------- -------------- ------------
   1  LYSOL    100 124.00    25.00     93.00     01/01/2015   02/01/2015
   1  LYSOL    100 124.00     5.00    117.80     02/01/2015   12/30/9999
   2 FINISH    220 110.00    25.00     82.50     01/01/2015   02/01/2015
   2 FINISH    220 110.00     5.00    104.50     02/01/2015   12/30/9999

  4 record(s) selected.
```

Step 3: Perform DML operations.

As with system-period temporal tables, you can specify time-range updates by using the FOR PORTION OF BUSINESS_TIME clause of the UPDATE statement to update records that fall within the range specified by the period begin and the period end columns.

If you want to offer an additional 5 percent discount (10 percent discount in total) on Lysol during the period February 01, 2015, to February 15, 2015, you can do so by executing the following command:

```
UPDATE SELLPRODUCT_BT
FOR PORTION OF BUSINESS_TIME FROM '2015-02-01' TO '2015-02-15'
SET (DISCOUNT, SELLPRICE) = (10, 111.6) WHERE ID=1
DB20000I  The SQL command completed successfully.
```

Continued

```
SELECT * FROM SELLPRODUCT_BT ORDER BY ID, BUSINESS_START

ID  NAME    WEIGHT PRICE   DISCOUNT SELLPRICE BUSINESS_START BUSINESS_END
--- ------ ------ ------- -------- --------- -------------- ------------
  1 LYSOL     100  124.00    25.00     93.00     01/01/2015   02/01/2015
  1 LYSOL     100  124.00    10.00    111.60     02/01/2015   02/15/2015
  1 LYSOL     100  124.00     5.00    117.80     02/15/2015   12/30/9999
  2 FINISH    220  110.00    25.00     82.50     01/01/2015   02/01/2015
  2 FINISH    220  110.00     5.00    104.50     02/01/2015   12/30/9999

  5 record(s) selected.
```

Notice that an additional row is inserted with new valid periods and that an existing row is updated with a new begin period to reflect the BUSINESS_TIME period for 5 percent discount coverage.

Similarly, if you want to delete a record from the application-period temporal table, use the DELETE command:

```
DELETE FROM SELLPRODUCT_BT FOR PORTION OF BUSINESS_TIME
   FROM '2015-02-01' TO '2015-02-10' WHERE ID=1
DB20000I  The SQL command completed successfully.

SELECT * FROM SELLPRODUCT_BT ORDER BY ID, BUSINESS_START

ID   NAME    WEIGHT PRICE  DISCOUNT SELLPRICE BUSINESS_START BUSINESS_END
---- ------ ------ ------ -------- --------- -------------- ------------
   1 LYSOL     100 124.00    25.00     93.00     01/01/2015   02/01/2015
   1 LYSOL     100 124.00    10.00    111.60     02/10/2015   02/15/2015
   1 LYSOL     100 124.00     5.00    117.80     02/15/2015   12/30/9999
   2 FINISH    220 110.00    25.00     82.50     01/01/2015   02/01/2015
   2 FINISH    220 110.00     5.00    104.50     02/01/2015   12/30/9999

  5 record(s) selected.
```

In the above example, the delete operation resulted in a row that is inserted due to partial range coverage during the DELETE command execution.

Step 4: Query the application-period temporal table.

As with system-period temporal tables, you can use any of the following period specifications in the FROM clause of a SELECT statement:

- FOR BUSINESS_TIME AS OF <ts1>: Enables you to query data as of a certain point in time.
- FOR BUSINESS_TIME FROM <ts1> TO <ts2>: Enables you to query data from a certain time ts1 to a certain time ts2.
- FOR BUSINESS_TIME BETWEEN <ts1> AND <ts2>: Enables you to query data between a range of times.

For example, to query data for the period between 01/01/2015 and 02/12/2015, run the SELECT statement, something like this:

```
SELECT NAME, PRICE, DISCOUNT, SELLPRICE, BUSINESS_START, BUSINESS_END
   FROM SELLPRODUCT_BT
   FOR BUSINESS_TIME BETWEEN '2015-01-01' AND '2015-02-12' WHERE ID =1

NAME       PRICE            DISCOUNT SELLPRICE    BUSINESS_START BUSINESS_END
---------- ------------ -------- ------------ -------------- ------------
LYSOL            124.00    25.00        93.00 01/01/2015     02/01/2015
LYSOL            124.00    10.00       111.60 02/10/2015     02/15/2015

  2 record(s) selected.
```

For the purpose of completion, Table 3.5 lists the differences between system-period and application-period temporal tables.

Table 3.5: System-period and application-period temporal table comparison

System-Period Temporal Table	Application-Period Temporal Table
This table maintains current versions of records in the base table and historical versions of records in a history table.	This table maintains in-effect business data.
This table includes a SYSTEM_TIME period with columns to capture the begin and end times when the data in a row is valid. It also uses it to maintain historical information.	This table includes a BUSINESS_TIME period with columns to capture the start and end of the validity period.
A history table is necessary.	A history table is not necessary.

Table 3.5: System-period and application-period temporal table comparison (continued)

System-Period Temporal Table	Application-Period Temporal Table
This table includes a transaction ID column to capture the start times for transactions that affect rows.	The transaction ID column is not necessary.
This table can have a referential integrity (RI) constraint defined; however, the constraints cannot be created on the history table.	This table can have a referential integrity (RI) constraint defined.
While retrieving data, you can use the FOR SYSTEM_TIME AS OF <ts1>, FOR SYSTEM_TIME FROM <ts1> TO <ts2>, or FOR SYSTEM_TIME BETWEEN <ts1> AND <ts2> clause of a SELECT statement.	While retrieving data, you can use the FOR BUSINESS_TIME AS OF <ts1>, FOR BUSINESS_TIME FROM <ts1> TO <ts2>, or FOR BUSINESS_TIME BETWEEN <ts1> AND <ts2> clause of a SELECT statement.
The ALTER TABLE ACTIVATE NOT LOGGED INITIALLY statement is not supported.	The ALTER TABLE ACTIVATE NOT LOGGED INITIALLY statement is not supported.
The TRUNCATE command is not supported.	The TRUNCATE command is supported.
Data movement utilities and commands need a MODIFIED BY clause while working on system-period temporal tables.	Data movement utilities and commands work normally.
You cannot run IMPORT or LOAD with the REPLACE clause.	You can run IMPORT or LOAD with the REPLACE clause.
This table cannot be an MQT.	This table can be an MQT.
The session's system time can be updated by using the SET CURRENT TEMPORAL SYSTEM_TIME registry variable.	The session's business time can be updated by using the SET CURRENT TEMPORAL BUSINESS_TIME registry variable.
You cannot perform an update or a delete operation when the session's system time registry is set to a NOT NULL value.	You can perform an update or a delete operation when the session's business time registry is set to a NOT NULL value.

Bitemporal Period Tables

A bitemporal table is a table that stores both the current version of records in the base table and history versions of records in a history table, along with storing in-effect business data. If you want to create a bitemporal table and configure it to work for history tracking and time-specific data storage capability, you can do so by performing the following steps:

Step 1: Include both a SYSTEM_TIME period and a BUSINESS_TIME period in the CREATE TABLE command.

Step 2: Create a history table to record the old rows.

Step 3: Add versioning to associate the link between the base and the history table.

Step 4: Define the WITHOUT OVERLAPS clause to a primary key, to a UNIQUE constraint, or to a UNIQUE INDEX statement to eliminate overlapping business-time periods for the same key:

```
CREATE TABLE sellproduct_bit
   (ID              INT NOT NULL,
    NAME            VARCHAR (10),
    WEIGHT          INT,
    PRICE           DECIMAL (10, 2),
    DISCOUNT        DECIMAL (5, 2),
    SELLPRICE       DECIMAL (10, 2),
    BUSINESS_START  DATE NOT NULL,
    BUSINESS_END    DATE NOT NULL,
    SYS_START       TIMESTAMP (12) GENERATED ALWAYS AS ROW BEGIN NOT NULL,
    SYS_END         TIMESTAMP (12) GENERATED ALWAYS AS ROW END NOT NULL,
    TXN_ID          TIMESTAMP (12) GENERATED ALWAYS AS TRANSACTION START ID
IMPLICITLY HIDDEN,
    PERIOD BUSINESS_TIME (BUSINESS_START, BUSINESS_END),
    PERIOD SYSTEM_TIME (SYS_START, SYS_END),
    PRIMARY KEY (ID, BUSINESS_TIME WITHOUT OVERLAPS))
DB20000I  The SQL command completed successfully.

CREATE TABLE sellproduct_bit_history LIKE
sellproduct_bit WITH RESTRICT ON DROP
DB20000I  The SQL command completed successfully.

ALTER TABLE sellproduct_bit ADD VERSIONING
      USE HISTORY TABLE SELLPRODUCT_BIT_HISTORY
DB20000I  The SQL command completed successfully.
```

A Word About SESSION Special Register

If you have an existing available application or any SQL batch script that you want to run on a DB2 10.1 system-period or application-period temporal table against a specific point in system time or business time, you can use the SET CURRENT TEMPORAL special register to eliminate the need to change the SQL statements to incorporate the FOR SYSTEM_TIME and FOR BUSINESS_TIME clause.

To set the special registry, you execute the SET command:

```
SET CURRENT TEMPORAL SYSTEM_TIME='2014-12-31-17.44.28.316318000000'
DB20000I  The SQL command completed successfully.
```

After you set the session's system time, any SQL statement run against a system-period temporal table automatically appends the FOR SYSTEM_TIME AS OF '2014-12-31-17.44.28.316318000000' clause.

For example, if you want to query the EMPLOYEE_ST table with the session's system time, execute a simple SELECT statement:

```
SELECT FIRSTNAME, SALARY, BAND, SYS_START FROM EMPLOYEE_ST

FIRSTNAME  SALARY       BAND  SYS_START
---------- ------------ ----- --------------------------------
COLIN          12000.00 A1    2014-12-31-17.44.28.316318000000

  1 record(s) selected.
```

To unset the registry variable, you can do so by executing this statement:

```
SET CURRENT TEMPORAL SYSTEM_TIME=NULL
DB20000I  The SQL command completed successfully.
```

Running the same SELECT statement without setting the session's system time registry will produce a different record set that looks something like the following:

```
SELECT FIRSTNAME, SALARY, BAND, SYS_START FROM EMPLOYEE_ST

FIRSTNAME  SALARY       BAND  SYS_START
---------- ------------ ----- --------------------------------
COLIN          12800.00 A2    2014-12-31-17.49.19.315851000000

  1 record(s) selected.
```

However, if you try deleting records from a system-period temporal table while the session's system time is active, you will get an SQL20535N error:

```
DELETE FROM EMPLOYEE_ST
SQL20535N  The data change operation "DELETE" is not supported for the tar-
get object "EMPLOYEE_ST" because of an implicit or explicit period specifi-
cation involving "SYSTEM_TIME". Reason code: "1".  SQLSTATE=51046
```

As with the session's system time, you can use the session's business time to set the default business period:

```
SET CURRENT TEMPORAL BUSINESS_TIME='2015-01-01'
DB20000I  The SQL command completed successfully.

SELECT NAME, PRICE, DISCOUNT, SELLPRICE, BUSINESS_START, BUSINESS_END
    FROM SELLPRODUCT_BT

NAME       PRICE        DISCOUNT SELLPRICE    BUSINESS_START BUSINESS_END
---------- ------------ -------- ------------ -------------- ------------
LYSOL            124.00    25.00        93.00 01/01/2015     02/01/2015
FINISH           110.00    25.00        82.50 01/01/2015     02/01/2015

  2 record(s) selected.
```

Unsetting the session's business time and running the same SELECT statement will produce results that look something like this:

```
SET CURRENT TEMPORAL BUSINESS_TIME=NULL
DB20000I  The SQL command completed successfully.

SELECT NAME, PRICE, DISCOUNT, SELLPRICE, BUSINESS_START, BUSINESS_END
    FROM SELLPRODUCT_BT"
```

Continued

```
NAME       PRICE        DISCOUNT SELLPRICE    BUSINESS_START BUSINESS_END
---------- ------------ -------- ------------ -------------- ------------
LYSOL            124.00     5.00       117.80 02/15/2015      12/30/9999
LYSOL            124.00    25.00        93.00 01/01/2015      02/01/2015
LYSOL            124.00    10.00       111.60 02/10/2015      02/15/2015
FINISH           110.00    25.00        82.50 01/01/2015      02/01/2015
FINISH           110.00     5.00       104.50 02/01/2015      12/30/9999

  5 record(s) selected.
```

If you update or delete rows in a table that contain business time while the session's business time registry is set, the UPDATE or DELETE statement affects only rows that are valid on the specified period. For example, if you try deleting records with the session's business time set to '2015-01-01', the DB2 database manager will add '2015-01-01' to the WHERE clause of the DELETE commands:

```
SET CURRENT TEMPORAL BUSINESS_TIME='2015-01-01'
DB20000I  The SQL command completed successfully.

SELECT * FROM SELLPRODUCT_BT

ID  NAME   WEIGHT PRICE  DISCOUNT SELLPRICE BUSINESS_START BUSINESS_END
--- ------ ------ ------ -------- --------- -------------- ------------
  1  LYSOL    100 124.00    25.00     93.00     01/01/2015   02/01/2015
  2 FINISH    220 110.00    25.00     82.50     01/01/2015   02/01/2015

  2 record(s) selected.

DELETE FROM SELLPRODUCT_BT
DB20000I  The SQL command completed successfully.
```

The above DELETE command is similar to performing a delete operation by using the DELETE FROM SELLPRODUCT_BT WHERE BUSINESS_START='2015-01-01' command:

```
SELECT * FROM SELLPRODUCT_BT

ID  NAME   WEIGHT PRICE  DISCOUNT SELLPRICE BUSINESS_START BUSINESS_END
--- ------ ------ ------ -------- --------- -------------- ------------

  0 record(s) selected.
```

Working with XML Data

DB2's pureXML technology unlocks the latent potential of XML by providing simple, efficient access to XML data with the same levels of security, integrity, and resiliency taken for granted with relational data. DB2's pureXML technology is available as an add-on feature to the DB2 Express Edition (EE), DB2 Workgroup Server Edition (WSE), and DB2 Enterprise Server Edition (ESE). However, it is part of DB2 Express-C, and the use of pureXML is included in the base DB2 Express-C license.

With pureXML, XML data is stored in a hierarchical structure that naturally reflects the structure of XML documents. This structure, along with innovative indexing techniques, allows DB2 to efficiently manage XML data while eliminating the complex and time-consuming parsing that is typically required to store XML data in a relational database. However, some restrictions apply when it comes to using pureXML:

- PureXML can be used only with single-partition databases.
- The use of any pureXML feature will prevent future use of the DPF that is available with DB2 ESE.
- PureXML cannot be used with the DB2 InfoSphere Warehouse edition because it uses DB2 ESE and DPF.

To use the pureXML feature, a database must be created using the UTF-8 code set. You specify the UTF-8 code set in the USING CODESET option of the CREATE DATABASE command.

If you want to create a database named XML_DB with a UTF-8 code set, you can do so by executing a CREATE DATABASE command that looks something like this:

```
CREATE DATABASE xml_db USING CODESET UTF-8 TERRITORY US
DB20000I  The CREATE DATABASE command completed successfully.
```

The XML Data Type and XML Column

To support pureXML, a new data type called XML was introduced with DB2 9. This data type defines columns that will store XML values. Each XML value stored must be a well-formed XML document, which looks something like this:

```
<?xml version="1.0" encoding="UTF-8" ?>
<customerinfo xmlns="http://crecord.dat" id="1000">
  <name>John Doe</name>
  <addr country="United States">
    <street>25 East Creek Drive</street>
    <city>Raleigh</city>
    <state-prov>North Carolina</state-prov>
    <zip-pcode>27603</zip-pcode>
  </addr>
  <phone type="work">919-555-1212</phone>
  <email>john.doe@xyz.com</email>
</customerinfo>
```

Most XML documents begin with an XML declaration, such as the following:

```
<?xml version="1.0" encoding="UTF-8" ?>
```

or

```
<?xml version="1.0"?>
```

The XML declaration is followed by one or more attributes and elements. All XML elements are enclosed with opening and closing tags, as this example shows:

```
<p>This is a paragraph</p>
<p>This is another paragraph</p>
```

Note that the opening and closing tags are case-sensitive—the tag *<Letter>* is different from the tag *<letter>*. Therefore, you must write opening and closing tags with the same case.

You normally use XML attributes to describe XML elements or to provide additional information about an element. Attributes are always contained within the start tag of an element, and attribute values must always be enclosed in double quotation marks. Here are some examples:

```
<file type="gif">

<person id="3344">
```

Attributes are handy in HTML, but in XML you should try to avoid them whenever you can express the same information by using elements. The following examples convey the same information:

```
<person sex="female">
    <firstname>Anna</firstname>
    <lastname>Smith</lastname>
</person>

<person>
   <sex>female</sex>
   <firstname>Anna</firstname>
   <lastname>Smith</lastname>
</person>
```

In the first example, SEX is an attribute. In the last example, SEX is an element.

To create tables with XML columns, you specify columns with the XML data type in the CREATE TABLE statement. (A table can have one or more XML columns.) Like a LOB column, an XML column holds only a descriptor of the column. The data itself is stored separately. Unlike for a LOB column, you do not specify a length when you define an XML column. So to create a table named CUSTOMER that contains an XML column named CUSTINFO, execute a CREATE TABLE statement that looks like this:

```
CREATE TABLE customer (custid   INTEGER NOT NULL, custinfo XML)
DB20000I  The SQL command completed successfully.
```

XML columns have the following restrictions:

- They cannot have a default value specified by the WITH DEFAULT clause; if the column is nullable, the default for the column is NULL.
- They cannot be referenced in CHECK constraints (except when you use a VALIDATED predicate).
- They cannot be referenced in generated columns.
- They cannot be included in typed tables and typed views.
- They cannot be used in an RCT.
- They cannot be used in an MDC table.
- They cannot be added to tables that have Type-1 indexes defined on them (note that Type-1 indexes are deprecated indexes; indexes created since DB2 UDB Version 8.1 are Type-2 indexes).
- They cannot be specified in the select list of scrollable cursors.
- They cannot be referenced in the triggered action of a CREATE TRIGGER statement.
- They cannot be included as columns of keys, including primary, foreign, and unique keys; dimension keys of MDC tables; sequence keys of RCTs; distribution keys; and data-partitioning keys.
- They cannot be used in a table with a distribution key.
- They cannot be part of any index except an index over XML data.
- They cause data blocking to be disabled when retrieving XML data.

Manipulating XML Data

Like traditional data, XML documents can be added to a database table, altered, removed, and retrieved using SQL DML statements (INSERT, UPDATE, DELETE, and SELECT). Typically, application programs manipulate XML documents (as defined in the XML 1.0 specification). When DML operations from an application program are performed, IBM recommends that XML data manipulation occurs through host variables, rather than literals, so that DB2 can use the host variable data type to determine some of the encoding information needed for processing. And although you can manipulate XML data by using XML, binary, or character types, IBM recommends that you use XML or binary types to avoid code page conversion issues.

XML data used in an application is often stored in a serialized string format—when this data is inserted into an XML column or when data in an XML column is updated, it must be converted to its XML hierarchical format. If the application data type you use is an XML data type, DB2 performs this operation implicitly. However, if the application data type is a character or binary data type, you must use the XMLPARSE () function to explicitly convert the data from its serialized string format to the XML hierarchical format during insert and update operations.

A simple INSERT statement that uses the XMLPARSE () function to insert a string value into an XML column named CUSTINFO in a table named CUSTOMERS might look something like this:

```
INSERT INTO customers (custinfo) VALUES
    (XMLPARSE (DOCUMENT '<name>John Doe</name>'
     PRESERVE WHITESPACE))
```

When you use the CLP to manipulate XML documents stored in XML columns, you can directly assign string data to XML columns without an explicit call to the XMLPARSE () function when performing insert, update, and delete operations. For example, say you want to add a record containing XML data to a table named CUSTOMER that has the following characteristics:

Column Name	Data Type
CUSTID	INTEGER
INFO	XML

You can do so by executing an INSERT statement from the CLP that looks something like this:

```
INSERT INTO customer VALUES (1000,
'<customerinfo xmlns="http://custrecord.dat" custid="1000">
  <name>John Doe</name>
  <addr country="United States">
    <street>25 East Creek Drive</street>
    <city>Raleigh</city>
    <state-prov>North Carolina</state-prov>
    <zip-pcode>27603</zip-pcode>
  </addr>
  <phone type="work">919-555-1212</phone>
  <email>john.doe@xyz.com</email>
</customerinfo>')
```

And if you want to update the XML data portion of this record from the CLP, execute an UPDATE statement similar to the following:

```
UPDATE customer SET custinfo =
'<customerinfo xmlns="http://custrecord.dat" custid="1000">
  <name>Jane Doe</name>
  <addr country="Canada">
    <street>25 East Creek Drive</street>
    <city>Raleigh</city>
    <state-prov>North Carolina</state-prov>
    <zip-pcode>27603</zip-pcode>
  </addr>
  <phone type="work">919-555-1212</phone>
  <email>jane.doe@xyz.com</email>
</customerinfo>'
WHERE XMLEXISTS ('declare default element namespace "http://custrecord.dat";
$info/customerinfo[name/text()="John Doe"]' PASSING custinfo as "info")
```

Finally, to delete the record from the CUSTOMER table, you execute a DELETE statement from the CLP:

```
DELETE FROM customer
WHERE XMLEXISTS ('declare default element namespace "http://custrecord.dat";
$info/customerinfo[name/text()="John Doe"]' PASSING custinfo as "info")
```

So how do you retrieve XML data once it has been stored in a table? With DB2, you can retrieve XML data by using an SQL query or one of the SQL/XML query functions available. When using SQL to query XML data, you can retrieve data only at the column level—in other words, an entire XML document must be retrieved. It is not possible to return fragments of a document by using SQL. To query within XML documents, you need to use XQuery.

XQuery is a functional programming language designed by the World Wide Web Consortium (W3C) to meet specific requirements for querying XML data. Unlike relational data, which is predictable and has a regular structure, XML data is often unpredictable, highly variable, sparse, and self-describing. Because the structure of XML data is unpredictable, the queries that are performed on XML data often differ from typical relational queries. For example, you might need to create XML queries that perform the following operations:

- Search XML data for objects that are at unknown levels of the hierarchy
- Perform structural transformations on the data (for example, you might want to invert a hierarchy)
- Return results that have mixed types

In XQuery, expressions are the main building blocks of a query. Expressions can be nested, and they form the body of a query. A query can also have a prolog that contains a series of declarations that define the processing environment for the query.

Thus, if you want to retrieve customer names for all customers who reside in North Carolina from XML documents stored in the CUSTINFO column of a table named CUSTOMER (assuming this table has been populated with the INSERT statement we looked at earlier), execute an XQuery expression that looks something like this:

```
XQUERY declare default element namespace "http://custrecord.dat"; for $info
in db2-fn:xmlcolumn('CUSTOMER.CUSTINFO')/customerinfo where $info/addr/
state-prov="North Carolina" return $info/name
```

And when you execute this XQuery expression from the CLP, it should return information that looks like this (again, assuming this table has been populated with the INSERT statement we looked at earlier):

```
1
-----------------------------------------------------------
<name xmlns="http://custrecord.dat">John Doe</name>
```

To remove the XML tags and return only the customer name, you execute an XQuery expression that looks like this instead:

```
XQUERY declare default element namespace "http://custrecord.dat"; for $info
in db2-fn:xmlcolumn('CUSTOMER.CUSTINFO')/customerinfo where $info/addr/
state-prov="North Carolina" return $info/name/text()
```

Now when you execute the XQuery expression from the CLP, it should return information that looks like this:

```
1
------------------------------------------------------------
John Doe
```

As mentioned previously, you can invoke XQuery expressions from SQL by using any of the following SQL/XML functions or predicates:

- **XMLQUERY()**. This is an SQL scalar function that enables you to execute an XQuery expression from within an SQL context. XMLQUERY () returns an XML value, which is an XML sequence. This sequence can be empty, or it can contain one or more items. You can also pass variables to the XQuery expression specified in XMLQUERY ().
- **XMLTABLE()**. This is an SQL table function that returns a table from the evaluation of XQuery expressions. XQuery expressions normally return values as a sequence; however, XMLTABLE () allows you to execute an XQuery expression and return values as a table instead. The table that is returned can contain columns of any SQL data type, including XML. The structure of the resulting table is defined by the COLUMNS clause of XMLTABLE ().
- **XMLEXISTS**. This predicate determines whether an XQuery expression returns a sequence of one or more items. If the XQuery expression specified in this predicate returns an empty sequence, XMLEXISTS returns FALSE; otherwise, TRUE is returned. You can use the XMLEXISTS predicate in the WHERE clauses of UPDATE, DELETE, and SELECT statements. This usage means that you can use values from stored XML documents to restrict the set of rows on which a DML statement operates.

By executing XQuery expressions from within the SQL context, you can:

- Operate on parts of stored XML documents instead of entire XML documents (only XQuery can query within an XML document; SQL alone queries at the whole document level)
- Enable XML data to participate in SQL queries
- Operate on both relational and XML data
- Apply further SQL processing to the returned XML values (for example, ordering results with the ORDER BY clause of a subselect)

Suppose you want to retrieve customer IDs and customer names for a table named CUSTOMER that has the following characteristics:

Column Name	Data Type
CUSTID	INTEGER
INFO	XML

You can do so (assuming this table has been populated with the INSERT statement we looked at earlier) by executing a SELECT statement from the CLP that looks something like this:

```
SELECT custid, XMLQUERY ('declare default element namespace "http://cus-
trecord.dat"; $d/customerinfo/name' passing CUSTINFO as "d") AS address FROM
customer
```

And when you execute this query, it should return information similar to the following:

```
CUSTID ADDRESS
------ ---------------------------------------------
  1000 <name xmlns="http://custrecord.dat">John Doe</name>
```

XML Indexes

Just as you can use an index over relational data to improve query performance, you can use an index over XML data to improve the efficiency of queries on XML documents that are stored in an XML column. In contrast to traditional relational indexes, where index keys consist of one or more columns that you specify, an index over XML data uses a particular XML pattern expression to index paths and values found in XML documents stored in a single column. The data type of that column must be XML.

To identify those parts of the document that will be indexed, you use an XML pattern to specify a set of nodes within the XML document. This pattern expression is similar to the path expression defined in the XQuery language, but it differs in that only a subset of the XQuery language is supported. Path expression steps are separated by the forward slash (/). You can also specify the double forward slash (//)—which is the abbreviated syntax for /descendant-or-self::node()/. In each step, you choose a forward axis (child::, @, attribute::, descendant::, self::, and descendant-or-self::), followed by an XML name or XML kind test. If you do not specify a forward axis, the child axis is used as the default. Figure 3.5 shows a simple XML pattern and how it is used to identify a specific value within an XML document.

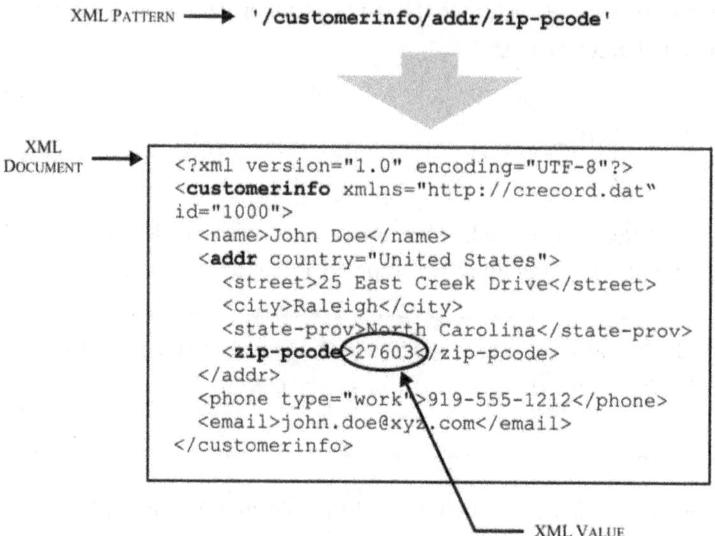

Figure 3.5: How to use an XML pattern to identify a specific value within an XML document

Instead of providing access to the beginning of a document, index entries in an index over XML data provide access to nodes within the document by creating index keys based on XML pattern expressions. And because multiple parts of an XML document can satisfy an XML pattern, you can insert multiple index keys into the index for a single document.

To create XML indexes, specify the GENERATE KEY USING XMLPATTERN clause of the CREATE INDEX SQL statement. The basic syntax for this optional clause is:

```
GENERATE KEY USING XMLPATTERN
<Namespace>
[XMLPattern]
AS [SQLDataType]
```

where:

Namespace — Identifies a valid namespace declaration to use to identify namespace prefixes when qualified names are used in the pattern expression specified

XMLPattern — Specifies a pattern expression that identifies the nodes to index; the pattern expression can contain any of the following XQuery components:

- The * (asterisk)—Specifies a pattern-matching character
- The / (forward slash)—Separates path expression steps

	• The // (double forward slash)—The abbreviated syntax for /descendant-or-self::node()/ • The child::—Specifies children of the context node; this is the default if no other forward axis is specified • The @—Specifies attributes of the context node; this is the abbreviated syntax for attribute:: • The attribute::—Specifies attributes of the context node • The descendant::—Specifies the descendants of the context node • The self::—Specifies just the context node itself • The descendant-or-self::—Specifies the context node and the descendants of the context node
SQLDataType	Specifies the SQL data type to which to convert indexed values before they are stored; the following values are valid for this parameter: VARCHAR(*Size*), DOUBLE, DATE, and TIMESTAMP

Thus, if you want to create an XML index by using postal zip code values found in XML column CUSTINFO in table CUSTOMER and store those values as DOUBLE values, execute a CREATE INDEX statement that looks something like this:

```
CREATE INDEX custindex ON customer (custinfo)
GENERATE KEY
USING XMLPATTERN '/customerinfo/addr/zip-pcode' AS SQL DOUBLE
```

However, to create an XML index by using address information found in XML column CUSTINFO in table CUSTOMER and store those values as VARCHAR values, you execute a CREATE INDEX statement similar to the following:

```
CREATE INDEX custindex ON customer (custinfo)
GENERATE KEY
USING XMLPATTERN /customerinfo/@addr' AS SQL VARCHAR (100)
```

In the first example, the index is created for an element; in the second, it is created for an attribute. Although it is possible to create XML indexes on attributes (or on the entire document, for that matter), performance can suffer. Therefore, it is usually better to create XML indexes on individual elements within an XML document.

Data Compression

In DB2, you have several forms of compression features available to optimize storage:

- Before DB2 9.1—value compression, MDC block indexes, and backup compression
- DB2 9.1—static row compression
- DB2 9.5—automatic dictionary creation process
- DB2 9.7—index, inline LOB, temporary table, XML, and replicated table compression
- DB2 10.1—adaptive compression and log archive compression

DB2 9.1—Static Row Compression

One of the most prominent features introduced in DB2 9.1 was the ability to reduce the amount of storage required to store table data by using data row compression. Although the primary purpose of data row compression is to save storage space, it can lead to significant disk I/O savings and higher buffer pool hit ratios as well. (More data can be cached in memory.) All of this can lead to an increase in performance, but not without some costs—extra CPU cycles are needed to compress and decompress the data. The storage savings and performance impact of data row compression are tied directly to the characteristics of the data within the database, the design of the database itself, how well the database has been tuned, and application workloads.

As the volume of data increases, the cardinality of that data tends to drop. As it turns out, there just are not that many truly "unique" things in the world. They may be unique when used in combination, but the basic elements themselves are not all that varied. Consider the periodic table of elements—everything in our world is made up of combinations of this rather small set of elements.

Apply the concept to data, and you find the same is true. For instance, according to the 2010 U.S. census, about 300 million people live in the United States of America. But there are only approximately 78,800 unique last names, resulting in very low cardinality with huge "clumps" in certain name sets. First names are even worse, coming in at around 6,600 (4,400 unique first names for females and 2,200 for males). The names of cities, streets, and addresses, as well as product names, descriptions, and attributes also tend to be highly redundant with low cardinality.

Data row compression works by searching for repeating patterns in the data and replacing the patterns with 12-bit symbols, which are stored along with the pattern they represent in a static dictionary. (Once this dictionary is created, it is stored in the table along with the compressed data and is loaded into memory whenever data in the table is accessed to aid in decompression.) DB2 does this by scanning an entire table and looking for repeating column values, as well as repeating patterns that span multiple columns in a row. DB2 also looks for repeating patterns that are substrings of a given column. However, just because a repeating pattern is found does not mean that the data is automatically compressed—data is compressed only where storage savings will be realized. Figure 3.6 illustrates how data row compression works.

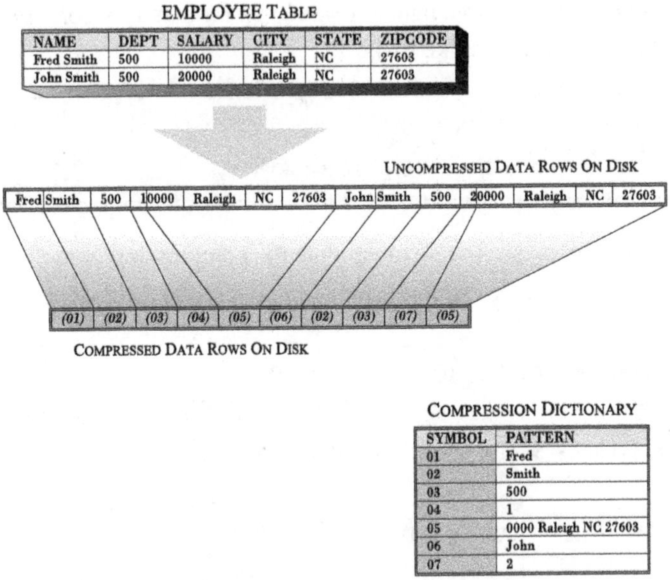

EMPLOYEE TABLE

NAME	DEPT	SALARY	CITY	STATE	ZIPCODE
Fred Smith	500	10000	Raleigh	NC	27603
John Smith	500	20000	Raleigh	NC	27603

UNCOMPRESSED DATA ROWS ON DISK

Fred	Smith	500	1	0000	Raleigh	NC	27603	John	Smith	500	2	0000	Raleigh	NC	27603

(01)	(02)	(03)	(04)	(05)	(06)	(02)	(03)	(07)	(05)

COMPRESSED DATA ROWS ON DISK

COMPRESSION DICTIONARY

SYMBOL	PATTERN
01	Fred
02	Smith
03	500
04	1
05	0000 Raleigh NC 27603
06	John
07	2

Figure 3.6: How DB2 9.1 static row compression works

To use data row compression with a table, you must satisfy two prerequisites:

1. Compression must be enabled at the table level.
2. A compression dictionary for the table must be built.

Enabling Static Row Compression

You enable compression at the table level by executing either the CREATE TABLE SQL statement or the ALTER TABLE statement with the COMPRESS YES option specified. For example, if you want to create a new table named EMPLOYEE and enable it for data row compression, execute a CREATE TABLE statement that looks something like this:

```
CREATE TABLE employee
    (name     VARCHAR (60),
     dept     CHAR (3),
     salary   DECIMAL (7, 2),
     city     VARCHAR (25),
     state    CHAR (2),
     zipcode  VARCHAR (10))
  COMPRESS YES
DB20000I  The SQL command completed successfully.
```

However, to enable an existing table named EMPLOYEE for data row compression, you execute an ALTER TABLE statement that looks like this:

```
ALTER TABLE employee COMPRESS YES
DB20000I  The SQL command completed successfully.
```

You can query the system catalog view to validate the compression mode:

```
SELECT
      SUBSTR (TABSCHEMA, 1, 10) AS TABSCHEMA,
      SUBSTR (TABNAME, 1, 12) AS TABNAME, COMPRESSION, ROWCOMPMODE
   FROM SYSCAT.TABLES WHERE TABNAME='EMPLOYEE'

TABSCHEMA  TABNAME      COMPRESSION ROWCOMPMODE
---------- ------------ ----------- -----------
MOHAN      EMPLOYEE     R           S

  1 record(s) selected.
```

In the above example, COMPRESSION R indicates row compression and ROWCOMPMODE S denotes static compression.

Building a Compression Dictionary

Although you can enable a table for static row compression at any time by setting its COMPRESS attribute to YES, data stored in the table will not be compressed until a compression dictionary has been built. To build a compression dictionary (and compress data in a table) you use an offline table reorganization operation. You initiate such an operation by executing the REORG command with either the KEEPDICTIONARY or the RESETDICTIONARY option specified. If you execute the REORG command with either option specified, and a compression dictionary does not exist, a new dictionary will be built. However, if you execute the REORG command with either option specified, and a dictionary already exists, data in the table will be reorganized and compressed, and the existing dictionary will be either re-created (RESETDICTIONARY) or left as it is (KEEPDICTIONARY).

Thus, if you want to create a new compression dictionary (and compress the existing data) for a table named EMPLOYEE that has been enabled for data row compression, you can do so by executing a REORG command that looks like this:

```
REORG TABLE employee RESETDICTIONARY
DB20000I  The REORG command completed successfully.
```

When you execute this command, data stored in the EMPLOYEE table will be analyzed, a compression dictionary will be constructed and stored at the beginning of the table, and the data will be compressed and written to the table directly behind the compression dictionary. Figure 3.7 illustrates how the EMPLOYEE table will look before and after data row compression is applied.

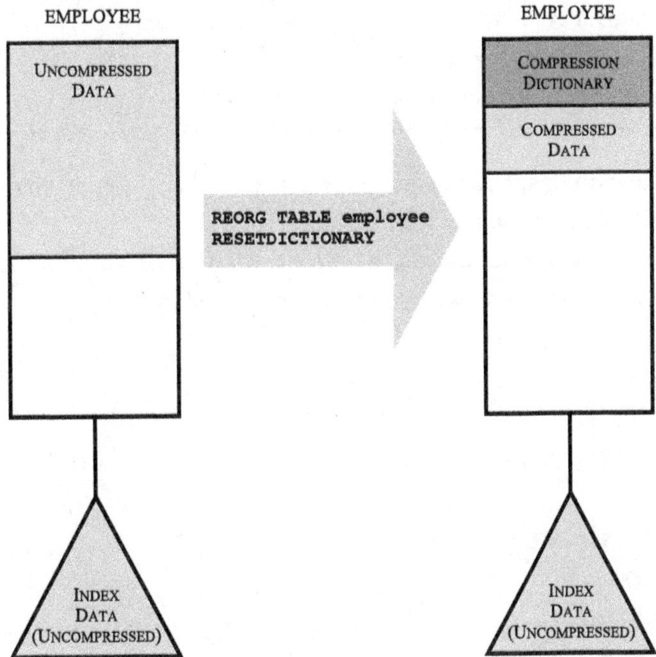

Figure 3.7: How data in a table is altered when a compression dictionary is built and data row compression is applied

Note that data row compression does not affect index data; only data stored on a page in a base table can be compressed. However, because records in a compressed table are moved between storage and memory in compressed form (the compression dictionary is moved into memory as well so that decompression can take place), records for compressed tables that are written to transaction log files will be compressed as well.

Storage Benefit Realization

Because you must use an offline reorganization operation to construct a compression dictionary and perform data compression, the initial overhead required to compress data can be quite high. Therefore, it can be beneficial to know which tables will benefit the most from data row compression and which tables will not. The Inspect utility can help you make that determination. To invoke the Inspect utility, you execute the INSPECT command. If you execute this command with the ROWCOMPESTIMATE option specified, the Inspect utility will examine each row in the table specified, build a compression dictionary from the data it finds, and then use this dictionary to estimate how much space will be saved if the data in the table is compressed.

Thus, if you want to estimate how much storage space will be saved if the data in a table named EMPLOYEE is compressed, execute an INSPECT command similar to the following:

```
INSPECT ROWCOMPESTIMATE TABLE NAME employee SCHEMA mohan
        RESULTS KEEP employee_comp.out
DB20000I  The INSPECT command completed successfully.
```

You can then use the db2inspf command to format the INSPECT command output (located in ~/sqllib/db2dump/DIAG0000), something like this:

```
db2inspf employee_comp.out employee_comp_formatted.out

DATABASE: SAMPLE
VERSION : SQL10013
2014-12-30-04.44.41.824894

Action: ROWCOMPESTIMATE TABLE
Schema name: MOHAN
Table name: EMPLOYEE
Tablespace ID: 2  Object ID: 4
Result file name: employee_comp.out

Table phase start (ID Signed: 4, Unsigned: 4; Tablespace ID: 2) : MOHAN.
EMPLOYEE

                                                                  Continued
```

```
        Data phase start. Object: 4  Tablespace: 2
        Row compression estimate results:
        Percentage of pages saved from compression: 86
        Percentage of bytes saved from compression: 86
        Compression dictionary size: 13312 bytes.
        Expansion dictionary size: 20832 bytes.
        INSPECT will not insert dictionary due to the current table status.
        Data phase end.
      Table phase end.
Processing has completed. 2014-12-30-04.44.42.684531
```

If you enable a table for data row compression (i.e., by setting the COMPRESS attribute to YES) before executing the INSPECT command, the compression dictionary that is built and used to estimate space savings will be written to the table, at the end of the existing data. Figure 3.8 illustrates how a table will look before and after the Inspect utility estimates storage savings if you enabled that table for data row compression before the estimate was acquired.

Once a data compression dictionary has been created and written to a table that has been enabled for data row compression, new records added to that table will be automatically compressed. The same is true for existing records that are modified. However, if the Inspect utility creates the compression dictionary for a table, preexisting data in the table will remain uncompressed until an offline reorganization operation is performed.

DB2 9.5—Automatic Dictionary Creation Process

If you enable a table for compression when you create that table, a feature introduced in DB2 9.5 called *automatic dictionary creation* (*ADC*) will build a compression dictionary automatically as soon as enough data has been stored in the table. The threshold at which ADC kicks in and begins constructing the compression dictionary depends upon the table's row size and how many records have been stored in it. At a minimum, at least 2 MB of data must be present in a table before a compression dictionary can be built.

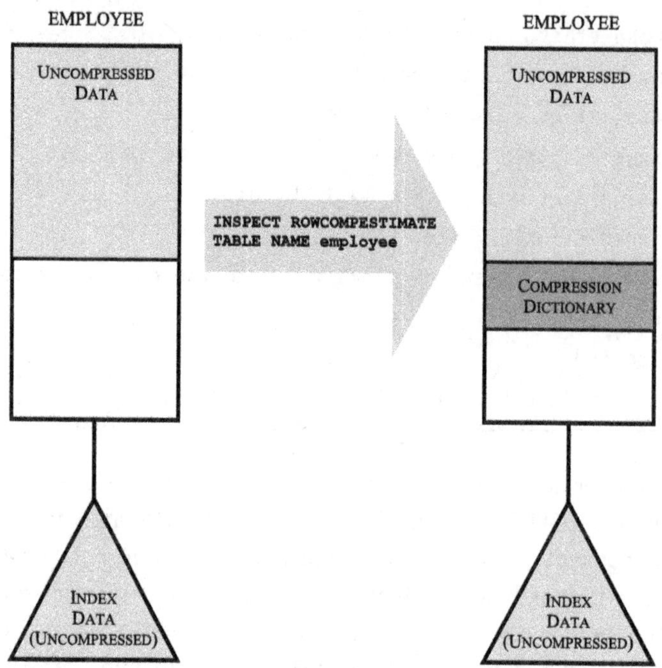

Figure 3.8: How data in a table is altered when the Inspect utility evaluates a table enabled for data row compression

DB2 9.5 provided a set of compression-related, simple SQL administrative procedures to determine the potential benefit of enabling compression on a table. One procedure was ADMIN_GET_TAB_COMPRESS_INFO, which has recently been deprecated. The recommendation is to use ADMIN_GET_TAB_COMPRESS_INFO table function instead. A sample command execution looks something like this:

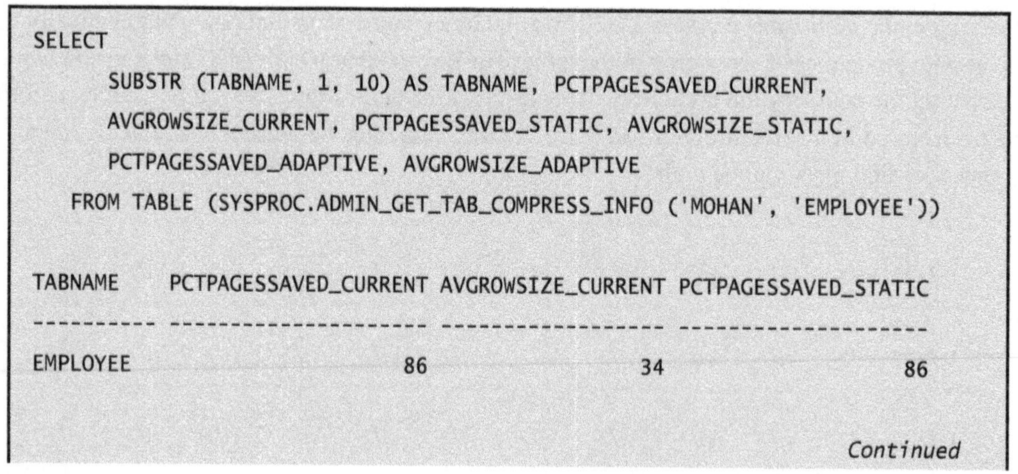

```
SELECT
      SUBSTR (TABNAME, 1, 10) AS TABNAME, PCTPAGESSAVED_CURRENT,
      AVGROWSIZE_CURRENT, PCTPAGESSAVED_STATIC, AVGROWSIZE_STATIC,
      PCTPAGESSAVED_ADAPTIVE, AVGROWSIZE_ADAPTIVE
   FROM TABLE (SYSPROC.ADMIN_GET_TAB_COMPRESS_INFO ('MOHAN', 'EMPLOYEE'))

TABNAME    PCTPAGESSAVED_CURRENT AVGROWSIZE_CURRENT PCTPAGESSAVED_STATIC
---------- --------------------- ------------------ --------------------
EMPLOYEE                      86                 34                   86

                                                                Continued
```

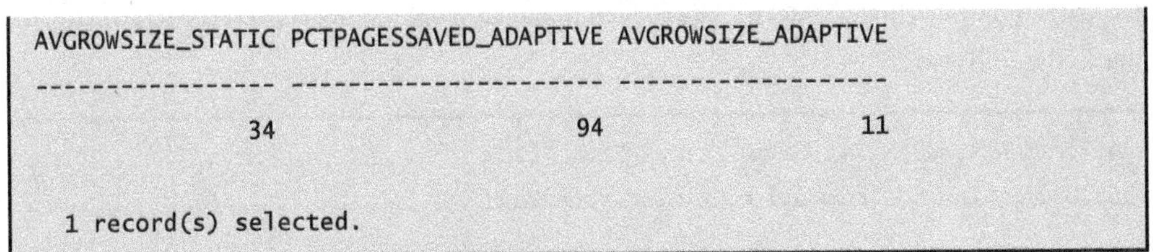

```
AVGROWSIZE_STATIC PCTPAGESSAVED_ADAPTIVE AVGROWSIZE_ADAPTIVE
----------------- ---------------------- -------------------
               34                     94                  11

  1 record(s) selected.
```

DB2 9.7—Increasing the Compression Landscape

In DB2 9.7, IBM introduced a stack of compression capabilities, including index compression, temporary table compression, inline large object compression, and XML object compression.

Index Compression

Many of the standard industry-specific applications consume considerable amounts of storage space to store indexes. In DB2 9.7, you can compress indexes, including indexes on declared or created temporary tables, to reduce storage costs. By default, index compression is enabled for compressed tables and disabled for uncompressed tables. You can also enable compression on existing indexes by using the ALTER INDEX ...COMPRESS YES command. The only indexes you cannot compress are MDC block indexes and XML path indexes.

You can use the ADMIN_GET_INDEX_COMPRESS_INFO table function to determine the potential index compression storage savings. The command looks something like this:

```
SELECT
      SUBSTR (INDNAME, 1, 30) AS INDNAME,
      COMPRESS_ATTR, INDEX_COMPRESSED, PCT_PAGES_SAVED, NUM_LEAF_PAGES_SAVED
   FROM TABLE (SYSPROC.ADMIN_GET_INDEX_COMPRESS_INFO ('T', 'MOHAN', 'EMPLOY-
EE', NULL, NULL)) AS t

INDNAM       COMPRESS_ATTR INDEX_COMPRESSED PCT_PAGES_SAVED NUM_LEAF_PAGES_
SAVED
------------ ------------- ---------------- --------------- ----------------
----
IX1_EMPLOYEE              N                N              69
816

  1 record(s) selected.
```

To enable compression on the IX1_EMPLOYEE index, execute the ALTER INDEX command, similar to the following:

```
ALTER INDEX MOHAN.IX1_EMPLOYEE COMPRESS YES
DB20000I  The SQL command completed successfully.

REORG INDEXES ALL FOR TABLE MOHAN.EMPLOYEE
DB20000I  The REORG command completed successfully.
```

LOB and XML Compression

LOBs and XML documents are generally stored in a location separate from the table row that references them. However, you can choose to store a LOB or XML document (up to 32 KB in size) inline in a base table row to simplify access to it. LOBs and XML documents that you store inline can be compressed along with other relational data. Additionally, XML data in the XML storage object of a table is eligible for compression if you use DB2 9.7 to create the XML columns and if you enable the table for data row compression. (XML columns created before DB2 9.7 are not eligible for compression).

Temporary Tables and Replication Support

With the DB2 Storage Optimization feature, temporary table compression is enabled by default. The DB2 Optimizer considers the storage savings and the SQL statement performance before actually compressing the temporary data for aggregated or ORDER BY clause queries. You can use the access plan or the db2pd command to see whether the optimizer used compression for temporary tables:

```
db2pd -db sample -temptable

System Temp Table Stats:
        Number of System Temp Tables      : 26066021
        Comp Eligible Sys Temps           : 5543
        Compressed Sys Temps              : 5274
        Total Sys Temp Bytes Stored       : 1356253552
        Total Sys Temp Bytes Saved        : 3405607604
        Total Sys Temp Compressed Rows    : 38004866
        Total Sys Temp Table Rows:        : 1163333695
```

Continued

```
User Temp Table Stats:
        Number of User Temp Tables      : 59
        Comp Eligible User Temps        : 59
        Compressed User Temps           : 0
        Total User Temp Bytes Stored    : 47448628
        Total User Temp Bytes Saved     : 0
        Total User Temp Compressed Rows : 0
        Total User Temp Table Rows:     : 400108
```

Starting from DB2 9.7, SQL replication, Q replication, and event publishing are supported from compressed and partitioned source tables to any target table. This is mainly done through enhancing the log read interface to read compressed log records and decompressing them before passing those records to the replication capture program at the source.

DB2 10.1—Adaptive Compression

In DB2 10.1, IBM introduced yet another data compression technique called *adaptive compression*. Adaptive row compression relies on a compression dictionary built at page level and compresses patterns within the page that are not part of the static dictionary. This way, adaptive compression not only yields a significantly better performance ratio but also adapts to changing data characteristics.

Table 3.6 shows the differences between static row compression (also called *classic compression*) and adaptive compression.

Table 3.6: Static and adaptive compression comparison

Static Row Compression	Adaptive Compression
This creates a global compression dictionary at table level.	This creates a local compression dictionary at page level.
This is the base-level compression required to enable adaptive compression.	This needs static row compression to be enabled before activating the adaptive compression.
This needs frequent REORG on the table to eliminate stale patterns.	This is dynamic in nature, and it always complements the classic/static row compression by using global dictionary patterns inside the local dictionary patterns.
The compression ratio is anywhere between 30 percent and 50 percent.	The compression ratio is anywhere between 50 percent and 80 percent.
This needs a little more maintenance, such as REORG and RUNSTATS, at regular intervals.	No maintenance is necessary.

Table 3.6: Static and adaptive compression comparison (continued)	
Static Row Compression	**Adaptive Compression**
Base data objects such as CHAR, VARCHAR, INTEGER, FLOAT, inline LOB, and inline XML data can be compressed.	Base data objects such as CHAR, VARCHAR, INTEGER, FLOAT, inline LOB, and inline XML data can be compressed.
The syntax to enable static compression is: CREATE TABLE ... COMPRESS YES STATIC or ALTER TABLE ... COMPRESS YES STATIC	The syntax to enable adaptive compression is: CREATE TABLE ... COMPRESS YES ADAPTIVE or ALTER TABLE ... COMPRESS YES ADAPTIVE
The ADMIN_GET_TAB_COMPRESS_INFO table function provides compression estimates.	The ADMIN_GET_TAB_COMPRESS_INFO table function provides compression estimates.
This is an add-on feature available as part of the Advanced Enterprise Server Edition and the Advanced Workgroup Server Edition.	This is an add-on feature and available as part of the Advanced Enterprise Server Edition and the Advanced Workgroup Server Edition.
The system catalog view statement SELECT SUBSTR (TABSCHEMA, 1, 10) AS TABSCHEMA, SUBSTR (TABNAME, 1, 12) AS TABNAME, COMPRESSION, ROWCOMPMODE FROM SYSCAT.TABLES WHERE TABNAME='<tabname>' can be used to validate the mode of compression. The ROWCOMPMODE S indicates static row compression.	The system catalog view statement SELECT SUBSTR (TABSCHEMA, 1, 10) AS TABSCHEMA, SUBSTR (TABNAME, 1, 12) AS TABNAME, COMPRESSION, ROWCOMPMODE FROM SYSCAT.TABLES WHERE TABNAME='<tabname>' can be used to validate the mode of compression. The ROWCOMPMODE A indicates adaptive compression.

Finally, you can compress the transaction archive log files in DB2 10.1 by updating the database configuration parameter, something like this:

```
UPDATE DB CFG FOR sample USING LOGARCHCOMPR1 ON LOGARCHCOMPR2 ON
DB20000I  The UPDATE DATABASE CONFIGURATION command completed successfully.
```

If you do not enable the database for archive logging or do not set the database configuration parameters LOGARCHMETH1 and LOGARCHMETH2, you will get an error similar to the following:

```
UPDATE DB CFG FOR sample USING LOGARCHCOMPR1 ON LOGARCHCOMPR2 ON
SQL1663W  Log archive compression is not fully enabled for "LOGARCHMETH1".
```

Chapter Summary

The objective of this chapter was to familiarize you with

- The relationship between the server, instance, and database
- The database creation and the directory structure for a nonpartitioned database
- The buffer pools and table spaces with design principles
- The DB2 storage hierarchy and storage groups
- The multi-temperature storage feature to optimize storage costs and application performance
- Range partitioning tables
- RCT
- MDC
- MQT
- The Time Travel Query feature by using the system-period and the application-period temporal tables
- The XML data operations and XML indexes
- The DB2 compression features such as classic (static) and adaptive compression algorithms

On completion of this chapter, you will be equipped with sufficient knowledge to answer the DB2 physical design questions in the certification exam. It is also highly recommended to complete the sample questions available at the end of the chapter.

Practice Questions

Question 1

An instance named db2inst1 exists on a server, and the dftdbpath database manager configuration parameter for that instance contains the value /home. If no databases exist on the server and you execute the following command:

```
CREATE DATABASE sample
```

Where will the metadata files for the database reside?

- A. In the /home/NODE0000/SQL00001 subdirectory
- B. In the /home/db2inst1/NODE0000/SQL00001 subdirectory
- C. In the /home/NODE0000/SAMPLE subdirectory
- D. In the /home/db2inst1/NODE0000/SAMPLE subdirectory

Question 2

Which feature is *not* automatically enabled when a new DB2 10.1 database is created?

- A. Automatic real-time statistics collection
- B. Self-tuning memory manager
- C. Data classic and adaptive row compression
- D. Automatic storage

Question 3

If you execute the following CREATE DATABASE command:

```
CREATE DATABASE sample ON C: USING CODESET UTF-8 TERRITORY US
RESTRICTIVE
```

Which privilege will be automatically granted to the group PUBLIC?

- A. No privileges are granted
- B. CONNECT, CREATETAB, BINDADD, and IMPLICIT_SCHEMA privileges on the database
- C. SELECT privilege on each system catalog table
- D. EXECUTE privilege on all procedures found in the SYSIBM schema

Question 4

If you execute the following CREATE DATABASE command:

```
CREATE DATABASE sales ON /data/db2fs1, /data/db2fs2
COLLATE USING IDENTITY
CATALOG TABLESPACE MANAGED BY SYSTEM USING ('/data/db2syscat');
```

Which statement is false about the resulting database?

❍ A. Automatic storage is enabled for the database.
❍ B. An SMS table space will be used to hold the system catalog.
❍ C. User data will be stored on /data/db2fs1 and /data/db2fs2.
❍ D. Metadata for the database will be stored on /data/db2fs2.

Question 5

Which command must be run before you can specify the value E:\DATA for the DBPATH ON parameter in the CREATE DATABASE command?

❍ A. db2set DB2_CREATE_DB_ON_PATH=YES
❍ B. UPDATE DB CFG FOR sample USING DFTDBPATH ON
❍ C. db2set DB2_OVERRIDE_BPF=50000
❍ D. db2set DB2LIBPATH=E:\DATA

Question 6

Which command converts an existing nonautomatic storage database named SAMPLE to use automatic storage?

❍ A. DROP DATABASE sample; CREATE DATABASE sample AUTOMATIC STORAGE YES
❍ B. CREATE STOGROUP sg_sample ON '/data/db2fs'
❍ C. db2set DB2_ENABLE_AUTOCONFIG_DEFAULT=YES
❍ D. ALTER DATABASE sample ADD STORAGE ON '/data/db2fs'

Question 7

Which statement is false about SMS table spaces?

- ❍ A. Regular data and long data cannot be split across multiple table spaces.
- ❍ B. Storage space is allocated by the operating system as it is needed.
- ❍ C. Containers can be added to or deleted from existing table spaces by using the ALTER TABLESPACE command.
- ❍ D. Only directory containers can be used for storage; file and device containers cannot be used.

Question 8

If you execute the following CREATE TABLESPACE statement:

```
CREATE REGULAR TABLESPACE ts_sales_8k
PAGESIZE 8 K
MANAGED BY SYSTEM USING
   ('/mnt/data1', '/mnt/data2', '/mnt/data3')
EXTENTSIZE 32
PREFETCHSIZE 128
```

How much space does DB2 allocate for the TS_SALES_8K table space when all existing pages in the table space become full?

- ❍ A. 8 KB
- ❍ B. 32 KB
- ❍ C. 128 KB
- ❍ D. 256 KB

Question 9

Which two of the following commands can you use to obtain detailed information, including status, about all table spaces that have been created for a database named SAMPLE?

- ❒ A. SELECT * FROM SYS.TABLESPACES
- ❒ B. LIST TABLESPACES SHOW DETAIL
- ❒ C. LIST TABLESPACE CONTAINERS SHOW DETAIL
- ❒ D. SELECT * FROM TABLE (MON_GET_TABLESPACE ('',-2)) AS TBSP
- ❒ E. GET SNAPSHOT FOR TABLESPACE CONTAINERS ON sample

Question 10

Which of the following is *not* a valid table space state?

- ❍ A. Load pending
- ❍ B. Online and not accessible
- ❍ C. Load in progress
- ❍ D. Offline and not accessible

Question 11

If you execute the following CREATE DATABASE command:

```
CREATE DATABASE payroll ON C:
```

Which command will add new storage containers to the PAYROLL database?

- ❍ A. ALTER TABLESPACE ADD STORAGE D:\data1, D:\data2
- ❍ B. ALTER DATABASE ADD STORAGE D:\data1, D:\data2
- ❍ C. ALTER STOGROUP IBMSTOGROUP ADD D:\data1, D:\data2
- ❍ D. ALTER DATABASE ADD CONTAINERS D:\data1, D:\data2

Question 12

Which option can you specify with the CREATE TABLESPACE statement to create a DMS table space that can automatically expand beyond its original storage definition?

- ❍ A. AUTORESIZE YES
- ❍ B. RESIZE YES
- ❍ C. EXTEND YES
- ❍ D. EXPAND YES

Question 13

Given the following CREATE TABLESPACE statement:

```
CREATE REGULAR TABLESPACE payroll_ts
MANAGED BY AUTOMATIC STORAGE
EXTENTSIZE 32
PREFETCHSIZE 128
```

Which statement is false?

- ❍ A. When created, the PAYROLL_TS table space will be a DMS table space with file containers.
- ❍ B. The database for which the PAYROLL_TS table space is to be created must be enabled for automatic storage.
- ❍ C. When created, the PAYROLL_TS table space will be an SMS table space with directory containers.
- ❍ D. The MANAGED BY AUTOMATIC STORAGE clause is unnecessary and could have been left out of the CREATE TABLESPACE command.

Question 14

Which statement will enable automatic storage in storage group SG_HOT for a given database SAMPLE, manage table space TS_SMALL_DATA, and remove all existing nonautomatic storage containers from the table space?

- ❍ A. ALTER TABLESPACE ts_small_data MANAGED BY AUTOMATIC STORAGE USING STOGROUP SG_HOT;
  ALTER TABLESPACE ts_small_data REBALANCE;
- ❍ B. ALTER TABLEPACE ts_small_data MANAGED BY DATABASE;
  ALTER TABLESPACE ts_small_data MANAGED BY AUTOMATIC STORAGE;
  ALTER TABLESPACE ts_small_data REBALANCE;
- ❍ C. ALTER TABLESPACE ts_small_data MANAGED BY AUTOMATIC STORAGE USE STOGROUP sg_hot;
  ALTER STOGROUP sg_hot DROP '/db2/filesystem1', '/db2/filesystem2';
  ALTER TABLESPACE my_ts REBALANCE;
- ❍ D. ALTER TABLESPACE ts_small_data MANAGED BY DATABASE USE STOGROUP sg_hot;
  ALTER STOGROUP sg_hot DROP '/db2/filesystem1', '/db2/filesystem2';
  ALTER TABLESPACE my_ts REBALANCE;

Question 15

An existing nonautomatic storage database named SAMPLE has been successfully converted to an automatic storage database. What must you do to convert any existing DMS table spaces to automatic storage table spaces?

- ❍ A. Execute the statement ALTER DATABASE sample CONVERT TO AUTOMATIC STORAGE IMMEDIATE.
- ❍ B. Execute the statement ALTER DATABASE sample CONVERT TABLESPACES TO AUTOMATIC STORAGE.
- ❍ C. Execute the ALTER TABLESPACE statement with the MANAGED BY STOGROUP clause specified for each DMS table space to be converted.
- ❍ D. Execute the ALTER TABLESPACE statement with the MANAGED BY AUTOMATIC STORAGE USING STOGROUP clause specified for each DMS table space to be converted.

Question 16

Which statement is false regarding the storage group?

- ❍ A. Only automatic storage table spaces can use storage groups.
- ❍ B. A storage group can associate with multiple table spaces; however, a table space can associate with only one storage group.
- ❍ C. Storage groups help segregate different classes of storage available to the database system.
- ❍ D. Both the DMS and SMS table spaces can use storage groups.

Question 17

Which table space is *not* created by default when you execute the CREATE DATABASE command?

- ❍ A. USERSPACE1
- ❍ B. TEMPSPACE1
- ❍ C. SYSCATSPACE
- ❍ D. SYSTOOLSSPACE

Question 18

Which command do you use to copy the data from an existing DMS table space to a newly created automatic storage table space, keeping the data unbroken for business use?

- ❍ A. The db2relocatedb utility
- ❍ B. The db2move utility
- ❍ C. The ADMIN_MOVE_TABLE_UTIL procedure
- ❍ D. The ADMIN_MOVE_TABLE procedure

Question 19

When you move a table space from an old storage group to a new storage group, what will be the state of the containers present in the old storage group?

- ❍ A. Storage must be defined
- ❍ B. Drop pending
- ❍ C. Table space deletion in progress
- ❍ D. Move pending

Question 20

Which command moves existing table space TBSP1 from storage group SG_HOT to SG_WARM without affecting the availability of the data in database SAMPLE?

- ❍ A. ALTER TABLESPACE tbsp1 USING STOGROUP sg_warm
- ❍ B. ALTER DATABASE sample MOVE STOGROUP sg_warm
- ❍ C. DROP TABLESPACE tbsp1; CREATE TABLESPACE tbsp1 USING STOGROUP sg_warm
- ❍ D. ALTER TABLESPACE tbsp1 MOVE USING STOGROUP sg_warm

Question 21

Which statement is false about global temporary tables?

- ❍ A. Indexes can be created on global temporary tables.
- ❍ B. Global temporary tables reside in user temporary table spaces.
- ❍ C. Statistics can be collected on global temporary tables.
- ❍ D. Global temporary tables are visible to all users connected to a database.

Question 22

A user named USER1 logs on to an AIX server and connects to a database named SAMPLE that belongs to an instance named DB2INST1 by executing the following command:

```
CONNECT TO sample USER db2admin USING ibmdb2
```

After connecting to the database, user USER1 creates a table by executing this statement:

```
CREATE TABLE test_tab (col1 INTEGER, col2 CHAR (12))
```

Assuming the CREATE TABLE statement executed successfully, in which schema was the table TEST_TAB created?

- ❍ A. ROOT
- ❍ B. DB2INST1
- ❍ C. USER1
- ❍ D. DB2ADMIN

Question 23

Which statement about schema objects is false?

- ❍ A. After connecting to a new database, all users who have successfully authenticated with the server can create a new schema.
- ❍ B. Like table spaces, schemas are used to physically group and store objects in a database.
- ❍ C. If a schema is explicitly created with the CREATE SCHEMA statement, the schema owner is granted CREATEIN, DROPIN, and ALTERIN privileges on the schema, as well as the ability to grant these privileges to other users.
- ❍ D. Ownership of a schema that is explicitly created can be assigned during the creation process.

Question 24

Which statement is false regarding range clustered tables?

- ❍ A. RCTs require less buffer cache because they rely on a special index for organizing data.
- ❍ B. Storage for an RCT must be preallocated and available when the table is created.
- ❍ C. RCTs can result in significant performance advantages during query processing because fewer I/O operations are needed.
- ❍ D. RCTs are created by specifying the ORGANIZE BY KEY SEQUENCE clause in a CREATE TABLE statement.

Question 25

Which statement will create a table named PARTS that is partitioned such that rows with part numbers that fall in the range of 0 to 33 are stored in one partition that resides in one table space, rows with part numbers in the range of 34 to 66 are stored in another partition that resides in another table space, and rows with part numbers in the range of 67 to 99 are stored in a third partition that resides in a third table space?

❍ A.
```
CREATE TABLE parts (partno INT, desc VARCHAR (25))
IN tbsp0, tbsp1, tbsp2
PARTITION BY (partno NULLS FIRST)
(STARTING 0 ENDING 33,
STARTING 34 ENDING 66,
STARTING 67 ENDING 99)
```

❍ B.
```
CREATE TABLE parts (partno INT, desc VARCHAR (25))
PARTITION BY (partno NULLS FIRST)
(PART part0 STARTING  0 ENDING 33,
PART part1 STARTING 34 ENDING 66,
PART part2 STARTING 67 ENDING 99)
```

❍ C.
```
CREATE TABLE parts (partno INT, desc VARCHAR (25))
PARTITION BY (partno NULLS FIRST
(STARTING 0 ENDING 33,
STARTING 34 ENDING 66,
STARTING 67 ENDING 99)
IN tbsp0, tbsp1, tbsp2)
```

❍ D.
```
CREATE TABLE parts (partno INT, desc VARCHAR(25))
PARTITION BY (partno NULLS FIRST)
(STARTING 0 ENDING 33 IN tbsp0,
STARTING 34 ENDING 66 IN tbsp1,
STARTING 67 ENDING 99 IN tbsp2)
```

Question 26

If you execute these statements in the following order:

```
CREATE TABLE sales
    (invoice_no    INTEGER,
     sales_date     DATE,
     sales_amt      NUMERIC(5,2))
    IN tbsp0, tbsp1, tbsp2, tbsp3
    PARTITION BY RANGE (sales_date NULLS FIRST)
        (STARTING '1/1/2014' ENDING '12/31/2014'
         EVERY 3 MONTHS);

CREATE INDEX sales_idx ON sales (invoice_no);
```

Which table spaces will contain the data for the SALES_IDX index?

- ❍ A. TBSP0
- ❍ B. TBSP1
- ❍ C. TBSP2
- ❍ D. TBSP0, TBSP1, TBSP2, TBSP3

Question 27

If you execute these statements in the following order:

```
CREATE TABLE sales
    (invoice_no    INTEGER,
     sales_date     DATE,
     sales_amt      NUMERIC(5,2))
    IN tbsp0, tbsp1, tbsp2, tbsp3
    PARTITION BY RANGE (sales_date NULLS FIRST)
        (STARTING '1/1/2014' ENDING '12/31/2014'
         EVERY 3 MONTHS);

CREATE INDEX sales_idx ON sales (invoice_no) PARTITIONED;
```

Which table spaces will contain the data for the SALES_IDX index?

- ❍ A. TBSP3
- ❍ B. TBSP2
- ❍ C. TBSP1
- ❍ D. TBSP0, TBSP1, TBSP2, TBSP3

Question 28

A partitioned table named SALES was created as follows:

```
CREATE TABLE sales
    (invoice_no    INTEGER,
     sales_date     DATE,
     sales_amt      NUMERIC(5,2))
     INDEX IN tbsp3
    PARTITION BY RANGE (sales_date NULLS FIRST)
        (STARTING FROM '1/1/2014' ENDING AT '3/31/2014' IN TBSP0,
         STARTING FROM '4/1/2014' ENDING AT '6/30/2014' IN TBSP1,
   STARTING FROM '7/1/2014' ENDING AT '9/30/2014' IN TBSP2,
         STARTING FROM '10/1/2014' ENDING AT '12/31/2014' IN TBSP3);

CREATE INDEX sales_idx ON sales (invoice_no) NOT PARTITIONED;
```

Which statement about the SALES_IDX index is true?

- ❍ A. The index SALES_IDX will be a nonpartitioned index and will be stored in table space TBSP3.
- ❍ B. The index SALES_IDX will be a nonpartitioned index and will be stored in table space TBSP0.
- ❍ C. The index SALES_IDX will contain four partitions, and all four partitions will be stored in table space TBSP0.
- ❍ D. The index SALES_IDX will contain four partitions; the first partition will be stored in table space TBSP0, the second in TBSP1, the third in TBSP2, and the fourth in TBSP3.

Question 29

A partitioned table named SALES was created as follows:

```
CREATE TABLE sales
    (invoice_no    INTEGER,
     sales_date     DATE,
     sales_amt      NUMERIC(5,2))
     INDEX IN tbsp3
    PARTITION BY RANGE (sales_date NULLS FIRST)
        (STARTING FROM '1/1/2014' ENDING AT '3/31/2014' IN TBSP0,
         STARTING FROM '4/1/2014' ENDING AT '6/30/2014' IN TBSP1,
         STARTING FROM '7/1/2014' ENDING AT '9/30/2014' IN TBSP2,
         STARTING FROM '10/1/2014' ENDING AT '12/31/2014' IN TBSP3);

CREATE INDEX sales_idx ON sales (invoice_no);
```

Which statement about the SALES_IDX index is true?

❍ A. The index SALES_IDX will be a nonpartitioned index and will be stored in table space TBSP3.

❍ B. The index SALES_IDX will be a nonpartitioned index and will be stored in table space TBSP0.

❍ C. The index SALES_IDX will contain four partitions, and all four partitions will be stored in table space TBSP0.

❍ D. The index SALES_IDX will contain four partitions; the first partition will be stored in table space TBSP0, the second in TBSP1, the third in TBSP2, and the fourth in TBSP3.

Question 30

When you use an ALTER TABLE ... DETACH operation to detach a data partition from a partitioned table, at what point does the newly detached data partition become accessible as a standalone table?

❍ A. After a SET INTEGRITY command is executed

❍ B. After the ALTER TABLE ... ATTACH to another table

❍ C. Immediately after the ALTER TABLE ... DETACH statement is executed

❍ D. Immediately after asynchronous index cleanup processing is completed for the data partition in the detach operation

Question 31

Which DB2 registry variable should you set to specify that 20 percent of each index page is to be left as free space when an index is built in the database?

- ❍ A. DB2_INDEX_FREE
- ❍ B. DB2_INDEX_PCTFREE_DEFAULT
- ❍ C. DB2_PARTITIONEDLOAD_DEFAULT
- ❍ D. DB2_ENABLE_AUTOCONFIG_DEFAULT

Question 32

If you execute the following statement:

```
CREATE TABLE sales_mdc
    (invoice_no       INTEGER,
     sales_date       DATE,
     sales_amt        NUMERIC(5,2),
     region           VARCHAR(10))
ORGANIZE BY DIMENSIONS (sales_date,region)
```

What indexes will be created for table SALES_MDC?

- ❍ A. One dimension-block index and one composite-block index
- ❍ B. One dimension-block index and two composite-block indexes
- ❍ C. Two dimension-block indexes and one composite-block index
- ❍ D. Two dimension-block indexes and two composite-block indexes

Question 33

Which statement about RCTs is true?

- ❍ A. RCTs can be used with the REORG utility.
- ❍ B. RCTs can be used with multiple-column keys.
- ❍ C. RCTs can be range partitioned tables.
- ❍ D. RCTs can be used with row compression.

Question 34

Which table type is *not* supported by the Load utility?

- ❍ A. Temporal tables
- ❍ B. Range partitioned tables
- ❍ C. Global temporary tables
- ❍ D. Multidimensional clustering tables

Question 35

Which statement is correct when describing RCTs as compared with regular base tables?

- ❍ A. RCTs require less logging, less buffer pool space, and less maintenance.
- ❍ B. RCTs require more logging, less buffer pool space, and more maintenance.
- ❍ C. RCTs require less logging, more buffer pool space, and no maintenance.
- ❍ D. RCTs require more logging, more buffer pool space, and no maintenance.

Question 36

Which statement about insert time clustering tables (ITCs) is true?

- ❍ A. ITC tables cannot be range partitioned tables.
- ❍ B. ITC table records are clustered based only on timestamp columns.
- ❍ C. The records in the ITC table are clustered according to the time they are inserted into the table.
- ❍ D. ITC table records are clustered based on a cluster index created on the timestamp column.

Question 37

If you execute these commands in the following order:

```
CREATE TABLE sales
    ( CUSTOMER          VARCHAR (80),
      SALES_AMOUNT      INTEGER,
      REGION            CHAR (5),
      YEAR              INTEGER,
      Volume            INTEGER,
      PERIOD            INTEGER,
      REC_LOAD_DT       TIMESTAMP )
ORGANIZE BY DIMENSIONS (CUSTOMER, REGION, YEAR);

CREATE TABLE sales_mqt AS
(SELECT SUM (SALES_AMOUNT) AS TOTAL_SUM, REGION
   FROM sales
   GROUP BY REGION)
   DATA INITIALLY DEFERRED REFRESH DEFERRED
   MAINTAINED BY SYSTEM;

SET INTEGRITY FOR SALES_MQT IMMEDIATE CHECKED;

REFRESH TABLE sales_mqt;
```

Which statement is true about MQT?

❍ A. The DML operations performed against the SALES table are automatically cascaded to the MQT table SALES_MQT.

❍ B. The DML operations performed against the SALES table are cascaded to the MQT table SALES_MQT only after a REFRESH TABLE command is executed.

❍ C. The SET INTEGRITY and REFRESH commands are not necessary to cascade the data from the base MDC table to the MQT.

❍ D. The MQT creation fails with error SQL20058N and reason code 8.

Question 38

Which statement about ITC tables is false?

❍ A. ITC tables can be compressed by using adaptive compression.

❍ B. Existing MDC tables can be easily converted to ITC tables.

❍ C. ITC tables can be created by using the CREATE TABLE ... ORGANIZE BY INSERT TIME command.

❍ D. ITC tables use block-based allocation and create dimension-block indexes on the implicit timestamp column.

Question 39

If you execute the following CREATE INDEX statements:

```
CREATE INDEX cust_zip_idx ON customer(custinfo)
GENERATE KEY
USING XMLPATTERN '/customerinfo/addr/zip-pcode'
AS SQL DOUBLE;

CREATE INDEX cust_city_idx ON customer(custinfo)
GENERATE KEY
USING XMLPATTERN '/customerinfo/addr/city'
AS SQL VARCHAR (40);
```

And you insert these XML documents into the CUSTOMER table:

```
<?xml version="1.0" encoding="UTF-8" ?>
<customerinfo xmlns="http://crecord.dat" id="1000">
  <name>John Doe</name>
  <addr country="United States">
    <street>25 East Creek Drive</street>
    <city>Raleigh</city>
    <state-prov>North Carolina</state-prov>
    <zip-pcode>27603</zip-pcode>
  </addr>
  <phone type="work">919-555-1212</phone>
  <email>john.doe@yahoo.com</email>
</customerinfo>

<?xml version="1.0" encoding="UTF-8" ?>
<customerinfo xmlns="http://crecord.dat" id="1010">
  <name>Jane Smith</name>
  <addr country="United States">
    <street>2120 Stewart Street</street>
    <city></city>
    <state-prov>South Carolina</state-prov>
    <zip-pcode>29501</zip-pcode>
  </addr>
  <phone type="work">843-555-3434</phone>
  <email>jane.smith@aol.com</email>
</customerinfo>
```

How many index keys will be generated?

❍ A. 1
❍ B. 2
❍ C. 3
❍ D. 4

Question 40

Which statement about XML indexes is true?

- ❍ A. XML indexes can contain relational data columns.
- ❍ B. An index over XML data can be used to improve the efficiency of XQuery expressions performed against XML columns.
- ❍ C. Unique XML indexes can be created by combining multiple XML columns.
- ❍ D. The entire contents of an XML document stored in an XML column are indexed.

Question 41

Which of the following must exist in order to use data row compression with a table?

- ❍ A. A compression index
- ❍ B. A compression dictionary
- ❍ C. A user-defined compression algorithm
- ❍ D. A table that contains only character data type columns

Question 42

Which statement is *not* valid regarding classic row compression?

- ❍ A. Data row compression can lead to disk I/O savings and improved buffer pool hit ratios.
- ❍ B. Compressing data at the row level is advantageous because it allows repeating patterns that span multiple columns within a row to be replaced with shorter symbols.
- ❍ C. Data row compression for a table can be enabled by executing the ALTER TABLE statement with the COMPRESS YES STATIC option specified.
- ❍ D. Only data in a table enabled for data row compression is compressed; data in corresponding indexes and transaction logs is not compressed.

Question 43

Which two utilities can you use to create a compression dictionary?

- ❒ A. reorg
- ❒ B. db2pd
- ❒ C. inspect
- ❒ D. runstats
- ❒ E. db2buildcd

Question 44

Which option can you use with the REORG command to construct a new compression dictionary before compressing data stored in a table?

- ❍ A. KEEPDICTIONARY
- ❍ B. RESETDICTIONARY
- ❍ C. GENERATEDICTIONARY
- ❍ D. NEWDICTIONARY

Question 45

Which two statements regarding the system-period temporal table are true when you create the history table by using the WITH RESTRICT ON DROP clause?

- ❒ A. When querying the time-period specification, only the history table is necessary.
- ❒ B. When querying the time-period specification, both the history table and the base temporal table are necessary.
- ❒ C. The history table can contain referential integrity constraints.
- ❒ D. The history table will be dropped automatically when the base temporal table is dropped.
- ❒ E. The history table will not be dropped automatically when the base temporal table is dropped.

Question 46

Which statement is true regarding temporary table compression?

- ❍ A. Temporary tables are automatically compressed using adaptive compression.
- ❍ B. Temporary tables are automatically compressed using static (classic) row compression.
- ❍ C. Users can run the ALTER TABLE ... COMPRESS YES command to compress temporary tables.
- ❍ D. The DB2 Optimizer determines which compression algorithm to use to compress temporary table based on the volume of data present.

Question 47

Which statement is true regarding adaptive row compression?

- ❍ A. Adaptive compression compresses temporary tables.
- ❍ B. Adaptive compression compresses data both at table level and at page level.
- ❍ C. Adaptive compression compresses tables and transaction logs.
- ❍ D. Adaptive compression compresses tables, indexes, transaction logs, table spaces, and database backups.

Question 48

Which statement enables index compression on table EMPLOYEE?

- ❍ A. ALTER TABLE employee COMPRESS YES ADAPTIVE
- ❍ B. ALTER TABLE employee COMPRESS TABLE AND INDEX YES
- ❍ C. ALTER TABLE employee COMPRESS ALL INDEXES
- ❍ D. ALTER TABLE employee COMPRESS ONLY INDEXES

Question 49

If you create table EMPLOYEE as follows:

```
CREATE TABLE employee
    (ID         INT,
     NAME       VARCHAR (20),
     CITY       VARCHAR (15),
     CONTACT_NO VARCHAR (15))
COMPRESS YES ADAPTIVE;
```

Which statement creates an index on the column ID of table EMPLOYEE that is enabled for compression?

- ❍ A. CREATE INDEX ix1_employee ON employee(ID);
- ❍ B. CREATE INDEX ix1_employee ON employee(ID); INDEX ix1_employee COMPRESS YES;
- ❍ C. CREATE INDEX ix1_employee ON employee(ID) COMPRESS NO;
- ❍ D. CREATE INDEX ix1_employee ON employee(ID); ALTER INDEX ix1_employee COMPRESS NO; REORG INDEX ix1_employee FOR TABLE employee;

Question 50

Which statement should you use to turn off row compression on table EMPLOYEE?

- ❍ A. ALTER TABLE employee COMPRESS NO; REORG TABLE employee;
- ❍ B. ALTER TABLE employee COMPRESS OFF; REORG TABLE employee;
- ❍ C. ALTER TABLE employee COMPRESS NO; RUNSTATS ON TABLE employee;
- ❍ D. ALTER TABLE employee COMPRESS OFF; RUNSTATS ON TABLE employee;

Answers

Question 1

The correct answer is **B**. Information about every DB2 database created is stored in a special hierarchical directory tree. Where this directory tree is actually created is determined by information you provide with the CREATE DATABASE command. If you provide no location information, this directory tree is created in the location specified by the DFTDBPATH DB2 database manager configuration parameter associated with the instance under which the database is being created.

The root directory of this hierarchical tree is assigned the name of the instance associated with the database. This directory will contain a subdirectory that has been assigned a name corresponding to the partition's node. If the database is a partitioned database, this directory will be named NODE*xxxx*, where *xxxx* is the unique node number that has been assigned to the partition; if the database is a nonpartitioned database, this directory will be named NODE0000. The node-name directory, in turn, will contain one subdirectory for each database that has been created, along with one subdirectory that includes the containers that will hold the database's data.

The name you assign to the subdirectory that holds the containers where the database's data resides is the same as that specified for the database; the name you assign to the subdirectory that contains the base files for the database corresponds to the database token that is assigned to the database during the creation process (the subdirectory for the first database created will be named SQL00001, the subdirectory for the second database will be named SQL00002, and so on).

Question 2

The correct answer is **C**. Whenever you create a new DB2 10.1 database, the following features are enabled by default:

- Automatic maintenance (database backups, table and index reorganization, data access optimization, and statistics profiling)
- Self-tuning memory manager (package cache, locking memory, sort memory, database shared memory, and buffer pool memory)
- Utility throttling

Question 3

The correct answer is **A**. Whenever you create a new database, by default the following authorities and privileges are granted automatically:

- DBADM authority along with CONNECT, CREATETAB, BINDADD, CREATE_NOT_FENCED, IMPLICIT_SCHEMA, and LOAD privilege are granted to the user who created the database.
- USE privilege on the table space USERSPACE1 is granted to the group PUBLIC.
- CONNECT, CREATETAB, BINDADD, and IMPLICIT_SCHEMA privileges are granted to the group PUBLIC.
- SELECT privilege on each system catalog table is granted to the group PUBLIC.
- EXECUTE privilege on all procedures in the SYSIBM schema is granted to the group PUBLIC.

- EXECUTE WITH GRANT privilege on all functions in the SYSFUN schema is granted to the group PUBLIC.
- BIND and EXECUTE privileges for each successfully bound utility are granted to the group PUBLIC.

However, if you specify the RESTRICTIVE clause with the CREATE DATABASE command, privileges are granted only to the database creator—no privileges are granted to the group PUBLIC.

Question 4

The correct answer is **D**. Automatic storage is enabled by default, and the storage paths /data/db2fs1 and /data/db2fs2 will hold table space containers used by automatic storage. And because no database path was specified, the metadata files associated with the database will be stored in the first storage path indicated as /data/db2fs1.

Question 5

The correct answer is **A**. On the Windows platform, the database path must be a drive letter only. If you want to specify a directory along with the drive letter, you must set the registry variable DB2_CREATE_DB_ON_PATH to YES. There is no database configuration parameter to set the default database path (this is a database manager configuration parameter). The DB2 registry variable DB2_OVERRIDE_BPF is often used to limit the size of the buffer pool during restore times. The DB2 registry variable DB2LIBPATH is frequently used to add a data client library during the federation setup.

Question 6

The correct answer is **B**. You can convert an existing nonautomatic storage database to use automatic storage by using the CREATE STOGROUP command:

```
CREATE STOGROUP sg_sample ON '/data/db2fs'
DB20000I  The SQL command completed successfully.
```

Dropping and re-creating the database on DB2 10.1 obviously creates an automatic storage database; however, you will lose the previously stored data, so this is not a wise step to follow. If you set the DB2 registry variable DB2_ENABLE_AUTOCONFIG_DEFAULT to YES, the DB2 database manager automatically invokes the Configuration Advisor after creating the database. The command ALTER DATABASE ... ADD STORAGE was available in DB2 9.7 and is deprecated in DB2 10.1.

Question 7

The correct answer is **C**. You cannot add more containers to an SMS table space (by using the ALTER TABLESPACE SQL statement) once the table space has been created. However, you can add more containers to a DMS table space after it has been created. When you add new containers, existing data can automatically be rebalanced across the new set of containers to retain optimal I/O efficiency.

Question 8

The correct answer is **D**. In DB2, the initial allocation of space for an object in a DMS table space is two extents; the initial allocation of space for an object in an SMS table space is one extent. In this example, one extent comprises thirty-two 8 KB pages or 256 KB (8 KB x 32 = 256 KB).

Question 9

The correct answers are **B** and **D**. You can obtain information about all table spaces that have been created for a particular database by executing the LIST TABLESPACES command. The syntax for this command is:

```
LIST TABLESPACES <SHOW DETAIL>
```

You can also obtain detailed information about all table spaces that have been created for a particular database by using the monitoring table function:

```
SELECT * FROM TABLE (MON_GET_TABLESPACE (' ', -2)) AS TBSP
```

The rest of the option commands are syntactically incorrect or deprecated in DB2 10.1.

Question 10

The correct answer is **B**. There is no state called Online and not accessible (a contradicting state, by the way).

Question 11

The correct answer is **C**. If a database is enabled for automatic storage (which is the default behavior in DB2), container and space management characteristics of its table spaces are determined by the DB2 database manager. And, although you can use the ALTER TABLESPACE command to add new containers to existing DMS table spaces, you cannot use it to add new containers to automatic storage table spaces. To perform this type of operation, you must use the ALTER STOGROUP or CREATE STOGROUP command instead. The basic syntax for this statement is:

```
ALTER STOGROUP [StorageGroupName] ADD '[StoragePath]' OR
  CREATE STOGROUP [StorageGroupName] ON '[StoragePath]'
```

Question 12

The correct answer is **A**. DMS table spaces consist of file containers or raw device containers, and their sizes are set when the containers are assigned to the table space. A table space is considered full when all of the space within the containers has been used. However, with DMS table spaces, you can add or extend containers by using the ALTER TABLESPACE statement to provide more storage space to a given table space.

DMS table spaces also have a feature called *autoresize*. As space is consumed in a DMS table space that can be automatically resized, the DB2 database manager can automatically extend one or more file containers associated with the table space. (SMS table spaces have similar capabilities for growing automatically, but the term *autoresize* is used exclusively for DMS.) You enable the autoresize feature of a DMS table space by specifying the AUTORESIZE YES option with the CREATE TABLESPACE statement that you use to create the table space. For example, you can use the following CREATE TABLESPACE statement to create an autoresized DMS table space:

```
CREATE TABLESPACE tbsp1 MANAGED BY DATABASE
     USING (FILE '/db2files/data1.dat' 10 M) AUTORESIZE YES
```

You can also enable the autoresize feature after a DMS table space has been created by executing the ALTER TABLESPACE statement with the AUTORESIZE YES option specified. For example:

```
ALTER TABLESPACE tbsp1 AUTORESIZE YES
```

Question 13

The correct answer is **C**. If a database is enabled for automatic storage, you can specify the MANAGED BY AUTOMATIC STORAGE clause with the CREATE TABLESPACE command to create an automatic storage table space (or you can omit this clause completely; in which case, automatic storage is implied). No container definitions are provided in this case because the DB2 database manager assigns the containers automatically.

Although automatic storage table spaces appear to be a different table space type, they are really just an extension of the existing SMS and DMS types. If the table space being created is a REGULAR or LARGE table space, it is created as a DMS with file containers. If the table space being created is a USER or SYSTEM TEMPORARY table space, it is created as a SMS with directory containers.

Question 14

The correct answer is **A**. You can convert a nonautomatic storage database to automatic storage by creating a storage group or by adding a storage path to the default storage group IBMSTOGROUP. You can then convert the table space to use automatic storage by executing the following command:

```
ALTER TABLESPACE TS_DMS_DATA MANAGED BY
AUTOMATIC STORAGE USING STOGROUP SG_HOT
DB20000I  The SQL command completed successfully.
```

To move the content from the old container to the new automatic storage path, use the REBALANCE command:

```
ALTER TABLESPACE TS_DMS_DATA REBALANCE
DB20000I  The SQL command completed successfully.
```

Question 15

The correct answer is **D**. You can use the ALTER TABLESPACE command to convert a DMS table space to automatic storage table space. A sample command looks something like this:

```
ALTER TABLESPACE TS_DMS_DATA MANAGED BY
AUTOMATIC STORAGE USING STOGROUP SG_HOT
DB20000I  The SQL command completed successfully.
```

Question 16

The correct answer is **D**. Only the automatic storage space table spaces can use storage groups. You can create multiple table spaces on a storage group; however, a table space should use only one storage group. The storage groups manage data based on the temperature by using the multi-temperature storage feature.

Question 17

The correct answer is **D**. When you create a database, it creates three table spaces:

- A regular table space named SYSCATSPACE, which stores the system catalog tables and views associated with the database
- A regular table space named USERSPACE1, which stores all user-defined objects (such as tables, indexes, and so on) along with user data, index data, and long value data
- A system temporary table space named TEMPSPACE1, which is a temporary storage area for operations such as sorting data, reorganizing tables, and creating indexes

Question 18

The correct answer is **D**. You can use the ADMIN_MOVE_TABLE procedure to move tables online without affecting the availability of the data. Using the db2relocatedb command will rename a database or relocate a database from one location to another. The db2move utility copies data from one table to another or from one schema to another. The ADMIN_MOVE_TABLE_UTIL works in conjunction with ADMIN_MOVE_TABLE by providing a mechanism to alter the user-defined values in ADMIN_MOVE_TABLE protocol table.

Question 19

The correct answer is **B**. When you move a table space from an old storage group to a new storage group or you drop an available storage path, the DB2 database manager does a reverse rebalance operation while moving the data from old to the new. When storage paths are in the Drop Pending state, the database manager performs a reverse rebalance, where movement of extents starts from the high watermark extent (the last possible extent containing data in the table space) and ends with extent 0.

You will see a table space with the "Storage must be defined" state while performing the redirect restore operation if you omit the set table space containers phase or specify an invalid path. The rest of the states are invalid states in DB2.

Question 20

The correct answer is **A**. You can use the ALTER TABLESPACE command to move the table spaces online from one storage group to another. The command looks something like this:

```
ALTER TABLESPACE tbsp1 USING STOGROUP sg_warm
DB20000I  The SQL command completed successfully.
```

You can also drop the current table space TBSP1 and re-create it on the specified storage group. However, you will lose the data present in the current TBSP1 table space. The commands ALTER DATABASE ... MOVE and ALTER TABLESPACE ... MOVE do not exist.

Question 21

The correct answer is **D**. A declared temporary table is a special table that holds temporary data on behalf of a single application. As with base tables, you can create indexes on and collect statistics for declared temporary tables. Unlike base tables, whose descriptions and constraints are stored in the system catalog tables of the database to which they belong, declared temporary tables are not persistent and can only be used by the application that creates them—and only for the life of the application. When the application that creates a declared temporary table terminates, the rows of the table are deleted, and the description of the table is dropped. (However, data stored in a temporary table can exist across transaction boundaries.)

Another significant difference focuses on where the data for each type of table is stored. Before an application can create and use a declared temporary table, a user must create at least one user temporary table space for the database the application will be working with, and the privileges needed to use that table space must be granted to the appropriate users. (User temporary table spaces are not created by default when a database is created.) Base tables, however, are created in regular table spaces. If you specify no table space when you create a base table, its data is stored in the table space USERSPACE1, which is created by default when you create a database.

Question 22

The correct answer is **D**. If you specify no schema or qualifier name when you create an object, that object is assigned to the default schema, which is usually the user ID of the individual who is currently connected to the database and is creating the object. In this example, the default schema is DB2ADMIN because the user ID was used to establish the database connection and to create the TEST_TAB table object.

Question 23

The correct answer is **B**. While table spaces physically store objects in a database, schemas logically classify and group other objects in the database, regardless of where they are physically stored.

Question 24

The correct answer is **A**. RCTs require less cache buffer allocation because there are no secondary objects to maintain. Indexes are not required nor are they supported.

Question 25

The correct answer is **D**. Data from a given table is partitioned into multiple storage objects based on the specifications you provide in the `PARTITION BY` clause of the `CREATE TABLE` statement. Thus, if you want to create a table named `DEPARTMENTS` that is partitioned such that rows with numerical values that fall in the range of 0 to 9 are stored in one partition that resides in one table space, rows with numerical values that fall in the range of 10 to 19 are stored in another partition that resides in another table space, and so on, you can do so by executing a `CREATE TABLE` SQL statement that looks something like this:

```
CREATE TABLE departments
    (dept_no   INT,
     desc      CHAR(3))
    PARTITION BY (dept_no NULLS FIRST)
        (STARTING  0 ENDING  9 IN tbsp0,
         STARTING 10 ENDING 19 IN tbsp1,
         STARTING 20 ENDING 29 IN tbsp2,
         STARTING 30 ENDING 39 IN tbsp3)
```

Question 26

The correct answer is **D**. By default, DB2 creates partitioned indexes. A partitioned index comprises a set of index partitions, each of which includes the index entries for a single data partition. Each index partition contains references only to data in its corresponding data partition.

Question 27

The correct answer is **D**. By default, DB2 creates partitioned indexes; however, you can specify the keyword `PARTITIONED` in the index creation command. A partitioned index consists of a set of index partitions, each of which includes the index entries for a single data partition. Each index partition contains references only to data in its corresponding data partition.

Question 28

The correct answer is **A**. By default, DB2 creates partitioned indexes; however, you can specify the keyword NOT PARTITIONED in the index creation command to store all the index keys in one table space. In this example, you specified the INDEX IN clause in the CREATE TABLE command, so all the index keys are stored in TBSP3.

Question 29

The correct answer is **D**. Even though you specified the INDEX IN clause in the CREATE TABLE command, the keyword NOT PARTITIONED or PARTITIONED takes priority. In this case, the default clause is PARTITIONED in the CREATE INDEX command, so the indexes are stored in their respective data table spaces.

Question 30

The correct answer is **D**. The data partition being detached is converted into a standalone table in the following two-phase process:

- The ALTER TABLE...DETACH PARTITION operation logically detaches the data partition from the partitioned table.
- An asynchronous partition detach (index cleanup) task converts the logically detached partition into a standalone table.

Question 31

The correct answer is **B**. You can use the DB2_INDEX_PCTFREE_DEFAULT registry variable to specify the percentage of each index page to leave as free space when building the index. The registry variable DB2_INDEX_FREE had functionality similar to DB2_INDEX_PCTFREE_DEFAULT; however, it is deprecated. The DB2_PARTITIONEDLOAD_DEFAULT registry variable lets you change the default behavior of the Load utility in an ESE environment when no ESE-specific load options are specified. The default value is YES, which indicates that in an ESE environment, if you do not specify ESE-specific load options, loading is attempted on all database partitions on which the target table is defined. When the value is NO, loading is attempted only on the database partition to which the Load utility is currently connected. If you set the DB2 registry variable DB2_ENABLE_AUTOCONFIG_DEFAULT to YES, the DB2 database manager automatically invokes the Configuration Advisor after creating the database.

Question 32

The correct answer is **C**. When you create an MDC table, you specify the dimensional key (or keys) along which to cluster the table's data. You can define each of the specified dimensions with one or more columns, the same as an index key. A dimension block index will be automatically created for each of the dimensions specified, and will be used to quickly and efficiently access data along each of the specified dimensions. The dimension blocks indexes point to extents instead of individual rows and are thus much smaller than regular indexes. These dimension block indexes can very quickly access only those extents of the table that contains particular dimension values. In addition, a block index will also be automatically created, containing all dimension key columns. The block index will maintain the clustering of the data during insert and update activity as well as provide quick and efficient access to the data.

A composite block index containing all dimension key columns is also created automatically. The composite block index maintains the clustering of data during insert and update activity. The composite block index is also used in query processing to access data in the table having particular dimension values.

Question 33

The correct answer is **B**. The RCT restrictions are as follows:

- RCT cannot be used in a pureScale environment.
- A partitioned table cannot be an RCT.
- Declared and created temporary tables cannot be RCTs.
- Automatic summary tables cannot be RCTs.
- The `LOAD` command is not supported.
- The `REORG` command is not supported.
- MDC and clustering indexes are not compatible with RCTs.
- Compression is not supported.
- Reverse scans on RCTs are not supported.
- The `IMPORT` command's `REPLACE` parameter is not supported.
- The `WITH EMPTY TABLE` clause is not supported on the `ALTER TABLE ... ACTIVATE NOT LOGGED INITIALLY` command.

Question 34

The correct answer is **C**. Declared global temporary tables are subject to some restrictions that do not apply to regular base tables. One restriction is that you cannot use the `IMPORT` and `LOAD` utilities to populate these tables.

Question 35

The correct answer is **A**. RCTs can result in significant performance advantages during query processing because fewer I/O operations are required. Additionally, RCTs require less cache buffer allocation because there are no secondary objects to maintain; indexes are not required nor are they supported.

Question 36

The correct answer is **C**. ITC tables provide an effective way of maintaining data clustering based on the insert time with easier space management. The characteristics of ITC tables are as follows:

- ITC table records are clustered based on their insert time.
- ITC tables have similar characteristics to MDC tables—they use block-based data allocation and a dimension block index. However, the data organization scheme is based on an implicitly created virtual dimension (record insert time) instead of explicitly stated dimension columns.
- ITC tables are created by using the `CREATE TABLE ... ORGANIZE BY INSERT TIME` clause.
- ITC tables' space reclamation can be done by executing the `REORG TABLE ... RECLAIM EXTENTS` command.
- ITC tables can be range partitioned tables.

Question 37

The correct answer is **B**. `DATA INITIALLY DEFERRED REFRESH DEFERRED` requires the `REFRESH TABLE` command to be executed to populate the MQT table from the base table.

Question 38

The correct answer is **B**. There is no straightforward command to convert an ITC table into a MDC table. You must identify the dimension columns, create an MDC table with the identified dimension columns, and then copy the data from the ITC table to the MDC table.

Question 39

The correct answer is **C**. When the documents specified are inserted into the `CUSTINFO` column of the `CUSTOMER` table, the values `27603` and `29501` will be added to the `CUST_ZIP_IDX` index and the value `Raleigh` will be added to the `CUST_CITY_IDX` index.

Question 40

The correct answer is **B**. Just as you can use an index over relational data to improve query performance, you can use an index over XML data to improve the efficiency of queries on XML documents that are stored in an XML column. In contrast to traditional relational indexes, where index keys consist of one or more columns you specify, an index over XML data uses a particular XML pattern expression to index paths and values found in XML documents stored in a single column—the data type of that column must be XML. All or part of the contents of an XML column can be indexed.

Question 41

The correct answer is **B**. To use data row compression with a table, you must satisfy two prerequisites:

- Compression must be enabled at the table level.
- A compression dictionary for the table must be built.

Question 42

The correct answer is **D**. Index data is also compressed when you enable compression on a table. However, because records in a compressed table are moved between storage and memory in compressed form (the compression dictionary is moved into memory as well so decompression can take place), records for compressed tables that are written to transaction log files will be compressed as well. To enable transaction log compression, use the `LOGARCHCOMPR1` and `LOGARCHCOMPR2` database configuration parameters.

Question 43

The correct answers are **A** and **C**. Although you can enable a table for data row compression at any time by setting its `COMPRESS` attribute to `YES`, you can force data stored in the table to create the compression dictionary by using the `REORG` and `INSPECT` commands.

Question 44

The correct answer is **B**. You can force a compression dictionary to build (and compress data in a table) by performing an offline table reorganization operation. You initiate such an operation by executing the `REORG` command with either the `KEEPDICTIONARY` or the `RESETDICTIONARY` option specified. If you execute the `REORG` command with either option specified and a compression dictionary does not exist, a new dictionary will be built. However, if you execute the `REORG` command with either option specified and a dictionary already exists, data in the table will be reorganized and compressed, and the existing dictionary will either be re-created (`RESETDICTIONARY`) or left as it is (`KEEPDICTIONARY`).

Question 45

The correct answers are **B** and **E**. When querying the time-period specification, you need both the base temporal table and its associated history table. Likewise, when you create a history table and specify the `WITH RESTRICT ON DROP` clause, the history table will not be dropped when the base temporal table is dropped. Otherwise, both the temporal and history tables will be dropped in a single `DROP TABLE` command.

Question 46

The correct answer is **B**. The temporary tables are always compressed by using the static row compression algorithm. Users cannot decide which tables are to be compressed and which are not.

Question 47

The correct answer is **B**. Adaptive row compression relies on a compression dictionary built at page level and compresses patterns within the page that are not part of the static dictionary.

Question 48

The correct answer is **A**. When you enable a table for compression, all the associated indexes are compressed by default. If you do not want to compress a specific index, specify the `COMPRESS NO` clause in the `CREATE INDEX` command.

Question 49

The correct answer is **A**. When you create a table with compression enabled, all the associated indexes will be compressed by default. So the index create command `CREATE INDEX ix1_employee ON employee (ID)` will inherit the index compression feature. If you do not want to compress a specific index, specify the `COMPRESS NO` clause in the `CREATE INDEX` command.

Question 50

The correct answer is **A**. To deactivate compression for a table, or to change from one type of row compression to another, issue an `ALTER TABLE` statement and perform an offline table reorganization by using the `REORG TABLE` command.

CHAPTER 4

Business Rules Implementation

This chapter will introduce you to the business rules that are used every day to define entities, attributes, relationships, and constraints at the database layer, instead of having them at the application layer. It will also contain topics that introduce you to the key system catalog tables, which describe the physical and logical structure of the data.

Exam Objectives

- Demonstrate the ability to understand various constraints and identify when and how to use NOT NULL constraints, DEFAULT constraints, CHECK constraints, UNIQUE constraints, referential integrity constraints, and informational constraints
- Demonstrate the ability to create base tables that contain one or more constraints
- Demonstrate the ability to identify how operations performed on the parent table of a referential integrity constraint are reflected in the child table of the constraint
- Demonstrate the ability to create and use triggers
- Demonstrate the ability use the SET INTEGRITY command
- Demonstrate the ability to examine the contents of the system catalog tables

Business Rules

A business rule is a statement that defines or constrains some characteristics of the business. According to the Business Rules Group (*www.businessrulesgroup.org*) organization, a business rule can belong to one of the following:

- Definitions of business terms (entity rules). An entity is a collection of information about things that are important to the business and worthy of capture. A business term has a specific meaning for a business in some designated context. This describes how people think about things and categorizes them based on behavior and dependency.
- Facts that relate terms to each other (relationship and cardinality rules). These express relationships between terms and define behaviors in specific situations.
- Constraints. Every organization constrains behavior in one way or another to prevent an action from taking place.
- Derivations. These define how organizations can transform knowledge in one form into another to derive facts or inferences.

This section focuses on the constraint rules. As in most businesses, data often must adhere to a certain set of rules and restrictions. For example, companies typically have a specific format and numbering sequence they use when generating purchase orders. Constraints allow you to place the logic needed to enforce such business rules directly in the database, rather than in applications that work with the database. Essentially, constraints are rules that govern how data values can be added to a table, as well as how those values can be modified once they have been added.

The following types of constraints are:

- NOT NULL
- DEFAULT
- CHECK
- UNIQUE
- Referential integrity
- Informational

Constraints are usually defined during table creation; however, constraints can also be added to existing tables by using the ALTER TABLE SQL statement.

Not Null Constraints

With DB2, you use NULL values (not to be confused with empty strings) to represent missing or unknown data or states. And by default, every column in a table will accept a NULL value. This allows you to add records to a table when not all the values that pertain to the record are known. However, at times, this behavior might be unacceptable (for example, a tax identification number might be required for every employee who works for a company). When such a situation arises, using the NOT NULL constraint can ensure that a particular column in a base table is never assigned a NULL value; once you have defined the NOT NULL constraint for a column, any operation that attempts to place a NULL value in that column will fail. Figure 4.1 illustrates how to use the NOT NULL constraint to avoid inserting a NULL value.

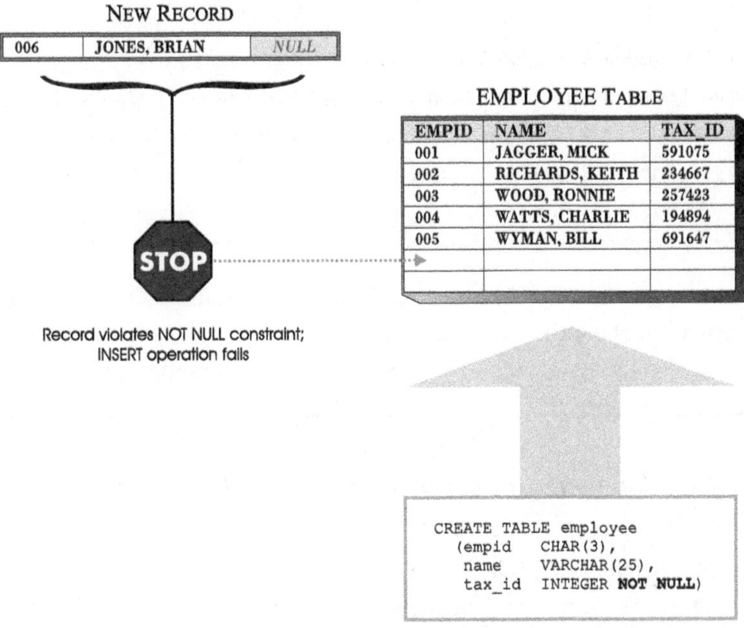

Figure 4.1: How the NOT NULL constraint prevents NULL values

Because NOT NULL constraints are associated with a specific column in a base table, they are usually defined during the table creation process or during the table alter process. The DB2 commands and the results for the above scenario are as follows:

```
CREATE TABLE employee
      (      EMPID       CHAR(3),
             NAME        VARCHAR(25),
             TAX_ID      INTEGER NOT NULL)
DB20000I The SQL command completed successfully.

INSERT INTO employee VALUES
      (001,'JAGGER, MICK', 591075),
```

Continued

```
      (002,'RICHARDS, KEITH', 234667),
      (003,'WOOD, RONNIE', 257423),
      (004,'WATTS, CHARLIE', 194894),
      (005,'WYMAN, BILL', 691647);
DB20000I The SQL command completed successfully.

INSERT INTO employee VALUES (006,'JONES, BRIAN', NULL)
DB21034E The command was processed as an SQL statement because it was not
a valid Command Line Processor command. During SQL processing it returned:
SQL0407N Assignment of a NULL value to a NOT NULL column "TBSPACEID=2, TA-
BLEID=258, COLNO=2" is not allowed. SQLSTATE=23502
```

If you are wondering what the TBSPACEID=2, TABLEID=258, and COLNO=2 are, they are all the metadata information about the table and the column in the system catalog table. You can query the system catalog tables or views by using a command something like:

```
SELECT
      VARCHAR (A.TABNAME, 10) TABNAME,
      VARCHAR (A.COLNAME, 10) COLNAME,
      A.COLNO, A.NULLS, B.TABLEID, B.TBSPACEID,
      VARCHAR (B.TBSPACE, 12) TBSPACE
   FROM SYSCAT.COLUMNS A, SYSCAT.TABLES B
   WHERE A.TABNAME=B.TABNAME AND A.COLNO=2 AND A.TABNAME='EMPLOYEE'

TABNAME    COLNAME    COLNO  NULLS TABLEID TBSPACEID TBSPACE
---------- ---------- ------ ----- ------- --------- ------------
EMPLOYEE   TAX_ID          2 N         258         2 USERSPACE1
```

Default Constraints

Just as there are times when it is objectionable to accept a NULL value, there may be times when it is desirable to have the system provide a specific value for you (for example, you might want to automatically assign the current date to a particular column whenever a new record is added to a table). In these situations, you can use the DEFAULT constraint to ensure that a particular column in a base table is assigned a predefined value (unless that value is overridden) each time a record is added to the table. The predefined value provided can be NULL (if the NOT NULL constraint has not been defined for the column), a user-supplied value compatible with the column's data type, or a value furnished by the DB2 database manager. Table 4.1 shows the default values that the DB2 database manager can provide for the various DB2 data types.

Table 4.1: DB2 default values

Column Data Type	Default Value Provided
Small integer (SMALLINT)	0
Integer (INTEGER or INT)	0
Decimal (DECIMAL, DEC, NUMERIC, or NUM)	0
Single-precision floating-point (REAL or FLOAT)	0
Double-precision floating-point (DOUBLE, DOUBLE PRECISION, or FLOAT)	0
Fixed-length character string (CHARACTER or CHAR)	A string of blank characters
Varying-length character string (CHARACTER VARYING, CHAR VARYING, or VARCHAR)	A zero-length string
Long varying-length character string (LONG VARCHAR)	A zero-length string
Fixed-length double-byte character string (GRAPHIC)	A string of blank characters
Varying-length double-byte character string (VARGRAPHIC)	A zero-length string
Long varying-length double-byte character string (LONG VARGRAPHIC)	A zero-length string
Date (DATE)	The system date at the time the record is added to the table (when a date column is added to an existing table; existing rows are assigned the date January 01, 0001)
Time (TIME)	The system time at the time the record is added to the table (when a time column is added to an existing table; existing rows are assigned the time 00:00:00)
Timestamp (TIMESTAMP)	The system date and time (including microseconds) at the time the record is added to the table (when a timestamp column is added to an existing table; existing rows are assigned a timestamp that corresponds to January 01, 0001 – 00:00:00.000000)
Binary large object (BLOB)	A zero-length string
Character large object (CLOB)	A zero-length string

Table 4.1: DB2 default values (continued)	
Column Data Type	**Default Value Provided**
Double-byte character large object (DBCLOB)	A zero-length string
XML document (XML)	Not applicable
Any distinct user-defined data type	The default value provided for the built-in data type that the distinct user-defined data type is based on (typecast to the distinct user-defined data type)
Adapted from Table 13 on page 140 of the DB2 SQL Reference, Volume 2 manual	

Figure 4.2 illustrates how to use the DEFAULT constraint to insert a default value when no data is supplied for the default column.

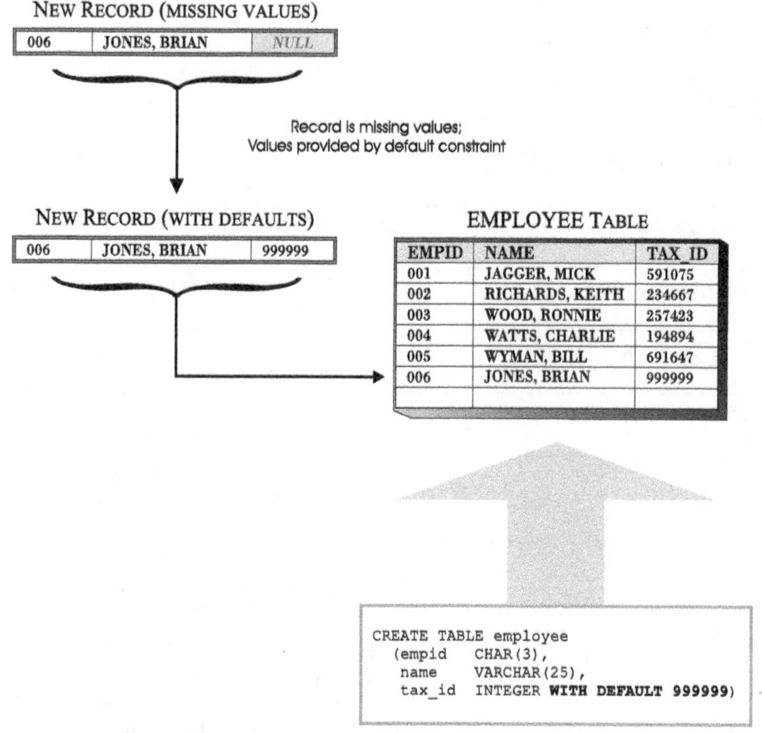

Figure 4.2: How to use the DEFAULT constraint to provide default data values

Like NOT NULL constraints, the DEFAULT constraints are associated with a specific column in a base table and are usually defined during the table creation process or changed during the table alter process.

The DB2 commands and the results for the above scenario are something like the following:

```
CREATE TABLE employee
      (     EMPID         CHAR(3),
            NAME          VARCHAR(25),
            TAX_ID        INTEGER WITH DEFAULT 999999)
DB20000I The SQL command completed successfully.

INSERT INTO employee VALUES
      (001,'JAGGER, MICK', 591075),
      (002,'RICHARDS, KEITH', 234667),
      (003,'WOOD, RONNIE', 257423),
      (004,'WATTS, CHARLIE', 194894),
      (005,'WYMAN, BILL', 691647)
DB20000I The SQL command completed successfully.

INSERT INTO employee (EMPID, NAME) VALUES (006,'JONES, BRIAN')
DB20000I  The SQL command completed successfully.

SELECT * FROM employee

EMPID NAME                      TAX_ID
----- ------------------------- -----------
1     JAGGER, MICK                   591075
2     RICHARDS, KEITH                234667
3     WOOD, RONNIE                   257423
4     WATTS, CHARLIE                 194894
5     WYMAN, BILL                    691647
6     JONES, BRIAN                   999999
```

Check Constraints

Sometimes, it is desirable to control which values will be accepted for a particular item and which values will not (for example, a company might decide that all nonexempt employees must be paid, at a minimum, the federal minimum wage). When this is the case, you can directly incorporate the logic needed to determine whether a value is acceptable into the data-entry program used to collect the data.

A better way to achieve the same objective is by defining a CHECK constraint for the column in the base table that is to receive the data value. You can use a CHECK constraint (also known as a *table check constraint*) to ensure that a particular column in a base table is never assigned an unacceptable value—once you have defined a CHECK constraint for a column, any operation that attempts to place a value in that column that does not meet specific criteria will fail.

CHECK constraints consist of one or more predicates (which are connected by the keywords AND or OR) collectively known as the *check condition*. This check condition is compared with the data values you provide, and the result of this comparison is returned as the value TRUE, FALSE, or Unknown. If the CHECK constraint returns the value TRUE, the value is acceptable, so it is added to the column. If, however, the CHECK constraint returns the value FALSE or Unknown, the operation attempting to place the value in the column fails, and all changes made by that operation are backed out. However, it is important to note that when the results of a particular operation are rolled back because of a CHECK constraint violation, the transaction that invoked that operation is not terminated, and other operations within that transaction are unaffected. Figure 4.3 illustrates how to use a simple CHECK constraint to control which data values are acceptable by a column.

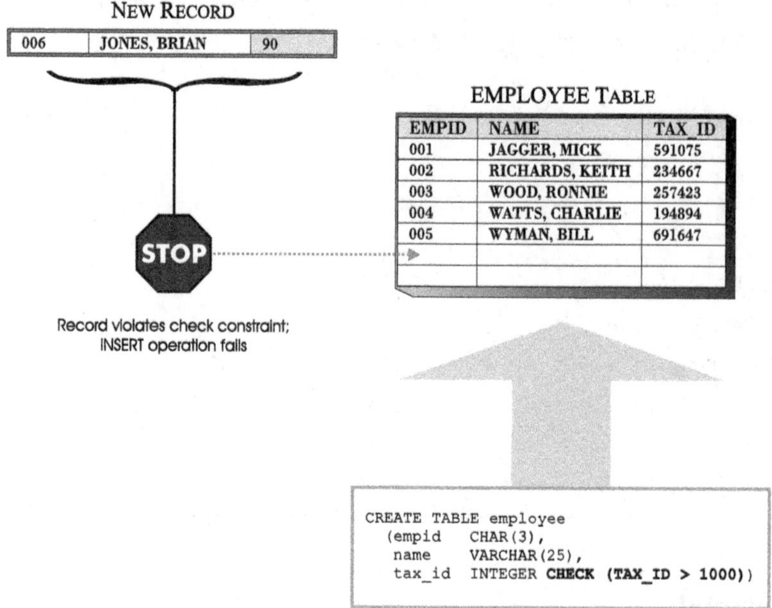

Figure 4.3: How to use the CHECK constraint to control what data values are acceptable

Like NOT NULL constraints and DEFAULT constraints, CHECK constraints are associated with a specific column in a base table and are usually defined during the table creation process or during the table alter process. The DB2 commands and the results for the above said scenario look something like this:

```
CREATE TABLE employee
      (     EMPID        CHAR(3),
            NAME         VARCHAR(25),
            TAX_ID       INTEGER CHECK (TAX_ID > 1000))
DB20000I The SQL command completed successfully.

INSERT INTO employee VALUES
      (001,'JAGGER, MICK', 591075),
      (002,'RICHARDS, KEITH', 234667),
      (003,'WOOD, RONNIE', 257423),
      (004,'WATTS, CHARLIE', 194894),
      (005,'WYMAN, BILL', 691647);
DB20000I The SQL command completed successfully.

INSERT INTO employee (EMPID, NAME, TAX_ID) VALUES (006,'JONES, BRIAN', 90)
DB21034E  The command was processed as an SQL statement because it was not
a valid Command Line Processor command.  During SQL processing it returned:
SQL0545N The requested operation is not allowed because a row does not
satisfy the check constraint "DATAMARTS.EMPLOYEE.SQL140717193343960". SQL-
STATE=23513
```

You can query the SYSIBM.CHECK_CONSTRAINTS system catalog table to capture the CHECK constraint information, as follows:

```
SELECT
      VARCHAR(CONSTRAINT_CATALOG,10)     CONSTRAINT_CATALOG,
      VARCHAR(CONSTRAINT_NAME,30)        CONSTRAINT_NAME,
      VARCHAR(CHECK_CLAUSE,40)           CHECK_CLAUSE
   FROM SYSIBM.CHECK_CONSTRAINTS
   WHERE
   CONSTRAINT_NAME='SQL140717193343960'
                                                              Continued
```

```
CONSTRAINT_CATALOG CONSTRAINT_NAME                    CHECK_CLAUSE
------------------ ------------------------------ --------------------
SAMPLE             SQL140717193343960             TAX_ID > 1000
```

Unique Constraints

By default, records added to a base table can have the same values assigned to any of the columns any number of times. As long as the records stored in the table do not contain information that is not be duplicated, this kind of behavior is acceptable. However, sometimes certain pieces of information that make up a record must be unique (for example, if an employee identification number is assigned to each individual that works for a particular company, each number must be unique—two employees must never have the same employee identification number).

In these situations, you can use the UNIQUE constraint to ensure that the values you assign to one or more columns when a record is added to a base table are always unique. Once you have defined a UNIQUE constraint for one or more columns, any operation that attempts to place duplicate values in those columns will fail. Figure 4.4 illustrates how to use the UNIQUE constraint.

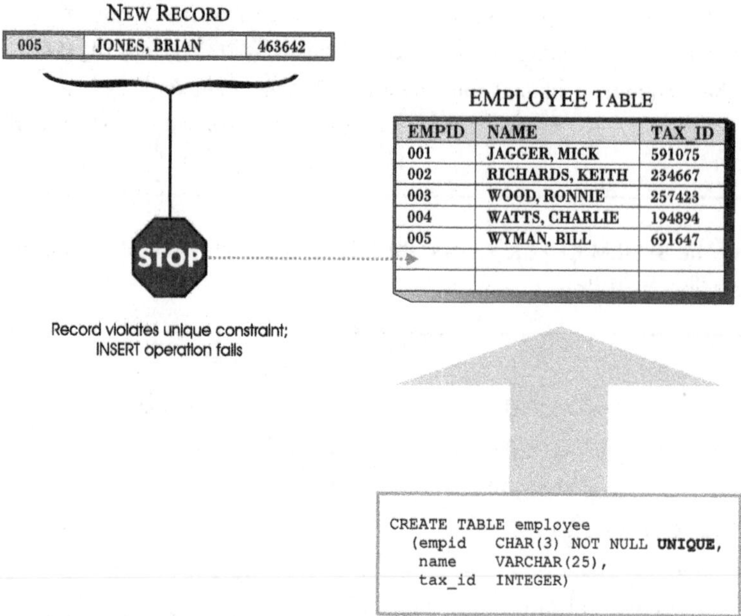

Figure 4.4: How to use the UNIQUE constraint to control the duplication of data values

Unlike NOT NULL constraints, DEFAULT constraints, and CHECK constraints, which can be associated with only a single column in a base table, UNIQUE constraints can be associated with either an individual column or a group of columns. However, each column in a base table can participate in only one UNIQUE constraint, regardless of how you group the columns. Like the other constraints, UNIQUE constraints are usually defined during the table creation process or during the table alter process. The DB2 commands and the results for the above scenario look something like this:

```
CREATE TABLE employee
      (     EMPID         CHAR(3)      NOT NULL UNIQUE,
            NAME          VARCHAR(25),
            TAX_ID        INTEGER)
DB20000I The SQL command completed successfully.

INSERT INTO employee VALUES
      (001,'JAGGER, MICK', 591075),
      (002,'RICHARDS, KEITH', 234667),
      (003,'WOOD, RONNIE', 257423),
      (004,'WATTS, CHARLIE', 194894),
      (005,'WYMAN, BILL', 691647)
DB20000I The SQL command completed successfully.

INSERT INTO employee
      (EMPID, NAME, TAX_ID) VALUES (005,'JONES, BRIAN', 463642)
DB21034E The command was processed as an SQL statement because it was not a
valid Command Line Processor command.  During SQL processing it returned:
SQL0803N One or more values in the INSERT statement, UPDATE statement, or
foreign key update caused by a DELETE statement are not valid because the
primary key, unique constraint or unique index identified by "1" constrains
table "DATAMARTS.EMPLOYEE" from having duplicate values for the index key.
SQLSTATE=23505
```

Regardless of when you define a UNIQUE constraint, when you create it, the DB2 database manager checks to determine whether an index for the columns that the UNIQUE constraint refers to already exists. If so, that index is marked as unique and system required (when an index is marked as system required, it cannot be dropped without dropping the constraint on the base table). If not, an appropriate index is created and marked as unique and system required. This index will then enforce uniqueness whenever new records are added to the columns for which the unique constraint was defined. As with other constraints, you can verify the unique rule by querying the system catalog views:

```
SELECT
      VARCHAR (INDSCHEMA, 8)          INDSCHEMA,
      VARCHAR (INDNAME, 20)           INDNAME,
      VARCHAR (TABNAME, 10)           TABNAME,
      UNIQUERULE,
      SYSTEM_REQUIRED
   FROM SYSCAT.INDEXES
   WHERE
   TABNAME='EMPLOYEE'

INDSCHEMA INDNAME              TABNAME    UNIQUERULE SYSTEM_REQUIRED
--------- -------------------- ---------- ---------- ---------------
SYSIBM    SQL140717202520710   EMPLOYEE   U                        1
```

Because no valid index was present on the EMPLOYEE table for the EMPID column, the DB2 database manager created the index SQL140717202520710 and marked it as system required. To provide a better naming convention, it is advisable to create an index and associate the UNIQUE constraint with the earlier created index, something like this:

```
CREATE TABLE employee
      (     EMPID       CHAR(3)     NOT NULL,
            NAME        VARCHAR(25),
            TAX_ID      INTEGER)
DB20000I The SQL command completed successfully.

INSERT INTO employee VALUES
      (001,'JAGGER, MICK', 591075),
      (002,'RICHARDS, KEITH', 234667),
      (003, 'WOOD, RONNIE', 257423),
                                                   Continued
```

```
      (004,'WATTS, CHARLIE', 194894),
      (005,'WYMAN, BILL', 691647);
DB20000I The SQL command completed successfully.

CREATE INDEX ix1_employee ON employee
            (EMPID ASC) ALLOW REVERSE SCANS
DB20000I The SQL command completed successfully.

ALTER TABLE employee ADD CONSTRAINT U1_EMPLOYEE UNIQUE (EMPID)
SQL0598W Existing index "DATAMARTS.IX1_EMPLOYEE" is used as the index for
the primary key or a unique key.  SQLSTATE=01550
```

The DB2 database manager is using the DATAMARTS.IX1_EMPLOYEE index to build the UNIQUE constraint on the table. You can also verify the unique rule in the system catalog view, as follows:

```
SELECT
      VARCHAR (INDSCHEMA, 8)    INDSCHEMA,
      VARCHAR (INDNAME, 20)     INDNAME,
      VARCHAR (TABNAME, 10)     TABNAME,
      UNIQUERULE,
      SYSTEM_REQUIRED
   FROM SYSCAT.INDEXES
   WHERE TABNAME='EMPLOYEE'

INDSCHEMA INDNAME              TABNAME    UNIQUERULE SYSTEM_REQUIRED
--------- -------------------- ---------- ---------- ---------------
DATAMARTS IX1_EMPLOYEE         EMPLOYEE   U                        1
```

A primary key, which we will look at next, is a special form of a UNIQUE constraint. Each table can contain only one primary key, and every column that defines a primary key must be assigned the NOT NULL constraint. In addition to ensuring that every record added to a table has some unique characteristic, primary keys allow tables to participate in referential constraints.

A table can have any number of UNIQUE constraints; however, a table cannot have more than one UNIQUE constraint defined on the same set of columns. Because UNIQUE constraints are enforced by indexes, all the limitations that apply to indexes (for example, a maximum of 64 columns with a combined length of 8,192 bytes is allowable; no column can have a large object, long character string data type) also apply to UNIQUE constraints.

Although a unique, system-required index can enforce a UNIQUE constraint, there is a distinction between defining a UNIQUE constraint and creating a unique index. Both enforce uniqueness, but a unique index allows NULL values and generally cannot be used in a referential constraint. A UNIQUE constraint, however, does not allow NULL values and can be referenced in a foreign key specification. (The value NULL means a column's value is undefined and distinct from any other value, including other NULL values.)

Referential Integrity Constraints

If you have worked with a relational database management system for any length of time, you are probably aware that data normalization is a technique used to ensure that only one way exists to get to a single fact. Data normalization is possible because two or more individual base tables can have some type of relationship with one another, and information stored in related base tables can be combined, if necessary, through a JOIN operation. This is where referential integrity constraints come into play. You use referential integrity constraints (also known as *referential constraints* and *foreign key constraints*) to define required relationships between two base tables.

To understand how referential constraints work, it helps to look at an example. Suppose you own a small auto parts store, and you use a database to keep track of your inventory on hand. Many of the parts you stock will work only with a specific make and model of automobile; therefore, your database has one table named MAKE to hold make information and another table named MODEL to hold model information. Because these two tables are related (every model must belong to a make), you can use a referential constraint to ensure that every record stored in the MODEL table has a corresponding record in the MAKE table. The relationship between these two tables is established by comparing values that are to be added to the MAKEID column of the MODEL table (known as the foreign key of the child table) with the values that currently exist for the set of columns that make up the primary key of the MAKE table (known as the parent key of the parent table).

To create the referential constraint just described, you define a primary key, using one or more columns in the MAKE table, and then define a foreign key for one or more corresponding columns in the MODEL table that reference the MAKE table's primary key. Assuming you use a column named MAKEID to create the primary key for the MAKE table and use a column also named MAKEID to create the foreign key for the MODEL table, the referential constraint created will look something like the one in Figure 4.5.

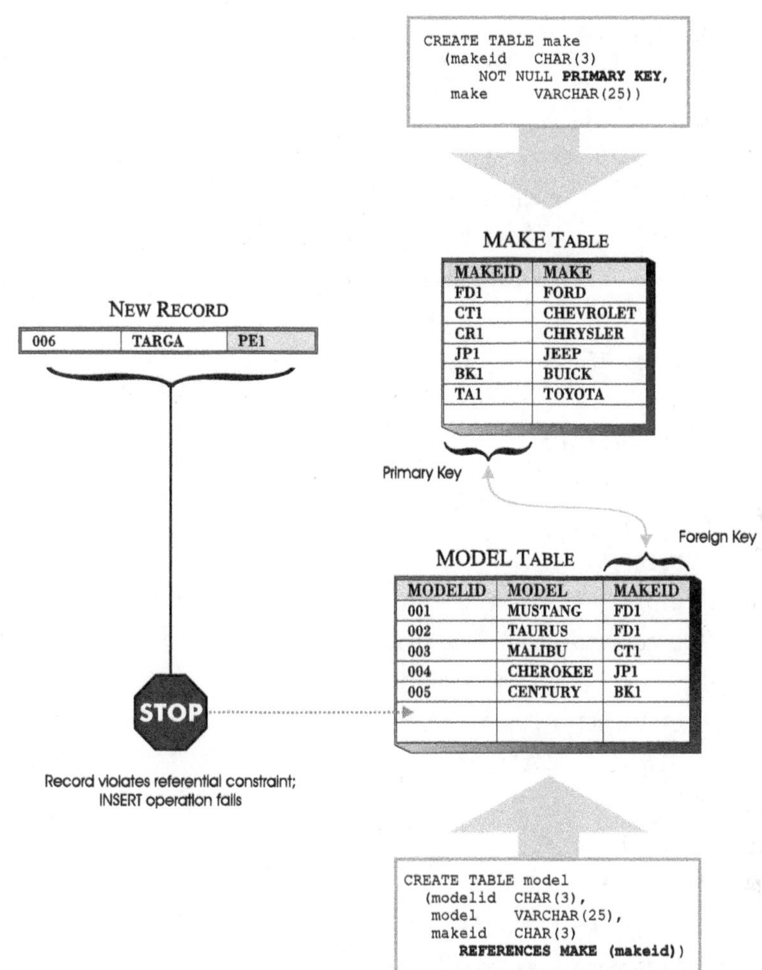

Figure 4.5: How to use a referential constraint to define a relationship between two tables

In this example, a single column defines the parent key and the foreign key of the referential constraint. However, as with UNIQUE constraints, you can use multiple columns to define both the parent and the foreign key of a referential constraint. The DB2 commands and the results for referential constraint example are as follows:

```
CREATE TABLE make
    (     MAKEID CHAR (3) NOT NULL PRIMARY KEY,
          MAKE VARCHAR(25))
```

Continued

```
DB20000I The SQL command completed successfully.

CREATE TABLE model
       (      MODELID      CHAR(3),
              MODEL        VARCHAR(25),
              MAKEID       CHAR(3) REFERENCES MAKE (MAKEID))
DB20000I The SQL command completed successfully.

INSERT INTO make VALUES
       ('FD1','FORD'),
       ('CT1','CHEVROLET'),
       ('CR1','CHRYSLER'),
       ('JP1','JEEP'),
       ('BK1','BUICK'),
       ('TA1','TOYOTA')
DB20000I The SQL command completed successfully.

INSERT INTO model VALUES
       ('001','MUSTANG', 'FD1'),
       ('002','TAURUS', 'FD1'),
       ('003','MALIBU', 'CT1'),
       ('004','CHEROKEE', 'JP1'),
       ('005','CENTURY', 'BK1')
DB20000I The SQL command completed successfully.
```

When you try inserting a record into the MODEL table, which has no matching value in the MAKE table, the MODEL table will fail with error SQL0530N:

```
INSERT INTO model VALUES ('006', 'TARGA', 'PE1')
DB21034E The command was processed as an SQL statement because it was not a
valid Command Line Processor command.  During SQL processing it returned:
SQL0530N The insert or update value of the FOREIGN KEY "DATAMARTS.MODEL.
SQL140718082508750" is not equal to any value of the parent key of the par-
ent table. SQLSTATE=23503
```

The referential constraint information can be captured through SYSCAT.REFERENCES and SYSCAT.TABCONST system catalog table views, as follows:

```
SELECT
      VARCHAR (CONSTNAME, 20)  CONSTNAME,
      VARCHAR (TABNAME, 10)    TABNAME,
      VARCHAR (REFKEYNAME, 20) REFKEYNAME,
      VARCHAR (REFTABNAME, 10) REFTABNAME,
      COLCOUNT,
      UPDATERULE,
      DELETERULE,
      VARCHAR (FK_COLNAMES, 7) FK_COLNAMES,
      VARCHAR (PK_COLNAMES, 7) PK_COLNAMES
   FROM SYSCAT.REFERENCES
   WHERE CONSTNAME='SQL140718082508750'

CONSTNAME            TABNAME    REFKEYNAME           REFTABNAME COLCOUNT
-------------------- ---------- -------------------- ---------- --------
SQL140718082508750   MODEL      SQL140718082508590   MAKE              1

UPDATERULE DELETERULE FK_COLNAMES PK_COLNAMES
---------- ---------- ----------- -----------
A          A          MAKEID      MAKEID

SELECT
      VARCHAR (CONSTNAME, 25) CONSTNAME,
      VARCHAR (TABNAME, 10) TABNAME,
      TYPE,
      ENFORCED,
      ENABLEQUERYOPT
   FROM SYSCAT.TABCONST
   WHERE TABNAME IN ('MAKE', 'MODEL')
```

Continued

```
CONSTNAME                  TABNAME    TYPE ENFORCED ENABLEQUERYOPT
-------------------------- ---------- ---- -------- --------------
SQL140718082508590         MAKE       P    Y        Y
SQL140718082508750         MODEL      F    Y        Y
```

Note: The names of the columns used to create the foreign key of a referential constraint do not have to be the same as the names of the columns used to create the primary key of the constraint (as was the case in the previous example). However, the data types used for the column or columns that make up the primary key and the foreign key of a referential constraint must be identical.

As you can see, referential constraints are much more complex than NOT NULL, DEFAULT, CHECK, and UNIQUE constraints. In fact, they can be so complex that a set of special terms is used to identify the individual components that can make up a single referential constraint. Although you may already be familiar with some of them, Table 4.2 shows the complete list of terms.

Table 4.2: Referential integrity constraint terminology

Term	Meaning
Unique key	A column or set of columns in which every row of values is different from the values of all other rows
Primary key	A special unique key that does not accept NULL values
Foreign key	A column or set of columns in a child table whose values must match those of a parent key in a parent table
Parent key	A primary key or unique key in a parent table that is referenced by a foreign key in a referential constraint
Parent table	A table that contains a parent key of a referential constraint (a table can be both a parent table and a dependent table of any number of referential constraints)
Parent row	A row in a parent table that has at least one matching row in a dependent table
Dependent or child table	A table that contains at least one foreign key that references a parent key in a referential constraint (a table can be both a dependent table and a parent table of any number of referential constraints)
Dependent or child row	A row in a dependent table that has at least one matching row in a parent table
Descendent table	A dependent table or a descendent of a dependent table
Descendent row	A dependent row or a descendent of a dependent row
Referential cycle	A set of referential constraints defined in such a way that each table in the set is a descendent of itself
Self-referencing table	A table that is both a parent table and a dependent table in the same referential constraint (the constraint is known as a *self-referencing constraint*)
Self-referencing row	A row that is a parent of itself

The primary reason for creating referential constraints is to guarantee that data integrity is maintained whenever one table object references another. As long as a referential constraint is in effect, the DB2 database manager ensures that for every row in a child table that has a value in any column that is part of a foreign key, a corresponding row exists in the parent table. So what happens when an SQL operation attempts to manipulate data in a way that violates a referential constraint? To answer this, let us look at how such operations can compromise data integrity if the checks and balances a referential constraint provides are not in place:

- An insert operation can add a row of data to a child table that does not have a matching value in the corresponding parent table. For example, using our MAKE/MODEL scenario, you might add a record to the MODEL table that does not have a corresponding value in the MAKE table.
- An update operation can change an existing value in a child table such that it no longer has a matching value in the corresponding parent table. For example, you might modify a record in the MODEL table so that it no longer has a corresponding value in the MAKE table.
- An update operation can change an existing value in a parent table, leaving rows in a child table with values that no longer match those in the parent table. For example, you might modify a record in the MAKE table such that records in the MODEL table no longer have a corresponding MAKE value.
- A delete operation can remove a value from a parent table, leaving rows in a child table with values that no longer match those in the parent table. For example, you might remove a record from the MAKE table, resulting in records in the MODEL table that no longer have a corresponding MAKE value.

The DB2 database manager can restrict these types of operations from being performed on tables that are part of a referential constraint, or it can attempt to carry out these actions in a way that will safeguard data integrity. In either case, DB2 uses a set of rules to control the operation's behavior:

- Insert Rule
- Update Rule
- Delete Rule

Each referential constraint has its own set of rules. You specify the way each rule is to be enforced during the referential constraint creation process.

The Insert Rule for Referential Constraints

The Insert Rule guarantees that a value can never be inserted into the foreign key of a child table unless a matching value exists in the corresponding parent key of the associated parent table. Any attempt to insert records into a child table that violates this rule will result in an SQL0530N error, and the insert operation will fail. In contrast, no checking occurs when records are added to the parent key of the parent table.

Creating the referential constraint itself will implicitly create the Insert Rule for the referential constraint. Figure 4.6 illustrates how a row that conforms to the Insert Rule for a referential constraint is successfully added to a child table.

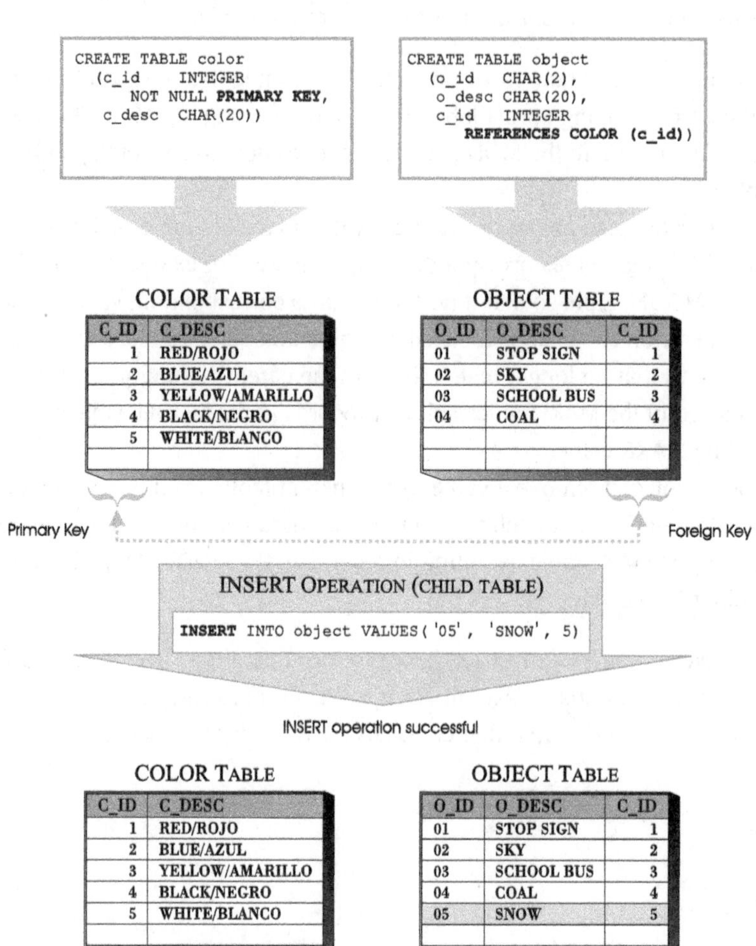

Figure 4.6: An insert operation that conforms to the Insert Rule of the referential constraint

Figure 4.7 illustrates how a row that violates the Insert Rule causes an insert operation to fail.

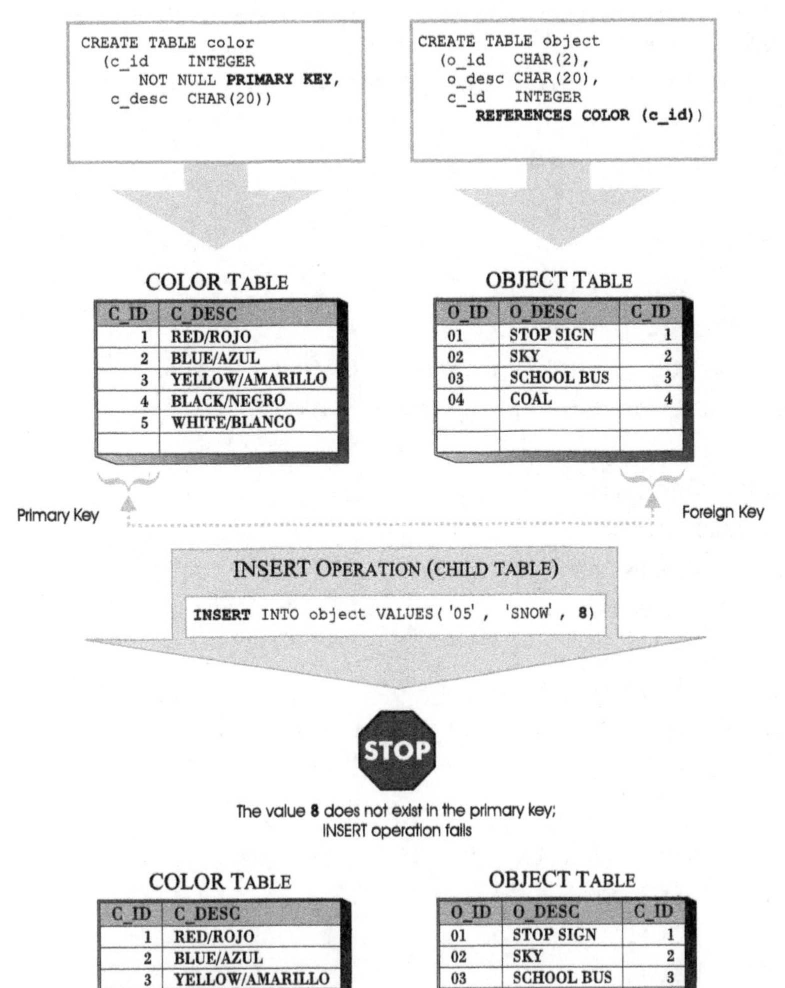

Figure 4.7: An insert operation that violates the Insert Rule of the referential constraint

The DB2 commands and the results for the above scenario are as follows:

```
CREATE TABLE color
      (     C_ID      INTEGER NOT NULL PRIMARY KEY,
            C_DESC    CHAR(20))
DB20000I The SQL command completed successfully.

CREATE TABLE object
      (     O_ID      CHAR(2),
            O_DESC    CHAR(20),
            C_ID      INTEGER REFERENCES COLOR (C_ID))
DB20000I The SQL command completed successfully.

INSERT INTO color VALUES
      (1, 'RED/ROJO'),
      (2, 'BLUE/AZUL'),
      (3, 'YELLOW/AMARILLO'),
      (4, 'BLACK/NEGRO'),
      (5, 'WHITE/BLANCO')
DB20000I The SQL command completed successfully.

INSERT INTO object VALUES
      ('01', 'STOP SIGN', 1),
      ('02', 'SKY', 2),
      ('03', 'SCHOOL BUS', 3),
      ('04', 'COAL', 4)
DB20000I The SQL command completed successfully.
```

A new record is successfully inserted into OBJECT table when it conforms to the Insert Rule of the referential constraint; when it does not, it returns SQL error SQL0530N:

```
INSERT INTO object VALUES
      ('05', 'SNOW', 5)
DB20000I The SQL command completed successfully.

INSERT INTO object VALUES
      ('05', 'SNOW', 8)
DB21034E The command was processed as an SQL statement because it was not
a valid Command Line Processor command. During SQL processing it returned:
SQL0530N The insert or update value of the FOREIGN KEY "DATAMARTS.OBJECT.
SQL140718151105830" is not equal to any value of the parent key of the par-
ent table. SQLSTATE=23503
```

It is important to note that because the Insert Rule exists, records must be inserted into the parent key of the parent table before corresponding records can be inserted into the child table. Going back to our MAKE/MODEL example, this means that you must add a record for a new MAKE to the MAKE table *before* adding a record that references the new MAKE to the MODEL table.

The Update Rule for Referential Constraints

The Update Rule controls how to process update operations performed against either table (child or parent) participating in a referential constraint. The following two types of behaviors are possible, depending on how you define the Update Rule:

- ON UPDATE RESTRICT. This definition ensures that whenever an update operation is performed on the parent table of a referential constraint, the value for the foreign key of each row in the child table will have the same matching value in the parent key of the parent table that it had before the update operation was performed.
- ON UPDATE NO ACTION. This definition ensures that whenever an update operation is performed on either table in a referential constraint, the value for the foreign key of each row in the child table will have a matching value in the parent key of the corresponding parent table; however, the value may not be the same as it was before the update operation occurred.

Figure 4.8 illustrates how the Update Rule is enforced with the ON UPDATE RESTRICT definition.

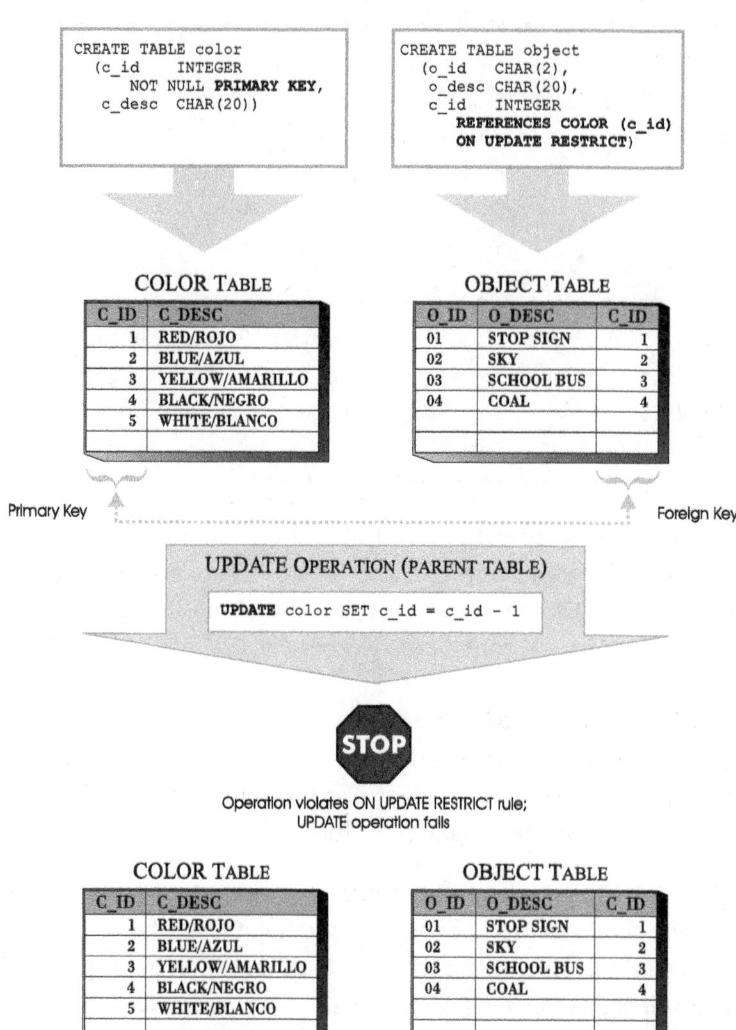

Figure 4.8: How ON UPDATE RESTRICT is enforced using the Update Rule of a referential constraint

When you try to update the C_ID column data, you will get error SQL0531N because updates are restrictive in this case:

```
UPDATE color SET C_ID=C_ID-1
DB21034E  The command was processed as an SQL statement because it was not
a valid Command Line Processor command.  During SQL processing it returned:
SQL0531N The parent key in a parent row of relationship "DATAMARTS.OBJECT.
SQL140718165922450" cannot be updated. SQLSTATE=23001
```

Figure 4.9 shows how the Update Rule is enforced when you use the ON UPDATE NO ACTION definition.

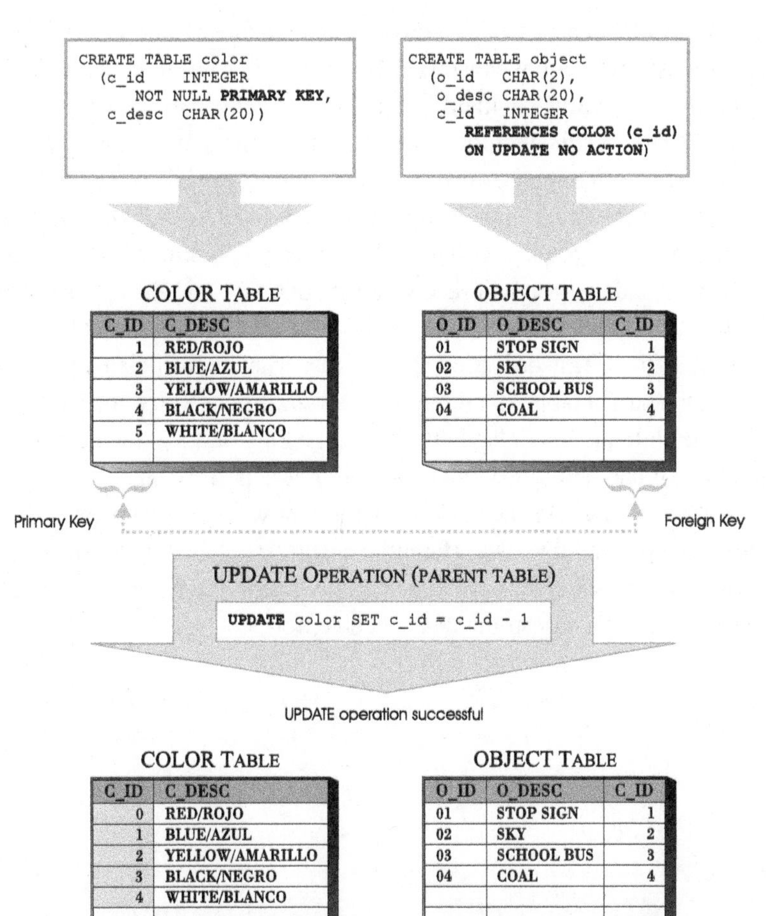

Figure 4.9: How ON UPDATE NO ACTION is enforced using the Update Rule of a referential constraint

Like the Insert Rule, the Update Rule for a referential constraint is implicitly created when the referential constraint itself is created. If no Update Rule definition is provided, the ON UPDATE NO ACTION definition is used by default. Regardless of which Update Rule definition you use, if the rule's condition is not met, the Update operation will fail, an error message will display, and any changes made to the data in either table participating in the referential constraint will be backed out.

The Delete Rule for Referential Constraints

The Delete Rule controls how to process delete operations performed against the parent table of a referential constraint. The following four types of behaviors are possible, depending on how you define the Delete Rule:

- ON DELETE CASCADE. This definition ensures that when a parent row is deleted from the parent table of a referential constraint, all dependent rows in the child table that have matching primary key values in their foreign key are deleted as well.
- ON DELETE SET NULL. This definition ensures that when a parent row is deleted from the parent table of a referential constraint, all dependent rows in the child table that have matching primary key values in their foreign key are located and their foreign key values are changed to NULL (if you try setting the foreign key column to a NOT NULL with ON DELETE SET NULL clause, you will receive error code SQL0629N, as the settings are contradicting each other). Other values for the dependent row are not affected.
- ON DELETE RESTRICT. This definition ensures that whenever a delete operation is performed on the parent table of a referential constraint, the value for the foreign key of each row in the child table will have the same matching value in the parent key of the parent table that it had before the delete operation was performed.
- ON DELETE NO ACTION. This definition ensures that whenever a delete operation is performed on the parent table of a referential constraint, the value for the foreign key of each row in the child table will have a matching value in the parent key of the parent table after the other referential constraints have been enforced.

Figure 4.10 illustrates how the Delete Rule is enforced with the ON DELETE CASCADE definition.

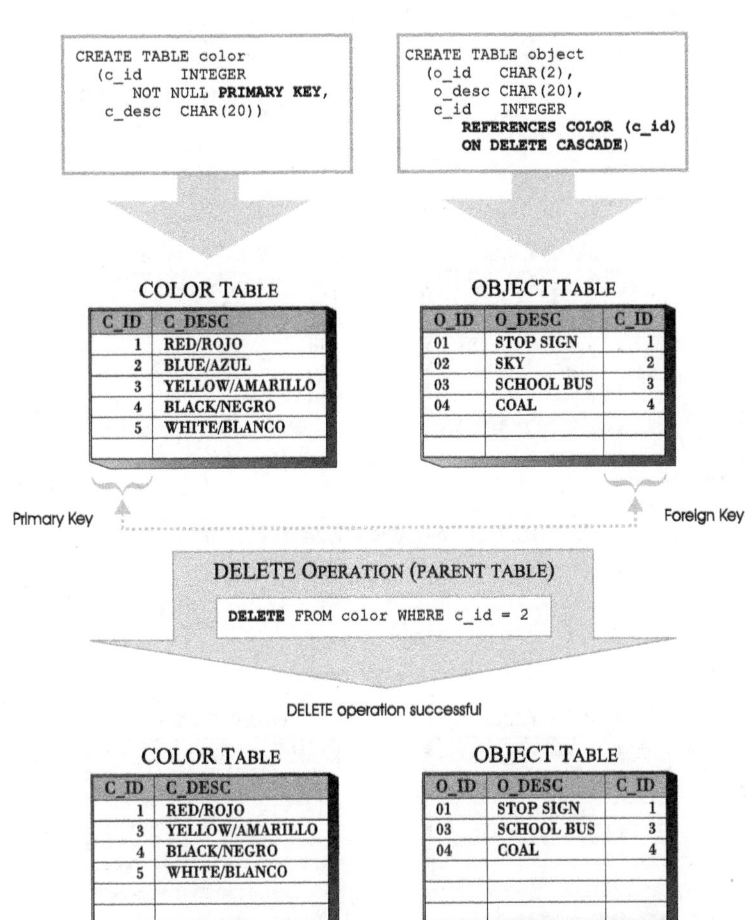

Figure 4.10: How ON DELETE CASCADE is enforced using the Delete Rule of a referential constraint

Figure 4.11 shows how the Delete Rule is enforced with the ON DELETE SET NULL definition.

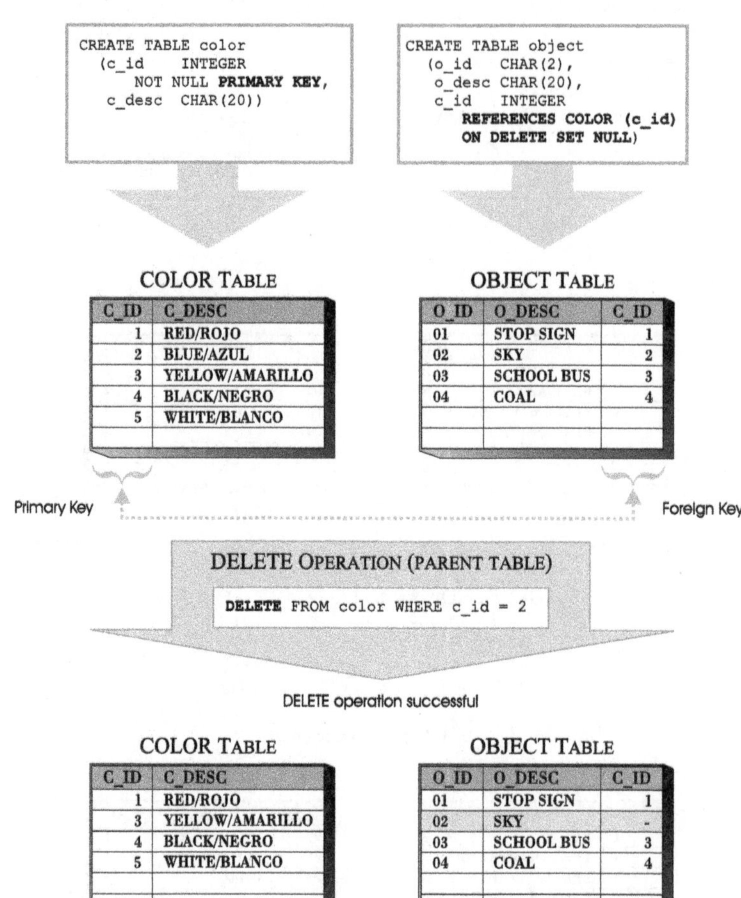

Figure 4.11: How ON DELETE SET NULL is enforced using the Delete Rule of a referential constraint

Figure 4.12 illustrates how the Delete Rule is enforced with the ON DELETE RESTRICT definition.

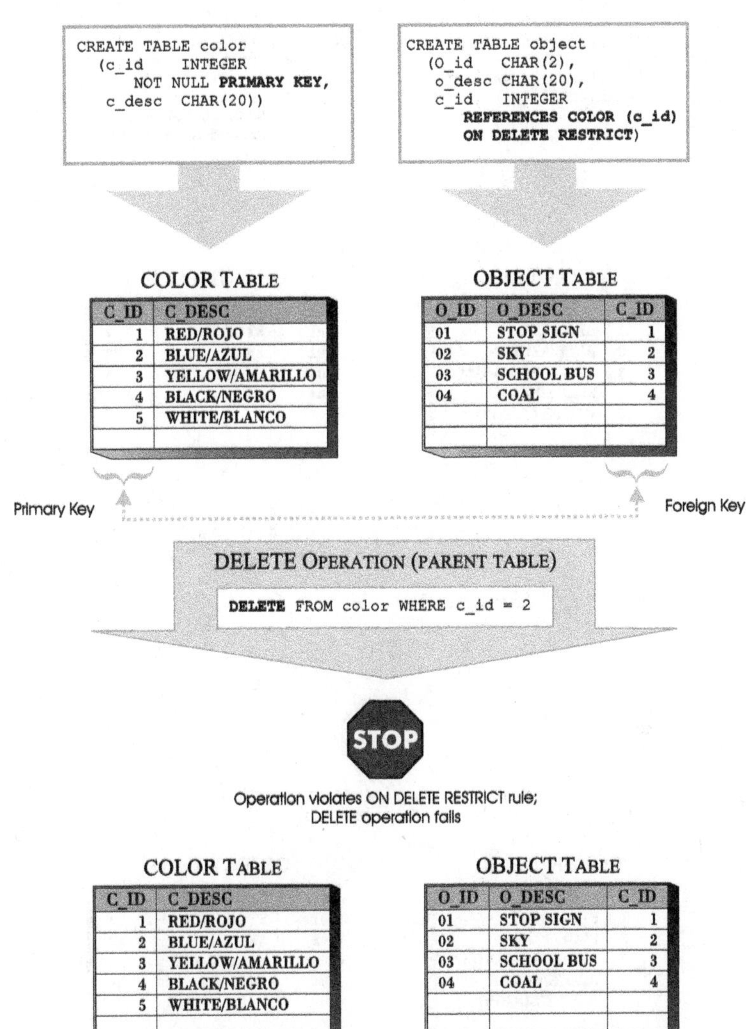

Figure 4.12: How ON DELETE RESTRICT is enforced using the Delete Rule of a referential constraint

Figure 4.13 illustrates how the Delete Rule is enforced with the ON DELETE NO ACTION definition.

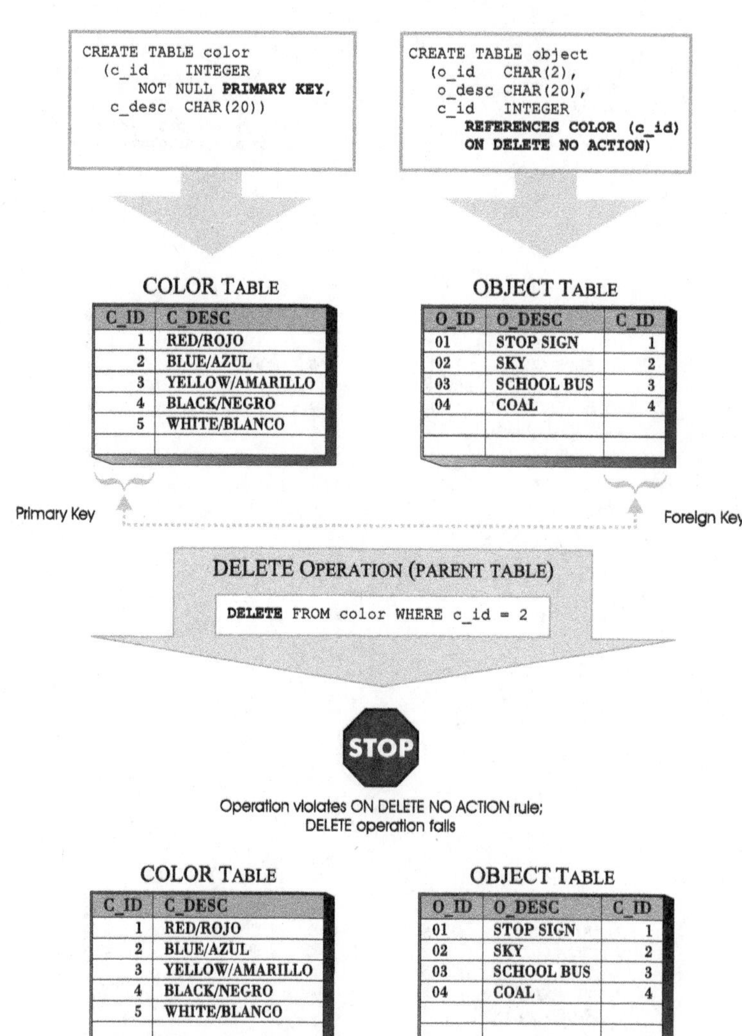

Figure 4.13: How ON DELETE NO ACTION is enforced using the Delete Rule of a referential constraint

In the case of ON DELETE RESTRICT and ON DELETE NO ACTION, the DELETE statement receives an SQL0532N error from the DB2 database manager.

The complete error message is as follows:

```
DELETE FROM color WHERE C_ID=2

DB21034E The command was processed as an SQL statement because it was not
a valid Command Line Processor command. During SQL processing it returned:
SQL0532N A parent row cannot be deleted because the relationship "DATAMARTS.
OBJECT.SQL140718183545500" restricts the deletion. SQLSTATE=23001
```

As with the Insert Rule and the Update Rule, when you create the referential constraint itself, the Delete Rule for a referential constraint is implicitly created. If no Delete Rule definition is provided, the ON DELETE NO ACTION definition is used by default. No matter which form of the Delete Rule you use, if the rule's condition is not met, an error message will display, and the delete operation will fail.

If you use the ON DELETE CASCADE Delete Rule, and the deletion of a parent row in a parent table causes the deletion of one or more dependent rows from the corresponding child table, the delete operation is said to have been propagated to the child table. In such a situation, the child table is *delete-connected* to the parent table. Because a delete-connected child table can also be the parent table in another referential constraint, a delete operation that is propagated to one child table can, in turn, be propagated to another child table, and so on. Thus, the deletion of one parent row from a single parent table can result in the deletion of several hundred rows from any number of tables, depending on how tables are delete-connected. Therefore, use the ON DELETE CASCADE Delete Rule with extreme caution when a hierarchy of referential constraints permeates a database.

Informational Constraints

The DB2 database manager automatically enforces all the constraints we have looked at so far whenever new data values are added to a table or existing data values are modified or deleted. As you might imagine, defining numerous constraints can require a considerable amount of system overhead to enforce those constraints, particularly when large amounts of data are loaded into a table.

If an application is coded in such a way that it validates data before inserting it into a DB2 database, it may be more efficient to create one or more informational constraints, as opposed to creating any of the other constraints. Unlike other constraints, informational constraints are not enforced during insert and update processing. However, the DB2 SQL optimizer will evaluate information provided by an informational constraint when considering the best access plan to use to resolve a query.

You define informational constraints by appending the keywords NOT ENFORCED ENABLE QUERY OPTIMIZATION to a normal constraint definition. Consequently, an informational constraint may result in better query performance, even though the constraint itself will not be used to validate data entry or modification. Figure 4.14 illustrates the behavior of a simple informational constraint.

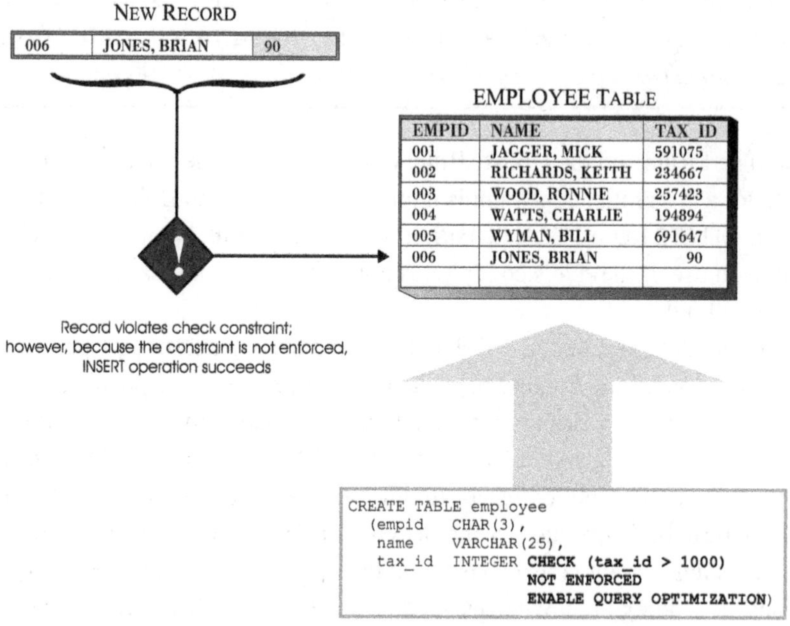

Figure 4.14: Behavior of a simple informational constraint

It is important to note that because the DB2 optimizer evaluates informational constraints when selecting the best data access plan to use to resolve a query, some queries may not return records that have been inserted into a table that violate one or more informational constraints.

For example, if you were to execute the SELECT query against the EMPLOYEE table in Figure 4.14, no records would be returned because the access plan chosen would assume that no records with a TAX_ID value less than 1,000 exist in the table:

```
SELECT * FROM employee WHERE TAX_ID=90

EMPID NAME                    TAX_ID
----- ----------------------- -----------

    0 record(s) selected.
```

However, executing SELECT without a filter predicate will return all of the data present in the table, as follows:

```
SELECT * FROM employee

EMPID NAME                     TAX_ID
----- ------------------------ ----------
1     JAGGER, MICK                 591075
2     RICHARDS, KEITH              234667
3     WOOD, RONNIE                 257423
4     WATTS, CHARLIE               194894
5     WYMAN, BILL                  691647
6     JONES, BRIAN                     90

  6 record(s) selected.
```

You can use the ALTER TABLE command to disable query optimization on the table:

```
ALTER TABLE employee ALTER CHECK SQL140718215507620
                                    DISABLE QUERY OPTMIZATION
```

The DB2 database manager will no longer use the constraint while retrieving the data from the table EMPLOYEE. Therefore, the results produced by querying the table will look like this:

```
SELECT * FROM EMPLOYEE WHERE TAX_ID=90

EMPID NAME                     TAX_ID
----- ------------------------ ----------
6     JONES, BRIAN                     90

  1 record(s) selected.
```

The Set Integrity Command

Although constraints provide a means of ensuring that some level of integrity is maintained as data is manipulated within a base table, their enforcement can prevent some types of operations from executing successfully. For example, suppose you want to bulk-load 10,000 rows of data into a base table by using the Load utility (which we will look at in more detail in Chapter 6, "DB2 Utilities"). If the data contains values that will violate a constraint that you have defined for the table into which the data is to be loaded, the operation will fail. Or suppose you want to add a new constraint to an existing table that already contains several hundred rows of data. If one or more rows in the table contain data values that violate the constraint you wish to add, any attempt to add the constraint will fail. In situations like these, it can be advantageous to suspend constraint checking just long enough to perform the desired operation. However, when you suspend constraint checking, at some point it must be resumed, and at that time, you must locate and deal with rows in the table that cause a constraint to be violated.

Constraint checking for a table can be suspended temporarily by executing the SET INTEGRITY SQL statement. When used to suspend constraint checking, the syntax for the simplest form of this statement is:

```
SET INTEGRITY FOR [TableName ,...] OFF <AccessMode>
```

where:

TableName — Identifies the name of one or more base tables for which to temporarily suspend constraint checking

AccessMode — Identifies whether the specified tables can be accessed in read-only mode while constraint checking is suspended; the following values are valid for this parameter: NO ACCESS and READ ACCESS—if no access mode is specified, NO ACCESS is used as the default

Thus, if you want to temporarily suspend constraint checking for table EMPLOYEE and deny read-only access to that table while constraint checking is turned off, execute a SET INTEGRITY statement:

```
SET INTEGRITY FOR employee OFF
```

Suspending constraint checking for a particular table places that table in the Set Integrity Pending state to indicate that it contains data that has not been checked and may not be free of constraint violations. While a table is in the Set Integrity Pending state, it cannot be used in select, insert, update, or delete operations, nor can it be used by any DB2 utility that needs to perform these types of operations. Furthermore, indexes cannot be created for a table while it is in the Set Integrity Pending state, and data stored in the table can be retrieved only if the access mode specified when the SET INTEGRITY statement was used to place the table in Set Integrity Pending state allows read-only access.

Just as one form of the SET INTEGRITY statement will temporarily suspend constraint checking, another form will resume it. In this case, the syntax for the simplest form of the SET INTEGRITY statement is:

```
SET INTEGRITY FOR [TableName] IMMEDIATE CHECKED
FOR EXCEPTION [IN [TableName] USE [ExceptionTable] ,...]
```

or

```
SET INTEGRITY FOR [[TableName] [ConstraintType] ,...] IMMEDIATE UNCHECKED
```

where:

TableName Identifies the name of one or more base tables for which to resume suspended constraint checking; these are also the base tables from which all rows that are in violation of a referential constraint or a check constraint are to be copied

ExceptionTable Identifies the name of a base table to which all rows that are in violation of a referential constraint or a check constraint are to be copied

ConstraintType Identifies the type of constraint checking to resume; the following values are valid for this parameter: FOREIGN KEY, CHECK, MATERIALIZED QUERY, GENERATED COLUMN, STAGING, and ALL

Thus, to resume constraint checking for the EMPLOYEE table you suspended constraint checking for in the previous example, execute a SET INTEGRITY statement that looks something like this:

```
SET INTEGRITY FOR employee IMMEDIATE CHECKED
```

When this particular form of the SET INTEGRITY statement is executed, the EMPLOYEE table is removed from the Set Integrity Pending state, and each row of data stored in the table is checked for constraint violations. If an offensive row is found, constraint checking is stopped, and the EMPLOYEE table is returned to the Set Integrity Pending state. However, consider the following form of the SET INTEGRITY statement:

```
SET INTEGRITY FOR employee IMMEDIATE CHECKED
FOR EXCEPTION IN employee USE bad_rows
```

When you execute this statement, each row found that violates one or more of the constraints that you have defined for the EMPLOYEE table will be copied to a table named BAD_ROWS, where it can be corrected and copied back to the EMPLOYEE table, if so desired.

However, if you execute the following form of the SET INTEGRITY statement, the EMPLOYEE table is taken out of the Set Integrity Pending state, and no constraint checking is performed:

```
SET INTEGRITY FOR employee ALL IMMEDIATE UNCHECKED
```

However, this is a very hazardous thing to do; you do it only if you have some independent means of ensuring that the EMPLOYEE table does not contain data that violates one or more constraints defined for the EMPLOYEE table.

Note: When a table is in the Set Integrity Pending state and you try to query it, you will receive an SQL0668N error:

```
SQL0668N  Operation not allowed for reason code "1" on table
"DATAMARTS.EMPLOYEE".SQLSTATE=57016
```

You can obtain the list of tables that are in the Set Integrity Pending state by running the following command:

```
SELECT SUBSTR (RTRIM (TABSCHEMA) ||'.'||RTRIM (TABNAME), 1, 50)
   FROM SYSCAT.TABLES WHERE STATUS = 'C';
```

When you complete the SET INTEGRITY check command on a table with an exception table, you will receive a warning message similar to this:

```
SQL3602W  Check data processing found constraint violations and moved them to
exception tables.  SQLSTATE=01603
```

You can make use the following UNIX shell script to automatically run the SET INTEGRITY check command on all the Set Integrity Pending tables in a database:

```
#!/bin/ksh
if [[ $# -gt 0 ]]
   then tables=$*
   else tables='db2 -x "SELECT SUBSTR(RTRIM(TABSCHEMA)||'.'||RTRIM (TABNAME), 1,
50) FROM SYSCAT.TABLES WHERE STATUS = 'C'"'
fi
for table in $tables
do
  echo 'db2 "SET INTEGRITY FOR ' $table 'IMMEDIATE CHECKED"'
  db2 "SET INTEGRITY FOR $table IMMEDIATE CHECKED"
done
exit
```

There are some rules to follow when creating the exception table:

- If the table is protected by a security policy, the exception table must be protected by the same security policy.
- The first "n" columns of the exception table are the same as the columns of the table being checked. All column attributes, including name, data type, and length, must be identical. For protected columns, the security label protecting the column must be the same in both tables.
- All columns of the exception table must be free of constraints and triggers. Constraints include referential integrity and CHECK constraints, as well as unique index constraints that could cause errors on insert.
- The "(n+1)" column of the exception table is an optional TIMESTAMP column. This serves to identify successive invocations of checking by the SET INTEGRITY statement on the same table, if the rows within the exception table have not been deleted before issuing the SET INTEGRITY statement to check the data. The timestamp precision can be any value from 0 to 12, and the value assigned will be the result of CURRENT TIMESTAMP special register.
- The "(n+2)" column must be of type CLOB (32 KB) or larger. This column is optional but recommended; it will provide the names of the constraints that the data within the row violates. If this column is not provided (as could be warranted if, for example, the original table had the maximum number of columns allowed), then only the row where the constraint violation was detected is copied.
- No additional columns are allowed.
- The exception table cannot be a range partition table, range clustered table, materialized query table, or staging table.

Creating Tables and Constraints

Although you can add constraints to an existing table by executing the ALTER TABLE SQL statement, you usually define them as part of the table creation process. Like many database objects, tables can be created by using IBM Data Studio SQL and Routine Development perspective or the IBM Data Studio Database Administration perspective or by using the CLP. In this section, we will concentrate more on the command syntax and executing it through the CLP instead of the IBM Data Studio editor.

Tables can also be created by using the CREATE TABLE SQL statement. In its simplest form, the syntax for this statement is:

```
CREATE TABLE [TableName] ([Element] ,...)
<IN [TablespaceName]>
<INDEX IN [TablespaceName]>
<LONG IN [TablespaceName]>
```

where:

TableName	Identifies the name to assign to the table to be created (a table name must be unique within the schema in which the table is to be defined)
Element	Identifies one or more columns, UNIQUE/primary key constraints, referential constraints, CHECK constraints, and informational constraints to include in the table definition; the syntax used for defining each of these elements varies according to the element being defined
TablespaceName	Identifies the table spaces in which to store the table and its regular data, indexes, or long/large object data

The basic syntax to define a column is:

```
[ColumnName] [DataType]
<NOT NULL>
<WITH DEFAULT <[DefaultValue] | CURRENT DATE |
CURRENT TIME | CURRENT TIMESTAMP | NULL>>
<UniqueConstraint>
<CheckConstraint>
<ReferentialConstraint>
```

where:

ColumnName Identifies the unique name to assign to the column that is to be created

DataType Identifies the data type (built-in or user-defined) to assign to the column to be created; the data type specified determines the kind of data values that can be stored in the column (Table 4.3 contains a list of the valid data type definitions)

DefaultValue Identifies the value to provide for the column in the event no value is supplied when an insert or update operation is performed against the table

UniqueConstraint Identifies a UNIQUE or primary key constraint to associate with the column

CheckConstraint Identifies a CHECK constraint to associate with the column

ReferentialConstraint Identifies a referential constraint to associate with the column

Table 4.3: Data type definitions that can be used with the CREATE TABLE statement

Data Type	Definition(s)
Small integer	SMALLINT
Integer	INTEGER INT
Big integer	BIGINT
Decimal	DECIMAL(*Precision, Scale*) DEC(*Precision, Scale*) NUMERIC(*Precision, Scale*) NUM(*Precision, Scale*) where *Precision* is any number between 1 and 31; *Scale* is any number between 0 and Precision
Single-precision floating-point	REAL FLOAT(*Precision*) where *Precision* is any number between 1 and 24
Double-precision floating-point	DOUBLE FLOAT(*Precision*) where *Precision* is any number between 25 and 53
Fixed-length character string	CHARACTER(*Length*) <FOR BIT DATA>* CHAR(*Length*) <FOR BIT DATA>* where *Length* is any number between 1 and 254
Varying-length character string	CHARACTER VARYING(*MaxLength*) <FOR BIT DATA>* CHAR VARYING(*MaxLength*) <FOR BIT DATA>* VARCHAR(*MaxLength*) <FOR BIT DATA>* where *MaxLength* is any number between 1 and 32,672
Long varying-length character string	LONG VARCHAR

<table>
<tr><th colspan="2">Table 4.3: Data type definitions that can be used with the CREATE TABLE statement (continued)</th></tr>
<tr><th>Data Type</th><th>Definition(s)</th></tr>
<tr><td>Fixed-length double-byte character string</td><td>GRAPHIC(Length)

where Length is any number between 1 and 127</td></tr>
<tr><td>Varying-length double-byte character string</td><td>VARGRAPHIC(MaxLength)

where MaxLength is any number between 1 and 16,336</td></tr>
<tr><td>Long varying-length double-byte character string</td><td>LONG VARGRAPHIC</td></tr>
<tr><td>Date</td><td>DATE</td></tr>
<tr><td>Time</td><td>TIME</td></tr>
<tr><td>Timestamp</td><td>TIMESTAMP</td></tr>
<tr><td>Binary large object</td><td>BINARY LARGE OBJECT(Size <K | M | G>)
BLOB(Size <K | M | G>)

where Size is any number between 1 and 2,147,483,647; if K (for kilobyte) is specified, Size is any number between 1 and 2,097,152; if M (for megabyte) is specified, Size is any number between 1 and 2,048; if G (for gigabyte) is specified, Size is any number between 1 and 2</td></tr>
<tr><td>Character large object</td><td>CHARACTER LARGE OBJECT(Size <K | M | G>)
CHAR LARGE OBJECT(Size <K | M | G>)
CLOB(Size <K | M | G>)

where Size is any number between 1 and 2,147,483,647; if K (for kilobyte) is specified, Size is any number between 1 and 2,097,152; if M (for megabyte) is specified, Size is any number between 1 and 2,048; if G (for gigabyte) is specified, Size is any number between 1 and 2</td></tr>
<tr><td>Double-byte character large object</td><td>DBCLOB(Size <K | M | G>)

where Size is any number between 1 and 1,073,741,823; if K (for kilobyte) is specified, Size is any number between 1 and 1,048,576; if M (for megabyte) is specified, Size is any number between 1 and 1,024; if G (for gigabyte) is specified, Size must be 1</td></tr>
<tr><td>XML document</td><td>XML</td></tr>
<tr><td>Label-based access control (LBAC) security label</td><td>DB2SECURITYLABEL</td></tr>
<tr><td colspan="2">*If the FOR BIT DATA option is used with any character string data type definition, the contents of the column to which the data type is assigned are treated as binary data. As a result, code page conversions are not performed if data is exchanged between other systems, and all comparisons made are done in binary, regardless of the collating sequence used by the database.</td></tr>
</table>

The syntax to create a UNIQUE or primary key constraint as part of a column definition is:

```
<CONSTRAINT [ConstraintName]> [UNIQUE | PRIMARY KEY]
```

where:

ConstraintName Identifies the unique name to assign to the constraint to be created

The syntax to create a CHECK constraint as part of a column definition is:

```
<CONSTRAINT [ConstraintName]> CHECK ([CheckCondition])
<ENFORCED | NOT ENFORCED>
<ENABLE QUERY OPTIMIZATION | DISABLE QUERY OPTIMIZATION>
```

where:

ConstraintName Identifies the unique name to assign to the constraint to be created
CheckCondition Identifies a condition or test that must evaluate to TRUE before a value can be stored in the column

And finally, the syntax to create a referential constraint as part of a column definition is:

```
<CONSTRAINT [ConstraintName]>
REFERENCES [PKTableName] <([PKColumnName] ,...)>
<ON UPDATE [RESTRICT | NO ACTION]>
<ON DELETE [CASCADE | SET NULL | RESTRICT | NO ACTION]>
<ENFORCED | NOT ENFORCED>
<ENABLE QUERY OPTIMIZATION | DISABLE QUERY OPTIMIZATION>
```

where:

ConstraintName Identifies the unique name to assign to the constraint to be created
PKTableName Identifies the name of the parent table that is to participate in the referential constraint
PKColumnName Identifies the column or columns that make up the parent key of the parent table that is to participate in the referential constraint

If you specify the NOT ENFORCED clause as part of a constraint's definition, an informational constraint will be created, and the constraint will not be enforced during insert and update processing. If you specify the ENABLE QUERY OPTIMIZATION clause, the DB2 optimizer will evaluate the information provided about the constraint when generating an access plan in response to a query. And using the ENABLE QUERY OPTIMIZATION clause will impose the constraint when

SELECT statements are issued against the table, and records stored in the table that do not conform to the constraint are not returned.

Therefore, to create a table containing three columns, two of which use an integer data type and one of which uses a fixed-length character string data type, you execute a CREATE TABLE SQL statement:

```
CREATE TABLE employee
    (empid  INTEGER,
     name   CHAR(50),
     dept   INTEGER)
```

If you want to create the same table such that the EMPID column had both the NOT NULL constraint and a primary key constraint associated with it, execute a CREATE TABLE statement that looks something like this:

```
CREATE TABLE employee
    (empid  INTEGER NOT NULL PRIMARY KEY,
     name   CHAR(50),
     dept   INTEGER)
```

Or you can add the primary key constraint later associating it to an existing unique index, as follows:

```
CREATE TABLE employee
    (empid  INTEGER NOT NULL,
     name   CHAR(50),
     dept   INTEGER)

CREATE UNIQUE INDEX pk_employee ON employee (EMPID ASC)
    COMPRESS YES ALLOW REVERSE SCANS

ALTER TABLE employee ADD PRIMARY KEY (EMPID)
```

To create the same table such that the DEPT column participates in a referential constraint with a column named DEPTID that resides in a table named DEPARTMENT, execute a CREATE TABLE statement that looks something like this:

```
CREATE TABLE employee
    (empid  INTEGER,
     name   CHAR(50),
     dept   INTEGER REFERENCES department (deptid))
```

And finally, if you want to create the same table such that the EMPID column has an informational constraint associated with it, you execute a CREATE TABLE statement similar to the following:

```
CREATE TABLE employee
    (empid  INTEGER NOT NULL
        CONSTRAINT inf_cs CHECK (empid BETWEEN 1 AND 100)
        NOT ENFORCED
        ENABLE QUERY OPTIMIZATION,
     name   CHAR(50),
     dept   INTEGER)
```

As you can see from these examples, a UNIQUE constraint, a CHECK constraint, a referential constraint, or an informational constraint that involves a single column can be defined as part of that particular column's definition. But what if you need to define a constraint that encompasses multiple columns in the table? Or what if you want to separate the constraint definitions from the column definitions? You do this by defining a constraint as another element, rather than as an extension to a single column's definition. The basic syntax to define a UNIQUE constraint as an individual element is:

```
<CONSTRAINT [ConstraintName]> [UNIQUE | PRIMARY KEY]
([ColumnName] ,...)
```

where:

ConstraintName	Identifies the unique name to assign to the constraint to be created
ColumnName	Identifies one or more columns that are to be part of the UNIQUE or primary key constraint to be created

The syntax to create a CHECK constraint as an individual element is the same as the syntax to create a CHECK constraint as part of a column definition:

```
<CONSTRAINT [ConstraintName]> CHECK ([CheckCondition])
<ENFORCED | NOT ENFORCED>
<ENABLE QUERY OPTIMIZATION | DISABLE QUERY OPTIMIZATION>
```

where:

ConstraintName	Identifies the unique name to assign to the constraint to be created
CheckCondition	Identifies a condition or test that must evaluate to TRUE before a value can be stored in the column

And finally, the syntax to create a referential constraint as an individual element is:

```
<CONSTRAINT [ConstraintName]>
FOREIGN KEY ([ColumnName] ,...)
REFERENCES [PKTableName] < ([PKColumnName] ,...)>
<ON UPDATE [NO ACTION | RESTRICT]>
<ON DELETE [CASCADE | SET NULL | NO ACTION | RESTRICT]>
<ENFORCED | NOT ENFORCED>
<ENABLE QUERY OPTIMIZATION | DISABLE QUERY OPTIMIZATION>
```

where:

ConstraintName	Identifies the unique name to assign to the constraint to be created
ColumnName	Identifies one or more columns that are to be part of the referential constraint to be created
PKTableName	Identifies the name of the parent table that is to participate in the referential constraint
PKColumnName	Identifies the column or columns that make up the parent key of the parent table that is to participate in the referential constraint

Thus, a table that was created by executing a CREATE TABLE statement as follows:

```
CREATE TABLE employee
    (empid  INTEGER NOT NULL PRIMARY KEY,
     name   CHAR(50),
     dept   INTEGER REFERENCES department(deptid))
```

can also be created by executing a CREATE TABLE statement that looks something like this:

```
CREATE TABLE employee
    (empid  INTEGER NOT NULL,
     name   CHAR(50)
     dept   INTEGER,
     PRIMARY KEY (empid),
     FOREIGN KEY (dept) REFERENCES department(deptid))
```

Creating Views with the Check Option

Views provide a different way of looking at the data stored in one or more base tables. Essentially, a view is a named specification of a result table that is populated whenever the view is referenced in an SQL statement. Each time a view is referenced, a query is executed, and the results are returned in a table-like format. Like base tables, views can be thought of as having columns and rows. And in most cases, you can retrieve data from a view the same way you can from a table. However, whether you can use a view in insert, update, and delete operations depends on how it was defined—views can be defined as insertable, updatable, deletable, and read-only.

Although views look and often behave like base tables, they do not have their own physical storage; therefore, they do not contain real data. Instead, views refer to data that is physically stored in other base tables. Only the view definition itself is actually stored in the database. In fact, when changes are made to the data presented in a view, the changes are actually made to the data stored in the base tables that the view references. Figure 4.15 shows the structure of a simple view, along with its relationship to two base tables.

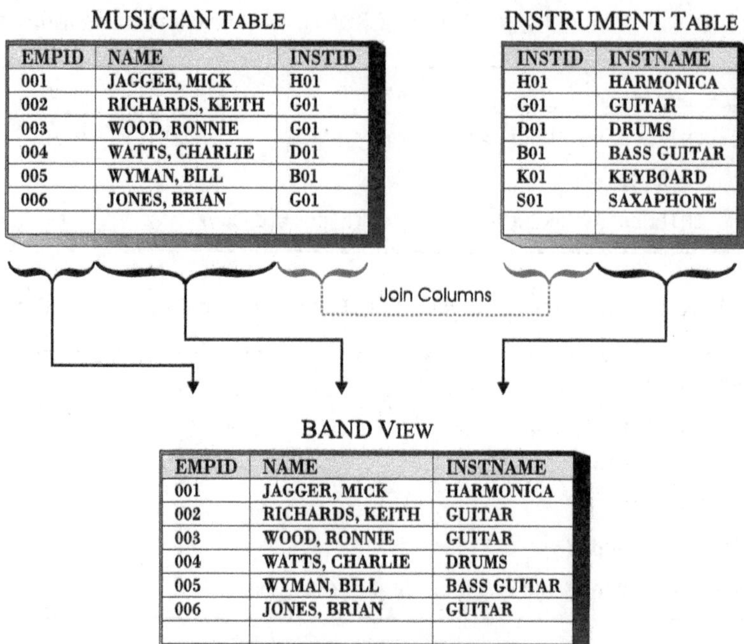

MUSICIAN TABLE

EMPID	NAME	INSTID
001	JAGGER, MICK	H01
002	RICHARDS, KEITH	G01
003	WOOD, RONNIE	G01
004	WATTS, CHARLIE	D01
005	WYMAN, BILL	B01
006	JONES, BRIAN	G01

INSTRUMENT TABLE

INSTID	INSTNAME
H01	HARMONICA
G01	GUITAR
D01	DRUMS
B01	BASS GUITAR
K01	KEYBOARD
S01	SAXAPHONE

BAND VIEW

EMPID	NAME	INSTNAME
001	JAGGER, MICK	HARMONICA
002	RICHARDS, KEITH	GUITAR
003	WOOD, RONNIE	GUITAR
004	WATTS, CHARLIE	DRUMS
005	WYMAN, BILL	BASS GUITAR
006	JONES, BRIAN	GUITAR

Figure 4.15: A simple database view that references two base tables

Because views allow different users to see different presentations of the same data, they are often used, together with view privileges, to control data access. For example, suppose you have a table that contains information about all employees who work for a particular company. You can give department managers access to this table via a view that allows them to see information only about the employees who work in their department. Members of the payroll department, however, can be granted access to the table via a view that allows them to see only the information needed to generate employee paychecks. Both sets of users have access to the same table; however, because each user works with a different view, it appears that the user is working with his or her own tables. By creating views and coupling them with the view privileges, a database administrator can have greater control over how individual users access specific pieces of data.

Note: Because there is no way to grant SELECT privileges on specific columns within a table (except by using row-level/column-level access control mechanisms), you can prevent users from accessing every column in a table by creating a result, summary, or declared temporary table that holds only the data a particular user needs—or by creating a view that contains only the table columns a user is allowed to access. Of the two options, a view is easier to implement and manage.

You can create or replace a view (if it is already present) by executing the CREATE OR REPLACE VIEW SQL statement. The basic syntax for this statement is:

```
CREATE OR REPLACE VIEW [ViewName]
<( [ColumnName] ,... )>
AS [SELECTStatement]
<WITH <LOCAL | CASCADED> CHECK OPTION>
```

where:

ViewName	Identifies the name to assign to the view to be created
ColumnName	Identifies the names of one or more columns to include in the view to be created; if a list of column names is specified, the number of column names provided must match the number of columns that will be returned by the SELECT statement used to create the view (if a list of column names is not provided, the columns of the view will inherit the names assigned to the columns returned by the SELECT statement used to create the view)
SELECTStatement	Identifies a SELECT SQL statement that, when executed, will produce data that will populate the view

Thus, to create a view that references all data stored in a table named DEPARTMENT and assign it the name DEPT_VIEW, execute a CREATE VIEW SQL statement:

```
CREATE VIEW dept_view AS SELECT * FROM department
```

However, if you want to create a view that references specific data values stored in a table named DEPARTMENT and assign it the name ADV_DEPT_VIEW, execute a CREATE VIEW SQL statement that looks something like this:

```
CREATE VIEW adv_dept_view
AS SELECT (dept_no, dept_name, dept_size)
    FROM department
    WHERE dept_size > 25
```

The view this statement creates will contain only department number, department name, and department size information for each department that has more than 25 people.

If you specify the WITH LOCAL CHECK OPTION clause in the CREATE VIEW SQL statement, insert and update operations performed against the newly created view are validated to ensure that all rows being inserted into or updated in the base table the view refers to conform to the view's definition (otherwise, the insert/update operation will fail). So what exactly does this mean?

Suppose you create a view by using the following CREATE VIEW statement:

```
CREATE VIEW priority_orders
AS SELECT * FROM orders WHERE response_time < 4
WITH LOCAL CHECK OPTION
```

Now, suppose a user tries to insert a record into this view that has a RESPONSE_TIME value of 6. The insert operation will fail with error code SQL0161N because the record violates the view's definition. Had the view not been created with the WITH LOCAL CHECK OPTION clause, the insert operation would have been successful, even though the new record would not have been visible to the view that was used to add it. Figure 4.16 illustrates how the WITH LOCAL CHECK OPTION clause works.

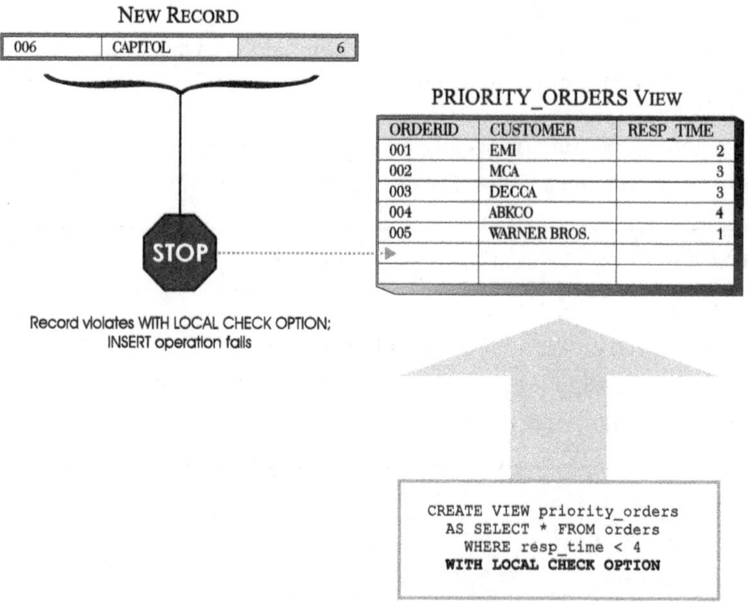

Figure 4.16: How the WITH LOCAL CHECK OPTION clause is used in a view's definition

Views created with the WITH LOCAL CHECK OPTION clause specified are referred to as *symmetric views* because every record that can be inserted into them can also be retrieved from them.

If you specify the WITH CASCADED CHECK OPTION clause in the CREATE VIEW SQL statement, the view created will inherit the search conditions of the parent view on which the view is based, and it will treat those conditions as one or more constraints that validate insert and update operations performed against the view. Additionally, every view created that is a child of the view that was created with the WITH CASCADED CHECK OPTION clause specified will inherit those constraints; the search conditions of both parent and child views are grouped together to form the constraints.

To better understand what this means, let us look at an example. Suppose you create a view by using the following CREATE VIEW statement:

```
CREATE VIEW priority_orders
AS SELECT * FROM orders WHERE response_time < 4
```

Now, suppose you create a second view by using this CREATE VIEW statement:

```
CREATE VIEW special_orders
AS SELECT * FROM priority_orders
WITH CASCADED CHECK OPTION
```

If a user tries to insert a record into the SPECIAL_ORDERS view that has a RESPONSE_TIME value of 6, the insert operation will fail with the same error code SQL0161N because the record violates the search condition of the PRIORITY_ORDERS view's definition (which is a constraint for the SPECIAL_ORDERS view). Figure 4.17 illustrates how the WITH CASCADED CHECK OPTION clause works.

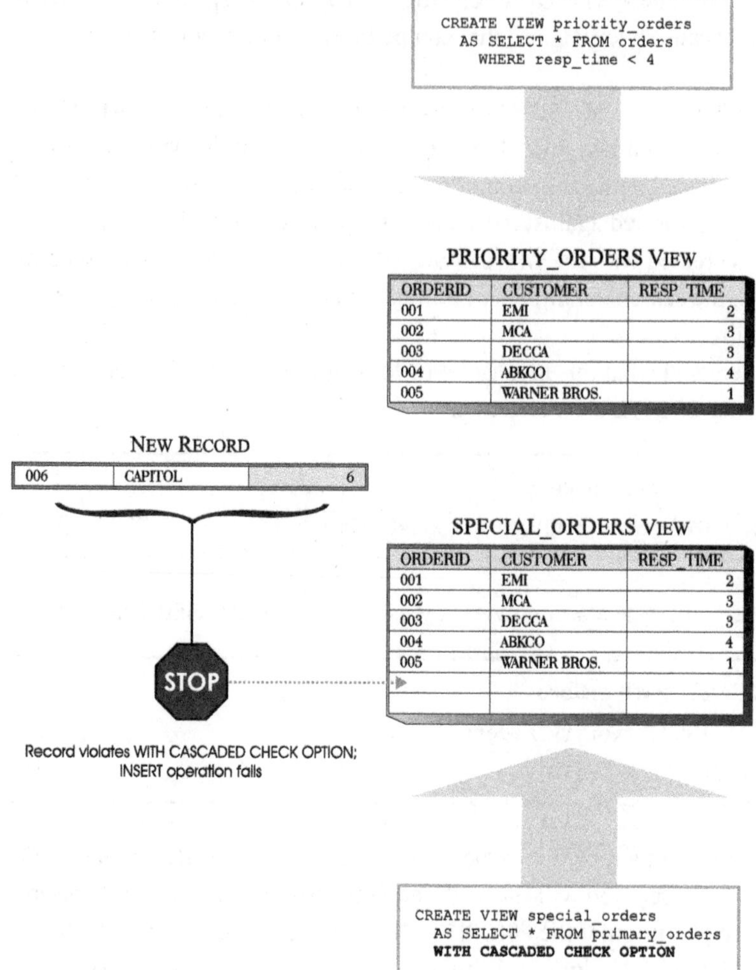

Figure 4.17: How the WITH CASCADED CHECK OPTION clause is used in a view's definition

A Word About Inoperative Views

An inoperative view is one that is no longer available and accessible to users and applications. A view can become inoperative when any of the following occur:

- A privilege on which the view definition is dependent is revoked, preventing access to one or more underlying base tables.
- An underlying view, table, alias, or function on which the view definition is dependent is dropped.
- A view on which the view definition is dependent becomes inoperative.

- The view's *superview* becomes inoperative (a superview is a typed view on which another typed view, known as a *subview*, is based).

Once a view becomes inoperative, you can follow these steps to recover it:

Step 1: Create the dropped parent object (view or a table) and then access the view to automatically activate it.

Step 2: Obtain the SQL statement you initially used to create the view by querying the TEXT column of the SYSCAT.VIEWS catalog view.

Step 3: Re-create the view by reexecuting the CREATE OR REPLACE VIEW statement (using the same view name and definition).

Step 4: Use the GRANT statement to regrant all privileges that were previously granted on the view. (Privileges granted on a view are revoked when the view is marked inoperative.)

If you do not wish to recover an inoperative view, you can explicitly drop it with the DROP VIEW statement. Alternatively, you can create a new view and assign it the same name as that of the inoperative view, but give it a different definition.

Let us look at the automatic object revalidation feature that was introduced in DB2 9.7. The database configuration parameter AUTO_REVAL controls the revalidation and invalidation semantics. You can set this configuration parameter online without restarting the database or the instance. This parameter can take any of the following values:

- IMMEDIATE
- DEFERRED
- DEFERRED_FORCE
- DISABLED

Setting the AUTO_REVAL configuration parameter to IMMEDIATE will revalidate all the dependent objects as soon as they become invalidated. Setting it to DEFERRED will revalidate all the dependent objects only after they are accessed the next time; until then, they are considered INVALID objects in the database. And setting the parameter to DEFERRED_FORCE will enable the CREATE WITH ERROR support feature, which allows creation of certain database objects (for example, views, functions, and triggers) even if the referenced object does not exist. For example, you can create a view on a table that never existed in the database. However, the database manager marks it as an INVALID view until you create a referenced base table. Setting AUTO_REVAL to DISABLED ensures that automatic object revalidation will never occur.

When the automatic object revalidation feature is enabled, views will never be marked inoperative. Instead, they are marked as INVALID and are automatically revalidated based on the

AUTO_REVAL configuration setting. You can query the SYSCAT.INVALIDOBJECTS system catalog view to understand the invalid object state.

Creating and Using Triggers

A trigger is a database object that can perform a set of actions in response to an insert, update, or delete operation on a specified table or view. Triggers are very useful in defining and enforcing the transitional business rules (rules that involve different states of data) centrally in the database, instead of defining them at multiple applications modules.

You can use triggers, along with referential constraints and CHECK constraints, to enforce data integrity rules. You can also use them to cause updates to other tables, to automatically generate or transform values for inserted or updated rows, or to invoke functions to perform tasks such as issuing alerts.

Five major components are associated with any trigger:

- The subject, on which the trigger is defined—basically, tables or views
- The event, which initiates the trigger—basically, an insert, update, or delete operation
- The activation time of the trigger—basically, a BEFORE or AFTER the event.
- The granularity, which specifies whether the trigger's actions are performed once for the statement or once for each of the affected rows—basically, a FOR EACH STATEMENT or FOR EACH ROW action
- The action, which the trigger performs—basically, one or more of the following elements:
  - » CALL statement
  - » DECLARE and/or SET variable statement
  - » WHILE and/or FOR loop
  - » IF, SIGNAL, ITERATE, LEAVE, and GET DIAGNOSTIC statements
  - » SELECT SQL statement
  - » INSERT, UPDATE, DELETE, and MERGE SQL statements (only for AFTER and INSTEAD OF triggers)

In DB2, triggers are classified as BEFORE, AFTER, or INSTEAD OF:

- BEFORE triggers are activated before an update or insert operation, and the values that are being updated or inserted can be changed before the database data is actually modified in the table. Generally, this trigger is used during data cleansing and modification. For example, if you are inserting a row into a table, the BEFORE trigger can check the integrity of the data. If the data does not adhere to the business rule, you can modify the data before it is inserted into the table.
- AFTER triggers are activated after an insert, update, or delete operation and are used to maintain relationship between data or to keep audit trail information. For example, if the

EMPLOYEE table has an insert operation due to a new hire, you can invoke an AFTER trigger to increase the number of employees in the COMPANY_STATS company statistics table.

- INSTEAD OF triggers define how to perform an insert, update, or delete operation on a view where these operations are otherwise not allowed. For example, suppose the HR department wants to update the salary for a set of people by using the V_EMPLOYEE view created on the EMPLOYEE table. Although the read-only view V_EMPLOYEE data cannot be modified, the underlying EMPLOYEE table data can. Thus, by using the INSTEAD OF trigger, you can ensure the business logic is triggered on the base table when an attempt is made to modify the read-only view data.

Triggers can be created or replaced (if it is already present) by executing the CREATE OR REPLACE TRIGGER SQL statement. The basic syntax for this statement is:

```
CREATE OR REPLACE TRIGGER [TriggerName]
<NO CASCADE>|<AFTER | BEFORE | INSTEAD OF> [TriggerEvent]
ON [TableName |ViewName]
REFERENCING <OLD AS | NEW AS | OLD TABLE AS | NEW TABLE AS>
            [CorrelationName |Identifier]
<FOR EACH ROW | FOR EACH STATEMENT>
<Action>
```

where:

TriggerName Identifies the name to assign to the trigger to be created

TriggerEvent Specifies to execute the triggered action associated with the trigger whenever one of the events is applied to the subject table or subject view

TableName Identifies the name of the table (subject) on which the trigger is defined

ViewName Identifies the name of the view (subject) on which the trigger is defined

CorrelationName Specifies a correlation name that identifies the row state before the triggering SQL operation

Identifier Specifies a temporary table name that identifies the set of affected rows before the triggering SQL operation

Action Specifies the action to perform when a trigger is activated; a triggered action consists of an SQL procedure statement and an optional condition for the execution of the SQL procedure statement

The following example illustrates a BEFORE trigger that is activated when an INSERT statement is executed on the EMPLOYEE table. According to the HR department's business rule, if the row being inserted has a NULL value for the column EMPSTARTDATE, then it should treat the employee start date as the next day. So the trigger EMPLOYEEJOINDATE assigns a value of the next day when it detects a NULL being inserted into the EMPSTARTDATE column of the EMPLOYEE table and continues with the insert operation:

```
CREATE OR REPLACE TRIGGER employeeJoinDate
    NO CASCADE BEFORE INSERT ON employee
    REFERENCING NEW AS N
    FOR EACH ROW
    MODE DB2SQL
    WHEN (N.EMPSTARTDATE IS NULL)
      SET N.EMPSTARTDATE = CURRENT DATE + 1 DAY
DB20000I  The SQL command completed successfully.

INSERT INTO employee
      (EMPID, EMPNAME, EMPPHONE, EMPDEPT, EMPADDRESS, EMPSTARTDATE)
      VALUES (001,'MILAN','07584203037','IS','VENUS, MANCHESTER', NULL)
DB20000I The SQL command completed successfully.

VALUES (CURRENT DATE)
      07/20/2014

1 record(s) selected.

SELECT * FROM employee

EMPID EMPNAME        EMPPHONE    EMPDEPT EMPADDRESS           EMPSTARTDATE
----- -------------- ----------- ------- -------------------- ------------
1     MILAN          07584203037 IS      VENUS, MANCHESTER    07/21/2014

1 record(s) selected.
```

In the following example, an AFTER trigger is activated when an INSERT statement is executed on the EMPLOYEE table. According to the HR department's business rule, if the row being inserted into the EMPLOYEE table is due to a new hire, the trigger statement will also update the employee head count in the company statistics table COMPANY_STATS:

```
CREATE OR REPLACE TRIGGER employeeNewHire
      NO CASCADE AFTER INSERT ON employee
      FOR EACH ROW
      MODE DB2SQL
      UPDATE COMPANY_STATS SET EMP_TCOUNT = EMP_TCOUNT + 1
DB20000I  The SQL command completed successfully.

SELECT * FROM COMPANY_STATS

EMP_TCOUNT  OFFICE_TCOUNT TURNOVER_TOTAL CEO
----------- ------------- -------------- --------------------
          1             1         200000 MILAN

  1 record(s) selected.

INSERT INTO EMPLOYEE

(EMPID, EMPNAME, EMPPHONE, EMPDEPT, EMPADDRESS, EMPSTARTDATE)
VALUES (002,'MOHAN','0161 6382409','IS','VENUS, MANCHESTER', NULL)
DB20000I The SQL command completed successfully.

SELECT * FROM COMPANY_STATS

EMP_TCOUNT  OFFICE_TCOUNT TURNOVER_TOTAL CEO
----------- ------------- -------------- --------------------
          2             1         200000 MILAN

  1 record(s) selected.
```

Continued

```
SELECT * FROM employee

EMPID EMPNAME EMPPHONE       EMPDEPT    EMPADDRESS          EMPSTARTDATE
----- ------- -------------- ---------- ------------------- --------------
1     MILAN   07584203037    IS         VENUS, MANCHESTER   07/21/2014
2     MOHAN   0161 6382409   IS         VENUS, MANCHESTER   07/21/2014

  2 record(s) selected.
```

Did the SELECT * FROM EMPLOYEE at the end of the example make you wonder? You are right—the INSERT INTO EMPLOYEE SQL statement triggered two trigger actions: one to insert EMPSTARTDATE and other to update EMP_TCOUNT. You can specify multiple triggers for a combination of table, event, or activation time. When more than one trigger exists for a particular table, event, and activation time, the order in which the triggers are activated is the same as the order in which they were created. Thus, the most recently created trigger is the last trigger to be activated.

Consider an example where the HR department wants to check for an employee pay raise before the salary change is actually made in the EMPLOYEE table. For any employee, if the pay raise is double the current salary, it must be recorded in the SALARY_AUDIT table for analysis purposes:

```
CREATE OR REPLACE TRIGGER employeeSalaryUpdate
      AFTER UPDATE OF salary ON employee
      REFERENCING NEW AS N OLD AS O
      FOR EACH ROW
      MODE DB2SQL
      WHEN (N.SALARY > O.SALARY * 2)
          INSERT INTO SALARY_AUDIT
                (EMPNO, OLD_SALARY, NEW_SALARY, RATING) VALUES
                (N.EMPID, O.SALARY, N.SALARY, N.RATING)

DB20000I  The SQL command completed successfully.
```

The following SQL statement extracts the information available in EMPLOYEE and salary_audit tables before activating the trigger employeeSalaryUpdate:

```
SELECT
      EMPID, VARCHAR (EMPNAME, 5) EMPNAME, EMPPHONE, EMPDEPT, EMPADDRESS,
      EMPSTARTDATE, SALARY, RATING
   FROM employee

EMPID EMPNAME EMPPHONE     EMPDEPT EMPADDRESS          EMPSTARTDATE SALARY RATING
----- ------- ----------- ------- ------------------- ------------ ------ ------
1     MILAN   07584203037        IS VENUS, MANCHESTER   07/21/2014   200000      1
2     MOHAN   0161 6382409       IS VENUS, MANCHESTER   07/21/2014   100000      1

  2 record(s) selected.

SELECT * FROM salary_audit

EMPNO       OLD_SALARY  NEW_SALARY  RATING
----------- ----------- ----------- -----------

  0 record(s) selected.
```

To activate the employeeSalaryUpdate trigger, update the salary column for Milan by tripling the salary:

```
UPDATE employee SET SALARY=600000 WHERE EMPID=1
DB20000I  The SQL command completed successfully.
```

And the trigger activation result is as follows:

```
SELECT * FROM salary_audit

EMPNO       OLD_SALARY  NEW_SALARY  RATING
----------- ----------- ----------- -----------
          1      200000      600000           1

  1 record(s) selected.
```

Triggers can also be used to raise errors through the SIGNAL statement and to prevent specific operations on the tables. For example, if the HR department rule is to disallow any pay raise that exceeds 300 percent, you can achieve this by using the trigger code, something like this:

```
CREATE TRIGGER salaryRaiseLimit
    AFTER UPDATE OF SALARY ON EMPLOYEE
    REFERENCING NEW AS N OLD AS O
    FOR EACH ROW
    WHEN (N.SALARY > O.SALARY * 3)
      SIGNAL SQLSTATE '75000' SET MESSAGE_TEXT='Salary increase>100%'
DB20000I  The SQL command completed successfully.

UPDATE employee SET SALARY=400000 WHERE EMPID=2;
DB21034E  The command was processed as an SQL statement because it was not
a valid Command Line Processor command.  During SQL processing it returned:
SQL0438N  Application raised error or warning with diagnostic text: "Salary
increase>100%". SQLSTATE=75000
```

You can use REFERENCING OLD_TABLE and NEW_TABLE transition tables whenever you need to work on the original and the modified result set in a trigger. For example, suppose the HR department rule is to disallow any pay raise in which the sum of the salary between the old and the new salary exceeds 200 percent. To achieve this, use the transition table trigger, something like this:

```
CREATE OR REPLACE TRIGGER TurnOverUpdate
  AFTER UPDATE OF salary ON employee
  REFERENCING NEW_TABLE AS N OLD_TABLE AS O
  FOR EACH ROW
  MODE DB2SQL
  WHEN ((SELECT SUM (SALARY) FROM N) > (SELECT SUM (SALARY) * 2 FROM O))
    SIGNAL SQLSTATE '76000' SET MESSAGE_TEXT='Company Level Pay Raise is
more than 200%'
DB20000I The SQL command completed successfully.
```

Continued

```
UPDATE employee SET SALARY = SALARY * 3
DB21034E  The command was processed as an SQL statement because it was not
a valid Command Line Processor command.  During SQL processing it returned:
SQL0438N Application raised error or warning with diagnostic text: "Company
Level Pay Raise is more than 200%". SQLSTATE=76000
```

When you use an INSTEAD OF trigger, the requested modified operation against the view is replaced by the trigger logic, which performs the operation on behalf of the view. From the application's perspective, this happens transparently, as it perceives that all operations are performed against the view. Only one INSTEAD OF trigger is allowed for each kind of operation on a given subject view.

Finally, a trigger definition cannot be modified when there is a need to change the trigger code. You will have to use the CREATE OR REPLACE command, which internally drops and re-creates the trigger. Otherwise, you can explicitly drop the trigger by using the DROP TRIGGER command and create it by using the CREATE TRIGGER command.

A Word About Multiple-Event Triggers

In DB2 10.1, you can create a multiple-event trigger to fire off a trigger action based on one of three possible triggering events—an INSERT, an UPDATE, or a DELETE statement—instead of creating a separate trigger for each event.

Multiple-event triggers are supported for both row-level triggers (FOR EACH ROW) and statement-level triggers (FOR EACH STATEMENT), which allows you to transform a complex business rule into sophisticated trigger logic. It also helps you greatly during the database migration process to migrate other database vendor products to DB2.

Consider an example where the HR department wants an audit log to be set for any insert, update, or delete operation on the EMPLOYEE table for the column SALARY. The code to do so looks something like this:

```
CREATE OR REPLACE TRIGGER employeeSalaryMulti
    AFTER INSERT OR DELETE OR UPDATE OF salary ON employee
    REFERENCING NEW AS N OLD AS O
    FOR EACH ROW
    MODE DB2SQL
    BEGIN
```

Continued

```
    INSERT INTO SALARY_AUDIT
           (EMPNO, OLD_SALARY, NEW_SALARY, RATING) VALUES
           (N.EMPID, O.SALARY, N.SALARY, N.RATING);--

    END
DB20000I The SQL command completed successfully.
```

The EMPLOYEE and SALARY_AUDIT table data extracts before triggering the event are as follows:

```
SELECT * FROM employee

EMPID EMPNAME EMPPHONE     EMPDEPT EMPADDRESS        EMPSTARTDATE SALARY RATING
----- ------- ------------ ------- ----------------- ------------ ------ ------
1     MILAN   07584203037       IS VENUS, MANCHESTER 07/21/2014   600000      1
2     MOHAN   0161 6382409      IS VENUS, MANCHESTER 07/21/2014   100000      1

  2 record(s) selected.

SELECT * FROM salary_audit

EMPNO       OLD_SALARY  NEW_SALARY  RATING
----------- ----------- ----------- -----------
          1      200000      600000           1
          2      100000      300000           1

  2 record(s) selected.
```

A new employee addition into the EMPLOYEE table, as below, will generate an event and trigger an action to insert a record in the SALARY_AUDIT table:

```
INSERT INTO employee VALUES (3, 'KENT', '8173520251','IS','USA', NULL,
       200000, 1)
DB20000I  The SQL command completed successfully.
```

Continued

```
SELECT * FROM salary_audit

EMPNO       OLD_SALARY  NEW_SALARY  RATING
----------- ----------- ----------- -----------
          1      200000      600000           1
          2      100000      300000           1
          3           -      200000           1

  3 record(s) selected.
```

Likewise, deleting or updating an entry in the EMPLOYEE table will generate an event and insert a record in the SALARY_AUDIT table, something like:

```
DELETE FROM employee WHERE EMPID=2
DB20000I  The SQL command completed successfully.

SELECT * FROM salary_audit

EMPNO       OLD_SALARY  NEW_SALARY  RATING
----------- ----------- ----------- -----------
          1      200000      600000           1
          2      100000      300000           1
          3           -      200000           1
          -      100000           -           -

  4 record(s) selected.


UPDATE employee SET SALARY = SALARY * 2 WHERE EMPID=3
DB20000I  The SQL command completed successfully.

SELECT * FROM salary_audit

                                           Continued
```

```
EMPNO       OLD_SALARY  NEW_SALARY  RATING
----------- ----------- ----------- -----------
          1      200000      600000           1
          2      100000      300000           1
          3           -      200000           1
          -      100000           -           -
          3      200000      400000           1

  5 record(s) selected.
```

A Word About the System Catalog

The system catalog consists of a set of special tables (and views) that includes information about all the objects within a database. These tables contain information about the definitions of the database objects (for example, tables, views, indexes, and packages) and security information about the type of access that users have to these objects. In Chapter 3, "Physical Design," you saw that the system catalog tables are created automatically when a new database is created. You cannot explicitly create or drop these tables, but you can control who has access to them.

Whenever an object is created, altered, or dropped, DB2 inserts, updates, or deletes records in the catalog that describe the object and how that object relates to other objects. Thus, if you want to obtain information about a particular database, often you can do so by connecting to that database and querying the system catalog. For example, to find out whether a table named EMPLOYEE must be reorganized to eliminate fragmentation, you execute a query against a system catalog table named SYSCAT.TABLES:

```
SELECT TABNAME, OVERFLOW FROM
    FROM SYSCAT.TABLES
    WHERE TABNAME = 'EMPLOYEE'
```

If the results of this query indicate that a high number of overflow records exists for the EMPLOYEE table, the data is fragmented, and the table probably needs to be reorganized. (We will look at how to reorganize a table in Chapter 6, "DB2 Utilities.")

However, if you want to know whether statistics have been collected for the EMPLOYEE table, you can execute a query against the system catalog, as follows:

```
SELECT CARD AS num_rows, STATS_TIME
   FROM SYSCAT.TABLES
   WHERE TABNAME = 'EMPLOYEE'
```

In this case, if the query returns a value of -1 instead of the number of rows stored in the EMPLOYEE table, statistics have not been collected. (We will look at how to collect statistics for a table in Chapter 6.)

To extract a trigger definition, you can use the SYSCAT.TRIGGERS system catalog view and generate the trigger code:

```
SELECT
      VARCHAR         (TRIGNAME, 20) TRIGNAME,
      VARCHAR         (TEXT, 400) TEXT
   FROM SYSCAT.TRIGGERS WHERE TRIGNAME='EMPLOYEEJOININDATE'

EMPLOYEEJOININDATE     CREATE OR REPLACE TRIGGER employeeJoinDate
        NO CASCADE BEFORE INSERT ON EMPLOYEE
        REFERENCING NEW AS N
        FOR EACH ROW
        MODE DB2SQL
        WHEN (N.EMPSTARTDATE IS NULL)
                SET N.EMPSTARTDATE = CURRENT DATE + 1 DAY

  1 record(s) selected.
```

It is possible to reconstruct any database object (for example, tables, views, indexes, sequences, triggers, stored procedures, constraints) by directly or indirectly using the system catalog information (other than executing a simple db2look command).

The possibilities are almost endless. To find out more about the tables in the system catalog and the information each table holds, refer to Appendix D, "Catalog Views," in the *IBM DB2 10.1 SQL Reference, Volume 1* (page 853) product documentation.

You can use the system catalog only to obtain information about a specific database. To obtain information at the system level, you must resort to executing administrative system commands or querying the administrative views. For example, to obtain information about the DB2 products that have been installed on a particular server, you must execute the system command db2ls -q -a (UNIX) or issue a query against the SYSIBMADM.ENV_PROD_INFO administrative view:

```
SELECT
       VARCHAR (INSTALLED_PROD,5) INSTALLED_PROD,
       VARCHAR(INSTALLED_PROD_FULLNAME,30) INSTALLED_PROD_FULLNAME,
       LICENSE_INSTALLED, VARCHAR(PROD_RELEASE,5) PROD_RELEASE,
       VARCHAR (LICENSE_TYPE,5) LICENSE_TYPE
   FROM SYSIBMADM.ENV_PROD_INFO;

                                                  LICENSE_  PROD_
INSTALLED_PROD INSTALLED_PROD_FULLNAME            INSTALLED RELEASE LICENSE_TYPE
-------------- ------------------------------ --------- ------- ------------
ESE            DB2_ENTERPRISE_SERVER_EDITION  Y         10.1    CPU

  1 record(s) selected.
```

Chapter Summary

The objective of this chapter was to familiarize you with

- What the business rules are and their importance in the real data world
- Various constraints within DB2 and making use of them to build the business rules at the database layer, instead of building them at the application layer
- The SET INTEGRITY command and the exception table to copy the business rule violated data
- Triggers and various types, along with HR partner business rules implementation
- The significance of system catalog tables and examining their content

On completion of this chapter, you will be equipped with sufficient knowledge to answer the business rules implementation questions in the certification exam. It is also highly recommended that you complete the sample questions at the end of the chapter.

Practice Questions

Question 1

What are informational constraints used for?

- ❍ A. To influence DB2 optimizer data access plan selection without slowing down DML operations
- ❍ B. To provide information to an application about any defined constraints
- ❍ C. To define nonchecked primary keys
- ❍ D. To influence the DB2 optimizer data access plans for foreign key–primary key relationships

Question 2

Consider the following CREATE TABLE statement:

```
CREATE TABLE department
      (     deptid      INTEGER,
            deptname    CHAR(25),
            budget      NUMERIC(12,2));
```

Which statement prevents two departments from being assigned the same DEPTID but allows NULL values?

- ❍ A. ALTER TABLE department ADD CONSTRAINT dpt_cst PRIMARY KEY (deptid)
- ❍ B. CREATE INDEX dpt_idx ON department(deptid)
- ❍ C. ALTER TABLE department ADD CONSTRAINT dpt_cst UNIQUE (deptid)
- ❍ D. CREATE UNIQUE INDEX dpt_idx ON department(deptid)

Question 3

Consider the following CREATE TABLE statement:

```
CREATE TABLE products
   ( prodid      INTEGER NOT NULL PRIMARY KEY,
     category    CHAR(3) CHECK(category IN ('323', '441', '615',
                 '832', '934')),
     description VARCHAR(200),
     quantity    INTEGER CHECK (quantity > 0),
     sellprice   NUMERIC(7,2) WITH DEFAULT,
     buyprice    NUMERIC(7,2) WITH DEFAULT,
   CONSTRAINT zeroloss CHECK (sellprice > buyprice))
```

Assuming the table is empty, which INSERT statement will succeed?

- ❍ A. INSERT INTO products (prodid, category, description, buyprice) VALUES (1, '832', 'medium white shirt', 6.99)
- ❍ B. INSERT INTO products (prodid, category, quantity, sellprice, buyprice) VALUES (2, '323', 5, 28.99, 26.99)
- ❍ C. INSERT INTO products (prodid, category, description, quantity) VALUES (1, '934', 'black shoe', 10)
- ❍ D. INSERT INTO products (prodid, category, description, quantity, sellprice, buyprice) VALUES (2, '615', 'dark blue socks', 3, 20.00, 25.65)

Question 4

Consider the following CREATE TABLE statement:

```
CREATE TABLE employee
      (    empid       INTEGER NOT NULL,
           name        VARCHAR(25),
           gender      CHAR(1) NOT NULL,
CONSTRAINT gender_ok CHECK(gender IN ('M', 'F')) NOT ENFORCED
ENABLE QUERY OPTIMIZATION)
```

What effect, if any, will the following command have when it is executed?

```
ALTER TABLE employee ALTER CHECK gender_ok
DISABLE QUERY OPTIMIZATION
```

❍ A. The GENDER_OK constraint will become an enforced CHECK constraint and will be used to check the validity of insert and update operations.

❍ B. The GENDER_OK constraint will become an enforced CHECK constraint, and any data in the EMPLOYEE table will be checked immediately for constraint violations.

❍ C. The DB2 optimizer's ability to use the GENDER_OK constraint for query optimization will be disabled.

❍ D. All data access plans that used the GENDER_OK constraint for query optimization will be marked inoperative.

Question 5

Consider the following CREATE TABLE statement:

```
CREATE TABLE employee
      (    empid       INTEGER NOT NULL,
           lname       VARCHAR(20),
           gender      CHAR(1) NOT NULL,
CONSTRAINT gender_ok CHECK(gender IN ('M', 'F')) NOT ENFORCED
ENABLE QUERY OPTIMIZATION)
```

And consider the following INSERT statement:

```
INSERT INTO employee VALUES (1, 'Smith', 'M'), (2, 'Doe', 'F'), (3,
'Jones', 'U')
```

Which query will return an empty result set?

❍ A. SELECT COUNT (gender) FROM employee

❍ B. SELECT * FROM employee WHERE gender = 'M'

❍ C. SELECT * FROM employee WHERE gender = 'F'

❍ D. SELECT * FROM employee WHERE gender = 'U'

Question 6

Which CREATE VIEW statement will ensure that every attempt to insert or update a record in table T1 via the view V1 must pass some criteria before the row can be inserted or updated?

- ❍ A. CREATE VIEW v1 AS SELECT c1, c2 FROM t1 WHERE c1 < 100
- ❍ B. CREATE VIEW v1 AS SELECT c1, c2 FROM t1 WHERE c1 < 100 ENFORCED
- ❍ C. CREATE VIEW v1 AS SELECT c1, c2 FROM t1 WHERE c1 < 100 WITH VALIDATION
- ❍ D. CREATE VIEW v1 AS SELECT c1, c2 FROM t1 WHERE c1 < 100 WITH LOCAL CHECK OPTION

Question 7

Which statement is *not* true concerning inoperative views?

- ❍ A. A view can become inoperative when a privilege the view definition is dependent upon is revoked.
- ❍ B. Privileges granted on a view are revoked when the view is marked inoperative.
- ❍ C. An inoperative view must be recovered before it can be dropped.
- ❍ D. An inoperative view can be re-created by reexecuting the statement initially used to create it (found in the TEXT column of the SYSCAT.VIEW catalog view).

Question 8

Consider the following table:

```
SALES

REGION                 SALES_REP_ID           AMOUNT
---------------------  ---------------------  -------------
East                   1200                           24000
East                   1420                           32000
West                   1200                           29000
South                  2120                           34000
```

If you execute the following SQL statements, how many rows will be returned by the last query?

```
CREATE UNIQUE INDEX indx1 ON sales(sales_rep_id);
INSERT INTO sales VALUES ('North', 1420, 27500);
SELECT * FROM sales;
```

❍ A. 3
❍ B. 4
❍ C. 5
❍ D. 6

Question 9

Which statement best describes the function of the db2ls command?

❍ A. It retrieves information about the DB2 products that have been installed on a particular server.
❍ B. It locks a DB2 system and limits access to users who hold System Administrator authority.
❍ C. It generates a list of all remote servers that have been cataloged on a client workstation.
❍ D. It returns the location of the system catalog for a particular database.

Question 10

Suppose you execute this query:

```
SELECT TABNAME, OVERFLOW
   FROM SYSCAT.TABLES
   WHERE TABNAME = 'SALES'
```

Which of the following can you determine based on the results?

- ❍ A. Whether the SALES table must be reorganized to reduce data fragmentation
- ❍ B. Whether the amount of memory available for sort operations must be increased
- ❍ C. Whether statistics for the SALES table must be updated
- ❍ D. Whether the size of the lock list must be increased to reduce the amount of lock escalations seen

Question 11

Suppose you execute the following query:

```
SELECT TABNAME, CARD, STATS_TIME
   FROM SYSCAT.TABLES
   WHERE TABNAME = 'EMPLOYEES'
```

Which of the following can you determine based on the results?

- ❍ A. Whether the EMPLOYEES table must be reorganized to reduce data fragmentation
- ❍ B. Whether the amount of storage available for the table space where the EMPLOYEES table resides must be increased
- ❍ C. Whether statistics for the EMPLOYEES table have been collected
- ❍ D. Whether storage space can be saved by enabling the EMPLOYEES table for data row compression

Question 12

Which statement about BEFORE triggers is false?

❍ A. A BEFORE trigger's action is executed for each row in the set of affected rows before the trigger event executes.

❍ B. A BEFORE trigger can be used to delete data in a database table.

❍ C. A BEFORE trigger is used to perform data cleansing and transformation to generate values for newly inserted rows.

❍ D. A BEFORE trigger cannot be used to modify data in a database table because BEFORE triggers are activated before the trigger event is applied to the database.

Question 13

What are the purposes of using the SET INTEGRITY command? (Choose two.)

❒ A. To take a table out of Set Integrity Pending state by performing the required integrity processing on the table

❒ B. To take a table out of Set Integrity Pending state by performing only CHECK constraint processing on the table

❒ C. To take a table out of Set Integrity Pending state without performing the required integrity processing on the table

❒ D. To take a table out of Set Integrity Pending state by performing only referential integrity constraint processing on the table

❒ E. To take a table out of Set Integrity Pending state by performing only referential integrity and CHECK constraint processing on the table

Question 14

You want to modify an existing view so that any rows that are inserted or updated with the view will not violate the SELECT statement used to create the view. What should you do?

❍ A. Alter the view and add the ENFORCE SELECT clause to the view definition.

❍ B. Drop and re-create the view with the WITH CHECK OPTION clause specified.

❍ C. Alter the view and add the WITH CHECK OPTION clause to the view definition.

❍ D. Create a new view with the same name and specify the ENFORCE SELECT clause.

Question 15

Consider the following statement:

```
CREATE TABLE employee
      (    empid         INTEGER NOT NULL PRIMARY KEY,
           empname       VARCHAR(20) NOT NULL,
           deptid        INTEGER NOT NULL,
           mgrname       VARCHAR(20),
           address       VARCHAR(20));
```

How many constraints are present in the EMPLOYEE table?

- ❍ A. 1
- ❍ B. 2
- ❍ C. 3
- ❍ D. 4

Question 16

What types of CHECK OPTIONS can you use to create the views? (Choose two.)

- ❒ A. Local
- ❒ B. Client
- ❒ C. Server
- ❒ D. Remote
- ❒ E. Cascaded

Question 17

Which statement about referential constraints is true?

- ❍ A. A referential constraint can be defined against a system catalog table.
- ❍ B. A referential constraint can be defined on both tables and views.
- ❍ C. A referential constraint is used to enforce business rules on one or more columns in one or more tables.
- ❍ D. A referential constraint is used to enforce business rules on how values in one or more columns in a table are to be referenced in a query.

Question 18

Which statement about the primary keys is true?

- A. A table can have multiple primary keys.
- B. A primary key accepts one, and only one, NULL value.
- C. A unique index, with matching columns of the primary key, must be created before a primary key can be created.
- D. A unique bidirectional index is automatically created for the columns of the primary key, if an appropriate unique index does not already exist.

Question 19

Consider the following command:

```
LOAD FROM employee.del OF DEL REPLACE INTO employee NONRECOVERABLE
```

Which statement must be executed before applications can query the newly loaded business rules' adhering data?

- A. SET INTEGRITY FOR employee IMMEDIATE CHECKED
- B. ALTER TABLE employee CHECK (COL IS VALIDATED)
- C. ALTER TABLE employee ALLOW READ ACCESS IMMEDIATE CHECKED
- D. SET INTEGRITY FOR employee IMMEDIATE UNCHECKED

Question 20

Which statement about triggers is false?

- A. A statement-level trigger fires only once for each SQL statement.
- B. A trigger's code block can be executed either before or after a triggering event.
- C. A row-level trigger fires once for each row that is affected by a triggering event.
- D. A table-level trigger fires once for each table that is affected by a triggering event.

Question 21

Which trigger activation time is invalid?

- ❍ A. AFTER trigger
- ❍ B. BEFORE trigger
- ❍ C. INTERMEDIATE trigger
- ❍ D. INSTEAD OF trigger

Question 22

Which statement about triggers is incorrect?

- ❍ A. You can create triggers on nicknames.
- ❍ B. You can create triggers on tables.
- ❍ C. You can create triggers on read-only views.
- ❍ D. You can create triggers on multiple columns of a table.

Question 23

A trigger definition can be modified by using which of the following?

- ❍ A. UPDATE TRIGGER command
- ❍ B. MODIFY TRIGGER command
- ❍ C. CREATE OR REPLACE command
- ❍ D. ALTER TRIGGER command

Question 24

Consider the following statements:

```
CREATE TABLE TEST (ID INT);
CREATE VIEW v1 AS SELECT id FROM test WHERE id > 20;
CREATE VIEW v2 AS SELECT id FROM v1 WITH CASCADED CHECK OPTION;
CREATE VIEW v3 AS SELECT id FROM v2 WHERE id < 50;
```

Which INSERT statement will fail?

- ❍ A. INSERT INTO v1 VALUES (10);
- ❍ B. INSERT INTO v2 VALUES (5);
- ❍ C. INSERT INTO v3 VALUES (50);
- ❍ D. INSERT INTO v3 VALUES (100);

Question 25

Which statement is false regarding a SET INTEGRITY exception table?

- ❍ A. The exception table definition must match the definition of the integrity checking table.
- ❍ B. The exception table can have two additional columns: one is TIMESTAMP and another is CLOB (32 KB).
- ❍ C. The exception table must also have similar constraints defined as in the integrity checking table.
- ❍ D. The exception table must not be created as range partition or range clustered tables.

Question 26

Which of the following can be referenced by a foreign key constraint? (Choose two.)

- ❒ A. Primary key constraint
- ❒ B. Identity column
- ❒ C. CHECK constraint
- ❒ D. UNIQUE constraint
- ❒ E. NOT NULL constraint

Answers

Question 1

The correct answer is **A**. Unlike other constraints, informational constraints are not enforced during insert and update processing. However, the DB2 SQL optimizer will evaluate information provided by an informational constraint when considering the best access plan to use to resolve a query. Consequently, an informational constraint may result in better query performance even though the constraint itself will not be used to validate data entry or modification. (You define informational constraints by appending the keywords `NOT ENFORCED ENABLE QUERY OPTIMIZATION` to a normal constraint definition.)

Question 2

The correct answer is **D**. By default, records that are added to a base table can have the same values assigned to any columns any number of times. You can use the `UNIQUE` constraint to ensure that the values assigned to one or more columns when a record is added to a base table are always unique. Once you have defined a `UNIQUE` constraint for one or more columns, any operation that attempts to place duplicate values in those columns will fail. `UNIQUE` constraints are usually defined during the table creation process, but can be added later with the `ALTER TABLE` SQL statement.

When a `UNIQUE` constraint is defined, the DB2 database manager determines whether an index for the columns the `UNIQUE` constraint refers to already exists. If so, that index is marked as being unique and system required. If not, an appropriate index is created and marked as being unique and system required. This index is then used to enforce uniqueness whenever new records are added to the columns the `UNIQUE` constraint was defined for.

Although a unique, system-required index is used to enforce a `UNIQUE` constraint, there is a distinction between defining a `UNIQUE` constraint and creating a unique index. Both enforce uniqueness, but a unique index allows `NULL` values and generally cannot be used in a referential constraint. A `UNIQUE` constraint, however, does not allow `NULL` values and can be referenced in a foreign key specification.

Question 3

The correct answer is **B**. The first `INSERT` statement will fail because the resulting `SELLPRICE` will be 0 (since no value was provided), and a `SELLPRICE` of 0 is less than a `BUYPRICE` of 6.99, which violates the `ZEROLOSS CHECK` constraint. The third `INSERT` statement will fail because the `CATEGORY '423'` is not in the set of values allowed for the `CATEGORY` column. Also, the resulting `SELLPRICE` and `BUYPRICE` will be 0 (since no value was provided), and a `SELLPRICE` of 0 is not greater than a `BUYPRICE` of 0, which violates the `ZEROLOSS CHECK` constraint. And finally, the last `INSERT` statement will fail because a `SELLPRICE` of 20.00 is less than a `BUYPRICE` of 25.65, which violates the `ZEROLOSS CHECK` constraint.

Question 4

The correct answer is **C**. To instruct the DB2 optimizer to ignore an informational constraint when selecting the best data access plan to use to resolve a query, you simply disable query optimization for the constraint. You can do this when you create the constraint, or you can do it later by executing an `ALTER TABLE` statement, identifying the constraint to alter, and specifying the `DISABLE QUERY OPTIMIZATION` option.

Question 5

The correct answer is **D**. Because the DB2 optimizer evaluates informational constraints when selecting the best data access plan to use to resolve a query, records that have been inserted into a table that violate one or more informational constraints may not be returned by some queries. Thus, if you were to execute the query `SELECT * FROM employee WHERE gender = 'U'` against the `EMPLOYEE` table shown, no records would be returned because the access plan chosen would assume that no records with a `GENDER` value of anything other than `'M'` or `'F'` exists in the table.

Question 6

The correct answer is **D**. If you specify the `WITH LOCAL CHECK OPTION` clause in the `CREATE VIEW` SQL statement (or select the **Local Check** option on the Create View dialog), insert and update operations performed against the view that is created are validated to ensure that all rows being inserted into or updated in the base table the view refers to conform to the view's definition (otherwise, the insert/update operation will fail). So what exactly does this mean? Suppose you created a view by using the following `CREATE VIEW` statement:

```
CREATE VIEW priority_orders
AS SELECT * FROM orders WHERE response_time < 4
WITH LOCAL CHECK OPTION
```

Now, suppose a user tries to insert a record into this view that has a `RESPONSE_TIME` value of 6. The insert operation will fail because the record violates the view's definition. Had the view not been created with the `WITH LOCAL CHECK OPTION` clause, the insert operation would have been successful, even though the new record would not be visible to the view that was used to add it.

Question 7

The correct answer is **C**. If you do not wish to recover an inoperative view, you can explicitly drop it with the `DROP VIEW` statement. Alternatively, you can create a new view and assign it the same name as that of the inoperative view, but give it a different definition.

Question 8

The correct answer is **C**. If the `UNIQUE` clause is specified when the `CREATE INDEX` statement is executed, rows in the table associated with the index to be created must not have two or more occurrences of the same values in the set of columns that make up the index key. If the base table the index is to be created for contains data, this uniqueness is checked when the DB2 database manager attempts to create the specified index—if records with duplicate values for the index key are found, the index will not be created. If no duplicates are found, the index is created and uniqueness is enforced each time an insert or update operation is performed against the table.

In this example, records with duplicate SALES_REP_ID numbers were found when the CREATE INDEX statement was executed, so the statement failed and the next insert operation was successful, bringing the total number of rows in the SALES table to 5.

Question 9

The correct answer is **A**. You can use the system catalog only to obtain information about a specific database. If you want to obtain information at the system level, you must resort to executing administrative system commands or querying the administrative views. For example, to obtain information about the DB2 products that have been installed on a particular server, you must execute the system command db2ls -q -a (if you are on a Linux or UNIX server).

Question 10

The correct answer is **A**. Whenever an object is created, altered, or dropped, DB2 inserts, updates, or deletes records in the catalog that describe the object and how that object relates to other objects. Thus, to obtain information about a particular database, you often can do so by connecting to that database and querying the system catalog. For example, suppose you want to find out whether a table named EMPLOYEES must be reorganized to eliminate fragmentation. You can do so by executing a query against a system catalog table named SYSCAT.TABLES:

```
SELECT TABNAME, OVERFLOW FROM
   FROM SYSCAT.TABLES
   WHERE TABNAME = 'EMPLOYEES'
```

If the results of this query indicate that a high number of overflow records exists for the EMPLOYEES table, the data is fragmented, and the table probably needs to be reorganized.

Question 11

The correct answer is **C**. The CARD column of SYSCAT.TABLES contains the number of rows found in each table the last time statistics were collected for the table. If this column has the value -1 instead of the number of rows stored in the table, statistics have not been collected. Also STATS_TIME will indicate when exactly the last update statistics were run on this table.

Question 12

The correct answer is **B**. The BEFORE triggers are activated before an update or insert operation, and the values that are being updated or inserted can be changed before the database data is actually modified in the table. Generally, this trigger is used during data cleansing and modification. For example, if you are inserting a row into a table, the BEFORE trigger can check the integrity of the data, and if the data does not abide by the business rule, you can modify the data before inserting it into the table. However, BEFORE triggers cannot be used to *delete* data as part of the trigger action.

Question 13

The correct answers are **A** and **C**. The purpose of using the SET INTEGRITY command is as follows:

- To temporarily suspend constraint checking for a table and deny read-only access to that table while constraint checking is turned off, you execute a statement that looks something like this:

```
SET INTEGRITY FOR employee OFF
```

- To resume constraint checking for a table for which constraint checking was suspended, you execute a statement that looks something like this:

```
SET INTEGRITY FOR employee IMMEDIATE CHECKED
```

- However, if you execute the following form of the SET INTEGRITY statement, the table is taken out of the Set Integrity Pending state, and no constraint checking is performed:

```
SET INTEGRITY FOR employee ALL IMMEDIATE UNCHECKED
```

- When you execute yet another form of the SET INTEGRITY command that uses the FOR EXCEPTION IN clause, the table is taken out of the Set Integrity Pending state, and constraint-violated rows are copied into an exception table. The statement looks something like this:

```
SET INTEGRITY FOR employee
IMMEDIATE CHECKED FOR EXCEPTION IN employee USE bad_rows
```

Question 14

The correct answer is **B**. When you want to change the definition of a view to include the WITH CHECK OPTION clause, the only way to do so is to drop and re-create the view using the CREATE OR REPLACE VIEW command, or by explicitly dropping the view using DROP VIEW and recreating it using the CREATE VIEW command.

Question 15

The correct answer is **D**. The EMPLOYEE table has four constraints—three NOT NULL constraints and one primary key referential integrity constraint.

Question 16

The correct answers are **A** and **E**. If you specify the WITH LOCAL CHECK OPTION clause in the CREATE VIEW SQL statement, insert and update operations performed against the view created are validated to ensure that all rows being inserted into or updated in the base table the view refers to conform to the view's definition (otherwise, the insert/update operation will fail).

If you specify the `WITH CASCADED CHECK OPTION` clause in the `CREATE VIEW` SQL statement, the view created will inherit the search conditions of the parent view on which the view is based, and it will treat those conditions as one or more constraints to use to validate insert and update operations that are performed against the view. Additionally, every view created that is a child of the view created with the `WITH CASCADED CHECK OPTION` clause specified will inherit those constraints; the search conditions of both parent and child views are grouped together to form the constraints.

Question 17

The correct answer is **C**. Referential integrity ensures that relationships between user tables remain consistent. When one table has a foreign key to another table, the concept of referential integrity states that you cannot add a record to the table that contains the foreign key unless a corresponding record exists in the primary table. It also includes the techniques known as *cascading update* and *cascading delete*, which ensure that changes made to the primary table are reflected in the foreign table. Referential constraints cannot be created on system catalog tables, system catalog views, or user created views, and they cannot recommend how to reference a query while building the business logic. Also, you cannot establish a referential constraint between a relational column and an element in an XML document.

Question 18

The correct answer is **D**. When you create a primary key, the DB2 database manager automatically creates a unique bidirectional index. If an appropriate unique index is present, then DB2 uses the existing index and marks it as system required. You can create one and only one primary key in a table; however, the primary key can have multiple columns defined. A primary key does not accept `NULL` values, but a unique index does accept one `NULL` value.

Question 19

The correct answer is **A**. It is always recommended to run the `SET INTEGRITY IMMEDIATE CHECK` command to ensure that data between multiple referencing tables is adhering to the business rules.

Question 20

The correct answer is **D**. There is no table-level trigger in the database management system. Five major components are associated with any trigger:

- The subject, on which the trigger is defined—basically, tables or views
- The event, which initiates the trigger—basically, an insert, update, or delete operation
- The activation time of the trigger—basically, a `BEFORE` or `AFTER` the event

- The granularity, which specifies whether the trigger's actions are performed once for the statement or once for the each of the affected rows—basically, a FOR EACH STATEMENT or FOR EACH ROW action
- The action, which the trigger performs—basically, one or more of the following elements:
  - CALL statement
  - DECLARE and/or SET variable statement
  - WHILE and/or FOR loop
  - IF, SIGNAL, ITERATE, LEAVE, and GET DIAGNOSTIC statements
  - SELECT SQL statement
  - INSERT, UPDATE, DELETE, and MERGE SQL statements (only for AFTER and INSTEAD OF triggers)

Question 21

The correct answer is **C**. Three trigger activation times are available in DB2:

- AFTER trigger
- BEFORE trigger
- INSTEAD OF trigger

Question 22

The correct answer is **A**. You can create triggers on the following objects:

- Tables (BEFORE and AFTER triggers); tables can have multiple columns referenced in the trigger
- Views (INSTEAD OF trigger)

Question 23

The correct answer is **C**. A trigger definition cannot be modified using any ALTER or UPDATE commands. To change it, you drop the current trigger by using the DROP TRIGGER command and create a new trigger with the newly modified definition by using either the CREATE TRIGGER command or the CREATE OR REPLACE TRIGGER command.

Question 24

The correct answer is **B**. The INSERT INTO v2 (view) command will fail due to the WITH CASCADED CHECK OPTION clause in the following CREATE VIEW statement:

```
CREATE VIEW v2 AS SELECT id FROM v1 WITH CASCADED CHECK OPTION;
```

That means the clause will check the data value conditions in the current view and in the parent views. Because the parent view v2 contains a condition in which ID column data must always be > 20, it did not allow you to insert 5 into it.

Question 25

The correct answer is **C**. You must follow some rules when creating the exception table:

- If the table is protected by a security policy, the exception table must be protected by the same security policy.
- The first "n" columns of the exception table are the same as the columns of the table being checked. All column attributes, including name, data type, and length, must be identical. For protected columns, the security label protecting the column must be the same in both tables.
- All columns of the exception table must be free of constraints and triggers. Constraints include referential integrity and `CHECK` constraints, as well as unique index constraints that may cause errors on insert.
- The "(n+1)" column of the exception table is an optional `TIMESTAMP` column. This serves to identify successive invocations of checking by the `SET INTEGRITY` statement on the same table, if the rows within the exception table have not been deleted before issuing the `SET INTEGRITY` statement to check the data. The timestamp precision can be any value from 0 to 12, and the value assigned will be the result of the `CURRENT TIMESTAMP` special register.
- The "(n+2)" column must be of type CLOB (32 KB) or larger. This column is optional but recommended; it will provide the names of the constraints that the data within the row violates. If this column is not provided (as could be warranted if, for example, the original table had the maximum number of columns allowed), then only the row where the constraint violation was detected is copied.
- No additional columns are allowed.
- The exception table cannot be a range partition table, range clustered table, materialized query table, or staging table.

Question 26

The correct answers are **A** and **D**. In DB2, primary key constraints and `UNIQUE` constraints can be referenced by a foreign key constraint.

CHAPTER 5

Monitoring DB2 Activity

This chapter will prepare you to monitor DB2 instances, databases, objects, and workloads. You will learn to use many of the monitor table functions and administrative views to collect and view data for systems, activities, and objects to monitor how well (or how poorly) your database system is operating. You will also be presented information designed to work with event monitors. At the end of the chapter, you will be able to troubleshoot database- and application-related issues using the available DB2 problem determination tools.

Exam Objectives

- ✓ Demonstrate knowledge of the various monitoring tools available with DB2
- ✓ Demonstrate the ability to use the monitoring table functions to collect activity data and analyze it
- ✓ Demonstrate the ability to use the workload management table functions to validate the health and efficiency of your system
- ✓ Demonstrate the ability to generate text reports of monitoring data by using the MONREPORT module
- ✓ Demonstrate the ability to create and activate event monitors, including capturing and analyzing event monitor data
- ✓ Demonstrate the ability to use the Explain facility to capture and analyze both comprehensive Explain information and Explain snapshot data

- ✓ Demonstrate the ability to use the problem determination tools available with DB2, including db2diag, db2fodc, db2pd, db2top, inspect, db2dart, db2mtrk, db2trc, and db2support
- ✓ Demonstrate the ability to use the operating system–specific problem determination tools to complement the DB2 problem determination
- ✓ Demonstrate the ability to use db2pdcfg to configure DB2 database for problem determination

The Database System Monitor

Database monitoring is a vital activity that, when performed regularly, provides continuous feedback on the health of a database system. Because database monitoring is such an integral part of database administration, DB2 comes equipped with a built-in monitoring utility known as the *database system monitor*. Although the name *database system monitor* suggests that only one monitoring tool is available, in reality the database system monitor consists of many distinct tools (monitoring table functions, administrative views, and event monitors) that you can use to capture and return system monitor information.

The monitoring table functions and administrative views allow you to capture a picture of a database's state (along with all database activity) at a specific point in time, whereas event monitors capture and log data as specific database events occur. Information collected by both tools is stored in entities that are referred to as *monitor elements* (or *data elements*), and each monitor element used is identified by a unique name and designed to store a certain type of information.

The following element types monitor elements used to store data:

- **Counter**. This keeps an accurate count of the number of times an activity or event has occurred. Counter values increase throughout the life of the monitor; often counter monitor elements are not resettable; however, they are reset on a successful database reactivation, the restart of a database, or the restart of the instance (for example, the total number of SQL statements executed against the database and total number of executions for each distinct SQL statement).
- **Gauge**. This indicates the current value for an item. Unlike counters, gauge values can go up or down, depending on the amount of database activity (for example, the number of applications currently connected to the database).
- **Watermark**. This signifies the highest (maximum) or lowest (minimum) value an item has seen since monitoring began (for example, the largest number of coordinator agents registered in the database instance).

- **Information**. This provides reference-type details of all monitoring activities performed (for example, buffer pool names, container names, database names and aliases, path details, SQL statements).
- **Timestamp**. This indicates the date and time an activity or event took place (for example, the date and time the first database connection was established). Timestamp values are provided as the number of seconds and microseconds that have elapsed since January 1, 1970.
- **Time**. This signifies the amount of time that was spent performing an activity or event (for example, the amount of time spent performing a sort operation). Time values are provided as the number of seconds and microseconds that have elapsed since the activity or event was started.

The database system monitor employs several methods for presenting the data collected. For both snapshot and event monitors, you have the option of storing all collected data in files or database tables, viewing it on screen, or processing it using a custom application. The database system monitor returns monitor data to a client application by using a self-describing data stream; with a snapshot monitoring application, you call the appropriate snapshot APIs (administrative view or table function) to capture a snapshot and then process the data stream returned. With an event monitoring application, you prepare to receive the data produced via a file or a named pipe, activate the appropriate event monitor, and process the data stream as it is received.

The Snapshot Monitor

Like DB2 administrative views, the snapshot monitor collects information about the state of a DB2 instance and the databases it controls at a specific point in time (i.e., at the time the snapshot is taken). Additionally, you can tailor the snapshot monitor to retrieve specific types of monitoring data (for example, configure the monitor to collect only information about buffer pools). Snapshots can be taken by executing the GET SNAPSHOT command from the DB2 CLP, by using the snapshot administrative views and/or snapshot table functions shown in the following sections, or by embedding the snapshot monitor APIs in a C or C++ application. Snapshots are useful for determining the status of a database system and, when taken at regular intervals, can provide valuable information to use to observe trends and identify potential problem areas.

Snapshot Monitor Switches

Often, the collection of database system monitor data introduces additional processing overhead. For example, to calculate the execution time of SQL statements, the DB2 database manager must call the operating system to obtain timestamps before and after every SQL statement is executed; these types of system calls are normally expensive. Another side effect of using the database system monitor is an increase in memory consumption—the DB2 database manager uses memory to store data collected for every monitor element tracked.

To help minimize the overhead involved in collecting database system monitor information, you can use a group of switches known as the *snapshot monitor switches* to control what information is collected when a snapshot is taken; the type and amount of information collected is determined by the way you have these snapshot monitor switches set. Each snapshot monitor switch has two settings: ON and OFF. When you set a snapshot monitor switch to OFF, monitor elements that fall under that switch's control do not collect information. The opposite is true if the switch is set to ON. (Keep in mind that a considerable amount of monitoring information is not under switch control and will always be collected regardless of how the snapshot monitor switches have been set.) Table 5.1 shows the snapshot monitor switches available, along with a description of the type of information that is collected when each has been set to ON.

Table 5.1: Snapshot monitor switches

Monitor Group	Monitor Switch	DB2 Database Manager Configuration Parameter	Information Provided
Buffer pools	BUFFERPOOL	dft_mon_bufferpool	Amount of buffer pool activity (i.e., number of read and write operations performed and the amount of time taken for each read/write operation)
Locks	LOCK	dft_mon_lock	Number of locks held and number of deadlock cycles encountered
Sorts	SORT	dft_mon_sort	Number of sort operations performed, size of heaps used, number of overflows encountered, and the amount of time taken for each sort operation performed
SQL statements	STATEMENT	dft_mon_stmt	SQL statement processing start time, SQL statement processing end time, and SQL statement identification
Tables	TABLE	dft_mon_table	Amount of table activity performed, such as number of rows read, number of rows written, and so on
Timestamps	TIMESTAMP	dft_mon_timestamp	Times and timestamp information
Transactions (units of work)	UOW	dft_mon_uow	Transaction start times, transaction completion times, and transaction completion status

Adapted from Table 119 on page 439 of the Database Monitoring Guide and Reference *manual*

By default, all of the switches in Table 5.1 are set to OFF, with the exception of the TIMESTAMP switch, which is set to ON.

Viewing Current Snapshot Monitor Switch Settings

Because the type and amount of information collected when a snapshot is taken is controlled, to some extent, by the way the snapshot monitor switches have been set, it is important that you know, before you take a snapshot, which snapshot monitor switches have been turned on and which remain off. So how can you determine the current setting of each snapshot monitor switch? The easiest way is by executing the GET MONITOR SWITCHES command from the DB2 CLP. The basic syntax for this command is:

```
GET MONITOR SWITCHES
<AT DBPARTITIONNUM [PartitionNum] | GLOBAL>
```

where:

PartitionNum Identifies the database partition (in a multipartitioned database environment) for which to obtain and display the status of the snapshot monitor switches

So if you want to obtain and display the status of the snapshot monitor switches for a single-partition database, execute a GET MONITOR SWITCHES command, similar to the following:

```
GET MONITOR SWITCHES
```

When this command is executed, you will most likely see output that looks something like this:

```
                    Monitor Recording Switches

Switch list for member 0
Buffer Pool Activity Information (BUFFERPOOL) = OFF
Lock Information                       (LOCK) = OFF
Sorting Information                    (SORT) = OFF
SQL Statement Information         (STATEMENT) = OFF
Table Activity Information            (TABLE) = OFF
Take Timestamp Information        (TIMESTAMP) = ON 08/27/2014
20:28:52.652196
Unit of Work Information                (UOW) = OFF
```

On close examination of this output, you will notice that the TIMESTAMP snapshot monitoring switch has been turned on and that all other switches are off. The timestamp value that follows the TIMESTAMP monitoring switch's state indicates the exact date and time the TIMESTAMP monitor switch was turned on.

Changing the State of Snapshot Monitor Switches

Once you know which snapshot monitor switches have been turned on and which have been turned off, you may find it necessary to change one or more switch settings before you start the monitoring process. To change snapshot monitor switch settings at the instance level, modify the appropriate DB2 database manager configuration parameters (see Table 5.1) with the UPDATE DATABASE MANAGER CONFIGURATION command. The snapshot monitor switch settings made at the instance level remain persistent across instance restarts. The snapshot monitor switch settings can be changed at the application level by calling the db2MonitorSwitches() API or by executing the UPDATE MONITOR SWITCHES command. The basic syntax for this command is:

```
UPDATE MONITOR SWITCHES USING [[SwitchID] ON | OFF ,...]
```

where:

SwitchID Identifies one or more snapshot monitor switches whose state is to be changed; the following values are valid for this parameter: BUFFERPOOL, LOCK, SORT, STATEMENT, TABLE, TIMESTAMP, and UOW

Thus, if you want to change the state of the LOCK snapshot monitor switch to ON at the application level, execute an UPDATE MONITOR SWITCHES command that looks like this:

```
UPDATE MONITOR SWITCHES USING LOCKS ON
```

Likewise, if you want to change the state of the BUFFERPOOL snapshot monitor switch to OFF, you execute an UPDATE MONITOR SWITCHES command:

```
UPDATE MONITOR SWITCHES USING BUFFERPOOL OFF
```

However, to change the state of the LOCK snapshot monitor switch to ON at the instance level, you execute an UPDATE DATABASE MANAGER CONFIGURATION command, as follows:

```
UPDATE DBM CFG USING DFT_MON_LOCK ON
```

Note: Setting snapshot monitor switches at the instance level affects all databases under the instance's control (i.e., every application that establishes a connection to a database under the instance's control will inherit the switch settings made in the instance's configuration), whereas setting monitor switches at the application level (i.e., using the UPDATE MONITOR SWITCH command) affects only the database with which a single application is interacting.

Capturing Snapshot Data

As soon as a database is activated or a connection to a database is established, the snapshot monitor begins collecting monitor data. Before the data collected can be viewed, a snapshot must be taken. You can take snapshots by embedding the db2GetSnapshot() API in an application program or by executing the GET SNAPSHOT command. The basic syntax for this command is:

```
GET SNAPSHOT FOR
[[DATABASE MANAGER | DB MANAGER | DBM] |
 ALL <DCS> DATABASES |
 ALL <DCS> APPLICATIONS |
 ALL BUFFERPOOLS |
 ALL REMOTE_DATABASES |
 ALL REMOTE_APPLICATIONS |
 ALL ON [DatabaseAlias] |
 <DCS> [DATABASE | DB] ON [DatabaseAlias] |
 <DCS> APPLICATIONS ON [DatabaseAlias] |
 <DCS> APPLICATION [APPLID AppID | AGENTID AgentID] |
 TABLES ON [DatabaseAlias] |
 TABLESPACES ON [DatabaseAlias] |
 LOCKS ON [DatabaseAlias] |
 BUFFERPOOLS ON [DatabaseAlias] |
 REMOTE DATABASES ON [DatabaseAlias] |
 REMOTE APPLICATIONS ON [DatabaseAlias]
 DYNAMIC SQL ON [DatabaseAlias] <WRITE TO FILE>]
```

where:

DatabaseAlias	Identifies the alias to assign to the database for which the snapshot monitor is to collect information
AppID	Identifies the application, by ID, for which the snapshot monitor is to collect information
AgentID	Identifies the application, by application handle, for which the snapshot monitor is to collect information

So if you want to take a snapshot that contains only data collected on locks being held by applications interacting with a database named SAMPLE, execute the GET SNAPSHOT command:

```
GET SNAPSHOT FOR LOCKS ON sample
```

And when this command is executed, you might see output that looks something like this:

```
              Database Lock Snapshot

Database name                              = SAMPLE
Database path                              = /data/db2inst1/NODE0000/
SQL00001/
                                             MEMBER0000/
Input database alias                       = SAMPLE
Locks held                                 = 5
Applications currently connected           = 2
Agents currently waiting on locks          = 1
Snapshot timestamp                         = 08/27/2014 21:40:51.167257

Application handle                         = 234
Application ID                             = *LOCAL.db2inst1.140827213902
Sequence number                            = 00001
Application name                           = db2bp
CONNECT Authorization ID                   = MOHAN
Application status                         = Lock-wait
                                                           Continued
```

```
Status change time                             =
Application code page                          = 1208
Locks held                                     = 2
Total wait time (ms)                           = 80954

  ID of agent holding lock                     = 228
  Application ID holding lock                  = *LOCAL.db2inst1.140827213834
  Lock name                                    = 0x03001600000000000000000054
  Lock attributes                              = 0x00000000
  Release flags                                = 0x00000000
  Lock object type                             = Table
  Lock mode                                    = Share Lock (S)
  Lock mode requested                          = Intention Exclusive Lock (IX)
  Name of tablespace holding lock              = IBMDB2SAMPLEREL
  Schema of table holding lock                 = MOHAN
  Name of table holding lock                   = T1
  Data Partition Id of table holding lock = 0
  Lock wait start timestamp                    = 08/27/2014 21:39:30.212745

List Of Locks
 Lock Name                   = 0x0100000001000000001004055D6
 Lock Attributes             = 0x00000000
 Release Flags               = 0x40000000
 Lock Count                  = 1
 Hold Count                  = 0
 Lock Object Name            = 0
 Object Type                 = Internal Variation Lock
 Mode                        = S
```

To take a snapshot that contains data collected on the database manager level, execute the GET SNAPSHOT command, as follows:

```
GET SNAPSHOT FOR DBM
```

And when this command is executed, you might see output that looks something like this:

```
              Database Manager Snapshot

Node type                                      = Enterprise Server Edition
with
                                                 local and remote clients
Instance name                                  = db2inst1
Number of members in DB2 instance              = 1
Database manager status                        = Active

Product name                                   = DB2 v10.1.0.3
Service level                                  = s130918 (IP23516)

Private Sort heap allocated                    = 0
Private Sort heap high watermark               = 0
Post threshold sorts                           = Not Collected
Piped sorts requested                          = 99
Piped sorts accepted                           = 99

Start Database Manager timestamp               = 08/27/2014 20:28:52.652196
Last reset timestamp                           =
Snapshot timestamp                             = 08/28/2014 11:15:42.552680

Remote connections to db manager               = 18
Remote connections executing in db manager     = 0
Local connections                              = 1
Local connections executing in db manager      = 0
Active local databases                         = 1

High watermark for agents registered           = 23
Agents registered                              = 23
Idle agents                                    = 0

                                                                 Continued
```

```
Committed private Memory (Bytes)                   = 19202048
Switch list for member 0
Buffer Pool Activity Information  (BUFFERPOOL) = ON  08/27/2014
21:40:08.919516
Lock Information                        (LOCK) = ON  08/27/2014
20:29:03.697165
Sorting Information                     (SORT) = ON  08/27/2014
21:40:24.745822
SQL Statement Information          (STATEMENT) = ON  08/27/2014
21:40:24.745821
Table Activity Information             (TABLE) = ON  08/27/2014
21:40:24.745822
Take Timestamp Information         (TIMESTAMP) = ON  08/27/2014
20:28:52.652196
Unit of Work Information                 (UOW) = ON  08/27/2014
21:40:24.745821

Agents assigned from pool                          = 2590
Agents created from empty pool                     = 25
Agents stolen from another application             = 0
High watermark for coordinating agents             = 23
Hash joins after heap threshold exceeded           = 0
OLAP functions after heap threshold exceeded       = 0

Total number of gateway connections                = 0
Current number of gateway connections              = 0
Gateway connections waiting for host reply         = 0
Gateway connections waiting for client request = 0
Gateway connection pool agents stolen              = 0

Node FCM information corresponds to                = 0
Free FCM buffers                                   = 128
Total FCM buffers                                  = 128
Free FCM buffers low watermark                     = 128
```

Continued

```
Maximum number of FCM buffers                    = 8192
Free FCM channels                                = 128
Total FCM channels                               = 128
Free FCM channels low watermark                  = 128
Maximum number of FCM channels                   = 8192

Memory usage for database manager:

  Node number                                    = 0
    Memory Pool Type                             = Other Memory
       Current size (bytes)                      = 104857600
       High watermark (bytes)                    = 105119744
       Configured size (bytes)                   = 149291008

  Node number                                    = 0
    Memory Pool Type                             = FCMBP Heap
       Current size (bytes)                      = 851968
       High watermark (bytes)                    = 851968
       Configured size (bytes)                   = 851968

  Node number                                    = 0
    Memory Pool Type                             = Database Monitor Heap
       Current size (bytes)                      = 851968
       High watermark (bytes)                    = 851968
       Configured size (bytes)                   = 393216
```

As a database administrator, it is important for you to understand every line of the above command output. This gives you enough information at one go, such as instance name, product name and version, number of remote connections, maximum number of agents and coordinator agents used concurrently in the database, FCM, and memory pool utilization.

Similarly, if you want a glance on the health of the database, you can execute this GET SNAPSHOT command:

```
GET SNAPSHOT FOR DB ON sample
```

And when this command is executed, you might see output that looks something like this:

```
                Database Snapshot

Database name                              = SAMPLE
Database path                              = /data/db2inst1/NODE0000/SQL00001/
                                             cMEMBER0000/
Input database alias                       = SAMPLE
Database status                            = Active
Catalog database partition number          = 0
Catalog network node name                  = gb01qa
Operating system running at database server = LINUXAMD64
Location of the database                   = Local
First database connect timestamp           = 08/28/2014 11:31:17.431890
Last reset timestamp                       =
Last backup timestamp                      = 08/24/2014 18:55:14.000000
Snapshot timestamp                         = 08/28/2014 11:38:46.031259

Number of automatic storage paths          = 1
Automatic storage path                     = /data
      Node number                          = 0
      State                                = In Use
      File system ID                       = 64768
      Storage path free space (bytes)      = 4441350144
      File system used space (bytes)       = 16629387264
      File system total space (bytes)      = 21137846272

High watermark for connections             = 20
Application connects                       = 27
Secondary connects total                   = 19
Applications connected currently           = 1
Appls. executing in db manager currently   = 0
Agents associated with applications        = 19
Maximum agents associated with applications = 20
Maximum coordinating agents                = 20
```

Like the database manager snapshot, the database snapshot contains key database information. It is highly recommended that you read through the command output.

While examining the syntax of the GET SNAPSHOT command, you may have noticed that different types of monitoring data can be captured when a snapshot is taken. This data includes the following:

- DB2 database manager data: information for an active instance
- Database data: information about one or more remote or local databases
- Application data: information about one or more applications
- Buffer pool data: information about buffer pool activity
- Table space data: information about the table spaces within a database
- Table data: information about the tables within a database
- Lock data: information about locks being held by applications
- Dynamic SQL data: point-in-time information about SQL statements being held in the SQL statement cache

The snapshot monitor switches, together with the options available with the GET SNAPSHOT command, will determine the type and volume of data that will be returned when a snapshot is taken. In fact, if a particular snapshot monitor switch has not been turned on, and a snapshot of the monitoring data associated with that switch is taken, the monitoring data captured may not contain any values at all.

To execute the GET SNAPSHOT command, you must be attached to an instance. If no instance attachment exists, an attachment to the default instance is made automatically. To obtain a snapshot of a remote instance, you must first attach to that instance.

Resetting Snapshot Monitor Counters

Earlier, you saw that one of the element types that monitor elements used to store data is a counter and that counter keeps a running total of the number of times an activity or event occurs. Thus, counter values increase throughout the life of the monitor. So when exactly does counting begin? Counting typically begins as soon as a snapshot monitor switch is turned on or when connection to a database is established (if you use instance-level monitoring, counting begins the first time an application establishes a connection to a database under the instance's control).

When you want to capture the workload or SQL statement throughput, it is desirable to reset all counters to zero without turning snapshot monitor switches off and back on, and without terminating and reestablishing database connections. By far, the easiest way to quickly reset all snapshot monitor counters to zero is by executing the RESET MONITOR command.

The basic syntax for this command is:

```
RESET MONITOR ALL
```

or

```
RESET MONITOR FOR <DCS> [DATABASE | DB] [DatabaseAlias]
```

where:

DatabaseAlias Identifies the alias to assign to the database for which to reset snapshot monitor counters

Thus, to reset the snapshot monitor counters for all databases under an instance's control to zero, you attach to that instance and execute the following RESET MONITOR command:

```
RESET MONITOR ALL
```

But if you want to reset just the snapshot monitor counters associated with a database named SAMPLE to zero, you execute a RESET MONITOR command that looks like this:

```
RESET MONITOR FOR DATABASE sample
```

However, you cannot selectively reset counters for a particular monitoring group that is controlled by a snapshot monitor switch by using the RESET MONITOR command. To perform this type of operation, you must turn the appropriate snapshot monitor switch off and back on or terminate and reestablish connections to the database.

Remember, each instance attachment has its own private view of the snapshot monitor data. If one user runs a reset monitor command or turns off a monitor switch, other users' views of the monitor data are not affected.

A Word About DB2 Monitoring Elements

DB2 provides various monitoring elements to examine and troubleshoot performance problems or to check the health of the database. The monitoring elements are categorized as follows:

- Request monitor elements. Also called *request metrics*, these measure the volume of work or effort spent by the database server as a whole to process the application requests, such as opening a connection from a client to the server and executing SQL statements. There are a few representative monitor elements for measuring overall system processing information, client/server processing information, common data server processing operations, and selected data server environments. Some examples are:

- » The total_rqst_time measures the time spent by requests in the data server, including the total processing and wait times.
- » The total_cpu_time measures the overall CPU usage in the data server.
- » The total_wait_time measures the overall wait time in the data server.
- » The client_idle_wait_time measures the time spent waiting for the next request from an open connection.
- » The tcpip_recv_volume measures the volume of data received by the data server from clients over the TCP/IP network.
- » The pool_data_l_reads measures the usage of buffer pool resources.
- » The pool_read_time provides information about the I/O processing.
- » The lock_wait_time provides information about the time database waited on locks.
- » The fcm_recv_wait_time measures total time spent waiting to receive data through Fast Communication Manager (FCM).

You can access the request metrics information by using a set of monitoring table functions and event monitors.

- **Activity monitor elements**. Also called *activity metrics*, these are a subset of request monitor elements. They measure data server processing related to executing activities, especially processing done to execute SQL statement sections, including locking, sorting, and row processing. You can access the activity metrics information by using a set of monitoring table functions.
- **Data object monitor elements**. These provide information about operations performed on specific database data objects, such as tables, indexes, buffer pools, table spaces, containers, locks, package cache, and FCM. You can access the current values for data monitor elements by using monitor table functions.
- **Monitor element collection levels**. These provide a control to activate or deactivate the data collection for the request monitor or data monitor elements. You can activate specific classes of monitor elements for the entire database by using the collection levels database configuration parameters mon_req_metrics, mon_act_metrics, and mon_obj_metrics. If you set this parameter to BASE, all metrics reported through unit of work, connection, service class, workload, package cache, buffer pool, table spaces, and container interfaces are collected for all the requests executed on the database server. And if you set this parameter to EXTENDED, it collects information at granular section levels.

- **Time-spent monitor elements.** These provide information about where time is spent in the system. The time is categorized into time spent waiting (lock wait time, buffer pool, or direct I/O) and processing (compiling, section processing, and committing or rolling back work).

Now that you know the basics of monitor elements, Table 5.2 lists few monitor elements and their usage.

Table 5.2: Sample monitor elements and their usage

Monitor Elements	How to you get this info?	Usage
(pool_index_p_reads) / (pool_index_l_reads)	Can be read from MON_GET_ BUFFERPOOL table function	Indicates the number of index pages read in from the table space container physically over logical reading from buffer pool; this shows the index table space buffer pool efficiency
(direct_reads) / (direct_read_reqs)	Can be read from many table functions, including MON_GET_ TABLESPACE table function	Indicates the number of sectors that are read by direct reads
(total_sort_time) / (total_sorts)	Can be read using one of the event monitor—database, connection, statements, and activities	Indicates the average elapsed time for each sort operation
(total_rqst_time – total_wait_time) / total_rqst_time	Can be read from many table functions, including MON_GET_ UNIT_OF_WORK	Indicates the percentage of time the database server spends actively working on the application requests
(rows_read) / (rows_returned)	Can be read from many table functions, including MON_GET_ ACTIVITY_DETAILS	Indicates the number of rows read from the database and number of rows returned to the application
lock_wait_time	Can be read from many table functions, including MON_GET_ PKG_CACHE_STMT	Indicates the total elapsed time spent waiting on locks
total_wait_time	Can be read from many table functions, including MON_GET_ CONNECTION_DETAILS	Indicates the total time spent waiting within the DB2 database server

Table Functions for Monitoring

The table functions are designed to collect and view data for systems, activities, and data objects at a specific point in time. The monitoring table functions use the newer lightweight, high-speed monitoring infrastructure introduced in DB2 9.7. The data for monitored elements are constantly accumulated in memory and available for querying. You can choose to receive data for a specific object or for all objects in the database. Remember, table functions are not actual tables—they are functions built around capturing information from many other sources. Before the DB2 9.7 release, the point-in-time monitoring data was accessed through snapshot monitoring, which was using a less efficient infrastructure.

The monitoring table functions are logically grouped according to the monitoring elements and are categorized as follows:

- Table functions for monitoring system information
- Table functions for monitoring activities
- Table functions for monitoring data objects
- Table functions for monitoring locks
- Table functions for monitoring system memory

Monitoring System Information

The system monitoring includes the complete volume of work and effort spent by the database server to process application requests. This provides a complete perspective of how the database server is performing as a whole and to particular subsets of the application requests.

The request monitor elements are aggregated across requests at various levels of the workload management (WLM) object hierarchy: by unit of work, by workload, by service class, and by connection. Table 5.3 lists the table functions for accessing the current system information.

Table 5.3: Table functions for monitoring system information

Table Function Name	Information Returned
MON_GET_SERVICE_SUBCLASS	Returns metrics for one or more service subclasses
MON_GET_SERVICE_SUBCLASS_DETAILS	Returns detailed metrics for one or more service subclasses in an XML document
MON_GET_WORKLOAD	Returns metrics for one or more workloads
MON_GET_WORKLOAD_DETAILS	Returns detailed metrics for one or more workloads in an XML document
MON_GET_UNIT_OF_WORK	Returns metrics for one or more units of work
MON_GET_UNIT_OF_WORK_DETAILS	Returns detailed metrics for one or more units of work in an XML document
MON_GET_CONNECTION	Returns metrics for one or more connections
MON_GET_CONNECTION_DETAILS	Returns detailed metrics for one or more connections in an XML document

The syntax to construct a query that references table functions for monitoring system information looks something like this:

```
SELECT * FROM TABLE ([FunctionName]
   ('[SystemInfoSepcifics]', [Member]) AS [CorrelationName]
```

where:

FunctionName	Identifies the monitoring table function name to use (i.e., one of the functions listed in Table 5.3)
SystemInfoSpecifics	Identifies the monitor table function system-specific information such as service superclass and subclass for which to retrieve monitored metrics data
Member	Identifies the member for which to collect monitored metrics data; you can specify -1 for the current member or -2 for all database members
CorrelationName	Identifies the name to assign to the result data set produced by the query

If you want to collect total CPU time spent in microseconds and the number of application requests completed for all the superclass and subclass in the system, execute the following query:

```
SELECT
      VARCHAR (SERVICE_SUPERCLASS_NAME, 30) AS SERVICE_SUPERCLASS,
      VARCHAR (SERVICE_SUBCLASS_NAME, 30) AS SERVICE_SUBCLASS,
      SUM (TOTAL_CPU_TIME) AS TOTAL_CPU,
      SUM (APP_RQSTS_COMPLETED_TOTAL) AS TOTAL_REQUESTS
   FROM TABLE (MON_GET_SERVICE_SUBCLASS ('','',-2)) AS T
GROUP BY SERVICE_SUPERCLASS_NAME, SERVICE_SUBCLASS_NAME
ORDER BY TOTAL_CPU DESC

SERVICE_SUPERCLASS           SERVICE_SUBCLASS   TOTAL_CPU    TOTAL_REQUESTS
---------------------------- ------------------ ------------ --------------
SYSDEFAULTUSERCLASS          SYSDEFAULTSUBCLASS    105778720          14262
SYSDEFAULTMAINTENANCECLASS   SYSDEFAULTSUBCLASS      4930433          25420
SYSDEFAULTSYSTEMCLASS        SYSDEFAULTSUBCLASS            0              0

  3 record(s) selected.
```

In the above example, CPU spent 105.77 seconds to complete 14,262 requests from the application in the service superclass SYSDEFAULTUSERCLASS across all the members in the DB2 instance.

To capture the locking and log information such as the number of deadlocks, lock wait times, number of lock waits, number of lock timeouts, number of lock escalations, and log buffer wait time (this is the agent spending time waiting for the space in the log buffer area in milliseconds) for a specific workload across all the members, execute this query:

```
SELECT
      VARCHAR (WORKLOAD_NAME, 30) AS WORKLOAD_NAME,
      SUM (DEADLOCKS) AS NUM_OF_DLOCKS,
      SUM (LOCK_WAIT_TIME) AS TOTAL_LOCK_WAIT_TIME,
      SUM (LOCK_WAITS) AS TOTAL_LOCK_WAITS,
      SUM (LOCK_TIMEOUTS) AS TOTAL_LOCK_TIMEOUTS,
      SUM (LOCK_ESCALS) AS TOTAL_LOCK_ESCALS,
      SUM (LOG_BUFFER_WAIT_TIME) AS LOG_BUF_WAIT
   FROM TABLE (MON_GET_WORKLOAD ('',-2)) AS t
GROUP BY WORKLOAD_NAME

                       NUM_OF_ TOTAL_LOCK_ TOTAL_      TOTAL_LOCK_ TOTAL_LOCK_ LOG_BUF_
WORKLOAD_NAME          DLOCKS  WAIT_TIME   LOCK_WAITS  TIMEOUTS    ESCALS      WAIT
---------------------- ------- ----------- ----------- ----------- ----------- --------
SYSDEFAULTUSERWORKLOAD       1       16784           2           0           0        0
SYSDEFAULTADMWORKLOAD        0           0           0           0           0        0

  2 record(s) selected.
```

If you want to view the unit of work characteristics such as total CPU time, total wait time, number of application requests, sort time and sort overflow, total SQL compile time, and total commit time on your database system, execute the following statement:

```
SELECT
      APPLICATION_HANDLE, UOW_ID, TOTAL_CPU_TIME, TOTAL_WAIT_TIME,
      APP_RQSTS_COMPLETED_TOTAL, TOTAL_SECTION_SORT_TIME, SORT_OVERFLOWS,
      TOTAL_COMPILE_TIME, TOTAL_COMMIT_TIME
   FROM TABLE (MON_GET_UNIT_OF_WORK (NULL, -1)) AS t
ORDER BY TOTAL_CPU_TIME DESC
```

To capture connection start time, total buffer pool read time in milliseconds, buffer pool logical reads, buffer pool physical reads, number of records returned, and data volume sent over the TCP/IP network for the current database connections, you can do so by executing the following query:

```
SELECT
      APPLICATION_HANDLE, CONNECTION_START_TIME, POOL_READ_TIME,
      POOL_DATA_L_READS, POOL_DATA_P_READS, ROWS_RETURNED,
      TCPIP_SEND_VOULME
   FROM TABLE (MON_GET_CONNECTION (CAST (NULL AS BIGINT), -2)) AS T
ORDER BY ROWS_RETURNED DESC

APPLICATION_                            POOL_READ_ POOL_DATA_ POOL_DATA_ ROWS_    TCPIP_SEND_
HANDLE       CONNECTION_START_TIME      TIME       L_READS    P_READS    RETURNED VOLUME
------------ -------------------------- ---------- ---------- ---------- -------- -----------
       43782 2014-08-23-16.07.16.304768        453       2207        153     4823      481561
       41979 2014-08-23-07.54.56.674879         99        139         26       76           0
       43748 2014-08-23-16.07.19.271656        110        472         27       15       10512

3 record(s) selected.
```

If you want to capture the same connection information by using the MON_GET_CONNECTION_DETAILS table function in an XML document format, execute this query:

```
SELECT
      CONMETRICS.APPLICATION_HANDLE,
      CONMETRICS.CONNECTION_START_TIME,
      CONMETRICS.POOL_READ_TIME,
      CONMETRICS.POOL_DATA_L_READS,
      CONMETRICS.POOL_DATA_P_READS,
      CONMETRICS.ROWS_RETURNED,
      CONMETRICS.TCPIP_SEND_VOLUME
FROM TABLE
      (MON_GET_CONNECTION_DETAILS (CAST (NULL AS BIGINT), -2)) AS CON_METRICS,
      XMLTABLE (XMLNAMESPACES (DEFAULT 'http://www.ibm.com/xmlns/prod/db2/mon'),
      '$CONMETRICS/db2_connection' PASSING XMLPARSE(DOCUMENT CON_METRICS.DETAILS)
      as "CONMETRICS" COLUMNS
                                                                    Continued
```

```
        APPLICATION_HANDLE INTEGER PATH 'application_handle',
        CONNECTION_START_TIME TIMESTAMP PATH 'connection_start_time',
        POOL_READ_TIME INT PATH 'system_metrics/pool_read_time',
        POOL_DATA_L_READS INT PATH 'system_metrics/pool_data_l_reads',
        POOL_DATA_P_READS INT PATH 'system_metrics/pool_data_p_reads',
        ROWS_RETURNED BIGINT PATH 'system_metrics/rows_returned',
        TCPIP_SEND_VOLUME BIGINT PATH 'system_metrics/tcpip_send_volume'
        ) AS CONMETRICS
ORDER BY ROWS_RETURNED DESC;

APPLICATION_                            POOL_READ_ POOL_DATA_ POOL_DATA_ ROWS_    TCPIP_SEND_
HANDLE       CONNECTION_START_TIME      TIME       L_READS    P_READS    RETURNED VOLUME
------------ -------------------------- ---------- ---------- ---------- -------- -----------
       41979 2014-08-23-07.54.56.674879        171        966         32      103           0
       44632 2014-08-23-20.13.58.440310          0         32          0       11           0

  2 record(s) selected.
```

The schema for the XML document that is returned in the DETAILS column is available in the file sqllib/misc/DB2MonRoutines.xsd, which you can use to expand the data selection in the function.

The database configuration parameter mon_req_metrics controls the data collection by the request monitor elements across the database server. You can set the parameter to one of the following values:

- NONE—No request monitor elements are collected.
- BASE—All request monitor elements are collected. This is the default value.
- EXTENDED—All request monitor elements are collected in a more granular level and are encapsulated in XML format.

Alternatively, you can control monitoring request metrics collection for individual WLM service classes by using the COLLECT REQUEST METRICS clause while creating or altering service classes.

To activate EXTENDED monitoring request metrics for the database SAMPLE, execute the UPDATE DB CFG command, as follows:

```
UPDATE DB CFG FOR sample USING MON_REQ_METRICS EXTENDED
DB20000I The UPDATE DATABASE CONFIGURATION command completed successfully.
```

However, if you want to alter an existing WLM service class, use the ALTER SERVICE CLASS command, something like this:

```
ALTER SERVICE CLASS SYSDEFAULTUSERCLASS COLLECT REQUEST METRICS EXTENDED
DB20000I  The SQL command completed successfully.
```

Monitoring Activities

The activity monitoring elements are a subset of the request monitor elements. The activity monitoring perspective focuses on the activities related to SQL statement execution. For activities in progress, activity metrics are accumulated in memory. For activities that are SQL statements, activity metrics are accumulated in the package cache. In the package cache, activity metrics are aggregated over all executions of each SQL statement section.

Table 5.4 lists the table functions for accessing the current activity information.

Table 5.4: Table functions for monitoring activity information

Table Function Name	Information Returned
MON_GET_ACTIVITY_DETAILS	Returns details about an activity including the SQL statement text when it is called
MON_GET_PKG_CACHE_STMT	Returns a point-in-time view of both static and dynamic SQL statements in the database package cache
MON_GET_PKG_CACHE_STMT_DETAILS	Returns detailed metrics for one more package cache

To find details about all the activities currently running in the system, use a query similar to the following:

```
WITH METRIC AS
  (SELECT *
      FROM TABLE (WLM_GET_WORKLOAD_OCCURRENCE_ACTIVITIES (NULL, -2))
         WHERE ACTIVITY_ID > 0)
      SELECT METRIC.APPLICATION_HANDLE, METRIC.ACTIVITY_ID,
             METRIC.UOW_ID, TOTAL_ACT_TIME, TOTAL_ACT_WAIT_TIME,
             SUBSTR (ACTMETRICS.STMT_TEXT, 1, 250) AS STMT_TEXT
         FROM METRIC, TABLE (MON_GET_ACTIVITY_DETAILS
           (METRIC.APPLICATION_HANDLE, METRIC.UOW_ID,
           METRIC.ACTIVITY_ID, -1)) AS ACTDETAILS,
                                                          Continued
```

```
        XMLTABLE (XMLNAMESPACES (DEFAULT
        'http://www.ibm.com/xmlns/prod/db2/mon'),
        '$ACTMETRICS/db2_activity_details' PASSING XMLPARSE (DOCUMENT
        ACTDETAILS.DETAILS) AS "ACTMETRICS"
      COLUMNS "STMT_TEXT" VARCHAR (1024) PATH 'stmt_text',
        "TOTAL_ACT_TIME" INTEGER PATH 'activity_metrics/total_act_time',
        "TOTAL_ACT_WAIT_TIME" INTEGER PATH
        'activity_metrics/total_act_wait_time')
        AS ACTMETRICS
```

```
APPLICATION_ ACTIVITY_ UOW_ TOTAL_   TOTAL_ACT_  STMT_TEXT
HANDLE       ID        ID   ACT_TIME WAIT_TIME
------------ --------- ---- -------- ----------- --------------------------------------
        2973         1   14        0           0 with "Scenario_Calendar_Dim"
                                                 as (select "Scenario_Calendar_Dim".
                                                 "SCENARIO_KEY" "SCENARIO_KEY" ,
                                                 "Scenario_Calendar_Dim".
                                                 "SCENARIO_CODE" "SCENARIO_CODE" ,
                                                 "Scenario_Calendar_Dim".
                                                 "SCENARIO_NAME" "SCENARIO_NAME" ,
                                                 "Scenario_Calendar_Dim"."CALENDAR_MONT
       61356         1  849        0           0 WITH METRIC AS (SELECT * FROM TABLE(WLM_
                                                 GET_WORKLOAD_OCCURRENCE_ACTIVITIES(NULL,
                                                 -2)) WHERE ACTIVITY_ID > 0)
                                                 SELECT METRIC.APPLICATION_HANDLE,
                                                 METRIC.ACTIVITY_ID, METRIC.UOW_ID,
                                                 TOTAL_ACT_TIME, TOTAL_ACT_WAIT_TIME,
                                                 SUBSTR(ACTMETRICS.STMT_TEXT,1,250)

2 record(s) selected.
```

In the above example, the WLM_GET_WORKLOAD_OCCURRENCE_ACTVITIES table function passes the activity information such as application handle, unit of work ID, and activity ID into the MON_GET_ACTIVITY_DETAILS table function to capture the currently executing SQL activity details. Unlike MON_GET_ACTIVITY_DETAILS returning the point-in-time view of the activities, MON_GET_PACKAGE_CACHE_STMT returns information about dynamic and static SQL statements since DB2 instance was stared.

If you want to capture expensive dynamic and static SQL statements that make heavy data reads over a period of time, use a query that looks something like this:

```
WITH SUM_REC_TAB (SUM_REC_READ) AS (
      SELECT SUM (ROWS_READ)
         FROM TABLE (MON_GET_PKG_CACHE_STMT (NULL, NULL, NULL, -2)) AS T)
SELECT
      SUBSTR (STMT_TEXT, 1, 20) AS STATEMENT,
      ROWS_READ,
      DECIMAL (100*(FLOAT (ROWS_READ)/ NULLIF (SUM_REC_TAB.SUM_REC_READ,0)),5,2)
        AS PCT_TOTAL_RECORDS_READ,
      ROWS_RETURNED,
      CASE
          WHEN ROWS_RETURNED > 0 THEN
             DECIMAL (FLOAT (ROWS_READ)/FLOAT (ROWS_RETURNED), 10, 2)
          ELSE -1
      END AS READ_EFFICIENCY,
      NUM_EXECUTIONS
   FROM TABLE (MON_GET_PKG_CACHE_STMT (NULL, NULL, NULL, -2)) AS T,
      SUM_REC_TAB ORDER BY ROWS_READ DESC FETCH FIRST 5 ROWS ONLY WITH UR

                                        PCT_TOTAL_   ROWS_      READ_       NUM_
STATEMENT                    ROWS_READ RECORDS_READ RETURNED   EFFICIENCY  EXECUTIONS
---------------------------- --------- ------------ -------------------- ----------
select count(*) from t1 w       294912        93.33        1    294912.00          1
select * from t1 where id        21058         6.66     4679         4.50          1
WITH SUM_REC_TAB (SUM_REC            0         0.00        5         0.00          1

  3 record(s) selected.
```

In the example query snippet, the total number of records read from the database are 315,970—out of which the first statement, SELECT COUNT (*) FROM t1, read 294,912 records; however, it returned only one record to the application. The second statement, SELECT * FROM t1 WHERE ID=2, read 21,058 records returning 4,679 records back to the application. For the read activity to be 100 percent efficient, READ_EFFICIENCY should always be less than 10. That means the SQL statement reads records only necessary for the application. You achieve this by having the right level of indexing on the underlying table. You can use the MON_GET_PKG_CACHE_STMT_DETAILS table function to extract similar information like that in the example query with more granular details in an XML format.

Like request monitoring elements, the database configuration parameter mon_act_metrics controls the data collected by the activity monitor elements across the database server. You can set the parameter to one of the following values:

- NONE—No request monitor elements are collected.
- BASE—All activity monitor elements are collected. This is the default value.
- EXTENDED—All activity monitor elements are collected in a more granular level and are encapsulated in XML format.

Alternatively, you can control monitoring activity metrics collection for individual WLM service classes by using the COLLECT ACTIVITY METRICS clause while creating or altering service classes.

If you want to activate EXTENDED monitoring activity metrics for the database SAMPLE, execute the UPDATE DB CFG command, as follows:

```
UPDATE DB CFG FOR sample USING MON_ACT_METRICS EXTENDED
DB20000I The UPDATE DATABASE CONFIGURATION command completed successfully.
```

However, to alter an existing WLM service subclass (note that a superclass cannot be updated for activity data), use the ALTER SERVICE CLASS command, something like this:

```
ALTER SERVICE CLASS SYSDEFAULTSUBCLASS UNDER SYSDEFAULTUSERCLASS COLLECT AC-
TIVITY DATA ON ALL WITH DETAILS
DB20000I  The SQL command completed successfully.
```

Monitoring Data Objects

The data object monitoring perspective focuses on providing information about operations performed on the data objects such as tables, indexes, buffer pools, table spaces, and containers. The monitor elements for a data object are incremented each time a request involves processing that object. For example, when you read data from a particular table, the metric for rows read is incremented each time you read that table. However, the historical data for data objects is not available.

Table 5.5 lists the table functions for accessing the data objects information.

Table 5.5: Table functions for monitoring data objects

Table Function Name	Information Returned
MON_GET_BUFFERPOOL	Returns monitor metrics for one or more table buffer pools
MON_GET_TABLESPACE	Returns monitor metrics for one or more table spaces
MON_GET_CONTAINERS	Returns monitor metrics for one or more table containers
MON_GET_TABLE	Returns monitor metrics for one or more tables
MON_GET_INDEX	Returns monitor metrics for one or more table indexes

The syntax to construct a query that references table functions for monitoring data objects is:

```
SELECT * FROM TABLE ([FunctionName]
('[ObjectSpecifics]', [Member]) AS [CorrelationName]
```

where:

FunctionName Identifies the monitoring table function name to use (i.e., one of the functions listed in Table 5.5)

FunctionSpecifics Identifies the monitor table function-specific object information such as buffer pool name, table space name, table schema name, table name, index schema name, and index name for which to retrieve monitored metrics data

Member Identifies the member for which to collect monitored metrics data; you can specify -1 for the current member or -2 for all database members

CorrelationName Identifies the name to assign to the result data set produced by the query

You can use the MON_GET_BUFFERPOOL table function to measure the efficiency of the buffer pools by means of the hit ratio. The highest possible hit ratio is 100 percent; that is, when every page requested by the application is always available in the buffer pool. If the pages that the application requests are not available in the buffer pool through the prefetching process, the hit ratio is 0 percent or less. In certain cases, a negative hit ratio means that the prefetcher brought pages into the buffer pool that are not subsequently referenced because the query stops before it reaches the end of the table space or the prefetched pages are stolen and reused by the DB2 process before the query can access them.

To compute the buffer pool hit ratio, you can use a query similar to this:

```
WITH BPMETRICS AS (
    SELECT
          BP_NAME,
          POOL_DATA_L_READS + POOL_TEMP_DATA_L_READS +
          POOL_INDEX_L_READS + POOL_TEMP_INDEX_L_READS +
          POOL_XDA_L_READS + POOL_TEMP_XDA_L_READS AS LOGICAL_READS,
          POOL_DATA_P_READS + POOL_TEMP_DATA_P_READS +
          POOL_INDEX_P_READS + POOL_TEMP_INDEX_P_READS +
          POOL_XDA_P_READS + POOL_TEMP_XDA_P_READS AS PHYSICAL_READS,
          MEMBER
       FROM TABLE (MON_GET_BUFFERPOOL ('',-2)) AS METRICS)
   SELECT
         VARCHAR (BP_nNAME, 20) AS BP_NAME,
         LOGICAL_READS,
         PHYSICAL_READS,
         CASE WHEN LOGICAL_READS > 0
         THEN DEC ((1 - (FLOAT (PHYSICAL_READS) / FLOAT (LOGICAL_READS))) *
                   100, 5, 2)
         ELSE NULL
         END AS HIT_RATIO,
         MEMBER
      FROM BPMETRICS

BP_NAME        LOGICAL_READS        PHYSICAL_READS        HIT_RATIO MEMBER
-------------- -------------------- -------------------- --------- ------
IBMDEFAULTBP                 726400                 4901     99.32      0
IBMSYSTEMBP4K                     0                    0         -      0
IBMSYSTEMBP8K                     0                    0         -      0
IBMSYSTEMBP16K                    0                    0         -      0
IBMSYSTEMBP32K                    0                    0         -      0

  5 record(s) selected.
```

In DB2, a table space is the most fundamental logical storage structure of the database. In most scenarios, you will need to find the table space attributes such as table space type, page size, prefetch size, rebalancing mode, storage type, state, used pages, available pages, and total pages. You can capture this information by using the LIST TABLESPACE SHOW DETAIL command; however, using the newer data object monitoring elements table function MON_GET_TABLESPACE will retrieve it all in one go, as follows:

```
SELECT
      VARCHAR (TBSP_NAME, 20) AS TBSP_NAME,
      PREFETCH_WAIT_TIME,
      POOL_DATA_P_READS,
      POOL_DATA_L_READS
   FROM TABLE (MON_GET_TABLESPACE ('',-2)) AS T
ORDER BY POOL_DATA_P_READS DESC

TBSP_NAME            PREFETCH_WAIT_TIME POOL_DATA_P_READS    POOL_DATA_L_READS
-------------------- ------------------ -------------------- -----------------
USERSPACE1                          367                 2101            114679
IBMDB2SAMPLEREL                       8                  222            302373
SYSCATSPACE                           0                  103               579
SYSTOOLSPACE                          0                   67            127551
IBMDB2SAMPLEXML                       0                   11               131
TEMPSPACE1                            0                    0                 0
SYSTOOLSTMPSPACE                      0                    0                 0

  7 record(s) selected.
```

In this example, the prefetch wait time shows how long an application spent waiting on an I/O server (prefetcher process) to finish loading pages from the table space container into the buffer pool. If the number of prefetch waits and prefetch wait time is considerably more, you will have to increase the I/O servers or check the storage input/output per second (IOPS) by using I/O testing tools.

The DB2 database manager provides the MON_GET_CONTAINER table function to complement the table space findings. Let us continue with the previous table space troubleshooting example.

You have identified that the USERSPACE1 table space has a higher prefetch wait time. So now you can drill down to the container level to identify the reason for the high prefetch time by using the following command:

```
SELECT
      VARCHAR (TBSP_NAME, 20) AS TBSPNAME,
      SUM (POOL_READ_TIME) AS POOL_READ_TIME,
      SUM (DIRECT_READS) AS DIRECT_READS,
      SUM (DIRECT_WRITES) AS DIRECT_WRITES,
      SUM (DIRECT_READ_TIME) AS DIRECT_READ_TIME,
      SUM (DIRECT_WRITE_TIME) AS DIRECT_WRITE_TIME
   FROM TABLE (MON_GET_CONTAINER ('',-2)) AS t
GROUP BY (TBSP_NAME);

                                                                   DIRECT_   DIRECT_
TBSPNAME          POOL_READ_TIME DIRECT_READS DIRECT_WRITES READ_TIME WRITE_TIME
---------------- -------------- ------------ ------------- --------- ----------
USERSPACE1                  5496       258278          1962     15321        328
IBMDB2SAMPLEREL              363           50            38         2          1
SYSCATSPACE                  243         2292           128        42         31
SYSTOOLSPACE                  76         1054             0      1651          0
IBMDB2SAMPLEXML               50            0             0         0          0
TEMPSPACE1                     0          166           172         0          1
SYSTOOLSTMPSPACE               0            0             0         0          0

  7 record(s) selected.
```

The potential reason for a fairly high prefetch wait time is that the large number of direct reads and direct writes may be due to high disk sorts or to many tables having LONG VARCHAR, LOB columns, or frequent backups happening on the table space USERSPACE1. You will have to set the mon_obj_metrics database configuration parameter to BASE or EXTENDED to activate collecting data object monitor elements reported by the above table functions.

Now that you have examined the table space container level, it is time to drill down to the table and index level to identify the objects causing high prefetch wait time in the USERSPACE1 table space:

```
SELECT SUBSTR (TABNAME, 1, 20) AS NAME, DIRECT_READS, DIRECT_WRITES
   FROM TABLE (MON_GET_TABLE ('', '', -1)) AS T
      WHERE TBSP_ID=2

NAME                 DIRECT_READS         DIRECT_WRITES
-------------------- -------------------- --------------------
T1                                 258278                 1962
  1 record(s) selected.
```

Because you have logically isolated the problem from a broader level to a specific object level, you can start looking at the solutions to reduce the direct reads and direct writes.

You can also use the MON_GET_TABLE table function to determine expensive table scans:

```
SELECT
      SUBSTR (TABNAME, 1, 25) AS NAME,
      TABLE_SCANS,
      ROWS_READ,
      ROWS_INSERTED,
      ROWS_DELETED
   FROM TABLE (MON_GET_TABLE ('', '', -1))
ORDER BY TABLE_SCANS DESC
FETCH FIRST 5 ROWS ONLY

NAME                      TABLE_SCANS ROWS_READ  ROWS_INSERTED ROWS_DELETED
------------------------- ----------- ---------- ------------- ------------
GDS_LEGALENT_STG               647967  362879440           560          560
GDS_HFM_LEGALENTITY_STG        623445  350394074           562          562
PLANT_JOB_LOG_DS               239779  775932707           143            0
EDW_VALIDATION_REPORTS_DS       67056    6306272             0            0
D_PLANT_FACTORY_HIER            58770 1540217316            40            0

  5 record(s) selected.
```

As usual, interpreting the output of a table function is fun and interesting. The total number of records in the table GDS_LEGALENT_STG is 560:

```
SELECT SUBSTR (TABNAME, 1, 20) AS TABLENAME, CARD
FROM SYSCAT.TABLES WHERE TABNAME='GDS_LEGALENT_STG'

TABLENAME            CARD
-------------------- --------------------
GDS_LEGALENT_STG                      560

  1 record(s) selected.
```

From the statistics, the data load must have happened only once, and this table is mostly used for data read purposes. The high number of table scans is because no indexes are present on the table, so you must identify and create the appropriate indexes.

In DB2, indexes are used for efficiently accessing data. You will always incur overheads maintaining indexes, and the overheads are:

- Additional storage is required to store index keys along with the actual data.
- Every insert on the table object page needs an additional insert on the index page.
- Table reorganization needs additional time to rebuild the indexes.
- In some situations, inefficient indexes can lead to lock timeouts and deadlocks.

It is always advisable to identify unused indexes from your database and consult application teams before taking any action on the used indexes.

You can use the MON_GET_INDEX table function to determine unused, inefficient indexes in the database. The command looks something like this:

```
SELECT
      VARCHAR (S.INDSCHEMA, 6) AS INDSCHEMA,
      VARCHAR (S.INDNAME, 30) AS INDNAME,
      T.INDEX_SCANS,
      T.INDEX_ONLY_SCANS
  FROM TABLE (MON_GET_INDEX ('','', -2)) AS T, SYSCAT.INDEXES AS S
  WHERE T.TABSCHEMA = S.TABSCHEMA AND
    T.TABNAME = S.TABNAME AND
```

Continued

```
    T.IID = S.IID AND
    T.INDEX_SCANS = 0 AND
    T.INDEX_ONLY_SCANS = 0
```

Unlike with unused indexes, if you want to find extremely efficient indexes in your database, execute a query similar to the following:

```
SELECT
      VARCHAR (S.INDSCHEMA, 6) AS INDSCHEMA,
      VARCHAR (S.INDNAME, 30) AS INDNAME,
      T.NLEAF,
      T.NLEVELS,
      T.INDEX_SCANS,
      T.INDEX_ONLY_SCANS,
      T.KEY_UPDATES,
      T.BOUNDARY_LEAF_NODE_SPLITS + T.NONBOUNDARY_LEAF_NODE_SPLITS AS PAGE_
SPLITS
   FROM TABLE (MON_GET_INDEX ('', '', -2)) AS T, SYSCAT.INDEXES AS S
ORDER BY T.INDEX_ONLY_SCANS DESC
FETCH FIRST 5 ROWS ONLY
```

Monitoring Locks

Understanding locking behavior is a crucial element in fighting the lock-wait and deadlock performance problems in a database. You can use lock object monitoring table functions to retrieve information about locks. Table 5.6 lists the table functions for accessing the lock objects information such as lock name, lock mode, lock status, lock waits, applications holding the lock, applications waiting to acquire the lock, and lock attributes.

Table 5.6: Table functions for monitoring locks

Table Function Name	Information Returned
MON_GET_LOCKS	Returns a list of all locks in the currently connected database
MON_GET_APPL_LOCKWAIT	Returns information about all locks that each application's agents connected to the current database are waiting to acquire

The following example illustrates the use of the lock table function to identify a locking issue in the database. In this case, two transactions—TR1 and TR2—are attempting to read and modify the data in a table T1, respectively. When both TR1 and TR2 are executing concurrently, TR2 stops processing. To capture the application handle, lock, and lock attributes, use the table functions listed in Table 5.6 to analyze potential locking problems:

```
SELECT
        LOCK_NAME,
        LOCK_STATUS,
        LOCK_MODE,
        LOCK_ATTRIBUTES,
        HLD_APPLICATION_HANDLE,
        REQ_APPLICATION_HANDLE
    FROM TABLE (MON_GET_APPL_LOCKWAIT (NULL, -2))

                                                             HLD_         REQ_
                                  LOCK_  LOCK_ LOCK_         APPLICATION_ APPLICATION_
LOCK_NAME                         STATUS MODE  ATTRIBUTES    HANDLE       HANDLE
-------------------------- ------ ----- -------------- ------------ ------------
03001600000000000000000054 W      S     0000000000400000        53165        53193

  1 record(s) selected.
```

You can use the MON_GET_LOCKS table function to identify the lock mode and the attributes such as update/insert row lock, locks acquired by the lock escalation process, and lock by repeatable read scan:

```
SELECT
        LOCK_STATUS,
        LOCK_ATTRIBUTES,
        APPLICATION_HANDLE
    FROM TABLE (MON_GET_LOCKS (
        CLOB ('<lock_name>03001600000000000000000054</lock_name>'), -2))

                                                                    Continued
```

```
LOCK_STATUS LOCK_ATTRIBUTES    APPLICATION_HANDLE
----------- ---------------- --------------------
G           0000000000000002                53310
W           0000000000000004                53316

  2 record(s) selected.
```

The LOCK_STATUS column G represents the application that is currently holding the lock, and W or C signifies the application that is currently waiting to acquire the lock. The LOCK_ATTRIBUTES column value 0000000000000002 indicates the lock acquired by lock escalation process and 0000000000000004 represents the RR lock.

You can use the MON_GET_ACTIVITY_DETAILS table function to capture the SQL statements for each application handle in question, and then work on identifying the solution to avoid the locking issues between them:

```
APPLICATION_HANDLE   ACTIVITY_ID UOW_ID      STMT_TEXT
-------------------- ----------- ----------- --------------
53310                2           1           SELECT * FROM t1 WITH RR
53316                1           3           UPDATE t1 SET id=100 WHERE id=2

  2 record(s) selected.
```

Monitoring System Memory

To see the amount of system memory in use on your database server, you can use system memory table functions. Table 5.7 lists the table functions for examining memory usage at the levels of memory sets, which are allocations of memory from the operating system. These functions should run locally on the server and do not support remotely cataloged databases.

Table 5.7: Table functions for monitoring system memory

Table Function Name	Information Returned
MON_GET_MEMORY_SET	Returns metrics from the allocated memory sets both at the instance level and at the active database level
MON_GET_MEMORY_POOL	Returns metrics from the memory pools contained within a memory set

If you want to view the memory utilization overall by database manager, database, applications, fenced mode process (FMP), and agents private memory, execute a query similar to the following:

```
SELECT
      VARCHAR (MEMORY_SET_TYPE, 20) AS SET_TYPE,
      VARCHAR (DB_NAME, 20) AS DBNAME,
      (MEMORY_SET_SIZE/1024) AS "MEMORY_SET_SIZE (MB)",
      (MEMORY_SET_USED/1024) AS "MEMORY_SET_USED (MB)",
      (MEMORY_SET_USED_HWM/1024) AS "MEMORY_SET_USED_HWM (MB)"
   FROM TABLE (MON_GET_MEMORY_SET (NULL, 'SAMPLE', -2));

                                           MEMORY_SET_ MEMORY_SET_
SET_TYPE    DBNAME   MEMORY_SET_SIZE (MB) USED (MB)   USED_HWM (MB)
---------- -------- -------------------- ----------- ------------
DBMS              -                  148         101          103
FMP               -                   22           1            1
PRIVATE           -                   25          18           51
DATABASE     SAMPLE                  157          78           79
APPLICATION  SAMPLE                  156           3            9

  5 record(s) selected.
```

To find a detailed level of memory utilization for each memory pool within the memory set, use the MON_GET_MEMORY_POOL table function:

```
SELECT
      VARCHAR (MEMORY_SET_TYPE, 10) AS SET_TYPE,
      VARCHAR (MEMORY_POOL_TYPE, 20) AS POOL_TYPE,
      VARCHAR (DB_NAME, 10) AS DBNAME,
      (MEMORY_POOL_USED/1024) AS "MEMORY_POOL_USED (MB)",
      (MEMORY_POOL_USED_HWM/1024) AS "MEMORY_POOL_USED_HWM (MB)"
   FROM TABLE (MON_GET_MEMORY_POOL ('DBMS', CURRENT_SERVER, -2));

                                                       Continued
```

```
SET_TYPE POOL_TYPE      DBNAME MEMORY_POOL_USED (MB) MEMORY_POOL_USED_HWM (MB)
-------- -------------- ------ -------------------- ------------------------
DBMS     FCM_LOCAL      -                         0                        0
DBMS     FCM_SESSION    -                         1                        1
DBMS     FCM_CHANNEL    -                         0                        0
DBMS     FCMBP          -                         0                        0
DBMS     FCM_CONTROL    -                        49                       50
DBMS     MONITOR        -                         0                        1
DBMS     RESYNC         -                         2                        2
DBMS     OSS_TRACKER    -                         1                        1
DBMS     APM            -                         2                        2
DBMS     KERNEL         -                        22                       22
DBMS     BSU            -                         4                        5
DBMS     SQL_COMPILER   -                         2                        2
DBMS     KERNEL_CONTROL -                         7                        7
DBMS     EDU            -                        11                       11

  14 record(s) selected.
```

Likewise, to find the detailed memory consumers for all memory sets, use this query:

```
SELECT
      VARCHAR (MEMORY_SET_TYPE, 10) AS SET_TYPE,
      VARCHAR (MEMORY_POOL_TYPE, 20) AS POOL_TYPE,
      VARCHAR (DB_NAME, 10) AS DBNAME,
      (MEMORY_POOL_USED/1024) AS "MEMORY_POOL_USED (MB)",
      (MEMORY_POOL_USED_HWM/1024) AS "MEMORY_POOL_USED_HWM (MB)"
   FROM TABLE (MON_GET_MEMORY_POOL (NULL, CURRENT_SERVER, -2));
```

Monitoring Routines

Using the monitoring routines table functions, you can measure the aggregated execution metrics for procedures, external procedures, functions, compiled functions and compiled triggers, and anonymous blocks since the database was activated. It also facilities in the problem determination process by listing subroutines and SQL statements that are executed within the routine. Table 5.8 lists the available table functions for routines.

Table 5.8: Table functions for monitoring routines	
Table Function Name	**Information Returned**
MON_GET_ROUTINE	Returns the execution metrics for routines in relational format
MON_GET_ROUTINE_DETAILS	Returns the detailed execution metrics for routines in an XML format
MON_GET_ROUTINE_EXEC_LIST	Returns a list of all statements and sections executed by routines
MON_GET_SECTION_ROUTINE	Returns a list of all subfunctions and subprocedures that might be invoked during the execution of the input section

To analyze stored procedure performance, you can execute the following query, which will show total CPU time consumption in microseconds:

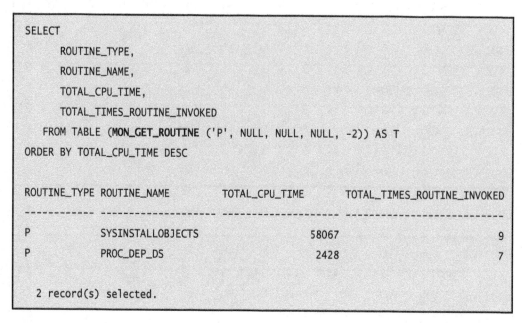

```
SELECT
      ROUTINE_TYPE,
      ROUTINE_NAME,
      TOTAL_CPU_TIME,
      TOTAL_TIMES_ROUTINE_INVOKED
   FROM TABLE (MON_GET_ROUTINE ('P', NULL, NULL, NULL, -2)) AS T
ORDER BY TOTAL_CPU_TIME DESC

ROUTINE_TYPE ROUTINE_NAME         TOTAL_CPU_TIME       TOTAL_TIMES_ROUTINE_INVOKED
------------ -------------------- -------------------- ---------------------------
P            SYSINSTALLOBJECTS                   58067                           9
P            PROC_DEP_DS                          2428                           7

  2 record(s) selected.
```

And if you want to extract detailed information for the procedure DB210.PROC_DEP_DS, execute this query:

```
SELECT
      B.*
   FROM
```

Continued

```
    TABLE (MON_GET_ROUTINE_DETAILS ('P', 'DB210', NULL, 'PROC_DEP_DS', -1)) AS A,
    TABLE (MON_FORMAT_XML_TIMES_BY_ROW (A.DETAILS)) AS B
ORDER BY
    TOTAL_TIME_VALUE DESC
FETCH FIRST 5 ROWS ONLY
```

To capture all the statements executed as part of the procedure DB210.PROC_DEP_DS, you can use this query:

```
SELECT
      SUBSTR (P.STMT_TEXT, 1, 45) AS TEXT
   FROM
      TABLE (MON_GET_ROUTINE_EXEC_LIST ('P', 'DB210', NULL, 'PROC_DEP_DS', -1)) AS T,
      TABLE (MON_GET_PKG_CACHE_STMT (NULL, NULL, NULL, -1)) AS P
WHERE
  T.EXECUTABLE_ID = P.EXECUTABLE_ID
```

As with other monitor collection settings, you need to set the routine data collection database configuration parameter mon_rtn_data to BASE and to collect the statement execution list information; you must set the mon_rtn_execlist database configuration parameter to BASE as well.

A few miscellaneous monitoring table functions are available in DB2 to retrieve information related to the fast communications manager (FCM) and the table space extent movement:

```
SELECT MEMBER, BUFF_FREE, BUFF_FREE_BOTTOM
   FROM TABLE (MON_GET_FCM (-2))

MEMBER BUFF_FREE            BUFF_FREE_BOTTOM
------ -------------------- --------------------
     0                  128                  128

  1 record(s) selected.
```

To measure traffic between the current member and the remote member in a database partitioning feature environment, use a query similar to the following:

```
SELECT
      MEMBER,
      CONNECTION_STATUS,
      SUM (TOTAL_BUFFERS_SENT) AS TOTAL_BUFFERS_SENT,
      SUM (TOTAL_BUFFERS_RCVD) AS TOTAL_BUFFERS_RCVD
   FROM TABLE (MON_GET_FCM_CONNECTION_LIST (-2)) AS T
GROUP BY MEMBER, CONNECTION_STATUS

MEMBER CONNECTION_STATUS TOTAL_BUFFERS_SENT   TOTAL_BUFFERS_RCVD
------ ----------------- -------------------- --------------------
     0 Active                      7962607027           6841368615
     1 Active                      1363528394           1142005164
     2 Active                       960820060            777595468
     3 Active                       952119928            794181684
     4 Active                      1025169470            811863878
   ...                                    ...                  ...
   ...                                    ...                  ...
    63 Active                      1218333556            857326505
    64 Active                      1049507135            813966152

  65 record(s) selected.
```

If you see an irregular FCM buffer sent and received between the multiple nodes, consider evenly redistributing the fact data across the node and evaluating the distribution keys to achieve collocated joins.

Whenever you want to monitor the progress of the ALTER TABLESPACE ... REDUCE command, you can use the MON_GET_EXTENT_MOVEMENT_STATUS table function to do so. This function returns information about the current extent being moved, the number of extents moved, the number of extents left to move, and the overall move time for all the extents moved in milliseconds.

The query looks something like this:

```
SELECT
      VARCHAR (TBSP_NAME, 20) AS TBSPNAME,
      CURRENT_EXTENT,
      NUM_EXTENTS_MOVED,
      NUM_EXTENTS_LEFT,
      TOTAL_MOVE_TIME
   FROM TABLE (MON_GET_EXTENT_MOVEMENT_STATUS ('', -2)) AS T
```

Functions Quick Reference

Table 5.9 provides a summary of table functions with corresponding monitor levels and database configuration parameters that controls monitoring data collection.

Table 5.9: Table functions summary

Table Function	Monitor Level	Database Configuration Parameter Control	WLM Service Class Setting
MON_GET_SERVICE_SUBCLASS MON_GET_SERVICE_SUBCLASS_DETAILS MON_GET_WORKLOAD MON_GET_WORKLOAD_DETAILS MON_GET_CONNECTION MON_GET_CONNECTION_DETAILS MON_GET_UNIT_OF_WORK MON_GET_UNIT_OF_WORK_DETAILS	Database server	mon_req_metrics	COLLECT REQUEST METRICS
MON_GET_ACTIVITY_DETAILS MON_GET_PKG_CACHE_STMT MON_GET_PKG_CACHE_STMT_DETAILS	Current executing activities	mon_act_metrics	COLLECT ACTIVITY METRICS
MON_GET_BUFFERPOOL MON_GET_TABLESPACE MON_GET_CONTAINER MON_GET_TABLE MON_GET_INDEX	Data object	mon_obj_metrics Always collected	None
MON_GET_LOCKS MON_GET_APPL_LOCKWAIT	Locks	Always collected	None
MON_GET_MEMORY_SET MON_GET_MEMORY_POOL	Database server	Always collected	None

Table 5.9: Table functions summary (continued)

Table Function	Monitor Level	Database Configuration Parameter Control	WLM Service Class Setting
MON_GET_ROUTINE MON_GET_ROUTINE_DETAILS MON_GET_ROUTINE_EXEC_LIST MON_GET_SECTION_ROUTINE	Functions, procedures, triggers	mon_rtn_data and mon_rtn_execlist	COLLECT REQUEST METRICS
MON_GET_FCM MON_GET_FCM_CONNECTION_LIST MON_GET_EXTENT_MOVEMENT_STATUS	FCM and table space	Always collected	None

Administrative Views for Monitoring

Starting at DB2 9.7 Fix Pack 1, a new set of administrative views is created in the SYSIBMADM schema to retrieve critical database monitoring information. Unlike monitoring table functions, administrative views do not require input parameters, and they always return data in relational format. Table 5.10 lists the monitoring administrative views based on the newer lightweight, high-speed monitoring solution.

Table 5.10: Monitoring administrative views

Admin View Name	Information Returned
MON_BP_UTILIZATION	Returns key monitoring metrics for buffer pools, including hit ratio and average read and write times across all the database partitions in the currently connected database
MON_CONNECTION_ SUMMARY	Returns key metrics for all connections, including the application handle, total commits, average amount of CPU time spent, and lock waits per activity in the currently connected database
MON_CURRENT_SQL	Returns key metrics for all activities that were submitted across all members of the database and have not yet been completed, including a point-in-time view of both dynamic and static SQL statements presently being executed in the currently connected database
MON_CURRENT_UOW	Returns key metrics for all units of work submitted across all members of the database, determines long-running units of work statements, and helps prevent performance problems
MON_DB_SUMMARY	Returns key metrics aggregated over all service classes across all members in the currently connected database and helps monitor the system in a high-level manner by providing a concise summary of the database
MON_LOCKWAITS	Returns information about agents working on behalf of applications that are waiting to obtain locks in the currently connected database (very useful when it comes to resolving locking problems)
MON_PKG_CACHE_ SUMMARY	Returns key metrics for both dynamic and static SQL statements in the cache, providing a high-level summary of the database package cache; the metrics returned are aggregated over all executions of the statement across all members of the database

Table 5.10: Monitoring administrative views (continued)	
Admin View Name	**Information Returned**
MON_SERVICE_ SUBCLASS_SUMMARY	Returns key metrics for all service subclasses in the currently connected database and helps monitor the system in a high-level manner, showing work executed per service class
MON_TBSP_UTILIZATION	Returns key monitoring metrics for table spaces in the currently connected database, including all table space attributes, utilization percentage, high watermark, and hit ratio
MON_WORKLOAD_ SUMMARY	Returns key metrics for all workloads in the currently connected database and helps monitor the system in a high-level manner, showing incoming work per workload

Identifying key performance indicators (KPIs) are very essential to validate database performance and functionality. Most of the newer DB2 monitoring administrative views provide precomputed KPI values, without requiring you to compute them as the older releases did.

Buffer Pool Hit Ratio and I/O Response Time

To capture performance metrics for buffer pools, such as data, index, and auxiliary storage objects' hit ratios and average buffer pool I/O response time, use a query similar to the following:

```
SELECT
      VARCHAR (BP_NAME, 30) AS BPOOL_NAME,
      DATA_HIT_RATIO_PERCENT,
      INDEX_HIT_RATIO_PERCENT,
      XDA_HIT_RATIO_PERCENT,
      AVG_PHYSICAL_READ_TIME,
      AVG_WRITE_TIME
FROM SYSIBMADM.MON_BP_UTILIZATION WHERE BP_NAME= 'IBMDEFAULTBP'

             DATA_HIT_     INDEX_HIT_    XDA_HIT_      AVG_PHYSICAL_ AVG_
BPOOL_NAME   RATIO_PERCENT RATIO_PERCENT RATIO_PERCENT READ_TIME     WRITE_TIME
------------ ------------- ------------- ------------- ------------- ----------
IBMDEFAULTBP         99.98         98.65         99.04             0          0

  1 record(s) selected.
```

For better end-user experience, the OLTP application database buffer pool hit ratios should always be greater than 95 percent; however, it varies in OLAP application databases due to large sequential scans. The average physical read time and average write time indicates I/O subsystem response time, which should be within 10 milliseconds.

Currently Running Expensive SQL Statement

Inefficient SQL statements are the real enemies of database administrators, so you should closely monitor the database server activities to identify those expensive SQL statements and take appropriate action at the right time. To capture the elapsed time since the activity began, total CPU time spent in timerons, activity type and state, efficiency of indexes present on the table, rough cost estimation of the query, and the actual SQL statement, you can use the following query:

```
SELECT
      APPLICATION_HANDLE,
      ELAPSED_TIME_SEC,
      VARCHAR (ACTIVITY_STATE, 10) AS ACTIVITY_STATE,
      VARCHAR (ACTIVITY_TYPE, 10) AS ACTIVITY_TYPE,
      TOTAL_CPU_TIME,
      (ROWS_READ/NULLIF (ROWS_RETURNED, 0)) AS INDEX_EFFICIENCY,
      QUERY_COST_ESTIMATE,
      SUBSTR (STMT_TEXT, 1, 100) AS STMT_TEXT
   FROM SYSIBMADM.MON_CURRENT_SQL
ORDER BY ELAPSED_TIME_SEC DESC

APPLICATION_ ELAPSED_ ACTIVITY_  ACTIVITY_ TOTAL_   INDEX_     QUERY_COST_
HANDLE       TIME_SEC STATE      TYPE      CPU_TIME EFFICIENCY ESTIMATE    STMT_TEXT
------------ -------- ---------- --------- -------- ---------- ----------- ---------
63096              32 IDLE       READ_DML     86037          4       21815 select *
                                                                            from t1
                                                                            where id=2
63079              13 IDLE       READ_DML     13945          1       20642 select *
                                                                            from t1

  2 record(s) selected.
```

Statements with a high ratio of ROWS_READ/ROWS_RETURNED indicate large table scans and possibly need indexes to fix them. In the above example, certainly SELECT * FROM t1 WHERE id=2 requires an index, as only about 25 percent of the records read were sent to the application.

You can just as well use the SYSIBMADM.MON_PKG_CACHE_SUMMARY administrative view to analyze the expensive SQL statement:

```
SELECT
      SECTION_TYPE,
      TOTAL_STMT_EXEC_TIME,
      AVG_STMT_EXEC_TIME,
      TOTAL_CPU_TIME,
      AVG_CPU_TIME,
      TOTAL_IO_WAIT_TIME,
      PREP_TIME,
      ROWS_READ_PER_ROWS_RETURNED,
      SUBSTR (STMT_TEXT, 1, 100) AS STMT_TEXT
   FROM SYSIBMADM.MON_PKG_CACHE_SUMMARY
ORDER BY TOTAL_CPU_TIME DESC
```

Current Lock-wait Chains in the Database

A common user symptom of a locking problem is an application hang. In most cases, a hang appears as lock wait within the database engine. Understanding the lock-wait event is key to fixing the problem permanently. You can access lock-wait information such as the application requesting the lock, the application holding the lock, lock-wait elapsed time, and related SQL statements by invoking the following query:

```
SELECT
      SUBSTR (HLD_APPLICATION_NAME, 1, 10) AS LOCK_HOLDING_APP,
      SUBSTR (HLD_USERID, 1, 10) AS LOCK_HOLDING_USER,
      SUBSTR (REQ_APPLICATION_NAME, 1, 10) AS LOCK_WAITING_APP,
      SUBSTR (REQ_USERID, 1, 10) AS LOCK_WAITING_USER,
      LOCK_MODE,
      LOCK_OBJECT_TYPE,
      SUBSTR (TABSCHEMA, 1, 10) AS TABSCHEMA,
      SUBSTR (TABNAME, 1, 10) AS TABNAME,
      SUBSTR (HLD_CURRENT_STMT_TEXT, 1, 20) AS STMT_HOLDING_LOCK,
```

Continued

```
      SUBSTR (REQ_STMT_TEXT, 1, 20) AS STMT_WAITING_LOCK,
      LOCK_WAIT_ELAPSED_TIME AS LOCK_WAIT_TIME
   FROM SYSIBMADM.MON_LOCKWAITS

LOCK_    LOCK_    LOCK_     LOCK_             LOCK_                     STMT_
HOLDING_ HOLDING_ WAITING_  WAITING_ LOCK_    OBJECT_  TAB     TAB     HOLDING_
APP      USER     APP       USER     MODE     TYPE     SCHEMA  NAME    LOCK
-------- ------- ---------  -------- -----    -------- ------  ----    --------
db2bp    MOHAN   db2bp      MOHAN    S        TABLE    MOHAN     T1    -

STMT_                LOCK_
WAITING_             WAIT_
LOCK                 TIME
-------------------- -----
update t1 set id=200    53


  1 record(s) selected.
```

Understanding Your Table Spaces

Table spaces are the logical grouping of containers. It is always beneficial to understand their operational performance statistics such as data, index, and XML data area (XDA) object hit ratio at a table-space level along with table-space utilization metrics. You can access the information by using a query similar to this:

```
SELECT
      SUBSTR (TBSP_NAME, 1, 10) AS TBSP_NAME,
      TBSP_TYPE,
      TBSP_CONTENT_TYPE,
      SUBSTR (TBSP_STATE, 1, 10) AS TBSP_STATE,
      TBSP_PAGE_SIZE,
      TBSP_EXTENT_SIZE,
```

Continued

```
      TBSP_USING_AUTO_STORAGE,
      TBSP_AUTO_RESIZE_ENABLED,
      (TBSP_TOTAL_SIZE_KB/1024) AS "TBSP_TOTAL_SIZE_KB (MB)",
      (TBSP_USABLE_SIZE_KB/1024) AS "TBSP_USABLE_SIZE_KB (MB)",
      TBSP_UTILIZATION_PERCENT,
      DATA_HIT_RATIO_PERCENT,
      INDEX_HIT_RATIO_PERCENT
   FROM SYSIBMADM.MON_TBSP_UTILIZATION
WHERE TBSP_NAME='USERSPACE1'


TBSP_NAME   TBSP_TYPE   TBSP_CONTENT_TYPE  TBSP_STATE  TBSP_PAGE_SIZE
----------  ----------  -----------------  ----------  --------------
USERSPACE1  DMS         LARGE              NORMAL                8192

TBSP_EXTENT_SIZE      TBSP_USING_AUTO_STORAGE  TBSP_AUTO_RESIZE_ENABLED
--------------------  -----------------------  ------------------------
                  32                        1                         1

TBSP_TOTAL_SIZE_KB (MB)  TBSP_USABLE_SIZE_KB (MB)  TBSP_UTILIZATION_PERCENT
-----------------------  ------------------------  ------------------------
                     15                        14                     96.61

DATA_HIT_RATIO_PERCENT  INDEX_HIT_RATIO_PERCENT
----------------------  -----------------------
                 99.85                    75.07

  1 record(s) selected.
```

In this example, the index hit ratio is unacceptable; the fact is, many tables are missing key indexes, so this is a good opportunity for you to fix them all.

Getting to Know Your Database Server

It is always recommended to know your entire database server performance with respect to the number of commits, number of rollbacks, number of application requests, overall requests, activity, I/O, and network wait times. You can use the SYSIBMADM.MON_DB_SUMMARY administrative view to determine the health of the database:

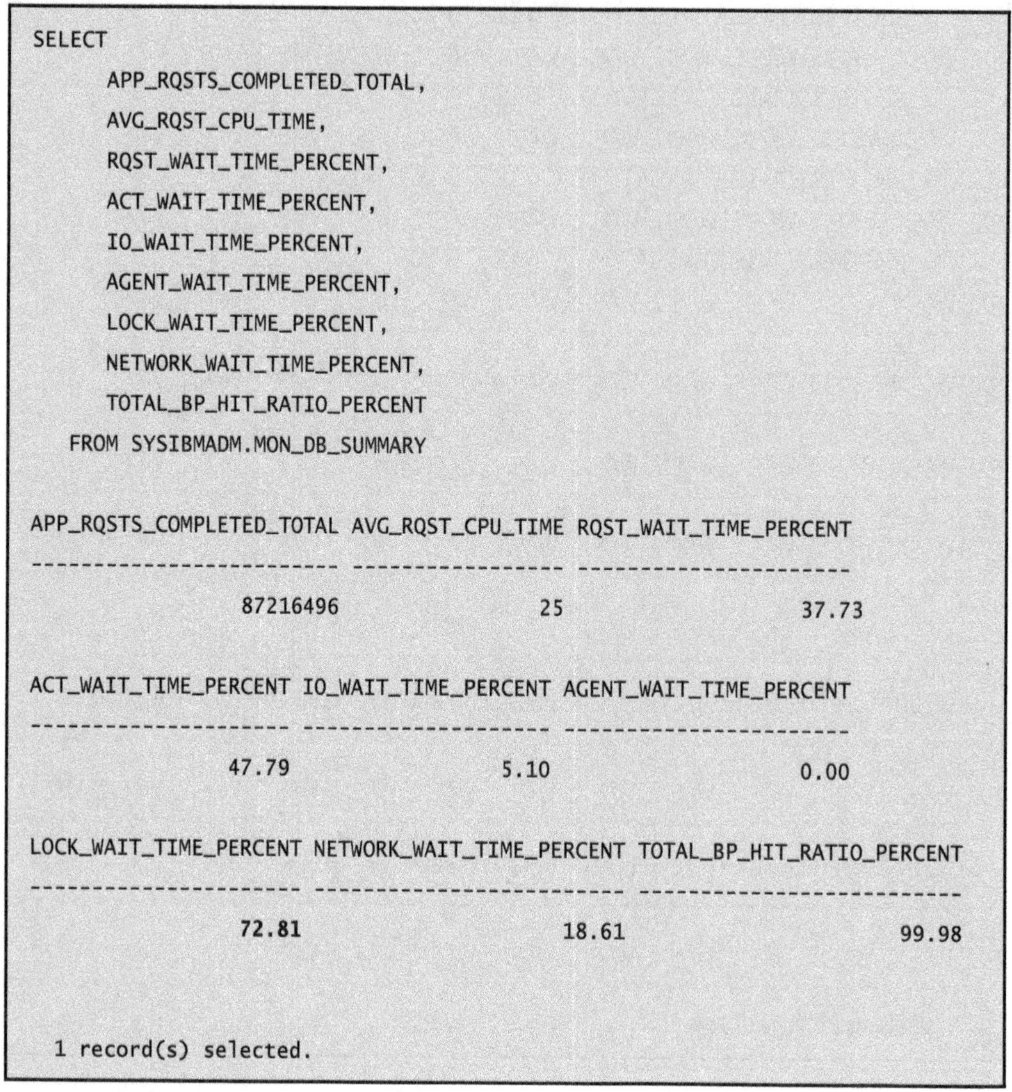

```
SELECT
      APP_RQSTS_COMPLETED_TOTAL,
      AVG_RQST_CPU_TIME,
      RQST_WAIT_TIME_PERCENT,
      ACT_WAIT_TIME_PERCENT,
      IO_WAIT_TIME_PERCENT,
      AGENT_WAIT_TIME_PERCENT,
      LOCK_WAIT_TIME_PERCENT,
      NETWORK_WAIT_TIME_PERCENT,
      TOTAL_BP_HIT_RATIO_PERCENT
   FROM SYSIBMADM.MON_DB_SUMMARY

APP_RQSTS_COMPLETED_TOTAL AVG_RQST_CPU_TIME RQST_WAIT_TIME_PERCENT
------------------------- ----------------- ----------------------
                 87216496                25                  37.73

ACT_WAIT_TIME_PERCENT IO_WAIT_TIME_PERCENT AGENT_WAIT_TIME_PERCENT
--------------------- -------------------- -----------------------
                47.79                 5.10                    0.00

LOCK_WAIT_TIME_PERCENT NETWORK_WAIT_TIME_PERCENT TOTAL_BP_HIT_RATIO_PERCENT
---------------------- ------------------------- --------------------------
                 72.81                     18.61                      99.98


  1 record(s) selected.
```

In this example, certainly lock-wait time is considerably higher and needs attention from the database administrator to identify the root cause.

Event Monitors

Whereas the snapshot monitors and table functions provide a method for recording information about the state of database activity at a given point in time, an scan record information about database activity when an event or transition occurs. Therefore, event monitors enable you to collect monitor data over time for events or activities that cannot be monitored using the snapshot monitors or other means.

For example, suppose you want to capture monitor data whenever a deadlock cycle occurs. If you are familiar with the concept of deadlocks, you may recall that a special process known as the *deadlock detector* runs quietly in the background and "wakes up" at predefined intervals to scan the locking system in search of a deadlock cycle. If a deadlock cycle exists, the deadlock detector randomly selects one of the transactions involved in the cycle to roll back and terminate. The transaction that is rolled back and terminated receives SQL error code SQL0911N reason code 2, all locks it had acquired are released, and the remaining transaction or transactions are then allowed to proceed.

Information about such a series of events cannot be captured by the snapshot monitor because, in all likelihood, the deadlock cycle will have been broken long before a snapshot can be taken. An event monitor, however, can capture such information because it is activated the moment the deadlock cycle is detected.

Unlike the snapshot and table monitor functions, which reside in the background and are always available, event monitors are special objects that you must create. To create event monitors, you execute the CREATE EVENT MONITOR SQL statement. The basic syntax for this statement is:

```
CREATE EVENT MONITOR [EventMonName]
FOR [DATABASE |
     BUFFERPOOLS |
     TABLESPACES |
     TABLES |
        LOCKING |
        UNIT OF WORK |
        ACTIVITIES |
        PACKAGE CACHE |
        STATISTICS |
        THRESHOLD VIOLATIONS |
     DEADLOCKS <WITH DETAILS> <HISTORY> <VALUES> |
                                                    Continued
```

```
     CONNECTIONS <WHERE [EventCondition]> |
     STATEMENTS <WHERE [EventCondition]>  |
     TRANSACTIONS <WHERE [EventCondition]> , ...] |
        CHANGE HISTORY <WHERE EVENT IN [EventControl]>]
WRITE TO [PIPE [PipeName] |
          TABLE (TABLE [TableName]) <BLOCKED | NONBLOCKED>|
          FILE [DirectoryName] <BLOCKED | NONBLOCKED>]
[MANUALSTART | AUTOSTART]
[ON DBPARTITIONNUM [PartitionNumber]]
[LOCAL | GLOBAL]
```

where:

EventMonName	Identifies the name to assign to the event monitor that is to be created
EventCondition	Identifies a condition that determines the CONNECTION, STATEMENT, or TRANSACTION events monitor data to collect
TableName	Identifies the name to assign to the database table where all event monitor data collected is to be written
EventControl	Identifies the event controls that specify which events the event monitor is to capture
PipeName	Identifies the name to assign to the named pipe where all event monitor data collected is to be written
DirectoryName	Identifies the name to assign to the directory where one or more files containing event monitor data are to be written
PartitionNumber	Identifies the database partition number or member on which the event monitor needs to collect the data in a partitioned database or pureScale environment

As you can see by examining the syntax of the CREATE EVENT MONITOR statement, when an event monitor is created, the type of event to be monitored must be specified. The DB2 supported event types are as follows:

- ACTIVITIES
- BUFFERPOOLS
- CONNECTIONS
- DATABASE
- DEADLOCKS
- DEADLOCKS WITH DETAILS

- DEADLOCKS WITH DETAILS HISTORY
- DEADLOCKS WITH DETAILS HISTORY VALUES
- STATEMENTS
- STATISTICS
- TABLES
- TABLESPACES
- THRESHOLD VIOLATIONS
- TRANSACTIONS
- UNIT OF WORK
- LOCKING
- PACKAGE CACHE
- CHANGE HISTORY

The location where all monitor data collected is to be written must be specified as well; output from an event monitor can be written to one or more database tables, one or more external files, a named pipe, or an unformatted event table. Table event monitors and pipe event monitors stream event records directly to the table or named pipe specified. File event monitors, however, stream event records to a series of eight-character numbered files that have the extension ".evt" (for example, 00000000.evt, 00000001.evt, 00000002.evt). You should consider the monitor data collected and stored in these files as being stored as one logical file even though the data is divided into smaller pieces. In other words, the start of the data stream is the first byte in the file named 00000000.evt; the end of the data stream is the last byte in the file named *nnnnnnnn*.evt.

Data collected by event monitors is streamed to buffers before it is externalized to disk (i.e., written to a table or file). If you specify the BLOCKED option, agents that generate an event being monitored will wait for an event buffer to be written to disk before continuing if it determines that both event buffers are full. As a result, although BLOCKED event monitors guarantee that no event monitor data will be lost, their behavior can increase application response time because any suspended agents (along with any dependent agents) will be allowed to run only when the event monitor buffers are clear. If you specify the NONBLOCKED option instead, an agent that generates an event being monitored will not wait for an event buffer to be written to disk before continuing if it determines that both event buffers are full. Thus, NONBLOCKED event monitors perform faster than BLOCKED event monitors but are subject to data loss on highly active systems. If you specify neither option, the event monitor created will be a BLOCKED event monitor.

If output from an event monitor is to be stored in one or more database tables, all target tables needed are automatically created when you execute the CREATE EVENT MONITOR statement. In case of a partitioned database, it is mandatory to choose a table space that is present across all partitions to create the event monitor tables. Likewise, if you want to monitor events across all the partitions, specify the monitoring scope as GLOBAL. On the other hand, if output from an event monitor is to be written to one or more external files or a named pipe, the output directory/named pipe you specify as the target location for the event monitor does not have to exist when you execute the CREATE EVENT MONITOR statement. However, it must exist and the DB2 database manager instance owner must be able to write to it at the time the event monitor is activated. The application monitoring the named pipe must also have opened the pipe for reading before the event monitor is activated.

So if you want to create an event monitor that captures the values of all application-level counters and writes them to a database table named TB_CON_EVENTMON every time an application that is connected to a database terminates its connection, execute a CREATE EVENT MONITOR command similar to the following:

```
CREATE EVENT MONITOR con_evmon FOR CONNECTIONS
WRITE TO TABLE CONN (TABLE TB_CON_EVENTMON)
DB20000I The SQL command completed successfully.
```

But if you want to create an event monitor that captures monitor data for both buffer pool and table space events and writes all data collected to a directory named /db2fs/dump/bptsmonitor, you execute a CREATE EVENT MONITOR command that looks something like this:

```
CREATE EVENT MONITOR bpts_evmon FOR BUFFERPOOLS, TABLESPACES
WRITE TO FILE '/db2fs/dump/bptsmonitor'
DB20000I The SQL command completed successfully.
```

Activating and Deactivating Event Monitors

The event monitors will begin collecting monitor data as soon as the database with which they are associated is activated or a connection to the database is established—provided the AUTOSTART option was specified when the event monitor was created. If you use the MANUALSTART option instead, or if you specify neither option (in which case, the MANUALSTART option is used by default), you must activate an event monitor before it will begin collecting data. You activate (and deactivate) event monitors by executing the SET EVENT MONITOR SQL statement. The basic syntax for this statement is:

```
SET EVENT MONITOR [EventMonName] STATE [MonitorState]
```

where:

EventMonName Identifies the name to assign to the event monitor whose state is to be altered

MonitorState Identifies the state in which to place the event monitor; if the event monitor is to be activated (i.e., placed in the active state), you must specify the value 1 for this parameter; if the event monitor is to be deactivated (i.e., placed in the inactive state), you must specify the value 0 for this parameter

Therefore, if you want to activate an event monitor named CON_EVMON that was created with the MANUALSTART option specified, execute a SET EVENT MONITOR statement:

```
SET EVENT MONITOR con_evmon STATE 1
```

However, to deactivate the CON_EVMON event monitor, you execute a SET EVENT MONITOR statement:

```
SET EVENT MONITOR con_evmon STATE 0
```

You can view the event monitor status created on the database by using a query something like the following:

```
SELECT
      SUBSTR (EVMONNAME, 1, 10) AS EVMONNAME,
      TARGET_TYPE,
      SUBSTR (TARGET, 1, 20) AS TARGET,
      MAXFILESIZE,
      BUFFERSIZE,
      AUTOSTART,
      EVMON_ACTIVATES
 FROM SYSCAT.EVENTMONITORS
```

Continued

```
           TARGET_                                                              EVMON_
EVMONNAME  TYPE    TARGET               MAXFILESIZE BUFFERSIZE AUTOSTART ACTIVATES
---------- ------- -------------------- ----------- ---------- --------- ---------
DB2DETAILD F       db2detaildeadlock            512          7 Y                 0
CON_EVMON  T                                      -          4 N                 0
BPTS_EVMON F       /db2fs/dump/bptsmoni        1000          4 N                 0

  3 record(s) selected.
```

Upon specific event monitor activation, you should see a value 1 in the column EVMON_ACTIVATES for a specific event.

When an event monitor is activated (started), it sits quietly in the background and waits for one of the events it is associated with to occur. Immediately after a monitored event takes place, the event monitor collects monitor data associated with the event that triggered it and writes all data collected to the event monitor's target location. Thus, the event itself controls when monitor data is collected—unlike with the snapshot monitor, an event monitor requires no special steps to capture the monitor data. Although the number of event monitors that you can define for a single database is unlimited, no more than 32 global event monitors and 128 local event monitors can be active at one time.

Forcing an Event Monitor to Generate Output Prematurely

Because some events do not activate event monitors as frequently as others, it may be desirable to force an event monitor to collect monitor data and write it to its target location *before* a monitor-triggering event takes place. In such situations, you can make an event monitor collect information early by executing the FLUSH EVENT MONITOR SQL statement. The basic syntax for this statement is:

```
FLUSH EVENT MONITOR [EventMonName] <BUFFER>
```

where:

EventMonName Identifies the name to assign to the event monitor that is to be forced to collect monitor data

By default, records that are written to an event monitor's target location prematurely are logged in the event monitor log and assigned a "partial record" identifier. However, if you specify the BUFFER option when you execute the FLUSH EVENT MONITOR statement, only monitor data that is present in the event monitor's active internal buffers is written to the event monitor's target location; partial records are not generated.

Thus, if you want to force an event monitor named CON_EVMON to collect monitor data and write it to its target location immediately, you would execute a FLUSH EVENT MONITOR statement:

```
FLUSH EVENT MONITOR con_evmon
DB20000I  The SQL command completed successfully.
```

Note that when event monitors are flushed, counters are not reset. This means that the event monitor record that would have been generated had you not used the FLUSH EVENT MONITOR statement to force event monitor data to be written will still be generated when the event monitor is triggered normally.

Viewing the Event Monitor Data

To view event monitor data that was written to files and named pipes, you must use the event monitor productivity tool. This text-based tool retrieves information from an event monitor data file or a named pipe and produces a formatted report. (Event monitor files and named pipes contain a binary stream of logical data groupings that must be formatted before they can be displayed.) You activate the event monitor productivity tool by executing the db2evmon command. The basic syntax for this command is:

```
db2evmon -db [DatabaseAlias] -evm [EventMonName]
```

or

```
db2evmon -path [EventMonTarget]
```

where:

DatabaseAlias	Identifies the alias to assign to the database where the event monitor whose data is to be displayed has been defined
EventMonName	Identifies the name to assign to the event monitor whose data is to be displayed
EventMonTarget	Identifies the location (directory or named pipe) to store data that an event monitor has collected

Thus, if you want to format and display all data collected by an event monitor named BPTS_EVMON that resides in a database named SAMPLE, execute a db2evmon command statement, as follows:

```
db2evmon -db sample -evm bpts_evmon
```

or

```
db2evmon -path /db2fs/dump/bptsmonitor
```

Event Types and Examples

Let us look at various event types available in DB2 10.1, along with the sort of information that they collect, when the data is actually collected, and real-time examples for each kind.

Event Monitor for the Database

This event monitor captures metrics and other monitor elements that reflect information about the database as a whole. Basically, it captures entire statistics for the database, such as application sections inserts, look-ups, catalog cache heap information, number of SQL statements committed in the database, database heap high watermark, number of data object changes, number of deadlocks, number of data reads and writes (insert, update, delete), lock attributes, transaction log archives, log write time, number of threshold violations, package cache information, buffer pool hit ratio, number of hash joins, and total sort time spent.

The database event monitor generates data at the time of database deactivation, so you will generally see an entry in the event monitor file or a record entry in the event monitor table. For example, to create and activate an event monitor for the database, use a CREATE EVENT MONITOR command similar to the following:

```
CREATE EVENT MONITOR db_evmon
FOR DATABASE
WRITE TO TABLE DB (TABLE DB210.TB_DB_EVENTMON IN USERSPACE1) BUFFERSIZE 16
  NONBLOCKED AUTOSTART
DB20000I The SQL command completed successfully.

SET EVENT MONITOR db_evmon STATE 1
DB20000I  The SQL command completed successfully.
```

The event monitor command creates a table DB210.DB_EVENTMON with 127 columns to record all database-related information. You can also use the db2evtbl command to generate event monitor target table definitions:

```
db2evtbl [-schema <SchemaName>] [-partitioned]
         -evm <EventMonitorName> <EventType> [, <EventType>]
```

where:

SchemaName	Identifies the schema name for the event monitor tables; if you do not specify this definition, it will provide unqualified table creation statements
EventMonitorName	Identifies the name for the event monitor to be created
EventType	Identifies the event type available on the FOR clause; currently, DB2 supports up to 15 types with subtypes for DEADLOCK; however, DEADLOCK and TRANSACTIONS event types are deprecated in DB2 10.1 and will be removed in future releases

Thus, if you want to create an event monitor for event type *database*, use a query similar to the following:

```
db2evtbl -schema DB210 -partitioned -evm db_evmon DATABASE
CREATE EVENT MONITOR db_evmon
          FOR DATABASE
          WRITE TO TABLE
                DB (TABLE DB210.DB_db_evmon
                              INCLUDES (APPL_SECTION_INSERTS,
                                        APPL_SECTION_LOOKUPS,
                                        ASYNC_RUNSTATS,
                                        BINDS_PRECOMPILES,
                                        BLOCKS_PENDING_CLEANUP,
                                        ...
                                        ...
                                        XQUERY_STMTS)),
                CONTROL (TABLE DB210.CONTROL_db_evmon
                              INCLUDES (EVENT_MONITOR_NAME,
                                        MESSAGE,
                                        MESSAGE_TIME));
```

You can modify the SQL statement before executing it on the system to create an event monitor.

The database event type supports three logical data groups: DB, CONTROL, and DBMEMUSE. The DBMEMUSE is a subset of DB, and CONTROL records the timestamp of the first database connection as well as the start time of the event monitor.

If you choose to create event monitors via the tables, you can view the monitor tables' information by using this listed query:

```
SELECT
      SUBSTR (EVMONNAME, 1, 10) AS EVMONNAME,
      SUBSTR (LOGICAL_GROUP, 1, 30) AS LOGICAL_GROUP,
      SUBSTR (TABSCHEMA, 1, 10) AS TABLESCHEMA,
      SUBSTR (TABNAME, 1, 20) ASS TABLENAME,
      PCTDEACTIVATE,
      TABOPTIONS
   FROM SYSCAT.EVENTTABLES

EVMONNAME  LOGICAL_GROUP TABSCHEMA TABNAME          PCTDEACTIVATE TABOPTIONS
---------- ------------- --------- ---------------- ------------- ----------
DB_EVMON   DB            DB210     DB_DB_EVMON                100 I
DB_EVMON   CONTROL       DB210     CONTROL_DB_EVMON           100 I
```

As with any other event monitor, you can use the SET EVENT MONITOR command to activate the newly created event monitor.

Event Monitor for Buffer Pools and Table Spaces

This event monitor captures metrics related to buffer pools and table spaces, such as the number of read and write requests (direct, logical, and physical) and the number of vector and block I/O requests for each available buffer pool and table space. The buffer pool and table space event monitors generate data at the time of database deactivation, so you will generally see an entry in the event monitor file or a record entry in the event monitor table.

For example, if you want to create an event monitor for buffer pools and table spaces, use the CREATE EVENT MONITOR command similar to the following:

```
CREATE EVENT MONITOR bptb_evmon
    FOR BUFFERPOOLS, TABLESPACES
```

Continued

```
    WRITE TO TABLE
    BUFFERPOOL (TABLE DB210.BUFFERPOOL_BPTB_EVMON IN USERSPACE1),
    TABLESPACE (TABLE DB210.TABLESPACE_BPTB_EVMON IN USERSPACE1) BUFFERSIZE 16
    NONBLOCKED AUTOSTART
SQL20173W The event monitor was created successfully but at least one event
monitor target table already exists.  SQLSTATE=01655
```

A target table can be used by only one event monitor. If the table is found to have already been defined, you will receive a warning message, as the example above shows. However, the newly created event monitor reuses the target tables only if the earlier created event monitor is dropped; otherwise, you will receive error message SQL20155N:

```
SQL20155N The specified event monitor target tables are invalid.  Reason
code = "8".  SQLSTATE=55049
```

Event Monitor for Tables

This event monitor captures metrics for tables, such as the rows read and written, the number of date object pages, and so on. The table event monitor generates data at the time of database deactivation, so you will generally see an entry per table in the event monitor file or a record entry per table in the event monitor table. For example, to create an event monitor for a table, use the CREATE EVENT MONITOR command, something like this:

```
CREATE EVENT MONITOR tb_evmon
        FOR TABLES
        WRITE TO TABLE
             TABLE (TABLE db210.TABLE_tb_evmon
                         INCLUDES (DATA_OBJECT_PAGES,
                                   DATA_PARTITION_ID,
                                   EVENT_TIME,
                                   EVMON_ACTIVATES,
                                   EVMON_FLUSHES,
                                   INDEX_OBJECT_PAGES,
                                   LOB_OBJECT_PAGES,
                                   LONG_OBJECT_PAGES,
                                                          Continued
```

```
                                    OVERFLOW_ACCESSES,
                                    PAGE_REORGS,
                                    PARTIAL_RECORD,
                                    ROWS_READ,
                                    ROWS_WRITTEN,
                                    TABLE_NAME,
                                    TABLE_SCHEMA,
                                    TABLE_TYPE,
                                    TABLESPACE_ID,
                                    XDA_OBJECT_PAGES ) ),
                  CONTROL (TABLE db210.CONTROL_tb_evmon
                            INCLUDES (EVENT_MONITOR_NAME,
                                    MESSAGE,
                                    MESSAGE_TIME ) )
DB20000I The SQL command completed successfully.
```

If you query the target table upon database reactivation, you will see something similar to the following:

```
SELECT DATA_OBJECT_PAGES, INDEX_OBJECT_PAGES, ROWS_READ, ROWS_READ,
       SUBSTR (TABLE_NAME, 1, 20) AS TABLE_NAME FROM DB210.TABLE_TB_EVMON

DATA_OBJECT_PAGES INDEX_OBJECT_PAGES ROWS_READ ROWS_READ TABLE_NAME
----------------- ------------------ --------- --------- --------------------
               33                 26         5         5 SYSTABLES
              199                103         5         5 SYSCOLUMNS
               68                100         6         6 SYSROUTINES
            17449                  0   9437184   9437184 T1
                1                  0         0         0 DB_DB_EVMON
                1                  6         1         1 SYSEVENTMONITORS
                1                  0         0         0 TABLE_TB_EVMON
                1                  0         0         0 CONTROL_TB_EVMON
                1                  8         4         4 SYSTRIGGERS
                1                  8        14        14 DEPARTMENT
                                                               Continued
```

```
 1          6      42      42 EMPLOYEE
 1          4       1       1 POLICY
33         26       3       3 SYSTABLES
24         15     347     347 SYSPLAN
 1         10       2       2 SYSDBAUTH
 1          0       0       0 DB_DB_EVMON
 1          0       0       0 CONTROL_DB_EVMON
 1          0       0       0 TABLESPACE_BPTB_EVMO
 1          6       2       2 SYSEVENTMONITORS
 1          0      12      12 TABLE_TB_EVMON
 1         14       1       1 SYSTABLESPACES
 1          0       0       0 CONTROL_TB_EVMON
 1         10      10      10 SYSROLEAUTH
 4          8       1       1 SYSVARIABLES
 1          8       1       1 SYSSTOGROUPS
 1          6     252     252 EMPLOYEE

26 record(s) selected.
```

Note that the table monitor not only captures the metrics for the application tables but also captures information for the system tables. If you decide to create an event monitor to write to a file, you can use an SQL statement like this:

```
CREATE EVENT MONITOR tb_filemon
FOR TABLES WRITE TO FILE '/data/dbeventmon'
MAXFILES 25 MAXFILESIZE 1024 NONBLOCKED APPEND
DB20000I  The SQL command completed successfully.
```

After a successful database deactivation and activation, files will be created at the specified location, as the following example shows. However, you will not able to read them until you format the file by using the db2evmon event monitor productivity tool command:

```
-rw-r----- 1 db2inst1 db2dadm    35 Aug 29 23:17 db2event.ctl
-rw-r--r-- 1 db2inst1 db2dadm 19724 Aug 29 23:17 00000000.evt
```

You can invoke the event monitor productivity tool command by executing a command similar to the following:

```
db2evmon -path /data/dbeventmon

Reading /data/dbeventmon/00000000.evt ...
--------------------------------------------------------------------------
                            EVENT LOG HEADER
  Event Monitor name: TB_FILEMON
  Server Product ID: SQL10013
  Version of event monitor data: 11
  Byte order: LITTLE ENDIAN
  Number of nodes in db2 instance: 1
  Codepage of database: 1208
  Territory code of database: 1
  Server instance name: db2inst1
--------------------------------------------------------------------------

--------------------------------------------------------------------------
  Database Name: SAMPLE
  Database Path: /data/db2inst1/NODE0000/SQL00001/MEMBER0000/
  First connection timestamp: 08/29/2014 23:17:26.935013
  Event Monitor Start time:   08/29/2014 23:34:57.412196
--------------------------------------------------------------------------
...
...
4) Table Event...
  Table schema: DB210
  Table name: T1
  Data partition id: 0

  Record is the result of a flush: FALSE
  Table type: User
  Data object pages: 17449
```

Continued

```
  Index object pages: 0
  Lob object pages: 0
  Long object pages: 0
  Rows read: 28311552
  Rows written: 0
  Overflow Accesses: 0
  Page reorgs: 0
  Tablespace id: 3
  Table event timestamp: 08/29/2014 23:35:32.560166
...
...
```

Event Monitor for Locking

This event monitor captures comprehensive information regarding applications engaged in locking events such as locking participants, lock attributes, application handles, objects involved, workload details, statement text, isolation levels, and optimization parameters. The locking event monitor generates data upon detection of any of the event types lock timeout, deadlock, and lock wait beyond a specified duration depending on the event monitor configuration.

Four key database configuration parameters are required to capture locking event information:

- Monitoring lock timeouts (mon_locktimeout)
- Monitoring deadlocks (mon_deadlock)
- Monitoring lock waits (mon_lockwait)
- Monitoring lock-waits threshold (mon_lw_thresh)

You can use the UPDATE DATABASE CONFIGURATION command to update these parameters to the correct values:

```
UPDATE DATABASE CONFIGURATION FOR sample USING
MON_LOCKTIMEOUT WITHOUT_HIST
MON_DEADLOCK WITHOUT_HIST
MON_LOCKWAIT WITHOUT_HIST
MON_LW_THRESH 5000000
DB20000I The UPDATE DATABASE CONFIGURATION command completed successfully.
```

To enable all the event types in one event monitor or to selectively build for and activate a specific locking event type, use an SQL statement similar to this:

```
CREATE EVENT MONITOR lk_evmon
     FOR LOCKING
     WRITE TO TABLE
          CONTROL (TABLE DB210.CONTROL_lk_evmon),
          LOCK (TABLE DB210.LOCK_lk_evmon),
          LOCK_PARTICIPANTS (TABLE DB210.LOCK_PARTICIPANTS_lk_evmon),
          LOCK_PARTICIPANT_ACTIVITIES (TABLE DB210.LOCK_PARTICIPANT_ACTIVITIES_lk_evmon),
          LOCK_ACTIVITY_VALUES (TABLE DB210.LOCK_ACTIVITY_VALUES_lk_evmon)
DB20000I  The SQL command completed successfully.

SET EVENT MONITOR lk_evmon STATE 1
DB20000I  The SQL command completed successfully.
```

The following example illustrates LOCKING event monitor usage by means of identifying a lock timeout issue in the database. In this case, two transactions—TR1 and TR2—are attempting to read and modify the data in a table T1 respectively. When both TR1 and TR2 are executing concurrently, TR2 stops processing.

So now let us capture the locking information by using the event monitor. Remember, though, that you can also use the monitoring table functions to identify the locking problems. However, it is quite difficult to extract the LOCKTIMEOUT information at the right time, unlike with event monitor captures based on an event instead of a point-in-time snapshot.

As the following example shows, transaction T2 received an error message in the application:

```
SQL0911N  The current transaction has been rolled back because of a deadlock
or timeout.  Reason code "68".  SQLSTATE=40001
```

It is the database administrators' responsibility to identify the SQL statements included in the lock timeout problem.

Now that you have the LOCKING event monitor enabled, it is just a question of querying the monitor table, something like this:

```
SELECT
     APPLICATION_HANDLE, PARTICIPANT_NO, PARTICIPANT_NO_HOLDING_LK,
```

Continued

```
      SUBSTR (TABLE_NAME, 1, 10) AS TABLE_NAME, ROLLED_BACK_PARTICIPANT_NO
   FROM DB210.LOCK_PARTICIPANTS_LK_EVMON

APPLICATION_HANDLE   PARTICIPANT_NO PARTICIPANT_NO_HOLDING_LK TABLE_NAME
-------------------- -------------- ------------------------- ----------
               10584              1                         2 T1
               10579              2                         - -

  2 record(s) selected.
```

The above output shows the application handles that were participating in the lock timeout and the object name, including the lock-waiting and lock-holding status. To know more about the SQL statement participating in the lock timeout, use a query similar to the following:

```
SELECT
      EFFECTIVE_ISOLATION, EVENT_TIMESTAMP, PARTICIPANT_NO, STMT_LOCK_TIME-
OUT,
      SUBSTR (STMT_OPERATION, 1, 30) AS STMT_OPERATION,
      SUBSTR (STMT_TEXT, 1, 32) AS STMT_TEXT
   FROM DB210.LOCK_PARTICIPANT_ACTIVITIES_LK_EVMON

EFFECTIVE_ISOLATION EVENT_TIMESTAMP            PARTICIPANT_NO STMT_LOCK_
TIMEOUT
------------------- -------------------------- -------------- -------------
---
CS                  2014-08-30-11.50.06.414495              1 300

STMT_OPERATION                          STMT_TEXT
--------------------------------------- ----------------------------------------
DML, Insert/Update/Delete               update T1 set CITY='NEW JERSEY'


  1 record(s) selected.
```

You can also use the LOCKING event monitor to find the deadlock (SQL0911N Reason code 2) participants by using a set of queries like the one in the previous example. To find the rollback application handle information, query the table DB210.LOCK_lk_evmon:

```
SELECT
     APPLICATION_HANDLE, PARTICIPANT_NO,
     PARTICIPANT_NO_HOLDING_LK,
     SUBSTR (TABLE_NAME, 1, 10) AS TABLE_NAME,
     ROLLED_BACK_PARTICIPANT_NO
   FROM DB210.LOCK_PARTICIPANTS_LK_EVMON lp
     INNER JOIN
     DB210.LOCK_lk_evmon ll
   ON
     lp.EVENT_ID=ll.EVENT_ID
     AND
     lp.EVENT_TYPE='DEADLOCK'

APPLICATION_                 PARTICIPANT_NO_              ROLLED_BACK_
HANDLE       PARTICIPANT_NO HOLDING_LK      TABLE_NAME  PARTICIPANT_NO
------------ -------------- --------------- ----------- --------------
          33              2               1          T1              2
          29              1               2          T2              2

  2 record(s) selected.


SELECT
      EFFECTIVE_ISOLATION, EVENT_TIMESTAMP,
      PARTICIPANT_NO, STMT_LOCK_TIMEOUT,
      SUBSTR (STMT_OPERATION, 1, 30) AS STMT_OPERATION,
      SUBSTR (STMT_TEXT, 1, 40) AS STMT_TEXT
   FROM DB210.LOCK_PARTICIPANT_ACTIVITIES_LK_EVMON WHERE EVENT_TYPE='DEADLOCK'
```

Continued

```
EFFECTIVE_ISOLATION EVENT_TIMESTAMP            PARTICIPANT_NO STMT_LOCK_TIMEOUT
------------------- -------------------------- -------------- -----------------
CS                  2014-08-30-20.31.59.546485              2               300
CS                  2014-08-30-20.31.59.546485              1               300

STMT_OPERATION                       STMT_TEXT
------------------------------------ ------------------------------------------
DML, Insert/Update/Delete            UPDATE T1 SET ID=30 WHERE NAME='COLIN'
DML, Insert/Update/Delete            UPDATE T2 SET ID=20 WHERE NAME='SIMON'

  2 record(s) selected.
```

Remember, the earlier deadlock event monitor DB2DETAILDEADLOCK and the lock timeout reporting feature DB2_CAPTURE_LOCKTIMEOUT db2 registry setting is deprecated in DB2 10.1.

As with lock timeout, you can also capture lock-wait events, such as any lock-wait exceed five seconds (controlled by the database configuration parameter setting mon_lw_threash), and capture them in the monitoring target tables. The event type is LOCKWAIT. You can use a similar set of commands as in the previous examples to analyze the events.

Sometimes, you might not want to wait for locks that cannot be obtained. You can use SET CURRENT LOCK TIMEOUT statement to change the CURRENT LOCK TIMEOUT special register value *before* and *after* executing your SQL statements:

```
SET CURRENT LOCK TIMEOUT NOT WAIT
  <Required transactions>
SET CURRENT LOCK TIMEOUT NULL
```

In such cases, the application will not be waiting until the locktimeout period to acquire locks on the required objects. However, the application receives SQLSTATE 40001 or 57033 error messages, which can very well be used to have a retry logic built in the application.

Finally, if you want to summarize the locking event occurrences on your database for last 24 hours, use a query that looks something like the following.

Locking events in the last 24 hours:

```
SELECT
      EVENT_ID, SUBSTR (EVENT_TYPE, 1, 12) AS EVENT_TYPE,
      EVENT_TIMESTAMP, DL_CONNS, ROLLED_BACK_PARTICIPANT_NO
   FROM DB210.LOCK_lk_evmon
WHERE EVENT_TIMESTAMP > (CURRENT TIMESTAMP - 1 DAY)
ORDER BY EVENT_ID, EVENT_TIMESTAMP

EVENT_ EVENT_      EVENT_                     DL_   ROLLED_BACK_
ID     TYPE        TIMESTAMP                  CONNS PARTICIPANT_NO
------ ----------- -------------------------- ----- --------------
     2 LOCKWAIT    2014-08-30-20.31.55.498480 -     -
     3 LOCKWAIT    2014-08-30-20.31.55.954476 -     -
     4 DEADLOCK    2014-08-30-20.31.59.546485 2     2
     5 LOCKWAIT    2014-08-30-22.14.43.802485 -     -
     6 LOCKTIMEOUT 2014-08-30-22.19.39.110504 -     -

  5 record(s) selected.
```

SQL statements that participated in the locking event in the last 24 hours:

```
SELECT
      SUBSTR (LP.EVENT_TYPE, 1, 12) AS EVENT_TYPE, LP.EVENT_TIMESTAMP,
      SUBSTR(LP.STMT_TEXT,1,40) AS STMT_TEXT
   FROM DB210.LOCK_PARTICIPANT_ACTIVITIES_LK_EVMON LP
     INNER JOIN
       DB210.LOCK_LK_EVMON LL ON LP.EVENT_ID=LL.EVENT_ID
       AND
       (LP.EVENT_TIMESTAMP > (CURRENT TIMESTAMP - 1 DAY))

EVENT_TYPE   EVENT_TIMESTAMP            STMT_TEXT
------------ -------------------------- ----------------------------------------
LOCKWAIT     2014-08-30-20.31.55.498480 UPDATE T2 SET ID=20 WHERE NAME='SIMON'
```

Continued

```
LOCKWAIT      2014-08-30-20.31.55.954476 UPDATE T1 SET ID=30 WHERE NAME='COLIN'
LOCKWAIT      2014-08-30-20.31.55.498480 UPDATE T1 SET ID=30 WHERE NAME='COLIN'
DEADLOCK      2014-08-30-20.31.59.546485 UPDATE T1 SET ID=30 WHERE NAME='COLIN'
LOCKWAIT      2014-08-30-20.31.55.954476 UPDATE T2 SET ID=20 WHERE NAME='SIMON'
DEADLOCK      2014-08-30-20.31.59.546485 UPDATE T2 SET ID=20 WHERE NAME='SIMON'
LOCKWAIT      2014-08-30-22.14.43.802485 SELECT * FROM T1 WITH RR
LOCKTIMEOUT   2014-08-30-22.19.39.110504 SELECT * FROM T1 WITH RR

  8 record(s) selected.
```

Event Monitor for a Unit of Work

This event monitor captures information related to transactions, such as start and end time of execution, workload and service class names under which they run, and packages or executable IDs for the statements and request metrics. The unit of work event monitor generates data upon completion of a transaction (unit of work).

Thus, if you want to create and activate an event monitor for event type unit of work, run SQL statements similar to the following:

```
CREATE EVENT MONITOR uow_evmon
           FOR UNIT OF WORK
           WRITE TO TABLE
              CONTROL (TABLE DB210.CONTROL_uow_evmon),
              UOW (TABLE DB210.UOW_uow_evmon),
              UOW_METRICS (TABLE DB210.UOW_METRICS_uow_evmon),
              UOW_PACKAGE_LIST (TABLE DB210.UOW_PACKAGE_LIST_uow_evmon),
              UOW_EXECUTABLE_LIST (
TABLE DB210.UOW_EXECUTABLE_LIST_uow_evmon)
DB20000I  The SQL command completed successfully.

SET EVENT MONITOR pkg_evmon STATE 1
DB20000I  The SQL command completed successfully.
```

Event Monitor for Activities

This event monitor captures information related to activities on the system, such as the execution of statements, resource consumption, and a complete activity metrics. The event data is generated upon completion of an activity that executed in a service class, workload, or work class that had its COLLECT ACTIVITY DATA option turned on.

Thus, if you want to create and activate an event monitor for event type activities, run SQL statements that look something like this:

```
CREATE EVENT MONITOR act_evmon
           FOR ACTIVITIES
           WRITE TO TABLE
                 CONTROL (TABLE DB210.CONTROL_act_evmon),
                 ACTIVITY (TABLE DB210.ACTIVITY_act_evmon),
                 ACTIVITYSTMT (TABLE DB210.ACTIVITYSTMT_act_evmon),
                 ACTIVITYVALS (TABLE DB210.ACTIVITYVALS_act_evmon),
                 ACTIVITYMETRICS (TABLE DB210.ACTIVITYMETRICS_act_evmon)
DB20000I  The SQL command completed successfully.

SET EVENT MONITOR act_evmon STATE 1
DB20000I  The SQL command completed successfully.
```

Event Monitor for the Package Cache

This event monitor captures a history of both dynamic and static SQL statements and related metrics that are no longer in the package cache. You can use this monitor when you need to examine performance metrics for statements that are no longer available in memory. It collects SQL statements and metrics aggregated over all executions of the section. The event data is generated whenever an entry is removed from the package cache.

Thus, to create and activate an event monitor for event type package cache, run SQL statements similar to the following:

```
CREATE EVENT MONITOR pkg_evmon
           FOR PACKAGE CACHE
           WRITE TO TABLE
             CONTROL (TABLE DB210.CONTROL_pkg_evmon),
             PKGCACHE (TABLE DB210.PKGCACHE_pkg_evmon),
             PKGCACHE_METRICS (TABLE DB210.PKGCACHE_METRICS_pkg_evmon),
             PKGCACHE_STMT_ARGS (TABLE DB210.PKGCACHE_STMT_ARGS_pkg_evmon)
```

Continued

```
DB20000I  The SQL command completed successfully.

SET EVENT MONITOR pkg_evmon STATE 1
DB20000I  The SQL command completed successfully.
```

You will find many ways to determine the problematic SQL statement by using the above said control tables.

To find the execution time, total number of sorts, rows read and modified, and associated SQL statement, use a query something like this:

```
SELECT
      STMT_EXEC_TIME, TOTAL_SORTS, ROWS_READ, ROWS_MODIFIED,
      SUBSTR (STMT_TEXT, 1, 50) AS STMT_TEXT
   FROM DB210.PKGCACHE_METRICS_PKG_EVMON PM
     INNER JOIN
   DB210.PKGCACHE_PKG_EVMON PP ON PM.EVENT_ID=pp.EVENT_ID
ORDER BY ROWS_READ DESC FETCH FIRST 10 ROWS ONLY
STMT_     TOTAL_ ROWS_READ ROWS_    STMT_TEXT
EXEC_TIME SORTS            MODIFIED
--------- ------ --------- --------- ------------- --------------------------------
      105      0   1638400         0 select count(*) from t3
      181      0   1048576         0 select * from t3
      803      0    393216    393216 insert into t3 select * from t3
      187      0    131064    131064 insert into t3 select * from t3
        4      6      6876         0 select coalesce(max(length(p.colname)),0)
        8      2      2292         0 select coalesce(max(length(p.colname)),0)
        3      5      1308         0 select STMT_EXEC_TIME, TOTAL_SORTS,
                                       COORD_STMT_EXE
        1      1      1146         0 select coalesce(max(length(p.colname)),0)
        6      1       965         0 SELECT DISTINCT a.schema, a.name,
                                       a.reorg_state, a
        1      0       739         0 DELETE FROM SYSTOOLS.HMON_ATM_INFO
                                       AS ATM WHERE NO

  10 record(s) selected.
```

Event Monitor for Statistics

This event monitor captures processing metrics related to workload management objects in the database. For example, you can use a statistics event monitor to understand CPU utilization over a time period for a given workload. The data is collected from the activities that executed within each WLM service class, workload, or work class that exists on the system at regular intervals defined by the wlm_collect_int database configuration parameter.

Thus, if you want to create and activate an event monitor for event type statistics, run SQL statements similar to the following:

```
CREATE EVENT MONITOR stat_evmon
          FOR STATISTICS
          WRITE TO TABLE
                CONTROL (TABLE DB210.CONTROL_stat_evmon),
                SCSTATS (TABLE DB210.SCSTATS_stat_evmon),
                SCMETRICS (TABLE DB210.SCMETRICS_stat_evmon),
                WCSTATS (TABLE DB210.WCSTATS_stat_evmon),
                WLSTATS (TABLE DB210.WLSTATS_stat_evmon),
                WLMETRICS (TABLE DB210.WLMETRICS_stat_evmon),
                QSTATS (TABLE DB210.QSTATS_stat_evmon),
                HISTOGRAMBIN (TABLE DB210.HISTOGRAMBIN_stat_evmon)
DB20000I The SQL command completed successfully.

SET EVENT MONITOR stat_evmon STATE 1
DB20000I The SQL command completed successfully.
```

Event Monitor for Threshold Violations

This event monitor captures specific thresholds that are exceeded during database operations. You can set the thresholds for a variety of things, including CPU time, the number of database connections, and the number of executing statements. It generates event data upon detection of a threshold violation.

Thus, to create and activate an event monitor for event type threshold violations, you can run these example SQL statements:

```
CREATE EVENT MONITOR tv_evmon
          FOR THRESHOLD VIOLATIONS
```

Continued

```
        WRITE TO TABLE
CONTROL (TABLE DB210.CONTROL_tv_evmon IN USERSPACE1 PCTDEACTIVATE 80),
THRESHOLDVIOLATIONS (
TABLE DB210.THRESHOLDVIOLATIONS_tv_evmon IN USERSPACE1 PCTDEACTIVATE 80)
DB20000I The SQL command completed successfully.

SET EVENT MONITOR tv_evmon STATE 1
DB20000I The SQL command completed successfully.
```

The PCTDEACTIVATE parameter specifies how full the table space must be before the event monitor automatically deactivates. This is applicable only when the event monitor control tables are created in an automatic storage or a DMS table space.

Event Monitor for Connections

This event monitor captures connection metrics, such as application name, authentication ID, client platform, connection protocol, number of reads and writes per connection, and CPU utilization. The event data is generated at the end of every connection.

Thus, if you want to create an event monitor for event type connections, run an SQL statement something like the following:

```
db2evtbl -schema DB210 -evm con_evmon CONNECTIONS

CREATE EVENT MONITOR con_evmon
           FOR CONNECTIONS
           WRITE TO TABLE
                 CONNHEADER (TABLE DB210.CONNHEADER_con_evmon
                               INCLUDES (AGENT_ID,
                                         APPL_ID,
                                         APPL_NAME,
                                         ...
                                         SEQUENCE_NO,
                                         TERRITORY_CODE)),
                 CONN (TABLE DB210.CONN_con_evmon
                               INCLUDES (ACC_CURS_BLK,
                                         AGENT_ID,
```

Continued

```
                                        APPL_ID,
                                        ...
                                        X_LOCK_ESCALS,
                                        XQUERY_STMTS)),
                  CONTROL (TABLE DB210.CONTROL_con_evmon
                              INCLUDES (EVENT_MONITOR_NAME,
                                        MESSAGE,
                                        MESSAGE_TIME))
DB20000I The SQL command completed successfully.
```

You can execute the command output to create the CONNHEADER, CONN, and CONTROL tables. Upon completion of the control table creation, you can activate the event monitor by executing the SET EVENT MONITOR command:

```
SET EVENT MONITOR con_evmon STATE 1
DB20000I The SQL command completed successfully.
```

Event Monitor for Statements

This event monitor captures the requests that are being made to the database as a result of the execution of SQL statements. It collects statement start time, end time, statement text, CPU time, number of records read and modified, and SQL Communication Area (SQLCA) structure. The event data is generated at four different phases, such as prepare, describe, open, and close. The most interesting data is usually during the close phase. However, an SQL statement that does large sorts may have high open times, or an SQL statement that takes a long time to prepare may have interesting data in the prepare phase.

Thus, if you want to create an event monitor for event type statements, run a command similar to the following:

```
db2evtbl -schema DB210 -evm stmt_evmon STATEMENTS

CREATE EVENT MONITOR stmt_evmon
        FOR STATEMENTS
        WRITE TO TABLE
            CONNHEADER (TABLE DB210.CONNHEADER_stmt_evmon
```

Continued

```
                             INCLUDES (AGENT_ID,
                                       APPL_ID,
                                       APPL_NAME,
                                       ...
                                       SEQUENCE_NO,
                                       TERRITORY_CODE)),
              STMT (TABLE DB210.STMT_stmt_evmon
                             INCLUDES (AGENT_ID,
                                       ...
                                       TOTAL_SORTS,
                                       USER_CPU_TIME)),
              CONTROL (TABLE DB210.CONTROL_stmt_evmon
                             INCLUDES (EVENT_MONITOR_NAME,
                                       MESSAGE,
                                       MESSAGE_TIME));
DB20000I The SQL command completed successfully.
```

You can execute the command output to create the CONNHEADER, STMT, and CONTROL tables. Upon completion of the control table creation, you can activate the event monitor by executing the SET EVENT MONITOR command:

```
SET EVENT MONITOR stmt_evmon STATE 1
DB20000I The SQL command completed successfully.
```

Event Monitor for Change History

This event monitor captures changes to the database and database manager configurations, DB2 registry settings, and data objects through DDL statements and execution of utilities. It generates event monitor data whenever the parameter value changes or when a DDL, command, or utility is completed.

Thus, if you want to create an event monitor for event type change history, run an SQL statement similar to the following:

```
CREATE EVENT MONITOR cghist_evmon
          FOR CHANGE HISTORY
```

Continued

```
          WHERE EVENT IN (DBCFG, DBCFGVALUES, DBMCFG, DBMCFGVALUES, REGVAR,
                          REGVARVALUES, DDLDATA, DDLFEDERATED, DDLMONITOR,
                          DDLSECURITY, DDLSTORAGE, DDLSQL, DDLXML, DDLWLM, REORG,
                          LOAD, BACKUP, RESTORE, ROLLFORWARD, RUNSTATS, MOVETABLE,
                          REDISTRIBUTE)
          WRITE TO TABLE
                CONTROL (TABLE DB210.CONTROL_cghist_evmon),
                CHANGESUMMARY (TABLE DB210.CHANGESUMMARY_cghist_evmon),
                EVMONSTART (TABLE DB210.EVMONSTART_cghist_evmon),
                DDLSTMTEXEC (TABLE DB210.DDLSTMTEXEC_cghist_evmon),
                TXNCOMPLETION (TABLE DB210.TXNCOMPLETION_cghist_evmon),
                DBDBMCFG (TABLE DB210.DBDBMCFG_cghist_evmon),
                REGVAR (TABLE DB210.REGVAR_cghist_evmon),
                UTILSTART (TABLE DB210.UTILSTART_cghist_evmon),
                UTILSTOP (TABLE DB210.UTILSTOP_cghist_evmon),
                UTILLOCATION (TABLE DB210.UTILLOCATION_cghist_evmon),
                UTILPHASE (TABLE DB210.UTILPHASE_cghist_evmon)
DB20000I  The SQL command completed successfully.
```

And you activate the event monitor by using the SET EVENT MONITOR command:

```
SET EVENT MONITOR cghist_evmon STATE 1
DB20000I  The SQL command completed successfully.
```

You can query the change summary information from change summary table DB210.
CHANGESUMMARY_CGHIST_EVMON:

```
SELECT APPLICATION_HANDLE, UTILITY_TYPE, EVENT_TIMESTAMP,SUBSTR(EVENT_TYPE,1,10)
       AS EVENT_TYPE FROM DB210.CHANGESUMMARY_CGHIST_EVMON

APPLICATION_HANDLE  UTILITY_TYPE     EVENT_TIMESTAMP            EVENT_TYPE
-------------------- ---------------- -------------------------- ----------
                3123                  2014-08-31-13.38.27.724691 EVMONSTART
                3123                  2014-08-31-13.38.27.737099 REGVARVALU
                                                                  Continued
```

```
              3123                          2014-08-31-13.38.27.743479 DBMCFGVALU
              3123                          2014-08-31-13.38.27.743771 DBCFGVALUE
              3123 RUNSTATS                 2014-08-31-13.41.09.988489 UTILSTART
              3123 RUNSTATS                 2014-08-31-13.41.10.140693 UTILSTOP
              3123                          2014-08-31-13.44.25.298828 DBCFG

  7 record(s) selected.
```

Note: The event monitors for deadlocks and transactions have been deprecated in DB2 10.1, so their use is no longer recommended. The suggestion is to use CREATE EVENT MONITOR FOR LOCKING and CREATE EVENT MONITOR FOR UNIT OF WORK to monitor deadlocks and transactions.

Event Monitors Quick Reference

Table 5.11 provides a summary of DB2 10.1 event monitors with corresponding logical data groups, data generation, and collection information and target table options.

Table 5.11: Event monitors summary

Event Monitor Name	Logical Data Groups	Event Monitor Properties
Database	DB, CONTROL, DBMEMUSE	Event data is generated when the last application disconnects from the database. You can direct this event monitor to write the monitor data into a formatted table, file, or pipe.
Buffer pool	BUFFERPOOL, CONTROL	Event data is generated at the time of database deactivation. It captures buffer pool performance metrics. You can direct this event monitor to write monitor data into a formatted table, file, or pipe.
Table spaces	TABLESPACE, CONTROL	Event data is generated at the time of database deactivation. It captures table space performance metrics. You can direct this event monitor to write monitor data into a table, file, or pipe.
Tables	TABLE, CONTROL	Event data is generated at the time of database deactivation. It captures table performance metrics. You can direct this event monitor to write monitor data into a formatted table, file, or pipe.

Table 5.11: Event monitors summary (continued)		
Event Monitor Name	**Logical Data Groups**	**Event Monitor Properties**
Locking	LOCK, LOCK_PARTICIPANTS, LOCK_PARTICIPANT_ ACTIVITIES, LOCK_ACTIVITY_VALUES, CONTROL	Event data is generated when the database manager detects lock timeout, deadlock, or lock waits beyond a specified duration. It captures application and lock information. You can direct this event monitor to write monitor data into a formatted table or an unformatted table.
Unit of work	UOW, UOW_METRICS, UOW_PACKAGE_LIST, UOW_EXECUTABLE_LIST, CONTROL	Event data is generated when a unit of work is completed. It captures resource performance information. You can direct this event monitor to write monitor data into a formatted table or an unformatted table.
Activities	ACTIVITY, ACTIVITYMETRICS, ACTIVITYSTMT, ACTIVITYVALS, CONTROL	Event data is generated when an activity is completed. It captures execution of individual statements. You can direct this event monitor to write monitor data into a formatted table, file, or pipe.
Package cache	PKGCACHE, PKGCACHE_METRICS, CONTROL	Event data is generated when an entry in removed from the package cache memory. It captures execution statistics for each SQL along with the statement text. You can direct this event monitor to write monitor data into a formatted table or an unformatted table.
Statistics	QSTATS, SCSTATS, SCMETRICS, WCSTATS, WLSTATS, WLMETRICS, HISTOGRAMBIN, CONTROL	Event data is generated automatically at regular intervals defined in the wlm_collect_int database configuration parameter. It captures processing metrics related to WLM. You can direct this event monitor to write monitor data into a formatted table, file, or pipe.
Threshold violations	THRESGHOLDVIOLATIONS, CONTROL	Event data is generated automatically when specific thresholds that you set are exceeded during the database operation. It captures processing metrics related to the system. You can direct this event monitor to write monitor data into a formatted table, file, or pipe.
Connections	CONNHEADER, CONN, CONTROL, CONNMEMUSE	Event data is generated when the connection ends to the database. It captures all application-level counters. You can direct this event monitor to write monitor data into a formatted table, file, or pipe.
Statements	CONNHEADER, STMT, SUBSECTION, CONTROL	Event data is generated when the statement ends the execution of the SQL statement. It captures all statement performance metrics, including SQLCA. You can direct this event monitor to write monitor data into a formatted table, file, or pipe.

Table 5.11: Event monitors summary (continued)

Event Monitor Name	Logical Data Groups	Event Monitor Properties
Change history	CHANGESUMMARY, EVMONSTART, TXNCOMPLETION, DDLSTMTEXEC, DBDBMCFG, REGVAR, UTILSTART, UTILSTOP, UTILPHASE, UTILLOCATION, CONTROL	Event data is generated when changes are made to the configuration parameters, database objects, or utilities command executions. It captures all changes made by the said commands. You can direct this event monitor to write monitor data into a formatted table only.

Reading Unformatted Event Data

The unformatted event (UE) table can store collected locking, package cache, and unit of work event monitoring data. When data is stored in an unformatted event table, it stores the event data in an internal binary format within an inline BLOB column, and this data cannot be read directly through an SQL statement the way formatted tables allow. So the data that has been collected by an event monitor and written to an unformatted event table can be viewed in one of two ways: by using a db2evmonfmt tool or by using the event monitor format table procedures.

The db2evmonfmt Tool

The Java-based, generic XML parser tool—db2evmonfmt—produces a readable text-based report from the UE tables. The basic command syntax is:

```
db2evmonfmt -d [DatabaseName] -ue [UeTable]
            -fxml | -ftext -ss [StyleSheet]
            -id [EventID]
            -type [EvenType]
            -hours [NumHours]
            -w [WorkloadName]
            -s [ServiceSubClass]
            -a [ApplName]
```

or

```
db2evmonfmt -f xmlfile < -fxml | -ftext [-ss StyleSheet] >
```

where:

DatabaseName	Identifies the alias to assign to the database where the UE monitor whose data is to be displayed has been defined
UeTable	Identifies the name to assign to the UE monitor table whose data is to be formatted
StyleSheet	Identifies the XSLT style sheet to use to transform the XML document
EventID	Identifies the event ID for which the matching events must be displayed
EvenType	Identifies the event type for which the matching events must be displayed
NumHours	Identifies the number of hours of events information that must be displayed
WorkLoadName	Identifies the workload name for which the matching events must be displayed
ServiceSubClass	Identifies the WLM service subclass for which the matching events must be displayed
ApplName	Identifies the application name for which the matching events must be displayed

There are a few tool-setup steps to follow before you start generating the intended reports:

Step 1: Create one or more event monitors by using the unformatted table option.

Create the one or more event monitors (locking, package cache, and unit of work event types) to write monitor data into unformatted event table. For example, for locking, the event monitor creation command looks something like this:

```
CREATE EVENT MONITOR uelk_evmon FOR LOCKING
WRITE TO UNFORMATTED EVENT TABLE (TABLE DB210.UE_LOCKING_EVENTS)
DB20000I  The SQL command completed successfully.
```

Activate the newly created event monitor by using the SET EVENT MONITOR command:

```
SET EVENT MONITOR act_evmon STATE 1
DB20000I  The SQL command completed successfully.
```

Step 2: Verify the environment variables on the database server.

Verify the Java class path by using the echo $CLASSPATH command from the operation system command shell.

You should see output similar to the following for the instance named db2inst1:

```
echo $CLASSPATH
/home/db2inst1/sqllib/java/db2java.zip:/home/db2inst1/sqllib/java/sqlj.zip:/
home/db2inst1/sqllib/function:/home/db2inst1/sqllib/java/db2jcc_license_
cu.jar:/home/db2inst1/sqllib/tools/clpplus.jar:/home/db2inst1/sqllib/tools/
antlr-3.2.jar:/home/db2inst1/sqllib/tools/jline-0.9.93.jar:/home/db2inst1/
sqllib/java/db2jcc.jar:.
```

Verify the UNIX or Windows environment variable LD_LIBRARY_PATH by using the echo or env operating system command. The output generally looks like the following on instance db2inst1:

```
env | grep -i LD_LIBRARY_PATH
LD_LIBRARY_PATH=/home/db2inst1/sqllib/lib64:/home/db2inst1/sqllib/lib32
```

Verify the UNIX or Windows environment variable PATH by using the echo or env operating system command. You should see output something like this on instance db2inst1:

```
echo $PATH
/home/db2inst1/bin:/usr/local/bin:/usr/bin:/bin:/usr/bin/X11:/usr/X11R6/
bin:/usr/games:/usr/lib64/jvm/jre/bin:/usr/lib/mit/bin:/usr/lib/mit/sbin:.:/
home/db2inst1/sqllib/bin:/home/db2inst1/sqllib/adm:/home/db2inst1/sqllib/
misc:/home/db2inst1/sqllib/db2tss/bin
```

Step 3: Verify the Java versions available on the system and always use the DB2 Java version. Java version on the system:

```
java -version
java version "1.4.2"
Java(TM) 2 Runtime Environment, Standard Edition (build 2.3)
IBM J9 VM (build 2.3, J2RE 1.4.2 IBM J9 2.3 Linux amd64-64
j9vmxa64142ifx-20110628 (JIT enabled)
J9VM - 20110627_85693_LHdSMr
JIT  - 20090210_1447ifx5_r8
GC   - 200902_24)
```

DB2 Java version:

```
/home/db2inst1/sqllib/java/jdk64/bin/java -version
java version "1.7.0"
Java(TM) SE Runtime Environment (build pxa6470-20110827_01)
IBM J9 VM (build 2.6, JRE 1.7.0 Linux amd64-64 20110810_88604 (JIT enabled,
AOT enabled)
J9VM - R26_Java726_GA_20110810_1208_B88592
JIT  - r11_20110810_20466
GC   - R26_Java726_GA_20110810_1208_B88592
J9CL - 20110810_88604)
JCL - 20110809_01 based on Oracle 7b147
```

Step 4: Compile the db2evmonfmt Java code.

Before you start compiling the Java source code, copy the source code from the samples directory to a directory on your instance home directory. For example:

```
mkdir $HOME/evmon_fmt (you could possibly create this on any scratch pad area)
```

Copy the Java source code for the db2evmonfmt tool from the path /home/db2inst1/sqllib/samples/java/jdbc to the newly created directory $HOME/evmon_fmt by using the following commands:

```
cp db2evmonfmt.java $HOME/evmon_fmt/
```

At this point, it is better for you to copy the XSLT style sheet files for locking, unit of work, and package cache event monitors from the same samples directory to the evmon_fmt:

```
cp DB2EvmonUOW.xsl DB2EvmonPkgCache.xsl DB2EvmonPkgCache.xsl $HOME/evmon_fmt/
```

It is essential to use the right compiler to compile the Java source code. It is always recommended to use DB2 Java binaries to compile the source code:

```
/home/db2inst1/sqllib/java/jdk64/bin/javac db2evmonfmt.java
```

Upon compiling the code, you will see .class files in your directory similar to the following:

```
-r-xr-xr-x 1 db2inst1 db2dadm 40360 Aug 31 17:49 db2evmonfmt.java
-r-xr-xr-x 1 db2inst1 db2dadm 59783 Aug 31 17:56 DB2EvmonUOW.xsl
-r-xr-xr-x 1 db2inst1 db2dadm 39491 Aug 31 17:56 DB2EvmonPkgCache.xsl
-r-xr-xr-x 1 db2inst1 db2dadm 46620 Aug 31 17:56 DB2EvmonLocking.xsl
-rw-r--r-- 1 db2inst1 db2dadm  1056 Aug 31 17:57 SimpleErrorHandler.class
-rw-r--r-- 1 db2inst1 db2dadm 16996 Aug 31 17:57 db2evmonfmt.class
```

Step 5: Run the tool.

You are now set to run the tool by using simple commands.
Next, you will create a lock timeout scenario to generate and analyze the report.

Application #1	**Application #2**
db2 +c "SELECT count(*) FROM t1 WITH RR" 1 ----------- 4 1 record(s) selected.	db2 "UPDATE t1 SET ID=100 WHERE NAME='MOHAN'" SQL0911N The current transaction has been rolled back because of a deadlock or timeout. Reason code "68". SQLSTATE=40001

Now that you have a lock timeout situation, run the tool by using the following command options to generate the text report based on the information collected in the unformatted event table DB210.UE_LOCKING_EVENTS:

```
/home/db2inst1/sqllib/java/jdk64/bin/java db2evmonfmt -d SAMPLE -ue
DB210.UE_LOCKING_EVENTS -ftext -hours 1 -type locktimeout

SELECT evmon.xmlreport FROM TABLE ( EVMON_FORMAT_UE_TO_XML( 'LOG_TO_
FILE',FOR EACH ROW OF ( SELECT * FROM DB21'0.UE_LOCKING_EVENTS  WHERE EVENT_
TIMESTAMP >= CURRENT_TIMESTAMP - 1 HOURS AND EVENT_TYPE = ? ORDER BY EVENT_
ID, EVENT_TIMESTAMP, EVENT_TYPE, MEMBER ))) AS evmon

                                                                   Continued
```

```
-------------------------------------------------------
Event ID                 : 2
Event Type               : LOCKTIMEOUT
Event Timestamp          : 2014-08-31-18.08.51.098510
Partition of detection : 0
-------------------------------------------------------


Participant No 1 requesting lock
----------------------------------
Lock Name              : 0x03001600000000000000000054
Lock wait start time : 2014-08-31-18.03.50.963146
Lock wait end time   : 2014-08-31-18.08.51.098510
Lock Type              : TABLE
Lock Specifics         :
Lock Attributes        : 00400000
Lock mode requested  : Intent Exclusive
Lock mode held         : Share
Lock Count             : 0
Lock Hold Count        : 0
Lock rrIID             : 0
Lock Status            : Waiting
Lock release flags   : 00000000
Tablespace TID         : 3
Tablespace Name        : IBMDB2SAMPLEREL
Table FID              : 22
Table Schema           : MOHAN
Table Name             : T1


Attributes             Requester                      Owner
-------------------- ----------------------------   ----------------------------
Participant No         1                              2
Application Handle     0177                           031
Application ID         *LOCAL.db2inst1.140831180351   *LOCAL.db2inst1.140831172446
```

Continued

```
Application Name      db2bp                         db2bp
Authentication ID     MOHAN                         MOHAN
Requesting AgentID    64                            22
Coordinating AgentID  64                            22
Agent Status          UOW Executing                 UOW Waiting
Application Action    No action                     No action
Lock timeout value    300                           0
Lock wait value       5000                          0
Workload ID           1                             1
Workload Name         SYSDEFAULTUSERWORKLOAD        SYSDEFAULTUSERWORKLOAD
Service subclass ID   13                            13
Service superclass    SYSDEFAULTUSERCLASS           SYSDEFAULTUSERCLASS
Service subclass      SYSDEFAULTSUBCLASS            SYSDEFAULTSUBCLASS
Current Request       Execute Immediate             Close Cursor
TEntry state          1                             1
TEntry flags1         00000000                      00000000
TEntry flags2         00000200                      00000200
Lock escalation       no                            no
Client userid
Client wrkstnname
Client applname
Client acctng
Utility ID



Current Activities of Participant No 1
----------------------------------------
Activity ID          : 1
Uow ID               : 1
Package Name         : SQLC2J25
Package Schema       : NULLID
Package Version      :
Package Token        : AAAAAWAd
```

Continued

```
Package Sectno      : 203
Reopt value         : none
Incremental Bind    : no
Eff isolation       : CS
Eff degree          : 0
Actual degree       : 1
Eff locktimeout     : 300
Stmt first use      : 2014-08-31-18.03.50.963106
Stmt last use       : 2014-08-31-18.03.50.963106
Stmt unicode        : no
Stmt query ID       : 0
Stmt nesting level  : 0
Stmt invocation ID  : 0
Stmt source ID      : 0
Stmt pkgcache ID    : 214748364801
Stmt type           : Dynamic
Stmt operation      : DML, Insert/Update/Delete
Stmt no             : 1
Stmt text           : UPDATE t1 SET ID=100 WHERE NAME='MOHAN'



Past Activities of Participant No 1
-------------------------------------
Activities not available

Current Activities of Participant No 2
----------------------------------------
Activities not available

Past Activities of Participant No 2
-------------------------------------
Activities not available
```

The output contains all the information required to analyze the cause for a lock timeout situation, including the following:

- Information about applications participating in the lock timeout, such as application handle, authorization ID, agent status, and SQL statements
- Information about locks, including the number of locks, type of lock, lock escalation conditions, and lock-wait threshold setting
- Information about the workload, including workload ID and service subclass

Table 5.12 shows the db2evmonfmt tool sample commands to generate reports for supported event types in the database SAMPLE.

Table 5.12: The db2evmonfmt command examples

Description	Command
Generate a lock timeout report in text format for the last 24 hours	java db2evmonfmt -d SAMPLE -ue <Lkt_UeTable> -ftext -hours 24 -type locktimeout
Generate a deadlock report in text format for the last 24 hours	java db2evmonfmt -d SAMPLE -ue <Dlk_UeTable> -ftext -hours 24 -type deadlock
Generate a lock-wait report in text format for the last 24 hours	java db2evmonfmt -d SAMPLE -ue <Lkw_UeTable> -ftext -hours 24 -type lockwait
Format an XML source file to generate a text format report for lock-wait for the last 5 hours	java db2evmonfmt -f lock.xml -ftext -type lockwait -hours 5
Generate all events that have occurred in the last 12 hours for the event package cache	java db2evmonfmt -d SAMPLE -ue Pkg_UeTable -ftext -hours 12
Generate all events that are part of workload HR in the last 8 hours	java db2evmonfmt -d SAMPLE -ue Pkg_UeTable -ftext -hours 8 -w HR
Generate all events that have occurred in the event unit of work in the style-sheet format	java db2evmonfmt -d SAMPLE -ue Uow_UeTable -ftext -ss Summary.xsl

Unformatted Event Data Format Table Functions

As with the db2evmonfmt tool, one other way to extract data from an unformatted event table is by using the following format table functions. With these procedures, you can control the output format by creating your own XSLT style sheets:

- SYSPROC.EVMON_FORMAT_UE_TO_XML ()
- SYSPROC.EVMON_FORMAT_UE_TO_TABLES ()

The EVMON_FORMAT_UE_TO_XML () table function extracts binary events from an unformatted event table and formats them into an XML document. The basic syntax for this table function is:

```
SYSPROC.EVMON_FORMAT_UE_TO_XML (
LOG_TO_FILE | LOG_PARTIAL_EVENTS |
SUPPRESS_PARTIAL_EVENTS_ERR | NULL> FOR EACH ROW OF (<FullSelect>))
```

where:

FullSelect Identifies the query that conforms to the rules of the SELECT statement

If the returning XML document is greater than 100 MB, which is the maximum size of each document returned by this table function, you can choose to write the XML document into a file by specifying the LOG_TO_FILE parameter in the table function. The file is written to the <xml_document_id>.xml file, where xml_document_id is a unique ID generated for each document. The output file is written to the diagpath. The option LOG_PARTIAL_EVENTS indicates that the table function is to write all the incomplete or partial events to a file. The option SUPPRESS_PARTIAL_EVENTS_ERR signifies that the table function ignores the SQL443N warning message when incomplete or partial events exist in the unformatted event table, and NULL indicates no options specified.

A sample command to extract the lock information from the UE table looks something like the following:

```
SELECT evmon.* FROM TABLE (
EVMON_FORMAT_UE_TO_XML (
NULL, FOR EACH ROW OF (
SELECT * FROM DB210.UE_LOCKING_EVENTS order by EVENT_TIMESTAMP))) AS evmon
```

The EVMON_FORMAT_UE_TO_TABLES () table function extracts data stored in an UE table and converts it into a set of relation tables. DB2 does the conversion of UE table data into relational tables in a two-step process. First, it converts the data to XML format by using the EVMON_FORMAT_UE_TO_XML procedure. Second, DB2 performs XML decomposition to covert the XML data into relational data.

The basic syntax for this table function is:

```
SYSPROC.EVMON_FORMAT_UE_TO_TABLES (
EventMonitorType, XSRSchema, XSRObjectName, XMLSchemaFile, TableSchema, TablespaceName,
Options [RECREATE_FORCE | RECREATE_ONERROR | PRUNE_UE_TABLE | UPGRADE_TABLE],
CommitCount, FullSelect)
```

where:

EventMonitorType Identifies the type of data to store in the UE table; the possible values are LOCKING, PKGCACHE, and UOW

XSRSchema Identifies the XML Schema Repository (XSR) object schema that describes how data from the UE file corresponds to columns in tables

XSRObjectName Identifies the XSR object name that describes how data from the UE file corresponds to columns in tables

XMLSchemaFile Identifies a fully qualified path to the XML schema document that describes the output produced by the event monitor

TableSchema Identifies the schema name where the event monitor relational tables are created

TablespaceName Identifies the table space where the relational tables are created

Options Identifies the options supported by the table function; you must delimit each option by using a semicolon character

RECREATE_FORCE Indicates that relational tables are dropped and re-created

RECREATE_ONERROR Indicates to drop and re-create relational tables in the following situations:

- XSR object not registered, but the tables exist
- Occurrence of decomposition failures and negative SQLCODES

PRUNE_UE_TABLE Specifies to prune any binary events that are successfully inserted into relational tables

UPGRADE_TABLES Upgrades the earlier created UE tables when the DB2 release contains a change

CommitCount Identifies the decomposition commit frequency:

- -1: Commits after every 100 successful documents are decomposed and is the default
- 0: Never Commit
- n: Commit after every *n* documents are successfully decomposed

FullSelect Identifies the query that conforms to the rules of the SELECT statement

A sample command to convert the lock information from an UE table into a set of relational tables looks similar to this:

```
CALL EVMON_FORMAT_UE_TO_TABLES
('LOCKING', NULL, NULL, NULL, 'DB210', NULL, NULL, -1,
'SELECT * FROM DB210.UE_LOCKING_EVENTS ORDER BY EDVENT_TIMESTAMP')
```

The above procedure call converts data and inserts it into the following four listed tables. If these tables do not exist, DB2 creates them during the procedure execution:

- LOCK_ACTIVITY_VALUES
- LOCK_PARTICIPANT_ACTIVITIES
- LOCK_PARTICIPANTS
- LOCK_EVENT

A Word About the MONREPORT Module

As you are aware, monitoring is a tedious task and requires time, effort, and experience. DB2 10.1 has many built-in modules providing an easy-to-use interface for performing a variety of useful operations, including database monitoring with the MONREPORT module. This module makes a database administrator's life easier by providing simple interface procedures to call to extract the monitoring data related to connections, statements, locks, and package cache without any profound investigation using the table functions. Table 5.13 shows available programs within the MONREPORT module.

Table 5.13: MONREPORT module procedures

Report Name	Procedure Name	Related Table Functions	Description
Summary report	MONREPORT. DBSUMMARY	MON_GET_SERVICE_ SUBCLASS, MON_GET_CONNECTION, MON_GET_WORKLOAD	Provides system and application performance metrics summary
Connection report	MONREPORT. CONNECTION	MON_GET_CONNECTION	Provides monitor data for each connection
Current application report	MONREPORT. CURRENTAPPS	MON_GET_CONNECTION, MON_GET_UNIT_OF_WORK, WLM_GET_SERVICE_CLASS_ AGENTS	Provides current state of processing of units of work, agents, and activities for each connection
Current SQL report	MONREPORT. CURRENTSQL	MON_GET_PKG_CACHE_STMT	Provides information about the top currently running activities
Package cache report	MONREPORT. PKGCACHE	MON_GET_PKG_CACHE_STMT	Provides top statement metrics by CPU, wait time, and so on

Table 5.13: MONREPORT module procedures (continued)

Report Name	Procedure Name	Related Table Functions	Description
Current lock-wait report	MONREPORT.LOCKWAIT	MON_GET_APPL_LOCKWAIT, MON_GET_CONNECTION, WLM_GET_SERVICE_CLASS_AGENTS	Provides information about current lock-wait processes

You can use these reports to troubleshoot SQL performance problems. To invoke the procedure, use a simple CALL command:

```
CALL MONREPORT.DBSUMMARY

  Result set 1
  --------------

  TEXT
  --------------------------------------------------------------------------------
  --------------------------------------------------------------------------------
  Monitoring report - database summary
  --------------------------------------------------------------------------------
  Database:                                  SAMPLE
  Generated:                                 09/06/2014 15:19:02
  Interval monitored:                        10

  ================================================================================
  ================================================================================
  Part 1 - System performance

  Work volume and throughput
  --------------------------------------------------------------------------------
                                  Per second              Total
                                  ---------------------   -----------------------
  TOTAL_APP_COMMITS               0                       0
  ACT_COMPLETED_TOTAL             24                      241
  APP_RQSTS_COMPLETED_TOTAL       0                       3
                                                                     Continued
```

```
TOTAL_CPU_TIME                     = 47982
TOTAL_CPU_TIME per request         = 15994

Row processing
  ROWS_READ/ROWS_RETURNED          = 0 (42/241)
  ROWS_MODIFIED                    = 0

Wait times
--------------------------------------------------------------------------------

-- Wait time as a percentage of elapsed time --

                                          %    Wait time/Total time
                                          ---  ----------------------------------
For requests                              0    45/10087
For activities                            0    37/10076

-- Time waiting for next client request --

CLIENT_IDLE_WAIT_TIME                 = 5016
CLIENT_IDLE_WAIT_TIME per second      = 501

-- Detailed breakdown of TOTAL_WAIT_TIME --

                               %    Total
                               ---  ---------------------------------------------
TOTAL_WAIT_TIME                100  45

I/O wait time
  POOL_READ_TIME               15   7
  POOL_WRITE_TIME              0    0
  DIRECT_READ_TIME             53   24
  DIRECT_WRITE_TIME            0    0
```

Continued

```
    LOG_DISK_WAIT_TIME            0    0
  LOCK_WAIT_TIME                  0    0
  AGENT_WAIT_TIME                 0    0
  Network and FCM
    TCPIP_SEND_WAIT_TIME          0    0
    TCPIP_RECV_WAIT_TIME          0    0
    IPC_SEND_WAIT_TIME            0    0
    IPC_RECV_WAIT_TIME            0    0
    FCM_SEND_WAIT_TIME            0    0
    FCM_RECV_WAIT_TIME            0    0
  WLM_QUEUE_TIME_TOTAL            0    0
  CF_WAIT_TIME                    0    0
  RECLAIM_WAIT_TIME               0    0
  SMP_RECLAIM_WAIT_TIME           0    0

  Component times
  --------------------------------------------------------------------------------
  -- Detailed breakdown of processing time --

                                      %                Total
                                      ---------------- -------------------------
  Total processing                    100              10042

  Section execution
    TOTAL_SECTION_PROC_TIME           0                13
      TOTAL_SECTION_SORT_PROC_TIME    0                0
  Compile
    TOTAL_COMPILE_PROC_TIME           0                4
    TOTAL_IMPLICIT_COMPILE_PROC_TIME  0                0
  Transaction end processing
    TOTAL_COMMIT_PROC_TIME            0                0
    TOTAL_ROLLBACK_PROC_TIME          0                0
  Utilities
    TOTAL_RUNSTATS_PROC_TIME          0                0
```

Continued

```
  TOTAL_REORGS_PROC_TIME            0                 0
  TOTAL_LOAD_PROC_TIME              0                 0

Buffer pool
--------------------------------------------------------------------------------
Buffer pool hit ratios

Type             Ratio            Reads (Logical/Physical)
---------------  ---------------  ---------------------------------------------
Data             99               1062/4
Index            100              28/0
XDA              0                0/0
Temp data        0                0/0
Temp index       0                0/0
Temp XDA         0                0/0
GBP Data         0                (0 - 0)/0
GBP Index        0                (0 - 0)/0
GBP XDA          0                (0 - 0)/0
LBP Data         99               (1068 - 10)/(1062 + 0)
LBP Index        100              (28 - 0)/(28 + 0)
LBP XDA          0                (0 - 0)/(0 + 0)

I/O
--------------------------------------------------------------------------------
Buffer pool writes
  POOL_DATA_WRITES         = 0
  POOL_XDA_WRITES          = 0
  POOL_INDEX_WRITES        = 0
Direct I/O
  DIRECT_READS             = 292
  DIRECT_READ_REQS         = 30
  DIRECT_WRITES            = 0
  DIRECT_WRITE_REQS        = 0
Log I/O
```

Continued

```
  LOG_DISK_WAITS_TOTAL  = 0

Locking
------------------------------------------------------------------------------
                        Per activity                  Total
                        -----------------------------  ---------------------
LOCK_WAIT_TIME          0                             0
LOCK_WAITS              0                             0
LOCK_TIMEOUTS           0                             0
DEADLOCKS               0                             0
LOCK_ESCALS             0                             0

Routines
------------------------------------------------------------------------------
                              Per activity            Total
                              -----------------------  -----------------------
TOTAL_ROUTINE_INVOCATIONS     1                       267
TOTAL_ROUTINE_TIME            41                      10066

TOTAL_ROUTINE_TIME per invocation   = 37

Sort
------------------------------------------------------------------------------
TOTAL_SORTS                         = 4
SORT_OVERFLOWS                      = 0
POST_THRESHOLD_SORTS                = 0
POST_SHRTHRESHOLD_SORTS             = 0

Network
------------------------------------------------------------------------------
Communications with remote clients
TCPIP_SEND_VOLUME per send          = 0          (0/0)
TCPIP_RECV_VOLUME per receive       = 0          (0/0)

                                                                     Continued
```

```
Communications with local clients
IPC_SEND_VOLUME per send            = 94         (189/2)
IPC_RECV_VOLUME per receive         = 163        (491/3)

Fast communications manager
FCM_SEND_VOLUME per send            = 0          (0/0)
FCM_RECV_VOLUME per receive         = 0          (0/0)

Other
-------------------------------------------------------------------------------
Compilation
  TOTAL_COMPILATIONS                = 2
  PKG_CACHE_INSERTS                 = 17
  PKG_CACHE_LOOKUPS                 = 17
Catalog cache
  CAT_CACHE_INSERTS                 = 3
  CAT_CACHE_LOOKUPS                 = 9
Transaction processing
  TOTAL_APP_COMMITS                 = 0
  INT_COMMITS                       = 0
  TOTAL_APP_ROLLBACKS               = 0
  INT_ROLLBACKS                     = 0
Log buffer
  NUM_LOG_BUFFER_FULL               = 0
Activities aborted/rejected
  ACT_ABORTED_TOTAL                 = 0
  ACT_REJECTED_TOTAL                = 0
Workload management controls
  WLM_QUEUE_ASSIGNMENTS_TOTAL       = 0
  WLM_QUEUE_TIME_TOTAL              = 0

DB2 utility operations
-------------------------------------------------------------------------------
  TOTAL_RUNSTATS                    = 0
  TOTAL_REORGS                      = 0
```

Continued

```
  TOTAL_LOADS                        = 0

================================================================================
Part 2 - Application performance drill down

Application performance database-wide
--------------------------------------------------------------------------------
TOTAL_CPU_TIME         TOTAL_       TOTAL_APP_     ROWS_READ +
per request            WAIT_TIME %  COMMITS        ROWS_MODIFIED
---------------------- -----------  -------------  ----------------------------
15994                  0            0              42

Application performance by connection
--------------------------------------------------------------------------------
APPLICATION_  TOTAL_CPU_TIME      TOTAL_       TOTAL_APP_    ROWS_READ +
HANDLE        per request         WAIT_TIME %  COMMITS       ROWS_MODIFIED
------------- ------------------- -----------  ------------  ------------
25246         15994               0            0             42

Application performance by service class
--------------------------------------------------------------------------------
SERVICE_      TOTAL_CPU_TIME      TOTAL_       TOTAL_APP_    ROWS_READ +
CLASS_ID      per request         WAIT_TIME %  COMMITS       ROWS_MODIFIED
--------      ------------------- -----------  ------------  ------------
11            0                   0            0             0
12            0                   0            0             0
13            15994               0            0             42

Application performance by workload
--------------------------------------------------------------------------------
WORKLOAD_     TOTAL_CPU_TIME         TOTAL_       TOTAL_APP_    ROWS_READ +
NAME          per request            WAIT_TIME %  COMMITS       ROWS_MODIFIED
------------- ---------------------- -----------  ------------  ------------
SYSDEFAULTADM 0                      0            0             0
SYSDEFAULTUSE 15994                  0            0             42
```

Continued

```
================================================================================
Part 3 - Member level information

- I/O wait time is
  (POOL_READ_TIME + POOL_WRITE_TIME + DIRECT_READ_TIME + DIRECT_WRITE_TIME).

       TOTAL_CPU_TIME         TOTAL_       RQSTS_COMPLETED_  I/O
MEMBER per request            WAIT_TIME %  TOTAL             wait time
------ ---------------------- -----------  ----------------  -----------------
0      15994                  0            3                 44


235 record(s) selected.

Return Status = 0
```

The above report is designed to answer system-level, application-level, and member-level data for most aspects of processing aggregated across the entire database.

A Word About DB2 WLM Monitoring

The key purpose of implementing the DB2 WLM is to achieve a stable and a predictable system for continuous business operation. DB2 has various WLM monitoring table functions to watch for any rogue queries, a change in the resource consumption pattern, and signs that the system remains in a healthy state. Table 5.14 shows the available workload management monitoring routines.

Table 5.14: DB2 WLM monitoring table functions

Routine Name	Description
WLM_GET_SERVICE_CLASS_ WORKLOAD_OCCURRENCES	Returns the list of all workload occurrences running on the system, including workload name, application name, and superclass and subclass names
WLM_GET_WORKLOAD_ OCCURRENCE_ACTIVITIES	Returns the list of all currently running activities submitted by the specified application
WLM_GET_SERVICE_CLASS_AGENTS	Returns the list of agents, fenced mode processes, and system entities, such as page cleaners and prefetchers, that are running in a specified service class

Table 5.14: DB2 WLM monitoring table functions (continued)	
Routine Name	**Description**
WLM_GET_SERVICE_SUPERCLASS_STATS	Returns aggregated connection information across service superclasses or across the members
WLM_GET_SERVICE_SUBCLASS_STATS	Returns aggregated connection information across service subclasses or across the members
WLM_GET_WORKLOAD_STATS	Returns summary information, including total activities completed, average execution time, activity throughput, total CPU time, and total CPU utilization for every combination of workload name and database member
WLM_GET_WORK_ACTION_SET_STATS	Returns total activity information for a work action set
WLM_GET_QUEUE_STATS	Returns total time spent, total queue size, and connection thresholds for one or more threshold queues

The syntax to construct a query that references table functions for monitoring WLM looks something like this:

```
SELECT * FROM TABLE ([FunctionName]
('[WLMSepcifics]', [Member]) AS [CorrelationName]
```

where:

FunctionName Identifies the monitoring table function name to use (i.e., one of the functions listed in Table 5.14)

WLMSpecifics Identifies the monitor table function WLM-specific information, such as the service superclass and subclass for which to retrieve monitored metrics data

Member Identifies the member for which to collect monitored metrics data; you can specify -1 for the current member or -2 for all database members

CorrelationName Identifies the name to assign to the result data set produced by the query

If you want to list the occurrences of workloads within the SYSDEFAULTUSERCLASS superclass and SYSDEFAULTSUBCLASS subclass across all the members of the instance, use an SQL statement similar to the following:

```
SELECT
      APPLICATION_HANDLE,
      VARCHAR (WORKLOAD_NAME, 30) AS WORKLOAD,
```

Continued

```
        VARCHAR (WORKLOAD_OCCURRENCE_STATE, 10) AS STATE,
        VARCHAR (SESSION_AUTH_ID, 16) AS SESSION_AUTH_ID,
        VARCHAR (APPLICATION_NAME, 10) AS APPL_NAME,
        COORD_ACT_COMPLETED_TOTAL,
        CONCURRENT_ACT_TOP
    FROM TABLE (WLM_GET_SERVICE_CLASS_WORKLOAD_OCCURRENCES ('SYSDEFAULTUSERCLASS',
'SYSDEFAULTSUBCLASS', -2)) AS T

APPLICATION_                                    SESSION_ APPL_  COORD_ACT_      CONCURRENT_
HANDLE       WORKLOAD              STATE    AUTH_ID  NAME   COMPLETED_TOTAL ACT_TOP
------------ --------------------- -------  -------- ------ --------------- ---------
       60494 SYSDEFAULTUSERWORKLOAD UOWEXEC EDWETLD  db2bp                0         1

  1 record(s) selected.
```

To understand the current activities running on the system, including the number of rows read, number of rows returned, and total CPU time, use an SQL statement that looks something like this:

```
SELECT
        T.APPLICATION_HANDLE,
        T.UOW_ID,
        T.ACTIVITY_ID,
        T.ACTIVITY_STATE,
        T.ACTIVITY_TYPE,
        T.TOTAL_CPU_TIME,
        T.ROWS_READ,
        T.ROWS_RETURNED,
        T.QUERY_COST_ESTIMATE,
        VARCHAR (P.STMT_TEXT, 200) AS STMT_TEXT
    FROM TABLE (WLM_GET_WORKLOAD_OCCURRENCE_ACTIVITIES (NULL, -1)) AS T
        INNER JOIN TABLE (MON_GET_PKG_CACHE_STMT (NULL, NULL, NULL, -1)) AS P
        ON T.EXECUTABLE_ID = P.EXECUTABLE_ID
```

Continued

```
APPLICATION_ UOW_ ACTIVITY_ ACTIVITY_ ACTIVITY_ TOTAL_    ROWS_  ROWS_    QUERY_COST
HANDLE        ID  ID        STATE     TYPE      CPU_TIME READ   RETURNED ESTIMATE
------------ ---- --------- --------- --------- -------- ------ -------- ----------
       60524    5         1 IDLE      READ_DML     30512 150673 150672   1217

STMT_TEXT
--------------------
select * from t3

  1 record(s) selected.
```

Analyzing SQL with the Explain Facility

When an SQL statement is submitted to the DB2 database engine for processing, the DB2 Optimizer will analyze it to produce what is known as an *access plan*. Each access plan contains detailed information about the strategy to use to execute the statement (such as whether to use indexes; the required sort methods, if any; the needed locks; and the join methods to use, if any). If you code the SQL statement in an application, the access plan is generated at precompile time (or at bind time if deferred binding is used), and an executable form of the access plan produced is stored in the system catalog as an object known as a *package*. If, however, you submit the statement from the CLP, or if the statement is a dynamic SQL statement in an application program (i.e., an SQL statement that is constructed at application run time), the access plan is generated at the time the statement is prepared for execution, and the access plan produced is stored temporarily in memory (in the global package cache) rather than in the system catalog.

Although you can use the monitoring table functions and event monitors to obtain information about how well (or poorly) some SQL operations perform, you cannot use the monitors to analyze how an SQL statement was optimized. To perform this type of analysis, you must be able to capture and view the information stored in an SQL statement's access plan, and that is where the DB2 Explain facility comes in.

The Explain facility allows you to capture and view detailed information about the access plan chosen for a particular SQL statement, along with performance information that you can use to help identify poorly written statements or a weakness in database design. Specifically, Explain data helps you understand how the DB2 database manager accesses tables and indexes to satisfy a query. You can also use Explain data to evaluate the results of any performance-tuning action taken. In fact, any time you change some aspect of the DB2 database manager, an SQL statement, or the database with which an SQL statement interacts, you should collect and examine Explain data to determine what effect, if any, your changes have had on performance.

The Explain Tables

Before Explain information can be captured, you must create a special set of tables known as the *Explain tables*. Table 5.15 shows each Explain table, along with the information it holds.

Table 5.15: Explain facility tables

Table Name	Contents
EXPLAIN_ARGUMENT	Contains the unique characteristics for each operator used, if there are any
EXPLAIN_INSTANCE	Contains basic information about the source of the SQL or XQuery statements being explained as well as information about the environment in which the explanation took place (the EXPLAIN_INSTANCE table is the main control table for all Explain information; each row of data in the other Explain tables is explicitly linked to one unique row in this table)
EXPLAIN_OBJECT	Contains information about the data objects required by the access plan generated for an SQL or XQuery statement
EXPLAIN_OPERATOR	Contains all the operators needed by the query compiler to satisfy the SQL or XQuery statement
EXPLAIN_PREDICATE	Contains information that identifies which predicates are applied by a specific operator
EXPLAIN_STATEMENT	Contains the text of the SQL or XQuery statement as it exists for the different levels of Explain information; the original SQL statement as entered by the user is stored in this table along with the version used by the DB2 Optimizer to choose an access plan to satisfy the SQL statement (the latter version may bear little resemblance to the original because it may have been rewritten or enhanced with additional predicates by the SQL precompiler)
EXPLAIN_STREAM	Contains information about the input and output data streams that exist between individual operators and data objects (the data objects themselves are represented in the EXPLAIN_OBJECT table, and the operators involved in a data stream reside in the EXPLAIN_OPERATOR table)
EXPLAIN_ACTUALS	Contains information about the SQL statement sections
EXPLAIN_ DIAGNOSTIC	Contains information about each diagnostic message produced for a particular instance of an explained statement in the EXPLAIN_STATEMENT table
EXPLAIN_ DIAGNOSTIC_DATA	Contains message token information for diagnostic messages that are recorded in the EXPLAIN_DIAGNOSTIC table
ADVISE_INDEX	Contains information about indexes recommended by the design advisor
ADVISE_INSTANCE	Contains information about the design advisor (db2avis) command execution, such as start time, end time, mode, and status
ADVISE_MQT	Contains information about MQT, such as the SQL statement that recommends MQT creation, column and row statistics, and refresh type
ADVISE_PARTITION	Contains information about the database partitions recommended by the design advisor
ADVISE_TABLE	Contains data definitions for table creation by using the design advisor recommendations for MQTs, MDCs, and database partitioning
ADVISE_WORKLOAD	Contains workload information, including SQL or XQuery statements
OBJECT_METRICS	Contains run-time information for each object that is referenced in a specific execution of a section at an explicit time

Typically, you use Explain tables in a development database to aid in application design, but not in production databases, where application code remains fairly static. Because of this, they are not created along with the system catalog tables as part of the database creation process. Instead, you must create Explain tables manually in the database with which the Explain facility will be used.

Fortunately, the process to create the Explain tables is pretty straightforward: using the CLP, you establish a connection to the appropriate database and execute a script named EXPLAIN.DDL, which is in the misc subdirectory of the sqllib directory where the DB2 software was initially installed. Alternatively, you can use the SYSINSTALLOBJECTS procedure to create the tables, similar to the following:

```
CALL SYSPROC.SYSINSTALLOBJECTS
('EXPLAIN', 'C', CAST (NULL AS VARCHAR (128)), 'DB210')


  Return Status = 0
```

Collecting Explain Data

The Explain facility comprises several individual tools, and not all tools require the same kind of Explain data. Therefore, two different types of Explain data can be collected:

- **Comprehensive Explain data**. Contains detailed information about SQL or XQuery statement access plan; this information is stored across several different Explain tables
- **Explain Snapshot data**. Contains the current internal representation of the SQL or XQuery statement, along with any related information; this information is stored in the SNAPSHOT column of the EXPLAIN_STATEMENT Explain table

And as you might imagine, you can collect both types of Explain data in a variety of ways. The methods available for collecting Explain data include the following:

- Executing the EXPLAIN SQL statement
- Setting the CURRENT EXPLAIN MODE special register
- Setting the CURRENT EXPLAIN SNAPSHOT special register
- Using the EXPLAIN bind option with the PRECOMPILE or BIND command
- Using the EXPLSNAP bind option with the PRECOMPILE or BIND command

The EXPLAIN SQL Statement

One way to collect both comprehensive Explain information and Explain snapshot data for a single, dynamic SQL statement is by executing the EXPLAIN SQL statement.

The basic syntax for this statement is:

```
EXPLAIN [ALL | PLAN | PLAN SELECTION]
<FOR SNAPSHOT | WITH SNAPSHOT>
FOR [SQLStatement]
```

where:

SQLStatement Identifies the SQL statement for which to collect Explain data or Explain snapshot data (the statement specified must be a valid INSERT, UPDATE, DELETE, SELECT, SELECT INTO, VALUES, or VALUES INTO SQL statement)

If you specify the FOR SNAPSHOT option with the EXPLAIN statement, only Explain snapshot information will be collected for the dynamic SQL statement specified. But if you specify the WITH SNAPSHOT option instead, both comprehensive Explain information and Explain snapshot data will be collected for the dynamic SQL statement specified. However, if you use neither option, only comprehensive Explain data will be collected; no Explain snapshot data will be produced.

Thus, if you want to collect only comprehensive Explain data for the SQL statement SELECT * FROM department, execute an EXPLAIN statement that looks like this:

```
EXPLAIN ALL FOR SELECT * FROM department
DB20000I  The SQL command completed successfully.
```

But if you want to collect only Explain snapshot data for the same SQL statement, you execute the following EXPLAIN statement:

```
EXPLAIN ALL FOR SNAPSHOT FOR SELECT * FROM department
DB20000I  The SQL command completed successfully.
```

And finally, to collect both comprehensive Explain data and Explain snapshot information for the SQL statement SELECT * FROM department, you execute this EXPLAIN statement:

```
EXPLAIN ALL WITH SNAPSHOT FOR SELECT * FROM department
DB20000I  The SQL command completed successfully.
```

It is important to note that the EXPLAIN statement does not execute the SQL statement specified, nor does it display the Explain information collected—you must use other Explain facility tools to view the information collected. (We will look at those tools shortly.)

The Special Registers

Although the EXPLAIN SQL statement is useful when you want to collect Explain or Explain snapshot information for a single dynamic SQL statement, it can become very time-consuming to use if a large number of SQL statements need to be analyzed. A better way to collect the same information for several dynamic SQL statements is by setting one or both of the special Explain facility registers provided before a group of dynamic SQL statements are executed. Then, as the statements are prepared for execution, Explain or Explain snapshot information is collected for each statement processed. The statements themselves, however, may or may not be executed.

The two Explain facility special registers that are used in this manner are CURRENT EXPLAIN MODE and CURRENT EXPLAIN SNAPSHOT. You set the CURRENT EXPLAIN MODE special register by using the SET CURRENT EXPLAIN MODE SQL statement, and you set the CURRENT EXPLAIN SNAPSHOT special register by using the SET CURRENT EXPLAIN SNAPSHOT SQL statement. The basic syntax for the SET CURRENT EXPLAIN MODE statement is:

```
SET CURRENT EXPLAIN MODE <=> [YES | NO | EXPLAIN]
```

And the basic syntax for the SET CURRENT EXPLAIN SNAPSHOT statement is:

```
SET CURRENT EXPLAIN SNAPSHOT <=> [YES | NO | EXPLAIN]
```

As you might imagine, setting both the CURRENT EXPLAIN MODE and the CURRENT EXPLAIN SNAPSHOT special registers to NO will disable the Explain facility, and no Explain data will be captured. But if you set either special register to EXPLAIN, the Explain facility will be activated, and comprehensive Explain information or Explain snapshot data (or both if both special registers have been set) will be collected each time a dynamic SQL statement is prepared for execution. However, the statements themselves are not executed. If you set either special register to YES, the behavior is the same as when you set the corresponding register to EXPLAIN, with one significant difference: the dynamic SQL statements for which Explain information is collected are executed as soon as the appropriate Explain/Explain snapshot data has been collected.

Table 5.16 summarizes the behavior each Explain special register setting has on the Explain facility and dynamic SQL statement processing.

Table 5.16: Explain facility tables

Explain Snapshot Values	Explain Mode Values: No	Explain Mode Values: Yes	Explain Mode Values: Explain
NO	• Explain facility is disabled. No Explain data is captured. Dynamic SQL statements are executed.	• Explain facility is enabled. Comprehensive Explain data is collected and written to the Explain tables. Dynamic SQL statements are executed.	• Explain facility is enabled. Comprehensive Explain data is collected and written to the Explain tables. Dynamic SQL statements are not executed.
YES	• Explain facility is enabled. Explain snapshot data is collected and written to the SNAPSHOT column of the EXPLAIN_STATEMENT Explain table. Dynamic SQL statements are executed.	• Explain facility is enabled. Comprehensive Explain data is collected and written to the Explain tables. Explain snapshot data is collected and written to the SNAPSHOT column of the EXPLAIN_STATEMENT Explain table. Dynamic SQL statements are executed.	• Explain facility is enabled. Comprehensive Explain data is collected and written to the Explain tables. Explain snapshot data is collected and written to the SNAPSHOT column of the EXPLAIN_STATEMENT Explain table. Dynamic SQL statements are not executed.
EXPLAIN	• Explain facility is enabled. Explain snapshot data is collected and written to the SNAPSHOT column of the EXPLAIN_STATEMENT Explain table. Dynamic SQL statements are not executed.	• Explain facility is enabled. Comprehensive Explain data is collected and written to the Explain tables. Explain snapshot data is collected and written to the SNAPSHOT column of the EXPLAIN_STATEMENT Explain table. Dynamic SQL statements are not executed.	• Explain facility is enabled. Comprehensive Explain data is collected and written to the Explain tables. Explain snapshot data is collected and written to the SNAPSHOT column of the EXPLAIN_STATEMENT Explain table. Dynamic SQL statements are not executed.

The EXPLAIN and EXPLSNAP Bind Options

So far, you have seen the ways in which comprehensive Explain information and Explain snapshot data can be collected for dynamic SQL statements. But often, database applications contain static SQL statements that must be analyzed as well. So how can you use the Explain facility to analyze static SQL statements coded in an embedded SQL application? To collect comprehensive Explain information or Explain snapshot data for both static and dynamic SQL statements that have been coded in an embedded SQL application, you must use the EXPLAIN and EXPLSNAP bind options.

The EXPLAIN bind option controls whether comprehensive Explain data is collected for SQL statements that have been coded in an embedded SQL application; the EXPLSNAP bind option controls whether Explain snapshot data is collected. You can specify one or both options as part of the PRECOMPILE command you use to precompile the source code file that contains embedded

SQL statements—if you use deferred binding, these options can be provided with the BIND command that will bind the embedded SQL application's bind file to a database.

You can assign both the EXPLAIN option and the EXPLSNAP option the value NO, YES, or ALL. Assigning both options the value NO (for example, EXPLAIN NO EXPLSNAP NO) will disable the Explain facility, and no Explain data will be captured. However, assigning either option the value YES will activate the Explain facility and collect comprehensive Explain information or Explain snapshot data (or both if both options are set to YES) for each static SQL statement encountered in the source code file; dynamic SQL statements will be ignored. If you assign either option the value ALL, the Explain facility will be activated, and comprehensive Explain information or Explain snapshot data (or both if both options are set) will be collected for every static and dynamic SQL statement found, even if the CURRENT EXPLAIN MODE or the CURRENT EXPLAIN SNAPSHOT special registers have been set to NO.

Table 5.17 summarizes the behavior the EXPLAIN bind option has on the Explain facility and on static and dynamic SQL statement processing when used in conjunction with the EXPLAIN MODE special register. Table 5.18 summarizes the behavior that the EXPLSNAP bind option has on the Explain facility and on static and dynamic SQL statement processing when used in conjunction with the EXPLAIN SNAPSHOT special register.

Table 5.17: Interaction of the EXPLAIN bind option and the EXPLAIN MODE special register

Explain Mode Special Register Values	EXPLAIN Bind Option Values: NO	EXPLAIN Bind Option Values: YES	EXPLAIN Bind Option Values: ALL
NO	• Explain facility is disabled. No Explain data is captured.	• Explain facility is enabled. Comprehensive Explain data is collected and written to the Explain tables for static SQL statements.	• Explain facility is enabled. Comprehensive Explain data is collected and written to the Explain tables for both static and dynamic SQL statements.
YES	• Explain facility is enabled. Comprehensive Explain data is collected and written to the Explain tables for dynamic SQL statements.	• Explain facility is enabled. Comprehensive Explain data is collected and written to the Explain tables for both static and dynamic SQL statements.	• Explain facility is enabled. Comprehensive Explain data is collected and written to the Explain tables for both static and dynamic SQL statements.
EXPLAIN	• Explain facility is enabled. Comprehensive Explain data is collected and written to the Explain tables for dynamic SQL statements. Dynamic SQL statements are not executed.	• Explain facility is enabled. Comprehensive Explain data is collected and written to the Explain tables for both static and dynamic SQL statements. Dynamic SQL statements are not executed.	• Explain facility is enabled. Comprehensive Explain data is collected and written to the Explain tables for both static and dynamic SQL statements. Dynamic SQL statements are not executed.

Table 5.18: Interaction of the EXPLSNAP bind option and the EXPLAIN SNAPSHOT special register

Explain Snapshot Special Register Values	EXPLSNAP Bind Option Values: NO	YES	ALL
NO	• Explain facility is disabled. No Explain data is captured.	• Explain facility is enabled. Explain snapshot data is collected and written to the SNAPSHOT column of the EXPLAIN_STATEMENT Explain table for static SQL statements.	• Explain facility is enabled. Explain snapshot data is collected and written to the SNAPSHOT column of the EXPLAIN_STATEMENT Explain table for both static and dynamic SQL statements.
YES	• Explain facility is enabled. Explain snapshot data is collected and written to the SNAPSHOT column of the EXPLAIN_STATEMENT Explain table for dynamic SQL statements.	• Explain facility is enabled. Explain snapshot data is collected and written to the SNAPSHOT column of the EXPLAIN_STATEMENT Explain table for both static and dynamic SQL statements.	• Explain facility is enabled. Explain snapshot data is collected and written to the SNAPSHOT column of the EXPLAIN_STATEMENT Explain table for both static and dynamic SQL statements.
EXPLAIN	• Explain facility is enabled. Explain snapshot data is collected and written to the SNAPSHOT column of the EXPLAIN_STATEMENT Explain table for dynamic SQL statements. Dynamic SQL statements are not executed.	• Explain facility is enabled. Explain snapshot data is collected and written to the SNAPSHOT column of the EXPLAIN_STATEMENT Explain table for both static and dynamic SQL statements. Dynamic SQL statements are not executed.	• Explain facility is enabled. Explain snapshot data is collected and written to the SNAPSHOT column of the EXPLAIN_STATEMENT Explain table for both static and dynamic SQL statements. Dynamic SQL statements are not executed.

Evaluating Explain Data

So far, you have concentrated on the various ways in which to collect comprehensive Explain and Explain snapshot data. You have also seen that once collected, this data is stored in one or more Explain tables. Although you can construct a query to retrieve this data, a better way to view collected Explain information is by using one of the Explain facility tools that have been designed specifically for presenting Explain information in a meaningful format. This set of tools consists of:

- The db2expln tool
- The db2exfmt tool
- The Visual Explain (access plan graph)

The db2expln Tool

Earlier, you saw that when a source code file containing embedded SQL statements is bound to a database (either as part of the precompile process or during deferred binding), the DB2 Optimizer analyzes each static SQL statement encountered and generates a corresponding access plan, which is then stored in the database in the form of a package. Given the name of the database, the name of the package, the ID of the package creator, and a section number (if the section number 0 is specified, all sections of the package will be processed), the db2expln tool will interpret and describe the access plan information for any package stored in a database's system catalog.

Because the db2expln tool works directly with a package and not with comprehensive Explain or Explain snapshot data, it is typically used to produce information about the access plans that have been chosen for packages for which Explain data has not been captured. However, because the db2expln tool can access only information that has been stored in a package, it can only describe the implementation of the final access plan chosen; it cannot provide information on how a particular SQL statement was optimized.

You can also use the db2expln tool to explain and optionally produce a graph of the access plan chosen by the DB2 Optimizer for a dynamic SQL statement. For example, if you want to view the access plan the Optimizer would select for the query "SELECT * FROM department", execute a db2expln command that looks something like this:

```
db2expln -d sample -t -g -statement "SELECT * FROM department"
```

And if you executed this command by using the SAMPLE database provided with DB2, you will see a report similar to the following:

```
DB2 Universal Database Version 10.1, 5622-044 (c) Copyright IBM Corp. 1991, 2011
Licensed Material - Program Property of IBM
IBM DB2 Universal Database SQL and XQUERY Explain Tool

DB2 Universal Database Version 10.1, 5622-044 (c) Copyright IBM Corp. 1991, 2011
Licensed Material - Program Property of IBM
IBM DB2 Universal Database SQL and XQUERY Explain Tool

******************** DYNAMIC ***************************************

==================== STATEMENT ==========================================

        Isolation Level          = Cursor Stability
        Blocking                 = Block Unambiguous Cursors
```

Continued

```
        Query Optimization Class = 5

        Partition Parallel       = No
        Intra-Partition Parallel = No

SQL Path                 = "SYSIBM", "SYSFUN", "SYSPROC",
     "SYSIBMADM","DB2INST1"


Statement:

  SELECT *
  FROM department


Section Code Page = 1208

Estimated Cost = 6.816431
Estimated Cardinality = 14.000000

Access Table Name = DB2INST1.DEPARTMENT  ID = 2,5
|  #Columns = 5
|  Avoid Locking Committed Data
|  May participate in Scan Sharing structures
|  Scan may start anywhere and wrap, for completion
|  Fast scan, for purposes of scan sharing management
|  Scan can be throttled in scan sharing management
|  Relation Scan
|  |  Prefetch: Eligible
|  Lock Intents
|  |  Table: Intent Share
|  |  Row  : Next Key Share
|  Sargable Predicate(s)
|  |  Return Data to Application
```

Continued

```
| | | #Columns = 5
Return Data Completion

End of section


Optimizer Plan:

     Rows
   Operator
     (ID)
     Cost

     14
   RETURN
    ( 1)
   6.81643
     |
     14
   TBSCAN
    ( 2)
   6.81643
     |
     14
  Table:
  DB2INST1.
  DEPARTMENT
```

The db2exfmt Tool

Unlike the db2expln tool, the db2exfmt tool works directly with comprehensive Explain or Explain snapshot data that has been collected and stored in the Explain tables. Given a database name and other qualifying information, the db2exfmt tool will query the Explain tables for information, format the results, and produce a text-based report that can be displayed directly on the terminal or written to an ASCII-formatted file.

The basic syntax for db2exfmt tool is:

```
db2exfmt [[-1] [-d <DatabaseName>] [-e <ExplainTblSchema>]
 [-f O | Y | C] -g [-x] [O [T | F] IC] [-l]
 [-n <PkgName>]  [-s <PkgSchema>] [-o <OutPutFile>] [-t]]
 [-u <User> <Password>] [-w <Timestamp>]
 [-# <SectionNum>] [-v <PkgVersion>] -h
```

where:

-1 Identifies default values for the command options; the defaults are -e %, -n %, -s %, -v %, -w, -1, and -# 0

DatabaseName Identifies the name of the database containing packages

ExplainTblSchema Identifies the schema for the Explain tables

-f Identifies the formatting flag and the options available, as follows:

- O: Specifies the operating summary
- Y: Forces the format option of the original statement even if EXPLAIN_TEXT contains formatting
- C: Indicates the compact mode, and the default is expanded mode for ease of reading

-g Identifies the graph plan; the valid options include:

- O: Generates a graph plan, only without formatting the table content
- T: Indicates total cost under each operator in a graph
- F: Specifies the first tuple cost in a graph
- I: Indicates I/O cost under each operator in a graph
- C: Specifies output cardinality of each operator in a graph

-l Identifies the case when processing package names

PkgName Identifies the package name for the Explain request and is case-sensitive

PkgSchema Identifies the package schema for the Explain request and is case-sensitive

OutPutFile Identifies the output file name

User Identifies the user name to connect to the database

Password Identifies the password to connect to the database

Timestamp	Identifies the timestamp for Explain; specify -1 to obtain the latest Explain plan
SectionNum	Identifies the section in the source SQL statement; specify 0 for all sections
PkgVersion	Identifies the package version of the Explain request; the default is %

For example, to generate a detailed report consisting of all Explain data that has been collected and stored in the SAMPLE database provided with DB2, you execute a db2exfmt command:

```
db2exfmt -d sample -1 -o db2exfmt.out
```

When this command is executed, a report will be produced and written to a file named db2exfmt.out. If you want to generate a detailed report for the SQL statement "SELECT * FROM department", execute the following command:

```
set current explain mode explain
DB20000I  The SQL command completed successfully.

!db2 -tvf SQL1.sql > SQL1.log

set current explain mode no
DB20000I  The SQL command completed successfully.

db2exfmt -d sample -g TIC -w -1 -s % -n % -# 0 -o db2exfmt.sql1.out
DB2 Universal Database Version 10.1, 5622-044 (c) Copyright IBM Corp. 1991, 2011
Licensed Material - Program Property of IBM
IBM DATABASE 2 Explain Table Format Tool

Connecting to the Database.
Connect to Database Successful.
Output is in db2exfmt.sql1.out.
Executing Connect Reset -- Connect Reset was Successful.
```

You can view the detailed report by using the vi editor in UNIX or by using Notepad in the Windows platform. The output will look something like this:

```
DB2 Universal Database Version 10.1, 5622-044 (c) Copyright IBM Corp. 1991, 2011
Licensed Material - Program Property of IBM
IBM DATABASE 2 Explain Table Format Tool

******************** EXPLAIN INSTANCE ********************

DB2_VERSION:       10.01.3
SOURCE_NAME:       SQLC2J25
SOURCE_SCHEMA:     NULLID
SOURCE_VERSION:
EXPLAIN_TIME:      2014-09-07-07.13.53.367009
EXPLAIN_REQUESTER: DB2INST1

Database Context:
----------------
        Parallelism:          None
        CPU Speed:            1.495757e-07
        Comm Speed:           100
        Buffer Pool size:     1000
        Sort Heap size:       256
        Database Heap size:   1200
        Lock List size:       4096
        Maximum Lock List:    10
        Average Applications: 1
        Locks Available:      13107

Package Context:
---------------
        SQL Type:           Dynamic
        Optimization Level: 5
        Blocking:           Block All Cursors
        Isolation Level:    Cursor Stability
```

Continued

```
---------------- STATEMENT 1  SECTION 201 ----------------
        QUERYNO:        2
        QUERYTAG:       CLP
        Statement Type:    Select
        Updatable:         No
        Deletable:         No
        Query Degree:      1

Original Statement:
SELECT
  *
FROM
  department

Optimized Statement:
-------------------
SELECT
  Q1.DEPTNO AS "DEPTNO",
  Q1.DEPTNAME AS "DEPTNAME",
  Q1.MGRNO AS "MGRNO",
  Q1.ADMRDEPT AS "ADMRDEPT",
  Q1.LOCATION AS "LOCATION"
FROM
  DB2INST1.DEPARTMENT AS Q1

Access Plan:
-----------
        Total Cost:             6.81643
        Query Degree:           1

      Rows
     RETURN
     (   1)
```

Continued

```
      Cost
       I/O
       |
       14
     TBSCAN
     (   2)
     6.81643
        1
       |
       14
 TABLE: DB2INST1
   DEPARTMENT
       Q1

Plan Details:
-------------


        1) RETURN: (Return Result)
                Cumulative Total Cost:          6.81643
                Cumulative CPU Cost:            76423
                Cumulative I/O Cost:            1
                Cumulative Re-Total Cost:       0.00386354
                Cumulative Re-CPU Cost:         25830
                Cumulative Re-I/O Cost:         0
                Cumulative First Row Cost:      6.81282
                Estimated Bufferpool Buffers:   1

                Arguments:
                ---------
                BLDLEVEL: (Build level)
                        DB2 v10.1.0.3 : s130918
                ENVVAR  : (Environment Variable)
                        DB2_INLIST_TO_NLJN=YES
```

Continued

```
            ENVVAR  : (Environment Variable)
                    DB2_REDUCED_OPTIMIZATION=YES
            HEAPUSE : (Maximum Statement Heap Usage)
                    80 Pages
            PREPTIME: (Statement prepare time)
                             9 milliseconds
            STMTHEAP: (Statement heap size)
                    8192

            Input Streams:
            -------------
                    2) From Operator #2

                            Estimated number of rows:       14
                            Number of columns:              5
                            Subquery predicate ID:          Not Applicable

                            Column Names:
                            ------------
                            +Q2.LOCATION+Q2.ADMRDEPT+Q2.MGRNO+Q2.DEPTNAME
                            +Q2.DEPTNO

...
...

Objects Used in Access Plan:
---------------------------

        Schema: DB2INST1
        Name:   DEPARTMENT
        Type:   Table
                        Time of creation:               2014-08-17-10.01.45.515467
                        Last statistics update:         2014-09-06-17.45.53.699943
```

Continued

```
Number of columns:                5
Number of rows:                   14
Width of rows:                    57
Number of buffer pool pages:      1
Number of data partitions:        1
Distinct row values:              No
Tablespace name:                  USERSPACE1
Tablespace overhead:              6.725000
Tablespace transfer rate:         0.080000
Source for statistics:            Single Node
Prefetch page count:              192
Container extent page count:      32
Table overflow record count:      0
Table Active Blocks:              -1
Average Row Compression Ratio:    0
Percentage Rows Compressed:       0
Average Compressed Row Size:      0
```

Visual Explain

Visual Explain is a GUI tool incorporated within IBM Data Studio to provide database administrators and application developers with the ability to view a graphical representation of the access plan that has been chosen for a particular SQL statement. In addition, Visual Explain allows you to do the following:

- See the database statistics that were used to optimize the SQL statement
- Determine whether an index was used to access table data (if an index was not used, Visual Explain can help you decide which columns might benefit from being indexed)
- View the effects of performance tuning by allowing you to make "before" and "after" comparisons
- Obtain detailed information about each operation that is performed by the access plan, including the estimated cost of each

However, you can use Visual Explain to view only Explain snapshot data. To view Explain data that has been collected and written to the Explain tables, you must use the `db2exfmt` tool instead.

Activating Visual Explain. One of the more common ways to activate Visual Explain is by generating Explain data for a dynamic SQL statement by using the Query Tuning dialog. Figure 5.1 illustrates the IBM Data Studio items you must select to activate the Query Tuning dialog. Figure 5.2 shows how the Query Advisor and Analysis Tools dialog might look when it has been populated with a simple query.

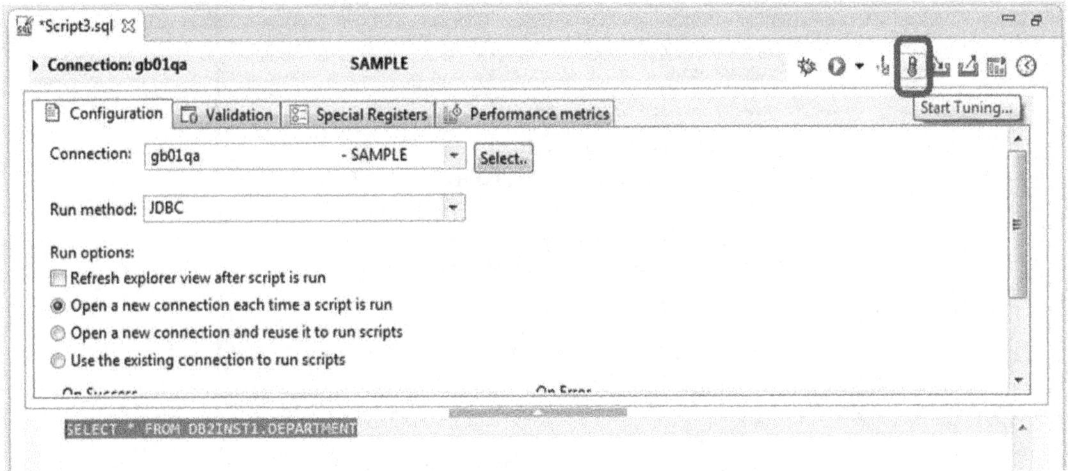

Figure 5.1: Activating the Query Tuning wizard

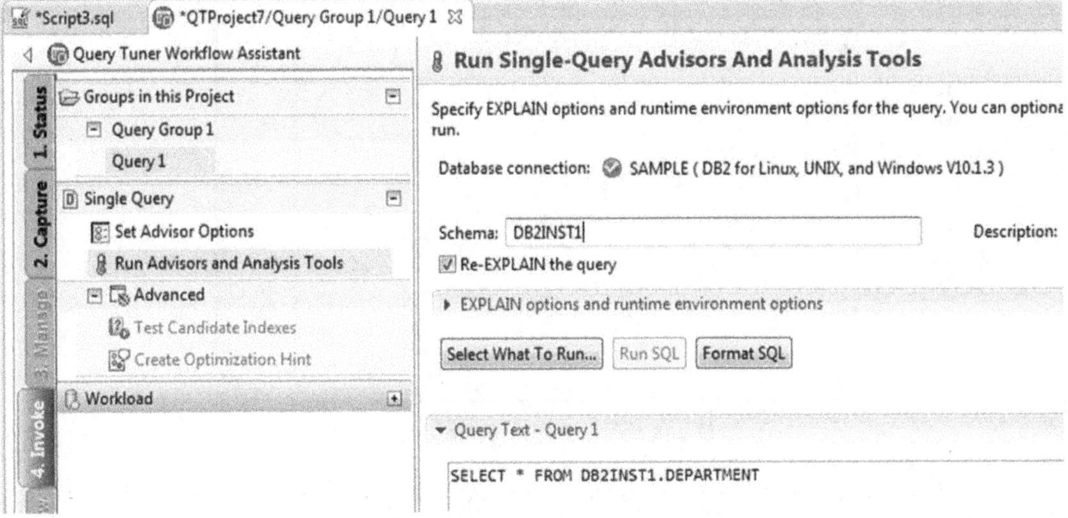

Figure 5.2: Query Advisor and Analysis Tools wizard

After the Query Advisor and Analysis Tools dialog opens, you can enter any dynamic SQL statement into the **Query Text** entry field. Then, when you click the **Select What To Run** button, you will see Analysis Tools options similar to those in Figure 5.3.

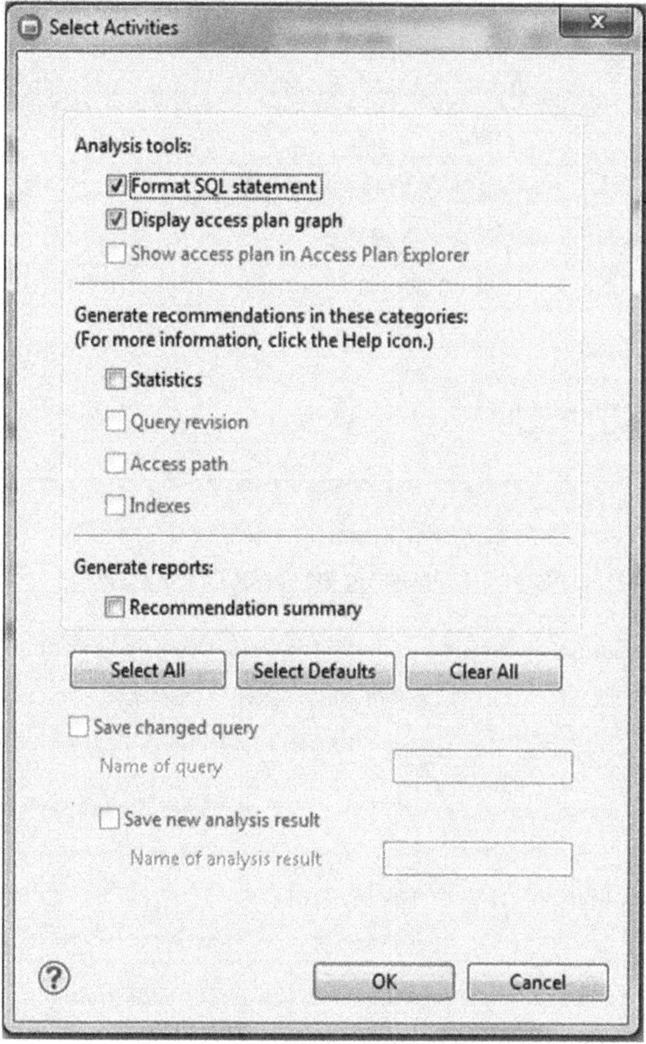

Figure 5.3: Select Activities wizard

Once you select activities to be performed on the database, you will see an access plan graph for the SQL statement supplied (Figure 5.4). When analyzing an access plan to identify the opportunities to improve an SQL statement's performance, click through the different object types to retrieve key information, such as node type, operator type, estimated cardinality, object type, and cumulative total cost, to understand the current optimization plan.

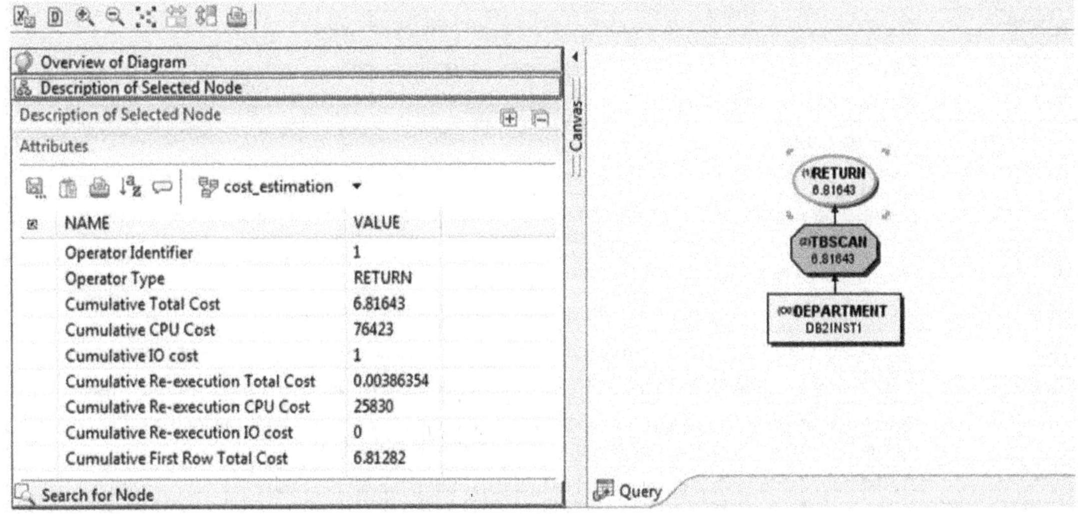

Figure 5.4: Access plan graph wizard

Visual Explain Output. As you can see in Figure 5.4, the output provided by Visual Explain consists of a hierarchical graph that represents the various components needed to process the access plan that has been chosen for a particular SQL statement. Each component is represented as a graphical object that is known as a *node*, and two types of nodes can exist:

- **Operator**. An operator node identifies either an action that must be performed on data or the output produced from a table or index.
- **Operand**. An operand node identifies an entity on which an operation is performed (for example, a table would be the operand of a table scan operator).

Typically, operand nodes identify tables, indexes, and table queues (you use table queues when using intrapartition parallelism), which are symbolized in the hierarchical graph by rectangles (tables), diamonds (indexes), and parallelograms (table queues). Operator nodes, however, identify anything from an insert operation to an index or table scan. Operator nodes, which are symbolized in the hierarchical graph by ovals, indicate how data is accessed, how tables are joined, and other factors such as whether a sort operation is to be performed. Table 5.19 lists the more common operators that can appear in an access plan hierarchical graph.

Table 5.19: DB2's common operators	
Definition	**Description**
DELETE	Deletes rows from a table
EISCAN	Scans a user-defined index to produce a reduced stream of rows
FETCH	Fetches columns from a table by using a specific record identifier
FILTER	Filters data by applying one or more predicates to it
GENROW	Generates a row
GRPBY	Groups rows by common values of designated columns or functions and evaluates set functions
HSJOIN	Represents a hash join, where two or more tables are hashed on the join columns (preferred method for joins performed in a decision support environment)
INSERT	Inserts rows into a table
IXAND	ANDs together the row identifier (RIDs) from two or more index scans
IXSCAN	Scans an index of a table with optional start/stop conditions, producing an ordered stream of rows
MSJOIN	Represents a merge join, where both outer and inner tables must be in join-predicate order
NLJOIN	Represents a nested loop join that accesses an inner table once for each row of the outer table (preferred method for joins performed in an OLTP environment)
PIPE	Transfers records from a complied table function during the debug mode
REBAL	Rebalance records between Symmetric Multiprocessing subagents
RETURN	Represents the return of data from the query to the user
RIDSCN	Scans a list of RIDs obtained from one or more indexes
RPD	Remote push-down operator defines a portion of the plan that is executed at a remote data source
SHIP	Retrieves data from a remote database source; used in the federated system
SORT	Sorts rows in the order of specified columns and optionally eliminates duplicate entries
TBFUNC	An in-stream table function operator used during SAS embedded processing
TBSCAN	Retrieves rows by reading all required data directly from the data pages
TEMP	Stores data in a temporary table to be read back out (possibly multiple times)
TQ	Transfers table data between database agents
UNION	Concatenates streams of rows from multiple tables
UNIQUE	Eliminates rows with duplicate values, for specified columns
UPDATE	Updates rows in a table
XISCAN	Uses index scan over XML data
XSCAN	Navigates XML elements to evaluate XPath expressions and to extract document elements if necessary
XANDOR	Optimizer uses applicable indexes by ANDing and ORing over XML data
ZZJOIN (ZigZag join)	Used when a fact table and two or more dimension tables are joined in a star schema

Arrows that illustrate how data flows from one node to the next connect all nodes in the hierarchical graph, and a RETURN operator normally terminates this path. Figure 5.4 shows how the hierarchical graph for an access plan that contains two different operator nodes (TBSCAN and RETURN) and one operand node (a table named DB2INST1.DEPARTMENT) might appear in Visual Explain or an access graph plan.

A Word About the DB2 Optimization Class

When you compile an SQL or XQuery statement, you can specify an optimization class that determines how the DB2 Optimizer will choose the most efficient access plan for that query. The optimization classes are differentiated by the number and type of optimization strategies that are considered in the compilation of the query. The possible values range from 0 to 9; in general, the higher classes cause the Optimizer to use more time and memory when selecting optimal access plans, which potentially results in better access plans and improved run-time performance.

You use the QUERYOPT precompile/bind option to specify the class of optimization techniques to use when preparing static SQL statements. If this option is not provided when an application is precompiled or bound to a database, the current value of the dft_queryopt database configuration file parameter is used as the default. You use the CURRENT QUERY OPTIMIZATION special register to control the class of optimization techniques to use when binding dynamic SQL statements. To change the value of the parameter, execute the SET CURRENT QUERY OPTIMIZATION SQL statement. The basic syntax for this statement is:

```
SET CURRENT QUERY OPTIMIZATION <=> [OptimizationLevel]
```

where:

OptimizationLevel Specifies the optimization level (class) to use when preparing dynamic SQL statements; this parameter must be set to one of the following values:

- 0: Specifies to use a minimal amount of optimization techniques when the Optimizer generates an access plan; this optimization class level is most suitable for simple dynamic SQL statements that access well-indexed tables
- 1: Specifies that the amount of optimization techniques to use when the Optimizer generates an access plan should be roughly equal to that provided by DB2 Version 1
- 2: Specifies that the amount of optimization techniques to use when the Optimizer generates an access plan should be higher than that provided by DB2 Version 1, but significantly less than the amount used by level 3 and higher
- 3: Specifies to use a moderate amount of optimization techniques when the Optimizer generates an access plan

- 5: Specifies to use a significant amount of optimization techniques when the Optimizer generates an access plan; for complex queries, heuristic rules are used to limit the amount of time spent selecting an access plan (whenever possible, queries will use summary tables instead of underlying base tables—this is the default optimization class that DB2 uses)
- 7: Specifies to use a significant amount of optimization techniques when the Optimizer generates an access plan; this level is similar to level 5; however, no heuristic rules are used to limit the amount of time spent selecting access plans for complex queries
- 9: Specifies to use the maximum amount of optimization techniques when the Optimizer generates an access plan; this optimization class can greatly expand the number of possible access paths that are evaluated before an access plan is chosen; for this reason, this class is typically used to process SQL statements that contain very complex and very long-running queries that are executed against very large tables

Therefore, if you want to instruct the DB2 Optimizer to use more optimization techniques than are normally used by default when generating access plans for dynamic SQL statements, execute a SET CURRENT QUERY OPTIMIZATION statement:

```
SET CURRENT QUERY OPTIMIZATION = 7
```

When you assign the CURRENT QUERY OPTIMIZATION special register a new value, a new class of query rewrite rules is enabled, and certain optimization variables are assigned appropriate values for the class. These query rewrite rules and optimization variables are then used during the preparation of dynamic SQL statements so that the optimum access plan for the statement is chosen. Note that you can assign the QUERYOPT precompile/bind the same values as the CURRENT QUERY OPTIMIZATION special register.

DB2 Troubleshooting Tools

Along with the database system monitors and the Explain facility, several others tools are available to help database administrators isolate and identify problems with a system, a database, or an application. This section explores many of the tools, including db2fodc, db2diag, db2pdcfg, db2bfd, db2mtrk, inspect, db2dart, db2top, db2pd, and db2support.

Obtaining Information About an Error Code

When the DB2 database manager returns an error code, you can use db2 "? <SQL Error Code>" to view the information about the error in detail. For example:

```
db2 "? SQL0911N"

SQL0911N  The current transaction has been rolled back because of a deadlock
or timeout. Reason code "<reason-code>".

Explanation:

The current unit of work was involved in an unresolved contention for use of
an object and had to be rolled back.

The reason codes are as follows:

2
         The transaction was rolled back due to a deadlock.
68
         The transaction was rolled back due to a lock timeout.
72
         The transaction was rolled back due to a DB2 Data Links Manager
         error during the transaction.
73
         The transaction was rolled back because a queuing threshold
         such as the CONCURRENTDBCOORDACTIVITIES threshold caused two or
         more activities to reach a deadlock state. For more
         information, see "CONCURRENTDBCOORDACTIVITIES threshold" in the
         DB2 Information Center.
The application was rolled back to the previous COMMIT.

                                                                 Continued
```

```
User response:

The changes associated with the unit of work must be entered again.

To help avoid deadlock or lock timeout, issue frequent COMMIT operations, if
possible, for a long-running application, or for an application likely to
encounter a deadlock.

Federated system users: the deadlock can occur at the federated server or at
the data source. There is no mechanism to detect deadlocks that span data
sources and potentially the federated system. It is possible to identify the
data source failing the request (refer to the problem determination guide to
determine which data source is failing to process the SQL statement).

Deadlocks are often normal or expected while processing certain combinations
of SQL statements. It is recommended that you design applications to avoid
deadlocks to the extent possible.

If a deadlock state was reached because of a queuing threshold such as the
CONCURRENTDBCOORDACTIVITIES threshold, increase the value of the queuing
threshold.

sqlcode: -911

sqlstate: 40001
```

Reason Codes

In some cases, an error message will contain a reference to what is known as a *reason code*. Reason codes are used when several different events can generate a single error code, and they provide additional information associated with the error code returned. For example, the error message associated with the error code SQL0911N looks something like this:

```
SQL0911N  The current transaction has been rolled back because of a deadlock
or timeout. Reason code "[ReasonCode]".
```

where:

ReasonCode Identifies the reason code associated with the error message; usually, this is a numerical value (for error code SQL0911N, *ReasonCode* can be the number 2, 68, 72, or 73)

The db2diag Utility

Essentially, the information in the administration notification log file and the DB2 diagnostic log file is easy to read once you understand the format used. However, searching through a large DB2 diagnostic log file can be time-consuming, particularly if the log file spans several months. To aid in problem determination, DB2 provides a utility that can filter and format the information available in the db2diag.log file. This utility is known as the db2diag utility, and you activate it by executing the db2diag command. Several options are available with this command. To find out more, execute any of the following commands from the DB2 CLP:

- db2diag -help—Provides a short description of the options available
- db2diag -h brief—Provides descriptions for all options without examples
- db2diag -h notes—Provides usage notes and restrictions
- db2diag -h examples—Provides a set of examples to help you get started
- db2diag -h tutorial—Provides examples for all options available
- db2diag -h all—Provides a comprehensive list of options available

If you see an error that looks something like the one in the next example with a ZRC hexadecimal number 0x86100025, you can use the db2diag command to extract detailed information for a specific ZRC, as follows:

```
2014-09-14-11.01.54.013828+000 E53480465E541        LEVEL: Error
PID      : 7533                    TID  : 46912912746816PROC : db2sysc 32
INSTANCE: db2inst1                   NODE : 032
EDUID    : 135                     EDUNAME: db2logmgr (SAMPLE) 32
FUNCTION: DB2 UDB, data protection services, sqlpgArchiveLogFile, probe:3160
MESSAGE : ZRC=0x86100025=-2045771739=SQLP_MEDIA_VENDOR_DEV_ERR
          "A vendor device reported a media error."

db2diag -rc 0x86100025

Input ZRC string '0x86100025' parsed as 0x86100025 (-2045771739).
```

Continued

```
ZRC value to map: 0x86100025 (-2045771739)

ZRC class :
        Critical Media Error (Class Index: 6)
Component:
        SQLP ; data protection services (Component Index: 16)
Reason Code:
        37 (0x0025)

Identifer:
        SQLP_MEDIA_VENDOR_DEV_ERR
Identifer (without component):
        SQLZ_RC_MEDIA_VENDOR_DEV_ERR

Description:
        A vendor device reported a media error.

Associated information:
        Sqlcode -2062
SQL2062N  An error occurred while accessing media "". Reason code: "".

        Number of sqlca tokens : 2
        Diaglog message number: 1
```

In the above example, clearly the problem is in the storage server, which needs a proper analysis and a fix.

First Occurrence Data Capture (FODC)

One of the most important diagnostic tools available with DB2 is a facility known as *First Occurrence Data Capture* (*FODC*). FODC runs quietly in the background until a significant event occurs, and at that time, diagnostic information about the event is automatically captured by the DB2 database manager and recorded in special ASCII-format files. This information contains crucial details that may help in the diagnosis and resolution of problems. And because this information is collected at the actual time an event takes place, the need to reproduce errors to obtain diagnostic information is greatly reduced or in some cases eliminated. The information that FODC captures is externalized in several different ways, including the following:

- **DB2 diagnostic log file entries**. Whenever a significant event occurs, an entry containing diagnostic information about that event is automatically recorded in a file named db2diag.log, which acts as the primary diagnostic log file for DB2.
- **Administration notification log entries**. When significant events occur, supplemental information for any SQL return code generated is written to the Windows Event Log (on Windows NT, Windows 2000, and Windows XP systems) or to a file named InstanceName.nfy—where InstanceName is the name of the instance that generated the information (on all other supported operating systems). This information is not cryptic and can be viewed with the Windows Event Viewer (on Windows systems) or with any text editor (on all other systems).
- **Dump files**. In some cases, when a DB2-specific process or thread fails, extra information is logged in external binary dump files (that are assigned a name based on the ID of the failing process/thread). These files are more or less unreadable and are intended to be forwarded to IBM Software Technical Support for interpretation.
- **DB2 event log**. Whenever an infrastructure event occurs in the system, it is recorded in the event log binary file in a circular fashion. This log file is replaced when the instance is restarted. If an instance crashes, a db2eventlog.xxx.crash file is generated. These files are intended for use by IBM Software Technical Support.
- **DB2 callout script (db2cos) output files**. When the database manager cannot continue processing the user or system request due to a panic, a trap, a segmentation violation, or an exception, the db2cos script is automatically invoked as part of FODC. The default db2cos script calls db2pd commands to collect information in an unlatched manner. The db2cos script is available at location ~sqllib/bin/. If you want to modify it, you can copy the db2cos script to ~sqllib/adm/ and change it by using the vi editor.
- **Trap files**. If the DB2 database manager cannot continue processing because a trap, a segmentation violation, or an exception has occurred, it generates a trap file that contains the sequence of function calls made for the last steps executed before the trap, segmentation violation, or exception event occurred.
- **Core files (UNIX only)**. If DB2 terminates abnormally on a UNIX platform, the operating system will generate a core file, which is a binary file that contains information similar to the information recorded in a DB2 trap file. Core files may also contain the entire memory image of the terminated DB2 process; the file size is controlled by the /etc/security/limits.conf UNIX limit configuration file.

FODC Information Location

By default, all FODC information collected on a UNIX platform is stored in the directory $HOME/sqllib/db2dump, where $HOME is the home directory of the instance owner. On Windows platforms, if the location of the instance directory has not been stored in the DB2INSTPROF environment variable, FODC information collected will be stored in the directory DB2Path\DB2Instance, where DB2Path is the path stored in the DB2PATH environment variable and DB2Instance is the value stored in the DB2INSTDEF environment variable (which is DB2 by default). But if the location of the instance directory has been stored in the DB2INSTPROF environment variable, FODC information will be stored in the directory Drive:\DB2InstProfile\DB2Instance, where Drive is the drive referenced in the DB2PATH environment variable, DB2InstProfile is the name of the instance profile directory, and DB2Instance is the value stored in the DB2INSTDEF environment variable.

However, where FODC information is actually recorded is controlled by the value of the diagpath or alt_diagpath parameter of a DB2 database manager instance's configuration file. Thus, if you want to store all FODC information in another location, you do so by changing the value of this parameter (which contains a null string when an instance is first created). You can also specify the FODC path through the FODCPATH registry variable or through the db2fodc -fodcpath command. Regardless of where FODC information is stored, it is up to the system administrator to ensure that the location used is cleaned periodically; DB2 does not automatically remove dump files, trap files, and core files that the FODC tool generates.

One or more of the following subdirectories is created under the FODC directory based on the FODC configuration and the outage type:

- DB2CONFIG—Contains DB2 configuration command output files
- DB2PD—Contains db2pd command output files
- DB2SNAPS—Contains snapshot command output files
- DB2TRACE—Contains db2 trace files
- OSCONFIG—Contains operating system configuration files
- OSSNAPS—Contains operating system monitor command output files
- OSTRACE—Contains operating system trace files

FODC Command Options

You can also capture the FODC diagnostic information by manually running the db2fodc command. The basic syntax for db2fodc is:

```
db2fodc <-hang | -perf | -cpu | -memory | -connections> <basic | full>
        <-db [DBName] | -alldbs>
```

Continued

```
<-dbpartitionnum [DBPartNum] | -alldbpartitionnums | -member  [MemberNum] |
   -host [HostList] | -allmembers>
<-timeout [TimeoutPeriod]>
<-fodcpath [FODCPath]>
<-indexerror [ScriptDir] <basic | full>
<-clp>
<-preupgrade>
<-hadr>
<-detect <connstatus=[ConStatus]> <condition=[Value]>
   <iteration=[Value]> <duration=[Value]> <sleeptime=[Value]>
   <interval=[Value]> <triggercount=[Value]> <off>>
```

where:

DBPartNum	Identifies the database partition number on which to issue the FODC diagnostic command
MemberNum	Identifies the member or members on which to issue the FODC diagnostic command
HostList	Identifies the host or hosts on which to issue the FODC diagnostic command
TimeoutPeriod	Identifies a timeout period for the callout script; if the timeout period has been reached before the callout script has finished executing, the callout script process will be killed—the default timeout period is unlimited
FODCPath	Identifies the path name to redirect all the db2fodc contents in which the entire FODC package will be created at this path
ScriptDir	Identifies the path name of the directory where db2cos_indexerror scripts reside
ConStatus	Identifies the connection status to detect in during problem investigation

To find the reasons for any hang situation, you can execute the following command:

```
db2fodc -hang basic
"db2fodc": List of active databases: "SAMPLE"


**********************WARNING***********************
*    This tool should be run with caution.         *
```

Continued

```
*     It can cause significant performance            *
*  degradation, especially on busy systems with a     *
*        high number of active connections            *
*                                                     *
*   Run times indicated below are estimates based     *
*  on test runs. Your actual run times might vary,    *
*   dependent on factors such as your hardware        *
*  specifications, operating system configuration,    *
*            and current workload                     *
*****************************************************

You have 10 seconds to cancel this script with Ctrl-C
You may interrupt execution at any time by issuing Ctrl-C
The script will then dump any active db2 trace, and inform
where to find the output files

Starting data collection for hang problem determination...
Sun Sep 14 10:56:49 GMT 2014

Collecting OS Configuration info (started at 10:56:49 AM)
Should complete in less than one minute
Finished at 10:56:50 AM

Collecting basic DB2 CONFIG info (started at 10:56:50 AM)
Should complete in less than one minute
Finished at 10:56:50 AM

Collecting OS monitor info: iteration 1 of 2 info (started at 10:56:50 AM)
Should complete in less than 6 minutes
Finished at 10:57:37 AM

Collecting OS monitor info: iteration 2 of 2 info (started at 10:58:07 AM)
Should complete in less than 6 minutes
Finished at 10:58:55 AM
```

Continued

```
Collecting OS kernel threads info (started at 10:58:55 AM)
Finished at 10:58:55 AM

Collecting OS trace info (started at 10:58:55 AM)
Should complete in less than 3 minutes
Finished at 10:58:55 AM

Collecting db2 trace info (started at 10:58:55 AM)
Estimated time to completion is 3 minutes (Ctrl-C to interrupt)
No db2fmp32 processes, issued trace init signal
formatting trace at 10:59:25 AM
Finished at 10:59:35 AM

Collecting Call stacks: iteration 1 of 2 info (started at 10:59:35 AM)
Waiting 2 minutes and 0 seconds for command to complete...
Finished at 11:01:36 AM

Collecting Call stacks: iteration 2 of 2 info (started at 11:01:36 AM)
Waiting 2 minutes and 0 seconds for command to complete...
Finished at 11:03:38 AM

Collecting db2pd info (started at 11:03:38 AM)
Should complete in 5-10 minutes (depending on your system load)
........Finished at 11:03:41 AM

.Collecting DB2 CONFIG info (started at 11:03:42 AM)
Estimated time to completion is 5 minutes (Ctrl-C to interrupt)
Finished at 11:03:43 AM

Output directory is /home/db2inst1/sqllib/db2dump/DIAG0000/FODC_Hang_2014-
09-14-10.56.19.574137_0000
Open db2fodc_hang.log in that directory for details of collected data
```

Figure 5.5 shows the number of files generated as part of db2fodc -hang command execution.

```
~/sqllib/db2dump/DIAG0000/FODC_Hang_2014-09-14-10.56.19.574137_0000> ls -ltr
drwxr-xr-x 2 db2inst1 db2dadm  4096 Sep 14 10:56 DB2SNAPS
drwxr-xr-x 2 db2inst1 db2dadm  4096 Sep 14 10:56 OSCONFIG
drwxr-xr-x 2 db2inst1 db2dadm  4096 Sep 14 10:58 OSSNAPS
drwxr-xr-x 2 db2inst1 db2dadm  4096 Sep 14 10:58 OSTRACE
-rw-r--r-- 1 db2inst1 db2dadm 34013 Sep 14 10:59 3692.000.processObj.txt
drwxr-xr-x 2 db2inst1 db2dadm  4096 Sep 14 11:03 DB2PD
drwxr-xr-x 2 db2inst1 db2dadm  4096 Sep 14 11:03 DB2CONFIG
drwxr-xr-x 2 db2inst1 db2dadm  4096 Sep 14 11:03 DB2TRACE
-rw-r--r-- 1 db2inst1 db2dadm  7181 Sep 14 11:03 db2fodc_hang.log
-rw-r--r-- 1 db2inst1 db2dadm 16112 Sep 14 11:01 3692.12.000.stack.txt
-rw-r--r-- 1 db2inst1 db2dadm 16238 Sep 14 11:01 3692.11.000.stack.txt
-rw-r--r-- 1 db2inst1 db2dadm 17350 Sep 14 11:01 3692.1.000.stack.txt
```

Figure 5.5: FODC directory structure and files

The DB2 Diagnostic Log File

Earlier, you saw that whenever a significant event occurs, an entry containing diagnostic information about that event is automatically recorded in a file named db2diag.log, which acts as the primary diagnostic log file for DB2. The db2diag.log file is an ASCII-format file made up of diagnostic records generated by the FODC tool and other DB2 engine components. Each record (or entry) in this file contains either information about a particular administrative event that has occurred or specific error information. Entries for administrative events are valuable because they indicate whether events such as backup and restore operations were started and, if so, whether they finished successfully. Entries for error information, however, are useful only when you are trying to diagnose an external symptom, or when the source of a particular error has been isolated and you are looking for more information (for example, an application receives an unexpected SQL code or a database crashes). If a database is behaving normally, informational message entries are not important and can usually be ignored.

Once created, the db2diag.log file grows continuously when you set the diagsize database manager configuration parameter to 0. As a result, the most recent entries are always found near the end of the file. If storage space for this file becomes an issue, you can delete the existing file—a new db2diag.log file will be created automatically the next time one is needed. When you set the diagsize database manager configuration parameter to a nonzero value, the DB2 database manager will create a series of diagnostic log files (also called *rotating diagnostic log files* named db2diag.*N*.log where *N* takes a starting value of 0 plus an auto-increment of 1) in the diagpath database manager configuration parameter location, each file growing until reaching the limited size.

The Administration Notification Log

The administration notification log (instance_name.nfy) is the repository from which you can obtain information about numerous database administration and maintenance activities, including the status of DB2 utilities, client application errors, and storage paths.

One noticeable difference about administration notification log entries as opposed to DB2 diagnostic log entries is the lack of confusing hex dumps. Meaningful, helpful messages that were reviewed and written with the help of real, professional DB2 database administrators (DB2 customers) are provided in their place. Most of these messages present supplemental information for each associated SQL return code value returned to an application or the CLP. Other messages provide notification of unexpected errors or asynchronous events, such as a crash, a signal from the operating system, or a suboptimal configuration. The format of administration notification log entries and DB2 diagnostic log entries are essentially identical. However, all messages written to the administration notification log use the end-user language specified during the installation process (messages written to the DB2 diagnostics log are always in English, regardless of the end-user language used).

As with the DB2 diagnostic log files, the rotation of notification log files arises when the diagsize database manager configuration parameter is set to a nonzero value. If you set diagsize to a nonzero value, that value specifies the combined total size of all rotating administration notification log files and all rotating diagnostic log files contained within the diagnostic data directory. For example, if a system with four database partitions has diagsize set to 1 GB, the maximum total size that the combined active notification and diagnostic logs can reach is 4 GB (4 x 1 GB).

Controlling How Much Information Is Collected

The type (which controls the amount) of administrative and diagnostic information recorded is also controlled by parameters (notifylevel and diaglevel) in a DB2 database manager instance's configuration file. Based on their current value, these parameters tell DB2 what type of administrative and diagnostic information to collect:

- 0: Do not collect administrative information and diagnostic data (not recommended).
- 1: Collect administrative information and diagnostic data for severe (fatal or unrecoverable) errors only.
- 2: Collect administrative information and diagnostic data for all types of errors (both severe and nonsevere) but not for warnings.
- 3: Collect administrative information and diagnostic data for all errors and warnings.
- 4: Collect administrative information and diagnostic data for all errors and warnings, including informational messages and other internal diagnostic information.

When an instance is first created, the notifylevel and diaglevel parameters in a DB2 database manager instance's configuration file are set to 3 by default, and DB2 collects administrative information and diagnostic data for errors and warnings whenever such events occur.

Interpreting the Notification and Diagnostic Log Entries

Every entry in the administration notification log file and the DB2 diagnostic log file begins with a specific set of values that are intended to help identify the particular event to which the entry corresponds. Because this block of information is recorded for all entries and because it is always recorded in a specific format, it is referred to as the *entry header*. Figure 5.6 illustrates how a typical administration notification log entry header looks.

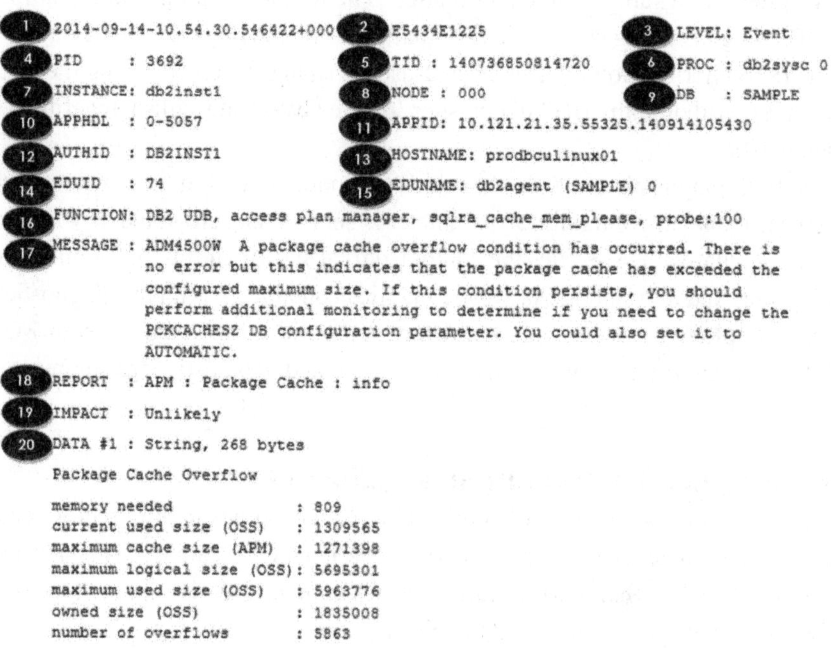

Figure 5.6: Individual components of an administration notification log/DB2 diagnostic log entry header

All entry headers consist of the following components (refer to the numbered bullets in Figure 5.6):

1. A timestamp that identifies when the entry was made
2. The db2diag.log file's record ID—this ID specifies the file offset at which the current message is being logged (for example, in E5434E1225, the file offset is 5434 and the message length is 1225 for the platform where the DB2 diagnostic log was created)
3. The diagnostic level associated with the error message—valid values are Info, Warning, Error, Severe, and Event

4. The unique identifier that the operating system has assigned to the db2sysc process—starting in DB2 9.5, DB2 operates with multiple threads rather than multiple processes in both Windows and UNIX environments; therefore, the process ID provided is usually that of the main DB2 executable
5. The unique identifier that the operating system has assigned to the thread that generated the entry
6. The name of the process that generated the entry
7. The name of the instance that generated the entry
8. The number that corresponds to the node that generated the entry—if you are using a nonpartitioned database, the node number will generally be 000; however, you can specify a nonzero partition number in the db2nodes.cfg file even in a single node partition database
9. The name of the database for which the entry was generated
10. The application handle assigned to the application for which the process that generated the event is working—this value consists of the coordinator partition number followed by the coordinator index number, separated by a dash
11. The unique identifier assigned to the application for which the process that generated the event is working—to find out more about a particular application ID, perform the following tasks:
    a. Use the LIST APPLICATIONS command on a DB2 server or the LIST DCS APPLICATIONS command on a DB2 Connect gateway to obtain a list of application IDs. Search this list for the application ID; once you have found it, you can obtain information about the client experiencing the error, such as its node name and TCP/IP address.
    b. Use the GET SNAPSHOT FOR APPLICATION command to view a list of application IDs.
    c. Use the SYSPROC.MON_GET_CONNECTION table function to view a list of application IDs.
    d. Execute the command db2pd -applications -db [DatabaseName].
12. The authorization ID of the user who was working with the instance or database when the entry was generated
13. The name of the server on which DB2 is running
14. The engine dispatchable unit ID, which you can find by using the command db2pd -edus
15. The name of the engine dispatchable unit
16. The product name DB2 UDB, component name access plan manager, and function name sqlra_cache_mem_pleaset that generated the message as well as the probe point [100] within the function—if the entry was generated by a user application that executed the db2AdminMsgWrite() API, this component of the entry header will read "User

Application"; applications can write messages to the administration notification log file and the DB2 diagnostic log file by invoking the db2AdminMsgWrite() API

To find out more about the type of activity performed by the function that produced the entry, look at the fourth letter of its name; the following shows some of the letters used in the fourth position of DB2 function names, along with the type of activity each function performs:

- **b:** Buffer pool management and manipulation
- **c:** Communications between clients and servers
- **d:** Data management
- **e:** Database engine processes
- **o:** Operating system calls (such as opening and closing files)
- **p:** Data protection (such as locking and logging)
- **r:** Relational database services
- **s:** Sorting operations
- **x:** Indexing operations
- **u:** Utility operations

In the entry in Figure 5.6, the fourth letter of the function named sqlra_cache_mem_pleaset, which is r, indicates that the message was generated by a function that was attempting to perform some type of relational database services operation.

17. A message that describes the event that was logged
18. Indicates the report is generated from the Package Cache application plug-in module
19. The impact level of the record returned—the possible values are NONE, UNLIKELY, POTENTIAL, IMMEDIATE, and CRITICAL
20. Data points from the report in (18)

The db2pdcfg Command

The DB2 problem determination configure (db2pdcfg) command enables you to influence the database system's behavior for problem determination purposes during a DB2 software failure. The basic syntax for the db2pdcfg command is:

```
db2pdcfg <-catch <clear | status | ['ErrorCode']> <-stack> <-db2cos>
<-db2stoptrc> <-lockname= [LockName]> <-locktype=[LockType]> >
<-cos <status | on | off | sleep= [NumSeconds] |    timeout= [NumSeconds] |
   count= [Count] | SQLO_SIG_DUMP>
<-dbmcfg>
                                                              Continued
```

```
<-dbcfg>
<-fodc <status | FODCPATH= [FODCPath] | DUMPCORE= [DumpCoreValue] |
   DUMPDIR = [DumpDirectory] | CORELIMIT = [CoreSize] | SERVICELEVEL= [ServiceValue]>
```

where:

ErrorCode	Identifies any specific SQLCODE, ZRC code, ADM, Deadlock, or Lock timeout error messages to capture, and indicates to invoke a db2cos script to dump out the information for analysis
LockName	Identifies the lock name for catching a specific lock
LockType	Identifies the lock type for catching a specific lock
NumSeconds	Identifies a sleep or wait time in seconds: • **sleep**—this is the amount of time to sleep between checking the size of the output generated by the db2cos script; the default is three seconds • **timeout**—this is the amount of time to wait before assuming the work is completed by the db2cos script; the default is 30 seconds
Count	Identifies the number of iterations to run the db2cos script during a database manager trap; the default value is 255
FODCPath	Identifies the fully qualified path to store the FODC data packages
DumpCoreValues	Identifies the values to enable or disable the operating system core file generation on UNIX systems; the valid values are AUTO, ON, and OFF
DumpDirectory	Identifies the fully qualified path to store the operating system core dump files
CoreSize	Identifies the maximum size of the core files created
ServiceValue	Identifies how to collect data during panics, traps, or specific errors that might indicate data corruption; the valid values are AUTOMATIC, BASIC, and FULL

As you can see, many options are available to customize your problem determination requirement by using the db2pdcfg command (a few examples follow).

To capture the information during any deadlock situation, set the catch flag to do so by executing this command:

```
db2pdcfg -catch -911, 2
Error Catch #2
   Sqlcode:         -911
```

Continued

```
    ReasonCode:      2
    ADMCode:         0
    DiagText:
    ZRC:             0
    ECF:             0
    Component ID:    0
    LockName:        Not Set
    LockType:        Not Set
    Current Count:   0
    Max Count:       255
    Bitmap:          0x661
    Action:          Error code catch flag enabled
    Action:          Execute /home/db2inst1/sqllib/adm/db2cos callout script
    Action:          Produce stack trace in db2diag.log
```

The error catch number shows that the number of catch flags is set, and the action shows how to invoke the db2cos command upon a database trap or an error.

If you want to display all the catch flags, execute the db2pdcfg command with no additional parameters:

```
db2pdcfg
Current PD Control Block Settings:

Error Catch #1
    Sqlcode:         -32479
    ReasonCode:      0
    ADMCode:         0
    DiagText:
    ZRC:             0
    ECF:             0
    Component ID:    0
    LockName:        Not Set
    LockType:        Not Set
    Current Count:   0
```

Continued

```
   Max Count:       255
   Bitmap:          0x461
   Action:          Error code catch flag enabled
   Action:          Execute /home/db2inst1/sqllib/adm/db2cos callout script
   Action:          Produce stack trace in db2diag.log
Error Catch #2
   Sqlcode:         -911
   ReasonCode:      2
   ADMCode:         0
   DiagText:
   ZRC:             0
   ECF:             0
   Component ID:    0
   LockName:        Not Set
   LockType:        Not Set
   Current Count:   0
   Max Count:       255
   Bitmap:          0x661
   Action:          Error code catch flag enabled
   Action:          Execute /home/db2inst1/sqllib/adm/db2cos callout script
   Action:          Produce stack trace in db2diag.log

db2cos is enabled for engine traps.
   PD Bitmap:       0x1800
   Sleep Time:      3
   Timeout:         300
   Current Count:   0
   Max Count:       255

Current bitmap value:  0x0

Instance is not in a sleep state

DB2 trap resilience is enabled.
```

Continued

```
    Current threshold setting :  0 ( disabled )
    Number of traps sustained : 0

Database Member 0

 FODC (First Occurrence Data Capture) options:
    Dump directory for large objects (DUMPDIR)= /home/db2inst1/sqllib/db-
2dump/DIAG0000/
    Service level (SERVICELEVEL)= AUTOMATIC (Effective: FULL)
    Dump Core files (DUMPCORE)= AUTO (Effective: ON)
    Current hard core file size limit = Unlimited
    Current soft core file size limit = Unlimited

EDU stats not available.
```

The db2bfd Command

You can use the DB2 bind file description tool to examine and verify the SQL statements within a bind file, as well as to display the precompile options used to create the bind file. To invoke the DB2 bind file description tool, execute the db2bfd command. The syntax for this command is:

```
db2bfd <-b> <-s> <-v> <-h> [BindFileName]
```

where:

BindFileName Identifies, by name, the bind file whose contents are to be retrieved and displayed

Table 5.20 describes all options shown with this command.

Table 5.20: db2bfd command options

Option	Meaning
-b	Specifies to display the bind file header
-s	Specifies to display the SQL statements in the bind file
-v	Specifies to display host variable declarations in the bind file
-h	Displays help information; specifying this option will ignore all other options and will display only the help information

Thus, if you want to see the contents of a bind file named db2cli.bnd, execute a db2bfd command that looks something like this:

```
db2bfd -b -s -v db2cli.bnd
```

And when you execute this command, the information returned will look something like this:

```
db2cli.bnd:  Header Contents

Header Fields:

Field           Value
-----           -----
releaseNum      0x800
Endian          0x4c
numHvars        3
maxSect         0
numStmt         4
optInternalCnt  4
optCount        9


Name                  Value
------------------    -----
Isolation Level       Cursor Stability
Creator               "NEWTON  "
App Name              "DB2CLI  "
Timestamp             "VAvBPXBc:2012/01/23 15:01:47:21"
Cnulreqd              Yes
Sql Error             No package
Validate              Bind
Date                  Default/local
Time                  Default/local

                                                   Continued
```

```
** All other options are using default settings as specified by the server
**



db2cli.bnd:  SQL Statements = 4

Line Sec Typ Var Len SQL statement text
---- --- --- --- --- ---------------------------------------------------
  11   0   5   0  21 BEGIN DECLARE SECTION
  15   0   2   0  19 END DECLARE SECTION
 104   0  19   1  19 CONNECT TO :H00001
 107   0  19   0  13 CONNECT RESET

db2cli.bnd: Host Variables = 3

Type SQL Data Type      Length Alias  Name_Len Name           UDT Name
---- --------------     ------ ------ -------- -------------- --------
 460 C STRING              129 H00001        7 dbAlias
 460 C STRING              129 H00002        4 user
 460 C STRING              129 H00003        4 pswd
```

The db2val Command

Sometimes you may have to recheck the previously installed DB2 files and instance setup during the troubleshooting process. You can use the DB2 validation (db2val) command to validate the current state of installation files, instance setup, database, and local connections. The basic syntax for db2val command is:

```
db2val  <-o> <-i [InstanceName]> | <-a> <-b [DBName]>
        <-t [TraceFile]> <-d> <-s> <-l [LogFile]>
```

where:

InstanceName Identifies the name of the instance to validate

DBName	Identifies the name of the database to validate
TraceFile	Identifies the fully qualified file name for the trace; this is valid only on UNIX systems
LogFile	Identifies the fully qualified file name to record the validation process and the result

If you want to validate the root installed instance db2inst1 and the database SAMPLE, run the command by using the root user on UNIX system, something like this:

```
db2val  -i db2inst1 -b sample

DBI1379I  The db2val command is running. This can take several minutes.
DBI1335I  Installation file validation for the DB2 copy installed at
      /opt/ibm/db2/V10.1 was successful.
DBI1339I  The instance validation for the instance db2inst1 was
      successful.
DBI1340I  Database validation for instance db2inst1 was successful.
DBI1343I  The db2val command completed successfully. For details, see
      the log file /tmp/db2val-140915_083319.log.
```

The validation result file will look like this:

```
Installation file validation for the DB2 copy installed at "/opt/ibm/db2/
V10.1" starts.

Task 1: Validating Installation file sets.
Status 1 : Success

Task 2: Validating embedded runtime path for DB2 executables and libraries.
Status 2 : Success

Task 3: Validating the accessibility to the installation path.
Status 3 : Success
```

Continued

```
Task 4: Validating the accessibility to the /etc/services file.
Status 4 : Success

DBI1335I  Installation file validation for the DB2 copy installed at
      /opt/ibm/db2/V10.1 was successful.

Installation file validation for the DB2 copy installed at "/opt/ibm/db2/
V10.1" ends.

Instance validation for "db2inst1" starts.

Task 5: Validating symbolic links in the instance directory.
Status 5 : Success

Task 6: Validating instance file ownership and permission.
Status 6 : Success

Task 7: Validating the accessibility to the /etc/services file.
Status 7 : Success

DBI1339I  The instance validation for the instance edwetld was successful.

Instance validation for "db2inst1" ends.

Database validation for instance "db2inst1" starts.

Task 8: Validating database connections using CLP command.

   Database Connection Information

 Database server        = DB2/LINUXX8664 10.1.3
 SQL authorization ID   = DB2INST1
 Local database alias   = SAMPLE

                                                              Continued
```

```
Status 8 : Success

DBI1340I  Database validation for instance db2inst1 was successful.

Database validation for instance "db2inst1" ends.

DBI1343I  The db2val command completed successfully. For details, see
      the log file /tmp/db2val-140915_083319.log.
```

The db2mtrk Command

The DB2 memory tracker utility produces a complete report of memory status for instances, databases, and agents. This utility provides the following information about memory pool allocation:

- Current size
- Maximum size (hard limit)
- Largest size (high watermark)
- Type (identifier indicating function for which memory will be used)
- Agent who allocated pool (only if the pool is private)

You invoke the DB2 memory tracker by executing the db2mtrk command. The syntax for this command is:

```
db2mtrk
<-i>
<-d>
<-a>
<-p <-m | -w>>
<-r [Interval] <Count>>
<-v>
<-h>
```

where:

Interval	Identifies the number of seconds to wait between subsequent calls to the DB2 memory tracker
Count	Identifies the number of times to repeat calls to the DB2 memory tracker

Table 5.21 describes all the other db2mtrk command options.

Table 5.21: db2mtrk command options	
Option	**Meaning**
-i	Specifies to collect and display information about instance-level memory
-d	Specifies to collect and display information about database-level memory
-a	Specifies to collect and display information about application-level memory
-p	Specifies to collect and display information about private memory
-m	Specifies to collect and display maximum values for each memory pool
-w	Specifies to collect and display a high watermark value for each memory pool
-v	Specifies to return verbose output
-h	Displays help information; specifying this option will ignore all other options and will display only the help information

Thus, if you want to see how memory is used by the instance and all the active databases on a system, execute a db2mtrk command similar to the following:

```
db2mtrk -i -d -v
```

Assuming a database named SAMPLE is active at the time you issue the db2mtrk command, the results produced should look something like this:

```
Tracking Memory on: 2014/09/15 at 09:12:09

Memory for instance

   Other Memory is of size 105316352 bytes
   FCMBP Heap is of size 851968 bytes
   Database Monitor Heap is of size 13959168 bytes
   Total: 120127488 bytes

Memory for database: SAMPLE

   Backup/Restore/Util Heap is of size 131072 bytes
   Package Cache is of size 1835008 bytes
```

Continued

```
Other Memory is of size 327680 bytes
Catalog Cache Heap is of size 1245184 bytes
Buffer Pool Heap (1) is of size 8781824 bytes
Buffer Pool Heap (System 32k buffer pool) is of size 851968 bytes
Buffer Pool Heap (System 16k buffer pool) is of size 589824 bytes
Buffer Pool Heap (System 8k buffer pool) is of size 458752 bytes
Buffer Pool Heap (System 4k buffer pool) is of size 393216 bytes
Shared Sort Heap is of size 65536 bytes
Lock Manager Heap is of size 17629184 bytes
Database Heap is of size 54067200 bytes
Application Heap (28) is of size 65536 bytes
Application Heap (27) is of size 65536 bytes
Application Heap (26) is of size 65536 bytes
Application Heap (25) is of size 65536 bytes
Application Heap (24) is of size 65536 bytes
Application Heap (23) is of size 65536 bytes
Application Heap (22) is of size 65536 bytes
Application Heap (21) is of size 65536 bytes
Application Heap (20) is of size 65536 bytes
Application Heap (19) is of size 65536 bytes
Application Heap (18) is of size 65536 bytes
Application Heap (17) is of size 65536 bytes
Application Heap (16) is of size 65536 bytes
Application Heap (15) is of size 65536 bytes
Application Heap (14) is of size 65536 bytes
Application Heap (13) is of size 65536 bytes
Application Heap (12) is of size 65536 bytes
Application Heap (11) is of size 196608 bytes
Application Heap (10) is of size 65536 bytes
Application Heap (9) is of size 65536 bytes
Application Heap (8) is of size 65536 bytes
Applications Shared Heap is of size 3407872 bytes
Total: 91291648 bytes
```

You can also use the Perl script to extract the total memory utilization by using something similar to the following:

```
db2mtrk -i -d -v | egrep '^Memory|Total:' |perl -ane 'BEGIN {$sum=0;}
$sum+=$1
if (/Total: (\d+) /); END {print "Total: ${sum}\n"; };'
Total: 211419136
```

The db2pd Command

You use the DB2 problem determination tool to obtain quick and immediate information from the DB2 database system memory sets, without acquiring any latches. Two benefits to collecting information without latching include faster data retrieval and no competition for engine resources. However, because the DB2 problem determination tool works directly with memory, it is possible to retrieve information that is changing as it is being collected; hence, the data retrieved might not be completely accurate. (A signal handler prevents the DB2 problem determination tool from aborting abnormally when changing memory pointers are encountered. However, this can result in messages such as "Changing data structure forced command termination" to appear in the output.) Nonetheless, this tool can be extremely helpful for problem determination.

You invoke the DB2 problem determination tool by executing the db2pd command. The basic syntax for this command is:

```
db2pd
<- version | -v >
<-inst>
<[-database | -db] [DatabaseName] ,...>
<-alldatabases | -alldbs>
<-full>
<-everything>
<-hadr [-db [DatabaseName] | -alldbs]>
<-utilities>
<-applications [-db [DatabaseName] | -alldbs]>
<-agents>
<-transactions [-db [DatabaseName] | -alldbs]>
<-bufferpools [-db [DatabaseName] | -alldbs]>
<-logs [-db [DatabaseName] | -alldbs]>
                                                    Continued
```

```
<-tablespaces [-db [DatabaseName] | -alldbs]>
<-dynamic [-db [DatabaseName] | -alldbs]>
<-static [-db [DatabaseName] | -alldbs]>
<-fcm>
<-memsets>
<-mempools>
<-memblocks>
<-dbmcfg>
<-dbcfg [-db [DatabaseName] | -alldbs]>
<-catalogcache [-db [DatabaseName] | -alldbs]>
<-tcbstats [-db [DatabaseName] | -alldbs]>
<-reorg [-db [DatabaseName] | -alldbs]>
<-recovery [-db [DatabaseName] | -alldbs]>
<-reopt [-db [DatabaseName] | -alldbs]>
<-osinfo>
<-storagepaths [-db [DatabaseName] | -alldbs]>
<-pages [-db [DatabaseName] | -alldbs]>
<-stack [all | [ProcessID]]>
<-repeat [Interval] <[Count]>>
<-command [CmdFileName]>
<-file [OutFileName]>
<-interactive>
<-h | -help>
```

where:

DatabaseName	Identifies, by name, the database with which the DB2 problem determination tool is to interact
ProcessID	Identifies the process, by ID, for which to produce a stack trace file
Interval	Identifies the number of seconds to wait between subsequent calls to the DB2 problem determination tool
Count	Identifies the number of time to repeat calls to the DB2 problem determination tool
CmdFileName	Identifies the name to assign to an ASCII-format file that contains the DB2 problem determination tool command options to use
OutFile	Identifies the name of the file to which to write information returned by the DB2 problem determination tool

Table 5.22 describes all the other db2pd command options.

Table 5.22: db2pd command options	
Option	**Meaning**
-version | -v	Specifies to collect and display the current version and service level of the installed DB2 product
-inst	Specifies to collect and display all instance-level information available
-alldatabases | -alldbs	Specifies that the utility is to attach to all memory sets of all available databases
-full	Specifies to expand all output to its maximum length (not specifying this option will truncate output to save space on the display)
-everything	Specifies to use all options and to collect and display information for all databases on all database partition servers that are local to the server
-hadr	Specifies to collect and display information about HADR
-utilities	Specifies to collect and display information about utilities
-applications	Specifies to collect and display information about applications
-agents	Specifies to collect and display information about agents
-transactions	Specifies to collect and display information about active transactions
-bufferpools	Specifies to collect and display information about buffer pools
-logs	Specifies to collect and display information about transaction log files
-locks	Specifies to collect and display information about locks
-tablespaces	Specifies to collect and display information about table spaces
-dynamic	Specifies to collect and display information about the execution of dynamic SQL statements
-static	Specifies to collect and display information about the execution of static SQL and packages
-fcm	Specifies to collect and display information about the fast communication manager
-memsets	Specifies to collect and display information about memory sets
-mempools	Specifies to collect and display information about memory pools
-memblocks	Specifies to collect and display information about memory blocks
-dbmcfg	Specifies to collect and display information about current DB2 database manager configuration parameter settings
-dbcfg	Specifies to collect and display information about current database configuration parameter settings
-catalogcache	Specifies to collect and display information about the catalog cache
-tcbstats	Specifies to collect and display information about tables and indexes
-reorg	Specifies to collect and display information about table and data partition reorganization
-recovery	Specifies to collect and display information about recovery activity
-reopt	Specifies to collect and display information about cached SQL statements that were reoptimized by using the REOPT ONCE option
-osinfo	Specifies to collect and display operating system information

Option	Meaning
-storagepaths	Specifies to collect and display information about the automatic storage paths defined for the database
-pages	Specifies to collect and display information about buffer pool pages
-stack	Specifies to collect and display stack trace information
-repeat	Specifies to repeat the command after the specified number of seconds for the specified number of times
-command	Specifies to execute db2pd commands that are stored in the specified file
-file	Specifies to write all information collected to the specified file
-interactive	Specifies to override values indicated for the DB2PDOPT environment variable when running the db2pd command
-help | -h	Displays help information; specifying this option will ignore all other options and will display only the help information

Table 5.22: db2pd command options (continued)

So if you want to determine which indexes are actually being used in the table S_PROD_BASELINE (table ID 5, table space ID 2) for accessing data in a database named SAMPLE, execute a db2pd command that looks something like this:

```
db2pd -db sample -tcbstats index 2 5

Database Member 0 -- Database SAMPLE -- Active -- Up 15 days 14:00:11 --
Date 2014-09-16-07.24.33.638978

TCB Table Information:
Address            TbspaceID TableID PartID MasterTbs MasterTab TableName
0x07800004721F2A80 2         5       n/a    18        5         S_PROD_BASELINE

SchemaNm ObjClass DataSize LfSize LobSize XMLSize
DB210    Perm     156627   0      0       0

TCB Table Stats:
Address            TableName       Scans UDI    PgReorgs NoChgUpdts Reads
0x07800004721F2A80 S_PROD_BASELINE 1     291673 950371   0          1378125598

                                                                  Continued
```

```
FscrUpdates Inserts Updates Deletes OvFlReads OvFlCrtes
416397      95760   4385694 6913    3700961   7366

TCB Index Stats:
Address            TableName        IID EmpPgDel RootSplits BndrySplts PseuEmptPg
0x07800004721FB6C0 S_PROD_BASELINE 1   0        0          0          0
0x07800004721FB6C0 S_PROD_BASELINE 6   0        0          0          0
0x07800004721FB6C0 S_PROD_BASELINE 3   0        0          0          0
0x07800004721FB6C0 S_PROD_BASELINE 4   0        0          0          0
0x07800004721FB6C0 S_PROD_BASELINE 2   2964     0          3152       3158
0x07800004721FB6C0 S_PROD_BASELINE 5   0        0          0          0

Scans   KeyUpdates InclUpdats NonBndSpts PgAllocs Merges PseuDels DelClean IntNodSpl
438543  4385694    0          6013       5698     0      4392508  4188968  26
0       0          0          30         28       0      1829     379      0
0       0          0          30         29       0      1829     379      0
0       0          0          30         29       0      1829     379      0
2875    4378773    0          118        667      0      4385587  3885573  1
6361255 0          0          192        184      0      6913     4119     1
```

The above output illustrates that the index ID 1 has been used 438,543 times and that index ID 6 has never been put into a data access plan. You can use this information to determine which indexes are unused.

To find out how many pages have been written to the transaction log files associated with a database named SAMPLE, execute a db2pd command that looks something like this:

```
db2pd -logs -db sample

Database Member 0 -- Database SAMPLE -- Active -- Up 15 days 14:01:41 --
Date 2014-09-16-07.26.03.639720

Logs:
Current Log Number            1382
Pages Written                 63
                                                          Continued
```

```
Cur Commit Disk Log Reads     0
Cur Commit Total Log Reads    0
Method 1 Archive Status       Success
Method 1 Next Log to Archive  1382
Method 1 First Failure        n/a
Method 2 Archive Status       n/a
Method 2 Next Log to Archive  n/a
Method 2 First Failure        n/a
Log Chain ID                  0
Current LSO                   5784101020
Current LSN                   0x000000000957096

Address            StartLSN         StartLSO   State      Size Pages Filename
0x00007FFFC568ACF8 00000000095670B 5779768001 0x00000000 1000 1000  S0001381.LOG
0x00007FFFC560BE18 0000000000956FF7 5783844001 0x00000000 1000 1000  S0001382.LOG
0x00007FFFC52987D8 0000000000000000 5787920001 0x00000000 1000 1000  S0001383.LOG
0x00007FFFC55DF2F8 0000000000000000 5791996001 0x00000000 1000 1000  S0001384.LOG
0x00007FFFC5598258 0000000000000000 5796072001 0x00000000 1000 1000  S0001385.LOG
```

If you want to know the fenced user ID for an instance, which is necessary during the instance migration activity, run a command similar to the following:

```
db2pd -fmp | grep -i fenced
Trusted Path:    /home/db2inst1/sqllib/function/unfenced
Fenced User:     db2fenc
```

To capture detailed information about all currently running transactions on the server, run the following command:

```
db2pd -db sample -transactions
```

The db2top Command

The DB2 monitoring (db2top) command is a built-in monitoring utility available within DB2 on Linux and AIX platforms. This is a very handy tool for viewing real-time monitoring data on the system. You invoke it by calling the db2top command in an interactive or in a batch mode. The basic syntax for the command is:

```
db2top
<-d [DBName]> <-n [NodeName]> <-V [ExplainSchema]> <-I [Interval]>
<-P [Member]> <-A> <-a> <-B> <-R> <-k> <-x> <-f [ReplayFile]>
<-b [BackgroundMode] <-s [MaxSamples]> <-D [Delimiter]>>
<-o [OutputFile]> <-C> <-m [Duration]> <-h >
```

where:

DBName	Identifies, by name, the database with which the db2top tool is to interact
NodeName	Identifies the logical partition number with which the db2top tool is to interact
ExplainSchema	Identifies the schema name for the default explain tables
Interval	Identifies the delay between the screen refreshes and is set in seconds
Member	Identifies the database partition number on which to issue the snapshot commands
ReplayFile	Identifies the snapshot collector file to use to run db2top in replay mode
BackgroundMode	Identifies the background mode options to run the db2top command; the valid options include d for database, l for sessions, t table spaces, b for buffer pools, T for tables, D for dynamic SQL statements, s for all the SQL statements, U for locks, u for utilities, F for federation, and m for memory pools
MaxSamples	Identifies the number of samples to capture while running the command in the background mode
Delimiter	Identifies the field delimiter while capturing data in the background mode
OutputFile	Identifies the output file name to record the information in the background mode
Duration	Identifies the duration in minutes to run the command in the background mode

To invoke the tool in an interactive mode on the SAMPLE database, execute a command similar to the following (Figure 5.7 shows the db2top interactive mode screen):

```
db2top -d sample
```

```
[-]20:33:10,refresh=2secs(0.001)
[d=Y,a=N,e=N,p=ALL]

######  ######   #####  ####### ####### ######   For help type h or ...
#     # #     # #     #    #       #    #     #  db2top -h: usage
#     # #     #       #    #       #    #     #
#     # ######   #####     #       #    # ######   Status: Active
#     # #     # #          #       #    # #        Uptime: 16d 03h:08m:48s
#     # #     # #          #       #    # #        Last backup
######  ######  #######    #       ####### #        2014/09/14 - 19:00:03

DB2 Interactive Snapshot Monitor V2.0
Use these keys to navigate:
d - Database              l - Sessions              a - Agent
t - Tablespaces           b - Bufferpools           T - Tables
D - Dynamic SQL           U - Locks                 m - Memory
s - Statements            p - Members               u - Utilities
A - HADR                  F - Federation            B - Bottlenecks
J - Skew monitor          q - Quit
```

Figure 5.7: db2top interactive mode screen

You can interactively select the appropriate option to view the monitoring data during the troubleshooting process. Click **h** to view the help at any point during the analysis.

If you want to run the command in the batch mode to collect the monitoring data in a file named db2top.collect.file for five minutes at five-seconds interval, execute a command similar to the following:

```
db2top -d sample -f db2top.collect.file -C -m 5 -i 5
[21:51:20] Starting DB2 snapshot data collector, collection every 5
second(s),
max duration 5 minute(s), max file growth/hour 500.0M, hit <CTRL+C> to can-
cel...
[21:51:20] Overridding previous occurence of 'db2top.collect.file'
[21:51:55] 1.1M written, time 35.037, 115.6M/hour
[21:52:30] 2.2M written, time 70.075, 115.6M/hour
[21:53:10] 3.5M written, time 110.116, 115.6M/hour
[21:53:55] 4.9M written, time 155.163, 115.6M/hour
[21:54:45] 6.5M written, time 205.214, 115.7M/hour
[21:55:40] 8.3M written, time 260.272, 115.7M/hour
[21:56:25] Max duration reached, 9.8M bytes, time was 305.319...
```

Continued

```
[21:56:25] Snapshot data collection stored in 'db2top.collect.file'
Exiting...
```

After collecting the data, if you want to play back the monitor data in analyze mode for dynamic SQL statements, you can do so by executing this command:

```
db2top -d sample -f db2top.collect.file  -b D -A

Analyzing objects doing the most 'SQL_Statement_HashValue' in function 'SQL'

*** End of input stream reached, size was 10279642...

--
-- Top twenty performance report for 'SQL' between 21:51:30 and 21:56:20
-- Sort criteria 'SQL_Statement_HashValue'
--

Rank Sql_Statement (first 30 char.) Percentage fromTime toTime   sum(SQL_Statement_HashValue)
---- ------------------------------ ---------- -------- -------- ----------------------------
   1 SET CURRENT LOCK TIMEOUT 5        1.1273% 21:51:30 21:56:20 9223372036854775749
   2 SET QUERY PATROLLER BYPASS = '    1.1215% 21:51:30 21:56:20 2950522435596591902
   3 SELECT POLICY FROM SYSTOOLS.PO    0.8018% 21:51:30 21:56:20 4189489065650141624

--
-- Performance report, breakdown by 300 seconds
--

fromTime sum(SQL_Statement_HashValue) Percentage Top Five in 300 seconds interval
-------- ---------------------------- ---------- +----------------------------
21:51:30         16363383538101509275    0.7960% |Rank|Percentage|Sql_Statement (first 30 char.)      |
                                    -          - |   1|   1.1273%|SET CURRENT LOCK TIMEOUT 5          |
                                    -          - |   2|   1.1215%|SET QUERY PATROLLER BYPASS = 'TRUE' |
                                    -          - |   3|   0.8018%|SELECT POLICY FROM SYSTOOLS.POLICY W|
                                                 +-------------------------------------------+
                                                                                   Continued
```

```
--
-- Performance report, breakdown by 0.5 hour
--

fromTime   sum(SQL_Statement_HashValue) Percentage Top Five in 0.5 hour interval
-------- ----------------------------- ---------- +-----------------------------------
21:51:30          16363383538101509275    0.7960% |Rank|Percentage|Sql_Statement (first 30 char.)    |
                                     -          - |   1|   1.1273%|SET CURRENT LOCK TIMEOUT 5         |
                                     -          - |   2|   1.1215%|SET QUERY PATROLLER BYPASS = 'TRUE|
                                     -          - |   3|   0.8018%|SELECT POLICY FROM SYSTOOLS.POLICY|
                                                      +------------------------------------------+
Exiting...
```

By default, db2top allows 100 MB data collection size per hour, and you can add a "streamsize" variable entry in the .db2toprc configuration file to increase the limit to 500 MB, as the following example shows. Various parameters are available to fine-tune the data collection, including colors, graphic, sessions order, and user-defined commands:

```
streamsize=500M
```

The db2trc Command

Sometimes, you may be asked to take a trace to analyze a recurring and reproducible problem. It is recommended to enable trace only when it is directed by a DB2 technical support representative; otherwise, turn off the trace to avoid any performance problems on the system. The DB2 trace works in two different stages. During stage 1, it collects information, and in stage 2, it parses the information into a readable format. The basic steps to capture a DB2 trace are as follows:

Step 1: Turn on DB2 trace to collect the information, and specify an 8 MB file limit:

```
db2trc on -l 8M -f db2trace.stage1.out
Trace is turned on
```

Step 2: Re-create the problem.

Step 3: Dump the information into a binary file:

```
db2trc dmp db2trace.dmp
Trace has been dumped to file "db2trace.dmp"
```

Step 4: Turn off the DB2 trace:

```
db2trc off
Trace is turned off
```

Step 5: Format the trace dump file into a text file and order it by the process or the thread:

```
db2trc fmt db2trace.dmp db2trace.fmt
Trace truncated                    : NO
Trace wrapped                      : YES
Total number of trace records      : 496
Number of trace records formatted : 496
```

The formatted file looks something like this:

```
<db2trc_header>
Marker                   :  @TRACE@
Trace version            :      7.0
Platform                 : Linux/X8664
Build level              : s130918
maxBufferSize            : 33554432 bytes (32 MB)
auxBufferSize            : 0 bytes (0 MB)
allocationCount          : 2
DB2TRCD pid              : 25073
Trace destination        : db2trace.stage1.out
...
</db2trc_header>
1       entry DB2 UDB buffer pool services sqlbClnrWritePages fnc (1.3.2.468.0)
        pid 3692 tid 140736972449536 cpid 24094 node 0
                                                                     Continued
```

```
        eduid 34 eduname db2pclnr
...
496     entry DB2 UDB oper system services sqloWaitEDUWaitPost cei (1.3.15.851.2)
        pid 3692 tid 140736867591936 cpid 24094 node 0
        eduid 59 eduname db2agent
        bytes 228

        Data1   (PD_TYPE_PTR,8) Pointer:
        0x00000002064affa0
        Data2   (PD_TYPE_SQLO_EDUWAITPOST,32) edu waitpost:
```

Step 6: Format the trace dump file into a text file and order it by the sequential flow:

```
db2trc flw db2trace.dmp db2trace.flw
Total number of trace records     : 496
Trace truncated                   : NO
Trace wrapped                     : YES
Number of trace records formatted : 41 (pid: 3692 tid 140736972449536 node: 0)
Number of trace records formatted : 36 (pid: 3692 tid 140736930506496 node: 0)
Number of trace records formatted : 36 (pid: 3692 tid 140736875980544 node: 0)
Number of trace records formatted : 36 (pid: 3692 tid 140736938895104 node: 0)
Number of trace records formatted : 36 (pid: 3692 tid 140736943089408 node: 0)
Number of trace records formatted : 14 (pid: 3692 tid 140737052141312 node: 0)
Number of trace records formatted : 9 (pid: 3692 tid 140737056335616 node: 0)
Number of trace records formatted : 54 (pid: 3692 tid 140736985032448 node: 0)
Number of trace records formatted : 54 (pid: 3692 tid 140736980838144 node: 0)
Number of trace records formatted : 54 (pid: 3692 tid 140736976643840 node: 0)
Number of trace records formatted : 27 (pid: 3692 tid 140736993421056 node: 0)
Number of trace records formatted : 54 (pid: 3692 tid 140736989226752 node: 0)
Number of trace records formatted : 11 (pid: 3692 tid 140737001809664 node: 0)
Number of trace records formatted : 8 (pid: 3692 tid 140737010198272 node: 0)
Number of trace records formatted : 22 (pid: 3692 tid 140737006003968 node: 0)
Number of trace records formatted : 4 (pid: 3692 tid 140736867591936 node: 0)
```

The Inspect Command

The inspect command checks the architectural integrity and page consistency within the database. This is a very useful command when it comes to validating the structures of tables and table spaces without taking the database offline. You can perform a check against the whole database, a table space, or a table.

If you want to inspect your database, you can do so by executing commands similar to the following:

```
CONNECT TO sample

   Database Connection Information

 Database server        = DB2/LINUXX8664 10.1.3
 SQL authorization ID   = DB2INST1
 Local database alias   = SAMPLE

INSPECT CHECK DATABASE RESULTS KEEP db_inspect.out
DB20000I  The INSPECT command completed successfully.
```

By default, the inspect command output is stored in the directory $HOME/sqllib/db2dump, where $HOME is the home directory of the instance owner. However, this can be controlled by the value of the diagpath or alt_diagpath parameter of a DB2 database manager instance's configuration file.

You will have to format the inspect command output file to make it human readable by using the db2inspf utility:

```
db2inspf db_inspect.out db_inspect.results.out
```

A sample result output looks something like this:

```
DATABASE: SAMPLE
VERSION : SQL10013
2014-09-17-11.55.33.578920

```

Continued

```
Action: CHECK DATABASE
Result file name: db_inspect.out

Database phase start.

  Storage Group file inspection phase start.
   Inspecting Storage Group ID: 0
  Storage Group file inspection phase end.

  Tablespace phase start. Tablespace ID: 0
   Tablespace name: SYSCATSPACE
   Tablespace Type: DMS - Database Managed Space; Extent size: 4; Page size: 8192;
   Number of containers: 1
...
    Table phase start (ID Signed: 6, Unsigned: 6; Tablespace ID: 0) :

      Data phase start. Object: 6  Tablespace: 0
      The index type is 2 for this table.
       Traversing DAT extent map, anchor 44.
       Extent map traversal complete.
       DAT Object Summary: Total Pages 263 - Used Pages 263 - Free Space 1 %
      Data phase end.

      Index phase start. Object: 6  Tablespace: 0
       Traversing INX extent map, anchor 176.
       Extent map traversal complete.
       INX Object Summary: Total Pages 139 - Used Pages 139
      Index phase end.

      LOB phase start. Object: 6  Tablespace: 0
       Traversing LOB extent map, anchor 52.
       Extent map traversal complete.
```

Continued

```
        Traversing LBA extent map, anchor 60.
        Extent map traversal complete.
        LOB Object Summary: Total Pages 0 - Used Pages 0
        LBA Object Summary: Total Pages 1 - Used Pages 0
       LOB phase end.
    Table phase end.
...
    Table phase start (ID Signed: 24, Unsigned: 24; Tablespace ID: 5) :

       Data phase start. Object: 24  Tablespace: 5
        Traversing DAT extent map, anchor 528.
        Extent map traversal complete.
        DAT Object Summary: Total Pages 1 - Used Pages 0 - Free Space 84 %
       Data phase end.
    Table phase end.
  Tablespace phase end.

  Tablespace phase start. Tablespace ID: 6
   Tablespace name: SYSTOOLSTMPSPACE
   Tablespace Type: SMS - System Managed Space; Extent size: 4; Page size: 8192;
   Number of containers: 1
   Container name: /home/db2inst1/db2inst1/NODE0000/SAMPLE/T0000006/C0000000.UTM
  The tablespace with ID 6 is of type temporary
  Tablespace phase end.
Database phase end.
Processing has completed. 2014-09-17-11.55.40.417505
```

The db2dart Command

You can use the DB2 database analysis and reporting tool to verify the architectural correctness of the database and the objects within it. You can also use this tool to exhibit the database control files' contents in order to extract the data from tables that might otherwise be inaccessible due to page-level corruptions. Unlike the inspect command, db2dart should be run only against a database having no connections because the command reads database data directly from disk. If the database has active connections, db2dart will not be aware of any changes made to the data pages and the control structures that are available in real memory, resulting in an inaccurate report, as the following example illustrates:

```
db2dart sample

FYI: An active connection to the database has been detected.
     False errors may be reported.
     Deactivate all connections and re-run to verify.

Warning: The database state is not consistent.
         False errors may be reported.

Warning: Errors reported about reorg rows may be due to the inconsistent
state of
the database.
                      DB2DART Processing completed with error!
                    Complete DB2DART report found in: SAMPLE.RPT
```

When you run the same command against a database with no active connections, the report will look something like this:

```
db2dart sample

         The requested DB2DART processing has completed successfully!
                  Complete DB2DART report found in: SAMPLE.RPT
```

The db2dart report is stored in the directory $HOME/sqllib/db2dump/DARTxxxx, where $HOME is the home directory of the instance owner. However, this can be controlled by the value of the diagpath or alt_diagpath parameter of a DB2 database manager instance's configuration file.

If you want to analyze only one table space, use a command something like the following instead of analyzing the entire database:

```
db2dart sample /ts /tsi 3
```

Similarly, if you want to analyze a table, you can execute this command:

```
db2dart sample /ts /tsi 3 /oi 10
```

To dump formatted table data in delimited ASCII format, use the command in this example:

```
db2dart sample /ddel
```

The db2support Tool

The db2support problem analysis and environment collection tool is a very handy command for extracting all diagnostic information, including db2diag.log, the notification log, trap files, lock list files, dump files, application snapshots, ODBC data sources, event monitors, getsadata, and various operating system command outputs. The basic command invocation is:

```
db2support . -d sample
```

The DB2 technical representative will generally supply db2support command options to collect a specific set of details for problem determination and troubleshooting.

Chapter Summary

The objective of this chapter was to familiarize you with

- The snapshot monitors switches and the monitoring elements
- The DB2 monitoring table functions to collect and view data for systems, activities, and data objects
- The DB2 administrative views and the use cases to capture a specific set of information, including buffer pool hit ratio, lock-wait chains, and so on
- The DB2 event monitors to record information about database activity when an event or a transition occurs
- The DB2 Explain facility to capture and view detailed information about the access plan chosen for a particular SQL statement
- Various DB2 troubleshooting tools, including FODC, db2pd, and db2pdcfg

On completion of this chapter, you will be equipped with sufficient knowledge to answer the DB2 monitoring questions in the certification exam. It is also highly recommended to complete the sample questions available at the end of the chapter.

Practice Questions

Question 1

A user issues the following commands:

```
UPDATE DBM CFG USING DFT_MON_SORT ON;
UPDATE MONITOR SWITCHES USING UOW ON;
UPDATE DBM CFG USING DFT_MON_TIMESTAMP ON;
UPDATE MONITOR SWITCHES USING BUFFERPOOL ON;
```

Assuming no other monitor switches have been set, if the DB2 instance is stopped and restarted, which of the following database monitor switches will be set?

❍ A. SORT, UOW
❍ B. UOW, BUFFERPOOL
❍ C. SORT, TIMESTAMP
❍ D. TIMESTAMP, BUFFERPOOL

Question 2

Which query can you use to obtain information about how buffer pools defined for a database named SAMPLE are being used?

❍ A. SELECT * FROM TABLE (MON_GET_BUFFERPOOL ('',-2)) AS bp_metrics
❍ B. SELECT * FROM SYSCAT.BUFFERPOOLS
❍ C. GET SNAPSHOT FOR DATABASE ON sample
❍ D. SELECT * FROM TABLE(MON_GET_BUFFERPOOL('sample', -1)) AS bp_metrics

Question 3

What is the RESET MONITOR command used for?

❍ A. To reset all snapshot monitor counters to zero
❍ B. To reset individual snapshot monitor counters to zero
❍ C. To turn all snapshot monitor switches off
❍ D. To turn all snapshot monitor switches except the TIMESTAMP switch off

Question 4

Which statement is false about DEADLOCK event monitors?

- ❍ A. The DEADLOCK event monitor is deprecated in DB2 10.1, and the recommendation is to use the LOCKING event monitor.
- ❍ B. The mon_deadlock database configuration parameter setting is essential to capture the deadlock events by using the LOCKING event monitor.
- ❍ C. The LOCKING event monitor data can be written to a regular formatted table, to an unformatted table, or to a pipe.
- ❍ D. When a LOCKING event monitor is created with an AUTOSTART clause, the event monitor will automatically be activated whenever the database partition on which the event monitor runs is activated.

Question 5

Which option can you specify with the CREATE EVENT MONITOR statement to indicate that each agent that generates an event being monitored will not wait for an event buffer to be externalized to disk before continuing if it determines that both event buffers are full?

- ❍ A. BLOCKED
- ❍ B. NONBLOCKED
- ❍ C. BUFFERED
- ❍ D. NONBUFFERED

Question 6

Which statement is false about event monitors?

- ❍ A. An unlimited number of event monitors may be defined.
- ❍ B. An event monitor must be activated before it will start collecting data.
- ❍ C. Up to but no more than 256 event monitors can be active simultaneously.
- ❍ D. An active event monitor must be stopped before it can be dropped.

Question 7

Which two utilities can you use to present Explain information in a meaningful format?

- ❒ A. db2bfd
- ❒ B. db2expln
- ❒ C. db2look
- ❒ D. db2exfmt
- ❒ E. db2advis

Question 8

If a query used in an OLTP environment joins two tables on their primary key, which operator will most likely represent this join in an access plan graph produced by Visual Explain?

- ❍ A. HSJOIN
- ❍ B. MSJOIN
- ❍ C. NLJOIN
- ❍ D. SJOIN

Question 9

If a query used in a decision support environment joins two tables, which operator will most likely represent this join in an access plan graph produced by Visual Explain?

- ❍ A. HSJOIN
- ❍ B. MSJOIN
- ❍ C. NLJOIN
- ❍ D. SJOIN

Question 10

Which command instructs the DB2 Optimizer to use the maximum amount of optimization techniques when generating data access plans for dynamic SQL statements that will interact with a database named SAMPLE?

- A. db2set –g DB2_QUERYOPT=9
- B. UPDATE DBM CFG USING QUERYOPT 9
- C. UPDATE DB CFG FOR sample USING QUERYOPT 9
- D. SET CURRENT QUERY OPTIMIZATION = 9

Question 11

Which command can you use to display the precompile options that were used to create a bind file?

- A. db2advis
- B. db2bfd
- C. db2mtrk
- D. db2rbind

Question 12

Which statement best describes the functionality of db2mtrk?

- A. It reports how memory is being managed by the self-tuning memory manager.
- B. It estimates the memory requirements for a database, based on values assigned to the memory-related database manager configuration parameters.
- C. It produces a report of memory status for instances, databases, and agents.
- D. It recommends memory-related database manager configuration parameter values that will improve memory utilization.

Question 13

Which command can you use to determine how many pages have been written to the transaction log files associated with a particular database?

❍ A. db2pd
❍ B. db2advis
❍ C. db2look
❍ D. db2mtrk

Question 14

Which statement is false about the DB2 problem determination tool (db2pd)?

❍ A. The db2pd tool can obtain quick and immediate information from the DB2 database system memory sets.
❍ B. The db2pd tool does not require a connection to an active database to obtain information about it.
❍ C. The db2pd tool can obtain information about an instance that has stopped prematurely.
❍ D. Because db2pd works directly with memory, it is possible to retrieve information that will change as it is being collected.

Question 15

What is the unit of measurement used to represent the estimated query execution cost in Visual Explain as well as in the Explain plan tools?

❍ A. Seconds
❍ B. Minutes
❍ C. CPU cycles in GHz
❍ D. Timerons

Question 16

After analyzing Explain plan data, you notice that a table scan is being performed instead of an index scan even though a valid cluster index exists. What must you do to use an available index during the data access?

- ❍ A. Run db2pd with the –reopt clause.
- ❍ B. Reorganize the table to cluster its data according to the cluster index and perform a RUNSTATS.
- ❍ C. Run the inspect command to check the architectural integrity of the base table.
- ❍ D. Run the db2mtrk command to check the memory usage on the server.

Question 17

Which command can you use to display only the severity messages from the DB2 diagnostic log file?

- ❍ A. db2support
- ❍ B. inspect
- ❍ C. db2diag
- ❍ D. db2dart

Question 18

Which statement about the db2pd tool is false?

- ❍ A. The command has changed to support the storage groups via the –storagegroups parameter.
- ❍ B. The command can monitor the progress of the database recovery by using the –recovery parameter.
- ❍ C. The command can monitor the run-time information about the lock owner and the lock waiter by using the –apinfo parameter.
- ❍ D. The command can retrieve information about the security audit logs.

Question 19

What information can you obtain by analyzing `db2exfmt` command output data?

- ❍ A. Access plan, optimized statement, total execution time in timerons
- ❍ B. Access plan, optimized statement, total execution time in minutes
- ❍ C. Access plan, optimized statement, total execution time in milliseconds
- ❍ D. Access plan, optimized statement, total execution time in seconds

Question 20

Which monitor element determines the time that an agent waits for log records to be flushed to disk?

- ❍ A. LOG_BUFFER_WAIT_TIME
- ❍ B. LOG_DISK_WAIT_TIME
- ❍ C. EVMON_FLUSHES
- ❍ D. LOG_WRITE_TIME

Question 21

Which is the best way to retrieve buffer pool metrics information?

- ❍ A. Ensure the MON_OBJ_METRICS configuration parameter is enabled, and query the BP_HITRATIO table function.
- ❍ B. Ensure the MON_ACT_METRICS configuration parameter is enabled, and query the BP_HITRATIO administrative view.
- ❍ C. Ensure the MON_OBJ_METRICS configuration parameter is enabled, and query the MON_GET_BUFFERPOOL table function.
- ❍ D. Ensure the MON_ACT_METRICS configuration parameter is enabled, and query the MON_GET_BUFFERPOOL administrative view.

Question 22

Which tool should you use to capture data during a potential hang situation?

- ❍ A. db2val
- ❍ B. db2dart
- ❍ C. db2mtrk
- ❍ D. db2fodc

Question 23

Which tool should you use to capture the lock-wait information?

- ❍ A. db2pdcfg
- ❍ B. db2pd
- ❍ C. db2mtrk
- ❍ D. db2top

Question 24

Which tool should you use to analyze a database for architectural integrity without taking the applications down?

- ❍ A. db2dart
- ❍ B. db2fodc
- ❍ C. inspect
- ❍ D. db2support

Question 25

Which procedure should you use to extract data from unformatted event table and convert it into XML document?

- ❍ A. EVMON_FORMAT_UE_TO_XML
- ❍ B. EVMON_FORMAT_UE_TO_TABLES
- ❍ C. UE_LOCKING_EVENTS
- ❍ D. MONREPORT module

Answers

Question 1

The correct answer is **C**. You can change snapshot monitor switch settings at the instance level by modifying the appropriate DB2 database manager configuration parameters with the UPDATE DATABASE MANAGER CONFIGURATION command. Snapshot monitor switch settings made at the instance level remain persistent across instance restarts. You can change snapshot monitor switch settings at the application level by executing the UPDATE MONITOR SWITCHES command. Switch settings made at the application level are not persistent across instance restarts.

Question 2

The correct answer is **A**. The monitor table function MON_GET_BUFFERPOOL () returns buffer pool metrics, including buffer pool logical data and index reads, physical data and index reads, blocked I/O configuration, and buffer pool read and write times. The catalog table SYSCAT.BUFFERPOOLS stores information about the page size, number of pages, block size information, and so on; however, it stores nothing about how the buffer pool is performing. The database snapshot command displays buffer pool aggregated information, but it does not display information specific to any buffer pool. The basic syntax for the table function MON_GET_BUFFERPOOL () is:

```
SELECT * FROM TABLE (MON_GET_BUFFERPOOL
('[BufferpoolName]', [Member]) AS bp_metrics
```

Question 3

The correct answer is **A**. At times, it may be desirable to reset all counters to zero without turning snapshot monitor switches off and back on, and without terminating and reestablishing database connections. The easiest way to quickly reset all snapshot monitor counters to zero is by executing the RESET MONITOR command.

Question 4

The correct answer is **C**. The locking event monitor data can only be written to a regular formatted table or to an unformatted event table. No options are available to write event monitor data to a pipe. Remember, the earlier deadlock event monitor and the lock timeout reporting feature DB2_CAPTURE_LOCKTIMEOUT db2 registry setting is deprecated in DB2 10.1. Instead, it is recommended to use the newly introduced LOCKING event monitor. Four key database configuration parameters are required to capture locking event information:

- Monitoring lock timeouts (mon_locktimeout)
- Monitoring deadlocks (mon_deadlock)
- Monitoring lock waits (mon_lockwait)
- Monitoring lock waits threshold (mon_lw_thresh)

Question 5

The correct answer is **B**. Data collected by event monitors is streamed to buffers before it is externalized to disk (i.e., written to a table or file). If you specify the `BLOCKED` option with the `CREATE EVENT MONITOR` command, agents that generate an event being monitored will wait for an event buffer to be written to disk before continuing if the agent determines that both event buffers are full. As a result, although `BLOCKED` event monitors guarantee that no event monitor data will be lost, their behavior can increase application response time because any suspended agents (along with any dependent agents) will only be allowed to run when the event monitor buffers are clear. If you specify the `NONBLOCKED` option instead, agents that generate an event being monitored will not wait for an event buffer to be written to disk before continuing if the agent determines that both event buffers are full. Thus, `NONBLOCKED` event monitors perform faster than `BLOCKED` event monitors, but they are subject to data loss on highly active systems. If you specify neither option, the event monitor created will be a `BLOCKED` event monitor.

Question 6

The correct answer is **C**. While there is no limit to the number of event monitors that you can define for a single database, no more than 128 event monitors can be active at one time.

Question 7

The correct answers are **B** and **D**. When Explain information is collected, the resulting data is stored in one or more Explain tables. You can construct a query to retrieve this data, but a better way to view the Explain information collected is by using one of the Explain facility tools that have been designed specifically for presenting Explain information in a meaningful format. This set of tools consists of:

- The `db2expln` tool
- The `db2exfmt` tool
- Visual Explain

Question 8

The correct answer is **C**. The `NLJOIN` operator in a Visual Explain access plan graph represents a nested-loop join that accesses an inner table once for each row of the outer table. Nested-loop joins are preferred for join operations performed in an OLTP environment.

Question 9

The correct answer is **A**. The `HSJOIN` operator in a Visual Explain access plan graph represents a hash join, where two or more tables are hashed on the join columns. Hash joins are preferred for join operations performed in a decision support environment.

Question 10

The correct answer is **D**. The `CURRENT QUERY OPTIMIZATION` special register controls the class of optimization techniques used when binding dynamic SQL statements. You can change the value by executing the `SET CURRENT QUERY OPTIMIZATION` SQL statement. The other options are incorrect because there is no registry called `DB2_QUERYOPT`, no `DBM CFG` called `QUERYOPT`, and no `DB CFG` called `QUERYOPT`.

Question 11

The correct answer is **B**. You can use the DB2 bind file description tool to examine and verify the SQL statements within a bind file, as well as to display the precompile options used to create the bind file. To invoke the DB2 bind file description tool, you execute the `db2bfd` command. The other options are incorrect because you use `db2advis` to invoke the design advisor, `db2mtrk` to track the current memory utilization, and `db2rbind` to rebind a package to the database.

Question 12

The correct answer is **C**. The DB2 memory tracker utility produces a complete report of memory status for instances, databases, and agents. This utility provides the following information about memory pool allocation:

- Current size
- Maximum size (hard limit)
- Largest size (high watermark)
- Type (identifier indicating function for which memory will be used)
- Agent that allocated pool (only if the pool is private)

You invoke the DB2 memory tracker by executing the `db2mtrk` command.

Question 13

The correct answer is **A**. You use the DB2 problem determination tool to obtain quick and immediate information from the DB2 database system memory sets, without acquiring any latches. You invoke the DB2 problem determination tool by executing the `db2pd` command.

If you want to determine how many pages have been written to the transaction log files associated with a database named `SAMPLE`, you execute a `db2pd` command that looks something like this:

```
db2pd -logs -db sample
```

Question 14

The correct answer is **C**. You use the DB2 problem determination tool (`db2pd`) to obtain quick and immediate information from the DB2 database system memory sets, without acquiring any latches. Two benefits to collecting information without latching include faster data retrieval and no competition for engine resources. However, because the DB2 problem determination tool works directly with memory, it is possible to retrieve information that is changing as it is being collected; hence, the data retrieved might not be completely accurate. (A signal handler prevents the DB2 problem determination tool from aborting abnormally when changing memory pointers are encountered. However, this can result in messages such as "Changing data structure forced command termination" to appear in the output produced.) Nonetheless, this tool can be extremely helpful for problem determination.

There is no minimum connection requirement for executing the db2pd command; if you specify a database-level option, that database must be active before the requested information can be returned. You cannot use the db2pd command to obtain information about a stopped instance.

Question 15

The correct answer is **D**. A timeron is an invented relative unit of measurement. Timeron values are determined by the Optimizer, based on internal values such as statistics that change as the database is used. As a result, the timeron values for an SQL or XQuery statement are not guaranteed to be the same every time an estimated cost in timerons is determined.

Question 16

The correct answer is **B**. During these circumstances, it is highly recommended to do the data reorganization by using the REORG TABLE...INDEX command according to the cluster index to place the data in sequential pages for better performance, followed by a RUNSTATS to let the Optimizer select recently reorganized data.

Question 17

The correct answer is **C**. You use the db2diag logs analysis tool for filtering and formatting the db2diag log files from the server. Various options are available to filter the data based on application ID, severity, function name, database, timestamp, and so on. Following are a few examples.

To display all severe error messages produced by the process with the process ID (PID) 17417 and on node 1 and 2, enter:

```
db2diag -g level=Severe,pid= 17417 -n 1,2
```

To display all severe error messages containing the database field, enter:

```
db2diag -g db:= -gi level=severe
```

To display severe errors logged for the last three days, enter:

```
db2diag -gi "level=severe" -H 3d
```

Question 18

The correct answer is **D**. The DB2 problem determination (db2pd) tool does not provide security log audit information, but it does provide most of the troubleshooting information, such as locks, lock-waits, currently running transactions, recovery status, REORG status, and so on.

Question 19

The correct answer is **A**. The Explain table format (`db2exfmt`) command generates information such operator summary, access plan graph, total cost under each operator in timerons, and cardinality of each operator in the graph.

Question 20

The correct answer is **B**. The `LOG_DISK_WAIT_TIME` monitor element determines the amount of time (in millisecond) an agent spends waiting for log records to be flushed to disk. You can also figure this out by dividing `LOG_WRITE_TIME` by `TOTAL_COMMITS`. The `LOG_BUFFER_WAIT_TIME` monitor element determines the amount of time (in milliseconds) an agent spends waiting for space in the log buffer. The `EVMON_FLUSHES` monitor element determines the number of times the `FLUSH EVENT MONITOR` SQL statement has been issued. The `LOG_WRITE_TIME` monitor element determines total elapsed time (in milliseconds) spent by the logger writing log data to the disk.

Question 21

The correct answer is **C**. DB2 provides various monitoring elements to examine and troubleshoot performance problems or to check the health of the database. The monitoring elements are categorized as follows:

- Request monitor elements
- Activity monitor elements
- Data object monitor elements
- Time-spent monitor elements

Starting with DB2 10.1, it is highly recommended to use the `MON_GET_BUFFERPOOL` table function (lightweight infrastructure) to retrieve buffer pool information. Because a buffer pool belongs to an object monitor element, you will have to set the `mon_obj_metrics` database configuration parameter to `BASE` or `EXTENDED` to activate collecting data object monitor elements reported by the above-said table function.

Question 22

The correct answer is **D**. One of the most important diagnostic tools available with DB2 is the FODC facility. The DB2 database manager calls the `db2fodc` command when there is a real problem in the database engine. If you want to invoke the `db2fodc` command during any hang situation, call it by executing a command that looks something like this:

```
db2fodc -hang
```

Question 23

The correct answer is **B**. The DB2 problem determination (db2pd) tool provides much troubleshooting information, including the lock-wait processes similar to the following:

```
db2pd -db sample -wlocks

Database Member 0 -- Database SAMPLE -- Active -- Up 0 days 03:00:02 --
Date 2014-09-22-14.11.38.388526

Locks being waited on :
AppHandl [nod-index] TranHdl Lockname                   Type       Mode Conv Sts
43209    [000-43209] 26      0300430000000000000000054 TableLock  ..S  G    45994
43207    [000-43207] 27      0300430000000000000000054 TableLock  .IX  W    45996

CoorEDU    AppName  AuthID   AppID
      db2bp    DB2INST1  *LOCAL.db2inst1.140922140729
      db2bp    DB2INST1  *LOCAL.db2inst1.140922140745
```

Question 24

The correct answer is **C**. The `inspect` command checks the architectural integrity and the page consistency within the database. This is a very useful command when it comes to validating the structures of tables and table spaces, without taking the database offline. You can perform a check against the whole database, a table space, or a table. Although `db2dart` does similar checks, it needs the application to be offline before starting the inspection.

Question 25

The correct answer is **A**. As with the `db2evmonfmt` tool, another way to extract data from an unformatted event table is by using the following format table functions:

- `SYSPROC.EVMON_FORMAT_UE_TO_XML ()`
- `SYSPROC.EVMON_FORMAT_UE_TO_TABLES ()`

The `EVMON_FORMAT_UE_TO_XML ()` table function extracts binary events from an unformatted event table and formats them into an XML document.

CHAPTER 6

DB2 Utilities

This chapter will introduce you to the various data movement and database maintenance utilities that are available in DB2. You will learn to use the DB2 Design Advisor to generate expert recommendations on indexes, MQTs, repartitioning of tables, MDC tables, and deletion of unused database objects. At the end of the chapter, you will also be able use online table maintenance procedures to copy a specific schema, its tables, and its objects.

Exam Objectives

- ✓ Demonstrate the ability to understand data movement file formats in DB2
- ✓ Demonstrate the ability to use the Export utility to extract data from a database and store it in an external file
- ✓ Demonstrate the ability to use the Import utility to transfer data from an external file to a database table
- ✓ Demonstrate the ability to use the Load utility to bulk-load data into a database table
- ✓ Demonstrate the ability to use the Continuous Data Ingest (CDI) utility to perform high-speed data loads into a database table
- ✓ Demonstrate the ability to choose the appropriate data-load utility based on business need
- ✓ Demonstrate the ability to use ADMIN_MOVE_TABLE and ADMIN_COPY_SCHEMA system stored procedures
- ✓ Demonstrate the ability to use the REORKCHK and REORG commands to locate and remove fragmentation in table space containers

- ✓ Demonstrate the ability to use the RUNSTATS, REBIND, and FLUSH PACKAGE CACHE commands to ensure that the DB2 Optimizer will always generate the best access plan for a given query and that applications will take advantage of new access plans when they are generated
- ✓ Demonstrate the ability to use the db2look, db2move, and db2batch commands
- ✓ Demonstrate the ability to use the db2relocatedb command to rename or move the database between the instances
- ✓ Demonstrate the ability to use the Design Advisor to generate expert performance recommendations on the database objects

Data Movement Utilities and File Formats

Although a database usually functions as a self-contained entity, at times it becomes necessary to exchange data with "the outside world." That is the purpose of DB2's data movement utilities. However, for data to be transferred between databases and external files, any external file used must be formatted in such a way that it can be processed by the DB2 data movement utilities.

Data Movement File Formats

The data movement utilities provided by DB2 (which we will look at shortly) recognize and support up to four different file formats:

- Delimited ASCII (DEL)
- Nondelimited or fixed-length ASCII (ASC)
- Worksheet File Format (WSF)
- PC Integrated Exchange Format (IXF)

But just what are these formats, how are they similar, and how do they differ? To answer these questions, let us look closer at each format supported.

Delimited ASCII (DEL)

The delimited ASCII file format is used extensively in many relational database management systems and software applications to exchange data with a wide variety of application products. With this format, data values typically vary in length, and a delimiter, which is a unique character (not found in the data values themselves), separates individual values and rows. Actually, delimited ASCII format files typically use three distinct delimiters:

- **Column delimiters**. These characters mark the beginning or end of a data value. (Usually, you associate each value with a particular column, based on its position in the file.)

Commas (,) are typically used as the column delimiter for delimited ASCII format files (in fact, such files are sometimes referred to as *comma separated variable/value*, or *CSV*, files and are often given a .csv extension). Vertical bars (|) are also commonly used as column delimiters; however, it is not the default.

- **Row delimiters.** These characters mark the end of a single record or row. On UNIX systems, you typically use the new line character (0x0A) as the row delimiter for a delimited ASCII format file; on Windows systems, you generally use the carriage return/linefeed characters (0x0D-0x0A) instead.
- **Character delimiters.** These characters mark the beginning and end of character data values. Double quotation marks (") are typically used as character delimiters for a delimited ASCII format files.

Generally, when data is written to a delimited ASCII file, rows are streamed into the file, one after another. The appropriate column delimiter separates each column's data values, the appropriate row delimiter separates individual rows (also called a *records*), and the appropriate character delimiters enclose all character and character string values. Numeric values are represented by their ASCII equivalent—the period character (.) denotes the decimal point (if appropriate); scientific notation (E) represents real values; the minus character (-) precedes negative values; and the plus character (+) may or may not precede positive values.

And because delimited ASCII files are written in ASCII, you can edit their contents with any simple text editor. This file format can be used to export data from database tables to external files, as well as to import or load data into database tables from externally compatible files.

Thus, if you used the comma character as the column delimiter, the carriage return/line feed character as the row delimiter, and the double quotation mark character as the character delimiter, the contents of a delimited ASCII file might look similar to the following:

```
10,"Headquarters",860,"Corporate","New York"
15,"Research",150,"Eastern","Boston"
20,"Legal",40,"Eastern","Washington"
38,"Support Center 1",80,"Eastern","Atlanta"
42,"Manufacturing",100,"Midwest","Chicago"
51,"Training Center",34,"Midwest","Dallas"
66,"Support Center 2",112,"Western","San Francisco"
84,"Distribution",290,"Western","Denver"
```

When you execute a SELECT statement on the WORKPLACES table, it looks something like this:

```
SELECT * FROM workplaces

NUMBER      NAME              EMPLOYEES   TYPE      CITY
----------- ----------------- ----------- --------- -------------
         10 Headquarters              860 Corporate New York
         15 Research                  150 Eastern   Boston
         20 Legal                      40 Eastern   Washington
         38 Support Center 1           80 Eastern   Atlanta
         42 Manufacturing             100 Midwest   Chicago
         51 Training Center            34 Midwest   Dallas
         66 Support Center 2          112 Western   San Francisco
         84 Distribution              290 Western   Denver

  8 record(s) selected.
```

Nondelimited ASCII (ASC)

The nondelimited ASCII file format is also used by a wide variety of software and database applications to exchange data with application products. With this format, data values have a fixed length, and the position of each value in the file determines to which column and row a particular value belongs. For this reason, nondelimited ASCII files are sometimes referred to as *fixed-length ASCII files*.

Typically, when data is written to a nondelimited ASCII file, rows are streamed into the file, one after another; each column's data values are written using a fixed number of bytes, and an appropriate row delimiter separates each individual row (record). On UNIX systems, the new line character (0x0A) typically acts as the row delimiter for nondelimited ASCII format files; on Windows systems, the carriage return/linefeed characters (0x0D-0x0A) act as the row delimiter instead. If a data value is smaller than the fixed length allotted for a particular column, it is padded with blanks until its length matches the length specified for the column.

As with delimited ASCII format files, numeric values are represented by their ASCII equivalent—the period character (.) denotes the decimal point (if appropriate); scientific notation (E) represents real values; the minus character (-) precedes negative values; and the plus character (+) may or may not precede positive values.

Thus, a simple nondelimited ASCII file might look something like this:

```
10Headquarters   860CorporateNew York
15Research       150Eastern  Boston
20Legal          40 Eastern  Washington
38Support Center 180Eastern  Atlanta
42Manufacturing  100Midwest  Chicago
51Training Center34 Midwest  Dallas
66Support Center 211Western  San Francisco
84Distribution   290Western  Denver
```

As with delimited ASCII files, you can edit the contents of nondelimited ASCII files with a simple text editor. You use this file format only to import or load data into database tables from externally compatible files.

Worksheet Format

The WSF is a special file format used exclusively by the Lotus 1-2-3 and Lotus Symphony spreadsheet products. Different releases of each of these products incorporate different features into the file formats they use for data storage; however, all releases use a common subset of features, and it is this subset that some of DB2's data movement utilities recognize and support. You cannot edit WSF with a simple text editor.

PC Integrated Exchange Format

The PC/IXF file format is a special file format used almost exclusively to move data between different DB2 databases (you cannot use this file format to move data between DB2 and other vendor databases). Typically, when data is written to a PC/IXF file, rows are streamed into the file, one after another, as an unbroken sequence of variable-length records. With this format, character data values are stored in their original ASCII representation (without additional padding), and numeric values are stored either as packed decimal values or as binary values, depending on the data type used to store them in the database. In addition to data, table definitions and associated index definitions are also stored in PC/IXF files. Thus, tables (along with any corresponding indexes) can be both defined and populated when you use this file format. As with WSF, you cannot edit PC/IXF files with a simple text editor.

Extracting Columnar Data from External Files

As you can see, the file format you use determines how data is physically stored in an external file. And the way data physically resides in a file determines the method that you must use to extract that data and map it to one or more columns of a table. With DB2, three mapping methods are used:

- The position method (METHOD P)
- The location method (METHOD L)
- The name method (METHOD N)

The Position Method

When you use the position method to extract data from an external file, columnar data values are identified by their indexed position within a single row; the first data value found is assigned the index position 1, the second data value found is assigned the index position 2, and so on. Figure 6.1 illustrates how the position method maps data values in an external file to columns in a table.

EMPLOYEE.DEL

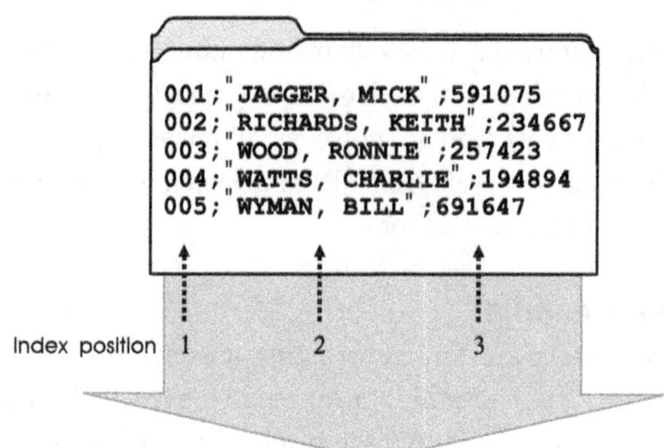

EMPLOYEE TABLE

EMPID	NAME	TAX_ID
001	JAGGER, MICK	591075
002	RICHARDS, KEITH	234667
003	WOOD, RONNIE	257423
004	WATTS, CHARLIE	194894
005	WYMAN, BILL	691647

Figure 6.1: Mapping columnar data by using the position method

Only data values in external files that use either the delimited ASCII (DEL) format or the PC/IXF format can be mapped using the position method.

The Location Method

When you use the location method to extract data from an external file, columnar data values are identified by a series of beginning and ending byte positions that, when combined, identify the location of a specific data value within a single row. Each byte position specified is treated as an offset from the beginning of the row (which is byte position 1), and two-byte positions are required to extract a single value. Figure 6.2 illustrates how the location method maps data values in an external file to columns in a table.

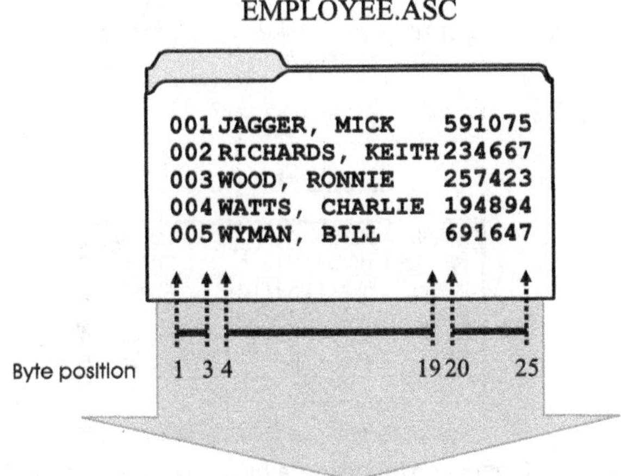

EMPLOYEE TABLE

EMPID	NAME	TAX_ID
001	JAGGER, MICK	591075
002	RICHARDS, KEITH	234667
003	WOOD, RONNIE	257423
004	WATTS, CHARLIE	194894
005	WYMAN, BILL	691647

Figure 6.2: Mapping columnar data by using the location method

Only data values in external files that use the nondelimited ASCII (ASC) format can be mapped with the location method.

The Name Method

When you use the name method to extract data from an external file, it is assumed that column names are stored in the file, and columnar data values are identified by the name of the column with which they are associated. Figure 6.3 illustrates how the name method maps data values in an external file to columns in a table.

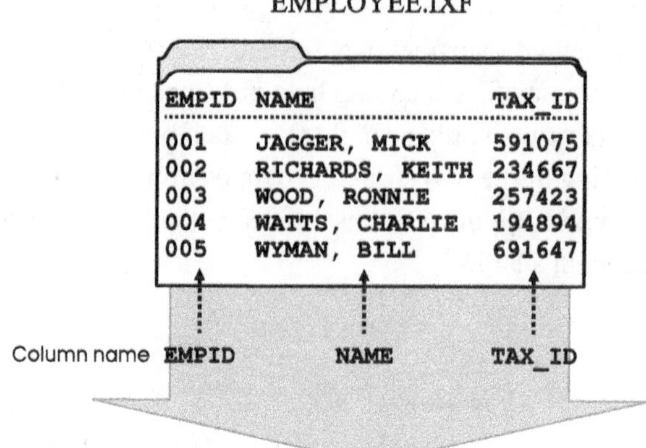

EMPLOYEE TABLE

EMPID	NAME	TAX_ID
001	JAGGER, MICK	591075
002	RICHARDS, KEITH	234667
003	WOOD, RONNIE	257423
004	WATTS, CHARLIE	194894
005	WYMAN, BILL	691647

Figure 6.3: Mapping columnar data by using the name method

Because DB2 expects column names to reside in the external file along with the data values themselves when the name method is used, only data values in external files that use the PC/IXF format can be mapped.

The DB2 Export Utility

The Export utility extracts data from a DB2 database table or view and externalizes it to a file, using the delimited ASCII (DEL) format, the WSF format, or the PC/IXF format. Such files can then provide data values to other databases (including the database from which the data was extracted) and software applications such as spreadsheets and word processors.

To successfully invoke the EXPORT command, you must have SYSADM authority at the instance level, DBADM authority at the database level, DATAACCESS authority at the database level, or CONTROL or SELECT privilege at the table or view level.

When you are exporting data from a table that has protected rows, the LBAC credentials held by your authorization ID might limit the rows that are exported. The records that your authorization ID does not have read access to will not be exported. However, no error or warning message is displayed. If the LBAC credentials do not allow reading from one or more protected columns included in the export, the export will fail with an error (SQLSTATE 42512).

One way to invoke the Export utility is by executing the EXPORT command. The basic syntax for this command is:

```
EXPORT TO [FileName] OF [DEL | WSF | IXF]
<LOBS TO [LOBPath ,...]>
<LOBFILE [LOBFileName ,...]>
<XML TO [XMLPath ,...]>
<XMLFILE [XMLFileName ,...]>
<MODIFIED BY [Modifier ,...]>
<METHOD N ([ColumnName ,...])>
<MESSAGES [MsgFileName]>
[SELECTStatement | XQueryExpression]
```

where:

FileName Identifies the name and location of the external file to which to export or copy data

LOBPath Identifies one or more locations to store LOB data values (if this option is specified, each LOB value will be stored in its own file at the location indicated)

LOBFileName Identifies one or more base names to use to name the files to which LOB data values are to be written; during an export operation, file names are constructed by appending a period (.) and a three-digit sequence number to the current base file name in this list, and then appending the generated file name to the large object data path specified (in LOBPath)—for example, if the current LOB path is the directory C:\LOBData and the current LOB file name is Value, the LOB files created will be C:\LOBData\Value.001.lob, C:\LOBData\Value.002.lob, and so on

XMLPath Identifies one or more locations to store XML documents (if this option is specified, each XML value will be stored in its own file at the location indicated)

XMLFileName Identifies one or more base names to use to name the files to which XML documents are to be written; during an export operation, file names are constructed by appending a period (.) and a three-digit sequence number to the current base file name in this list and then appending the generated file name to the XML data path specified (in XMLPath)—for example, if the current XML path is the directory C:\XMLData, and the current XML file name is Value, the XML files created will be C:\XMLData\Value.001.xml, C:\XMLData\Value.002.xml, and so on

Modifier	Identifies one or more options to use to override the default behavior of the Export utility (Table 6.1 contains a list of valid modifiers)
ColumnName	Identifies one or more column names to write to the external file to which data is to be exported
MsgFileName	Identifies the name and location of an external file to which messages produced by the Export utility are to be written as the export operation is performed
SELECTStatement	Identifies a SELECT SQL statement that, when executed, will retrieve the data to copy to an external file
XQueryExpression	Identifies an XQuery expression that, when executed, will retrieve the data to copy to an external file

A simple EXPORT command looks something like this:

```
EXPORT TO employee.del OF DEL
MESSAGES employee.msg
SELECT * FROM employee

SQL3104N  The Export utility is beginning to export data to file "employee.del".

SQL3105N  The Export utility has finished exporting "5" rows.
```

The following output file, employee.del, has default file-type modifiers; that is, character strings enclosed by quotation marks ("), column values separated by commas (,) and rows separated by carriage return (0x0A or CHR(10):

```
"1  ","JAGGER, MICK",591075
"2  ","RICHARDS, KEITH",234667
"3  ","WOOD, RONNIE",257423
"4  ","WATTS, CHARLIE",194894
"5  ","WYMAN, BILL",691647
```

Table 6.1 list the most commonly used file-type modifiers for the EXPORT command.

Table 6.1: File-type modifiers recognized by the EXPORT command		
Modifier	**Description**	**File Format**
lobsinfile	Indicates to write LOB data values to the locations specified by the LOBS TO clause; otherwise, LOB data is sent to the same location as the data file produced	Delimited ASCII (DEL), WSF, and PC/IXF
lobsinsepfiles	Indicates to write each LOB value to a separate file; by default, multiple values are concatenated together in the same file	Delimited ASCII (DEL), WSF, and PC/IXF
xmlinsepfiles	Indicates to write each XML document (XQuery Data Model, or QDM, instance) to a separate file; by default, multiple values are concatenated together in the same file	Delimited ASCII (DEL), WSF, and PC/IXF
xmlnodeclaration	Indicates to write XML documents without an XML declaration tag; by default, XML documents are exported with an XML declaration tag at the beginning that includes an encoding attribute	Delimited ASCII (DEL), WSF, and PC/ IXF
xmlchar	Indicates to write XML documents by using the character code page; the character code page is the value specified by the codepage modifier, or the application code page if this modifier is not specified; by default, XML documents are written in Unicode	Delimited ASCII (DEL), WSF, and PC/IXF
xmlgraphic	Indicates to encode and write XML documents in the UTF-16 code page, regardless of the application code page or character code page specified with the codepage modifier	Delimited ASCII (DEL), WSF, and PC/IXF
chardel*x* where *x* is any valid delimiter character	Identifies a specific character to use as a character delimiter; the default character delimiter is a double quotation mark (") character; the character specified is used in place of the double quotation mark to enclose a character string	Delimited ASCII (DEL)
codepage=*x* where *x* is any valid code page identifier	Identifies the code page of the data contained in the output data set produced; character data is converted from the application code page to the code page specified during the export operation	Delimited ASCII (DEL) and PC/ IXF
coldel*x* where *x* is any valid delimiter character	Identifies a specific character to use as a column delimiter; the default column delimiter is a comma (,) character; the character specified is used in place of a comma to signal the end of a column	Delimited ASCII (DEL)
decplusblank	Indicates to prefix positive decimal values with a blank space instead of a plus sign (+); the default action is to prefix positive decimal values with a plus sign	Delimited ASCII (DEL)
decpt*x* where *x* is any valid delimiter character	Identifies a specific character to use as a decimal point character; the default decimal point character is a period (.) character; the character specified is used in place of a period as a decimal point character	Delimited ASCII (DEL)
nochardel	Indicates not to surround column data by character delimiters—this option should not be specified if the data is intended to be imported or loaded using DB2; it is provided to support vendor data files that do not have character delimiters, and improper usage might result in data loss or corruption—this option cannot be specified with the chardelx or nodoubledel modifiers; these are mutually exclusive options	Delimited ASCII (DEL)

Table 6.1: File-type modifiers recognized by the EXPORT command (continued)		
Modifier	**Description**	**File Format**
nodoubledel	Indicates not to recognize double character delimiters	Delimited ASCII (DEL)
striplzeros	Indicates to remove leading zeros from all exported decimal columns	Delimited ASCII (DEL)
timestampformat="*x*" where *x* is any valid combination of date and time format elements	Identifies how to format date, time, and timestamp values before they are written to an external file Using the following date and time elements will create the format string provided with this modifier: YYYY—Year (four digits ranging from 0000 to 9999) M—Month (one or two digits ranging from 1 to 12) MM—Month (two digits ranging from 1 to 12; mutually exclusive with M) D—Day (one or two digits ranging from 1 to 31) DD—Day (two digits ranging from 1 to 31; mutually exclusive with D) DDD—Day of the year (three digits ranging from 001 to 366; mutually exclusive with other day or month elements) H—Hour (one or two digits ranging from 0 to 12 for a 12-hour system, and 0 to 24 for a 24-hour system) HH—Hour (two digits ranging from 0 to 12 for a 12-hour system, and 0 to 24 for a 24-hour system; mutually exclusive with H) M—Minute (one or two digits ranging from 0 to 59) MM—Minute (two digits ranging from 0 to 59; mutually exclusive with M) S—Second (one or two digits ranging from 0 to 59) SS—Second (two digits ranging from 0 to 59; mutually exclusive with S) SSSSS—Second of the day after midnight (5 digits ranging from 00000 to 86399; mutually exclusive with other time elements) UUUUUU—Microsecond (6 digits ranging from 000000 to 999999) TT—Meridian indicator (AM or PM) An example of a valid timestamp format string is: "YYYY/MM/DD HH:MM:SS.UUUUUU"	Delimited ASCII (DEL)
nodoubledel	Indicates not to recognize double character delimiters	Delimited ASCII (DEL)
1	Specifies to create a WSF file that is compatible with Lotus 1-2-3 Release 1 or Lotus 1-2-3 Release 1a; by default, WSF files that are compatible with Lotus 1-2-3 Release 1 or Lotus 1-2-3 Release 1a are generated unless otherwise indicated	WSF
2	Specifies to create a WSF file that is compatible with Lotus Symphony Release 1.0 is to be created	WSF
3	Specifies to create a WSF file that is compatible with Lotus 1-2-3 Version 2 or Lotus Symphony Release 1.1 is to be created	WSF
4	Specifies to create a WSF file containing DBCS characters is to be created	WSF
Adapted from Tables 10–12 of the IBM DB2 10.1 Command Reference		

So if you want to export data stored in a table named DEPARTMENT to a PC/IXF file named department.ixf, execute the EXPORT command:

```
EXPORT TO department.ixf OF IXF
MESSAGES department.msgs
SELECT * FROM department
```

When data to be exported contains LOB values, by default only the first 32 KB of each LOB value are actually written to the file containing the exported data—LOB values that are greater than 32 KB in size will be truncated. As you might imagine, this presents quite a problem if LOB values are greater than 32 KB in size. When you override this default behavior (by using the lobsinfile or the lobsinsepfiles modifier) and provide the Export utility with one or more locations to which LOB data values are to be written, each LOB value encountered will be stored, in its entirety, in its own file (which is assigned a name that either the user or the Export utility provides).

Thus, if you want to export data stored in a table named EMPLOYEE to a delimited ASCII (DEL) format external file named employee.del, and all large object values stored in the PHOTO column of this table are written to individual files, you can do so by executing an EXPORT command:

```
EXPORT TO C:\employee.del OF DEL
LOBS TO C:\lobfiles
LOBFILE e_photo
MODIFIED BY lobsinsepfiles coldel;
MESSAGES exp_msgs.txt
SELECT * FROM employee
```

When executed, this command will do the following:

- Retrieve all data values stored in the table named EMPLOYEE.
- Copy all non-LOB values retrieved from the EMPLOYEE table to a delimited ASCII (DEL) format external file named employee.del (this file will reside in the root directory on drive C:).
- Copy each LOB value retrieved from the PHOTO column to its own file (each file created will reside in a directory named lobfiles that is located on drive C:).
- Record all messages produced by the Export utility to a file named exp_msgs.txt (which will reside in the current working directory).

Figure 6.4 illustrates this export operation.

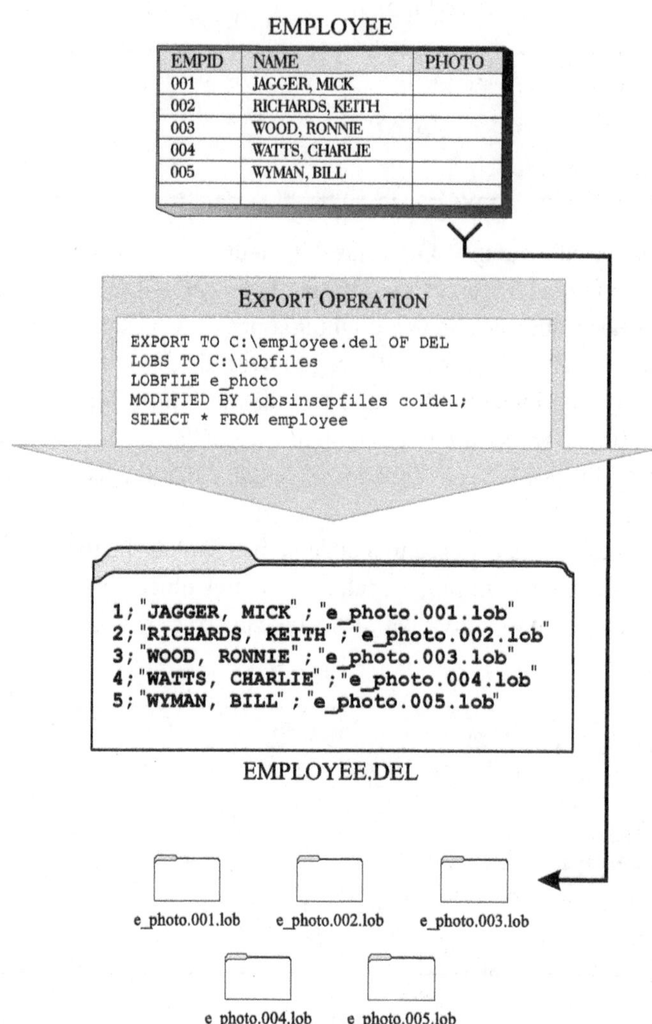

Figure 6.4: An export operation in which LOB values are stored in individual files

As with LOB data, XML data can be written to a file along with other exported data, or each XML document stored in a table can be copied to its own file (which is assigned a name that either the user or the Export utility provides). Figure 6.5 illustrates a simple export operation in which XML documents are processed in this manner.

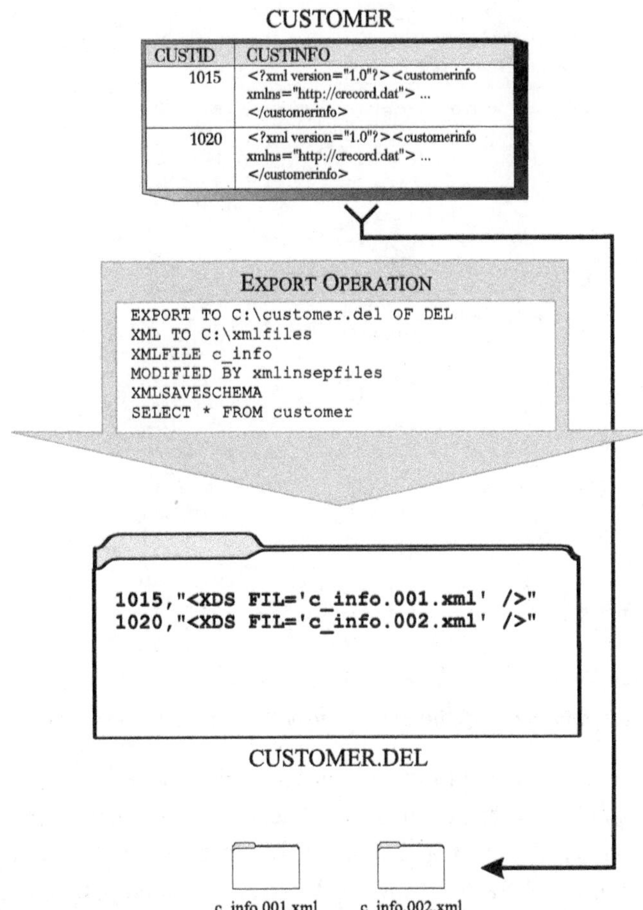
CUSTOMER
CUSTID
CUSTINFO
1015
<?xml version="1.0"?><customerinfo xmlns="http://crecord.dat"> ... </customerinfo>
1020
<?xml version="1.0"?><customerinfo xmlns="http://crecord.dat"> ... </customerinfo>
EXPORT OPERATION
EXPORT TO C:\customer.del OF DEL
XML TO C:\xmlfiles
XMLFILE c_info
MODIFIED BY xmlinsepfiles
XMLSAVESCHEMA
SELECT * FROM customer
1015,"<XDS FIL='c_info.001.xml' />"
1020,"<XDS FIL='c_info.002.xml' />"
CUSTOMER.DEL
c_info.001.xml
c_info.002.xml

Figure 6.5: An export operation in which XML values are stored in individual files

Figure 6.6 displays the IBM Data Studio menu items (**Administrative Perspective -> Database (SAMPLE) -> Tables**) that you must select to activate the Export Table wizard. It is important to note that regardless of whether you use the EXPORT command or the Export Table wizard to export data, a database connection must be established before the Export utility is invoked. Additionally, you use the Cursor Stability isolation level to bind the Export utility to a database so that its use does not prohibit other applications and users from accessing a table while data is being exported.

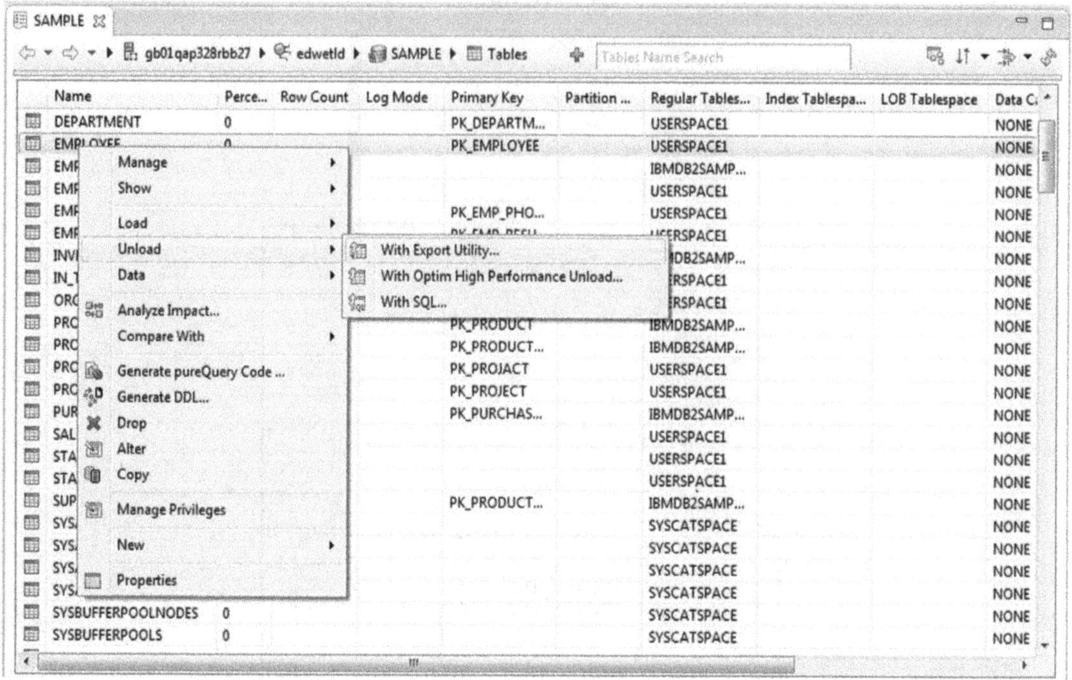

Figure 6.6: Invoking the Export utility through IBM Data Studio

Figure 6.7 shows the file name and format options available in the Export Utility wizard within IBM Data Studio. By opening the Target window, you can also choose the document code page from three options: Unicode, Character, and Graphic. The Options window in Figure 6.8 lets you select a column delimiter, character string delimiter, and decimal point character along with a timestamp format. Finally, you can write customized SQL statements for export in the Source window, as Figure 6.9 illustrates.

The DB2 Import Utility

Just as there are times when it is beneficial to copy data stored in a table or view to an external file, there can be times when it is advantageous to copy data stored in an external file to a database table or updatable view. One way to copy data from an external file to a database is by using DB2's Import utility. The Import utility reads data directly from an external file (provided the file is written in a format that DB2 supports) and inserts it in a specific table or updatable view.

To successfully invoke the IMPORT command, you must have SYSADM authority at the instance level, DBADM authority at the database level, or SELECT, UPDATE, INSERT, DELETE, or CONTROL object privileges. You need to have CREATETAB authority at the database level and USE privilege at the table space level to run the IMPORT command with the REPLACE_CREATE clause.

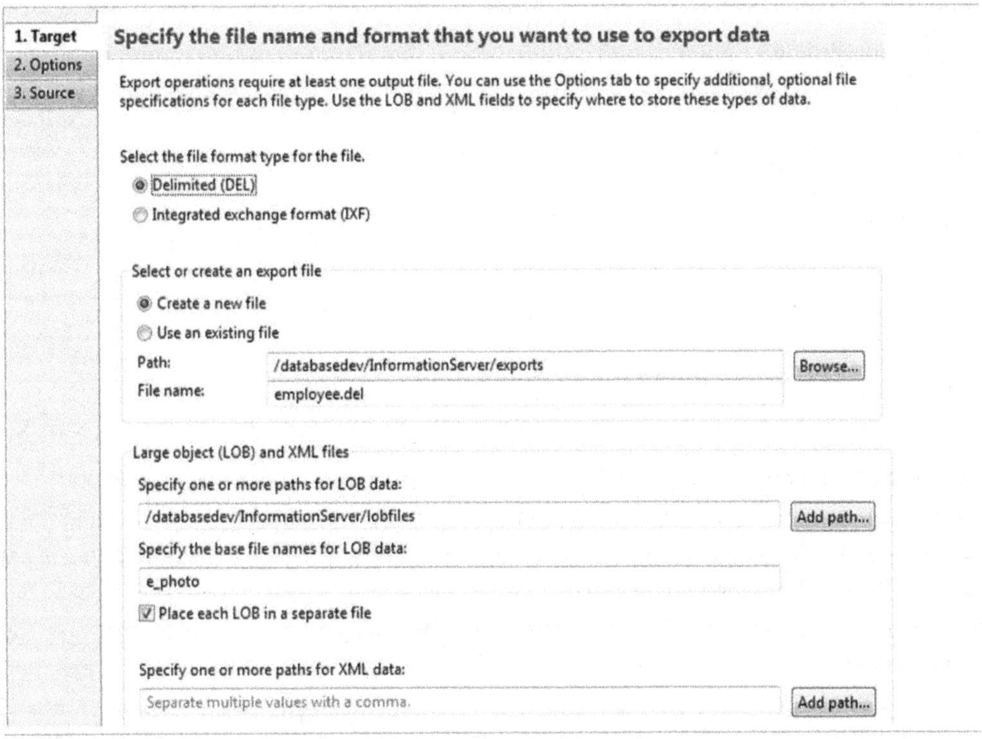

1. Target
2. Options
3. Source

Specify the file name and format that you want to use to export data

Export operations require at least one output file. You can use the Options tab to specify additional, optional file specifications for each file type. Use the LOB and XML fields to specify where to store these types of data.

Select the file format type for the file.

- (•) Delimited (DEL)
- ( ) Integrated exchange format (IXF)

Select or create an export file

- (•) Create a new file
- ( ) Use an existing file

Path: /databasedev/InformationServer/exports [Browse...]

File name: employee.del

Large object (LOB) and XML files

Specify one or more paths for LOB data:

/databasedev/InformationServer/lobfiles [Add path...]

Specify the base file names for LOB data:

e_photo

[x] Place each LOB in a separate file

Specify one or more paths for XML data:

Separate multiple values with a comma. [Add path...]

Figure 6.7: Export—file name and data format

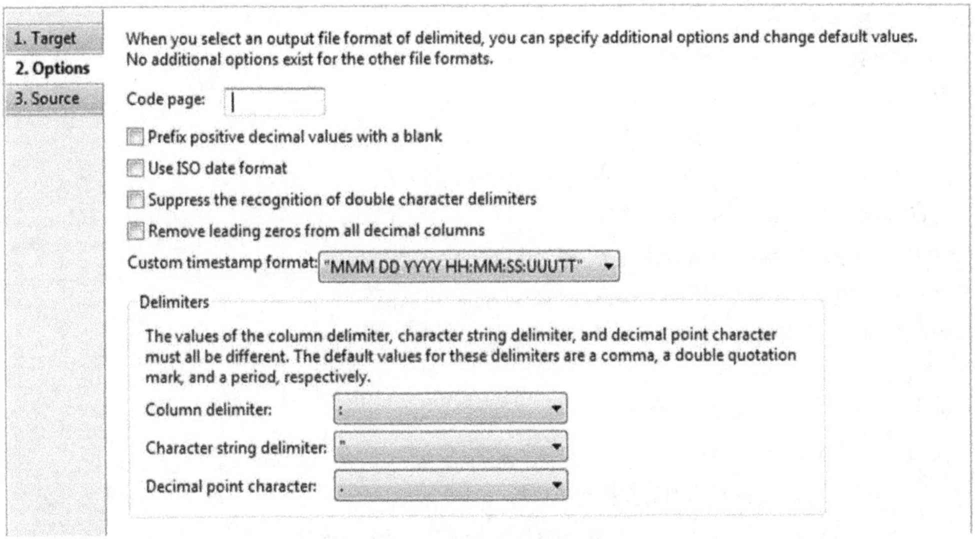

1. Target
2. Options
3. Source

When you select an output file format of delimited, you can specify additional options and change default values. No additional options exist for the other file formats.

Code page:

- [ ] Prefix positive decimal values with a blank
- [ ] Use ISO date format
- [ ] Suppress the recognition of double character delimiters
- [ ] Remove leading zeros from all decimal columns

Custom timestamp format: "MMM DD YYYY HH:MM:SS:UUUTT"

Delimiters

The values of the column delimiter, character string delimiter, and decimal point character must all be different. The default values for these delimiters are a comma, a double quotation mark, and a period, respectively.

Column delimiter: :

Character string delimiter: "

Decimal point character: .

Figure 6.8: Export—delimiter options

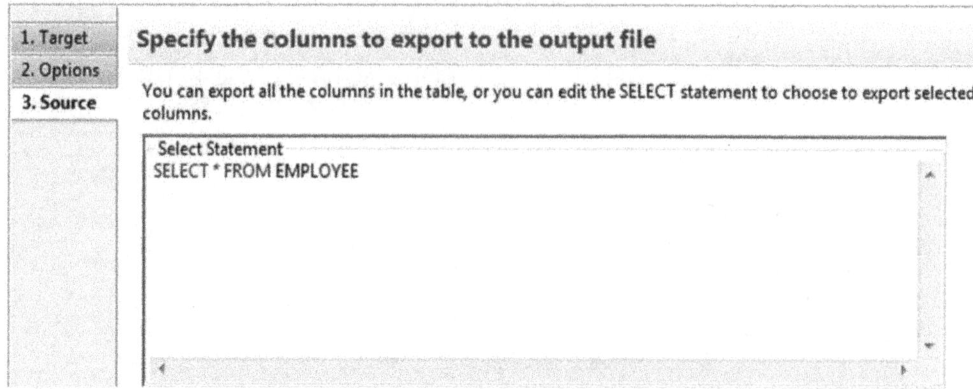

Figure 6.9: Export—customize the data selection

If you want to import data into a table that has protected columns, you must have LBAC credentials that allow write access to all protected columns in the table. To import data into a table that has protected rows, you must have been granted a security label for write access that is part of the security policy protecting the table.

You can invoke the Import utility by executing the IMPORT command. The basic syntax for this command is:

```
IMPORT FROM [FileName] OF [DEL | ASC | WSF | IXF]
<LOBS FROM [LOBPath ,...]>
<XML FROM [XMLPath ,...]>
<MODIFIED BY [Modifier ,...]>
<Method>
<XML PARSE [STRIP | PRESERVE] WHITESPACE>
<XMLVALIDATE USING [XDS | SCHEMA [SchemaID]]>
<ALLOW NO ACCESS | ALLOW WRITE ACCESS>
<COMMITCOUNT [CommitCount] | COMMITCOUNT AUTOMATIC>
<RESTARTCOUNT | SKIPCOUNT [RestartCount]>
<WARNINGCOUNT [WarningCount]>
<NOTIMEOUT>
<MESSAGES [MsgFileName]>
[CREATE | INSERT | INSERT_UPDATE | REPLACE | REPLACE_CREATE]
    INTO [TableName] <([ColumnName ,...])>
    <IN [TSName] <INDEX IN [TSName]> <LONG IN [TSName]>>
```

where:

FileName	Identifies the name and location of the external file from which to import (copy) data
LOBPath	Identifies one or more locations to store LOB data values that are to be imported
XMLPath	Identifies one or more locations to store XML documents that are to be imported
Modifier	Identifies one or more options to use to override the default behavior of the Import utility (Table 6.2 contains a list of valid modifiers)
Method	Identifies the method (location, name, or position) to use to extract data values from the source external files specified and map them to one or more columns of the target table/updatable view indicated; the syntax you use to specify each method varies (more about this syntax a little later)
SchemaID	Identifies the XML schema/SQL identifier against which to validate XML documents being imported; when you validate XML documents in this manner, the SCH attribute of the XML Data Specifier (XDS) is ignored
CommitCount	Identifies the number of rows of data (records) to copy to the table/updatable view specified before a commit operation is performed (use COMMITCOUNT AUTOMATIC instead for import operations that fail because transaction logs become full)
RestartCount	Identifies the number of rows of data to skip in the external file specified; you typically use this option when an earlier import operation failed—by skipping rows that have already been successfully imported into a table/updatable view, one import operation can essentially continue where another import operation left off
WarningCount	Identifies the number of warnings to allow before the import operation is stopped; (if you specify the file to be imported or the target table incorrectly, the Import utility will generate a warning for each row that it attempts to import)—if this parameter is set to 0 or not specified, the import operation will continue regardless of the number of warnings issued
MsgFileName	Identifies the name and location of an external file to which to write messages produced by the Import utility as the import operation is performed
TableName	Identifies the name to assign to the table or updatable view to which data is to be imported (copied); this cannot be the name of a system catalog table or view
ColumnName	Identifies one or more specific columns (by name) to which to import data
TSName	Identifies the table space in which to store the table and its regular data, indexes, and long data/large object data if the table specified is to be created

A simple IMPORT command and a sample output look something like the following:

```
IMPORT FROM department.del OF DEL
MESSAGES department.msg
INSERT INTO department

SQL3109N  The utility is beginning to load data from file "department.del".

SQL3110N  The utility has completed processing.  "14" rows were read from the
input file.

SQL3221W  ...Begin COMMIT WORK. Input Record Count = "14".

SQL3222W  ...COMMIT of any database changes was successful.

SQL3149N  "14" rows were processed from the input file.  "14" rows were
successfully inserted into the table.  "0" rows were rejected.


Number of rows read         = 14
Number of rows skipped      = 0
Number of rows inserted     = 14
Number of rows updated      = 0
Number of rows rejected     = 0
Number of rows committed    = 14
```

Table 6.2 lists the most commonly used file type modifiers for the IMPORT command.

Table 6.2: File type modifiers recognized by the IMPORT command

Modifier	Description	File Format
compound=*x* where *x* is any number between 1 and 100	Indicates to use non-atomic compound SQL to insert the data read from a file into a table/updatable view and to include a specific number of statements (between 1 and 100) in the compound SQL block; this modifier cannot be used when INSERT_UPDATE mode is used and is incompatible with the following modifiers: usedefaults, identitymissing, identityignore, generatedmissing, and generatedignore	Delimited ASCII (DEL), nondelimited ASCII (ASC), WSF, and PC/IXF

Table 6.2: File type modifiers recognized by the IMPORT command (continued)		
Modifier	**Description**	**File Format**
generatedignore	Indicates that although data for all generated columns is present in the file being imported, this data should be ignored; instead, the Import utility should replace all generated data values found with its own generated values; this modifier is incompatible with the generatedmissing modifier	Delimited ASCII (DEL), nondelimited ASCII (ASC), WSF, and PC/IXF
generatedmissing	Indicates that data for generated columns is missing from the file being imported and that the Import utility should generate an appropriate value for each missing value encountered; this modifier is incompatible with the generatedignore modifier	Delimited ASCII (DEL), nondelimited ASCII (ASC), WSF, and PC/IXF
identityignore	Indicates that although data for all identity columns is present in the file being imported, this data should be ignored. Instead, the Import utility should replace all identity column data found with its own generated values; this modifier is incompatible with the identitymissing modifier	Delimited ASCII (DEL), nondelimited ASCII (ASC), WSF, and PC/IXF
identitymissing	Indicates that data for identity columns is missing from the file being imported and that the Import utility should generate an appropriate value for each missing value encountered; this modifier is incompatible with the identityignore modifier	Delimited ASCII (DEL), nondelimited ASCII (ASC), WSF, and PC/IXF
implicitlyhiddeninclude	Indicates that the input data file contains data for the implicitly hidden columns and that this data will also be imported; this modifier cannot be used with the implicitlyhiddenmissing modifier	Delimited ASCII (DEL), nondelimited ASCII (ASC), WSF, and PC/IXF
implicitlyhiddenmissing	Specifies that the input data file does not contain data for the implicitly hidden columns and that the utility will generate values for those hidden columns; this modifier cannot be used with the implicitlyhiddeninclude modifier	Delimited ASCII (DEL), nondelimited ASCII (ASC), WSF, and PC/IXF
lobsinfile	Indicates that LOB data values are stored in their own files	Delimited ASCII (DEL), nondelimited ASCII (ASC), WSF, and PC/IXF
no_type_id	Indicates to convert data for typed tables to a single nontyped subtable; this modifier is valid only when importing data into a single subtable of a table hierarchy	Delimited ASCII (DEL), nondelimited ASCII (ASC), WSF, and PC/IXF

Table 6.2: File type modifiers recognized by the IMPORT command (continued)		
Modifier	**Description**	**File Format**
nodefaults	Indicates that if the source column data for a target table column is not provided, and if the target table column is not nullable, default values are not to be imported; if this modifier is not used, and a source column data value for one of the target table columns is not provided, one of the following will occur: • If a default value is found for the column, the default value will be imported. • If the column is nullable, and a default value is not found for that column, a NULL value is stored in the column. • If the column is not nullable, and a default value is not found, an error is returned, and the Import utility stops processing.	Delimited ASCII (DEL), nondelimited ASCII (ASC), WSF, and PC/IXF
norowwarnings	Indicates to suppress all warning messages about rejected rows	Delimited ASCII (DEL), nondelimited ASCII (ASC), WSF, and PC/IXF
periodignore	Indicates that data for the period columns is present in the data file but should be ignored; when this modifier is specified, all period column values are generated by the utility; this modifier cannot be used with the periodmissing modifier	Delimited ASCII (DEL), nondelimited ASCII (ASC), WSF, and PC/IXF
periodmissing	Specifies that the input data file contains no data for the period columns; when this modifier is specified, all period column values are generated by the utility; this modifier cannot be used with the periodignore modifier	Delimited ASCII (DEL), nondelimited ASCII (ASC), WSF, and PC/IXF
rowchangetimestampignore	Specifies that data for the row change timestamp column is present in the data file but should be ignored; this results in all ROW CHANGE TIMESTAMP being generated by the utility—the behavior will be the same for both GENERATED ALWAYS and GENERATED BY DEFAULT columns, so for GENERATED ALWAYS columns, no rows will be rejected—this modifier cannot be used with the rowchangetimestampmissing modifier	Delimited ASCII (DEL), nondelimited ASCII (ASC), WSF, and PC/IXF
rowchangetimestampmissing	Specifies that the input data file contains no data for the row change timestamp column (not even NULLs) and will therefore generate a value for each row—the behavior will be the same for both GENERATED ALWAYS and GENERATED BY DEFAULT columns—this modifier cannot be used with the rowchangetimestampignore modifier	Delimited ASCII (DEL), nondelimited ASCII (ASC), WSF, and PC/IXF

Table 6.2: File type modifiers recognized by the IMPORT command (continued)		
Modifier	**Description**	**File Format**
seclabelchar	Indicates to store security labels in the input source file in the string format for security label values rather than in the default encoded numeric format (the Import utility converts each security label found into the internal format as it is loaded; if a string is not in the proper format, the row is not imported, and a warning is returned; if the string does not represent a valid security label that is part of the security policy protecting the table, then the row is not imported, and a warning is returned); this modifier cannot be used if the seclabelname modifier is specified	Delimited ASCII (DEL), nondelimited ASCII (ASC), WSF, and PC/IXF
eclabelname	Indicates to identify security labels in the input source file by their name rather than by the default encoded numeric format (the Import utility will convert the name to the appropriate security label if it exists; if no security label exists with the indicated name for the security policy protecting the table, the row is not imported and a warning is returned); this modifier cannot be used if the seclabelchar modifier is specified	Delimited ASCII (DEL), nondelimited ASCII (ASC), WSF, and PC/IXF
transactionidignore	Specifies that data for the TRANSACTION START ID column is present in the data file but should be ignored; when this modifier is specified, the value for the TRANSACTION START ID column is generated by the utility; this modifier cannot be used with the transactionidmissing modifier	Delimited ASCII (DEL), nondelimited ASCII (ASC), WSF, and PC/IXF
transactionidmissing	Specifies that the input data file contains no data for the TRANSACTION START ID columns; when this modifier is specified, the value for the TRANSACTION START ID column is generated by the utility; this modifier cannot be used with the transactionidignore modifier	Delimited ASCII (DEL), nondelimited ASCII (ASC), WSF, and PC/IXF
usedefaults	Indicates to generate default values for the column if the source column data for a target table column is not provided and if the target table column has a defaults constraint; if this modifier is not used, and a source column data value for one of the target table columns is not provided, one of the following will occur: • If the column is nullable, a NULL value is stored in the column. • If the column is not nullable, and a default value cannot be generated, the row is rejected.	Delimited ASCII (DEL), nondelimited ASCII (ASC), WSF, and PC/IXF
codepage=*x* where *x* is any valid code page identifier	Identifies the code page of the data contained in the output data set produced; character data is converted from the application code page to the code page specified during the import operation	Delimited ASCII (DEL) and nondelimited ASCII (ASC)

Table 6.2: File type modifiers recognized by the IMPORT command (continued)		
Modifier	**Description**	**File Format**
dateformat=*x* where *x* is any valid combination of date format elements	Identifies how to format date values stored in the source file; using the following date elements will create the format string provided with this modifier: • YYYY—Year (four digits ranging from 0000 to 9999) • M—Month (one or two digits ranging from 1 to 12) • MM—Month (two digits ranging from 1 to 12; mutually exclusive with M) • D—Day (one or two digits ranging from 1 to 31) • DD—Day (two digits ranging from 1 to 31; mutually exclusive with D) • DDD—Day of the year (three digits ranging from 001 to 366; mutually exclusive with other day or month elements) Examples of valid date format strings include the following: "D-M-YYYY" "MM.DD.YYYY" "YYYYDDD"	Delimited ASCII (DEL) and nondelimited ASCII (ASC)
implieddecimal	Indicates that the column definition is to determine the location of an implied decimal point—the Import utility is not to assume that the decimal point is at the end of the value (default behavior);.for example, if this modifier is specified, the value 12345 would be loaded into a DECIMAL(8,2) column as 123.45, not as 12345.00	Delimited ASCII (DEL) and nondelimited ASCII (ASC)
timeformat=*x* where *x* is any valid combination of time format elements	Identifies how to format time values stored in the source file; using the following time elements will create the format string provided with this modifier: • H—Hour (one or two digits ranging from 0 to 12 for a 12-hour system, and 0 to 24 for a 24-hour system) • HH—Hour (two digits ranging from 0 to 12 for a 12-hour system, and 0 to 24 for a 24-hour system; mutually exclusive with H) • M—Minute (one or two digits ranging from 0 to 59) • MM—Minute (two digits ranging from 0 to 59; mutually exclusive with M) • S—Second (one or two digits ranging from 0 to 59) • SS—Second (two digits ranging from 0 to 59; mutually exclusive with S) • SSSSS—Second of the day after midnight (5 digits ranging from 00000 to 86399; mutually exclusive with other time elements) • TT—Meridian indicator (am or pm) Examples of valid time format strings include: "HH:MM:SS" "HH.MM TT" "SSSSS"	Delimited ASCII (DEL) and nondelimited ASCII (ASC)

Table 6.2: File type modifiers recognized by the IMPORT command (continued)		
Modifier	**Description**	**File Format**
timestampformat=*x* where *x* is any valid combination of date and time format elements	Identifies how to format timestamp values stored in the source file; using the following date and time elements will create the format string provided with this modifier: • YYYY—Year (four digits ranging from 0000 to 9999) • M—Month (one or two digits ranging from 1 to 12) • MM—Month (two digits ranging from 1 to 12; mutually exclusive with M) • D—Day (one or two digits ranging from 1 to 31) • DD—Day (two digits ranging from 1 to 31; mutually exclusive with D) • DDD—Day of the year (three digits ranging from 001 to 366; mutually exclusive with other day or month elements) • H—Hour (one or two digits ranging from 0 to 12 for a 12-hour system, and 0 to 24 for a 24-hour system) • HH—Hour (two digits ranging from 0 to 12 for a 12-hour system, and 0 to 24 for a 24-hour system; mutually exclusive with H) • M—Minute (one or two digits ranging from 0 to 59) • MM—Minute (two digits ranging from 0 to 59; mutually exclusive with M) • S—Second (one or two digits ranging from 0 to 59) • SS—Second (two digits ranging from 0 to 59; mutually exclusive with S) • SSSSS—Second of the day after midnight (5 digits ranging from 00000 to 86399; mutually exclusive with other time elements) • UUUUUU—Microsecond (6 digits ranging from 000000 to 999999) • TT—Meridian indicator (am or pm) An example of a valid timestamp format string is: "YYYY/MM/DD HH:MM:SS.UUUUUU"	Delimited ASCII (DEL) and nondelimited ASCII (ASC)
usegraphiccodepage	Indicates to store data being imported into graphic or double-byte character large object (DBCLOB) columns in the graphic code page; the rest of the data is assumed to be stored in the character code page—the Import utility determines the character code page either through the codepage modifier, if it is specified, or through the code page of the application if the codepage modifier is not specified; this modifier must not be specified with delimited ASCII (DEL) files created by the Export utility—those files contain data encoded in only one code page	Delimited ASCII (DEL) and nondelimited ASCII (ASC)
xmlchar	Specifies to encode XML documents in the character code page; this modifier is useful for processing XML documents that are encoded in the specified character code page but do not contain an encoding declaration	Delimited ASCII (DEL) and nondelimited ASCII (ASC)
xmlgraphic	Indicates to encode XML documents in the graphic code page specified; this modifier is useful for processing XML documents that are encoded in a specific graphic code page but do not contain an encoding declaration	Delimited ASCII (DEL) and nondelimited ASCII (ASC)

Table 6.2: File type modifiers recognized by the IMPORT command (continued)		
Modifier	**Description**	**File Format**
chardel*x* where *x* is any valid delimiter character	Identifies a specific character to use as a character delimiter; the default character delimiter is a double quotation mark (") character; the character specified is used in place of the double quotation mark to enclose a character string	Delimited ASCII (DEL)
coldel*x* where *x* is any valid delimiter character	Identifies a specific character to use as a column delimiter; the default column delimiter is a comma (,) character; the character specified is used in place of a comma to signal the end of a column	Delimited ASCII (DEL)
decplusblank	Indicates to prefix positive decimal values with a blank space instead of a plus sign (+); the default action is to prefix positive decimal values with a plus sign	Delimited ASCII (DEL)
decpt*x* where *x* is any valid delimiter character	Identifies a specific character to use as a decimal point character; the default decimal point character is a period (.) character; the character specified is used in place of a period as a decimal point character	Delimited ASCII (DEL)
delprioritychar	Indicates that the priority for evaluating delimiters is to be character delimiter, record delimiter, column delimiter rather than record delimiter, character delimiter, column delimiter (which is the default); this modifier is typically used with older applications that depend on the other priority	Delimited ASCII (DEL)
keepblanks	Indicates to retain all leading and trailing blanks found for each column that has a data type of CHAR, VARCHAR, LONG VARCHAR, or CLOB; if this modifier is not specified, all leading and trailing blanks that reside outside character delimiters are removed, and a NULL is inserted into the table for all missing data values found	Delimited ASCII (DEL)
nochardel	Indicates that the Import utility is to assume all bytes found between the column delimiters to be part of the column's data (character delimiters will be parsed as part of column data); this modifier should not be specified if DB2 exported the data (unless the nochardel modifier was specified at export time)—it is provided to support vendor data files that do not have character delimiters, and improper usage might result in data loss or corruption—this modifier cannot be specified with chardelx, delprioritychar, or nodoubledel; these are mutually exclusive options	Delimited ASCII (DEL)
nodoubledel	Indicates not to recognize double character delimiters	Delimited ASCII (DEL)
nochecklengths	Indicates that the Import utility is to attempt to import every row in the source file, even if the source data has a column value that exceeds the size of the target column's definition; such rows can be successfully imported if code page conversion causes the source data to shrink in size (for example, 4-byte EUC data in a source file can shrink to 2-byte DBCS data in the target table and require half the space); this option is particularly useful if it is known in advance that the source data will always fit in a column despite mismatched column definitions/sizes	Non-delimited ASCII (ASC) and PC/IXF

Table 6.2: File type modifiers recognized by the IMPORT command (continued)		
Modifier	**Description**	**File Format**
nullindchar=*x* where *x* is any valid character	Identifies a specific character to use as a null indicator value; the default null indicator is Y—this modifier is case-sensitive for EBCDIC data files, except when the character is an English letter (for example, if the null indicator character is specified as N, then the n is also recognized as a null indicator)	Non-delimited ASCII (ASC)
reclen=*x* where *x* is any number between 1 and 32,767	Indicates to read a specific number of characters from the source file for each row found; new-line characters are to be ignored instead of being used to indicate the end of a row	Non-delimited ASCII (ASC)
striptblanks	Indicates to truncate all leading and trailing blanks found for each column that has a data type of VARCHAR, LONG VARCHAR, VARGRAPHIC, or LONG VARGRAPHIC; this modifier is incompatible with the striptnulls modifier	Non-delimited ASCII (ASC)
striptnulls	Indicates to truncate all leading and trailing nulls (0x00 characters) found for each column that has a data type of VARCHAR, LONG VARCHAR, VARGRAPHIC, or LONG VARGRAPHIC; this modifier is incompatible with the striptblanks modifier	Non-delimited ASCII (ASC)
forcein	Indicates that the Import utility is to accept data despite code page mismatches (in other words, to suppress translation between code pages); fixed-length target columns are checked to verify that they are large enough to hold the data unless the nochecklengths modifier has been specified	PC/IXF
indexixf	Indicates that the Import utility is to drop all indexes currently defined on the existing table and is to create new indexes by using the index definitions stored in the IXF formatted source file; this modifier can be used only when the contents of a table are being replaced, and it cannot be used with a view	PC/IXF
indexschema=*x* where *x* is a valid schema name	Indicates that the Import utility is to assign all indexes created to the schema specified—if this modifier is used, and no schema name is provided, all indexes created will be assigned to the default schema for the user ID that is associated with the current database connection; if this modifier is not used, all indexes created will be assigned to the schema identified in the IXF formatted source file	PC/IXF
forcecreate	Specifies to create a table with possible missing or limited information after an import operation returns the error code SQL3311N	PC/IXF
Adapted from Tables 13-18 of the IBM DB2 10.1 Command Reference		

Earlier, you saw that three methods are used to map data values in external files to columns in a table: the location method, the name method, and the position method.

The syntax to indicate the use of the location method to extract data values from the external file specified is:

```
METHOD L ( [ColumnStart] [ColumnEnd] ,... )
    <NULL INDICATORS ( [NullIndColNumber ,...] )>
```

where:

ColumnStart	Identifies the starting position of one or more data values in the nondelimited ASCII (ASC) formatted file from which to retrieve values
ColumnEnd	Identifies the ending position of one or more data values in the nondelimited ASCII (ASC) formatted file from which to retrieve values
NullIndColNumber	Identifies the position of one or more data values to treat as null indicator variables for column data values in the nondelimited ASCII (ASC) formatted file from which to retrieve values

The syntax to indicate the use of the name method to extract data values from the external file specified is:

```
METHOD N ( [ColumnName ,...] )
```

where:

ColumnName	Identifies one or more unique names to assign to columns in the PC/IXF formatted file from which to retrieve values

And the syntax to indicate the use of the position method to extract data values from the external file specified is:

```
METHOD P ( [ColumnPosition ,...] )
```

where:

ColumnPosition	Identifies the indexed position of one or more columns in the delimited ASCII (DEL) or PC/IXF formatted file from which to retrieve values

You may also have noticed that the following five options are available with the IMPORT command to control how the target table data to be copied will be altered by the import operation:

- **CREATE.** When you use the CREATE option, the target table is created along with all of its associated indexes, and data is then imported into the new table. This option also allows you to control in which table space the new table will be created. However, you can use this option only when importing data from PC/IXF formatted files.
- **INSERT.** With the INSERT option, data is inserted into the target table (which must already exist). Imported data is appended to any data that already exists.
- **INSERT_UPDATE.** When you use the INSERT_UPDATE option, data is either inserted into the target table (which must already exist) or used to update existing rows (if the row being imported has a primary key value that matches that of an existing record). Existing records will be updated only if the target table you specify has a primary key defined.
- **REPLACE.** With the REPLACE option, any existing data is deleted from the target table (which must already exist); then the new data is inserted. (You cannot use this option if the target table contains a primary key that is referenced by a foreign key in another table.)
- **REPLACE_CREATE.** When you use the REPLACE_CREATE option, any existing data is deleted from the target table if it already exists, and then the new data is inserted. However, if the target table does not exist, it is created along with all of its associated indexes, and data is then imported into the new table. As you might imagine, this option can be used only when importing data from PC/IXF formatted files. (You cannot use this option if the target table contains a primary key that is referenced by a foreign key in another table.)

Thus, if you want to import data stored in a PC/IXF format external file named DEPT.IXF to a new table named DEPARTMENT, you execute an IMPORT command:

```
IMPORT FROM C:\dept.ixf OF IXF
MESSAGES imp_msgs.txt
CREATE INTO department IN hr_space1
```

As previously mentioned, when data that is to be exported contains LOB values, by default only the first 32 KB of each LOB value are actually written to the file containing the exported data. To override this behavior, you use the lobsinfile or lobsinsepfiles modifier and provide the Export utility with one or more locations to which LOB data values are to be written. In this case, each LOB value found will be stored, in its entirety, in its own file that is assigned a name that either the user or the Export utility provides. You can also import LOB values that reside in individual files by using the appropriate modifier (lobsinfile). And because the names and locations of files containing LOB data values are stored in the source data file (assuming the

Export utility produced the source data file) along with other data, this information does not have to be provided to the Import utility to retrieve the LOB data values.

Thus, to import data stored in a delimited ASCII (DEL) format external file named employee.del, along with LOB data values stored in individual files, to a table named EMPLOYEE, execute an IMPORT command:

```
IMPORT FROM C:\employee.del OF DEL
LOBS FROM C:\lobfiles
MODIFIED BY lobsinfile coldel;
MESSAGES imp_msgs.txt
INSERT INTO employee
```

When executed, this command will do the following:

- Retrieve all data values stored in a delimited ASCII (DEL) format external file named employee.del (this file resides in the root directory on drive C:).
- Locate all LOB values referenced in the file named employee.del and retrieve each value from its own file (each file is expected to reside in a directory named lobfiles located on drive C:).
- Insert all data values retrieved from both the file named employee.del and the individual LOB data files into a table named EMPLOYEE (which already exists).
- Record all messages produced by the Import utility to a file named imp_msgs.txt (which will reside in the current working directory).

Figure 6.10 illustrates this import operation.

You can retrieve and copy XML documents stored in individual files to a table in a similar manner. Figure 6.11 illustrates a simple import operation in which XML documents are processed this way. To import XML files, use the XML FROM option to specify one or more paths where XML files are stored. You can also choose how the XML documents are parsed: PRESERVE or STRIP WHITESPACE options. If you do not specify the XMLPARSE option, the parsing behavior for XML documents will be determined by the CURRENT IMPLICIT XMLPARSE OPTION special register and its initial value set to STRIP WHITESPACE. When you insert or update an XML document, you can possibly validate the structure, content, and data type of the XML document by using XMLVALIDATE option within the IMPORT command.

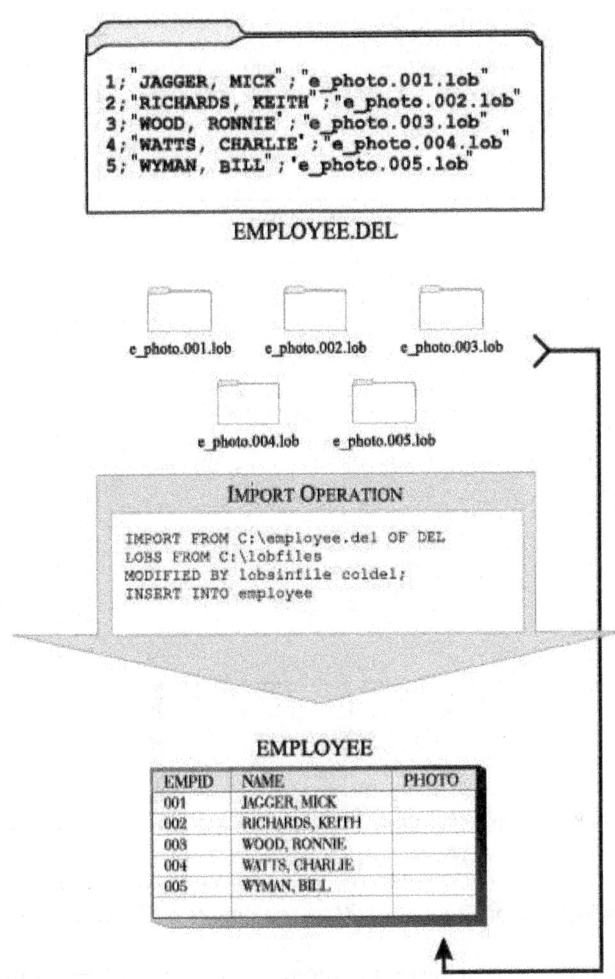

Figure 6.10: An import operation in which LOB values are stored in individual files

You can also import data stored in external files by using the Import Table wizard within IBM Data Studio, which you activate by selecting the appropriate action from the Administration Perspective. Figure 6.12 illustrates how to activate the Import Table dialog; Figure 6.13 shows file formats and the import modes along with import file absolute path.

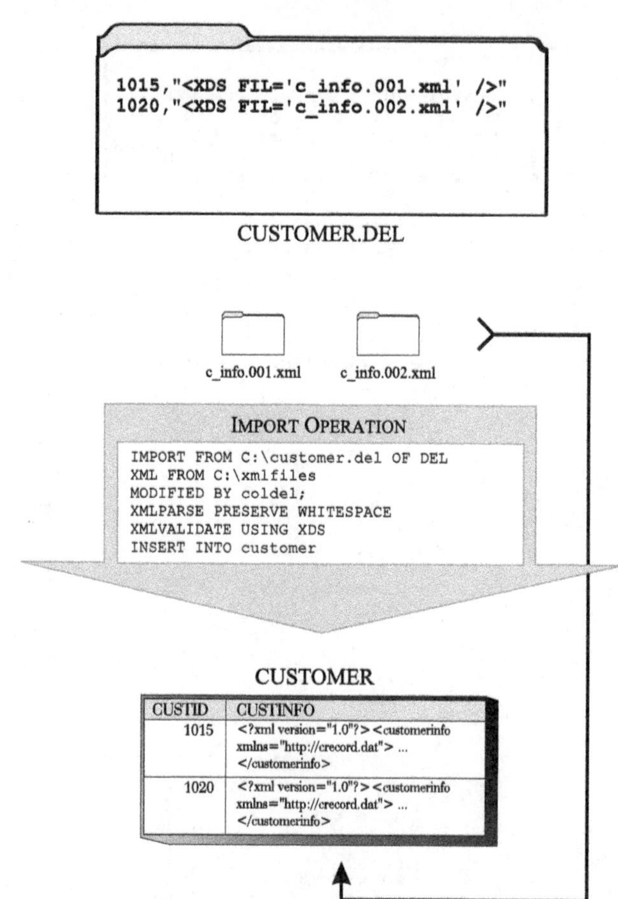

Figure 6.11: Import operation in which XML documents are stored in individual files

Figure 6.14 shows the behavior of various column types such as identityignore, identitymissing, generatedignore, generatedmissing, rowchangetimestampignore, and rowchangetimestampmissin. It also lets you specify one or more directories that contain LOB and XML data. You can also choose to insert DEFAULT values for missing data.

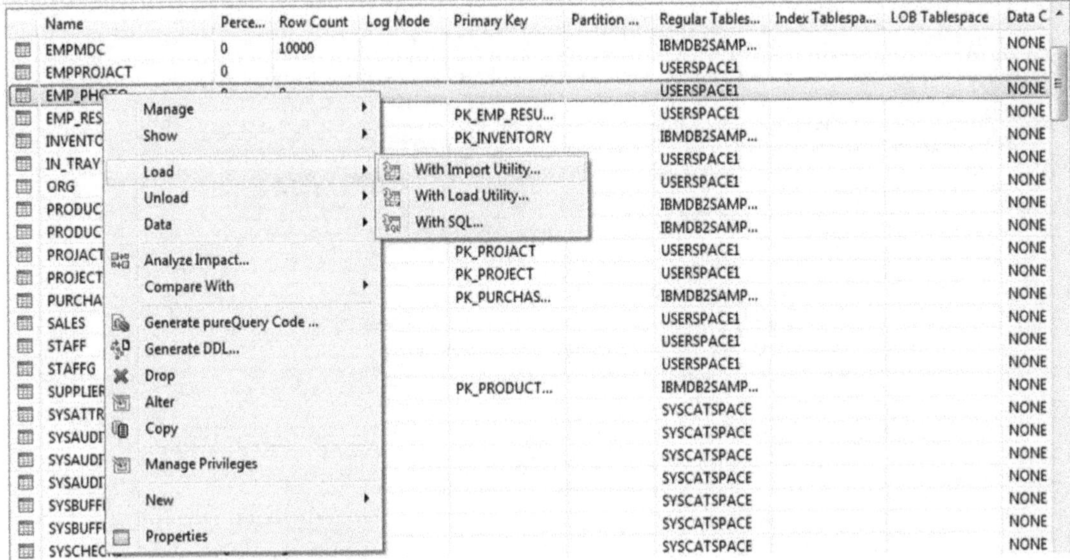

Figure 6.12: Invoking the Import utility through IBM Data Studio

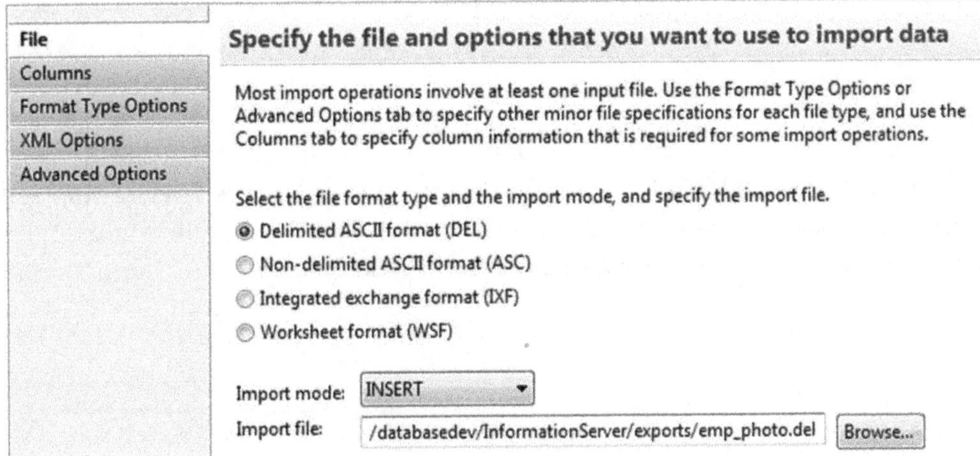

Figure 6.13: Import—file options

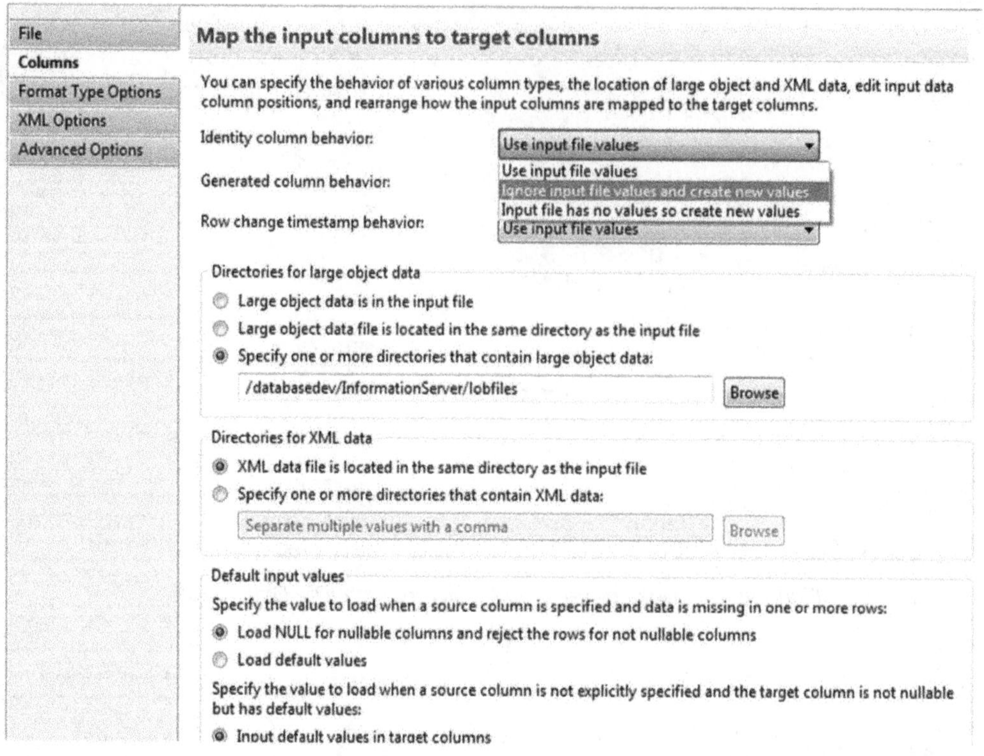

Figure 6.14: Import—column options

Figure 6.15 displays available date, time, and timestamp formats to choose along with the data code page and graphic code page for data imported into graphic and DBCLOB columns. You can choose specific delimiters while loading DEL file format data into a table.

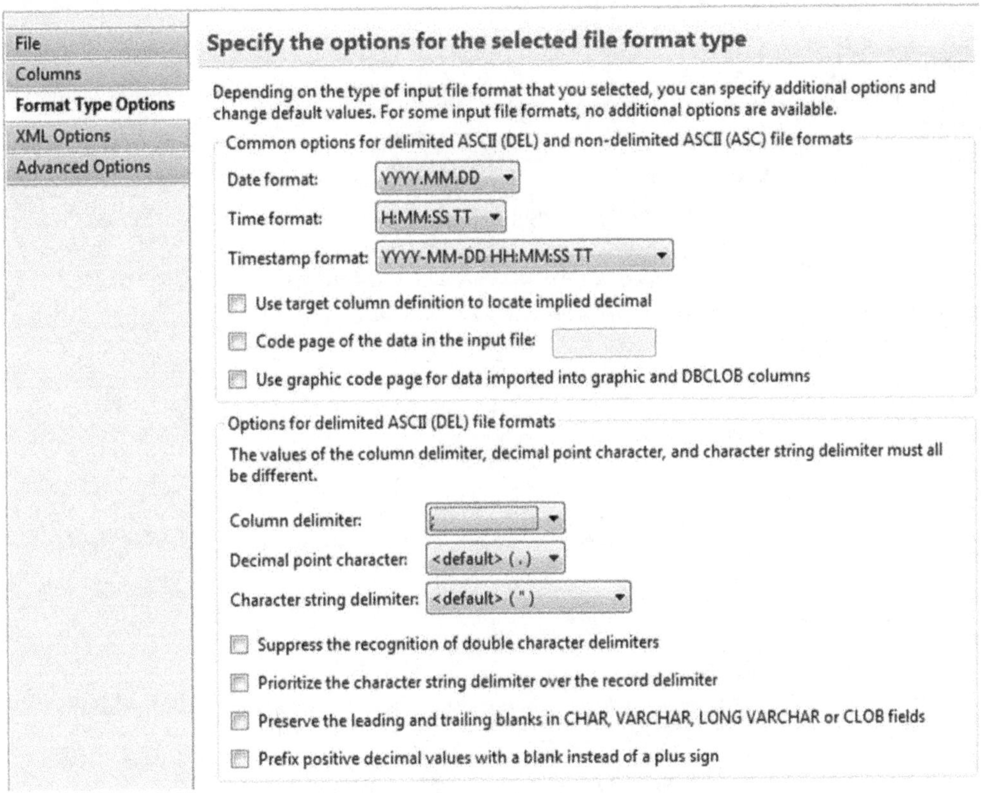

File
Columns
Format Type Options
XML Options
Advanced Options

Specify the options for the selected file format type

Depending on the type of input file format that you selected, you can specify additional options and change default values. For some input file formats, no additional options are available.

Common options for delimited ASCII (DEL) and non-delimited ASCII (ASC) file formats

Date format: YYYY.MM.DD
Time format: H:MM:SS TT
Timestamp format: YYYY-MM-DD HH:MM:SS TT

- [ ] Use target column definition to locate implied decimal
- [ ] Code page of the data in the input file:
- [ ] Use graphic code page for data imported into graphic and DBCLOB columns

Options for delimited ASCII (DEL) file formats

The values of the column delimiter, decimal point character, and character string delimiter must all be different.

Column delimiter:
Decimal point character: <default> (.)
Character string delimiter: <default> (")

- [ ] Suppress the recognition of double character delimiters
- [ ] Prioritize the character string delimiter over the record delimiter
- [ ] Preserve the leading and trailing blanks in CHAR, VARCHAR, LONG VARCHAR or CLOB fields
- [ ] Prefix positive decimal values with a blank instead of a plus sign

Figure 6.15: Import—format type options

Figure 6.16 shows the XML options available to choose while loading data into a table having one or more XML columns. You can select either **Preserve white space** or **Remove white space**. The following XMLVALIDATE options validate XML document content, structure, and data type against a schema:

- **USING XDS**. The XML documents are validated against the XML schema identified by the XDS. When you invoke XML validation with the USING XDS clause, the schema to use to perform validation will be determined by the SCH (a fully qualified SQL identifier of the XML schema) attribute of the XDS. The SCH information is generally stored in the SYSCAT. XSROBJECTS system catalog table.
- **USING SCHEMA**. The XML documents are validated against the XML schema with the specified SQL identifier.
- **USING SCHEMALOCATION HINTS**. The XML documents are validated against the schemas identified by XML schema location hints in the source XML documents.

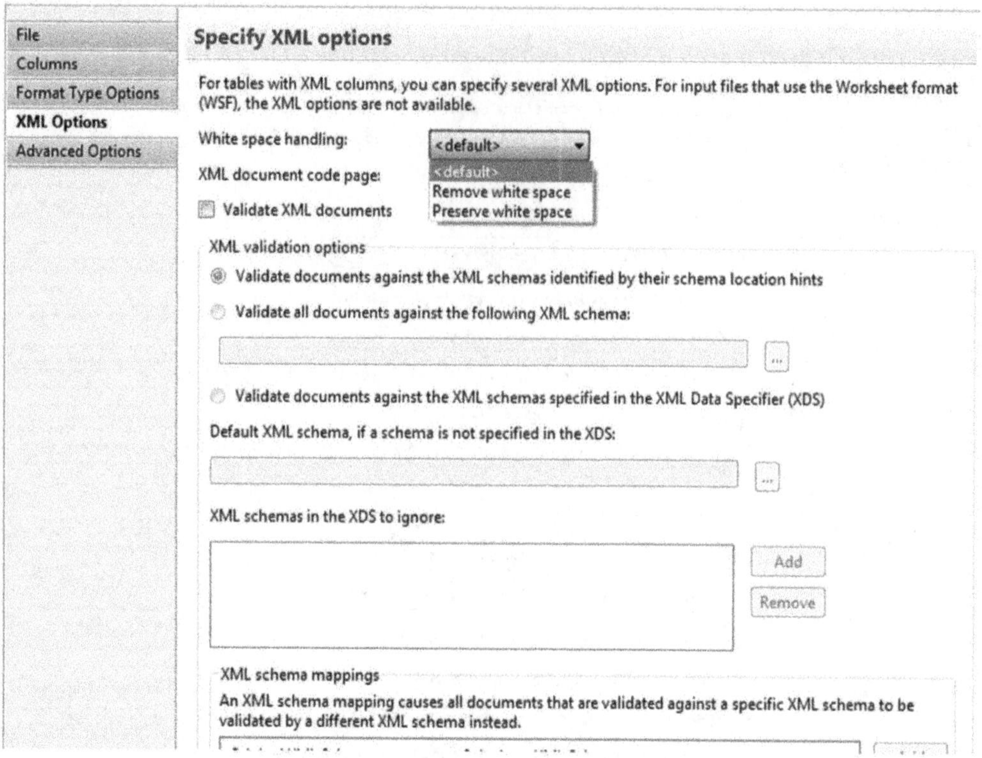

Figure 6.16: Import—XML options

Figure 6.17 illustrates advanced options available to specify while loading the data through the IMPORT command. There are three commit options:

- **Use database server setting.** The Import utility loads data into a table through insert SQL statements, and it executes COMMIT statement only after finishing the whole data load operation. Remember, the IMPORT operation logs every insert in the transaction log.
- **Automatically commit.** The database manager determines the COMMIT frequency based on the available active transaction log space, the available locklist memory, and the maxlocks setting to avoid lock escalations. This is equivalent to specifying COMMITCOUNT AUTOMATIC in the command.
- **Commit after processing number of rows.** This option lets you choose the number of inserts after which the database manager forces a COMMIT to release lock memory and the active transaction log space. This is equivalent to specifying COMMITCOUNT <number> in the command.

Two table access options are available while loading the data through import operation.

- **Restrict all access**. This runs import operations in an offline mode. An exclusive (X) lock on the target table is acquired before any rows are inserted. This generally affects concurrent applications accessing the table data, and this is IMPORT's default behavior.
- **Allow write access**. This runs import operations in an online mode. An intent exclusive (IX) lock on the target table is acquired when the first row is inserted. This facilitates concurrent applications accessing the table data. However, this is not compatible with REPLACE, CREATE, and REPLACE_CREATE import options because it needs an exclusive lock to replace or create table data or table.

The other advanced options are:

- **Start import after record number**. This specifies to start an import operation at record *n*+1, where the first *n* records are being skipped. This is equivalent to SKIPCOUNT *n* or RESTARTCOUNT *n* in the IMPORT command.
- **Maximum number of rows to import**. This specifies *n* number of records in the file to be imported into the table; it can be an insert or an update. This is equivalent to ROWCOUNT *n* in the IMPORT command.
- **Stop the import after a set number of warnings**. This specifies *n* number of warning messages after which the import operation stops running. This is equivalent to WARNINGCOUNT *n* in the IMPORT command.
- **Reduce overhead with compound SQL**. This specifies *x* number of non-atomic compound SQL statements to insert the data into a table and the number *x* positions between 1 and 100 inclusive. This is equivalent to COMPOUND *x* in the IMPORT command.
- **Suppress all warnings about rejected rows**. This specifies to generate no warnings about any rejected rows. This is equivalent to NOROWWARNINGS in the IMPORT command.
- **Do not time out while waiting for locks**. This specifies that the Import utility will not time out while waiting for locks. This option supersedes the locktimeout database configuration parameter. Other applications are not affected.

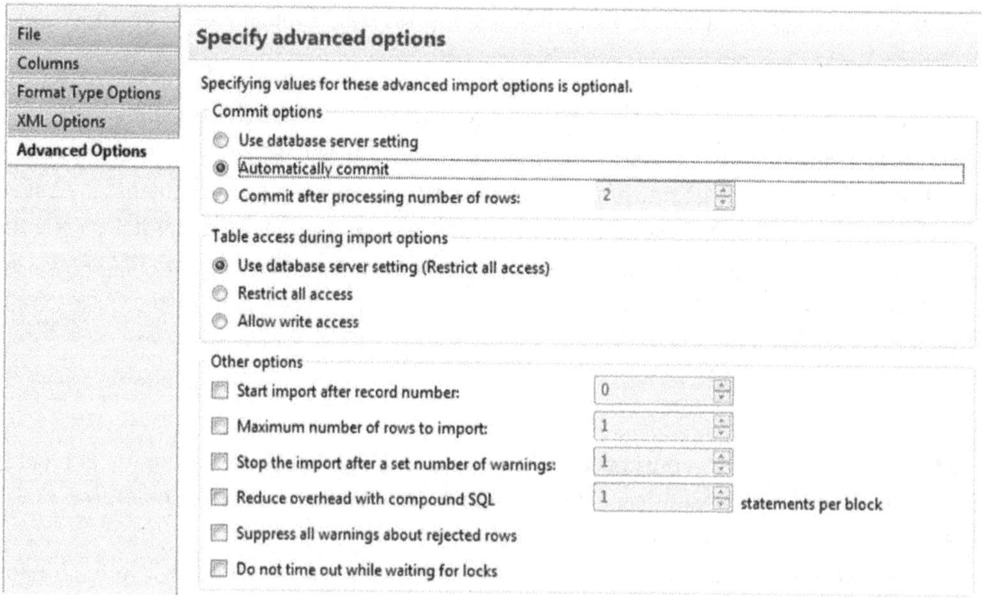

Figure 6.17: Import—advanced options

Figure 6.18 shows the command edit and run options. When you click the **Run** button, the DB2 database manager runs an IMPORT command with the appropriate command clauses by using the SYSPROC.ADMIN_CMD built-in ADMIN stored procedure:

```
CALL SYSPROC.ADMIN_CMD ( '
IMPORT FROM "/databasedev/InformationServer/exports/emp_photo.del" OF DEL
LOBS FROM "/home/edwetld/lobdata"
MODIFIED BY dateformat="YYYY.MM.DD"
timeformat="H:MM:SS TT"
timestampformat="YYYY-MM-DD HH:MM:SS TT"
coldel;
COMMITCOUNT AUTOMATIC
MESSAGES ON SERVER
INSERT INTO DATAMARTS.EMP_PHOTO');
```

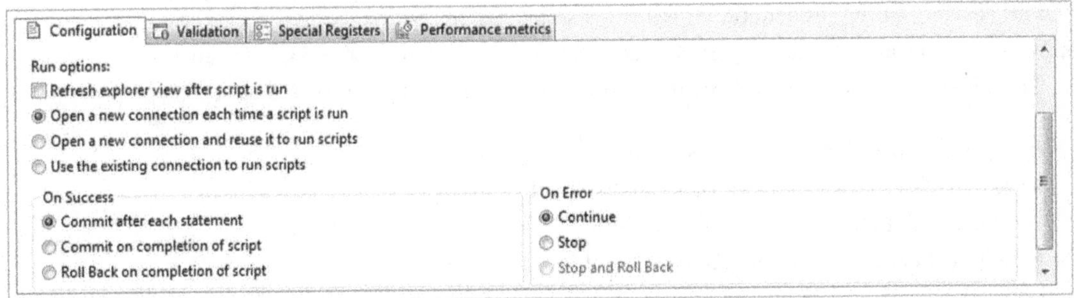


```
CALL SYSPROC.ADMIN_CMD( 'IMPORT FROM "/databasedev/InformationServer/exports/emp_photo.del" OF DEL LOBS FROM "/databasede
```

Figure 6.18: Import—run options

Note: You might have experienced the SQL0964C (Transaction Log Full) condition while running the IMPORT command due to running out of active log space in the database. This can well be controlled by DB2 registry variable DB2_FORCE_APP_ON_MAX_LOG and the IMPORT command's commit clause COMMITCOUNT, as in Table 6.3.

Table 6.3: Avoiding the transaction log full conditions

DB2_FORCE_APP_ON_MAX_LOG	COMMITCOUNT	Database Manager Behavior
FALSE	AUTOMATIC	The DB2 database manager determines a COMMITCOUNT value that avoids SQL0964C by looking at the active log space available.
FALSE	*n*	The DB2 database manager attempts to resolve the SQL0964C condition by performing unconditional commits and reattempting the inserts/updates.
TRUE (default)	AUTOMATIC or *n*	The import operation will fail if it encounters an SQL9064C error and the DB2 datatbase manager made no attempts to resolve it.

A Word About the ADMIN_CMD () Stored Procedure

Although you can invoke most of the utilities provided with DB2 from the IBM Data Studio or by executing the appropriate command from the DB2 CLP or an operating system prompt, there may be times when you want to invoke a utility from an embedded SQL, CLI, or Java application. For this reason, most DB2 commands have a corresponding application programming interface (API). Unfortunately, the source code needed to use some of these APIs can be quite complex, and all the APIs available are used primarily in C and C++ applications. A simpler approach is to use the

ADMIN_CMD () stored procedure, which is a special system built-in stored procedure that allows applications to run select administrative commands by using the CALL SQL statement.

You must have one of the following authorities to execute the ADMIN_CMD () stored procedure:

- EXECUTE privilege on the procedure
- DATAACCESS authority at the database level
- DBADM authority at the database level
- SQLADM authority at the database level

You can invoke the following commands by using the ADMIN_CMD () stored procedure:

- ADD CONTACT
- ADD CONTACTGROUP
- AUTOCONFIGURE
- BACKUP (online only)
- DESCRIBE
- DROP CONTACT
- DROP CONTACTGROUP
- EXPORT
- FORCE APPLICATION
- IMPORT
- INITIALIZE TAPE
- LOAD
- PRUNE HISTORY/LOGFILE
- QUIESCE DATABASE
- QUIESCE TABLESPACES FOR TABLE
- REDISTRIBUTE
- REORG INDEXES/TABLE
- RESET ALERT CONFIGURATION
- RESET DATABASE CONFIGURATION
- RESET DATABASE MANAGER CONFIGURATION
- REWIND TAPE
- RUNSTATS
- SET TAPE POSITION
- UNQUIESCE DATABASE
- UPDATE ALERT CONFIGURATION
- UPDATE CONTACT

- UPDATE CONTACTGROUP
- UPDATE DATABASE CONFIGURATION
- UPDATE DATABASE MANAGER CONFIGURATION
- UPDATE HEALTH NOTIFICATION CONTACT LIST
- UPDATE HISTORY

Thus, if you want to use the ADMIN_CMD() stored procedure to export data stored in a table named STAFF to a PC/IXF format, external file named staff.ixf, you can do so by connecting to the database that contains the STAFF table and executing a CALL SQL statement:

```
CALL SYSPROC.ADMIN_CMD ('EXPORT TO staff.ixf OF IXF
                        MESSAGES ON SERVER SELECT * FROM staff')
```

Because the ADMIN_CMD() stored procedure runs on the server, messages produced by the utility being executed are generated on the server; the MESSAGES ON SERVER option available with some commands indicates that any message file used is to be created on the server. Additionally, command execution status is returned in the SQL communications area (SQLCA) data structure associated with the CALL statement used.

If the execution of the administrative command is successful, and the command returns more than execution status, the additional information is returned in the form of one or more result data sets. For example, if the EXPORT command is executed successfully, a result data set is returned that contains information about the number of rows that were successfully exported. (The actual result set information returned is documented with each command.) It is important to note that you can retrieve result set information by using the CLP or with JDBC and DB2 CLI applications, but not with embedded SQL applications.

If the execution of an administrative command is not successful, the ADMIN_CMD () stored procedure will return an SQL20397W warning message, along with a result set containing details about the reason for the failure. Therefore, any application that uses the ADMIN_CMD () procedure should check the SQLCA return code that the procedure call generates. If the return code is greater than or equal to 0, a result set was produced and should be retrieved for evaluation.

Interestingly, the procedure ADMIN_CMD () supports two commands that the CLP does not support:

- GET STMM TUNING
- UPDATE STMM TUNING

command reads the catalog tables to report the user-preferred STMM current STMM tuning member number. A value of -1 indicates that to run the self-tuning memory manager:

```
OC.ADMIN_CMD ('GET STMM TUNING MEMBER')

  Result set 1
  --------------

  USER_PREFERRED_NUMBER CURRENT_NUMBER
  --------------------- --------------
                     -1             -1

  1 record(s) selected.

  Return Status = 0
```

For compatibility purposes, you can replace MEMBER by DBPARTITIONNUM in the command to run the procedure on DB2 9.7, or as follows:

```
CALL SYSPROC.ADMIN_CMD ('GET STMM TUNING DBPARTITIONNUM')

  Result set 1
  --------------

  USER_PREFERRED_NUMBER CURRENT_NUMBER
  --------------------- --------------
                      1              1

  1 record(s) selected.

  Return Status = 0
```

The UPDATE STMM TUNING command updates the user-preferred STMM tuning databa
member number. This setting makes much sense in DB2 DPF and DB2 pureScale systems:

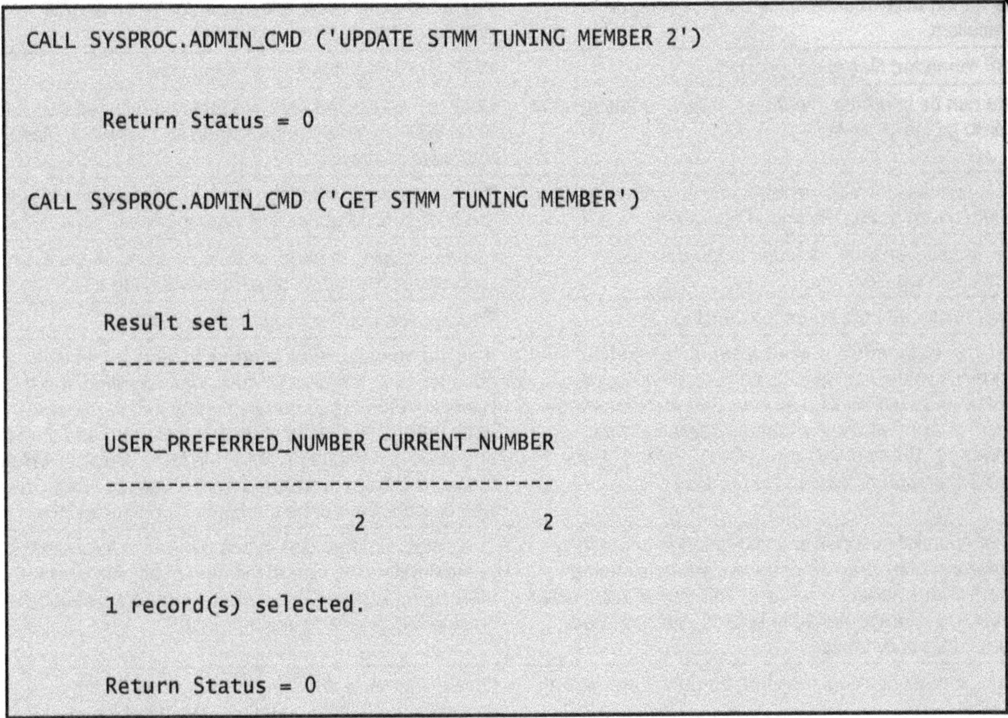

```
CALL SYSPROC.ADMIN_CMD ('UPDATE STMM TUNING MEMBER 2')

        Return Status = 0

CALL SYSPROC.ADMIN_CMD ('GET STMM TUNING MEMBER')


        Result set 1
        --------------

        USER_PREFERRED_NUMBER CURRENT_NUMBER
        --------------------- --------------
                            2              2

        1 record(s) selected.

        Return Status = 0
```

The DB2 Load Utility

Like the Import utility, the Load utility reads data directly from an external file (provided the file is written in a format that DB2 supports) and stores it in a specific table. However, unlike with the Import utility, when you use the Load utility, the table to which data is to be copied must already exists in the database before the load operation is initiated. Table 6.4 lists other differences between the Import utility and the Load utility.

Table 6.4: Differences between the Import utility and the Load utility

Import Utility	Load Utility
The Import utility is slow when processing large amounts of data because it calls parallel INSERT statements in the background.	The Load utility is significantly faster than the Import utility when processing large amounts of data because it writes formatted pages directly into the database's storage containers.
Tables and indexes can be created from IXF format files.	Tables and indexes must exist before data can be loaded into them.

Table …etween the Import utility and the Load utility (continued)

Import Utility	Load Utility
… use of intrapartition	The Load utility takes full advantage of intrapartition parallelism on SMP workstations.
… are supported.	WSF formatted files are not supported.
…nported into tables, views, or aliases that …ables or views.	Data can be loaded only into tables or aliases that refer to tables—data cannot be loaded into views or aliases that refer to views.
Table spaces in which the table and its indexes reside remain online during the import operation.	Table spaces in which the table and its indexes reside are taken offline during the load operation.
Row transactions are recorded in the database's transaction log files.	Minimal logging is performed—row transactions are not recorded in the database's transaction log files.
Triggers can be fired during processing.	Triggers are not fired during processing.
If an import operation is interrupted, and a commit frequency value was specified, the table will remain usable, and it will contain all rows that were inserted up to the moment the last commit operation was performed. The user has the option of restarting the import operation or leaving the table as it is.	If a load operation was interrupted, and a consistency point (commit frequency) value was specified, the table remains in the "Load pending" state and cannot be used until (1) the load process is restarted, and the load operation is completed, or (2) the table space in which the table resides is restored from a backup image that was created before the load operation was initiated.
The amount of free disk space needed to import data is approximately the size of the largest index being imported plus about 10 percent. This space is allocated from system temporary table spaces that have been defined for the database.	The amount of free disk space needed to load data is approximately the size of the sum of all indexes for the table being loaded. This space is temporarily allocated outside the database environment.
All constraint checking is performed during processing.	Only uniqueness checking is performed during processing. All other constraint checking (check constraints, referential integrity constraints, etc.) must be performed after the load operation has completed using the SET INTEGRITY SQL statement.
The keys of each row are inserted into the appropriate index during an import operation.	All keys are sorted during a load operation, and the indexes are rebuilt when the load phase of the load operation has completed.
Statistics for the affected table must be manually collected (by issuing the RUNSTATS command) after an import operation is performed.	Statistics for the affected table can be collected and updated during a load operation.
Data can be imported into a host database through DB2 Connect.	Data cannot be loaded into a host database.
Data files to be imported must reside on the workstation from which the Import facility is invoked.	Data files and named pipes that will provide the data to be loaded must reside on the same workstation where the database receiving the data resides.
A backup image is not created during an import operation. Because the Import utility uses SQL inserts, the DB2 database manager logs all processing, and no backup images are required to reproduce the import operation if a failure occurs.	A backup image (copy) can be created during a load operation by using the COPY YES option.

Table 6.4: Differences between the Import utility and the Load utility (continued)	
Import Utility	**Load Utility**
The Import utility makes limited use of intrapartition parallelism.	The Load utility takes full advantage of intrapartition parallelism on SMP workstations.
Hierarchical data is supported.	Hierarchical data is not supported.
Numeric data must be stored as character representations.	Numeric data (other than DECIMAL data) can be stored and loaded either in binary form or as character representations. DECIMAL data can be stored and loaded in packed decimal or zoned decimal form or as character representations.
Data conversion between code pages is not performed.	Character data (and numeric data expressed as characters) can be converted from one code page to another during processing.
No FASTPARSE support provided.	FASTPARSE support is provided. (FASTPARSE provides reduced data checking of user-supplied data.)
No BINARYNUMERICS support is provided.	BINARYNUMERICS support is provided.
No PACKEDDECIMAL support is provided.	PACKEDDECIMAL support is provided.
No ZONEDDECIMAL support is provided.	ZONEDDECIMAL support is provided.
Cannot override columns defined as GENERATED ALWAYS.	Can override columns defined as GENERATED ALWAYS by using the GENERATEDIGNORE and IDENTITYIGNORE file type modifiers.
No support for importing into MQTs is provided.	Support for loading into MQTs is provided.
XML documents can be imported into XML columns.	XML documents can be loaded; however, LOBs and XML data can only be read from the server side
Adapted from Appendix B on page 257 of the IBM DB2 10/1 Data Movement Utilities Guide and Reference	

The most important difference between the Import utility and the Load utility is the way in which each utility moves data between an external file and a database table. The Import utility copies data by using SQL insert or update operations. As a result, each row processed must be checked for constraint compliance, and all activity that the Import utility performs is recorded in the database's transaction log files.

The Load utility, however, inserts data into a table by building data pages consisting of several individual rows of data and writing those pages directly to the table space containers that the target table uses for data storage. Once the utility has constructed and written all data pages to the appropriate table space containers, it rebuilds all existing primary and unique indexes associated with the target table, and deletes all rows that violate primary or unique key constraints defined for the table (and copies them to an exception table, if provided). Because pages of data are written instead of individual rows, changes made to the target table are not recorded in the database's transaction log files. As a result, overall performance is typically faster. However, because changes made to a table by the Load utility are not logged, if a database failure occurs, the loaded

performing a roll-forward recovery operation. To get around this generate a backup copy of all data loaded so that it can be quickly

es of a Load Operation

ad operation consists of four distinct phases:

- Load phase
- Build phase
- Delete phase
- Index copy phase

Load phase. Four things happen during the load phase: data is read from the source file specified and loaded into the appropriate target table, index key values and table statistics are collected, point of consistency information is recorded, and invalid data is placed into dump files. Point of consistency information serves as a checkpoint for the Load utility—in the event the load operation is interrupted during execution of the load phase and restarted, the operation will continue from the last consistency point established. As part of updating point of consistency information, the Load utility writes a message to the appropriate message file identifying the current number of records that have been successfully loaded. You can use this information to pick up where the load operation left off if a failure occurs or to monitor the load operation's progress. The LOAD QUERY TABLE command monitors the progress/status of a load operation.

Build phase. During the build phase, indexes associated with primary and unique keys defined for the table that was loaded are updated with the index key values that were collected and sorted during the load phase. This is also when statistical information about the table and its indexes is updated, if appropriate.

Because the beginning of the build phase is recorded as a point of consistency, if the load operation is interrupted during execution of the build phase and restarted, the operation will be restarted at the beginning of the build phase—the load phase will not have to be repeated.

Delete phase. During the delete phase, all rows that violated primary and unique key constraints defined on the target table are removed and copied to an exception table (if appropriate), and a message about each offending row is written to the appropriate message file so that you can modify and manually copy it to the target table later. These are the only table constraints that are checked. To check loaded data for additional constraint violations, you should turn off constraint checking (with the SET INTEGRITY SQL statement) before starting the load operation and then turn it back on and perform constraint checking immediately (again, with the SET INTEGRITY statement) after the load operation has completed.

The beginning of the delete phase is also recorded as a point of consistency. Thus, if a load operation is interrupted during execution of the delete phase and restarted, the operation will be restarted at the beginning of the delete phase—the load phase and the build phase do not have to be repeated.

Index copy phase. During the index copy phase, index data is copied from the system temporary table space used to the table space where the index data associated with the table that was loaded is to reside. It is important to note that this phase is executed only if you execute the LOAD command with the ALLOW READ ACCESS and USE [*TablespaceName*] options specified.

Performing a Load Operation

Now that you have seen how the Load utility differs from the Import utility, and how the Load utility copies data stored in an external file to a database table, let us look at how to invoke the Load utility. You invoke the Load utility by executing the LOAD command. The basic syntax for this command is:

```
LOAD <CLIENT> FROM [FileName OF [DEL | ASC | IXF] |
    PipeName | Device | CursorName OF CURSOR ,...]
<LOBS FROM [LOBPath ,...]>
<MODIFIED BY [Modifier ,...]>
<Method>
<SAVECOUNT [SaveCount]>
<ROWCOUNT [RowCount]>
<WARNINGCOUNT [WarningCount]>
<MESSAGES [MsgFileName]>
<TEMPFILES PATH [TempFilesPath]>
[INSERT | REPLACE | RESTART | TERMINATE]
INTO [TableName] < ([ColumnName ,...])>
<FOR EXCEPTION [ExTableName]>
<STATISTICS [NO | USE PROFILE]>
<NONRECOVERABLE | COPY YES TO [CopyLocation ,...]>
<WITHOUT PROMPTING>
<DATA BUFFER [Size]>
<INDEXING MODE [AUTOSELECT | REBUILD | INCREMENTAL |
    DEFERRED]>
<ALLOW NO ACCESS | ALLOW READ ACCESS <USE [TmpTSName]>>
<SET INTEGRITY PENDING CASCADE [IMMEDIATE | DEFERRED]>
```

where:

FileName	Identifies the name and location of one or more external files from which to load (copy) data
PipeName	Identifies the name of one or more named pipes from which to load data
Device	Identifies the name of one or more devices from which to load data
CursorName	Identifies the name of one or more cursors from which to load data
LOBPath	Identifies one or more locations to store LOB data values to be loaded
Modifier	Identifies one or more options to use to override the default behavior of the Load utility (Table 6.5 contains a list of valid modifiers)
Method	Identifies the method (location, name, or position) to use to extract data values from the source external files specified and map them to one or more columns of the target table indicated; the syntax you use to specify each method varies
SaveCount	Identifies the number of rows of data (records) to copy to the target table specified before the Load utility will establish a new point of consistency
RowCount	Identifies the actual number of rows of data to load in the specified external files, named pipes, devices, and cursors
WarningCount	Identifies the number of warning conditions the Load utility should ignore before terminating the load operation
MsgFileName	Identifies the name and location of an external file to which to write messages that the Load utility produces as the load operation is performed
TempFilesPath	Identifies the location to store temporary files that the Load utility might need
TableName	Identifies the name to assign to the table into which to load data (this cannot be the name of a system catalog table)
ColumnName	Identifies one or more specific columns (by name) into which to load data
ExTableName	Identifies the name to assign to the table to which to copy all rows that violate unique index or primary key constraints defined for the target table specified
CopyLocation	Identifies the directory or device that is to store a backup copy of all data loaded into the target table
Size	Identifies the number of 4 KB pages to use as buffered storage space for transferring data within the Load utility
TmpTSName	Identifies the system temporary table space in which to build shadow copies of indexes before they are copied to the appropriate regular table space for final storage during the Index Copy phase of a load operation

Table 6.5 lists the most commonly used file type modifiers for the LOAD command.

Table 6.5: File type modifiers recognized by the LOAD command		
Modifier	**Description**	**File Format**
anyorder	This modifier indicates that the preservation of source data order is not required This will yield significant performance increases on SMP systems. This modifier is not supported if SAVECOUNT > 0 because data must be loaded in sequence for crash recovery (after a consistency point has been taken) to work properly.	Delimited ASCII (DEL), nondelimited ASCII (ASC), and PC/IXF
generatedignore	This modifier indicates that although data for all generated columns is present in the file being loaded, to ignore this data. Instead, the Load utility should replace all generated data values found with its own generated values. This modifier is incompatible with the generatedmissing modifier.	Delimited ASCII (DEL), nondelimited ASCII (ASC), and PC/IXF
generatedmissing	This modifier indicates that data for generated columns is missing from the file being loaded and that the Load utility should generate an appropriate value for each missing value encountered. This modifier is incompatible with the generatedignore modifier.	Delimited ASCII (DEL), nondelimited ASCII (ASC), and PC/IXF
generatedoverride	This modifier indicates that the Load utility is to accept explicit, non-NULL data values for all generated columns in the table (contrary to the normal rules for these types of columns). This modifier is useful when migrating data from another database system or when loading a table from data that was recovered by using the DROPPED TABLE RECOVERY option of the ROLLFORWARD DATABASE command. This modifier is incompatible with the generatedignore and generatedmissing modifiers.	Delimited ASCII (DEL), nondelimited ASCII (ASC), and PC/IXF
identityignore	This modifer indicates that although data for all identity columns is present in the file being loaded, to ignore this. Instead, the Load utility should replace all identity column data found with its own generated values. This modifier is incompatible with the identitymissing modifier.	Delimited ASCII (DEL), nondelimited ASCII (ASC), and PC/IXF
identitymissing	This modifier indicates that data for identity columns is missing from the file being loaded and that the Load utility should generate an appropriate value for each missing value encountered. This modifier is incompatible with the identityignore modifier.	Delimited ASCII (DEL), nondelimited ASCII (ASC), and PC/IXF

Table 6.5: File type modifiers recognized by the LOAD command (continued)		
Modifier	**Description**	**File Format**
identityoverride	This modifier indicates that the Load utility is to accept explicit, non-NULL data values for all identity columns in the table (contrary to the normal rules for these types of columns). This modifier is useful when migrating data from another database system or when loading a table from data that was recovered by using the DROPPED TABLE RECOVERY option of the ROLLFORWARD DATABASE command. Use this modifier only when an identity column that was defined as GENERATED ALWAYS is present in the table that is to be loaded. This modifier is incompatible with the identityignore and identitymissing modifiers.	Delimited ASCII (DEL), nondelimited ASCII (ASC), and PC/IXF
indexfreespace=*x* where *x* is a number between 0 and 99 (percent)	This modifier indicates to leave a percentage of each index page as free space when loading indexes that are associated with the table being loaded.	Delimited ASCII (DEL), nondelimited ASCII (ASC), and PC/IXF
lobsinfile	This modifier indicates to store LOB data values in their own files.	Delimited ASCII (DEL), nondelimited ASCII (ASC), and PC/IXF
noheader	This modifier indicates that the Load utility is to skip the header verification code (applicable only to load operations performed on tables that reside in a single-node node group) when processing the source data file.	Delimited ASCII (DEL), nondelimited ASCII (ASC), and PC/IXF
norowwarnings	This modifier indicates to suppress warning messages about rejected rows.	Delimited ASCII (DEL), nondelimited ASCII (ASC), and PC/IXF
pagefreespace=*x* where *x* is a number between 0 and 100 (percent)	This modifier indicates to leave a percentage of each data page associated with the table being loaded as free space.	Delimited ASCII (DEL), nondelimited ASCII (ASC), and PC/IXF
seclabelchar	This modifier indicates to store security labels in the input source file in the string format for security label values rather than in the default encoded numeric format. (The Load utility converts each security label found into the internal format as it is loaded. If a string is not in the proper format, the row is not loaded, and a warning is returned. If the string does not represent a valid security label that is part of the security policy protecting the table, then the row is not loaded, and a warning is returned.) This modifier is incompatible with the seclabelname modifier.	Delimited ASCII (DEL), nondelimited ASCII (ASC), and PC/IXF
seclabelname	This modifier indicates to specify security labels in the input source file by their name rather than the default encoded numeric format. (The Load utility will convert the name to the appropriate security label if it exists. If no security label exists with the indicated name for the security policy protecting the table, the row is not loaded, and a warning is returned.) This modifier is incompatible with the seclabelchar modifier.	Delimited ASCII (DEL), nondelimited ASCII (ASC), and PC/IXF

Table 6.5: File type modifiers recognized by the LOAD command (continued)		
Modifier	**Description**	**File Format**
totalfreespace=*x* where *x* is a number between 0 and 100 (percent)	This modifier indicates to append a percentage of the total number of data pages used by the table being loaded to the end of the table and to treat as free space.	Delimited ASCII (DEL), nondelimited ASCII (ASC), and PC/IXF
usedefaults	This modifier indicates that if the source column data for a target table column is not provided, and if the target table column has a defaults constraint, to generate default values for the column. If this modifier is not used, and a source column data value for one of the target table columns is not provided, one of the following will occur: • If the column is nullable, a NULL value is stored in the column. • If the column is not nullable, and a default value cannot be generated, and the row is rejected.	Delimited ASCII (DEL), nondelimited ASCII (ASC), and PC/IXF
codepage=*x* where *x* is any valid code page identifier	This modifier identifies the code page of the data contained in the output data set produced. Character data is converted from the application code page to the code page specified during the load operation.	Delimited ASCII (DEL) and nondelimited ASCII (ASC)
dateformat=*x* where *x* is any valid combination of date format elements	This modifier identifies how to format date values stored in the source file. The following date elements will create the format string provided with this modifier: • YYYY—Year (four digits ranging from 0000 to 9999) • M—Month (one or two digits ranging from 1 to 12) • MM—Month (two digits ranging from 1 to 12; mutually exclusive with M) • D—Day (one or two digits ranging from 1 to 31) • DD—Day (two digits ranging from 1 to 31; mutually exclusive with D) • DDD—Day of the year (three digits ranging from 001 to 366; mutually exclusive with other day or month elements) Examples of valid date format strings include the following: "D-M-YYYY" "MM.DD.YYYY" "YYYYDDD"	Delimited ASCII (DEL) and nondelimited ASCII (ASC)
dumpfile=*x* where *x* is a fully qualified name of a file	This modifier identifies the name and location of an exception file to which to write rejected rows. The contents of a dump file are written to disk in an asynchronous buffered mode. If a load operation fails or is interrupted, you will not know with certainty the number of records committed to disk, and consistency cannot be guaranteed after a LOAD RESTART. You can only assume a dump file to be complete for load operations that start and finish in a single pass. This modifier does not support file names with multiple file extensions (for example, dumpfile=/home/DUMP.FILE is acceptable; dumpfile=/home/DUMP.LOAD.FILE is not).	Delimited ASCII (DEL) and nondelimited ASCII (ASC)

Table 6.5: File type modifiers recognized by the LOAD command (continued)		
Modifier	**Description**	**File Format**
dumpfileaccessall	This modifier grants read access to OTHERS when a dump file is created. This modifier is only valid when • it is used in conjunction with the dumpfile modifier, • the user has SELECT privilege on the target table specified, and • it is used on a DB2 server database partition that resides on a UNIX operating system.	Delimited ASCII (DEL) and nondelimited ASCII (ASC)
fastparse	This modifier indicates to perform reduced syntax checking on user-supplied column values. (This can yield significant performance increases). Use of this modifier guarantees tables to be architecturally correct, and the Load utility performs sufficient data checking only to prevent a segmentation violation or trap from occurring.	Delimited ASCII (DEL) and nondelimited ASCII (ASC)
implieddecimal	This modifier indicates that the location of an implied decimal point is to be determined by the column definition—the Load utility is not to assume that the decimal point is at the end of the value (default behavior). For example, if you specify this modifier, the value 12345 will be loaded into a DECIMAL (8,2) column as 123.45, not as 12345.00.	Delimited ASCII (DEL) and nondelimited ASCII (ASC)
timeformat=*x* where *x* is any valid combination of time format elements	This modifier identifies how to format time values stored in the source file. The following time elements will create the format string provided with this modifier: • H—Hour (one or two digits ranging from 0 to 12 for a 12-hour system, and 0 to 24 for a 24-hour system) • HH—Hour (two digits ranging from 0 to 12 for a 12-hour system, and 0 to 24 for a 24-hour system; mutually exclusive with H) • M—Minute (one or two digits ranging from 0 to 59) • MM—Minute (two digits ranging from 0 to 59; mutually exclusive with M) • S—Second (one or two digits ranging from 0 to 59) • SS—Second (two digits ranging from 0 to 59; mutually exclusive with S) • SSSSS—Second of the day after midnight (5 digits ranging from 00000 to 86399; mutually exclusive with other time elements) • TT—Meridian indicator (am or pm) Examples of valid time format strings include the following: "HH:MM:SS" "HH.MM TT" "SSSSS"	Delimited ASCII (DEL) and nondelimited ASCII (ASC)

Table 6.5: File type modifiers recognized by the LOAD command (continued)

Modifier	Description	File Format
timestampformat=*x* where *x* is any valid combination of date and time format elements	This modifier identifies how to format timestamp values stored in the source file. The following date and time elements will create the format string provided with this modifier: • YYYY—Year (four digits ranging from 0000 to 9999) • M—Month (one or two digits ranging from 1 to 12) • MM—Month (two digits ranging from 1 to 12; mutually exclusive with M) • D—Day (one or two digits ranging from 1 to 31) • DD—Day (two digits ranging from 1 to 31; mutually exclusive with D) • DDD—Day of the year (three digits ranging from 001 to 366; mutually exclusive with other day or month elements) • H—Hour (one or two digits ranging from 0 to 12 for a 12-hour system, and 0 to 24 for a 24-hour system) • HH—Hour (two digits ranging from 0 to 12 for a 12-hour system, and 0 to 24 for a 24-hour system; mutually exclusive with H) • M—Minute (one or two digits ranging from 0 to 59) • MM—Minute (two digits ranging from 0 to 59; mutually exclusive with M) • S—Second (one or two digits ranging from 0 to 59) • SS—Second (two digits ranging from 0 to 59; mutually exclusive with S) • SSSSS—Second of the day after midnight (5 digits ranging from 00000 to 86399; mutually exclusive with other time elements) • UUUUUU—Microsecond (6 digits ranging from 000000 to 999999) • TT—Meridian indicator (am or pm) An example of a valid timestamp format string is: "YYYY/MM/DD HH:MM:SS.UUUUUU"	Delimited ASCII (DEL) and nondelimited ASCII (ASC)
usegraphiccodepage	This modifier indicates to store data being loaded into graphic or DBCLOB columns in the graphic code page. The rest of the data is assumed to be stored in the character code page. The Load utility determines the character code page either through the codepage modifier if it is specified, or through the code page of the application if the codepage modifier is not specified. This modifier must not be specified with delimited ASCII (DEL) files created by the Export utility—those files contain data encoded in only one code page.	Delimited ASCII (DEL) and nondelimited ASCII (ASC)
chardel*x* where *x* is any valid delimiter character	This modifier identifies a specific character to use as a character delimiter. The default character delimiter is a double quotation mark (") character. The character specified is used in place of the double quotation mark to enclose a character string.	Delimited ASCII (DEL)

Table 6.5: File type modifiers recognized by the LOAD command (continued)		
Modifier	**Description**	**File Format**
coldel*x* where *x* is any valid delimiter character	This modifier identifies a specific character to use as a column delimiter. The default column delimiter is a comma (,) character. The character specified is used in place of a comma to signal the end of a column.	Delimited ASCII (DEL)
decplusblank	This modifier indicates to prefix positive decimal values with a blank space instead of a plus sign (+). The default action is to prefix positive decimal values with a plus sign.	Delimited ASCII (DEL)
decpt*x* where *x* is any valid delimiter character	This modifier identifies a specific character to use as a decimal point character. The default decimal point character is a period (.) character. The character specified is used in place of a period as a decimal point character.	Delimited ASCII (DEL)
delprioritychar	This modifier indicates that the priority for evaluating delimiters is to be character delimiter, record delimiter, column delimiter rather than record delimiter, character delimiter, column delimiter (which is the default). This modifier is typically used with older applications that depend on the other priority.	Delimited ASCII (DEL)
keepblanks	This modifier indicates to retain all leading and trailing blanks found for each column that has a data type of CHAR, VARCHAR, LONG VARCHAR, or CLOB. If you do not specify this modifier, all leading and trailing blanks that reside outside character delimiters are removed, and a NULL is inserted into the table for all missing data values found.	Delimited ASCII (DEL)
nochardel	This modifier indicates that the Load utility is to assume all bytes found between the column delimiters to be part of the column's data. (Character delimiters will be parsed as part of column data.) Do not specify this modifier if DB2 exported the data (unless the nochardel modifier was specified at export time). It is provided to support vendor data files that do not have character delimiters. Improper usage might result in data loss or corruption. This modifier is incompatible with chardelx, delprioritychar, or nodoubledel. These are mutually exclusive options.	Delimited ASCII (DEL)
nodoubledel	This modifier indicates to ignore double character delimiters.	Delimited ASCII (DEL)

<table>
<tr><th colspan="3">Table 6.5: File type modifiers recognized by the LOAD command (continued)</th></tr>
<tr><th>Modifier</th><th>Description</th><th>File Format</th></tr>
<tr><td>binarynumerics</td><td>This modifier indicates to store numeric (but not DECIMAL) data in binary format rather than as character representations. When you use this modifier, the following conditions apply:<ul><li>No conversion between data types is performed, with the exception of BIGINT, INTEGER, and SMALLINT.</li><li>Data lengths must match their target column definitions.</li><li>FLOAT values must be in IEEE floating point format.</li><li>The byte order of the binary data stored in the source file is assumed to be big-endian, regardless of the server platform used. (Little-endian computers—Intel-based PCs, VAX workstations, and so on—store the least significant byte (LSB) of a multibyte word at the lowest address in a word and the most significant byte (MSB) at the highest address. Big-endian computers —machines based on the Motorola 68000a series of CPUs, such as Sun, Macintosh, and so on—do the opposite: the MSB is stored at the lowest address, and the LSB is stored at the highest address.)</li><li>NULLs cannot be present in the data for columns that are affected by this modifier—blanks (normally interpreted as NULL) are interpreted as a binary value.</li></ul></td><td>Nondelimited ASCII (ASC)</td></tr>
<tr><td>nochecklengths</td><td>This modifier indicates that the Load utility is to attempt to load every row found in the source, even if the source data has a column value that exceeds the size of the target column's definition. Such rows can be successfully loaded if code page conversion causes the source data to shrink in size. For example, 4-byte EUC data found in a source file could shrink to 2-byte DBCS data in the target table and require half the space. This option is particularly useful if you know in advance that the source data will always fit in a column despite mismatched column definitions/sizes.</td><td>Nondelimited ASCII (ASC) and PC/IXF</td></tr>
<tr><td>nullindchar=x where x is any valid character</td><td>This modifier identifies a specific character to use as a null indicator value. The default null indicator is the letter Y. This modifier is case-sensitive for EBCDIC data files, except when the character is an English letter. For example, if the null indicator character is specified to be the letter N, then the letter n is also recognized as a null indicator.</td><td>Nondelimited ASCII (ASC)</td></tr>
<tr><td>packeddecimal</td><td>This modifier indicates to store numeric DECIMAL data in packed decimal format rather than as character representations.
When you use this modifier, the following apply:<ul><li>The byte order of the binary data stored in the source file is assumed to be big-endian, regardless of the server platform used.</li><li>NULLs cannot be present in the data for columns that are affected by this modifier—blanks (normally interpreted as NULL) are interpreted as a binary value.</li></ul></td><td>Nondelimited ASCII (ASC)</td></tr>
</table>

Table 6.5: File type modifiers recognized by the LOAD command (continued)		
Modifier	**Description**	**File Format**
reclen=*x* where *x* is any number between 1 and 32,767	This modifier indicates to read a specific number of characters from the source file for each row found, and to ignore new-line characters used to indicate the end of a row.	Nondelimited ASCII (ASC)
striptblanks	This modifier indicates to truncate all leading and trailing blanks found for each column that has a data type of VARCHAR, LONG VARCHAR, VARGRAPHIC, or LONG VARGRAPHIC. This modifier is incompatible with the striptnulls modifier.	Nondelimited ASCII (ASC)
striptnulls	This modifier indicates to truncate all leading and trailing nulls (0x00 characters) found for each column that has a data type of VARCHAR, LONG VARCHAR, VARGRAPHIC, or LONG VARGRAPHIC. This modifier is incompatible with the striptblanks modifier.	Nondelimited ASCII (ASC)
zoneddecimal	This modifier indicates to store numeric DECIMAL data in zoned decimal format rather than as character representations. When you use this modifier, the following conditions apply: • Half-byte sign values can be one of the following: "+" = 0xC 0xA 0xE 0xF "-" = 0xD 0xB • Supported values for digits are 0x0 to 0x9. • Supported values for zones are 0x3 and 0xF.	Nondelimited ASCII (ASC)
forcein	This modifier indicates that the Load utility is to accept data despite code page mismatches (in other words, to suppress translation between code pages). Fixed-length target columns are checked to verify that they are large enough to hold the data unless the nochecklengths modifier has been specified.	PC/IXF
Adapted from Tables 32–36 of the IBM DB2 10.1 Command Reference		

As with the Import utility, you can use one of three methods to map data values in external files to columns in a table: the location method, the name method, and the position method. The syntax to indicate that the location method is to be used to extract data values from the external file specified is:

```
METHOD L ( [ColumnStart] [ColumnEnd] ,... )
   <NULL INDICATORS ( [NullIndColNumber ,...] )>
```

where:

ColumnStart Identifies the starting position of one or more data values in the nondelimited ASCII (ASC) formatted file from which to retrieve values

ColumnEnd Identifies the ending position of one or more data values in the nondelimited ASCII (ASC) formatted file from which to retrieve values

NullIndColNumber Identifies the position of one or more data values to treat as null indicator variables for column data values in the nondelimited ASCII (ASC) formatted file from which to retrieve values

The syntax to indicate that the name method is to be used to extract data values from the external file specified is:

```
METHOD N ( [ColumnName ,...] )
```

where:

ColumnName Identifies one or more unique names assigned to columns in the PC/IXF formatted file from which to retrieve values

And the syntax to indicate that the position method is to be used to extract data values from the external file specified is:

```
METHOD P ( [ColumnPosition ,...] )
```

where:

ColumnPosition Identifies the indexed position of one or more columns in the delimited ASCII (DEL) or PC/IXF formatted file from which to retrieve values

As you can see, four different options are available with the LOAD command that control how the load operation will affect the table data to be copied to. These options include the following:

- **INSERT**. When you use the INSERT option, data is appended to the target table (which must already exist).
- **REPLACE**. With the REPLACE option, any existing data is deleted from the target table (which must already exist), and then the new data is loaded.
- **RESTART**. When you use the RESTART option, any previous load operation that failed or was terminated is continued, starting from the last recorded point of consistency. With this option, the LOAD command specified must be identical to the LOAD command used to initiate the previous load operation (with the exception of the RESTART option specification).
- **TERMINATE**. When you use the TERMINATE option, the current load operation is terminated, and any changes made are backed out if that load operation was started with the INSERT option. If the load operation being terminated was started with the REPLACE option specified, data in the target table is truncated.

So if you want to load data stored in a PC/IXF format external file named dept.ixf into an existing table named DEPARTMENT, execute a LOAD command that looks something like this:

```
LOAD FROM C:\dept.ixf OF IXF
MESSAGES load_msgs.txt
INSERT INTO department
```

However, if you want to load data stored in a PC/IXF format external file named emp_photo.ixf, along with LOB data values stored in individual files, into a table named EMP_PHOTO and then update the statistics for the EMP_PHOTO table and its associated indexes, execute a LOAD command similar to the following:

```
LOAD FROM C:\emp_photo.ixf OF IXF
LOBS FROM C:\lob_data
MODIFIED BY lobsinfile
MESSAGES load_msgs.txt
REPLACE INTO emp_photo
STATISTICS USE PROFILE
```

In this case, you must execute the LOAD command with the REPLACE option specified; statistics cannot be collected if you execute the LOAD command with any option other than the REPLACE option. Additionally, a statistics profile for the EMP_PHOTO table must already exist (statistics profiles are created by executing the RUNSTATS command, which we will look at shortly). If a profile does not exist, and the Load utility is instructed to collect statistics, a warning is returned, and statistics are not collected.

Now, suppose you want to load data stored in a delimited ASCII (DEL) format external file named dept.del into an existing table named DEPARTMENT, while allowing other transactions to read data that existed in the DEPARTMENT table before you initiated the load operation. You can do so by executing a LOAD command that looks something like this:

```
LOAD FROM C:\dept.del OF DEL
MESSAGES load_msgs.txt
INSERT INTO department
ALLOW READ ACCESS
```

It is important to note that while this load operation is in process, the data residing in the table before the load operation was started will be accessible to other transactions when data is loaded with ALLOW READ ACCESS. If, for some reason, the load operation fails, the original data in the table will remain available for read access.

To load data stored in a delimited ASCII (DEL) format external file named emp.del into an existing table named EMPLOYEE, in such a way that records violating constraints that have been defined for the EMPLOYEE table are written to a table named EMP_EXP, you can execute a LOAD command that looks something like this:

```
LOAD FROM C:\emp.del OF DEL
MODIFIED BY dumpfile=C:\employee.dmp
MESSAGES load_msgs.txt
INSERT INTO employee
FOR EXCEPTION emp_exp
```

In this case, any record found that violates a constraint that has been defined for the EMPLOYEE table will be loaded into the EMP_EXP table, rather than the EMPLOYEE table. Exception table should have same number of columns, column data types, and column nullability attributes as the target table to be loaded. Additionally, you might want to add an optional timestamp (to record the deletion timestamp from the target table) and CLOB (32 KB—to record the load error messages) columns to the exception table.

You can create exception table emp_exp in the table space TS_SMALL_DATA by using the CREATE TABLE command:

```
CREATE TABLE emp_exp LIKE employee IN TS_SMALL_DATA
```

Even though TIMESTAMP and CLOB (32 KB) are optional, if you want to add them to the above table, you can do so by executing the ALTER TABLE command:

```
ALTER TABLE emp_exp
        ADD COLUMN rec_ts   TIMESTAMP
        ADD COLUMN rec_log_msg     CLOB(32K)
```

The following example illustrates the LOAD with an exception table in place. The EMPLOYEE (target) table structure is:

```
CREATE TABLE employee (
                "ID"            INTEGER NOT NULL PRIMARY KEY,
                  "NAME"        VARCHAR(10) ,
                  "ADDRESS"     VARCHAR(20) ,
                  "SALARY"      INTEGER )
                  IN "TS_SMALL_DATA"
```

The data file emp.del that is ready to be loaded into employee is:

```
----------------------------
ID NAME     ADDRESS SALARY
----------------------------
1,"MOHAN","VENUS UK",10000
2,"MILAN","VENUS UK",20000
3,"COLIN","VENUS UK",20000
,"KENT","USA",20000
1,"NELSON","USA",20000
----------------------------
```

If you look closely at the data, the fourth record has a NULL value for the ID that violates a NOT NULL constraint in the target table EMPLOYEE, and the fifth record has a duplicate ID that violates the PRIMARY KEY constraint in the target table EMPLOYEE.

Let us perform a data load by using this command:

```
LOAD FROM emp.del OF DEL
MODIFIED BY dumpfile=c:\employee.dmp
MESSAGES load_msgs.txt
INSERT INTO employee FOR EXCEPTION emp_exp

Number of rows read         = 5
Number of rows skipped      = 0
```

Continued

```
Number of rows loaded        = 4
Number of rows rejected      = 1
Number of rows deleted       = 1
Number of rows committed     = 5

SQL3107W  At least one warning message was encountered during LOAD processing.
```

If you now query the tables EMPLOYEE and EMP_EXP, you will find something like:

```
SELECT * FROM employee

ID          NAME       ADDRESS              SALARY
----------- ---------- -------------------- -----------
          1 MOHAN      VENUS UK                   10000
          2 MILAN      VENUS UK                   20000
          3 COLIN      VENUS UK                   20000

  3 record(s) selected.

SELECT * FROM emp_exp

ID NAME     ADDRESS    SALARY     REC_TS                     REC_LOAD_MSG
-- -------- ---------- ---------- ------------- ---------- ----------------
1  NELSON   USA        20000      2014-08-04-20.37.34.457684 00001I0000500001

  1 record(s) selected.
```

And if you look at employee.dmp.load.000, it will look similar to the following:

```
,"KENT","USA",20000
```

So effectively, the records that are violating the NOT NULL constraint recorded in the dump file and the records that are violating the UNIQUE or PRIMARY KEY constraint are deleted from target table and inserted into the exception table.

Loading XML Data

You can use the Load utility to load large volumes of XML data into tables. When loading data into XML columns, use the XML FROM clause to specify the paths of the input XML data files. To load relational data from delimited ASCII file product.del and XML data from XML files located in c:\xmlpath into the PRODUCT table, execute the LOAD command something like this:

```
LOAD FROM product.del OF DEL
XML FROM c:\xmlpath
MESSAGES product_load.msg
INSERT INTO product

SQL3501W  The table space(s) in which the table resides will not be placed
in backup pending state since forward recovery is disabled for the database.

SQL3039W  The memory available to LOAD for DATA BUFFER prohibits full LOAD
parallelism.  Load parallelism of "2" will be used

SQL3109N  The utility is beginning to load data from file
"C:\xmlpath\PRODUCT.del".

SQL3500W  The utility is beginning the "LOAD" phase at time "08/04/2014
22:03:02.562026".

SQL3519W  Begin Load Consistency Point. Input record count = "0".

SQL3520W  Load Consistency Point was successful.

SQL3110N  The utility has completed processing.  "4" rows were read from the
input file.

SQL3519W  Begin Load Consistency Point. Input record count = "4".

SQL3520W  Load Consistency Point was successful.
```

Continued

```
SQL3515W  The utility has finished the "LOAD" phase at time "08/04/2014
22:03:02.673052".

SQL3500W  The utility is beginning the "BUILD" phase at time "08/04/2014
22:03:02.673427".

SQL3213I  The indexing mode is "REBUILD".

SQL3515W  The utility has finished the "BUILD" phase at time "08/04/2014
22:03:02.822823".


Number of rows read         = 4
Number of rows skipped      = 0
Number of rows loaded       = 4
Number of rows rejected     = 0
Number of rows deleted      = 0
Number of rows committed    = 4
```

During the load, you will not be able to collect distribution statistics for the columns of type XML.

Loading from a CURSOR

The Load utility supports a CURSOR-type load, where you can specify the CURSOR file type when using the LOAD command, and load the results of an SQL query directly into a target table without creating an intermediate exported file. Additionally, you can load data from another database by referencing a DB2 federation nickname within the SQL query by using the DATABASE option within the DECLARE CURSOR statement. To execute a LOAD FROM CURSOR CLP command, first declare a cursor against the SQL statement that you intend to load, and then use that cursor name in the LOAD command similar to the following:

```
DECLARE mycursor CURSOR FOR SELECT * FROM employee
LOAD FROM mycursor OF CURSOR INSERT INTO employee2
```

Loading from a Pipe

As with LOAD FROM CURSOR, you can also use an operating system pipe to load data into a target table without creating an intermediate exported file. Additionally, you can load data from another remote database by using the catalog and the operating system pipe instead of creating an intermediate exported file and copying it across the servers. When using the PIPE file type, you must have already created the pipe at the operating system layer by using the mkfifo command. Let us take a close look at each step.

Step 1: Create an operating system pipe in the target server:

```
mkfifo datapipe
ls -ltr datapipe
prw-r--r--  1 bculinux bcuigrp     0 2014-08-05 16:32 datapipe
```

Step 2: Catalog the source database in the target server:

```
CATALOG TCPIP NODE snode REMOTE sourcedbServer SERVER 50001
CATALOG DATABASE sourcedb AT NODE snode
```

Step 3: Connect to the source database remotely from the target server:

```
CONNECT TO sourcedb user <username> using <password>
```

Step 4: Export data from source database and write it to one end of the pipe (datapipe):

```
EXPORT TO datapipe OF DEL MODIFIED BY COLDEL,
       MESSAGES CUSTOMERS.msg SELECT * FROM customers
```

Step 5: Connect locally to the target database:

```
CONNECT TO targetdb
```

Step 6: Use the LOAD command to read data from other end of the pipe and load data into the target table:

```
LOAD FROM datapipe OF DEL MODIFIED BY COLDEL,
        MESSAGES CUSTOMERS.msg INSERT INTO customers
```

Step 7: After the data load process, delete the pipe created in step 1:

```
rm datapipe
```

A Nonrecoverable Load Operation

When your database is archive-logging enabled and you perform a NO COPY load operation on a table, the underlying table space will remain in Backup Pending state. If the table space is not backed up, the database manager will not allow any DML operations on the table space to occur; however, read-only operations are allowed to run.

In the business process, if there are cases where you need to load data from external source systems into a staging table before performing any transformation, you could possibly use the NONRECOVERABLE clause to avoid backing up the table spaces for every load run. When you specify this clause, the load transaction will be marked as nonrecoverable, and it will not be possible to recover the data by a subsequent roll-forward operation. An attempt to perform a roll-forward operation will cause the utility to skip the transaction and will mark the table into which data was being loaded as invalid. After the roll-forward operation, such tables can only be dropped and recreated.

If you have performed a NONRECOVERABLE load on a data partition of a range partition table, a subsequent roll-forward operation will mark the specific data partition as invalid instead of invalidating the whole table. This enables you to detach the invalid partitions from the base table and access the remaining data partitions data. The relevant invalid object error codes and the steps to resolve them are as follows:

```
SELECT * FROM staging.jde_gl_incr_stg
For table "STAGING.JDE_GL_INCR_STG" an object "547" in table space "4" can-
not be
accessed. SQLSTATE=55019
```

To find the invalid partition in the base range partition table, use the SQL statement something like:

```
SELECT
VARCHAR (DATAPARTITIONNAME, 15) DATAPARTITIONNAME,
VARCHAR (TABNAME, 30) TABLENAME
FROM SYSCAT.DATAPARTITIONS WHERE TBSPACEID=4 AND PARTITIONOBJECTID=547

DATAPARTITIONNAME TABLENAME
----------------- ------------------------------
201403107         JDE_GL_INCR_STG

  1 record(s) selected.
```

Once you have the data partition name, use the ALTER TABLE command to detach it from the parent table:

```
ALTER TABLE staging.jde_gl_incr_stg
DETACH PART 201403107 INTO TABLE staging.jde_gl_incr_stg_201403107
DB20000I  The SQL command completed successfully.
```

If your database is circular-logging enabled, by default the LOAD command runs in NONRECOVERABLE mode, which is the only mode supported.

Monitoring a Load Operation

You can use the LIST UTILITIES command or the LOAD QUERY command to monitor the progress of the load operation. The LIST UTILITIES SHOW DETAIL command displays all the active utilities running on the instance. If you want to see a specific table load operation, execute the LOAD QUERY TABLE command:

```
LIST UTILITIES SHOW DETAIL


ID                               = 365
Type                             = LOAD
```

Continued

```
Database Name                    = SAMPLE
Partition Number                 = 0
Description                      = [LOADID: 815.2014-08-05-09.57.29.999409.0
                                   (4;341)]
                                   [*N0.db2inst1.140805083726] OFFLINE LOAD
                                   DEL
                                   AUTOMATIC INDEXING INSERT NON-RECOVERABLE
                                   DATASTORE.STOCK_AVAILABILITY_DS
Start Time                       = 08/05/2014 09:57:30.029518
State                            = Executing
Invocation Type                  = User
Progress Monitoring:
   Phase Number                  = 1
      Description                = SETUP
      Total Work                 = 0 bytes
      Completed Work             = 0 bytes
      Start Time                 = 08/05/2014 09:57:30.029524

   Phase Number [Current]        = 2
      Description                = LOAD
      Total Work                 = 25517033 rows
      Completed Work             = 258604 rows
      Start Time                 = 08/05/2014 09:57:31.088683

   Phase Number                  = 3
      Description                = BUILD
      Total Work                 = 3 indexes
      Completed Work             = 0 indexes
      Start Time                 = Not Started
```

The above command output shows that a load was performed on the database SAMPLE at 08/05/2014 09:57:30.029518; it also lists the command in the top description section. You can easily monitor the progress of the load by looking at the phases in the progress monitoring section. If no indexes are present on the target table, you will see only the setup and load phases.

To specifically monitor a table load (this is the case on a busy analytic database with terabytes of data where many load processes runs in parallel), use the LOAD QUERY command:

```
LOAD QUERY TABLE datastore.stock_availability_ds

SQL3530I  The Load Query utility is monitoring "LOAD" progress on partition "0".

SQL3109N  The utility is beginning to load data from file
"/stage/DATASTORE.STOCK_AVAILABILITY_DS.del".

SQL3500W  The utility is beginning the "LOAD" phase at time "08/05/2014
09:57:31.092533".

SQL3519W  Begin Load Consistency Point. Input record count = "0".

SQL3520W  Load Consistency Point was successful.

SQL3532I  The Load utility is currently in the "LOAD" phase.


Number of rows read         = 13023126
Number of rows skipped      = 0
Number of rows loaded       = 13023126
Number of rows rejected     = 0
Number of rows deleted      = 0
Number of rows committed    = 0
Number of warnings          = 0

Tablestate:
  Load in Progress
```

The Set Integrity Command

Following a load operation, the loaded table might be in Set Integrity Pending state to check for referential integrity and check constraints. However, the load process will generally check for invalid data for NOT NULL columns and UNIQUE or PRIMARY KEY constraints during the delete phase. You can use SET INTEGRITY command to check a table for constraint violations and take the table out of set integrity pending state:

```
SET INTEGRITY FOR TABLE datastore.stock_availability_ds IMMEDIATE CHECKED
```

There are various options available for this command, which are discussed in detail in Chapter 4, "Business Rules Implementation," in the "Set Integrity Command" section.

Note: The Load utility can also delete all records in a table without generating corresponding log records. Simply specify the null device (on UNIX this is /dev/null; on Windows it is nul) as the input file. For example:

```
LOAD FROM /dev/null OF DEL REPLACE INTO department (on UNIX)
LOAD FROM nul OF DEL REPLACE INTO department (on Windows)
```

You can use the above trick to get the table out of the Load Pending state (SQL0668N reason code 3) by using the TERMINATE clause:

```
LOAD FROM /dev/null OF DEL TERMINATE INTO department (on UNIX)
```

In addition, you can use the TRUNCATE command (introduced in DB2 9.7) to delete all the records in a table with minimal logging.

Certification Tips: Only users with System Administrator (SYSADM) authority, Database Administrator (DBADMN) authority, or Load (LOAD) authority and INSERT privilege on all tables referenced are allowed to load data by using the INSERT option (or to restart or terminate INSERT load operations). Only users with SYSADM authority, DBADMN authority, or LOAD authority and INSERT and DELETE privileges on all tables referenced are allowed to load data by using the REPLACE option (or to restart or terminate REPLACE load operations). And only users with SYSADM authority, DBADMN authority, or INSERT privilege on the exception table used are allowed to perform load operations in which invalid rows are written to an exception table.

Data stored in external files can also be loaded by using the Load Table wizard within IBM Data Studio, which you activate by selecting the appropriate action from the Administration perspective. Figure 6.19 shows how to activate the Load Table dialog; the remaining selections are similar to those in Data Studio's Import window.

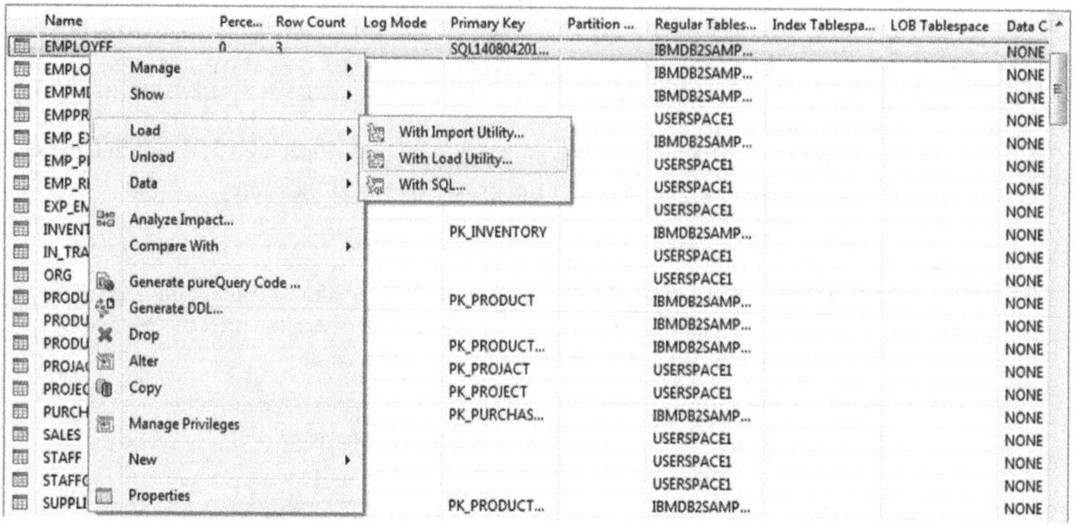

Figure 6.19: Invoking the Load utility through IBM Data Studio

The DB2 Ingest Utility

Modern data warehouse environments demand a continuous data streaming from multiple data sources to ensure timely access to business-critical data in real time. The other key requirements of data warehouse systems are:

- Concurrent data access with minimal or no locking behavior
- High fault tolerance and data recoverability enablement
- The ability to perform data transformations during the data streaming phase

The Ingest utility (also known as *Continuous Data Ingest*, or *CDI*) is a high-speed, client-side, highly configurable, multithreaded DB2 utility that streams data from files and pipes into DB2 target tables by using SQL-like commands. Because the Ingest utility can move large amounts of real-time data without locking the target table, you do not need to choose between the data currency and availability.

The DB2 Ingest utility meets the current modern data warehouse expectations through several key capabilities:

- **Concurrent data access**. You can run concurrent SQL statements against the DB2 tables that are being loaded because the Ingest utility always uses row-level locking. You do not have to choose between tweaking data concurrency and data availability through isolation levels as before.

- **Exception handling**. You can copy rejected records to a file or table, or discard them based on the business rule. If any data load failed operations, the data can easily be recovered by restarting the ingest operation from the last commit point.
- **Data transformations**. You can apply the data transformation techniques while continuously pumping data into DB2 tables.
- **Database partition aware**. You can insert data directly into the appropriate partition in parallel instead of processing the whole data set through a coordinator partition. This is similar to the IBM Information Server Enterprise Stage.
- **Extensive DML support**. You can use INSERT, UPDATE, DELETE, REPLACE, and MERGE operations while streaming data into the data warehouse system. These DML operations can be used during the data transformation.
- **Configure anywhere**. The Ingest utility is part of the DB2 client feature (no additional licenses are necessary) and is very flexible and easily configurable. It is possible to install and configure the Ingest utility on an existing DB2 server, a dedicated ingest server, an existing shared Extract, Transform, and Load (ETL) server, or a coordinator node on the DPF system.
- **Data format support**. You can load data from delimited ASCII (DEL), nondelimited ASCII (ASC), columns in various orders and formats, positional text, and binary data file formats.
- **Various table support**. You can load data into regular tables, nicknames, MDC and insert time clustering (ITC) tables, range partitioned tables, range clustered tables (RCT), MQT, temporal tables, and updatable views.

Figure 6.20 shows the Ingest utility architecture. The data from source systems is exported into files or named pipes, which are then streamed into the Ingest utility as input sources. The data is then ingested into target data warehouse system through a three-step process:

1. **Transport**. The transporter thread reads data from the data source and puts records on the formatter queues. For insert and merge operations, there is one transporter thread for each input source (for example, one thread for each input file). For update and delete operations, there is only one transporter thread.
2. **Format**. The formatter parses each record available in the formatter queue, converts the data into the format that DB2 database systems require, and places each formatted record on one of the flusher queues for that record's partition. The number of formatter threads is specified by the NUM_FORMATTERS ingest configuration parameter and by default is set to (number of logical CPUs)/2.

3. **Flush.** The flusher issues the SQL statements to perform the ingest operations on the data warehouse target tables. The number of flushers for each partition is specified by the NUM_FLUSHERS_PER_PARTITION ingest configuration parameter and by default is set to max (1, ((number of logical CPUs)/2)/(number of partitions)).

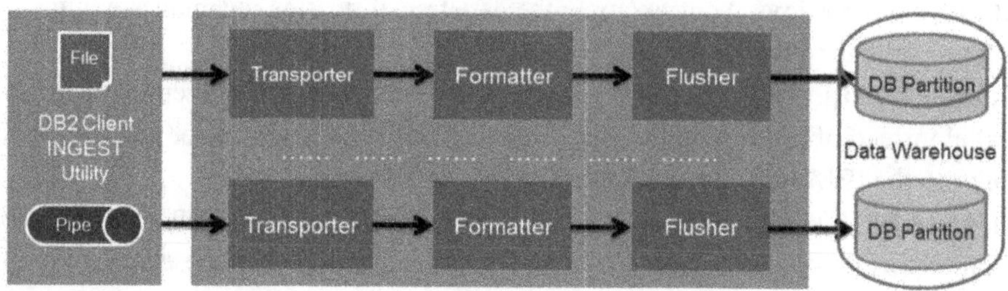

Figure 6.20: Ingest utility architecture

You invoke the Ingest utility by executing the INGEST command. The basic syntax for this command is:

```
INGEST [DATA] FROM FILE [FileName] | PIPE [PipeName]
<FORMAT DELIMITED | POSITIONAL>
<DUMPFILE|BADFILE [ExFileName]>
<EXCEPTION TABLE [ExTableName]>
<WARNINGCOUNT n>
<MESSAGES MsgFileName>
[RESTART | CONTINUE | TERMINATE]
[INSERT | REPLACE | UPDATE | DELETE | MERGE]
INTO [TableName]
```

where:

FileName	Specifies the name and location of the external file from which to ingest data
PipeName	Specifies the name of the pipe from which to ingest data
ExFileName	Specifies the name of the file to which to write rows rejected by the formatters
ExTableName	Specifies the table to which to write rows inserted by the Ingest utility and rejected by DB2 with certain SQLSTATEs
MsgFileName	Specifies the name of the file to record informational, warning, and error messages

TableName Specifies the target DB2 tables into which to write the Ingest utility flusher process

Before invoking the Ingest utility, it is mandatory to create ingest control table SYSTOOLS.INGESTRESTART. You can create this table through the SYSINSTALLOBJECTS () procedure or by using the data definition of the object:

```
CALL SYSPROC.SYSINSTALLOBJECTS ('INGEST', 'C', 'SYSTOOLSPACE','SYSTOOLS')

  Return Status = 0
```

or

```
CREATE TABLE SYSTOOLS.INGESTRESTART (
       JOBID                VARCHAR (256)        NOT NULL,
       APPLICATIONID        VARCHAR (256)        NOT NULL,
       FLUSHERID            INT                  NOT NULL,
       FLUSHERDISTID        INT                  NOT NULL,
       TRANSPORTERID        INT                  NOT NULL,
       BUFFERID             BIGINT               NOT NULL,
       BYTEPOS              BIGINT               NOT NULL,
       ROWSPROCESSED        INT                  NOT NULL,
       PRIMARY KEY
       (JOBID,
       FLUSHERID,
       TRANSPORTERID,
       FLUSHERDISTID))
IN SYSTOOLSPACE
```

If you want to ingest data stored in a DEL format external file named employee.del into table EMPLOYEE, you can do so by executing the INGEST command:

```
INGEST FROM FILE employee.del
FORMAT DELIMITED
INSERT INTO EMPLOYEE
```

Continued

```
SQL2979I  The ingest utility is starting at "08/07/2014 17:03:07.017299".
SQL2914I  The ingest utility has started the following ingest job:
"DB21001:20140807.170307.017299:00003:00011".

Number of rows read          = 3
Number of rows inserted      = 3
Number of rows rejected      = 0

SQL2980I  The ingest utility completed successfully at timestamp "08/07/2014
17:03:08.416668"
```

In the above INGEST command, the default delimiter is a comma (,). If you want to override the comma (,) with a semicolon (;), specify the DELIMITED BY ';' clause.

If the LOCKLIST database memory area exhausts, you must fine-tune the database configuration parameters similar to the following (the later sections will discuss the performance tuning aspects of INGEST command):

```
INGEST FROM FILE employee.del
FORMAT DELIMITED BY ','
INSERT INTO employee
SQL2979I  The ingest utility is starting at "08/07/2014 17:16:28.965618".
SQL2914I  The ingest utility has started the following ingest job:
"DB21001:20140807.171628.965618:00003:00011".
SQL2965I  The following warning or error occurred issuing the SQL "INSERT"
statement on table "MOHAN.EMPLOYEE".
SQL0912N  The maximum number of lock requests has been reached for the
database. Reason code = "1"  SQLSTATE=57011
SQL2977I  Because of the previous error, the ingest utility will exit.

Number of rows read          = 393216
Number of rows inserted      = 6000
Number of rows rejected      = 0

                                                            Continued
```

```
SQL2902I  The ingest utility completed at timestamp "08/07/2014
17:16:32.935864". Number of errors: "1". Number of warnings: "0".

UPDATE DB CFG FOR sample USING LOCKLIST 30000 MAXLOCKS 80
DB20000I  The UPDATE DATABASE CONFIGURATION command completed successfully.

INGEST FROM FILE employee.del
FORMAT DELIMITED BY ','
INSERT INTO employee
SQL2979I  The ingest utility is starting at "08/07/2014 17:27:36.172956".
SQL2914I  The ingest utility has started the following ingest job:
"DB21001:20140807.172736.172956:00003:00011".

Number of rows read          = 393216
Number of rows inserted      = 393216
Number of rows rejected      = 0

SQL2980I  The ingest utility completed successfully at timestamp "08/07/2014
17:27:41.716126"
```

Formatting the Input Values

In the real world, the input file is not always in a format for the DB2 database to process directly. In those cases, you can use ingest parsing capability to parse and format the input file data into a DB2-compatible data set. This is beneficial when working with files from other source systems that have different ways of representing specific data types such as timestamp and decimal:

```
INGEST FROM FILE myinputfile.txt
FORMAT DELIMITED BY '|'
(
$field1 INTEGER EXTERNAL,
$field2 DATE 'yyyy/mm/dd',
$field3 CHAR (32)
)
INSERT INTO mytable VALUES ($field1, $field2, $field3)
```

In the above command, the Ingest utility parses the data from file myinputfile.txt, converts the DATE format for field2 of the file, and inserts it into table MYTABLE. The EXTERNAL keyword is used with numeric field types such as INTEGER, DECIMAL to indicate that the field value is specified in ASCII rather than in binary.

The following example shows the data in the input file myinputfile.txt. Notice that the DATE data type format is not DB2 compatible. However, when INGEST streams data into the DB2 table, it converts the DATE column data to a DB2-compatible format:

```
1|2013/01/27|"MOHAN"
2|2013/02/28|"MILAN"
3|2013/03/21|"COLLINS"
```

The INGEST command output is:

```
SQL2979I  The ingest utility is starting at "08/07/2014 19:54:45.979772".
SQL2914I  The ingest utility has started the following ingest job:
"DB21001:20140807.195445.979772:00003:00012".

Number of rows read          = 3
Number of rows inserted      = 3
Number of rows rejected      = 0

SQL2980I  The ingest utility completed successfully at timestamp "08/07/2014
19:54:47.276151"
```

The actual data in the table after the INGEST command execution is as follows:

```
SELECT * FROM mytable

ID          JOIN_DATE  NAME
----------- ---------- ------------------------------
          1 01/27/2013 MOHAN
          2 02/28/2013 MILAN
          3 03/21/2013 COLLINS

  3 record(s) selected.
```

Let us look at an interesting ingest behavior. Assume the table structure for mytable2 is:

```
CREATE TABLE mytable2 (
c1 VARCHAR(32),
c2 INTEGER GENERATED BY DEFAULT AS IDENTITY,
c3 INTEGER GENERATED ALWAYS AS (c2 + 1))
```

The data in the delimited ASCII file myinputfile2 is:

```
"UNITED STATES",10,1
"UNITED KINGDOM",20,2
```

The INGEST command to insert the data into target table mytable2 is something like this:

```
INGEST FROM FILE myinputfile2.txt FORMAT DELIMITED INSERT INTO mytable2
SQL2979I  The ingest utility is starting at "08/07/2014 20:18:02.964778".
SQL2914I  The ingest utility has started the following ingest job:
"DB21001:20140807.201802.964778:00003:00013".

Number of rows read          = 2
Number of rows inserted      = 2
Number of rows rejected      = 0

SQL2980I  The ingest utility completed successfully at timestamp "08/07/2014
20:18:04.313926"

SELECT * FROM mytable2
C1                               C2          C3
-------------------------------- ----------- -----------
UNITED STATES                             10          11
UNITED KINGDOM                            20          21

  2 record(s) selected.
```

The DB2 Ingest utility automatically modifies the VALUES list in the INSERT based on the target table definition. For the above table definition, the VALUES list will be something like VALUES ($C1, $C2, DEFAULT).

As the next example shows, the Ingest utility can process multiple input files in a single command:

```
INGEST FROM FILE myinputfile2.txt, myinputfile2.txt, myinputfile4.txt FORMAT
DELIMITED
INSERT INTO mytable2
SQL2979I  The ingest utility is starting at "08/07/2014 20:42:21.253631".
SQL2914I  The ingest utility has started the following ingest job:
"DB21001:20140807.204221.253631:00003:00013".

Number of rows read         = 6
Number of rows inserted     = 6
Number of rows rejected     = 0

SQL2980I  The ingest utility completed successfully at timestamp "08/07/2014
20:42:22.589056"
```

Ingesting Data from a Pipe

You can ingest data into the target DB2 table by using an operating system pipe instead of using external files. This avoids having to create large amounts of input files on the source server and copying it over to the Ingest utility server. The basic steps are as follows:

Step 1: Create an operating system pipe on the target server by using the mkfifo command (UNIX):

```
mkfifo datapipe
```

Step 2: Catalog the source database as remote on the target server or on the Ingest utility server:

```
CATALOG TCPIP NODE snode REMOTE sourcedbServer SERVER 50001
CATALOG DATABASE sourcedb AT NODE snode
```

Step 3: Connect to the source database remotely from the target server:

```
CONNECT TO sourcedb user <username> using <password>
```

Step 4: Export data from the source database and write it to one end of the pipe (datapipe):

```
EXPORT TO datapipe OF DEL MODIFIED BY COLDEL,
       MESSAGES CUSTOMERS.msg SELECT * FROM customers
```

Step 5: Connect locally to the target database:

```
CONNECT TO targetdb
```

Step 6: Use the INGEST command to read data from the other end of the pipe and load data into the target table:

```
INGEST FROM datapipe FORMAT DELIMITED
       INSERT INTO customers
```

Step 7: After the data load process, delete the pipe created in step 1:

```
rm datapipe
```

DML Operations

With the Ingest utility, you can use insert, update, delete, replace, and merge DML operations to stream the source data into the target DB2 tables. The sample command for the update operation is:

```
INGEST FROM FILE myinputfile5.txt
       FORMAT DELIMITED
            ($id            INTEGER EXTERNAL,
             $join_date     DATE 'yyyy/mm/dd',
             $name          CHAR (32))
       BADFILE exp_update.txt
```

Continued

```
        MESSAGES exp_update.msg
        UPDATE mytable3
               SET (NAME, JOIN_DATE) = ($name, $join_date)
        WHERE ID=$id
```

The input data file and current records in mytable3 will look something like this:

```
1,2013/01/27,"MOHAN KUMAR"
2,2013/02/28,"MILAN MOHAN"
3,2013/03/21,"KENT COLLINS"
4,2012/03/20,"COLIN CHAPMAN"
5,2012/03/22,"HAMDI ROUMANI"

SELECT * FROM mytable3

ID          JOIN_DATE  NAME
----------- ---------- --------------------------------
          1 01/27/2013 MOHAN
          2 02/28/2013 MILAN
          3 03/21/2013 COLLINS
```

Notice that the input data file record entries have two additional records compared with the table data. Those records will be rejected because no matching records are in the base table to update:

```
INGEST FROM FILE myinputfile5.txt
        FORMAT DELIMITED
        ($id INTEGER EXTERNAL,
        $join_date DATE 'yyyy/mm/dd',
        $name CHAR (32))
BADFILE exp_update.txt
MESSAGES exp_update.msg
UPDATE mytable3 SET (NAME, JOIN_DATE) = ($name, $join_date) WHERE ID=$id
```

Continued

```
Number of rows read          = 5
Number of rows updated       = 3
Number of rows rejected      = 2
SQL2901I The ingest utility completed at timestamp "08/07/2014 22:04:49.367472".
Number of errors: "0". Number of warnings: "3". Message file: "exp_update.msg".
```

The message file shows information about why two records have been rejected and displays the Ingest configuration automatic setting:

```
SQL2903W  Configuration parameter "NUM_FLUSHERS_PER_PARTITION" has been
automatically adjusted to the following value: "1". Reason code= "12"
SQL2979I  The ingest utility is starting at "08/07/2014 22:04:48.109911".
SQL2914I  The ingest utility has started the following ingest job:
"DB21001:20140807.220448.109911:00003:00012".
SQL2905I  The following error occurred issuing the SQL "UPDATE" statement on table
"MOHAN.MYTABLE3" using data from line "4" of input file
"myinputfile.txt". SQL0100W  No row was found for FETCH, UPDATE or DELETE; or the
result of a query is an empty table.  SQLSTATE=02000

SQL2905I  The following error occurred issuing the SQL "UPDATE" statement on table
"MOHAN.MYTABLE3" using data from line "5" of input file
"myinputfile.txt". SQL0100W  No row was found for FETCH, UPDATE or DELETE; or the
result of a query is an empty table.  SQLSTATE=02000

SQL2902I  The ingest utility completed at timestamp "08/07/2014
22:04:49.367472". Number of errors: "0". Number of warnings: "3".
```

Finally, the records in the base table after the update ingest operation look like this:

```
ID          JOIN_DATE  NAME
----------- ---------- --------------------------------
          1 01/27/2012 MOHAN KUMAR
          2 02/28/2012 MILAN MOHAN
```

Continued

```
        3 03/21/2012 KENT COLLINS


  3 record(s) selected.
```

Similarly, the Ingest utility commands for delete, merge, and replace operations are as follows:

```
INGEST FROM FILE myinputfile6.txt
       FORMAT DELIMITED
            ($id            INTEGER EXTERNAL,
             $join_date     DATE 'yyyy/mm/dd',
            $name           CHAR (32))
       BADFILE exp_delete.txt
       MESSAGES exp_delete.msg
       DELETE FROM mytable4  WHERE ID=$id


INGEST FROM FILE myinputfile7.txt
       FORMAT DELIMITED
            ($id            INTEGER EXTERNAL,
             $join_date     DATE 'yyyy/mm/dd',
            $name           CHAR (32))
       BADFILE exp_merge.txt
       MESSAGES exp_merge.msg
       MERGE INTO mytable5 on (ID = $id)
       WHEN MATCHED THEN
             UPDATE SET (NAME, JOIN_DATE) = ($name, $join_date)
       WHEN NOT MATCHED THEN
             INSERT VALUES ($id, $name, $join_date)


INGEST FROM FILE myinputfile8.txt
        FORMAT DELIMITED
             ($id               INTEGER EXTERNAL,
```

Continued

```
        $join_date      DATE 'yyyy/mm/dd',
        $name           CHAR (32))
    BADFILE exp_replace.txt
    MESSAGES exp_replace.msg
    REPLACE INTO mytable6
```

DB2 Ingest Parameters

The Ingest utility has its own configuration parameter settings, which affect only later INGEST commands in the same CLP session but not INGEST commands in other CLP sessions.

The command syntax to update the Ingest utility parameter is:

```
INGEST SET <PARAMETER> <VALUE>

Examples:
INGEST SET COMMIT_COUNT 1000
INGEST SET COMMIT_PERIOD 60
INGEST SET RETRY_COUNT 20
INGEST SET RETRY_PERIOD 30
```

Table 6.6 lists the Ingest configuration parameters; these settings affect only at the session level.

Table 6.6: DB2 Ingest utility parameters

Parameter	Default and Range	Description
commit_count	0 [0 to 32 BIT SIGNED INT]	This specifies the number of rows each flusher writes in a single transaction before issuing a commit. It should always be multiples of 1,000; if not, DB2 will round it to nearest multiple.
commit_period	1 [0 to 2 678 400]	This specifies the number of seconds between committed transactions. At each flush, the Ingest utility checks for the number of seconds since the last commit; if it is greater than or equal to the setting of commit_period, it issues a commit command.
num_flushers_per_partition	MAX(1,((CPU/2)/PARTITION)) [0 to System CPU's]	This specifies the number of flushers to allocate for each database partition. When there is a delete, merge, or update operation, this parameter will be adjusted to 0 or 1 to avoid the deadlock situation (SQL2903W).
num_formatters	MAX(1,CPU/2) [0 to System CPU's]	This specifies the number of formatters to allocate. If you specify the DUMPFILE or BADFILE clause in the INGEST command to record the bad records in the same order as they appear in the input file, you must set this parameter to 1.

Table 6.6: DB2 Ingest utility parameters (continued)

Parameter	Default and Range	Description
pipe_timeout	600 [0 to 2 678 400]	This specifies the maximum number of seconds to wait for data when the input source is a pipe. When you set this parameter to 0, the Ingest utility waits indefinitely.
retry_count	0 [0 to 1000]	This specifies the number of times to retry a failed but recoverable transaction.
retry_period	0 [0 to 2 678 400]	This specifies the number of seconds to wait before retrying a failed but recoverable transaction.
shm_max_size	1 [1 to System Memory]	This specifies the maximum size of Interprocess communication (IPC) shared memory in bytes. Because the Ingest utility runs on the client, this memory is allocated on the client machine.

Handling Ingest Data Problems

The Ingest utility supports copying rejected records to a file or table or discarding them, as Figure 6.21 shows. A record can be rejected for many reasons, such as out-of-range numeric values, incompatible data types, or invalid date format. You can specify what the INGEST command does with rows rejected by the Ingest utility (using the DUMPFILE option) or by DB2 (using the EXCEPTION TABLE option). Remember, rejected records do not cause the INGEST command to fail; the command will generally continue with ingesting valid records from the source input.

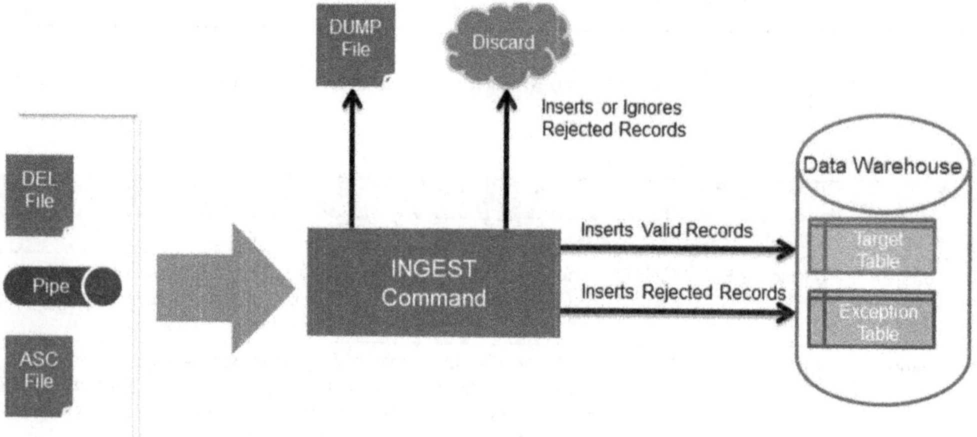

Figure 6.21: Ingest utility error handling

The following example intentionally places some invalid records in the data file myinputfile9.txt:

```
PROD1|product 1|10|5|3
PROD2|product 2|15|5|3
PROD3|product 3|20|15|3
PROD4|product 4|5|3|2
PROD5|product 5|7|2|1
PROD6|product 6|A|0|0
```

To populate the myinputfile9.txt file data into the target table mytable7 having a CHECK (TOTAL_PRICE > 10) constraint, you execute this INGEST command:

```
INGEST DATA FROM FILE myinputfile9.txt
       FORMAT DELIMITED BY '|'
       ($prod_id            CHAR (8),
        $description        CHAR (32),
        $price              DECIMAL (5, 2) EXTERNAL,
        $sales_tax          DECIMAL (4, 2) EXTERNAL,
        $shipping           DECIMAL (3, 2) EXTERNAL)
DUMPFILE dump_mytable7.txt
EXCEPTION TABLE exp_mytable7
MESSAGES msg_mytable7.msg
INSERT INTO mytable7 (PROD_ID, DESCRIPTION, TOTAL_PRICE)
VALUES ($prod_id, $description, $price + $sales_tax + $shipping)


Number of rows read         = 6
Number of rows inserted     = 3
Number of rows rejected     = 3

SQL2901I  The ingest utility completed at timestamp "08/08/2014
10:20:11.187482". Number of errors: "3". Number of warnings: "0".    Message file:
"msg_mytable7.msg".
```

In the above example, DUMPFILE specifies that rows rejected by the formatters due to data type mismatch are to be written to the file dump_mytable7.txt. The content of this file will look something like:

```
PROD6|product 6|A|0|0
```

EXCEPTION TABLE indicates that rows rejected by the formatter due to constraint checking are to be written to the table exp_mytable7. The content of this table will look similar to this:

```
PROD_ID  DESCRIPTION                       TOTAL_PRICE
-------- --------------------------------- -----------
PROD4    product 4                               10.00
PROD5    product 5                               10.00
```

MESSAGES specifies the file that is to receive informational, warning, and error messages. In the above example, all messages were recorded in msg_mytable7.msg, and the file content looks something like:

```
SQL2979I  The ingest utility is starting at "08/08/2014 10:20:09.946252".
SQL2914I  The ingest utility has started the following ingest job:
"DB21001:20140808.102009.946252:00003:00015".
SQL2922I  The following warning or error occurred while formatting data from line "6"
of input file "myinputfile9.txt".
SQL2927N  The field value in line "6" and field "3" cannot be converted to the value
type: "DECIMAL".

SQL2905I  The following error occurred issuing the SQL "INSERT" statement on table
"MOHAN.MYTABLE7" using data from line "4" of input file
"myinputfile9.txt".
SQL0545N  The requested operation is not allowed because a row does not
satisfy the check constraint "MOHAN.MYTABLE7.SQL140808101045490".
SQLSTATE=23513

                                                                       Continued
```

```
SQL2905I  The following error occurred issuing the SQL "INSERT" statement on table
"MOHAN.MYTABLE7" using data from line "5" of input file
"myinputfile9.txt".
SQL0545N  The requested operation is not allowed because a row does not
satisfy the check constraint "MOHAN.MYTABLE7.SQL140808101045490".
SQLSTATE=23513

SQL2902I  The ingest utility completed at timestamp "08/08/2014
10:20:11.187482". Number of errors: "3". Number of warnings: "0".
```

Finally, the data that is ingested into the target table mytable7 is:

```
SELECT * FROM mytable7

PROD_ID  DESCRIPTION                      TOTAL_PRICE
-------- -------------------------------- -----------
PROD1    product 1                              18.00
PROD2    product 2                              23.00
PROD3    product 3                              38.00
```

Recovering a Failed Ingest Command

The INGEST command is considered complete only when it reaches the end of the source file or the pipe. Under any other circumstances, the Ingest utility considers the command execution as incomplete, and these conditions include:

- The utility cannot read the input file due to an I/O error.
- A critical DB2 system error indicates that the job is not functioning as expected.
- The INGEST command is killed or terminates abnormally.

If an INGEST command fails, you can restart it by reissuing the command with the RESTART CONTINUE clause. The Ingest utility will then start the operation from the last commit point.

To simulate a failed INGEST command, you can run the following specified statement and do a forceful kill by using CTRL +C:

```
INGEST DATA FROM FILE myinputfile10.txt
FORMAT DELIMITED BY '|'
(       $prod_id            CHAR(8),
        $description        CHAR(32),
        $price              DECIMAL(5,2) EXTERNAL,
        $sales_tax          DECIMAL(4,2) EXTERNAL,
        $shipping           DECIMAL(3,2) EXTERNAL)
BADFILE dump_mytable7.txt
EXCEPTION TABLE exp_mytable7
MESSAGES msg_mytable7.msg
RESTART NEW 'myjob9'
INSERT INTO mytable7 (PROD_ID, DESCRIPTION, TOTAL_PRICE)
                      VALUES($prod_id, $description, $price + $sales_tax + $shipping)
^C
Number of rows read           = 884520
Number of rows inserted       = 261000
Number of rows rejected       = 0

SQL2901I  The ingest utility completed at timestamp "08/08/2014
12:36:25.175011". Number of errors: "2". Number of warnings: "0".    Message file:
"msg_mytable7.msg".
```

You can look at the message file to identify the real cause (in this specific case, the problem is CTRL +C):

```
SQL2979I  The ingest utility is starting at "08/08/2014 12:36:19.897239".
SQL2914I  The ingest utility has started the following ingest job: "myjob9".
SQL2965I  The following warning or error occurred issuing the SQL "INSERT"
statement on table "MOHAN.MYTABLE7".
```

Continued

```
SQL0952N  Processing was cancelled due to an interrupt.  SQLSTATE=57014
SQL2977I  Because of the previous error, the ingest utility will exit.

SQL0952N  Processing was cancelled due to an interrupt.  SQLSTATE=57014
SQL2902I  The ingest utility completed at timestamp "08/08/2014
12:36:25.175011". Number of errors: "2". Number of warnings: "0".
```

If you want to restart the failed job, you can use the command something like:

```
INGEST DATA FROM FILE myinputfile10.txt
FORMAT DELIMITED BY '|'
(       $prod_id            CHAR(8),
        $description        CHAR(32),
        $price              DECIMAL(5,2) EXTERNAL,
        $sales_tax          DECIMAL(4,2) EXTERNAL,
        $shipping           DECIMAL(3,2) EXTERNAL)
BADFILE dump_mytable7.txt
EXCEPTION TABLE exp_mytable7
MESSAGES msg_mytable7.msg
RESTART CONTINUE 'myjob9'
INSERT INTO mytable7 (PROD_ID, DESCRIPTION, TOTAL_PRICE)
                    VALUES($prod_id, $description, $price + $sales_tax +
$shipping)

Number of rows read          = 655613
Number of rows inserted      = 623520
Number of rows rejected      = 0

SQL2980I  The ingest utility completed successfully at timestamp "08/08/2014
13:26:27.149012"
```

If you do not want to restart a failed job, you can terminate it by using the RESTART TERMINATE option in the INGEST command to clear all the log records.

Monitoring Ingest Operations

Like other DB2 database utilities, the Ingest utility has two simple commands to monitor the progress:

- INGEST LIST
- INGEST GET STATS FOR <id>

These commands must be run on the same machine running the Ingest utility. The commands syntax and the output results are:

```
INGEST LIST

Ingest job ID                = myjob9
Ingest temp job ID           = 1
Database Name                = SAMPLE
Target table                 = MOHAN.MYTABLE7
Input type                   = FILE
Start Time                   = 08/08/2014 13:44:56.259299
Running Time                 = 00:00:00
Number of records processed = 0

DB20000I  The INGEST LIST command completed successfully.
```

The INGEST LIST command displays Ingest job name, and if none is specified, DB2 will allocate a job ID (for example, DB21001:20140808.135651.893482:00003:00012). The Ingest temp job ID is necessary to run the INGEST GET STATS command:

```
INGEST GET STATS FOR 1

Ingest job ID               = myjob9
Database Name               = SAMPLE
Target table                = MOHAN.MYTABLE7

                                                    Continued
```

```
Overall           Overall           Current           Current
ingest rate       write rate        ingest rate       write rate
(records/second)  (writes/second)   (records/second)  (writes/second)   Total records
----------------- ----------------- ----------------- ----------------- --------------
           176904             85800            884520            429000         429000

DB20000I  The INGEST GET STATS command completed successfully.
```

If you want to continuously monitor the ingest operation at regular intervals until the completion, you can run the following INGEST GET STATS command:

```
INGEST GET STATS FOR 1 EVERY 1 SECONDS

Ingest job ID                = myjob9
Database Name                = SAMPLE
Target table                 = MOHAN.MYTABLE7

Overall           Overall           Current           Current
ingest rate       write rate        ingest rate       write rate
(records/second)  (writes/second)   (records/second)  (writes/second)   Total records
----------------- ----------------- ----------------- ----------------- --------------
           176904             81800            884520            409000         409000
           147420            100666                 0            195000         604000
           126360            112428                 0            183000         787000
           110565            110565                 0             97520         884520

DB20000I  The INGEST GET STATS command completed successfully.
```

Ingest Performance Tuning Tips

The Ingest utility runs the ingest process in parallel using multiple threads. You will need to fine-tune lock and transaction log database configuration parameters to effectively use the multithread parallel architecture.

The locklist and maxlocks parameters are essential to speed up the ingest operation. If you do not set these parameters correctly, you might encounter performance problems and in some cases received the SQL0912N (The maximum number of lock requests has been reached for the database) error. The recommendation is to set these parameters to AUTOMATIC to let the database manager manage lock resources.

Define ingest fields to be the same data type as their corresponding column types in the target table. This specifically avoids data conversion overhead. It is always advisable to understand your workload and the target tables. For tables with a small row size, increase the commit_count value, and for tables with a large row size, reduce the commit_count value in the ingest parameter setting.

Unlike Load, Ingest does fast inserts producing many transaction logs. Be sure to review the workload and transaction log parameters such as logprimary, logfilsz and logbufsz.

Comparison Between Ingest, Load, and Import Utilities

Table 6.7 summarizes key differences between Ingest, Import, and Load utilities.

Table 6.7: DB2 utilities comparison: Import vs. Ingest vs. Load

Attribute	Import	Ingest	Load
Speed	Slow—uses sequential insert statements	Fast—uses parallel insert threads	Very fast—writes formatted pages directly into table space containers
Concurrency	High—sometimes escalates to table level lock	Very high—row-level locking	Low—allows read-only operations
Transaction logging	Every record change is logged	Every record change is logged	Very minimal logging
Behavior on failure	Rollback, and table is accessible	Rollback, and table is accessible	Table will remain in Load Pending state
LOBs and XML data	Supported data type	Unsupported data type	Supported data type
Utility type	Server side	Client side	Server side
Triggers activation	Yes	Yes	No
Constraint validation	Yes	Yes	Only UNIQUE keys are validated
Is table space backup necessary?	No	No	Yes—but No if run using NONRECOVERABLE clause or with COPY YES
Utility throttling	Can use UTIL_IMPACT_PRIORITY or util_impact_lim to throttle the utility	No impact	Can use UTIL_IMPACT_PRIORITY or util_impact_lim to throttle the utility
Data type support	Supports LOB and XML data types	Does not support LOB and XML data types	Supports LOB and XML data types

Ingest Utility Limitations

Be aware of a few limitations when using the Ingest utility:

- It supports ingest operations only against DB2 Linux, UNIX, and Windows systems.
- It does not support operations on typed tables, types view, and DGTT.

- It does not support operations on tables having BLOB, CLOB, LOB, DBCLOB, XML, or structured or user-defined data type columns.
- It does not assign a value to a column defined as GENERATED ALWAYS.
- It does not assign a combination of default values to a column defined as GENERATED BY DEFAULT AS IDENTITY.
- The LIST HISTORY command does not show the ingest operation.
- UTIL_IMPACT_PRIORITY cannot be used.
- It does not support DB2 special registers except CURRENT SCHEMA, CURRENT TEMPORAL SYSTEM_TIME, and CURRENT TEMPORAL BUSINESS_TIME.

Other DB2 Data Movement Options

DB2 has several other features to move data within and between databases:

- Move online or offline tables by using the SYSPROC.ADMIN_MOVE_TABLE () procedure.
- Create a copy of a schema by using the SYSPROC.ADMIN_COPY_SCHEMA () procedure.
- Relocate a database by using the db2relocatedb command.
- Create a copy of a table or schema by using db2move and extracting DDL by using the db2look commands.

The SYSPROC.ADMIN_MOVE_TABLE () Procedure

In the past (well before DB2 9.7), to move an existing table from one table space to another due to a change in storage characteristics requirements such as changing the extent size with a particular table or changing the type of table space for a particular table (SMS, DMS, or automatic storage), required several steps. You had to either export the table's data to an external file, drop and re-create the table in the desired table space, and then populate the newly created table with the data stored in the external file or create the table with a different name on the desired table space and copy the data using the INSERT INTO... SELECT * FROM SQL statement and rename the table at the end. With DB2 9.7 onward, you can easily move tables, indexes, long data, and LOB data from one table space to another by using the ADMIN_MOVE_TABLE () procedure, so no more manual DBA tasks to move a table.

This procedure moves data stored in an existing table to a new table that has the same name but may have been defined in a different table space. You can also use this procedure to change the MDC (ORGANIZE BY DIMENSION) specification for a table, alter the ITC (ORGANIZE BY INSERT TIME) specification for a table, modify a table's partitioning keys (DISTRIBUTE BY HASH), change the range partitioning (PARTITION BY RANGE) specification for a table, add or remove columns from a table, alter a column's data type (provided the new data type is compatible with the data type being used), or create a new compression dictionary for a table that has deep compression enabled. Furthermore, the table can remain online and accessible while these operations are being performed.

Figure 6.8 shows different phases of the ADMIN_MOVE_TABLE () procedure operation.

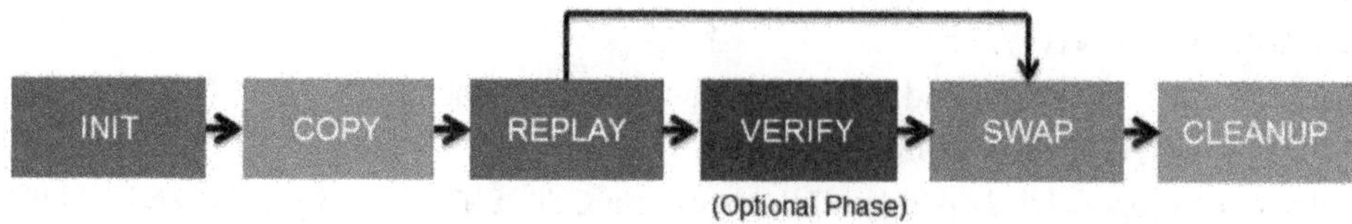

Figure 6.22: ADMIN_MOVE_TABLE phases

- **INIT**. This phase initializes all the objects required for the operation, including the staging table that is necessary for capturing all the data changes during the move.
- **COPY**. This phase creates a copy of the source table according to the current definition and copies the data into the target table. Any DML operation occurring on the source table during the move is captured in the staging table. By default, all the indexes on the target table are created at the end of the COPY phase. If you want to create the indexes before the data copy, you can specify the COPY_WITH_INDEXES clause to do so.
- **REPLAY**. This phase replays all the changes captured in the staging table into the target table just before swapping the source and target tables.
- **VERIFY**. This is an optional phase that checks the table contents between source and target to make sure they are identical before the swap. This process acquires a shared lock on both source and target tables to perform a comparison. If the table has a unique index, this phase compares unique index values between columns that are in tables. Otherwise, it compares all values between all the columns except LONG, LOB, and XML columns. This is an expensive operation, so use it only when absolutely necessary.
- **SWAP**. This phase performs a swapping of source and target tables. The source table will be taken offline briefly to complete the REPLAY.
- **CLEANUP**. This phase drops all the intermediate tables created during the online move such as the staging table, any non-unique indexes, and triggers. This can also be called to perform a cleanup when the online table move failed during the SWAP phase.

When you invoke the ADMIN_MOVE_TABLE () procedure, a shadow copy of the table to move is created in the table space specified (you can also create the target table manually beforehand). This procedure also creates a staging table and set of triggers to capture data changes made on the source table during the move operation. Data is then copied from the source to the target by using either INSERT FROM CURSOR or LOAD FROM CURSOR. Once the data has been copied, changes captured in the staging table are replayed against the target table to bring it up to date. During this phase, the source table is briefly taken offline to rename it. By default, the source table is then dropped; however, it can be kept and renamed by using the KEEP option.

The ADMIN_MOVE_TABLE () procedure will move any indexes, triggers, views, and constraints that have been defined on the table being moved. It is important to remember that this procedure requires additional storage for the target and staging tables, as well as additional transaction log requirements due to triggers being fired to capture the data changes in source table.

The ADMIN_MOVE_TABLE () procedure syntax is:

```
CALL SYSPROC.ADMIN_MOVE_TABLE (
[TableSchema],
[SourceTable],
[TargetDataTS],
[TargetIndexTS],
[TargetLongTS],
[MDC_Columns],
[PartitionKeys],
[DataPartitions],
[ColumnDefs],
[Options,...],
[Operations])
```

or

```
CALL SYSPROC.ADMIN_MOVE_TABLE (
[TableSchema],
[SourceTable],
[TargetTable],
[Options,...],
[Operations])
```

where:

TableSchema	Specifies the name of the schema which contains the table to move and is case-sensitive
SourceTable	Specifies the name of the table to move and is case-sensitive
TargetName	Specifies the name of an existing table to use as the target table during the move
TargetDataTS	Specifies the new data table space for the target table

TargetIndexTS	Specifies the new index table space for the target table
TargetLongTS	Specifies the new LOB object table space for the target table
MDC_Columns	Specifies the dimension columns for MDC and ITC tables; if the value provided does not begin with ORGANIZE BY, it treats the columns as MDC dimension columns; for ITC tables, the values should be ORGANIZE BY INSERT TIME
PartitionKeys	Specifies the column names for the partition keys on the target table
DataPartitions	Specifies the range partition specification for the target tables
ColumnDefs	Specifies the new column definitions for the target table and allows you to change the column type as long as it is compatible with the current type
Options	Specifies one or more options for the stored procedure to use; the following list of options is case-sensitive:

- **KEEP** retains a copy of the original source table under a different name.
- **COPY_USE_LOAD** uses ADMIN_CMD () (when you do not specify the COPY_USE_LOAD option) or a LOAD with NONRECOVERABLE option through the db2Load API (when you specify COPY_USE_LOAD).
- **COPY_WITH_INDEXES** creates indexes before copying the source table data into target; however, the default is to create the indexes after copying the source table.
- **FORCE** causes the SWAP phase to ignore checking the source table definition changes.
- **NO_STATS** does not start RUNSTATS on the target table.
- **COPY_STATS** copies the statistics information from the source to the target. This may not be accurate when you move the table to a table space having a different page size.
- **NO_AUTO_REVAL** prevents automatic revalidation of objects (triggers, views) and creates them after the table move.
- **REORG** performs an offline REORG on the target table before the SWAP phase.
- **NO_TARGET_LOCKSIZE_TABLE** does not retain the LOCKSIZE table option on the target table during the COPY and SWAP phase.
- **CLUSTER** makes the read happen by using the ORDER BY clause on the source table.
- **NON_CLUSTER** makes the read happen without using the ORDER BY clause on the source table.
- **LOAD_MSGPATH** specifies the load message file path.

- **LOAD_TEMPPATH** specifies the load temporary file path.
- **ALLOW_RLBAC** moves a table that has the LBAC security label specified.

Operations Specifies which operation the stored procedure is to execute:

- **MOVE** performs the entire table move (INIT, COPY, REPLAY, and SWAP).
- **INIT**, **COPY**, **REPLAY**, **VERIFY**, **SWAP**, and **CLEANUP** perform as in Figure 6.22.
- **REDIRECT** forwards changes directly to the target table instead of capturing the changes in the staging table.
- **REVERT** reverts to the original behavior wherein the staging table captures the changes.
- **CANCEL** cancels a multistep table move while between phases, or cancels a failed table move operation.

There are two ways to invoke the ADMIN_MOVE_TABLE () procedure, as the procedure syntax shows. You can rely on the procedure to create the target table, or you can create the target table with the necessary changes to the columns, such as adding new columns or changing the column data type that is compatible with the source table column data type. Let us look at each technique with an example.

In the following example, the ADMIN_MOVE_TABLE () procedure is moving the table MOHAN. EMP_PHOTO to different table spaces, namely TS_SMALL_DATA for data, TS_SMALL_INDEX for indexes, and TS_LOB_DATA for LOB columns. The invocation and the results are:

```
CALL SYSPROC.ADMIN_MOVE_TABLE
('MOHAN',
'EMP_PHOTO',
'TS_SMALL_DATA',
'TS_SMALL_INDEX',
'TS_LOB_DATA',
'',
'',
'',
'',
'',
'MOVE')
```

Continued

```
Result set 1
--------------

KEY                              VALUE
-------------------------------- ----------------------------------------
AUTHID                           MOHAN
CLEANUP_END                      2014-08-09-17.06.11.868296
CLEANUP_START                    2014-08-09-17.06.11.759876
COPY_END                         2014-08-09-17.06.11.139883
COPY_OPTS                        NON_CLUSTER
COPY_START                       2014-08-09-17.06.11.038316
COPY_TOTAL_ROWS                  24
INDEXNAME                        IX1_EMP_PHOTO
INDEXSCHEMA                      MOHAN
INDEX_CREATION_TOTAL_TIME        0
INIT_END                         2014-08-09-17.06.10.827127
INIT_START                       2014-08-09-17.06.09.891880
REPLAY_END                       2014-08-09-17.06.11.634378
REPLAY_START                     2014-08-09-17.06.11.140233
REPLAY_TOTAL_ROWS                0
REPLAY_TOTAL_TIME                0
STATUS                           COMPLETE
SWAP_END                         2014-08-09-17.06.11.719530
SWAP_RETRIES                     0
SWAP_START                       2014-08-09-17.06.11.670976
UTILITY_INVOCATION_ID            01000000A900000008000000000000000020140809
                                 17061082788000000000
VERSION                          10.01.0003

22 record(s) selected.

Return Status = 0
```

The results for any ADMIN_MOVE_TABLE () procedure invocation are recorded in the table SYSTOOLS.ADMIN_MOVE_TABLE, which you can query by using this command:

```
SELECT
VARCHAR (TABSCHEMA, 5) AS TABSCHEMA,
VARCHAR (TABNAME, 10) AS TABNAME,
VARCHAR (KEY, 25) AS KEY,
VARCHAR (VALUE, 30) AS VALUE
FROM SYSTOOLS.ADMIN_MOVE_TABLE

TABSCHEMA TABNAME    KEY                       VALUE
--------- ---------- ------------------------- ------------------------------
MOHAN     EMP_PHOTO  REPLAY_END                2014-08-09-17.06.11.634378
MOHAN     EMP_PHOTO  SWAP_START                2014-08-09-17.06.11.670976
MOHAN     EMP_PHOTO  SWAP_END                  2014-08-09-17.06.11.719530
MOHAN     EMP_PHOTO  SWAP_RETRIES              0
MOHAN     EMP_PHOTO  CLEANUP_START             2014-08-09-17.06.11.759876
MOHAN     EMP_PHOTO  CLEANUP_END               2014-08-09-17.06.11.868296
MOHAN     EMP_PHOTO  STATUS                    COMPLETE
MOHAN     EMP_PHOTO  AUTHID                    MOHAN
MOHAN     EMP_PHOTO  VERSION                   10.01.0003
MOHAN     EMP_PHOTO  INIT_START                2014-08-09-17.06.09.891880
MOHAN     EMP_PHOTO  INDEXSCHEMA               MOHAN
MOHAN     EMP_PHOTO  INDEXNAME                 IX1_EMP_PHOTO
MOHAN     EMP_PHOTO  INIT_END                  2014-08-09-17.06.10.827127
MOHAN     EMP_PHOTO  UTILITY_INVOCATION_ID     01000000A900000008000000000000
MOHAN     EMP_PHOTO  COPY_START                2014-08-09-17.06.11.038316
MOHAN     EMP_PHOTO  COPY_OPTS                 NON_CLUSTER
MOHAN     EMP_PHOTO  COPY_TOTAL_ROWS           24
MOHAN     EMP_PHOTO  COPY_END                  2014-08-09-17.06.11.139883
MOHAN     EMP_PHOTO  REPLAY_START              2014-08-09-17.06.11.140233
MOHAN     EMP_PHOTO  INDEX_CREATION_TOTAL_TIME 0
MOHAN     EMP_PHOTO  REPLAY_TOTAL_ROWS         0
MOHAN     EMP_PHOTO  REPLAY_TOTAL_TIME         0

  22 record(s) selected.
```

The ADMIN_MOVE_TABLE () procedure can also move the original table into an already existing target table that has an additional column:

```
Source table: CREATE TABLE mohan.employee
(EMPID       CHAR (3),
                    NAME          VARCHAR (25),
                    TAX_ID        INTEGER NOT NULL)

Target table: CREATE TABLE mohan.new_employee
                   (EMPID         CHAR (3),
                    NAME          VARCHAR (25),
                    TAX_ID        INTEGER NOT NULL,
                    ADDRESS       VARCHAR (20),
                    RATING        SMALLINT);
```

The ADMIN_MOVE_TABLE () command will look like this:

```
CALL SYSPROC.ADMIN_MOVE_TABLE ('MOHAN', 'EMPLOYEE', 'NEW_EMPLOYEE', '',
'MOVE')

  Result set 1
  --------------

  KEY                              VALUE
  -------------------------------- ---------------------------------------
  AUTHID                           MOHAN
  CLEANUP_END                      2014-08-09-17.32.07.283581
  CLEANUP_START                    2014-08-09-17.32.07.154177
  COPY_END                         2014-08-09-17.32.06.503661
  COPY_OPTS                        ARRAY_INSERT,NON_CLUSTER
  COPY_START                       2014-08-09-17.32.06.448170
  COPY_TOTAL_ROWS                  5
  INDEXNAME
  INDEXSCHEMA
                                                                 Continued
```

```
INIT_END                                2014-08-09-17.32.06.311068
INIT_START                              2014-08-09-17.32.05.723878
PAR_COLDEF                              using a supplied target table so COLDEF
                                        could be different
REPLAY_END                              2014-08-09-17.32.07.061977
REPLAY_START                            2014-08-09-17.32.06.503990
REPLAY_TOTAL_ROWS                       0
REPLAY_TOTAL_TIME                       0
STATUS                                  COMPLETE
SWAP_END                                2014-08-09-17.32.07.099224
SWAP_RETRIES                            0
SWAP_START                              2014-08-09-17.32.07.071796
UTILITY_INVOCATION_ID                   01000000B000000008000000000000000201408
                                        09173206311812000000000
VERSION                                 10.01.0003

22 record(s) selected.

Return Status = 0
```

You can now see two new columns added in the table with the default values:

```
EMPID NAME                    TAX_ID     ADDRESS              RATING
----- ----------------------- ---------- -------------------- ------
1     JAGGER, MICK                591075 -                         -
2     RICHARDS, KEITH             234667 -                         -
3     WOOD, RONNIE                257423 -                         -
4     WATTS, CHARLIE              194894 -                         -
5     WYMAN, BILL                 691647 -                         -

  5 record(s) selected.
```

However, if you add a new column along with a constraint such as NOT NULL, the ADMIN_MOVE_TABLE () procedure will report an error (SQL2105N reason code 30) to define the default value for the NOT NULL column.

You can use the SYSPROC.ADMIN_MOVE_TABLE_UTIL () procedure to modify the online move table procedure attributes. The procedure syntax is:

```
SYSPROC.ADMIN_MOVE_TABLE_UTIL (
        [TableSchema],
        [TableName],
        [Action],
        [Key],
        [Value])
```

where:

TableSchema — Identifies the name of the schema which contains the table to move and is case-sensitive

TableName — Identifies the name of the table to move and is case-sensitive

Action — Identifies the action for the procedure to execute:

- **UPSERT** updates the corresponding value with the new value parameter if the specified TABSCHEMA.TABNAME.KEY exists in the ADMIN_MOVE_TABLE protocol table. Otherwise, it inserts the key and value pair into the ADMIN_MOVE_TABLE protocol table.
- **DELETE** deletes the specified key and value pair from the ADMIN_MOVE_TABLE protocol table if the specified TABSCHEMA.TABNAME. KEY exists in the ADMIN_MOVE_TABLE protocol table.

Key — Identifies the key to UPSERT or DELETE in the ADMIN_MOVE_TABLE procedure:

- **COMMIT_AFTER_N_ROWS** insert or updates will commit after this many records during the COPY phase.
- **DEEPCOMPRESSION_SAMPLE** specifies how much data (in KB) is sampled when creating a dictionary for compression if the source table has compression enabled.
- **COPY_ARRAY_SIZE** specifies the array size for COPY_ARRAY_INSERT.
- **COPY_INDEXSCHEMA** specifies the schema of the index to use to cluster the data on the target table during the COPY phase.

- **COPY_INDEXNAME** specifies the name of the index to use to cluster the data on the target table during the COPY phase.
- **REPLAY_MAX_ERR_RETRIES** specifies the maximum retry count for errors (lock timeouts or deadlocks) that may occur during the REPLAY phase.
- **REPLAY_THRESHOLD** specifies that, for a single iteration of the REPLAY phase, if the number of rows applied to the staging table is less than this value, to stop REPLAY, even if new entries are made in the meantime.
- **REORG_USE_TEMPSPACE** allows you to specify a temporary table space for the USE clause of the REORG command if you call the REORG option in the table move.
- **SWAP_MAX_RETRIES** specifies the maximum number of retries allowed during the SWAP phase.

Value Identifies the actual values for the key

If you want to change the commit count value to 20, follow these steps:

Step 1: Invoke the ADMIN_MOVE_TABLE () procedure to copy the EMPLOYEE table in the INIT phase:

```
CALL SYSPROC.ADMIN_MOVE_TABLE ('MOHAN','EMPLOYEE','','','','','','','','','INIT')

  Result set 1
  --------------

  KEY                              VALUE
  -------------------------------- ---------------------------------------
  AUTHID                           MOHAN
  INDEXNAME
  INDEXSCHEMA
  INIT_END                         2014-08-09-18.17.32.399352
  INIT_START                       2014-08-09-18.17.31.636489
  STAGING                          EMPLOYEEACUUk1s
  STATUS                           COPY
  TABNAME_IN_CATALOG               EMPLOYEE
  TARGET                           EMPLOYEEACUUk1t
```

Continued

```
  UTILITY_INVOCATION_ID
01000000BB00000008000000000000000000201408091817324001850000000
  VERSION                             10.01.0003

  11 record(s) selected.

  Return Status = 0
```

Step 2: Modify the compression sampling attribute COMMIT_AFTER_N_ROWS by invoking the ADMIN_MOVE_TABLE_UTIL () procedure:

```
CALL SYSPROC.ADMIN_MOVE_TABLE_UTIL
('MOHAN','EMPLOYEE','UPSERT','COMMIT_AFTER_N_ROWS','20')
Return Status = 0
```

Step 3: Invoke ADMIN_MOVE_TABLE with remaining the phases to complete the copy:

```
CALL SYSPROC.ADMIN_MOVE_TABLE ('MOHAN','EMPLOYEE','','','','','','','','','COPY')
CALL SYSPROC.ADMIN_MOVE_TABLE ('MOHAN','EMPLOYEE','','','','','','','','','REPLAY')
CALL SYSPROC.ADMIN_MOVE_TABLE ('MOHAN','EMPLOYEE','','','','','','','','','SWAP')
```

SYSPROC.ADMIN_COPY_SCHEMA () Procedure

With ADMIN_COPY_SCHEMA () procedure, you can copy a specific database schema and associated objects to a new target schema by using the same object names as in the source schema but with the target schema qualifier. The syntax for the copy schema procedure is:

```
SYSPROC.ADMIN_COPY_SCHEMA (
            [SourceSchema],
            [TargetSchema],
            [CopyMode],
            [ObjectOwner],
            [SourceTBSP],
            [TargetTBSP],
            [ErrorTableSchema],
            [ErrorTable])
```

where:

SourceSchema	Specifies the name of the schema whose objects are to be copied
TargetSchema	Specifies the name of the unique schema name to create the copied objects into; you cannot specify an already existing schema as a target schema
CopyMode	Specifies the mode of copy operation, and the valid options are: • **DDL** creates empty copies of all supported objects from source schema. • **COPY** creates empty copies of all supported objects from the source schema and loads data by using the NONRECOVERABLE clause. • **COPYNO** is similar to the COPY option, but calls LOAD with the COPYNO clause.
ObjectOwner	Specifies the authorization ID to use as the owner of the copied objects
SourceTBSP	Specifies a list of source table spaces for the copy, separated by commas
TargetTBSP	Specifies a list of target table spaces for the copy, separated by commas
ErrorTableSchema	Specifies the schema name of a table containing error information for objects that could not be copied
ErrorTable	Specifies the name of a table containing error information for objects that could not be copied

To copy all the tables contained in schema MOHAN to MILAN, you can follow these simple steps:

Step 1: List the tables available in schema MOHAN:

```
LIST TABLES FOR SCHEMA MOHAN

Table/View                      Schema          Type  Creation time
------------------------------- --------------- ----- --------------------
EMPLOYEE                        MOHAN           T     2014-08-09-19.01.19.166800
EMP_PHOTO                       MOHAN           T     2014-08-09-17.06.09.986805
NEW_EMPLOYEE                    MOHAN           T     2014-08-09-17.36.24.373251
```

Step 2: Invoke procedure ADMIN_COPY_SCHEMA () to copy all schema objects:

```
CALL SYSPROC.ADMIN_COPY_SCHEMA ('MOHAN', 'MILAN', 'COPY', NULL, '', ' ',
'ERRORSCHEMA', 'ERRORNAME')

  Value of output parameters
  --------------------------
  Parameter Name  : ERRORTABSCHEMA
  Parameter Value : -

  Parameter Name  : ERRORTABNAME
  Parameter Value : -

  Return Status = 0
```

Step 3: Validate the copy by listing the tables in the new schema MILAN:

```
LIST TABLES FOR SCHEMA MILAN

Table/View                      Schema          Type  Creation time
------------------------------- --------------- ----- --------------------
EMPLOYEE                   MILAN           T     2014-08-09-19.17.02.545801
EMP_PHOTO                  MILAN           T     2014-08-09-19.17.02.655610
NEW_EMPLOYEE               MILAN           T     2014-08-09-19.17.03.000894

  3 record(s) selected.
```

Relocate a Database by Using db2relocatedb

The relocate database command is handy for renaming a database or for relocating database table space containers or database log directories. You must deactivate the target database before running the db2relocatedb command to modify the metadata and associated control files.

The command syntax is:

```
db2relocatedb -f [ConfigFileName]
```

where:

ConfigFileName Specifies the name of the file containing the configuration information required for database relocation

The db2relocatedb command essentially allows you to change the various database characteristics, including:

- The database name
- The database path
- The instance associated with the database
- Each node database name in a DPF environment
- The active log path associated with the database (newlogpath)
- The container paths for the table space
- The storage paths for the database
- The failure archive log path (failarchpath)
- The archive log paths associated with the database (logarchmenth1 and logarchmenth2)
- The active mirror log path associated with the database (mirrorlogpath)
- The overflow log path associated with the database (overflowlogpath)

The format of the configuration file is simple to use:

```
DB_NAME=oldName,newName
DB_PATH=oldPath,newPath
INSTANCE=oldInst,newInst
NODENUM=nodeNumber
LOG_DIR=oldDirPath,newDirPath
CONT_PATH=oldContPath1,newContpath1
..
STORAGE_PATH=oldStoragePath1,newStoragePath1
..
FAILARCHIVE_PATH=newDirPath
LOGARCHMETH1=newDirPath
LOGARCHMETH2=newDirPath
MIRRORLOG_PATH=newDirPath
OVERFLOWLOG_PATH=newDirPath
```

Now that you are aware of the command and configuration file syntax, let us try renaming database SAMPLE to NEWDB by using the following configuration file:

```
db2relocatedb.1.cfg
DB_NAME=SAMPLE,NEWDB
DB_PATH=/home/db2inst1
INSTANCE=db2inst1
```

To change the database names, you need to follow a few steps:

Step 1: Make sure to turn off applications and to deactivate the database:

```
DEACTIVATE DB sample
DB20000I  The DEACTIVATE DATABASE command completed successfully.
```

Step 2: Alter the table space containers or automatic storage paths to match the new database name. In this example, SAMPLE database table spaces are located in /home/db2inst1/NODE0000/SAMPLE and need to be changed to /home/db2inst1/ NODE0000/NEWDB. You can achieve this by moving the files from one location to another in UNIX and renaming the path in Windows:

```
mkdir /home/db2inst1/db2inst1/NODE0000/NEWDB
/home/db2inst1/db2inst1/NODE0000/SAMPLE> mv * ../NEWDB (UNIX)
```

Step 3: Invoke the db2relocatedb command:

```
db2relocatedb -f db2relocatedb.1.cfg
Files and control structures were changed successfully.
Database was catalogued successfully.
DBT1000I  The tool completed successfully.
```

Step 4: Verify the database rename by listing the DB DIRECTORY and connecting to it:

```
LIST DB DIRECTORY
CONNECT TO newdb
LIST TABLESPACES SHOW DETAIL
```

If you want to rename a database on a two-node partition database (DPF), you must execute the above steps for each logical partition, something like this:

db2relocatdb.part0.cfg	db2relocatdb.part1.cfg
DB_NAME=BCUDB,NEWDB	**DB_NAME=BCUDB,NEWDB**
DB_PATH=/db2fs	DB_PATH=/db2fs
INSTANCE=bculinux	INSTANCE=bculinux
Move relevant files as shown above	Move relevant files as shown above
export DB2NODE=0	export DB2NODE=1
db2 TERMINATE	db2 TERMINATE
db2relocatedb -f b2relocatedb.part0.cfg	db2relocatedb -f db2relocatedb.part1.cfg

If you want to change the database directory from /home/db2instl to /database, execute the steps by using the configuration file similar to the following:

```
db2relocatedb.2.cfg
DB_NAME=NEWDB
DB_PATH=/home/db2inst1,/database/
INSTANCE=db2inst1
```

Step 1: Make sure to turn off applications and to deactivate the database:

```
DEACTIVATE DB newdb
DB20000I  The DEACTIVATE DATABASE command completed successfully.
```

Step 2: Identify the ~/NODExxxx/SQLyyyyy directory mapping to a database by using any of the following commands:

```
LIST DB DIRECTORY ON /home/db2inst1
Database alias                          = NEWDB
 Database name                          = NEWDB
```

Continued

```
Database directory                        = SQL00001
Database release level                    = f.00
Comment                                   =
Directory entry type                      = Home
Catalog database partition number         = 0
Database member number                    = 0
```

or by using the LIST ACTIVE DATABASES command:

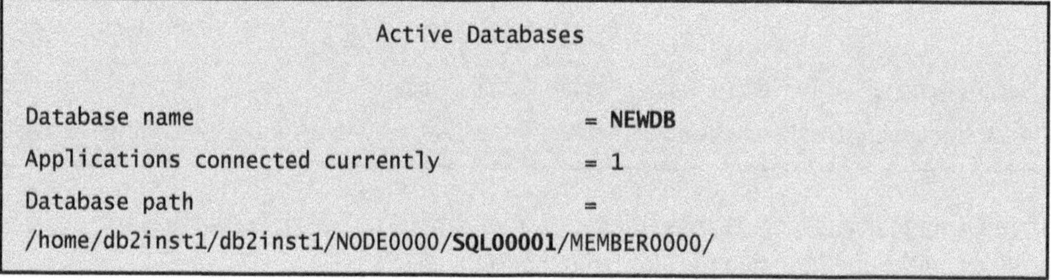

```
                         Active Databases

Database name                                 = NEWDB
Applications connected currently              = 1
Database path                                 =
/home/db2inst1/db2inst1/NODE0000/SQL00001/MEMBER0000/
```

Step 3: Move SQL00001 and sqldbdir to the new location and execute the db2relocatedb command:

```
mv /home/db2inst1/db2inst1/NODE0000/SQL00001 /database/db2inst1/NODE0000/
mv /home/db2inst1/db2inst1/NODE0000/sqldbdir /database/db2inst1/NODE0000/

db2relocatedb -f db2relocatedb.2.cfg
Files and control structures were changed successfully.
Database was catalogued successfully.
DBT1000I  The tool completed successfully.
```

Step 4: Verify the database rename by listing the DB DIRECTORY and connecting to it:

```
LIST DB DIRECTORY
CONNECT TO newdb
LIST TABLESPACES SHOW DETAIL
```

You can use the following sample db2relocatedb configuration file to move a database between instances (on the same server or between servers):

```
db2relocatedb.3.cfg
DB_NAME=NEWDB
DB_PATH=/database
INSTANCE=db2inst1,db2inst2
```

You can build similar db2relocatedb configuration files to move the container paths and the storage groups between the file systems.

The db2move and db2look Commands

It is easy to see how you can use the Export utility together with the Import utility or the Load utility to copy a table from one database to another. But what if you want to copy several tables or an entire database? In this case, you can copy data on a table-by-table basis by using the Export and Import or Load utilities (if PC/IXF formatted files are used, the table structure and any associated indexes will be copied as well), but a more efficient way to copy an entire DB2 database is by using the db2move utility.

This utility queries the system catalog tables of the specified database and compiles a list of all user tables found. It then exports the contents and table structure of each table in the database to individual PC/IXF formatted files. The set of files produced can then be imported or loaded to another DB2 database on the same system, or they can be transferred to another workstation and be imported or loaded to a DB2 database residing there.

You can run the db2move utility in one of four different modes: Export, Import, Load, or Copy. When run in Export mode, db2move invokes the Export utility to extract data from one or more tables and externalize it to PC/IXF formatted files. It also produces a file named db2move.lst that contains the names of all tables processed, along with the names of the files to which each table's data was written. Additionally, the db2move utility may also produce one or more message files that contain warning or error messages that were generated as a result of the Export operation.

If you run db2move in Import mode, it will invoke the Import utility to re-create each table and its associated indexes by using information stored in PC/IXF formatted files. When run in this mode, the file db2move.lst establishes a link between the PC/IXF formatted files needed and the tables into which data is to be imported.

Running in Load mode enables db2move to invoke the Load utility to populate tables that already exist with data stored in PC/IXF formatted files. (You should never use the Load mode to populate an empty database that does not contain table definitions.) Again, the file db2move.lst establishes a link between the PC/IXF formatted files needed and the tables into which data is to be loaded.

Unfortunately, you can use the db2move utility to move only table and index objects. If the database you need to migrate contains other objects such as aliases, views, triggers, UDTs, UDFs, and so on, you must also duplicate those objects in the target database if you want to have an identical copy of the source database. This is where the db2look utility comes in. When invoked, db2look can reverse-engineer an existing database and produce a set of DDL SQL statements, which you can then use to re-create all the data objects found in the database that was analyzed. The db2look utility can also collect environment registry variable settings, configuration parameter settings, and statistical (RUNSTATS) information on the source system, which you can use to duplicate those settings on the target system.

Certification Tips: You can extract the statistics from a source system in mimic mode by using the command db2look -d <dbname> -z <schema> -t <tabname> -m -c -r -o statsfile.in and replicate it on the target test system while troubleshooting any production issue by running command db2 -tvf statsfile.in.

Database Maintenance Utilities

Along with moving data between a database and external files, a database administrator must often do routine maintenance on a database to keep it running at optimum performance. This section examines some of those utilities and the functions they perform.

The REORGCHK Utility

The way in which data is physically distributed across table space containers can have a significant impact on how applications that access the data perform. And the way data is distributed is controlled primarily by the insert, update, and delete operations that are executed against tables. For example, a series of insert operations will try to distribute data pages contiguously across table space containers. However, a subsequent delete operation may leave empty pages in storage that, for some reason, are never refilled. Or an update operation performed on a variable-length column may cause an entire row to be written to another page because a larger column value no longer allows the record to fit on the original page. In both cases, internal gaps are created in the underlying table space containers. As a consequence, the DB2 database manager may have to read more physical pages into memory to retrieve the data needed to satisfy a query.

So how do you know how much storage space the data is currently using, and how much is free but part of an unusable gap? You can obtain this information by taking advantage of DB2's

REORGCHK utility. When executed, this utility generates statistics on a database and analyzes those statistics to determine whether one or more tables need to be reorganized (which will cause any existing internal gaps to be removed).

You invoke the REORGCHK utility by executing the REORGCHK command, usually from the DB2 CLP. The basic syntax for this command is:

```
REORGCHK
<UPDATE STATISTICS | CURRENT STATISTICS>
<ON TABLE USER |
    ON SCHEMA [SchemaName] |
    ON TABLE [USER | SYSTEM | ALL | [TableName]>
```

where:

SchemaName Identifies the name to assign to a schema whose objects are to be analyzed to determine whether they must be reorganized

TableName Identifies the name to assign to a specific table to analyze to determine whether it must be reorganized

So to generate statistics for all tables that reside in the PAYROLL schema and have those statistics analyzed to determine whether one or more tables must be reorganized, you execute a REORGCHK command:

```
REORGCHK UPDATE STATISTICS ON SCHEMA payroll
```

The REORG Utility

Upon careful evaluation of the REORGCHK utility's output, you may discover that one or more tables or indexes must be reorganized. If that is the case, you can reorganize them by using DB2's REORG utility. The REORG utility eliminates gaps in table space containers by retrieving the data stored in a table and one or more of its associated indexes and rewriting it onto defragmented, physically contiguous pages in storage. (The REORG utility works much the way a disk defragmenter works.) The REORG utility can also physically order the data rows of the table to mirror the logical order presented by a particular index, thereby increasing the cluster ratio of the specified index. This behavior has an attractive side effect—if the DB2 database manager finds that the data needed to resolve a query is stored in contiguous storage space and already ordered, the overall performance of the query will be improved because the seek time required to retrieve the data will be shorter. You can also use the REORG utility to convert Type-1 indexes to Type-2 indexes.

You invoke the REORG utility by executing the REORG command. The basic syntax for this command is:

```
REORG TABLE [TableName]
<INDEX [IndexName]>
<ALLOW READ ACCESS | ALLOW NO ACCESS>
<USE [TmpTSName]>
<INDEXSCAN>
<LONGLOBDATA <USE [LongTSName]>>
<KEEPDICTIONARY | RESETDICTIONARY>
```

or

```
REORG TABLE [TableName]
<INDEX [IndexName]>
INPLACE
[ALLOW READ ACCESS | ALLOW NO ACCESS]
<NOTRUNCATE TABLE>
[START | RESUME]
```

or

```
REORG TABLE [TableName]
<INDEX [IndexName]>
INPLACE
[STOP | PAUSE]
```

or

```
REORG [INDEXES ALL FOR TABLE [SrcTableName] |
       INDEX [SrcIndexName] <FOR TABLE [SrcTableName]>]
<ALLOW READ ACCESS | ALLOW WRITE ACCESS | ALLOW NO ACCESS>
<CLEANUP ONLY ALL | CLEANUP ONLY PAGES | CONVERT>
```

where:

TableName	Identifies the name to assign to the table whose physical layout is to be reorganized
IndexName	Identifies the name to assign to the associated index to use to order the data stored in the table that is to be reorganized; (if you do not specify an index name, the data in the table is reorganized without any regard to order)
TmpTSName	Identifies the system temporary table space in which the DB2 database manager is to temporarily store a copy of the table to be reorganized; (if you do not specify a table space name, the DB2 database manager will store a working copy of the table to be reorganized in the same table space in which the table resides)
LongTSName	Identifies the temporary table space that the DB2 database manager is to use for rebuilding long data; (if you do not specify a table space name, the DB2 database manager will rebuild long data objects in the table space where they reside)
SrcTableName	Identifies the name to assign to the table whose associated indexes are to be reorganized
SrcIndexName	Identifies the name to assign to the index whose physical layout is to be reorganized

Specifying the CLEANUP ONLY option will perform a cleanup operation rather than a full reorganization. As a result, indexes will not be rebuilt, and any freed pages will be available only for reuse by the indexes defined on the table specified.

Thus, if you want to reorganize the data for table EMPLOYEE and physically order the data to match the order in index EMPNO_PK, you can do so by executing a REORG command:

```
REORG TABLE employee INDEX empno_pk
```

However, to reorganize table MKT_VALUE and cluster its rows based on index MKT_INDX, you execute the following command:

```
REORG TABLE mkt_value INDEX mkt_indx USE tbspace1
```

If you want to reorganize table STAGING.JDE_AB_STG on the only one-range partition, you execute this command:

```
REORG TABLE staging.jde_ab_stg ON DATA PARTITION 201300191_180
```

The RUNSTATS Utility

Among other things, the system catalog tables for a database can contain statistical information such as the number of rows stored in a table, the way tables and indexes use storage space, and the number of unique values in a particular column. The DB2 Optimizer uses such information when deciding on the best access plan to use to obtain data in response to a query. (Whenever an SQL statement is sent to the DB2 database manager for processing, the DB2 Optimizer reads the system catalog tables to determine the size of each table referenced, the characteristics of each column referenced, and whether indexes have been defined for the tables/columns referenced and to obtain other similar information. Using this information, the DB2 Optimizer then determines the best access path to take to satisfy the needs of the SQL statement.) Therefore, if the information the DB2 Optimizer requires is missing or out of date, the access plan chosen may cause the SQL statement to take longer to execute than necessary. Having valid information available becomes more crucial as the complexity of the SQL statement increases—with simple statements, there are usually a limited number of choices; with complex statements, the number of choices increases dramatically.

Before DB2 Version 9, the information the DB2 Optimizer used was not automatically updated as changes were made to a database. Instead, you had to update this information periodically by manually running DB2's RUNSTATS utility. Starting with DB2 Version 9, automatic statistics collection (part of DB2's automated table maintenance feature discussed in Chapter 2, "DB2 Server Management," in the "DB2 Autonomic Computing Features" section) is enabled by default when a new database is created. As long as automatic statistics collection remains enabled, DB2 will automatically execute the RUNSTATS utility in the background to ensure that the most current database statistics are available.

If automatic statistics collection is disabled, you can invoke the RUNSTATS utility by executing the RUNSTATS command. The basic syntax for this command is:

```
RUNSTATS ON TABLE [TableName]
USE PROFILE
<UTIL_IMPACT_PRIORITY [Priority]>
```

or

```
RUNSTATS ON TABLE [TableName] FOR
<<SAMPLED> DETAILED>
[INDEXES | INDEX]
[[IndexName,...] | ALL]
<EXCLUDING XML COLUMNS>
<ALLOW READ ACCESS | ALLOW WRITE ACCESS>
<SET PROFILE NONE | SET PROFILE <ONLY> | UPDATE PROFILE
    <ONLY>>
<UTIL_IMPACT_PRIORITY [Priority]>
```

or

```
RUNSTATS ON TABLE [TableName]
<ON ALL COLUMNS |
    ON KEY COLUMNS> |
    ON COLUMNS [ColumnName ,...] |
    ON ALL COLUMNS AND COLUMNS [ColumnName ,...] |
    ON KEY COLUMNS AND COLUMNS [ColumnName ,...]>
<WITH DISTRIBUTION>
<EXCLUDING XML COLUMNS>
<AND <<SAMPLED> DETAILED>
    [INDEXES | INDEX]
    [[IndexName,...] | ALL]>
<EXCLUDING XML COLUMNS>
<ALLOW READ ACCESS | ALLOW WRITE ACCESS>
<SET PROFILE NONE | SET PROFILE <ONLY> | UPDATE PROFILE
    <ONLY>>
<UTIL_IMPACT_PRIORITY [Priority]>
```

where:

TableName	Identifies the name to assign to the table for which to collect statistical information; this can be any base table, including a volatile table
IndexName	Identifies the name to assign to one or more associated indexes for which to collect statistical information

ColumnName	Identifies the name to assign to one or more columns for which to collect statistical information
Priority	Specifies to throttle the RUNSTATS utility such that it executes at a specific rate so that its effect on concurrent database activity can be controlled; you can assign this parameter a numerical value within the range of 1 to 100, with 100 representing the highest priority and 1 representing the lowest

Thus, if you want to collect statistics for table EMPLOYEE (which resides in schema PAYROLL) along with all of its associated indexes and allow read-only access to the table while statistics are being gathered, you can do so by executing a RUNSTATS command:

```
RUNSTATS ON TABLE payroll.employee
FOR INDEXES ALL ALLOW READ ACCESS
```

However, to collect basic statistics, and distribution statistics are collected for all eligible columns of table DEPARTMENT (which resides in schema PAYROLL), you execute a RUNSTATS command that looks something like this:

```
RUNSTATS ON TABLE payroll.department
ON ALL COLUMNS WITH DISTRIBUTION DEFAULT
```

You can perform statistics collection on some columns and not on others. For example, columns with data types such as LONG VARCHAR and CLOB are ineligible.

The Rebind Utility

Earlier, you saw that the DB2 Optimizer uses the statistical information produced by the RUNSTATS utility to select the best access plan to use to obtain data in response to a query. Because the DB2 Optimizer generates an access plan each time a dynamic SQL statement is prepared for execution, applications using dynamic SQL may see performance improvements immediately after new statistical information has been produced. Unfortunately, that is not the case for applications that use static SQL. That is because the DB2 Optimizer generates access plans for static SQL statements only when the package that contains those statements is bound to the database. Therefore, for existing packages to exploit new statistical information produced by the RUNSTATS utility, you must rebind them to the database so that the DB2 Optimizer will evaluate the new information and formulate new access plans (which may or may not perform better that the original access plan).

The easiest way to rebind an existing package—provided the application source code used to produce the package has not changed—is by executing the REBIND command. The basic syntax for this command is:

```
REBIND <PACKAGE> [PackageName]
<VERSION [Version]>
RESOLVE [ANY | CONSERVATIVE]
<REOPT NONE | REOPT ONCE | REOPT ALWAYS>
```

where:

PackageName Identifies the name to assign to the package to rebind
IndexName Identifies a specific version of the package to rebind

If you specify the REOPT NONE option, the access path for SQL statements containing host variables, parameter markers, or special registers will not be optimized using real values—default estimates for these variables/markers/registers will be used instead. If you specify the REOPT ONCE option, the access path for SQL statements containing host variables, parameter markers, or special registers will be optimized using real values when the statement is first executed. And finally, if you specify the REOPT ALWAYS option, the access path for SQL statements containing host variables, parameter markers, or special registers will be optimized using real values each time the statement is executed.

Thus, to rebind package EMP_MGMT, you execute a REBIND command:

```
REBIND PACKAGE emp_mgmt
```

Flushing the Package Cache

If a dynamic SQL statement is prepared, and its corresponding access plan is placed in memory *before* new statistical information is collected, and if the application that uses the statement is coded such that the statement is prepared once and executed multiple times, that particular statement will not be able to exploit the new statistical information produced by the RUNSTATS utility until it is reprepared. Typically, this behavior is acceptable. However, if the new statistical information could result in significant performance gains, you may wish to take advantage of the new information immediately, as opposed to waiting for the cached package to be rebuilt.

The FLUSH PACKAGE CACHE SQL statement provides database administrators with the ability to remove cached dynamic SQL statement packages from memory (the package cache) by invalidating them. The invalidation of a cached dynamic SQL statement package has no effect on current users of the statement; however, once you invalidate a package, any new requests for the statement with which the invalidated package was associated will cause the DB2 Optimizer to reprocess the statement, which in turn will produce a new cached package (which may or may not contain a more efficient access plan). The basic syntax for the FLUSH PACKAGE CACHE statement is:

```
FLUSH PACKAGE CACHE DYNAMIC
```

Once this statement is executed, any cached packages associated with dynamic SQL statements that are currently in use will be allowed to continue to exist in the package cache until their current user no longer needs them; the next new user of the same statement will force the DB2 database manager to implicitly prepare the statement, and the new user will then execute the new version of the cached dynamic SQL statement.

Performance-related Utilities

Along with data movement utilities and maintenance utilities, DB2 provides additional tools that can help pinpoint performance bottlenecks and make recommendations for additional data objects that can improve overall performance. This section looks at some of those utilities and the functions they perform.

The db2batch Utility

Benchmark testing is a normal part of the application development life cycle. Ideally, it is a team effort that involves both application developers and database administrators. Typically, two different types of benchmark tests are run to obtain two different kinds of information:

- A transaction-per-second benchmark determines the throughput capabilities of the DB2 database manager under certain limited laboratory conditions.
- An application benchmark tests throughput capabilities under conditions that mirror production conditions.

Benchmarking can also be helpful in understanding how the DB2 database manager responds under varying conditions. For example, you can create scenarios that test deadlock handling, utility performance, different methods of loading data, transaction rate characteristics as more users are added, and the effect of using a new release of DB2 software, just to name a few.

Benchmarking is performed by developing a test scenario and then running the scenario several times, capturing key information during each run. You can develop an elaborate application specifically for this purpose, but a simpler approach is to take advantage of DB2's db2batch utility. The db2batch utility is a simple benchmark tool that reads SQL statements and

XQuery expressions from either an ASCII format file or standard input; dynamically prepares, describes, and executes the statements and expressions found; and returns a result set that includes, among other things, the timing for the execution.

You invoke the db2batch utility by executing the db2batch command. The basic syntax for this command is:

```
db2batch
<-d [DatabaseAlias]>
<-f [InFile]>
<-a [Authorization]>
<-m [ParametersFile]>
<-t [Delimiter]>
<-r [OutFile] <,SummaryFile>>
<-c [on | off]>
<-i [short | long | complete]>
<-g [on | off]>
<-w [32768 | ColumnWidth]>
<-time [on | off]>
<-msw MonSwitch [hold | on | off]>
<-mss Snapshot>
<-iso [RR | RS | CS | UR]>
<-v [on | off]>
<-s [on | off]>
<-q [off | on | del]>
<-l TermDelimiter>
<-h>
```

where:

DatabaseAlias	Identifies, by alias, the database against which to apply SQL statements and XQuery statements; if you do not specify this option, the value of the DB2DBDFT environment variable is used
InFile	Identifies the name to assign to an ASCII format file that contains SQL statements and XQuery expressions that constitute the benchmark workload
Authorization	Specifies the authentication ID (or user ID) and password, separated by a forward slashes (/),to use to establish a connection to the database specified

ParametersFile Identifies the input file containing parameter values to bind to any SQL statement parameter markers used before executing a statement

Delimiter Specifies a single character that is to act as a column separator (specify -t TAB for a tab column delimiter or -t SPACE for a space column delimiter; by default, a space is used when you set the -q on option, and a comma is used when you set the -q del option)

OutFile Identifies an output file to which to write query results

SummaryFile Identifies an output file to which to write summary information

ColumnWidth Specifies the maximum column width of the result data set produced, with an allowable range of 0 to 2 GB; data is truncated to this width when displayed, unless the data cannot be truncated

MonSwitch Identifies a specific snapshot monitor switch to set; valid values for this parameter are uow, statement, table, bufferpool, lock, sort, timestamp, and all

Snapshot Identifies the type of snapshots to take after each statement or block is executed (depending on the value of the -g option); valid values for this parameter are applinfo_all, dbase_applinfo, dcs_applinfo_all, db2, dbase, dbase_all, dcs_dbase, dcs_dbase_all, dbase_remote, dbase_remote_all, agent_id, dbase_appls, appl_all, dcs_appl_all, dcs_appl_handle, dcs_dbase_appls, dbase_appls_remote, appl_remote_all, dbase_tables, appl_locks_agent_id, dbase_locks, dbase_tablespaces, bufferpools_all, dbase_bufferpools, dynamic_sql, and all

TermDelimiter Specifies one or two characters to serve as a termination character (delimiter); the default is a semicolon (;)

Table 6.8 lists all other db2batch command options.

Table 6.8: db2batch command options

Option	Meaning
-c	This option indicates whether to automatically commit changes resulting from each SQL statement or XQuery expression executed.
-i	This option indicates which time intervals to measure. SHORT indicates that db2batch is to measure the elapsed time required to run each statement. LONG specifies that db2batch is to measure the elapsed time required to run each statement, including any overhead between statements. COMPLETE indicates that db2batch is to measure the elapsed time required to run each statement and report the times needed to prepare, execute, and fetch data separately.
-g	This option specifies whether to report timing by block or by statement. ON indicates to take a snapshot for the entire block and to report only block timing in the summary table. OFF indicates to take a snapshot and to report summary table timing for each statement executed in the block.
-iso	This option specifies the isolation level to use, which determines how transactions are locked and isolated from other processes while the data is being accessed. By default, db2batch uses the Repeatable Read (RR) isolation level.

Table 6.8: db2batch command options (continued)

Option	Meaning
-v	This option indicates to run db2batch in verbose mode. (Information is sent to standard error during query processing.)
-s	This option specifies whether to stop running db2batch when a noncritical error occurs.
-q	This option specifies how to return query results. OFF indicates to return query results and all associated information to standard output (stdout). ON specifies to return only query results in nondelimited ASCII format. DEL indicates to return only query results in delimited ASCII format.
-h | -u | -?	This option displays help information. When you specify this option, all other options are ignored, and only the help information is displayed.

The easiest way to conduct benchmark testing with the db2batch utility is by constructing a file that contains one or more queries that represent a typical workload and providing that file's contents as input to the db2batch command. Such a file might look something like this:

```
-- File Name: wkload.sql
-- Execution Command:
--       db2batch -d sample -f test.sql -r results.txt
---------------------------------------------------------
--#SET PERF_DETAIL 1
--#SET ROWS_OUT 5

-- This query lists employees, the name of their department
-- and the number of activities to which they are assigned
-- for employees who are assigned to more than one activity
-- less than full-time.

--#COMMENT Query 1
SELECT lastname, firstnme,
       deptname, count(*) AS num_act
FROM employee, department, emp_act
WHERE employee.workdept = department.deptno AND
      employee.empno = emp_act.empno AND
      emp_act.emptime < 1
GROUP BY lastname, firstnme, deptname
HAVING count(*) > 2;
```

Once such a file is created, you can conduct benchmark testing by executing a db2batch command (assuming the file containing the workload is named wkload.sql, and the workload is to be run against a database named SAMPLE):

```
db2batch -d sample -f test.sql -r results.txt
```

When you execute this command, results that db2batch collects will be recorded in a file named results.txt, which you can review after each benchmark run.

The DB2 Design Advisor

Earlier, you saw how you can use the RUNSTATS utility to update system catalog statistics and force the DB2 Optimizer to use those statistics to provide optimum access plans in response to a query or XQuery expression. Another factor that can have great influence on access plan selection is the existence (or nonexistence) of appropriate indexes.

So how do you decide when having an index would be beneficial, and how do you determine what indexes should exist? If you have a lot of experience with database and database application design, these decisions may be easy to make. However, if you have relatively little experience in this area, or if you want to validate the decisions you have already made, you can turn to DB2's Design Advisor.

The Design Advisor is a special tool that identifies indexes, MQTs, MDCs, and the repartitioning of tables that may help improve query performance in your database environment. Using current database statistics, the DB2 Optimizer, snapshot monitor information, and/or a specific query or set of SQL statements (known as a workload) you provide, the Design Advisor recommends one or more indexes that will improve query or workload performance. In addition, the indexes/MQTs/MDCs/partitions recommended, the statistics derived for them, and the DDL statements required to create them can be written to a user-created table named ADVISE_INDEX, if so desired.

You invoke the Design Advisor by executing the db2advis command. The basic syntax for this command is:

```
db2advis [-d | -db] [DatabaseName]
<-w [WorkloadName]>
<-s "[SQLStatement]">
<-i [InFile]>
<-g>
                                        Continued
```

```
<-qp>
<-a [UserID] </[Password]>
<-m [AdviseType ,...]>
<-l [DiskLimit]>
<-t "[MaxAdviseTime]">
<-k [high | med | low | off]>
<-h>
<-p>
<-o [OutFile]>
```

where:

DatabaseName	Identifies, by name, the database with which the Design Advisor is to interact
WorkloadName	Identifies the name of the workload to analyze to determine whether to create new indexes, MQTs, or MDCs
SQLStatement	Identifies a single SQL statement to analyze to determine whether to create new indexes, MQTs, or MDCs
InFile	Identifies the name to assign to an ASCII format file that contains a set of SQL statements to analyze to determine whether to create new indexes, MQTs, or MDCs
UserID	Identifies the authentication ID (or user ID) to use to establish a connection to the database specified
Password	Identifies the password to use to establish a connection to the database specified
AdviseType	Specifies one or more types of recommendations for which the Design Advisor is to analyze; valid values for this parameter include the following: I (index), M (MQTs and indexes on the MQTs), C (convert standard tables to MDC tables), and P (repartitioning of existing tables)
DiskLimit	Identifies the maximum amount of storage space, in megabytes, that is available for all indexes, MQTs, and MDCs in the existing schema
MaxAdviseTime	Identifies the maximum amount of time, in minutes, in which the Design Advisor will be allowed to conduct an analysis; when this time limit is reached, the Design Advisor will stop all processing
OutFile	Identifies the name of the file to which to write the DDL needed to create the indexes/MQTs/MDCs recommended

Table 6.9 lists all other db2advis command options.

Table 6.9: db2advis command options

Option	Meaning
-g	This option specifies to retrieve the SQL statements that make up the workload from a dynamic SQL snapshot. If combined with the -p parameter, the SQL statements remain in the ADVISE_WORKLOAD table.
-qp	This option specifies that the workload is coming from the DB2 Query Patroller.
-k	This option specifies to what degree to compress the workload. Compression allows the advisor to reduce the complexity of the advisor's execution while achieving similar results to those the advisor could provide when the full workload is considered. HIGH indicates that the advisor will concentrate on a small subset of the workload. MED specifies that the advisor will concentrate on a medium-sized subset of the workload. LOW stipulates that the advisor will concentrate on a larger subset of the workload. OFF indicates that no compression will occur and to consider every query.
-p	This option specifies to retain the plans that were generated while running the Design Advisor in the Explain tables. This option causes the workload for -qp and -g to be saved in the ADVISE_WORKLOAD table and the workload query plans that use the final recommendation to be saved in the Explain tables.
-h	This option displays help information. When you specify this option, all other options are ignored, and only the help information is displayed.

The easiest way to determine whether an index, MQT, or MDC will improve a workload's performance is by constructing a file that contains one or more queries that represent a typical workload and providing that file's contents as input to the db2advis command. Such a file might look something like this:

```
-- File Name: wkload.sql
-- Execution Command:
--        db2advis -d sample -i db2advis.sql -t 5

-- Evaluate the following set of statements 100 times
--#SET FREQUENCY 100
SELECT COUNT(*) FROM employee;
SELECT * FROM employee WHERE lastname='HAAS';

-- Evaluate the following statement once
--#SET FREQUENCY 1
SELECT AVG(bonus), AVG(salary) FROM employee
   GROUP BY workdept ORDER BY workdept;
```

Once such a file is created, you can conduct analysis by executing a db2advis command:

```
db2advis -d sample -i db2advis.sql -t 5
```

When this command is executed, the results might look something like this:

```
Using user id as default schema name. Use -n option to specify schema
execution started at timestamp 2014-08-10-08.40.59.542947
found [3] SQL statements from the input file
Recommending indexes...
total disk space needed for initial set [   0.076] MB
total disk space constrained to         [  34.120] MB
Trying variations of the solution set.
  2  indexes in current solution
 [9683.0000] timerons  (without recommendations)
 [2121.0000] timerons  (with current solution)
 [78.10%] improvement


--
--
-- LIST OF RECOMMENDED INDEXES
-- ===========================
-- index[1],    0.064MB
   CREATE INDEX "MOHAN"."IDX1408100846320" ON "MOHAN"."EMPLOYEE"
   ("LASTNAME" ASC, "COMM" ASC, "BONUS" ASC, "SALARY"
   ASC, "BIRTHDATE" ASC, "SEX" ASC, "EDLEVEL" ASC, "JOB"
   ASC, "HIREDATE" ASC, "PHONENO" ASC, "WORKDEPT" ASC,
   "MIDINIT" ASC, "FIRSTNME" ASC, "EMPNO" ASC) ALLOW
   REVERSE SCANS COLLECT SAMPLED DETAILED STATISTICS;
   COMMIT WORK ;
-- index[2],    0.013MB
   CREATE INDEX "MOHAN"."IDX1408100848120" ON "MOHAN"."EMPLOYEE"
   ("WORKDEPT" ASC, "SALARY" ASC, "BONUS" ASC) ALLOW
   REVERSE SCANS COLLECT SAMPLED DETAILED STATISTICS;
```

Continued

```
    COMMIT WORK ;

--
-- RECOMMENDED EXISTING INDEXES
-- ============================
-- RUNSTATS ON TABLE "MOHAN"."EMPLOYEE" FOR SAMPLED DETAILED INDEX "MOHAN"."XEMP2" ;
-- COMMIT WORK ;

--
-- UNUSED EXISTING INDEXES
-- ============================
-- ===========================
--
-- ====ADVISOR DETAILED XML OUTPUT=============
-- ==(Benefits do not include clustering recommendations)==
--
....
....

    -- ====ADVISOR DETAILED XML OUTPUT=============
    --
    98 solutions were evaluated by the advisor
    DB2 Workload Performance Advisor tool is finished.
```

A Word About the DBMS_UTILITY Module

DB2 introduced modules in version 9.7. These modules provide a way to group related database objects such as functions, procedures, types, and variables in one object. Table 6.10 shows various built-in modules available within DB2 for application reuse.

Table 6.10: Available DB2 modules	
Module Name	**Description**
DBMS_ALERT	This module provides a set of procedures for registering alerts, sending alerts, and receiving alerts.
DBMS_DDL	This module provides the capability to obfuscate DDL objects such as routines, triggers, views, or PL/SQL packages. Obfuscation allows the deployment of SQL objects to a database without exposing the procedural logic.

Table 6.10: Available DB2 modules (continued)	
Module Name	**Description**
DBMS_JOB	This module provides procedures for creating, scheduling, and managing jobs.
DBMS_LOB	This module provides the capability to operate on large objects.
DBMS_OUTPUT	This module provides a set of procedures to place and receive messages from the message buffer.
DBMS_PIPE	This module provides a set of routines for sending messages through a pipe (IPC) within the same DB2 instance.
DBMS_SQL	This module provides a set of procedures for executing dynamic SQL and therefore supports various DML or DDL statements.
DBMS_UTILITY	This module provides various utility programs (discussed in the next section).
MONREPORT	This module provides a set of procedures for retrieving a variety of monitoring data and for generating text reports.
UTL_DIR	This module provides a set of routines for maintaining directory aliases that are used with the UTL_FILE module.
UTL_FILE	This module provides a set of routines for reading from and writing to files on the database server's file system.
UTL_MAIL	This module provides the capability to send e-mail.
UTL_SMTP	This module provides the capability to send e-mail over the Simple Mail Transfer Protocol (SMTP).

You can use DBMS_UTILITY programs to perform analysis on tables and indexes, finding the dependency between the objects and so on. Table 6.11 shows available programs within the DBMS_UTILITY module.

Table 6.11: DBMS_UTILITY programs	
Object	**Description**
DBMS_UTILITY.ANALYZE_DATABASE	This stored procedure provides the capability to gather statistics on tables, clusters, and indexes in the database
DBMS_UTILITY.ANALYZE_PART_OBJECT	This stored procedure provides the capability to gather statistics on a partitioned table or index.
DBMS_UTILITY.ANALYZE_SCHEMA	This stored procedure provides the capability to gather statistics on tables, clusters, and indexes in the specified schema.
DBMS_UTILITY.CANONICALIZE	This stored procedure performs various operations on an input string.
DBMS_UTILITY.COMMA_TO_TABLE_LNAME DBMS_UTILITY.COMMA_TO_TABLE_UNCL	These stored procedures convert a comma-delimited list of names into an array of names. Each entry in the list becomes an element in the array.
DBMS_UTILITY.COMPILE_SCHEMA	This stored procedure provides the capability to recompile all functions, procedures, triggers, and packages in a schema.
DBMS_UTILITY.DB_VERSION	This stored procedure returns the version number of the database.

Table 6.11: DBMS_UTILITY programs (continued)	
Object	**Description**
DBMS_UTILITY.EXEC_DDL_STATEMENT	This stored procedure provides the capability to execute a DDL command.
DBMS_UTILITY.GET_CPU_TIME	This function returns the CPU time in hundredths of a second from some arbitrary point in time.
DBMS_UTILITY.GET_DEPENDENCY	This stored procedure provides the capability to list all objects that are dependent upon the given object.
DBMS_UTILITY.GET_HASH_VALUE	This function provides the capability to compute a hash value for a given string.
DBMS_UTILITY.GET_TIME	This function provides the capability to return the current time in hundredths of a second.
DBMS_UTILITY.NAME_RESOLVE	This stored procedure provides the capability to obtain the schema and other membership information of a database object. Synonyms are resolved to their base objects.
DBMS_UTILITY.NAME_TOKENIZE	This stored procedure parses a name into its component parts. Names without double quotation marks are put in uppercase, and double quotation marks are stripped from names with double quotation marks.
DBMS_UTILITY.TABLE_TO_COMMA_LNAME DBMS_UTILITY.TABLE_TO_COMMA_UNCL	These stored procedures convert an array of names into a comma-delimited list of names. Each array element becomes a list entry.
DBMS_UTILITY.VALIDATE	This stored procedure provides the capability to change the state of an invalid routine to valid.

In the past, if you wanted to identify object dependencies within the database, you could parse the db2look -d <dbname> -e command output for the whole database to determine the dependency. This activity is made simple by introducing the DBMS_UTILITY.GET_DEPENDENCY () procedure. With this procedure, you can find the dependency on a function, index, package, procedure, sequence, table, trigger, view, and LOB.

Let us find the dependency on the SYSTOOLS.STMG_DBSIZE_INFO table in the database by invoking the following command:

```
SET SERVEROUTPUT ON
DB20000I  The SET SERVEROUTPUT command completed successfully.

CALL DBMS_UTILITY.GET_DEPENDENCY ('TABLE', 'SYSTOOLS','STMG_DBSIZE_INFO')"

  Return Status = 0

DEPENDENCIES ON SYSTOOLS.STMG_DBSIZE_INFO
------------------------------------------------------------------
*TABLE SYSTOOLS.STMG_DBSIZE_INFO ()
```

Chapter Summary

The objective of this chapter was to familiarize you with

- The DB2 data movement utilities file formats
- The DB2 data movement utility commands and the use-case scenarios
- The DB2 Ingest utility and its business benefits in data warehouse environments
- The ADMIN_MOVE_TABLE () and ADMIN_COPY_SCHEMA () system stored procedures syntax and their usage
- The DB2 database maintenance utilities such as REORGCHK, RUNSTATS, and REORG
- The DB2 performance utilities such as db2batch and db2advis

On completion of this chapter, you will be equipped with sufficient knowledge to answer DB2 Utilities questions in the certification exam. It is also highly recommended to complete the sample questions available at the end of the chapter.

Practice Questions

Question 1

Which of the following is not a method by which the Export utility can be invoked?

- ❍ A. IBM Data Studio
- ❍ B. CLP
- ❍ C. ADMIN_CMD stored procedure
- ❍ D. db2look command

Question 2

Which IMPORT command option will cause the Import utility to acquire a table-level lock after every commit?

- ❍ A. ALLOW NO ACCESS
- ❍ B. ALLOW READ ACCESS
- ❍ C. ALLOW WRITE ACCESS
- ❍ D. ALLOW FULL ACCESS

Question 3

Which operation *cannot* be performed on a table that contains a primary key that is referenced by a foreign key in another table?

- ❍ A. IMPORT ... INSERT
- ❍ B. IMPORT ... REPLACE
- ❍ C. IMPORT ... INSERT_UPDATE
- ❍ D. IMPORT ... CREATE

Question 4

Which LOAD command modifier can you use when working with identity column data?

- ❍ A. IDENTITYRESET
- ❍ B. IDENTITYOVERRIDE
- ❍ C. IDENTITYSUPRESS
- ❍ D. IDENTITYRETAIN

Question 5

Which IMPORT command option can you use to prevent an import operation from filling up a database's transaction log files and failing?

- ❍ A. ALLOW NO ACCESS
- ❍ B. NOTIMEOUT
- ❍ C. COMMITCOUNT AUTOMATIC
- ❍ D. ALLOW WRITE ACCESS

Question 6

A database administrator wants to delete all records found in a table named DEPARTMENT. If the DEPARTMENT table resides in a database that is stored on an AIX server, which command can the DBA use to accomplish this objective?

- ❍ A. LOAD FROM null OF DEL INSERT INTO department
- ❍ B. LOAD FROM null OF DEL REPLACE INTO department
- ❍ C. LOAD FROM /dev/null OF DEL INSERT INTO department
- ❍ D. LOAD FROM /dev/null OF DEL REPLACE INTO department

Question 7

Given the following command:

```
LOAD FROM salesdata.del OF DEL INSERT INTO sales
MODIFIED BY DELPRIORITYCHAR
ALLOW READ ACCESS
STATISTICS USE PROFILE
```

Which statement is false?

- ❍ A. During the load operation, statistics will be collected, and the statistics profile for the SALES table and its associated indexes will be updated; if a statistics profile does not exist, one will be created.
- ❍ B. Only data in the SALES table that existed before the invocation of the LOAD command can be read by other applications while the load operation is in progress.
- ❍ C. The priority for evaluating delimiters is character delimiter, record delimiter, column delimiter rather than record delimiter, character delimiter, column delimiter.
- ❍ D. If the load operation aborts, the original data stored in the SALES table will be accessible for read access.

Question 8

Which command can you use to display the status of a load operation?

- ❍ A. LOAD STATUS
- ❍ B. LOAD MESSAGES
- ❍ C. LOAD QUERY
- ❍ D. LOAD STATISTICS

Question 9

The table EMPLOYEES was created by executing the following command:

```
CREATE TABLE employees (empid  INTEGER NOT NULL PRIMARY KEY,
                        name   VARCHAR(25))
```

Assume the file employee.del contains the following data:

```
100, "SIMON WOODCOCK"
100, "KENT COLLINS"
200, "COLIN CHAPMAN"
300, "ROGER SANDERS"
400, "ROUMANI HAMDI"
```

If the following commands are executed:

```
CREATE TABLE emp_exp LIKE EMPLOYEES
LOAD FROM empdata.del OF DEL INSERT INTO EMPLOYEE FOR EXECPTION
emp_exp
```

Which statement is true?

- ❍ A. The table EMPLOYEES will contain four rows; the table EMP_EXP will be empty.
- ❍ B. The table EMPLOYEES will contain five rows; the table EMP_EXP will contain five rows.
- ❍ C. The table EMPLOYEES will contain four rows; the table EMP_EXP will contain one row.
- ❍ D. The table EMPLOYEES will contain five rows; the table EMP_EXP will contain one row.

Question 10

In which of the following scenarios should you use the LOAD utility instead of the Import utility?

- ❍ A. You need to add data to a table, and any associated triggers must be fired.
- ❍ B. You need to add a large amount of data to a table quickly without incurring a significant amount of transaction logging.
- ❍ C. You need to add data stored in a WSF formatted file to a table.
- ❍ D. You need to add a large amount of data to a table and enforce constraint checking during population.

Question 11

Which set of steps can you use to build a test database that has the same structure and statistics of a production database, but with limited data for testing?

- ❍ A. Extract the data from the production database by using the db2move utility (Export mode).
  Create a test database and populate it by using the db2move utility (Import mode).
- ❍ B. Generate the SQL needed to create the objects in the production database by using the db2look utility.
  Create a test database and run the script produced by db2look to create the database objects.
  Extract the data from the production database by using the db2move utility (Export mode).
  Populate the test database by using the db2move utility (Import mode).
  Run the RUNSTATS utility on each table in the test database.
- ❍ C. Run the RUNSTATS utility on each table in the production database.
  Generate the SQL needed to create the objects in the production database and reproduce the statistics profile by using the db2look utility.
  Create a test database and run the script produced by `db2look` to create the database objects and duplicate the statistics.
  Insert, import, or load test data into the database.
- ❍ D. Generate the SQL needed to create the objects in the production database by using the db2look utility.
  Create a test database and run the script produced by db2look to create the database objects.
  Load test data into the database by using the LOAD command with the STATISTICS USE PROFILE option specified so that statistics will be collected.

Question 12

Which task is the db2batch utility best suited for?

- ❍ A. Benchmarking SQL and XQuery operations.
- ❍ B. Copying 50 tables created under a single schema from one database to another.
- ❍ C. Reorganizing table data and clustering its rows.
- ❍ D. Updating access plan information stored in packages.

Question 13

In an attempt to improve query performance, a database administrator created an index for a table named EMPLOYEE, which contains 500,000 records. Performance of ad hoc queries run against the EMPLOYEE table has improved, but performance of a batch application that runs at night has not improved. Which of operation should correct this problem?

- ❍ A. REORGCHK
- ❍ B. REORG
- ❍ C. FLUSH PACKAGE CACHE
- ❍ D. REBIND

Question 14

Which of the following illustrates the proper order in which to use the DB2 data management utilities?

- ❍ A. RUNSTATS, REORG table, REORG indexes, REORGCHK, REBIND
- ❍ B. RUNSTATS, REORGCHK, REORG table, REORG indexes, RUNSTATS, REBIND
- ❍ C. REORGCHK, REORG indexes, REORG table, RUNSTATS, REBIND
- ❍ D. RUNSTATS, REBIND, REORGCHK, REORG table, REORG indexes, RUNSTATS

Question 15

Which command invokes the Design Advisor and instructs it to make recommendations for a database named SAMPLE, based on information collected by the snapshot monitor?

- ❍ A. db2advis –d SAMPLE –k
- ❍ B. db2advis –d SAMPLE –qp
- ❍ C. db2advis –d SAMPLE –g
- ❍ D. db2advis –d SAMPLE –h

Question 16

The Design Advisor can be used to analyze SQL from which two of the following choices?

- ❒ A. The EXPLAIN_STATEMENT table
- ❒ B. A file containing a workload
- ❒ C. The SYSIBM.SYSPLANS system catalog table
- ❒ D. The EXPLAIN_STREAM table
- ❒ E. The ADVISE_WORKLOAD table

Question 17

Which table type is *not* supported by the Load utility?

- ❍ A. A global temporary table
- ❍ B. An ITC
- ❍ C. A range partitioned table
- ❍ D. An MDC table

Question 18

Which data movement utility is suitable for moving and processing large amounts of real-time data into the data warehouse without affecting availability?

- ❍ A. LOAD WITH NO ACCESS
- ❍ B. SQL or Q replication
- ❍ C. INGEST
- ❍ D. IMPORT WITH COMMITCOUNT AUTOMATIC

Question 19

What does the FLUSH PACKAGE CACHE statement do?

- ❍ A. It invalidates all dynamic SQL statements from the package cache.
- ❍ B. It invalidates only inactive SQL statements from the package cache.
- ❍ C. It saves dynamic SQL statements stored in the package cache to an external file.
- ❍ D. It causes all SQL statements in the package cache that are currently in use to be recompiled.

Question 20

The following commands are executed against database SAMPLE, which has been configured to use archival logging:

```
BACKUP DATABASE sample ONLINE TO /db2backup;
CONNECT TO sample;
LOAD FROM data.del OF DEL INSERT INTO employee NONRECOVERABLE;
```

Which statement is *true*?

- ❍ A. Upon a successful completion of the load, the table EMPLOYEE is placed into Backup Pending state.
- ❍ B. During the load operation, a copy of the data is made and the table will be active.
- ❍ C. After a database restore and a roll-forward operation, the newly loaded nonrecoverable data is made available in the database and the table is active.
- ❍ D. After a database restore and a roll-forward operation, the newly loaded nonrecoverable data is marked unavailable and can only be dropped and re-created.

Question 21

Which statement is true about using the RUNSTATS command to update index statistics?

- ❍ A. It should always be a full index scan.
- ❍ B. It can be accomplished by sampling the index.
- ❍ C. It must be executed against all indexes for the table.
- ❍ D. It must be executed along with the table.

Question 22

What can you use to provide input to the Design Advisor?

- ❍ A. A query workload file
- ❍ B. A DDL file with the current definition
- ❍ C. db2nodes.cfg
- ❍ D. Database configuration file SQLDBCONF

Question 23

Which statement describes the best way to minimize the impact of a RUNSTATS operation?

- ❍ A. Execute the RUNSTATS command with INDEXES ALL option specified.
- ❍ B. Execute the RUNSTATS command with the WITH DISTRIBUTION option specified.
- ❍ C. Execute the RUNSTATS command with the DETAILED UNSAMPLED option specified.
- ❍ D. Execute the RUNSTATS command with TABLESAMPLE option specified.

Question 24

If the following command is executed on an archive logging–enabled database named SAMPLE:

```
LOAD FROM data.del OF DEL INSERT INTO employee
FOR EXCEPTION exp_employee ALLOW NO ACCESS;
```

Which statement is true?

- ❍ A. All rejected records will be inserted into the table EXP_EMPLOYEE.
- ❍ B. The associated table space will not be kept in Backup Pending state after the load operation.
- ❍ C. While the LOAD command is executing, other transactions can both read and write into table EMPLOYEE.
- ❍ D. DB2 database manager creates the exception table EXP_EMPLOYEE during the load operation.

Question 25

Which tool can mimic the statistics for tables by capturing statistics from a production database and replicating it in a test database?

- ❍ A. The EXPORT TABLE with RUNSTATS option in production and the IMPORT TABLE with RUNSTATS option in test system
- ❍ B. db2move to copy SYSCAT.TABLES information from production to test
- ❍ C. db2look
- ❍ D. db2mimic

Question 26

Which of the following can you use to move data from one table space to another while the data remains online and available for access?

- ❍ A. The db2move command
- ❍ B. The db2relocatedb command
- ❍ C. The ADMIN_MOVE_TABLE () procedure
- ❍ D. The ADMIN_MOVE_TABLE_UTIL () procedure

Question 27

Which statement is true about the ADMIN_MOVE_TABLE () procedure?

- ❍ A. The ADMIN_MOVE_TABLE () procedure immediately applies all changes that occur to data in the source table during the move operation to the target table.
- ❍ B. The ADMIN_MOVE_TABLE () procedure stores all changes that occur to data in the source table during the move to a user-supplied staging table so the changes can be replayed against the target table when the move is complete.
- ❍ C. If the ADMIN_MOVE_TABLE () procedure is used to move data in a source table to a target table that was created beforehand, the target table is renamed upon a successful data copy.
- ❍ D. If the ADMIN_MOVE_TABLE () procedure is invoked with the KEEP option specified, the source table will remain, and if the target table is to be created automatically, a name that is different from that of the active table must be specified for the target table.

Question 28

Which statement about the REORGCHK command is true?

- ❍ A. It cannot be run against the system catalog.
- ❍ B. It automatically calls RUNSTATS by default.
- ❍ C. It cannot be run against MDC tables.
- ❍ D. It automatically calls REORG if it is determined that a reorganization is necessary.

Question 29

What is the purpose of specifying the RESTART CONTINUE option in an INGEST command?

- ❍ A. To terminate a failed INGEST command.
- ❍ B. To restart a failed INGEST command from the beginning.
- ❍ C. To clean up the log records of a failed INGEST command.
- ❍ D. To restart a failed INGEST command from the last commit point.

Question 30

Which two commands can you use to monitor the ingest operation?

- ❒ A. LIST UTILITIES SHOW DETAIL
- ❒ B. INGEST LIST
- ❒ C. GET SNAPSHOT FOR INGEST
- ❒ D. INGEST GET STATS FOR <id>
- ❒ E. GET SNAPSHOT FOR ALL APPLICATIONS

Answers

Question 1

The correct answer is **D**. You can invoke most of the utilities that are provided with DB2 from IBM Data Studio or by executing the appropriate command from the DB2 CLP or an operating system prompt. And because most DB2 commands have a corresponding API, you can invoke them from an embedded SQL or a CLI application as well. However, the source code needed to use some of these APIs can be quite complex, and all of the APIs are designed to be used primarily in C and C++ applications. Another approach is to use the `ADMIN_CMD ()` stored procedure, which is a special stored procedure that allows applications to run select administrative commands by using the `CALL` SQL statement. The `ADMIN_CMD ()` stored procedure also allows you to invoke utilities from Java applications—something that cannot be done easily with the APIs.

Question 2

The correct answer is **C**. If you execute the `IMPORT` command with the `ALLOW WRITE ACCESS` option specified, the `Import` utility will request a table lock after every commit operation is performed. This can cause an import operation to run slowly in environments that have high concurrency. That is not the case if you specify the `ALLOW NO ACCESS` option. No `ALLOW READ ACCESS` and `ALLOW FULL ACCESS` options are available in DB2.

Question 3

The correct answer is **B**. When you use the `Import` utility's `REPLACE` option, any existing data is deleted from the target table (which must already exist), and then the new data is inserted. You cannot use this option if the target table contains a primary key that is referenced by a foreign key in another table.

When you use the `INSERT` option, data is inserted into the target table (which must already exist). Imported data is appended to any data that already exists. When the `INSERT_UPDATE` option is used, data is either inserted into the target table (which must already exist) or used to update existing rows (if the row being imported has a primary key value that matches that of an existing record). Existing records will only be updated if the target table specified has a primary key defined. When you use the `CREATE` option, the target table is created along with all of its associated indexes, and then data is imported into the new table.

Question 4

The correct answer is **B**. You use the `LOAD` command modifiers—`IDENTITYIGNORE`, `IDENTITYMISSING`, and `IDENTITYOVERRIDE`–when loading identity column data.

The `IDENTITYIGNORE` modifier indicates that although data for all identity columns is present in the file being loaded, this data should be ignored, and the `Load` utility should replace all identity column data found with its own generated values. The `IDENTITYMISSING` modifier specifies that data for identity columns is missing from the file being loaded and that the `Load` utility should generate an appropriate value for each missing value encountered. The IDENTITYOVERRIDE modifier indicates that the Load utility is to accept explicit, non-NULL data values for all identity columns in the table. This modifier is useful when migrating data from another database system, or when loading a table from data that was recovered by using the ROLLFORWARD DATABASE command's DROPPED TABLE RECOVERY option. Use this modifier only when an identity column that was defined as GENERATED ALWAYS is present in the table that is to be loaded.

Question 5

The correct answer is **C**. The IMPORT command's COMMITCOUNT option specifies the number of rows of data (records) to copy to the table or updatable view specified before a commit operation is performed. You use the COMMITCOUNT AUTOMATIC option for import operations that fail because transaction logs become full. This guarantees that transaction logs do not become full of uncommitted data.

Question 6

The correct answer is **D**. You use the Load utility to delete all records in a table without generating corresponding log records by specifying the null device as the input file and invoking the LOAD with the REPLACE option specified. On UNIX, the null device is /dev/null; on Windows, it is nul). Thus, the you can execute the following commands to delete all records found in a table named DEPARTMENT:

```
LOAD FROM /dev/null OF DEL REPLACE INTO department (UNIX)
LOAD FROM nul OF DEL REPLACE INTO department (Windows)
```

Question 7

The correct answer is **A**. Statistics cannot be collected if you execute the LOAD command with any option other than the REPLACE option specified. Additionally, a statistics profile for the SALES table must already exist (statistics profiles are created by executing the RUNSTATS command); the Load utility will not create one. If a profile does not exist and the Load utility is instructed to collect statistics, a warning is returned statistics are not collected.

Question 8

The correct answer is **C**. The LOAD QUERY command monitors the progress and status of a load operation. There are no LOAD STATUS, LOAD MESSAGES, or LOAD STATISTICS commands.

Question 9

The correct answer is **C**. During the delete phase of a load operation, any rows that violated primary or unique key constraints defined on the target table are removed and copied to an exception table (if appropriate), and a message about each offending row is written to the appropriate message file so that you can modify and manually move that row to the target table in the future. Because the data in this example contains two records that have an employee ID value of 100 and the EMPID column in the EMPLOYEES is a primary key, the first record will be loaded into the EMPLOYEES table, and the second will be moved to the EMP_EXP table.

Question 10

The correct answer is **B**. The Load utility is significantly faster than the Import utility when processing large amounts of data because the Load utility writes formatted pages directly into the database's storage containers. Additionally, when you use the Load utility, a minimal amount of logging is performed—individual row transactions are not recorded in the database's transaction log files.

WSF formatted files are not supported by the Load utility, triggers are not fired during load processing, and only uniqueness checking is performed during processing. You must perform all other constraint checking (check constraints, referential integrity constraints, and so on) after the load operation has completed by using the SET INTEGRITY SQL statement.

Question 11

The correct answer is **C**. The db2move utility queries the system catalog tables of the specified database and compiles a list of all user tables found. It then exports the contents and table structure of each table in the database to individual PC/IXF formatted files. The set of files produced can then be imported or loaded to another DB2 database on the same system, or they can be transferred to another workstation and be imported or loaded to a DB2 database residing there. Thus, you can use db2move to copy the entire contents of a database from one location to another.

One limitation of the db2move utility is that you can use it only to duplicate table and index objects. If the database to duplicate contains other objects such as aliases, views, triggers, UDTs, UDFs, and so on, you must duplicate those objects in the target database as well if you want to have an identical copy of the source database. That is where the db2look utility comes in. When invoked, db2look can reverse-engineer an existing database and produce a set of DDL SQL statements, which you can then use to re-create all data objects found in the database that was analyzed. The db2look utility can also collect environment registry variable settings, configuration parameter settings, and statistical (RUNSTATS) information on the source system, which can be used to duplicate those settings on the target system.

In this scenario, you want to copy only a portion of the data, and you want to copy the statistics from the production database to the test database. Therefore, you cannot use db2move to move the date; instead, you must use db2look to duplicate the objects and statistics found in the production database and then add the appropriate amount of data to the tables.

Question 12

The correct answer is **A**. The db2batch utility is a simple benchmark tool that reads SQL statements and XQuery expressions from either an ASCII format file or standard input; dynamically prepares, describes, and executes the statements and expressions found; and returns a result set that includes, among other things, the timing of the execution. It is best to use db2move for copying 50 tables from one database to another, REORG for reorganizing table data and clustering its rows, and REBIND for updating access plan information stored in packages.

Question 13

The correct answer is **D**. Because the DB2 Optimizer generates an access plan each time a dynamic SQL statement is prepared for execution, applications using dynamic SQL may see performance improvements immediately after new statistical information has been produced. Unfortunately, that is not the case for applications that use static SQL. That is because the DB2 Optimizer only generates access plans for static SQL statements when the package that contains those statements is bound to the database. Therefore, for existing packages to exploit new statistical information produced by the RUNSTATS utility, you must rebind them to the database so the DB2 Optimizer will evaluate the new information and formulate new access plans (which may or may not perform better that the original access plan). The easiest way to rebind an existing package—provided the application source code used to produce the package has not changed—is by executing the REBIND command.

Question 14

The correct answer is **B**. The RUNSTATS utility should be run immediately after any of the following occur:

- A large number of insert, update, or delete operations are performed against a specific table.
- An import operation is performed.
- A load operation is performed.
- One or more columns are added to an existing table.
- A new index is created.
- A table or index is reorganized.

It is also a good idea to run the RUNSTATS utility before running the REORGCHK utility. If the query response is slow because fragmentation and statistics are not current, the REORGCHK utility may report that a table or index reorganization operation is unnecessary when it really is. Upon careful evaluation of the REORGCHK utility's output, you may discover that one or more tables or indexes need to be reorganized. If that is the case, you can reorganize the tables, followed by the indexes, using DB2's REORG utility. After you reorganize data, statistics should be collected again and any packages that are associated with the table should be rebound (using the REBIND utility) so the DB2 Optimizer can generate new data access plans using the new statistics information collected.

Question 15

The correct answer is **C**. The Design Advisor is a special tool that identifies indexes, MQTs, and MDCs that may help improve query performance in your database environment. You invoke the Design Advisor by executing the db2advis command; the -g option of the db2advis command specifies to analyze the SQL statements that make up the workload and to retrieve them from a dynamic SQL snapshot.

The -k option specifies to what degree to compress the workload. (Compression allows the advisor to reduce the complexity of the advisor's execution while achieving similar results to those the advisor could provide when the full workload is considered.) The -qp option indicates that the workload is coming from the DB2 Query Patroller, and the -h option displays help information.

Question 16

The correct answers are **B** and **E**. The Design Advisor recommends one or more indexes that would improve query or workload performance using current database statistics, the DB2 Optimizer, snapshot monitor information, and/or a specific query or set of SQL statements (known as a workload) you provide. The indexes/MQTs/MDCs recommended, the statistics derived for them, and the DDL statements required to create them can be written to a user-created table named ADVISE_INDEX, if so desired.

If you execute the db2advis command with the -p option specified, the plans that were generated while running the Design Advisor will be saved in the ADVISE_WORKLOAD table, and the workload query plans that use the final recommendation will be written to the Explain tables. However, input for the Design Advisor does not come from the Explain tables.

Question 17

The correct answer is **A**. Global temporary tables cannot be used with the LOAD, IMPORT, or INGEST command. Table 6.12 lists the complete supported table types.

Table 6.12: DB2-supported table types for Ingest, Load, and Import

Table type	Ingest	Load	Import
Detached table	Not supported	Not supported	Not supported
Global temporary table	Not supported	Not supported	Not supported
MDC or ITC table	Supported	Supported	Supported
MQT that is maintained by user	Supported	Supported	Supported
Nickname	Supported	Not supported	Supported
Range-clustered table	Supported	Not supported	Supported
Range-partitioned table	Supported	Supported	Supported
Summary table	Supported	Supported	Supported
Temporal table	Supported	Supported	Supported
Typed table	Not supported	Not supported	Supported
Untyped (regular) table	Supported	Supported	Supported
Updatable view (except typed view)	Supported	Not supported	Supported

Question 18

The correct answer is **C**. The `Ingest` utility is a high-speed, client-side, highly configurable, multithreaded DB2 utility that streams data from files and pipes into DB2 target tables by using SQL-like commands. Because the `Ingest` utility can move large amounts of real-time data without locking the target table, you do not need to choose between the data currency and availability. `LOAD WITH NO ACCESS` does not allow users to access the table until it finishes, and SQL and Q replication can replicate one or more tables between the source and target systems to capture the data changes; however, these are not designed to move large amount of data at one go because they do call `INSERT/UPDATE/DELETE/MEGRE` internally in sequence. `IMPORT WITH COMMITCOUNT AUTOMATIC`, even though this option allows other users to access the target table, it takes very long to process the data load due to sequential, multiple `INSERT`s threads.

Question 19

The correct answer is **A**. The `FLUSH PACKAGE CACHE` statement invalidates all cached dynamic SQL statements in the package cache. This invalidation causes the next request for any SQL statement that matches an invalidated cached dynamic SQL statement to be compiled instead of reused from the package cache.

Question 20

The correct answer is **D**. When you specify thte `NONRECOVERABLE` option in the `LOAD` command, all the transaction on the `EMPLOYEE` table will be marked as nonrecoverable, and it will not be possible to recover the data by a subsequent roll-forward operation. If there an attempt to perform a roll-forward operation, the utility will skip the transaction and will mark the table into which data was being loaded as invalid. After the roll-forward operation, such tables can only be dropped and re-created.

When you load data with `NONRECOVERABLE`, table spaces will not be placed in Backup Pending state. However, when you load without `NONRECOVERABLE` or `COPY YES` options, the table spaces will be placed in Backup Pending state. A copy of the table can be made with the `COPY YES` option.

Question 21

The correct answer is **B**. You can collect the statistics only for the specific index by sampling the data using the option `INDEXSAMPLE`. It is not necessary to scan all the indexes before updating the system catalog table. The `FOR INDEXES` clause collects and updates statistics for the indexes only. If no table statistics had been previously collected on the table, basic table statistics are also collected.

Question 22

The correct answer is **A**. You can invoke the design advisor on database SAMPLE by using the command `db2advis -d sample -i db2advis.sql -t 5`. You could pass the workload file as an input to the advisor to generate expert recommendation on indexes, MQT, MDC, and partitions. The DB2 advisor does not accept DDLs, `db2nodes.cfg` (DPF configuration file), and the database configuration parameter file.

Question 23

The correct answer is **D**. To minimize the performance impact of the RUNSTATS utility, follow these guidelines:

- Limit the columns for which statistics are collected by using the COLUMNS clause. Many columns are never referenced by predicates in the query workload, so they do not require statistics.
- Limit the columns for which distribution statistics are collected if the data tends to be uniformly distributed. Collecting distribution statistics requires more CPU and memory than collecting basic column statistics. However, determining whether the values for a column are uniformly distributed requires either having existing statistics or querying the data. This approach also assumes that the data remains uniformly distributed as the table is modified.
- Limit the number of pages and rows processed by using page- or row-level table sampling (by specifying the TABLESAMPLE SYSTEM or TABLESAMPLE BERNOULLI clause) and by using page- or row-level index sampling (by specifying INDEXSAMPLE SYSTEM or INDEXSAMPLE BERNOULLI clause). Start with a 10 percent page-level sample by specifying TABLESAMPLE SYSTEM (10) and INDEXSAMPLE SYSTEM (10). Check the accuracy of the statistics and whether system performance has degraded due to changes in access plan. If it has degraded, try a 10 percent row-level sample instead by specifying TABLESAMPLE BERNOULLI (10). Likewise, experiment with the INDEXSAMPLE parameter to obtain the right rate for index sampling. If the accuracy of the statistics is insufficient, increase the sampling amount. When using RUNSTATS page- or row-level sampling, use the same sampling rate for tables that are joined. This is important to ensure that the join column statistics have the same level of accuracy.
- Collect index statistics during index creation by specifying the COLLECT STATISTICS option on the CREATE INDEX statement. This approach is faster than performing a separate RUNSTATS operation after the index is created. It also ensures that the new index has statistics generated immediately after creation to allow the optimizer to accurately estimate the cost of using the index.
- Collect statistics when executing the LOAD command with the REPLACE option. This approach is faster than performing a separate RUNSTATS operation after the load operation has completed. It also ensures that the table has the most current statistics immediately after the data is loaded to allow the optimizer to accurately estimate the cost of using the table.

Question 24

The correct answer is **A**. In this case, any record that violates a constraint that has been defined for the EMPLOYEE table will be loaded into the EXP_EMPLOYEE table, rather than the EMPLOYEE table. Exception table should have same number of columns, column data types, and column nullability attributes as the target table to be loaded. In addition, you might want to add an optional timestamp (to record the deletion timestamp from the target table) and CLOB (32 KB) (to record the load error messages) columns to the exception table. Exception tables will not be created by the database manager. Because this load has no COPY YES or NONRECOVERABLE, table space will be placed in Backup Pending state if archive logging is enabled in the database.

Question 25

The correct answer is C. You can use this db2look command to mimic the statistics between the systems:

```
db2look -d <dbname> -z <schema> -t <tabname> -m -c -r -o statsfile.in
```

You cannot export the system catalog tables from one and import it to another by using either db2move or EXPORT/IMPORT commands. There is no command called db2mimic.

Question 26

The correct answer is C. You can use the SYSPROC.ADMIN_MOVE_TABLE () procedure to move the table online, as this example shows:

```
CALL SYSPROC.ADMIN_MOVE_TABLE
('MOHAN',
'EMP_PHOTO',
'TS_SMALL_DATA',
'TS_SMALL_INDEX',
'TS_LOB_DATA',
'',
'',
'',
'',
'',
'MOVE')
```

The db2move command creates a copy of the table in the same database or on a different database, but it does not move it. You can use db2relocatedb to perform the following set of actions:

- Change the database name
- Change the database path
- Reassociate the database with another instance
- Change each node database name in a DPF environment
- Change the new log path directory
- Change the container paths
- Change the storage paths
- Change the failarchpath
- Change the logarchmenth1 and logarchmenth2
- Change the mirrorlogpath and overflow log path

The SYSPROC.ADMIN_MOVE_TABLE_UTIL () procedure complements the ADMIN_MOVE_TABLE () procedure by modify the online move table procedure attributes; however it cannot act on a table on its own.

Question 27

The correct answer is **C**. When you invoke the ADMIN_MOVE_TABLE () procedure, a shadow copy of the table to move is created in the table space specified (you can also create the target table manually beforehand). This procedure also creates a staging table and set of triggers to capture any data changes made on the source table during the move operation. Data is then copied from the source to the target by using either INSERT FROM CURSOR or LOAD FROM CURSOR. Once the data has been copied, changes captured in the staging table are replayed against the target table to bring it up to date. During this phase, the source table is briefly taken offline to rename it. By default, the source table is then dropped; however, it can be kept and renamed by using the KEEP option.

Question 28

The correct answer is **B**. If you run REORGCHK with the UPDATE STATISTICS clause, DB2 will call RUNSTATS internally to perform the statistics updates. It can even be run on system catalog tables and MDCs. However, REORGCHK cannot invoke REORG automatically.

Question 29

The correct answer is **D**. The INGEST command is considered complete only when it reaches the end of the source file or the pipe. Under any other circumstances, the Ingest utility considers the command execution as incomplete, and these conditions include:

- The utility is unable to read the input file due to an I/O error.
- A critical DB2 system error indicates that the job is not functioning as expected.
- The INGEST command is killed or terminates abnormally.

If an INGEST command fails, you can restart it by reissuing the command with the RESTART CONTINUE clause. The Ingest utility will then start the operation from the last commit point.

Question 30

The correct answers are **B** and **D**. The Ingest utility has two simple commands to monitor the progress:

- INGEST LIST
- INGEST GET STATS FOR <id>

These commands must be run on the same machine running the Ingest utility. Neither the LIST UTILITIES nor the SNAPSHOTS can capture the progress of INGEST command.

CHAPTER 7

High Availability

This chapter will introduce you to the backup and recovery tools that are available with DB2 and will show you how to back up a database regularly and restore a database if it becomes damaged or corrupted. It will also introduce you to the DB2 advanced features, such as High Availability and Disaster Recovery (HADR) with read on standby (ROS) and multiple standby databases.

Exam Objectives

- ✓ Demonstrate the ability to understand the various transaction logging features
- ✓ Demonstrate the ability to configure a database log mirror
- ✓ Demonstrate the ability to understand the various types of database recovery features as well as when and how to use each
- ✓ Demonstrate the ability to create and use database-level and table space–level backup images
- ✓ Demonstrate the ability to return a damaged or corrupt database to its previous state at any given point in time
- ✓ Demonstrate the ability to understand how and when an invalid index is re-created
- ✓ Demonstrate the ability to understand and implement the HADR feature
- ✓ Demonstrate the ability to configure HADR with ROS
- ✓ Demonstrate the ability to understand and implement HADR with multiple standby databases

- ✓ Demonstrate the ability to suspend and resume database I/O and to initialize a split mirror copy of a database
- ✓ Demonstrate the ability to understand pureScale architecture and basic operations

Transactions

A transaction (also known as a unit of work) is a sequence of one or more SQL operations grouped together as a single unit, usually within an application process. A given transaction can perform any number of SQL operations—from one operation to many hundreds or even thousands, depending on what is considered a "single step" within your business logic.

The initiation and termination of a single transaction defines points of data consistency within a database; either the effects of all operations performed within a transaction are applied to the database and made permanent (committed), or the effects of all operations performed are backed out (rolled back), and the database is returned to its previous state before the transaction was initiated.

Generally, transactions are initiated the first time an executable SQL statement is executed after a connection to a database has been made or immediately after a preexisting transaction has been terminated. Once initiated, transactions can be implicitly terminated using a feature known as *automatic commit* (in which case, each executable SQL statement is treated as one transaction, and any changes that statement makes are applied to the database if the statement executes successfully, or they are discarded if the statement fails), or transactions can be explicitly terminated by executing the COMMIT or the ROLLBACK SQL statement. The basic syntax for these two statements is:

```
COMMIT
```

and

```
ROLLBACK
```

When you use the COMMIT statement to terminate a transaction, all changes made to the database since the transaction began are made permanent. However, when you use the ROLLBACK statement, all changes made are backed out, and the database is returned to its prior state just before the transaction began. Figure 7.1 shows the effects of terminating a transaction with a COMMIT statement.

EMPLOYEE TABLE
(BEFORE TRANSACTION)

EMPID	NAME
001	JAGGER, MICK
002	RICHARDS, KEITH
003	WOOD, RONNIE

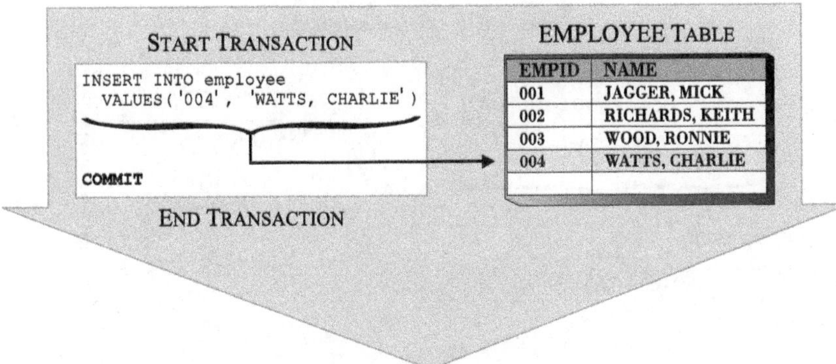

EMPLOYEE TABLE
(AFTER TRANSACTION)

EMPID	NAME
001	JAGGER, MICK
002	RICHARDS, KEITH
003	WOOD, RONNIE
004	WATTS, CHARLIE

Figure 7.1: Terminating a transaction with the COMMIT SQL statement

Figure 7.2 shows the effects of terminating a transaction with a ROLLBACK statement.

EMPLOYEE TABLE
(BEFORE TRANSACTION)

EMPID	NAME
001	JAGGER, MICK
002	RICHARDS, KEITH
003	WOOD, RONNIE

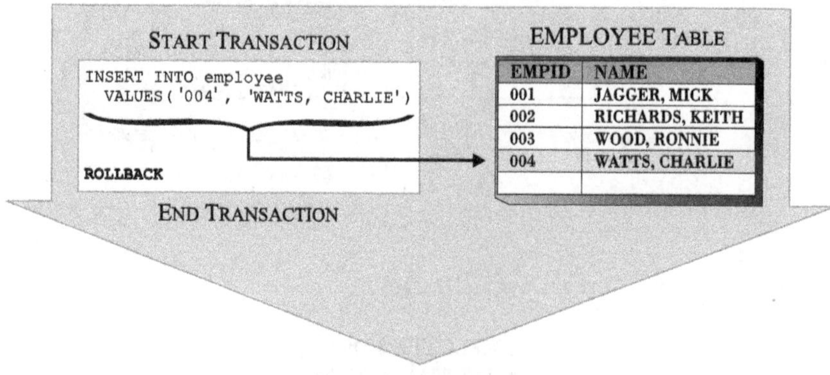

EMPLOYEE TABLE
(AFTER TRANSACTION)

EMPID	NAME
001	JAGGER, MICK
002	RICHARDS, KEITH
003	WOOD, RONNIE

Figure 7.2: Terminating a transaction with the ROLLBACK SQL statement

It is important to remember that commit and rollback operations have an effect only on changes that have been made within the transaction they terminate. So to evaluate the effects of a series of transactions, you must be able to identify where each transaction begins as well as when and how each transaction is terminated. Figure 7.3 evaluates the effects of a series of transactions.

Changes made by a transaction that have not been committed are usually inaccessible to other users and applications (unless the Uncommitted Read isolation level is used) and can be backed out with a rollback operation. However, once a transaction's changes are committed, they become accessible to all other users and applications and can be removed only by executing new SQL statements (within a new transaction). So what happens if a system failure occurs or an application abnormally ends before a transaction's changes can be committed? To answer that question, we must first examine how data changes are made and how transactions are logged.

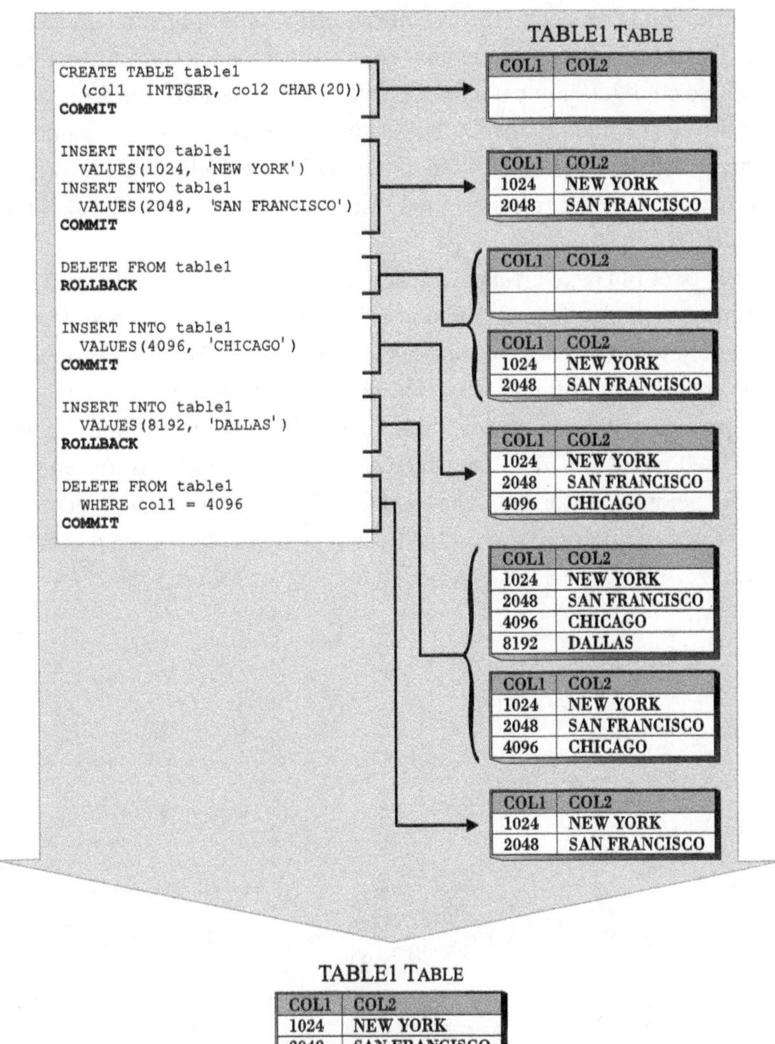

Figure 7.3: Evaluating the effects of a series of transactions

Transaction Logging

So just what is transaction logging and how does it work? Transaction logging is simply a process used to keep track of changes made to a database (by a transaction), *as they occur*. Each time you perform an update or a delete operation, the page containing the record to be updated or deleted is retrieved from storage and copied to the appropriate buffer pool, where it is then modified by the update/delete operation. (If an insert operation creates a new record, it creates that record directly in the appropriate buffer pool.) Once the record has been modified (or inserted), a record reflecting the modification/insertion is written to the log buffer, which is simply another designated storage area in memory. (The actual amount of memory reserved for the log buffer is controlled by the logbufsz database configuration parameter.) If you perform an insert operation, a record containing the new row is written to the log buffer; if you perform a delete operation, a record containing the row's original values is written to the log buffer; and if you perform an update operation, a record containing the row's original values, combined with the row's new values, is written to the log buffer.

Whenever buffer pool I/O page cleaners are activated, the log buffer becomes full, or a transaction is terminated (by being committed or rolled back), all records residing in the log buffer are immediately written to one or more log files stored on disk. This is done to minimize the number of log records that might get lost if a system failure occurs. As soon as all log records associated with a particular transaction have been externalized to one or more log files, the effects of the transaction itself are recorded in the database (i.e., executed against the appropriate table space containers for permanent storage). The modified data pages remain in memory, where they can be quickly accessed, if necessary—eventually, they will be overwritten as newer pages are retrieved from storage. You can see the transaction logging process in Figure 7.4.

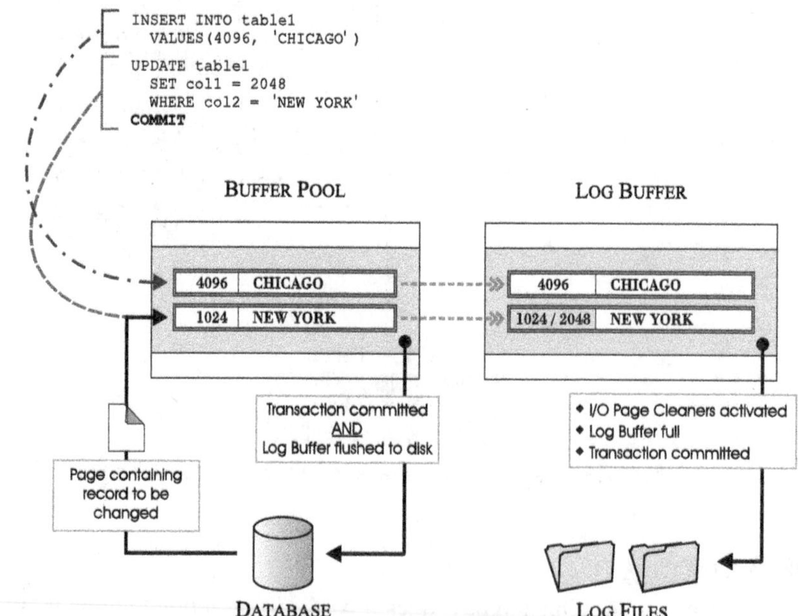

Figure 7.4: The transaction logging process

Because multiple transactions may be working with a database at any given time, a single log file may contain log records that belong to several different transactions. Therefore, to keep track of which log records belong to which transactions, every log record is assigned a special "transaction identifier" that ties it to the transaction that created it. The use of transaction IDs allows log records associated with a particular transaction to be written to one or more log files at any time, without impacting data consistency—eventually, the execution of the COMMIT or ROLLBACK statement that terminates the transaction will be logged as well.

Because log records are externalized frequently and because changes made by a particular transaction are only externalized to the database when the transaction itself is successfully terminated, the ability to return a database to a consistent state after a failure occurs is guaranteed. When you restart the database, log records are analyzed, and each record that has a corresponding COMMIT record is reapplied to the database; every record that lacks a corresponding COMMIT record is either ignored or backed out (which is why "before" and "after" information is recorded for all update operations).

Transaction Logging Strategies

When you first create a database, 13 primary log files are allocated (without an intervention of the Configuration Advisor; however, if you invoke the Configuration Advisor while creating the database, the Configuration Advisor will decide the number of primary logs to be created) as part of the creation process. On Linux, UNIX, and Windows platforms, these log files are 1,024 4-KB pages in size. However, the number of primary log files used, along with the amount of data each is capable of holding, is controlled by the logprimary and logfilsiz parameters in the database configuration file. The way in which all log files are used is determined by the logging strategy chosen for the database. Two very different strategies known as *circular logging* and *archival logging* are available within DB2.

Circular Logging

When you use circular logging, records stored in the log buffer are written to transaction log files in a circular sequence. Log records are written to the current "active" log file, and when that log file becomes full, it is marked as "unavailable." Then, DB2 makes the next log file in the sequence the active log file and begins writing log records to it; when that log file becomes full, the process is repeated. In the meantime, as transactions are terminated and their effects are externalized to the database, their corresponding log records are released because they are no longer needed. When all records stored in an individual log file are released, that file is marked as "reusable," and the next time it becomes the active log file, its contents are overwritten with new log records.

Although primary log files are not marked reusable in any particular order (they are marked reusable when they are no longer needed), they must be written to in sequence. So what happens when the logging process cycles back to a primary log file that is marked as unavailable?

When this occurs, the DB2 database manager will allocate what is known as a *secondary log file* and begin writing log records to it. As soon as the secondary log file becomes full, the DB2 database manager will poll the primary log file again, and if its status is still unavailable, another secondary log file is allocated and filled. This process will continue until either the desired primary log file becomes reusable or the number of secondary log files created matches the number of secondary log files allowed (designated by the logsecond database configuration parameter). If the former occurs, the DB2 database manager will begin writing log records to the appropriate primary log file, and logging will pick up where it left off in the logging sequence. In the meantime, log records stored in the secondary log files are eventually released, and when all connections to the database have been terminated, any secondary log files that were created are destroyed. However, if the maximum numbers of secondary log files allowed have been allocated, and the desired primary log file is still unavailable, all database activity will stop, and the following message will be generated:

```
SQL0964C The transaction log for the database is full.
```

By default, up to 12 secondary log files will be created (without an intervention of the Configuration Advisor; however, if you invoke the Configuration Advisor while creating the database, the Configuration Advisor will decide the number of secondary logs to be created), and their size will be the same as that of each primary log file used. Figure 7.5 illustrates circular logging. By default, when you create a new database, circular logging is the logging strategy used.

Archival Logging

As with circular logging, when you use archival logging (also known as *log retention logging* or *LOGRETAIN mode logging*), log records stored in the log buffer are written to the primary log files that have been preallocated. However, unlike with circular logging, these log files are never reused. Instead, when all records stored in an individual log file are released, that file is marked as "archived" rather than as "reusable," and the only time it is used again is if it is needed for a roll-forward recovery operation. When all the primary log files become full, the DB2 database manager allocates a new set of primary log files. This process continues as long as sufficient disk space is available, the number of transaction logs on the server reaches 256 (logprimary + logsecond), and they are classified according to their current state and storage location.

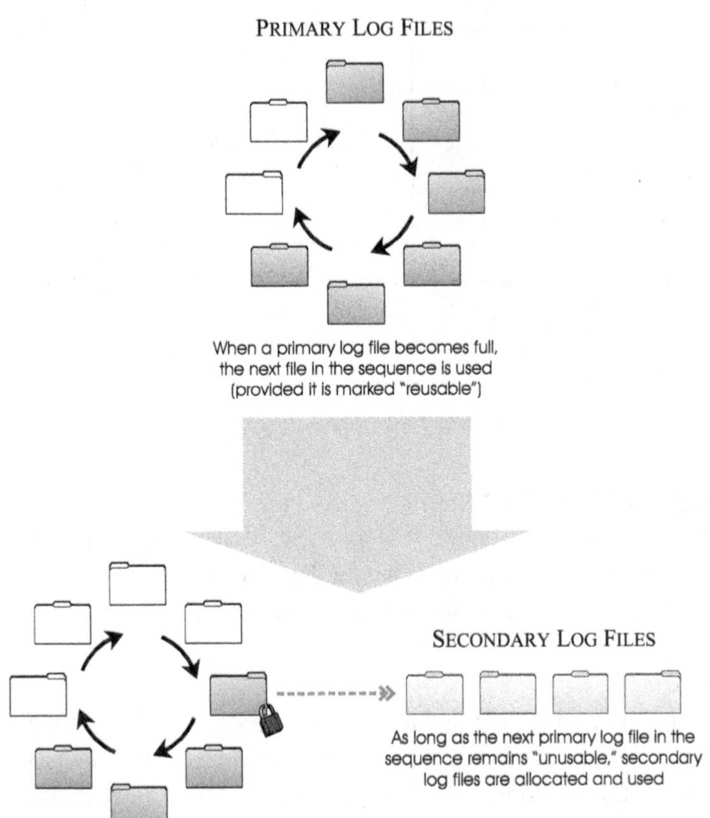
PRIMARY LOG FILES
When a primary log file becomes full, the next file in the sequence is used (provided it is marked "reusable")
SECONDARY LOG FILES
As long as the next primary log file in the sequence remains "unusable," secondary log files are allocated and used

Figure 7.5: Circular logging

Log files containing records associated with transactions that have not yet been committed or rolled back are known as *active log files* and reside in the active log directory (or device); log files containing records associated with completed transactions (i.e., transactions that have been externalized to the database) that are in the active log directory are called *online archive log files*; and log files containing records that are associated with completed transactions that have been moved to a storage location other than the active log directory are referred to as *offline archive log files*. Offline archive files can be copied to their storage location automatically by assigning the appropriate value (USEREXIT, DISK, TSM, or VENDOR) to the logarchmeth1 or logarchmeth2 database configuration parameter. Figure 7.6 illustrates archival logging.

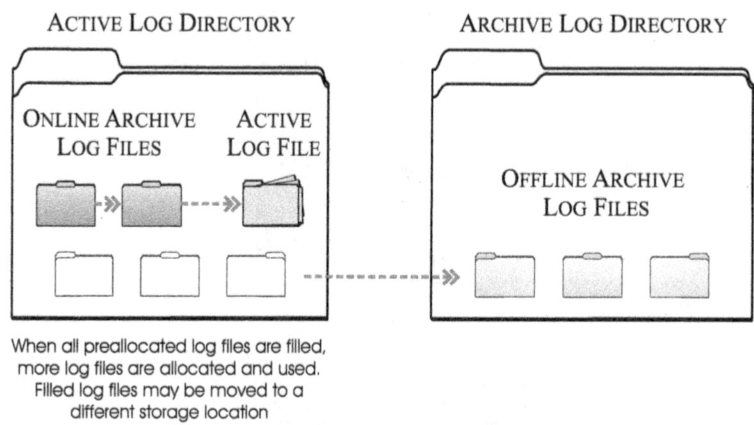
ACTIVE LOG DIRECTORY
ARCHIVE LOG DIRECTORY
ONLINE ARCHIVE LOG FILES
ACTIVE LOG FILE
OFFLINE ARCHIVE LOG FILES
When all preallocated log files are filled, more log files are allocated and used. Filled log files may be moved to a different storage location

Figure 7.6: Archival logging

Other Logging Considerations

Along with specifying the logging strategy to employ, several database configuration parameters can be used to control a database's logging behavior. Be sure to consider the following items when configuring a database for transaction log management.

Infinite Logging

You would think that you could avoid running out of log space simply by configuring a database to use a large number of secondary log files if needed. However, the maximum number of primary and secondary log files allowed (logprimary + logsecond) is 256, and if the size of your log files is relatively small, you can still run out of log space quickly when transaction workloads become heavy. Furthermore, you want to avoid allocating a large number of secondary log files if possible because performance is affected each time a log file has to be allocated. Ideally, you want to allocate enough primary log files to handle most situations, and you want to use just enough secondary log files to handle peaks in transaction workloads.

If you are concerned about running out of log space, and you want to avoid allocating a large number of secondary log files, you can configure a database to use what is known as *infinite logging*. To enable infinite logging, you simply set the logsecond database configuration parameter to -1. With infinite logging, whenever DB2 runs out of logprimary logs, instead of failing with "active log space full," it will archive logs that are still active and proceed to allocate (rename) a new log. This way, the number of logs in the active log path is still satisfied.

To use infinite logging, a database must be configured to use archival logging; infinite logging can affect performance hugely if one or many longer-running transactions must be rolled back and the log files needed have already been archived.

Dual Logging

In DB2, you have the ability to configure a database such that the database manager will simultaneously create and update active log files in two different locations. If you store active log files in one location and mirror them in another, separate location, database activity can continue if a disk failure or human error causes log files in one location to become inaccessible. (Mirroring log files may also aid in database recovery.) To enable log file mirroring, you simply assign the fully qualified name of the mirror log location (path) to the mirrorlogpath database configuration parameter. Ideally, the mirror log path should refer to a physical location (disk) that does not get a large amount of disk I/O and that is separate from the physical location used to store primary log files.

If an error is encountered during attempts to write to either the active log path or the mirror log path, the DB2 database manager will mark the failing path as "bad," write a message to the administration notification log, and write subsequent log records to the remaining "good" log path only. When DB2 allocates storage for its next primary log file, the DB2 database manager will make a second attempt to write to both log paths. If successful, dual logging will continue. If not, DB2 will not attempt to use the bad path again until the next log file is accessed for the first time. There is no attempt to synchronize the log paths, but DB2 keeps track of each access error that occurs, so that the correct paths will be used when log files are archived. If a failure occurs while writing to the remaining good path, the database shuts down.

Dual logging will not be allowed if you set the newlogpath database configuration parameter value to a raw device as an active log file storage location. When you set both the mirrorlogpath and the logarchmeth2 database configuration parameter values, then logarchmeth2 archives the log files from mirrorlogpath instead of archiving the logs from the active log path newlogpath location.

Controlling How "Disk Full" Errors Are Handled

When archival logging is used and archived log files are not copied (and renamed) from the active log directory to another location, the disk where the active log directory resides can quickly become full. Therefore, by default, transactions will receive a disk full error and be rolled back. But what if, instead of the current transaction being terminated, you were given the chance to manually move or delete files to make more room available? That is the purpose behind the blk_log_dsk_ful database configuration parameter.

If you set this parameter to YES, applications will hang if the DB2 database manager receives a disk full error when it attempts to create a new log file in the active log directory. The DB2 database manager will then try to create the log file every five minutes until it succeeds—after each attempt, a message is written to the administration notification log. (The only way that you can confirm that an application is hung because of a disk full condition is to monitor this log.) Until the log file is successfully created, applications attempting to insert or update data will not be permitted to commit their transactions. Read-only queries may not be directly affected;

however, if a query needs to access data that is locked by an update request or a data page that is fixed in the buffer pool by the updating application, read-only queries will also appear to hang.

To resolve a disk full situation, you simply move old log files to another location or enlarge the current file system. Once the needed space becomes available, the database manager can create new log files, and all hung applications will be able to continue processing.

Database Recovery Concepts

Over time, a database can encounter any number of problems, including power interruptions, storage media failure, application abnormal termination, or a site disaster. All of these issues can result in database failure, and each failure scenario requires a different recovery action.

The concept of backing up a database is the same as that of backing up any other set of data files: you make a copy of the data and store it on a different medium, where it can be accessed in the event the original becomes damaged or destroyed. The simplest way to back up a database is to shut it down to ensure that no further transactions are processed, and then back it up using the backup utility provided with DB2. Once a backup image has been created, you can use it to rebuild the database, if for some reason it becomes damaged or corrupted.

The process of rebuilding a database is known as *recovery*, and four types of recovery are available with DB2:

- Crash recovery
- Version recovery
- Roll-forward recovery
- Disaster recovery

Crash Recovery

When an event or condition causes a database or the DB2 database manager to end abnormally, one or more transaction failures may result. Conditions that can cause transaction failure include the following:

- A power failure at the workstation where the DB2 database manager is running
- A serious operating system error
- A hardware failure such as memory corruption, disk failure, CPU failure, or network failure

When a transaction failure occurs, all work done by partially completed transactions that had not yet been externalized to the database are lost. As a result, the database may be left in an inconsistent state (and therefore will be unusable). Crash recovery is the process of returning such a database to a consistent and usable state. You perform crash recovery by using information stored in the transaction log files to complete any committed transactions that were in memory (but had not yet been externalized to storage) when the transaction failure occurred, roll back any incomplete transactions found, and purge any uncommitted transactions from memory. Once a database is returned to a consistent and usable state, it has attained what is known as a *point of consistency*. Figure 7.7 illustrates crash recovery.

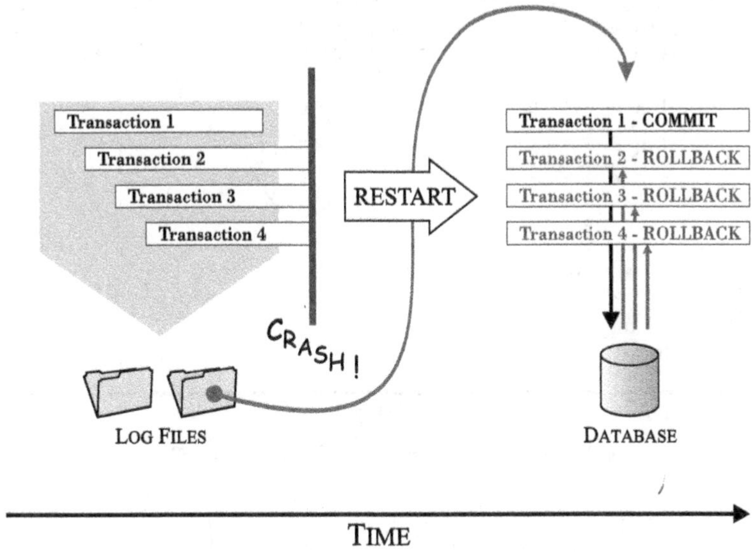

Figure 7.7: The crash recovery process

Version Recovery

Version recovery is the process of returning a database to the state it was in at the time a particular backup image was made. You perform version recovery by replacing the current version of a database with a previous version, using a copy that was made with a backup operation—you rebuild the entire database by using a backup image that was created earlier. Unfortunately, performing version recovery will lose all changes made to the database since the backup image used was created. Figure 7.8 illustrates version recovery.

Roll-forward Recovery

Roll-forward recovery takes version recovery one step further by rebuilding a database or one or more individual table spaces, using a backup image and replaying information stored in transaction log files to return the database/table spaces to the state they were in at an exact point in time. To perform a roll-forward recovery operation, you must have archival logging enabled, have either a full backup image of the database or a complete set of table space backup images available, and have access to all archived log files created since the backup images were made. Figure 7.9 illustrates the roll-forward recovery process.

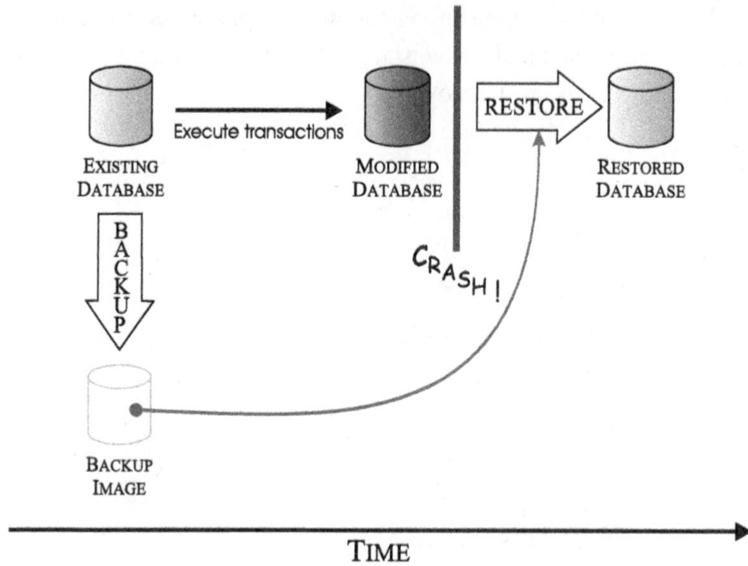

Figure 7.8: The version recovery process

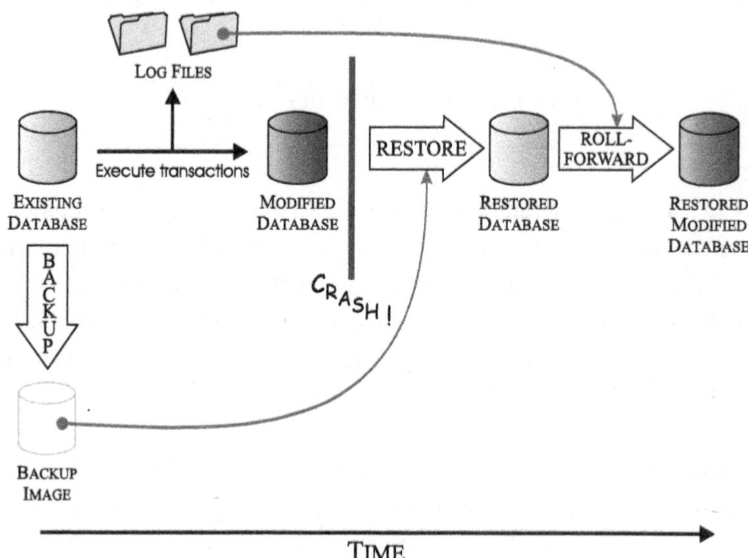

Figure 7.9: The roll-forward recovery process

Disaster Recovery

Disaster recovery (DR) consists of set of associated processes, policies, and procedures that restore the database to a different site in the event of a natural or human-induced disaster.

DB2 provides you with many robust features to enable a smooth DR process between the sites, or computers. Two of these features are:

- HADR data replication
- SQL or Q Replication for specific schemas or set of tables

DB2 also supports storage-level mirroring, such as Peer-to-Peer Remote Copy (PPRC), providing data recovery capability in the event of a disaster. We will discuss HADR in greater detail in the "High Availability and Disaster Recovery" section.

Tip: In case of a power failure, you can bring the database back to a consistent state by using crash recovery. Version recovery and roll-forward recovery are generally required when a disk failure or a database corruption occurs. Disaster recovery can also be used in the case of a disk failure or corrupt database (with HADR delayed replay feature) to avoid application outages.

Recoverable and Nonrecoverable Databases

Although any DB2 database can be recovered from a backup image, whether a database is considered recoverable is determined by the values of the database's logarchmeth1 and logarchmeth2 configuration parameters. When you set both of these configuration parameters to OFF—which is the default—circular logging is used, and the database is considered nonrecoverable. A database is deemed recoverable when crash recovery, version recovery, *and* roll-forward recovery are possible. Table 7.1 shows other differences between recoverable and nonrecoverable databases.

Table 7.1: Differences between recoverable and unrecoverable databases

Recoverable Database	Nonrecoverable Database
Archive logging is used.	Circular logging is used.
The database can be backed up at any time, regardless of whether applications are connected to it and transactions are in progress.	The database can be backed up only when all connections to it have been terminated.
The entire database can be backed up, or individual table spaces can be backed up. Table spaces can also be restored independently.	The entire database must be backed up; table space–level backups are not supported.
A damaged database can be returned to the state it was in at any point in time; crash recovery, version recovery, and roll-forward recovery are supported.	A damaged database can be returned only to the state it was in at the time the last backup image was taken; only crash recovery and version recovery are supported.

Deciding whether a database should be recoverable or nonrecoverable is based on several factors:

- If a database supports read-only operations, it can be nonrecoverable; because no transactions will be logged, roll-forward recovery is not necessary.
- If relatively few changes will be made to a database, and if all changes made can be easily re-created, it may be desirable to leave the database nonrecoverable.
- If numerous changes will be made to a database, or if it would be difficult and time consuming to re-create all changes made, the database should be recoverable.

Online Versus Offline Backup and Recovery

From a backup and recovery perspective, a database is considered to be either online or offline. When a database is offline, other applications and users cannot gain access to it; when a database is online, just the opposite is true. You can perform backup and recovery operations against a nonrecoverable database only while it is offline. Recoverable databases, though, can be backed up at any time, regardless of whether the database is offline or online. However, before you can restore any database (recoverable or nonrecoverable), you must first take it offline.

When you perform an online backup operation, archival logging ensures that all changes made while the backup image is being made are captured and can be re-created with a roll-forward recovery operation. Additionally, you can do online backup operations against individual table spaces as well as entire databases. And, unlike with full database version recovery operations, you can perform table space version recovery operations and table space roll-forward recovery operations while a database remains online—provided the table space that contains the system catalog is not the table space being recovered. During an online table space backup operation, the table space being backed up remains available for use, and all modifications to the data stored in that table space are recorded in the transaction log files. However, when you perform an online restore or online roll-forward recovery operation against a table space, the table space itself is taken offline and is unavailable for use until the restore/roll-forward recovery operation is complete.

Incremental and Delta Backup and Recovery

As the size of a database grows, the time and hardware needed to back up and recover the databases also increase substantially. Thus, creating full database and table space backup images is not always the best approach when dealing with large databases because the storage requirements for multiple copies of such backup images can be enormous. A better alternative is to create a full backup image periodically and one or more incremental backup images more frequently. An incremental backup is a backup image that contains only pages that have been updated since the previous backup image was made. Along with updated data and index pages, each incremental backup image also includes all of the initial database metadata (such as database configuration, table space definitions, recovery history file) that is normally in a full database backup image.

Two types of incremental backup images can be produced: incremental and delta. An incremental backup image is a copy of all database data that has changed since the most recent successful full backup image was created. An incremental backup image is also known as a *cumulative* backup image because the last incremental backup image in a series of incremental backup images made over a period of time will contain the contents of all of the previous incremental backup images. The predecessor of an incremental backup image is always the most recent successful full backup image of the same object.

A delta backup image, however, is a copy of all database data that has changed since the last successful backup (full, incremental, or delta) of the database or table space in question. For this reason, a delta backup image is also known as a *differential*, or *noncumulative*, backup image. The predecessor of a delta backup image is the most recent successful backup image that contains a copy of each object found in the delta backup image.

The one thing that incremental and delta backup images have in common is that before either type of backup image can be created, a full backup image must already exist. Where they differ is both in their creation (usually, delta backup images are smaller and can be created faster than incremental backup images) and in how they are used for recovery. When you take incremental backup images, database recovery involves restoring the database by using the most recent full backup image available and applying the most recent incremental backup image produced. However, when you take delta backup images, database recovery involves restoring the database by using the most recent full backup image available and applying each delta backup image produced since the full backup image used was made, in the order in which they were created.

Let us look at an example to understand incremental and delta backups. Suppose an organization's database backup policy is to take full online backups on a Sunday, incremental backups on Wednesday, and delta on rest of the days (as follows) to effectively use the storage on the backup device.

Backup Name	Backup Description	Day
BKUP1	Full Online Backup	Sunday
BKUP2	Delta Backup	Monday
BKUP3	Delta Backup	Tuesday
BKUP4	Incremental Backup	Wednesday
BKUP5	Delta Backup	Thursday
BKUP6	Delta Backup	Friday
BKUP7	Delta Backup	Saturday

A full online backup consists of a full database image, and Monday's delta backup image constitutes data changes made between Sunday and Monday. Likewise, Tuesday's delta backup image consists of data changes made between Monday and Tuesday. The Wednesday incremental backup image comprises data changes made between Sunday and Wednesday because that incremental backup will always be referenced from the full backup. The Thursday delta backup image consists of data changes made between Wednesday and Thursday.

Performing a Crash Recovery Operation

Earlier, you saw that whenever transaction processing is interrupted by an unexpected event (such as a power failure), the database that the transaction was interacting with at the time is placed in an inconsistent state. Such a database will remain in an inconsistent state and will be unusable until a crash recovery operation returns it to some point of consistency. (An inconsistent database will notify users and applications that it is unusable via a return code and error message that is generated each time an attempt to activate it or establish a connection to it is made.)

One way of initiating crash recovery is by executing the RESTART DATABASE command from the DB2 CLP. The basic syntax for this command is:

```
RESTART [DATABASE | DB] [DatabaseAlias]
<USER [UserName] <USING [Password]>>
<DROP PENDING TABLESPACES ([TS_Name], ... )>
<WRITE RESUME>
```

where:

DatabaseAlias	Identifies the alias assigned to the database that is to be returned to a consistent and usable state
UserName	Identifies the name assigned to a specific user who is to perform the crash recovery operation
Password	Identifies the password that corresponds to the name of the user who is to perform the crash recovery operation
TS_Name	Identifies the name assigned to one or more table spaces to disable and place in Drop Pending state during the crash recovery process

If a problem occurs with a table space container during the restart process, you can use the DROP PENDING TABLESPACES ([TS_Name]) option to place one or more table spaces in Drop Pending state. Doing so allows the database to be successfully restarted, after which the offending table space can be dropped and, if necessary, re-created. You can find a list of troubled table space names in the administration notification log if a database restart operation fails because of table space container problems.

When only one system temporary table space is in the database, and that table space is placed in Drop Pending state, a new system temporary table space must be created immediately following a successful database restart operation.

In the event that all database I/O is suspended at the time a crash occurred, you can use the RESTART command's WRITE RESUME option to resume database I/O as part of the crash recovery process (suspended operations are discussed in the section "Backing Up a Database with Split Mirroring").

Thus, to perform a crash recovery operation on an unusable database named SAMPLE, execute a RESTART command that looks something like this:

```
RESTART DATABASE sample
```

However, if you want to perform a crash recovery operation on a database named SAMPLE and place a table space named TEMPSPACE1 in Drop Pending state, you could do so by executing a RESTART command that looks something like this:

```
RESTART DATABASE sample
DROP PENDING TABLESPACES (TEMPSPACE1)
```

You can also initiate a crash recovery operation for a particular database by selecting the **Restart** action from the **Manage Database** option in IBM Data Studio. Figure 7.10 shows the IBM Data Studio menu items you must select to perform a crash recovery operation on an unusable database.

It is possible to configure a database in such a way that the database manager will automatically perform crash recovery, if necessary, when an application or user attempts to establish a connection to it. To do so, you assign the value ON to the autorestart database configuration parameter. The DB2 database manager checks the state of a database the first time an application or user tries to establish a connection to the database, and if the database manager determines that the database is in an inconsistent state, it executes the RESTART command automatically if the autorestart database configuration parameter is set to ON.

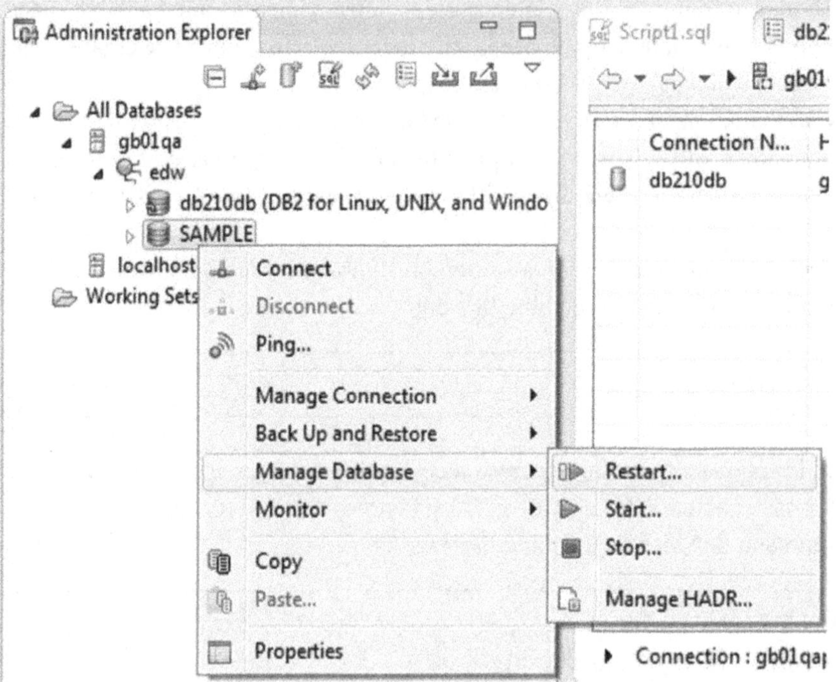

Figure 7.10: Initiating a crash recovery operation from IBM Data Studio

It is important to note that if DB2 database manager perform a crash recovery operation on a recoverable database (i.e., a database that has been configured to support roll-forward recovery operations), and an error occurs during the recovery process that is attributable to an individual table space, that table space will be taken offline and will no longer be accessible until it is repaired. This has no effect on crash recovery itself, and upon completion of the crash recovery operation, all other table spaces in the database will be accessible, and connections to the database can be established—provided the table space that is taken offline is not the table space that contains the system catalogs. If the table space containing the system catalogs is taken offline, it must be repaired before any connections to the database will be permitted.

A Word About Soft Checkpoints

As mentioned earlier, the DB2 database manager performs crash recovery by using information stored in the transaction log files to roll back all incomplete transactions and complete any committed transactions that are still in memory (but have not yet been externalized to storage) when a transaction failure occurs. As you might imagine, large transaction log files for a database can take quite a while to scan the entire log and check for corresponding rows in the database. However, it is usually not necessary to scan the entire log because records recorded at the beginning of a log file are typically associated with transactions that have been completed and have already been externalized to the database. Furthermore, if these records can be skipped, the amount of time required to recover a crashed database can be greatly reduced.

That is where a mechanism known as the *soft checkpoint* comes in. The DB2 database manager uses a log control file to determine which records from a specific log file need to be applied to the database. This log control file is written to disk periodically, and the frequency at which this file is updated is determined by the value of the `softmax` database configuration parameter. Once the log control file is updated, the soft checkpoint information stored in it establishes where in a transaction log file crash recovery should begin; all records in a log file that precede the soft checkpoint are assumed to be associated with transactions that have already been written to the database and are ignored.

Backup and Recovery

Although using crash recovery can resolve inconsistency problems that result from power interruptions or application failures, it cannot handle problems that arise when the storage media that hold a database's files become corrupted or fail. To handle these types of problems, some kind of backup and recovery program must be put in place.

A database recovery strategy must include a regular schedule for making database backup images and, in the case of partitioned database systems, include making backup images whenever the system is scaled (i.e., whenever database partition servers are added or dropped). Additionally, the strategy must ensure that all information needed is available when database recovery is necessary, and it must include procedures for restoring command scripts, applications, UDFs, stored procedure code in operating system libraries, load copies, and database data. To help with such a strategy, DB2 provides four utilities that you can use to facilitate backing up and restoring a database:

- The Backup utility
- The Restore utility
- The Roll-forward utility
- The Recover utility

The DB2 Backup Utility

The single most important item you can possess that will prevent catastrophic data losses in the event storage media become corrupted or fail is a database backup image. A database backup image is essentially a copy of an entire database that includes its metadata, objects, data, and transaction logs. Once created, a backup image can be used at any time to return a database to the exact state it was in at the time the backup image was made (version recovery). A good database recovery strategy ensures that backup images are created regularly and that backup copies of critical data are retained in a secure location and on different storage media from that used to house the database. Depending on the logging method you use (circular or archival), you can make database backup images when a database is offline or while other users and applications are connected to it. To back up a database while it is online, archival logging must be enabled.

You can create a backup image of a DB2 database, or a table space within a DB2 database, by executing the BACKUP DATABASE command. The basic syntax for this command is:

```
BACKUP [DATABASE | DB] [DatabaseAlias]
<USER [UserName] <USING [Password]>>
<TABLESPACE ([TS_Name],...)
<ONLINE>
<INCREMENTAL <DELTA>>
<TO [Location] | USE TSM <OPTIONS [TSMOptions]>>
<WITH [NumBuffers] BUFFERS>
<BUFFER [BufferSize]>
<PARALLELISM [ParallelNum]>
<COMPRESS>
<UTIL_IMPACT_PRIORITY [Priority]>
<INCLUDE LOGS | EXCLUDE LOGS>
<WITHOUT PROMPTING>
```

where:

DatabaseAlias Identifies the alias assigned to the database for which a backup image will be created

UserName Identifies the name assigned to a specific user who is to perform the backup operation

Password Identifies the password that corresponds to the name of the user who is to perform the backup operation

TS_Name Identifies the name assigned to one or more specific table spaces to create backup images for

Location Identifies the directory or device in which to store the created backup image

TSMOptions Identifies options that the Tivoli Storage Manager (TSM) is to use during the backup operation

NumBuffers Identifies the number of buffers to use to perform the backup operation (by default, two buffers are used if this option is not specified)

BufferSize	Identifies the size, in pages, of each buffer used to perform the backup operation (by default, the value of the backbufsz DB2 database manager configuration parameter determines the size of each buffer used by the Backup utility)
ParallelNum	Identifies the number of table spaces that can be read in parallel during the backup operation
Priority	Indicates to throttle the Backup utility such that it executes at a specific rate, so that its effect on concurrent database activity can be controlled; you can assign this parameter a numerical value within the range of 1 to 100, with 100 representing the highest priority and 1 representing the lowest

Specifying the INCREMENTAL option will produce an incremental backup image, which is a copy of all data that has changed since the last successful full backup image was made. When you specify the INCREMENTAL DELTA option, a delta backup image will be produced—a delta backup image is a copy of all data that has changed since the last successful backup image of any type (full, incremental, or delta) was made.

Thus, to create a full backup image of a database named SAMPLE that is currently offline and store the image created in a directory named backups on logical disk drive E: on Windows or the */db2backup* file system on Linux, you would execute a BACKUP DATABASE command that looks something like this:

```
BACKUP DATABASE sample USER db2admin USING
ibmdb2 TO /db2backup COMPRESS
```

However, to create an incremental backup image of a table space named USERSPACE1 and store the image created in a directory named BACKUPS on logical disk drive E: on Windows or the */db2backup* file system on Linux while the image's associated database (named SAMPLE) remains online, execute a BACKUP DATABASE command that looks something like this:

```
BACKUP DATABASE sample USER db2admin USING
ibmdb2 TABLESPACE (userspace1) ONLINE
INCREMENTAL TO /db2backup COMPRESS
```

Keep in mind that you can create table space backup images only when using archival logging. If you use circular logging instead, table space backups are not supported. The incremental backup image can be taken only after setting the TRACKMOD database configuration parameter to YES.

You can also create a backup image of a database or one or more table spaces by using IBM Data Studio. To activate the Backup wizard, select the **Back Up** and **Restore** action, followed by the **Back Up** option, as in Figure 7.11.

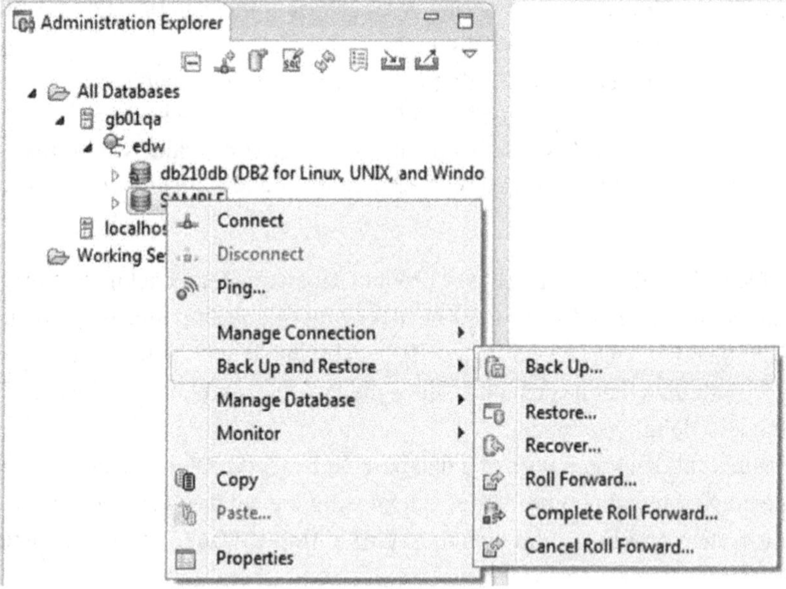

Figure 7.11: Invoking the Backup wizard from IBM Data Studio

Figure 7.12 shows how the first page of the Backup wizard might look immediately after activation.

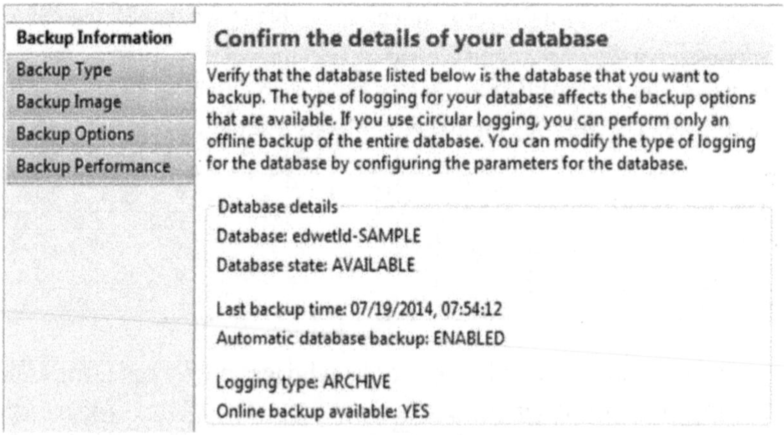

Figure 7.12: The first page of the IBM Data Studio Backup wizard

If your database is circular logging enabled, you will see no options available in the Backup Type window. Figure 7.13 displays backup types (full or table space level) that you can select when the database is set to archival logging.

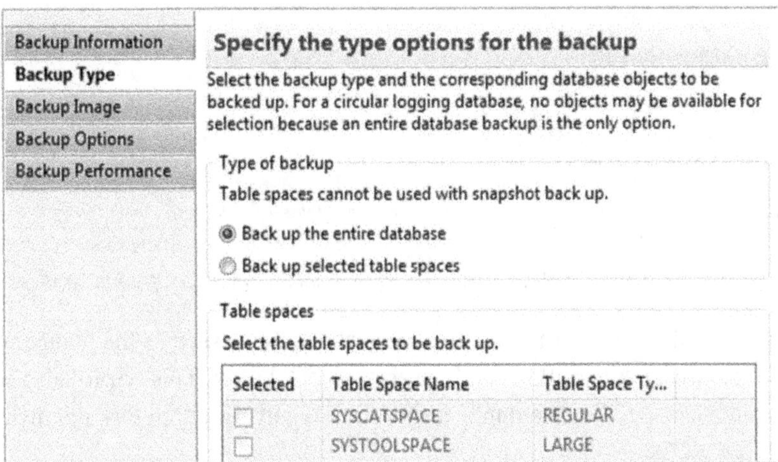

Figure 7.13: The IBM Data Studio Backup wizard's Backup Type window

Figure 7.14 shows media types supported by DB2 (external tape, TSM, NFS or local file system, TSM, XBSA, and other vendor specifics) and options to add a backup device or the file system path in the Backup Image window.

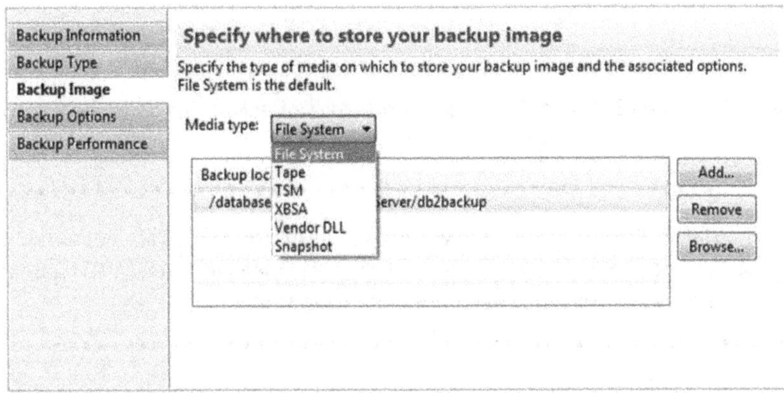

Figure 7.14: The IBM Data Studio Backup wizard's Backup Image window

Figure 7.15 illustrates backup options supported within DB2. You can select a full, incremental, or delta backup and choose to compress it to effectively use the storage.

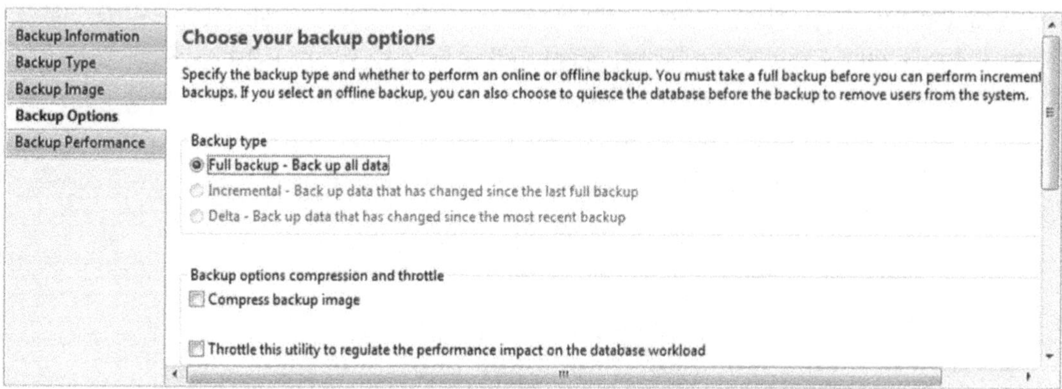

Figure 7.15: The IBM Data Studio Backup wizard's Backup Options window

Figure 7.16 shows the database Backup Performance options, such as the number of sessions, the number of database backup buffers, and the size of each buffer. This wizard also lets you effectively use a device-specific data duplication compression algorithm through media controller options (DEDUP_DEVICE).

Figure 7.16: The IBM Data Studio Backup wizard's Backup Performance window

Note: Only users with System Administrator (SYSADM) authority, System Control (SYSCTRL) authority, or System Maintenance (SYSMAINT) authority are allowed to back up a database or its table spaces.

Tip: In DB2, temporary table space data is never backed up; however, the metadata about the temporary table spaces is recorded in the database backup image.

Dropped Table Recovery

You might seldom drop a table that contains data you still need. If so, consider making your critical tables recoverable following a drop table operation by using the following steps.

Step 1: Make sure your table space is DROPPED TABLE RECOVERY enabled. You can enable it using the CREATE TABLESPACE or ALTER TABLESPACE command:

```
ALTER TABLESPACE USERSPACE1 DROPPED TABLE RECOVERY ON
```

Step 2: Verify the DROP_RECOVERY setting in the system catalog table:

```
SELECT VARCHAR(TBSPACE,20) AS TBSPACE, DROP_RECOVERY FROM SYSCAT.TABLESPACES

TBSPACE              DROP_RECOVERY
-------------------- -------------
SYSCATSPACE          N
TEMPSPACE1           N
USERSPACE1           Y
SYSTOOLSPACE         Y
SYSTOOLSTMPSPACE     N
```

Step 3: Back up your database to test the drop recovery feature:

```
BACKUP DATABASE sample ONLINE COMPRESS
Backup successful. The timestamp for this backup image is : 20140706224734
```

Step 4: Create a table in the drop recovery–enabled table space and insert data into it:

```
CREATE TABLE employee_rec
(ID INT, NAME VARCHAR(20)) COMPRESS YES IN USERSPACE1;
DB20000I  The SQL command completed successfully.

INSERT INTO employee_rec VALUES
(1,'MOHAN'), (2,'MILAN'), (3,'SUMAN'), (4,'COLIN'), (5,'NELSON')
```

Continued

```
SELECT * FROM employee_rec

ID          NAME
----------- --------------------
          1 MOHAN
          2 MILAN
          3 SUMAN
          4 COLIN
          5 NELSON

  5 record(s) selected.
```

Step 5: Drop the table for the recovery test:

```
DROP TABLE employee_rec
DB20000I  The SQL command completed successfully.
```

Step 6: Use the LIST HISTORY command to extract the dropped table information, including the DDL:

```
LIST HISTORY DROPPED TABLE ALL FOR sample

                    List History File for sample

Number of matching file entries = 1


                                               Earliest Current
 Op Obj Timestamp+Sequence Type Dev Log      Log     Backup ID
 -  --- ------------------ ---- --- -------- ------- ------------------------
 D  T   20140706230156                                000000003006e8000020110
----------------------------------------------------------------------------
                                                                   Continued
```

```
"MOHAN"."EMPLOYEE_REC" resides in 1 tablespace(s):

00001 USERSPACE1
-----------------------------------------------------------------------------
   Comment: DROP TABLE
Start Time: 20140706230156
  End Time: 20140706230156
    Status: A
-----------------------------------------------------------------------------
 EID: 127

DDL: CREATE TABLE "MOHAN"."EMPLOYEE_REC" ( "ID" INTEGER , "NAME" VARCHAR(20) )
          COMPRESS YES ADAPTIVE IN "USERSPACE1" ;
-----------------------------------------------------------------------------
```

Step 7: Restore the table space where the dropped recovery table was residing:

```
RESTORE DATABASE sample TABLESPACE (USERSPACE1)
DB20000I  The RESTORE DATABASE command completed successfully.
```

Step 8: Perform a roll-forward with a RECOVER DROPPED TABLE clause:

```
ROLLFORWARD DATABASE sample TO END OF LOGS AND COMPLETE RECOVER DROPPED TABLE
000000003006e8000020110 TO /home/mohan/


                              Rollforward Status

 Input database alias                   = sample
 Number of members have returned status = 1

 Member ID                              = 0
 Rollforward status                     = not pending
```

Continued

```
  Next log file to be read                  =
  Log files processed                       = -
  Last committed transaction                = 2014-07-06-23.01.56.000000 UTC

DB20000I  The ROLLFORWARD command completed successfully.
```

Step 9: Create the table EMPLOYEE_REC by using the DDL from the LIST HISTORY command and import the data residing in the /home/mohan/NODE0000/ directory:

```
CREATE TABLE "MOHAN"."EMPLOYEE_REC" ( "ID" INTEGER , "NAME" VARCHAR(20) )
      COMPRESS YES ADAPTIVE IN "USERSPACE1" "
DB20000I  The SQL command completed successfully.


IMPORT FROM data OF DEL INSERT INTO "MOHAN"."EMPLOYEE_REC"

SQL3109N The utility is beginning to load data from file "data".

SQL3110N The utility has completed processing. "5" rows were read from
the input file.

SQL3221W ...Begin COMMIT WORK. Input Record Count = "5".

SQL3222W ...COMMIT of any database changes was successful.

SQL3149N "5" rows were processed from the input file. "5" rows were
successfully inserted into the table. "0" rows were rejected.


Number of rows read         = 5
Number of rows skipped      = 0
Number of rows inserted     = 5
Number of rows updated      = 0
Number of rows rejected     = 0
                                                          Continued
```

```
Number of rows committed    = 5

SELECT * FROM employee_rec


ID          NAME
----------- --------------------
          1 MOHAN
          2 MILAN
          3 SUMAN
          4 COLIN
          5 NELSON

  5 record(s) selected.
```

The Restore Utility

Earlier, you saw that version recovery is the process that returns a database to the state it was in at the time a backup image was made. This means that for you to perform a version recovery operation, at least one backup image must exist and be available. So just how do you initiate a version recovery operation? The most common way is by executing the RESTORE DATABASE command. The basic syntax for this command is:

```
RESTORE [DATABASE | DB] [DatabaseAlias]
<USER [UserName] <USING [Password]>>
<REBUILD WITH [TABLESPACE ([TS_Name] ,... )] |
    [ALL TABLESPACES IN [DATABASE | IMAGE]]
        <EXCEPT TABLESPACE ([TS_Name] ,... )>>
[TABLESPACE ([TS_Name] ,... ) <ONLINE> |
   HISTORY FILE <ONLINE>> |
   COMPRESSION LIBRARY <ONLINE>> |
   LOGS <ONLINE>]
<INCREMENTAL <AUTO | AUTOMATIC | ABORT>>
<FROM [SourceLocation] | USE TSM <OPTIONS [TSMOptions]>>
<TAKEN AT [Timestamp]>
                                                    Continued
```

```
<TO [TargetLocation]>
<DBPATH ON [TargetPath]>
<TRANSPORT [STAGE IN StagingAlias] [USING STOGROUP StoGroupName]]
<INTO [TargetAlias]> <LOGTARGET [LogsLocation]>
<NEWLOGPATH [LogsLocation]>
<WITH [NumBuffers] BUFFERS>
<BUFFER [BufferSize]>
<REPLACE HISTORY FILE>
<REPLACE EXISTING>
<REDIRECT <GENERATE SCRIPT [ScriptFile]>>
<PARALLELISM [ParallelNum]>
<WITHOUT ROLLING FORWARD>
<WITHOUT PROMPTING>
```

or

```
RESTORE [DATABASE | DB] [DatabaseName]
[CONTINUE | ABORT]
```

where:

DatabaseAlias	Identifies the alias assigned to the database associated with the backup image to use to perform a version recovery operation
UserName	Identifies the name assigned to a specific user who is to perform the version recovery operation
Password	Identifies the password that corresponds to the name of the user who is to perform the version recovery operation
TS_Name	Identifies the name assigned to one or more specific table spaces to restore from a backup image (if the table space name has changed since the backup image was made, specify the new name)
SourceLocation	Identifies the directory or device in which to store the backup image to be used for version recovery
TSMOptions	Identifies options that TSM is to use during the version recovery operation
Timestamp	Identifies a timestamp to use as search criterion when looking for a particular backup image to use for version recovery (specifying no

	timestamp will assume that only one backup image is stored at the source location indicated)
TargetLocation	Identifies the directory in which to store the storage containers for the database that will be created, if the backup image is to be used to create a new database and automatic storage is used
TargetPath	Identifies the directory in which to store the metadata for the database that will be created, if the backup image is to be used to create a new database and automatic storage is used
StagingAlias	Identifies the temporary staging database for the transport operation
StoGroupName	Identifies the target storage group for all the automatic storage table spaces being transported
TargetAlias	Identifies the alias to assign to the new database to be created
LogsLocation	Identifies the directory or device in which to store log files for the new database
NumBuffers	Identifies the number of buffers to use to perform the version recovery operation (by default, two buffers are used if this option is not specified)
BufferSize	Identifies the size, in pages, of each buffer used to perform the backup operation (by default, the value of the restbufsz DB2 database manager configuration parameter determines the size of each buffer used by the Restore utility)
ScriptFile	Identifies the name of the file to which to write all commands needed to perform a redirected restore operation
ParallelNum	Identifies the number of table spaces that can be read in parallel during the version recovery operation

Thus, if you want to restore a database named SAMPLE (which already exists), using a full backup image stored in a directory named BACKUPS on logical disk drive E: on Windows, you could do so by executing a RESTORE DATABASE command that looks something like this:

```
RESTORE DATABASE sample
USER db2admin USING ibmdb2
FROM E:\backups
REPLACE EXISTING WITHOUT PROMPTING
```

However, if you want to restore a table space named USERSPACE1 from an incremental backup image stored in a directory named BACKUPS on logical disk drive E: while the database it is associated with (named SAMPLE) remains online, you would execute a RESTORE DATABASE command that looks something like this:

```
RESTORE DATABASE sample
USER db2admin USING ibmdb2
TABLESPACE (USERSPACE1) ONLINE
INCREMENTAL
FROM E:\backups
```

Each full database backup image contains, among other things, a copy of the database's recovery history file. However, when an existing database is restored from a full database backup image, the existing recovery history file is not overwritten. But what if the recovery history file for the database happens to be corrupted? Can the recovery history file be restored as well, given that a copy exists in the database backup image? The answer is yes. Using a special form of the RESTORE DATABASE command, you can restore *just* the recovery history file from a database backup image. Such a RESTORE DATABASE command looks something like this:

```
RESTORE DATABASE sample
HISTORY FILE
FROM E:\backups
```

It is also possible to create an entirely new database from a full database backup image, effectively cloning an existing database. Thus, you could create a new database named SAMPLE_2 that is an exact duplicate of a database named SAMPLE, using a backup image stored in a directory named BACKUPS on logical disk drive E: by executing a RESTORE DATABASE command that looks something like this:

```
RESTORE DATABASE sample
USER db2admin USING ibmdb2
FROM E:\backups
INTO sample2
```

It is important to note that if you use a backup image to create a new database, the recovery history file stored in the backup image will become the recovery history file for the new database.

You can also perform any of the restore/recovery operations just described (along with many others) using IBM Data Studio. Figure 7.17 shows the Data Studio menu items that you must select to activate the Restore Database wizard.

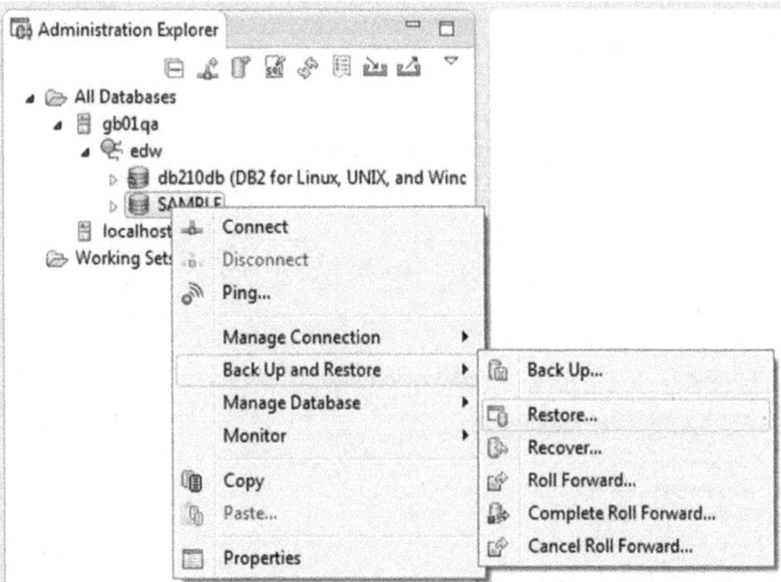

Figure 7.17: Invoking the Restore Data wizard from IBM Data Studio

Figure 7.18 illustrates how the first page of the Restore Database wizard's Restore Type window might look immediately after activation. You can choose to restore on an existing current database or to a new database.

In Figure 7.19, you can see that the Restore Objects wizard provides many restore options, including restoring the entire database, restoring only the history file, or restoring one or more table spaces. It also enables you to choose the restore image from the available backup images in the table format, as in Figure 7.20.

Restore Type
Restore Objects
Restore Containers
Restore Options

Select the type of restore

Database details
Database: SAMPLE
Last backup time: 07/27/2014 19:00:03
Logging type: ARCHIVE

Restore target
Restore the backup to the current database
Restore the backup to a different database

Database name and location
Database name: SAMPLE2
Database location (for Windows, if DB2_CREATE_DB_ON_PATH is not set or set to NO, the location must only be a letter drive):
Browse...

Figure 7.18: Restore Type wizard

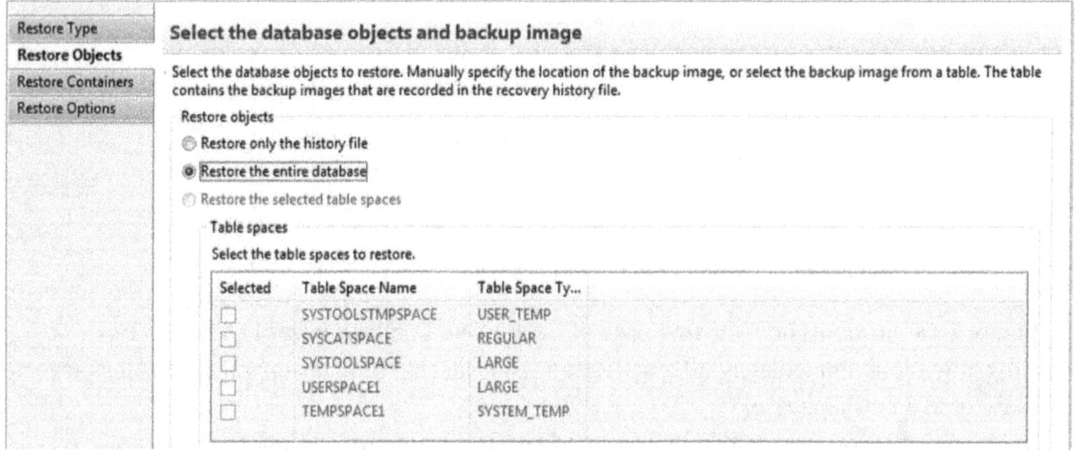

Figure 7.19: Restore Objects wizard

Figure 7.21 shows the Restore Containers wizard, which you can use to perform redirected restore operations by setting system-managed and database-managed table space containers to an available path on the server. The redirected restore operation will be discussed in more detail in the next section.

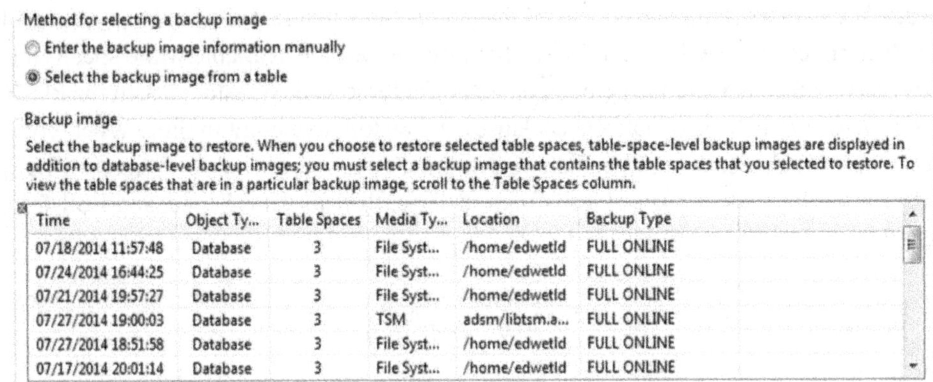

Figure 7.20: Restore Backup Image table

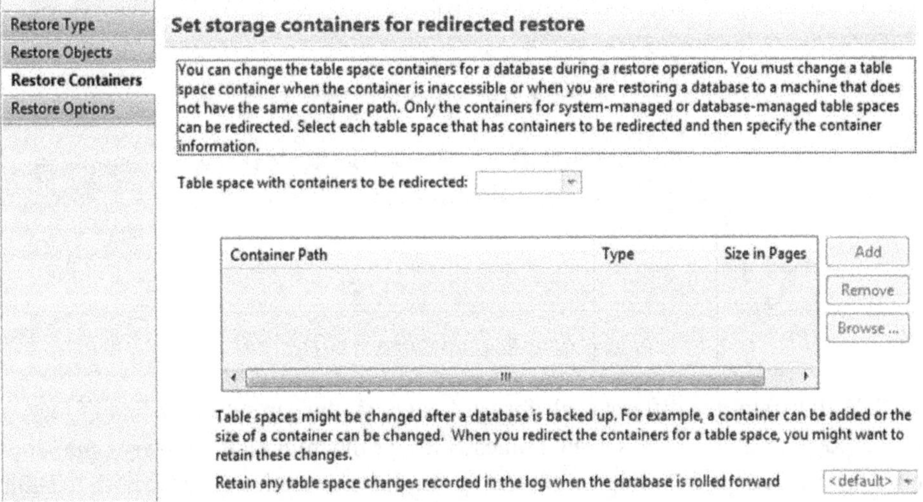

Figure 7.21: Restore Containers wizard

Figure 7.22 displays the Restore Options wizard, which consists of options for replacing the database history file, specifying the active log path (newlogpath database configuration parameter), and designating the path to extract the logs within the database backup image (this applies when you take a backup with the INCLUDE LOGS option and is the default behavior).

You can choose to forcefully terminate all the connections before restoring by selecting the **Remove all connections** check box. Two roll-forward options are available while specifying the restore: restore the database only (that means the database will be restored with the RESTORE command's WITHOUT ROLLING FORWARD clause) and restore to a point in time. When you choose to restore the database to a specific point in time, three more window options will display in the left pane of the Restore wizard: Roll-forward Type, Roll-forward Scope, and Roll-forward Final State.

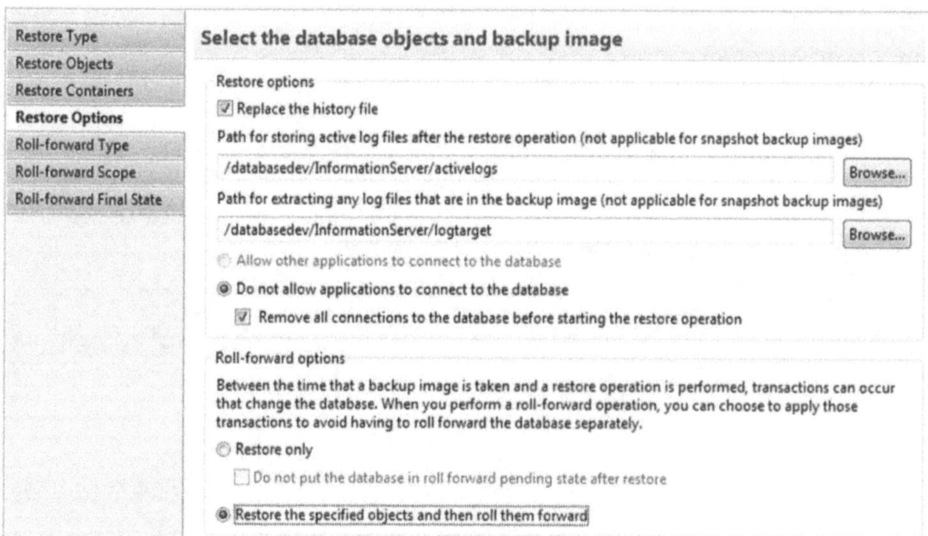

Figure 7.22: Restore Options wizard

Figure 7.23 illustrates the different roll-forward options; you can select the end of logs, a point in time (local or UTC and associated timestamp), or the minimum recovery time. You can also choose the archive log location, such as using the default location (newlogpath location), disabling the retrieval of archive logs (it basically uses END OF BACKUP to complete the roll-forward), and specifying an alternative path to find the archive logs (generally the log target path).

Figure 7.24 shows Roll-forward Scope in terms of which object you would like to roll-forward (an entire database or a particular table space). This wizard also helps you recover dropped tables by providing a dropped table recovery option.

Figure 7.25 shows the final states of Roll-forward, which the wizard allows you to choose. If you want to keep the database in the Roll-forward Pending state to apply more transaction logs in the future as part of the log shipping disaster recovery process, you could select **Leave in roll-forward pending state**, and if you want to activate the database to allow connections, opt for **Complete the roll-forward operation and return to the active state**.

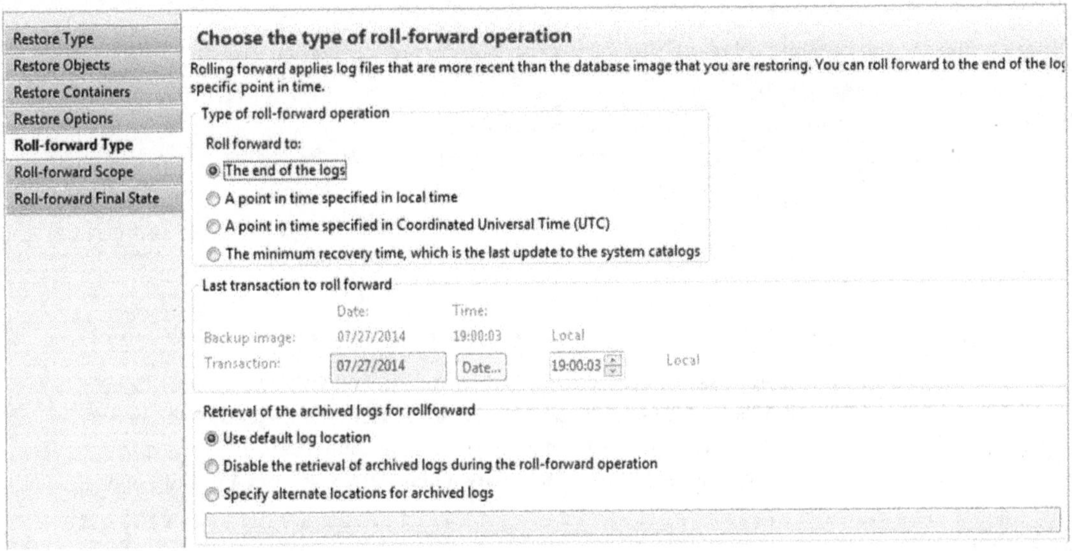

Figure 7.23: Restore Roll-forward Type wizard

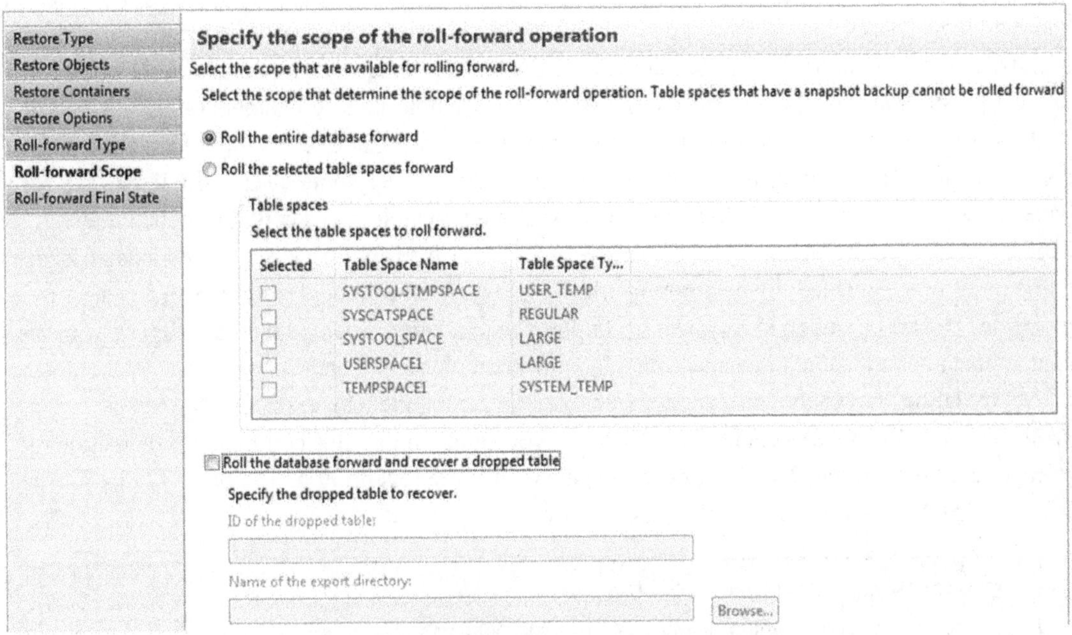

Figure 7.24: Restore Roll-forward Scope wizard

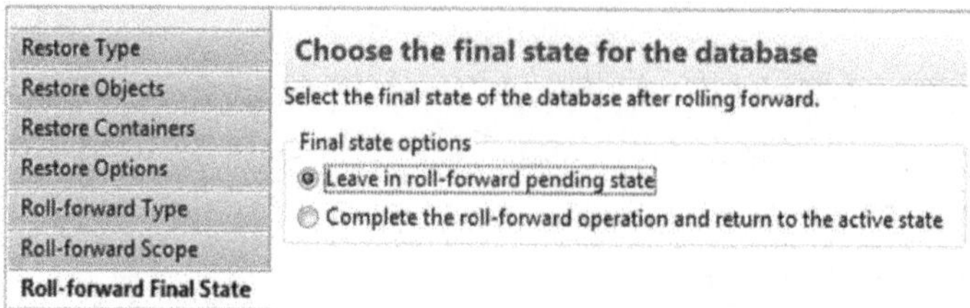

Figure 7.25: Restore Roll-forward Final State wizard

Note: Only users with System Administrator (SYSADM), System Control (SYSCTRL), or System Maintenance (SYSMAINT) authority are allowed to restore a database or table spaces from a backup image. Only users with SYSADM and SYSCTRL authority are allowed to create a new database from a backup image.

Redirected Restore Operation

As you might imagine, a full backup image of a database contains, among other things, information about all table spaces that have been defined for the database, including specific information about each table space container being used at the time the backup image was made. During a version recovery operation, a check is performed to verify that all table space containers referenced by the backup image exist and are accessible. If this check determines that one or more of the table space containers needed is no longer available or accessible, the recovery operation will fail, and the database will not be restored. When this happens, all invalid table space containers encountered can be redefined at the beginning of the recovery process (this is not necessary when a database is automatic storage enabled) by performing what is known as a redirected restore. You can also use a redirected restore operation to restore a backup image to a target machine that is different from the source machine or to store table space data in a different physical location.

You redefine unavailable or inaccessible table space containers by executing the SET TABLESPACE CONTAINERS command. However, you cannot apply this command to the automatic storage table spaces; the DB2 database manager will handle redefinition. The basic syntax for the SET TABLESPACE CONTAINERS command is:

```
SET TABLESPACE CONTAINERS FOR [TS_ID]
[(REPLAY | IGNORE) ROLLFORWARD CONTAINER OPERATIONS]
USING [AUTOMATIC STORAGE | (PATH '[Container]' ,...) |
  ([FILE | DEVICE] '[Container]' [ContainerSize] ,...)]
```

where:

TS_ID	Identifies the identification number assigned to the table space for which to provide new storage containers
Container	Identifies one or more containers to use to store the data associated with the table space specified
ContainerSize	Identifies the number of pages to store in the table space container specified

The steps to perform a redirected restore operation are as follows:

Step 1: Start the redirected restore operation by executing the RESTORE DATABASE command with the REDIRECT option specified. When you specify this option, each invalid table space container encountered is flagged, and all table spaces that reference invalid table space containers are placed in the Restore Pending state. To display a list of all table spaces affected, execute the LIST TABLESPACES command. At some point, you should see a message that looks something like this:

```
SQL1277W A redirected restore operation is being performed. During a table
space restore, only table spaces being restored can have their paths
reconfigured. During a database restore, storage group storage paths and DMS
table space containers can be reconfigured.
DB20000I The RESTORE DATABASE command completed successfully.
```

Step 2: Specify the storage group paths for the database to restore by using the SET STOGROUP PATHS command

or

Specify new table space containers for each table space placed in Restore Pending state by executing a SET TABLESPACE CONTAINERS command for each appropriate table space. Keep in mind that SMS table spaces can use only PATH containers, whereas DMS table spaces can use only FILE or DEVICE containers. And all the AUTOMATIC STORAGE PATHs will automatically be set by DB2.

Step 3: Complete the redirected restore operation by executing the RESTORE DATABASE command again with the CONTINUE option specified.

To simplify things, you can code all these steps in a UNIX shell script or Windows batch file, which you can then execute from a system prompt.

Such a file would look something like this:

```
RESTORE DATABASE sample FROM '/db2backup'
TAKEN AT 20130629092421 ON '/database'
DBPATH ON '/database' INTO sample2
REDIRECT WITHOUT PROMPTING;
SET TABLESPACE CONTAINERS FOR 4 USING (PATH '/database/temp/ts_temp_16k');
SET TABLESPACE CONTAINERS FOR 7 USING (FILE '/database/index/ts_index_16k ' 2000);
RESTORE DATABASE sample CONTINUE;
```

From DB2 9.1 onward, you can use the RESTORE DATABASE command's REDIRECT GENERATE SCRIPT option to automatically create the restore script file. You can then modify the script produced, and run the script to perform the redirected restore operation. For example, to generate a redirected restore script based on an existing backup image of a database named SAMPLE that resides on a Linux server, execute a RESTORE DATABASE command that looks something like this:

```
RESTORE DATABASE SAMPLE FROM
/db2backup TAKEN AT 20130629092421 ON /database
INTO SAMPLE2 REDIRECT GENERATE SCRIPT redirect_SAMPLE.ddl;
```

Tip: While performing a database restoration from one system to another, you set the DB2 registry variable DB2_RESTORE_GRANT_ADMIN_AUTHORITIES to YES to grant SECADM, DBADM, DATAACCESS, and ACCESSCTRL privileges on the target database to the user who is to perform the restore operation.

Note: In addition to providing new storage containers for table spaces when older table space containers are inaccessible or are no longer present, a redirected restore can also add new containers to existing SMS table spaces. The ALTER TABLESPACE command does not allow you to add new storage containers to existing SMS table spaces; a redirected restore provides a workaround to this limitation.

Database Rebuild Operation

In earlier versions of DB2, we were supposed to have full, incremental, and delta backup images to recover the database from any failure. With the DB2 9.1 database rebuild feature, you can rebuild an entire database by using a set of table space–level backups, which means that you no longer have to take a full database backup. Also, this feature provides the capability to rebuild the database with very limited table spaces at the start and add the remaining as required. In a critical recovery situation, you may need to bring certain table spaces online faster than others to make your application available to the business.

Table 7.2 illustrates some rebuild recovery scenarios based on the business requirement and the database recovery type.

Table 7.2: Rebuild database recovery scenarios

Recovery Requirement	Backup Media Type	Method
Entire database recovery	• Online/offline full database backup • Table space–level backup • Incremental/delta backup • Associated transaction logs	REBUILD WITH ALL
Certain table spaces recovery only	• Online/offline full database backup • Table space–level backup • Incremental/delta backup • Associated transaction logs	REBUILD WITH TABLESPACE
Entire database recovery on a different file system	Online full database backup and associated transaction logs	REBUILD WITH ALL ....REDIRECT
Entire database recovery or certain table spaces recovery only	Offline unrecoverable database backup	The above specified options are all valid for an unrecoverable database REBUILD operation without a roll-forward; however, in case of certain table space recovery, table spaces not restored can no longer be recovered.

The steps to perform a rebuild of database SAMPLE that has six table spaces—SYSCATSPACE, USERSPACE1, TEMPSPACE1, IBMDB2SAMPLEREL, IBMDB2SAMPLEXML, and SYSTOOLSPACE—are as follows:

Step 1: Start the restore/rebuild operation on application critical table space USERSPACE1. You must include SYSCATSPACE in the first rebuild because this table space holds all the system catalog information:

```
RESTORE DATABASE sample
REBUILD WITH TABLESPACE (SYSCATSPACE, USERSPACE1)
TAKEN AT 20130630124123
LOGTARGET /db2backup/logs
```

Step 2: Execute the ROLLFORWARD DATABASE (you will see details in later pages) command to apply any changes recorded in the transaction log:

```
ROLLFORWARD DATABASE sample
TO END OF LOGS AND STOP
OVERFLOW LOG PATH (/db2backup/logs)
```

Now, you should see a message that looks something like this:

```
SQL1271W Database "SAMPLE" is recovered but one or more table spaces are
offline on members or nodes "0".
```

At this stage, the SAMPLE database is connectable. The LIST TABLESPACES command will show you the status of each table space. You should see SYSCATSPACE, TEMPSPACE1, USERSPACE1, and SYSTOOLSPACE in state *0x0000* (normal) and IBMDB2SAMPLEREL and IBMDB2SAMPLEXML in state *0x0100* (restore pending).

Step 3: Start the second phase of the restore operation to restore the IBMDB2SAMPLEREL and IBMDB2SAMPLEXML table spaces, followed by a ROLLFORWARD command. You can do this activity online without affecting the application connections and the functionality:

```
RESTORE DATABASE sample TABLESPACE (IBMDB2SAMPLEXML, IBMDB2SAMPLEREL) TAKEN
AT 20130630124123;

ROLLFORWARD DATABASE sample TO END OF LOGS AND STOP TABLESPACE
(IBMDB2SAMPLEXML, IBMDB2SAMPLEREL) OVERFLOW LOG PATH (/db2backup/logs)

Rollforward Status

Input database alias                    = sample
Number of members have returned status  = 1

Member ID                               = 0
Rollforward status                      = not pending
Next log file to be read                =
                                                                Continued
```

```
Log files processed                        = -
Last committed transaction                 = 2013-06-30-12.41.25.000000 UTC

DB20000I  The ROLLFORWARD command completed successfully.
```

Now, you should see all the table spaces of database SAMPLE in the Normal state.

The DB2 Roll-forward Utility

When you use a backup image to restore a damaged or corrupted database, you can return the database only to the state it was in at the time the backup image was made. Therefore, all changes made to the database after the backup image was created will be lost when a version recovery operation is performed. To return a database to the state it was in at any given point in time, you must use roll-forward recovery instead. And to perform a roll-forward recovery operation, the database must be recoverable (that is, the database must be configured to use archival logging), you must have a full backup image of the database available (REBUILD is an exception), and you must have access to all archived log files that have been created since the last backup image (full, incremental, or delta) was made.

Roll-forward recovery starts out as a version recovery operation. However, where a version recovery operation will leave a nonrecoverable database in a Normal state, the same operation will leave a recoverable database in Roll-forward Pending state (unless you specify the WITHOUT ROLLING FORWARD option with the RESTORE DATABASE command that you used to recover the database). At that point, either the database can be taken out of Roll-forward Pending state (in which case, all changes made to the database since the backup image used for version recovery was made will be lost), or information stored in the database's transaction log files can be replayed to return the database to the state it was in at any given point in time.

The process of replaying transactions stored in archived log files is known as *rolling the database forward*. One way to roll a database forward is by executing the ROLLFORWARD DATABASE command. The basic syntax for this command is:

```
ROLLFORWARD [DATABASE | DB] [DatabaseAlias]
<USER [UserName] <USING [Password]>>
<TO [PointInTime] <USING [UTC | LOCAL] TIME>
    <AND [COMPLETE | STOP]> |
        END OF LOGS <AND [COMPLETE | STOP]> |
        COMPLETE |
```

Continued

```
        STOP |
        CANCEL |
        QUERY STATUS <USING [UTC | LOCAL] TIME>>
<TABLESPACE ONLINE |
   TABLESPACE <( [TS_Name] ,... )> <ONLINE>>
<OVERFLOW LOG PATH ([LogDirectory] ,...)>
<RECOVER DROPPED TABLE [TableID] TO [Location]>
```

where:

DatabaseAlias	Identifies the alias assigned to the database to roll forward
UserName	Identifies the name assigned to a specific user who is to perform the roll-forward operation
Password	Identifies the password that corresponds to the name of the user who is to perform the roll-forward operation
PointInTime	Identifies a specific point in time, identified by a timestamp value in the form *yyyy-mm-dd-hh.mm.ss.nnnnnn* (year, month, day, hour, minutes, seconds, micro seconds), to which that the database is to be rolled forward (only transactions that took place before and up to the date and time specified will be reapplied to the database)
TS_Name	Identifies the name assigned to one or more specific table spaces to roll forward (if the table space name has changed since the backup image used to restore the database was made, specify the new name)
LogDirectory	Identifies the directory that contains offline archived log files to use to perform the roll-forward operation
TableID	Identifies a specific table (by ID) that was dropped earlier to restore as part of the roll-forward operation (to obtain the table ID, examine the database's recovery history file)
Location	Identifies the directory to which to write files containing dropped table data when the table is restored as part of the roll-forward operation

Specifying the AND COMPLETE, AND STOP, COMPLETE, or STOP option (actually STOP and COMPLETE options are synonyms for each other) will return the database to Normal state when the roll-forward operation has completed. Otherwise, the database will remain in Roll-forward Pending state. (When a recoverable database is restored from a backup image, it is automatically placed in Roll-forward Pending state unless you use the WITHOUT ROLLING FORWARD option with the RESTORE DATABASE command; while a database is in Roll-forward Pending state, users and applications cannot access it.)

If you specify the QUERY STATUS option, a list of the log files used to perform the roll-forward recovery operation, along with the next archive file required, and the timestamp (in UTC) of the last committed transaction since roll-forward processing began is returned.

Thus, to perform a roll-forward recovery operation on a database named SAMPLE that was just restored from a backup image, execute a ROLLFORWARD DATABASE command that looks something like this:

```
ROLLFORWARD DATABASE sample TO END OF LOGS AND STOP
```

However, if you want to perform a roll-forward recovery operation on a table space (this can be activated only when you intend to do a table space recovery instead of a full database recovery) named TS_SMALL_DATA in a database named SAMPLE by reapplying transactions that were performed against the table space on or before June 1, 2013, you would execute a ROLLFORWARD DATABASE command that looks something like this:

```
ROLLFORWARD DATABASE sample TO 2013-06-01-00.00.00.0000
AND STOP TABLESPACE (TS_SMALL_DATA)
```

It is important to note that the time value you specify is interpreted as a Coordinated Universal Time (UTC)—otherwise known as Greenwich Mean Time (GMT)—value. If a ROLLFORWARD DATABASE command that looks something like the following had been executed instead, the time value specified would have been interpreted as a local time value:

```
ROLLFORWARD DATABASE sample TO 2013-06-01-00.00.00.0000 USING LOCAL TIME AND
STOP TABLESPACE (TS_SMALL_DATA)
```

Note: When you roll a table space forward to a specific point in time, the time you specify must be greater than the minimum recovery time recorded for the table space. You can obtain this time by executing the following command:

```
SELECT VARCHAR (TBSP_NAME, 30) AS TBSP_NAME, TABLESPACE_MIN_RECOVERY_TIME
   FROM TABLE (MON_GET_TABLESPACE ('',-2)) AS T;
```

Among other things, this command returns the earliest point in time to which each table space can be rolled forward. (The minimum recovery time is updated when DDL statements are run against a table space or against tables stored in a table space.) A table space must be rolled forward to at least the minimum recovery time so that it becomes synchronized with the information in the system catalog tables. If recovering more than one table space, you must roll each table space forward to at least the highest minimum recovery time of all the table spaces being recovered.

Tip: When restoring a database from a source server having a higher memory configuration to a target server having a lower memory configuration, you might receive an SQL1218N error during a roll-forward operation or during the database activation due to memory constraints on the target server. The workaround is to set the DB2_OVERRIDE_BPF registry variable on the target server to a small number of buffer pool pages to avoid the database manager attempting to allocate large buffer pools consuming all the server memory.

To temporarily change all the buffer pool sizes in the database to 5,000 pages, use this command:

```
db2set DB2_OVERRIDE_BPF=5000
```

To temporarily change the number of pages only for the BUFFERPOOL ID 1 in the database to 5,000 pages, use this command:

```
db2set DB2_OVERRIDE_BPF=1,5000
```

The DB2_OVERRIDE_BPF setting will not affect the DB2 system buffer pools.

If you want to roll a table space forward to a specific point in time, and a table in the table space participates in a referential integrity constraint with another table that resides in another table space, roll both table spaces forward simultaneously to the same point in time. If you do not, the child table in the referential integrity relationship will be placed in Set Integrity Pending state at the end of the roll-forward recovery operation, and constraint checking will have to be performed on the table before it can be used.

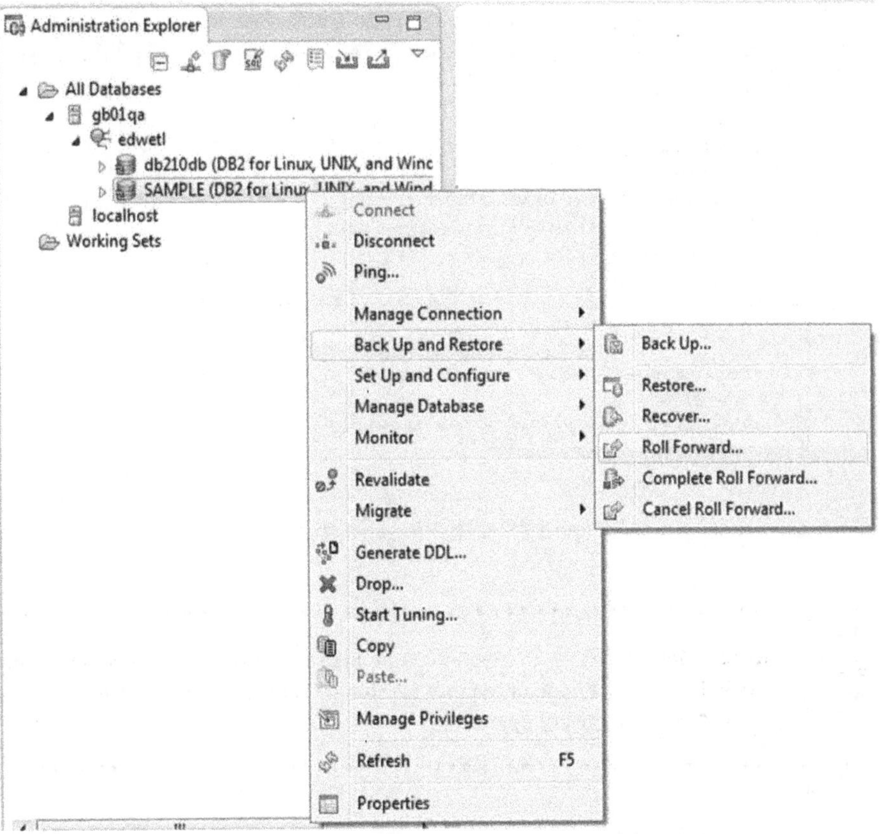

Figure 7.26: Invoking the Roll-forward wizard from IBM Data Studio

You can also initiate a roll-forward recovery operation by using the Roll-forward wizard, which you can activate by selecting the **Roll Forward** action from the **Backup and Restore** menu in IBM Data Studio. Figure 7.26 shows the Data Studio menu items you must select to activate the Roll-forward wizard.

Figure 7.27 shows how the first page of the Roll-forward wizard might look immediately after activation. As you can see, this wizard provides many roll-forward window options, such as Roll-forward Type, Roll-forward Scope, and Roll-forward Final State, similar to what was discussed in the Restore section.

Roll-forward Type
Roll-forward Scope
Roll-forward Final State

Choose the type of roll-forward operation

Rolling forward applies log files that are more recent than the database image that you are restoring. You can roll forward to the end of the logs or to a specific point in time.

Type of roll-forward operation

Roll forward to:

The end of the logs

A point in time specified in local time

A point in time specified in Coordinated Universal Time (UTC)

The minimum recovery time, which is the last update to the system catalogs

Last transaction to roll forward

Date: Time:

Backup image: 07/27/2014 19:00:03 Local

Transaction: 07/27/2014 Date... 19:00:03 Local

Retrieval of the archived logs for rollforward

Use default log location

Disable the retrieval of archived logs during the roll-forward operation

Specify alternate locations for archived logs

Browse...

Figure 7.27: Roll-forward steps

Note: Only users with System Administrator (SYSADM), System Control (SYSCTRL), or System Maintenance (SYSMAINT) authority are allowed to perform a roll-forward recovery operation.

A Word About the Recovery History File

In Chapter 3, "Physical Design," you saw that a special file, known as the *recovery history file*, is created as part of the database creation process. This file's purpose is to log historical information about specific actions that are performed against the database with which the file is associated. Specifically, records are written to the recovery history file whenever you perform any of the following actions:

- A backup image of any type is created
- A version recovery operation is performed either on the database or on one of its table spaces
- A table is loaded, using the Load utility
- A roll-forward recovery operation is performed either on the database or on one of its table spaces
- A table space is altered, renamed, or both

- A table space is quiesced
- Data in a table is reorganized, using the REORG utility
- Statistics for a table are updated, using the RUNSTATS utility
- A table is deleted (dropped)
- A log file is archived

In addition to identifying the performed event, each entry in the recovery history file identifies the date and time the event occurred, how the event took place, the table spaces and tables affected and, if the action was a backup operation, the storage location of the resulting backup image, along with information on how to access this image. And because the recovery history file contains image location information for each backup image, it acts as a tracking and verification mechanism during version recovery operations.

The recovery history file sits quietly in the background and the DB2 database manager is responsible for managing its contents, so a database administrator rarely has to interact with it. However, two commands—LIST HISTORY and PRUNE HISTORY—provide a way to both view the contents of a database's recovery history file and remove one or more entries stored in it. Additionally, if the recovery history file for a database becomes corrupt, it is possible to restore just the recovery history file from a database backup image.

Note: To easily view information from the recovery history files, use the SYSIBMADM.DB_HISTORY administrative view instead of reading through the file. This administrative view also returns information from the history files from all the database partitions in a Database Partitioning Feature environment.

The DB2 Recover Utility

Earlier, you saw how using the RESTORE DATABASE command can return a database to the state it was in at the time a backup image was made, and how using the ROLLFORWARD DATABASE command can replay information recorded in a database's transaction to restore the database from a full database backup image. This process is pretty straightforward. However, if you have a full database backup image and several incremental backup images, delta backup images, or table space backup images, the process can be a little complicated. That is where DB2's Recover utility comes in.

The Recover utility performs the necessary restore and roll-forward operations to recover a database to a specific point in time, based on information it finds in the recovery history file. To invoke the Recover utility, execute the RECOVER DATABASE command. The basic syntax for this command is:

```
RECOVER [DATABASE | DB] [DatabaseAlias]
<TO [PointInTime] <USING [UTC | LOCAL] TIME> |
    END OF LOGS>
<USER [UserName] <USING [Password]>>
<USING HISTORY FILE ([HistoryFile])>
<OVERFLOW LOG PATH ([LogDirectory] ,...)>
<RESTART>
```

where:

DatabaseAlias	Identifies the alias assigned to the database associated with the backup image to use to perform a version recovery operation
PointInTime	Identifies a specific point in time, identified by a timestamp value in the form *yyyy-mm-dd-hh.mm.ss.nnnnnn* (year, month, day, hour, minutes, seconds, micro seconds), to which to roll the database forward (only transactions that occur before and up to the specified date and time will be reapplied to the database)
UserName	Identifies the name assigned to the specific user who is to perform the recovery operation
Password	Identifies the password that corresponds to the name of the user who is to perform the recovery operation
HistoryFile	Identifies the name assigned to the recovery history log file that the Recovery utility is to use
LogDirectory	Identifies the directory that contains offline archived log files to use to perform the roll-forward portion of the recovery operation

Thus, to perform a full recovery operation on a database named SAMPLE (which already exists) by using information stored in the recovery history file, you could do so by executing a RECOVER DATABASE command that looks something like this:

```
RECOVER DATABASE sample TO END OF LOGS
```

However, if you want to restore a database named SAMPLE and roll it forward to an extremely old point in time that the current recovery history file no longer contains, you would execute a

RECOVER DATABASE command that looks something like this (assuming you have a copy of an older recovery history file):

```
RECOVER DATABASE sample TO 2013-06-30-20.09.34.000000
USING HISTORY FILE (/db2backup/db2rhist.asc)
```

It is important to note that if the Recover utility successfully restores a database, but for some reason fails while attempting to roll it forward, the Recover utility will attempt to continue the previous recover operation, without redoing the restore phase. If you want to force the Recover utility to redo the complete restore, you execute the RECOVER DATABASE command with the RESTART option specified. There is no way to explicitly restart a recovery operation from a point of failure.

Rebuilding Invalid Indexes

So far we have looked at ways to recover data in the event the storage media holding a database's files become corrupted or fail. But what if only indexes are damaged, and a database's data is unaffected (which could be the case if data and indexes are stored in separate table spaces and only the physical device where index data is stored fails)? In this situation, the affected indexes are invalidated and can be recovered by being re-created once the faulty media has been replaced.

Whenever the DB2 database manager detects that an index is no longer valid, it automatically attempts to rebuild it. However, the point in time at which the DB2 database manager attempts to rebuild an invalid index is controlled by the indexrec parameter of the database or the DB2 database manager configuration file. This parameter has three possible settings:

- SYSTEM. Invalid indexes are to be rebuilt at the time specified in the indexrec parameter of the DB2 database manager configuration file. This setting is valid only for database configuration files.
- RESTART. Invalid indexes are to be rebuilt, either explicitly or implicitly, when the database is restarted (i.e., when crash recovery is performed on the database).
- ACCESS. Invalid indexes are to be rebuilt the first time they are accessed after they have been marked as being invalid.

So when is the best time to rebuild invalid indexes? If the time required to perform a crash recovery operation on a database is not a concern, it is better to let the DB2 database manager rebuild invalid indexes while it is in the process of returning the database to a consistent state. The time needed to restart a database will be longer because of the index re-creation process, but once the database has been restored, query processing will not be affected. However, crash recovery will be performed faster if indexes are rebuilt as they are accessed, though users may experience a decrease in performance—queries against tables that contain associated invalid indexes will have to wait for the invalid indexes to be rebuilt before they can be processed. Furthermore, unexpected locks may be acquired and held long after an invalid index has been re-created, especially if the transaction that caused the index re-creation to occur is not committed (or rolled back) for some time.

Although you can use the indexrec parameter of the database or the DB2 database manager configuration file to control when indexes are rebuilt as part of a crash recovery operation, indexrec has no effect on how indexes are rebuilt during roll-forward recovery operations. To control that behavior, you must assign the appropriate value to the logindexbuild database configuration parameter. This parameter has two possible settings:

- ON. Index creation, re-creation, and reorganization operations are to be recorded in the database's transaction log files so that indexes can be reconstructed during roll-forward recovery operations or HADR log replay operations.
- OFF. Index creation, re-creation, and reorganization operations will not be recorded in the database's transaction log files.

If you set the LOG INDEX BUILD table attribute to its default value of NULL, DB2 will use the value specified for the logindexbuild database configuration parameter. If you set the LOG INDEX BUILD table attribute to ON or OFF, the value specified for the logindexbuild database configuration parameter will be ignored.

Backing Up a Database with Split Mirroring

It was mentioned earlier that as databases increase in size and as heavy usage demands require databases to be available 24 x 7, the time and hardware needed to back up and restore a database can grow substantially. Backing up an entire database or several table spaces of a large database can put a strain on system resources, require a considerable amount of additional storage space (to hold the backup images), and reduce the availability of the database system (particularly if the system has to be taken offline to be backed up). Therefore, a popular alternative to creating and maintaining backup images of high-availability databases is to use what is known as a *split mirror*.

A split mirror is an "instantaneous" copy of a database that is made by mirroring the disk or disks that contain the database's data and splitting the mirror when a backup copy of the database is required. Mirroring is the process of writing all database data to two separate disks (or disk subsystems) simultaneously; one disk/subsystem holds the database data, and the other holds an exact copy (known as a mirror) of the primary disk/subsystem being used. Splitting a mirror simply involves separating the primary and secondary copies of the database from each other. Split mirroring provides the following advantages:

- The overhead required to create backup images of the database is eliminated.
- Entire systems can be cloned very quickly.
- It provides a fast implementation of idle standby failover.

To further enhance split mirroring, DB2 offers a way to temporarily suspend (and later resume) all database I/O so that a mirror can be split without having to take a database offline. The command that provides this functionality is SET WRITE, and the syntax for this command is:

```
SET WRITE SUSPEND FOR DATABASE [INCLUDE LOGS | EXCLUDE LOGS]
```

Therefore, if you want to temporarily suspend all I/O for a database, you would do so by establishing a connection to that database and executing a SET WRITE command that looks like this:

```
SET WRITE SUSPEND FOR DATABASE
```

When executed, the SET WRITE SUSPEND FOR DATABASE INCLUDE LOGS command causes the DB2 database manager to suspend all write operations to table space containers and log files (if the EXCLUDE LOGS clause is specified within the SET WRITE SUSPEND command, logs will not be suspended for write operations) that are associated with the current database. The suspension of writes to table spaces and log files is intended to prevent partial page writes from occurring until the suspension is removed. All operations, apart from online backup and restore operations will function normally while database writes are suspended. That is because read-only transactions are not suspended and can continue working with a write-suspended database provided they do not require I/O processing; applications can continue to perform insert, update, and delete operations with data that has been cached in the database's buffer pools, but new pages cannot be read from disk. Additionally, new database connections can be established to a write-suspended database if the system catalog pages required to authenticate the connections already reside in a buffer pool. Optionally, you can use the FLUSH BUFFERPOOLS ALL statement before the SET WRITE SUSPEND command to minimize the recovery time of the standby database.

Once you suspend the database for write operations, create one or more split mirrors from the primary database by using the appropriate operating system and storage commands.

To resume I/O for a write-suspended database at any time, execute a SET WRITE command that looks like this:

```
SET WRITE RESUME FOR DATABASE
```

When executed, the SET WRITE RESUME FOR DATABASE command causes the DB2 database manager to lift all write suspensions and to allow write operations to table space containers and log files associated with the current database to continue.

Note: You can execute the SET WRITE RESUME FOR DATABASE command from any other session, so there is no limitation around executing it from the same connection session from which the SET WRITE SUSPEND FOR DATABASE command was issued.

You can determine the state of I/O write operations on the database by viewing the SUSPEND_IO database configration parameter or by using the MON_GET_TABLESPACE table function. Let us run through the steps on database SAMPLE to see what the outcomes are.

Step 1: Connect to the primary database SAMPLE:

```
CONNECT TO sample;
   Database Connection Information

 Database server        = DB2/LINUXX8664 10.1.3
 SQL authorization ID   = MOHAN
 Local database alias   = SAMPLE
```

Step 2: Flush the data from the buffer pool to the disk from the primary database:

```
FLUSH BUFFERPOOLS ALL
DB20000I  The SQL command completed successfully.
```

Step 3: Suspend the I/O write operations on the primary database:

```
SET WRITE SUSPEND FOR DATABASE EXCLUDE LOGS
DB20000I  The SET WRITE command completed successfully.
```

Step 4: Check the status of the table spaces:

```
SELECT VARCHAR(TBSP_NAME, 30) AS TBSP_NAME, VARCHAR(TBSP_STATE,30) AS
TBSP_STATE FROM TABLE(MON_GET_TABLESPACE('',-2)) AS T

TBSP_NAME                      TBSP_STATE
------------------------------ ------------------------------
SYSCATSPACE                    SUSPEND_WRITE
TEMPSPACE1                     SUSPEND_WRITE
USERSPACE1                     SUSPEND_WRITE
SYSTOOLSPACE                   SUSPEND_WRITE
SYSTOOLSTMPSPACE               SUSPEND_WRITE

  5 record(s) selected.
```

You can also validate this by using the GET DB CFG command:

```
GET DB CFG FOR sample | grep -i SUSPEND
Database is in write suspend state           = YES
```

Step 5: Create one or more split mirrors from the primary database by using the appropriate operating system and storage commands.

Step 6: Resume the I/O write operations on the primary database:

```
SET WRITE RESUME FOR DATABASE
DB20000I  The SET WRITE command completed successfully.
```

Initializing a Split Mirror with db2inidb

Before you can use a split mirror copy of a DB2 database, you must first initialize it by executing the system command db2inidb. The syntax for this command is:

```
db2inidb [DatabaseAlias]
AS [SNAPSHOT | MIRROR | STANDBY]
<RELOCATE USING [ConfigFile]>
```

where:

DatabaseAlias	Identifies the alias assigned to the database that the split mirror copy to initialize is to reference
ConfigFile	Indicates to relocate database files contained in the split mirror copy according to information stored in the specified configuration file

As you can see, a split mirror database copy can be initialized in one of three ways:

- SNAPSHOT. The split mirror copy of the database will be initialized as a read-only clone of the primary database.
- MIRROR. The split mirror copy of the database will be initialized as a backup image to use to restore the primary database.
- STANDBY. The split mirror copy of the database will be initialized and placed in Roll-forward Pending state so that it can be continuously synchronized with the primary database. (New logs from the primary database can be retrieved and applied to the copy of the database at any time.) You can then use the standby copy of the database in place of the primary database if, for some reason, the primary database goes down.

Thus, if you want to initialize a split mirror copy of a database named SAMPLE and make it a backup image to use to restore the primary database, you would execute a db2inidb command that looks like this:

```
db2inidb SAMPLE AS MIRROR
```

High Availability Disaster Recovery (HADR)

HADR is a DB2 database replication feature that provides a high-availability solution for both partial and complete site failures. HADR protects against data loss by replicating data changes from a source database, called the *primary*, to one or more target databases, called the *multiple standby databases*. In an HADR environment, applications can access the current primary database—synchronization with the standby databases occurs by rolling forward transaction log data that is generated on the primary database and shipped to the standby databases. And with HADR, you can choose the level of protection you want from potential loss of data by specifying one of four synchronization modes: synchronous (SYNC), near synchronous (NEARSYNC), asynchronous (ASYNC), and super asynchronous (SUPERASYNC).

HADR's design minimizes the impact to a database system when a partial or a complete site failure occurs. A hardware, network, or software (DB2 or operating system) malfunction can cause a partial site failure. Without HADR, a partial site failure requires restarting the server and the instance where one or more DB2 databases reside. The length of time it takes to restart the server and the instance is unpredictable. If the transaction load was heavy at the time of the partial site failure, it can take several minutes to return a database to a consistent state and make it available for use. With HADR, the principal standby database can take over in seconds. Furthermore, you can redirect the clients that were using the original primary database to the standby database (which is now the new primary database) by implementing the automatic client reroute feature or by retrying logic in the applications that interact with the database.

After the failed original primary server is repaired, it can rejoin the HADR pair as a standby database if both copies of the database can be made consistent. And once the original primary database is reintegrated into the HADR pair as the standby database, you can switch the roles so that the original primary database again functions as the primary database. This is known as a *failback operation.*

A complete site failure can occur when a disaster, such as a fire, destroys the entire site. Because HADR uses TCP/IP to communicate between a primary and the standby databases, the databases can reside in multiple, different locations. For example, your primary database might be at your head office in one city, whereas your principal standby database is at your sales office in another city and auxiliary databases are in marketing office in another city. If a disaster occurs at the primary site, data availability is maintained by having the remote standby database take over as the primary database.

Requirements for HADR Environments

For you to achieve optimal performance with HADR, the system hosting the standby databases will consist of the same hardware and software as the system where the primary database resides. If the system hosting the standby databases has fewer resources than the system hosting the primary database, the standby database may not be able to keep up with the transaction load that the primary database generates. This can cause the standby databases to fall behind or the performance of the primary database to suffer. But more important, if a failover situation occurs, the new primary database may not have the resources needed to adequately service the client applications. And because buffer pool operations performed on the primary database are replayed on the standby database, it is important that the primary and standby database servers have the same amount of memory.

IBM recommends that you use identical host computers for the HADR primary and standby databases. If possible, make sure they are from the same vendor and have the same architecture. Furthermore, the operating system on the primary and standby database servers should be the same version, including patch level. You can violate this rule for a short time during a rolling upgrade, but use extreme caution when doing so. A TCP/IP interface must also exist between the HADR host machines, and be sure to use a high-speed, high-capacity network to connect the two.

The DB2 software installed on both the primary and the standby database server must have the same bit size (32 or 64), and the version of DB2 you use for the primary and standby databases must be identical; for example, both must be either version 10.1 or version 10.5. During rolling upgrades, the modification level (for example, the fix pack level) of the database system for the standby databases can be later than that of the primary database for a short while. However, do not keep this configuration for an extended period. The primary and standby databases will not connect to each other if the modification level of the database system for the primary database is later than that of the standby databases. Therefore, you must always apply fix packs to the standby database systems first.

Both the primary and the standby databases must be single-partition databases, and they all must have the same database name; however, they do not have to be stored on the same database path. Also make sure that the amount of storage space allocated for transaction log files is the same on both the primary and the standby database servers—the use of raw devices for transaction logging is not supported. (Only the current primary database will perform archival logging.)

Table space properties such as table space name, table space type (DMS, SMS, or Automatic Storage), table space page size, table space size, container path, container size, and container type (raw device, file, or directory) must be identical on the primary and standby databases. When you issue a table space statement such as CREATE TABLESPACE, ALTER TABLESPACE, or DROP TABLESPACE on the primary database, it is replayed on the standby databases. Therefore, you must ensure that the table space containers involved with such statements exist on both systems before you issue the table space statement on the primary database. If you create a table space on the primary database, and log replay fails on the standby database because the containers are not available, the primary database will not receive an error message stating that the log replay failed on the standby and all the future writes to this table space can no longer be replayed on the standby. Automatic storage databases are fully supported, including replication of ALTER STOGROUP, RENAME STOGROUP, DROP STOGROUP, and deprecated ALTER DATABASE statements. Similar to table space containers, the specified storage paths must exist on both the primary and the standby servers.

Additionally, once you have established the HADR environment, the following restrictions apply:

- Self-tuning memory manager (STMM) can be run only on the current primary database.
- Backup operations cannot be performed on the standby database.
- Redirected restore is not supported. That is, HADR does not support redirecting table space containers. However, database directory and log directory changes are supported.
- Load operations with the COPY NO option specified are not supported.
- Nonlogged operations, such as database configuration parameter and recovery history file changes will not be replicated to standby servers.
- Clients cannot connect to the standby database unless you have the ROS feature enabled.
- HADR does not support infinite logging and does not fully support federation server.

Table 7.3 shows HADR features at different DB2 version levels and their synchronization mode support, if any.

Table 7.3: HADR feature compatibility matrix			
Feature	**DB2 Version**	**Support**	**Synchronization Mode**
HADR on pureScale	DB2 9.8	No	Not applicable
HADR on pureScale	DB2 10.1	No	Not applicable
HADR Read on Standby	DB2 9.7	Yes	SYNC, NEARSYNC, ASYNC, SUPERASYNC
HADR Multiple Standbys	DB2 10.1	Yes	Principal standby—All Auxiliary standby—SUPERASYNC only

Read on Standby Feature

Starting with DB2 9.7, you can use the ROS capability to offload your read-only operations on the standby server in your HADR solution without affecting the log shipping process. This feature reduces your HADR solution's total cost of ownership (TCO) by utilizing the standby system resources for actual read-only types of business processing and freeing the primary system for additional workload.

The ROS feature is supported in all four HADR synchronization modes (SYNC, NEARSYNC, ASYNC, and SUPERASYNC).

Enabling the ROS Feature

You can enable ROS on the HADR standby database by setting the DB2 instance-level registry variable DB2_HADR_ROS to ON and subsequently restarting the standby instance:

```
db2set DB2_HADR_ROS=ON
```

Data Concurrency on the Active Standby Database

The only isolation level that is supported on the active standby database is Uncommitted Read (UR). Any application requesting more than UR will receive the SQL1773N reason code = 1 error.

You can avoid getting this message by using explicit statement isolation or by setting the DB2 instance-level registry DB2_STANDBY_ISO to UR.

Replay-Only Window on the Active Standby Database

When an HADR active standby database is replaying the DDL log records or maintenance operations such as REORG, the standby database enters into the replay-only window. When the standby is in the replay-only window, all the existing connections are terminated, and new connections are blocked with an error SQL1776N reason code = 4.

You can check the replay-only window status and the start time by using the db2pd command. The following example snippet shows the command output:

```
db2pd -db DB210DB -hadr

Database Member 0 -- Database DB210DB -- Active Standby -- Up 0 days 01:12:41 --
Date 2013-07-07-13.31.04.929726

                            HADR_ROLE = STANDBY
                          REPLAY_TYPE = PHYSICAL
                        HADR_SYNCMODE = SUPERASYNC
                           STANDBY_ID = 0
                        LOG_STREAM_ID = 0
                           HADR_STATE = REMOTE_CATCHUP
                  PRIMARY_MEMBER_HOST = 10.110.20.5
                     PRIMARY_INSTANCE = db2i10
                       PRIMARY_MEMBER = 0
                  STANDBY_MEMBER_HOST = 10.112.0.1
                     STANDBY_INSTANCE = db2i10
                       STANDBY_MEMBER = 0
                  HADR_CONNECT_STATUS = CONNECTED
             HADR_CONNECT_STATUS_TIME = 07/07/2013 12:18:27.054651 (1373199507)
          HEARTBEAT_INTERVAL(seconds) = 30
                HADR_TIMEOUT(seconds) = 120
        TIME_SINCE_LAST_RECV(seconds) = 1
             PEER_WAIT_LIMIT(seconds) = 0
           LOG_HADR_WAIT_CUR(seconds) = 0.000
    LOG_HADR_WAIT_RECENT_AVG(seconds) = 0.020026
   LOG_HADR_WAIT_ACCUMULATED(seconds) = 1712.670
                  LOG_HADR_WAIT_COUNT = 118073
SOCK_SEND_BUF_REQUESTED,ACTUAL(bytes) = 0, 16384
SOCK_RECV_BUF_REQUESTED,ACTUAL(bytes) = 0, 87380
            PRIMARY_LOG_FILE,PAGE,POS = S0000661.LOG, 7, 2941696503
            STANDBY_LOG_FILE,PAGE,POS = S0000661.LOG, 7, 2941696503
                                                                   Continued
```

```
                 HADR_LOG_GAP(bytes) = 0
 STANDBY_REPLAY_LOG_FILE,PAGE,POS = S0000661.LOG, 7, 2941696503
     STANDBY_RECV_REPLAY_GAP(bytes) = 43
                  PRIMARY_LOG_TIME = 07/07/2013 13:16:17.000000 (1373202977)
                  STANDBY_LOG_TIME = 07/07/2013 13:16:17.000000 (1373202977)
           STANDBY_REPLAY_LOG_TIME = 07/07/2013 13:16:17.000000 (1373202977)
     STANDBY_RECV_BUF_SIZE(pages) = 4300
         STANDBY_RECV_BUF_PERCENT = 0
        STANDBY_SPOOL_LIMIT(pages) = 0
              PEER_WINDOW(seconds) = 0
         READS_ON_STANDBY_ENABLED = Y
 STANDBY_REPLAY_ONLY_WINDOW_ACTIVE = Y
  STANDBY_REPLAY_ONLY_WINDOW_START = 07/07/2013 13:20:26.000000 (1373203226)
STANDBY_REPLAY_ONLY_WINDOW_TRAN_COUNT = 1
```

Read On Standby Restrictions

As the name suggests, the HADR ROS feature allows you to run read-only workloads on HADR active standby databases. In addition to the read-only restriction, this feature has limitations to be aware of before designing your solution around the ROS feature, as Table 7.4 shows.

Table 7.4: HADR ROS restrictions

ROS Limitation	SQL Error Code
Write operations are not supported on ROS databases.	SQL1773N reason code 5
The standby database is inaccessible during the replay-only window, which means user connections terminate during the primary database DDL changes and maintenance operations.	SQL1776N reason code 4
Only supported isolation level for the data-read operation is Uncommitted Read (UR); other isolation level operations receive the error message.	SQL1773N reason code 1
Declared temporary tables (DGTTs) are not supported on the standby.	SQL1773N reason code 4
Created global temporary tables (CGTTs) access from the active standby database is not supported, and any attempt to do so will receive an error message.	SQL1773N reason code 4
Tables created with Not Logged Initially (NLI) cannot be accessed from the active standby, and any attempts to access those will receive an error message.	SQL1477N
Queries on the standby can make use only of an SMS system temporary table space; if you have created only a DMS system temporary table space in the primary, make sure to create one SMS system temporary table space for the standby's use—otherwise, the application will receive an error message.	SQL1773N reason code 5
Explain tools are not supported on the active standby.	SQL1773N reason code 5

Table 7.4: HADR ROS restrictions (continued)	
ROS Limitation	**SQL Error Code**
The self-tuning memory manager is not supported.	Not applicable
The active standby database cannot participate in the federation server setup.	Not applicable
Database backup and quiesce operations are not supported.	Not applicable

HADR Multiple Standbys

Starting with DB2 10.1, HADR provides a combination of local high availability and remote disaster recovery for a single database multisite-data-replication solution. Additionally, integrating a multiple standby setup with the new HADR enhancements, log spooling, and delayed replay allows for quick recovery from any errant transaction.

To enable the HADR multiple standby setup, you use the HADR_TARGET_LIST new database configuration parameter along with the traditional HADR parameters. The number of entries specified by this parameter on the primary database determines the number of standbys a primary database has in the setup. In DB2 10.1, the number of supported standbys is three: one principal standby and two auxiliary standby databases.

All the traditional HADR features and functionalities work with multiple standbys as well; for example, ROS can be enabled on any standby, and any standby can become the HADR primary by a graceful or forced manual takeover. Remember, the IBM Tivoli System Automation for Multiplatforms (TSA MP) automated takeover can happen only between the primary and the principal standby.

HADR provides four transaction log shipping synchronization modes to balance performance and data protection. Table 7.5 lists the information on the synchronization modes, performance, and data protection level.

Table 7.5: HADR synchronization modes, performance, and data protection comparison			
Mode	**Description**	**Performance**	**Data Protection**
SYNC	Log writes on the primary are considered successful only when the log data has been shipped and written to the physical log file on the standby.	Compromised	Greatest
NEARSYNC	Log writes on the primary are considered successful only when the log data has been written to the main memory on the standby.	Balanced	Balanced
ASYNC	Log writes on the primary are considered successful only when the log data has been delivered to the TCP layer of the primary server.	Greater	Compromised
SUPERASYNC	Log writes on the primary have no dependency on the standby.	Greatest	Highly Compromised

You can see the similarities and dissimilarities between the principal standby and the auxiliary standby databases in Table 7.6.

Table 7.6: HADR principal and auxiliary standby databases

Principal Standby	Auxiliary Standby
Supports ROS feature	Supports ROS feature
Only one standby database can act as the principal standby	Maximum of two standby databases can act as auxiliary standbys
Synchronization is through a TCP/IP direct connection	Synchronization is through a TCP/IP direct connection
Time delayed log shipping is supported	Time delayed log shipping is supported
TSA MP automated failover is supported	Only a manual failover is supported
All four synchronization modes are supported	Only SUPERASYNC synchronization mode is supported

Setting Up an HADR Multiple Standby Environment

The process of setting up an HADR environment is fairly straightforward. After ensuring that the systems you intend to use as primary and standby servers are identical and that a TCP/IP connection exists between them, you simply perform the following tasks, in the following order.

Step 1: Determine the host name, host IP address, and the service name or port number for both the primary and the standby database servers.

If a server has multiple network interfaces, ensure that the HADR host name or IP address maps to the intended interface. You will need to allocate separate HADR ports for each protected database—these cannot be the same as the ports that have been allocated to the instance. The host name can map to only one IP address.

Step 2: Create the principal standby and auxiliary standby databases by restoring a backup image or initializing a split mirror copy of the database that is to serve as the primary database.

It is recommended that you do not issue the ROLLFORWARD DATABASE command on the standby databases after the restore operation or split mirror initialization. The results of performing a roll-forward recovery operation might differ slightly from replaying the logs on the standby databases by using HADR. If the primary and standby databases are not identical when HADR is started, an error will occur.

When you set up the standby databases by using the RESTORE DATABASE command, it is recommended that you use the REPLACE HISTORY FILE option—but avoid using the following options: TABLESPACE, INTO, REDIRECT, and WITHOUT ROLLING FORWARD.

When setting up the standby databases by using the db2inidb utility, do not use the SNAPSHOT or MIRROR options. You can specify the RELOCATE USING option to change one or more of the following configuration attributes: instance name, log path, or database path. However, you must not change the database name or the table space container paths.

Step 3: Set the HADR configuration parameters on the primary, principal standby, and auxiliary standby databases.

After the standby databases have been created, you must set the HADR configuration parameters listed in Table 7.7 before starting HADR.

Table 7.7: HADR-specific database configuration parameters

Parameter	Description
HADR_LOCAL_HOST	Specifies the local host for HADR TCP communication.
HADR_LOCAL_SVC	Specifies the TCP service name or port number for which the local HADR process accepts connections.
HADR_REMOTE_HOST	Specifies the TCP/IP host name or IP address of the remote HADR node.
HADR_REMOTE_SVC	Specifies the TCP service name or port number that the remote HADR node will use.
HADR_REMOTE_INST	Specifies the instance name of the remote HADR server.
HADR_TIMEOUT	Specifies the time (in seconds) that the HADR process waits before considering a communication attempt to have failed.
HADR_TARGET_LIST	Specifies the host and port names of all the standbys in the multiple standby HADR setup. The first standby that you specify in the parameter is considered to be the principal HADR standby database.
HADR_SYNCMODE	Specifies the synchronization mode to use for HADR.
HADR_SPOOL_LIMIT	Specifies a limit on how much is spooled or written to disk if the log receive buffer (DB2_HADR_BUF_SIZE) fills up. The default value is 0, which means no spooling; a value of -1 means unlimited spooling.
HADR_REPLAY_DELAY	Specifies the delayed replay in seconds to keep the standby database at a point in time that is earlier than that of the primary database. You can set this parameter only on a standby database that is in SUPERASYNC synchronization mode.
HADR_PEER_WINDOW	Specifies the peer window for the connection between the primary and its principal standby database. The peer window is not applicable to auxiliary standby databases because they are always in SUPERASYNC mode.

Figure 7.28 shows the demonstration setup, where the host dbserver1 is the primary database server at data center 1, host dbserver2 is the principal standby database server at data center 2, and host dbserver3 is the auxiliary standby database server at data center 3.

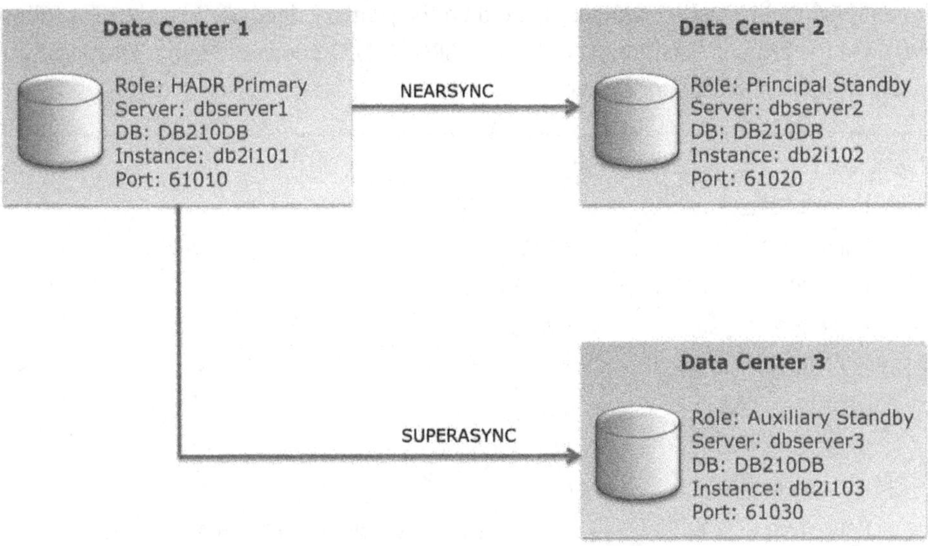

Figure 7.28: HADR multiple standby setup

Table 7.8 lists the respective host name, instance name, port number, and other HADR parameter information.

Table 7.8: HADR-multiple standby configuration

Parameter	Data Center 1	Data Center 2	Data Center 3
HADR_LOCAL_HOST	dbserver1	dbserver2	dbserver3
HADR_LOCAL_SVC	61010	61020	61030
HADR_REMOTE_HOST	db2server2	dbserver1	dbserver1
HADR_REMOTE_SVC	61020	61010	61010
HADR_REMOTE_INST	db2i102	db2i101	db2i103
HADR_TIMEOUT	120	120	120
HADR_TARGET_LIST	dbserver2:61020| dbserver3:61030	dbserver1:61010| dbserver3:61030	dbserver2:61020| dbserver1:61010
HADR_SYNCMODE	NEARSYNC	NEARSYNC	SUPERASYNC
HADR_SPOOL_LIMIT	0	0	0
HADR_REPLAY_DELAY	0	0	0
HADR_PEER_WINDOW	0	0	0

Start configuring the standby databases and then the primary database by using the following commands. On the principal standby, the HADR_TARGET_LIST command's first entry is always the primary server and associated port number.

```
UPDATE DB CFG FOR DB210DB USING
      HADR_LOCAL_HOST          dbserver2
      HADR_LOCAL_SVC           61020
      HADR_REMOTE_HOST         dbserver1
      HADR_REMOTE_SVC          61010
      HADR_REMOTE_INST         db2i101
      HADR_TIMEOUT             120
      HADR_SYNCMODE            NEARSYNC
      HADR_PEER_WINDOW         0
      HADR_TARGET_LIST         dbserver1:61010|dbserver3:61030
```

On the auxiliary standby, the HADR_TARGET_LIST command's first entry is always the principal standby, then the primary, and then the other auxiliary standby (if any).

```
UPDATE DB CFG FOR DB210DB USING
      HADR_LOCAL_HOST             dbserver3
      HADR_LOCAL_SVC              61030
      HADR_REMOTE_HOST            dbserver1
      HADR_REMOTE_SVC             61010
      HADR_REMOTE_INST            db2i101
      HADR_TIMEOUT                120
      HADR_SYNCMODE               SUPERASYNC
      HADR_PEER_WINDOW            0
      HADR_TARGET_LIST            dbserver2:61020|dbserver1:61010
```

On the primary, the HADR_TARGET_LIST command's first entry is always the principal standby and then the auxiliary standbys.

```
UPDATE DB CFG FOR DB210DB USING
      HADR_LOCAL_HOST             dbserver1
```

Continued

```
HADR_LOCAL_SVC            61010
HADR_REMOTE_HOST          dbserver2
HADR_REMOTE_SVC           61020
HADR_REMOTE_INST          db2i102
HADR_TIMEOUT              120
HADR_SYNCMODE             NEARSYNC
HADR_PEER_WINDOW          0
HADR_TARGET_LIST          dbserver2:61020|dbserver3:61030;
```

Step 4: Connect to the standby instances and start HADR on the principal and auxiliary standby databases.

To start HADR, you execute the START HADR command. The basic syntax for this command is:

```
START HADR ON [DATABASE | DB] [DatabaseAlias]
<USER [UserName] <USING [Password]>>
AS [PRIMARY <BY FORCE> | SECONDARY]
```

where:

DatabaseAlias	Identifies the alias assigned to the database for which to start HADR.
UserName	Identifies the name assigned to a specific user who is to start HADR.
Password	Identifies the password that corresponds to the name of the user who is to start HADR.

Thus, if you want to start HADR on a database named DB210DB and indicate that it is to act as a standby database, you could do so by executing a START HADR command that looks something like this:

```
START HADR ON DATABASE db210db AS STANDBY;
```

Step 5: Connect to the primary instance and start HADR on the primary database.

In this case, you would execute a START HADR command that looks something like this:

```
START HADR ON DATABASE db210db AS PRIMARY;
```

You can also set up an HADR environment by using the IBM Data Studio HADR setup wizard. To activate this wizard, right-click the database and select the **Set Up and Configure** action, as Figure 7.29 shows.

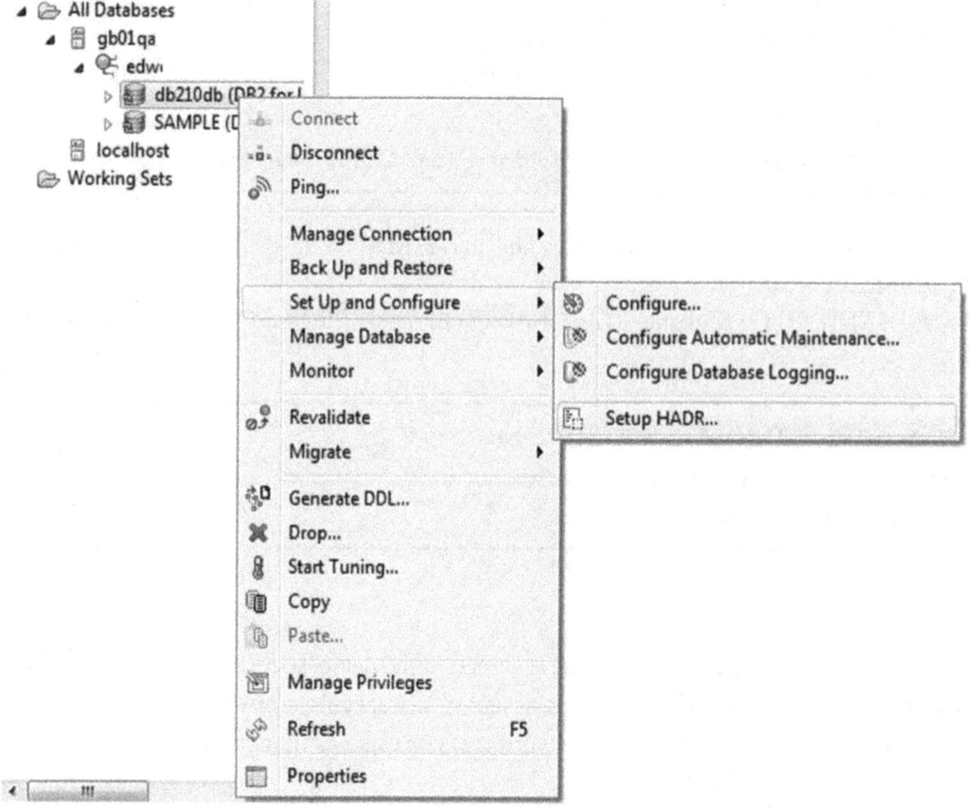

Figure 7.29: Invoking the Set Up HADR Databases wizard from Data Studio

Once an HADR environment has been established, the following operations will be replicated automatically in the standby database whenever they are performed on the primary database:

- Execution of DDL statements (CREATE, ALTER, DROP)
- Execution of DML statements (INSERT, UPDATE, DELETE)
- Buffer pool operations
- Table space operations
- Online reorganization
- Offline reorganization
- Changes to metadata for stored procedures and UDFs

HADR does not replicate stored procedure and UDF object and library files. If this type of replication is needed, you must physically create the files on identical paths on both the primary and standby databases. If the standby database cannot find the referenced object or library file, the stored procedure or UDF invocation will fail on the standby database.

Nonlogged operations, such as changes to database configuration parameters and to the recovery history file, are not replicated to the standby database.

Note: You can use the db2pd -db *<dbname>* -hadr or the MON_GET_HADR table function to monitor HADR status. The auxiliary standby databases will always be in REMOTE_CATCHUP state due to SUPERASYNC synchronization mode.

```
db2 "SELECT HADR_ROLE, STANDBY_ID, HADR_STATE, PRIMARY_MEMBER_HOST,
STANDBY_MEMBER_HOST FROM TABLE (MON_GET_HADR (NULL))"

HADR_ROLE   STANDBY_ID HADR_STATE        PRIMARY_MEMBER_HOST  STANDBY_MEMBER_HOST
----------- ---------- ----------------- -------------------- -------------------
PRIMARY              1 PEER              10.110.20.5          10.110.7.6
PRIMARY              2 REMOTE_CATCHUP    10.110.20.5          10.112.0.1
 2 record(s) selected.
```

Load Operations and HADR

Load operations present a special problem for HADR. Because load operations are not recorded in a database's transaction log files, whether a load operation can be duplicated is dependent on whether a copy of the loaded data was saved as part of the load process (which is the case if you specify the COPY YES option of the LOAD command). If you specify COPY YES when performing a load operation on the primary database, the command will execute on the primary database, and the data will be replicated to the standby database—provided the load copy image created can be accessed by the standby database via the path or device supplied with the LOAD command. If the standby database cannot access the load copy image, the table space in which the table is stored is marked invalid on the standby database, and the standby database will stop replaying log records that pertain to this table space.

To ensure that the load operation can access the copy on the standby database, it is recommended that you use a shared location for the load copy image output file location specified with the COPY YES option. Alternatively, you can deactivate the standby database while doing the load operation, perform the load operation on the primary database, place a copy of the resulting output file in the standby path, and then activate the standby database.

If you execute a load operation on the primary database and specify the NONRECOVERABLE option, data will be loaded into the appropriate table in the primary database, the corresponding table on the standby database will be marked invalid, and the standby database will stop replaying log records that pertain to this table. You can reissue the LOAD command with the COPY YES and REPLACE options specified to restore the table on the standby database, or you can drop the table and recover the space.

Because HADR does not support the execution of a load operation with the COPY NO option specified, an attempt to perform such an operation is automatically converted to a load operation that behaves as if the NONRECOVERABLE option was specified. To prevent this behavior, you can set the DB2_LOAD_COPY_NO_OVERRIDE registry variable on the primary database to COPY YES, in which case all load operations performed will behave as if the COPY YES option were specified. When setting this variable, make sure that the device or directory you specify on the primary database can be accessed by the standby database via the same path, device, or load library.

Load operations against primary databases in an HADR environment can have an effect on indexes as well as tables and table spaces. If you perform a load operation on the primary database and specify the COPY YES option, affected indexes will be replicated as follows:

- If you set the indexing mode to REBUILD and assign the table being loaded the LOG INDEX BUILD attribute, or if you assign the table being loaded the DEFAULT attribute and set the logindexbuild database configuration parameter on the primary database to ON, the primary database will include the rebuilt index object in the copy file so that the standby database can replicate the index object. If the index object on the standby database is marked invalid before the load operation is performed, it will become usable again after the load operation as a result of the index rebuild.
- If you set the indexing mode to INCREMENTAL and assign the table being loaded the LOG INDEX BUILD attribute, or if you assign the table being loaded the NULL attribute and set the logindexbuild database configuration parameter on the primary database to ON, the index object on the standby database is updated only if it is not marked invalid before the load operation. Otherwise, the index is marked invalid on the standby database.
- IBM recommends that you set the logindexbuild database configuration parameter to ON for HADR databases to ensure that complete information is logged for index creation, re-creation, and reorganization. Although this means that index builds might take longer on the primary system and that more log space may be required, the indexes will be rebuilt on the standby system during HADR log replay and will be available when a failover takes place. If index operations on the primary system are not logged, and a failover occurs, any invalid

indexes that remain after the failover is complete will have to be rebuilt before they can be accessed—while indexes are being re-created, they cannot be accessed by any application.

A Word About DB2 HA Instance Configuration Utility (db2haicu)

The DB2 high availability instance configuration utility (db2haicu) is an interactive, text-based utility you use to configure and administer highly available databases in a clustered environment. This utility uses the TSA MP cluster manager to configure a shared database instance.

The utility takes the database instance, cluster environment, and cluster manager as inputs and then configures the instance for high availability failover. The input can be supplied either in interactive mode or by using an XML input file. All the parameters to the db2haicu are case-sensitive and must be in lowercase. The basic syntax is:

```
db2haicu [ -f XML-input-file ]
[ -disable ]
[ -delete  [ dbpartitionnum dbpartnum-list | hadrdb dbname ] ]
```

where:

XML-input-file	Specifies cluster domain details in an input XML file to the db2haicu command
-disable	Ceases high availability on a database manager instance; to reconfigure a ceased database manager instance for high availability, you must rerun the db2haicu utility
-delete	Deletes resource groups in the current database manager instance; to limit the deletion only to a specific partition group in a database-partition-featured instance, use the dbpartitionnum *dbpartnum-list* clause; to delete resource groups for a HADR database, use the hadrdb *dbname* clause

DB2 pureScale—An Overview

The pureScale is a DB2 9.8 feature that provides a scalable active-active configuration that transparently delivers high throughput and continuous availability for any business-critical system. From an architectural standpoint, DB2 pureScale leverages the architecture and design principles of the DB2 z/OS sysplex, which was introduced in early 1990s.

Figure 7.30 shows the pureScale components, which are broadly classified into:

- DB2 members
- Cluster caching facility (CF)
- Shared storage
- Cluster services and interconnect

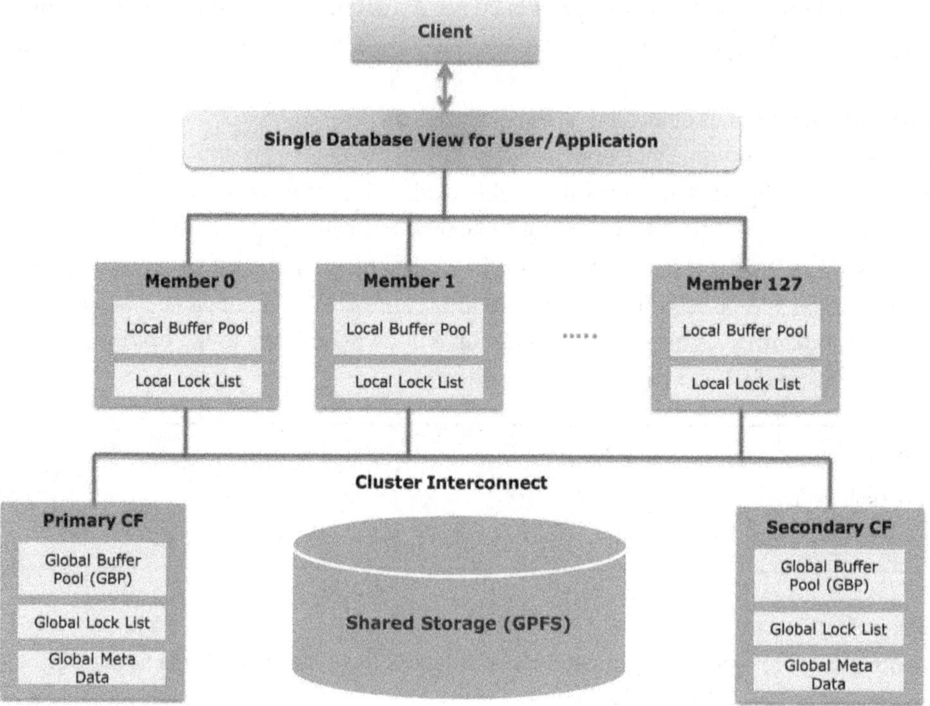

Figure 7.30: DB2 pureScale components

A DB2 member is the core processing engine within the pureScale cluster. You can install it on a physical host, logical partition of a physical machine (LPAR), or virtual machine. Each database member has a defined home host and can accept client connections only on the home host. If home host is not functional, the database member will fail and be started on a guest host (other member host in the cluster) in *restart light* mode to complete the member crash recovery. This activity completes the rollback of uncommitted changes and deallocates the locks held by the failed member.

A DB2 member can be in one of the following states:

- STARTED. The member is started on the home host and is functioning normally.
- STOPPED. The member has been stopped by the administrator.
- RESTARTING. The member is starting after a crash recovery on the home host or on the guest host.
- WAITING_FOR_FAILBACK. The member is running in restart light mode on a guest host and waiting to failback to the home host to function normally. In this state, the member will not accept any client connection.

- ERROR. The member could not be started on the home host or on the guest host, and it needs administrator attention to resolve the problem.

A pureScale cluster facilitates data sharing and concurrency control between its multiple database members, using the concept of a cluster caching facility (CF). The CF is a software application managed by DB2 cluster services to facilitate centralized coordination of locking through a Global Lock Manager (GLM) and centralized page caching through a Global Buffer Pool (GBP). At bare minimum, a pureScale environment will require one CF; however, two CFs configured as primary and secondary will eliminate a single point of failure. The GLM's function is to prevent conflicting access to the same object data by multiple members through a physical lock. The DB2 members hold the physical locks, and the transaction within a member holds the logical locks.

The Local Lock Manager (LLM), the lock manager within each DB2 member, requests the physical lock from the GLM before granting a logical lock to a transaction. The purpose of the Global Lock List (GLL) is to track the lock requests made by the LLMs of active database members.

By using the GBP, the DB2 database manager keeps page caching consistent across all members and coordinates the copies of pages that might exists across the members' Local Buffer Pools (LBP).

A CF can be in one of the following states:

- PRIMARY. The CF is functioning normally as the primary.
- PEER. This is the secondary CF, which is ready to assume the primary in case the current primary CF fails.
- STOPPED. The CF has been stopped by the administrator.
- RESTARTING. The CF is restarting due to a `db2start` command or after a failure occurred.
- BECOMING_PRIMARY. The CF will take over the primary CF role if no other primary CF is running in the pureScale cluster.
- CATCHUP. This is the intermediate state of the nonprimary CF before that CF can copy all the relevant information, including the GBP, GLL, and reach PEER state.
- ERROR. The CF could not be started on any host on the instance, and it needs administrator attention to resolve the problem.

As you may be already aware, the DB2 pureScale cluster operates on a shared disk architecture. The disk subsystem is accessed by all members within the pureScale cluster; therefore, this subsystem must allow concurrent read/write operations from all members. To maintain the data files' integrity and consistency, a clustered file system called IBM General Parallel File System (GPFS) is being used in the pureScale implementation.

To support fast communication, the DB2 members, CFs, and the storage are connected by using a high-speed interconnect called Infiniband, which supports Remote Direct Memory Access (RDMA) and User Direct Access Programming Library (uDAPL).

Note: The DB2 pureScale feature is supported on AIX, SUSE, and Red Hat Linux operating systems on Power 6, Power 7, System X (x3650 M3, x3690 X5, x3850 X5), and BladeCenter HS22 servers.

Working with a pureScale Cluster

Now that you have seen the components of DB2 pureScale cluster, it is also imperative to know the basic commands and utilities to work with pureScale environments. The commands are classified into three categories:

- Operations
- Maintenance
- Monitoring

Operations

Table 7.9 provides a quick view of basic pureScale operation capabilities and associated commands.

Table 7.9: The pureScale operation commands

Operation Element	Commands, Admin Views, or Table Functions
Querying the cluster status	db2instance –list
Starting the CF	db2start cf [*cf-identifier*] where *cf-identifier* is the CF's numeric identifier
Stopping the CF	db2stop cf [*cf-identifier*] where *cf-identifier* is the CF's numeric identifier
Querying CF status	SYSIBMADM.DB2_CF DB2 administrative view DB2_GET_INSTANCE_INFO table function
Starting the DB2 member	db2start member [*member-identifier*] where *member-identifier* is the member's numeric identifier
Stopping the DB2 member	db2stop member [*member-identifier*] where *member-identifier* is the member's numeric identifier
Querying the member status	SYSIBMADM.DB2_MEMBER DB2 administrative view
Activating the database	ACTIVATE DATABASE [*dbname*] where *dbname* is the database to be activated
Deactivating the database	DEACTIVATE DATABASE [*dbname*] where *dbname* is the database to be deactivated

Table 7.9: The pureScale operation commands (continued)

Operation Element	Commands, Admin Views, or Table Functions
Quiescing a DB2 member	db2stop member [*member-identifier*] quiesce where *member-identifier* is the member's numeric identifier
Unquiescing a DB2 member	db2start member [*member-identifier*] quiesce where *member-identifier* is the member's numeric identifier
Quiescing a database	QUIESCE DATABASE
Unquiescing a database	UNQUIESCE DATABASE
Quiescing an instance	QUIESCE INSTANCE [*instance-name*] where *instance-name* is the instance to be quiesced
Unquiescing an instance	UNQUIESCE INSTANCE [*instance-name*] where *instance-name* is the instance to be quiesced
Obtaining the CF system resource information	SELECT * FROM SYSIBMADM.ENV_CF_SYS_RESOURCES;
Obtaining information about the cluster hosts	SELECT * FROM SYSIBMADM.DB2_CLUSTER_HOST_STATE; *and* SELECT * FROM TABLE(DB2_GET_CLUSTER_HOST_STATE('hostname')) as T

Maintenance

Table 7.10 provides a quick view of basic pureScale maintenance capabilities and associated commands.

Table 7.10: The pureScale maintenance commands

Maintenance Element	Commands, Admin Views, or Table Functions
Adding a DB2 member	db2iupdt –add –m [hostname] –mnet [netname] [instance-name]
Removing a DB2 member	db2iupdt –drop –m [hostname] [instance-name]
Adding a CF server	db2iupdt –add –cf [hostname] –cfnet [netname] [instance-name]
Removing a CF server	db2iupdt –drop –cf [hostname] [instance-name]
Placing a DB2 member host into a maintenance mode	1. db2stop member [member-identifier] quiesce 2. db2stop instance on [hostname] 3. db2cluster –cm –enter –maintenance 4. db2cluster –cfs –enter –maintenance
Resuming a maintenance mode from a DB2 member	1. db2cluster –cm –exit –maintenance 2. db2cluster –cfs –exit –maintenance 3. db2start instance on [hostname] 4. db2start member [member-identifier]
Placing a cluster into maintenance mode	1. db2stop instance on [hostname] 2. db2cluster –cm –enter –maintenance –all 3. db2cluster –cfs -enter –maintenance –all 4. db2start instance on [hostname] 5. db2start
Database backup	BACKUP DATABASE [*dbname*]
Database restore	RESTORE DATABASE [*dbname*]

Monitoring

Table 7.11 provides a quick view of basic pureScale monitoring capabilities and associated commands.

Table 7.11: The pureScale monitoring commands

Monitoring Element	Commands, Admin Views, or Table Functions
Obtaining the GBP hit ratio for all data and index pages	WITH GBP AS (SELECT BP_NAME, POOL_DATA_GBP_L_READS+POOL_INDEX_GBP_L_READS AS LOGICAL_READS POOL_DATA_GBP_P_READS+POOL_INDEX_GBP_P_READS AS PHYSICAL_READS, MEMBER FROM TABLE(MON_GET_BUFFERPOOL('',-2)) AS METRICS) SELECT VARCHAR(BP_NAME,20) AS BP_NAME, LOGICAL_READS, PHYSICAL_READS, CASE WHEN LOGICAL_READS > 0 THEN DEC(((FLOAT(LOGICAL_READS) -FLOAT(PHYSICAL_READS))/ FLOAT(LOGICAL_READS)) * 100,5,2) ELSE NULL END AS HIT_RATIO, MEMBER FROM GBP;
Determining the performance metrics for one or more connections	SELECT MEMBER, APPLICATION_HANDLE, TOTAL_SORTS, TOTAL_COMPILE_TIME, TOTAL_CPU_TIME, TOTAL_WAIT_TIME, LOG_BUFFER_WAIT_TIME, ROWS_READ, ROWS_RETURNED, TCPIP_SEND_VOLUME FROM TABLE(MON_GET_CONNECTION(CAST(NULL AS BIGINT), -2)) AS T ORDER BY TOTAL_CPU_TIME DESC
Determining the lock performance for each connection	SELECT MEMBER, SUM(LOCK_ESCALS_GLOBAL) AS LOCK_ESCALS, SUM(LOCK_TIMEOUTS_GLOBAL) AS LOCK_TIMEOUTS, SUM(LOCK_WAIT_TIME_GLOBAL) AS LOCK_WAIT_TIME, SUM(LOCK_WAITS) AS LOCK_WAITS FROM TABLE (MON_GET_CONNECTION('',-2)) GROUP BY MEMBER;

Table 7.11: The pureScale monitoring commands (continued)

Monitoring Element	Commands, Admin Views, or Table Functions
Obtaining the CF metrics	SELECT ID AS CFID, SUBSTR(DB_NAME, 1,8) AS DBNAME, CURRENT_CF_GBP_SIZE, CONFIGURED_CF_GBP_SIZE, TARGET_CF_GBP_SIZE, CURRENT_CF_LOCK_SIZE, CONFIGURED_CF_LOCK_SIZE, TARGET_CF_LOCK_SIZE, CURRENT_CF_SCA_SIZE, CONFIGURED_CF_SCA_SIZE, TARGET_CF_SCA_SIZE FROM TABLE(MON_GET_CF(cast(NULL as integer))) AS CAMETRICS ORDER BY CFID;

Chapter Summary

Every day, database and operating system administrators across the globe are executing numerous DB2 high availability tasks. However, to successfully manage the system, thorough knowledge of the major functions is mandatory. The objective of this chapter was to familiarize you with the following:

- Various transaction logging features
- Various types of database recovery features available within DB2
- Database backup categories and the usage of each
- HADR feature concepts and implementation
- Implementation techniques for HADR with multiple standby databases
- DB2 pureScale architecture and basic operations

On completion of this chapter, you will be equipped with sufficient knowledge to answer the high availability questions in the certification exam. It is also highly recommended that you complete the sample questions available at the end of the chapter.

Practice Questions

Question 1

Which command can you use to enable dual logging for a database named SAMPLE?

- A. db2set DB2_NEWLOGPATH=1
- B. UPDATE DB CFG FOR sample USING failarchpath D:\logs_copy
- C. UPDATE DB CFG FOR sample USING mirrorlogpath D:\logs_copy
- D. UPDATE DB CFG FOR sample USING logarchmeth2 MIRRORPATH:D:\logs_copy

Question 2

What will happen if you execute the following SQL statement?

```
UPDATE DB CFG FOR sample USING BLK_LOG_DSK_FUL YES
```

- A. The SAMPLE database will be configured to use infinite logging.
- B. The SAMPLE database will not automatically allocate additional storage space when the active log directory becomes full.
- C. Log files for the SAMPLE database will be backed up automatically whenever a full backup image of the SAMPLE database is made.
- D. Transactions running against the SAMPLE database will be suspended.

Question 3

A power failure occurred while several applications were interacting with a database named SAMPLE. When power was restored, the database could not be restarted because a user temporary table space named USER_TMPTS was damaged. What must you do to successfully recover the database?

- A. Restart the database by executing the command RESTART DATABASE sample DROP PENDING TABLESPACES (USER_TMPTS); drop and re-create the USER_TMPTS table space.
- B. Restart the database by executing the command RESTART DATABASE sample DROP PENDING TABLESPACES; re-create the USER_TMPTS table space.
- C. Restart the database by executing the command RESTART DATABASE sample DROP TABLESPACE (USER_TMPTS); re-create the USER_TMPTS table space.
- D. Restart the database by executing the command RESTART DATABASE sample RECREATE TABLESPACES (USER_TMPTS).

Question 4

What type of recovery operation do you use to reapply transactions that were committed but not externalized to storage, to roll back transactions that were externalized to storage but not committed, and to purge transactions from memory that were neither committed nor externalized to storage?

- ❍ A. Disaster recovery
- ❍ B. Crash recovery
- ❍ C. Version recovery
- ❍ D. Roll-forward recovery

Question 5

Which command will restore a database by using information found in the recovery history log file?

- ❍ A. RESTART DATABASE
- ❍ B. RESTORE DATABASE
- ❍ C. RECOVER DATABASE
- ❍ D. REBUILD DATABASE

Question 6

While cleaning up files stored on an older Windows server, a database administrator finds a shell script that contains the following commands:

```
db2 "RESTORE DATABASE sample FROM C:\backups TO D:\DB_DIR INTO sample2 REDIRECT"
db2 "SET TABLESPACE CONTAINERS FOR 0 USING (PATH 'D:\DB_DIR\SYSTEM')"
db2 "SET TABLESPACE CONTAINERS FOR 1 USING (PATH 'D:\DB_DIR\TEMP')"
db2 "SET TABLESPACE CONTAINERS FOR 2 USING (PATH 'D:\DB_DIR\USER')"
db2 "RESTORE DATABASE sample CONTINUE"
```

What was this file designed to perform?

- ❍ A. A multiple table-space recovery operation
- ❍ B. A reverted restore operation
- ❍ C. A partial table-space reconstruction operation
- ❍ D. A redirected restore operation

Question 7

If a database named SAMPLE was backed up on Sunday, which command will produce a backup image on Wednesday that contains a copy of just the data that has changed since the backup image on Sunday was created?

- ❍ A. BACKUP DATABASE sample INCREMENTAL TO C:\backups
- ❍ B. BACKUP DATABASE sample DELTA TO C:\backups
- ❍ C. BACKUP DATABASE sample DELTA INCREMENTAL TO C:\backups
- ❍ D. BACKUP DATABASE sample INCREMENTAL DELTA TO C:\backups

Question 8

Which command can you use to back up a database named PAYROLL, in such a way that workloads against the database are not affected by more than 25 percent?

- ❍ A. BACKUP DATABASE payroll ONLINE TO D:\backups UTIL_IMPACT_PRIORITY 25
- ❍ B. BACKUP DATABASE payroll ONLINE TO D:\backups UTIL_IMPACT_LIM 25
- ❍ C. BACKUP DATABASE payroll ONLINE TO D:\backups UTIL_IMPACT_PRIORITY 75
- ❍ D. BACKUP DATABASE payroll ONLINE TO D:\backups UTIL_IMPACT_PRIORITY 75

Question 9

Which statement about incremental backups is false?

- ❍ A. The predecessor of an incremental backup image is always the most recent successful full backup image of the same object (database or table space).
- ❍ B. Database recovery involves restoring the database by using the most recent full backup image available and applying each incremental backup image produced since the last full backup, in the order in which they were created.
- ❍ C. Before an incremental backup image can be created, a full backup image must already exist.
- ❍ D. Along with updated data and index pages, each incremental backup image also contains all the initial database metadata that normally resides in a full database backup image.

Question 10

Which of the following is *not* needed to recover a database to a specific point in time?

❍ A. Access to a full database backup image
❍ B. Access to a backup copy of the recovery history file
❍ C. Access to archive log files produced since a backup image was made
❍ D. Access to all delta backup images produced since the last full backup image was made

Question 11

Which statement about roll-forward recovery is false?

❍ A. Table space roll-forward recovery cannot be accomplished while users are connected to the database.
❍ B. Recovery must be to a point in time that is greater than the minimum recovery time obtained with the MON_GET_TABLESPACE table function.
❍ C. Recovery to a specific point in time can only be done on a database that is using archival logging.
❍ D. By default, all recovery times specified are interpreted as Coordinated Universal Time (UTC)—otherwise known as Greenwich Mean Time (GMT)—values.

Question 12

You execute the following command in an attempt to return a database named SAMPLE to the state it was in at 9:30 a.m. on July 1, 2013:

```
ROLLFORWARD DB sample TO 2013-07-01-09.30.00.000000 AND STOP
```

During execution, this error was returned:

```
SQL4970N Roll-forward recovery on database SAMPLE cannot reach
the specified stop point (end-of-log or point-in-time) because of
missing or corrupted log file(s) on database partition(s) "0". Roll-
forward recovery processing has halted on log file S0000007.LOG.
```

Which option can you add to the ROLLFORWARD command to resolve the problem?

❍ A. END OF LOGS
❍ B. OVERFLOW LOG PATH
❍ C. ALTERNATE LOG PATH
❍ D. MIRROR LOG PATH

Question 13

A database named COMPANY was backed up on June 1. On June 15, the following SQL statement was executed:

```
RENAME TABLESPACE emp_info TO hr_info
```

On July 1, a failed operation made recovery of the HR_INFO table space necessary. Which command must you use to roll forward the table space?

- ❍ A. ROLLFORWARD DATABASE company TO END OF LOGS AND STOP TABLESPACE (emp_info)
- ❍ B. ROLLFORWARD DATABASE company TO END OF LOGS AND STOP TABLESPACE (hr_info)
- ❍ C. ROLLFORWARD DATABASE company TO END OF LOGS AND STOP TABLESPACE (emp_info TO hr_info)
- ❍ D. ROLLFORWARD DATABASE company TO END OF LOGS AND STOP TABLESPACE (RENAME emp_info TO hr_info)

Question 14

Which command can cause queries against a database named SAMPLE that use indexes to run slower than usual the first time they are executed after a crash recovery operation has been performed?

- ❍ A. UPDATE DBM CFG USING INDEXREC ACCESS; UPDATE DB CFG FOR sample USING INDEXREC ACCESS;
- ❍ B. UPDATE DBM CFG USING INDEXREC SYSTEM; UPDATE DB CFG FOR sample USING INDEXREC FIRSTEXEC;
- ❍ C. UPDATE DBM CFG USING INDEXREC RESTART; UPDATE DB CFG FOR sample USING INDEXREC RESTART;
- ❍ D. UPDATE DBM CFG USING INDEXREC FIRSTEXEC; UPDATE DB CFG FOR sample USING INDEXREC SYSTEM;

Question 15

Which command will ensure that index creation, re-creation, and reorganization operations against a database named SAMPLE will be logged so that indexes can be reconstructed during roll-forward recovery operations or HADR log replay procedures?

- ❍ A. UPDATE DB CFG FOR sample USING INDEXREC ON
- ❍ B. UPDATE DB CFG FOR sample USING LOGINDEXMAINT ON
- ❍ C. UPDATE DB CFG FOR sample USING INDEXOPS ON
- ❍ D. UPDATE DB CFG FOR sample USING LOGINDEXBUILD ON

Question 16

In a split mirror environment, which command do you use to initialize a mirrored copy of a database named MYDB as a read-only clone of the primary database?

- ❍ A. db2inidb mydb AS SNAPSHOT
- ❍ B. db2inidb mydb AS MIRROR
- ❍ C. db2inidb mydb AS DUPLICATE
- ❍ D. db2inidb mydb AS STANDBY

Question 17

Given two servers named SVR1 and SVR2 with a database named SALES on SVR1, in what order should you perform the following steps to set up an HADR environment using SVR2 as a standby server?

a) Back up the SALES database on SVR1.
b) Determine the host name, host IP address, and the service name or port number for SVR1 and SVR2.
c) Start HADR on SVR2.
d) Set the HADR configuration parameters on SVR1 and SVR2.
e) Restore the SALES database on SVR2.
f) Start HADR on SVR1.

- ❍ A. b, a, e, d, f, c
- ❍ B. b, d, f, c, a, e
- ❍ C. b, a, e, d, c, f
- ❍ D. f, c, b, d, a, e

Question 18

Which of the following is *not* a requirement for an HADR environment?

❍ A. The operating system on the primary server and the standby server must be the same (including fix pack level).

❍ B. The database path on the primary server and the standby server must be the same.

❍ C. The DB2 software version and bit size (32 or 64) used on the primary server and the standby server must be the same.

❍ D. Table spaces and table space containers on the primary server and the standby server must be identical.

Question 19

You set the LOG INDEX BUILD attribute for a table named EMPLOYEES to ON just before populating the table with a load operation. If the database the EMPLOYEES table resides in has been configured for HADR, what will happen when the database fails over to the standby server?

❍ A. Indexes defined for the EMPLOYEES table can be rebuilt.

❍ B. Insert operations on the standby server (after the failover to the standby server) will take longer.

❍ C. Indexes defined for the EMPLOYEES table will not be rebuilt.

❍ D. An attempt to create a unique index on the EMPLOYEES table (after the failover to the standby server) will fail.

Question 20

A database administrator has HADR enabled and wants to do a load operation on the primary server. If the LOAD command is executed with the COPY YES option specified and the copy of the loaded data created is written to a location that cannot be accessed by the standby database via the path provided with the LOAD command, what will happen?

- ❍ A. The load operation will fail on both the primary and the standby server.
- ❍ B. The load operation will automatically be converted to COPY NO, and the standby database will be marked corrupt.
- ❍ C. The table space in which the table is stored is marked invalid on the standby database, and the standby server will stop replaying log records that pertain to this table space.
- ❍ D. The table space in which the table is stored is marked invalid on the primary database, and the primary server will stop sending log records that pertain to this table space to the standby server.

Question 21

Company ABC has an HADR production environment and wants to isolate most of the expensive read-only SQL operations on the standby by using the read on standby (ROS) feature. How do you enable the ROS feature in this case?

- ❍ A. Set the DB2 registry variable DB2_HADR_ROS to ON.
- ❍ B. Set the DB2 registry variable DB2_HADR_SOSNDBUF to ON.
- ❍ C. Set the DB2 registry variable DB2_HADR_PEER_WAIT_LIMIT to ON.
- ❍ D. Set the DB2 registry variable DB2_HADR_NO_IP_CHECK to ON.

Question 22

Which HADR synchronization mode has the shortest transaction response time, but also the highest probability of transaction losses if the primary system fails?

- ❍ A. SYNC
- ❍ B. NEARSYNC
- ❍ C. ASYNC
- ❍ D. SUPERASYNC

Question 23

The DBA of company ABC wants to recover the HR.EMPLOYEE table, which was created in a drop table recovery–enabled table space, without affecting other application users and in minimal time. What is the correct procedure for the DBA to follow?

- ❍ A. Restore the database from the database backup image taken before the table was dropped, and execute the ROLLFORWARD DATABASE command with the RECOVER DROPPED TABLE option to restore the table space and the table HR.EMPLOYEE.
- ❍ B. Recover the database with the RECOVER DROPPED TABLE option to recover the table space and the table HR.EMPLOYEE.
- ❍ C. Restore the table space by using the database backup or the table space–level backup image taken before the table was dropped, and execute the ROLLFORWARD DATABASE command with RECOVER DROPPED TABLE option to restore the table space and the table HR.EMPLOYEE.
- ❍ D. Use IBM Data Studio to extract the dropped table in IXF format from the backup image taken before the table was dropped, re-create the table, and import the data.

Question 24

Which DB2 feature or product offers a breakthrough clustering technology for an OLTP environment, along with client reroute and connection-based workload capabilities?

- ❍ A. Database Partitioning Feature
- ❍ B. HADR
- ❍ C. pureScale
- ❍ D. DB2 Workload Manager

Question 25

Company ABC is running DB2 10.1 on a clustered environment. Which command do you use to administer the cluster environment?

- ❍ A. db2haicu
- ❍ B. lssam
- ❍ C. db2instance–list
- ❍ D. db2cluster

Question 26

Company ABC wants to restore a database with a subset of its original table spaces. What do you suggest?

- ❍ A. Perform a database RESTORE specifying the REBUILD WITH ALL TABLESPACES option and a set of table spaces required to be available to the business.
- ❍ B. Perform a database RESTORE specifying the REBUILD WITH option and a set of table spaces required to be available to the business.
- ❍ C. Perform a database RESTORE specifying the REBUILD WITH ALL TABLESPACES IN DATABASE option and a set of table spaces required to be available to the business.
- ❍ D. Perform a database RESTORE specifying the REBUILD WITH ALL TABLESPACES IN IMAGE option and a set of table spaces required to be available to the business.

Question 27

Company ABC is planning to implement an OLTP application infrastructure stack by using the DB2 pureScale feature for better application availability and scalability. Which file system is recommended for pureScale implementation?

- ❍ A. Network File System (NFS) with IBM N-series
- ❍ B. UNIX File System (UFS)
- ❍ C. IBM General Parallel File System (GPFS)
- ❍ D. Veritas File System (VxFS)

Question 28

Which is *not* a valid state in the DB2 member?

- ❍ A. WAITING_FOR_FAILBACK
- ❍ B. RESTARTING
- ❍ C. STARTED
- ❍ D. WAITING_FOR_FAILOVER

Question 29

Which is *not* a valid state in the cluster caching facility (CF)?

- ❍ A. PEER
- ❍ B. STOPPED
- ❍ C. BECOMING_SECONDARY
- ❍ D. PRIMARY

Question 30

Which two statements are true about the database restore operation in DB2 10.1? (Choose two.)

- ❒ A. A DBA can restore a database from a Linux environment into an AIX environment.
- ❒ B. Table space–level restoration is always done offline.
- ❒ C. A database restore operation requires an exclusive connection, and no applications can perform any operation during the restore.
- ❒ D. In the case of a table space restore operation, the specific table space will not be usable until the operation has completed.
- ❒ E. A DBA can restore a database from 64-bit architecture onto a 32-bit architecture system.

Question 31

Which isolation level is supported on the HADR active standby read-only database?

- ❒ A. Read Stability
- ❒ B. Repeatable Read
- ❒ C. Uncommitted Read
- ❒ D. Cursor Stability
- ❒ E. Currently Committed (CUR_COMMIT)

Question 32

Which two conditions can cause a replay-only window on the HADR active standby read-only database?

- ❒ A. Bulk data inserts on the primary
- ❒ B. REORG database maintenance on the primary
- ❒ C. DDL changes on the primary
- ❒ D. Bulk data inserts on the standby
- ❒ E. DDL changes on the standby

Question 33

Which statement is false regarding HADR auxiliary standby functionality in a multiple standby environment?

- ❍ A. Supports the ROS feature
- ❍ B. Supports a maximum of two auxiliary standbys
- ❍ C. Supports only a manual HADR failover
- ❍ D. Supports all four HADR synchronization modes

Question 34

Which statement is false regarding HADR principal standby functionality in a multiple standby environment?

- ❍ A. Supports the ROS feature
- ❍ B. Supports a maximum of two principal standbys
- ❍ C. Supports both manual and TSA HADR failover
- ❍ D. Supports all four HADR synchronization modes

Question 35

How do you force isolation levels requested by applications and statements running on an active HADR standby to be Uncommitted Read (UR) at all times?

- ❍ A. Set the DB2 registry variable DB2_STANDBY_ISO to UR.
- ❍ B. Set the DB2 registry variable DB2_HADR_ROS to ON.
- ❍ C. Set the DB2 registry variable DB2_HADR_NO_IP_CHECK to ON.
- ❍ D. Update the database configuration parameter CUR_COMMIT to UR on the standby.

Question 36

Company ABC wants to implement a delayed replay on the HADR standby. Which two key parameters must you set on the standby to achieve the delayed replay?

- ❒ A. Update the database configuration parameter HADR_PEER_WINDOW=0 on the standby database.
- ❒ B. Update the database configuration parameter HADR_REPLAY_DELAY=7200 on the standby database.
- ❒ C. Update the database configuration parameter HADR_SYNCMODE=SUPERASYNC on the standby database.
- ❒ D. Update the database configuration parameter HADR_SYNCMODE=ASYNC on the standby database.
- ❒ E. Update the database configuration parameter HADR_SPOOL_LIMIT=-1 on the standby database.

Question 37

The DBA of company ABC is managing a HADR multiple standby environment having one primary, one principal standby, and one auxiliary standby. The DBA uses the MON_GET_HADR table function to monitor the HADR status. What will be the HADR_STATE for the auxiliary standby database?

- ❍ A. Local Catchup state
- ❍ B. Remote Catchup state
- ❍ C. Remote Catchup Pending state
- ❍ D. PEER state

Question 38

How many maximum DB2 pureScale members can you have in one setup?

❍ A. 127
❍ B. 128
❍ C. 129
❍ D. 256

Question 39

How many maximum DB2 pureScale CFs can you have in one setup?

❍ A. 0
❍ B. 1
❍ C. 2
❍ D. 3

Question 40

Company ABC has a pureScale setup with the following configuration:

- Two DB2 members
- One DB2 CF
- One IBM GPFS

What is your recommendation to company ABC for effective pureScale operation?

❍ A. Add an additional DB2 member.
❍ B. Add an additional GPFS.
❍ C. Remove one DB2 member from the cluster.
❍ D. Add an additional CF.

Question 41

Which db2haicu utility option ceases high availability on a database manager instance?

- ❍ A. db2haicu –delete
- ❍ B. db2haicu –disable
- ❍ C. db2haicu –cease
- ❍ D. db2haicu –f [xml-input file] –cease

Question 42

What kind of high availability solution is the DB2 HADR?

- ❍ A. Shared disk
- ❍ B. Shared nothing
- ❍ C. Shared everything
- ❍ D. Only high available or only disaster recovery

Question 43

Which two DB2 functions are not supported in a pureScale environment?

- ❒ A. Health monitor
- ❒ B. Update statistics
- ❒ C. Incremental backup
- ❒ D. Event monitor
- ❒ E. Deadlock monitor

Question 44

What kind of solution is DB2 pureScale?

- ❍ A. Shared disk
- ❍ B. Shared nothing
- ❍ C. Shared everything
- ❍ D. Shared CPU

Question 45

Which table function can you use to obtain the Group Buffer Pool hit ratio in a pureScale environment?

- ❍ A. MON_GET_CONNECTION
- ❍ B. MON_GET_CF
- ❍ C. MON_GET_BUFFERPOOL
- ❍ D. DB2_GET_INSTANCE_INFO

Question 46

During a database restore from one instance to another, which setting in DB2 10.1 is necessary to grant DBADM, SECADM, DATAACCESS, and CONTROL privileges to the user issuing the restore operation?

- ❍ A. Set the DB2 registry variable DB2_RESTORE_GRANT_ADMIN_AUTHORITIES=YES before starting the database restoration process.
- ❍ B. Set the DB2 registry variable DB2_COMPATIBILITY_VECTOR to NULL before starting the database restoration process.
- ❍ C. Set the DB2 registry variable DB2_LIMIT_FENCED_GROUP to ON before starting the database restoration process.
- ❍ D. Run the command GRANT DBADM ON DATABASE after the database restore, and grant SECADM, DATAACCESS, and CONTROL privileges.

Question 47

How does DB2 manage the concurrency in a pureScale cluster environment?

- ❍ A. Using the Global Lock Manager
- ❍ B. Using the Local Lock Manager
- ❍ C. Using the Global Buffer Pool
- ❍ D. Using the Local Buffer Pool

Question 48

What additional locking mechanism is introduced in a DB2 pureScale environment to manage concurrency control?

- ❍ A. Logical locks
- ❍ B. Physical locks
- ❍ C. Row locks
- ❍ D. Column locks

Question 49

Which synchronization mechanism is used between primary and secondary CF servers?

- ❍ A. SYNC
- ❍ B. ASYNC
- ❍ C. NEARSYNC
- ❍ D. Duplexing

Question 50

Which command fails to start the respective pureScale cluster component?

- ❍ A. db2start CF 129
- ❍ B. db2start add CF 130
- ❍ C. db2start member 3
- ❍ D. db2start member 127

Answers

Question 1

The correct answer is **C**. To enable log file mirroring, you simply assign the fully qualified name of the mirror log location (path) to the `mirrorlogpath` database configuration parameter. Ideally, the mirror log path should refer to a physical location (disk) that does not see a large amount of disk I/O and that is separate from the physical location used to store primary log files.

Question 2

The correct answer is **D**. When archival logging is used, and archived log files are not moved from the active log directory to another location, the disk where the active log directory resides can quickly become full. By default, when this happens, transactions will receive a disk full error and be rolled back. If you set the `blk_log_dsk_ful` database configuration parameter to YES, applications will hang (instead of rolling back the current transaction) if the DB2 database manager receives a disk full error when it attempts to create a new log file in the active log directory. (This gives you the opportunity to manually move or delete files to make more room available.) The DB2 database manager will then attempt to create the log file every five minutes until it succeeds—after each attempt, a message is written to the administration notification log.

Question 3

The correct answer is **A**. If a problem occurs with a table space container during the restart process, you can use the `DROP PENDING TABLESPACES ([TS_Name])` option to place one or more table spaces in Drop Pending state. This allows the database to be successfully restarted, after which the offending table space can be dropped and, if necessary, re-created. You can find a list of troubled table space names in the administration notification log, if a database restart operation fails because of table space container problems.

Question 4

The correct answer is **B**. When a transaction failure occurs, all work done by partially completed transactions that have not yet been externalized to the database is lost. As a result, the database might be left in an inconsistent state (and therefore will be unusable). *Crash recovery* is the process used to return such a database to a consistent and usable state. To perform crash recovery, you use information stored in the transaction log files to complete any committed transactions that were in memory (but had not yet been externalized to storage) when the transaction failure occurred, roll back any incomplete transactions, and purge any uncommitted transactions from memory.

Question 5

The correct answer is **C**. The `Recover` utility performs the restore and roll-forward operations needed to recover a database to a specific point in time, based on information found in the recovery history file. You invoke the `Recovery` utility by executing the `RECOVER DATABASE` command.

Question 6

The correct answer is **D**. When invalid table space containers are encountered, you can redefine them at the beginning of the recovery process by performing what is known as a *redirected restore*. You can also use a redirected restore operation to restore a backup image to a target machine that is different than the source machine, or to store table space data in a different physical location.

Question 7

The correct answer is **D**. As the size of a database grows, the time and hardware needed to back up and recover the databases also increases substantially. Thus, creating full database backup images is not always the best approach when dealing with large databases because the storage requirements for multiple copies of such backup images can be enormous. A better alternative is to create a full backup image periodically and one or more *incremental backup* images more frequently. An incremental backup is a backup image that contains only pages that have been updated since the previous backup image was made.

Question 8

The correct answer is **A**. You use the `BACKUP DATABASE` command's `UTIL_IMPACT_PRIORITY` option to indicate that the execution of a backup operation is to be throttled such that its effect on concurrent database activity can be controlled. You can assign this parameter a numerical value within the range of 1 to 100, with 100 representing the highest priority and 1 representing the lowest. Backup operations that have been assigned a `UTIL_IMPACT_PRIORITY` value of 25 will affect database workloads by 25 percent and will take longer to complete; backup operations that have been assigned a `UTIL_IMPACT_PRIORITY` value of 75 will affect database workloads by 75 percent and will finish sooner.

Question 9

The correct answer is **B**. When incremental backup images are taken, database recovery involves restoring the database by using the most recent full backup image available and applying the most recent incremental backup image produced. However, when delta backup images are taken, database recovery involves restoring the database by using the most recent full backup image available and applying each delta backup image produced since the full backup image used was made, in the order in which they were created.

Question 10

The correct answer is **B**. Roll-forward recovery takes version recovery one step further by rebuilding a database or one or more individual table spaces by using a backup image, and then replaying information stored in transaction log files to return the database or table spaces to the state they were in at an exact point in time. To perform a roll-forward recovery operation, you must enable archival logging, have a full backup image of the database available, and have access to all archived log files that have been created since the full backup image was made.

Question 11

The correct answer is **A**. Table space roll-forward recovery operations can be performed on individual table spaces while a database remains online. However, before a database can be restored, it must first be taken offline. Therefore, roll-forward recovery can be accomplished while users are connected to the database—but only at the table space level.

Question 12

The correct answer is **B**. The `OVERFLOW LOG PATH` option of the `ROLLFORWARD DATABASE` command identifies the directory that contains offline archived log files (including `S0000007.LOG`) that are to be used to perform the roll-forward operation. The `Roll-forward` utility searches the active log directory first, and then searches the directory specified with the `OVERFLOW LOG PATH` option for log files needed to perform a roll-forward recovery operation.

Question 13

The correct answer is **B**. If you want to restore a table space from a backup image and the table space name has changed since the backup image was created, you reference the table space by its new name. Table space metadata is stored in an external file, and DB2 uses the information stored in this file to correctly identify the table space to restore.

Question 14

The correct answer is **A**. Whenever the DB2 database manager detects that an index is no longer valid, it automatically attempts to rebuild it. However, the point in time at which the DB2 database manager attempts to rebuild an invalid index is controlled by the `INDEXREC` parameter of the database or the DB2 database manager configuration file.

Question 15

The correct answer is **D**. Although you can use the `indexrec` parameter of the database or the DB2 database manager configuration file to control when indexes are rebuilt as part of a crash recovery operation, doing so has no effect on how indexes are rebuilt during roll-forward recovery operations. To control that behavior, you must assign the appropriate value to the `logindexbuild` database configuration parameter.

Question 16

The correct answer is **A**. Before you can use a DB2 database's split mirror copy, it must first be initialized. To initialize a split mirror database copy, execute the system command `db2inidb`.

Question 17

The correct answer is **C**. After ensuring the systems to use as the primary and secondary servers are identical and that a TCP/IP connection exists between them, you can establish an HADR environment by performing the following tasks, in the following order:

1. Determine the host name, host IP address, and the service name or port number for both the primary and the secondary database servers.
2. Create the standby database by restoring a backup image or initializing a split mirror copy of the database that is to serve as the primary database.
3. Set the HADR configuration parameters on both the primary and the standby databases.
4. Connect to the standby instance and start HADR on the standby database.
5. Connect to the primary instance and start HADR on the primary database.

Question 18

The correct answer is **B**. Both the primary and the standby databases must be single-partition databases, and they both must have the same database name; however, they do not have to be stored on the same database path.

Question 19

The correct answer is **A**. Load operations against primary databases in an HADR environment can have an effect on indexes, tables, and table spaces.

Question 20

The correct answer is **C**. Because load operations are not recorded in a database's transaction log files, whether a load operation can be duplicated depends upon whether a copy of the loaded data was saved as part of the load process (which is the case if you specified the `LOAD` command's `COPY YES` option). If you perform a load operation on the primary database and specify the `COPY YES` option, the command will execute on the primary database and the data will be replicated to the standby database—provided the copy of the loaded data created can be accessed by the standby database via the path or device supplied with the `LOAD` command. If the standby database cannot access the data, the table space in which the table is stored is marked invalid on the standby database, and the standby database will stop replaying log records that pertain to this table space.

Question 21

The correct answer is **A**. You can enable the ROS on the HADR standby database by using the DB2 instance–level registry variable DB2_HADR_ROS. The steps involved are:

Step 1: Set the registry variable.

```
db2set DB2_HADR_ROS=ON
```

Step 2: Deactivate the standby database.

```
DEACTIVATE DB HADRDB
```

Step 3: Stop HADR on the standby database.

```
STOP HADR ON DATABASE HADRDB
```

Step 4: Stop and start the standby DB2 instance.

```
db2stop; db2start
```

Step 5: Start HADR on the standby database.

```
START HADR ON DATABASE HADRDB AS STANDBY
```

Question 22

The correct answer is **D**. SUPERASYNC synchronization mode has the shortest transaction response time because primary transaction commits have no dependency on the standby commit. And in the meantime, if a system failure occurs, SUPERASYNC is highly susceptible to data loss. Table 7.5 lists the detail for each synchronization mode.

Question 23

The correct answer is **C**. To recover the HR.EMPLOYEE table, it is always faster to restore the associated table space instead of restoring the complete database. This helps you in two ways: other application users except HR schema users will not be affected, and table space restoration will be quicker.

Question 24

The correct answer is **C**. DB2 pureScale is built using Reliable Scalable Cluster Technology (RSCT) and Tivoli System Automation (TSA), providing automatic heartbeat detection and automatic client reroute facilities. The automatic client reroute is an IBM Data Server feature that redirects client application connections from a failed DB2 member to another DB2 member within a pureScale system, so applications can continue their work with minimal interruption. Also, the built-in automatic workload balancing feature distributes work in a balanced fashion among the DB2 members.

Question 25

The correct answer is **A**. You use the `db2haicu` utility to configure and administer the DB2 cluster environment. You use the commands `lssam`, `db2instance -list`, and `db2cluster` to investigate the states of Tivoli System Automation for Multiplatform.

Question 26

The correct answer is **B**. The suggested way is to perform a database rebuild with a specific set of table spaces, instead of rebuilding all the table spaces. Answer A is incorrect because you cannot specify specific table spaces in the `REBUILD WITH ALL TABLESPACES` option. Answers C and D will restore the database with all the table spaces that are known to the database during image restoration.

Question 27

The correct answer is **D**. The only currently supported file system for pureScale is the IBM General Parallel File System.

Question 28

The correct answer is **D**. There is no WAITING_FOR_FAILOVER state available within a DB2 member, as the failover is instantaneous in case of system problems.

Question 29

The correct answer is **C**. There is no BECOMING_SECONDARY state available within the CF. However, there is the BECOMING_PRIMARY state, in which the CF will take over the primary CF role if no other primary CF is running in the pureScale cluster.

Question 30

The correct answers are **C** and **D**. The full database restore operation requires an exclusive connection to the database and does not allow any other application to connect. In case of a user table space restore operation, the table space will not be available to the user until the operation is completed. However, if the restore pertains to the system catalog table space, the whole database will not be available for the application to connect. Answer A is incorrect due to byte order difference between big endian (AIX) and little endian (Linux) architectures. Answer E is incorrect because you can successfully restore a database from a 32-bit system to a 64-bit system, but vice-versa is not allowed.

Question 31

The correct answer is **C**. The only isolation level that is supported on the Read on Standby HADR database is Uncommitted Read (UR). Any application requests other than UR will receive an error SQL1773N reason code 1. DBA can enforce the UR isolation level on the standby by setting the DB2 registry variable DB2_STANDBY_ISO=UR. When you set the CUR_COMMIT database configuration parameter to ON, all the queries will return the data's committed value when the query is submitted.

Question 32

The correct answers are **B** and **C**. The database table reorganization, index reorganization, or DDL change activities initiates the replay-only window, and any attempts to connect to the active standby database during this period will receive error SQL1776N reason code 4. You can monitor this by using the db2pd command.

Example:

```
db2pd -db db210db -hadr

Database Member 0 -- Database DB210DB -- Active Standby -- Up 24 days 06:58:01 --
Date 2013-07-31-19.16.24.410579
....
....
                 READS_ON_STANDBY_ENABLED = Y
     STANDBY_REPLAY_ONLY_WINDOW_ACTIVE = Y
      STANDBY_REPLAY_ONLY_WINDOW_START = 07/31/2013 19:16:16.000000 (1375298176)
STANDBY_REPLAY_ONLY_WINDOW_TRAN_COUNT = 1
```

Note that load, RUNSTATS, and database backup operations will not initiate the replay-only window.

The bulk database insert and DDL changes are not supported on the active standby, so D and E are incorrect answers.

Question 33

The correct answer is **D**. The only supported synchronization mode for auxiliary standby is SUPERASYNC. You can see the supported modes in Table 7.6.

Question 34

The correct answer is **B**. The HADR multiple standby functionality supports only one principal standby. The rest of the information is available in Table 7.6.

Question 35

The correct answer is A. The only isolation level supported on the ROS HADR database is Uncommitted Read (UR). Any application requests other than UR will receive an error SQL1773N reason code 1. DBA can enforce the UR isolation level on the standby by setting the DB2 registry variable DB2_STANDBY_ISO=UR. The registry setting B2_HADR_ROS is to enable the ROS. The registry setting DB2_HADR_NO_IP_CHECK is for network address translation support. When you set the CUR_COMMIT database configuration parameter to ON, all the queries will return the data's committed value when the query is submitted.

Question 36

The correct answers are **B** and **C**. To implement a delayed replay, you set the HADR_REPLAY_DELAY parameter; the only supported HADR synchronization mode is SUPERASYNC. Setting HADR_REPLAY_DELAY to 7200 will delay the log replay on the standby by two hours.

Question 37

The correct answer is **B**. The HADR auxiliary standby database will always be in the REMOTE_CATCHUP state irrespective of the HADR_LOG_GAP between the primary and the auxiliary standby. In the following example, standby member 10.112.0.1 is the auxiliary standby server.

```
db2 "SELECT HADR_ROLE, STANDBY_ID, HADR_STATE, PRIMARY_MEMBER_HOST, STANDBY_MEMBER_
HOST FROM TABLE (MON_GET_HADR (NULL))"

HADR_ROLE STANDBY_ID HADR_STATE        PRIMARY_MEMBER_HOST  STANDBY_MEMBER_HOST
--------- ---------- ----------------- -------------------- -------------------
PRIMARY            1 PEER                      10.110.20.5           10.110.7.6
PRIMARY            2 REMOTE_CATCHUP            10.110.20.5           10.112.0.1
  2 record(s) selected.
```

Question 38

The correct answer is **B**. The maximum number of supported pureScale DB2 members is 128 (0–127).

Question 39

The correct answer is **C**. The maximum number of supported pureScale DB2 CF servers is two (128, 129). At bare minimum, you can have only one primary CF; however, you need two CFs (primary and secondary) to eliminate a single point of failure.

Question 40

The correct answer is **D**. At a minimum, you can have only one primary CF; however, you need two CFs (primary and secondary) to eliminate a single point of failure. Condering the requirement of company ABC, it is recommended to have an additional CF installed for an effective pureScale operation.

Question 41

The correct answer is **B**. When you disable cluster operations by using the `db2haicu -disable` option, high availability on the database manager ceases. However, using the `-delete` option will remove all the cluster policies from the instance. Answers C and D are incorrect command syntaxes.

Question 42

The correct answer is **B**. HADR is a shared nothing architecture, as you will be using separate servers to set up primary and standby databases. No resources are shared between the servers.

Question 43

The correct answers are **A** and **C**. Currently, delta backup, incremental backup, and health monitors are not support in a pureScale environment.

Question 44

The correct answer is **A**. The pureScale cluster solution uses a shared disk architecture to share common data between the DB2 members. However, other system components, such as memory and processors, are not shared between the members of the cluster.

Question 45

The correct answer is **C**. The `MON_GET_BUFFERPOOL` function determines the Group Buffer Pool hit ratio. You use table function `MON_GET_CONNECTION` to determine the performance metrics for one or more connections, `MON_GET_CF` to obtain the CF metrics, and `DB2_GET_INSTANCE_INFO` to query the CF status.

Question 46

The correct answer is **A**. While performing a database restoration from one system to another, you set the DB2 registry variable `DB2_RESTORE_GRANT_ADMIN_AUTHORITIES` to `YES` to grant `SECADM`, `DBADM`, `DATAACCESS`, and `ACCESSCTRL` privileges on the target database to the user who is to perform the restore operation. Setting the `DB2_COMPATIBILITY_VECTOR` to `NULL` has no effect on the database and is generally used for database compatibility purposes between Oracle and DB2, or Sybase and DB2. The `DB2_LIMIT_FENCED_GROUP` setting is available on Microsoft Windows to restrict the privilges of the `db2fmp` process to the privilges assigned to the `DB2USERS` group. DB2 will not let you complete answer D after the restoration process.

Question 47

The correct answer is **A**. The Global Lock Manager manages the concurrency in the pureScale cluster environment by keeping track of the lock requests made by the Local Lock Managers of active database members. The Group Buffer Pool keeps page caching consistent across all the members and coordinates the copies of pages that might exists across the members' Local Buffer Pools.

Question 48

The correct answer is **B**. The physical locks (p-locks) are introduced in pureScale to control multiple DB2 members' concurrent access to the physical pages. You can apply these p-locks in either shared or exclusive mode, and they are managed by the CF's Global Lock Manager.

Question 49

The correct answer is **D**. Duplexing is the method CF uses to keep both the primary and the secondary up to date to allow transparent takeovers between the primary and secondary CFs. Other synchronization modes are HADR synchronization modes.

Question 50

The correct answer is **B**. Because pureScale supports only two CF servers—ID 128 and ID 129—a command attempt to start 130 would fail with error SQL1542N: "Adding the CF failed because the maximum number of CFs in the DB2 instance has been reached."

CHAPTER 8

DB2 Security

This chapter will introduce you to the security model available in DB2. You will learn to use many of the DB2 security features, including roles, trusted contexts, trusted connections, row and column access control, and label-based access control to protect data and database objects against unauthorized access and modification. At the end of the chapter, you will also be able use the DB2 audit facility to monitor the data access.

Exam Objectives

- ✓ Demonstrate the ability to identify the methods to use to restrict access to data stored in a DB2 database
- ✓ Demonstrate the ability to identify the authorization levels used by DB2
- ✓ Demonstrate the ability to identify the privileges used by DB2
- ✓ Demonstrate the ability to identify how to grant specific authorizations and privileges to a user or group
- ✓ Demonstrate the ability to simplify the administration and management of privileges by using roles
- ✓ Demonstrate the ability to identify how to revoke specific authorizations and privileges from a user or group
- ✓ Demonstrate the ability to create and use trusted contexts and trusted connections between database and application servers
- ✓ Demonstrate the ability to implement column or row permissions by using row and column access control (RCAC)

- ✓ Demonstrate the ability to create and activate column masks
- ✓ Demonstrate the ability to implement label-based access control (LBAC)

Controlling Database Access

Identity theft—a crime in which someone wrongfully obtains another person's personal data (such as a Social Security number, bank account number, or credit card number) and uses it in some way that involves fraud or deception for economic gain—is the fastest-growing crime in our nation today. Criminals are stealing information by overhearing conversations made on cell phones, by reading faxes and emails, by hacking into computers, by waging telephone and email scams, by stealing wallets and purses, by stealing discarded documents from trash bins, by stealing mail, and by taking advantage of careless online shopping and banking habits. But more frightening is the fact that studies show that up to 70 percent of all identity theft cases are inside jobs—perpetrated by a coworker or an employee of a business you patronize. In these cases, all that is needed is access to your personal data, which the perpetrator can often find in a company database.

Every database management system must be able to protect data against unauthorized access and modification. DB2 uses a combination of external security services and internal access control mechanisms to perform this vital task. In most cases, three different levels of security are employed. The first level controls access to the instance under which a database was created, the second controls access to the database itself, and the third controls access to the data and data objects that reside within the database.

Authentication

The first security portal most users must pass through on their way to gaining access to a DB2 instance or database is a process known as *authentication*. The purpose of authentication is to verify that users really are who they say they are. Normally, an external security facility that is not part of DB2 performs the authentication. This security facility may be part of the operating system (as is the case with AIX, Solaris, Linux, HP-UX, Windows Server 2008/2012, and many others), may be a separate add-on product (for example, Distributed Computing Environment [DCE] Security Services), or may not exist at all (which is the case with Windows 95, Windows 98, and Windows Millennium Edition). If a security facility does exist, it must be presented with two specific items before a user can be authenticated: a unique user ID and a corresponding password. The user ID identifies the user to the security facility, and the password, which is information known only by the user and the security facility, verifies that the user is indeed who he or she claims to be.

Where Does Authentication Occur?

Because DB2 can reside in environments composed of multiple clients, gateways, and servers, each of which may be running on a different operating system, deciding where authentication is to take place can be a daunting task. To simplify things, DB2 uses a parameter called authentication in the DB2 database manager configuration file to determine how and where users are authenticated. Such a file is associated with every instance, and the value you assign to this parameter, often referred to as the *authentication type*, is set initially when an instance is created. On the server side, the authentication type is specified during the instance creation process (you can update it anytime with an instance restart); on the client side, the authentication type is specified when a remote database is cataloged. Only one authentication type exists for each instance, and it controls access to that instance as well as to all databases that fall under that instance's control.

With DB2 10.1, the following authentication types are available:

- **SERVER.** Authentication occurs at the server workstation by using the security facility that the server's operating system provides. The user ID and password that the user enters to attach to an instance or connect to a database are compared with the user ID and password combinations stored at the server to determine whether the user is permitted to access the instance or database. By default, this is the authentication type used when an instance is first created.
- **SERVER_ENCRYPT.** Authentication occurs at the server workstation by using the security facility that the server's operating system provides. However, the user ID and password that the user enters to attach to an instance or connect to a database stored on the server may be encrypted at the client workstation before it is sent to the server workstation for validation.
- **CLIENT.** Authentication occurs at the client workstation or database partition where a client application is invoked by using the security facility that the client's operating system provides, assuming one is available. If no security facility is available, authentication is handled in a slightly different manner. The user ID and password that the user enters to attach to an instance or connect to a database are compared with the user ID and password combinations stored at the client or node to determine whether the user is permitted to access the instance or the database.
- **KERBEROS.** Authentication occurs at the server workstation by using a security facility that supports the Kerberos security protocol. This protocol performs authentication as a third-party service by using conventional cryptography to create a shared secret key. The key becomes the credentials used to verify the identity of the user whenever local or network services are requested; this eliminates the need to pass a user ID and password across the network as ASCII text. (If both the client and the server support the Kerberos security protocol, the user ID and password that the user enters to attach to an instance or connect to a database are encrypted at the client workstation and sent to the server for validation.) Note that the KERBEROS authentication type is supported only on clients and servers that

are using anything later than the Windows 2000, Windows XP, or Windows NT operating system. In addition, both client and server workstations must belong either to the same Windows domain or to trusted domains.

- **KRB_SERVER_ENCRYPT**. Authentication occurs at the server workstation by using either the KERBEROS or the SERVER_ENCRYPT authentication method. If the client's authentication type is set to KERBEROS, authentication is performed at the server using the Kerberos security system. However, if the client's authentication type is set to anything other than KERBEROS, or if the Kerberos authentication service is unavailable, the server acts as if the SERVER_ENCRYPT authentication type was specified, and the rules of this authentication method apply.
- **DATA_ENCRYPT**. Authentication occurs at the server workstation by using the SERVER_ENCRYPT authentication method. In addition, all user data is encrypted before it is passed from client to server and from server to client.
- **DATA_ENCRYPT_CMP**. Authentication occurs at the server workstation by using the SERVER_ENCRYPT authentication method; all user data is encrypted before it is passed from client to server and from server to client. In addition, this authentication type provides compatibility for down-level products that do not support the DATA_ENCRYPT authentication type. Such products connect by using the SERVER_ENCRYPT authentication type, and user data is not encrypted.
- **GSSPLUGIN**. Authentication occurs at the server workstation by using a Generic Security Service Application Program Interface (GSS-API) plug-in. If the client's authentication type is not specified, the server returns a list of server-supported plug-ins (in the srvcon_gssplugin_list database manager configuration parameter) to the client. The client then selects the first plug-in it finds in the client plug-in directory from the list. If the client does not support any plug-in in the list, the client is authenticated by using the KERBEROS authentication method.
- **GSS_SERVER_ENCRYPT**. Authentication occurs at the server workstation by using either the GSSPLUGIN or the SERVER_ENCRYPT authentication method. That is, if client authentication occurs through a GSS-API plug-in, the client is authenticated using the first client-supported plug-in found in the list of server-supported plug-ins. If the client does not support any of the plug-ins found in the server-supported plug-in list, the client is authenticated with the KERBEROS authentication method. If the client does not support the Kerberos security protocol, the client is authenticated using the SERVER_ENCRYPT authentication method.

Note that if the authentication type used by the client workstation encrypts user ID and password information before sending it to a server for authentication (i.e., SERVER_ENCRYPT, KRB_SERVER_ENCRYPT, and so on), you must configure the server to use a compatible authentication method. Otherwise, it will not be able to process the encrypted data received, and an error will occur.

It is also important to note that if you do not specify the authentication type for a client workstation, the SERVER_ENCRYPT authentication method is used by default. If such a client tries to communicate with a server that does not support the SERVER_ENCRYPT authentication method, the client will attempt to use the authentication type that the server is using—provided you have configured the server to use only one authentication type. If the server supports multiple authentication types, an error will be generated.

Security Plug-ins

In DB2 10.1, authentication is done by using security plug-ins. A security plug-in is a dynamically loadable library that provides authentication security services. DB2 supports two mechanisms for plug-in authentication:

- **User ID and password authentication**. This involves authentication using a user ID and password. You implement the following authentication types by using user ID/password authentication plug-ins:
  - CLIENT
  - SERVER
  - SERVER_ENCRYPT
  - DATA_ENCRYPT
  - DATA_ENCRYPT_CMP
- **GSS-API authentication**. GSS-API was formally known as Generic Security Service Application Program Interface, Version 2 (IETF RFC2743) and Generic Security Service API Version 2: C-Bindings (IETF RFC2744). You implement the following authentication types by using GSS-API authentication plug-ins:
  - KERBEROS
  - GSSPLUGIN
  - KRB_SERVER_ENCRYPT
  - GSS_SERVER_ENCRYPT

KRB_SERVER_ENCRYPT and GSS_SERVER_ENCRYPT support both GSS-API authentication and user ID/password authentication; however, GSS-API authentication is the preferred authentication type.

Each plug-in can be used independently or in conjunction with one or more of the other plug-ins. For example, you might specify only a server authentication plug-in to use and allow DB2 to use the defaults for client and group authentication. Alternatively, you might specify only a group or client authentication plug-in. The only situation that requires both a client and server plug-in is for GSS-API authentication. (In some cases—for example, if you are using Microsoft Active Directory to validate a user—you may need to create your own custom security plug-in and make it available for DB2 to use.)

You enable the security plug-in by setting the following database manager configuration parameters:

- **CLNT_PW_PLUGIN**. Specifies the name of the client user ID and password plug-in
- **CLNT_KRB_PLUGIN**. Specifies the name of the client Kerberos plug-in
- **GROUP_PLUGIN**. Specifies the name of the group plug-in
- **LOCAL_GSSPLUGIN**. Specifies the name of the local authorization plug-in
- **SRV_PLUGIN_MODE**. Specifies the server plug-in mode
- **SRVCON_GSSPLUGIN_LIST**. Specifies the server list of the GSS plug-in
- **SRVCON_PW_PLUGIN**. Specifies the name of the server user ID and password plug-in
- **SRVCON_AUTH**. Specifies the server connection authentication
- **AUTHENTICATION**. Specifies the authentication mechanism

If you do not supply the values for these parameters, the default behavior for DB2 10.1 is to use a user ID/password plug-in that implements an operating-system-level mechanism for authentication.

Trusted and Untrusted Clients

If you configure both the server and the client to use the CLIENT authentication type, authentication occurs at the client workstation (if the database is a nonpartitioned database) or at the database partition from which the client application is invoked (if the database is a partitioned database) by using the security facility that the client workstation's operating system provides. But what happens if the client workstation is using an operating system that does not contain a tightly integrated security facility, and no separate add-on security facility has been made available? Does such a configuration compromise security? The answer is no.

However, in such environments, the DB2 database manager for the instance at the server must be able to determine which clients will be responsible for validating users and which clients will be forced to let the server handle user authentication. To make this distinction, clients that use an operating system that contains a tightly integrated security facility (for example, OS/390, VM, VSE, MVS, AS/400, Windows NT, Windows 2000, Windows 2003, Windows 2008, Windows 2012, and all supported versions of UNIX) are classified as trusted clients, whereas clients that use an operating system that does not provide an integrated security facility (for example, Windows 95, Windows 98, and Windows Millennium Edition) are treated as untrusted clients.

The trust_allclnts parameter of a DB2 database manager configuration file helps the DB2 database manager, for an instance on a server, anticipate whether to treat its clients as trusted or untrusted. If this configuration parameter is set to YES (which is the default), the DB2 database manager assumes that any client that accesses the instance is a trusted client and that some form of authentication will take place at the client. However, if you set this configuration parameter to NO, the DB2 database manager assumes that one or more untrusted clients will try to access the server; therefore, all users must be authenticated at the server. (Setting this configuration parameter to DRDAONLY will treat only MVS, OS/390, VM, VSE, and OS/400 clients as trusted clients.) Note that, regardless of how the trust_allclnts parameter is set, whenever an untrusted client attempts to access an instance or a database, user authentication always occurs at the server.

In some situations, it may be desirable to authenticate users at the server, even when untrusted clients will not be used. In such situations, you can set the trust_clntauth configuration parameter of a DB2 database manager configuration file to control where to validate trusted clients. When the default value for this parameter (which is CLIENT) is accepted, authentication for trusted clients will take place at the client workstation. If, however, you change the value for this parameter to SERVER, authentication for all trusted clients will occur at the server.

Authorities and Privileges

Once a user has been authenticated, and an attachment to an instance or a connection to a database has been established, the DB2 database manger evaluates any authorities and privileges that have been assigned to the user to determine what operations the user is allowed to do. Privileges convey the rights to execute certain actions against specific database resources (such as tables and views). Authorities convey a set of privileges or the right to perform high-level administrative, maintenance, and utility operations on an instance or a database.

You can assign authorities and privileges directly to a user, or they can be obtained indirectly from the authorities and privileges that you have assigned to a group of which the user is a member. Together, authorities and privileges act to control access to the DB2 database manager for an instance, to one or more databases running under that instance's control, and to a particular database's objects. Users can work only with those objects for which they have been given the appropriate authorization—that is, the required authority or privilege. Figure 8.1 provides a hierarchical view of the authorities and privileges that DB2 10 recognizes.

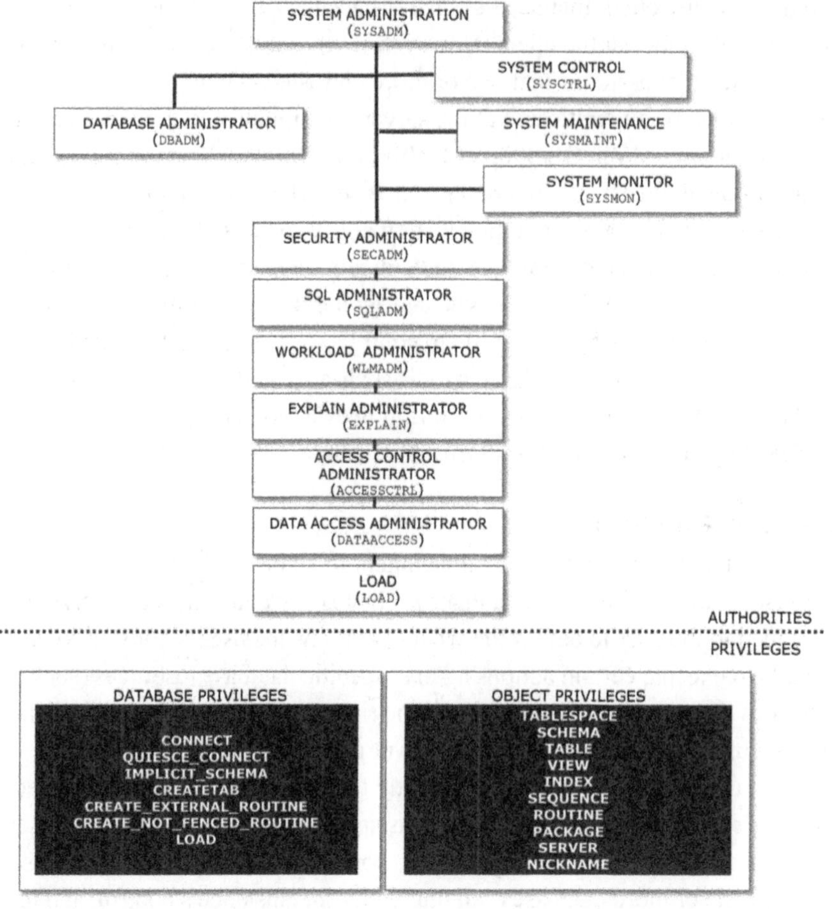

Figure 8.1: Hierarchy of the authorities and privileges available with DB2 10.1

Authorities

DB2 10 uses 12 different authorities to control how users perform administrative and maintenance operations against an instance or a database:

- System Administrator (SYSADM) authority
- System Control (SYSCTRL) authority
- System Maintenance (SYSMAINT) authority
- System Monitor (SYSMON) authority
- Database Administrator (DBADM) authority
- Security Administrator (SECADM) authority
- SQL Administrator (SQLADM) authority
- Workload Management Administrator (WLMADM) authority

- Explain Administrator (EXPLAIN) authority
- Access Control Administrator (ACCESSCTRL) authority
- Data Access Administrator (DATAACCESS) authority
- Non-Administrator Database (LOAD) authority

Four of these apply to the DB2 database manager instance (and to all databases that are under that instance's control), whereas eight apply only to specific databases within a particular instance. You assign the instance-level authorities only to groups; the names of the groups possessing these authorities are stored in the DB2 database manager configuration file that is associated with the instance. Conversely, you assign the database-level authorities to individual users and, in some cases, groups; groups and users having database-level authorities are recorded in the system catalog tables of the database to which the authority applies.

System Administrator Authority

SYSADM authority is the highest level of administrative authority available. Users who have this authority can run any DB2 utility, execute any DB2 command, and perform any SQL or XQuery operation that does not attempt to access data protected by LBAC. Users with this authority also have the ability to control all database objects within an instance, including databases, database partition groups, buffer pools, table spaces, schemas, tables, views, indexes, aliases, servers, data types, functions, procedures, triggers, packages, and event monitors. Additionally, users who have this authority are allowed to perform the following tasks:

- Upgrade (migrate) an existing database from a previous version of DB2 to a new DB2 version
- Modify the parameter values of the DB2 database manager configuration file associated with an instance—including specifying which groups have SYSADM, SYSCTRL, SYSMAINT, and SYSMON authority; the DB2 database manager configuration file controls the amount of system resources allocated to a single instance
- Grant DBADM authority and SECADM authority to individual users and groups
- Revoke DBADM authority and SECADM authority from individual users and groups

You assign SYSADM authority only to a group by storing the appropriate group name in the sysadm_group parameter of the DB2 database manager configuration file associated with an instance. (You do this by executing an UPDATE DATABASE MANAGER CONFIGURATION command with the SYSADM_GROUP parameter specified, along with the name of the group that is to receive SYSADM authority.) Individual membership in the group itself is controlled through the security facility provided by the operating system used on the workstation where the instance has been defined. Users who possess SYSADM authority are responsible both for controlling the DB2 database manager associated with an instance and for ensuring the safety and integrity of the data contained in databases that fall under the instance's control.

System Control Authority

SYSCTRL authority is the highest level of system or instance control authority available. Users who have this authority can perform maintenance and utility operations both on a DB2 database manager instance and on any databases that fall under that instance's control. However, because SYSCTRL authority allows special users to maintain an instance that contains sensitive data that they most likely do not have the right to view or modify, users who are granted this authority do not implicitly receive authority to access the data stored in the databases that are controlled by the instance. However, because a connection to a database is required in order to perform some of the utility operations, users possessing SYSCTRL authority for a particular instance also receive the privileges needed to connect to each database under that instance's control.

Users with SYSCTRL authority (or higher) are allowed to perform the following tasks:

- Update a database, node, or Distributed Connection Services (DCS) directory (by cataloging/uncataloging databases, nodes, or DCS databases)
- Modify the parameter values in one or more database configuration files (a database configuration file controls the amount of system resources that are allocated to a single database during normal operation)
- Force users off the system
- Create or drop a database
- Create, alter, or drop a table space
- Make a backup image of a database or a table space
- Restore an existing database by using a backup image
- Restore a table space by using a backup image
- Create a new database from a database backup image
- Perform a roll-forward recovery operation on a database
- Start or stop a DB2 database manager instance
- Run a trace on a database operation
- Take database system monitor snapshots by using monitor table functions for a DB2 database manager instance or any database under the instance's control
- Query the state of a table space
- Update recovery history log files
- Quiesce (restrict access to) a table space
- Reorganize a table
- Collect catalog statistics by using the RUNSTATS utility

As with SYSADM authority, you assign SYSCTRL authority only to a group by storing the appropriate group name in the sysctrl_group parameter of the DB2 database manager configuration file associated with a particular instance. (You do this by executing an UPDATE DATABASE MANAGER CONFIGURATION command with the SYSCTRL_GROUP parameter specified, along with the name of the group that is to receive SYSCTRL authority.) Again, individual membership in the group itself is controlled through the security facility that is used on the workstation where the instance has been defined.

System Maintenance Authority

SYSMAINT authority is the second highest level of system or instance control authority available. Users who hold this authority can perform maintenance and utility operations both on a DB2 database manager instance and on all databases that fall under that instance's control. SYSMAINT authority allows special users to maintain a database that contains sensitive data that they most likely do not have the right to view or modify. Therefore, users who are granted this authority do not implicitly receive authority to access the data stored in the databases on which they are permitted to perform maintenance. However, because a connection to a database must exist before some utility operations can be performed, users possessing SYSMAINT authority for a particular instance automatically receive the privileges needed to connect to each database that falls under that instance's control.

Users with SYSMAINT authority (or higher) are allowed to perform the following tasks:

- Modify the parameter values of one or more DB2 database configuration files
- Make a backup image of a database or a table space
- Restore an existing database by using a backup image
- Restore a table space by using a backup image
- Perform a roll-forward recovery operation on a database
- Start or stop a DB2 database manager instance
- Run a trace on the database operation
- Take database system monitor snapshots by using monitor table functions for a DB2 database manager instance or any database under the instance's control
- Query the state of a table space
- Update recovery log history files
- Quiesce (restrict access to) a table space
- Reorganize a table
- Collect catalog statistics by using the RUNSTATS utility

As with SYSADM and SYSCTRL authorities, you assign SYSMAINT authority only to a group by storing the appropriate group name in the sysmaint_group parameter of the DB2 database manager configuration file associated with a particular instance. (You do this by executing an UPDATE DATABASE MANAGER CONFIGURATION command with the SYSMAINT_GROUP parameter specified, along with the name of the group that is to receive SYSMAINT authority.) Again, individual membership in the group itself is controlled through the security facility that is used on the workstation where the instance has been defined.

System Monitor Authority

SYSMON authority is the third highest level of system or instance control authority available with DB2. Users who hold this authority can take system monitor snapshots by using monitor table functions for a DB2 database manager instance and for one or more databases that fall under that instance's control. SYSMON authority allows special users to monitor the performance of a database that contains sensitive data that they most likely do not have the right to view or modify. Therefore, users who possess this authority do not implicitly receive authority to access the data stored in the databases on which they are permitted to collect snapshot monitor information. However, because a connection to a database must exist before the snapshot monitor SQL table functions can be used, users having SYSMON authority for a particular instance automatically receive the privileges needed to connect to each database under that instance's control.

Users with SYSMON authority (or higher) are allowed to perform the following tasks:

- Obtain the current settings of the snapshot monitor switches
- Modify the settings of one or more snapshot monitor switches
- Reset all counters used by the snapshot monitor
- Obtain a list of active databases
- Obtain a list of active applications, including DCS applications
- Collect snapshot monitor data
- Use the snapshot monitor table functions

As with SYSADM, SYSCTRL, and SYSMAINT authority, you assign SYSMON authority only to a group by storing the appropriate group name in the sysmon_group parameter of the DB2 database manager configuration file associated with a particular instance. (You do this by executing an UPDATE DATABASE MANAGER CONFIGURATION command with the SYSMON_GROUP parameter specified, along with the name of the group that is to receive SYSMON authority.) Again, individual membership in the group itself is controlled through the security facility that is used on the workstation where the instance has been defined.

Database Administrator Authority

DBADM authority is the second highest level of administrative authority available (just below SYSADM authority). Users who have this authority can run most DB2 utilities, issue database-specific DB2 commands, perform most SQL and XQuery operations, and access data stored in any table in a database—provided that data is not protected by LBAC and that DATAACCESS authority is not revoked. To access data protected by LBAC, users must have the appropriate LBAC credentials. However, they can perform these functions only on the database for which they hold DBADM authority.

Additionally, users with DBADM authority (or higher) are allowed to perform the following tasks:

- Read database log files
- Create, activate, and drop event monitors
- Query the state of a table space
- Update recovery history log files
- Quiesce (restrict access to) a table space
- Reorganize a table
- Collect catalog statistics by using the RUNSTATS utility

Unlike with SYSADM, SYSCTRL, SYSMAINT, and SYSMON authority, you can assign DBADM authority to both individual users and groups by executing the appropriate form of the GRANT SQL statement (which we will look at shortly). When you give a user DBADM authority for a particular database, that user automatically receives all database privileges available for that database as well.

Note: Anytime a user with SYSADM or SYSCTRL authority creates a new database, that user automatically receives DBADM, SECADM, ACCESSCTRL, and DATAACCESS authority on that database. Furthermore, if a user with SYSADM or SYSCTRL authority creates a database and is later removed from the SYSADM or SYSCTRL group (i.e., the user's SYSADM or SYSCTRL authority is revoked), the user retains DBADM, SECADM, ACCESSCTRL, and DATAACCESS authority for that database until it is explicitly revoked.

Security Administrator Authority

SECADM authority is a special database level of authority that allows special users to configure various LBAC elements to restrict access to one or more tables that contain data to which they most likely do not have access themselves. Users who possess this authority do not implicitly receive authority to access the data stored in the databases for which they manage data access. In fact, users with SECADM authority are allowed to perform only the following tasks:

- Grant and revoke all database level authorities, including DBADM, SECADM, DATAACCESS, ACCESSSCTRL, EXPLAIN, SQLADM, WLMADM, and LOAD
- Create, drop, grant, and revoke security objects such as security policies, security labels, trusted contexts, and roles
- Grant and revoke LBAC rule exemptions
- Grant and revoke SETSESSIONUSER privileges (by using the GRANT SETSESSIONUSER SQL statement)
- Transfer ownership of any object not owned by the SECADM (by executing the TRANSFER OWNERSHIP SQL statement)

No other authority, including SYSADM authority, provides a user with these abilities. You assign SYSADM authority only to individual users; you cannot assign it to groups (including the group PUBLIC). To make this assignment, a system administrator executes the appropriate form of the GRANT SQL statement, and only users with SYSADM authority are allowed to grant this authority.

SQL Administrator Authority

SQLADM authority is needed to monitor and tune the SQL statements. Users with SQLADM are allowed to perform the following tasks:

- Create, drop, or flush event monitors
- Generate Explain data by using EXPLAIN
- Flush the optimization profile cache
- Perform table and index reorganization
- Perform RUNSTATS on the table and indexes
- Enable or disable event monitors
- Flush the package cache and prepare SQL statements

SQLADM can execute certain clauses of the following workload management commands:

- ALTER SERVICE CLASS on collect aggregate activity data, request data, and request metrics
- ALTER THRESHOLD on collect activity data
- ALTER WORK ACTION SET on collect activity data and aggregate activity data
- ALTER WORKLOAD on activity metrics, aggregate activity data, lock timeout, lock wait, and unit of work data

Users who hold SECADM or ACCESSCTRL authority can grant SQLADM authority to a user, a group, a role, or PUBLIC. If the DB2AUTH registry variable is set to SQLADM_NO_RUNSTATS_

REORG, users with SQLADM authority will not be able to perform REORG or RUNSTATS operations on tables or indexes.

Workload Management Administrator

WLMADM authority is required to manage workload objects for a specific database. Users with WLMADM are allowed to perform the following tasks:

- Create, alter, drop, and comment on the following WLM objects:
  - Service classes
  - Thresholds
  - Work action sets
  - Work class sets
  - Workloads
  - Histogram templates
- Grant and revoke workload privileges
- Execute built-in workload management routines

Users possessing SECADM or ACCESSCTRL authority can grant this authority to a user, a group, a role, or PUBLIC.

Explain Administrator Authority

EXPLAIN authority is needed to explain query access plans without actually gaining access to data for a specific database. Users with EXPLAIN are allowed to perform the following tasks:

- Generate access plan information for SQL statements
- Prepare the SQL statements
- Perform a DESCRIBE on the output of a SELECT statement or of an XQuery statement

Users who hold SECADM or ACCESSCTRL authority can grant this authority to a user, a group, a role, or PUBLIC.

Access Control Administrator Authority

ACCESSCTRL authority is required to grant and revoke privileges on objects within a database. Users with ACCESSCTRL are allowed to perform the following tasks:

- Grant and revoke SELECT privileges on the system catalog tables and views
- Grant and revoke all privileges on table, table space, view, index, nickname, package, routine (except DB2 audit routines), schema, sequence, server, global variables, and XML schema repository (XSR) objects

- Grant and revoke database privileges, including BINDADD, CONNECT, CREATETAB, CREATE_EXTERNAL_ROUTINE, CREATE_NOT_FENCED_ROUTINE, IMPLICIT_SCHEMA, LOAD, and QUIESCE_CONNECT
- Grant and revoke administrative authorities, including EXPLAIN, SQLADM, and WLMADM

Only the security administrator can assign ACCESSCTRL to a user, a group, or a role.

Data Access Administrator Authority

DATAACCESS authority is needed to grant or revoke data access privileges to data within a specific database. Users with DATAACCESS are allowed to perform the following tasks:

- Grant or revoke LOAD authority on the database
- Grant or revoke SELECT privileges on tables, including system catalog tables, views, MQTs, and nicknames
- Grant or revoke INSERT privileges on tables, views, MQTs, and nicknames
- Grant or revoke DELETE privileges on tables, views, MQTs, and nicknames
- Grant or revoke UPDATE privileges on tables, views, MQTs, and nicknames
- Grant or revoke EXECUTE privileges on all packages and routines except DB2 audit routines

Only the security administrator can grant DATAACCESS authority to a user, a group, or a role.

Nonadministrator (LOAD) Database Authority

LOAD authority is a special database level of administrative authority that has a much smaller scope than DBADM authority. Users who have LOAD authority, along with INSERT and in some cases DELETE privileges, on a particular table are allowed to bulk-load data into that table by using either the AutoLoader utility (db2atld command) or the LOAD command/API. LOAD authority permits special users to perform bulk-load operations against a database with which they most likely cannot do anything else. This authority provides a way for database administrators to allow more users to perform special database operations, such as ETL operations, without having to sacrifice control.

In addition to being able to load data into a database table, users with LOAD authority (or higher) are allowed to perform the following tasks:

- Query the state of a table space by using the LIST TABLESPACES command
- Quiesce (restrict access to) a table space
- Perform bulk-load operations by using the Load utility (if exception tables are used as part of a load operation, the user must have INSERT privileges on the exception tables used as well as have INSERT privileges on the table being loaded)
- Collect catalog statistics by using the RUNSTATS utility

As with DBADM authority, you can assign LOAD authority to both individual users and groups by executing the appropriate form of the GRANT SQL statement.

Privileges

As mentioned earlier, privileges convey the rights to perform certain actions on specific database resources to both individual users and groups. With DB2 10.1, two distinct types of privileges exist: database privileges and object privileges.

Database Privileges

Database privileges apply to a database as a whole, and in many cases, they act as a second security checkpoint that must be cleared before access to data is provided. Figure 8.2 shows the different types of database privileges.

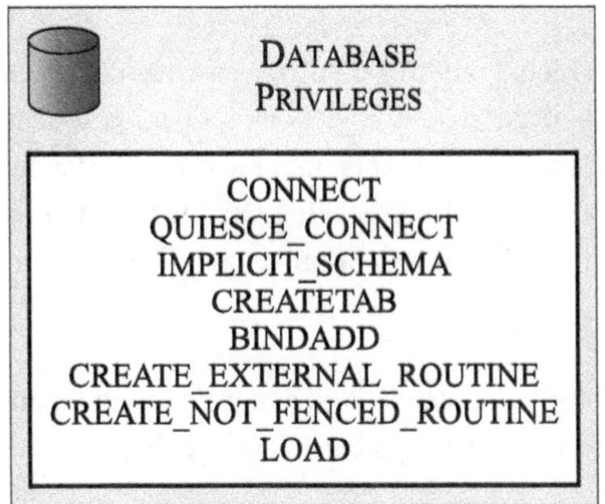

Figure 8.2: Database privileges available with DB2

As you can see in Figure 8.2, eight different database privileges exist:

- **CONNECT**. Allows a user to establish a connection to the database
- **QUIESCE_CONNECT**. Allows a user to establish a connection to the database while it is in a quiesced state (i.e., while access to it is restricted)
- **IMPLICIT_SCHEMA**. Allows a user to create a new schema in the database implicitly by creating an object and assigning that object a schema name that is different from any of the schema names that already exist in the database
- **CREATETAB**. Allows a user to create new tables in the database
- **BINDADD**. Allows a user to create packages in the database (by precompiling embedded SQL application source code files against the database or by binding application bind files to the database)

- **CREATE_EXTERNAL_ROUTINE.** Allows a user to create UDFs and procedures and store them in the database so that other users and applications can use them
- **CREATE_NOT_FENCED_ROUTINE.** Allows a user to create unfenced UDFs and procedures and store them in the database (unfenced UDFs and stored procedures are considered "safe" enough to be run in the DB2 database manager operating environment's process or address space; unless a UDF or procedure is registered as unfenced, the DB2 database manager insulates the UDF's or procedure's internal resources in such a way that they cannot be run in the DB2 database manager's address space)
- **LOAD.** Allows a user to bulk-load data into one or more existing tables in the database

At a minimum, a user must have CONNECT privileges on a database before working with any object contained in that database.

Object Privileges

Unlike database privileges, which apply to a database as a whole, object privileges pertain only to specific objects within a database. These objects include table spaces, schemas, tables, views, indexes, sequences, routines, packages, servers, and nicknames. Because the nature of each database object varies, the individual privileges that exist for each object can vary as well. The following sections describe the different sets of object privileges that are available with DB2 10.

Table Space Privileges

Table space privileges control what users can and cannot do with a particular table space. (Table spaces control where data in a database physically resides.) Figure 8.3 shows the only table space privilege available.

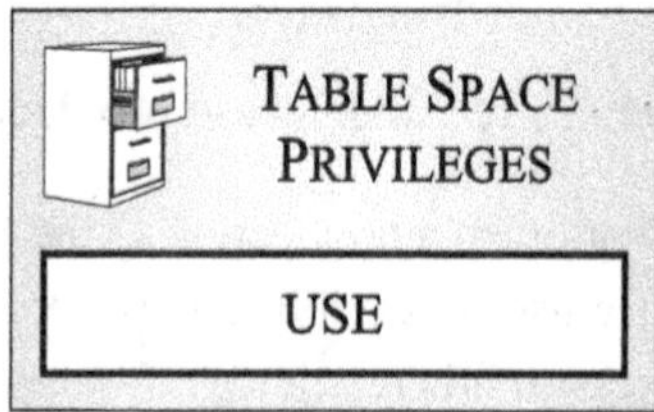

Figure 8.3: Table space privilege available with DB2

As you can see in Figure 8.3, only one table space privilege exists. That privilege is the USE privilege, which, when granted, allows a user to create tables and indexes in the table space. The owner of a table space (usually the individual who created the table space) automatically receives the USE privilege for that table space. The USE privilege cannot be used to provide a user with the ability to create tables in the SYSCATSPACE table space or in any temporary table space that might exist.

Schema Privileges

Schema privileges control what users can and cannot do with a particular schema. (A schema is an object that logically classifies and groups other objects in the database. Most objects are named by using a naming convention that consists of a schema name, followed by a period, followed by the object name.) Figure 8.4 shows the different types of schema privileges.

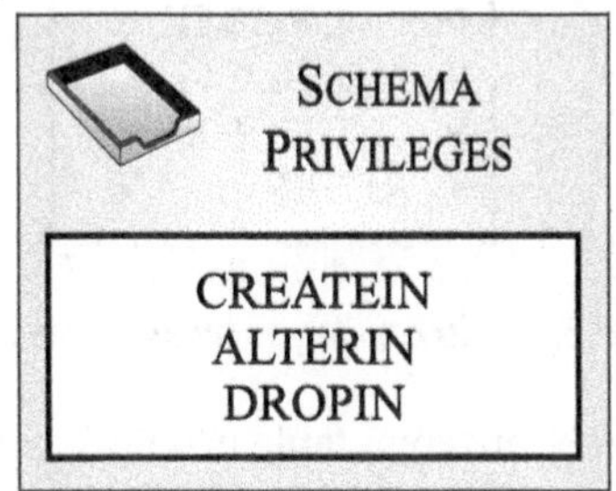

Figure 8.4: Schema privileges available with DB2

As you can see in Figure 8.4, three different schema privileges exist:

- **CREATEIN**. Allows a user to create objects within the schema
- **ALTERIN**. Allows a user to change the comment associated with any object in the schema or to alter any object that resides within the schema
- **DROPIN**. Allows a user to remove (drop) any object within the schema

Objects that can be manipulated within a schema include tables, views, indexes, packages, user-defined data types, UDFs, triggers, stored procedures, and aliases. The owner of a schema (usually the individual who created the schema) automatically receives all privileges available for that schema, along with the right to grant any combination of those privileges to other users and groups.

Table Privileges

Table privileges control what users can and cannot do with a particular table in a database. (A table is a logical structure that presents data as a collection of unordered rows with a fixed number of columns.) Figure 8.5 shows the different types of table privileges.

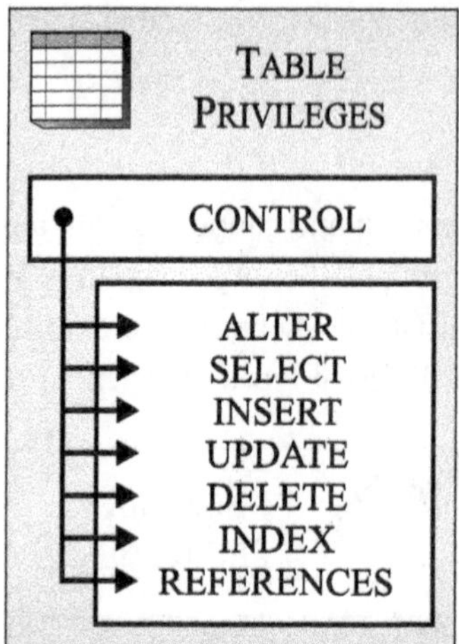

Figure 8.5: Table privileges available with DB2

As you can see in Figure 8.5, eight different table privileges exist:

- **CONTROL.** Provides a user with every table privilege available, allows the user to remove (drop) the table from the database, and gives the user the ability to grant and revoke one or more table privileges (except the CONTROL privilege) to and from other users and groups
- **ALTER.** Allows a user to execute the ALTER TABLE SQL statement against the table; in other words, it allows a user to add columns to the table, add or change comments associated with the table or any of its columns, create or drop a primary key for the table, create or drop a UNIQUE constraint for the table, create or drop a CHECK constraint for the table, and create or drop triggers for the table (provided the user holds the appropriate privileges for every object referenced by the trigger)
- **SELECT.** Allows a user to execute a SELECT SQL statement against the table; in other words, this privilege allows a user to retrieve data from a table, create a view that references the table, and run the Export utility against the table
- **INSERT.** Allows a user to execute the INSERT SQL statement against the table; in other words, it allows a user to add data to the table and run the Import utility against the table
- **UPDATE.** Allows a user to execute the UPDATE SQL statement against the table; in other words, this privilege allows a user to modify data in the table (this privilege can be granted for the entire table or limited to one or more columns within the table)
- **DELETE.** Allows a user to execute the DELETE SQL statement against the table; in other words, it allows a user to remove rows of data from the table
- **INDEX.** Allows a user to create an index for the table
- **REFERENCES.** Allows a user to create and drop foreign key constraints that reference the table in a parent relationship (this privilege can be granted for the entire table or limited to

one or more columns within the table, in which case only those columns can participate as a parent key in a referential constraint)

The owner of a table (usually the individual who created the table) automatically receives all privileges available for that table (including the CONTROL privilege), along with the right to grant any combination of those privileges (except the CONTROL privilege) to other users and groups. If you later revoke the CONTROL privilege from the table owner, all other privileges that were automatically granted to the owner for that particular table are not automatically revoked. Instead, you must explicitly revoke them in one or more separate operations.

View Privileges

View privileges control what users can and cannot do with a particular view. (A view is a virtual table residing in memory that provides an alternative way of working with data that is in one or more base tables. For this reason, you can use views to prevent access to select columns in a table.) Figure 8.6 shows the different types of view privileges.

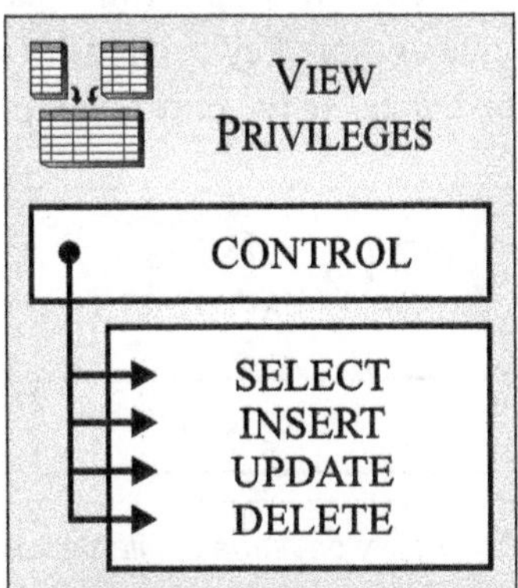

Figure 8.6: View privileges available with DB2

As you can see in Figure 8.6, five different view privileges exist:

- **CONTROL**. Provides a user with every view privilege available, allows the user to remove (drop) the view from the database, and gives the user the ability to grant and revoke one or more view privileges (except the CONTROL privilege) to and from other users and groups
- **SELECT**. Allows a user to retrieve data from the view, create a second view that references the view, and run the Export utility against the view
- **INSERT**. Allows a user to execute the INSERT SQL statement against the view; in other words, it permits a user to add data to the view

- **UPDATE.** Allows a user to execute the UPDATE SQL statement against the view; in other words, it permits a user to modify data in the view (this privilege can be granted for the entire view or limited to one or more columns within the view)
- **DELETE.** Allows a user to execute the DELETE SQL statement against the view; in other words, this privilege permits a user to remove rows of data from the view

To create a view, a user must hold the appropriate privileges (at a minimum, the SELECT privilege) on each base table the view references. The owner of a view (usually the individual who created the view) automatically receives all privileges available—with the exception of the CONTROL privilege—for that view, along with the right to grant any combination of those privileges (except CONTROL privilege) to other users and groups. A view owner will receive the CONTROL privilege for a view only if he or she also holds the CONTROL privilege for every base table the view references.

Index Privileges

Index privileges control what users can and cannot do with a particular index. (An index is an ordered set of pointers that refer to one or more key columns in a base table; you use indexes to improve query performance.) Figure 8.7 shows the only index privilege available.

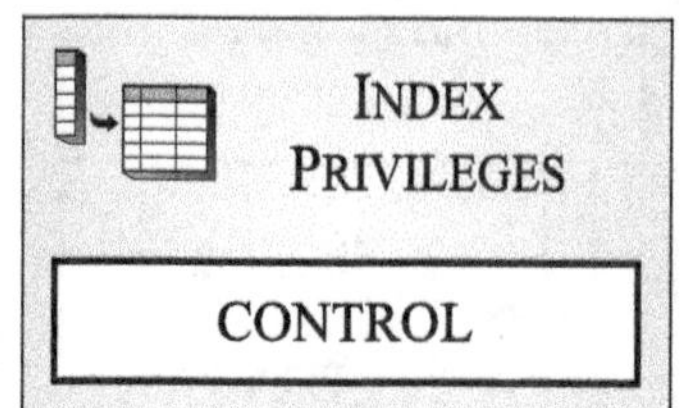

Figure 8.7: Index privilege available with DB2

As you can see in Figure 8.7, only one index privilege exists. That privilege is the CONTROL privilege, which, when granted, allows a user to remove (drop) the index from the database. Unlike the CONTROL privilege for other objects, the CONTROL privilege for an index does not give a user the ability to grant and revoke index privileges to and from other users and groups. That is because the CONTROL privilege is the only index privilege available, and only users who hold SYSADM or DBADM authority are allowed to grant and revoke CONTROL privileges for an object. The owner of an index (usually the individual who created the index) automatically receives CONTROL privilege for that index.

Sequence Privileges

Sequence privileges control what users can and cannot do with a particular sequence. (A sequence is an object that can generate values automatically. Sequences are ideal for generating unique key values, and you can use them to avoid the possible concurrency and performance problems that can occur when unique counters residing outside the database are used for data generation.) Figure 8.8 shows the different types of sequence privileges.

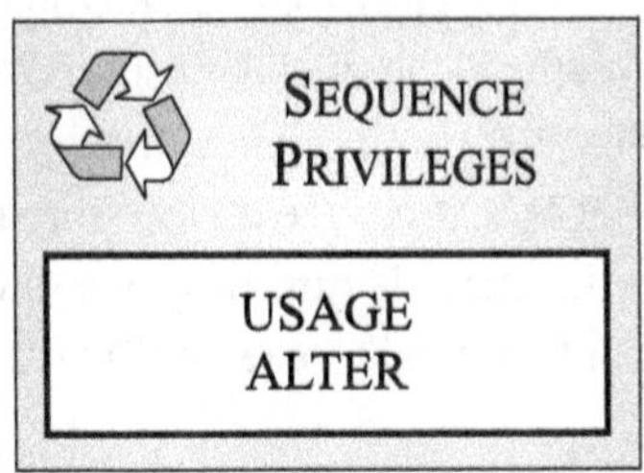

Figure 8.8: Sequence privileges available with DB2

As you can see in Figure 8.8, two different sequence privileges exist:

- **USAGE.** Allows a user to use the PREVIOUS VALUE and NEXT VALUE expressions associated with the sequence (the PREVIOUS VALUE expression returns the most recently generated value for the specified sequence; the NEXT VALUE expression returns the next value for the specified sequence)
- **ALTER.** Allows a user to perform administrative tasks such as restarting the sequence, changing the increment value for the sequence, and adding or modifying the comment associated with the sequence

The owner of a sequence (usually the individual who created the sequence) automatically receives all privileges available for that sequence, along with the right to grant any combination of those privileges to other users and groups.

Routine Privileges

Routine privileges control what users can and cannot do with a particular routine. (A routine can be a UDF, a stored procedure, or a method that several different users can invoke.) Figure 8.9 shows the only routine privilege.

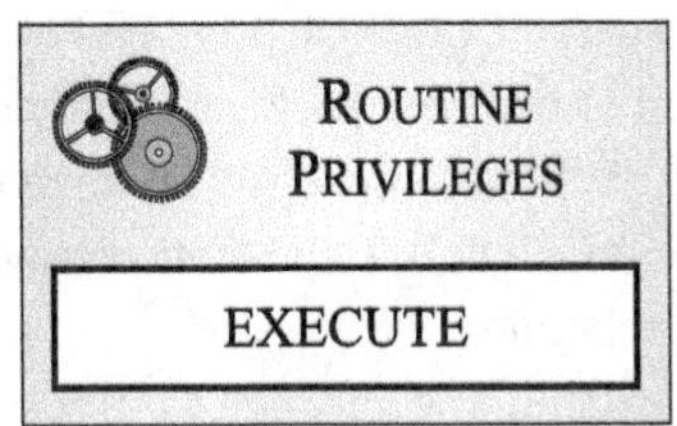

Figure 8.9: Routine privilege available with DB2

As you can see in Figure 8.9, only one routine privilege exists. That privilege is the EXECUTE privilege, which, when granted, allows a user to invoke the routine, create a function that is sourced from the routine (provided the routine is a function), and reference the routine in any DDL SQL statement (for example, CREATE VIEW and CREATE TRIGGER). Before a user can invoke a routine (UDF, stored procedure, or method), he or she must hold both the EXECUTE privilege on the routine and any privileges required by that routine. Thus, to execute a stored procedure that queries a table, a user must hold both the EXECUTE privilege on the stored procedure and the SELECT privilege on the table against which the query is run. However, the owner of a routine (usually the individual who created the routine) automatically receives EXECUTE privilege for that routine.

Package Privileges

Package privileges control what users can and cannot do with a particular package. (A package is an object that contains the information that the DB2 database manager needs to process SQL statements in the most efficient way possible on behalf of an embedded SQL application.) Figure 8.10 shows the different types of package privileges.

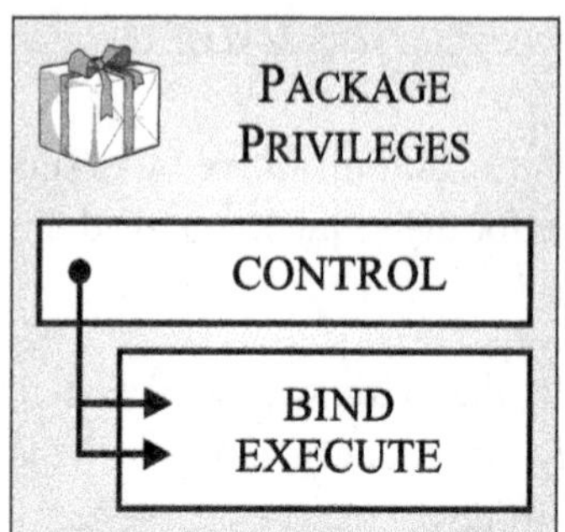

Figure 8.10: Package privileges available with DB2

As you can see in Figure 8.10, three different package privileges exist:

- **CONTROL**. Provides a user with every package privilege available, allows the user to remove (drop) the package from the database, and gives the user the ability to grant and revoke one or more table privileges (except the CONTROL privilege) to and from other users and groups
- **BIND**. Allows a user to rebind or add new package versions to a package that has already been bound to a database (in addition to the BIND package privilege, a user must hold the privileges needed to execute the SQL statements that make up the package before the package can be successfully rebound)
- **EXECUTE**. Allows a user to execute the package (a user who has EXECUTE privilege for a particular package can execute that package, even if the user does not have the privileges needed to execute the SQL statements stored in the package; that is because all privileges

needed to execute the SQL statements are implicitly granted to the package user—note that for privileges to be implicitly granted, the creator of the package must hold privileges as an individual user or as a member of the group PUBLIC, not as a member of another named group)

The owner of a package (usually the individual who created the package) automatically receives all privileges available for that package (including the CONTROL privilege), along with the right to grant any combination of those privileges (except the CONTROL privilege) to other users and groups. If you later revoke the CONTROL privilege from the package owner, all other privileges that were automatically granted to the owner for that particular package are not automatically revoked. Instead, you must explicitly revoke them in one or more separate operations.

Server Privileges

Server privileges control what users can and cannot do with a particular federated database server. (A DB2 federated system is a distributed computing system that consists of a DB2 server, known as a *federated server*, and one or more data sources to which the federated server sends queries. Each data source consists of an instance of some supported relational database management system—such as Oracle—plus the database or databases that the instance supports.) Figure 8.11 shows the only server privilege.

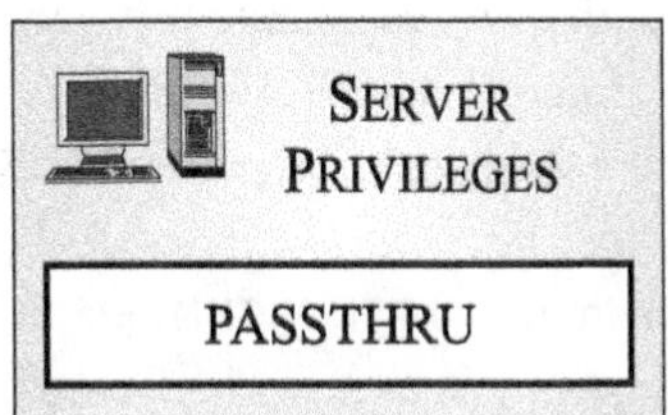

Figure 8.11: Server privilege available with DB2

As you can see in Figure 8.11, only one server privilege exists. That privilege is the PASSTHRU privilege, which, when granted, allows a user to issue DDL and DML SQL statements (as pass-through operations) directly to a data source via a federated server.

Nickname Privileges

Nickname privileges control what users can and cannot do with a particular nickname. (When a client application submits a distributed request to a federated database server, the server forwards the request to the appropriate data source for processing. However, such a request does not identify the data source itself; instead, it references tables and views within the data source by using nicknames that map to specific table and view names in the data source. Nicknames are not alternate names for tables and views in the same way that aliases are; instead, they are pointers by which a federated server references external objects.) Figure 8.12 shows the different types of nickname privileges.

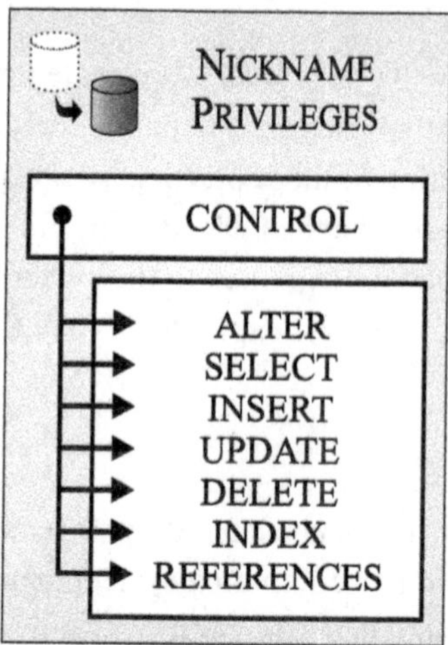

Figure 8.12: Nickname privileges available with DB2

As you can see in Figure 8.12, eight different nickname privileges exist:

- **CONTROL**. Provides a user with every nickname privilege available, allows the user to remove (drop) the nickname from the database, and gives the user the ability to grant and revoke one or more nickname privileges (except the CONTROL privilege) to and from other users and groups
- **ALTER**. Allows a user to execute the ALTER NICKNAME SQL statement against the table; in other words, this privilege permits a user to change column names in the nickname, add or change the DB2 data type to which a particular nickname column's data type maps, and specify column options for a specific nickname column
- **SELECT**. Allows a user to execute a SELECT SQL statement against the nickname; in other words, it permits a user to retrieve data from the table or view within a federated data source to which the nickname refers
- **INSERT**. Allows a user to execute the INSERT SQL statement against the nickname; in other words, this privilege permits a user to add data to the table or view within a federated data source to which the nickname refers
- **UPDATE**. Allows a user to execute the UPDATE SQL statement against the nickname; in other words, this privilege permits a user to modify data in the table or view within a federated data source to which the nickname refers (this privilege can be granted for the entire table or limited to one or more columns within the table to which the nickname refers)

- **DELETE**. Allows a user to execute the DELETE SQL statement against the nickname; in other words, it permits a user to remove rows of data from the table or view within a federated data source to which the nickname refers
- **INDEX**. Allows a user to create an index specification for the nickname
- **REFERENCES**. Allows a user to create and drop foreign key constraints that reference the nickname in a parent relationship

The owner of a nickname (usually the individual who created the table) automatically receives all privileges available for that nickname (including the CONTROL privilege), along with the right to grant any combination of those privileges (except the CONTROL privilege) to other users and groups. If you later revoke the CONTROL privilege from the nickname owner, all other privileges that were automatically granted to the owner for that particular table are not automatically revoked. Instead, you must explicitly revoke them in one or more separate operations.

Granting Authorities and Privileges

Users (and in some cases groups) can obtain database-level authorities and database/object privileges in three different ways:

- **Implicitly**. When a user creates a database, that user implicitly receives DBADM authority for that database, along with most database privileges available. Likewise, when a user creates a database object, that user implicitly receives all privileges available for that object, along with the ability to grant any combination of those privileges (with the exception of the CONTROL privilege) to other users and groups. Privileges can also be implicitly given whenever a higher-level privilege is explicitly granted to a user (for example, if you explicitly give a user the CONTROL privilege for a table space, the user will implicitly receive the USE privilege for that table space as well). Remember that such implicitly assigned privileges are not automatically revoked when you revoke the higher-level privilege that caused them to be granted.
- **Indirectly**. Indirectly assigned privileges are usually associated with packages; when a user executes a package that requires additional privileges that the user does not have (for example, a package that deletes a row of data from a table requires the DELETE privilege on that table), the user is indirectly given those privileges for the express purpose of executing the package. Indirectly granted privileges are temporary and do not exist outside the scope in which they are granted.
- **Explicitly**. Database-level authorities, database privileges, and object privileges can be explicitly given to or taken from an individual user or a group of users by anyone who has the authority to do so. To grant privileges explicitly on most database objects, a user must have SYSADM or DBADM authority or CONTROL privileges on that object. Alternately, a user can explicitly grant any privilege that user was assigned with the WITH GRANT OPTION

specified. To grant CONTROL privilege for any object, a user must have SYSADM or DBADM authority; to grant SYSADM or DBADM authority, a user must have SYSADM authority.

Granting Authorities and Privileges from IBM Data Studio

One way to explicitly grant and revoke database-level authorities, as well as many of the object privileges available, is by using the manage privileges dialogs that IBM Data Studio provides. You activate these dialogs by highlighting the appropriate database or object name in the Data Studio panes and selecting **Manage Privileges** from the corresponding object menu. Figure 8.13 shows the menu items that you must select in IBM Data Studio to activate the **Manage Privileges** option for a particular table.

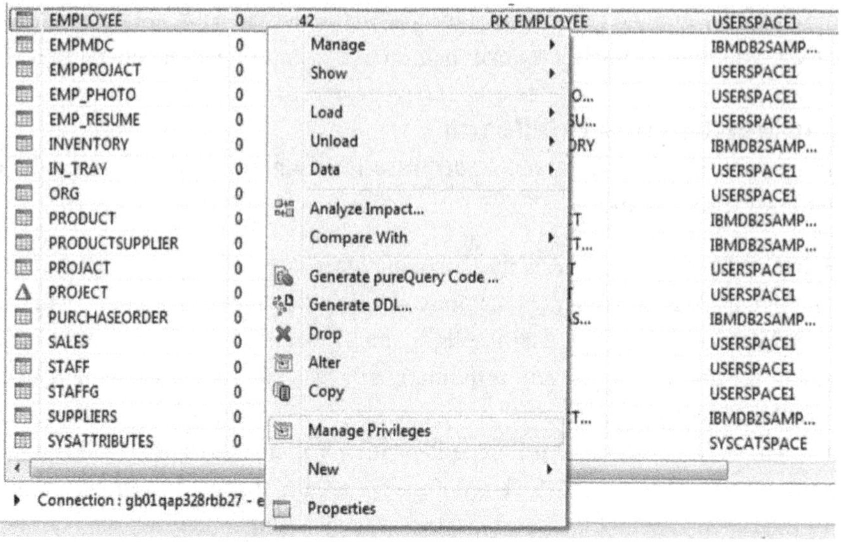

Figure 8.13: Invoking the Table privileges dialog from IBM Data Studio

Figure 8.14 illustrates how the Table Privileges dialog might look immediately after a table is first created. (A single check mark under a privilege means that the individual or group has been granted that privilege; a double check mark indicates that the individual or group has also been granted the ability to give that privilege to other users and groups.)

To assign privileges to an individual user from the Table Privileges dialog (or a similar authorities or privileges dialog), you simply identify a particular user by highlighting the user's entry in the recognized users list—if the desired user is not in the list, you can add the user by clicking the **Grant New Privilege** button; selecting **Grantee Type** as a user, group, role, or public; and assigning **Grantee** the required privileges, as in Figure 8.15.

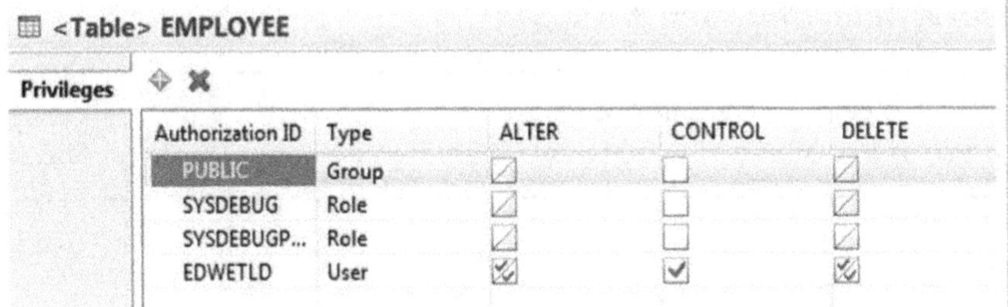

Figure 8.14: The Table privileges dialog

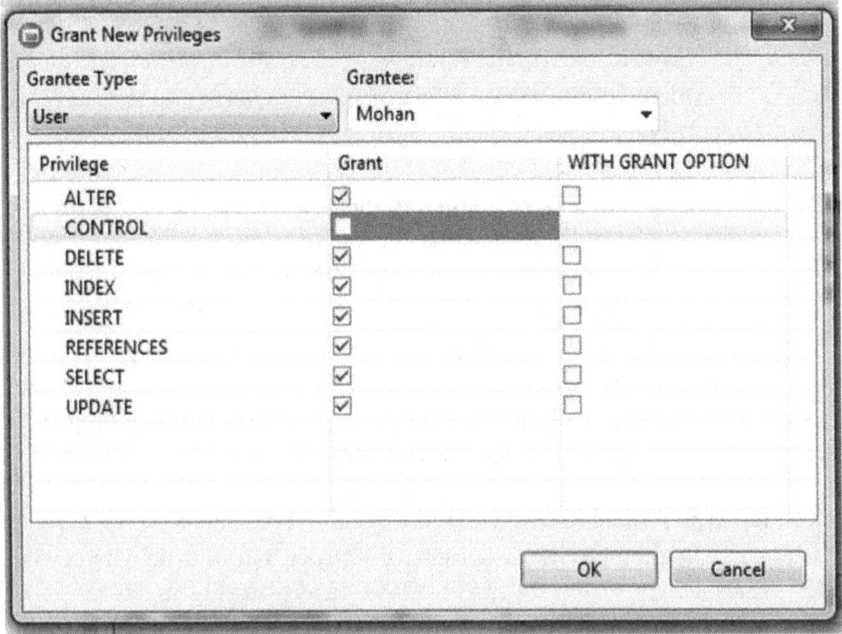

Figure 8.15: Grant New Privileges dialog

Granting Authorities and Privileges with the GRANT command

You can explicitly give database-level authorities and database/object privileges to users and groups by executing the appropriate form of the GRANT SQL statement. The syntax for the GRANT SQL statement varies according to the authority or privilege you are granting. The following subsections show the syntax used to grant each database-level authority and database/object privilege available.

Database-level Authorities and Privileges

```
GRANT [Privilege, ...] ON DATABASE
TO [Recipient, ...]
```

where:

Privilege	Identifies one or more database privileges to give to one or more users and groups; the following values are valid for this parameter: DBADM, SECADM, CONNECT, CONNECT_QUIESCE, IMPLICIT_SCHEMA, CREATETAB, BINDADD, CREATE_EXTERNAL_ROUTINE, CREATE_NOT_FENCED_ROUTINE, and LOAD
Recipient	Identifies the name of the users, groups, and roles to receive the database privileges specified; the value you specify for the Recipient parameter can be any combination of the following: • <USER> [*UserName*]. Identifies a specific user to receive the privileges specified • <GROUP> [*GroupName*]. Identifies a specific group to receive the privileges specified • <ROLE> [*RoleName*]. Identifies a specific role to receive the privileges specified
PUBLIC	Indicates to grant the privileges specified to the group PUBLIC—(all users are members of the group PUBLIC)

No user-checking is performed to ensure that the Recipient parameter values are valid. Therefore, it is possible to grant privileges to users, groups, or roles that do not yet exist.

Table Space Privileges

```
GRANT USE OF TABLESPACE [TablespaceName]
TO [Recipient, ...]
<WITH GRANT OPTION>
```

where:

TablespaceName	Identifies the table space with which to associate the USE privilege
Recipient	Identifies the name of the users and groups to receive the USE privilege; again, the value you specify for the Recipient parameter can be

any combination of the following: <USER> [*UserName*], <GROUP> [*GroupName*], <ROLE> [*RoleName*], and PUBLIC.

If you specify the WITH GRANT OPTION clause, each Recipient is given the ability to grant the privilege received to others.

Schema Privileges

```
GRANT [Privilege, ...] ON SCHEMA [SchemaName]
TO [Recipient, ...]
<WITH GRANT OPTION>
```

where:

Privilege	Identifies one or more schema privileges to give to one or more users and groups; the following values are valid for this parameter: CREATIN, ALTERIN, and DROPIN
SchemaName	Identifies by name the schema with which to associate all schema privileges specified
Recipient	Identifies the name of the users, groups, and roles to receive the schema privileges specified; the value you specify for the Recipient parameter can be any combination of the following: <USER> [*UserName*], <GROUP> [*GroupName*], <ROLE> [*RoleName*], and PUBLIC

Table Privileges

```
GRANT [ALL <PRIVILEGES> |
      Privilege <( ColumnName, ... )> , ...]
ON TABLE [TableName]
TO [Recipient, ...]
<WITH GRANT OPTION>
```

where:

Privilege	Identifies one or more table privileges to give to one or more users and groups; the following values are valid for this parameter: CONTROL, ALTER, SELECT, INSERT, UPDATE, DELETE, INDEX, and REFERENCES

ColumnName Identifies by name one or more specific columns with which to associate UPDATE or REFERENCES privileges; you use this option only when the Privilege parameter contains the value UPDATE or REFERENCES

TableName Identifies by name the table with which to associate all table privileges specified

Recipient Identifies the name of the users, groups, and roles to receive the table privileges specified; the value you specify for the Recipient parameter can be any combination of the following: <USER> [*UserName*], <GROUP> [*GroupName*], <ROLE> [*RoleName*], and PUBLIC

Note that only users who hold SYSADM or DBADM authority are allowed to grant the CONTROL privilege for a table. For this reason, when you specify the ALL PRIVILEGES clause, all table privileges *except* the CONTROL privilege are granted to each Recipient; you must grant the CONTROL privilege separately.

View Privileges

```
GRANT [ALL <PRIVILEGES> |
      Privilege <( ColumnName, ... )>  , ...]
ON [ViewName]
TO [Recipient, ...]
<WITH GRANT OPTION>
```

where:

Privilege Identifies one or more view privileges to give to one or more users and groups; the following values are valid for this parameter: CONTROL, SELECT, INSERT, UPDATE, and DELETE

ColumnName Identifies by name one or more specific columns with which to associate UPDATE privileges; you use this option only when the Privilege parameter contains the value UPDATE

ViewName Identifies by name the view with which to associate all view privileges specified

Recipient Identifies the name of the users, groups, and roles to receive the view privileges specified; the value you specify for the Recipient parameter can be any combination of the following: <USER> [*UserName*], <GROUP> [*GroupName*], <ROLE> [*RoleName*], and PUBLIC

Again, only users who hold SYSADM or DBADM authority are allowed to grant the CONTROL privilege for a table. Therefore, when you specify the ALL PRIVILEGES clause, all view privileges *except* the CONTROL privilege are granted to each Recipient; you must grant the CONTROL privilege separately.

Index Privileges

```
GRANT CONTROL ON INDEX [IndexName]
TO [Recipient, ...]
```

where:

IndexName	Identifies by name the index with which to associate the CONTROL privilege
Recipient	Identifies the name of the users, groups, and roles to receive the CONTROL privilege; the value you specify for the Recipient parameter can be any combination of the following: <USER> [*UserName*], <GROUP> [*GroupName*], <ROLE> [*RoleName*], and PUBLIC

Sequence Privileges

```
GRANT [Privilege, ...] ON SEQUENCE [SequenceName]
TO [Recipient, ...]
<WITH GRANT OPTION>
```

where:

Privilege	Identifies one or more sequence privileges to give to one or more users and groups; the following values are valid for this parameter: USAGE and ALTER
SequenceName	Identifies by name the sequence with which to associate all sequence privileges specified
Recipient	Identifies the name of the users, groups, and roles to receive the sequence privileges specified; again, the value you specify for the Recipient parameter can be any combination of the following: <USER> [*UserName*], <GROUP> [*GroupName*], <ROLE> [*RoleName*], and PUBLIC

Routine Privileges

```
GRANT EXECUTE ON [RoutineName |
                  FUNCTION <SchemaName.> * |
                  METHOD * FOR [TypeName] |
                  METHOD * FOR <SchemaName.> * |
                  PROCEDURE <SchemaName.> *]
TO [Recipient, ...]
<WITH GRANT OPTION>
```

where:

RoutineName	Identifies by name the routine (UDF, method, or stored procedure) with which to associate the EXECUTE privilege
TypeName	Identifies by name the type in which to find the specified method
SchemaName	Identifies by name the schema in which to grant the EXECUTE privilege to all functions, methods, or procedures—including those that may be created in the future
Recipient	Identifies the name of the users, groups, and roles to receive the EXECUTE privilege; the value you specify for the Recipient parameter can be any combination of the following: <USER> [*UserName*], <GROUP> [*GroupName*], <ROLE> [*RoleName*], and PUBLIC

Package Privileges

```
GRANT [Privilege, ...] ON PACKAGE <SchemaName.>[PackageID] TO [Recipient, ...]
<WITH GRANT OPTION>
```

where:

Privilege	Identifies one or more package privileges to give to one or more users and groups; the following values are valid for this parameter: CONTROL, BIND, and EXECUTE
SchemaName	Identifies by name the schema in which to find the specified package
PackageName	Identifies by name the package with which to associate all package privileges specified
Recipient	Identifies the name of the users, groups, and roles to receive the package privileges specified; the value you specify for the Recipient parameter

can be any combination of the following: <USER> [*UserName*], <GROUP> [*GroupName*], <ROLE> [*RoleName*], and PUBLIC (DB2 for Linux, UNIX, and Windows does not allow users to grant package privileges to themselves)

Server Privileges

```
GRANT PASSTHRU ON SERVER [ServerName]
TO [Recipient, ...]
```

where:

ServerName Identifies by name the server with which to associate the PASSTHRU privilege

Recipient Identifies the name of the users, groups, and roles to receive the PASSTHRU privilege; the value you specify for the Recipient parameter can be any combination of the following: <USER> [*UserName*], <GROUP> [*GroupName*], <ROLE> [*RoleName*], and PUBLIC

Nickname Privileges

```
GRANT [ALL <PRIVILEGES> |
       Privilege <( ColumnName, ... )>  , ...]
ON [Nickname]
TO [Recipient, ...]
<WITH GRANT OPTION>
```

where:

Privilege Identifies one or more nickname privileges to give to one or more users and groups; the following values are valid for this parameter: CONTROL, ALTER, SELECT, INSERT, UPDATE, DELETE, INDEX, and REFERENCES

ColumnName Identifies by name one or more specific columns with which to associate UPDATE or REFERENCES privileges; you use this option only when the Privilege parameter contains the value UPDATE or REFERENCES

Nickname Identifies by name the nickname with which to associate all privileges specified

Recipient Identifies the name of the users, groups, and roles to receive the nickname privileges specified; the value you specify for the Recipient parameter can be any combination of the following: <USER> [*UserName*], <GROUP> [*GroupName*], <ROLE> [*RoleName*], and PUBLIC

Only users who hold SYSADM or DBADM authority are allowed to grant the CONTROL privilege for a nickname. Therefore, when you specify the ALL PRIVILEGES clause, all nickname privileges *except* the CONTROL privilege are granted to each Recipient; you must grant the CONTROL privilege separately.

GRANT SQL Statement Examples

Now that you have seen the basic syntax for the various forms of the GRANT SQL statement, let us look at some examples.

Example 1. A server has a group named BINDER. Give the group BINDER the ability to bind applications to the database SAMPLE:

```
CONNECT TO sample;
GRANT BINDADD ON DATABASE TO GROUP binder;
```

Example 2. Grant all table privileges available for the table PAYROLL.EMPLOYEE (except the CONTROL privilege) to the group PUBLIC:

```
GRANT ALL PRIVILEGES ON TABLE payroll.employee TO PUBLIC
```

Example 3. Give user USER1 and user USER2 the privileges needed to perform DML operations on the table DEPARTMENT by using the view DEPTVIEW:

```
GRANT SELECT, INSERT, UPDATE, DELETE ON deptview
TO USER user1, USER user2
```

Example 4. Give user JOHN the privileges required to query the table INVENTORY, along with the ability to give these privileges to other users whenever appropriate:

```
GRANT SELECT ON TABLE inventory TO USER john
WITH GRANT OPTION
```

Example 5. Grant user USER1 the ability to run an embedded SQL application that requires a package named GET_INVENTORY:

```
GRANT EXECUTE ON PACKAGE get_inventory TO USER user1
```

Example 6. Give user USER1 the ability to use a stored procedure named PAYROLL.CALC_SALARY in a query:

```
GRANT EXECUTE ON PROCEDURE payroll.calc_salary TO user1
```

Example 7. Give user USER1 and group GROUP1 the ability to define a referential constraint between the tables EMPLOYEE and DEPARTMENT by using column EMPID in table EMPLOYEE as the parent key:

```
GRANT REFERENCES (empid) ON TABLE employee TO USER user1, GROUP group1
```

Example 8. Grant the group PUBLIC the ability to modify information stored in the ADDRESS and HOME_PHONE columns of the table EMP_INFO:

```
GRANT UPDATE (address, home_phone) ON TABLE emp_info TO PUBLIC
```

Example 9. Give the group APPGRP the ability to create tables and load data into the database SAMPLE:

```
CONNECT TO sample;
GRANT CREATETAB, LOAD ON DATABASE TO GROUP appgrp;
```

Example 10. Give the user ICEBI the ability to use and alter the sequence DATAMARTS.COMPOSITION_SEQ:

```
GRANT USAGE, ALTER ON SEQUENCE datamarts.composition_seq TO USER icebi;
```

Revoking Authorities and Privileges with the REVOKE SQL Statement

Just as there is an SQL statement to grant database-level authorities and database/object privileges, there is an SQL statement to revoke these authorities and privileges. This statement is the REVOKE SQL statement, and as with GRANT, the syntax for REVOKE varies according to the authority or privilege you are revoking. The following sections show the syntax to revoke each database-level authority and database/object privilege.

Database-level Authorities and Privileges

```
REVOKE [Privilege, ...] ON DATABASE
FROM [Forfeiter, ...] <BY ALL>
```

where:

Privilege — Identifies one or more database privileges to revoke; valid values are: DBADM, SECADM, CONNECT, CONNECT_QUIESCE, IMPLICIT_SCHEMA, CREATETAB, BINDADD, CREATE_EXTERNAL_ROUTINE, CREATE_NOT_FENCED_ROUTINE, and LOAD

Forfeiter — Identifies the name of the users, groups, and roles that are to lose the database privileges specified; the value you specify for the *Forfeiter* parameter can be any combination of the following:

- <USER> [*UserName*]. Identifies a specific user from whom to revoke the privileges specified
- <GROUP> [*GroupName*]. Identifies a specific group from which to revoke the privileges
- <ROLE> [*RoleName*]. Identifies a specific role from which to revoke the privileges

PUBLIC — Indicates to revoke the privileges specified from the group PUBLIC (all users are members of the group PUBLIC)

The BY ALL clause is optional and is provided as a courtesy for administrators who are familiar with the syntax of the DB2 for OS/390 REVOKE SQL statement. Whether it is included or not, all privileges indicated will be revoked from all users and groups specified.

Note that when you revoke DBADM authority, privileges held on objects in the database by the *Forfeiter* you specify are not automatically revoked. The same is true for all other database authorities that were implicitly and automatically granted when DBADM authority was granted.

Table Space Privileges

```
REVOKE USE OF TABLESPACE [TablespaceName]
FROM [Forfeiter, ...] <BY ALL>
```

where:

TablespaceName — Identifies by name the table space with which to associate the USE privilege

Forfeiter — Identifies the name of the users, groups, and roles that are to lose the USE privilege; again, the value you specify for the *Forfeiter* parameter can be any combination of the following: <USER> [*UserName*], <GROUP> [*GroupName*], <ROLE> [*RoleName*], and PUBLIC

Schema Privileges

```
REVOKE [Privilege, ...] ON SCHEMA [SchemaName]
FROM [Forfeiter, ...] <BY ALL>
```

where:

Privilege — Identifies one or more schema privileges to revoke from one or more users or groups; the following values are valid for this parameter: CREATIN, ALTERIN, and DROPIN

SchemaName — Identifies by name the schema with which to associate all schema privileges specified

Forfeiter — Identifies the name of the users, groups, and roles that are to lose the schema privileges specified; the value you specify for the *Forfeiter* parameter can be any combination of the following: <USER> [*UserName*], <GROUP> [*GroupName*], <ROLE> [*RoleName*], and PUBLIC

Table Privileges

```
REVOKE [ALL <PRIVILEGES> |
        Privilege, ...]
ON TABLE [TableName]
FROM [Forfeiter, ...] <BY ALL>
```

where:

Privilege — Identifies one or more table privileges to revoke from one or more users or groups; the following values are valid for this parameter: CONTROL, ALTER, SELECT, INSERT, UPDATE, DELETE, INDEX, and REFERENCES

TableName Identifies by name the table with which to associate all table privileges specified

Forfeiter Identifies the name of the users, groups, and roles that are to lose the table privileges specified; the value you specify for the *Forfeiter* parameter can be any combination of the following: <USER> [*UserName*], <GROUP> [*GroupName*], <ROLE> [*RoleName*], and PUBLIC

Note that only users who hold SYSADM or DBADM authority are allowed to revoke the CONTROL privilege for a table. For this reason, when you specify the ALL PRIVILEGES clause, all table privileges *except* the CONTROL privilege are revoked from each *Forfeiter*; you must revoke the CONTROL privilege separately.

View Privileges

```
REVOKE [ALL <PRIVILEGES> |
        Privilege, ...]
ON [ViewName]
FROM [Forfeiter, ...] <BY ALL>
```

where:

Privilege Identifies one or more view privileges to revoke from one or more users or groups; the following values are valid for this parameter: CONTROL, SELECT, INSERT, UPDATE, and DELETE

ViewName Identifies by name the view with which to associate all view privileges specified

Forfeiter Identifies the name of the users, groups, and roles that are to lose the view privileges specified; the value you specify for the *Forfeiter* parameter can be any combination of the following: <USER> [*UserName*], <GROUP> [*GroupName*], <ROLE> [*RoleName*], and PUBLIC

Again, only users who hold SYSADM or DBADM authority are allowed to revoke the CONTROL privilege for a table. For this reason, when you specify the ALL PRIVILEGES clause, all table privileges *except* the CONTROL privilege are revoked from each *Forfeiter*; you must revoke the CONTROL privilege separately.

Index Privileges

```
REVOKE CONTROL ON INDEX [IndexName]
FROM [Forfeiter, ...] <BY ALL>
```

where:

IndexName Identifies by name the index with which to associate the CONTROL privilege

Forfeiter Identifies the name of the users, groups, and roles that are to lose the CONTROL privilege; the value you specify for the *Forfeiter* parameter can be any combination of the following: <USER> [*UserName*], <GROUP> [*GroupName*], <ROLE> [*RoleName*], and PUBLIC

Sequence Privileges

```
REVOKE [Privilege, ...] ON SEQUENCE [SequenceName]
FROM [Forfeiter, ...] <BY ALL>
```

where:

Privilege Identifies one or more sequence privileges to revoke from one or more users or groups; the following values are valid for this parameter: USAGE and ALTER

SequenceName Identifies by name the sequence with which to associate all sequence privileges specified

Forfeiter Identifies the name of the users, groups, and roles that are to lose the sequence privileges specified; the value you specify for the *Forfeiter* parameter can be any combination of the following: <USER> [*UserName*], <GROUP> [*GroupName*], <ROLE> [*RoleName*], and PUBLIC

Routine Privileges

```
REVOKE EXECUTE ON [RoutineName |
                  FUNCTION <SchemaName.> * |
                  METHOD * FOR [TypeName] |
                                                        Continued
```

```
                    METHOD * FOR <SchemaName.> * |
                    PROCEDURE <SchemaName.> *]
FROM [Forfeiter, ...] <BY ALL>
RESTRICT
```

where:

RoutineName	Identifies by name the routine (UDF, method, or stored procedure) with which to associate the EXECUTE privilege
TypeName	Identifies by name the type in which to find the specified method
SchemaName	Identifies by name the schema from which to revoke the EXECUTE privilege for all functions, methods, or procedures—including those that may be created in the future
Forfeiter	Identifies the name of the users, groups, and roles that are to lose the EXECUTE privilege; the value you specify for the *Forfeiter* parameter can be any combination of the following: <USER> [*UserName*], <GROUP> [*GroupName*], <ROLE> [*RoleName*], and PUBLIC

The RESTRICT clause guarantees that the EXECUTE privilege will not be revoked if the routine specified is used in a view, trigger, constraint, index, SQL function, SQL method, or transform group or is referenced as the source of a sourced function. Additionally, the EXECUTE privilege will not be revoked if the loss of the privilege would prohibit the routine definer from executing the routine (i.e., if the user who created the routine is identified as a *Forfeiter*).

Package Privileges

```
REVOKE [Privilege, ...] ON PACKAGE <SchemaName.>[PackageID]
FROM [Forfeiter, ...] <BY ALL>
```

where:

Privilege	Identifies one or more package privileges to revoke from one or more users or groups; the following values are valid for this parameter: CONTROL, BIND, and EXECUTE
SchemaName	Identifies by name the schema in which to find the specified package
PackageName	Identifies by name the specific package with which to associate all package privileges specified

Forfeiter Identifies the name of the users, groups, and roles that are to lose the package privileges specified; the value you specify for the *Forfeiter* parameter can be any combination of the following: <USER> [*UserName*], <GROUP> [*GroupName*], <ROLE> [*RoleName*], and PUBLIC

Server Privileges

```
REVOKE PASSTHRU ON SERVER [ServerName]
FROM [Forfeiter, ...] <BY ALL>
```

where:

ServerName Identifies by name the server with which to associate the PASSTHRU privilege

Forfeiter Identifies the name of the users, groups, and roles that are to lose the PASSTHRU privilege; the value you specify for the *Forfeiter* parameter can be any combination of the following: <USER> [*UserName*], <GROUP> [*GroupName*], <ROLE> [*RoleName*], and PUBLIC

Nickname Privileges

```
REVOKE [ALL <PRIVILEGES> |
        Privilege, ...]
ON [Nickname]
FROM [Forfeiter, ...] <BY ALL>
```

where:

Privilege Identifies one or more nickname privileges to revoke from one or more users or groups; the following values are valid for this parameter: CONTROL, ALTER, SELECT, INSERT, UPDATE, DELETE, INDEX, and REFERENCES

Nickname Identifies by name the nickname with which to associate all privileges specified

Forfeiter Identifies the name of the users, groups, and roles that are to lose the nickname privileges specified; the value you specify for the *Forfeiter* parameter can be any combination of the following: <USER> [*UserName*], <GROUP> [*GroupName*], <ROLE> [*RoleName*], and PUBLIC

Only users who hold SYSADM or DBADM authority are allowed to revoke the CONTROL privilege for a nickname. For this reason, when you specify the ALL PRIVILEGES clause, all nickname privileges *except* the CONTROL privilege are revoked from each *Forfeiter*; you must revoke the CONTROL privilege separately.

REVOKE SQL Statement Examples

Now that you have seen the basic syntax for the various forms of the REVOKE SQL statement, let us look at some examples.

Example 1. A server has a group named BINDER. Remove the ability to connect to the database named SAMPLE from the group BINDER:

```
CONNECT TO sample;
REVOKE CONNECT ON DATABASE FROM GROUP binder;
```

Example 2. Revoke all table privileges available for the table DEPARTMENT (except the CONTROL privilege) from the user USER1 and the group PUBLIC:

```
REVOKE ALL PRIVILEGES ON TABLE department FROM USER user1, GROUP PUBLIC
```

Example 3. Take away user USER1's ability to use a UDF named CALC_BONUS:

```
REVOKE EXECUTE ON FUNCTION calc_bonus FROM user1
```

Example 4. Revoke user USER1's ability to modify information stored in the ADDRESS and HOME_PHONE columns of the table EMP_INFO:

```
REVOKE UPDATE (address, home_phone) ON TABLE emp_info FROM user1 BY ALL
```

Example 5. Take away USER1's ability to read data stored in a table named INVENTORY:

```
REVOKE SELECT ON TABLE inventory FROM user1
```

Example 6. Prevent users in the group PUBLIC from adding or changing data stored in a table named EMPLOYEE:

```
REVOKE INSERT, UPDATE ON TABLE employee FROM PUBLIC
```

Example 7. Revoke the APPGRP group's ability to create tables and load data into the database SAMPLE:

```
CONNECT TO sample;
REVOKE CREATETAB, LOAD ON DATABASE FROM GROUP appgrp;
```

Example 8. Take away the ICEBI user's ability to use and alter the sequence DATAMARTS .COMPOSITION_SEQ:

```
REVOKE USAGE, ALTER ON SEQUENCE datamarts.composition_seq FROM USER icebi;
```

Requirements for Granting and Revoking Authorities and Privileges

Not only do authorization levels and privileges control what a user can and cannot do, but they also control what authorities and privileges a user is allowed to grant and revoke. Table 8.1 lists the authorities and privileges that a user who has a specific authority level or privilege is allowed to grant and revoke.

Table 8.1: Requirements for granting and revoking authorities and privileges

If a User Holds...	The User Can Grant...	The User Can Revoke...
SYSADM authority	SYSCTRL authority SYSMAINT authority SYSMON authority DBADM authority SECADM authority LOAD authority Any database privilege Any object privilege, including the CONTROL privilege	SYSCTRL authority SYSMAINT authority SYSMON authority DBADM authority SECADM authority LOAD authority Any database privilege Any object privilege, including the CONTROL privilege
SYSCTRL authority	The USE table space privilege	The USE table space privilege
SYSMAINT authority	No authorities or privileges	No authorities or privileges
SYSMON authority	No authorities or privileges	No authorities or privileges

Table 8.1: Requirements for granting and revoking authorities and privileges (continued)		
If a User Holds...	**The User Can Grant...**	**The User Can Revoke...**
DBADM authority	Any database privilege Any object privilege, including the CONTROL privilege	Any database privilege Any object privilege, including the CONTROL privilege
SECADM authority	DBADM authority SQLADM authority WLMADM authority EXPLAIN authority ACCESSCTRL authority DATAACCESS authority	DBADM authority SQLADM authority WLMADM authority EXPLAIN authority ACCESSCTRL authority DATAACCESS authority
SQLADM authority	No authorities or privileges	No authorities or privileges
WLMADM authority	No authorities or privileges	No authorities or privileges
EXPLAIN authority	No authorities or privileges	No authorities or privileges
ACCESSCTRL authority	SQLADM authority WLMADM authority EXPLAIN authority SELECT on the system catalog table All privileges on tables, table spaces, views, indexes, nicknames, packages, routines, schemas, sequences, servers, global variables, and XSR objects	SQLADM authority WLMADM authority EXPLAIN authority SELECT on the system catalog table All privileges on tables, table spaces, views, indexes, nicknames, packages, routines, schemas, sequences, servers, global variables, and XSR objects
DATAACCESS authority	No authorities or privileges	No authorities or privileges
LOAD authority	No authorities or privileges	No authorities or privileges
CONTROL privilege on an object (but no other authority)	All privileges available (with the exception of the CONTROL privilege) for the object on which the user holds the CONTROL privilege	All privileges available (with the exception of the CONTROL privilege) for the object on which the user holds the CONTROL privilege
A privilege on an object that was assigned with the WITH GRANT OPTION option specified	The same object privilege that was assigned with the WITH GRANT OPTION option specified	No authorities or privileges

Authorities and Privileges Needed to Perform Common Tasks

So far, we have identified the authorities and privileges that are available, and we have examined how to grant and revoke these authorities and privileges. But to use authorities and privileges effectively, you must be able to determine which authorities and privileges are appropriate for an individual user and which are not. Often, a blanket set of authorities and privileges is assigned to an individual based on his or her job title and job responsibilities. Then, as the individual begins to work with the database, you can modify the set of authorities and privileges he or she has as appropriate. Table 8.2 lists some of the more common job titles used, along with the tasks that usually accompany them and the authorities and privileges needed to perform those tasks.

Table 8.2: Common job titles, tasks, authorities, and privileges needed		
Job Title	**Tasks**	**Authorities/Privileges Needed**
Department administrator	Oversees the departmental system; designs and creates databases	SYSCTRL authority or SYSADM authority (if the department has its own instance)
Security administrator	Grants authorities and privileges to other users and revokes them, if necessary	SYSADM authority or DBADM authority (SECADM authority if label-based access control is used)
Database administrator	Designs, develops, operates, safeguards, and maintains one or more databases	DBADM authority over one or more databases and SYSMAINT authority, or in some cases SYSCTRL authority over the instances that control the databases
System operator	Monitors the database and performs routine backup operations; also performs recovery operations if needed	SYSMAINT authority or SYSMON authority
Application developer/ programmer	Develops and tests database/DB2 database manager application programs; may also create test tables and populate them with data	CONNECT and CREATE_TAB privileges for one or more databases, BINDADD and BIND privileges on one or more packages, one or more schema privileges for one or more schemas, and one or more table privileges for one or more tables; CREATE_EXTERNAL_ROUTINE privilege for one or more databases may also be required
User analyst	Defines the data requirements for an application program by examining the database structure using the system catalog views	CONNECT privilege for one or more databases and SELECT privilege on the system catalog views
End user	Executes one or more application programs	CONNECT privilege for one or more databases and EXECUTE privilege on the package associated with each application used; if an application program contains dynamic SQL statements, SELECT, INSERT, UPDATE, and DELETE privileges for one or more tables may be needed as well
Information center consultant	Defines the data requirements for a query user; provides the data needed by creating tables and views and by granting access to one or more database objects	DBADM authority for one or more databases
Application user	Executes application programs such as procedures, functions, and modules; performs one or more insert, update, delete operations on the application tables	DATAACCESS privilege for one or more databases
Query user	Issues SQL statements (usually from the CLP) to retrieve, add, update, or delete data (may also save results of queries in tables)	CONNECT privilege on one or more databases; SELECT, INSERT, UPDATE, and DELETE privilege on each table used; and CREATEIN privilege on the schema in which tables and views are to be created

Role-based Access Control

Recently, role-based security has emerged as a preferred way to protect organizations' information assets. With this access control mechanism, you grant the privileges to roles instead of granting directly to the user's authorization IDs. A role is a database object that groups together one or more privileges and can be assigned to users, groups, PUBLIC, or other roles.

If you want to create a role called TESTER, use the CREATE ROLE command something like this:

```
CREATE ROLE TESTER
DB20000I  The SQL command completed successfully.
```

All DB2 privileges and authorities that you can grant within a database you can also grant to a role. For example, a role can be granted any of the following authorities and privileges:

- Database privileges, including DBADM, SECADM, DATAACCESS, ACCESSCTRL, SQLADM, WLMADM, LOAD, IMPLICIT_SCHEMA, CONNECT, CREATETAB, CREATE_NOT_FENCED, BINDADD, CREATE_EXTERNAL_ROUTINE, and QUIESCE_CONNECT
- Any database object privilege, including SELECT, INSERT, UPDATE, DELETE, CONTROL, EXECUTE, and USE

Once you create a role, you can associate set of privileges to a role by using the GRANT command:

```
GRANT SELECT, INSERT ON TABLE EMPLOYEE TO ROLE TESTER
DB20000I  The SQL command completed successfully.
```

After creating a role, the security administrator can grant a role to a user, group, or another role. Additionally, the security administrator can delegate the management of membership in a role to an authorization ID by using the WITH ADMIN OPTION clause. The basic syntax for the GRANT ROLE command is:

```
GRANT ROLE <RoleName>
TO [USER | GROUP | ROLE | PUBLIC] <AuthorizationID>
[WITH ADMIN OPTION]
```

where:

RoleName	Identifies the role name to grant
AuthorizationID	Identifies a list of authorization IDs of one or more users, groups, or roles; however, an authorization ID cannot grant a privilege or authority to itself

To delegate the management of membership in the role TESTER to SIMON, execute the GRANT command:

```
GRANT ROLE TESTER TO USER SIMON WITH ADMIN OPTION
DB20000I  The SQL command completed successfully.
```

Likewise, you can use the REVOKE command to revoke a role from a user, group, or another role. The basic syntax for REVOKE ROLE command is:

```
REVOKE [ADMIN OPTION FOR] ROLE <RoleName>
FROM [USER | GROUP | ROLE | PUBLIC] <AuthorizationID>
[BY ALL]
```

where:

RoleName	Identifies the role name to revoke
AuthorizationID	Identifies a list of authorization IDs of one or more users, groups, or roles

For example, if you want to revoke the role TESTER from user SIMON, execute the REVOKE command:

```
REVOKE ROLE TESTER FROM USER SIMON
DB20000I  The SQL command completed successfully.
```

A Comparison Between Roles and Groups

Both roles and operating system groups function the same way with little dissimilarity between the two, as Table 8.3 shows.

Table 8.3: Comparison between roles and groups

Roles	Groups
It is a collection of privileges, and a user effectively inherits those privileges when a role is granted to a user.	It is a collection of users with a given set of privileges to the group.
It is created and managed within the database engine by SYSADM or SECADM users.	It is created and managed within the operating system engine or in LDAP by operating-system or AD administrators.
Privileges and authorities granted to roles are considered when creating views, MQTs, SQL routines, triggers, and packages containing static SQL.	Privileges and authorities granted to groups are not considered when creating views, MQTs, SQL routines, triggers, and packages containing static SQL.
Roles cannot own database objects.	Groups cannot own database objects.
Roles cannot be used to grant instance-level authorities such as SYSADM, SYSCTRL, SYSMAINT, and SYSMON.	Groups can be used to grant instance-level authorities such as SYSADM, SYSCTRL, SYSMAINT, and SYSMON.
Role maintenance can be delegated by using the WITH ADMIN OPTION clause in the GRANT ROLE command.	The group maintenance can only be done through a user having the UNIX root privilege.

A Word About Data Encryption

Most of today's regulations and standards are concerned largely with the protection of private data at the storage level, during the transaction's execution, and while it transits over the network. Implementing a sound data protection strategy in an organization can be a daunting task. However, the global regulations and standards in Table 8.4 are making it easier to implement the data protection policies effectively.

Table 8.4: Global regulations and standards

Regulation/Standard	Focus
Payment Card Industry Data Security Standards (DSS)	Protection of payment card information during processing, transit, and storage
Gramm-Leach-Bliley Act (GLBA)	Protection of private data in the financial industries
Sarbanes-Oxley Act (SOX)	Protection of private data related to financial reporting in public companies
Health Insurance Portability and Accountability Act (HIPAA)	Protection of private data related to patient health
Data Protection Act (DPA) of 1984	Protection of personal information in the UK
Personal Information Protection and Electronic Documents Act (PIPEDA)	Protection of personal information in Canada

DB2 10.1 supports data encryption at different levels—at disk and while the data is in transit through the network.

You can use the encryption built-in functions to encrypt data at disk level within the database tables and use decrypt built-in functions while displaying the data. Remember that only CHAR, VARCHAR, and FOR BIT DATA can be encrypted using these functions. Table 8.5 lists more information about these encryption built-in functions.

Table 8.5: Encryption and decryption built-in scalar functions

Built-in Function Name	Description	Basic Command Syntax
ENCRYPT	This scalar function encrypts data by using a password-based encryption method. It also accepts a password hint as an argument to help data owners remember the password. Once data is encrypted, the only way to decrypt it is by using the correct password.	ENCRYPT (<DataStringExp>, <PasswordStringExp>, <PasswordHintExp>) where: • DataStringExp identifies the data that needs encryption. • PasswordStringExp identifies the password used to encrypt the data. • PasswordHintExp identifies the hint to help data owners remember the password.
DECRYPT_CHAR	This scalar function decrypts data that was encrypted by using the ENCRYPT function, and it always returns VARCHAR data.	DECRYPT_CHAR(<EncryptedData>, <PasswordStringExp>) where: • EncryptedData identifies the data that needs decryption. • PasswordStringExp identifies the password used while encrypting the data.
DECRYPT_BIN	This scalar function decrypts unstructured data such as images that were encrypted by using the ENCRYPT function, and it always returns VARCHAR FOR BIT DATA.	DECRYPT_BIN(<EncryptedData>, <PasswordStringExp>) where: • EncryptedData identifies the data that needs decryption. • PasswordStringExp identifies the password used while encrypting the data.
GETHINT	This scalar function returns an encapsulated password hint to help data owners remember passwords when they forget them.	GETHINT(<EncryptedData>) where: • EncryptedData identifies the data that needs a password hint to be found.

There are two levels of implementation—*column level* and *row-column level* for encrypting data at the storage level using the ENCRYPT scalar function. Column-level encryption encrypts a given column's data with the password specified in the ENCRYPTION PASSWORD special register.

It is always advisable to use one common password for all the rows in the table, as this example shows:

```
CREATE TABLE EMPLOYEE_ENCRYPT
(     EMPNO INT NOT NULL,
NAME VARCHAR (30),
SSN VARCHAR (30) FOR BIT DATA) IN USERSPACE1
DB20000I  The SQL command completed successfully.

SET ENCRYPTION PASSWORD 'ABCD1234$'
DB20000I  The SQL command completed successfully.

INSERT INTO EMPLOYEE_ENCRYPT VALUES (1, 'SIMON WOODCOCK', ENCRYPT ('123-45-6789'))
DB20000I  The SQL command completed successfully.

INSERT INTO EMPLOYEE_ENCRYPT VALUES (2, 'HAMDI ROUMANI', ENCRYPT ('123-45-6790'))
DB20000I  The SQL command completed successfully.

INSERT INTO EMPLOYEE_ENCRYPT VALUES (3, 'COLIN CHAPMAN', ENCRYPT ('123-45-6791'))
DB20000I  The SQL command completed successfully.

SELECT * FROM EMPLOYEE_ENCRYPT

EMPNO NAME                     SSN
----- ------------------------ ---------------------
    1 SIMON WOODCOCK           x'080AF6FFB804A0D513EE7D3CB879F1CBF1CB9003C8B7D942'
    2 HAMDI ROUMANI            x'086A96FFB804A0D513EE7D3CB879F1CBA29FFA3991B00BF9'
    3 COLIN CHAPMAN            x'082BD5FFB804A0D513EE7D3CB879F1CB0F0C0C241889EA3C'

  3 record(s) selected.

SET ENCRYPTION PASSWORD 'ABCD1234$'
DB20000I  The SQL command completed successfully.
```

Continued

```
SELECT EMPNO,NAME, DECRYPT_CHAR(SSN) AS SSN FROM EMPLOYEE_ENCRYPT

EMPNO NAME                      SSN
----- ------------------------ ---------------------
    1 SIMON WOODCOCK            123-45-6789
    2 HAMDI ROUMANI             123-45-6790
    3 COLIN CHAPMAN             123-45-6791

  3 record(s) selected.
```

If you try setting a password other than the one that was set earlier, you will receive an error something like this:

```
SET ENCRYPTION PASSWORD 'abcd1234$'
DB20000I  The SQL command completed successfully.

SELECT EMPNO,NAME, DECRYPT_CHAR(SSN) AS SSN FROM EMPLOYEE_ENCRYPT

EMPNO NAME                      SSN
----- ------------------------ ---------------------
SQL20145N  The decryption function failed. The password used for decryption
does not match the password used to encrypt the data.  SQLSTATE=428FD
```

Unlike with column-level encryption, if you want to encrypt data by using many different passwords, use row-column level encryption, as in the following example:

```
INSERT INTO EMPLOYEE_ENCRYPT (EMPNO, NAME, SSN) VALUES (1, 'SIMON WOODCOCK',
   ENCRYPT ('123-45-6789', 'POIU09876$'))
DB20000I  The SQL command completed successfully.

INSERT INTO EMPLOYEE_ENCRYPT VALUES (2, 'HAMDI ROUMANI', ENCRYPT ('123-45-6790',
   'abcd12345&'))
DB20000I  The SQL command completed successfully.
```

Continued

```
INSERT INTO EMPLOYEE_ENCRYPT VALUES (3, 'COLIN CHAPMAN', ENCRYPT ('123-45-6791',
   'xectqazw121£'))
DB20000I  The SQL command completed successfully.

SELECT * FROM EMPLOYEE_ENCRYPT
EMPNO NAME                      SSN
----- ------------------------- ---------------------
    1 SIMON WOODCOCK            x'08867AFFB804A0D55CEE84FCF583C506E6821167BB2B2D56'
    2 HAMDI ROUMANI             x'084BB5FFB804A0D51F3DD84B979734E4BD08A6E518D04A5E'
    3 COLIN CHAPMAN             x'08E51BFFB804A0D5AB48994A3422BF9F5C7FD72D89339010'

  3 record(s) selected.


SELECT EMPNO,NAME, DECRYPT_CHAR(SSN, 'POIU09876$') AS SSN FROM EMPLOYEE_ENCRYPT
       WHERE EMPNO=1
EMPNO NAME                      SSN
----- ------------------------- ---------------------
    1 SIMON WOODCOCK            123-45-6789

1 record(s) selected.
```

To encrypt data in transit over the network, you can use DATA_ENCRYPT authentication mechanism or Secure Sockets Layer (SSL) support. The solution works only when both the DB2 client and the server support DATA_ENCRYPT configuration or SSL setup.

If you want to enable encryption through DATA_ENCRYPT, set the database manager configuration AUTHENTICATION to DATA_ENCRYPT both at the server side and at the client side by using the sample commands below.

On the DB2 server side:

```
UPDATE DBM CFG USING AUTHENTICATION DATA_ENCRYPT
DB20000I  The UPDATE DATABASE MANAGER CONFIGURATION command completed
successfully.
```

On the DB2 client side:

```
CATALOG DB SAMPLE AT NODE SMPLNODE AUTHENTICATION DATA_ENCRYPT
DB20000I  The CATALOG DATABASE command completed successfully.
DB21056W  Directory changes may not be effective until the directory cache is
refreshed.
```

To implement SSL, refer to "Configuring Secure Sockets Layer (SSL) support in a DB2 instance" at the DB2 10.1 IBM Knowledge Center.

Trusted Contexts and Trusted Connections

In a three-tier application model having a web server, an application server, and a database server, the middle tier such as IBM WebSphere Application Server (WAS) is responsible for authenticating users who are running the client applications and managing the interactions with the database server. All the users—for example, Eric, Jason, Simon, Colin, and Hamdi—are connecting to the application server by using their own user IDs. However, the connection from the application server to the database server is normally done through a common application user ID such as AppUser, as Figure 8.16 shows.

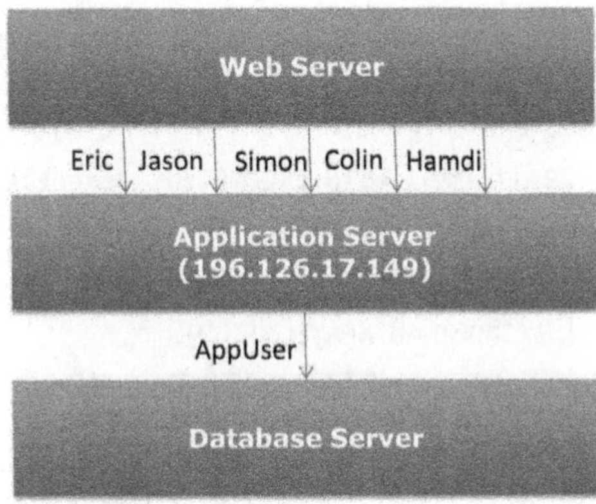

Figure 8.16: Three-tier application model and context switch

This raises several security concerns:

- Loss of user identity and accountability. For access control and audit purposes, organizations today prefer to know the identity of the actual user accessing the database and transactions that he or she is performing on the database.

- Overgranting of privileges. In most cases, the middle-tier application ID will have CONTROL privilege on all the tables and will have EXECUTE privilege on all the functions and packages. This creates the security threat of enabling users who do not need access to certain information to obtain access to that data.
- Weakened security. In addition to the overgranting privilege issue, the middle-tier application ID can access all the resources that might be accessed by user requests. If the application ID is ever compromised, all those resources are exposed.

The DB2's trusted context feature addresses these problems. A trusted context is a database object that defines a trust relationship for a connection between the database and an external entity such as an application server. The trust relationship is built based on the following set of attributes:

- **Authorization ID**. Identifies the user who establishes a connection to the database
- **IP address or domain name**. Identifies the host name from which a database connection is established to the database server
- **Data stream encryption**. Identifies the data stream's minimum level of encryption between the database server and the client

A person holding SECADM authority can create a trusted context by using the CREATE TRUSTED CONTEXT command. The basic syntax is:

```
CREATE TRUSTED CONTEXT <ContextName>
BASED ON CONNECTION USING SYSTEM AUTHID <AuthorizationID>
ATTRIBUTES (ADDRESS <IPAddress> [WITH ENCRYPTION <EncryptionValue>])
[NO DEFAULT ROLE | DEFAULT ROLE <RoleName> [ENABLE|DISABLE]]
WITH USE FOR [<UseAuthorizationID> | ROLE <UseRoleName>]
[WITH AUTHENTICATION | WITHOUT AUTHENTICATION]
```

where:

ContextName	Identifies the name of the trusted context
AuthorizationID	Identifies the system authorization ID to use in establishing a trusted context
IPAddress	Identifies the IP address value to associate with the ADDRESS trust attribute; this must be an IPv4, an IPv6, or a secure domain name
EncryptionValue	Identifies the level of encryption of the data stream or network encryption for a specific IP address; the valid values are NONE, LOW, and HIGH

RoleName	Identifies the role name to associate with a trusted connection based on a trusted context
UseAuthorizationID	Identifies the authorization ID that can use the trusted connection
UseRoleName	Identifies the role to use for the user when a trusted connection is using the trusted context

Let us create a trusted context TCXU1 to allow the application user APPUSER to connect to the database SAMPLE only from IP address 196.126.17.149 and associate the role developer to it:

```
CREATE ROLE developer
DB20000I  The SQL command completed successfully.

GRANT SELECT ON TABLE MOHAN.EMPLOYEE TO ROLE developer
DB20000I  The SQL command completed successfully.

CREATE TRUSTED CONTEXT TCXU1
BASED UPON CONNECTION USING SYSTEM AUTHID APPUSER
ATTRIBUTES (ADDRESS '196.126.17.149 ')
DEFAULT ROLE developer ENABLE;
DB20000I  The SQL command completed successfully.
```

If you try to connect to database SAMPLE and run the SELECT statement from IP address 196.126.17.149, you will see something like the following:

```
CONNECT TO sample USER AppUser
Enter current password for AppUser:

   Database Connection Information

 Database server        = DB2/LINUXX8664 10.1.3
 SQL authorization ID   = APPUSER
 Local database alias   = SAMPLE
```

Continued

```
SELECT COUNT (*) AS COUNT FROM MOHAN.EMPLOYEE"

COUNT
-----------
         42

  1 record(s) selected.
```

Likewise, a connection and a SELECT statement from IP address 196.126.19.150 will result in an error similar to this:

```
CONNECT TO sample USER AppUser
Enter current password for AppUser:

   Database Connection Information

 Database server        = DB2/LINUXX8664 10.1.3
 SQL authorization ID   = APPUSER
 Local database alias   = SAMPLE

SELECT COUNT (*) AS COUNT FROM MOHAN.EMPLOYEE"
SQL0551N  "APPUSER" does not have the required authorization or privilege to
perform operation "SELECT" on object "MOHAN.EMPLOYEE".  SQLSTATE=42501
```

It is evident from the above result that by combining the capabilities of trusted contexts and roles, you can control where a user connects to the database from and obtains access to the database objects.

To create a trusted context to allow user Jason to connect from the IP address 196.126.17.149 and allow the connection to switch from Jason to Eric without authentication and to Colin with authentication, execute the CREATE TRUSTED CONTEXT command, something like this:

```
CREATE TRUSTED CONTEXT TCXU2
BASED UPON CONNECTION USING SYSTEM AUTHID JASON
DEFAULT ROLE DEVELOPER
ENABLE
```

Continued

```
ATTRIBUTES (ADDRESS '196.126.17.149')
WITH USE FOR ERIC WITHOUT AUTHENTICATION,
COLIN WITH AUTHENTICATION
DB20000I  The SQL command completed successfully.
```

Securing Data with Label-based Access Control

Earlier, you saw that authentication is performed at the operating system level to verify that users are who they say they are, and that authorities and privileges control access to a database and the objects and data that reside within it. Views, which allow different users to see different presentations of the same data, can be used in conjunction with privileges to limit access to specific columns. But what if your security requirements dictate that you create and manage several hundred views? Or, more important, what if you want to restrict access to individual rows in a table? The solution for these situations is label-based access control (LBAC).

LBAC is a security feature that uses one or more security labels to control who has read access and who has write access to individual rows and columns in a table. The United States and many other governments use LBAC models in which hierarchical classification labels such as CONFIDENTIAL, SECRET, and TOP SECRET are assigned to data based on its sensitivity. Access to data labeled at a certain level (for example, SECRET) is restricted to those users who have been granted that level of access or higher. With LBAC, you can construct security labels to represent any criteria your company uses to determine who can read or modify particular data values. And LBAC is flexible enough to handle the simplest to the most complex criteria.

One problem with the traditional security methods DB2 uses is that security administrators and DBAs have access to sensitive data stored in the databases they oversee. To solve this problem, LBAC-security administration tasks are isolated from all other tasks—only users with SECADM authority are allowed to configure LBAC elements.

Implementing Row-level LBAC

Before you implement a row-level LBAC solution, you need to have a thorough understanding of the security requirements. Suppose you have a database that contains company sales data, and you want to control how senior executives, regional managers, and sales representatives can access data stored in a table named SALES. Security requirements might dictate that access to this data should comply with these rules:

- Senior executives are allowed to view, but not update, all records in the table.
- Regional managers are allowed to view and update only records that were entered by sales representatives who report to them.
- Sales representatives are allowed to view and update only records of the sales they made.

Once you know the security requirements, you must then define the appropriate security policies and labels, create an LBAC-protected table (or alter an existing table to add LBAC protection), and grant the proper security labels to the appropriate users.

Defining a Security-label Component

Security-label components represent criteria to use to decide whether a user should have access to specific data. Three types of security label components exist:

- A set is a collection of elements (character string values) where the order in which each element appears is not important.
- An array is an ordered set that can represent a simple hierarchy. In an array, the order in which the elements appear is important—the first element ranks higher than the second, the second ranks higher than the third, and so on.
- A tree represents a more complex hierarchy that can have multiple nodes and branches.

To create security-label components, you execute one of the following CREATE SECURITY LABEL COMPONENT SQL statements:

```
CREATE SECURITY LABEL COMPONENT [ComponentName]
SET {StringConstant,...}
```

or

```
CREATE SECURITY LABEL COMPONENT [ComponentName]
ARRAY [StringConstant,...]
```

or

```
CREATE SECURITY LABEL COMPONENT [ComponentName]
TREE (StringConstant ROOT < StringConstant UNDER StringConstant >)]
```

where:

ComponentName	Identifies the name to assign to the security-label component being created
StringConstant	Identifies one or more string constant values that make up the valid array, set, or tree of values that the security-label component being created will use

Thus, to create a security-label component named SEC_COMP that contains a set of values whose order is insignificant, you execute a CREATE SECURITY LABEL COMPONENT statement like this:

```
CREATE SECURITY LABEL COMPONENT sec_comp
SET {'CONFIDENTIAL', 'SECRET', 'TOP_SECRET'}
```

To create a security-label component that contains an array of values listed from highest to lowest order, execute a CREATE SECURITY LABEL COMPONENT statement, as follows:

```
CREATE SECURITY LABEL COMPONENT sec_comp
ARRAY ['MASTER_CRAFTSMAN', 'JOURNEYMAN', 'APPRENTICE']
```

And to create a security-label component that contains a tree of values that describe a company's organizational chart, you execute a CREATE SECURITY LABEL COMPONENT statement something like this:

```
CREATE SECURITY LABEL COMPONENT sec_comp
TREE ('EXEC_STAFF' ROOT,
          'N_MGR' UNDER 'EXEC_STAFF',
          'E_MGR' UNDER 'EXEC_STAFF',
          'S_MGR' UNDER 'EXEC_STAFF',
          'W_MGR' UNDER 'EXEC_STAFF',
          'C_MGR' UNDER 'EXEC_STAFF',
          'SALES_REP1' UNDER 'N_MGR',
          'SALES_REP2' UNDER 'W_MGR')
```

Defining a Security Policy

Security policies determine exactly how LBAC is to protect a table. Specifically, a security policy identifies the following:

- What security-label components to use in the security labels that will be part of the policy
- What rules to use when security-label components are compared (at this time, only one set of rules is supported: DB2LBACRULES)
- Which optional behaviors to use when accessing data protected by the policy

Every LBAC-protected table must have one and only one security policy associated with it. Rows and columns in that table can be protected only with security labels that are part of that security policy; all protected data access must adhere to the rules of that policy. You can have multiple security policies within a single database, but you cannot have more than one security policy protecting any given table.

To create a security policy, execute the CREATE SECURITY POLICY SQL statement, as follows:

```
CREATE SECURITY POLICY [PolicyName]
COMPONENTS [ComponentName ,...]
WITH DB2LBACRULES
<[OVERRIDE | RESTRICT] NOT AUTHORIZED WRITE SECURITY LABEL>
```

where:

PolicyName	Identifies the name to assign to the security policy being created
ComponentName	Identifies, by name, one or more security-label components that are to be part of the security policy being created

The [OVERRIDE | RESTRICT] NOT AUTHORIZED WRITE SECURITY LABEL option specifies the action to take when a user who is not authorized to write the security label explicitly specified with INSERT and UPDATE statements attempts to write data to the protected table. By default, the value of a user's security label, rather than an explicitly specified security label, is used for write access during insert and update operations (OVERRIDE NOT AUTHORIZED WRITE SECURITY LABEL). If you use the RESTRICT NOT AUTHORIZED WRITE SECURITY LABEL option, insert and update operations will fail if the user is not authorized to write the explicitly specified security label to the protected table.

Therefore, to create a security policy named SEC_POLICY that is based on the SEC_COMP security-label component created earlier, execute a CREATE SECURITY POLICY statement that looks something like this:

```
CREATE SECURITY POLICY sec_policy
COMPONENTS sec_comp
WITH DB2LBACRULES
```

Defining Security Labels

Security labels describe a set of security criteria and are used to protect data against unauthorized access or modification. A security administrator grants security labels to users who are allowed to access or modify protected data; when users attempt to access or modify protected data, their security label is compared to the security label protecting the data to determine whether the access or modification is permitted. Every security label is part of exactly one security policy, and a security label must exist for each security-label component in the security policy.

You create security labels by executing the CREATE SECURITY LABEL SQL statement. The syntax for this statement is:

```
CREATE SECURITY LABEL [LabelName]
[COMPONENT [ComponentName] [StringConstant] ,...]
```

where:

LabelName	Identifies the name to assign to the security label being created; the name you specify must be qualified with a security policy name and must not match an existing security label for the security policy indicated
ComponentName	Identifies, by name, a security label component that is part of the security policy specified as the qualifier for the LabelName parameter
StringConstant	Identifies one or more string constant values that are valid elements of the security-label component specified in the ComponentName parameter

Thus, to create a set of security labels for the security policy named SEC_POLICY that was created earlier, you execute a set of CREATE SECURITY LABEL statements that looks something like this:

```
CREATE SECURITY LABEL sec_policy.exec_staff
COMPONENT sec_comp 'EXEC_STAFF'

CREATE SECURITY LABEL sec_policy.n_mgr
COMPONENT sec_comp 'N_MGR'

CREATE SECURITY LABEL sec_policy.e_mgr
COMPONENT sec_comp 'E_MGR'

CREATE SECURITY LABEL sec_policy.s_mgr
COMPONENT sec_comp 'S_MGR'
```

Continued

```
CREATE SECURITY LABEL sec_policy.w_mgr
COMPONENT sec_comp 'W_MGR'

CREATE SECURITY LABEL sec_policy.c_mgr
COMPONENT sec_comp 'C_MGR'

CREATE SECURITY LABEL sec_policy.sales_rep1
COMPONENT sec_comp 'SALES_REP1'

CREATE SECURITY LABEL sec_policy.sales_rep2
COMPONENT sec_comp 'SALES_REP2'
```

Creating a LBAC-Protected Table

Once you have defined the security policy and labels needed to enforce your security requirements, you are ready to create a table and configure it for LBAC protection. To configure a new table for row-level LBAC protection, you include a column with the data type DB2SECURITYLABEL in the table's definition and associate a security policy with the table by using the SECURITY POLICY clause of the CREATE TABLE SQL statement.

So to create a table named SALES and configure it for row-level LBAC protection using the security policy named SEC_POLICY created earlier, you execute a CREATE TABLE statement that looks something like this:

```
CREATE TABLE corp.sales (
     sales_rec_id     INTEGER NOT NULL,
     sales_date       DATE WITH DEFAULT,
     sales_rep        INTEGER,
     region           VARCHAR(15),
     manager          INTEGER,
     sales_amt        DECIMAL(12,2),
     margin           DECIMAL(12,2),
     sec_label        DB2SECURITYLABEL)
   SECURITY POLICY sec_policy
```

To configure an existing table named SALES for row-level LBAC protection using a security policy named SEC_POLICY, execute an ALTER TABLE statement similar to the following:

```
ALTER TABLE corp.sales
    ADD COLUMN sec_label DB2SECURITYLABEL
    ADD SECURITY POLICY sec_policy
```

However, before you can execute such an ALTER TABLE statement, you must possess a security label for write access that is part of the security policy that will protect the table (which, in this case is SEC_POLICY). Otherwise, you will not be able to create the DB2SECURITYLABEL column.

Granting Security Labels to Users

Once you have defined the security policy and labels needed to enforce your security requirements and have enabled a table for LBAC protection, you must grant the proper security labels to the appropriate users and indicate whether they are to have read access, write access, or full access to data that is protected by that label. You grant security labels to users by executing a special form of the GRANT SQL statement. The syntax for this form of the GRANT statement is:

```
GRANT SECURITY LABEL [LabelName]
TO USER [UserName]
[FOR ALL ACCESS | FOR READ ACCESS | FOR WRITE ACCESS]
```

where:

LabelName	Identifies the name of an existing security label; you must qualify the name you specify with the security policy name that was used when the security label was created
UserName	Identifies the name of the user to whom to grant the security label

Thus, to give a user named USER1 the ability to read data protected by the security label SEC_POLICY.EXEC_STAFF, execute a GRANT statement that looks like this:

```
GRANT SECURITY LABEL sec_policy.exec_staff
TO USER user1 FOR READ ACCESS
```

Putting Row-level LBAC into Action

To enforce the security requirements listed earlier, you must first give users the ability to perform DML operations against the SALES table. You accomplish this by executing the following GRANT statements, as a user with SYSADM or DBADM authority:

```
GRANT ALL PRIVILEGES ON TABLE corp.sales TO exec_staff
GRANT ALL PRIVILEGES ON TABLE corp.sales TO n_manager
GRANT ALL PRIVILEGES ON TABLE corp.sales TO e_manager
GRANT ALL PRIVILEGES ON TABLE corp.sales TO s_manager
GRANT ALL PRIVILEGES ON TABLE corp.sales TO w_manager
GRANT ALL PRIVILEGES ON TABLE corp.sales TO c_manager
GRANT ALL PRIVILEGES ON TABLE corp.sales TO sales_rep1
GRANT ALL PRIVILEGES ON TABLE corp.sales TO sales_rep2
```

Next, you must grant the proper security labels to the appropriate users and indicate whether they are to have read access, write access, or full access to data that is protected by that label. You do this by executing the following GRANT statements, but this time as a user with SECADM authority:

```
GRANT SECURITY LABEL sec_policy.exec_staff
TO USER exec_staff FOR READ ACCESS

GRANT SECURITY LABEL sec_policy.n_mgr
TO USER n_manager FOR ALL ACCESS

GRANT SECURITY LABEL sec_policy.e_mgr
TO USER e_manager FOR ALL ACCESS

GRANT SECURITY LABEL sec_policy.s_mgr
TO USER s_manager FOR ALL ACCESS

GRANT SECURITY LABEL sec_policy.w_mgr
TO USER w_manager FOR ALL ACCESS
```

Continued

```
GRANT SECURITY LABEL sec_policy.c_mgr
TO USER c_manager FOR ALL ACCESS

GRANT SECURITY LABEL sec_policy.sales_rep1
TO USER sales_rep1 FOR ALL ACCESS

GRANT SECURITY LABEL sec_policy.sales_rep2
TO USER sales_rep2 FOR ALL ACCESS
```

Now, suppose user SALES_REP1 adds three rows to the SALES table by executing the following SQL statements:

```
INSERT INTO corp.sales VALUES (1, DEFAULT, 1, 'NORTH', 5,
     1000.50, 500.00,
     SECLABEL_BY_NAME ('SEC_POLICY', 'SALES_REP1'))

INSERT INTO corp.sales VALUES (2, DEFAULT, 1, 'NORTH', 5,
     2000.00, 400.00,
     SECLABEL_BY_NAME ('SEC_POLICY', 'SALES_REP1'))

INSERT INTO corp.sales VALUES (3, DEFAULT, 1, 'NORTH', 5,
     4500.90, 850.00,
     SECLABEL_BY_NAME ('SEC_POLICY', 'SALES_REP1'))
```

SALES_REP1 possesses read and write access to the table via the SEC_POLICY.SALES_REP1 security label, so the statements execute successfully. Next, user SALES_REP2 adds two more rows to the SALES table by executing the following SQL statements:

```
INSERT INTO corp.sales VALUES (4, DEFAULT, 1, 'WEST', 20,
     1000.50, 500.00,
     SECLABEL_BY_NAME('SEC_POLICY', 'SALES_REP2'))

INSERT INTO corp.sales VALUES (5, DEFAULT, 1, 'WEST', 20,
     3200.00, 600.00,
     SECLABEL_BY_NAME('SEC_POLICY', 'SALES_REP2'))
```

SALES_REP2 also holds read and write access to the table via the SEC_POLICY.SALES_REP2 security label, so the rows are successfully inserted.

Now, when user EXEC_STAFF queries the SALES table, all five records entered will appear (because the security label SEC_POLICY.EXEC_STAFF is the highest level in the security policy's security-label component tree). However, if user EXEC_STAFF attempts to insert additional records or update an existing record, an error will be generated because user EXEC_STAFF is allowed only to read the data (only read access was granted).

When user N_MANAGER queries the table, only records entered by the user SALES_REP1 will display; the user W_MANAGER will see only records entered by the user SALES_REP2; and the users E_MANAGER, S_MANAGER, and C_MANAGER cannot view any records at all. (SALES_REP1 reports to N_MANAGER, SALES_REP2 reports to W_MANAGER, and no other managers have a sales representative reporting to them.)

And finally, when SALES_REP1 or SALES_REP2 queries the SALES table, they will see only the records they personally entered. Likewise, they can update only the records they entered.

Implementing Column-level LBAC

To understand how to use column-level LBAC, assume you want to control how human resources (HR) staff members, managers, and employees will access data stored in a table named EMPLOYEES. For this scenario, the security requirements are as follows:

- All employees can view name, gender, department, and phone number information.
- Only managers and HR staff members can see hire date, salary, and bonus information (in addition to name, gender, department, and phone number information).
- Only HR staff members can view employee ID and Social Security number information. Additionally, HR staff members are the only users who can create and modify employee records.

Once again, after you have identified the security requirements, the next steps are to define the appropriate security component, policies, and labels; create the table that will house the data; alter the table to add LBAC protection; and grant the proper security labels to the appropriate users.

Defining a Security-label Component

Because an array of values, listed from highest to lowest order, is the best way to implement the security requirements just outlined, you can create the security component needed by executing a CREATE SECURITY LABEL COMPONENT statement (as a user with SECADM authority) that looks something like this:

```
CREATE SECURITY LABEL COMPONENT sec_comp
ARRAY ['CONFIDENTIAL', 'CLASSIFIED', 'UNCLASSIFIED']
```

Defining a Security Policy

After you have created the appropriate security-label component, you can create a security policy named SEC_POLICY that is based on the SEC_COMP security-label component by executing the following CREATE SECURITY POLICY statement (as a user with SECADM authority):

```
CREATE SECURITY POLICY sec_policy
COMPONENTS sec_comp
WITH DB2LBACRULES
```

Defining Security Labels

Earlier, you saw that security labels are granted to users who are allowed to access or modify LBAC-protected data. When users attempt to access or modify protected data, their security label is compared with the security label protecting the data to determine whether to permit the access or modification. But before you can grant security labels, you must first define them.

To create a set of security labels for the security policy named SEC_POLICY that was just created, you execute the following set of CREATE SECURITY LABEL statements (as a user with SECADM authority):

```
CREATE SECURITY LABEL sec_policy.confidential
COMPONENT sec_comp 'CONFIDENTIAL'

CREATE SECURITY LABEL sec_policy.classified
COMPONENT sec_comp 'CLASSIFIED'

CREATE SECURITY LABEL sec_policy.unclassified
COMPONENT sec_comp 'UNCLASSIFIED'
```

Remember that every security label is part of exactly one security policy, and a security label must exist for each security-label component in that security policy.

Creating an LBAC-Protected Table

As previously discussed, to configure a new table for row-level LBAC protection, you must associate a security policy with the table being created by using the SECURITY POLICY clause of the CREATE TABLE SQL statement. The same is true for column-level LBAC protection.

Therefore, to create a table named EMPLOYEES and associate it with a security policy named SEC_POLICY, you must execute a CREATE TABLE statement that looks something like this:

```
CREATE TABLE hr.employees (
     emp_id    INTEGER NOT NULL,
     f_name    VARCHAR(20),
     l_name    VARCHAR(20),
     gender    CHAR(1),
     hire_date DATE WITH DEFAULT,
     dept_id   CHAR(5),
     phone     CHAR(14),
     ssn       CHAR(12),
     salary    DECIMAL(12,2),
     bonus     DECIMAL(12,2))
    SECURITY POLICY sec_policy
```

Granting Security Labels to Users

To enforce the security requirements identified earlier, you must give users the ability to perform the appropriate DML operations against the EMPLOYEES table. You do this by executing the following GRANT SQL statements (as a user with SYSADM or DBADM authority):

```
GRANT ALL PRIVILEGES ON TABLE hr.employees TO hr_staff
GRANT SELECT ON TABLE hr.employees TO manager1
GRANT SELECT ON TABLE hr.employees TO employee1
```

Finally, you must grant the proper security label to the appropriate users and indicate whether they are to have read access, write access, or full access to data that is protected by that label. To accomplish this, you execute a set of GRANT statements (as a user with SECADM authority) that look something like this:

```
GRANT SECURITY LABEL sec_policy.confidential
TO USER hr_staff FOR ALL ACCESS

                                                Continued
```

```
GRANT SECURITY LABEL sec_policy.classified
TO USER manager1 FOR READ ACCESS

GRANT SECURITY LABEL sec_policy.unclassified
TO USER employee1 FOR READ ACCESS
```

Creating LBAC-Protected Columns

Once you have defined the security policy and labels needed to enforce your security requirements and have granted the appropriate privileges and security labels to users, you are ready to modify the table associated with the security policy and configure its columns for column-level LBAC protection. You do this by executing an ALTER TABLE statement:

```
ALTER TABLE hr.employees
     ALTER COLUMN emp_id SECURED WITH confidential
     ALTER COLUMN f_name SECURED WITH unclassified
     ALTER COLUMN l_name SECURED WITH unclassified
     ALTER COLUMN gender SECURED WITH unclassified
     ALTER COLUMN hire_date SECURED WITH classified
     ALTER COLUMN dept_id SECURED WITH unclassified
     ALTER COLUMN phone SECURED WITH unclassified
     ALTER COLUMN ssn SECURED WITH confidential
     ALTER COLUMN salary SECURED WITH classified
     ALTER COLUMN bonus SECURED WITH classified
```

Here is where things get a little tricky. If you try to execute the above ALTER TABLE statement as a user with SYSADM or SECADM authority, the operation will fail, and you will receive an error message similar to the following:

```
SQL20419N  For table "HR.EMPLOYEES", authorization ID "MOHAN" does not have
LBAC credentials that allow using the security label
   "SEC_POLICY.CONFIDENTIAL" to protect column "EMP_ID".  SQLSTATE=42522
```

That is because the only user who can secure a column with the CONFIDENTIAL security label is a user who holds *write access* to data that is protected by that label. In our scenario, this is the user HR_STAFF. So what happens when user HR_STAFF attempts to execute the preceding ALTER TABLE statement? It completes the ALTER TABLE command execution with incorrect security labels association, such as updating all the column security labels to CONFIDENTIAL, as follows:

```
CREATE TABLE HR.EMPLOYEES (
EMP_ID INTEGER COLUMN SECURED WITH CONFIDENTIAL NOT NULL,
F_NAME VARCHAR (20) COLUMN SECURED WITH CONFIDENTIAL,
L_NAME VARCHAR (20) COLUMN SECURED WITH CONFIDENTIAL,
GENDER CHAR (1) COLUMN SECURED WITH CONFIDENTIAL,
HIRE_DATE DATE COLUMN SECURED WITH CONFIDENTIAL WITH DEFAULT,
DEPT_ID CHAR (5) COLUMN SECURED WITH CONFIDENTIAL,
PHONE CHAR (14) COLUMN SECURED WITH CONFIDENTIAL,
SSN CHAR (12) COLUMN SECURED WITH CONFIDENTIAL,
SALARY DECIMAL (12, 2) COLUMN SECURED WITH CONFIDENTIAL,
BONUS DECIMAL (12, 2) COLUMN SECURED WITH CONFIDENTIAL)
SECURITY POLICY SEC_POLICY
```

LBAC Rule Set—DB2LBACRULES

An LBAC rule set is a predefined set of rules that is used when comparing security labels. Currently, only one LBAC rule set is supported (DB2LBACRULES), and as you have just seen, this rule set prevents both write-up and write-down behavior. (Write-up and write-down apply only to ARRAY security-label components and only to write access.) Write-up is when the security label protecting data to which you are attempting to write is higher than the security label you have been granted; write-down is when the security label protecting data is lower.

Which rules are used when two security labels are compared is dependent on the type of component used (SET, ARRAY, or TREE) and the type of access being attempted (read or write). Table 8.6 lists the rules in the DB2LBACRULES rules set, identifies the component each rule is used for, and describes how the rule determines whether to block access.

Table 8.6: Summary of LBAC rules

Rule Name Component	Component	Access	Access is blocked when this condition is met
DB2LBACREADARRAY	ARRAY	Read	The user's security label is lower than the protecting security label.
DB2LBACREADSET	SET	Read	There are one or more protecting security labels that the user does not hold.

Table 8.6: Summary of LBAC rules (continued)			
Rule Name Component	**Component**	**Access**	**Access is blocked when this condition is met**
DB2LBACREADTREE	TREE	Read	None of the user's security labels is equal to or an ancestor of one of the protecting security labels.
DB2LBACWRITEARRAY	ARRAY	Write	The user's security label is either higher than or lower than the protecting security label.
DB2LBACWRITESET	SET	Write	There are one or more protecting security labels that the user does not hold.
DB2LBACWRITETREE	TREE	Write	None of the user's security labels is equal to or an ancestor of one of the protecting security labels.
Adapted from Table 11 on pages 169–170 of the IBM DB2 Version 10.1 for Linux, UNIX, and Windows Database Security Guide.			

LBAC Rule Exemptions

So how can you secure the remaining columns in the EMPLOYEES table with the appropriate security labels? The security administrator must first grant user HR_STAFF an exemption to one or more security policy rules. When a user holds an exemption on a particular security policy rule, that rule is not enforced when the user attempts to access data that is protected by that security policy.

You grant security policy exemptions by executing the GRANT EXEMPTION ON RULE SQL statement (as a user with SECADM authority). The syntax for this statement is:

```
GRANT EXEMPTION ON RULE [Rule] ,...
FOR [PolicyName]
TO USER [UserName]
```

where:

Rule	Identifies one or more DB2LBACRULES security policy rules for which to grant exemptions; the following values are valid for this parameter: DB2LBACREADARRAY, DB2LBACREADSET, DB2LBACREADTREE, DB2LBACWRITEARRAY WRITEDOWN, DB2LBACWRITEARRAY WRITEUP, DB2LBACWRITESET, DB2LBACWRITETREE, and ALL (if an exemption is held for every security policy rule, the user will have complete access to all data protected by that security policy)
PolicyName	Identifies the security policy for which to grant the exemption
UserName	Identifies the name of the user to whom to grant the exemptions specified

Thus, to grant an exemption to the DB2LBACWRITEARRAY rule in the security policy named SEC_POLICY created earlier to a user named HR_STAFF, you execute a GRANT EXEMPTION statement that looks something like this:

```
GRANT EXEMPTION ON RULE DB2LBACWRITEARRAY
WRITEDOWN FOR sec_policy
TO USER hr_staff
```

Once you grant this exemption along with the appropriate security label, user HR_STAFF will be able to execute the ALTER TABLE statement shown earlier without generating an error. Alternatively, you can use the following CREATE TABLE statement to create the EMPLOYEES table and protect each column with the appropriate security label, provided user HR_STAFF has the privileges needed to create the table:

```
CREATE TABLE hr.employees (
     emp_id      INTEGER NOT NULL SECURED WITH confidential,
     f_name      VARCHAR(20) SECURED WITH unclassified,
     l_name      VARCHAR(20) SECURED WITH unclassified,
     gender      CHAR(1) SECURED WITH unclassified,
     hire_date   DATE WITH DEFAULT SECURED WITH classified,
     dept_id     CHAR(5) SECURED WITH unclassified,
     phone       CHAR(14) SECURED WITH unclassified,
     ssn         CHAR(12) SECURED WITH confidential,
     salary      DECIMAL(12,2) SECURED WITH classified,
     bonus       DECIMAL(12,2) SECURED WITH classified)
  SECURITY POLICY sec_policy
```

Putting Column-level LBAC into Action

Now that you have established a column-level LBAC environment, let us see what happens when different users try to access data stored in protected columns of the EMPLOYEES table. Suppose the user HR_STAFF adds three rows to the EMPLOYEES table by executing the following SQL statements:

```
INSERT INTO hr.employees VALUES(1, 'Colin', 'Chapman', 'M',
    DEFAULT, 'A01', '919-555-1212', '111-22-3333',
    72000.50, 9500.00)
```

Continued

```
INSERT INTO hr.employees VALUES(2, 'Simon', 'Woodcock', 'M',
    DEFAULT, 'A01', '919-555-3434', '222-33-4444',
    72100.75, 9400.00)

INSERT INTO hr.employees VALUES(3, 'Paul', 'Smith', 'M',
    DEFAULT, 'C03', '919-555-5656', '333-44-5555',
    39250.00, 3500.00)
```

User HR_STAFF1 holds read and write access to all columns in the table (via the SEC_POLICY .CLASSIFIED security label and the DB2LBACWRITEARRAY WRITEDOWN exemption), so the statements are executed successfully. If user HR_STAFF attempts to query the table, the user will be able to see every column and every row because he or she possesses the highest security level in the array.

Now, when user MANAGER1 attempts to read every column in the table, an error will be generated stating that the user does not have read access to the column SSN. However, MANAGER1 will be able to execute the following query because the user has read access to each column specified:

```
SELECT f_name, l_name, hire_date, salary, bonus
FROM hr.employees
```

Now, if user EMPLOYEE1 attempts to execute the same query, an error will be generated stating that he or she does not have read access to the column BONUS.

But an attempt by EMPLOYEE1 to execute the following query will be successful:

```
SELECT f_name, l_name, gender, dept_id, phone
FROM hr.employees
```

Additionally, if user MANAGER1 or user EMPLOYEE1 attempts to insert additional records or update existing information, that user will receive an error stating that he or she does not have permission to perform the operation against the table.

Combining Row-level and Column-level LBAC

At times, you may want to limit an individual user's access to a specific combination of rows and columns. When this is the case, you must include a column with the data type DB2SECURITYLABEL in the table's definition, add the SECURED WITH [*SecurityLabel*] option to each column in the table's definition, and associate a security policy with the table by using the SECURITY POLICY clause of the CREATE TABLE SQL statement or the ADD SECURITY POLICY clause of the ALTER TABLE statement. Typically, you will also create two security-label components—one for rows and one for columns—and use both components to construct the security policy and labels needed.

For example, assume that you create two security-label components by executing the following commands:

```
CREATE SECURITY LABEL COMPONENT scom_level
ARRAY ['CONFIDENTIAL', 'CLASSIFIED', 'UNCLASSIFIED'];

CREATE SECURITY LABEL COMPONENT scom_country
TREE ('NA' ROOT, 'CANADA' UNDER 'NA', 'USA' UNDER 'NA');
```

You then create a security policy by executing a CREATE SECURITY POLICY command that looks something like this:

```
CREATE SECURITY POLICY sec_policy
COMPONENTS scom_level, scom_country
WITH DB2LBACRULES
```

Next, you create corresponding security labels by executing commands similar to the following:

```
CREATE SECURITY LABEL sec_policy.confidential
COMPONENT scom_level 'CONFIDENTIAL';

CREATE SECURITY LABEL sec_policy.uc_canada
COMPONENT scom_level 'UNCLASSIFIED'
COMPONENT scom_country 'CANADA';

CREATE SECURITY LABEL sec_policy.uc_us
COMPONENT scom_level 'UNCLASSIFIED'
COMPONENT scom_country 'USA';
```

Finally, after associating the appropriate security labels with individual columns, you grant the proper security label to each user and conduct a few tests to ensure data access is controlled as expected.

Row and Column Access Control

DB2 10.1 introduced RCAC as an additional data-security feature to limit data access to those users who have a real business need to know the data—this feature is also termed as *fine-grained access control* (*FGAC*). Unlike LBAC, RCAC is a general-purpose security model that works with your own security rules to complement the table privileges.

You can implement RCAC by using the following database objects:

- **Row permission.** Expresses a row-access control rule for a specific table and describes what set of rows a user has access to
- **Column mask.** Expresses a column-access control rule for a specific column in a table and describes what column values a user is permitted to see and under what conditions

Implementing Row Permissions

A user having SECADM authority can create row permission on a table by using the CREATE PERMISSION command. The basic syntax is:

```
CREATE <OR REPLACE> PERMISSION [PermissionName] ON [TableName]
FOR ROWS WHERE [SearchCondition] ENFORCED FOR ALL ACCESS
<ENABLE | DISABLE>
```

where:

PermissionName	Identifies the name of the permission, including the explicit or implicit qualifier
TableName	Identifies the name of the table on which to create the row permission—it must not be a nickname; a created or declared global temporary table, view, alias, or synonym; a typed table; or system catalog tables
SearchCondition	Identifies a condition that can be true or false for a row of the table; this follows the same rules used by the search condition in a WHERE clause of a subselect query

Earlier, you saw that to configure a new table for row-level or column-level LBAC protection, you must associate a security policy with the table being created by using the SECURITY POLICY clause of the CREATE TABLE SQL statement. However, to configure a new table for RCAC, there is no need to associate any policy with the table. The following steps show how to configure RCAC.

Creating the Tables

You can create the tables with no additional security clause. The sample EMPLOYEES and DEPARTMENT tables are as follows:

```
CREATE TABLE hr.employees (
     emp_id                     INTEGER NOT NULL,
     f_name                     VARCHAR(20),
     l_name                     VARCHAR(20),
     gender                     CHAR(1),
     hire_date                  DATE WITH DEFAULT,
     dept_id                    CHAR(5),
     phone                      CHAR(14),
     ssn                        CHAR(12),
     salary                     DECIMAL(12,2),
     bonus                      DECIMAL(12,2))
DB20000I  The SQL command completed successfully.

CREATE TABLE hr.department (
     dept_id                     CHAR(5),
     dept_name                   CHAR(20),
     dept_hr                     CHAR(20),
     hr_director                 CHAR(20))
DB20000I  The SQL command completed successfully.
```

Loading the Data

You can load the data before creating the row permissions. If you want to load the data after creating the row permissions, you will need to consider the INSERT behavior under RCAC:

```
INSERT INTO hr.employees VALUES
(1, 'MOHAN','KUMAR','M', CURRENT DATE, '00001',
'7584203037', '123-456-7891', 17000.00, 34000.00),
(2, 'MILAN','MOHAN','M', CURRENT DATE, '00001',
'7032698085', '123-456-9810', 12000.00, 24000.00),
```

Continued

```
(3, 'ROBERTS','COLLINS','M', CURRENT DATE-1 year, '00002',
'8931218799', '123-456-0001', 18000.00, 38000.00),
(4, 'COLIN','CHAPMAN','M', CURRENT DATE-6 months, '00001',
'9856594996', '123-126-4321', 18000.00, 38000.00),
(5, 'SIMON','WOODCOCK','M', CURRENT DATE, '00002',
'7584208737', '123-561-7898', 18000.00, 38000.00),
(6, 'HAMDI','ROUMANI','M', CURRENT DATE, '00001',
'7584608535', '123-061-8901', 18000.00, 38000.00)
DB20000I  The SQL command completed successfully.
```

Creating Roles and Row Permissions

In the current scenario, the HR managers can access information only for those employees from their own department. All HR managers (Jason, Colin) are members of the HRMGR role. The HR director can access all employees' information across all departments. All HR directors (Eric) are members of the HRDIRECTOR role. A user with SECADM authority can create the roles and row permissions:

```
CREATE ROLE HRMGR
DB20000I  The SQL command completed successfully.

CREATE ROLE HRDIRECTOR
DB20000I  The SQL command completed successfully.

GRANT ROLE HRMGR TO USER JASON, COLIN
DB20000I  The SQL command completed successfully.

GRANT ROLE HRDIRECTOR TO USER ERIC
DB20000I  The SQL command completed successfully.

GRANT SELECT, INSERT, UPDATE, DELETE ON TABLE HR.EMPLOYEES
 TO ROLE HRMGR, HRDIRECTOR
DB20000I  The SQL command completed successfully.
```

The business requirement is to allow the department HR managers to see their respective department employees' data and to permit the HR director to see the entire employees' data. Row permission is created accordingly for each group of personnel (HR managers and HR directors) in the HR department:

```
CREATE PERMISSION HR.DEPT_MGR_ACCESS ON HR.EMPLOYEES
 FOR ROWS WHERE VERIFY_ROLE_FOR_USER
 (SESSION_USER,'HRMGR') = 1 AND
    DEPT_ID = (SELECT DEPT_ID FROM HR.DEPARTMENT WHERE DEPT_HR=SESSION_USER)
ENFORCED FOR ALL ACCESS
ENABLE
DB20000I  The SQL command completed successfully.

CREATE PERMISSION HR.DEPT_DIRECTOR_ACCESS ON HR.EMPLOYEES
 FOR ROWS WHERE VERIFY_ROLE_FOR_USER (SESSION_USER,'HRDIRECTOR') = 1
 ENFORCED FOR ALL ACCESS
 ENABLE
DB20000I  The SQL command completed successfully.
```

When the row permission is enabled, it is not enforced until you activate the row access control at the row level. You do this by executing the ALTER TABLE command:

```
ALTER TABLE HR.EMPLOYEES ACTIVATE ROW ACCESS CONTROL
DB20000I  The SQL command completed successfully.
```

Putting RCAC into Action

When Jason connects to the database and executes the SELECT command, he will see only data for DEPT_ID 00001, as follows:

```
CONNECT TO SAMPLE USER jason
Enter current password for jason:

   Database Connection Information

                                                    Continued
```

```
 Database server        = DB2/LINUXX8664 10.1.3
 SQL authorization ID   = JASON
 Local database alias   = SAMPLE

SELECT EMP_ID,F_NAME,DEPT_ID,SSN, SALARY FROM HR.EMPLOYEES

EMP_ID      F_NAME     DEPT_ID SSN         SALARY
----------- ---------- ------- ----------- -------------
          1 MOHAN      00001   123-456-7891       17000.00
          2 MILAN      00001   123-456-9810       12000.00
          4 COLIN      00001   123-126-4321       18000.00
          6 HAMDI      00001   123-061-8901       18000.00

  4 record(s) selected.
```

Likewise, Colin will see only data for DEPT_ID 00002:

```
CONNECT TO SAMPLE USER colin
Enter current password for colin:

   Database Connection Information

 Database server        = DB2/LINUXX8664 10.1.3
 SQL authorization ID   = COLIN
 Local database alias   = SAMPLE

SELECT EMP_ID,F_NAME,DEPT_ID,SSN, SALARY FROM HR.EMPLOYEES

EMP_ID      F_NAME     DEPT_ID SSN         SALARY
----------- ---------- ------- ----------- -------------
          3 ROBERTS    00002   123-456-0001       18000.00
          5 SIMON      00002   123-561-7898       18000.00

  2 record(s) selected.
```

And when Eric connects to the database and executes the SELECT command, he will see all the records, something like this:

```
CONNECT TO SAMPLE USER eric
Enter current password for eric:

   Database Connection Information

 Database server        = DB2/LINUXX8664 10.1.3
 SQL authorization ID   = ERIC
 Local database alias   = SAMPLE

SELECT EMP_ID,F_NAME,DEPT_ID,SSN, SALARY FROM HR.EMPLOYEES

EMP_ID      F_NAME     DEPT_ID SSN          SALARY
----------- ---------- ------- ------------ --------------
          1 MOHAN      00001   123-456-7891       17000.00
          2 MILAN      00001   123-456-9810       12000.00
          3 ROBERTS    00002   123-456-0001       18000.00
          4 COLIN      00001   123-126-4321       18000.00
          5 SIMON      00002   123-561-7898       18000.00
          6 HAMDI      00001   123-061-8901       18000.00

  6 record(s) selected.
```

Understanding the DML Behavior Under RCAC

The DML behavior is fairly simple: if you cannot perform a SELECT to specify a type of record, you cannot perform an INSERT, an UPDATE, or a DELETE on that record.

For example, for DEPT_ID 00001, either the HR manager responsible for that department or the HR director can insert a new record into the HR.EMPLOYEES table. In this scenario, either Jason or Eric can perform the insert operations, as follows:

```
CONNECT TO SAMPLE USER jason
Enter current password for jason:

   Database Connection Information
```

Continued

```
 Database server        = DB2/LINUXX8664 10.1.3
 SQL authorization ID   = JASON
 Local database alias   = SAMPLE

INSERT INTO HR.EMPLOYEES VALUES (7, 'MARK','HAMILTON','M', CURRENT DATE,
'00001','7804408021','321-001-0001', 19000.00, 38000.00)"
DB20000I  The SQL command completed successfully.
```

Similarly, when Jason tries to insert a record for DEPT_ID 00002, he receives an SQL20471N error, something like this:

```
INSERT INTO HR.EMPLOYEES VALUES (8, 'KAREN','BOUSTEAD','F',CURRENT DATE,
'00002','7801648819','321-001-0002',18000.00,37000.00)"
DB21034E  The command was processed as an SQL statement because it was
not a valid Command Line Processor command.  During SQL processing it
returned:SQL20471N  The INSERT or UPDATE statement failed because a
resulting row did not satisfy row permissions.  SQLSTATE=22542
```

Deactivating the Row Access Control

If you want to deactivate row access control for any reason, execute the ALTER TABLE command, similar to the following:

```
ALTER TABLE HR.EMPLOYEES DEACTIVATE ROW ACCESS CONTROL
DB20000I  The SQL command completed successfully.
```

Creating Column Masks

As previously discussed, you use row permissions to limit access to records. If the business requirement is to limit access or mask data at the column level, you can do so by using column masks. A user having SECADM authority can create column masks on a table by using the CREATE MASK command. The basic syntax is:

```
CREATE <OR REPLACE> MASK [MaskName] ON [TableName]
FOR COLUMN [ColumnName] RETURN [CaseExpression]
<ENABLE | DISABLE>
```

where:

MaskName	Identifies the name of the column mask, including the explicit or implicit qualifier
TableName	Identifies the name of the table on which to create the column mask—it must not be a nickname; a created or declared global temporary table, view, alias, or synonym; a typed table; or system catalog tables
ColumnName	Identifies the column to which the mask applies; the column name must be an unqualified name and must not have any existing masks on that column—the column must not be a LOB, XML, or a generated column
CaseExpression	Identifies the CASE expression to evaluate to determine the value to return for the column

Using the previous HR.EMPLOYEES example, if the business requirement is to allow the payroll department to see the Social Security number (SSN) in entirety, the welfare department to see only the last four digits of SSN, and the communications department to see nothing from SSN, you can do so by executing the CREATE MASK command:

```
CREATE MASK HR.EMP_SSN_MASK ON HR.EMPLOYEES
  FOR COLUMN SSN RETURN
    CASE WHEN (VERIFY_ROLE_FOR_USER (SESSION_USER,'PAYROLL') = 1)
                                  THEN SSN
         WHEN (VERIFY_ROLE_FOR_USER (SESSION_USER,'WELFARE') = 1)
                                  THEN 'XXX-XX-' || SUBSTR (SSN, 8, 4)
         ELSE NULL
    END
  ENABLE
DB20000I  The SQL command completed successfully.

ALTER TABLE HR.EMPLOYEES ACTIVATE COLUMN ACCESS CONTROL
DB20000I  The SQL command completed successfully.
```

When a payroll user runs a SELECT query on HR.EMPLOYEES, he or she will see data similar to the following:

```
CONNECT TO SAMPLE USER hamdi
Enter current password for hamdi:
```

Continued

```
  Database Connection Information

 Database server        = DB2/LINUXX8664 10.1.3
 SQL authorization ID   = HAMDI
 Local database alias   = SAMPLE

SELECT EMP_ID,F_NAME,DEPT_ID,SSN, SALARY FROM HR.EMPLOYEES

EMP_ID      F_NAME     DEPT_ID SSN          SALARY
----------- ---------- ------- ------------ -------------
          1 MOHAN      00001   123-456-7891       17000.00
          2 MILAN      00001   123-456-9810       12000.00
          3 ROBERTS    00002   123-456-0001       18000.00
          4 COLIN      00001   123-126-4321       18000.00
          5 SIMON      00002   123-561-7898       18000.00
          6 HAMDI      00001   123-061-8901       18000.00
          7 MARK       00001   321-001-0001       19000.00
          8 KAREN      00002   321-001-0002       18000.00

  8 record(s) selected.
```

When a welfare user runs a SELECT query on HR.EMPLOYEES, he or she will see data something like this:

```
CONNECT TO SAMPLE USER jason
Enter current password for jason:

   Database Connection Information

 Database server        = DB2/LINUXX8664 10.1.3
 SQL authorization ID   = JASON
 Local database alias   = SAMPLE

                                                   Continued
```

```
SELECT EMP_ID,F_NAME,DEPT_ID,SSN, SALARY FROM HR.EMPLOYEES

EMP_ID      F_NAME     DEPT_ID SSN          SALARY
----------- ---------- ------- ------------ -------------
          1 MOHAN      00001   XXX-XX-7891       17000.00
          2 MILAN      00001   XXX-XX-9810       12000.00
          3 ROBERTS    00002   XXX-XX-0001       18000.00
          4 COLIN      00001   XXX-XX-4321       18000.00
          5 SIMON      00002   XXX-XX-7898       18000.00
          6 HAMDI      00001   XXX-XX-8901       18000.00
          7 MARK       00001   XXX-XX-0001       19000.00
          8 KAREN      00002   XXX-XX-0002       18000.00

  8 record(s) selected.
```

Similarly, when a communications user runs a SELECT query on HR.EMPLOYEES, he or she will see data something like the following:

```
CONNECT TO SAMPLE USER eric
Enter current password for eric:

   Database Connection Information

 Database server        = DB2/LINUXX8664 10.1.3
 SQL authorization ID   = ERIC
 Local database alias   = SAMPLE

SELECT EMP_ID,F_NAME,DEPT_ID,SSN, SALARY FROM HR.EMPLOYEES

EMP_ID      F_NAME     DEPT_ID SSN          SALARY
----------- ---------- ------- ------------ -------------
          1 MOHAN      00001   -                 17000.00
          2 MILAN      00001   -                 12000.00
          3 ROBERTS    00002   -                 18000.00
```

Continued

```
4 COLIN        00001    -                    18000.00
5 SIMON        00002    -                    18000.00
6 HAMDI        00001    -                    18000.00
7 MARK         00001    -                    19000.00
8 KAREN        00002    -                    18000.00

8 record(s) selected.
```

If you want to deactivate the column mask on a table, execute the ALTER TABLE command:

```
ALTER TABLE HR.EMPLOYEES DEACTIVATE COLUMN ACCESS CONTROL
DB20000I  The SQL command completed successfully.
```

Built-in Scalar Functions

As you have already seen in earlier RCAC examples, you have three built-in scalar functions available to express conditions in row permissions and column masks. Table 8.7 describes the functions to verify the membership of a user in a given role or group.

Table 8.7: Built-in RCAC scalar functions

Built-in Function Syntax	Description
VERIFY_ROLE_FOR_USER (SESSION_USER, [RoleNameExp])	Returns a value that indicates whether any of the roles associated with the authorization ID identified by the SESSION_USER special register are in (or contain any of) the role names specified by the list of RoleNameExp arguments
VERIFY_GROUP_FOR_USER(SESSION_USER, [GroupNameExp])	Returns a value that indicates whether any of the groups associated with the authorization ID identified by the SESSION_USER special register are in (or contain any of) the group names specified by the list of GroupNameExp arguments
VERIFY_TRUSTED_CONTEXT_ROLE_FOR_USER(SESSION_USER, [RoleNameExp])	Returns a value that indicates that the authorization ID identified by the SESSION_USER special register has acquired a role under a trusted connection associated with some trusted context and that role is in (or contained in any of) the role names specified by the list of RoleNameExp arguments

Advantages of Using RCAC

Using RCAC provides various advantages:

- All column or row access rules are stored centrally in the system catalog tables.
- No database user is inherently exempted from the RCAC rules, including DATAACCESS authority.
- Rules are created and managed centrally through SECADM authority.

- No matter how data is accessed, whether it is through SQL tools (e.g., IBM Data Studio, Toad) or through an application, all approaches are subject to RCAC rules.
- No application changes are necessary to use this additional layer of data security.
- This enables multitenancy when it comes to cloud computing solutions, where several independent customers or business units can share a single database table without being aware of one another.
- The application of enabled column masks does not interfere with the operations of other clauses within the statement, such as the WHERE, GROUP BY, HAVING, SELECT DISTINCT, and ORDER BY.
- RCAC will have no impact on LOAD, REORG, RUNSTATS, and BACKUP operations.

Note: Functions and triggers must be deemed secure before they can be called with row and column access control definitions. To create a secured UDF or alter an existing UDF to be secured, the developer must possess CREATE_SECURE_OBJECT authority.

The DB2 Audit Facility

DB2 has a range of authentication and authorization control mechanisms to establish rules and control access to sensitive data. However, to protect data against and discover unknown or unacceptable behaviors, you can monitor data access by using the DB2 audit facility.

The DB2 audit facility generates, and allows you to maintain, an audit trail for a series of predefined database events. The records generated from this facility are kept in an audit log file. The analysis of these records can reveal usage patterns that identify system misuse. Once they are identified, you can perform actions to reduce or eliminate such system misuse.

The audit facility provides the ability to audit at both instance level and database level, independently recording all instance- and database-level activities with separate logs for each. User holding SYSADM authority can use the db2audit tool to configure the audit at the instance level as well as to control the audit information. You can also use the db2audit tool to archive or extract both instance and database audit logs to and from archive locations.

Table 8.8 lists the categories of events available for auditing.

Table 8.8: Categories of events available in db2audit tool

Event	Command Option	Description
Audit	audit	Generates records when audit settings are changed or when the audit log is accessed
Authorization checking	checking	Generates records during authorization checking of attempts to access or manipulate DB2 database objects or functions

Table 8.8: Categories of events available in db2audit tool (continued)		
Event	**Command Option**	**Description**
Object maintenance	objmaint	Generates records when database objects are created or dropped
Security maintenance	secmaint	Generates records when database/object privileges or DBADM authority is granted or revoked; records are also generated when the database manager security configuration parameters sysadm_group, sysctrl_group, or sysmaint_group are modified
System administration	sysadmin	Generates records when operations requiring SYSADM, SYSMAINT, or SYSCTRL authority are performed
User validation	validate	Generates records when users are authenticated or system security information is retrieved
Operation context	context	Generates records to show the operation context when an instance operation is performed
Execute	execute	Generates records during the execution of SQL statements

DB2 provides a set of stored procedures to archive audit logs, locate logs of interest, and extract data into delimited files for analysis. The procedures include:

- SYSPROC.AUDIT_ARCHIVE
- SYSPROC.AUDIT_LIST_LOGS
- SYSPROC.AUDIT_DELIM_EXTRACT

Users with SECADM authority can grant EXECUTE privilege on the above listed stored procedures to another user, enabling the security administrator to delegate these tasks.

db2audit Tool Command

At the instance level, a user with SYSADM authority can start or stop the audit facility by using the db2audit command:

```
db2audit stop
AUD0000I  Operation succeeded.


db2audit start
AUD0000I  Operation succeeded.
```

If you want to view the current instance-level audit settings and status, use the db2audit command with the describe option, like this:

```
db2audit describe
DB2 AUDIT SETTINGS:

Audit active: "TRUE "
Log audit events: "FAILURE"
Log checking events: "FAILURE"
Log object maintenance events: "FAILURE"
Log security maintenance events: "FAILURE"
Log system administrator events: "FAILURE"
Log validate events: "FAILURE"
Log context events: "NONE"
Return SQLCA on audit error: "FALSE "
Audit Data Path: ""
Audit Archive Path: ""

AUD0000I  Operation succeeded.
```

The above output indicates that the audit facility is not configured on the current instance. To configure it, execute the db2audit command, as follows:

```
db2audit configure scope all status both datapath "/backup/auditlogs/"

AUD0000I  Operation succeeded.

db2audit describe
DB2 AUDIT SETTINGS:

Audit active: "TRUE "
Log audit events: "BOTH"
Log checking events: "BOTH"
Log object maintenance events: "BOTH"
Log security maintenance events: "BOTH"
Log system administrator events: "BOTH"
```

Continued

```
Log validate events: "BOTH"
Log context events: "BOTH"
Return SQLCA on audit error: "FALSE "
Audit Data Path: "/backup/auditlogs/"
Audit Archive Path: ""

AUD0000I  Operation succeeded.
```

Once the above command is executed, you can see the audit file at the specified data path location:

```
/home/edwetld/auditlogs> ls -ltr
Total 40
-rw------- 1 db2inst1 db2dadm  8392 Dec  2 03:16 db2audit.db.SAMPLE.log.0
-rw------- 1 db2inst1 db2dadm 25907 Dec  2 03:25 db2audit.instance.log.0
```

If you want to archive the audit logs, you can do so by executing the db2audit command with an archive command option, something like this:

```
db2audit archive database sample to /backup/archiveauditlogs

Member   DB Partition   AUD      Archived or Interim Log File
Number   Number         Message
-------- -------------- -------- ----------------------------------------
       0              0 AUD0000I db2audit.db.SAMPLE.log.0.20141202033403

AUD0000I  Operation succeeded.
```

And if you want to convert the archive audit log to a readable format, you execute this command:

```
db2audit extract delasc to /backup/delauditlogs from files /backup/
   archiveauditlogs/db2audit.db.SAMPLE.log.0.20141202033403

AUD0000I  Operation succeeded.
```

You can see all the converted delimited ASCII files and a sample output file:

```
-rw-rw-rw- 1 db2inst1 db2dadm    0 Dec  2 03:36 auditlobs
-rw-rw-rw- 1 db2inst1 db2dadm  187 Dec  2 03:45 validate.del
-rw-rw-rw- 1 db2inst1 db2dadm    0 Dec  2 03:45 sysadmin.del
-rw-rw-rw- 1 db2inst1 db2dadm    0 Dec  2 03:45 secmaint.del
-rw-rw-rw- 1 db2inst1 db2dadm    0 Dec  2 03:45 objmaint.del
-rw-rw-rw- 1 db2inst1 db2dadm    0 Dec  2 03:45 execute.del
-rw-rw-rw- 1 db2inst1 db2dadm  409 Dec  2 03:45 context.del
-rw-rw-rw- 1 db2inst1 db2dadm    0 Dec  2 03:45 checking.del
-rw-rw-rw- 1 db2inst1 db2dadm    0 Dec  2 03:45 audit.del

cat validate.del
"2014-12-02-03.28.04.992641","VALIDATE","AUTHENTICATION",2,0,"SAMPLE","db2in
st1","MOHAN","db2inst1",,,"*LOCAL.db2inst1.141202032805","db2bp","DATA_ENCRY
PT",,,,,"IBMOSauthserver",,,,,,,,,,
```

Because the DB2 audit facility works independently of the DB2 instance, it will remain active even if the instance is stopped.

AUDIT SQL Statements

A user holding SECADM authority can create audit policies by using the CREATE AUDIT POLICY command to audit a specific set of objects within the database. You can associate the following objects with an audit policy:

- An entire database
- Tables
- Trusted contexts
- Authorization IDs representing users, groups, or roles
- Authorities—SYSADM, SECADM, DBADM, SQLADM, WLMADM, ACCESSCTRL, DATAACCESS, SYSCTRL, SYSMAINT, and SYSMON

If you want to audit all SQL access to the data in the table HR.EMPLOYEES, you can do so by creating a security policy and associating the policy to the respective table, something like this:

```
CREATE AUDIT POLICY SENSITIVEDATA_POLICY CATEGORIES EXECUTE STATUS BOTH ERROR
TYPE AUDIT
DB20000I  The SQL command completed successfully.

COMMIT
DB20000I  The SQL command completed successfully.

AUDIT TABLE HR.EMPLOYEES USING POLICY SENSITIVEDATA_POLICY
DB20000I  The SQL command completed successfully.

COMMIT
DB20000I  The SQL command completed successfully.
```

Likewise, if you want to audit all the activities performed by the SYSADM or DBADM authority, you can create a policy similar to the following:

```
CREATE AUDIT POLICY ADMIN_POLICY CATEGORIES EXECUTE STATUS BOTH, SYSADMIN STATUS
BOTH ERROR TYPE AUDIT
DB20000I  The SQL command completed successfully.

COMMIT
DB20000I  The SQL command completed successfully.

AUDIT SYSADM, DBADM USING POLICY ADMIN_POLICY
DB20000I  The SQL command completed successfully.

COMMIT
DB20000I  The SQL command completed successfully.
```

To extract the AUDIT statement data, use the db2audit command as illustrated in the "db2audit Tool Command" section.

A Word About the System Catalog for Security Information

Now that you have decent knowledge about various authorities and privileges in DB2, it is beneficial to know where all this security information is stored, how to retrieve it, and what system catalog objects you should consider restricting access to other users.

Table 8.9 lists the views and table functions that contain information about privileges held by users, roles, and object ownership:

Table 8.9: Views and table functions that contain privileges information

Catalog View, Administrative Views, and Table Functions	Description	Restrict Access to PUBLIC and Other Users
SYSCAT.COLAUTH	Stores the column privileges	Yes
SYSCAT.DBAUTH	Stores the database privileges	Yes
SYSCAT.INDEXAUTH	Stores the index privileges	Yes
SYSCAT.MODULEAUTH	Stores the module privileges	
SYSCAT.PACKAGEAUTH	Stores the package privileges	Yes
SYSCAT.PASSTHRUAUTH	Stores the server privileges	Yes
SYSCAT.ROLEAUTH	Stores the role privileges	
SYSCAT.ROUTINEAUTH	Stores the routine privileges	Yes
SYSCAT.SCHEMAAUTH	Stores the schema privileges	Yes
SYSCAT.SEQUENCEAUTH	Stores the sequence privileges	Yes
SYSCAT.SURROGATEAUTHIDS	Stores the authorization IDs for which another authorization ID can act as a substitute	Yes
SYSCAT.TABAUTH	Stores the table and view privileges	Yes
SYSCAT.TBSPACEAUTH	Stores the table space privileges	Yes
SYSCAT.VARIABLEAUTH	Stores the variable privileges	
SYSCAT.WORKLOADAUTH	Stores the workload privileges	
SYSCAT.XSROBJECTAUTH	Stores the XSR object privileges	
SYSCAT.SECURITYLABELS	Stores the LBAC security-label information	
SYSCAT.SECURITYLABELACCESS	Stores the LBAC security-label access information	
SYSCAT.SECURITYLABEL COMPONENTS	Stores the LBAC security-label component information	
SYSCAT.SECURITYLABEL COMPONENTELEMENTS	Stores the element value for each security-label component	
SYSCAT.SECURITYPOLICIES	Stores security policy information	
SYSCAT.SECURITYPOLICY COMPONENTRULES	Stores read and write access rules for a security-label component of the security policy	
SYSCAT.SECURITYPOLICY EXEMPTIONS	Stores information about the security policy exemption that was granted to a database authorization ID	

Table 8.9: Views and table functions that contain privileges information (continued)		
Catalog View, Administrative Views, and Table Functions	**Description**	**Restrict Access to PUBLIC and Other Users**
SYSIBMADM.AUTHORIZATIONIDS	Administrative view returns a list of all the users, roles, and groups that exist in the database catalog of the currently connected server	Yes
SYSIBMADM.OBJECTOWNERS	Administrative view returns all object ownership information for every authorization ID of type USER that owns an object and that is defined in the system catalog of the currently connected server	Yes
SYSIBMADM.PRIVILEGES	Administrative view returns all explicit privileges for all authorization IDs defined in the system catalog of the currently connected database server	Yes
AUTH_GET_INSTANCE_AUTHID	Built-in scalar function returns the authorization ID of the instance owner	
AUTH_LIST_AUTHORITIES_FOR_AUTHID	Table function returns all authorities held by the authorization ID, either found in the database configuration file or granted to an authorization ID directly or indirectly through a group or a role	
AUTH_LIST_GROUPS_FOR_AUTHID	Table function returns the list of groups of which the given authorization ID is a member	
AUTH_LIST_ROLES_FOR_AUTHID	Function returns the list of roles in which the given authorization ID is a member	

Chapter Summary

The objective of this chapter was to familiarize you with

- The authentication and authorization mechanisms available in DB2
- The granting and revoking authorities and privileges in DB2
- The role-based access control and the differences between roles and groups
- The data encryption and decryption functions available in DB2
- The trusted context and trusted connections concepts
- The LBAC and RCAC mechanisms available in DB2
- The DB2 audit facility and its usage

On completion of this chapter, you will be equipped with sufficient knowledge to answer the DB2 security questions in the certification exam. It is also highly recommended that you complete the sample questions available at the end of the chapter.

Practice Questions

Question 1

Which of the following is *not* a security mechanism used to control access to DB2 data?

- ❍ A. Authorization
- ❍ B. Privileges
- ❍ C. Validation
- ❍ D. Authentication

Question 2

Which of the following identifies users who have SYSMAINT authority?

- ❍ A. The DB2 registry
- ❍ B. The DB2 database manager configuration
- ❍ C. The database configuration
- ❍ D. The system catalog

Question 3

Which database privilege is *not* automatically granted to the group PUBLIC when a database is created?

- ❍ A. CONNECT
- ❍ B. BINDADD
- ❍ C. IMPLICIT_SCHEMA
- ❍ D. CREATE_EXTERNAL_ROUTINE

Question 4

User USER1 needs to remove a view named ORDERS_V, which is based on a table named ORDERS, from the SALES database. Assuming user USER1 does not hold any privileges, which privilege must you grant before user USER1 will be allowed to drop the view?

- ❍ A. DROP privilege on the ORDERS table
- ❍ B. CONTROL privilege on the ORDERS table
- ❍ C. DROP privilege on the ORDERS_V view
- ❍ D. CONTROL privilege on the ORDERS_V view

Question 5

Which of the following identifies how authentication is performed for an instance?

- ❍ A. The operating system used by the instance
- ❍ B. The communications configuration used by the instance
- ❍ C. The DB2 registry
- ❍ D. The DB2 database manager configuration

Question 6

The following SQL statement is executed:

```
GRANT ALL PRIVILEGES ON TABLE employee TO USER user1
```

Assuming user USER1 has no other authorities or privileges, which action is USER1 allowed to perform?

- ❍ A. Drop an index on the EMPLOYEE table
- ❍ B. Grant all privileges on the EMPLOYEE table to other users
- ❍ C. Alter the table definition
- ❍ D. Drop the EMPLOYEE table

Question 7

A user named USER1 possesses DBADM authority. Assuming you have granted no other authorities or privileges and have revoked all privileges from the group PUBLIC, if you execute the following SQL statement:

```
REVOKE DBADM ON DATABASE FROM user1
```

What authorities or privileges will user USER1 have?

- ❍ A. CONNECT
- ❍ B. ACCESSCTRL
- ❍ C. CREATETAB
- ❍ D. NONE

Question 8

User USER1 wants to call an SQL stored procedure that dynamically retrieves data from a table. Which two privileges must user USER1 have to invoke the stored procedure?

- ❒ A. EXECUTE privilege on the stored procedure
- ❒ B. CALL privilege on the stored procedure
- ❒ C. SELECT privilege on the table from which the stored procedure retrieves data
- ❒ D. EXECUTE privilege on the package for the stored procedure
- ❒ E. SELECT privilege on the stored procedure

Question 9

Which privilege allows a user to remove a foreign key that has been defined for a table?

- ❍ A. ALTER privilege on the table
- ❍ B. DELETE privilege on the table
- ❍ C. DROP privilege on the table
- ❍ D. UPDATE privilege on the table

Question 10

Which privilege allows a user to generate a package for an embedded SQL application and store it in a database?

- ❍ A. BIND
- ❍ B. BINDADD
- ❍ C. CREATE_EXTERNAL_ROUTINE
- ❍ D. CREATE_NOT_FENCED_ROUTINE

Question 11

Which statement about DB2 security is false?

- ❍ A. A custom security plug-in must be created if you use Microsoft Active Directory to validate users.
- ❍ B. Only users with SECADM authority can grant and revoke SETSESSIONUSER privileges.
- ❍ C. Users and groups must exist before they can be granted privileges.
- ❍ D. If a user holding SELECT privilege on a table creates a view based on that table and that user's SELECT privilege is later revoked, the view will become inoperative.

Question 12

User USER1 has the privileges required to invoke a stored procedure named GEN_RESUME. User USER2 needs to be able to call the procedure—user USER1 and all members of the group PUBLIC should no longer be allowed to call the procedure. Which command can you use to accomplish this?

- ❍ A. GRANT EXECUTE ON ROUTINE gen_resume TO user2 EXCLUDE user1, PUBLIC
- ❍ B. GRANT EXECUTE ON PROCEDURE gen_resume TO user2; REVOKE EXECUTE ON PROCEDURE gen_resume FROM user1, PUBLIC;
- ❍ C. GRANT CALL ON ROUTINE gen_resume TO user2 EXCLUDE user1, PUBLIC
- ❍ D. GRANT CALL ON PROCEDURE gen_resume TO user2; REVOKE CALL ON PROCEDURE gen_resume FROM user1, PUBLIC;

Question 13

Which of the following is *not* used to limit access to individual rows in a table that is protected by LBAC?

❍ A. One or more security profiles
❍ B. A security policy
❍ C. One or more security labels
❍ D. A DB2SECURITYLABEL column

Question 14

Which statement about LBAC is false?

❍ A. LBAC can restrict access to individual rows and columns.
❍ B. Users who hold different LBAC security labels will get different results when they execute the same query.
❍ C. Only users with SECADM authority are allowed to create security policies and security labels.
❍ D. Security-label components represent criteria that you can use to decide whether a user should have access to specific data.

Question 15

Which SQL statement allows user USER1 to write to LBAC-protected columns that have been secured with an LBAC label that indicates a lower level of security than USER1 holds?

❍ A. GRANT EXCEPTION ON RULE DB2LBACWRITEARRAY WRITEDOWN FOR sec_policy TO USER user1
❍ B. GRANT EXEMPTION ON RULE DB2LBACWRITEARRAY WRITEDOWN FOR sec_policy TO USER user1
❍ C. GRANT EXCEPTION ON RULE DB2LBACWRITEARRAY WRITEUP FOR sec_policy TO USER user1
❍ D. GRANT EXEMPTION ON RULE DB2LBACWRITEARRAY WRITEUP FOR sec_policy TO USER user1

Question 16

Which statement about the SERVER_ENCRYPT authentication setting is true?

❍ A. The user ID and password will be encrypted.
❍ B. The user ID will be encrypted.
❍ C. The user ID, password, and data will be encrypted.
❍ D. The password will be encrypted.

Question 17

Which DB2 authority can monitor and tune the SQL statements?

❍ A. WLMADM
❍ B. EXPLAIN
❍ C. ACCESSCTRL
❍ D. SQLADM

Question 18

Which DB2 authority is necessary to create, alter, and drop workload management objects?

❍ A. DATAACCESS
❍ B. WLMADM
❍ C. ACCESSCTRL
❍ D. SQLADM

Question 19

Which statement about the characteristics of a role is true?

❍ A. Users having SECADM authority create and manage roles.
❍ B. Roles can own the database objects.
❍ C. You can use roles to grant SYSADM, SYSCTRL, SYSMAINT, and SYSMON authorities.
❍ D. Privileges and authorities granted to groups are not considered when creating views, MQTs, SQL routines, triggers, and packages containing static SQL.

Question 20

Which administrative authority is necessary to grant ACCESSCTRL, DATAACCESS, SQLADM, or SECADM authority to other users?

- ❍ A. SYSMAINT
- ❍ B. SYSCTRL
- ❍ C. SECADM
- ❍ D. SYSMON

Question 21

Which statement about SECADM authority is false?

- ❍ A. SECADM users can grant and revoke LBAC rule exemptions.
- ❍ B. SECADM can only be granted to individual users.
- ❍ C. PUBLIC can receive SECADM authority either directly or indirectly.
- ❍ D. Only users with SYSADM authority are allowed to grant SECADM authority to others.

Question 22

Which authority can revoke SECADM authority?

- ❍ A. SYSADM
- ❍ B. ACCESSCTRL
- ❍ C. DBADM
- ❍ D. SECADM

Question 23

Which two of the following security-label components can you use with LBAC?

- ❒ A. Array
- ❒ B. Tree
- ❒ C. Forest
- ❒ D. Range
- ❒ E. DB2SECURITYLABEL

Question 24

Which is *not* a valid statement about the RCAC feature?

- ❍ A. Users with SECADM authority cannot be exempt from RCAC rules.
- ❍ B. You can activate and deactivate RCAC when needed by using the ALTER TABLE command.
- ❍ C. RCAC is a more powerful security mechanism than LBAC.
- ❍ D. When a result set is restricted due to the RCAC rules defined on a table, no warnings or errors messages are returned.

Question 25

The following statements are run on the database SAMPLE:

```
CREATE MASK HR.EMP_SSN_MASK ON HR.EMPLOYEES
  FOR COLUMN SSN RETURN
    CASE WHEN (VERIFY_ROLE_FOR_USER (SESSION_USER,'PAYROLL') = 0)
                THEN SSN
          ELSE NULL
    END
  ENABLE;

ALTER TABLE HR.EMPLOYEES ACTIVATE COLUMN ACCESS CONTROL;
```

Which statement about the SSN column is true?

- ❍ A. Values stored in the SSN column are visible to all users.
- ❍ B. Values stored in the SSN column are visible to all users except the PAYROLL role users.
- ❍ C. Values stored in the SSN column are visible only to the PAYROLL role users.
- ❍ D. Values stored in the SSN column are not visible to any users.

Question 26

Who can execute CREATE ROW PERMISSION and CREATE MASK commands?

- ❍ A. SYSMON
- ❍ B. SECADM
- ❍ C. ACCESSCTRL
- ❍ D. SQLADM

Question 27

Which of the following is *not* a valid event in the DB2 audit facility?

- ❍ A. execute
- ❍ B. sysmaint
- ❍ C. objmaint
- ❍ D. sysadmin

Question 28

What authorization is needed to use the AUDIT statement to create an audit policy?

- ❍ A. DBADM
- ❍ B. SYSADM
- ❍ C. SECADM
- ❍ D. SYSMAINT

Question 29

Which authorities can you audit with the AUDIT statement?

- ❍ A. SECADM, DBADM, SYSMAINT, and SYSCTRL can be audited, but SYSADM cannot.
- ❍ B. SYSADM, DBADM, SYSMAINT, and SYSCTRL can be audited, but SECADM cannot.
- ❍ C. SYSADM, SECADM, DBADM, SQLADM, ACCESSCTRL, and DATAACCESS can be audited.
- ❍ D. DBADM, SYSMAINT, ACCESSCTRL, and DATAACCESS can be audited, but SYSADM and SECADM cannot.

Question 30

Which of the following is *not* a security table function?

- ❍ A. SYSIBMADM.PRIVILEGES
- ❍ B. AUTH_LIST_AUTHORITIES_FOR_AUTHID
- ❍ C. AUTH_LIST_GROUPS_FOR_AUTHID
- ❍ D. AUTH_LIST_ROLES_FOR_AUTHID

Answers

Question 1

The correct answer is **C**. The first security portal most users must pass through on their way to gaining access to a DB2 instance or database is a process known as *authentication*. The purpose of authentication is to verify that users really are who they say they are. Once a user has been authenticated and an attachment to an instance or a connection to a database has been established, the DB2 database manger evaluates any authorities and privileges that have been assigned to the user to determine what operations the user is allowed to perform. *Privileges* convey the rights to perform certain actions against specific database resources (such as tables and views). *Authorities* convey a set of privileges or the right to perform high-level administrative and maintenance/utility operations on an instance or a database.

Question 2

The correct answer is **B**. As with SYSADM, SYSCTRL, and SYSMON authority, you can assign SYSMAINT authority only to a group. You make this assignment by storing the appropriate group name in the `sysmaint_group` parameter of the DB2 database manager configuration file that is associated with a particular instance.

Question 3

The correct answer is **D**. To connect to and work with a particular database, a user must have the authorities and privileges needed to use that database. Therefore, whenever a new database is created, unless otherwise specified, the following authorities and privileges are automatically granted:

- DBADM authority along with CONNECT, CREATETAB, BINDADD, CREATE_NOT_FENCED, IMPLICIT_SCHEMA, and LOAD privileges are granted to the user who created the database.
- USE privilege on the table space USERSPACE1 is granted to the group PUBLIC.
- CONNECT, CREATETAB, BINDADD, and IMPLICIT_SCHEMA privileges are granted to the group PUBLIC.
- SELECT privilege on each system catalog table is granted to the group PUBLIC.
- EXECUTE privilege on all procedures in the SYSIBM schema is granted to the group PUBLIC.
- EXECUTE WITH GRANT privilege on all functions in the SYSFUN schema is granted to the group PUBLIC.
- BIND and EXECUTE privileges for each successfully bound utility are granted to the group PUBLIC.

Question 4

The correct answer is **D**. The CONTROL view privilege provides a user with every view privilege available, allows the user to remove (drop) the view from the database, and gives the user the ability to grant and revoke one or more view privileges (except the CONTROL privilege) to and from other users and groups.

Question 5

The correct answer is **D**. Because DB2 can reside in environments consisting of multiple clients, gateways, and servers, each of which may be running on a different operating system, deciding where authentication is to occur is determined by the value you assign to the `authentication` parameter in each DB2 database manager configuration file. The value you assign to this parameter, often referred to as the *authentication type*, is set initially when an instance is created. (On the server side, the authentication type is specified during the instance creation process; on the client side, the authentication type is specified when a remote database is cataloged.) Only one authentication type exists for each instance, and it controls access to that instance, as well as to all databases that fall under that instance's control.

Question 6

The correct answer is **C**. The `GRANT ALL PRIVILEGES` statement gives `USER1` the following privileges for the `EMPLOYEE` table: `ALTER`, `SELECT`, `INSERT`, `UPDATE`, `DELETE`, `INDEX`, and `REFERENCES`. To drop an index, `USER1` must have `CONTROL` privilege on the index—not the table the index is based on. `USER1` cannot grant privileges to other users because the `WITH GRANT OPTION` clause was not specified with the `GRANT ALL PRIVILEGES` statement used to give `USER1` table privileges. And to drop the `EMPLOYEE` table, `USER1` must have `CONTROL` privilege on the table—`CONTROL` privilege is not granted with the `GRANT ALL PRIVILEGES` statement.

Question 7

The correct answer is **B**. When you grant users `DBADM` authority for a particular database, they automatically receive all database privileges available for that database (`CONNECT`, `CONNECT_QUIESCE`, `IMPLICIT_SCHEMA`, `CREATETAB`, `BINDADD`, `CREATE_EXTERNAL_ROUTINE`, `CREATE_NOT_FENCED_ROUTINE`, and `LOAD`). When you revoke `DBADM` authority, all other database authorities that were implicitly and automatically granted upon granting `DBADM` authority are not automatically revoked. The same is true for privileges held on objects in the database.

Question 8

The correct answers are **A** and **C**. Before users can invoke a routine (UDF, stored procedure, or method), they must hold both `EXECUTE` privilege on the routine and any privileges that routine requires. Thus, to execute a stored procedure that queries a table, a user must hold both `EXECUTE` privilege on the stored procedure and `SELECT` privilege on the table the query is run against.

Package privileges control what users can and cannot do with a particular package. (A package is an object that contains the information the DB2 database manager needs to process SQL statements in the most efficient way possible on behalf of an embedded SQL application.)

Question 9

The correct answer is **A**. The ALTER table privilege allows a user to execute the ALTER TABLE SQL statement against a table. In other words, this privilege permits a user to add columns to the table, add or change comments associated with the table or any of its columns, create or drop a primary key for the table, create or drop a UNIQUE constraint for the table, create or drop a CHECK constraint for the table, and create triggers for the table (provided the user holds the appropriate privileges for every object referenced by the trigger).

The UPDATE privilege allows a user to execute the UPDATE SQL statement against the table. In other words, this privilege permits a user to modify data in the table. The DELETE privilege allows a user to execute the DELETE SQL statement against the table. In other words, it allows a user to remove rows of data from the table.

Question 10

The correct answer is **B**. The BINDADD database privilege allows a user to create packages in the database (by precompiling embedded SQL application source code files against the database or by binding application bind files to the database).

The BIND package privilege permits a user to rebind or add new package versions to a package that has already been bound to a database. (In addition to the BIND package privilege, a user must hold the privileges needed to execute the SQL statements that make up the package before the package can be successfully rebound.) The CREATE_EXTERNAL_ROUTINE database privilege allows a user to create UDFs and procedures and store them in the database so that other users and applications can use them. The CREATE_NOT_FENCED_ROUTINE database privilege allows a user to create unfenced UDFs and procedures and store them in the database. (Unfenced UDFs and stored procedures are UDFs/procedures that are considered "safe" enough to be run in the DB2 database manager operating environment's process or address space. Unless a UDF or procedure is registered as unfenced, the DB2 database manager insulates the UDF's or procedure's internal resources in such a way that they cannot be run in the DB2 database manager's address space.)

Question 11

The correct answer is **C**. The GRANT statement does not check to ensure that the names of users and groups that are to be granted authorities and privileges are valid. Therefore, it is possible to grant authorities and privileges to users and groups that do not exist.

Question 12

The correct answer is **B**. The syntax to grant the only stored procedure privilege available is:

```
GRANT EXECUTE ON [RoutineName] |
                 [PROCEDURE <SchemaName.> *]
TO [Recipient, ...]
<WITH GRANT OPTION>
```

The syntax to revoke the only stored procedure privilege available is:

```
REVOKE EXECUTE ON [RoutineName |
                  [PROCEDURE <SchemaName.> *]
FROM [Forfeiter, ...] <BY ALL>
RESTRICT
```

Thus, the proper way to grant and revoke stored procedure privileges is by executing the GRANT EXECUTE and REVOKE EXECUTE statements.

Question 13

The correct answer is **A**. To restrict access to rows in a table using LBAC, you must define a security-label component, define a security policy, create one or more security labels, create an LBAC-protected table or alter an existing table to add LBAC protection (by adding the security policy to the table and defining a column that has the DB2SECURITYLABEL data type), and grant the proper security labels to the appropriate users. There are no LBAC security profiles.

Question 14

The correct answer is **C**. SECADM authority is a special database level of authority that allows special users to configure various LBAC elements to restrict access to one or more tables that contain data to which they most likely do not have access themselves. Users with SECADM authority are allowed to perform the following tasks:

- Create and drop security policies
- Create and drop security labels
- Grant and revoke security labels to/from individual users (by using the GRANT SECURITY LABEL and REVOKE SECURITY LABEL SQL statements)
- Grant and revoke LBAC rule exemptions
- Grant and revoke SETSESSIONUSER privileges (by using the GRANT SETSESSIONUSER SQL statement)
- Transfer ownership of any object not owned by the security administrator (by executing the TRANSFER OWNERSHIP SQL statement)

No other authority provides a user with these abilities, including SYSADM authority.

Question 15

The correct answer is **B**. When a user holds an exemption on an LBAC security policy rule, that rule is not enforced when the user attempts to read or write data that is protected by that security policy.

You grant security policy exemptions by executing the `GRANT EXEMPTION ON RULE` SQL statement (as a user with `SECADM` authority). The syntax for this statement is:

```
CREATE EXEMPTION ON RULE [Rule] ,...
FOR [PolicyName]
TO USER [UserName]
```

Thus, to grant an exemption to the `DB2LBACWRITEARRAY` rule in a security policy named `SEC_POLICY` to a user named `USER1`, you execute a `GRANT EXEMPTION` statement that looks something like this:

```
GRANT EXEMPTION ON RULE DB2LBACWRITEARRAY
WRITEDOWN FOR sec_policy TO USER user1
```

Question 16

The correct answer is **A**. Authentication occurs at the server workstation by using the security facility that the server's operating system provides. However, the user ID and password that the user enters to attach to an instance or connect to a database stored on the server may be encrypted at the client workstation before it is sent to the server workstation for validation.

Question 17

The correct answer is **D**. `SQLADM` authority is required to monitor and tune the SQL statements. Users with `SQLADM` authority are allowed to perform the following tasks:

- Create, drop, or flush event monitors
- Generate Explain data by using `EXPLAIN`
- Flush the optimization profile cache
- Perform table and index reorganization
- Perform `RUNSTATS` on the table and indexes
- Enable or disable event monitors
- Flush the package cache and prepare SQL statements

Question 18

The correct answer is **B**. WLMADM authority is required to manage workload objects for a specific database. Users with WLMADM authority are allowed to perform the following tasks:

- Create, alter, drop, and comment on the following WLM objects:
  - Service classes
  - Thresholds
  - Work action sets
  - Work class sets
  - Workloads
  - Histogram templates
- Grant and revoke workload privileges
- Execute built-in workload management routines

Question 19

The correct answer is **A**. The true characteristics of roles are:

- SECADM users create and manage roles within the database engine.
- Privileges and authorities you grant to roles are considered when creating views, MQTs, SQL routines, triggers, and packages containing static SQL. Roles cannot own database objects.
- Roles cannot grant instance-level authorities such as SYSADM, SYSCTRL, SYSMAINT, and SYSMON.
- You can delegate the role maintenance by using the WITH ADMIN OPTION clause in the GRANT ROLE command.

Question 20

The correct answer is **C**. SECADM can grant and revoke all database-level authorities, including DBADM, SECADM, DATAACCESS, DATAACCESS, ACCESSSCTRL, EXPLAIN, SQLADM, WLMADM, and LOAD. Users with SYSMAINT, SYSMON, and SYSCTRL authority cannot grant authority to others.

Question 21

The correct answer is **C**. SECADM authority can be granted only by the security administrator (who holds SECADM authority) and can be granted to a user, a group, or a role. PUBLIC cannot obtain the SECADM authority directly or indirectly.

Question 22

The correct answer is **D**. SECADM authority can be granted or revoked only by the security administrator (who holds SECADM authority) and can be granted to a user, a group, or a role. And by default, a user with SYSADM authority will have SECADM authority.

Question 23

The correct answers are **A** and **B**. A security-label component represents criteria that you can use to decide whether a user should have access to specific data. Three types of security-label components exist:

- A set is a collection of elements (character string values) where the order in which each element appears is not important.
- An array is an ordered set that can represent a simple hierarchy. In an array, the order in which the elements appear is important—the first element ranks higher than the second, the second ranks higher than the third, and so on.
- A tree represents a more complex hierarchy that can have multiple nodes and branches.

Question 24

The correct answer is **C**. LBAC is a more powerful security mechanism compared with RCAC. LBAC is mainly used in defense applications and RCAC in commercial applications. No database user is inherently exempt from the RCAC rules, including DATAACCESS and SECAM authorities. You can easily activate and deactivate RCAC by using this set of commands:

```
ALTER TABLE <SCHEMA>.<TABLENAME> ACTIVATE ROW ACCESS CONTROL
ALTER TABLE <SCHEMA>.<TABLENAME> DEACTIVATE ROW ACCESS CONTROL
```

When a result set is restricted due to the RCAC rules defined on a table, no warnings or errors messages are returned.

Question 25

The correct answer is **B**. The CREATE MASK command works in two cases for HR.EMP_SSN_MASK for the column SSN:

- When the session user role is PAYROLL, that user will see a NULL value in SSN column values.
- When the session user role is other than PAYROLL, that user will see the actual SSN values.

Question 26

The correct answer is **B**. Only a user having SECADM authority can execute the CREATE MASK and CREATE ROW PERMISSION commands.

Question 27

The correct answer is **B**. The event sysmaint is an incorrect event for the DB2 audit facility.

Question 28

The correct answer is **C**. Users holding SECADM authority can create audit policies by using the CREATE AUDIT POLICY command to audit specific set of objects within the database. You can associate the following objects with an audit policy:

- An entire database
- Tables
- Trusted contexts
- Authorization IDs representing users, groups, or roles
- Authorities—SYSADM, SECADM, DBADM, SQLADM, WLMADM, ACCESSCTRL, DATAACCESS, SYSCTRL, SYSMAINT, and SYSMON

Question 29

The correct answer is **C**. You can audit the authorities SYSADM, SECADM, DBADM, SQLADM, WLMADM, ACCESSCTRL, DATAACCESS, SYSCTRL, SYSMAINT, and SYSMON by using the AUDIT statement.

Question 30

The correct answer is **A**. The AUTH_LIST_AUTHORITIES_FOR_AUTHID, AUTH_LIST_GROUPS_FOR_AUTHID, and AUTH_LIST_ROLES_FOR_AUTHID are scalar table functions, and SYSIBMADM.PRIVILEGES is an administrative view for security.

CHAPTER 9

Connectivity and Networking

This chapter introduces you to the process of configuring communications and cataloging for remote databases, remote data servers, and Database Connection Services (DCS) databases. It also contains topics that introduce you to DB2 discovery and management of connections to System z and System i host databases.

Exam Objectives

- ✓ Demonstrate the ability to understand the communications protocols within DB2
- ✓ Demonstrate the ability to configure connections between the DB2 database server and clients
- ✓ Demonstrate the ability to configure and use DB2 discovery for administration servers, instances, and databases
- ✓ Demonstrate the ability to manage connections to System z and System i host databases
- ✓ Demonstrate the ability to configure Lightweight Directory Access Protocol (LDAP) connections
- ✓ Demonstrate the ability to identify and resolve any client/server connectivity problems

Configuring Communications

In a typical client/server environment, databases hosted on a server are accessed by applications running on remote client workstations by using what is known as a *distributed connection.* In addition to providing client applications with a way to access a centralized database located on a remote server, a distributed connection helps administrators manage databases and servers remotely.

To communicate with a server, each client must use the specific type of communications protocol recognized by the server to perform desired tasks. Similarly, each server must have a communications protocol matrix to serve inbound requests from clients appropriately. In most cases, the operating system on both client and server machines provides the communications protocol support needed; however, in few cases, a separate add-on product might be required to provide necessary protocol support. In either case, you must configure both clients and servers to use a communications protocol supported by DB2. DB2 10.1 supports the following communications protocols:

- Transmission Control Protocol/Internet Protocol (TCP/IP)—both IPv4 and IPv6 are supported. Table 9.1 lists the differences between IPv4 and IPv6.
- Named pipe—This is a first-in first-out (FIFO) unidirectional or bi-directional pipe for communications between the server and one or more clients. This protocol is supported on the Windows platform.
- Secure Sockets Layer (SSL) and Transport Layer Security (TLS)—These are the most widely used protocols to establish a secured private communications channel between the clients, such as CLI, CLP, and the DB2 server.

Table 9.1: IPv4 versus IPv6 communications protocol

IPv4	IPv6
It consists of a four-part structure.	It consists of an eight-part structure.
It uses 32 bits for the IP address.	It uses 128 bits for the IP address.
It supports 4.294 billion Internet devices.	It supports 3.4028236692093846346337460743177e+38 Internet devices—literally unlimited!
It is represented by using decimals; for example: 10.111.19.110.	It is represented by using hexadecimal numbers separated by a colon; for example: 2000:0db8:4545:3::08ed:afe6:82ef.

When you install DB2 on a client or server, DB2 will detect all communications protocols installed on the client/server and will start serving connections coming in on those protocols. During installation, information about each supported communications protocol is collected and stored in the configuration files for both the DAS instance and the default instance as they are created. Unfortunately, this information is not updated automatically when a new protocol is activated or when an existing protocol is reconfigured. Instead, you must manually reconfigure each instance for any changes to the protocol to take effect.

Manually Configuring DB2 Server Communications

The easiest way to manually configure communications or make communications configuration changes is by using the Set Up and Configure dialog, which you can activate by selecting the appropriate action from the instance or the database menu in IBM Data Studio. Figure 9.1 shows the Data Studio menu items you must select to activate the Set Up and Configure communications dialog. Figure 9.2 illustrates how the Set Up and Configure communications dialog might be used to configure the TCP/IP protocol for a particular instance.

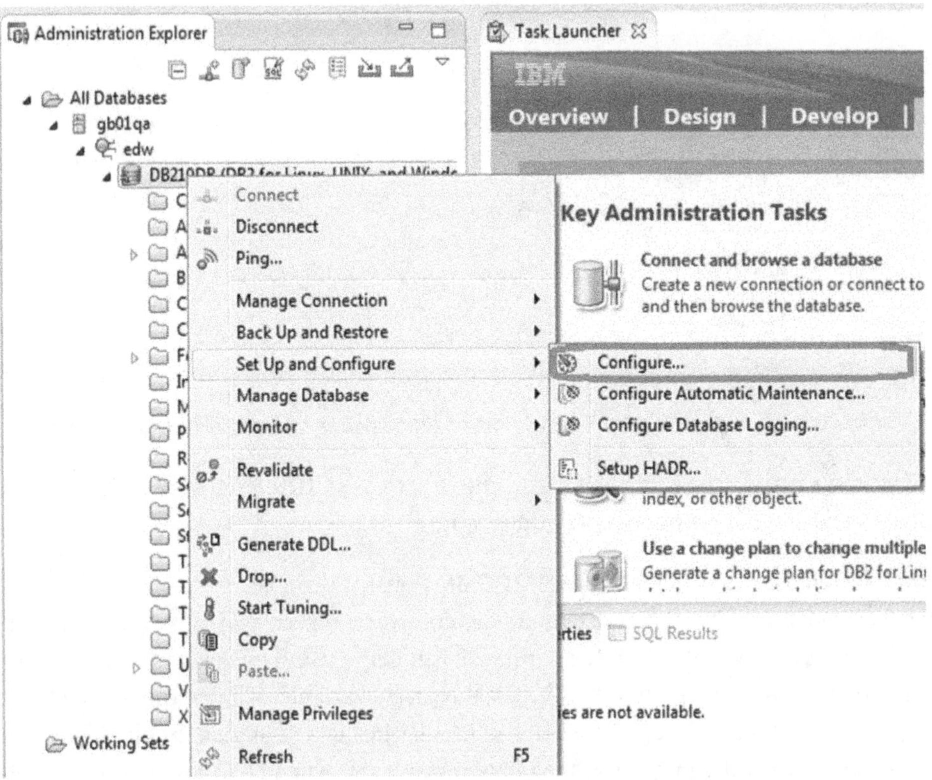

Figure 9.1: Set Up and Configure menu in IBM Data Studio

The **Configure** option launches the "Modify instance and database configuration parameters" page. In the Communication section, you can set the svcename parameter to a valid TCP/IP port number or valid services name, which is available in the /etc/services file in UNIX and %SystemRoot%\system32\drivers\etc\services in Windows operating systems.

If you change the svcename instance configuration in the menu in Figure 9.2, an asterisk (*) will appear to the left of the altered parameter to highlight the change.

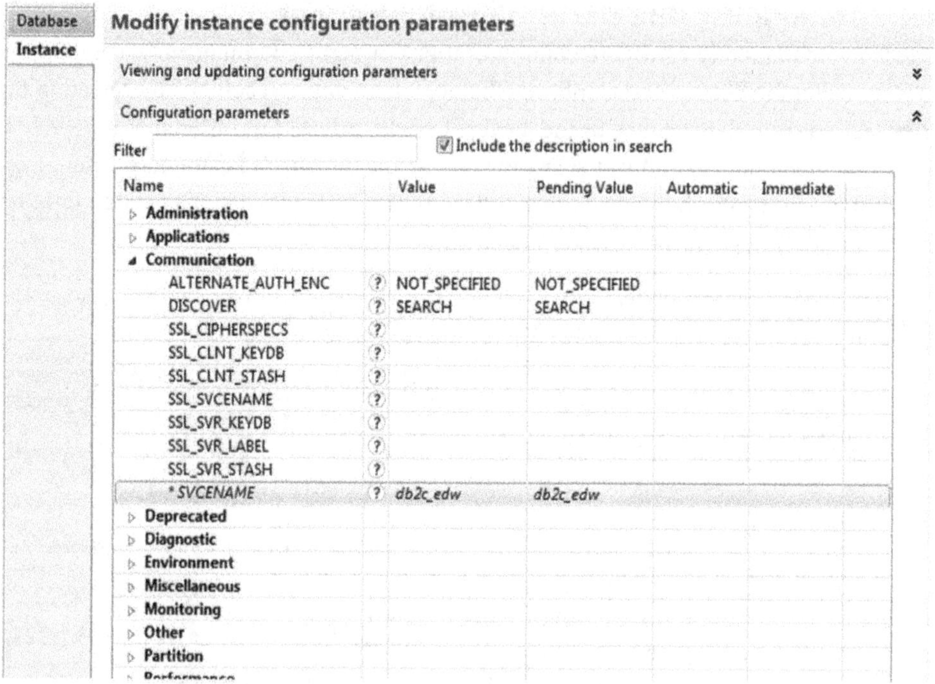

Database
Instance

Modify instance configuration parameters

Viewing and updating configuration parameters

Configuration parameters

Filter [ ] Include the description in search

Name	Value	Pending Value	Automatic	Immediate
▷ Administration				
▷ Applications				
◢ Communication				
ALTERNATE_AUTH_ENC	? NOT_SPECIFIED	NOT_SPECIFIED		
DISCOVER	? SEARCH	SEARCH		
SSL_CIPHERSPECS	?			
SSL_CLNT_KEYDB	?			
SSL_CLNT_STASH	?			
SSL_SVCENAME	?			
SSL_SVR_KEYDB	?			
SSL_SVR_LABEL	?			
SSL_SVR_STASH	?			
*SVCENAME	? db2c_edw	db2c_edw		
▷ Deprecated				
▷ Diagnostic				
▷ Environment				
▷ Miscellaneous				
▷ Monitoring				
▷ Other				
▷ Partition				

Figure 9.2: Configuring the TCP/IP port or the services name in IBM Data Studio

An alternative way to configure communications is to use CLP commands or the operating system command shell by using the following steps:

Step 1: Assign the value TCPIP to the DB2COMM registry variable.

Whenever you manually configure communications for a server, you must update the value of the DB2COMM registry variable before an instance can begin using the desired communications protocol. The values you assign to the DB2COMM registry variable will determine which communications managers to activate when a particular instance is started. Setting the DB2COMM registry variable incorrectly may generate one or more errors when DB2 attempts to start protocol support during instance initialization.

To assign the DB2COMM registry variable the value TCPIP, execute a db2set command that looks something like this:

```
db2set DB2COMM=TCPIP
```

Step 2: Assign the name of the TCP/IP port that the database server will use to receive communications from remote clients to the svcename parameter of the DB2 database manager configuration file.

Be sure to set the svcename parameter to the service name associated with the main connection port, or to the port number itself, so that when the database server is started, it can determine which port to listen on for incoming connection requests. You set this parameter by executing an UPDATE DATABASE MANAGER CONFIGURATION command that looks something like this:

```
UPDATE DBM CFG USING SVCENAME db2c_db2inst1
```

Step 3: Update the services file on the database server, if appropriate.

The TCP/IP services file identifies the ports on which server applications will listen for client requests. If you specified a service name in the svcename parameter of the DB2 database manager configuration file, you must add the appropriate service name-to-port number/protocol mapping to the services file on the server. If you specified a port number in the svcename parameter, you do not need update the services file.

The default location of the services file depends on the operating system used. On UNIX systems, the services file is named services and is located in the /etc directory; on Windows systems, the services file is located in %SystemRoot%\system32\drivers\etc. An entry in the services file for DB2 might look something like this:

```
# DB2 instance db2inst1
db2c_db2inst1    50012/tcp
DB2_db2inst1     60004/tcp
DB2_db2inst1_1   60005/tcp
DB2_db2inst1_2   60006/tcp
DB2_db2inst1_END 60007/tcp
```

In the above /etc/services file snippet, db2c_db2inst1 service TCP/IP port is reserved for communications between the client and the DB2 server. The remaining services TCP/IP port ranges are reserved for database partition communications in a DPF system.

Step 4: Restart the database instance to activate the newly added services name:

```
FORCE APPLICATIONS ALL
DEACTIVATE DB <dbname>
!db2stop
!db2start
ACTIVATE DB <dbname>
```

DB2 Directory Files

The DB2 instances and associated databases can reside locally on a server anywhere on the network. Each DB2 instance must know where databases that fall under its control are physically located, as well as how to establish connections to those databases on behalf of users and applications over the network. To keep track of this information, DB2 uses a special set of files known as *directory files* (or *directories*). Four types of directories exist:

- System database directory
- Local database directory
- Node directory
- Database Connection Services (DCS) directory

The System Database Directory

The system database directory resides in a file named `sqldbdir` that is created automatically in the path `DBPATH/<instancename>/NODE0000/sqldbdir` (for a UNIX environment) when the first database for an instance is created. Information about the new database is then recorded in the system database directory, and as additional databases are cataloged, information about those databases is recorded as well. Each entry recorded in the system database directory contains the following information:

- The name assigned to the database when the database was created (or explicitly cataloged)
- The alias assigned to the database (which is the same as the database name if no alias was specified when the database was created/cataloged)
- Descriptive information about the database (if that information is available)
- The location of the local database directory file that contains additional information about the database
- The location of the database itself:
  - » A remote entry describes a database that resides on another node.
  - » An indirect entry describes a database that is local. Databases that reside on the same node as the system database directory are thought to indirectly reference the home entry (to a local database directory) and are considered indirect entries.
  - » A home entry indicates that the database directory is on the same path as the local database directory.
  - » An LDAP entry indicates that the database location information is stored on an LDAP server.
- Other system information, including the code page the database was created under

You can view the contents of the system database directory or a local database directory file by executing the LIST DATABASE DIRECTORY command. The syntax for this command is:

```
LIST [DATABASE | DB] DIRECTORY <ON [Location]>
```

where:

Location Identifies the drive or directory where one or more databases are stored

If you do not specify a location when you execute this command, the contents of the system database directory file will be displayed. However, if you specify a location, the contents of the local database directory file that exists at that particular location will be displayed:

```
LIST DATABASE DIRECTORY

 System Database Directory

 Number of entries in the directory = 1

Database 1 entry:

 Database alias                       = DB210DB
 Database name                        = DB210DB
 Local database directory             = /database
 Database release level               = f.00
 Comment                              =
 Directory entry type                 = Indirect
 Catalog database partition number    = 0
 Alternate server hostname            =
 Alternate server port number         =
```

The Local Database Directory

Anytime a DB2 database is created in a new location (i.e., a drive or a directory), a local database directory file is also created at that location. Information about that database is then recorded in the local database directory, and as other databases are created in that location, information about those databases is recorded in the local database directory as well. Thus, although only one system database directory exists for a particular instance, several local database directories can exist, depending upon how databases have been distributed across the available storage.

Each entry recorded in a local database directory contains the following information:

- The name assigned to the database when the database was created (or explicitly cataloged)
- The alias assigned to the database (which is the same as the database name, if no alias was specified when the database was created/cataloged)
- Descriptive information about the database (if that information is available)
- The name of the root directory of the hierarchical tree used to store information about the database
- Other system information, including the code page the database was created under

As mentioned earlier, you can view the contents of a local database directory file by executing the LIST DATABASE DIRECTORY command:

```
LIST DATABASE DIRECTORY ON /database

 Local Database Directory on /database

 Number of entries in the directory = 1

Database 1 entry:

 Database alias                       = DB210DB
 Database name                        = DB210DB
 Database directory                   = SQL00001
 Database release level               = f.00
 Comment                              =
 Directory entry type                 = Home
 Catalog database partition number    = 0
 Database member number               = 0
```

The Node Directory

Unlike the system database directory and the local database directory, which you use to keep track of which databases exist and where they are stored, the node directory contains information that identifies how and where to find remote systems or instances. A node directory file is created on each client the first time a remote server or instance is cataloged. As other remote instances or servers are cataloged, information about them is recorded in the node directory as well. Entries in the node directory are then used along with entries in the system database directory to make connections and instance attachments to DB2 databases stored on remote servers.

Each entry recorded in the node directory contains the following information:

- The name assigned to the node when the node was explicitly cataloged
- Descriptive information about the node (if that information is available)
- The operating system used at the remote database server (optional)
- The communications protocol to use to communicate between the client workstation and the remote database server
- The TCP/IP host name or the remote TCP/IP address of the node where the remote database resides (if the protocol used is TCP/IP)
- The TCP/IP service name or the port number of the remote instance (if the protocol used is TCP/IP)

To view the contents of the node directory file, execute the LIST NODE DIRECTORY command. The syntax for this command is:

```
LIST <ADMIN> NODE DIRECTORY <SHOW DETAIL>
```

If you specify the ADMIN option when you execute this command, information about administration servers will be displayed:

```
LIST NODE DIRECTORY SHOW DETAIL

 Node Directory

 Number of entries in the directory = 1

Node 1 entry:

 Node name                          = ISASNODE
 Comment                            =
 Directory entry type               = LOCAL
 Protocol                           = TCPIP
 Hostname                           = prodbcuadm01
                                                          Continued
```

```
Service name                      = 50001
Remote instance name              =
System                            =
Operating system type             = None
```

The Database Connection Services Directory

Using an add-on product called DB2 Connect, it is possible for DB2 for Linux, UNIX, and Windows clients to establish a connection to a DRDA application server, such as:

- DB2 for z/OS databases on System z architecture host computers
- DB2 for VM and VSE databases on System z architecture host computers
- DB2 databases on AS/400 and System i computers

Because the information needed to connect to DRDA host databases is different from the information used to connect to LAN-based databases, information about remote host databases is kept in a special directory known as the *Database Connection Services* (*DCS*) directory. If an entry in the DCS directory has a database name that corresponds to the name of a database stored in the system database directory, the specified application requester (which, in most cases, is DB2 Connect) can forward SQL requests to the database that resides on a remote DRDA server.

You can view the contents of the DCS directory file by executing the LIST DCS DIRECTORY command. The syntax for this command is:

```
LIST DCS DIRECTORY
```

It is important to note that the DCS directory only exists if the DB2 Connect product has been installed.

Cataloging Remote Servers and Databases

Once you have configured a server for communications, any client that wishes to access a database on the server must be configured to communicate with the server. But that is just the first step. You must also add entries for both the server and the remote database to the system database and node directories on the client. (Entries must also be added to the DCS directory if the client intends to connect to a System z or System i database via the DB2 Connect software.) You add entries to DB2's directories by using a process known as *cataloging*.

Cataloging a DB2 Database

Because a database is implicitly cataloged as soon as it is created, most users never have to be concerned with the cataloging process. However, if you want to access a database stored on a remote server, you will need to become familiar with the tools that you can use to catalog DB2 databases. Fortunately, cataloging a database is a relatively straightforward process and can be done using IBM Data Studio or by executing the CATALOG DATABASE command.

By highlighting the **All Databases** object in the objects pane of IBM Data Studio and right-clicking the mouse button, you can open a menu that contains a list of options for database objects. To invoke the dialog used to catalog databases, select **New Connection to a database** from this menu, as Figure 9.3 shows.

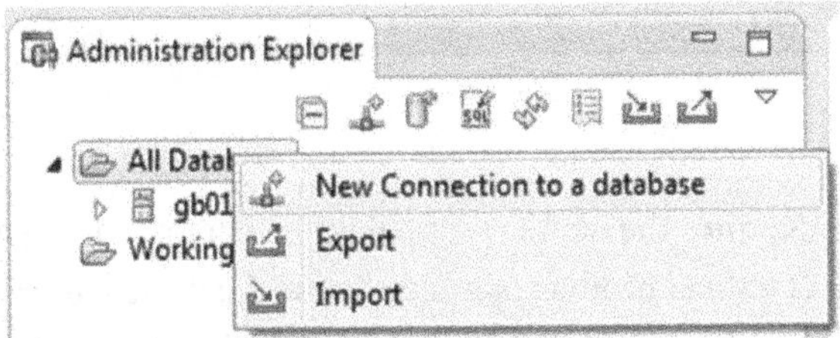

Figure 9.3: New Connection to a database option in IBM Data Studio

When you enter the connection parameters such as database name, host name or the IP address, and the port number, IBM Data Studio internally creates a catalog and establishes a connection with the database instance and the database by using the user credentials supplied. This information is recorded in the org.eclipse.datatools.connectivity directory and is used only by the IBM Data Studio client for future connections. However, other applications cannot use this internal catalog information to connect to the DB2 database server. Figure 9.4 shows the connection parameters required in IBM Data Studio.

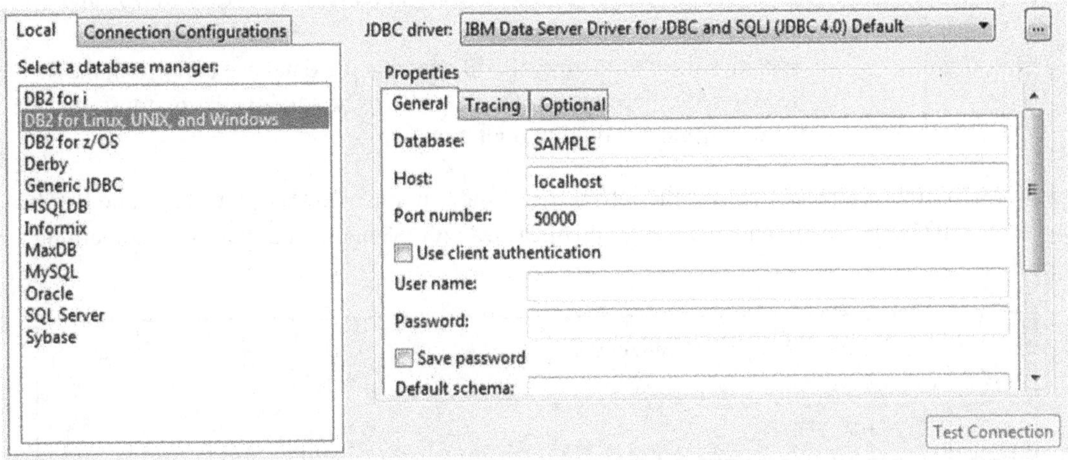

Figure 9.4: Connection parameters in IBM Data Studio

To configure connectivity between the application server and the database server, you can catalog a database by executing the command. The syntax for this command is:

```
CATALOG [DATABASE | DB] [DatabaseName]
<AS [Alias]> CATALOG DATABASE
<ON [Path] | AT NODE [NodeName]>
<AUTHENTICATION [AuthenticationType]>
<WITH "[Description]">
```

where:

DatabaseName	Identifies the name assigned to the database to be cataloged
Alias	Identifies the alias to assign to the database when it is cataloged
Path	Identifies the location (drive and/or directory) where the directory hierarchy and files associated with the database to catalog are physically stored
NodeName	Identifies the node where the database to catalog resides; the node name you specify must match an entry in the node directory file (i.e., the name corresponds to a node that has already been cataloged)
AuthenticationType	Identifies where and how authentication is to take place when a user attempts to access the database; the following values are valid for this parameter: SERVER, CLIENT, SERVER_ENCRYPT, KERBEROS TARGET PRINCIPAL [*PrincipalName*] (where *PrincipalName* is the fully qualified Kerberos principal name for the target server), DATA_ENCRYPT, and GSSPLUGIN
Description	Specifies the comment that will describe the database entry to make in the database directory for the database to be cataloged; you must enclose the description in double-quotation marks

Thus, to catalog a local database that physically resides in the directory /database and that has the name DB210DB, you would execute a CATALOG DATABASE command that looks something like this:

```
CATALOG DATABASE db210db AS db2demo
ON /database
AUTHENTICATION SERVER
```

And if you want to catalog a remote database that physically resides on a different server over the network, execute a CATALOG NODE command and CATALOG DATABASE command that looks something like this (this requires you to run the CATALOG NODE command before the CATALOG DATABASE command, and is discussed in the next section):

```
CATALOG DATABASE remotedb AT NODE bcunode AUTHENTICATION SERVER
```

The command LIST DB DIRECTORY shows the cataloged information with the database release level and the directory entry type as indirect (local) or remote:

```
Database 1 entry:

 Database alias                        = DB210DB
 Database name                         = DB210DB
 Local database directory              = /database
 Database release level                = f.00
 Comment                               =
 Directory entry type                  = Indirect
 Catalog database partition number     = 0
 Alternate server hostname             =
 Alternate server port number          =

Database 2 entry:

 Database alias                        = REMOTEDB
 Database name                         = REMOTEDB
 Node name                             = BCUNODE
 Database release level                = f.00
 Comment                               =
 Directory entry type                  = Remote
 Authentication                        = SERVER
 Catalog database partition number     = -1
 Alternate server hostname             =
 Alternate server port number          =
```

The database release level is an internal DB2 release level extracted from the "database manager configuration release level" of the server's database manager configuration file—in the case of DB2 10.1, it is set to a hexadecimal value 0x0f00. Table 9.2 shows the different DB2 versions and database release levels.

Table 9.2: DB2 internal release levels

DB2 Version	Database Release Level
DB2 8	a.00
DB2 9	b.00
DB2 9.5	c.00
DB2 9.7	d.00
DB2 9.8	e.00
DB2 10.1	f.00
DB2 10.5	10.00

If you want a remote database to be cataloged, you will need to catalog the node (server) and then the database, as the next section explains.

Cataloging a Remote DB2 Node (Server)

The process of cataloging nodes (servers) is significantly different from the process of cataloging databases. Instead of being explicitly cataloged as needed, nodes are usually implicitly cataloged whenever a remote database is cataloged via IBM Data Studio. However, if you desire to explicitly catalog a particular node (server), you can do so by executing the CATALOG ... NODE command that corresponds to the communications protocol that will be used to access the server being cataloged. Several forms of the CATALOG ... NODE command are available, including:

```
CATALOG LOCAL NODE
CATALOG LDAP NODE
CATALOG NAMED PIPE NODE
CATALOG TCPIP NODE
```

All of these commands' syntax is very similar, the major difference being that many of the options available with each are specific to the communications protocol for which the command has been tailored. Because TCP/IP is probably the most common communications protocol in use today, let us take a look at the syntax for that form of the CATALOG ... NODE command.

The syntax for the CATALOG TCPIP NODE command is:

```
CATALOG <ADMIN> [TCPIP | TCPIP4 | TCPIP6] NODE [NodeName]
REMOTE [IPAddress | HostName]
SERVER [ServiceName | PortNumber]
<SECURITY SOCKS>
<REMOTE INSTANCE [InstanceName]>
<SYSTEM [SystemName]>
<OSTYPE [SystemType]>
<WITH "[Description]">
```

where:

NodeName	Identifies the alias to assign to the node to be cataloged; this is an arbitrary name created on the user's workstation and is used to identify the node
IPAddress	Identifies the IP address of the server where the remote database that you are trying to communicate with resides
HostName	Identifies the host name as it is known to the TCP/IP network (this is the name of the server where the remote database that you are trying to communicate with resides)
ServiceName	Identifies the service name that the DB2 database manager instance on the server uses to communicate
PortNumber	Identifies the port number that the DB2 database manager instance on the server uses to communicate
InstanceName	Identifies the name of the server instance to make an attachment to
SystemName	Identifies the DB2 system name used to identify the server workstation
SystemType	Identifies the type of operating system in use on the server workstation; the following values are valid for this parameter: AIX, WIN, HPUX, SUN, OS390, OS400, VM, VSE, and LINUX
Description	Specifies the comment that will describe the node entry to make in the node directory for the node being cataloged; you must enclose the description in double-quotation marks

If you want to catalog a node for an AIX server named db2host that has a DB2 instance named db2inst1 that listens on port 50001 and assign it the alias PRDNODE, you would execute a CATALOG TCPIP NODE command that looks something like this:

```
CATALOG TCPIP NODE PRDNODE
REMOTE db2host
SERVER 50001
OSTYPE AIX
WITH "A remote AIX TCP/IP node"
```

To view the node catalog information, use LIST NODE DIRECTORY command:

```
LIST NODE DIRECTORY

 Node Directory

 Number of entries in the directory = 2

Node 1 entry:

 Node name                          = PRDNODE
 Comment                            = A remote AIX TCP/IP node
 Directory entry type               = LOCAL
 Protocol                           = TCPIP
 Hostname                           = db2host
 Service name                       = 50001
```

Note: To catalog a node for a Linux server that has the IPv4 address 192.0.32.67 and a DB2 instance named db2inst1 that is listening on port 50001 and assign it the alias ip4_node, execute a CATALOG TCPIP NODE command that looks something like this:

```
CATALOG TCPIP4 NODE ipv4_node
REMOTE 192.0.32.67
```

Continued

```
SERVER 50001
OSTYPE LINUX
WITH "A remote Linux TCP/IP-IPv4 node"
```

However, if you want to catalog a node for a Linux server that has the IPv6 address 1080:0:0:0:8:800:200C:417A and a DB2 instance named db2inst1 that is listening on port 50001, and assign it the alias ipv6_node, you would execute a CATALOG TCPIP NODE command that looks something like this:

```
CATALOG TCPIP6 NODE ipv6_node
REMOTE 1080:0:0:0:8:800:200C:417A
SERVER 50001
OSTYPE LINUX
WITH "A remote Linux TCP/IP-IPv6 node"
```

Cataloging a DCS Database

The process for cataloging a DCS database is very similar to that for cataloging a regular DB2 database. You catalog a DCS database by executing the CATALOG DCS DATABASE command. The syntax for this command is:

```
CATALOG DCS [DATABASE | DB] [Alias]
<AS [TargetName]>
<AR [LibraryName]>
<PARMS "[ParameterString]">
<WITH "[Description]">
```

where:

Alias	Identifies the alias of the target database to catalog; this name must match an entry in the system database directory associated with the remote node
TargetName	Identifies the name of the target host database to catalog (if the host database to catalog resides on an OS/390 or a z/OS server, specify the *TargetName* to refer to a DB2 for z/OS subsystem identified by its LOCATION NAME or one of the alias LOCATION names defined on the z/OS server; you can determine the LOCATION NAME by logging in to TSO and issuing the SQL query SELECT CURRENT SERVER FROM SYSIBM.SYSDUMMY1)

LibraryName	Identifies the name of the application requester library to load and use to access the remote database listed in the DCS directory
ParameterString	Identifies the parameter string to pass to the application requestor when it is invoked; you must enclose the parameter string in double-quotation marks
Description	Specifies the comment that will describe the database entry to make in the DCS directory for the database to be cataloged; you must enclose the description in double-quotation marks

Thus, if you want to catalog a DB2 for z/OS database residing in the DSN_ZDB subsystem on the z/OS server that has the name PAYROLL and assign it the alias dsn_zdb, you would execute a CATALOG DCS DATABASE command that looks something like this:

```
CATALOG DCS DATABASE payroll
AS dsn_zdb
WITH "DB2 for z/OS LOCATION NAME DSN_ZDB"
```

It is important to note that an entry for the database alias db2zdb also has to exist in the system database directory before the entry in the DCS database directory can be used to connect to the z/OS database.

Binding Utilities and Applications

Before DB2-specific utilities and applications such as Import, Export, and CLP can be used with a database that resides on a remote database server, they must be "bound" to the database. During the binding process, a package—an object that includes all the information needed to process specific SQL statements used by a utility or an application—is created and stored in the database. In a network environment, if you are using multiple clients that run on different operating systems or are at different versions or service levels of DB2, you must bind the utilities once for each operating system and DB2 version combination.

To bind DB2 utilities and applications to a database that is residing remotely on a server, perform the following steps:

Step 1: Go to the directory on the DB2 server where the DB2-specific utility and application bind files are stored. On Linux and UNIX, these bind files are in the $HOME/sqllib/bnd of the instance user; on Windows, they are in the bnd subdirectory of the sqllib directory where DB2 was installed.

Step 2: Using the CLP, establish a connection to the database by executing a CONNECT command as follows:

```
CONNECT TO [dbname] USER [username] USING [password]
```

where:

dbname	Identifies the name of the database that needs db2 utilities to be bound using the BIND command
username	Identifies the name of the user who is present on the remote database server and has BINDADD privileges
password	Identifies the password for the user who is present on the remote database server

Step 3: Bind the DB2-specific utilities and applications to the database by executing the following commands from the CLP:

```
BIND @db2ubind.lst MESSAGES $HOME/ubind.msg BLOCKING ALL GRANT PUBLIC
BIND @db2cli.lst MESSAGES $HOME/clibind.msg BLOCKING ALL GRANT PUBLIC
```

The file db2ubind.lst contains a list of the bind files (.bnd) required to create packages for DB2's database utilities; the file db2cli.lst contains a list of the bind files (.bnd) needed to create packages for the DB2 Call Level Interface (CLI) and the DB2 ODBC driver. The previous statement specifies to create three CLI large packages and to have multiple connections access them concurrently. When you execute these two commands, all messages the Bind utility produces will be written to files named ubind.msg and clibind.msg, and the group PUBLIC will receive EXECUTE and BINDADD privileges for each resulting package.

Step 4: Terminate the connection to the database by executing the CONNECT RESET or TERMINATE command from the CLP.

By default, DB2 creates three dynamic WITH HOLD CLI packages in the database. When you have more than three concurrent connections running DB2 utilities, increase the number of packages by specifying the CLIPKG clause:

```
BIND @db2cli.lst MESSAGES $HOME/clibind.msg
   BLOCKING ALL GRANT PUBLIC CLIPKG 20
```

To verify the number of dynamic WITH HOLD CLI packages created on the database for cursor stability isolation, run the following SQL statement on the target database:

```
SELECT SUBSTR (PKGNAME, 1, 10) as PKGNAME FROM SYSCAT.PACKAGES
WHERE PKGNAME LIKE 'SYSLH2%'

PKGNAME
-----------
SYSLH200
SYSLH201
...
...
SYSLH20F
SYSLH210
SYSLH211
SYSLH212
SYSLH213

  20 record(s) selected.
```

The BINDADD privilege is necessary to create packages on the remote database. The creator of a package automatically has the CONTROL privilege on that package and retains this privilege even if the BINDADD authority is subsequently revoked. Execute the following command to grant authority for a specific user to create packages on the database server:

```
GRANT BINDADD ON DATABASE TO USER [username]
```

A Word About the db2schema.bnd File

When you create or migrate a database on a Linux, UNIX, or Windows DB2 server, a file named db2schema.bnd is automatically bound to the database as part of the database creation or migration process. This bind file exists only on these types of servers and is used to create a package that provides system catalog function support. If, for some reason, this package is missing (for example, a fix pack was applied on the server, the package was intentionally dropped by a user, or an SQL1088W warning was generated when a database was created or migrated), the db2schema.bnd file must be rebound to the database (stored locally on the server).

On Linux and UNIX workstations, the db2schema.bnd bind file is in the sqllib/bnd subdirectory of the home directory of the instance user; on Windows workstations, this bind file is in the bnd subdirectory of the sqllib directory where DB2 was installed. To bind this file to a database, simply execute a BIND command that looks something like this:

```
BIND db2schema.bnd BLOCKING ALL GRANT PUBLIC
```

When binding utilities and applications to a System z or System i database server in order to configure a DB2 Connect server so that it can access a database stored on a System z or System i host, *never* include the db2schema.bnd file in the set of files being bound. Attempting to do so can lead to corruption of data in the host database.

Configuring Communications to System z and System i

Before you can access data stored in a DB2 for z/OS or a DB2 for i5/OS database, you must configure TCP/IP communications between the client that is running DB2 Connect and a System z or System i host. Then you must catalog the remote server and the database. In other words, you must perform the following steps (from the DB2 Connect server):

1. Configure TCP/IP communications on the DB2 Connect server.
2. Catalog the TCP/IP node.
3. Catalog the System z or System i database as a DCS database.
4. Catalog the System z or System i database.
5. Bind utilities and applications to the System z or System i database server.

Most of the steps to establish a connection between a DB2 Connect and a System z or System i host database are identical to the steps to configure a client so that it can access a database stored on a remote server. The most significant difference between the two processes is the step that requires you to catalog the host database as a DCS database and the step that requires you to bind DB2 utilities and applications to the System z or System i host database by using the ddcsmvs.lst and ddsc400.lst list files.

DB2 Discovery

It is easy to see how manually configuring communications between clients and servers can become a difficult process, especially in complex network environments. And, as you have just seen, establishing communications between clients and servers is only the beginning. Before a client can send requests to a DB2 server for processing, both the server and the database stored on the server must be cataloged on the client as well.

DB2 Discovery allows you to easily catalog a remote server and a database and set up a distributed connection between a client and a server without having to know any detailed communications-specific information. Here is how DB2 Discovery works.

When invoked from a client, DB2 Discovery broadcasts a discovery request over the network, and each DB2 server on the network that has been configured to support the discovery process responds by returning a list of instances found on the server, information about the communications protocol each instance supports, and a list of databases that reside within each instance. You can then use IBM Data Studio to import the catalog information for any instance or database returned by the discovery process by following these steps:

Step 1: Open the **Administration Explorer** tab and select the **Import** option to import the connections, as Figure 9.5 shows.

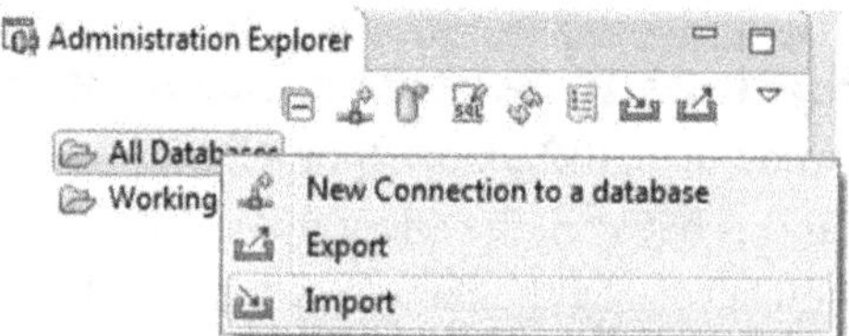

Figure 9.5: Importing connections by using IBM Data Studio

Step 2: In the resulting Import Connect Profiles window (see Figure 9.6), select the **Local file** option.

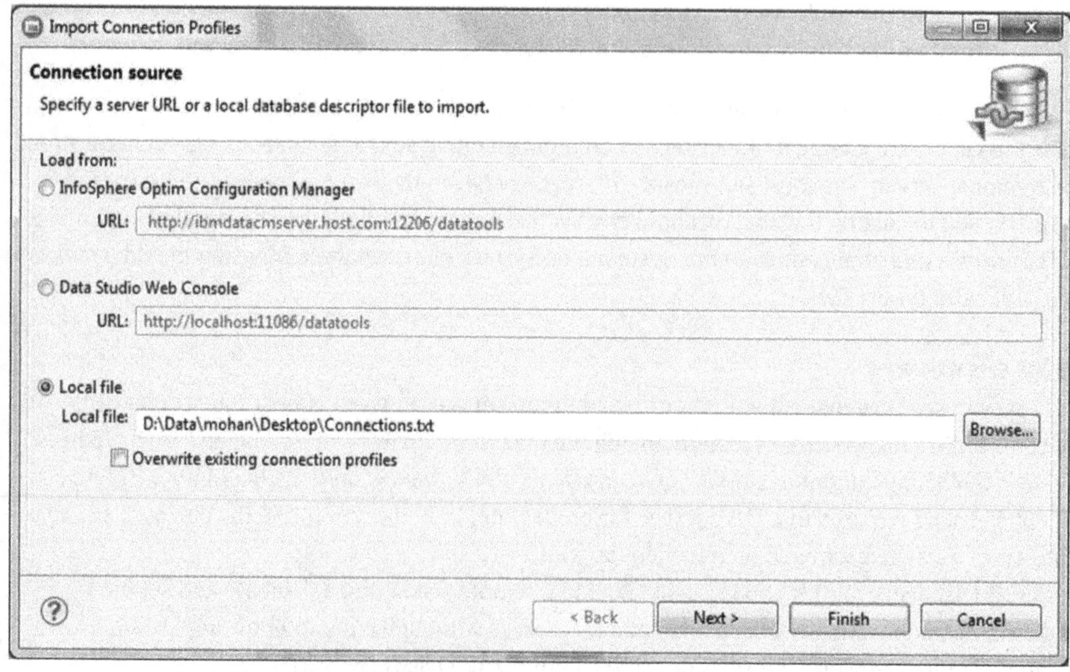

Figure 9.6: Importing using the Local file option in IBM Data Studio

Step 3: Now, choose the connection profiles you want to import by marking the check box next to the listed connections, as in Figure 9.7.

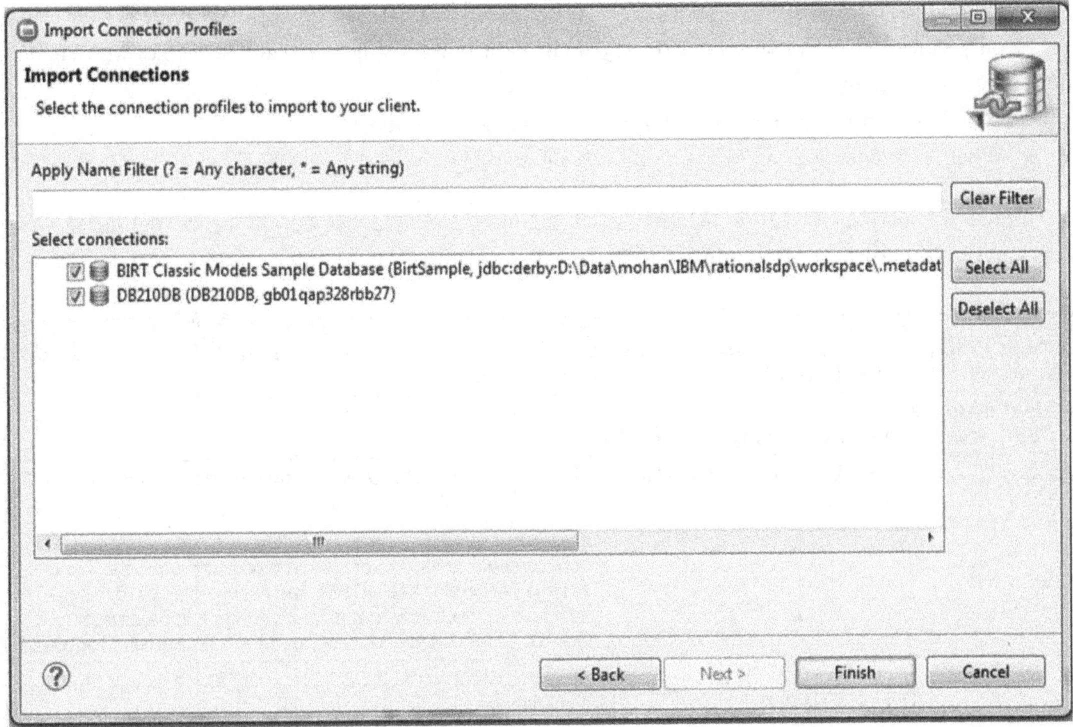

Figure 9.7: Selecting the databases or instances to import

To process a discovery request, DB2 Discovery can use one of two methods: search or known. The search discovery method will search the entire network for valid DB2 servers and databases and will return a list of all servers, instances, and databases found to the client, along with the communications information needed to catalog and connect to each one. In contrast, the known discovery method will search the network for a specific server by using a specific communications protocol. (Because the client knows the name of the server and the communications protocol used by that server, the server is said to be "known" by the client.) Again, when the known discovery method locates the specified server, it returns a list of all instances and databases found on the server to the client, along with the information needed to catalog and connect to each one.

Whether a client can launch a DB2 Discovery request and, if so, how, and whether a particular server will respond and, if so, how, are determined by the values of parameters found in the configuration file for the DAS instance, the DB2 database manager configuration file for each instance (both on the client and on the server), and the database configuration file for each database within an instance.

Specifically, these parameters control:

- Whether a client can launch a DB2 Discovery request
- Whether DB2 Discovery can locate a server and, if so, whether it can locate the server only when using the search discovery method or when using either the search or known discovery method
- Whether an instance can be located with a discovery request
- Whether a database can be located with a discovery request

Table 9.3 describes the DAS instance, DB2 instance, and database configuration parameters that you use to control the behavior of DB2 Discovery.

Table 9.3: Configuration parameters that control DB2 Discovery behavior

Parameter	Values/Default	Description
Client Instance (DB2 Database Manager Configuration File)		
discover	DISABLE, KNOWN, or SEARCH Default: SEARCH	Identifies the DB2 Discovery action that the client instance will use. If you set this parameter to SEARCH, the client instance can issue either search or known discovery requests; if you set this parameter to KNOWN, the client instance can issue only known discovery requests; if you set this parameter to DISABLE, the client instance cannot issue discovery requests.
discover_inst	ENABLE or DISABLE Default: ENABLE	Specifies whether other DB2 Discovery requests can detect this instance.
Server DAS Instance (see Note below Table 9.3) ***(DAS Configuration File)***		
discover	DISABLE, KNOWN, or SEARCH Default: SEARCH	Identifies the DB2 Discovery action to use when the server is started. If you set this parameter to SEARCH, the server will respond to both search and known discovery requests; if you set this parameter to KNOWN, the server will respond only to known discovery requests; if you set this parameter to DISABLE, the server will not respond to discovery requests.
Server Instance (DB2 Database Manager Configuration File)		
discover	DISABLE, KNOWN, or SEARCH Default: SEARCH	Identifies the DB2 Discovery action that the server instance will use. If you set this parameter to SEARCH, the server instance can issue either search or known discovery requests; if you set this parameter to KNOWN, the server instance can issue only known discovery requests; if you set this parameter to DISABLE, the server instance cannot issue discovery requests.

Table 9.3: Configuration parameters that control DB2 Discovery behavior (continued)		
Parameter	**Values/Default**	**Description**
discover_inst	ENABLE or DISABLE Default: ENABLE	Identifies whether information about a particular instance found on a server will be included in the server's response to a discovery request. If this parameter is set to ENABLE, the server will include information about the instance in its response to both search and known discovery requests. If this parameter is set to DISABLE, the server will not include information about the instance (and will not include information about any databases that come under the instance's control) in its response to discovery requests. This parameter provides a way to hide an instance and all of its databases from DB2 Discovery.
Server Database (Database Configuration File)		
discover_db	ENABLE or DISABLE Default: ENABLE	Identifies whether information about a particular database on a server will be included in the server's response to a discovery request. If you set this parameter to ENABLE, the server will include information about the database in its response to both search and known discovery requests. However, if you set this parameter to DISABLE, the server will not include information about the database in its response to discovery requests. This parameter provides a way to hide an individual database from DB2 Discovery.

Note: DAS has been deprecated in DB2 9.7 and will actually be removed in the future releases. Because DAS is no longer an essential component within DB2, it is not supported in DB2 pureScale environments.

As you can see, it is possible to enable or disable DB2 Discovery at the server level, instance level, and database level, as well as to control how clients and servers initiate discovery requests. It is also possible to configure a server so that DB2 Discovery will not detect one or more of its instances or databases when discovery requests are made. Figure 9.8 shows how you can use the configuration parameters that control DB2 Discovery's behavior to prevent DB2 Discovery from detecting certain instances and databases stored on a server.

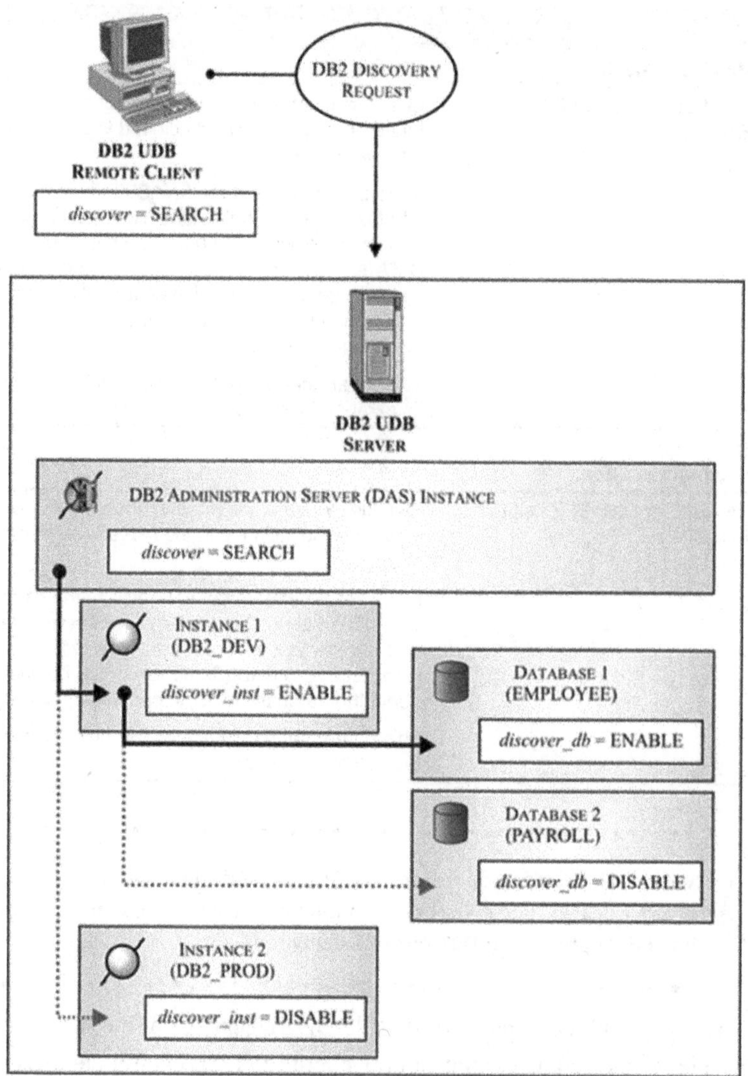

Figure 9.8: Controlling which instances and databases DB2 Discovery can detect (in this example, the server, Instance 1, and Database 1 will be returned by a discovery request; Instance 2 and Database 2 will not)

Fast Communications Manager (FCM)

In a partitioned database environment, most communications between database partitions is handled by the Fast Communications Manager (FCM). During instance creation, a number of ports equal to the number of participating DB2 logical partitions on each server will be reserved in the /etc/services file on the Linux and UNIX platform and in the %SystemRoot%\system32\

drivers\etc\services file on Windows. FCM uses these ports for communications. You can reserve the ports by using the following format:

```
DB2_InstanceName
DB2_InstanceName_1
DB2_InstanceName_2
DB2_InstanceName_END
```

Consider an example of an IBM Smart Analytics System (ISAS) having one admin node (server) and four data nodes (servers), with each data node hosting eight logical partitions. You will need to reserve eight ports in the /etc/services file to facilitate FCM daemons to communicate within the members.

FCM uses 4 KB buffers for internal communications between database partitions and database servers; the actual number of 4 KB buffers used for each database partition is controlled by the fcm_num_buffers DB2 database manager configuration parameter. By default, this parameter is assigned the value AUTOMATIC, which means that FCM monitors resource usage periodically and incrementally releases resources if they are not used within 30 minutes. If DB2 cannot allocate the number of resources needed when an instance is started, it scales back the configuration values incrementally until the instance is successfully started.

If you have multiple logical nodes on the same machine, you might find it beneficial to assign a value to this parameter. And if you have assigned a value to this parameter, you might find it necessary to increase the value if you run out of message buffers because of the number of users on the system, the number of database partition servers on the system, or the complexity of the applications being used. However, before attempting to manually configure memory for the FCM, it is recommended that you start with the automatic setting for both the fcm_num_buffers (number of FCM buffers) and the fcm_num_channels (number of FCM channels) DB2 database manager configuration parameters. Then use the system monitor to evaluate FCM activity to determine whether this setting is appropriate. You can obtain system monitor information for FCM by using the administrative view or the table function, as follows:

Administrative View:

```
SELECT
        BUFF_FREE,
        BUFF_FREE_BOTTOM,
        MEMBER
```

Continued

```
    FROM SYSIBMADM.SNAPFCM ORDER BY MEMBER

BUFF_FREE            BUFF_FREE_BOTTOM     MEMBER
-------------------- -------------------- ------
                 128                  128      0
```

Table Function:

```
SELECT * FROM TABLE (SYSPROC.SNAP_GET_FCM (0)) AS T

SNAPSHOT_TIMESTAMP          BUFF_FREE            BUFF_FREE_BOTTOM
-------------------------- -------------------- --------------------
2014-05-18-12.32.09.701010                   128                  128

CH_FREE              CH_FREE_BOTTOM       DBPARTITIONNUM MEMBER
-------------------- -------------------- -------------- ------
                 128                  127              0      0
```

To determine whether the number of FCM buffers in use is appropriate, it is important to examine the current allocation of the number of FCM buffers as well as the maximum number of FCM buffers that have been allocated. You can then compare these numbers; if the percentage of free FCM buffers drops below 10 percent, DB2 may run out of available buffers, indicating that you should increase the number of FCM buffers in use.

If you want to set the fcm_num_buffers parameter to a specific value as well as AUTOMATIC, and you do not want the DB2 system controller thread to drop the buffer size below the specified value, set the DB2_FCM_SETTINGS registry variable as:

```
db2set DB2_FCM_SETTINGS=FCM_CFG_BASE_AS_FLOOR:YES
```

It is important to note that if you are using multiple database partitions on the same server, one pool of buffers is shared by all logical database partitions on the same machine. In this case, you determine the size of the pool by multiplying the fcm_num_buffers value by the number of logical database partitions defined on that physical machine.

Note: If you want to determine the memory allocation to the FCM component on the server, use the MON_GET_FCM table function, as follows:

```
SELECT (SUM (buff_total)*4/1024/1024) AS "FCM Memory Allocation in GB"
   FROM TABLE (MON_GET_FCM (-2))
```

To find the actual FCM memory usage, use this function:

```
SELECT (SUM (buff_total*4) - SUM (buff_free*4))/1024 AS "FCM Actual Memory Usage in MB"
   FROM TABLE (MON_GET_FCM (-2))
```

Configuring LDAP Connections

Lightweight Directory Access Protocol (LDAP) is an industry standard application protocol for accessing, updating, and maintaining the distributed directory services over the network. An LDAP directory greatly simplifies the deployment and maintenance of client/server applications. With DB2, clients must know the location of the DB2 data server—such as host name/IP address, database name, and port number—to access the server. You can accomplish this by using the method discussed in the section "Cataloging Remote Servers and Databases"; however, this is a tedious task when it comes to maintaining numerous database servers within an organization.

LDAP offers an effective way of handling the database server information in one central location, and any changes or additions are made in that location. All application clients refer to the LDAP directory for information about the database location and the port number. Figure 9.9 shows the data flow between the LDAP server, the DB2 client, and the DB2 database server.

Each database server instance publishes its presence to the LDAP server by inserting or updating the database information in the LDAP directory. During a database connection, the catalog information for the server is retrieved from the LDAP directory, and the client uses this information to connect to the server. Hence, the client is no longer required to store this information locally on the machine in node and database directories.

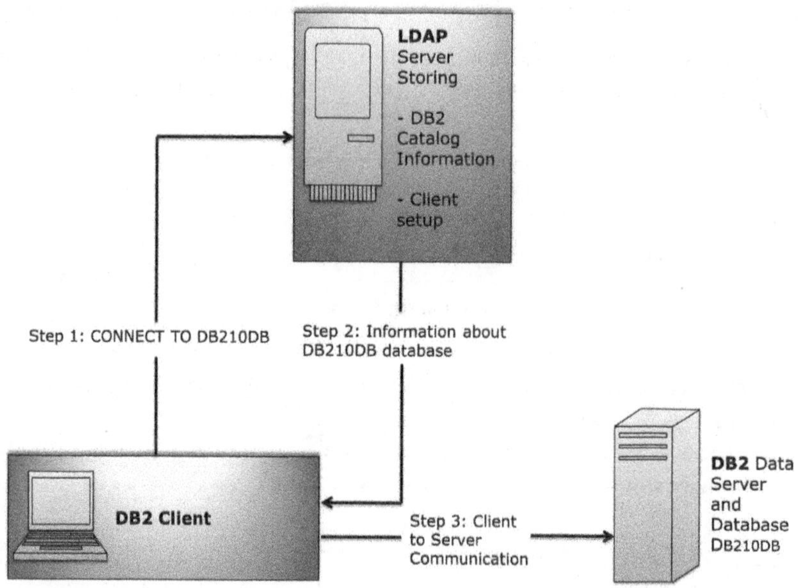

Figure 9.9: Data flow between LDAP, the DB2 client, and the DB2 server

To improve directory access performance during the client reconnection, a caching mechanism exists so that the client must search the LDAP directory server once. After the information is retrieved from the LDAP directory, it is cached on the local client computer based on the dir_cache database manager configuration parameter's value and the DB2LDAPCACHE registry variable. You use the dir_cache database manager configuration parameter to store the database, node, and DCS directory files in a memory cache—dir_cache is available until an application closes all the connections. Whereas using the DB2LDAPCACHE registry variable will store the database, node, and DCS directory files in local database directories. Table 9.4 shows the differences between DB2LDAPCACHE and dir_cache.

Table 9.4: DB2LDAPCACHE and dir_cache parameter differences

DB2LDAPCACHE	dir_cache	Caching Information
No	No	Connection always reads information from LDAP.
No	Yes	Connection information is read from LDAP once and stored in the DB2 memory cache.
Yes	Yes/No	Connection information is read from LDAP once and stored in the DB2 local database, node, and DCS directories.

Registering the DB2 Server with LDAP

Each DB2 server instance must be registered in LDAP to publish the connectivity information that the client application uses to connect to the DB2 server instance. When registering an instance of the database server, you must specify a node name, which the client will then use when it connects or attaches to the server.

You issue the REGISTER command from the DB2 server, as follows:

```
REGISTER DB2 SERVER IN LDAP
AS [ldap_node_name]
PROTOCOL TCPIP
```

where:

ldap_node_name	Identifies the node name for each DB2 server and must be unique within the LDAP directory

You can also issue the REGISTER command remotely for any DB2 server by using this command:

```
REGISTER DB2 SERVER IN LDAP
AS [ldap_node_name]
PROTOCOL TCPIP
HOSTNAME [db2_host_name]
SVCENAME [tcpip_service_name]
REMOTE [db2_server_name]
INSTANCE [db2_instance_name]
```

where:

ldap_node_name	Identifies the node name for each DB2 server and must be unique within the LDAP directory
db2_host_name	Identifies the host name of the server that you intend to register in the LDAP directory
tcpip_service_name	Identifies the service name or the port number at which DB2 is listening on the DB2 server; you can retrieve this by using the DBM CFG command on the server
db2_server_name	Identifies the host name of the server; in regard to TCPIP configuration, both the host name and remote servers' names must be same
db2_instance_name	Identifies the DB2 instance name on the server that you intend to register in LDAP directory

Registering the DB2 Database with LDAP

During the creation of a database within an instance registered in the LDAP directory, the database is automatically registered in LDAP. This registration allows remote client connections to the database without having to catalog the database and node locally on the client system. When a client attempts to connect to a database, if the database does not exist in the database directory on the local client system, the LDAP directory is searched for the connection information and cached locally based on the DB2LDAPCACHE and dir_cache settings.

You can use the CATALOG command to manually register the database in the LDAP directory:

```
CATALOG LDAP DATABASE [dbname]
AT NODE [ldap_node_name]
WITH "[description for the LDAP database]"
```

where:

dbname	Identifies the name of the database to register in the LDAP directory
ldap_node_name	Identifies the node name for each DB2 server and must be unique within the LDAP directory

Deregistering the DB2 Server from LDAP

Deregistration of an instance from the LDAP directory also removes the node, alias, and associated database objects referring to the instance.

You can use the DEREGISTER command to remove the DB2 server information from the LDAP directory:

```
DEREGISTER DB2 SERVER
IN LDAP NODE <[ldap_node_name]>
```

where:

ldap_node_name	Identifies the LDAP node name for the DB2 server that you intend to deregister and is unique within LDAP directory

Deregistering the DB2 Database from LDAP

The LDAP registered database is automatically deregistered from LDAP when the database is dropped from the DB2 server or when the owning instance is deregistered from the LDAP directory.

To remove the DB2 database information from the LDAP directory, use the UNCATALOG command:

```
UNCATALOG LDAP DATABASE [dbname]
```

where:

dbname Identifies the name of the database to deregister from the LDAP directory

Troubleshooting Communications Errors

After configuring a client or DB2 Connect server to communicate with a remote database, try to connect to the database to verify that you have configured everything properly. Assuming everything has been configured correctly, a test connection to the remote database should be successful. However, if a test connection results in an error, take the following actions to determine why the error occurred:

1. Verify that the remote database server is available over the corporate network. Try to *ping* the server from the client machine command shell by using the IP address or the host name of the database server. If no network or the server problem exists, you should generally see 0 percent packet loss. If the round-trip time is extremely high during the ping test, verify the number of hops and the time between hops from client to the server by using the command tracert (Windows) or traceroute (UNIX—root privilege is necessary).
2. Verify that the client can access the port to connect to the database instance on the server by using the Telnet command telnet <hostname/ipaddress> <portnumber>.
3. Verify that the remote database is available. Try connecting to the remote database at the server. If you cannot connect to the database locally, bring the database online and try connecting to it again from the client. If you can connect to the database locally, the problem is somewhere else.
4. Ensure that the remote database server is configured to receive incoming connections via the desired protocol. Make certain that the DB2COMM registry variable at both the client and the server have a matching value. (You can do this by executing the command db2set at both machines.) Verify that the svcename parameter of the DB2 database manager configuration file on the server has been assigned the correct name of the TCP/IP port that the database server will use to receive communications from remote clients, and ensure that the services file on the database server has a matching entry. Finally, make sure you run netstat | grep -i <servicename> to watch the DB2 listener state [ESTABLISHED, TIME_WAIT]. If other clients are having problems connecting to this server, chances are that the DB2COMM registry variable and/or the svcename configuration parameter have

been set incorrectly—or that the services file does not have a matching entry. If other clients can connect to the server, the problem lies somewhere else.

5. Verify that the node has been cataloged correctly at the client. Make sure the port number used to catalog the remote server has a matching entry in the services file on the remote server. (The easiest way to test this is by attaching to the node.)
6. Verify that the DCS database has been cataloged correctly at the client. If the remote database resides on a System z or System i server, it must have an entry in the DCS database directory. Check the DCS database directory to see whether the database has been cataloged correctly. (Make sure the local database alias and the remote database names specified were not accidently switched when the DCS database was cataloged; the target database name should refer to the subsystem's LOCATION name on z/OS.)
7. Verify that the database has been cataloged correctly at the client. A database must be cataloged in the system database directory on a client before connections can be made to it. Furthermore, if the remote database resides on a System z or System i server, you must catalog it in both the DCS database directory and the system database directory. Check the system database directory to see whether the database has been cataloged correctly. (Make sure the local database alias and the remote database/DCS database names specified were not accidently switched when the database was cataloged. Also, make sure there is a corresponding node entry in the node directory.)
8. Verify that DB2 Discovery has been configured correctly at the server. If you are trying to use DB2 Discovery and cannot locate a particular server, instance, or database, check the appropriate configuration parameters to determine whether DB2 Discovery requests can detect the server, instance, or database.

Chapter Summary

The objective of this chapter was to familiarize you with the following:

- The client/server communications methods and protocols available in DB2 Linux, UNIX, Windows, and DB2 for z/OS
- How to catalog and uncatalog remote nodes and remote databases
- How to control the behavior of the DB2 Discovery process by using configuration parameters
- The significance of FCM within the DB2 server
- How to register the DB2 node and the database with LDAP
- The common communications errors and ways to resolve them

On completion of this chapter, you will be equipped with sufficient knowledge to answer the communications and networking questions in the certification exam. It is also highly recommended that you complete the sample questions available at the end of the chapter.

Practice Questions

Question 1

Which command will successfully catalog a node for a Linux server that has the IP address 1080:0:0:0:8:800:200C:417A and an instance that is listening on port 50000?

❍ A. CATALOG TCPIP NODE rmt_server
REMOTE 1080:0:0:0:8:800:200C:417A
SERVER 50000
OSTYPE LINUX

❍ B. CATALOG TCPIP2 NODE rmt_server
REMOTE 1080:0:0:0:8:800:200C:417A
SERVER 50000
OSTYPE LINUX

❍ C. CATALOG TCPIP4 NODE rmt_server
REMOTE 1080:0:0:0:8:800:200C:417A
SERVER 50000
OSTYPE LINUX

❍ D. CATALOG TCPIP6 NODE rmt_server
REMOTE 1080:0:0:0:8:800:200C:417A
SERVER 50000
OSTYPE LINUX

Question 2

After applying a fix pack to a DB2 server, which two of the following commands should you execute to create new packages for the DB2 utilities and CLI/ODBC driver?

❒ A. BIND db2util.bnd BLOCKING ALL GRANT PUBLIC
❒ B. BIND @db2ubind.lst MESSAGES bind.msg GRANT PUBLIC
❒ C. BIND @db2cli.lst MESSAGES bind.msg GRANT PUBLIC
❒ D. BIND @db2odbc.lst MESSAGES bind.msg GRANT PUBLIC
❒ E. BIND db2schema.bnd BLOCKING ALL GRANT PUBLIC

Question 3

Which statement is true regarding client/server database connectivity?

- ❍ A. Remote connections can be made between the DB2 client and server by using Interprocess Communication (IPC).
- ❍ B. Loopback connections can be made by using the TCP/IP protocol between the client and server.
- ❍ C. The DB2 client running a lower version of DB2 can establish a local/remote connection to a DB2 server.
- ❍ D. A remote connection can be established between the DB2 client and server by using the TCPIP protocol.

Question 4

An instance named db2inst1 and a database named SAMPLE reside on a server named DB2SERVER1. Which two of the following commands must you execute before both the instance and the database can be detected by a DB2 discovery request?

- ❒ A. db2set DISCOVER_INST=ENABLE
- ❒ B. UPDATE DBM CFG USING DISCOVER_INST ENABLE
- ❒ C. db2set DISCOVER_DB=ENABLE
- ❒ D. UPDATE DB CFG FOR sample USING DISCOVER_DB ENABLE
- ❒ E. UPDATE DBM CFG USING DISCOVER_DATABASE ENABLE

Question 5

A DB2 for UNIX server has two instances named DB2INST1 and DB2INST2. Both the instances have a database named SAMPLE. What can you do to prevent a DB2 Discovery operation from detecting the DB2INST1 instance and its database SAMPLE?

- ❍ A. Set the DISCOVER_DB database configuration parameter for the database SAMPLE in the instance DB2INST1 to DISABLE.
- ❍ B. Set the DISCOVER DB2 Administration Server (DAS) configuration parameter on the client to DISABLE.
- ❍ C. Set the DISCOVER_DB database manager configuration parameter for the instance DB2INST2 to ENABLE.
- ❍ D. Set the DISCOVER_INST database manager configuration parameter for the instance DB2INST1 to DISABLE.

Question 6

Which database configuration parameter must you set to DISABLE to prevent clients from detecting a database with a DB2 discovery request?

- ❍ A. DISCOVER
- ❍ B. DISCOVERY
- ❍ C. DISCOVER_DB
- ❍ D. DISCOVER_DATABASE

Question 7

Although everyone else in the HR department can connect to a remote database named PAYROLL from their workstations, one employee cannot, even though he is supplying the correct user ID and password. What is most likely the cause of the problem?

- ❍ A. DB2COMM is not set correctly on the remote database server.
- ❍ B. DB2COMM is not set correctly on the employee's workstation.
- ❍ C. The PAYROLL database was not cataloged correctly on the server.
- ❍ D. The PAYROLL database was not cataloged correctly on the employee's workstation.

Question 8

No one in the HR department can connect to a remote database named PAYROLL from his or her workstation. Preliminary investigation shows that the network has no problems, the instance on the server is active, TCP/IP is running normally on both the clients and the servers, and users are trying to connect with valid user IDs and passwords. What is most likely the cause of the problem?

- ❍ A. DB2COMM is not set correctly on the remote database server.
- ❍ B. The remote instance's authentication type has not been set to CLIENT.
- ❍ C. The DAS has not been started on the remote database server.
- ❍ D. The PAYROLL database was not cataloged correctly on each employee's workstation.

Question 9

What are two types of DB2 Discovery requests that a client can make?

- ❒ A. KNOWN
- ❒ B. SEARCH
- ❒ C. HASHMAP
- ❒ D. LOOKUP
- ❒ E. TRUSTED

Question 10

While attempting to connect to a database named SAMPLE, which is a DB2 for z/OS database, from a Windows DB2 client, an employee received the following message: *SQL1013N The database alias name or database name "SAMPLE" could not be found.* Other employees in the same department can connect to the database without any problem. Close examination shows that the entries for the server and the database in the node and system database directories are the same on everyone's workstation. Which of the following actions should you perform to resolve the problem?

- ❍ A. Stop and restart the instance on the z/OS server.
- ❍ B. Uncatalog and recatalog the database in the system database directory.
- ❍ C. Catalog the database in the remote database directory.
- ❍ D. Catalog the database in the Database Connection Services (DCS) directory.

Question 11

In a DB2 Connect configuration between a UNIX client and a z/OS server, the following commands were executed:

```
CATALOG TCPIP NODE node001 REMOTE hostnm01.us.mycorp.com SERVER 446;
CATALOG DATABASE payroll AT NODE node001 AUTHENTICATION DCS;
```

Later, an error occurred while the client was trying to connect to the PAYROLL database in the DSN_DB_1 subsystem on the z/OS server. Close examination shows that the entry for the server in the node directory is correct and that the subsystem's LOCATION NAME on z/OS is DSN_DB_1. Which command, if executed, should resolve the problem?

- ❍ A. CATALOG DCS DATABASE dsn_db_1 AS payroll
- ❍ B. CATALOG DCS DATABASE payroll AS dsn_db_1
- ❍ C. CATALOG DCS DATABASE payroll_db AS payroll
- ❍ D. CATALOG DCS DATABASE payroll AS payroll_db AR dsn_db_1

Question 12

A database administrator obtained the following information about a UNIX DB2 server:

- Instance name: db2inst1
- Port number: 50001
- Service name: db2c_db2inst1
- Host name: db2server1
- Host TCP/IP address: 10.205.15.100
- DB2COMM=TCPIP
- Database name: SAMPLE

In an attempt to establish connectivity between a Windows DB2 client and the DB2 server, the following commands were executed from the Windows client:

```
CATALOG TCPIP NODE node001 REMOTE db2server1 SERVER 50001;
CATALOG DATABASE sample AT NODE node001;
```

However, when an attempt was made to connect to the database, an error occurred. Which action should you perform to resolve the problem?

❍ A. Catalog the database SAMPLE in the local database directory.
❍ B. Add the entry db2c_db2inst1 50001/tcp to the services file on the UNIX server.
❍ C. Catalog the database SAMPLE in the DCS directory.
❍ D. Add the entry DB2_db2inst1_0 10.205.15.100 to the services file on the UNIX server.

Question 13

A database administrator is attempting to catalog a DB2 for z/OS server from a DB2 for Linux, UNIX, and Windows server. The communications protocol that the DBA will use is TCP/IP. What should the administrator do if he or she cannot connect to a database on the DB2 for z/OS server?

❍ A. Ping the server where the DB2 for z/OS database resides and verify that the server has been cataloged correctly.
❍ B. Verify the process db2tcpcm is running on the server and that the server has been cataloged correctly.
❍ C. Verify that the Distributed Data Facility (DDF) is running and that the server has been cataloged correctly.
❍ D. Verify that the Distributed Connection Facility (DCF) is running and that the server has been cataloged correctly.

Question 14

Which two of the following items are *not* required to establish a TCP/IP connection to a DB2 for z/OS database from a DB2 for Linux, UNIX, and Windows server?

❒ A. Host name
❒ B. Port number
❒ C. Database name (target and local)
❒ D. Subsystem ID
❒ E. Logical Unit (LU)

Question 15

Which two server authentication methods are supported by transparent Lightweight Directory Access Protocol (LDAP)?

❒ A. CLIENT
❒ B. SERVER
❒ C. KERBEROS
❒ D. DATA_ENCRYPT
❒ E. KERBEROS_PLUGIN

Question 16

Which DB2 registry variable do you use to configure your DB2 instance to use transparent LDAP authentication?

❍ A. DB2AUTH
❍ B. DB2LDAPCACHE
❍ C. DIR_CACHE
❍ D. AUTHENTICATION

Answers

Question 1

The correct answer is **D**. Nodes (servers) are usually cataloged implicitly whenever a remote database is cataloged via IBM Data Studio. However, if you want to explicitly catalog (i.e., add an entry to the node directory for a particular server), you can do so by executing a CATALOG...NODE command that corresponds to the communications protocol that will access the server being cataloged. The syntax for the CATALOG TCPIP NODE command is:

```
CATALOG <ADMIN> [TCPIP | TCPIP4 | TCPIP6] NODE [NodeName]
REMOTE [IPAddress | HostName]
SERVER [ServiceName | PortNumber]
<SECURITY SOCKS>
<REMOTE INSTANCE [InstanceName]>
<SYSTEM [SystemName]>
<OSTYPE [SystemType]>
<WITH "[Description]">
```

where:

NodeName	Identifies the alias to assign to the node to be cataloged; this is an arbitrary name created on the user's workstation and is used to identify the node
IPAddress	Identifies the IP address of the server where the remote database that you are trying to communicate with resides
HostName	Identifies the host name, as it is known to the TCP/IP network (this is the name of the server where the remote database that you are trying to communicate with resides)
ServiceName	Identifies the service name that the DB2 database manager instance on the server uses to communicate
PortNumber	Identifies the port number that the DB2 database manager instance on the server uses to communicate
InstanceName	Identifies the name of the server instance to make an attachment to
SystemName	Identifies the DB2 system name used to identify the server workstation
SystemType	Identifies the type of operating system in use on the server workstation; the following values are valid for this parameter: AIX, WIN, HPUX, SUN, OS390, OS400, VM, VSE, and LINUX
Description	A comment that describes the node entry that will be made in the node directory for the node being cataloged; you must enclose the description in double-quotation marks

Thus, to catalog a node for a Linux server that has the IPv6 address 1080:0:0:0:8:800:200C:417A and an instance that is listening on port 50000, you would execute a CATALOG TCPIP NODE command that looks something like this:

```
CATALOG TCPIP NODE rmt_server
REMOTE 1080:0:0:0:8:800:200C:417A
```

```
SERVER 50000
OSTYPE LINUX
```

However, if you want to catalog a node for a Linux server that has the IPv4 address 192.0.32.67 and an instance that is listening on port 50000, you would execute a `CATALOG TCPIP NODE` command that looks like this:

```
CATALOG TCPIP NODE rmt_server
REMOTE 192.0.32.67
SERVER 50000
OSTYPE LINUX
```

Question 2

The correct answers are **B** and **C**. The file `db2ubind.lst` contains a list of the bind files (`.bnd`) needed to create packages for DB2's database utilities; the file `db2cli.lst` contains a list of the bind files (`.bnd`) required to create packages for the DB2 Call Level Interface (CLI) and the DB2 ODBC driver. When you execute these two commands, all messages that the `Bind` utility produces will be written to a file named `bind.msg`, and the group `PUBLIC` will receive `EXECUTE` and `BINDADD` privileges for each resulting package.

The `db2schema.bnd` bind file is used to create a package that provides system catalog function support and is often used with DB2 Connect.

Question 3

The correct answer is **D**. To establish a connection between the client and server systems, it is mandatory to pass the data packets over the network. The industry standard communications protocols are TCP/IP version 4 and version 6.

Interprocess Communication (IPC) does not support the data movement over the network; however, it supports data flow within the system internal process. The loopback connection is a connection made to a local database as if it were a remote database. This is basically used to troubleshoot connectivity problems. The command syntax to catalog loopback node and the database is:

```
CATALOG TCPIP NODE loopnode REMOTE myhostname SERVER db2c_DB2
CATALOG DATABASE sample AS LSAMPLE AT NODE loopnode
```

It is recommended that you run the DB2 client version equivalent to the DB2 server version to avoid functionality issues between the client driver and the server.

Question 4

The correct answers are **B** and **D**. If you set the `discover_inst` DB2 database manager configuration parameter to `ENABLE`, information about the corresponding instance will be returned in response to both search and known discovery requests. If you set the `discover_db` database configuration parameter to `ENABLE`, information about the corresponding database will be returned in response to both search and known discovery requests. DB2 database manager configuration parameters are set by executing the command UPDATE DBM CFG [*Parameter*] [*Value*]; database configuration parameters are set by executing the command UPDATE DB CFG FOR [DBAlias] USING [*Parameter*] [*Value*].

Question 5

The correct answer is **D**. If you set the discover_inst DB2 database manager configuration parameter for the instance DB2INST1 to DISABLE, information about the instance and the database will not be returned in response to a DB2 discovery request. If you set the discover_db database configuration parameter to DISABLE, then the database will not be returned in response to a DB2 discovery request; however, it does return the instance information. The discover DB2 administration server parameter must be set at the server level instead of at the client level.

Question 6

The correct answer is **C**. If you set the discover_db database configuration parameter to DISABLE, information about the corresponding database will not be returned in response to a DB2 discovery request. If the discover_inst DB2 database manager configuration parameter for the instance the database resides under has been set to DISABLE, then this is not required. If you set the discover_inst DB2 database manager configuration parameter to DISABLE, information about the corresponding instance will not be returned in response to a DB2 discovery request.

Question 7

The correct answer is **D**. To communicate with a server, each client must use some type of communications protocol recognized by the server. Likewise, each server must use some type of communications protocol to detect inbound requests from clients. Both clients and servers must be configured to use a communications protocol recognized by DB2.

Whenever you manually configure communications for a server, you must update the value of the DB2COMM registry variable before an instance can begin using the desired communications protocol. The value you assign to the DB2COMM registry variable will determine which communications managers to activate when a particular instance is started. (Setting the DB2COMM registry variable incorrectly may generate one or more errors when DB2 attempts to start protocol support during instance initialization.)

After you have configured a server for communications, any client that wishes to access a database on the server must contain additional entries for both the server and the remote database to the system database and node directories on the client. (You must also add entries to the DCS directory if the client intends to connect to a System z or System i database via DB2 Connect.) Entries are added to DB2's directories using a process known as *cataloging*.

In this example, because everyone else in the HR department can connect to the PAYROLL database, the DB2COMM registry variable must be set correctly on the server. The same is true about the way the PAYROLL database was cataloged on the server—since everyone else can connect to the database, the database must be cataloged correctly. The value assigned to the DB2COMM registry variable on the client has no effect because the node directory entry specifies the communications protocol and port number to use to connect to the server. So, that is not the problem either. Therefore, the problem must be that either the server (node) or the database has been cataloged incorrectly on the client.

Question 8

The correct answer is **A**. To communicate with a server, each client must use some type of communications protocol recognized by the server. Likewise, each server must use some type of communications protocol to detect inbound requests from clients. Both clients and servers must be configured to use a communications protocol recognized by DB2.

Whenever you manually configure communications for a server, you must update the value of the `DB2COMM` registry variable before an instance can begin using the desired communications protocol. The value you assign to the `DB2COMM` registry variable will determine which communications managers to activate when a particular instance is started.

In this example, because everyone in the HR department cannot connect to the `PAYROLL` database, the problem is most likely that the `DB2COMM` registry variable has not been assigned the value `TCPIP`.

Question 9

The correct answers are **A** and **B**. To process a discovery request, DB2 Discovery can use one of two methods: search or known. When you use the search discovery method, the entire network is searched for valid DB2 servers and databases, and a list of all servers, instances, and databases found is returned to the client, along with the communications information needed to catalog and connect to each one. In contrast, when you use the known discovery method, the network is searched for a specific server by using a specific communications protocol. (Because the client knows the name of the server and the communications protocol used by that server, the server is said to be "known" by the client.) Again, when the specified server is located, a list of all instances and databases found on the server is returned to the client, along with the information needed to catalog and connect to each one.

Question 10

The correct answer is **D**. To access a remote database from a client workstation, you must catalog the database in the system database directory of both the client and the server, *and* you must catalog the server workstation in the client's node directory. (The entry in the node directory tells the DB2 database manager how to connect to the server to obtain access to the database stored there.) Because the information required to connect to DRDA host databases is different from the information used to connect to LAN-based databases, information about remote host or System i databases is kept in a special directory known as the *Database Connection Services* (*DCS*) directory. If an entry in the DCS directory has a database name that corresponds to the name of a database stored in the system database directory, the specified application requester (which in most cases is DB2 Connect) can forward SQL requests to the database that resides on a remote DRDA server. If no record exists for a System z or System i database in the DCS directory, no database connection can be established.

Question 11

The correct answer is **B**. You catalog a DCS database by executing the CATALOG DCS DATABASE command. The syntax for this command is:

```
CATALOG DCS [DATABASE | DB] [Alias]
<AS [TargetName]>
<AR [LibraryName]>
<PARMS "[ParameterString]">
<WITH "[Description]">
```

where:

Alias	Identifies the alias of the target database to catalog; this name must match an entry in the system database directory associated with the remote node
TargetName	Identifies the name of the target host database to catalog (if the host database to catalog resides on an OS/390 or z/OS server, specify the *TargetName* to refer to a DB2 for z/OS subsystem identified by its LOCATION NAME or one of the alias LOCATION names defined on the z/OS server; to determine the LOCATION NAME, log in to TSO and issue the following SQL query by using one of the available query tools: SELECT CURRENT SERVER FROM SYSIBM.SYSDUMMY1)
LibraryName	Identifies the name of the application requester library to load and use to access the remote database listed in the DCS directory
ParameterString	Identifies a parameter string to pass to the application requestor when it is invoked; you must enclose the parameter string in double-quotation marks
Description	A comment that describes the database entry to make in the DCS directory for the database to be cataloged; you must enclose the description in double-quotation marks

Thus, if you want to catalog a DB2 for z/OS database residing in the DSN_DB_1 subsystem on the z/OS server that has the name PAYROLL_DB and assign it the alias PAYROLL, you would execute a CATALOG DCS DATABASE command that looks something like this:

```
CATALOG DCS DATABASE payroll
AS dsn_db_1
WITH "DB2 for z/OS LOCATION NAME DSN_DB_1"
```

Question 12

The correct answer is **B**. If you want to configure a server to use TCP/IP, you would perform the following steps (in any order):

Step 1: Assign the value TCPIP to the DB2COMM registry variable.

You assign the DB2COMM registry variable the value TCPIP by executing a db2set command that looks something like this:

```
db2set DB2COMM=TCPIP
```

Step 2: Assign the name of the TCP/IP port that the database server will use to receive communications from remote clients to the `svcename` parameter of the DB2 database manager configuration file. You set this parameter by executing an `UPDATE DATABASE MANAGER CONFIGURATION` command that looks something like this:

```
UPDATE DBM CFG USING SVCENAME db2c_db2inst1
```

Step 3: Update the services file on the database server, if appropriate.

The TCP/IP services file identifies the ports on which server applications will listen for client requests. If you specified a service name in the `svcename` parameter of the DB2 database manager configuration file, you must add the appropriate service name-to-port number/protocol mapping to the services file on the server. If you specified a port number in the `svcename` parameter, you do not need to update the services file.

The default location of the services file depends on the operating system used: on UNIX systems, the services file is named `services` and is located in the `/etc` directory; on Windows systems, the services file is located in `%SystemRoot%\system32\drivers\etc`. An entry in the services file for DB2 might look something like this:

```
db2c_db2inst1        50001/tcp
```

After you have configured a server for communications, any client that wishes to access a database on the server must contain additional entries for both the server and the remote database to the system database and node directories on the client.

In this example, because the server and database were cataloged correctly on the Windows client, the most likely cause of the problem was that the services file on the UNIX server lacked an entry for the DB2 service name and port.

Question 13

The correct answer is **C**. Once you have configured a server for communications, any client that wishes to access a database on the server must be configured to communicate with the server. To catalog a remote server using TCP/IP, you must provide, among other things, the host name as it is known to the TCP/IP network. (This is the name of the server where the remote database that you are trying to communicate with resides.) When you catalog a DB2 for z/OS remote server, the host name will appear in the DSNL004I message (DOMAIN=hostname) when the DDF is started—provided the target database has been set up for TCP/IP communications; the DDF is required for TCP/IP communications with DB2 on z/OS servers.

Question 14

The correct answers are **D** and **E**. Any client that wishes to access a database on a remote server must be configured to communicate with that server. But that is just the first step. You must add entries for both the server and the remote database to the system database and node directories on the client. You add entries to DB2's directories by using a process known as *cataloging*.

To explicitly catalog a remote server, you execute the `CATALOG ... NODE` command that corresponds to the communications protocol that will be used to access the server being cataloged.

To catalog a database, you execute the CATALOG DATABASE command. The syntax for the CATALOG TCPIP NODE command is:

```
CATALOG <ADMIN> [TCPIP | TCPIP4 | TCPIP6] NODE [NodeName]
REMOTE [IPAddress | HostName]
SERVER [ServiceName | PortNumber]
<SECURITY SOCKS>
<REMOTE INSTANCE [InstanceName]>
<SYSTEM [SystemName]>
<OSTYPE [SystemType]>
<WITH "[Description]">
```

where:

NodeName	Identifies the alias to assign to the node to be cataloged; this is an arbitrary name created on the user's workstation and is used to identify the node
IPAddress	Identifies the IP address of the server where the remote database that you are trying to communicate with resides
HostName	Identifies the host name as it is known to the TCP/IP network (this is the name of the server where the remote database that you are trying to communicate with resides)
ServiceName	Identifies the service name that the DB2 database manager instance on the server uses to communicate
PortNumber	Identifies the port number that the DB2 database manager instance on the server uses to communicate
InstanceName	Identifies the name of the server instance to make an attachment to
SystemName	Identifies the DB2 system name used to identify the server workstation
SystemType	Identifies the type of operating system in use on the server workstation; the following values are valid for this parameter: AIX, WIN, HPUX, SUN, OS390, OS400, VM, VSE, and LINUX.
Description	Specifies the comment that will describe the node entry to make in the node directory for the node being cataloged; you must enclose the description in double-quotation marks

The syntax for the CATALOG DATABASE command is:

```
CATALOG [DATABASE | DB] [DatabaseName]
<AS [Alias]>
<ON [Path] | AT NODE [NodeName]>
<AUTHENTICATION [AuthenticationType]>
<WITH "[Description]">
```

where:

DatabaseName	Identifies the name assigned to the database to be cataloged
Alias	Identifies the alias to assign to the database when it is cataloged
Path	Identifies the location (drive and directory) where the directory hierarchy and files associated with the database to catalog are physically stored

NodeName	Identifies the node where the database to catalog resides; the node name you specify must match an entry in the node directory file (i.e., it must correspond to a node that has already been cataloged)
AuthenticationType	Identifies where and how authentication is to take place when a user attempts to access the database; the following values are valid for this parameter: SERVER, CLIENT, SERVER_ENCRYPT, KERBEROS TARGET PRINCIPAL [*PrincipalName*] (where *PrincipalName* is the fully qualified Kerberos principal name for the target server), DATA_ENCRYPT, and GSSPLUGIN.
Description	Specifies the comment that will describe the database entry to make in the database directory for the database to be cataloged; you must enclose the description in double-quotation marks

Question 15

The correct answers are **B** and **D**. SERVER, SERVER_ENCRYPT, and DATA_ENCRYPT are the authentication methods supported by transparent LDAP. To configure transparent LDAP authentication on your DB2 instance:

1. Set the DB2 registry variable DB2AUTH to OSAUTHDB.
2. Set the authentication on the database server instance to any one of the following:
   - SERVER
   - SERVER_ENCRYPT
   - DATA_ENCRYPT
3. Use the default values for CLNT_PW_PLUGIN, GROUP_PLUGIN, and SRVCON_PW_PLUGIN database manager configuration parameters.
4. Restart the DB2 instance.

Question 16

The correct answer is **A**. To configure transparent LDAP authentication on your DB2 instance:

1. Set the DB2 registry variable DB2AUTH to OSAUTHDB.
2. Set the authentication on the database server instance to any one of the following:
   - SERVER
   - SERVER_ENCRYPT
   - DATA_ENCRYPT
3. Use the default values for CLNT_PW_PLUGIN, GROUP_PLUGIN, and SRVCON_PW_PLUGIN DBM CFG parameters.
4. Restart the DB2 instance.

You use the DB2 registry variable DB2LDAPCACHE and the database manager configuration parameter DIR_CACHE to configure the LDAP directory information caching at the client location.

DB2LDAPCACHE	DIR_CACHE	Caching Information
No	No	Connection always reads information from LDAP.
No	Yes	Connection information is read from LDAP once and stored in the DB2 memory cache.
Yes	Yes/No	Connection information is read from LDAP once and stored in the DB2 local database, node and DCS directories.

CHAPTER 10

DB2 10.5 Exam Crash Course

This chapter will bridge your DB2 10 knowledge to 10.5 PF4 (Cancun) and provide important information for configuring and managing DB2 servers, instances, and databases running DB2 10.5. It also explores in some detail the new features and enhancements introduced in V10.5.

The purpose of this chapter is to add to the knowledge and information gained from reading and studying the nine chapters before it. You will learn about many of the DB2 BLU Acceleration features designed to improve system availability and performance for business analytics solutions, as well as how to plan, design, configure, and manage columnar workloads (BLU).

This chapter will also cover significant advances in IBM DB2 cluster technology (pureScale), including a significant CF feature introduced in FP5 (provided in the fix pack after Cancun). In addition, you will learn how to install and configure the IBM Optim Query Workload Tuner to obtain expert recommendations for managing query workload performance in BLU environments, as well as how to properly deploy shadow tables.

Exam Objectives

- ✓ Demonstrate the ability to configure a DB2 workload for an analytics system
- ✓ Demonstrate the ability to use autonomic features in DB2 10.5 BLU Acceleration
- ✓ Demonstrate the ability to understand the new DB2 software packaging
- ✓ Demonstrate the ability to use configuration parameters introduced in 10.5
- ✓ Demonstrate the ability to understand the DB2 10.5 BLU Acceleration seven big ideas

- ✓ Demonstrate the ability to use expression-based indexes and statistics for those indexes
- ✓ Demonstrate the ability to understand new SQL enhancements
- ✓ Demonstrate the ability to understand and use new monitoring elements for BLU
- ✓ Demonstrate the ability to understand pureScale enhancements in DB2 10.5
- ✓ Demonstrate the ability to understand how shadow tables work and how to deploy them
- ✓ Demonstrate the ability to understand and use DB2 10.5 compression features
- ✓ Demonstrate the ability to understand `db2dsdriver.cfg`
- ✓ Demonstrate the ability to convert row-organized tables to columnar-organized tables
- ✓ Demonstrate the ability to understand DB2 Advanced Copy Services (ACS) customized scripts
- ✓ Demonstrate the ability to set up and configure DB2 JSON

DB2 Server Management

This section reviews specific DB2 10.5 enhancements that affect server management, with a focus on tasks and operations normally performed by server administrators.

Product Packaging

Starting with 10.5, IBM changed the product packaging for DB2. To fully understand the changes, remember these three easy points:

1. IBM reduced available packages from nine to six.
2. All packages with the word "Advanced" in the name contain all of the available features except the Advanced Recovery Feature, which is the only feature separately priced.
3. Enterprise and Workgroup Editions are packaged the same. Workgroup has size restrictions.

Table 10.1 shows a list of features in the Advanced Editions.

Table 10.1: Tools and features included in Advanced Editions	
BLU Acceleration	pureScale
Database Partitioning Feature	Optim Performance Manager
Optim Configuration Manager	pureQuery
WHS Design Studio	WHS SQL Warehouse Tool
WHS Mining and text Analytics	Cognos 10.2 (5 users)
WHS Cubing Services	MQ/CDC Replication

Table 10.1: Tools and features included in Advanced Editions (continued)	
Adaptive Compression	solidDB and solidDB UC
DB2 Connect	Continuous Data Ingest
Tivoli System Automation	SQL Replication
Optim Query Workload Tuner	Warehouse Model Packs
Work Load Manager	Data Architect (10 users)

If a feature is included on all products, it is not listed. For information about which package is right for your specific situation, please search under "DB2 Database Product Editions" in the IBM Knowledge Center for DB2 10.5 (*www-01.ibm.com/support/knowledgecenter*). To find features by editions in the IBM Knowledge Center for 10.5, search under "Functionality in DB2 feature and DB2 product editions."

Making Sense of It All

IBM DB2 has one shared cluster solution, called *pureScale*. Two product packages are licensed to run it: Advanced Enterprise Server Edition (AESE) with product identifier "db2aese" and Advanced Workgroup Server Edition (AWSE) with product identifier "db2awse". The Workgroup Server Edition (WSE) and Enterprise Server Edition (ESE) are row-organized, non-clustered products.

Starting with IBM DB2 pureScale 9.8 or 10.1, many features were licensed separately under the product Enterprise Server Edition ("db2ese"):

```
Product name:                    "DB2 Enterprise Server Edition"
License type:                    "CPU Option"
Expiry date:                     "Permanent"
Product identifier:              "db2ese"
Version information:             "10.1"
Enforcement policy:              "Soft Stop"
Features:
DB2 Storage Optimization:        "Not licensed"
DB2 pureScale:                   "Licensed"
```

Product packages "db2aese" and "db2awse" can run in three different modes: cluster (DSF), non-cluster (ESE), or partitioned (DPF):

```
Product name:                  "DB2 Advanced Enterprise Server Edition"
License type:                  "CPU Option"
Expiry date:                   "Permanent"
Product identifier:            "db2aese"
Version information:           "10.5"
Enforcement policy:            "Soft Stop"
```

Think of AESE-C or AWSE-C as the cluster mode product, also referred to as pureScale, and AESE or AWSE as the non-cluster mode product (ESE).

What applies to AESE-C also applies to AWSE-C but on a smaller scale, and what applies to AESE also applies to AWSE but on a smaller scale. Table 10.2 shows what solutions the product packages can run on.

Table 10.2: What can run DPF, BLU, or pureScale

Product Package and Mode	Identified in This Chapter As	BLU Capable	pureScale Capable	DPF Capable
Enterprise Server Edition	ESE	No	No	No
Workgroup Server Edition	WSE	No	No	No
Advanced Enterprise Server Edition with BLU	AESE	Yes	No	No
Advanced Enterprise Server Edition–Cluster	AESE-C	No	Yes	No
Advanced Enterprise Server Edition–Partitioned	AESE-D	No	No	Yes
Advanced Workgroup Server Edition with BLU	AWSE	Yes	No	No
Advanced Workgroup Server Edition–Cluster	AWSE-C	No	Yes	No
Advanced Workgroup Server Edition–Partitioned	AWSE-D	No	No	Yes

You can use the db2ls command to display all or only installed products and features on a server. Can you tell from the following example who installed the products? The command lists the installer's UID, which in this case is root. Now that DB2 products can be installed by nonroot, using db2ls to display such information may prove useful:

```
db2ls -a
```

Continued

```
Install Path             Level    Fix Pack   Install Date                     Installer UID
----------------------------------------------------------------------------------------
/opt/ibm/db2/V10.5       10.5.0.3   3a       Tue Jul 29 11:44:35 2014 CDT           0
/opt/ibm/db2/V10.5/FP4   10.5.0.4   4        Wed Aug 13 11:10:41 2014 CDT           0
/opt/ibm/db2/V10.5_01    10.5.0.4   4        Tue Aug 19 13:13:42 2014 CDT           0
```

The db2ls command provides additional information, such as the product package installed and the detail features that make up the package:

```
db2ls -q -p -b /opt/ibm/db2/V10.5_01

Install Path : /opt/ibm/db2/V10.5_01
Product Response File ID              Level    Fix Pack   Product Description
--------------------------------------------------------------------------------
DB2_SERVER_EDITION                  10.5.0.4     4        DB2 Server Edition

db2ls -q -b /opt/ibm/db2/V10.5

Install Path : /opt/ibm/db2/V10.5

Feature Response File ID              Level    Fix Pack   Feature Description
--------------------------------------------------------------------------------
BASE_CLIENT                         10.5.0.3    3a        Base client support
JAVA_SUPPORT                        10.5.0.3    3a        Java support
SQL_PROCEDURES                      10.5.0.3    3a        SQL procedures
BASE_DB2_ENGINE                     10.5.0.3    3a        Base server support
CONNECT_SUPPORT                     10.5.0.3    3a        Connect support
DB2_DATA_SOURCE_SUPPORT             10.5.0.3    3a        DB2 data source support
SPATIAL_EXTENDER_SERVER_SUPPORT     10.5.0.3    3a        Spatial Extender server
JDK                                 10.5.0.3    3a        IBM Software Development
LDAP_EXPLOITATION                   10.5.0.3    3a        DB2 LDAP support
INSTANCE_SETUP_SUPPORT              10.5.0.3    3a        DB2 Instance Setup
ACS                                 10.5.0.3    3a        Integrated Flash Copy
SPATIAL_EXTENDER_CLIENT_SUPPORT     10.5.0.3    3a        Spatial Extender client
```

Continued

```
COMMUNICATION_SUPPORT_TCPIP        10.5.0.3   3a    Communication support
APPLICATION_DEVELOPMENT_TOOLS      10.5.0.3   3a    Base application
DB2_UPDATE_SERVICE                 10.5.0.3   3a    DB2 Update Service
REPL_CLIENT                        10.5.0.3   3a    Replication tools
DB2_SAMPLE_DATABASE                10.5.0.3   3a    Sample database source
TEXT_SEARCH                        10.5.0.3   3a    DB2 Text Search
ORACLE_DATA_SOURCE_SUPPORT         10.5.0.3   3a    Oracle data source
FIRST_STEPS                        10.5.0.3   3a    First Steps
GUARDIUM_INST_MNGR_CLIENT          10.5.0.3   3a    Guardium Installation
```

If you want to display the location and content of the global registry, use the db2greg command (think of it as the software IRS):

```
==> db2greg -dump
S,DB2,9.8.0.5,/opt/IBM/db2/V9.8/FP5,,,5,0,,1341607379,0
V,DB2GPRF,DB2SYSTEM,srvxxdb2t001,/opt/IBM/db2/V9.8/FP5,
V,INSTPROF,db2blu01,/db2sd_20120706135722,-,-
V,DEFAULT_INSTPROF,DEFAULT,/db2sd_20120706135722,-,-
V,GPFS_CLUSTER,NAME,db2cluster_20120706135720.abc.com,-,DB2_CREATED
V,PEER_DOMAIN,NAME,db2domain_20120706135757,-,DB2_CREATED
S,GPFS,3.5.0.4,/usr/lpp/mmfs,-,-,0,0,-,1366409310,0
S,TSA,3.2.7.1,/opt/IBM/tsamp,-,-,0,0,-,1366409310,0
S,DB2,10.1.0.2,/opt/IBM/db2/V10/FP2,,,2,0,,1366409661,0
V,DB2GPRF,DB2SYSTEM,srvxxdb2t001,/opt/IBM/db2/V10/FP2,
I,DB2,10.1.0.2,db2blu01,/db/home/db2blu01/sqllib,,1,0,/opt/IBM/db2/V10/FP2,
V,DB2GPRF,DB2INSTDEF,db2blu01,/opt/IBM/db2/V10/FP2,
```

The -dump option shows the complete contents of the global registry. The above output is from a pureScale 9.8 FP5 deployment back in 2012. The server is srvxxdb2t001 and the instance is db2blu01.

The -g option displays the location of the global registry file:

```
db2greg -g
/var/db2/global.reg
```

The -getservrec option shows the details for that specific field, which in this case is the GPFS service:

```
db2greg -getservrec Service=GPFS
Retrieved record:
   Service      = |GPFS|
   Version      = |3.5.0.4|
   InstallPath = |/usr/lpp/mmfs|
   GCFModule    = |-|
   Comment      = |-|
   FixpackNum   = 0
   InstallerUID  = 0
   InterimFixLetter   = -
   Timestamp   = 1366409310
   SpecialInstallNumber   = 0
```

A Server for BLU

BLU Acceleration can run on any hardware or operating system that DB2 supports, but there are strengths and weaknesses for each. The definitive catch phrase for BLU server sizing has to be "go big or go home."

When selecting a platform, keep the following points in mind:

- More is better.
- The platform should allow more cores per socket.
- It should have more hardware threads per core.
- POWER8 has eight threads per core.
- The platform should have more memory (RAM).
- It should have more processor registers.
- POWER8 has 64 registers per core.
- Fast processors are better than slow ones.
- Virtual images can provide quick provisioning of resources, but you will need to be careful of virtualization limits.
- Virtual = Sharing and BLU is the proverbial bully, so be sure to set the maximum CPU/core and memory for the server.
- Appliances such as PureFlex or PureApplication provide quick provisioning and isolation as well as large disk storage volumes.

- You can run OLTP and analytical workloads on the same server, but it is best to isolate analytical workloads even from each other.
  - » **Option 1**: BLU and OLTP workloads on separate servers
    - This is the best option.
    - It minimizes risk to workloads.
    - You have fewer controls to manage, configure, and set up.
    - It offers the best security.
    - It provides ease of resource and capacity management.
  - » **Option 2:** One server with separate DB2 instances
    - This is a good option.
    - You set DB2 instance resources to guarantee each instance receives specific levels of server resources.
    - This option allows registry/instance controls you can manage, configure, and set up.
    - It offers good security.
    - It uses the local extract, transform, and load (ETL) process if OLTP is the source for BLU analytical data.
  - » **Option 3:** One server, one instance, one or more databases
    - You can implement this option, but it is not recommended.
    - It requires setting resource limits at the DB level.
    - Instance-level changes that require an instance cycle take down all databases along with the instance.
    - Instance upgrades affect all databases.
    - This option allows a join between OLTP (row) and BLU (column) tables.
    - One SQL query can access both table types without federation (one DB).
    - It uses ETL if OLTP is the source for BLU analytical data and the data is contained within one database.
    - This option enables single-instruction, multiple-data (SIMD) processing on the same server and instance where OLTP workloads might run.

On Linux systems, you can execute `cat /proc/cpuinfo | grep -i sse`. However, just because the processors have the vector instructions, this does not mean that software running on the server is using SIMD. You must set the compiler to enable vector instructions, and the software has to be written to take advantage of vector instructions.

If you create the DB2 instance and start it, it will inform you whether SIMD is enabled in the `db2diag.log`. Sizing a server for BLU workloads or for mixed workloads is not an exact science. This is a good reason to select a platform that you can expand. Start out small, somewhere between 16 and 24 cores with 64 to 128 GB of RAM, and build outward as you add workloads. Try to maintain an 8 GB per core RAM ratio as you expand the server.

BLU Autonomics

The BLU feature from IBM in DB2 10.5 is the first to be designed with autonomics. When originally released, pureScale required Automatic Storage Manager (ASM), but nothing else.

BLU automates configuration and operational settings with consideration given for varying server sizes. Much of the required workload-maintenance tasks for row-based workloads have been automated.

Configuration Autonomics

You can completely configure a BLU environment by setting a few configuration parameters. If you set the instance registry variable DB2_WORKLOAD=ANALYTICS, all databases created with this setting in place will have the following parameters:

```
Degree of parallelism                    (DFT_DEGREE)       = ANY
Default tablespace extentsize (pages)    (DFT_EXTENT_SZ)    = 4
Default table organization               (DFT_TABLE_ORG)    = COLUMN
Database page size                                          = 32768
```

Databases created before the registry setting change will have the row-based defaults and, if needed, will require manual modification.

To build a mix of row- and column-configured databases, begin with the instance configured for row. Build the row-based databases you need, set the DB2_WORKLOAD=ANALYTICS registry setting, and then restart the instance and create the database configured for column.

When running a DB2 instance with row- and column-organized databases, configure the database manager and database configuration settings for column workloads. Row workloads (OLTP) will run fine in a column-configured DB2 instance, but not vice versa.

The three critical database configuration settings for BLU workloads are SHEAPTHRES_SHR, SORTHEAP, and DATABASE_MEMORY, out of which DATABASE_MEMORY is set to AUTOMATIC. The DB2 database configuration manager will set the initial values for SHEAPTHRES_SHR and SORTHEAP based on server resources at the time of database creation.

On a 64 GB RAM server, set the database manager configuration, as follows:

```
SHEAPTHRES_SHR       = 1266237
SORTHEAP             = 63311
DATABASE_MEMORY      = AUTOMATIC (9729422)
```

However, on a 128 GB RAM server, you use these settings:

```
SHEAPTHRES_SHR          = 2581763
SORTHEAP                = 129088
DATABASE_MEMORY         = AUTOMATIC (13980817)
```

You must periodically review sort performance, with the goal being a standard service level for sorts. A good service level for sorts is 95 percent on one pass, meaning that 95 percent of all sorts are processed in memory and do not require disk storage. All sorting in the database is row based.

The recommended value for BLU workloads is 40–50 percent of the DATABASE_MEMORY value for SHEAPTHRES_SHR and 5–20 percent of SHEAPTHRES_SHR for SORTHEAP, depending on the number of concurrent sort requests, with 5 percent for a large number of concurrent sorts and 20 percent for a low number.

A good starting point for the 128 GB server in the previous example is:

```
SHEAPTHRES_SHR          = 5592326
SORTHEAP                = 671079
DATABASE_MEMORY         = AUTOMATIC (13980817)
```

Keep the instance configuration setting for SHEAPTHRES to 0, which is the preferred value. Remember, this setting manages more than sorts but includes all working memory. This will allow SHEAPTHRES_SHR to control both private and shared sort memory.

For BLU databases, the automatic maintenance settings are different from row-organized databases with the one exception being automatic reorganization (AUTO_REORG) = ON for column-organized databases. Two other recommended database configuration settings for statistics collection are AUTO_STATS_VIEWS and AUTO_SAMPLING, which you should turn on.

Proper statistics collection generally results in positive performance gains, but it is possible to have some negative results. Thus, monitor the performance of the workloads to ensure the impact is positive and make changes as required.

Operational Autonomics

The UTIL_HEAP_SZ is the third critical database setting. While columnar tables support full DML, data is primarily populated through the Load or Ingest utilities.

The Load utility for column tables has three phases. The first is the analysis phase, in which the entire input is processed for compression keys. The second and third phases are the same for all loads.

Note: INSTANCE_MEMORY or DATABASE_MEMORY does not restrict the UTIL_HEAP_SZ. Memory in the pool is released when it is no longer needed.

When you create a new database under DB2_WORKLOAD=ANALYTICS, the UTIL_HEAP_SZ is set to AUTOMATIC (<some size value>). On a 64 GB server, the initial setting is AUTOMATIC (827738), or 3.157 GB, and the default setting is 5 percent of RAM.

A good setting for a typical BLU installation is between four million and six million 4 KB pages. An undersized utility heap can significantly affect the compression efficiency of load processes and therefore the performance of BLU queries. When a load process begins, it acquires the full utility heap memory. If a second concurrent load is started, memory will be removed from the first load and given to the second load. This process will continue for the number of concurrent loads executed.

Statistical Collection

For column-organized tables, both compression and statistics are managed automatically and internally. It is not possible to turn them on or off. This is why when the compression dictionary or statistics are being initially seeded, it is important to process the entire data set.

Let us consider an example to understand the logic and effect. Assume you want to build a column-organized table and have 12 months of data, with each month being in one file. You could set up 12 load commands, one for each file, and use the LOAD INSERT command to load the data into your column-organized table.

This approach will certainly work; however, a better way is to load all 12 files by using one LOAD INSERT command. That way, the analysis phase of the LOAD command has the full breadth of data to review in making final compression key selections.

Statistical updates to the catalog representing the column-organized table will occur with each LOAD INSERT. Thus, the results should be an accurate representation of the data regardless of how it is loaded.

Space Management

It is well documented that with DB2_WORKLOAD=ANALYTICS set, disk storage space management is performed automatically for column-organized tables. Let us look at how this works and what it does.

DB2 has for a long time performed what is called *logical deletion* of rows. This is different from *pseudodeletion*, because in logical deletion, the space occupied by the deleted row on the data page can be overwritten with an inserted row, while pseudodeleted rows are not available until additional cleanup operations are performed.

For column-organized tables, data is pseudodeleted; for row organized tables, it is logically deleted. Thus, for column-organized tables, space reclaims are performed at the extent level, and the extent space is returned to the table space for use with any defined table.

Note: When you set AUTO_MAINT and AUTO_REORG database configuration settings to ON, space reclamations are performed for column-organized tables automatically.

For information regarding building and managing table spaces, see the "Physical Design" section later in the chapter. You can find information about utilities specific to management of table spaces and tables in the "Utilities: Converting Row Tables to Column" section.

Autonomic Workloads

The WLM settings are automatically defined for all databases created. However, the settings are enabled by default only for columnar default databases. Remember as you read this that all databases have these objects defined:

- Two workloads are defined: one for administration activities and one for user queries. These are SYSDEFAULTUSERWORKLOAD and SYSDEFAULTADMWORKLOAD with evaluation orders of 1 and 2, respectively.
- A work action set named SYSDEFAULTUSERWAS is created with an action name called SYSMAPMANAGEDQUERIES and a work class called SYSMANAGEDQUERIES and assigned to the service superclass named SYSDEFAULTUSERCLASS, to which everything except administration workloads default.

The work class set (WCS) basically identifies all read workloads that have a timeron cost greater than 150000, and this is evaluation order 1. A timeron is a relative unit of measure determined by the DB2 Optimizer based on internal cost values as a weighted sum of I/O and processor costs.

To establish a usage-based concurrent query threshold of <*n*>, use SYSDEFAULTCONCURRENT where <*n*> is determined by the number of cores at the time of database creation. Concurrent requests over <*n*> are queued up. If the instance is deployed on virtual hardware and the size of the image changes after the database is created, use AUTOCONFIGURE APPLY NONE to obtain new recommendations:

```
Current and Recommended Values for System WLM Objects

Description                                     Current Value       Recommended Value
------------------------------------------------------------------------------------
Work Action SYSMAPMANAGEDQUERIES Enabled        = Y                 Y
Work Action Set SYSDEFAULTUSERWAS Enabled       = Y                 Y
Work Class SYSMANAGEDQUERIES Timeroncost        = 1.50000E+05       1.50000E+05
Threshold SYSDEFAULTCONCURRENT Enabled          = Y                 Y
Threshold SYSDEFAULTCONCURRENT Maxvalue         = 15                15
```

You can use the ALTER THRESHOLD command to apply a new value. For example:

```
ALTER THRESHOLD SYSDEFAULTCONCURRENT WHEN CONCURRENTDBCOORDACTIVITIES > 18
   STOP EXECUTION;
```

For row-organized databases, this threshold is disabled, but for column-organized databases, it is enabled. Remember, if you set DB2_WORKLOAD=ANALYTICS and a database is created, this concurrent threshold will be enabled even for row-based workloads. The idea is that 150,000 timerons will prevent most row workloads from being selected. The opposite is also true, meaning DB2_WORKLOAD=<blank> is set and you manually change the database manager and database configuration. However, this concurrent threshold would be disabled, requiring you to alter and enable it manually.

The pureScale Model

The *pureScale feature* is now installable on commodity hardware with supported versions of UNIX, but again there are strengths and weaknesses for each. The two main differences between the varying architectures are interconnect communications and member recovery.

Three supported interconnect communications methods are available:

- RDMA protocol over an InfiniBand (IB) network
- RDMA protocol over a Converged Ethernet (RoCE) network
- TCP/IP protocol over an Ethernet (TCP/IP) network

The order in which these methods are listed is also the order of performance. Remote Direct Memory Access (RDMA) is a set of instructions that allows servers to access each other's memory. It is fast and cheap.

Note: InfiniBand offers the lowest latency and highest bandwidth with RDMA support. Some Ethernet adapters support RDMA and some do not.

So the question is, how will you run transactional workloads?

Best fit means workloads will find the best place to run in the cluster. Connections and transactions will load-balance across the entire cluster. *Control* means workloads will be assigned to specific members within the cluster. This configuration can be one of two options: Active or Active/Standby. Table 10.3 compares best-fit workloads with control workloads.

Table 10.3: Best-fit versus control workloads

Consideration	Best-fit	Control
Capacity Management:		
Cluster	Yes	No
Server	N/A	Yes
HADR Active/Standby configuration	N/A	Yes
Cluster resource aware	Yes	N/A
Availability Management:		
Cluster	Yes	N/A
Server	N/A	Yes
Highest reliability level	Yes	No
Highest interconnect communication level	Yes	No
Add Member—workloads automatically rebalance	Yes	No
Drop Member—workloads automatically rebalance	Yes	No
Server Upgrade—hardware or OS—no workload impact	Yes	Maybe

When selecting a platform to run pureScale, remember the following points:

1. RDMA is required for any best-fit environment in which performance is important.
2. Ethernet is slower than InfiniBand and has less bandwidth.
3. PureData does not have a Power version. PureFlex does.
4. PureData does not support cluster communication load-balancing. PureFlex can be set up with load balancing.
5. PureData comes preconfigured for pureScale.
6. PureFlex must be configured.
7. PureApplication cannot run pureScale.
8. Do-it-yourself (DIY) cluster offers the greatest reward but with the highest risk.
9. You get what you pay for. There is no shortcut to building a HA/performing pureScale cluster.

10. Virtualization is not the same as logical partitioning (LPAR). By definition, virtualization is the hardware sharing of multiple images. Virtualization requires VIO and N-Port ID Virtualization (NPIV) deployment because it means sharing I/O cards, Ethernet cards, and internal BUS across multiple images.

    You can configure LPARs to also share hardware and require VIO and NPIV deployment. However, given enough hardware, you can configure multiple partitions that share nothing except power to the server. Figure 10.1 shows a pureScale cluster built on LPARs.

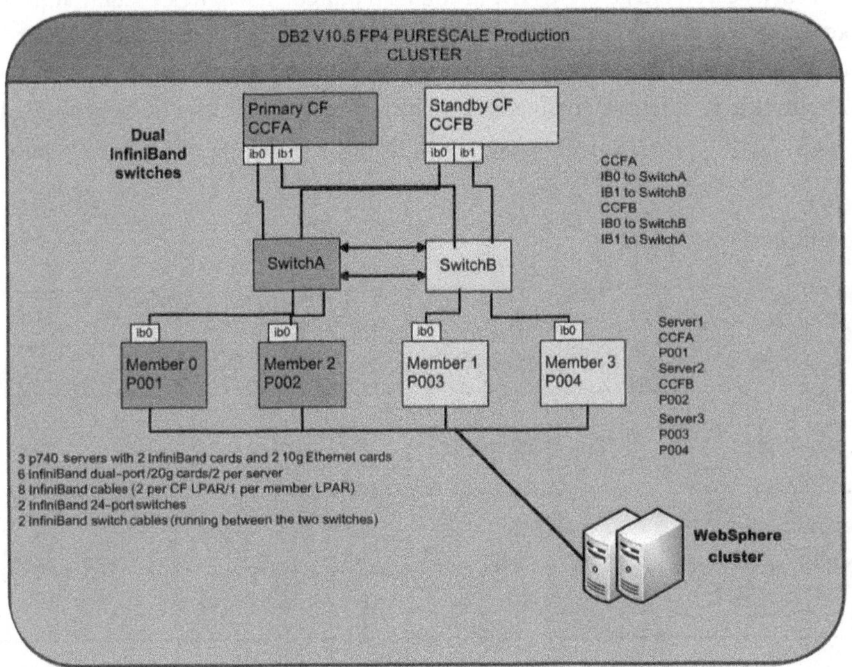

Figure 10.1: pureScale cluster built on LPARs

Installing DB2

You can apply one method of installation for DB2 whether you are building a single instance or a pureScale cluster. This will allow you to follow the same general process for both pureScale and non-pureScale deployments. The software bundles are deployed as a separate operation from the creation of the instance.

Preinstallation Information

The DB2 install bundle can come in different forms, such as a zip file download, a DVD, or an ISO file. This software install bundle is copied to the target server and unzipped.

On UNIX systems, DB2 product installations are no longer operating system packages. Therefore, you can no longer use tools like rpm and installp. The file could be placed in /opt/ibm/db2, in a separate location like /tmp, or in something you created such as /ibm/software.

On UNIX systems, the db2setup program will require the following:

- /tmp requires 2 GB of free space
- /var requires 2 GB of free space (pureScale)

You need to create the UNIX accounts and groups in support of this installation.

As root on each server, create the UNIX accounts required. Though not required, it is a good idea to make the UID and GID settings the same for these accounts across every server in the pureScale cluster. Non-pureScale clusters have only one server, so there is no concern.

To install pureScale, run these commands on one server in the cluster and obtain the GID and UID values. Then for all the other servers, add the parameters -G for groupadd and -U for useradd.

Step 1: Add the UNIX group:

```
Location /opt/ibm/db2/V10.5_02
UNIX Prompt: ==> groupadd <INSTANCE GROUP>
```

Step 2: Add the UNIX ID for the DB2 instance:

```
Location /opt/ibm/db2/V10.5_02 :
UNIX Prompt: ==> useradd -d /db/home/<DB2INSTANCE> -G <INSTANCE GROUP>
                 -p <PASSWORD> -s <UNIX SHELL> <DB2INSTANCE>
```

Step 3: Add the UNIX group for the fenced user:

```
Location /opt/ibm/db2/V10.5_02/FP4/instance :
UNIX Prompt: ==> groupadd <FENCED GROUP>
```

Step 4: Add the UNIX ID for the fenced user:

```
Location /opt/ibm/db2/V10.5_02/FP4/instance :
UNIX Prompt: ==> useradd -d /db/home/<FENCED USER> -G <FENCED GROUP>
                 -p <PASSWORD> -s <UNIX SHELL> <FENCED USER>
```

Step 5: Set the passwords to never expire and ulimits to unlimited for <DB2INSTANCE> and <FENCED USER> accounts.

Step 6: Set the kernel settings on each server as required.

db2setup Information

The GUI mode is the preferred method of installing DB2. Running in GUI mode from a remote Windows laptop requires setting the DISPLAY variable. For example, "export DISPLAY=<hostname>:10,0" where <hostname> is the database server host name where you want to install the software. In some cases, 'localhost' is allowed.

On the UNIX server, edit the "/etc/ssh/sshd_config" file, as follows:

```
X11DisplayOffset 10
X11UseLocalhost yes
X11Forwarding yes
```

To execute db2setup, you must have an SSH client. Cygwin (*www.cygwin.org*), an open-source product, provides full UNIX shell functionality on Windows. You start an XWin service in which to run xterm and, from within an xterm window, execute "ssh <user>@<hostname>" to access the remote server.

A nice feature of Cygwin XWin is that when you execute SSH to access the remote server, XWin will set the DISPLAY variable automatically.

Putty (*www.putty.org*) is another open-source tool that provides a remote SSH client interface for accessing UNIX servers from Windows. Let us look at the installation steps for using Cygwin 1.11.2. (*x.cygwin.com*):

1. Start XServer (this provides X11).
2. Start an xterm session.
3. Right-click XServer and select Applications, then Xterm.
4. Execute from the command line "ssh root@<servername or IP>".
5. Execute from the command line "env | grep -i display" to see whether the DISPLAY variable is set. If the DISPLAY variable is set, you are ready to execute "db2setup".

Note: The UNIX server must have X11 installed. For example, on Linux systems you can run "yum grouplist" to see which group packages are installed. On Redhat, the best way to install X11 is to install just the group Desktop by running the command "yum -y groupinstall "Desktop"".

Response File (Silent) Mode

If you want to install DB2 by using a response file, run the db2setup -r <rsp.file> command. Currently, both db2setup and db2_install methods are supported, but because db2setup is the preferred method, it is the only one presented here. The db2_install method is deprecated and could be removed in a future release.

Within the execution of db2setup, it is possible to perform all the necessary steps to create the DB2 instance for both AESE-C and AESE environments. Even if you select this method, it is a good idea to know how to create a DB2 instance apart from any software installation.

The Installation Process

Step 1: Obtain and place the required DB2 installation bundle on the target server. If you do not have the software, you can download it from *www-01.ibm.com/software/data/db2/linux-unix-windows/downloads.html.*

Step 2: Place the DB2 installation bundle on the server at the location where the contents are to be unzipped. For UNIX, place the file in the location where you want to unzip it. Database Services Flexible Architecture (DSFA) guidelines recommend using /db/admin/tmp and creating a directory at this location for the specific release. If you are installing FP4, place the zip file at /db/admin/tmp/db2/V10.5/fp4.

For Windows, you do the same thing as recommended for UNIX. This example uses the D drive; however, you can use any drive besides C. The mount point db is created under the D drive. The folder admin\tmp is created, and the zip file is placed at this location and unzipped.

You have now set up the DB2 data server on Windows by using basically the same standards as UNIX.

Execute "gunzip <zip file from IBM>" to unzip the file, or on Windows you extract the contents to this location. On UNIX, the contents should look something like this:

```
db2  db2checkCOL_readme.txt  db2checkCOL.tar.gz  db2ckupgrade  db2_deinstall
db2_install  db2ls  db2prereqcheck  db2setup  ibm_im  installFixPack  nlpack
```

Step 3: Before running db2setup or the Windows setup program, execute the db2prereqcheck command to make sure you have met the server requirements for running DB2.

Step 4: Install the DB2 software by using db2setup. To install the DB2 software on each server in the same location, you will use a response file. The response file may be different depending on what you will install.

The response file that installs everything looks like this:

```
PROD=DB2_SERVER_EDITION
LIC_AGREEMENT=ACCEPT
FILE=/opt/ibm/db2/V10.5
INSTALL_TYPE=COMPLETE
```

However, a response file that performs a basic installation looks like this:

```
PROD=DB2_SERVER_EDITION
LIC_AGREEMENT=ACCEPT
FILE=/opt/ibm/db2/V10.5
INSTALL_TYPE=TYPICAL
```

The command executed on the server by user "root" is `db2setup -r <rsp.file>`.

Step 5: Create the DB2 instance.

For non-pureScale deployments, you can create instances on the server by using this command:

```
db2icrt -s ese -u <fenced_user> <instance_name>
```

You must create the UNIX or Windows accounts *<fenced_user>* and *<instance_name>* before running the above command.

For pureScale only, follow these steps:

Step 1: Perform steps 1–4 on all servers in the cluster.

You can use the following response file:

```
PROD=DB2_SERVER_EDITION
LIC_AGREEMENT=ACCEPT
FILE=/opt/ibm/db2/V10.5
INSTALL_TYPE=COMPLETE
```

Step 2: Create a pureScale instance.

The server (Member) where you execute the db2icrt command is called the *initial install host* (*IIH*). Let us run the commands db2icrt and db2iupdt once for each new member to add, plus the second standby cluster facility (CF).

Assume you have the following set of servers:

```
CFSERVER1     CF128 Primary CF Server
CFSERVER2     CF129 Secondary CF Server
MEMSERVER1    DB2 Member 0
MEMSERVER2    DB2 Member 1
MEMSERVER3    DB2 Member 2
```

On each server, make sure the /etc/hosts file is the same across them all. Placing these entries in the /etc/hosts file allows the servers to resolve the names without an external DNS server. Just be sure you modify these in the event that either an IP address or name change occurs.

```
# List of hosts in DB2 pureScale cluster
114.37.132.1 cfserver1.<domain> cfserver1
114.37.132.2 cfserver2.<domain> cfserver2
114.37.132.3 memserver1.<domain> memserver1
114.37.132.4 memserver2.<domain> memserver2
114.37.132.5 memserver3.<domain> memserver3
# List of RoCE adapters in DB2 pureScale cluster
10.100.1.1 cfserver1-roce0.<domain> cfserver1-roce0
10.100.2.1 cfserver1-roce1.<domain> cfserver1-roce1
10.100.1.2 cfserver2-roce0.<domain> cfserver2-roce0
10.100.2.2 cfserver2-roce1.<domain> cfserver2-roce1
10.100.1.3 memserver1-roce0.<domain> memserver1-roce0
10.100.2.3 memserver1-roce1.<domain> memserver1-roce1
10.100.1.4 memserver2-roce0.<domain> memserver2-roce0
10.100.2.4 memserver2-roce1.<domain> memserver2-roce1
10.100.1.5 memserver3-roce0.<domain> memserver3-roce0
10.100.2.5 memserver3-roce1.<domain> memserver3-roce1
```

Note: Some sources use -ib to represent RDMA over InfiniBand versus the Ethernet -roce. Our example will use Ethernet. The diagram in the pureScale model contains an InfiniBand design example.

Before running the db2icrt command, you need two GPFS drives: one for INSTANCE_SHARE and the other for the TIEBREAKER disk. Also make sure the <fenced user> and <instance name> UNIX accounts with the same UID and GID are created across all servers before running the db2icrt and db2iupdt commands.

On server MEMSERVER3, as the root user, execute the following command:

```
db2icrt -s dsf -cf CFSERVER1 -cfnet CFSERVER1-roce0, CFSERVER1-roce1
-m MEMSERVER3 -mnet MEMSERVER3-roce0, MEMSERVER3-roce1
-instance_share_dev /dev/hdisk6
-tbdev /dev/hdisk3
-u <fence_user>
<instance_name>
```

Now run the db2iupdt command to add the other members and the second CF:

```
db2iupdt -d -add -m MEMSERVER1:MEMSERVER1-roce0,MEMSERVER1-roce1
<instance_name>
db2iupdt -d -add -m MEMSERVER2:MEMSERVER2-roce0,MEMSERVER2-roce1
<instance_name>
db2iupdt -d -add -cf CFSERVER2:cfserver2-roce0,cfserver2-roce1
<instance_name>
```

Managing Access to the Database Server

DB2 relies on the operating system to authenticate users. Authentication can occur through the local operating system or through a single sign-on (SSO) solution like Microsoft Active Directory or IBM Tivoli Identity Manager.

Regardless of the tools you use to manage DB2, you must decide which accounts to require, and then based on the tools, determine how to define and manage those accounts.

Four basic categories of access are available for any database:

1. **Service category**. This pertains to those who service the database environments and are responsible for its continued support. These are generally administrators or specialized service providers such as monitoring or backup/restore.
2. **Development category**. This relates to those who build and support the applications that use the database. The rights of this group can vary from environment to environment and from company to company. This group generally will have read-only access to data in production and, in some cases, might be restricted to only specific columns. In development environments, this group might have full DML-level access but limited DDL access.
3. **Application category**. These are the applications that access the database. Access rights are typically determined by design decisions and corporate policies. Most companies, for example, have policies restricting any DDL operations from within deployed application code. Users in this case obtain access to the application, and the application accesses the database. Whatever tested features are deployed within the application are available to its authorized users.
4. **Power user category**. These are users who access the database directly, usually through some supported client interface. In many cases, these users are running untested SQL queries directly against production databases. This category is by far the most difficult to manage and is probably the category of highest focus today. The whole concept of "free the data" centers on getting information into the hands of decision makers within any organization.

Groups, Roles, User IDs

A user ID is the string that identifies the user to the database, as in the command line statement "`db2 connect to DB1 user <userid>`". The operating system authenticates this user ID through a DB2 program named `db2ckpw`. A UNIX or Windows login account is a user ID in this context.

When you define a user ID, you assign it to one or more groups. Groups are defined to identify a collection of users that have the same general role or responsibility. In the following UNIX example, the user ID is `db2inst1` and has been assigned to three groups: `db2inst1` (primary) and `dba` and `db2das` (secondary). This is true on Windows systems as well.

```
uid=508(db2inst1) gid=510(db2inst1) groups=510(db2inst1),500(dba),505(db2das)
```

The DBA can assign access rights in the database either to `db2inst1` (user) or to any or all three of the groups (`db2inst1`, `dba`, `db2das`). Again in this context, a database group is equal to a UNIX or Windows group. On Windows, for example, two important groups are created when DB2 is installed: DB2ADMNS and DB2USERS.

Within the database, it is possible to assign users or groups to roles. For example, you could set up the role SP_ADM with the necessary rights to manage stored procedures but only in specific schemas:

```
CREATE ROLE SP_ADM@
COMMENT ON ROLE SP_ADM IS 'Manages Stored Procedures'@
GRANT CONNECT, SQLADM ON DATABASE TO ROLE SP_ADM@
GRANT CREATEIN, DROPIN, ALTERIN ON SCHEMA PAYROLL TO ROLE SP_ADM@
```

Once the role is defined, you can assign it to users or groups.

The "Physical Design" section later in this chapter discusses this more in depth. At this point, understand that you can group accounts in many ways. For example, you can group all PAYROLL DB users into a group called PAYROLL_USERS. All DBAs supporting database PAYROLL can be grouped and called PAYROLL_DBADM. This will allow the DBA to control access rights at the group level.

Creating the Group and User IDs for One DB2 Instance

As root, <db2instance> is the UNIX user ID (SYSADM) that runs all the DB2 system processes, <db2edu> is the UNIX user ID that runs all fenced processes, and <db2group> is the UNIX management group that supports all DB2 processes.

In the following example, use:

- db2inst1 as the DB2 instance (DB2INSTANCE)
- db2fenc1 as the DB2 fenced account (DB2EDU)
- dbagrp as the UNIX group to which all DBAs are assigned

Step 1: Create the HOME directory:

```
mkdir -p /db/home/db2inst1
mkdir -p /db/home/db2fenc1
```

Step 2: Create UNIX accounts and groups as required.

On AIX (smitty is a very good admin tool), add group dbagrp: "mkgroup -'A' dbagrp" or "smitty group".

Next, add user db2inst1: "smitty user", or use the following command:

```
"mkuser pgrp='dbagrp' home='/db/home/db2inst1'
shell='/bin/ksh' gecos='DB2 Instance Owner' "
```

To add user db2fenc1, execute this command:

```
"mkuser pgrp='dbagrp' home='/db/home/db2fenc1' shell='/bin/ksh'
gecos='DB2 EDU Owner' "
```

On Linux, add group db2grp: "groupadd db2grp", and then add user db2inst1:

```
"useradd -d /db/home/db2inst1 -G dbagrp -s /bin/ksh db2inst1"
```

Now add user db2fenc1:

```
"useradd -d /db/home/db2fenc1 -G dbagrp -s /bin/ksh db2fenc1"
```

Step 3: Set the password for the new accounts:

```
passwd db2inst1
passwd db2fenc1
```

Step 4: Set passwords to never expire for both users.

Step 5: Set ulimit settings to unlimited for both users.

BLU Technology

This section presents the seven base technologies that deliver IBM DB2 BLU Acceleration:

- Columnar-organized data
- In-memory
- SIMD
- Compression
- Buffer pool manager
- Multi-core parallelism
- Data skipping

Because more competing ideas and strategies are available today, knowing what not to do is often more important than knowing what to do. So this section will look closely at different solutions and provide some key points to help you make informed decisions.

Columnar-Organized Data

DB2 organizes data as rows or as columns. A single data page will contain data from one table organized by rows or from one column, as Figure 10.2 and Figure 10.3 show.

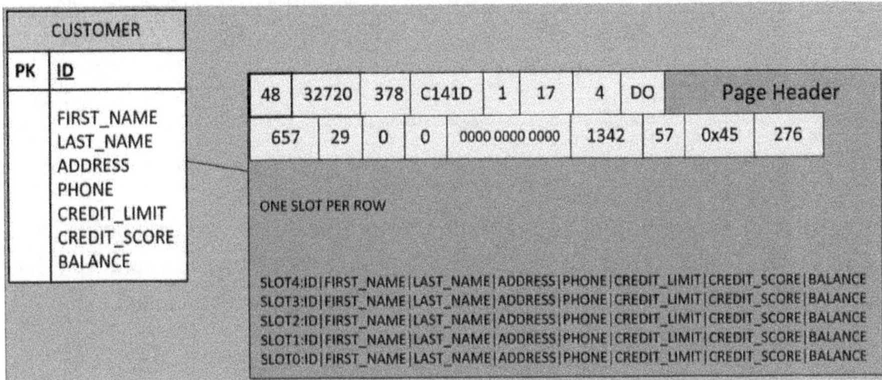

Figure 10.2: Row-organized data

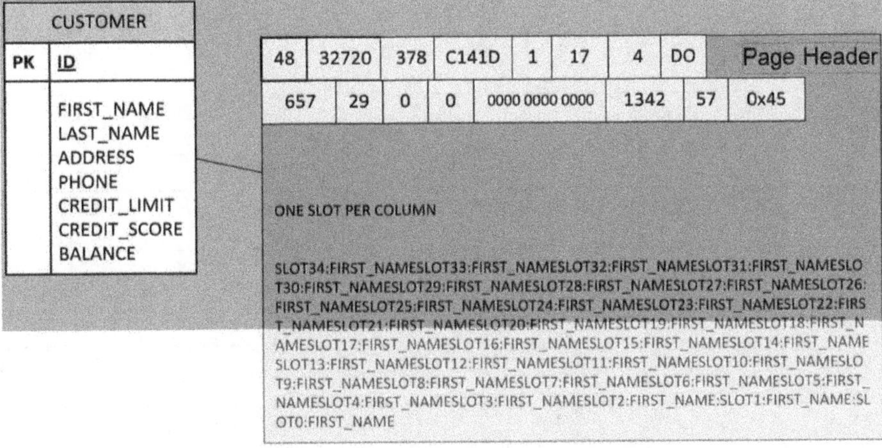

Figure 10.3: Column-organized data

Data is deleted or inserted but never updated in a column-organized table. The currently committed (CC) isolation level is supported in column-organized pages by keeping track of both current and previous copies of the slot. Table 10.4 displays the contents of a data page.

Table 10.4: Contents of a data page			
BPS Page Header	**Data Page Header**	**Row Slot**	**Column Slot**
PAGE OFFSET	SLOT COUNT	Offset location	Offset location
PAGE LENGTH	FREE SPACE	Record length	Record length
LSN	TOTAL RESERVE SPACE	Compressed record	Record type (Multiple types)
OBJECT PAGE NUMBER	YOUNGEST RESERVE SPACE	Actual length	Flags
POOL PAGE NUMBER	TID	Record type (FIXEDVAR)	Ordinal
OBJECT ID	FREE SPACE OFFSET	Flags	Records
OBJECT TYPE	MAX RECORD SIZE		Prev RID
	DPG FLAGE		Next RID
	PAGE DICTIONARY SLOT		

So if you convert a row-organized table to column, will the number of data pages increase or decrease? The answer is that it depends largely on the number of rows and columns in the table. TABLE1, TABLE2, and TABLE3 saw a sharp reduction in the number of pages, while TABLE4 has a very small increase. You can see the actual tables in Table 10.5.

Table 10.5: Actual tables (FP3a)											
Table	**Column Count**	**Pages with Rows**	**Row Count**	**Avg Row Size**	**Max Row Size**	**PCT Rows Comp**	**PCT Pages Saved**	**M PGS**	**Col Object Size (KB)**	**Data Object Size (KB)**	**Index Object Size (KB)**
ROW_ TABLE1	6	352	309,064	31	492	99.98	59	0		11,520	5504
COL_ TABLE1	6	134	309,064	-1	-1	-1	14	596	73,728	32,768	16,384
ROW_ TABLE2	7	37	48,411	20	190	98	66	0	0	1,408	1,152
COL_ TABLE2	7	14	48,411	-1	-1	-1	63	24	81,920	16,384	16,384
ROW_ TABLE3	11	9	5,372	40	268	100	57	0		512	512
COL_ TABLE3	11	13	5,372	-1		-1	0	9	114,688	16,384	16,384
ROW_ TABLE4	40	361,370	137,671,308	81	317	100	55	0		18,108,800	2,635,520
COL_ TABLE4*	20*	152,296	137,671,308	-1	-1	-1	69	10	5,136,384	16,384*	24,576

The row and column tables for TABLE1, TABLE2, and TABLE3 are identical. No changes were made; they were just organized differently. The column encoding percentages were 100 percent, with the exception of the unique column identifier, which was populated by using the GENERATE_UNIQUE() function. The reason is that CHAR() and VARCHAR() were not supported in FP3a (see FP4 in Table 10.6).

Column-organized TABLE3 was not built as a straight copy. The row-organized TABLE4 was normalized into two different columnar tables. ROW_TABLE4 contained both measures and characteristics, therefore normalizing the data into a dimension column table and a fact column table. The entire process took fewer than eight hours and loaded both tables at around 8 MB rows per minute.

Table 10.6: Actual tables (FP4)

Table	Column Count	Pages with Rows	Row Count	PCT Rows Compressed	PCT Pages Saved	MPAGES	Col Object Size(KB)	Data Object Size(KB)	Index Object Size(KB)
COL_TABLE4_ FACT	24	188,944	137,671,308	-1	66	6	5,234,688	16,384	24,576

With FP4, you get all data types for the synopsis table with CHAR() and VARCHAR() up to 1,000 characters. Table 10.7 shows the column-organized tables built in FP4. Notice the increases in MPAGES and the increases in pages saved.

Table 10.7: Actual tables with increased MPAGES (FP4)

Table	Column Count	Pages with Rows	Row Count	PCT Rows Compressed	PCT Pages Saved	MPAGES	Col Object Size(KB)
COL_TABLE1	6	119	309,064	-1	19	569	73,728
COL_TABLE2	11	13	5,372	-1	0	9	114,688
COL_TABLE3	7	14	48,411	-1	63	24	81,920
COL_TABLE4	20	145,491	137,671,308	-1	71	33	4,759,552
COL_TABLE4_ FACT	24	177,012	137,671,308	-1	68	33	5,783,552

In Memory

In the world of databases, everything takes place in memory with the exception of external LOBs. So exactly what does *in memory* mean and how is it different?

Memory is a layered resource that becomes more expensive and less resident the closer it gets to the processor. Access speeds to L3 cache are 15 times faster and to L1 cache are 170 times faster than main memory. Although this has not changed over the years, in-memory residency time for data in RAM has. The thought a few years ago was that any RAM page not referenced in, say, one second should not be in RAM.

Some DBAs put all the data in RAM and leave it there to avoid I/O. Even though memory access is faster than disk access, accessing data that is not needed is bad regardless of where the data resides.

Solutions are available that require data to be less than or equal to RAM, or at some level the technology fails to achieve the performance desired. As you can see from the diagram in Figure 10.4, memory is needed for every processor instruction executed, but not every processor instruction is of equal significance because not every workload executed has the same importance.

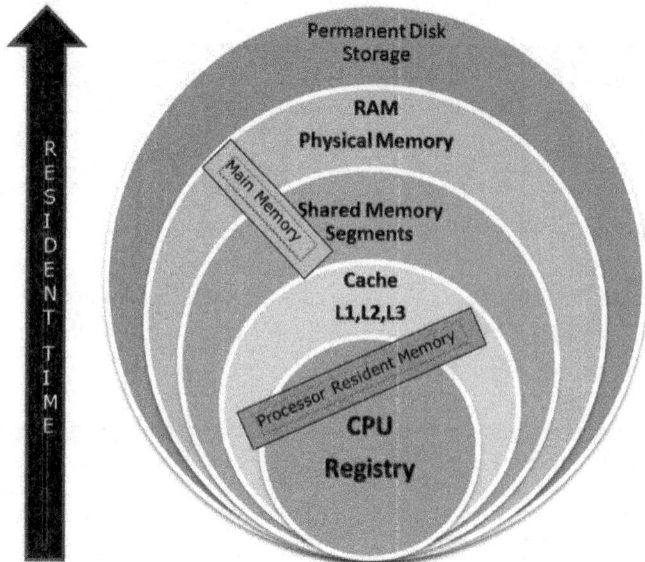

Figure 10.4: Memory residency

BLU Acceleration is a just-in-time solution providing required data at the speed of thought. This is the right approach in managing any resource as fluid as data.

Managing Database Memory

A measured factor used in performance analysis of every database is *page residency*. This is the time a database page remains in physical memory (RAM). After setting performance baselines, be sure to maintain the ratio of data to memory. As data grows, increase physical memory to maintain the ratio:

```
Memory Ratio = Physical DB Data Size to BufferPool Storage
```

You can divide database transaction execution time into compute, I/O, and network time. A local transaction (one executed from the same server where the database resides) has no network time. A transaction in which all database pages are in memory has no I/O time. So in this case, the transaction execution time equals compute time.

Note: Data pages that are pinned in memory or accessed frequently will remain in memory and will experience no I/O.

So for workloads executed in the database, what is the memory requirement? To answer this, simply run the same workload in a structured test and increase buffer pool storage until no physical I/O is issued.

Is each SQL statement executed in a database of equal importance to the overall body of work delivered? In most cases, you have classifications of work executed in a database. So again, why load into memory data you do not need? In addition, why implement a technology that will fail in the event all data will not fit into physical RAM?

A diskless database, in which a database stores data only in memory and never on disk storage, would keep data in two or three different memory locations for redundancy. In the case of a scheduled shutdown, the data would be written to disk only for the purpose of reading it after the database management system is restarted.

However, this scenario may never happen because database software manages data, and in-memory databases will be required to provide these same management services (for example, simple transactional recovery, locking, security, versioning, and data integrity). Also, moving database files to solid state drive (SSD) or flash storage is safer and is closer to in-memory performance.

For physical memory to have real business impact, it needs the following (also, see Figure 10.5):

- Placement where the business code is running (local memory)
- Organization or structure specific to the business objects being processed
- Sized and managed locally based on the workload
- N-active cache coherency with dynamic scalability

If you properly configure memory allocation for a database, placing the entire database into physical RAM will result in no measurable performance difference for important workloads over a reasonable execution time.

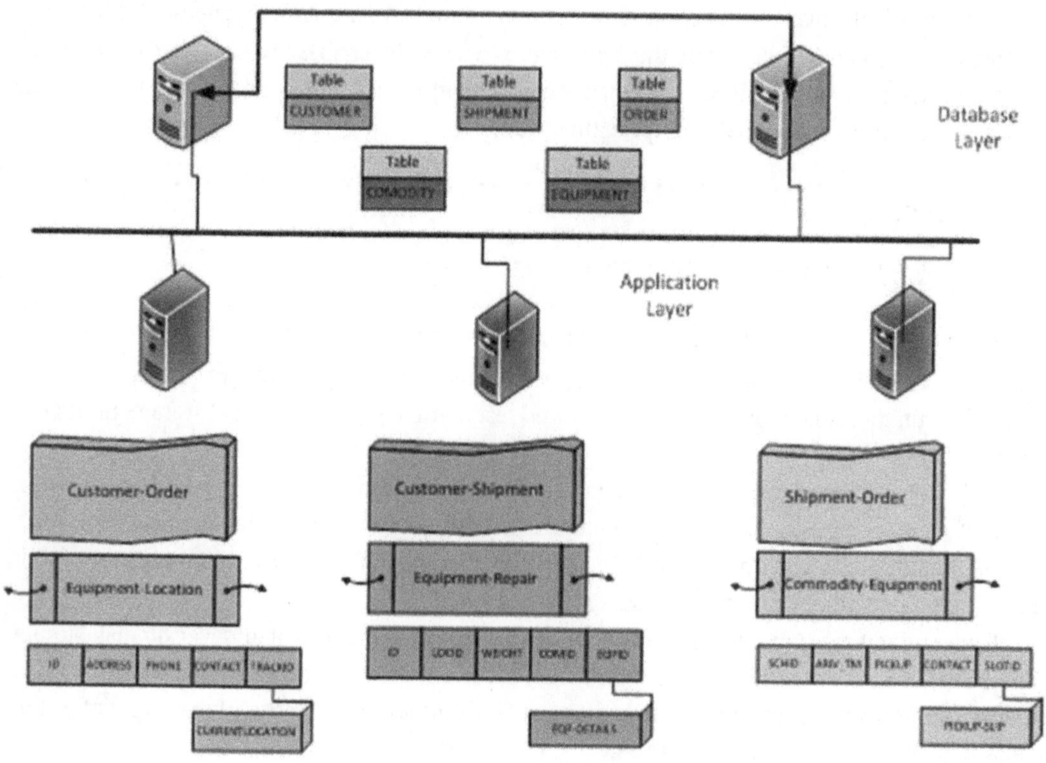

Figure 10.5: Memory planning

Single-Instruction, Multiple-Data (SIMD)

Most data is processed in scalar operations by using one CPU instruction for each piece of data. SIMD is handled through array processing with one instruction for 128 bits of data.

If you want to determine whether an SIMD instruction set is available on a server, create a `db2` instance and start it. In the `db2diag.log` file, you will see the server's characteristics, which will include SIMD, if available:

```
CPU: total:24 online:24 Cores per socket:12 Threading degree per core:1 SIMD:Y
```

Alternatively, you can write some C code and execute a SIMD instruction to see if it works.

Compression

Compression has a rich technological history. Row compression using a variant of the Lempel-Ziv algorithm got the ball rolling. Then, IBM marketed deep compression before introducing adaptive compression in DB2 10.1. With DB2 10.5, we get actionable compression.

Adaptive compression provides table- and page-level compression dictionaries, so that if row compression does not get the job done, page-level compression will. Actionable compression allows data to be processed more efficiently in its compressed form.

The key effectiveness of any compression technique is how long the data will remain compressed. The longer values can remain compressed, the better.

IBM DB2 10.5 keeps data and index keys compressed through processing, including grouping and many predicate operations, allowing the data to stay compressed longer. The longer data is compressed, the better the performance, and that is why it is called *acceleration*.

The only difference between the following two CREATE TABLE statements is how they are organized:

```
CREATE TABLE ROW_TBL (OBJECT_NAME VARCHAR (1000) NOT NULL,
                      OBJECT_VALUE VARCHAR (5000)) ORGANIZE BY ROW
CREATE TABLE COLUMN_TBL (OBJECT_NAME VARCHAR (1000) NOT NULL,
                         OBJECT_VALUE VARCHAR (5000)) ORGANIZE BY COLUMN
```

Assume you load the data in Figure 10.6 into both tables and then execute this command:

```
select object_value from <table> where object_name = 'Street'
```

When you use scalar operations, each database page is loaded into the buffer pool and then into CPU cache. The equal (=) operation is then performed against each row, one instruction per row. So a table scan of 14 rows will result in 14 instructions. If you place an index on column Name, only two rows will match and two instructions will be executed.

Using array operations (SIMD) will move data into CPU cache 128-bit registers and will execute one equal (=) instruction.

While the index access scalar operation may be faster in this example, what if the table has 50 billion rows, or if every page that contains Street is known and indexed? With these two changes, column is orders of magnitude faster. If you compress Name to 100 percent, all 14 rows could fit and be executed by using one instruction.

To recap, a columnar table does not have user-defined indexes, so there are no indexes to maintain. If you want to search Object_Value or Object_Name, you will need two indexes. With columnar tables, both Object_Value and Object_Name have pages, and you access only those pages containing the values for which you are searching. Table 10.8 lists the limitations for columnar tables.

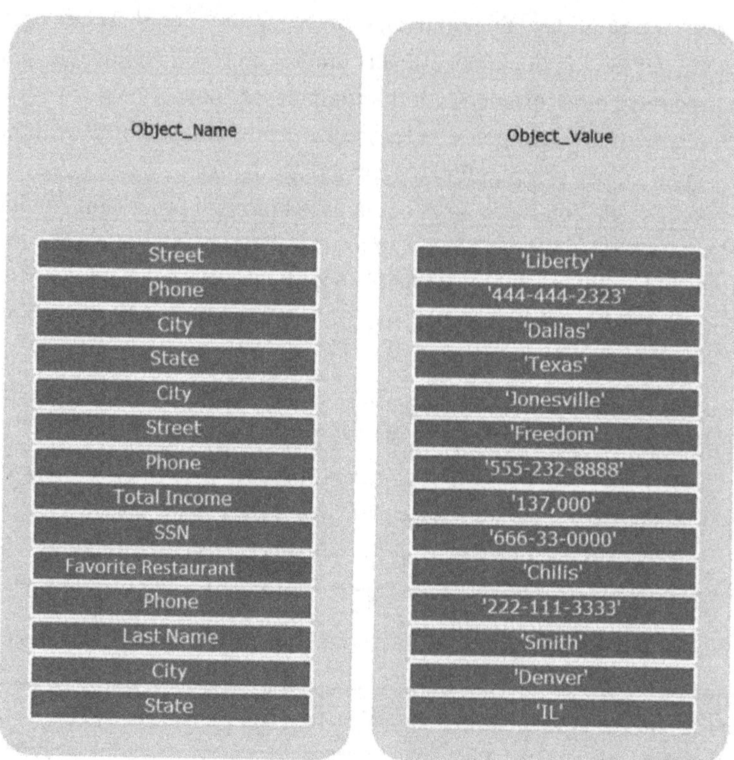

Figure 10.6: Name/value pairs

Table 10.8: Columnar table limitations

Restriction	Description
GENERATED ALWAYS AS	Cannot define "generated" columns
COMPRESS YES	Is the default; cannot be specified
CREATE INDEX	Cannot create user-defined indexes
RUNSTATS	Unnecessary; collected automatically
Range partitioned table	Not supported
APPEND MODE	Not supported
CREATE TRIGGER	Not supported

Buffer Pool Manager

Keeping data in memory that is required for transactional workloads is one significant key to performance. Data pages and index pages move in and out of buffer storage, with the basic idea being to keep only what is needed in memory. Asynchronous page fetching can overtake buffer pool space because of the volume of pages scanned. Techniques to avoid this included limiting the buffer pool space that asynchronous prefetching could take, which allowed synchronous processing to have buffer pool space also.

DB2 has deployed many different page-caching techniques to manage buffer pool storage. You might recognize some of these, such as most recently used (MRU), least recently used (LRU), first-in first-out (FIFO), or last-in last-out (LILO).

With columnar tables, everything is a scan, so a new approach in managing the buffer pool was needed. With DB2 10.5, IBM introduces a new technique called *scan-friendly page caching (SFPC)*, which you can see in Figure 10.7 and Figure 10.8.

Note: Remember, only those pages containing column values are loaded.

However, all data is not uniform. In some cases, the values being scanned may be significantly larger than the amount of buffer pool storage available. In the example in Figure 10.7, 'Smith' will not fit entirely in the buffer pool, which means pages will be victimized, leaving the last pages loaded in the pool. If you start a second scan, the process will repeat itself with those pages still in the pool being victims first. This process will repeat itself continuously with no caching hits.

If you reserve the first 25 percent as victimless pages when 'Smith' is processed, when the 'Smith' process is finished, the first 25 percent of pages will remain in the buffer pool (see Figure 10.8). If you execute a second scan on 'Smith', the first 25 percent will already be cached, and the second scan will leave the first 25 percent in the buffer pool. As these scans continue, the caching percentages should increase.

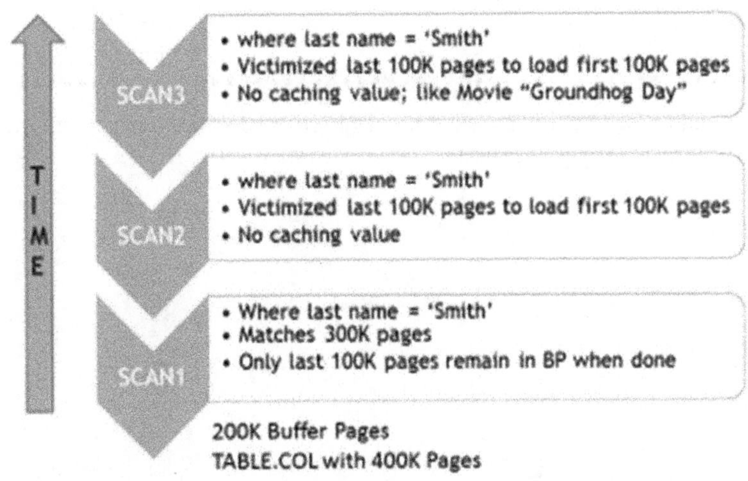

Figure 10.7: Victimized pages in the buffer pool

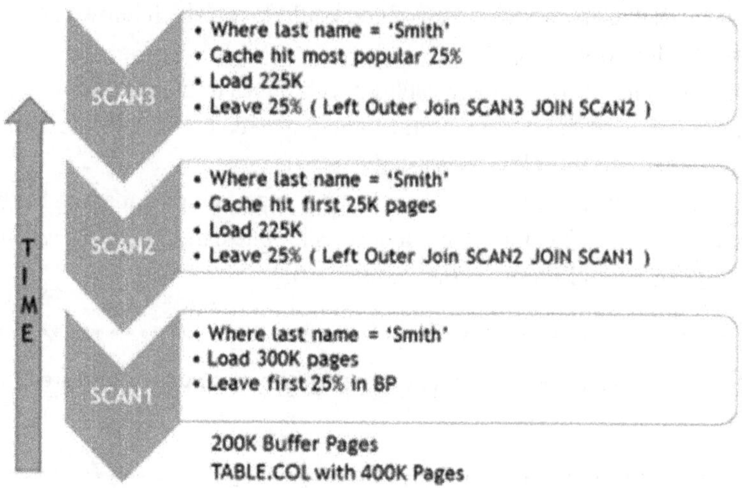

Figure 10.8: Reserving the first 25 percent as victimless pages

Multi-Core Parallelism

With IBM DB2 BLU, the bigger the better. If you provide a resource to BLU, it will use it.

So how do you know what size server you need? One way to determine this is to run the same workload on increasing resources until the workload no longer improves in execution time. With a virtual server, this is possible. Here is a formula that sums this up: BLU TIME IMPROVES = COMPRESSION (~100%) + REGISTERS + H-THREADS + MEMORY.

Note: Remember, if compression is poor, all the hardware in the world will not help.

Think for a second as BLU being a drag racer. In Figure 10.9, BLU has all engines running waiting for the red light to turn green (SQL).

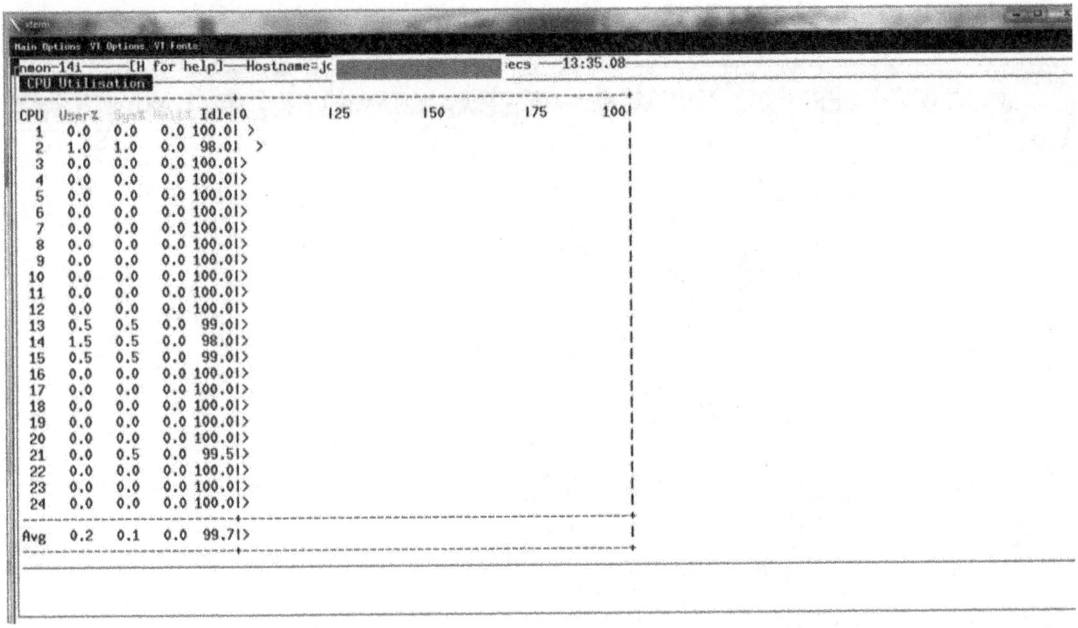

```
Main Options  VT Options  VT Fonts
nmon-14i——[H for help]——Hostname=jc                ecs ——13:35.08——
 CPU Utilisation
CPU  User%  Sys%  Wait%  Idle|0          |25          |50          |75          100|
  1   0.0   0.0   0.0 100.0| >
  2   1.0   1.0   0.0  98.0|  >
  3   0.0   0.0   0.0 100.0|>
  4   0.0   0.0   0.0 100.0|>
  5   0.0   0.0   0.0 100.0|>
  6   0.0   0.0   0.0 100.0|>
  7   0.0   0.0   0.0 100.0|>
  8   0.0   0.0   0.0 100.0|>
  9   0.0   0.0   0.0 100.0|>
 10   0.0   0.0   0.0 100.0|>
 11   0.0   0.0   0.0 100.0|>
 12   0.0   0.0   0.0 100.0|>
 13   0.5   0.5   0.0  99.0|>
 14   1.5   0.5   0.0  98.0|>
 15   0.5   0.5   0.0  99.0|>
 16   0.0   0.0   0.0 100.0|>
 17   0.0   0.0   0.0 100.0|>
 18   0.0   0.0   0.0 100.0|>
 19   0.0   0.0   0.0 100.0|>
 20   0.0   0.0   0.0 100.0|>
 21   0.0   0.5   0.0  99.5|>
 22   0.0   0.0   0.0 100.0|>
 23   0.0   0.0   0.0 100.0|>
 24   0.0   0.0   0.0 100.0|>
Avg   0.2   0.1   0.0  99.7|>
```

Figure 10.9: Idle server

Figure 10.10 shows BLU when the light turns green (one SQL statement is running).

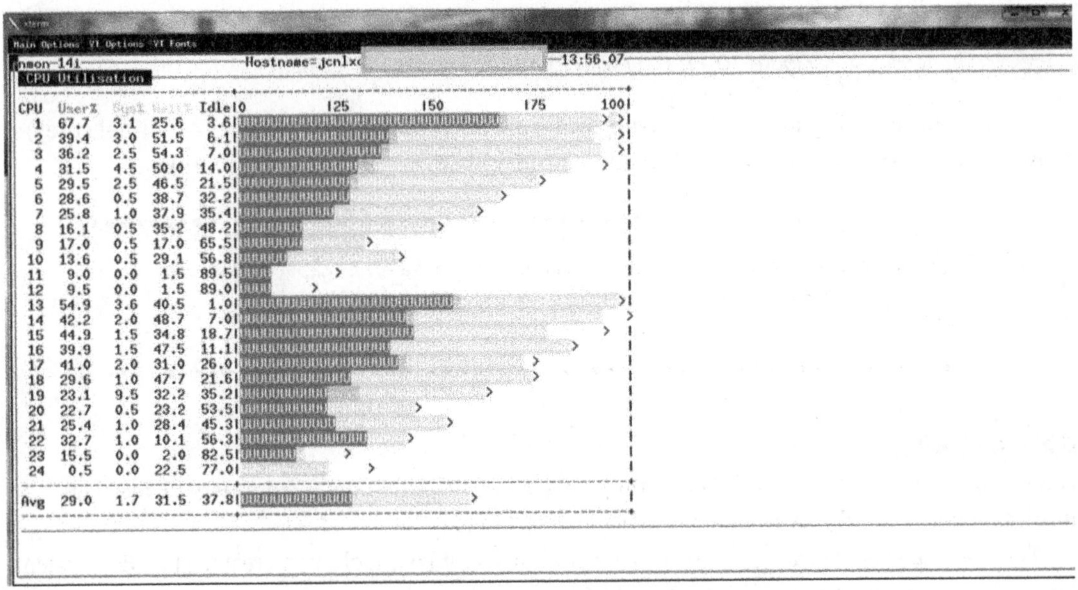

```
Main Options  VT Options  VT Fonts
nmon-14i——————Hostname=jcnlx                ——13:56.07——
 CPU Utilisation
CPU  User%  Sys%  Wait%  Idle|0          |25          |50          |75          100|
  1  67.7   3.1  25.6   3.6|UUUUUUUUUUUUUUUUUUUUUUUUUUUUUUUUU  > >|
  2  39.4   3.0  51.5   6.1|UUUUUUUUUUUUUUUUUUU                  >|
  3  36.2   2.5  54.3   7.0|UUUUUUUUUUUUUUUUUU                   >|
  4  31.5   4.5  50.0  14.0|UUUUUUUUUUUUUUU                   >  |
  5  29.5   2.5  46.5  21.5|UUUUUUUUUUUUUU               >       |
  6  28.6   0.5  38.7  32.2|UUUUUUUUUUUUUU           >           |
  7  25.8   1.0  37.9  35.4|UUUUUUUUUUUU            >            |
  8  16.1   0.5  35.2  48.2|UUUUUUUU            >                |
  9  17.0   0.5  17.0  65.5|UUUUUUUU      >                      |
 10  13.6   0.5  29.1  56.8|UUUUUU             >                 |
 11   9.0   0.0   1.5  89.5|UUUU      >                          |
 12   9.5   0.0   1.5  89.0|UUUU     >                           |
 13  54.9   3.6  40.5   1.0|UUUUUUUUUUUUUUUUUUUUUUUUUUU          >|
 14  42.2   2.0  48.7   7.0|UUUUUUUUUUUUUUUUUUUUU                 >
 15  44.9   1.5  34.8  18.7|UUUUUUUUUUUUUUUUUUUUUU           >   |
 16  39.9   1.5  47.5  11.1|UUUUUUUUUUUUUUUUUUU              >    |
 17  41.0   2.0  31.0  26.0|UUUUUUUUUUUUUUUUUUUU          >       |
 18  29.6   1.0  47.7  21.6|UUUUUUUUUUUUUU                >       |
 19  23.1   9.5  32.2  35.2|UUUUUUUUUUU             >            |
 20  22.7   0.5  23.2  53.5|UUUUUUUUUUU         >                |
 21  25.4   1.0  28.4  45.3|UUUUUUUUUUUU            >            |
 22  32.7   1.0  10.1  56.3|UUUUUUUUUUUUUUUU      >              |
 23  15.5   0.0   2.0  82.5|UUUUUUU      >                       |
 24   0.5   0.0  22.5  77.0|              >                      |
Avg  29.0   1.7  31.5  37.8|UUUUUUUUUUUUUU               >       |
```

Figure 10.10: BLU with one SQL statement running

In Figure 10.11, you see four SQL statements trying to run simultaneously.

```
Main Options  VT Options  VT Fonts
nmon-14i        Hostname=jcnlx            14:12.48
 CPU Utilisation
CPU User%  Sys%  Wait%  Idle|0       |25       |50       |75      100|
  1 78.2   1.6  19.7   0.5|
  2 85.9   0.5  12.6   1.0|
  3 76.9   0.5  22.1   0.5|
  4 80.4   0.5  18.6   0.5|
  5 84.9   0.5  11.6   3.0|
  6 80.0   0.5  17.5   2.0|
  7 78.6   0.0  20.4   1.0|
  8 75.0   0.5  22.5   2.0|
  9 73.2   0.5  22.2   4.0|
 10 72.9   0.5  21.6   5.0|
 11 68.7   1.0  26.4   4.0|
 12 82.1   1.0  11.4   5.5|
 13 79.5   2.6  17.9   0.0|
 14 86.6   0.5  11.4   1.5|
 15 79.5   0.5  19.5   0.5|
 16 85.5   1.0  13.0   0.5|
 17 79.9   1.0  18.1   1.0|
 18 87.9   0.5  10.1   1.5|
 19 88.5   0.5   9.5   1.5|
 20 73.1   1.5  24.9   0.5|
 21 80.5   0.5  18.5   0.5|
 22 73.0   1.0  24.5   1.5|
 23 73.6   1.0  17.9   7.5|
 24 70.1   1.5  27.4   1.0|
Avg 79.0   0.8  18.3   1.9|
Warning: Some Statistics may not shown
```

Figure 10.11: BLU with four SQL statements running

As you can see in Figure 10.11, a 12-physical core VMware/Red Hat server (24 virtual cores) shows only 1.9 percent idle. This is difficult to accomplish with any database workload.

Note: Monitoring CPU busy as an operational alert or capacity indicator will not work for BLU workloads or for pureScale CF workloads.

Data Skipping

Data skipping is the process of locating only the pages containing data your query needs. The information to make this work resides in a synopsis table.

There is one synopsis table for every user column-organized table you create. The DB2 system builds and maintains the synopsis table, which is also a column-organized table placed in the sysibm schema. DB2 creates the synopsis table in the same table spaces as the user column table.

Because system indexes are also created, the table definition should include a separate index table space. LOB objects are not supported yet, so you do not need a long table space.

The synopsis table contains metadata that identifies which column pages to skip. This is accomplished by recording in the synopsis table a column's minimum and maximum values in groups of 1,024 rows.

Consider the following query:

```
where COL4 between 230 and 240
```

In this case, TSN 7168 through 8191 will be scanned. Tuple Sequence Number (TSN) helps in the assembling of the row from the column data. Table 10.9 shows a synopsis of the table's contents.

Table 10.9: Synopsis of the table's contents

TSNMIN	TSNMAX	COL1 MIN	COL1 MAX	COL2 MIN	COL2 MAX	COL3 MIN	COL3 MAX	COL4 MIN	COL4 MAX
0	1023	14.18	30.41	20.67	131199.05	-99.00	1.44	96	176
1024	2047	14.78	26.68	435.89	130476.19	-99.00	1.84	92	199
2048	3071	14.75	32.84	133.16	120558.08	-99.00	1.76	92	177
3072	4095	14.50	31.55	69.36	121059.78	-99.00	2.32	95	199
4096	5119	13.34	30.28	132.78	131320.18	-99.00	1.68	83	224
5120	6143	11.91	30.05	95.92	130477.57	-99.00	1.76	95	184
6144	7167	12.92	30.70	137.72	131315.95	-99.00	1.68	84	210
7168	8191	9.46	29.14	224.27	120468.21	-99.00	1.44	83	243
8192	9215	9.03	27.23	9.70	120693.83	-99.00	1.68	67	180
9216	10239	14.78	27.26	250.55	131145.08	-99.00	1.52	93	209

Note: The smallest grouping of pages in the synopsis table is around 1,000 pages. The length limit for CHAR and VARCHAR is 1,000 characters. Starting with DB2 V10.5, FP4 Cancun supports most data types.

Deep Dive into BLU

Let us look closely at how to set up an environment to run both BLU and OLTP workloads. Note that you have plenty of flexibility to build and manage BLU in your environment differently. (Several terms used in this book have the same meaning in the scope of this discussion: BLU, BLU Acceleration, columnar, organize by column, and in memory.)

BLU Acceleration is super analytics, super easy. The following list explains how:

1. Install and configure the DB2 instance and database the same, whether row or column. Simply install the software that has BLU licensed.
2. Both columnar and row workloads can run in the same database (not preferred).
3. Existing utilities work with both row and column (for example, Load and Reorg).
4. Converting row-organized tables to column-organized tables is easy.
5. Using shadow tables, DB2 will decide which is best, column or row, to execute a query. No changes to your application are required.
6. No RUNSTATS commands are needed.
7. There are no user indexes to maintain.
8. More is better, but less will work! All data does not have to fit into RAM, and you do not have to guess at the size beforehand and purchase hardware you will never use. You can grow the platform as you increase the work.
9. Full DML capabilities with column-organized tables are supported.

Because of the shift toward automation with ASM and STMM, BLU Acceleration and pureScale are now built on these managers.

Following are the database requirements for column-organized tables:

- The database must have ASM enabled.
- Table spaces must have automatic space reclaim enabled.
- Identity or Identity-16 bit must be used.
- The code set must be Unicode.
- No pureScale is involved.
- No DPF is involved.
- A UNIX operating system (Linux or AIX) is required.
- A db2aese or db2awse license is needed.
- SORTHEAP and SHEAPTHRES_SHR cannot be STMM controlled.
- UTIL_HEAP_SZ is automatic, but you need to set the default size between 1 MB and 6 MB pages.

Note: DB2_WORKLOAD=ANALYTICS is not listed above because it is not required; however, it does make setup easier for BLU.

If you want to identify all column-organized tables in a database that are user defined, execute the following SQL query:

```
SELECT TABSCHEMA, TABNAME FROM SYSCAT.TABLES
WHERE TABLEORG = 'C' AND TABSCHEMA <> 'SYSIBM'
```

To obtain a list of row-organized user tables, use TABLEORG = 'R'.

Separate Row and Column Instances on a Database Server

Assume you have a database server (virtual, LPAR, or bare metal) that has 16 cores and 96 GB of RAM. Your plan is to dedicate resources to each DB2 instance based on the server size in a 75/25 percent split. Table 10.10 shows the column and row workloads on the server.

Table 10.10: One server for both column and row workloads

Instance	CPU	Memory	I/O
db2blu01	12	72	Normal
db2row01	4	24	WLM I/O PREFETCH READ HIGH

You create and start the instance db2blu01 by using this command:

```
db2icrt -s ese -u db2fenc1 db2blu01
```

Checking the db2diag.log, you see that SIMD is enabled:

```
==> grep -i 'SIMD' db2diag.log
CPU: total:12 online:12 Cores per socket:1 Threading degree per core:1
SIMD:Y
BLU: HW SIMD enabled: SCAN(Y), ARITH(Y), HASH(Y), CPU(0)
```

To create and start the instance db2row01, execute the following command:

```
db2icrt -s ese -u db2fenc2 db2row01
```

You plan to set up BLU workloads to run in the db2blu01 instance and OLTP (row) in the db2row01 instance.

For db2blu01, set the registry parameters:

```
DB2TCP_CLIENT_KEEPALIVE_TIMEOUT=15
DB2_KEEP_AS_AND_DMS_CONTAINERS_OPEN=ON
DB2_OPT_MAX_TEMP_SIZE=10240
DB2_ENABLE_AUTOCONFIG_DEFAULT=YES
DB2TCP_CLIENT_CONTIMEOUT=30
DB2_WORKLOAD=ANALYTICS
DB2_SKIPINSERTED=ON
DB2_USE_ALTERNATE_PAGE_CLEANING=ON
DB2_SMS_TRUNC_TMPTABLE_THRESH=0
DB2_FORCE_APP_ON_MAX_LOG=TRUE
DB2_EVALUNCOMMITTED=ON
DB2_LOGGER_NON_BUFFERED_IO=ON
DB2_DISABLE_FLUSH_LOG=OFF
DB2_SKIPDELETED=ON
DB2_BINSORT=YES
DB2_PRED_FACTORIZE=YES
DB2MEMDISCLAIM=YES
DB2ENVLIST=EXTSHM
DB2COMM=TCPIP
DB2_PARALLEL_IO=*
DB2AUTOSTART=NO
```

For db2row01, set the registry parameters:

```
DB2TCP_CLIENT_KEEPALIVE_TIMEOUT=15
DB2_KEEP_AS_AND_DMS_CONTAINERS_OPEN=ON
DB2_OPT_MAX_TEMP_SIZE=10240
DB2_ENABLE_AUTOCONFIG_DEFAULT=YES
DB2TCP_CLIENT_CONTIMEOUT=30
DB2_SKIPINSERTED=ON
DB2_USE_ALTERNATE_PAGE_CLEANING=ON
```

Continued

```
DB2_SMS_TRUNC_TMPTABLE_THRESH=0
DB2_FORCE_APP_ON_MAX_LOG=TRUE
DB2_EVALUNCOMMITTED=ON
DB2_LOGGER_NON_BUFFERED_IO=ON
DB2_DISABLE_FLUSH_LOG=OFF
DB2_SKIPDELETED=ON
DB2_BINSORT=YES
DB2_PRED_FACTORIZE=YES
DB2MEMDISCLAIM=YES
DB2ENVLIST=EXTSHM
DB2COMM=TCPIP
DB2_PARALLEL_IO=*
DB2AUTOSTART=NO
```

You create database db2row01:OLTPDB and db2blu01:BLUDB with the same script but set the correct values for each database. Each database has five STOGROUPS and 10 data paths. Four buffer pools are defined in each database.

The script output for BLUDB will look like this:

```
CREATE DATABASE BLUDB ON '/db/ts01','/db/ts02','/db/ts03','/db/ts04' DBPATH
ON '/db/home' USING CODESET UTF-8 TERRITORY en_US COLLATE USING IDENTITY
DB20000I  The CREATE DATABASE command completed successfully.

CONNECT TO BLUDB
Database Connection Information

 Database server        = DB2/LINUXX8664 10.5.4
 SQL authorization ID   = DB2INST1
 Local database alias   = BLUDB

CREATE STOGROUP T2_DATA ON '/db/ts04','/db/ts03','/db/ts02','/db/ts01'
OVERHEAD 0.17 DEVICE READ RATE 4096  SET AS DEFAULT
DB20000I  The SQL command completed successfully.
                                                              Continued
```

```
CREATE STOGROUP T2_INDX ON '/db/ts01','/db/ts02','/db/ts03','/db/ts04'
OVERHEAD 0.17 DEVICE READ RATE 4096
DB20000I  The SQL command completed successfully.

ALTER DATABASE BLUDB ADD STORAGE ON '/db/tstemp01','/db/tstemp02',
'/db/tstemp03','/db/tstemp04'
DB20000I  The SQL command completed successfully.

CREATE STOGROUP TEMP ON '/db/tstemp04','/db/tstemp03','/db/tstemp02',
'/db/tstemp01' OVERHEAD 0.35 DEVICE READ RATE 8192
DB20000I  The SQL command completed successfully.


ALTER DATABASE BLUDB ADD STORAGE ON '/db/ts05s','/db/ts06s'
DB20000I  The SQL command completed successfully.

CREATE STOGROUP T1_DATA ON '/db/ts05s','/db/ts06s' OVERHEAD 0.10
DEVICE READ RATE 12048
DB20000I  The SQL command completed successfully.

CREATE STOGROUP T1_INDX ON '/db/ts06s','/db/ts05s' OVERHEAD 0.10
DEVICE READ RATE 12048
DB20000I  The SQL command completed successfully.

CREATE BUFFERPOOL "BP00_32K" IMMEDIATE DATABASE PARTITION GROUP
IBMDEFAULTGROUP SIZE 10240 PAGESIZE 32K
DB20000I  The SQL command completed successfully.

CREATE BUFFERPOOL "BP01_32K" IMMEDIATE DATABASE PARTITION GROUP
IBMDEFAULTGROUP SIZE 102400 PAGESIZE 32K
DB20000I  The SQL command completed successfully.
```

Continued

```
CREATE BUFFERPOOL "BPT01_32K" IMMEDIATE DATABASE PARTITION GROUP
IBMTEMPGROUP SIZE 51200 PAGESIZE 32K
DB20000I  The SQL command completed successfully.

CREATE BUFFERPOOL "BPT01_04K" IMMEDIATE DATABASE PARTITION GROUP
IBMTEMPGROUP SIZE 51200 PAGESIZE 4K
DB20000I  The SQL command completed successfully.
```

The database BLUDB now has the following database configuration:

```
Degree of parallelism                          (DFT_DEGREE) = ANY
Default tablespace extentsize (pages)          (DFT_EXTENT_SZ) = 4
Default table organization                     (DFT_TABLE_ORG) = COLUMN
Database page size                                  = 32768
```

The database OLTPDB now has this database configuration:

```
Degree of parallelism                          (DFT_DEGREE) = 1
Default tablespace extentsize (pages)          (DFT_EXTENT_SZ) = 32
Default table organization                     (DFT_TABLE_ORG) = ROW
Database page size                                  = 4096
```

You should set some common best-practice values for all DB2 databases, so do this for both of the databases you just created:

```
BLK_LOG_DSK_FUL      YES
DIAGPATH             /db/messagelog/<DB2INSTANCE>
NEWLOGPATH           /db/activelog/<DB2INSTANCE>
OVERFLOWLOGPATH      /db/overflowlog/<DB2INSTANCE>
LOCKTIMEOUT          30 ( Or approperate value just not -1 )
TRACKMOD              YES
LOGFILSIZ            <Depends on load>
LOGPRIMARY           <Depends on UOW sizes>
LOGSECOND            <Depends on UOW sizes>
LOCKLIST             <Good initial size to avoid lock escalation> AUTO
```

The storage groups defined to each database are as follows:

- T1_DATA is Tier 1 storage for data with two data paths both defined to SSD.
- T1_INDX is Tier 1 storage for indexes with two data paths both defined to SSD.
- T2_DATA is set as the default and is Tier 2 storage for data with four data paths defined to hard-disk drive (HDD).
- T2_INDX is Tier 2 storage for indexes with four data paths defined to HDD. TEMP is for system temporary table spaces that are the only SMS-defined table spaces in the database.

Removing the generated system table space TEMPSPACE1 cannot be done until you create a 4 KB system temporary table space. Regardless of the purpose of a DB2 database, always create both a 4 KB and 32 KB system temporary table space, as in the following example. You can create other sizes, such as 8 KB or 16 KB, but they are not required.

```
CREATE SYSTEM TEMPORARY TABLESPACE "XXT0004K"
  IN DATABASE PARTITION GROUP "IBMTEMPGROUP"
  PAGESIZE 4K
  MANAGED BY AUTOMATIC STORAGE USING STOGROUP TEMP
  BUFFERPOOL BPT01_04K
  NO FILE SYSTEM CACHING;

CREATE SYSTEM TEMPORARY TABLESPACE "XXT0032K"
  IN DATABASE PARTITION GROUP "IBMTEMPGROUP"
  PAGESIZE 32K
  MANAGED BY AUTOMATIC STORAGE USING STOGROUP TEMP
  BUFFERPOOL BPT01_32K
  NO FILE SYSTEM CACHING;

DROP TABLESPACE TEMPSPACE1;
```

You also need to create DMS user table spaces so you can create tables and indexes. Both of these are in the Tier 1 storage pools, which means both containers are on SSD:

```
CREATE LARGE TABLESPACE "XXA10100" IN DATABASE PARTITION GROUP
"IBMDEFAULTGROUP" PAGESIZE 32K MANAGED BY AUTOMATIC STORAGE USING STOGROUP
T1_DATA INITIALSIZE 6 G EXTENTSIZE 4 INCREASESIZE 6 G MAXSIZE 24 G
BUFFERPOOL BP01_32K NO FILE SYSTEM CACHING ;
```

Continued

```
CREATE LARGE TABLESPACE "XXDX10100" IN DATABASE PARTITION GROUP
"IBMDEFAULTGROUP" PAGESIZE 32K MANAGED BY AUTOMATIC STORAGE USING STOGROUP
T2_INDX INITIALSIZE 5 G EXTENTSIZE 4 INCREASESIZE 5 G MAXSIZE 15 G
BUFFERPOOL BP01_32K NO FILE SYSTEM CACHING ;
```

Both of these are in the Tier 2 storage pools, meaning both containers are on HDD:

```
CREATE LARGE TABLESPACE "XXA20100" IN DATABASE PARTITION GROUP
"IBMDEFAULTGROUP" PAGESIZE 32K MANAGED BY AUTOMATIC STORAGE USING STOGROUP
T2_DATA INITIALSIZE 6 G EXTENTSIZE 4 INCREASESIZE 6 G MAXSIZE 24 G
BUFFERPOOL BP01_32K NO FILE SYSTEM CACHING ;

CREATE LARGE TABLESPACE "XXX20100" IN DATABASE PARTITION GROUP
"IBMDEFAULTGROUP" PAGESIZE 32K MANAGED BY AUTOMATIC STORAGE USING STOGROUP
T2_INDX INITIALSIZE 5 G EXTENTSIZE 4 INCREASESIZE 5 G MAXSIZE 15 G
BUFFERPOOL BP01_32K NO FILE SYSTEM CACHING ;
```

Notice in the table space naming, the two examples above use "A" for data and "X" for index table spaces; they also group SSD table spaces beginning with 10100 through 19900 and group HDD with 20100 through 29900.

Now you need to set the DBM and database configurations based on your physical partitioning scheme to isolate these two workloads. For db2blu01, keep the instance within 72 GB of RAM. For everything except UTIL_HEAP_SZ, that is possible.

Set the INSTANCE_MEMORY to 71 GB and leave 1 GB for the operating system or other allocations:

```
Global instance memory (4KB)          (INSTANCE_MEMORY) = 18612224
```

For the DATABASE_MEMORY, leave it set to AUTOMATIC:

```
Size of database shared memory (4KB)  (DATABASE_MEMORY) = AUTOMATIC(3444462)
```

There are three other critical database configuration settings for BLU workloads. Two of the settings are not automatic: SHEAPTHRES_SHR and SORTHEAP. Not only are they *not* automatic, but they cannot even be set to AUTOMATIC for column-organized tables.

For BLUDB, set SHRAPTHRES_SHR at 50 percent of the DATABASE_MEMORY size, and set SORTHEAP at 10 percent of SHRAPTHRES_SHR as a starting point:

```
SHEAPTHRES_SHR = 1722231
SORTHEAP = 172223
```

UTIL_HEAP_SZ is critical to a successful operation of BLU workloads. While columnar tables support full DML, data is populated primarily through the Load or Ingest utilities.

The Load utility for column tables has three phases. The first is the Analyze phase in which the entire input is processed for compression keys. The second and third phases are the same for all loads.

UTIL_HEAP_SZ is not restricted by INSTANCE_MEMORY or by DATABASE_MEMORY. Memory in the pool is released when no longer needed.

A good setting for a typical BLU installation is between 4 MB and 6 MB pages. An undersized utility heap can significantly affect the compression efficiency of a load and therefore the performance of BLU queries.

When a load process begins, it acquires the full utility heap memory. If a second concurrent load is started, memory will be taken from the first load and given to the second load. This process will continue for the number of concurrent loads executed.

For BLUDB, set UTIL_HEAP_SZ to 4 MB AUTOMATIC:

```
Utilities heap size (4KB)   (UTIL_HEAP_SZ) = AUTOMATIC(4000000)
```

At this point, stop and start your instance to be sure everything is fresh and ready:

```
db2stop force
db2start
```

Now, turn your attention to db2row01, which is your OLTP workload instance. Set the INSTANCE_MEMORY to (24–1) GB:

```
Global instance memory (4KB)   (INSTANCE_MEMORY) = 6029312
```

For the DATABASE_MEMORY, leave it AUTOMATIC:

```
Size of database shared memory (4KB)  (DATABASE_MEMORY) = AUTOMATIC(2024800)
```

You can adjust the rest of the DBM and DB settings as required for the workloads' demands. There is no need to change any of the STMM settings for OLTPDB.

You have one more important setting to do for success: cap the number of cores each DB2 instance can consume. If you do not, there is a good chance db2row01 will have trouble getting enough CPU. So set MAX_QUERYDEGREE to 12 for db2blu01 and 4 for db2row01.

When you set DB2_WORKLOAD=ANALYTICS, intraparallelism is automatically set even though the DBM settings shows No. But if MAX_QUERYDEGREE is anything other than ANY, you must set INTRA_PARALLEL=YES manually for column-organized workloads to work:

```
db2blu01
Maximum query degree of parallelism      (MAX_QUERYDEGREE) = 12
Enable intra-partition parallelism       (INTRA_PARALLEL)  = YES

db2row01
Maximum query degree of parallelism      (MAX_QUERYDEGREE) = 4
```

Once you cycle both instances, you should be ready to run successfully both OLTP and columnar (analytical) workloads on the same server.

If you have a slowdown in OLTP read transactions due in part to the heavy read activity on the disk drives, you can set up a work class on DML READ and set the prefetch (I/O) priority higher. This may help prevent row prefetch reads from waiting behind column prefetch reads.

BLU Social

You can get started with BLU in three ways: with BLU Central (*www.ibmbluhub.com/get-blu*), with BLU in the Cloud (*www-01.ibm.com/software/data/dashdb*), or with BLU Trial Download (IBM ID is required—*www14.software.ibm.com/webapp/iwm/web/preLogin.do?source=swg-dm-db2trial&S_CMP-BLUhub*).

Physical Design

This section reviews the DB2 10.5 tasks that a DBA performs. You have a functioning instance and are ready to build your databases and manage them. The primary focus of this section will be BLU, significant advances in pureScale, and business rule changes introduced in DB2 10.5.

Statistical Collection

In some cases, the statistics associated with RUNSTATS are collected, and in other cases they are not. Using table functions, it is possible to determine whether statistics collections are executing or are waiting to run.

Real-time statistics collection (RTS) output is stored in the statistics cache and can be used by database agents for subsequent statements. The cached statistics are later written to the database catalog by a daemon process in servicing a WRITE_STATS request.

A COLLECT_STATS request can be issued by a db2agent process during a statement compilation because of any of the following factors:

- The allotted collection time is less than the time to complete a synchronous full unsampled collection.
- RTS determined that new statistics would be helpful but are not required for the SQL statement being processed.
- RTS determined that a synchronous fabrication is preferred.
- RTS determined that a samples synchronous collection is preferred because of the size of the table.

You can use the following SQL query to gather status information for RTS processing:

```
SELECT QUEUE_POSITION,
       REQUEST_STATUS,
       REQUEST_TYPE,
       OBJECT_TYPE,
       VARCHAR (OBJECT_SCHEMA, 10) AS SCHEMA,
       VARCHAR (OBJECT_NAME, 10) AS NAME
FROM TABLE (MON_GET_RTS_RQST()) AS T
ORDER BY QUEUE_POSITION, SCHEMA, NAME
```

There are three possible statuses for REQUEST_STATUS: EXECUTING, QUEUED, or PENDING. At most, you can have one table with EXECUTING status. RTS checks for PENDING requests every five minutes and places the requests on the run queue.

To gather status information for automatic RUNSTATS asynchronous processing, execute the following SQL query:

```
SELECT QUEUE_POSITION,
       OBJECT_TYPE,
       OBJECT_STATUS,
       VARCHAR (OBJECT_SCHEMA, 10) AS SCHEMA,
       VARCHAR (OBJECT_NAME, 10) AS NAME
```

Continued

```
FROM TABLE (MON_GET_AUTO_RUNSTATS_QUEUE ()) AS T
ORDER BY QUEUE_POSITION
```

An asynchronous collection of statistics for a table will display as OBJECT_STATUS of JOB_SUBMITTED, while other tables awaiting evaluation will have a status of EVALUATION_PENDING. Automatic statistics profiling (ASP) was deprecated in DB2 10.1 and is disconnected in 10.5. It is replaced with the Statistics Advisor in Data Studio.

Databases

Before you start building databases, consider these points. BLU and pureScale require databases with ASM enabled. Both also require Unicode code sets and IDENTITY or IDENTITY_16BIT collation. For column-organized tables, you must define table spaces with automatic space reclaim enabled.

Note: The default is AUTOMATIC, and removal of AUTOMATIC STORAGE NO is a good possibility soon.

You use the CREATE DATABASE command to create the database. The following example has four STORAGE PATHS for the database DB_COL: '/db/ts01', '/db/ts02', '/db/ts03', '/db/ts04'. The DB_HOME or DBPATH is '/db/home', which is the same location as the INSTHOME:

```
CREATE DATABASE DB_COL ON '/db/ts01','/db/ts02','/db/ts03','/db/ts04' DBPATH
ON '/db/home' USING CODESET UTF-8 TERRITORY en_US COLLATE USING IDENTITY
DB20000I  The CREATE DATABASE command completed successfully.
```

For pureScale databases, the command is the same:

```
CREATE DATABASE DB_ROW ON '/ds/ts01','/ds/ts02','/ds/ts03', '/ds/ts04'
DBPATH ON '/db2sd_20120706154522' ;
DB20000I  The CREATE DATABASE command completed successfully.
```

The default collation is IDENTITY, and the code set is UTF-8. The INSTANCE SHARE SQLLIB is generated when the instance is created and is identified by the mount point 'db2sd_<timestamp of creation>'.

The pureScale DBPATHs are GPFS file systems. So for the pureScale CREATE DATABASE command, all mount points that you specify on the command are shared across all members of the cluster.

Note: pureScale supports only row-organized tables today. There is no difference in how a BLU database is created versus a standard row database if you use ASM, STMM, Unicode, and IDENTITY. The difference is in how you configure them and by what means.

Storage Groups

Storage groups provide a good way to manage table space containers. The CREATE STORAGE GROUP statement creates a new storage group within a database, assigns container paths, and records the definition and attributes in the catalog. You should define OVERHEAD and DEVICE READ RATE in the storage group and not in the table space. Only one storage group within the database can have the SET AS DEFAULT attribute. Any table space created as MANAGED BY AUTOMATIC STORAGE without USING STOGROUP will be assigned to the default storage group automatically.

A storage group must have at least one storage path. You can specify multiple storage paths (up to 128) in quotation marks separated by commas. Storage paths are valid file systems mounted and accessible based on the operating system. You cannot drop storage paths from storage groups in pureScale.

To create a storage group, execute the CREATE STOGROUP command. This syntax for this command is:

```
CREATE STOGROUP StorageGroupName
  ON StoragePaths
  OVERHEAD OverheadRate
  DEVICE READ RATE ReadRate
  <SET AS DEFAULT>
```

where:

StorageGroupName	Identifies the unique name of the storage group
StoragePaths	Identifies the storage paths
OverheadRate	Identifies the number of milliseconds to use to determine the cost of I/O
ReadRate	Identifies the transfer rate in megabytes per second

To add storage paths or change attributes, and in ESE (LUW) to drop storage paths, use the ALTER STOGROUP statement. Newly added storage paths will be used by newly created table spaces. Use the ALTER TABLESPACE REBALANCE statement to redistribute existing table space containers across all the paths in the storage group.

Add the storage path to the storage group by using the ALTER STOGROUP statement:

```
ALTER STOGROUP DATA ADD '/db/ts06/data' ;
```

When you drop storage paths from a storage group, the status of the storage group will be changed to DROP PENDING until all table space containers using the path are redistributed across the remaining paths. Any new table spaces created will not use the dropped path. Once the path is no longer in use, the status of the storage group will be changed to NORMAL and the path will be removed.

Drop the storage path from the storage group by using ALTER STOGROUP statement:

```
ALTER STOGROUP DATA DROP '/db/ts06/data' ;
```

Table Spaces

Table spaces consist of chunks of disk space called *containers*. Tables and indexes are assigned to table spaces either implicitly or explicitly. Using the CREATE TABLESPACE statement will define a new table space within the database, assign containers, and record the table space definition and attributes in the catalog.

You can manage table spaces by using SYSTEM(SMS), DATABASE(DMS), or AUTOMATIC STORAGE(AS). pureScale supports only AUTOMATIC STORAGE(AS). Each of these management types manages disk space differently as data is changed. In ESE (LUW) databases, it is typical to define all table spaces as DMS except for SYSTEM TEMPORARY table spaces, which are defined as SMS.

Consider the syntax of the following CREATE LARGE TABLESPACE command:

```
CREATE LARGE TABLESPACE TablespaceName
   IN DATABASE PARTITION GROUP GroupName
   PAGESIZE PageSize
   MANAGED BY ManagementType
   <USING STOGROUP StorageGroupName>
   EXTENTSIZE ExtentSize
```

Continued

```
PREFETCHSIZE AUTOMATIC
BUFFERPOOL BufferPoolName
AUTORESIZE YES
INITIALSIZE InitialSize
INCREASESIZE IncreaseSize
MAXSIZE MaxSize
NO FILE SYSTEM CACHING
DATA TAG NONE
```

where:

TablespaceName	Identifies the unique name of the table space
GroupName	Identifies the database partition group
PageSize	Identifies the page size (4 KB, 8 KB, 16 KB, or 32 KB)
ManagementType	Identifies the management type (SYSTEM, DATABASE, or AUTOMATIC STORAGE)
StorageGroupName	Identifies the storage group; only ASM
ExtentSize	Identifies the allocation extent size
BufferPoolName	Identifies the buffer pool
InitialSize	Identifies the allocated size at creation
IncreaseSize	Identifies the growth size
MaxSize	Identifies the maximum allocation size

If you want to change the attributes of a table space, use the ALTER TABLESPACE statement. You can alter almost all the attributes of a table space except for extent size, page size, and initial size. In pureScale, the storage group of a table space cannot be altered. To move it to a different storage group, you must drop and re-create the table space.

Tables

Row- and column-organized tables can reside in the same database. You should define the database configuration settings for column if any column-organized tables are defined.

As previously discussed, using registry parameter DB2_WORKLOAD=ANALYTICS will set up everything for column processing with the exception of SHEAPTHRES_SHR and SORTHEAP. The UTIL_HEAP_SZ is set to AUTOMATIC, but you may need to increase the initial size manually.

The following is a CREATE TABLE statement for a row-organized table with adaptive compression:

```
CREATE TABLE XX.TMILES_MTHLY
(
  TEQUIP_NM      CHARACTER(4)       NOT NULL,
  TEQUIP_NBR     CHARACTER(10)      NOT NULL,
  ML_DT          DATE               NOT NULL,
  ONLN_LD_ML     DECIMAL(9, 0)      NOT NULL      DEFAULT ,
  ONLN_MTY_ML    DECIMAL(9, 0)      NOT NULL      DEFAULT ,
  OFLN_LD_ML     DECIMAL(9, 0)      NOT NULL      DEFAULT ,
  OFLN_MTY_ML    DECIMAL(9, 0)      NOT NULL      DEFAULT
) IN TBLTS1 INDEX IN INDXTS1 LONG IN LONGTS1
  COMPRESS YES ADAPTIVE
  ORGANIZE BY ROW;
```

It is recommended to always specify the ORGANIZE BY clause in all CREATE TABLE statements you build. The COMPRESS clause is valid only for row-organized tables and for all CREATE INDEX statements. The keyword ADAPTIVE is acceptable only for row-organized tables.

The following is a CREATE TABLE statement for a column-organized table:

```
CREATE TABLE XX.TSHOW_DIM
(
  SHOW_RCD_ID           CHARACTER(13) FOR BIT DATA NOT NULL,
  SEG_NBR               SMALLINT        NOT NULL,
  TYP_NBR_CD            VARCHAR(6)      NOT NULL,
  INSP_SDT              DATE            NOT NULL,
  INSP_STRT_MP_NBR      DECIMAL(9, 2)   NOT NULL,
  INSP_END_MP_NBR       DECIMAL(9, 2)   NOT NULL,
  INSP_STM              TIME            NOT NULL,
  SHOW_INSP_TS          TIMESTAMP       NOT NULL,
                                                       Continued
```

```
  SHOW_INSP_SFTWR_NBR    VARCHAR(60)     NOT NULL,
  LST_MAINT_ID           VARCHAR(128)    NOT NULL      DEFAULT CURRENT_USER,
  LST_MAINT_TS           TIMESTAMP       NOT NULL      DEFAULT
) IN TBLTS2 INDEX IN INDXTS2
  ORGANIZE BY COLUMN;
```

Note: Notice the index table space in the definition. Although column-organized tables have indexes, they do not have user-defined ones.

This table has two indexes:

```
CREATE INDEX SYSIBM.SQL140826105252217531
  ON XX.TSHOW_DIM
    (SQLNOTAPPLICABLE ASC, SQLNOTAPPLICABLE ASC)
  PCTFREE 0
  ALLOW REVERSE SCANS
  COMPRESS YES
  INCLUDE NULL KEYS
  PAGE SPLIT HIGH
```

and

```
CREATE UNIQUE INDEX XX.PK_TSHOW_DIM
  ON XX.TSHOW_DIM
    ( SHOW_RCD_ID ASC )
  ALLOW REVERSE SCANS
  COMPRESS YES
  INCLUDE NULL KEYS
```

The unique index above was created in support of the following ALTER TABLE statement to add a primary key:

```
ALTER TABLE XX.TSHOW_DIM
  ADD CONSTRAINT PK_TSHOW_DIM PRIMARY KEY
    (SHOW_RCD_ID)
    ENFORCED
```

In Table 10.11, you can see the index details.

Table 10.11: Index details

Name*	Schema*	Columns*	Unique Rule	Index Type*	Remarks	Compression*
SQL140826105252217531	SYSIBM	+SQLNOTAPPLICABLE +SQLNOTAPPLICABLE	Duplicates Allowed	CPMA		Yes
PK_TSHOW_DIM	XX	+SHOW_RCD_ID	Primary Index	REG = Regular		Yes

The index type CPMA is *Column Page Map Index*. These two indexes are defined on table TSHOW_DIM.

Note: For every column-organized table, a synopsis table is also created in the SYSIBM schema that has a CPMA index as well.

The table and index are automatically created when the column-organized table is created:

```
CREATE TABLE SYSIBM.SYN140826105251930187_TSHOW_DIM
(
  SHOW_RCD_IDMIN          CHARACTER(13) FOR BIT DATA     NOT NULL,
  SHOW_RCD_IDMAX          CHARACTER(13) FOR BIT DATA     NOT NULL,
  SEG_NBRMIN              SMALLINT             NOT NULL,
  SEG_NBRMAX              SMALLINT             NOT NULL,
  TYP_NBR_CDMIN           VARCHAR(6)           NOT NULL,
```

Continued

```
    TYP_NBR_CDMAX            VARCHAR(6)      NOT NULL,
    INSP_SDTMIN              DATE            NOT NULL,
    INSP_SDTMAX              DATE            NOT NULL,
    INSP_STRT_MP_NBRMIN      DECIMAL(9, 2)   NOT NULL,
    INSP_STRT_MP_NBRMAX      DECIMAL(9, 2)   NOT NULL,
    INSP_END_MP_NBRMIN       DECIMAL(9, 2)   NOT NULL,
    INSP_END_MP_NBRMAX       DECIMAL(9, 2)   NOT NULL,
    INSP_STMMIN              TIME            NOT NULL,
    INSP_STMMAX              TIME            NOT NULL,
    SHOW_INSP_TSMIN          TIMESTAMP       NOT NULL,
    SHOW_INSP_TSMAX          TIMESTAMP       NOT NULL,
    SHOW_INSP_SFTWR_NBRMIN   VARCHAR(60)     NOT NULL,
    SHOW_INSP_SFTWR_NBRMAX   VARCHAR(60)     NOT NULL,
    LST_MAINT_IDMIN          VARCHAR(128)    NOT NULL        DEFAULT CURRENT_USER,
    LST_MAINT_IDMAX          VARCHAR(128)    NOT NULL        DEFAULT CURRENT_USER,
    LST_MAINT_TSMIN          TIMESTAMP       NOT NULL        DEFAULT ,
    LST_MAINT_TSMAX          TIMESTAMP       NOT NULL        DEFAULT ,
    TSNMIN                   BIGINT          NOT NULL,
    TSNMAX                   BIGINT          NOT NULL
)
    IN XXA20100
    INDEX IN XXX20100
    ORGANIZE BY COLUMN@

    CREATE INDEX SYSIBM.SQL140826105252367212
    ON SYSIBM.SYN140826105251930187_TSHOW_DIM
      ( SQLNOTAPPLICABLE ASC, SQLNOTAPPLICABLE ASC )
    PCTFREE 0
    ALLOW REVERSE SCANS
    COMPRESS YES
    INCLUDE NULL KEYS
    PAGE SPLIT HIGH
```

The following CREATE TABLE statement was executed on a db2aese licensed row-organized default database and failed:

```
CREATE TABLE xx.table1 (COL1 INTEGER) ORGANIZED BY COLUMN
SQL1668N  The operation failed because the operation is not supported with
this environment. Reason code: "9".
```

Note: If you want to leave the default database as row and still be able to create column-organized tables, you must remove SORTHEAP and SHEAPTHRES_SHR from STMM's control.

Remember, the default for CREATE DATABASE is AUTOMATIC for these two settings. The default setting for SORTHEAP and SHEAPTHRES_SHR is AUTOMATIC:

```
db2 get db cfg for db_row | grep -i sort
 Sort heap thres for shared sorts (4KB) (SHEAPTHRES_SHR) = AUTOMATIC(143266)
 Sort list heap (4KB)                         (SORTHEAP) = AUTOMATIC(7163)
```

You can change it to the following:

```
db2 get db cfg for db_row | grep -i sort
 Sort heap thres for shared sorts (4KB) (SHEAPTHRES_SHR) = 655360
 Sort list heap (4KB)                         (SORTHEAP) = 10240

CREATE TABLE xx.table1 (COL1 INTEGER) ORGANIZED BY COLUMN
DB20000I  The SQL command completed successfully.
```

Random Key Indexes

Ascending numeric keys can cause performance bottlenecks for heavy insert processing. This bottleneck issue becomes even more pronounced in cluster technologies like pureScale.

Consider the following table/index example:

```
CREATE TABLE XX.TEQCMPNT_MEAS
(
  EQCMPNT_MEAS_ID   BIGINT      NOT NULL,
  MSG_ID            BIGINT      NOT NULL,
  ,,,
  CRET_TS           TIMESTAMP   NOT NULL   DEFAULT
) IN DATATS001 INDEX IN INDXTS001
  COMPRESS YES ADAPTIVE
  ORGANIZE BY ROW
CREATE UNIQUE INDEX XX.PK_TEQCMPNT_MEAS
  ON XX.TEQCMPNT_MEAS
    ( EQCMPNT_MEAS_ID ASC )
  ALLOW REVERSE SCANS
  COMPRESS YES
  INCLUDE NULL KEYS
ALTER TABLE XX.TEQCMPNT_MEAS
  ADD CONSTRAINT PK_TEQCMPNT_MEAS PRIMARY KEY
    (EQCMPNT_MEAS_ID)
    ENFORCED
```

When you are evaluating performance, if the system identifies that lock/latch contention is occurring on the index during insert processing, converting the primary key index into a RANDOM index may improve performance significantly:

```
CREATE UNIQUE INDEX XX.PK_TEQCMPNT_MEAS
  ON XX.TEQCMPNT_MEAS
    ( EQCMPNT_MEAS_ID RANDOM )
  ALLOW REVERSE SCANS
  COMPRESS YES
  INCLUDE NULL KEYS
```

The MSG_ID column is also an ascending numeric key, but you should not change the index defined on it because it is a 1-M foreign key relationship with scan/set processing. Only indexes involved in direct read should be considered for randomization.

Index on Expression

Data stored in the database is mixed case. Nothing in the application will prevent lowercase names, and no triggers have been defined to force all searchable data to uppercase or lowercase.

Users input data into the system, and some enter an uppercase first letter for the name and some do not. Some users even enter the entire name in uppercase.

If you want to identify or locate a specific user in the system, execute a search function similar to this:

```
SELECT CUST_ADDR
FROM XX.CUSTOMER
WHERE UPPER(CUST_NAME) = 'CECIL'
```

The following SQL query runs poorly because CUST_NAME is not indexable in this example, and an index scan zero match is executed if an index on CUST_NAME exists:

```
CREATE TABLE xx.customer
(CUST_NAME VARCHAR (100),
 CUST_ADDR VARCHAR (100),
 CUST_CITY VARCHAR (100)
) ORGANIZE BY ROW

CREATE INDEX xx.ix_cust_1 ON xx.customer (CUST_NAME ASC)

INSERT INTO xx.customer VALUES ('Adams','Road1','City1')
INSERT INTO xx.customer VALUES ('ADams','Road2','City2')
INSERT INTO xx.customer VALUES ('bones','Road3','City3')
INSERT INTO xx.customer VALUES ('BONES','Road4','City4')
INSERT INTO xx.customer VALUES ('CECIL','Road5','City5')
INSERT INTO xx.customer VALUES ('cecil','Road6','City6')
INSERT INTO xx.customer VALUES ('dawson','Road7','City7')
INSERT INTO xx.customer VALUES ('DAWson','Road8','City8')
INSERT INTO xx.customer VALUES ('ZaUs','Road9','City9')
```

When you execute the above SELECT SQL query, you will see output from the Data Studio Query Workload Tuner that looks like this:

```
Avoid table space scan (Operator ID = 3) on table XX.CUSTOMER. The table is
accessed by a table space scan. Consider running the Statistics Advisor,
because the updated statistics might improve the access path. Also, consider
running the Index Advisor to determine whether creating an index might
improve the access path. Click here to see the access plan operator.
```

Figure 10.12 illustrates the Visual Explain dynamic graph produced by Data Studio.

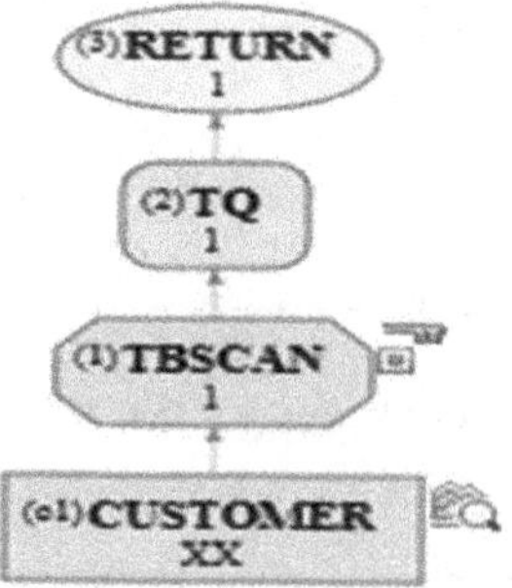

Figure 10.12: Graphical Explain

Replacing the index with an index expression shows that the new index is used and the table scan is removed:

```
CREATE INDEX XX.IX_CUST_1
  ON XX.CUSTOMER
    (UPPER (CUST_NAME) ASC)
  ALLOW REVERSE SCANS
  COMPRESS NO
  INCLUDE NULL KEYS
```

In Figure 10.13, you can see the Visual Explain graph displaying an index.

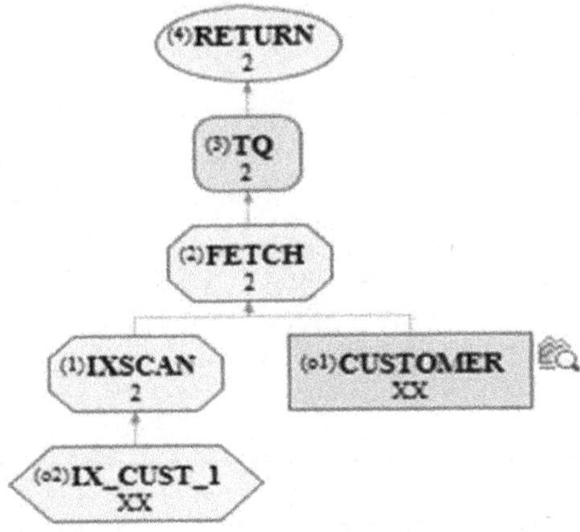

Figure 10.13: Graphical Explain with index

Extended Row Size

The extended row size feature, which is new in DB2, allows a single row to span multiple pages with a maximum length of 1,048,319 bytes. If a row length will be larger than its current page size (maximum of 4005 for 4096 pages), increase the size of the page up to the maximum before allowing the row to extend past one page. To allow rows to span multiple pages, set the database configuration parameter EXTENDED_ROW_SZ to enable, which is the default:

```
update db cfg for db_row using EXTENDED_ROW_SZ enable
DB20000I  The UPDATE DATABASE CONFIGURATION command completed successfully.
```

Let us look at a simple example. Currently, the database setting EXTENDED_ROW_SZ is disabled:

```
Extended row size support                 (EXTENDED_ROW_SZ) = DISABLE
```

The CREATE TABLE command follows and fails on execution:

```
create table xx.longrow
( stringcol varchar(30000)
, my_xml  xml
, stringcol2  varchar(30000)
```

Continued

```
, letter_nbr bigint
, lst_maint_ts timestamp default
) in userts32K

Error:2014-09-14 08:49:24.334664 0:00:00.000: Lookup Error - DB2 Database
Error: ERROR [54010] [IBM][DB2/LINUXX8664] SQL0670N  The statement failed
because the row size of the resulting table would have exceeded the row size
limit. Limit: "32677". Table space: "USERTS32K".
2: create table xx.longrow
```

Now, change the database setting to enable and execute the CREATE TABLE command again:

```
update db cfg for db_row using EXTENDED_ROW_SZ enable
DB20000I  The UPDATE DATABASE CONFIGURATION command completed successfully.
Extended row size support              (EXTENDED_ROW_SZ) = ENABLE
```

This time the CREATE TABLE statement executed successfully. You inserted a single row successfully, and the statistics for the table show the maximum row length to be 64,125.

Note: When you enable EXTENDED_ROW_SZ, any data that does not fit within the maximum row size is stored as a LOB, which can negatively impact performance.

JSON

IBM DB2 10.5 FP1 introduced JSON support. DB2 JSON provides a complete storage/persistence solution for JSON documents. The solution combines application server-side components with JSON enhancements and functions in the DB2 engine.

This configuration provides a NoSQL API that uses DB2 to store, retrieve, modify, parse, and index JSON documents in DB2. The application server-side component is Java based. So a Java API is included that allows native Java applications to exercise all the JSON capabilities directly.

For applications written in other languages, the solution also provides the Wire Listener Gateway (WLG) between MongoDB applications and a DB2 database server. This allows Mongo applications written in a supported language (such as Java, Node.js, or PyMongo) or that use the Mongo CLI to communicate with a DB2 database with no code changes. (Java applications can use the Wire Listener but may find advantage in using the Java API methods directly.)

DB2 JSON is simple to implement and maintain. The interface is contained within the nosqljson.jar file.

The following requirements are necessary to implement JSON support:

- DB2 10.5.0.1 or higher Java client
- The jar files listed below (which are included) as well as startup scripts and documentation
- DFT_TABLE_ORG = ROW
- DB2 database at 10.5 FP1 or higher
- Java in shell PATH (Java 1.5 64-bit or higher)
- CLASSPATH jar files:
  - db2jcc.jar (Java client)
  - nosqljson.jar (DB2 noSQL JSON)
  - wplistener.jar (Wire Protocol Listener)
  - js.jar (Rhino JavaScript engine—not required if only using Java methods directly)

Required for command shell:

- Proper authority
- CREATE TABLE and CREATE FUNCTION in schema SYSTOOLS or DBADM on the target database

Configuring the Database

The preferred database is one with automatic storage, code set UTF-8, and page size 32 KB. As the DB2 instance owner, configure the database for UNIX and Windows systems as follows.

On UNIX

Execute <DB2INSTALL PATH>/json/bin/db2nosql.sh.

If running a remote command, execute the following:

```
db2nosql.sh -user <USER> -hostName <HOSTNAME> -port <PORT> -db <DBNAME>
-password <PASSWORD>
```

If running a local command, execute this instead:

```
db2nosql.sh -db <DBNAME>
```

On Windows

Execute <DB2INSTALL PATH>/json/bin/db2nosql.bat.

If running a remote command, execute the following:

```
db2nosql.bat -user <USER> -hostName <HOSTNAME> -port <PORT> -db <DBNAME>
-password <PASSWORD>
```

If running a local command, execute this instead:

```
    db2nosql.bat -db <DBNAME>
When prompted enter
    enable(true)
```

The following is an example of the output:

```
db2nosql.sh
JSON Command Shell Setup and Launcher.
This batch script assumes your JRE is 1.5 and higher. 1.6 will mask your
password.
Type db2nosql.sh -help to see options
Enter DB:db3a_row

IBM DB2 NoSQL JSON API 1.1.0.0 build 1.3.44
Licensed Materials - Property of IBM
(c) Copyright IBM Corp. 2013 All Rights Reserved.

nosql>Type your JSON query and hit <ENTER>
nosql>Type help() or help for usage information. All commands are case
sensitive.
Meta-data tables and functions for NoSQL JSON have not been created or have
been created incorrectly.
 Please run 'enable(true)' to create them.
```

Continued

```
  You must have the correct admin privileges.
  Run 'enable(false)' to see the SQL that will be used.

nosql>nosql>enable(true)
nosql>Executing SQL...
Database artifacts created successfully.
```

Managing JSON

You can control several of JSON's features by using the nosql.properties file. Although you can place this file anywhere on the application server, you must include its location in the shell's CLASSPATH (see the IBM Knowledge Center for details). Table 10.12 lists the NoSQL properties.

Table 10.12: NoSQL properties

Property	Definition
nosql.asyncMaxThreadCount	Max number of asynchronous threads
nosql.connectionPoolSize	JDBC connection pool size
nosql.tracefile	Trace file name
nosql.tracelevel	Level of trace output
nosql.statementCacheSize	Internal statement cache size
nosql.afg.includeID	Aggregation query adds _id field if no custom_id is specified
nosql.caseSensitiveNames	Schema/collection as case-sensitive
nosql.multiTypedID	Enabled support for multiple _id fields to be different types for documents in the same collection

Working with Data Studio V4.1.1

Data Studio V4.1.1 can be a central development and support product for your organization. Some key business uses are stored procedure development, database administration, SQL analysis, and workload analysis.

Several IBM products use the Eclipse framework, including the Rational tools. Eclipse is built upon the concept of perspectives. A *perspective* is a view of the world, which in this case is DB2. In Data Studio V4.1.1, DB2 provides 24 perspectives, with the capability to also build custom ones. Figure 10.14 shows the perspectives in the Open Perspective window.

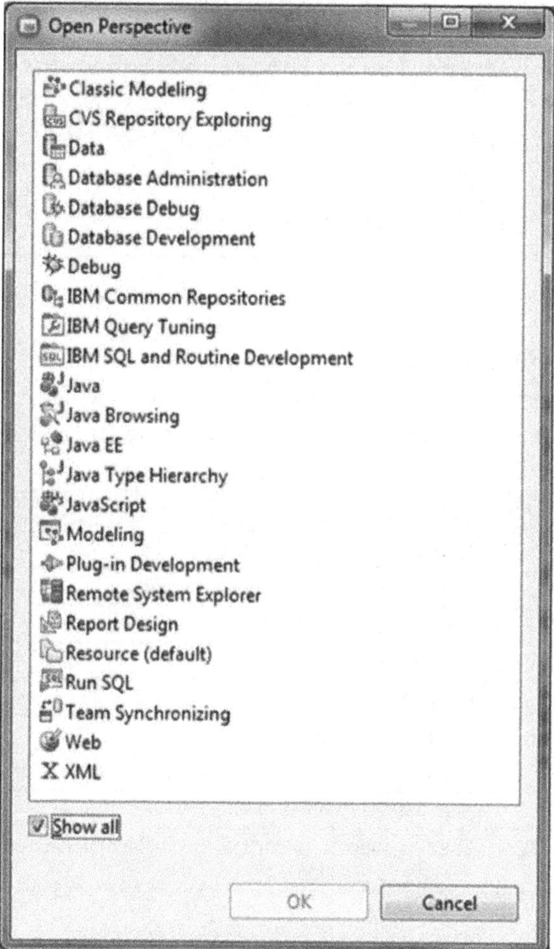

Figure 10.14: Open Perspective window

Configuring a DB2 Database

Data Studio provides five configuration wizards (see Figure 10.15).

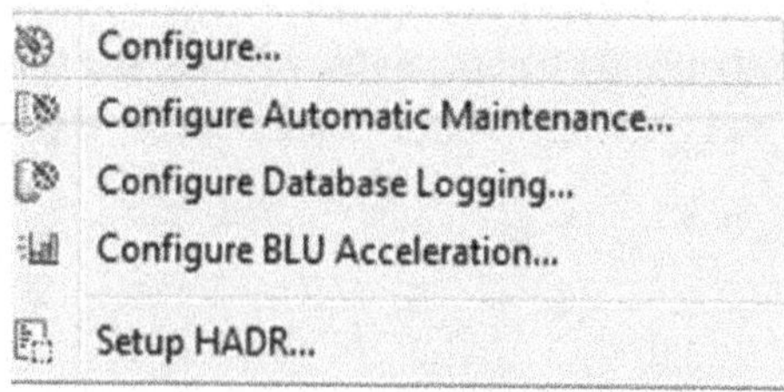

Figure 10.15: Configuration wizards

The Configure Parameters wizard in Figure 10.16 shows the database configuration settings and identifies them based on several key factors, including **Automatic**, **Immediate**, and **Deprecated**. It builds the commands as changes are made.

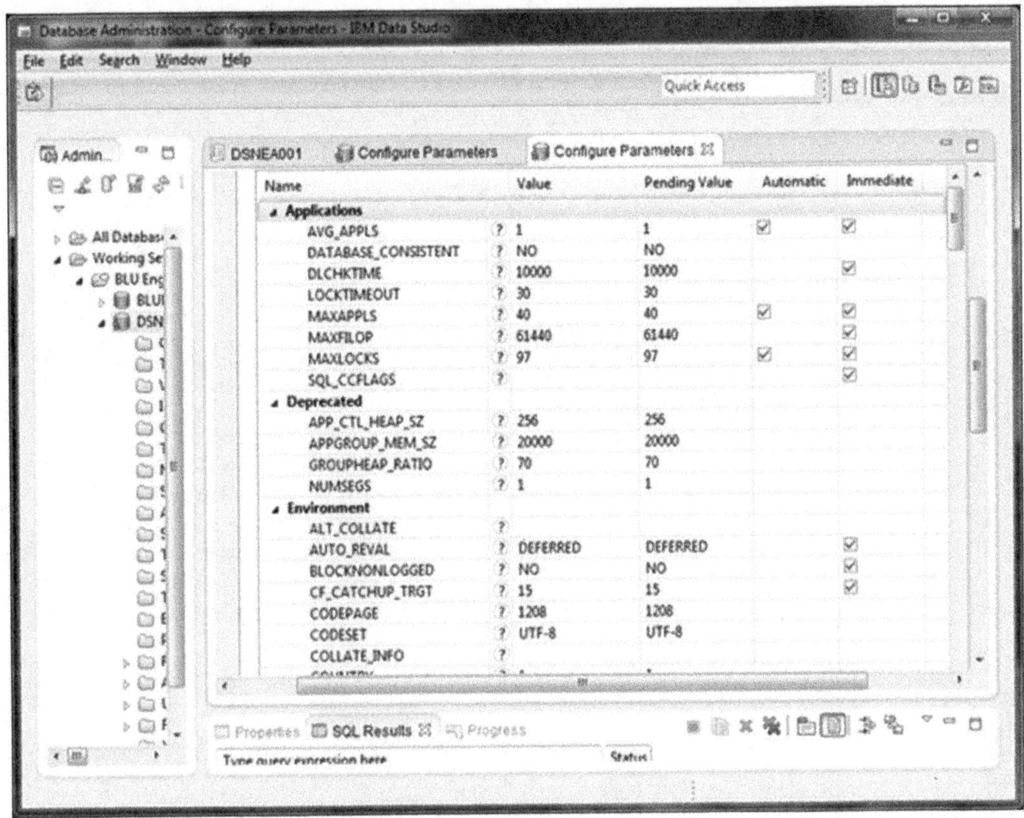

Figure 10.16: Database properties in the Configure Parameters Wizard

The second wizard is Configure Automatic Maintenance. As Figure 10.17 illustrates, this wizard allows changes to the database's automatic maintenance configuration settings, the definition of both an online and offline scheduling window, and the policy definitions for RUNSTATS, REORG, and backups.

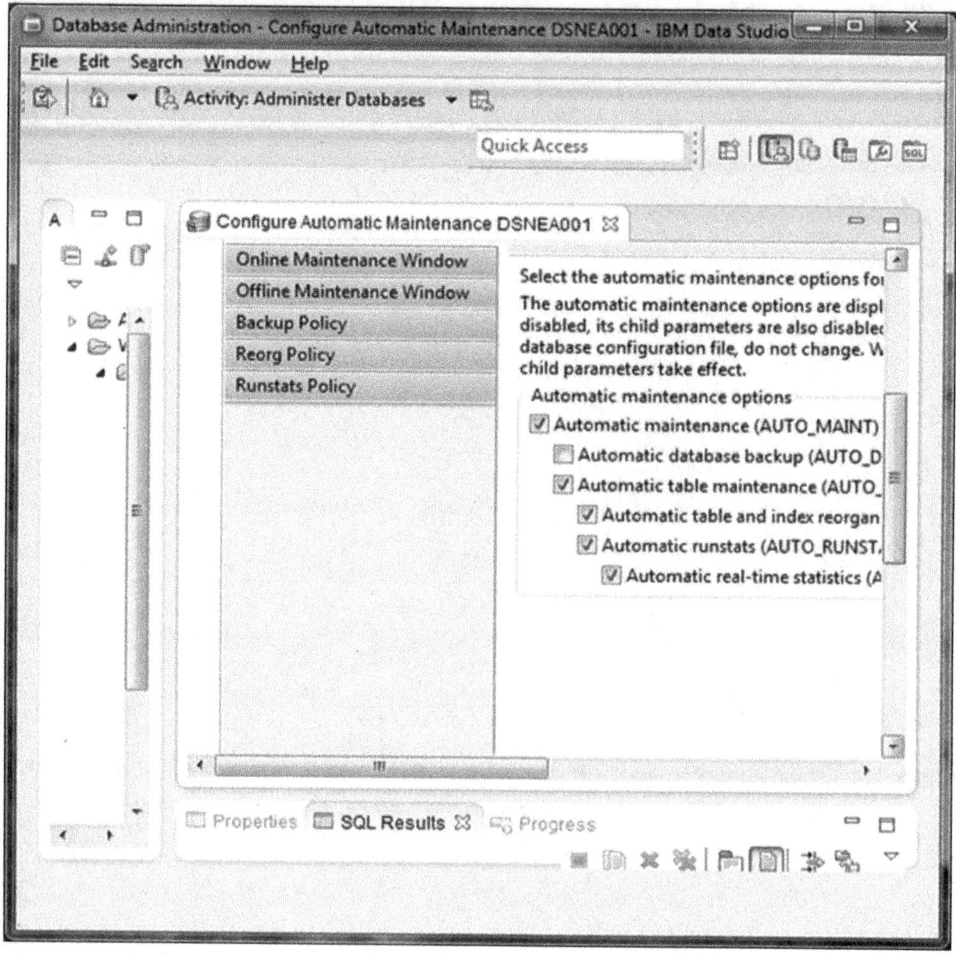

Figure 10.17: Configure Automatic Maintenance wizard

Settings for the **Online** and **Offline Maintenance Window** of operation can be either "allow" or "prevent" based. You can set the window as specific days of the week or to a combination of days of the week and days during the month. In Figure 10.18, the **Online Maintenance Window** is 14 hours long, beginning at 6:00 and ending at 20:00 Monday through Friday.

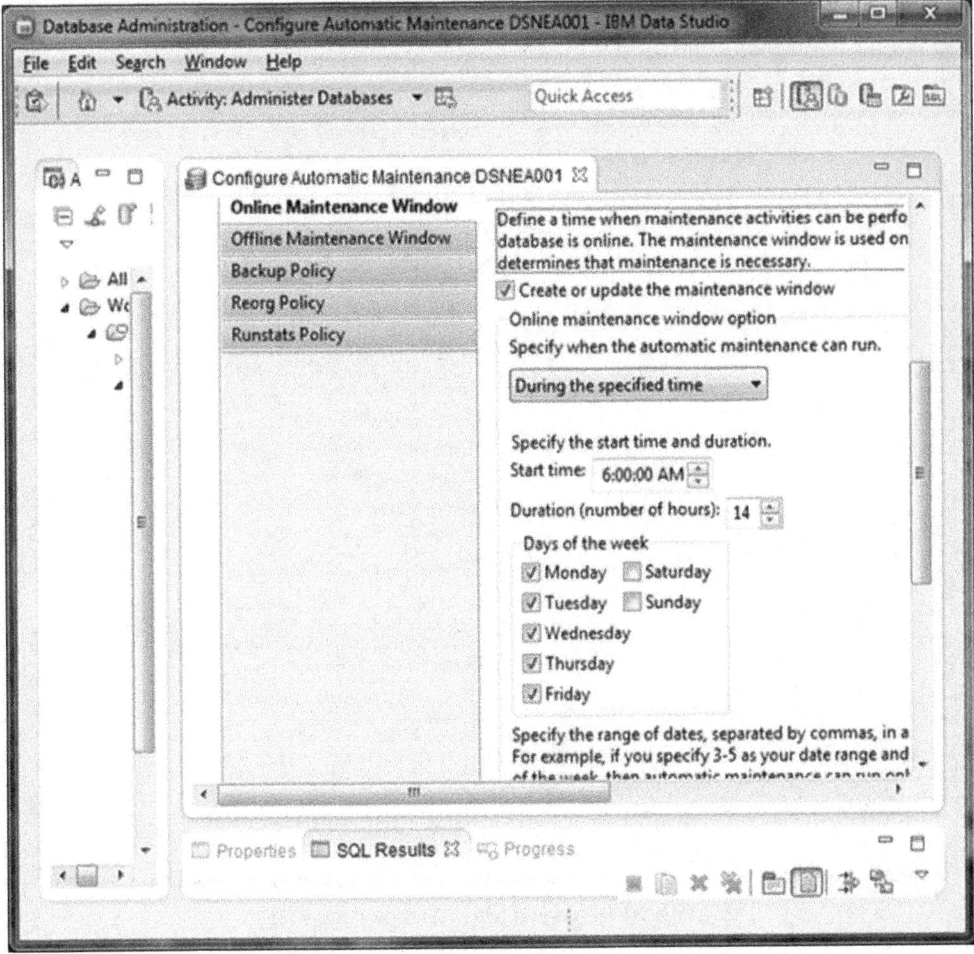

Figure 10.18: Online maintenance schedule

In Figure 10.19, the **Offline Maintenance Window** has a start time of 21:00 (9:00 p.m.) and a duration of seven hours for all seven days of the week.

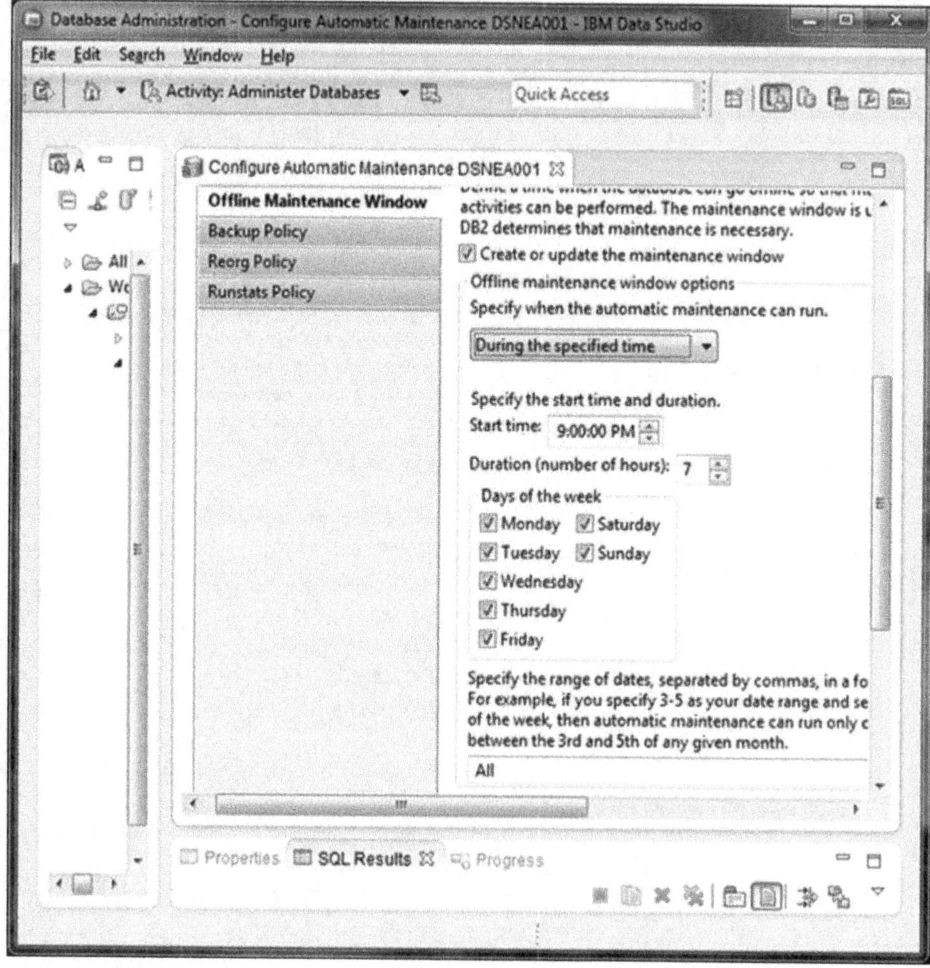

Figure 10.19: Offline Maintenance schedule

For the **Backup Policy**, Figure 10.20 shows an online backup will occur at least once per day with no more than 250 GB of log space taken between backups. The backup will be sent to TSM.

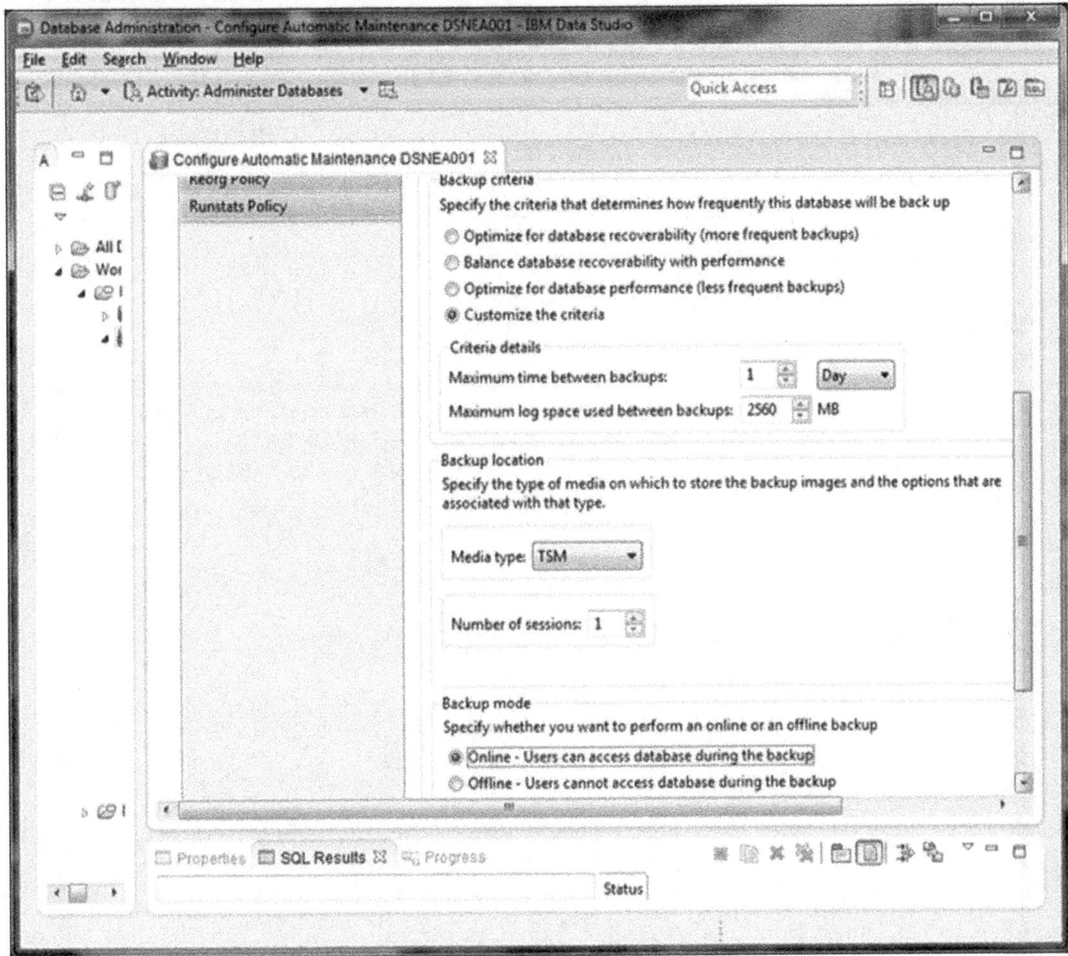

Figure 10.20: Backup schedule

Next, you set **Reorg Policy** to limit the table sizes to 40 GB and to allow REORG to be executed on all tables, including system tables (see Figure 10.21). For compressed tables, select the **Keep Compression data dictionary** option; for indexes, opt to perform the work online.

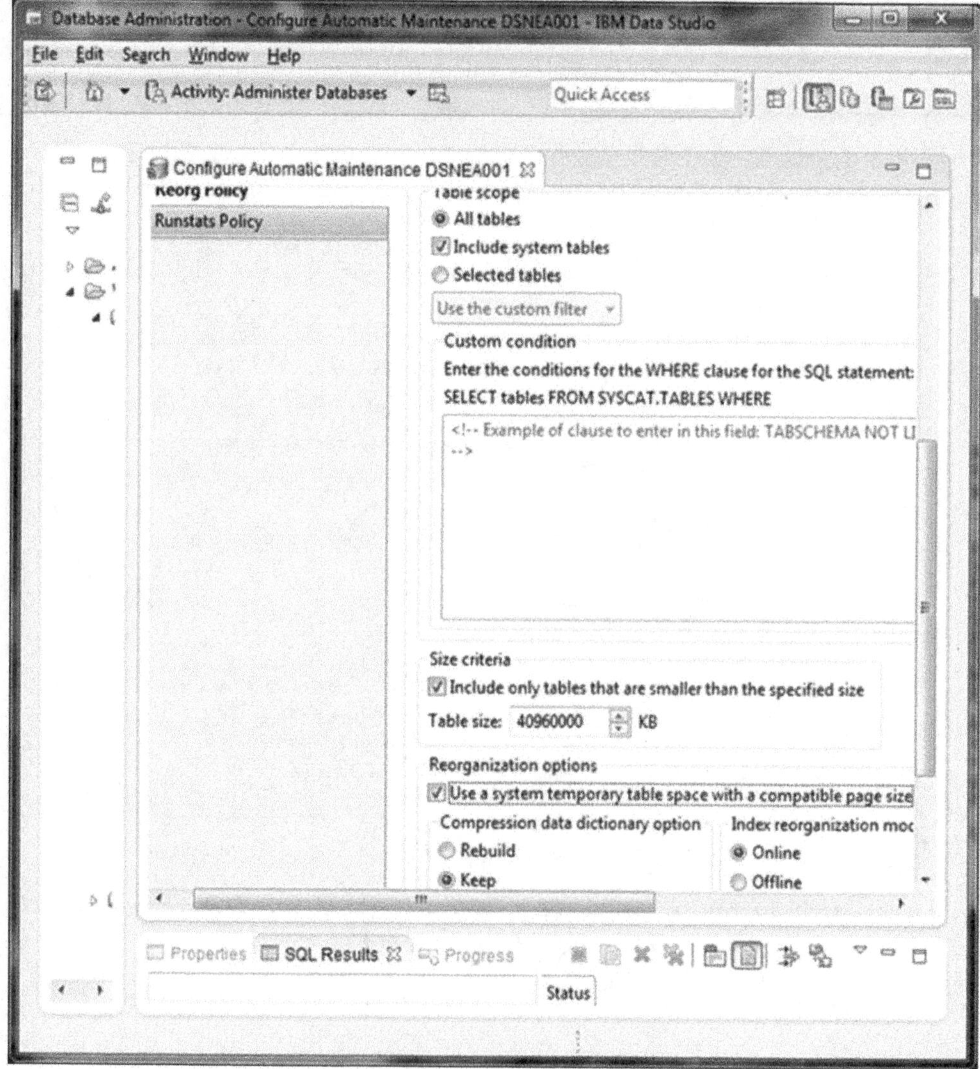

Figure 10.21: Reorg Policy schedule

In Figure 10.22, you set **Runstats Policy** to be all tables.

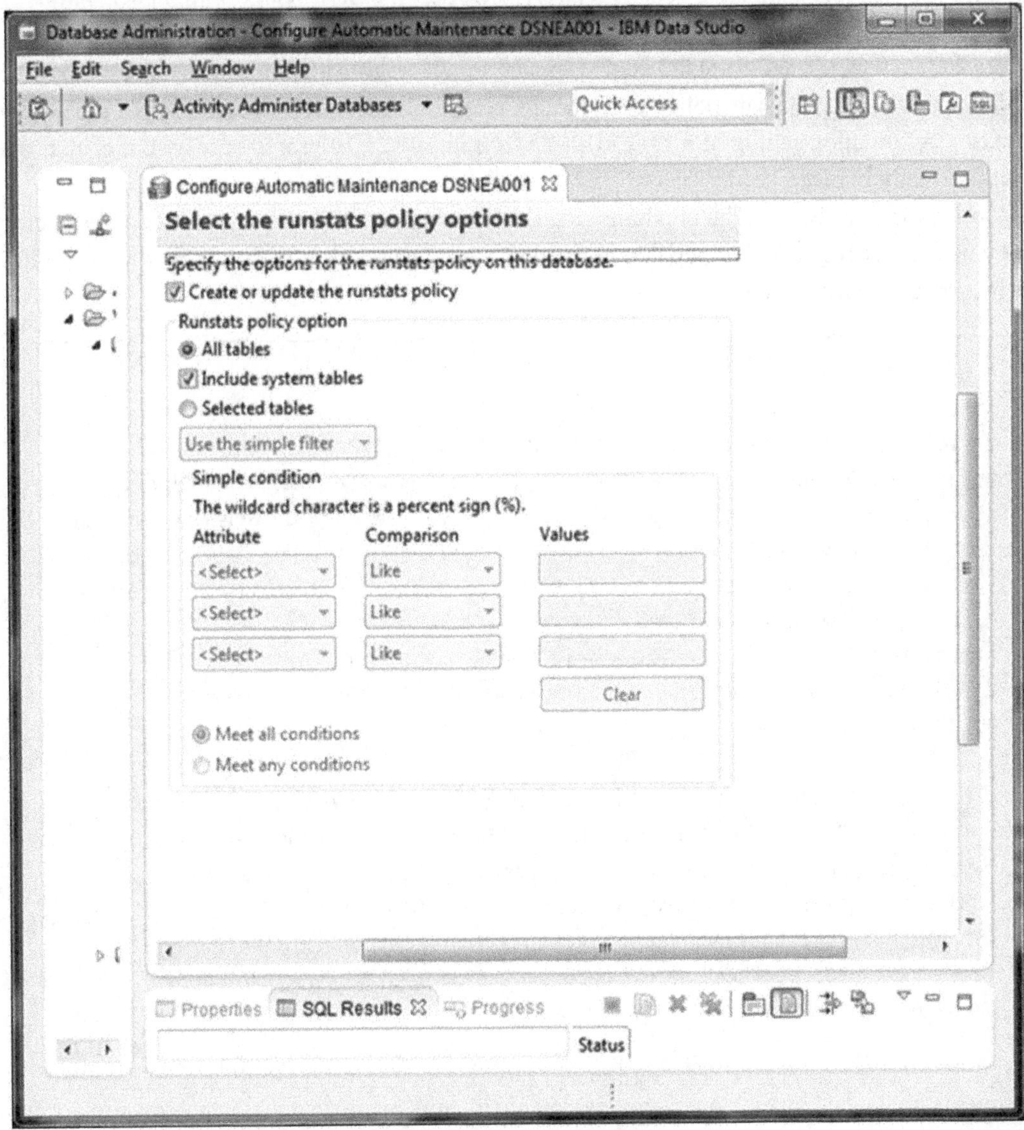

Figure 10.22: Runstats policy

You execute the following generated commands to set up this maintenance plan for your database. The example commands specify a MAINTENANCE_WINDOW policy with both an online and an offline window, an AUTO_BACKUP policy for online backups to occur daily or when log activity reaches 2621440 pages, and an AUTO_REORG policy for all tables with online REORG of indexes.

Notice there is no Runstats policy even though one was selected. The reason is that the database configuration setting of AUTO_RUNSTATS is in effect; therefore, a policy that includes all tables is already in place.

Currently in Data Studio, the maximum log duration value that you can specify on the **Backup Policy** window is 10240 MB. Keep that in mind so that you change it before executing the policy commands to the size desired:

```
CONNECT TO sample;

CALL SYSPROC.AUTOMAINT_SET_POLICY ('MAINTENANCE_WINDOW', BLOB('<?xml
version="1.0" encoding="UTF-8"?><DB2MaintenanceWindows xmlns="http://www
.ibm.com/xmlns/prod/db2/autonomic/config"><OnlineWindow Occurrence="During"
startTime="06:00:00" duration="14"><DaysOfWeek> Mon Tue Wed Thu Fri
</DaysOfWeek><DaysOfMonth>All</DaysOfMonth><MonthsOfYear> All</MonthsOfYear>
</OnlineWindow><OfflineWindow Occurrence="During" startTime="21:00:00"
duration="7"><DaysOfWeek> All</DaysOfWeek><DaysOfMonth>All
</DaysOfMonth><MonthsOfYear> All</MonthsOfYear></OfflineWindow>
</DB2MaintenanceWindows> ') )

CALL SYSPROC.AUTOMAINT_SET_POLICY ( 'AUTO_BACKUP', BLOB('<?xml
version="1.0" encoding="UTF-8"?><DB2AutoBackupPolicy xmlns="http://
www.ibm.com/xmlns/prod/db2/autonomic/config"><BackupOptions mode=
"Online"><BackupTarget><TSMBackupTarget numberOfSessions="1" />
</BackupTarget></BackupOptions><BackupCriteria numberOfFullBackups="1"
timeSinceLastBackup="24" logSpaceConsumedSinceLastBackup="2621440"/>
</DB2AutoBackupPolicy> ') )

CALL SYSPROC.AUTOMAINT_SET_POLICY ( 'AUTO_REORG', BLOB('<?xml version="1.0"
encoding="UTF-8"?><DB2AutoReorgPolicy xmlns="http://www.ibm.com/xmlns/
prod/db2/autonomic/config"><ReorgOptions dictionaryOption="Keep"
indexReorgMode="Online" useSystemTempTableSpace="true"/><ReorgTableScope
maxOfflineReorgTableSize="40960000"><FilterClause /></ReorgTableScope >
</DB2AutoReorgPolicy> ') );

CONNECT RESET;
```

Tuning SQL

Query Workload Tuner is a component of Data Studio that you use to run query analysis to identify performance issues and fix them. One way to get started is to use the Task Launcher window and select **Tune**, as Figure 10.23 shows.

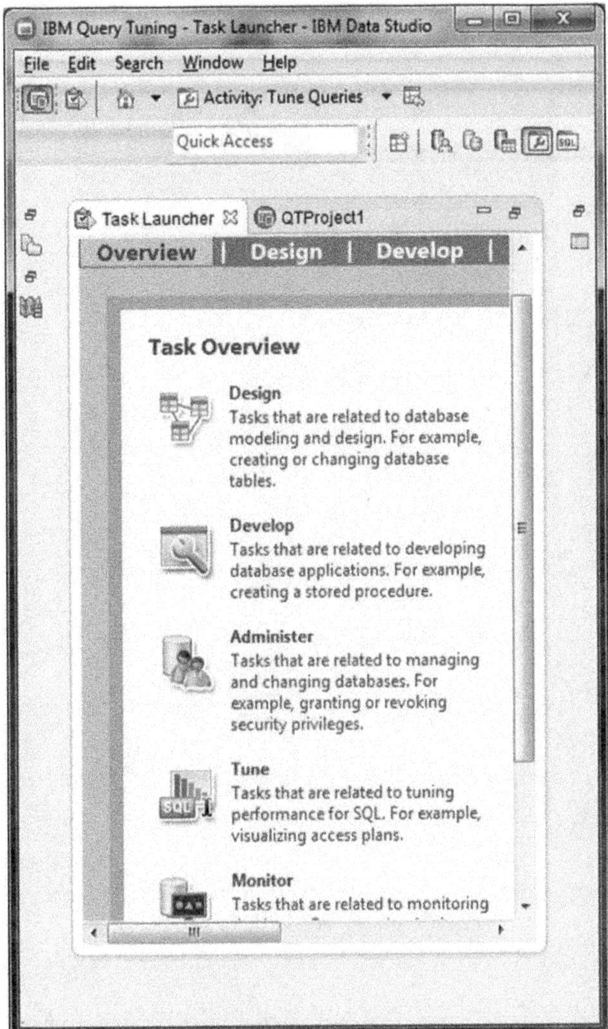

Figure 10.23: Task Launcher

In the next window, select **Start tuning** (see Figure 10.24).

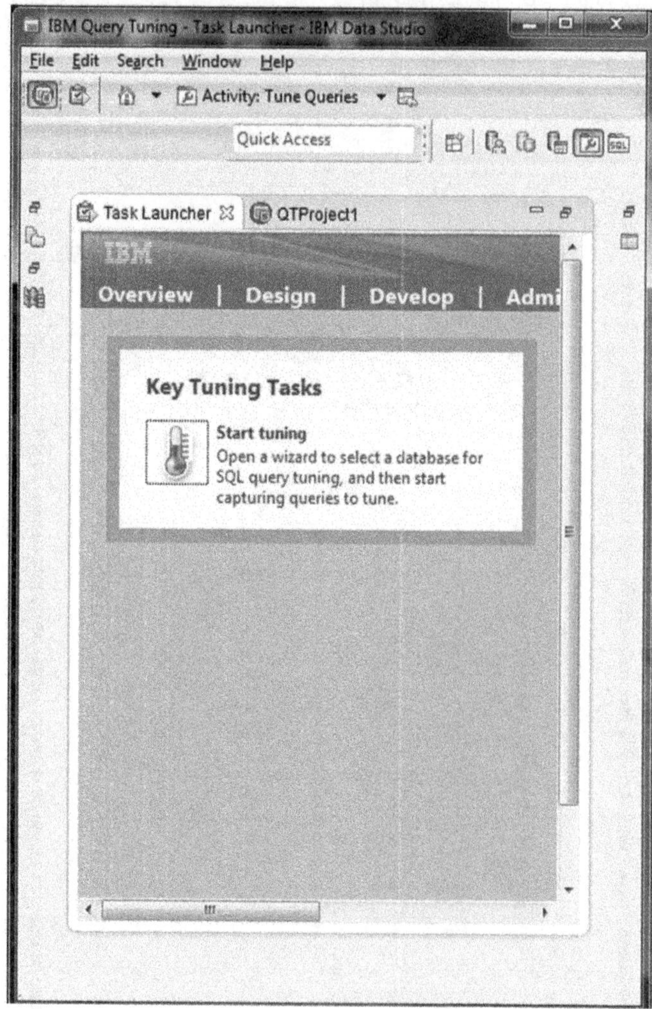

Figure 10.24: Start tuning option

A project is created and the Input SQL Text window is opened, as in Figure 10.25.

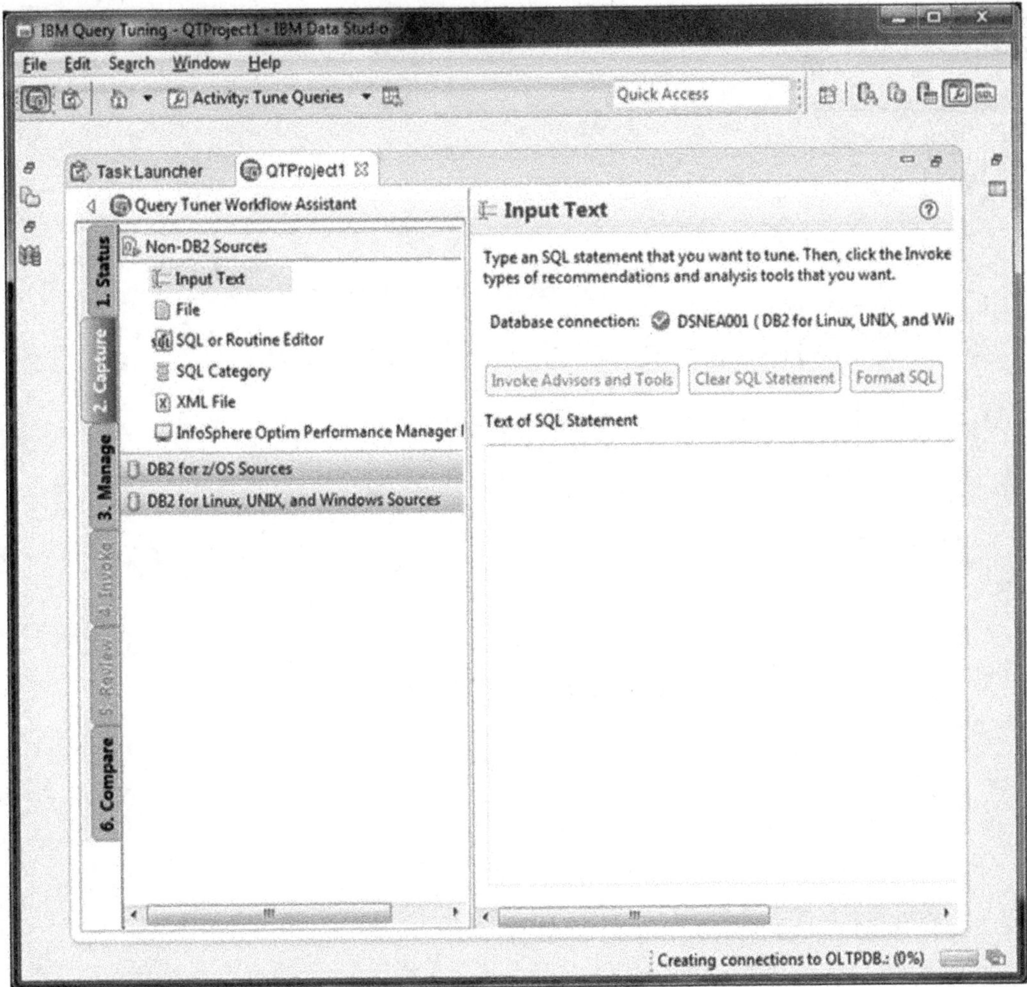

Figure 10.25: Workflow Assistant with Input Text option

Click **File** to capture the SQL statements stored in a file (see Figure 10.26).

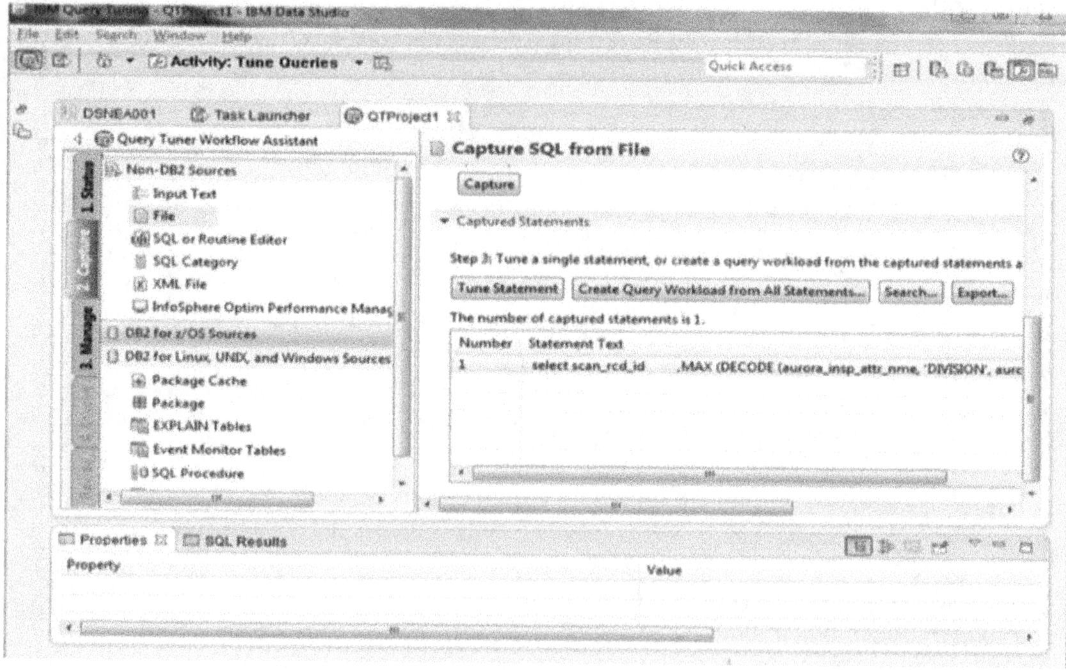

Figure 10.26: Reading SQL from a file

Click **Tune Statement**, then **Select What to Run**. For this example, click the **Select All** button in Figure 10.27.

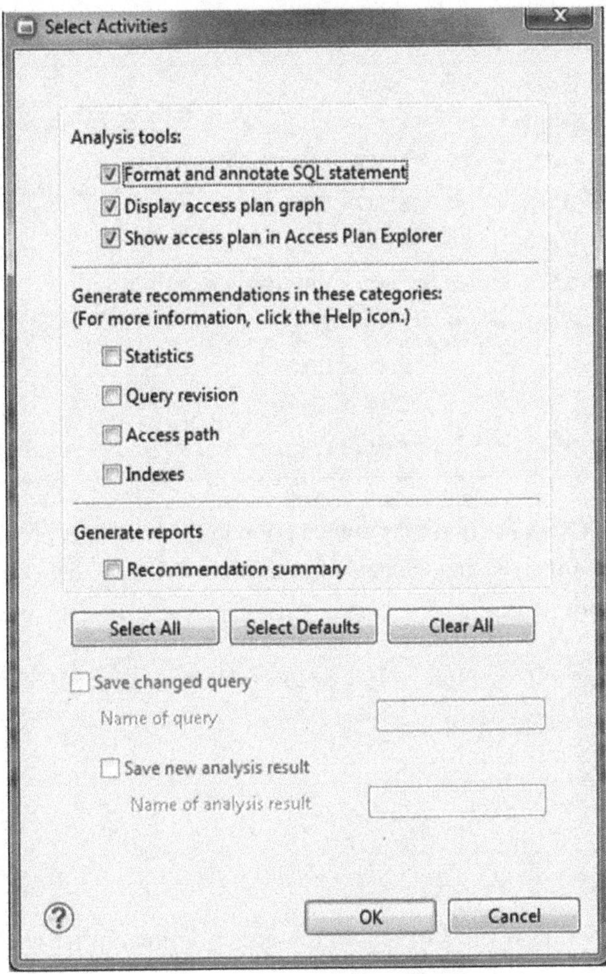

Figure 10.27: Activities selection

The SQL query being tuned looks like this:

```
SELECT F.SCAN_RCD_ID,
       F.TIE_LGTH,
       A.INSP_ATTR_VAL,
       D.TIE_MP_NBR
  FROM XXX.TTIE_FACT F, XXX.TTIE_DIM D, XXX.tattr_dim A
 WHERE      F.TIE_RCD_ID = D.TIE_RCD_ID
       AND A.SCAN_RCD_ID = F.SCAN_RCD_ID
       AND F.TIE_LGTH BETWEEN 108.6 AND 108.7
       AND insp_attr_nme IN ('DIVISION',
                             'SUBDIVISION',
                             'LINESEGMENT',
                             'TRACK');
```

In Figure 10.28, the **Open Formatted Query** option in the left panel provides a detailed description of the tables involved and the data organization. Clicking the icon will open the contents in a new window.

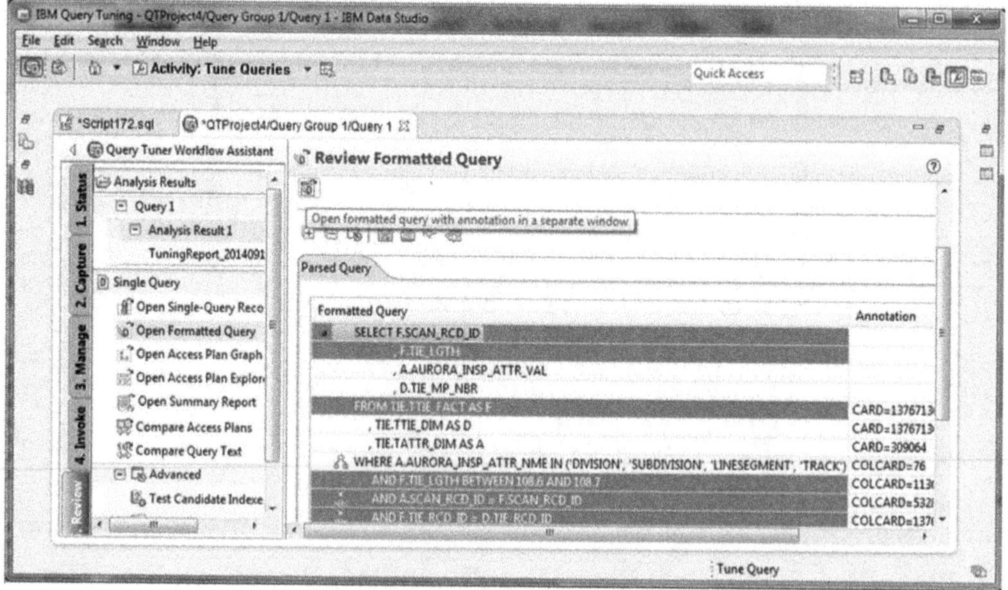

Figure 10.28: Analysis results

Figure 10.29 shows a snippet of the data, such as statistical information and skewed comments about specific columns in the WHERE clause.

Statistics	Comments
CARD=137671308 NPAGES=177012 ORGANIZATION=C	
CARD=137671308 NPAGES=145491 ORGANIZATION=C	
CARD=309064 NPAGES=119 ORGANIZATION=C	
COLCARD=76 MAX_FREQ=2.25%	TIE.TATTR_DIM.AURORA_INSP_ATTR_NME contain(s)...
COLCARD=1136 MAX_FREQ=(missing)	
COLCARD=5328/5328 MAX_FREQ=0.2%/(missing)	TIE.TATTR_DIM.SCAN_RCD_IDTIE.TTIE_FACT.SCAN_R...
COLCARD=137671308/137671308 MAX_FREQ=(missing)	TIE.TTIE_DIM.TIE_RCD_ID contain(s) skewed data

Figure 10.29: Table and column statistics

Let us look at the graphical Explain in Figure 10.30. Again, open it in a new window.

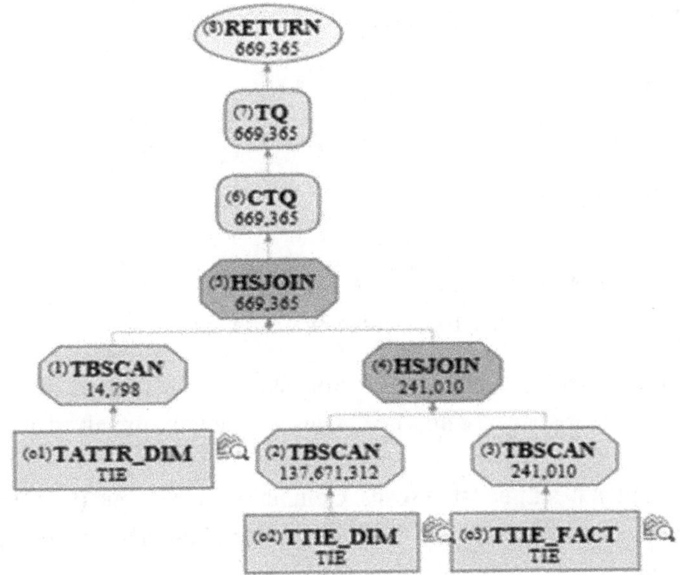

Figure 10.30: Graphical Explain example

Starting with TTIE_FACT, you see the analysis has produced a recommendation (see Figure 10.31).

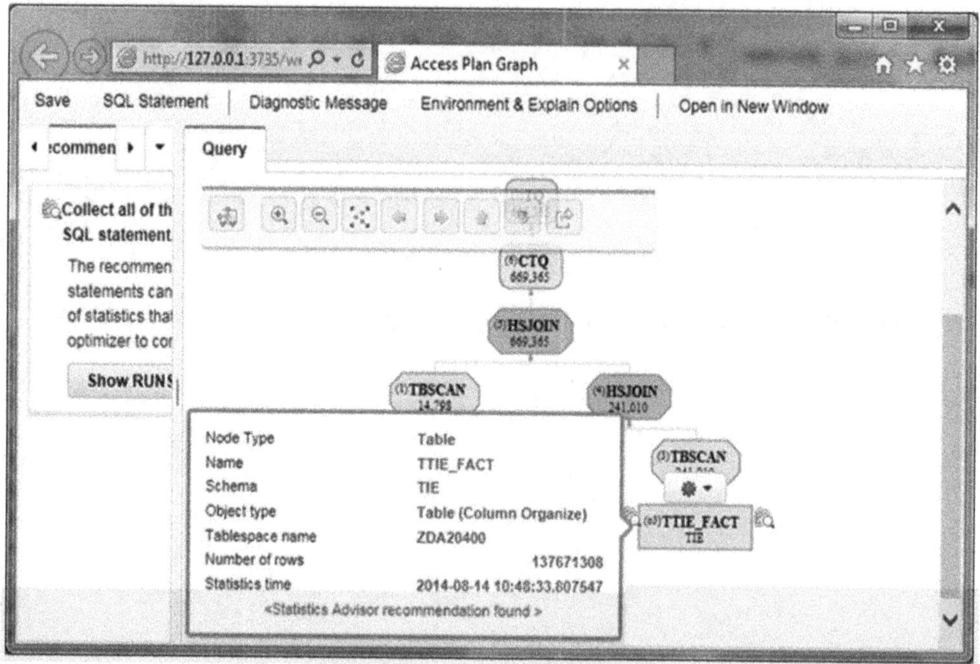

Figure 10.31: Table recommendation

The Statistics Advisor is recommending collecting statistics on all three tables in this query. However, this is not necessary because all three tables are column-organized and statistics collection is automatic.

Notice that this Explain has three table scans. Columnar Table Queue (CTQ) is the handoff point between column and row processing. Some query operations such as sorting are performed on row-organized data.

In this case, there are no sort operations in the execution plan. The result set formation is occurring and is returned to the requestor in row format.

As Figure 10.32 illustrates, CTQ is followed by Table Queue (TQ) and then Return.

What happens to the overall plan if you add DISTINCT? Nothing, because the UNIQUE process is performed on column data. But what happens to the overall plan if you add ORDER BY? As Figure 10.33 shows, you get an Access Plan Advisor recommendation and a sort operation after the data is converted from column to row organization.

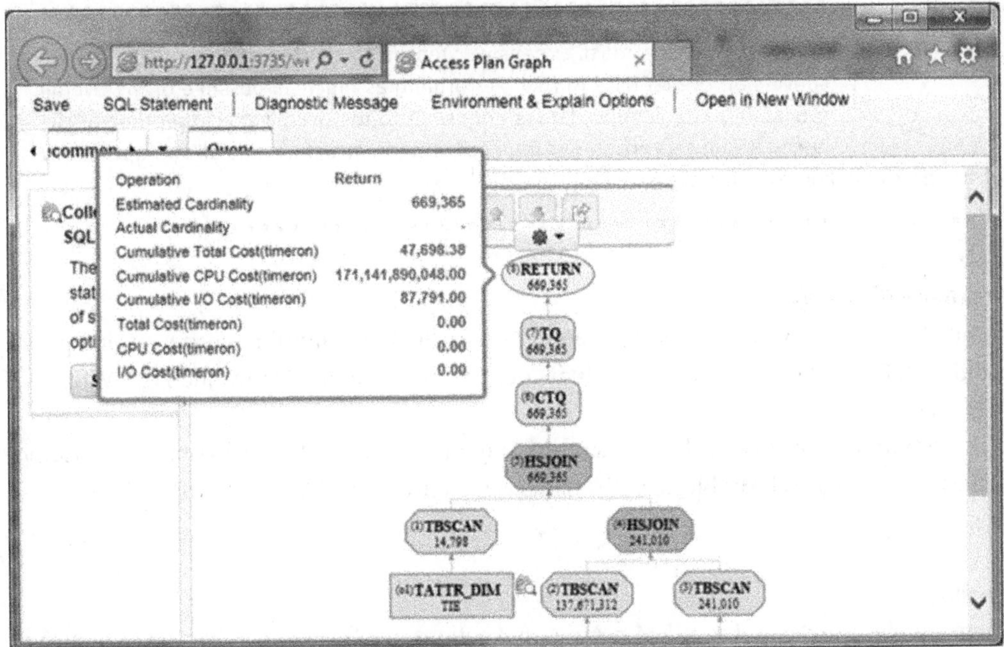

Figure 10.32: Return statistics

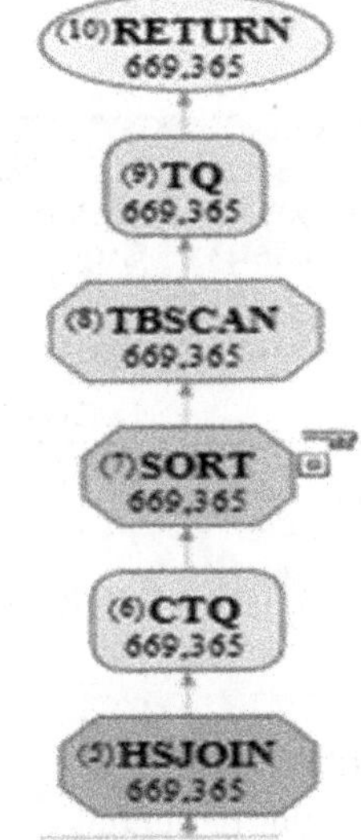

Figure 10.33: Graphical Explain with sort

Note: Perhaps the most expensive step in processing columnar data is the conversion of that data to row. Performing as much as possible of the overall processing as columnar data is important to the overall execution time of the query. Result sets are always returned as a row structure, and all sort operations are performed on row structures.

Workload Management

For years, DB2 has provided the DB2 governor as a method of controlling resources and priority. In addition, DB2 contains WLM features in its operations, including UNIX and DB2 WLM components.

This section will identify the keys to successfully implementing WLM and provide specific examples. To manage WLM objects in the database requires WLMADM- or DBADM-level access.

Planning

Before we undertake deploying WLM policies and actions, we first need a clear set of goals. Is there already in place a clear set of Service Level Agreements (SLAs)? Are the workloads grouped into classifications by importance? Regardless of the goals, is it possible for them to be quantified?

A good way to map out the WLM definitions is to build a workload matrix something like that in Table 10.13.

Table 10.13: WLM planning

Evaluation Order	Workload Name	App Name	System User	Session User	Session Group	Session Role	Client User ID	Client App Name	Client Work Station
1	Tier1				Tier1Grp				
2	Tier2				Tier2Grp				
3	Tier3				Tier3Grp				

Once you have the workload matrix completed, follow these steps to define the WLM policies:

- Create the workload definitions.
- Create service classes for the identified workloads.
- Create work classes based on thresholds or actions.
- Relate the work classes to the service classes by using REMAP and MAP actions.
- Obtain baseline performance measures before activating WLM.
- Activate WLM policies and gather performance measures to compare.

WLM Objects

As Table 10.14 shows, WLM consists of six objects.

Table 10.14: WLM objects

Object Name	Catalog Information	Functions
Service class	SERVICECLASSES SYSSERVICECLASSES	WLM_GET_SERVICE_SUPERCLASS_STATS WLM_GET_SERVICE_SUBCLASS_DETAILS WLM_GET_SERVICE_SUBCLASS_STATS WLM_GET_SERVICE_SUBCLASS MON_GET_SERVICE_SUBCLASS_DETAILS MON_GET_SERVICE_SUBCLASS_STATS MON_GET_SERVICE_SUPERCLASS_STATS
Workload	WORKLOAD WORLOADAUTH WORKLOADCONNATTR SYSWORKLOADAUTH SYSWORKLOADCONNATTR SYSWORKLOADS	MON_GET_WORKLOAD MON_GET_WORKLOAD_DETAILS MON_GET_WORKLOAD_STATS WLM_GET_SERVICE_CLASS_OCCURRENCES WLM_GET_SERVICE_CLASS_WORKLOAD_ OCCURRENCES
Threshold	SYSTHRESHOLDS	
Work class	WORKCLASSES WORKCLASSSETS WORKCLASSATTRIBUTES SYSWORKCLASSSETS	MON_GET_WORK_ACTION_SET_STATS
Work action	WORKACTIONSETS WORKACTIONS SYSWORKACTIONS	WLM_GET_WORK_ACTION_SET_STATS
Histogram	HISTOGRAMTEMPLATEBINS HISTOGRAMTEMPLATES HISTOGRAMTEMPLATEUSE	

WLM DDL administers these objects and is different from other DB2 DDL. WLM DDL is executed in the order it is issued. Only one WLM DDL can be uncommitted at a time. All subsequent DDL waits until the active DDL is committed or rolled back. Each DDL must be followed by a COMMIT or ROLLBACK statement. Neither XA transactions nor z/OS is supported.

Classes

There are two groups of classes: service and work. A *service class* is an execution classification in which resources are assigned and managed. All work runs in a service class, and you assign the resources by creating a relationship between a workload and either a superclass or a subclass. To establish the relationship, use either a threshold action (REMAP ACTIVITY) or a work action (MAP ACTIVITY).

Any workload not explicitly related to a service class defaults to SYSTEMDEFAULTUSERCLASS, which is a superclass. A service class that has no parent is called a *superclass* (think of it as a work domain).

This example creates three service classes for PRODUCTION and one for TEST:

```
CREATE SERVICE class Tier1
COMMIT
CREATE service class Tier2
COMMIT
CREATE service class Tier3
COMMIT
CREATE service class Test
COMMIT
```

A *work class* identifies database activity based on the activities' attributes. Database activities such as load, DML, read, write, call, and DDL are definable to a work class. You can also define a work class on predictive elements—for example, on estimated cost (timerons). This allows work to be classified and managed before it starts running.

Work classes are grouped into *work class sets*. You create a work class set by using the CREATE WORK CLASS SET statement. A second way to create work classes is with the ALTER WORK CLASS SET ADD command:

```
CREATE WORK CLASS SET COLUMN_QUERIES ( WORK CLASS TIER3_CPU_COST WORK TYPE
DML FOR TIMERONCOST FROM 150000 TO UNBOUNDED )

CREATE WORK CLASS SET LARGE_RESULTSET_QUERIES ( WORK CLASS LARGE_RESULTS
WORK TYPE DML FOR CARDINALITY FROM 20000 TO UNBOUNDED )

CREATE WORK CLASS SET FAVOR_WRITES ( WORK CLASS DML_WRITES WORK TYPE WRITE )

ALTER WORK CLASS SET FAVOR_WRITES ADD WORK CLASS TIER1_CPU_COST WORK TYPE
WRITE FOR TIMERONCOST FROM 0 TO 100
```

Workloads

You group transactions into workloads either by origin (connection attributes) or by characteristics of the transaction, such as cost, type, or object access. Two default workloads are created at database creation. All user transactions you execute are placed in a workload called SYSTEMDEFAULTUSERWORKLOAD, and administration requests are assigned to SYSTEMDEFAULTADMWORKLOAD. A workload simply identifies the work you want to manage.

This example creates eight workloads, assigning some to work groups and others to an individual user:

```
CREATE WORKLOAD WL_TIER1 SESSION_USER GROUP ('TIER1GRP')
SERVICE CLASS TIER1
COMMIT
CREATE WORKLOAD WL_TIER2 SESSION_USER GROUP ('TIER2GRP')
SERVICE CLASS TIER2
COMMIT
CREATE WORKLOAD WL_TIER3 SESSION_USER GROUP ('TIER3GRP')
SERVICE CLASS TIER3
COMMIT
CREATE WORKLOAD WL_TIE SYSTEM_USER ('ENTIESUP')
SERVICE CLASS TIER1
COMMIT
CREATE WORKLOAD WL_ROW SYSTEM_USER ('ROWUSER')
SERVICE CLASS TIER1
COMMIT
CREATE WORKLOAD WL_COLUMN SYSTEM_USER ('COLUSER')
SERVICE CLASS TIER2
COMMIT
CREATE WORKLOAD WL_PROD SESSION_USER GROUP ('PRODGRP')
SERVICE CLASS TIER2
COMMIT
CREATE WORKLOAD WL_TEST SESSION_USER GROUP ('TESTGRP')
SERVICE CLASS TEST
COMMIT
```

Let us walk through a simple example. Change the service class TEST to a lower prefetch priority:

```
ALTER SERVICE CLASS TEST PREFETCH PRIORITY LOW
COMMIT
```

Create a new service class called CUST_WEB and assign it to the superclass TIER1:

```
CREATE SERVICE CLASS CUST_WEB UNDER TIER1
COMMIT
```

Create a new threshold called MAXSERVICECLASSCONNECTIONS to limit the number of concurrent connections to the database to 20:

```
CREATE THRESHOLD MAXSERVICECLASSCONNECTIONS FOR SERVICE CLASS CUST_WEB
UNDER TIER1 ACTIVITIES
ENFORCEMENT DATABASE WHEN TOTALMEMBERCONNECTIONS > 20 STOP EXECUTION
COMMIT
```

Create a second MAXSERVICECLASSCONNECTIONS threshold and assign it to superclass TEST. It will limit concurrent connections to 100:

```
CREATE THRESHOLD MAXSERVICECLASSCONNECTIONS FOR SERVICE CLASS TEST ACTIVITIES
ENFORCEMENT DATABASE PARTITION
WHEN TOTALSCMEMBERCONNECTIONS > 100 STOP EXECUTION
COMMIT
```

So the workload WL_TEST SESSION_USER will be limited to 100 concurrent connections, and WL_TIER1 will be limited to 20.

Changing a Database's Code Set

Both BLU and pureScale require databases to be Unicode, so you should create all new databases as Unicode. Chances are good that the requirement to convert data to a Unicode code set will happen. Because a database cannot be altered to a different code set, this will mean you must unload and load the data.

In the past, string units of character data have been stored in a relational database in bytes. So for a single-byte character set (SBCS), each character represents one byte. The string unit of the column data type is a byte, sometimes referred to as an *octet*.

The byte approach can be problematic when moving from an SBCS to a multibyte character set (MBCS), as the representation of a character can be more than one byte depending on the encoding. This can result in truncation of string data because the length of the target Unicode column is too small for the encoded MBCS data.

You can set the encoding method at the session level, the database level, or the column level. OCTETS encoding can be set for any database code set. CODEUNITS16 and CODEUNITS32 are allowed only in Unicode databases.

As previously stated, OCTETS string units are byte-length units. CODEUNITS16 string units are Unicode UTF-16 code sets and are double-byte–length units, and CODEUNITS32 string units are Unicode UTF-32 and are character-length units.

At the session level, execute the following command:

```
SET NLS_STRING_UNITS = Encoding
```

At the database level, use this UPDATE command:

```
UPDATE DB CFG FOR SAMPLE USING STRING_UNITS Encoding
```

where Encoding is OCTETS, CODEUNITS16, or CODEUNITS32.

At the column level, execute the CREATE TABLE or ALTER TABLE statement:

```
CREATE TABLE TEST_ENCODING
      (STR_COL VARCHAR(2000 CODEUNITS32),
       STR_CLOB CLOB(1M OCTETS),
       STR_GRAPH GRAPHIC(63 CODEUNITS32)
      )
  ALTER TABLE TEST_ENCODING
  ALTER COLUMN STR_COL SET DATA TYPE VARCHAR(3000 OCTETS)
```

Using Export

When moving data between databases with different code sets, you can use the EXPORT command with MODIFIED BY CODEPAGE=*CodePage*, where CodePage is the code page value of the target database (for example, a valid code page for UTF-8 is 1208).

To migrate data from a non-Unicode database to a Unicode database, follow these steps:

Step 1: Remove access to the source database.

Step 2: Export the data by using the Export utility. For all export statements, use a modifier code page and set it to the target code page used.

Step 3: Dump the DDL by using db2look.

Step 4: Dump the configurations that include the registry, DBM, and database.

Step 5: Drop the source database.

Step 6: Re-create the source database by using the CREATE DATABASE command as Unicode and by using ASM, which is now the default.

Step 7: Execute DDL from db2look output to create the required objects. If using the column-level method, make the encoding changes in the file before executing.

Step 8: Run the configurations for the registry, DBM, and database.

Step 9: *Optional*: Set SYSTEM_UNITS to the required encoding.

Step 10: Stop and start the DB2 instance to make all changes active.

Step 11: Import and load the data.

Step 12: *Optional*: Set NLS_STRING_UNITS to the desired encoding for each import or load session.

Step 13: *Optional*: Collect statistics and rebind as needed.

Note: IBM DB2 10.5 FP4 (Cancun) is required to use the SYSTEM_UNITS or NLS_STRING_UNITS method.

Shadow Tables

The idea behind shadow tables is good parenting where DB2 is the parent. The DBA builds the table structures, and DB2 decides on a query by query basis where best to run.

Think of a dynamic query as having two doors: row and MQT column. When you submit a SELECT statement, components of DB2 guide the request to the appropriate door. DB2 Analytics Accelerator for z/OS (old IDAA) does this by using DB2/Z as the parent and Netezza as the column door. This solution has a minimum latency of one minute.

With shadow tables, you begin by using a standard OLTP (row) database. For specific tables within this database, you want to add a possible columnar solution for queries accessing the target table, without making application changes.

You do the work to identify key opportunities where columnar tables might improve throughput. Once you have identified them, you make changes to isolate those workloads and control risks by allowing only those workloads to run across either row- or column-organized tables. One reason for this is that not all workloads can handle an in-sync delay (latency) between the row and column side. To keep the MQT-column side up to date with the row side, use IBM InfoSphere Data Replication–Change Data Capture (InfoSphere CDC) in a unidirectional manner.

Deploying Shadow Tables

To get shadow tables working requires significant knowledge about InfoSphere Data Replication. This section provides sufficient information to enable you to deploy and run shadow tables.

You will need three additional software products, all of which are already licensed as part of the requirement to run BLU. This license provides DB2 LUW to DB2 LUW replication; for shadow tables, it is replication within a single DB2 instance.

Software Requirements

You can learn how to download software for IBM DB2 10.5 for Linux, UNIX, and Windows at *www-01.ibm.com/support/docview.wss?uid=swg21638030*. You can find a helpful PDF document entitled "Bringing BLU Acceleration performance to OLTP environments with Shadow Tables" at *public.dhe.ibm.com/ps/products/db2/info/vr105/pdf/en_US/shadowtablesdb21050.pdf#nameddest=C0061672*.

There are two URLs you should save. One is Passport Advantage, which is the place to go to download licensed software under your customer agreement (*www-01.ibm.com/software/howtobuy/passportadvantage/?lnk=ftpl*). The second important URL is IBM Fix Central, where you can find all the fix packs for IBM products (*www-933.ibm.com/support/fixcentral/options*). The Fix Central site for replication products is *www-933.ibm.com/support/fixcentral/options?selectionBean.selectedTab=find&selection=ibm%2fInformation+Management%3bibm%2fInformation+Management%2fIBM+InfoSphere+Data+Replication*.

Table 10.15 lists the required software. Select the software for the correct target operating system.

Table 10.15: CDC requirement for shadow tables
IBM InfoSphere Data Replication–CDC DB2 10.2.1
IBM InfoSphere Data Replication–CDC Fix Pack 15 or higher
IBM InfoSphere Data Replication–CDC for Access Server 10.2.1
IBM InfoSphere Data Replication–CDC for Access Server 10.2.1 Fix Pack 5 or higher
IBM InfoSphere Data Replication–CDC for Management Console 10.2.1 for Windows

The software installation is usually straightforward, but there are a few things to remember:

Install the software in the above-listed order. Do not configure the instance until you are installing Access Server Fix Pack 5. It will prompt you to configure.

Before installing any software, create the accounts and groups that will run the software and manage the subscriptions. The software is not installed or executed by root.

In the following examples, db2cdc01 is the UNIX account that will execute and maintain the software. The UNIX group cdcadmin as well as the secondary group DB2 SYSADM are also assigned to db2cdc01.

For the example, you will install all the software on Linux Red Hat 6 except for the Management Console, which must be installed on Windows. The UNIX software requires 32-bit support libraries be installed on the server. As root, you can execute "yum install gtk2.i686" to install the required x86 32-bit libraries. A file system named /db/cdc will store the replication software on UNIX, and you will assign ownership to db2cdc01.

Install the data replication software on the DB2 instance server where you will configure shadow tables. You can install the Access Server on UNIX or Windows on a separate central server to support multiple DB2 instances. In the example, you will install the Access Server on the DB2 instance server in the same install directory path as the data replication product.

The tools use two TCP/IP ports, and in the installation you will accept the defaults.

Now that you have an idea about how to install the software, let us go through an installation in detail.

Database Requirements

The database requirements are basically the same as for BLU but without DB2_WORKLOAD=ANALYTICS. SORTHEAP and SHEAPTHRES_SHR cannot be automatic, but they still need to be significantly large. UTIL_HEAP_SZ can be automatic but must be more than 1 MB pages. Table 10.16 shows the shadow table database requirements.

Table 10.16: Shadow table database requirements
Unicode plus IDENTITY or IDENTITY_16BIT
Automatic Storage Management
Automatic table maintenance, including statistics and space reclaim Auto_runstats and auto_reorg
DB2_WORKLOAD=""
Connection stored procedure
InfoSphere Data Replication–CDC subscription mirroring
DB2_EXTENDED_OPTIMIZATION add OPT_SORTHEAP_EXCEPT_COL db2set DB2_EXTENDED_OPTIMIZATION="OPT_SORTHEAP_EXCEPT_COL <SORTHEAP>"
ORGANIZE BY ROW
SHEAPTHRES_SHR = 50% of DATABASE_MEMORY
SORTHEAP = 50% of SHEAPTRHES_SHR
UTIL_HEAP_SZ large enough and Automatic

Table 10.16: Shadow table database requirements (continued)
Archive logging
SYSTOOL objects have to be created and properly granted

Identifying Workloads That May Benefit from Shadow Tables

Table 10.17 lists the processing criteria to consider as potential candidates for shadow tables.

Table 10.17: Workload identification

Table size	Row organized >= 5 MB rows
Integrated workloads	Must have mixed workloads from the same initiation point; some decision-support or warehouse-like queries mixed in with OLTP
Latency aware	Select workloads okay with some latency
Near real-time requirements	Dashboard like; cannot be 24 hours old
Reasonable IUD volumes	Not 100 percent IUD; needs some manageable rates
MQT restrictions	Okay with the added MQT restrictions
Queries: dynamic selects	• Zero matching index scans • Table scans • Returns few columns • Limited sorting • No joins or only between column tables

Note: Notice that query execution time is not listed. You will learn why it is not a little later.

A Database for Shadow Tables

Before you can set up and use shadow tables, you must configure the database correctly. The sectión "Database Requirements" lists all the requirements.

Let us assume that you have a standard OLTP database that is already defined with Unicode, IDENTITY, and ASM. If STMM is active, you need to remove SORTHEAP and SHEAPTHRES_SHR from being automatically managed:

```
db2 "update db cfg for <dbname> using
       SHEAPTHRES_SHR <50% database_memory>"
db2 "update  db cfg for <dbname> using
        sortheap <10-20% sheapthres_shr>"
```

Next, verify that automatic maintenance is turned on and that archive logging and UTIL_HEAP_SZ is at least 1 MB pages:

```
LOGARCHMETH1 = DISK:/db/archivelog/db2row01/oltpdb/
UTIL_HEAP_SZ = AUTOMATIC(1000000)

Automatic maintenance                          (AUTO_MAINT) = ON
   Automatic database backup               (AUTO_DB_BACKUP) = OFF
   Automatic table maintenance             (AUTO_TBL_MAINT) = ON
     Automatic runstats                     (AUTO_RUNSTATS) = ON
       Real-time statistics               (AUTO_STMT_STATS) = ON
       Statistical views                 (AUTO_STATS_VIEWS) = ON
       Automatic sampling                   (AUTO_SAMPLING) = ON
     Automatic reorganization                  (AUTO_REORG) = ON
```

Set the registry parameter DB2_EXTENDED_OPTIMIZATION by adding OPT_SORTHEAP_EXCEPT_COL:

```
db2set DB2_EXTENDED_OPTIMIZATION="OPT_SORTHEAP_EXCEPT_COL 10240"
```

To create the SYSTOOLS tables in support of shadow tables, run the following command:

```
CALL SYSPROC.SYSINSTALLOBJECTS('REPL_MQT','C',null,null) ;
```

You grant PUBLIC CREATEIN authority on schema SYSTOOLS and select access to any user running shadow workloads on SYSTOOLS.REPL_MQT_LATENCY table. Only CDC replication should be updating this table.

Creating a Shadow Table

You begin with a row-organized table that has been identified as having workloads that might benefit from column organization. You create an MQT column-organized table that matches the current row table. Using Data Studio, select **Create MQT**, as Figure 10.34 shows.

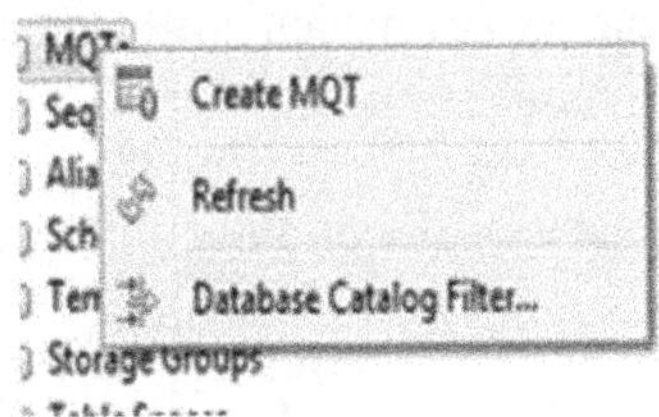

Figure 10.34: Create MQT option

MQT is defined as column organized, optimized, and maintained with replication control (see Figure 10.35).

<Column-organized materialized query tab.

General
Columns
Privileges
Table Spaces
SQL
Documentation

Name: TDTL_STG
Schema: TIE_COL
Table organization: Column
Refresh: DEFERRED
Optimize query: ☑
Maintained by: REPLICATION

Figure 10.35: MQT settings

You enter the SELECT statement used by replication to match up columns between two tables, as in Figure 10.36. The licensed use of InfoSphere Data Replication–CDC for shadow tables restricts the copying of data to nontranslation. So for all practical purposes, it is a one-to-one column copy.

Connection : 10.23.20.100 - db2row01 - OLTPDB

Properties | SQL Results | Progress

<Column-organized materialized query table> TDTL_STG

General
Columns
Privileges
Table Spaces
SQL
Documentation

Expression: SELECT * FROM TIE.TDTL_STG

Figure 10.36: MQT population SELECT

To identify unique rows, set a primary key, which must match the source and target exactly (see Figure 10.37).

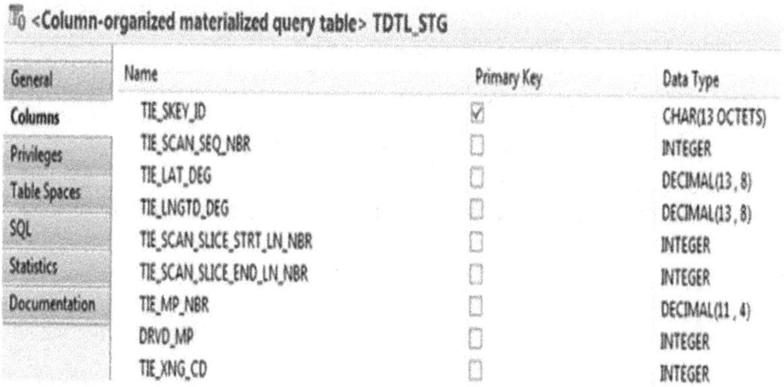

<Column-organized materialized query table> TDTL_STG

General | Columns | Privileges | Table Spaces | SQL | Statistics | Documentation

Name	Primary Key	Data Type
TIE_SKEY_ID	☑	CHAR(13 OCTETS)
TIE_SCAN_SEQ_NBR	☐	INTEGER
TIE_LAT_DEG	☐	DECIMAL(13, 8)
TIE_LNGTD_DEG	☐	DECIMAL(13, 8)
TIE_SCAN_SLICE_STRT_LN_NBR	☐	INTEGER
TIE_SCAN_SLICE_END_LN_NBR	☐	INTEGER
TIE_MP_NBR	☐	DECIMAL(11, 4)
DRVD_MP	☐	INTEGER
TIE_XNG_CD	☐	INTEGER

Figure 10.37: Selecting a primary key

The DDL is generated and executed to create the MQT:

```
CREATE TABLE TIE_COL.TDTL_STG ( DTL_RCD_ID, SCAN_RCD_ID, TIE_SCAN_SEQ_NBR,
TIE_LAT_DEG, TIE_LNGTD_DEG, TIE_SCAN_SLICE_STRT_LN_NBR, TIE_SCAN_SLICE_END_
LN_NBR, TIE_MP_NBR, TIE_XNG_CD, TIE_SWITCH_CD, TIE_BRDG_CD, TIE_GUARD_RAIL_
CD, TIE_TYP_CD, TIE_SPCNG_IN, TIE_SCAN_CUM_DISTN_FT, TIE_PLT_CUT_FSLR_IN,
TIE_PLT_CUT_GSLR_IN, TIE_PLT_CUT_GSRR_IN, TIE_PLT_CUT_FSRR_IN, TIE_PLT_CUT_
DIFF_LR_IN, TIE_PLT_CUT_DIFF_RR_IN, TIE_RJT_CD, TIE_LFT_TIE_PLT_TYP_CD,
TIE_RGHT_TIE_PLT_TYP_CD, TIE_LFT_WDTH_PXL, TIE_RGHT_WDTH_PXL, TIE_LGTH,
TIE_SKEW_ANGLE, TIE_LFT_FLD_ADZ_DPTH_IN, TIE_LFT_GAGE_ADZ_DPTH_IN, TIE_
RGHT_FLD_ADZ_DPTH_IN, TIE_RGHT_GAGE_ADZ_DPTH_IN, TIE_COND_SCOR_CD, TIE_TQI_
WGHTD_SCOR, TIE_BLST_CVR_PCT, TIE_GPS_QOS_CD, TIE_CURV_DEG, LST_MAINT_ID,
LST_MAINT_TS, INT_MP ) AS
( SELECT * FROM TIE.TDTL_STG )
DATA INITIALLY DEFERRED
REFRESH DEFERRED
MAINTAINED BY REPLICATION
ORGANIZE BY COLUMN
IN XXA10300 INDEX IN XXX10300;
                                                              Continued
```

```
SET INTEGRITY FOR TIE_COL.TDTL_STG ALL IMMEDIATE UNCHECKED;

ALTER TABLE TIE_COL.TDTL_STG ADD CONSTRAINT TDTL_STG_PK
PRIMARY KEY ( DTL_RCD_ID );

GRANT SELECT ON TABLE TIE_COL.TDTL_STG TO USER SHADOW;
```

Note: Create shadow tables in separate table spaces:

- Pagesize 32 KB
- Extentsize 4
- Prefetch Automatic

Define both data and index table spaces. Do this also for all column-organized tables. Then, use separate buffer pools for column- and row-organized tables.

Creating a Data Store

At this point, you have the replication engine and the Access Server running and have created the MQT column shadow table. Now you must create the subscription service that will populate the MQT and keep the MQT in sync with the row table.

Log in to the Access Server by using the account you created when you installed the Access Server software. If one was not created, you can create it now by using dmcreateuser, which is in the install path bin directory.

Run the command with the UNIX account that installed the software. In this example, it is db2cdc01. In the UNIX command prompt, execute the following command:

```
/dmcreateuser cdcadmin 'cdc admin' 'admin cdc' <password> sysadmin true
false true
```

On a Windows server, you have the **Management Console** icon, as Figure 10.38 shows. Launch it and log in to the Access Server.

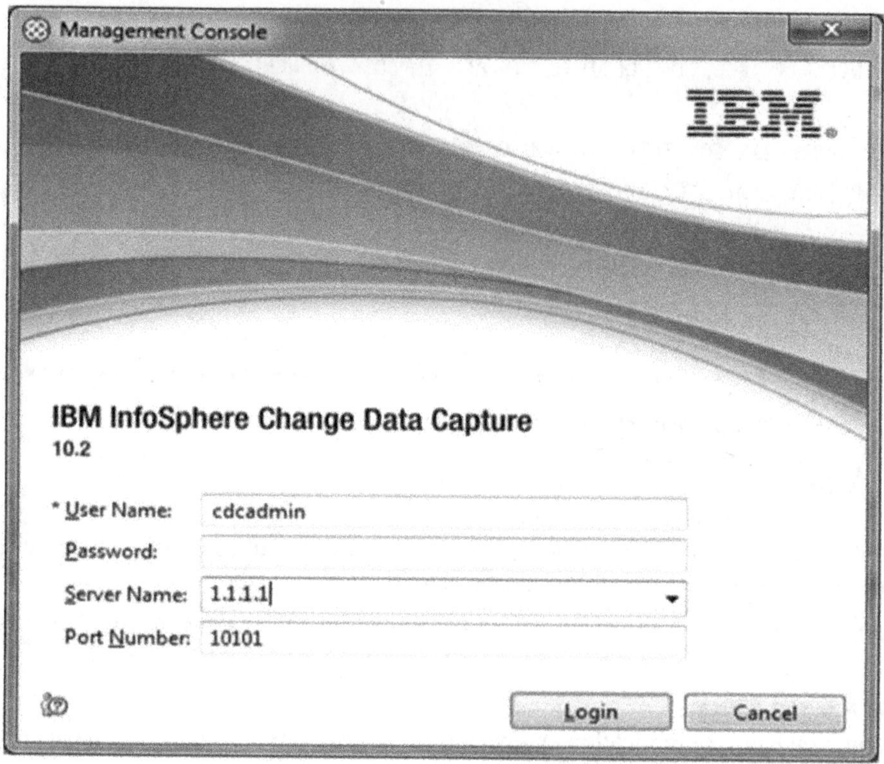

Figure 10.38: CDC login screen

Next, you need to define a data store via the **Datastore Management** tab in Figure 10.39. The data store identifies to the Access Server the source and target databases. For shadow tables, the source and target will be the same.

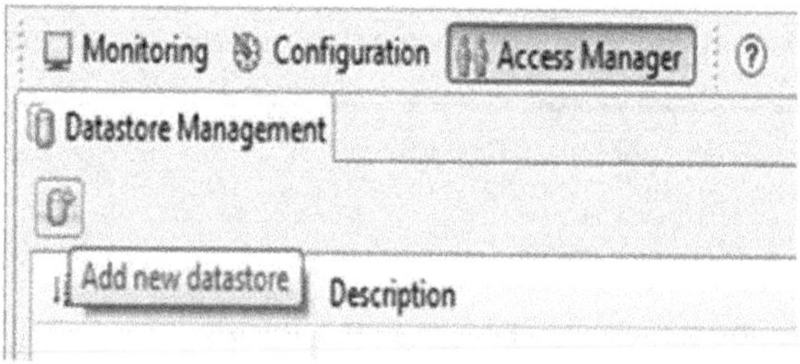

Figure 10.39: Adding a data store

The data store name is TIE and the communication type is JDBC. As Figure 10.40 illustrates, the port is the one you defaulted to during installation (10901).We will use the connection ID and password of the UNIX account that installed the software (see Figure 10.41).

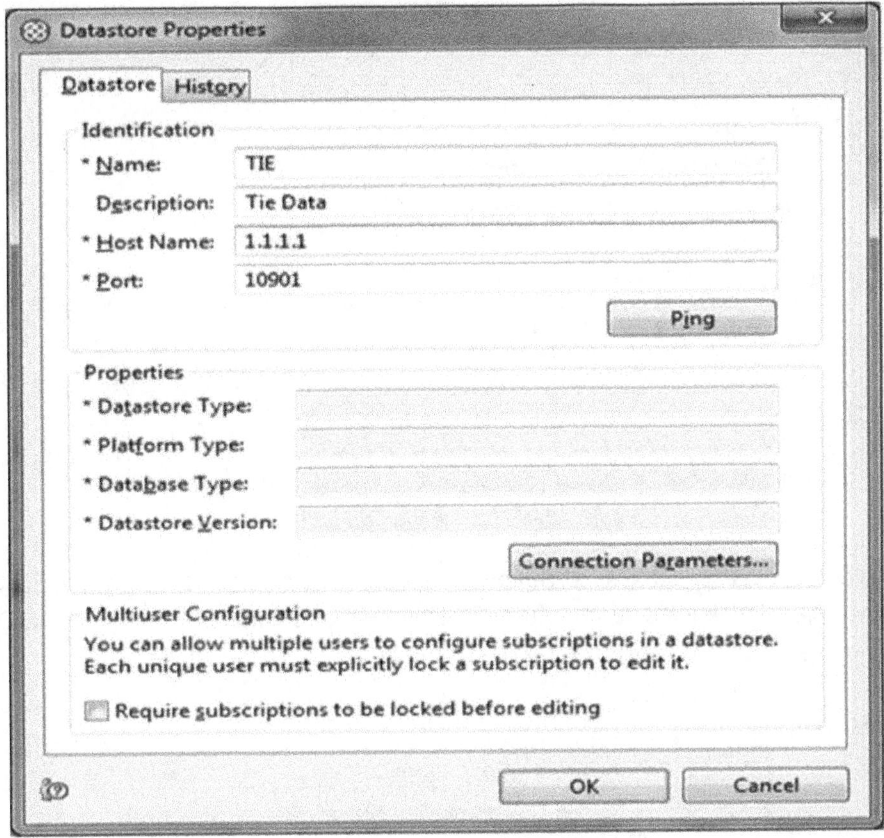

Figure 10.40: Datastore Properties screen

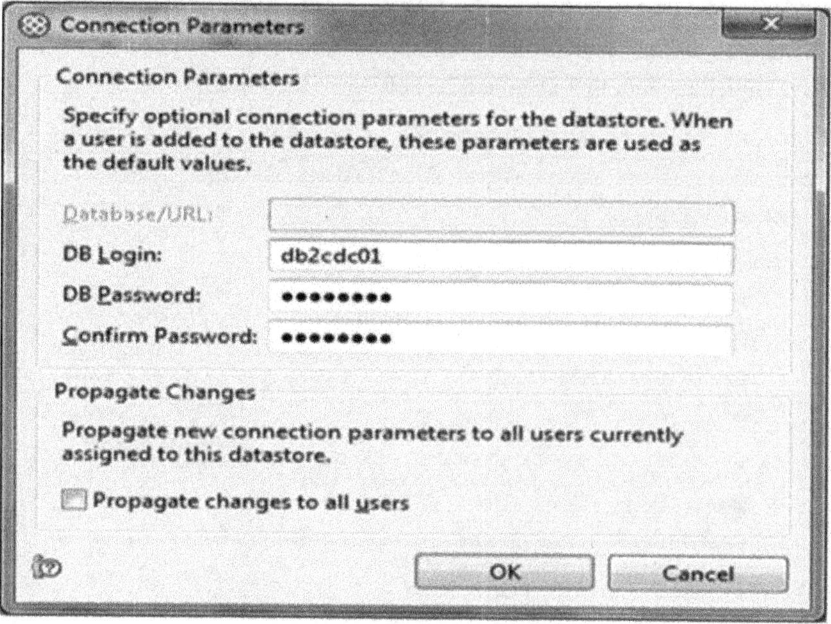

Figure 10.41: Connection parameters

Before you can begin creating subscriptions, you need to be sure you have a required system parameter set. Right-click the data store just created and select **Properties**. In Figure 10.42, you can see the data store access properties for this example.

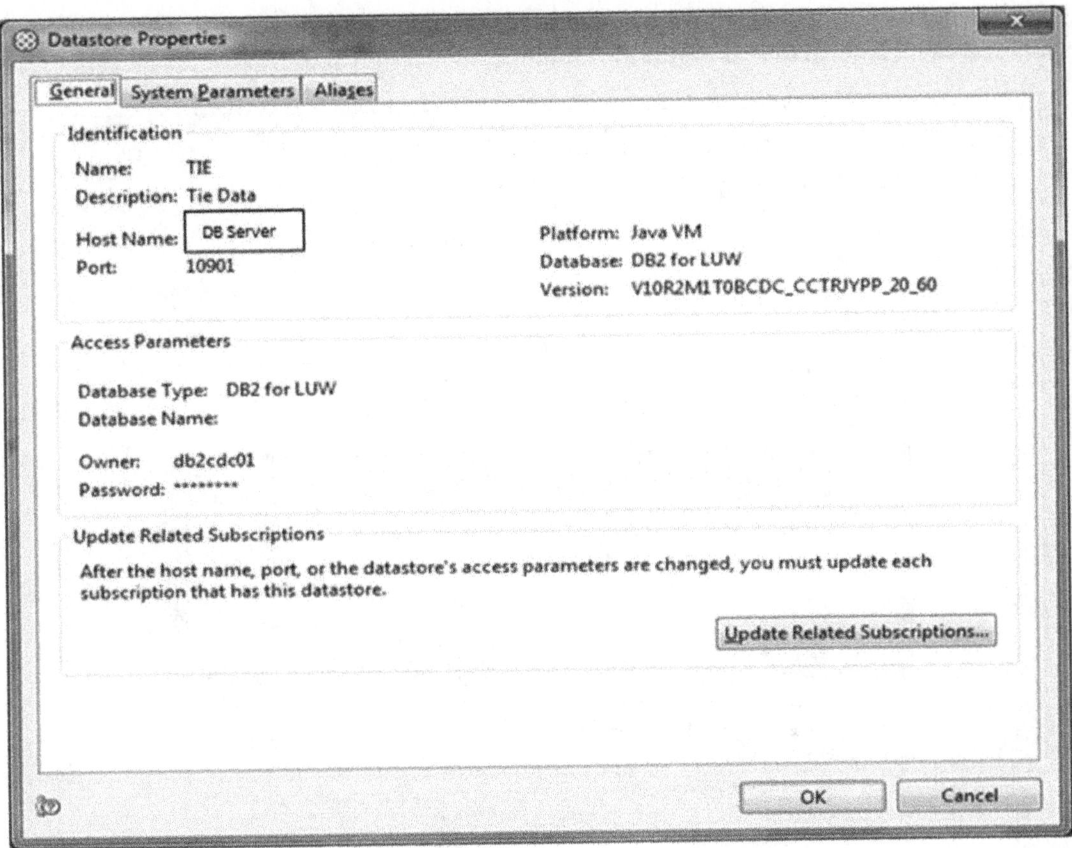

Figure 10.42: Data store access properties

Select the **System Parameters** tab, then look for **maintain_replication_mqt_latency_table** and make sure it is set to true, as Figure 10.43 shows.

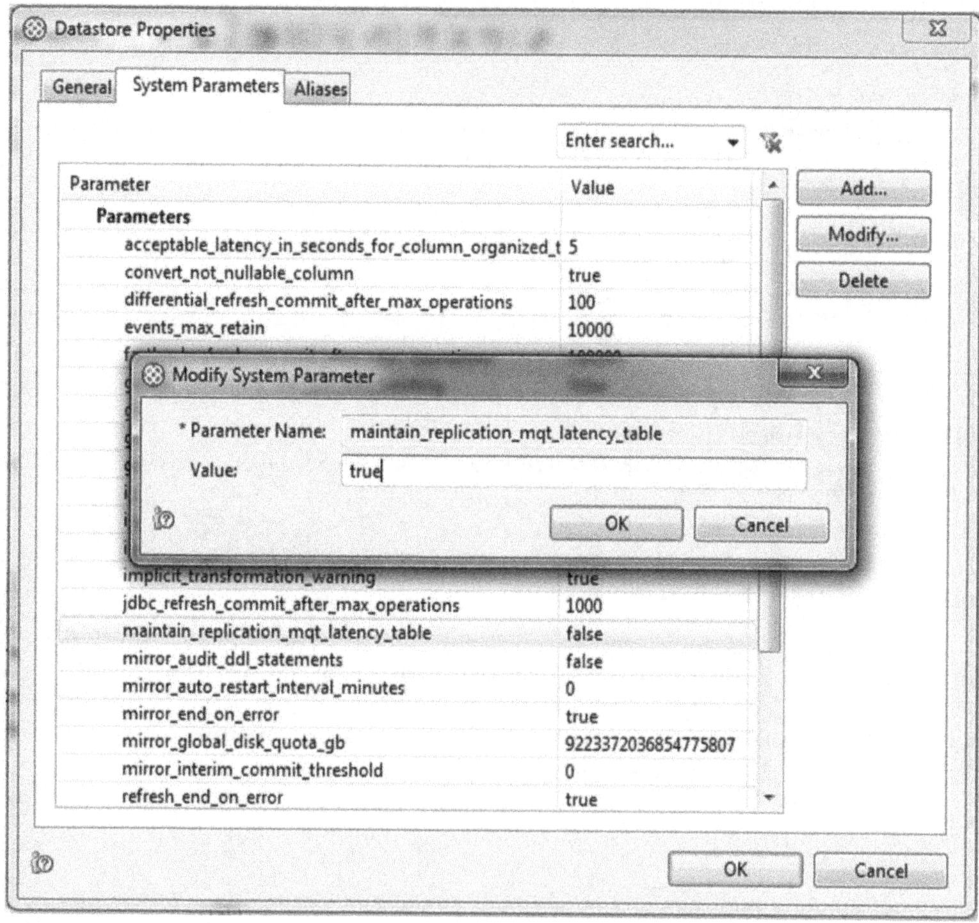

Figure 10.43: Setting the required system parameter

If you change it, be sure to stop and start replication so the change will take effect.

Creating a Subscription

Now you are ready to create the subscription. Click the **Configuration** tab; the second icon to the left is **Create new subscription** (see Figure 10.44).

Because the subscriptions all have the same source and target, the message in Figure 10.45 will display when you create the subscription. Click **Yes** and continue.

Also, the prompt in Figure 10.46 will ask whether you want to map tables. Click **Yes** and continue.

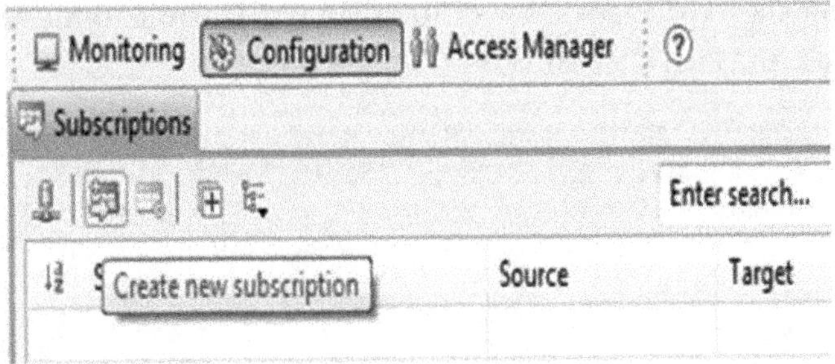

Figure 10.44: Creating a new subscription

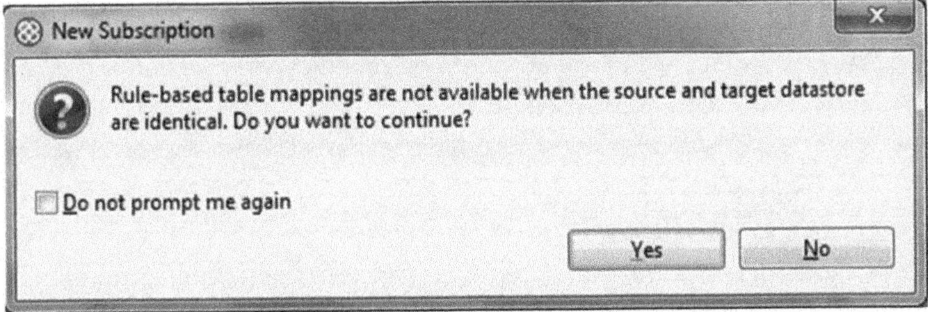

Figure 10.45: "Target and source are identical" message on New Subscription

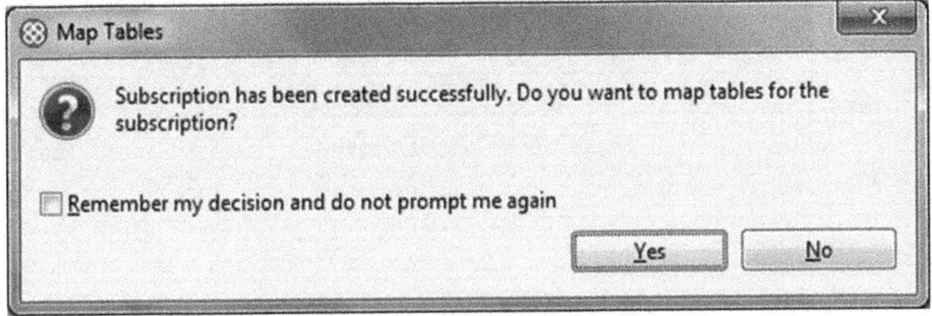

Figure 10.46: Map Tables prompt

On the Select Mapping Type page in Figure 10.47, choose **Custom Table Mapping** and **Standard** for the type, and then click **Next**.

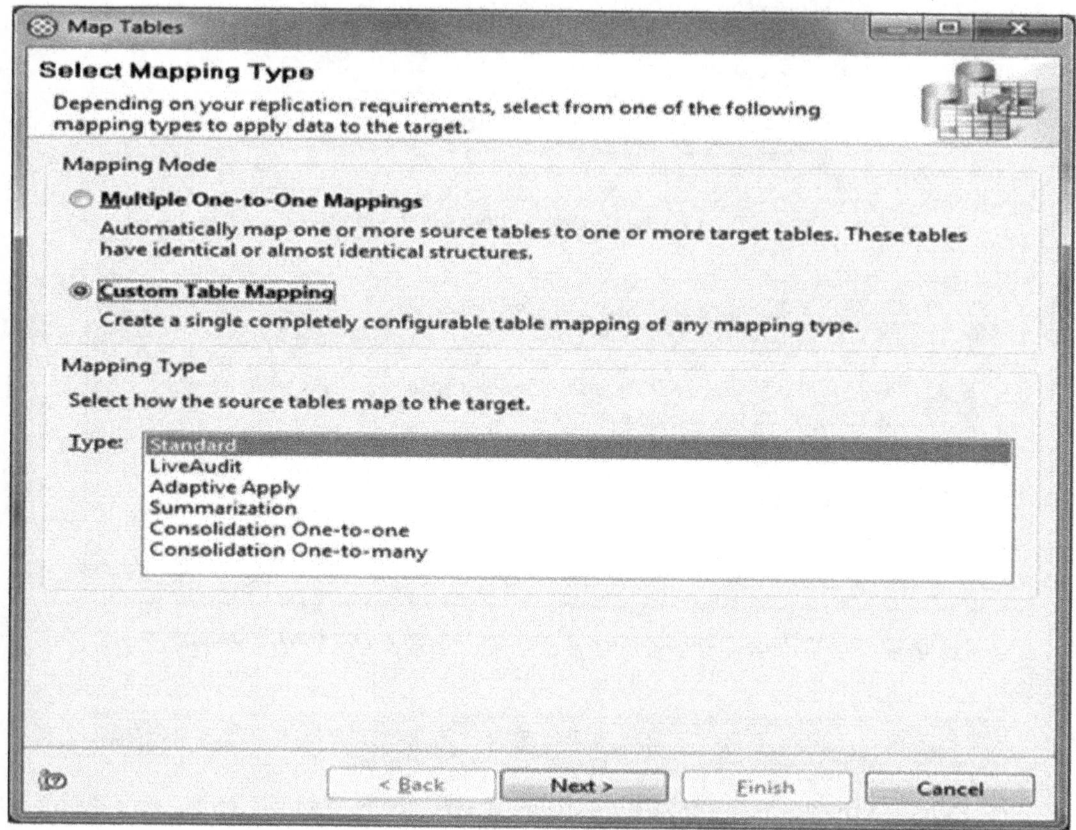

Figure 10.47: Custom mapping

In the next two windows, select the source and target tables. Only the target window (Figure 10.48) is presented here.

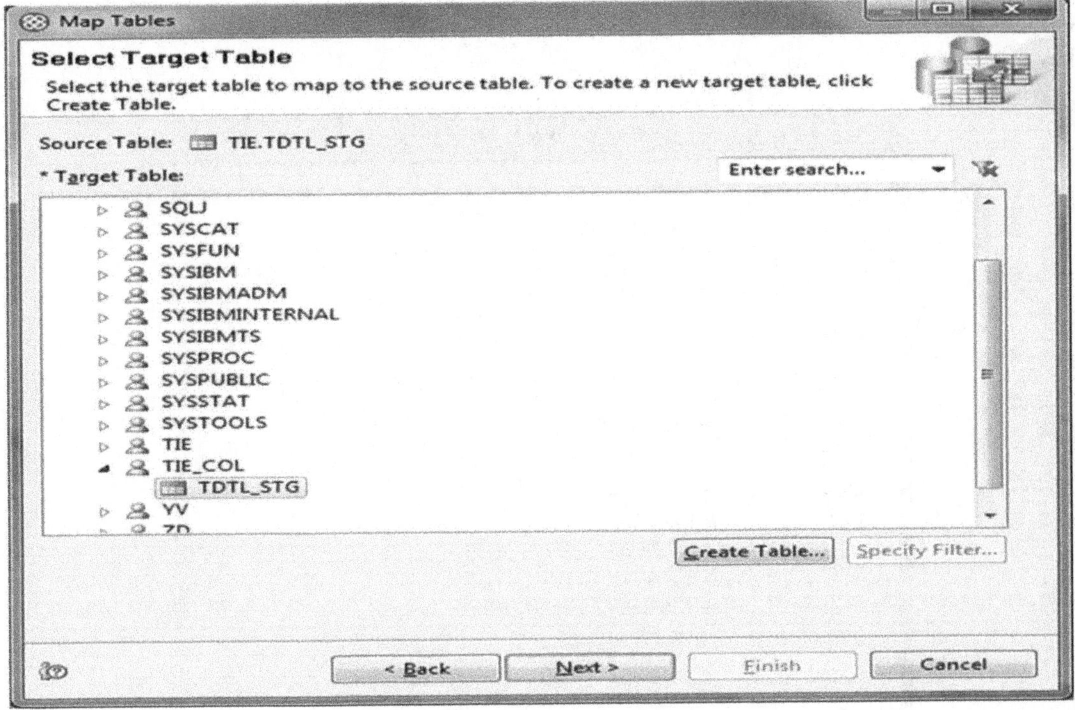

Figure 10.48: Select Target Table wizard

The Specify Key window in Figure 10.49 is where you select the primary key. By default, all columns are checked (your unique primary key should not be every column in the table). You can highlight all the columns and click "toggle" to switch them all off, and then select the one or two columns you need to identify the primary key. Remember, the two tables must match primary keys exactly.

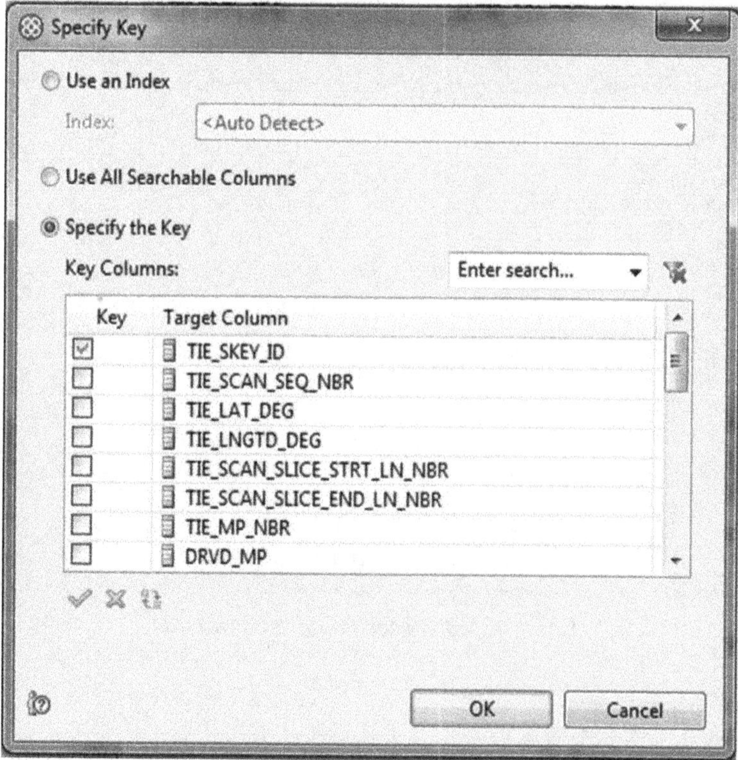

Figure 10.49: Selecting the index or key to use for mapping rows

Next is the replication method (see Figure 10.50), which you can change later if needed.

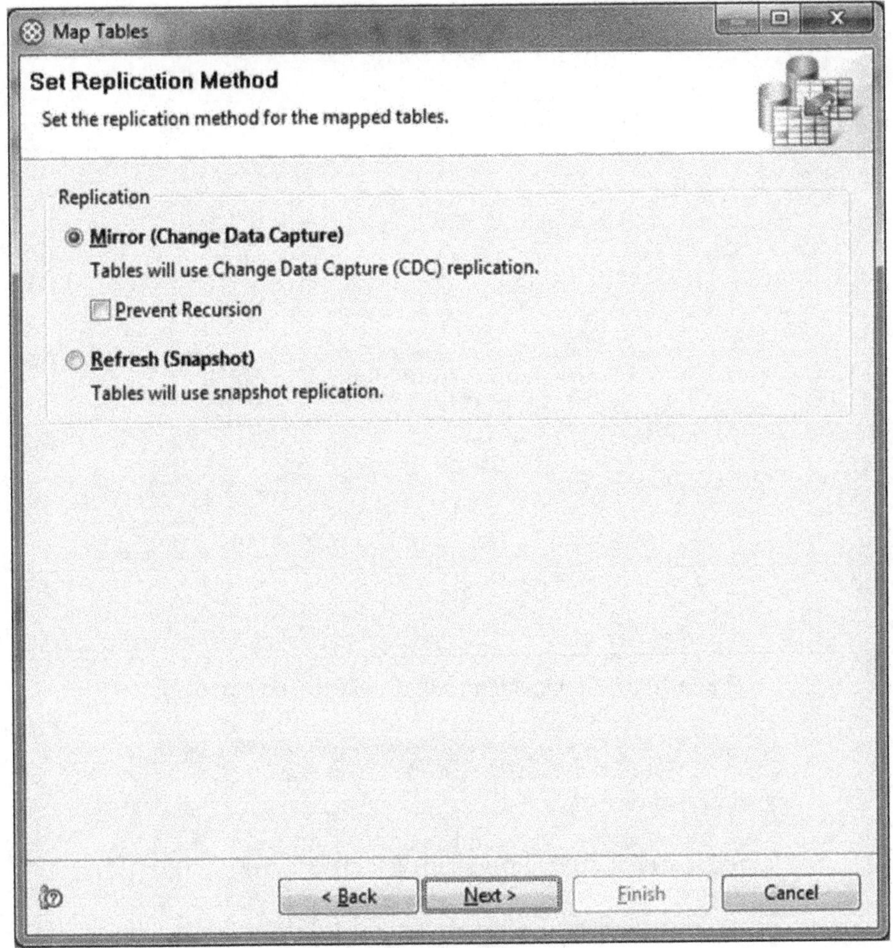

Figure 10.50: Set Replication Method

In the configuration window in Figure 10.51, select the column mapping as **Auto Map** and then choose **Name to Name** (Figure 10.52).

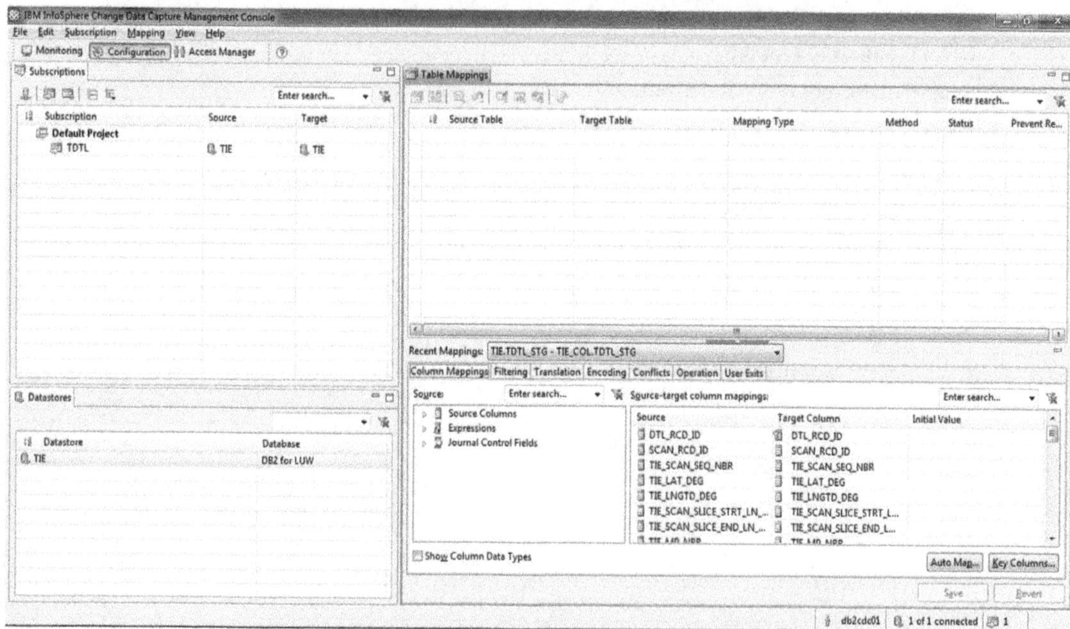

Figure 10.51: Configuration setup—using Auto Mapping

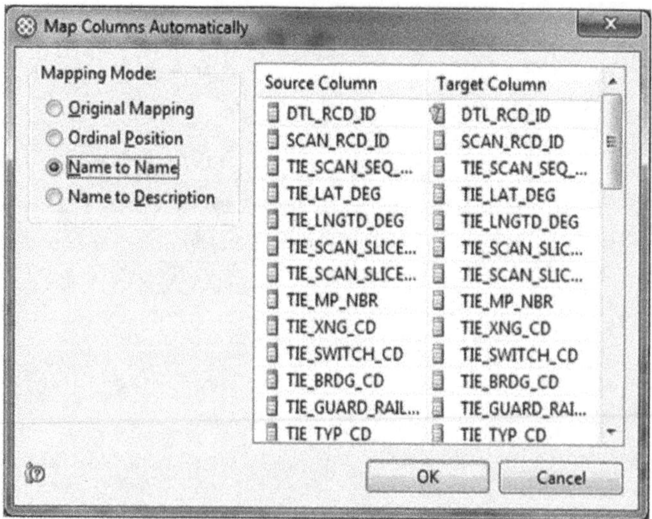

Figure 10.52: AutoMap columns by name

To recap, you have defined the MQT table and have set up a subscription service to replicate data between the row and MQT tables. At this point, MQT is empty and row table has, say, 150 MB rows.

You now need to use FastLoad to initially populate the MQT and then set up ongoing replication so the two tables stay in sync. Right-click the subscription and click **Start Refresh**, as Figure 10.53 shows.

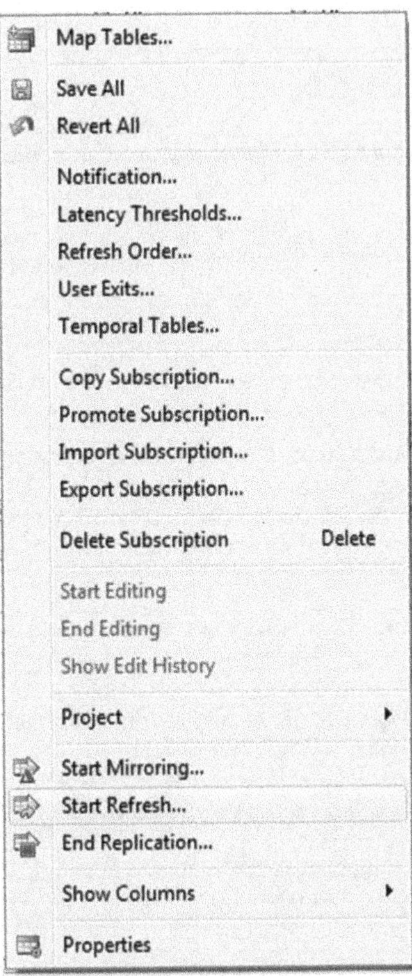

Figure 10.53: Starting the table refresh

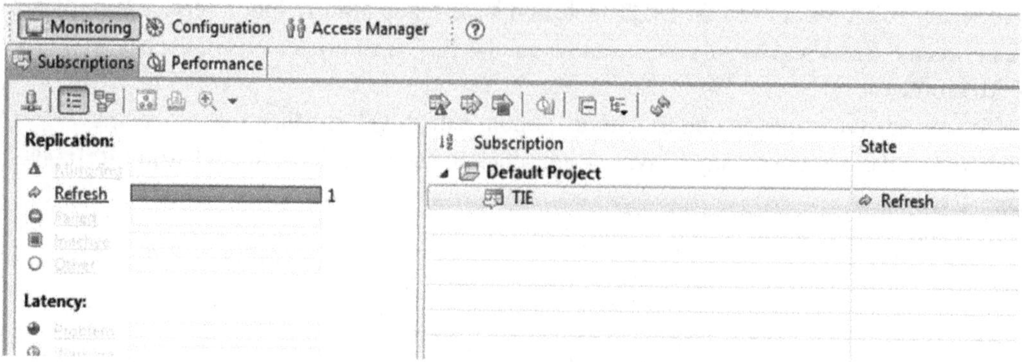

Figure 10.54: Monitoring status of refresh

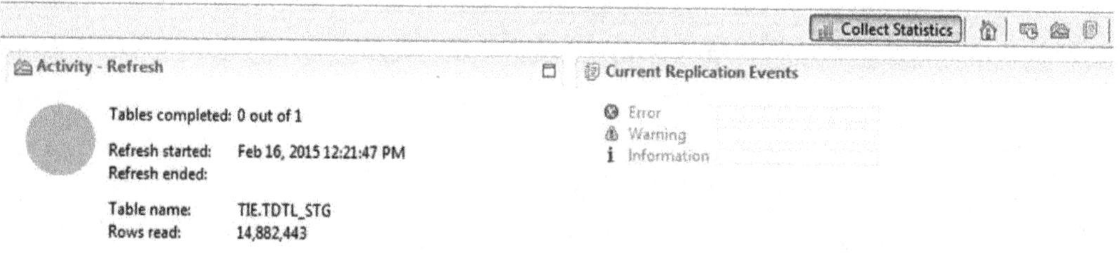

Figure 10.55: Overview refresh statistics

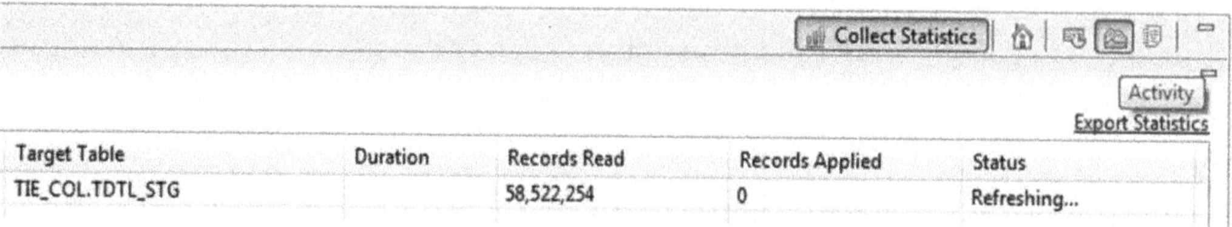

Figure 10.56: Activity refresh statistics

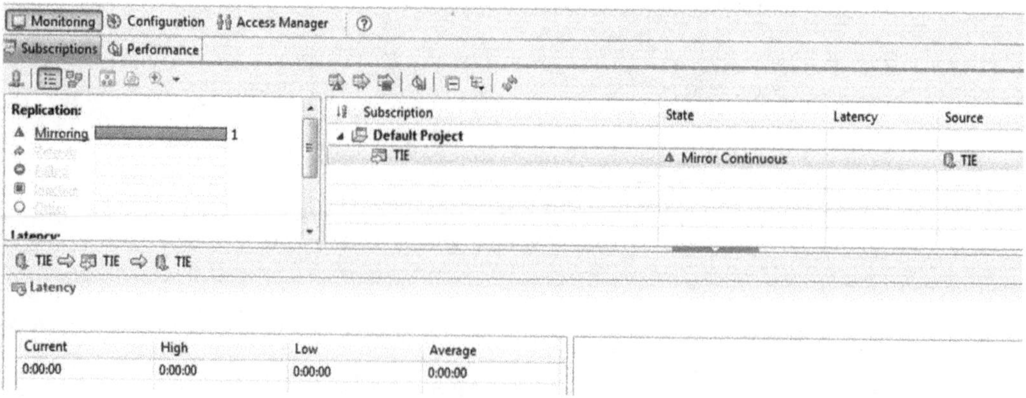

Figure 10.57: Monitoring status of the mirrored table

Switch to the **Monitoring** tab to see the status of the subscription as "refreshed" (see Figure 10.54).

To see the status of the refresh event for this subscription, click the **Collect Statistics** tab followed by the **Overview** in Figure 10.55 or the **Activity** tab in Figure 10.56.

Once the refresh is complete, set the ongoing replication to **Mirroring**, as Figure 10.57 shows. Changes to the row table data are now replicated to the MQT.

The DB2 objects created should include the synopsis table as well as both the synopsis index and the primary key (unique) index.

Check the latency table to see whether replication is updating the table with information related to the gap between row and MQT:

```
Select * from systools.repl_mqt_latency ;
COMMIT_POINT DELAY_OFFSET
1411338130     0
```

Putting Shadow Tables to Work

On the server, a dmts64-java process is using about 2 GB of RAM with 9 GB total space, and a dmaccessserver-java process is using about 512 MB. Before you began, you identified a few workloads you thought would benefit from column-organized data. These workloads are executed by users through a connection to the database. Figure 10.58 shows the process to implement to identify and direct these requests.

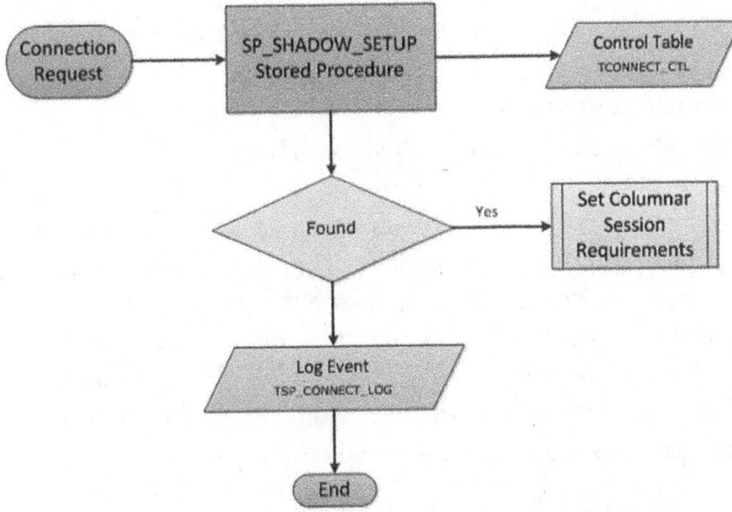

Figure 10.58: Shadow table workflow diagram

Connections have specific characteristics just as workloads do. So the way you create WLM objects to manage specific workloads, you will do the same for shadow tables.

You can set a new database parameter to force execution of a stored procedure when a connection request is made. The purpose of this stored procedure is to identify the workloads you want as candidates for shadow tables and set the required connection properties to allow them to run columnar.

In this example, you have a DB2 connection SYSTEM_AUTH_ID named shadow that you want to make eligible for execution against the MQT columnar shadow tables you set up. The stored procedure logs execution events to a table, so it is easy to see which ones are shadow eligible and which ones are not. It is also possible to insert, update, or delete rows in the TCONNECT_CTL table to control the actual setting of columnar requirements.

The UPDATE DB CFG command is added to the front and back of the script because you cannot drop the stored procedure that is defined to the database CONNECT_PROC parameter. CONNECT_PROC is a dynamic database parameter.

The stored procedure SP_SHADOW_SETUP checks for matching values in TCONNECT_CTL for SYSTEM_AUTH_ID and CLIENT_HOSTNAME. If either are a match, it sets the required values for potential columnar processing.

You can improve the overall control of this process by moving the Refresh Age setting to the control table, thereby allowing you to dynamically control the setting and have custom levels depending on the user or workstation.

The script output from creating the objects in the above diagram looks like this:

```
UPDATE DB cfg for oltpdb using CONNECT_PROC ""
DB20000I  The UPDATE DATABASE CONFIGURATION command completed successfully.

DROP TABLE XX.TSP_CONNECT_LOG
DB20000I  The SQL command completed successfully.

CREATE TABLE XX.TSP_CONNECT_LOG ( CONNECT_LOG_ID          CHAR(13) FOR BIT
DATA , APPLNAME                    VARCHAR(128) , CLIENT_USERID   VARCHAR(128) ,
SYSTEM_AUTH_ID       VARCHAR(128) , SESSION_AUTH_ID  VARCHAR(128) ,
CLIENT_HOSTNAME  VARCHAR(255) , CLIENT_PORT_NUMBER     INTEGER ,
RAN_COL                    CHAR(1) , LST_MAINT_TS           TIMESTAMP DEFAULT ) IN
XXA10100 INDEX IN XXX10100 COMPRESS YES ADAPTIVE organize by row
DB20000I  The SQL command completed successfully.

                                                                Continued
```

```
DROP TABLE XX.TCONNECT_CTL
DB20000I  The SQL command completed successfully.

CREATE TABLE XX.TCONNECT_CTL ( CONNECT_CTL_ID        CHAR(13) FOR BIT DATA ,
VAR_NME             VARCHAR(128) , VAR_VALUE           VARCHAR(255) ,
LST_MAINT_TS          TIMESTAMP DEFAULT ) IN XXA10100 INDEX IN XXX10100
COMPRESS YES ADAPTIVE organize by row
DB20000I  The SQL command completed successfully.

INSERT INTO XX.TCONNECT_CTL(CONNECT_CTL_ID,VAR_NME,VAR_VALUE)
VALUES(generate_unique(),'SYSTEM_AUTH_ID','TESTSHADOW')
DB20000I  The SQL command completed successfully.

DROP PROCEDURE XX.SP_SHADOW_SETUP
DB20000I  The SQL command completed successfully.

CREATE OR REPLACE  PROCEDURE XX.SP_SHADOW_SETUP()
BEGIN
     DECLARE V_APPLNAME           VARCHAR(128) ;
     DECLARE V_CLIENT_USERID      VARCHAR(128) ;
     DECLARE V_SYSTEM_AUTH_ID     VARCHAR(128) ;
     DECLARE V_SESSION_AUTH_ID    VARCHAR(128) ;
     DECLARE V_CLIENT_HOSTNAME    VARCHAR(255) ;
     DECLARE V_CLIENT_PORT_NUMBER        INTEGER ;
     DECLARE V_IS_COL              CHAR(1) ;
     SET V_APPLNAME = ( SELECT APPLICATION_NAME FROM
TABLE(SYSPROC.MON_GET_CONNECTION(MON_GET_APPLICATION_HANDLE(),-1)) );
     SET V_CLIENT_USERID = ( SELECT CLIENT_USERID FROM
TABLE(SYSPROC.MON_GET_CONNECTION(MON_GET_APPLICATION_HANDLE(),-1)) );
     SET V_SYSTEM_AUTH_ID = ( SELECT SYSTEM_AUTH_ID FROM
TABLE(SYSPROC.MON_GET_CONNECTION(MON_GET_APPLICATION_HANDLE(),-1)) );
     SET V_SESSION_AUTH_ID = ( SELECT SESSION_AUTH_ID FROM
TABLE(SYSPROC.MON_GET_CONNECTION(MON_GET_APPLICATION_HANDLE(),-1)) );
     SET V_CLIENT_HOSTNAME = ( SELECT CLIENT_HOSTNAME FROM
TABLE(SYSPROC.MON_GET_CONNECTION(MON_GET_APPLICATION_HANDLE(),-1)) );
```

Continued

```
    SET V_CLIENT_PORT_NUMBER = ( SELECT CLIENT_PORT_NUMBER FROM
TABLE(SYSPROC.MON_GET_CONNECTION(MON_GET_APPLICATION_HANDLE(),-1)) );
    SET V_IS_COL = 'N' ;

    if ( ( SELECT 1 FROM XX.TCONNECT_CTL WHERE VAR_NME = 'SYSTEM_AUTH_ID'
AND VAR_VALUE = V_SYSTEM_AUTH_ID OR VAR_NME = 'CLIENT_HOSTNAME' AND
VAR_VALUE = V_CLIENT_HOSTNAME ) > 0 ) THEN
      CALL SYSPROC.ADMIN_SET_INTRA_PARALLEL('YES') ;
      SET CURRENT DEGREE 'ANY' ;
      SET CURRENT MAINTAINED TYPES REPLICATION ;
      SET CURRENT REFRESH AGE 500 ;
      SET V_IS_COL = 'Y' ;
    END IF ;

  INSERT INTO XX.TSP_CONNECT_LOG(CONNECT_LOG_ID,APPLNAME,CLIENT_
USERID,SYSTEM_AUTH_ID,SESSION_AUTH_ID,CLIENT_HOSTNAME,CLIENT_PORT_
NUMBER,RAN_COL)  VALUES(generate_unique(),V_APPLNAME,V_CLIENT_USERID
V_SYSTEM_AUTH_ID,V_SESSION_AUTH_ID,V_CLIENT_HOSTNAME,V_CLIENT_PORT_NUMBER,
V_IS_COL) ;
  COMMIT ;

END
DB20000I  The SQL command completed successfully.

GRANT EXECUTE ON PROCEDURE XX.SP_SHADOW_SETUP to PUBLIC
DB20000I  The SQL command completed successfully.

UPDATE DB cfg for oltpdb using CONNECT_PROC "XX.SP_SHADOW_SETUP"
DB20000I  The UPDATE DATABASE CONFIGURATION command completed successfully.
```

What You Have

User shadow executes several SQL dynamic SELECT statements. The database is ready to identify those queries and determine, based on latency and cost, whether running on the MQT column table is an option.

The overall process after the user connects to the database and submits a dynamic SELECT statement is as follows:

1. Is the user SYSTEM_AUTH_ID in your control table? For user shadow, yes.
2. Is the latency between row and MQT table less than what is defined in the stored procedure (500)? Yes.
3. Is the timeron cost better on MQT? If not, then run on row table.

Note: Catalog statistics are vital to successful determination of the optimizer and therefore selection of the correct door for the queries to open.

The Verification Process

You want to take selected, SQL statements and explain them to verify whether they meet the required 150 KB timeron cost. Then, you run some that do and some that do not to be sure the system is behaving correctly. In addition, you run the SQL statements under different connection accounts to make sure that only shadow works.

The model to explain the queries is as follows:

```
SET CURRENT MAINTAINED TYPES REPLICATION ;
SET CURRENT REFRESH AGE 500 ;

explain plan for < sql statement for testing > ;
```

Query 1 looks like this:

```
SELECT DTL_RCD_ID, LAT_DEG, LNGTD_DEG, SCAN_SLICE_STRT_LN_NBR,
  SCAN_SLICE_END_LN_NBR, MP_NBR,XNG_CD, SWITCH_CD,
  BRDG_CD, GUARD_RAIL_CD,TYP_CD, RJT_CD,
  LFT_TIE_PLT_TYP_CD, RGHT_PLT_TYP_CD, LGTH, COND_SCOR_CD,
  TQI_WGHTD_SCOR, BLST_CVR_PCT,GPS_QOS_CD, INT_MP
FROM XXX.TDTL_STG
```

Continued

```
WHERE
  SCAN_SLICE_STRT_LN_NBR > 10 and
  SCAN_SLICE_END_LN_NBR < 2000 and
  MP_NBR between 108.6 and 108.7
with ur ;

The extended optimizer returned the following information:
Diagnostic Identifier:     1
Diagnostic Details:
EXP0148W  The following MQT or statistical view was considered in query
matching: "XXX_COL "."TDTL_STG".
Diagnostic Identifier:     2
Diagnostic Details:
EXP0149W  The following MQT was used (from those considered) in query
matching: "XXX_COL "."TDTL_STG".
Here is the access plan.  We know the MQT was selected because of the CTQ
step and the CO-Table label at the bottom.
Access Plan:
-----------
Total Cost:        63461.2
Query Degree: 12
        Rows
       RETURN
       (   1)
        Cost
         I/O
         |
      0.487566
       CTQ
       (   2)
       63461.2
     1.29071e+06
         |
      0.487566
       TBSCAN
```

Continued

```
        (   3)
        63461.2
      1.29071e+06
           |
      1.37671e+08
   CO-TABLE: XXX_COL
         TDTL_STG
            Q1
```

And query 2 looks like this:

```
SELECT DTL_RCD_ID, LAT_DEG, LNGTD_DEG, SCAN_SLICE_STRT_LN_NBR,
SCAN_SLICE_END_LN_NBR,MP_NBR,XNG_CD,SWITCH_CD,BRDG_CD,          GUARD_RAIL_CD,
TYP_CD, RJT_CD, LFT_TIE_PLT_TYP_CD,          RGHT_TIE_PLT_TYP_CD, LGTH,
COND_SCOR_CD, TQI_WGHTD_SCOR,          BLST_CVR_PCT, GPS_QOS_CD, INT_MP
FROM TIE.TDTL_STG
where INT_MP = 100
fetch first 1000 rows only    with ur ;
```

Query 2 also ran on MQT, and its access plan is as follows:

```
Total Cost:         458.961
Query Degree: 12
Rows
    RETURN
        (   1)
         Cost
          I/O
           |
         1000
        CTQ
        (   2)
        458.961
                                                                Continued
```

```
        14368.1
           |
          1000
         TBSCAN
         (   3)
        41227.1
      1.29071e+06
           |
      1.37671e+08
   CO-TABLE: XXX_COL
        TDTL_STG
           Q1
```

Reducing the number of columns returned will significantly decrease the overall cost of columnar processing. It should also make it a better choice.

Query 3 is the same as query 2, only with fewer columns selected:

```
SELECT MP_NBR,
 FROM TIE.TDTL_STG
WHERE INT_MP = 100
FETCH FIRST 1000 ROWS ONLY
with ur ;
```

The MQT was selected and the overall cost dropped to 209.876, a reduction of more than 50 percent.

In query 4, the SQL is exactly as in query 3 above, but you created an index on INT_MP. The access plan for row should be a one-column matching index scan, which is likely significantly better than columnar.

The access plan looks like this:

```
Access Plan:
-----------
Total Cost:          5.33195
Query Degree: 12
```

Continued

```
Rows
           RETURN
           (   1)
            Cost
             I/O
              |
            1000
           LTQ   -- Intra-partition parallelism
           (   2)
           5.33195
           175.246
              |
            1000
           FETCH
           (   3)
           398.207
           13711.3
         /---+----\
     90573.2     1.37671e+08
     IXSCAN   TABLE: XXX
     (   4)      TDTL_STG
     36.3676         Q1
     58.6059
        |
   1.37671e+08
 INDEX: XXX
   XD2_DTL_STG
       Q1

Extended Diagnostic Information:
--------------------------------


Diagnostic Identifier:    1
```

Continued

```
Diagnostic Details:         EXP0079W  The following MQT was not used in the
                            final access plan, because the plan cost with this
                            MQT was more expensive or a better candidate was
                            available: "XXX_COL "."TDTL_STG".
Diagnostic Identifier:      2
Diagnostic Details:         EXP0148W  The following MQT or statistical view was
                            considered in query matching: "XXX_COL "."TDTL_STG".
```

So how did the elapse time performance compare? Table 10.18 shows the query comparison.

Table 10.18: Query comparison

Query	Row Elapse Time (Seconds)	Column Elapse Time (Seconds)
1	102.133	43.457
2	99.699	19.530
3	7.029	5.579
4 (index)	.785	N/A

Note: So why did you not put execution time of the row queries as a requirement for selecting workloads? The optimizer did a good job of comparing row versus column, so eliminating quick row queries is not necessary.

Currently, it appears that statistic collection for MQT column tables is not automatic regardless of the settings you have on the database. Make sure to check that both row and MQT column objects have valid and up-to-date statistics.

Note: When loading significant data into the row parent of a shadow table, it is recommended to collect statistics for the shadow table manually by running the RUNSTATS utility. This is especially true if workloads will be executed immediately after the load process is completed. There is a time lag between the data load and the real-time statistics collector operation. If the loading process is performed in batch in a maintenance window where workloads will not be executed for hours, the RTS function will perform the needed work:

```
CALL SYSPROC.ADMIN_CMD('RUNSTATS ON TABLE XXX_COL.TDTL_STG  ON ALL COLUMNS  AND
DETAILED INDEXES ALL') ;
```

Utilities: Converting Row Tables to Column

There are a few ways to convert row-organized tables to column. Before you review them, you need to remember several key points. Conversion to column is a one-way street. No reversal back to row is available, so take the necessary precautions. In many cases, the row-organized tables will be placed in table spaces not properly configured for column; therefore, it is recommended to move the converted table to a new, properly defined table space. This will also allow the move operation to perform more efficiently.

Several types of tables cannot be converted:

- RCTs
- Typed tables
- MQTs
- Declared global temporary tables
- Created global temporary tables
- Table with XML or LOB columns
- Tables in nonautomatic storage table spaces
- Tables with generated columns

ADMIN_MOVE_TABLE

You can use the ADMIN_MOVE_TABLE stored procedure to move a row-organized table and, in the process, convert it to column organized. Some restrictions apply:

- Foreign key constraints cannot be enforced.
- Check constraints cannot be enforced.
- Primary key constraint cannot be defined.

In the following example, the SCH1.TATTR_STG table is moved to XXA10500 for data and XXX10500 for indexes and converted to column organized in the process. If you want to move the table but not copy it, use the COPY_USE_LOAD option:

```
CALL SYSPROC.ADMIN_MOVE_TABLE('SCH1','TATTR_STG','XXA10500','XXX10500','XXDA10500',
'ORGANIZE BY COLUMN','','','','COPY_USE_LOAD','MOVE');
```

db2convert

The db2convert is an executable program wrapper for ADMIN_MOVE_TABLE, with a few nice features included. It is possible to convert all the tables in a database with one command, although doing so might not be recommended.

Using the -force parameter will convert all tables, including range partition tables, MDC, and ITC tables:

```
==> db2convert -d mydb
```

You can also stop execution in specific phases. For example, -stopbeforeswap will halt the move operation at swap, preventing INIT, COPY, and REPLAY phases until the requestor responds to the prompt. This will allow the requestor to perform an online backup before continuing.

The -check option allows the user to run the db2convert program for validation without making any changes. This is a helpful way to make sure all conditions are met before actually running the program.

Following are a few examples:

```
Example1: Trigger error
db2convert.ksh

Conversion notes for exceptional table(s)
-----------------------------------------
Table: SCH1.TDTL_STG:
-Cannot convert: triggers are not supported with column-organized tables.

Example2: db2convert.ksh
Conversion notes for exceptional table(s)
-----------------------------------------
Table: SCH1.TDTL_STG:
-Foreign keys will be applied to the new, column-organized table as NOT ENFORCED.
-Secondary indexes will be dropped from the table.

Enter 1 to proceed with the conversion.
Enter 2 to quit.
```

Reclaiming Deleted Space in Column-Organized Tables

Column-organized tables have no clustering index, so traditional REORG operations are unnecessary except when used for recovering pseudodeleted rows. You can execute the command manually, but it is automatically performed with AUTO_REORG. Extents recovered can be used by any column-organized tables in the table space.

To reclaim extents, execute a REORG command similar to the following:

```
REORG TABLE <TABLENAME> RECLAIM EXTENTS ;
```

PureScale

IBM DB2 pureScale cluster technology is by far the most significant achievement in database technology in the past 10 years. PureScale was introduced in 2010 as IBM DB2 9.8. Running pureScale can result in cost savings by providing the following features:

- Endless scalability
- No wasted capacity
- No idle standby server cost
- No DBA time spent moving databases between servers
- Ability to add capacity with no downtime
- Ability to manage resources at the cluster level or at member subsets
- Autonomics free up DBA time to work on business requirements
- Higher availability and becoming higher with each release
- Easier servicing, as it can typically be done at the member level with no disruption of service

How does pureScale compare with server virtualization of DB2 workloads? Table 10.19 lists the comparison, but note that these are not competing technologies. PureScale can run on virtual images. Also note that we are discussing only database workloads, specifically DB2 (assumes pureScale is running on bare metal or dedicated LPARs).

Table 10.19: pureScale versus virtualization comparison

Measure	pureScale	Virtualization
Add capacity (memory/CPU)—no outage	Yes	
Performance	Yes	
All workloads		Yes
Scalability—unlimited	Yes	
No wasted resources	Yes	
Provisioning—initial planning and setup		Yes
Workers with experience		Yes
Resolving performance issues	Yes	
Complexity—can be dependent on hardware	Yes	
Cost savings for database workloads	Yes	

A move to pureScale means changing how data is managed. For share-nothing architectures, most business workloads are managed in isolation. This generally means workloads are separated by server, instance, and database. For large UNIX/Windows shops, this appears in explosive growth with support and management issues.

Some companies have attacked this problem with virtualization. This resulted in switching one problem for another without addressing the explosive growth problem. Providing images instead of servers made provisioning faster, but the challenges around size, performance, capacity, and core product upgrades like ESX presented a new brand of management opportunities.

Virtualization's main selling point is monetary savings. But quickly, most of us who supported it realized the only way to truly save money was to overprovision the resources. Once we started doing that, a host of hard-to-diagnose performance issues kept us working almost round the clock.

In a pureScale environment, consider managing data at the schema level; however, this may require making changes to how database software is developed in your organization. For example, using nonqualified table names in the JDBC calls will allow you to control and set the schema name at execution. This in turn provides schema versioning opportunities.

You may also need to make changes regarding data placement as it relates to table and table space mapping. You can perform recovery or copy operations at the schema level. Keeping cross-schema references to a minimum will make recovery simpler and easier. Using this schema method will allow more granular backup procedures, which you can tailor at the schema level as well.

With DB2 10.5, IBM introduced several key enhancements. One area of primary focus is availability, and many of the enhancements reduce scheduled outages and improve recovery operations. This section looks closely at these new features.

Rolling Upgrades

Beginning with DB2 10.5 FP4, IBM increased availability with rolling upgrades. A DB2 release contains two markers that identify it. One is an architecture level and the other is a code level. Each release of DB2 has a specific code level, while the architecture level may remain the same. These are referred to as the *Current Effective Architecture Level* (*CEAL*) and *Current Effective Code Level* (*CECL*).

If you want to show the markers for any release, execute the following command:

```
Unix Prompt: ==> installFixPack -show_level_info

Code level         =  Version:10 Release:5 Modification:0 Fixpack:4
Architecture level =  Version:10 Release:5 Modification:0 Fixpack:4
```

Continued

```
Section level      =  Version:10 Release:5 Modification:0 Fixpack:4

Supports online update = Yes


Minimum committed code level required for online install =
   Version:10 Release:5 Modification:0 Fixpack:1
The execution completed successfully.
For more information, see the DB2 installation log at
"/tmp/installFixPack.log.21485".
DBI1070I Program installFixPack completed successfully.
```

As Figure 10.59 illustrates, the online (rolling) upgrade process is fairly simple. Each cluster you intend to upgrade has a CECL level, which must be the same across all members and CFs. As you upgrade each member and CF, their individual CECL level changes to the new release CECL. Once all are upgraded to the release CECL level, the cluster CECL level is changed to match.

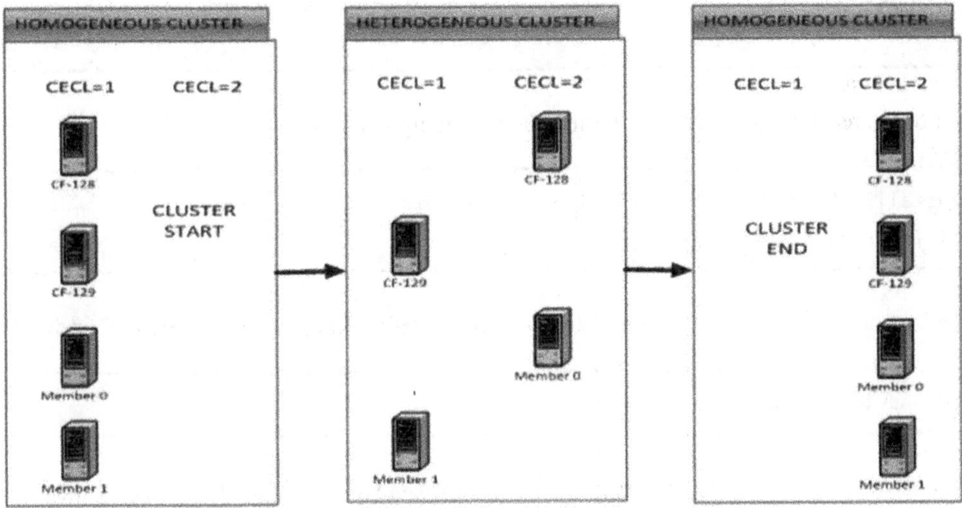

Figure 10.59: Online rolling fix pack upgrades

Online (Rolling) Upgrade of a PureScale Cluster

You can upgrade the pureScale software either online or offline, but the following steps provide details for the online method only.

Step 1: Place the uncompressed fix pack on a file system accessible to all members and CFs.

Step 2: Run the following command on each member one at a time:

```
installFixPack -p FP-install-path -I instance-name -online -l log-file-name
-t trace-file-name
```

Make sure the software has been successfully installed on all members before continuing to the CF.

Step 3: Apply the fix pack to the secondary CF by using the command in step 2.

Confirm that the secondary CF is in the peer state before continuing. Use the db2instance -list command to verify that it is.

Step 4: Apply the fix pack to the primary CF by using the command in step 2.

Step 5: Check that all members and CFs have properly been upgraded by executing this command:

```
installFixPack -check_commit -I instance-name
```

Step 6: Commit the upgrade by running the following command:

```
installFixPack -commit_level -I instance-name -l log-file-name
-t trace-file-name
```

Step 7: Apply the changes to the existing database DB2 catalog by executing db2updv105:

```
db2updv105 -d <dbname>
```

Options such as -o (Oracle compatibility views) and -a (force all functions to execute) might be needed.

Checking the Progress and Status of the Upgrade

During the upgrade process, you can obtain status information by running this command:

```
db2pd -ruStatus

ROLLING UPDATE STATUS:
                          Disk Value                                               Memory Value

Record Type        = INSTANCE
ID                 = 0
Code Level         = V:10 R:5 M:0 F:4 I:0 SB:0 (0x0A05000400000000)  Not Applicable
Architecture Level = V:10 R:5 M:0 F:4 I:0 SB:0 (0x0A05000400000000)  Not Applicable
State              = [NONE]
Last updated       = 2014/09/19:21:20:11

Record Type        = MEMBER
ID                 = 0
Code Level         = V:10 R:5 M:0 F:4 I:0 SB:0 (0x0A05000400000000)
                     V:10 R:5 M:0 F:4 I:0 SB:0 (0x0A05000400000000)
CECL               = V:10 R:5 M:0 F:4 I:0 SB:0 (0x0A05000400000000)
                     V:10 R:5 M:0 F:4 I:0 SB:0 (0x0A05000400000000)
Architecture Level = V:10 R:5 M:0 F:4 I:0 SB:0 (0x0A05000400000000)
                     V:10 R:5 M:0 F:4 I:0 SB:0 (0x0A05000400000000)
CEAL               = V:10 R:5 M:0 F:4 I:0 SB:0 (0x0A05000400000000)
                     V:10 R:5 M:0 F:4 I:0 SB:0 (0x0A05000400000000)
Section Level      = V:10 R:5 M:0 F:4 I:0 SB:0 (0x0A05000400000000)
                     V:10 R:5 M:0 F:4 I:0 SB:0 (0x0A05000400000000)
State              = [NONE]
Last updated       = 2014/09/18:11:28:42

Record Type        = CF
ID                 = 128
Code Level         = V:10 R:5 M:0 F:4 I:0 SB:0 (0x0A05000400000000)  Not Applicable
Architecture Level = V:10 R:5 M:0 F:4 I:0 SB:0 (0x0A05000400000000)  Not Applicable
State              = [NONE]
Last updated       = 2014/09/19:13:02:06

Record Type        = CF
ID                 = 129
Code Level         = V:10 R:5 M:0 F:4 I:0 SB:0 (0x0A05000400000000)  Not Applicable
Architecture Level = V:10 R:5 M:0 F:4 I:0 SB:0 (0x0A05000400000000)  Not Applicable
State              = [NONE]
Last updated       = 2014/09/19:12:04:10
```

Another way to obtain instance code information is by using the table function "ENV_GET_INSTANCE_CODE_LEVEL":

```
SELECT architecture_level_disk, code_level_disk
FROM TABLE("SYSPROC"."ENV_GET_INSTANCE_CODE_LEVELS"()) AS UDF
FOR FETCH ONLY
ARCHITECTURE_LEVEL_DISK                          CODE_LEVEL_DISK
------------------------------------------------ ---------------------------------
V:10 R:5 M:0 F:4 I:0 SB:0                        V:10 R:5 M:0 F:4 I:0 SB:33113
V:10 R:5 M:0 F:4 I:0 SB:0                        V:10 R:5 M:0 F:4 I:0 SB:33113
V:10 R:5 M:0 F:4 I:0 SB:0                        V:10 R:5 M:0 F:4 I:0 SB:33113
V:10 R:5 M:0 F:4 I:0 SB:0                        V:10 R:5 M:0 F:4 I:0 SB:33113
V:10 R:5 M:0 F:4 I:0 SB:0                        V:10 R:5 M:0 F:4 I:0 SB:33113
V:10 R:5 M:0 F:4 I:0 SB:0                        V:10 R:5 M:0 F:4 I:0 SB:33113
```

Online (Rolling) Upgrade of PureScale in a HADR Configuration

To perform this upgrade method, you use the same steps as previously listed, with a few additional items to consider:

1. Upgrade the standby cluster completely—all members and CFs.
2. Upgrade the members in the standby cluster before upgrading the standby CF, as discussed in the previous section, but leave the current replay member until last.
3. Verify that all members and CFs are upgraded on the standby cluster before performing any work on the primary cluster.
4. Upgrade the primary cluster the same way as in the previous section.
5. The cluster is considered *homogenous* only after both clusters are completely upgraded.

Adding a PureScale Member

With DB2 10.5, it is now possible to expand the capacity of a pureScale cluster without requiring an outage. You can add a pureScale member or CF to an existing server or to a new server. The process is basically the same as that for adding a second CF or members after the initial member and CF.

A new server will require all the initial installation steps and network configuration changes to add routing within the cluster. For this discussion, assume the server has been properly configured and cabled.

You want to add a new bare metal server with a two-LPAR configuration, with each LPAR having equal resources and dedicated network adapters. Now might be a good time to review "Installing DB2" in the "pureScale model" section because you will be adding to that configuration.

Step 1: Change the /etc/hosts files on all LPARs in the cluster to reflect the two LPAR additions.

The following /etc/hosts file shows the current configuration:

```
CFSERVER1            CF128 Primary CF Server
CFSERVER2            CF129 Secondary CF Server
MEMSERVER1           DB2 Member 0
MEMSERVER2           DB2 Member 1
MEMSERVER3           DB2 Member 2
# List of hosts in DB2 pureScale cluster
114.37.132.1 cfserver1.<domain> cfserver1
114.37.132.2 cfserver2.<domain> cfserver2
114.37.132.3 memserver1.<domain> memserver1
114.37.132.4 memserver2.<domain> memserver2
114.37.132.5 memserver3.<domain> memserver3
# List of RoCE adapters in DB2 pureScale cluster
10.100.1.1 cfserver1-roce0.<domain> cfserver1-roce0
10.100.2.1 cfserver1-roce1.<domain> cfserver1-roce1
10.100.1.2 cfserver2-roce0.<domain> cfserver2-roce0
10.100.2.2 cfserver2-roce1.<domain> cfserver2-roce1
10.100.1.3 memserver1-roce0.<domain> memserver1-roce0
10.100.2.3 memserver1-roce1.<domain> memserver1-roce1
10.100.1.4 memserver2-roce0.<domain> memserver2-roce0
10.100.2.4 memserver2-roce1.<domain> memserver2-roce1
10.100.1.5 memserver3-roce0.<domain> memserver3-roce0
10.100.2.5 memserver3-roce1.<domain> memserver3-roce1
```

You want to add MEMSERVER4 and MEMSERVER5. So the new /etc/hosts file will look as follows and will be placed on every LPAR in the cluster:

```
CFSERVER1            CF128 Primary CF Server
CFSERVER2            CF129 Secondary CF Server
MEMSERVER1           DB2 Member 0
MEMSERVER2           DB2 Member 1
MEMSERVER3           DB2 Member 2
MEMSERVER4           DB2 Member 3
MEMSERVER5           DB2 Member 4
# List of hosts in DB2 pureScale cluster
114.37.132.1 cfserver1.<domain> cfserver1
114.37.132.2 cfserver2.<domain> cfserver2
114.37.132.3 memserver1.<domain> memserver1
114.37.132.4 memserver2.<domain> memserver2
114.37.132.5 memserver3.<domain> memserver3
114.37.132.6 memserver4.<domain> memserver4
114.37.132.7 memserver5.<domain> memserver5
# List of RoCE adapters in DB2 pureScale cluster
10.100.1.1 cfserver1-roce0.<domain> cfserver1-roce0
10.100.2.1 cfserver1-roce1.<domain> cfserver1-roce1
10.100.1.2 cfserver2-roce0.<domain> cfserver2-roce0
10.100.2.2 cfserver2-roce1.<domain> cfserver2-roce1
10.100.1.3 memserver1-roce0.<domain> memserver1-roce0
10.100.2.3 memserver1-roce1.<domain> memserver1-roce1
10.100.1.4 memserver2-roce0.<domain> memserver2-roce0
10.100.2.4 memserver2-roce1.<domain> memserver2-roce1
10.100.1.5 memserver3-roce0.<domain> memserver3-roce0
10.100.2.5 memserver3-roce1.<domain> memserver3-roce1

10.100.1.6 memserver4-roce0.<domain> memserver4-roce0
10.100.2.6 memserver4-roce1.<domain> memserver4-roce1
10.100.1.7 memserver5-roce0.<domain> memserver5-roce0
10.100.2.7 memserver5-roce1.<domain> memserver5-roce1
```

Notice that each component of your pureScale cluster has two entries. This is because you are using "dual pathing" for high availability through redundancy. Also with InfiniBand and DIY configurations, it is possible to load-balance these paths for high bandwidth and capacity.

Step 2: Verify that passwordless SSH is working. You can do this from any of the existing servers to the new servers by executing `ssh <to be added server>` as the DB2 instance owner. So in this example, from server `MEMSERVER1`, execute `ssh MEMSERVER4` as `db2inst1`.

Step 3: Place the DB2 installation bundle on servers `MEMSERVER4` and `MEMSERVER5` and execute `db2setup -r <response file>` on each.

Step 4: Verify the homogenous status of the cluster software by running this command:

```
installFixPack -check_commit -I instance-name
```

It is also possible to check the status by executing the following SQL query:

```
SELECT architecture_level_disk, code_level_disk
FROM TABLE("SYSPROC"."ENV_GET_INSTANCE_CODE_LEVELS"()) AS UDF
FOR FETCH ONLY;
```

Step 5: Now you can add the two new members one at a time by using `db2iupdt`:

```
db2iupdt -d -add -m MEMSERVER4:MEMSERVER4-roce0,MEMSERVER4-roce1
<instance name>
db2iupdt -d -add -m MEMSERVER5:MEMSERVER5-roce0,MEMSERVER5-roce1
<instance name>
```

Adding a Member When HADR Is Involved

The process is altered only slightly for adding a member to a pureScale cluster that is part of a cluster HADR configuration. You basically perform the work first on the standby cluster and then on the primary cluster.

Step 1: Make `/etc/hosts` changes on the standby cluster servers.

Step 2: Test to be sure passwordless SSH is set up.

Step 3: Place the installation DB2_BUNDLE on the new server, and run the following command to add the DB2 binaries and linkages to the new server:

```
db2setup -r <response file>
```

Step 4: Always check the cluster status before executing the db2iupdt command. The cluster must be in a homogenous state before you can add a member:

```
installFixPack -check_commit -I instance-name
```

Step 5: Add the new member to the standby cluster by running db2iupdt:

```
db2iupdt -d -add -m member_id -mnet <SERVERNAME>:<SERVERNAME>-roce0,
<SERVERNAME>-roce1 <instance_name>
```

Note the use of roce to indicate RDMA over Ethernet. Dual paths are defined for redundancy and to eliminate a single point of failure.

Step 6: Make the necessary database configuration settings for HADR:

```
update db cfg for <db_name> member <member_id> using <hadr_local_host>
<standby_member_host>
update db cfg for <db_name> member <member_id> using <hadr_local_svc>
<standby_member_port>
```

Step 7: Add the new member to the primary cluster by executing this command:

```
db2iupdt -d -add -m member_id -mnet <SERVERNAME>:<SERVERNAME>-roce0,
<SERVERNAME>-roce1 <instance_name>
```

Note that here you must see the same member_id you used for the standby cluster.

Step 8: Make the necessary database configuration settings for HADR on the primary cluster:

```
update db cfg for <db_name> member <member_id> using <hadr_local_host>
<primary_member_host>
update db cfg for <db_name> member <member_id> using <hadr_local_svc>
<primary_member_port>
```

If you run the db2instance -list command now, the standby and the primary member will not display. This is because the command is not activated on the primary and is not defined yet to the cluster on the standby.

Step 9: Activate the new member on the primary cluster. Either connect to the database on the new node or execute the activate database command:

```
db2 "activate db <db_name>"
```

Explicit Hierarchical Locking (EHL)

In DB2 10.5, IBM significantly increased the value proposition of pureScale with explicit hierarchical locking (EHL). In pureScale, dirty pages in local buffer pools are "registered" in the CF. Think of it as a hotel registry where guests are database pages and hotel floors are pureScale logical members.

When the guests arrive, they are asked whether they will remain in their rooms until checkout. If yes, then no need to update the hotel registry for this room or for this guest. However, if they exit their rooms and move about the hotel during their stay, you will want to keep track of their use of the hotel facilities.

You can turn on EHL by using this command:

```
db2 "update db cfg for <DB_NAME> using OPT_DIRECT_WRKLD YES immediate"
```

To turn off EHL (the default), use this one:

```
db2 "update db cfg for <DB NAME> using OPT_DIRECT_WRKLD NO immediate"
```

Once EHL is active, DB2 tracks access to tables and partitions. If DB2 determines, over a period of time (minutes), that only one member is accessing this table or partition, DB2 will stop coordinating local member events with the CF for this table or partition. This can reduce overhead and make the local process run faster. At any time, should a different member request access to the table or partition, coordination will begin with the CF for this table or partition.

Turning on and off coordination with the CF for a table or partition is an expensive operation and must be avoided. You can do so by restricting insert/update/delete activity against a table or partition to a single member.

The following example has an insert process that runs continuously against the table; no updates/deletes are run against this table. You have partitioned the table across the three members of your cluster. With EHL off, page and lock registration will occur—but with EHL on, it will not.

```
CREATE TABLE TABLE_MEAS
(
  EQP_MEAS_ID     BIGINT        NOT NULL,
  MSG_ID          BIGINT        NOT NULL,
  EQP_SEQ_NB      SMALLINT,
  .
  .
  .
  CRET_CLUSTER_MEMBER INTEGER  NOT NULL  DEFAULT CURRENT NODE,
  .
  .
  .
)
PARTITION BY RANGE ( CRET_CLUSTER_MEMBER NULLS LAST )
(
 PARTITION PART0 STARTING 0 INCLUSIVE ENDING 0 INCLUSIVE IN TSD301 INDEX IN TSX301,
 PARTITION PART1 STARTING 1 INCLUSIVE ENDING 1 INCLUSIVE IN TSD302 INDEX IN TSX302,
 PARTITION PART2 STARTING 2 INCLUSIVE ENDING 2 INCLUSIVE IN TSD303 INDEX IN TSX303
)
COMPRESS YES ADAPTIVE
APPEND MODE YES
ORGANIZE BY ROW ;
```

Member Sets

PureScale has the ability to isolate workloads that do not relate well. Member Sets identifies the schizophrenic nature of customers and specifically DBAs, in that with clusters, you have community and with Member Sets you have a colony. At one point you want to share, and the next moment you want to send workloads to their own rooms.

So using WLM, you basically want to separate the members into colonies (for example, members 0,3 for batch workloads exclusive and members 1,2 for OLTP workloads inclusive—or BLU/shadow workloads on members 0,2,4,6 and all other workloads on members 1,3,5).

If you want to create a new Member Set, use a new stored procedure named SYSPROC.WLM_CREATE_MEMBER_SUBSET. To alter an existing Member Set, use new stored procedure SYSPROC.WLM_ALTER_MEMBER_SUBSET.

The SYSPROC.WLM_CREATE_MEMBER_SUBSET looks something like this:

```
call sysproc.wlm_create_member_subset('COLUMN_SUBSET',
<databaseAlias>COLDB</databaseAlias>,
<inclusiveSubset>no</inclusiveSubset>,
'(0,2,4,6)' ) ;

call sysproc.wlm_create_member_subset('ROW_SUBSET',
<databaseAlias>ROWDB</databaseAlias>,
<inclusiveSubset>yes</inclusiveSubset>,
'(1,3,5)' ) ;
```

Note: The above code snippet requires DBADM or WLMADM authority to execute.

PureScale Workload Management: Real-World Example

It is Thursday afternoon around 3:00 p.m. when you receive a call about a high-visibility project, which is scheduled to go live on Friday evening. There seems to be an issue regarding insert processing performance. After hours of discussion with the development team, you learn that this problem was just identified because no volume tests had been executed. In Java, you have 10 parallel threads all inserting into one table:

```
CREATE TABLE XXX.BIG_INSERT_LOAD
( PK_COLUMN          BIGINT NOT NULL,
```

Continued

```
   TEXT_INFO          VARCHAR(3200),
   CREATE_TS          TIMESTAMP DEFAULT CURRENT_TIMESTAMP
) IN TS1 INDEX IN TS2
   COMPRESS YES ADAPTIVE
   ORGANIZE BY ROW ;
```

It has been reported that insert processing in ESE is 5 KB rows per second, while in pureScale it is under 2 KB rows per second. You set up tests to confirm the reported findings and discover that with one Java thread in pureScale, the rate is around 4 KB rows per second, but with each additional Java parallel thread the totals drop. The development team has informed you that the target to achieve must be over 26 KB rows inserted per second for the project to be successful.

You make the normal Java changes, including setting the batch size to an optimal value. So something must be slowing pureScale insert processing. A simple check of the number of reclaims and the average time wait for each gives you the answer.

The pureScale cluster is three active members. The `values(current member) ;` returns the current member number of the active connection. Each Java connection object will return the current member, but it is too late in the deployment/release cycle for any coding changes. So the development team tells you to do whatever you need to do without requiring code modifications.

The plan is to create target member tables so that the insert processing can occur with no CF collisions. Each cluster member (0,1,2) will have its own table:

```
CREATE TABLE XXX.BIG_INSERT_LOAD_MEM0
( PK_COLUMN          BIGINT NOT NULL,
  TEXT_INFO          VARCHAR(3200),
  CREATE_TS          TIMESTAMP DEFAULT CURRENT_TIMESTAMP
) IN TS1 INDEX IN TS2
  COMPRESS YES ADAPTIVE
  ORGANIZE BY ROW ;

CREATE TABLE XXX.BIG_INSERT_LOAD_MEM1
( PK_COLUMN          BIGINT NOT NULL,
  TEXT_INFO          VARCHAR(3200),
  CREATE_TS          TIMESTAMP DEFAULT CURRENT_TIMESTAMP
) IN TS3 INDEX IN TS4
                                                    Continued
```

```
  COMPRESS YES ADAPTIVE
  ORGANIZE BY ROW ;


CREATE TABLE XXX.BIG_INSERT_LOAD_MEM2
( PK_COLUMN          BIGINT NOT NULL,
  TEXT_INFO          VARCHAR(3200),
  CREATE_TS          TIMESTAMP DEFAULT CURRENT_TIMESTAMP
) IN TS5 INDEX IN TS6
  COMPRESS YES ADAPTIVE
  ORGANIZE BY ROW ;

CREATE VIEW XXX.BIG_INSERT_LOAD AS
SELECT * FROM XXX.BIG_INSERT_LOAD_MEM0
UNION ALL
SELECT * FROM XXX.BIG_INSERT_LOAD_MEM1
UNION ALL
SELECT * FROM XXX.BIG_INSERT_LOAD_MEM2
;
```

You create an INSTEAD OF INSERT trigger to capture the Java inserts and direct them to the correct table depending on where the connection is established. This enables you to keep your default of allowing workloads to float across the cluster:

```
CREATE TRIGGER XXX.II_BIG_INSERT_LOAD
INSTEAD OF INSERT ON XXX.BIG_INSERT_LOAD
REFERENCING NEW as NEW
FOR EACH ROW
BEGIN ATOMIC
    DECLARE V_CURRENT_MEMBER  INTEGER ;
    SET V_CURRENT_MEMBER = CURRENT MEMBER ;
    IF V_CURRENT_MEMBER = 0
    then
        INSERT INTO XXX.BIG_INSERT_LOAD_MEM0(PK_COLUMN,TEXT_INFO,CREATE_TS)
        VALUES ( NEW.PK_COLUMN, NEW.TEXT_INFO, NEW.CREATE_TS ) ;
```

```
        ELSE IF V_CURRENT_MEMBER = 1
        Then
            INSERT INTO XXX.BIG_INSERT_LOAD_MEM1(PK_COLUMN,TEXT_INFO,CREATE_TS)
            VALUES ( NEW.PK_COLUMN, NEW.TEXT_INFO, NEW.CREATE_TS ) ;
        ELSE IF V_CURRENT_MEMBER = 2
        then
            INSERT INTO XXX.BIG_INSERT_LOAD_MEM2(PK_COLUMN,TEXT_INFO,CREATE_TS)
            VALUES ( NEW.PK_COLUMN, NEW.TEXT_INFO, NEW.CREATE_TS ) ;
        ELSE SIGNAL SQLSTATE '90000'
             SET MESSAGE_TEXT = 'Invalid Member' ;
        END IF ; -- 2
        END IF ; -- 1
        END IF ; -- 0
    END @
```

So without changing any application code, you have set up INSERTs and SELECTs to operate as originally designed, but the INSERTs will perform much better.

The final results for the insert processing exceeded 36 KB rows inserted per second.

Should you turn on EHL? In this case, EHL will reduce CPU and traffic to the CF for this insert process. However, it will do so at the cost of being able to use the group buffer pool (GBP) as a secondary caching level for SELECTs against the table. Instead, you can monitor the read hit ratios with EHL off, and then later turn EHL on to see whether the read hit ratios worsen and the read I/O counts increase.

Backup and Restore Enhancements

DB2 10.5 FP4 Cancun provides incremental and delta incremental backups for pureScale topologies. After you change your pureScale topology (for example, dropping a member or after restoring to a non-superset topology), an offline backup is no longer required. Also when restoring an ESE (LUW) database to pureScale, you can perform an incremental online or offline backup instead of a full offline backup.

Using Backup and Restore to Migrate a Database

The ability to use the backup and restore enhancements to move a database to pureScale or from pureScale to ESE (LUW) depends largely on whether the applications accessing the data can be down. Assume for now that the data can be unavailable long enough to complete the migration.

It is now possible to back up and restore databases between non-pureScale and pureScale databases. Backup and restore operations are also supported between pureScale environments of different topologies. When backup and restore operations are between pureScale and non-pureScale environments, you must perform offline full backups.

You should execute all backups and restores from the same logical member. The file `db2nodes.cfg` in SQLLIB will contain the node numbers associated with the topology. For ESE (LUW) topologies, this will most likely be zero (0). You execute the restore from this backup, if run on a pureScale cluster, from member `0`.

When all the members of the source pureScale cluster topology are present in the target pureScale cluster topology, the target pureScale cluster topology is referred to as a *superset of the source cluster topology*. In this case, only roll-forward operations are allowed, which also means it is the only case in which you can use an online backup of the source.

If the target cluster topology is not a superset of the source cluster topology, but there is at least one member in common, any topology change will require either an incremental or a full backup, and only full offline backups of the source database will work.

Table 10.20 lists the different backup and restore options.

Table 10.20: Backup and restore options

Source	Target	Superset	Backup	Roll-forward	Target Backup Required	DB2 Software Levels
ESE	PS	N/A	Offline	N/A	Yes	Same version/release
PS	ESE	N/A	Offline	N/A	Yes	Same version/release
PS	PS	Yes	Online	Yes	No	Same version/release
PS	PS	No	Offline	N/A	Yes	Same version/release

Prerequisites to Moving a Database to PureScale

There are three prerequisites to moving databases from ESE (LUW) to pureScale. Most of these are related to the database requirements of pureScale.

Non-Unicode Database

PureScale requires that you define the database by using a Unicode code set. You cannot modify the code set of a database; therefore, you must create a new database in order to change the code set. You do this by creating a Unicode code set database and migrating the data from the non-Unicode database. See "Changing a Database's Code Set" in the "Physical Design" section for more information on how to move data between different code sets.

When you are creating a new database to satisfy the Unicode requirement, it is recommended you satisfy any and all prerequisites at the same time. Furthermore, it is strongly recommended you make the necessary changes while the database is still in ESE (LUW). Make sure the container assignments are correctly placed and the storage groups are properly defined before performing the source database backup.

When a new database is created as AUTOMATIC STORAGE YES, the default storage group is IBMSTOGROUP. You should define all table spaces as MANAGED BY AUTOMATIC STORAGE and assign them to a proper storage group.

Once the database is ready, execute db2checkSD to verify whether it is eligible for pureScale. Correct any issues reported and run the command again until no issues are reported.

Unicode Database Defined as AUTOMATIC STORAGE NO

A database that is defined AUTOMATIC STORAGE NO will not have any storage groups defined. You must define at least one storage group before table spaces can be defined as MANAGED BY AUTOMATIC STORAGE.

Create at least one storage group. When you execute the CREATE STOGROUP statement in a database defined as AUTOMATIC STORAGE NO, the following changes occur:

1. The database is altered to AUTOMATIC STORAGE YES.
2. The storage group is set to default.

Basically, creating the first storage group in the database will convert the database to AUTOMATIC STORAGE YES. However, this is not reversible. You cannot drop the default storage group, which means you must always define one storage group as the default.

For more information about how to use storage groups, see "Storage Groups" under the "Physical Design" section. For more information about table spaces, see "Table Spaces" under the "Physical Design" section.

All table spaces should be converted to MANAGED BY AUTOMATIC STORAGE. For DMS table spaces, you can accomplish this by using the ALTER TABLESPACE statement or the SET TABLESPACE statement during a redirected restore. You cannot alter SMS table spaces in this way, so you will need to re-create them.

Database Configuration Settings

Because pureScale is more restrictive than ESE (LUW) today, some database configuration settings if used in ESE (LUW) must be changed before migrating to pureScale. The list of restrictions can also vary depending on the target pureScale software level.

The db2checkSD process will check the source database for compatibility issues, so make sure you correct all problems before performing a backup and attempting to migrate to pureScale.

Mapping Container Paths ESE (LUW) to PureScale

One prerequisite is common to any database migration. Table space containers must be allocated on mounted file systems at the target server. If the file systems are the same on the source and target servers, no change is required. In many cases, however, the placement of the containers will change; therefore, the source file system must be translated to a target file system.

PureScale accesses data stored in containers allocated on shared file systems managed by GPFS software. A source ESE (LUW) database uses table space containers allocated on nonshared file systems. The best and easiest way to manage table space containers is by using storage groups. It is also the easiest way to map file systems source to the target server.

During the redirected restore process, you will use the SET STOGROUP statement to alter the paths assigned to the storage groups. Assume that in your ESE (LUW) database, you have created the following storage group:

```
CREATE STOGROUP DATA
  ON '/db/ts01/db2inst1/data',
      '/db/ts02/db2inst1/data',
      '/db/ts03/db2inst1/data',
      '/db/ts04/db2inst1/data'
  OVERHEAD 0.75
  DEVICE READ RATE 800.
  SET AS DEFAULT;
```

The paths defined to the DATA storage group are on local disks mounted on the database server. When you restore this database into a pureScale cluster, you will need to modify these paths to point to your shared file systems.

After the initial restore database command, you will change the paths using this statement:

```
SET STOGROUP PATHS FOR DATA ON '/ds/ts01/data','/ds/ts02/data','/ds/ts03/
data','/ds/ts04/data' ;
```

Note: Make sure when moving to pureScale that you have done everything correctly, especially when it comes to table spaces and storage groups. Table space rebalance is not supported in pureScale, nor are many alterations to storage groups or table spaces. If the move is to ESE (LUW), making corrections after the restore is fine.

Backup and Restore Examples

Now let us look at four backup and restore examples that focus on the previously discussed scenarios.

In the first example, the source ESE (LUW) database is named SAMPLE and the pureScale target database is NEWDB:

```
CREATE DATABASE SAMPLE
  AUTOMATIC STORAGE YES
  ON '/db/home'
  DBPATH ON '/db/home/db2inst1'
  ALIAS SAMPLE
  USING CODESET UTF-8 TERRITORY US
  COLLATE USING SYSTEM_819_US
  PAGESIZE 4096
  NUMSEGS 1
  DFT_EXTENT_SZ 32
  CATALOG TABLESPACE
    MANAGED BY
    AUTOMATIC STORAGE
    EXTENTSIZE 4
    PREFETCHSIZE -1
    OVERHEAD -1
    TRANSFERRATE -1
    NO FILE SYSTEM CACHING
    AUTORESIZE YES
    INITIALSIZE 32 M
  USER TABLESPACE
    MANAGED BY
    AUTOMATIC STORAGE
    EXTENTSIZE 32
    PREFETCHSIZE -1
    OVERHEAD -1
```

Continued

```
    TRANSFERRATE -1
    NO FILE SYSTEM CACHING
    AUTORESIZE YES
    INITIALSIZE 32 M
  TEMPORARY TABLESPACE
    MANAGED BY
    AUTOMATIC STORAGE
    EXTENTSIZE 32
    PREFETCHSIZE -1
    OVERHEAD -1
    TRANSFERRATE -1
    NO FILE SYSTEM CACHING

CREATE STOGROUP IBMSTOGROUP
  ON '/db/home'
  OVERHEAD 6.725
  DEVICE READ RATE 100.
  SET AS DEFAULT;

#/usr/bin/ksh -p
db2 "restore database sample from /ds/exp
     dbpath on /db2sd_20141123121420
     into newdb REDIRECT
     without rolling forward without prompting"
db2 "SET STOGROUP PATHS FOR IBMSTOGROUP ON
     '/ds/ts01/data','/ds/ts02/data','/ds/ts03/data','/ds/ts04/data'"
db2 "restore database sample continue"
db2checkSD newdb
db2 "backup database newdb to /dev/null"
**  There are two backup statements here because of a known bug **"
db2 "backup database newdb to /dev/null"
db2 "connect to newdb"
```

In the second example, the pureScale database NEWDB is the source and the ESE (LUW) database SAMPLE is the target:

```
CREATE DATABASE NEWDB
  AUTOMATIC STORAGE YES
  ON '/ds/ts04/indx', '/ds/ts03/indx', '/ds/ts02/indx', '/ds/ts01/indx',
'/ds/tstemp04', '/ds/tstemp03', '/ds/tstemp02', '/ds/tstemp01', '/ds/ts04',
'/ds/ts03', '/ds/ts02', '/ds/ts01', '/ds/ts04/data', '/ds/ts03/data',
'/ds/ts02/data', '/ds/ts01/data'
DBPATH ON '/db2sd_20141123121420/db2inst1'
ALIAS NEWDB
  USING CODESET UTF-8 TERRITORY US
  COLLATE USING SYSTEM_819_US
  PAGESIZE 4096
  NUMSEGS 1
  DFT_EXTENT_SZ 32
  RESTRICTIVE
  CATALOG TABLESPACE
    MANAGED BY
    AUTOMATIC STORAGE
    EXTENTSIZE 32
    PREFETCHSIZE 128
    OVERHEAD 7.5
    TRANSFERRATE 0.06
    NO FILE SYSTEM CACHING
    AUTORESIZE YES
    INITIALSIZE 32 M
    INCREASESIZE 256 M
    MAXSIZE 24576 M

CREATE STOGROUP IBMSTOGROUP
  ON '/ds/ts01',
     '/ds/ts02',
     '/ds/ts03',
     '/ds/ts04'
```

Continued

```
CREATE STOGROUP INDX
  ON '/ds/ts04/indx',
     '/ds/ts03/indx',
     '/ds/ts02/indx',
     '/ds/ts01/indx'
  OVERHEAD 0.75
  DEVICE READ RATE 800

CREATE STOGROUP DATA
  ON '/ds/ts01/data',
     '/ds/ts02/data',
     '/ds/ts03/data',
     '/ds/ts04/data'
  OVERHEAD 0.75
  DEVICE READ RATE 800
  SET AS DEFAULT

CREATE STOGROUP TMP1
  ON '/ds/tstemp01',
     '/ds/tstemp02',
     '/ds/tstemp03',
     '/ds/tstemp04'
  OVERHEAD 0.75
  DEVICE READ RATE 800

#/usr/bin/ksh -p
db2 "restore database newdb from /db/exp
     dbpath on /db/home/db2inst1
     into sample REDIRECT
     without rolling forward without prompting"
db2 "SET STOGROUP PATHS FOR IBMSTOGROUP ON
     '/db/ts01/data','/db/ts02/data','/db/ts03/data','/db/ts04/data'"
```

Continued

```
db2 "SET STOGROUP PATHS FOR DATA ON
     '/db/ts01/data','/db/ts02/data','/db/ts03/data','/db/ts04/data'"
db2 "SET STOGROUP PATHS FOR INDX ON
     '/db/ts04/indx','/db/ts03/indx','/db/ts02/indx','/db/ts01/indx'"
db2 "SET STOGROUP PATHS FOR TMP1 ON
     '/db/tstemp01','/db/tstemp02','/db/tstemp03','/db/tstemp04'"
db2 "restore database newdb continue"
db2checkSD sample
db2 "backup database sample to /dev/null"
db2 "connect to sample"
```

In example 3, the source members are (0,1); the target members are (0,2) and are not a superset.

```
The backup is run from Source:Member 0:
db2snd1@xxxaxdb2d005:/ds/exp
==> db2 "backup db sample to /ds/exp"
Backup successful. The timestamp for this backup image is : 20140925113659

Restore Run from Target:Member 0
db2inst1@xxxaxdb2d007:/ds/exp
==> db2 "restore db sample from /ds/exp without rolling forward"
DB20000I  The RESTORE DATABASE command completed successfully.

db2inst1@xxxaxdb2d007:/ds/exp
==> db2 "backup db sample to /ds/exp"
Backup successful. The timestamp for this backup image is : 20140925131104
```

In example 4, the source members are (0,1,2), and the target members are (0,1,2,3) and are a superset:

```
db2snd1@xxxaxdb2d005:/ds/exp
==> db2 "backup db sample to /ds/exp online include logs"
Backup successful. The timestamp for this backup image is : 20140926100320
```

Continued

```
db2inst1@xxxaxdb2d007:/ds/exp
==> db2 "restore db sample from /ds/exp on /db/home/db2inst1 logtarget
/ds/overflowlogs"
DB20000I  The RESTORE DATABASE command completed successfully.

db2inst1@xxxaxdb2d007:/ds/exp
==> db2 "rollfoward db sample to end of logs overflow log
path(/ds/overflowlogs)"
DB20000I  The ROLLFORWARD DATABASE command completed successfully.
```

Supporting Multiple Databases in pureScale

Sometimes, it might be necessary to create more than one database in a pureScale topology. Many of the reasons used years ago to create multiple databases no longer apply, and in a pureScale topology, there are even fewer reasons to create multiple databases. Also, in many cases, a separate pureScale cluster/instance can be justified over adding databases to an existing cluster.

A single pureScale cluster can support up to 200 databases. The maximum number of database activations per cluster is 512. Thus, in a four-member cluster, the maximum value for database manager NUMDB is 128. If member crash recovery (MCR) is required, the number of parallel database recoveries is the lesser value of NUMDB or registry setting DB2_MCR_RECOVERY_PARALLELISM_CAP. When only one database is active, set DB2_DATABASE_CF_MEMORY=100 and CF_DB_MEM_SZ= <CF_MEM_SZ> AUTOMATIC.

If you are running a pureScale instance with multiple active databases, the challenge is in managing CF resources. CF_MEM_SZ is not configurable online, so setting it to AUTOMATIC is the best option. However, you can configure the other important CF settings online. CF_DB_MEM_SZ must always be less than CF_MEM_SZ and less than or equal to the sum of CF_GBP_SZ, CF_LOCK_SZ, and CF_SCA_SZ. The sum of CF_DB_MEM_SZ for all databases in the cluster should be less than or equal to CF_MEM_SZ. Avoid increasing the sum of CF_DB_MEM_SZ values above that of CF_MEM_SZ. If you need to increase a CF_DB_MEM_SZ of one of the databases so that the sum exceeds CF_MEM_SZ, you must first reduce the value of CF_DB_MEM_SZ in one or more of the other databases to offset the increase.

CF Self-Tuning Memory Feature

Before IBM DB2 10.5 FP5, the available settings for registry parameter DB2_DATABASE_CF_MEMORY were -1 or a fixed percentage. In the multiple database configuration, setting DB2_DATABASE_CF_MEMORY=-1 will cause each active database to receive an equal share of

CF resources. This might be fine to do in your environment, but it has two significant concerns. Both -1 and a fixed percentage are based on the number of active databases. In the case of -1, the system sets the percentage for you based on the database manager setting NUMDB, which requires a global instance cycle to change. *Global instance cycle* means all members of the cluster must be down at the same time for the setting to change.

With DB2 10.5 FP5, IBM introduces CF self-tuning memory (autonomics for CF memory). To activate this feature, you set the registry parameter DB2_DATABASE_CF_MEMORY=AUTO and set the database manager parameter CF_MEM_SZ=*<90% of the RAM on the CF Server>* AUTOMATIC. The feature provides two ways of managing CF memory resources.

If you want fewer variations to the active databases' CF footprint, the first step is to set the database configuration parameters:

- CF_DB_MEM_SZ=<Percentage * CF_MEM_SZ>
- CF_GBP_SZ=<.80 * CF_DB_MEM_SZ> AUTOMATIC
- CF_LOCK_SZ=<.15 * CF_DB_MEM_SZ> AUTOMATIC
- CF_SCA_SZ=<.05 * CF_DB_MEM_SZ> AUTOMATIC

The sum (CF_DB_MEM_SZ) for all active databases in the instance should be less than or equal to CF_MEM_SZ. The (CF_GBP_SZ+CF_LOCK_SZ+CF_SCA_SZ) should be equal to CF_DB_MEM_SZ.

The CF self-tuning feature will make memory adjustments based on workloads for CF_GBP_SZ, CF_LOCK_SZ, and CF_SCA_SZ within the memory boundary of CF_DB_MEM_SZ. This prevents one active database workload from affecting another active database based on CF memory resources.

If you want the CF self-tuning feature to adjust the CF memory assigned to each active database based on workloads, set CF_DB_MEM_SZ=*<Percentage * CF_MEM_SZ>* AUTOMATIC. It is important to properly set the database manager parameter NUMDB to a reasonable value, which is probably not the default of 32. Instead, set NUMDB to the number of expected active databases or to a reasonable growth target. If CF_MEM_SZ is set to AUTOMATIC, the CF self-tuning feature will adjust the CF memory amount if RAM changes are made to CF servers.

Monitoring DB2 Activity

In DB2 10.5, IBM added monitoring elements to help you understand columnar processing, HADR processing, sort processing, backup, and index creation. For detailed information about DB2 monitoring, see Chapter 5, "Monitoring DB2 Activity."

Columnar Monitoring

Tables 10.21–10.26 list the new monitor elements for columnar processing.

Table 10.21: Data page reads	
Element	**Description**
POOL_COL_L_READS	Logical data pages reads
POOL_COL_P_READS	Physical data pages reads
POOL_COL_LBP_PAGES_FOUND	Data pages found in local buffer pool
POOL_ASYNC_COL_READS	Asynchronous data pages reads
POOL_ASYNC_COL_READ_REQS	Asynchronous data pages requests
POOL_ASYNC_COL_LBP_PAGES_FOUND	Asynchronous data pages found in local buffer pool
OBJECT_COL_L_READS	Object logical data pages reads
OBJECT_COL_P_READS	Object physical data pages reads
OBJECT_COL_GBP_L_READS	Object logical group buffer pool reads
OBJECT_COL_GBP_P_READS	Object physical group buffer pool reads
OBJECT_COL_GBP_INVALID_PAGES	Object global buffer pool invalid pages
OBJECT_COL_LBP_PAGES_FOUND	Object logical buffer pool hit
OBJECT_COL_GBP_INDEP_PAGES_FOUND_IN_LBP	Object independent global buffer pool hit in logical buffer pool
POOL_QUEUED_ASYNC_COL_REQS	Queued asynchronous requests
POOL_QUEUED_ASYNC_COL_PAGES	Queued asynchronous pages
POOL_FAILED_ASYNC_COL_REQS	Queued asynchronous requests
SKIPPED_PREFETCH_COL_P_READS	Skipped prefetch physical reads
SKIPPED_PREFETCH_UOW_COL_P_READS	Skipped prefetch UOW physical reads

Table 10.22: Data page writes	
Element	**Description**
POOL_COL_WRITE	Column writes
POOL_ASYNC_COL_WRITES	Asynchronous column writes

Table 10.23: Column table sizes	
Element	**Description**
COL_OBJECT_L_SIZE	Object logical size (KB) allocated space
COL_OBJECT_P_SIZE	Object physical size (KB) used space
COL_OBJECT_L_PAGES	Object logical pages

Table 10.24: Column times	
Element	**Description**
TOTAL_COL_TIME	Column elapse time (ms)
TOTAL_COL_PROC_TIME	Column processing nonwait time (ms)
TOTAL_COL_EXECUTIONS	Times column-organized data was accessed

Table 10.25: Column sorts

Element	Description
TOTAL_HASH_GRPBYS	Column GRPBYS
ACTIVE_HAPS_GRPBYS	Active column GRPBYS
HASH_GRPBY_OVERFLOWS	Column GRPBYS times disk used
POST_THRESHOLD_HASH_GRPBYS	Times limited by shared or private sortheap
ACTIVE_HASH_GRPBYS_TOP	Maximum concurrent column GRPBYS

Table 10.26: Column sortheap vector memory

Element	Description
ACTIVE_COL_VECTOR_CONSUMERS	Active column consumers
ACTIVE_COL_VECTOR_CONSUMERS_TOP	Maximum concurrent active column consumers
POST_THRESHOLD_COL_VECTOR_CONSUMERS	Consumers requesting sort memory after heap exceeded
TOTAL_COL_VECTOR_CONSUMERS	Total column consumers

Metrics are grouped into the following categories: request, activity, object, and ratio. The monitor interfaces in Table 10.27 present these metrics.

Table 10.27: Interfaces that report request metrics

Interfaces
MON_GET_DATABASE
MON_GET_DATABASE_DETAILS
MON_GET_WORKLOAD
MON_GET_WORKLOAD_DETAILS
MON_GET_UNIT_OF_WORK
MON_GET_UNIT_OF_WORK_DETAILS
MON_GET_SERVICE_SUBCLASS
MON_GET_SERVICE_SUBCLASS_DETAILS
MON_GET_CONNECTION
MON_GET_CONNECTION_DETAILS
EVMON_FORMAT_UE_TO_XML
MON_FORMAT_XML_METRICS_BY_ROW
Unit of Work event monitor
Statistics event monitor

The following is one example view set up to report database metrics at the detail level:

```
CREATE OR REPLACE VIEW XXX.MON_DB_DETAIL
( MEMBER, TOTAL_CONS, LOCK_TIMEOUTS, DEADLOCKS, CF_WAITS, CF_WAIT_TIME,
  MAX_CONS, MAX_COOR_AGENTS, MAX_AGENTS, DS_LOCKWAITS, DS_LOCKWAIT_TIME,
  TOTAL_CON_REQS, TOTAL_CON_REQ_TIME, TOTAL_CON_AUTHS,
  TOTAL_CON_AUTH_TIME,TOTAL_CON_AUTH_PROC_TIME, TOTAL_CON_REQ_PROC_TIME,
  LOCK_WAITS, TOTAL_CPU_TIME, COL_EXECS, COL_PROC_TIME, TOTAL_COL_TIME,
  PREFETCH_WAIT_TIME, PREFETCH_WAITS, RECLAIM_WAIT_TIME,ROWS_READ,
  DIRECT_READS, DIRECT_READ_REQS, DIRECT_READ_TIME, ROWS_DELETED,
  ROWS_UPDATED, ROWS_INSERTED, ROWS_RETURNED, LOGICAL_INDEX_READS,
  PHYSICAL_INDEX_READS,LOGICAL_LBP_HITS, TOTAL_REORGS, TOTAL_REORG_PROC_TIME,
  TOTAL_REORG_TIME, FAILED_SQL_COUNT, FILES_CLOSED, LOCK_ESCALS,
  LOCK_ESCALS_GLOBAL, LOCK_ESCALS_LOCKLIST, LOCK_ESCALS_MAXLOCKS,
  LOCK_LIST_IN_USE, LOCKWAITS, LOCKWAITS_GLOBAL, LOCKWAIT_TIME,
  LOCKWAIT_TIME_GLOBAL
) AS
SELECT wlm.member as member
,detm.total_cons as total_cons
,detm.LOCK_TIMEOUTS as lock_timeouts
,detm.deadlocks as deadlocks
,detm.cf_waits as cf_waits
,detm.cf_wait_time as cf_wait_time
,detm.connections_top as max_cons
,detm.coord_agents_top as max_coor_agents
,detm.agents_top as max_agents
,detm.data_sharing_remote_lockwait_count as ds_lockwaits
,detm.data_sharing_remote_lockwait_time as ds_lockwait_time
,detm.total_connect_requests as total_con_reqs
,detm.total_connect_request_time as total_con_req_time
,detm.total_connect_authentications as total_con_auths
,detm.total_connect_authentication_time as total_con_auth_time
,detm.total_connect_authentication_proc_time as total_con_auth_proc_time
```

Continued

```
,detm.total_connect_request_proc_time as total_con_req_proc_time
,detm.num_locks_waiting as lock_waits
,detm.total_cpu_time as total_cpu_time
,detm.total_col_executions as col_execs
,detm.total_col_proc_time as col_proc_time
,detm.total_col_time as total_col_time
,detm.prefetch_wait_time as prefetch_wait_time
,detm.prefetch_waits as prefetch_waits
,detm.reclaim_wait_time as reclaim_wait_time
,detm.rows_read as rows_read
,detm.direct_reads as direct_reads
,detm.direct_read_reqs as direct_read_reqs
,detm.direct_read_time as direct_read_time
,detm.rows_deleted as rows_deleted
,detm.rows_updated as rows_updated
,detm.rows_inserted as rows_inserted
,detm.rows_returned as rows_returned
,detm.pool_index_l_reads as Logical_index_reads
,detm.pool_index_p_reads as Physical_index_reads
,detm.pool_index_lbp_pages_found as Logical_lbp_hits
,detm.total_reorgs as Total_Reorgs
,detm.total_reorg_proc_time as Total_Reorg_proc_time
,detm.total_reorg_time as Total_Reorg_time
,detm.failed_sql_stmts as Failed_SQL_COUNT
,detm.files_closed as Files_Closed
,detm.LOCK_ESCALS as lock_escals
,detm.LOCK_ESCALS_GLOBAL as lock_escals_global
,detm.LOCK_ESCALS_LOCKLIST as lock_escals_locklist
,detm.LOCK_ESCALS_MAXLOCKS as lock_escals_maxlocks
,detm.LOCK_LIST_IN_USE as lock_list_in_use
,detm.LOCK_waits as lockwaits
,detm.LOCK_waits_global as lockwaits_global
,detm.LOCK_wait_time as lockwait_time
,detm.LOCK_wait_time_global as lockwait_time_global
```

Continued

```
FROM TABLE(MON_GET_DATABASE_DETAILS(-2)) AS WLM,
XMLTABLE (XMLNAMESPACES
( DEFAULT 'http://www.ibm.com/xmlns/prod/db2/mon'),'$detmetric/db2_database'
  PASSING XMLPARSE(DOCUMENT WLM.DETAILS) as "detm"
COLUMNS "TOTAL_CONS" BIGINT PATH 'system_metrics/total_cons'
 ,"DEADLOCKS" BIGINT PATH 'system_metrics/deadlocks'
 ,"CONNECTIONS_TOP" BIGINT PATH 'system_metrics/connections_top'
 ,"COORD_AGENTS_TOP" BIGINT PATH 'system_metrics/coord_agents_top'
 ,"AGENTS_TOP" BIGINT PATH 'system_metrics/agents_top'
 ,"DATA_SHARING_REMOTE_LOCKWAIT_COUNT" BIGINT PATH
'system_metrics/data_sharing_remote_lockwait_count'
 ,"DATA_SHARING_REMOTE_LOCKWAIT_TIME" BIGINT PATH
'system_metrics/data_sharing_remote_lockwait_time'
 ,"TOTAL_CONNECT_REQUESTS" BIGINT PATH 'system_metrics/total_connect_requests'
 ,"TOTAL_CONNECT_REQUEST_TIME" BIGINT PATH
'system_metrics/total_connect_request_time'
 ,"TOTAL_CONNECT_REQUEST_PROC_TIME" BIGINT PATH
'system_metrics/total_connect_request_proc_time'
 ,"TOTAL_CONNECT_AUTHENTICATIONS" BIGINT PATH
'system_metrics/total_connect_authentications'
 ,"TOTAL_CONNECT_AUTHENTICATION_TIME" BIGINT PATH
'system_metrics/total_connect_authentication_time'
 ,"TOTAL_CONNECT_AUTHENTICATION_PROC_TIME" BIGINT PATH
'system_metrics/total_connect_authentication_proc_time'
 ,"TOTAL_COL_EXECUTIONS" BIGINT PATH 'system_metrics/total_col_executions'
 ,"TOTAL_COL_PROC_TIME" BIGINT PATH 'system_metrics/total_col_proc_time'
 ,"TOTAL_COL_TIME" BIGINT PATH 'system_metrics/total_col_time'
 ,"ROWS_READ" BIGINT PATH 'system_metrics/rows_read'
 ,"ROWS_DELETED" BIGINT PATH 'system_metrics/rows_deleted'
 ,"ROWS_INSERTED" BIGINT PATH 'system_metrics/rows_inserted'
 ,"ROWS_UPDATED" BIGINT PATH 'system_metrics/rows_updated'
 ,"ROWS_RETURNED" BIGINT PATH 'system_metrics/rows_returned'
 ,"NUM_LOCKS_WAITING" BIGINT PATH 'system_metrics/lock_waits'
 ,"TOTAL_CPU_TIME" BIGINT PATH 'system_metrics/total_cpu_time'
```

Continued

```
  ,"DIRECT_READS" BIGINT PATH 'system_metrics/direct_reads'
  ,"DIRECT_READ_REQS" BIGINT PATH 'system_metrics/direct_read_reqs'
  ,"DIRECT_READ_TIME" BIGINT PATH 'system_metrics/direct_read_time'
  ,"PREFETCH_WAIT_TIME" BIGINT PATH 'system_metrics/prefetch_wait_time'
  ,"PREFETCH_WAITS" BIGINT PATH 'system_metrics/prefetch_waits'
  ,"RECLAIM_WAIT_TIME" BIGINT PATH 'system_metrics/reclaim_wait_time'
  ,"POOL_INDEX_L_READS" BIGINT PATH 'system_metrics/pool_index_l_reads'
  ,"POOL_INDEX_P_READS" BIGINT PATH 'system_metrics/pool_index_p_reads'
  ,"POOL_INDEX_LBP_PAGES_FOUND" BIGINT PATH
'system_metrics/pool_index_lbp_pages_found'
  ,"TOTAL_REORGS" BIGINT PATH 'system_metrics/total_reorgs'
  ,"TOTAL_REORG_TIME" BIGINT PATH 'system_metrics/total_reorg_time'
  ,"TOTAL_REORG_PROC_TIME" BIGINT PATH 'system_metrics/total_reorg_proc_time'
  ,"FAILED_SQL_STMTS" BIGINT PATH 'system_metrics/failed_sql_stmts'
  ,"FILES_CLOSED" BIGINT PATH 'system_metrics/files_closed'
  ,"LOCK_ESCALS" BIGINT PATH 'system_metrics/lock_escals'
  ,"LOCK_ESCALS_GLOBAL" BIGINT PATH 'system_metrics/lock_escals_global'
  ,"LOCK_ESCALS_LOCKLIST" BIGINT PATH 'system_metrics/lock_escals_locklist'
  ,"LOCK_ESCALS_MAXLOCKS" BIGINT PATH 'system_metrics/lock_escals_maxlocks'
  ,"LOCK_LIST_IN_USE" BIGINT PATH 'system_metrics/lock_list_in_use'
  ,"LOCK_TIMEOUTS" BIGINT PATH 'system_metrics/lock_timeouts'
  ,"LOCK_WAITS" BIGINT PATH 'system_metrics/lock_waits'
  ,"LOCK_WAITS_GLOBAL" BIGINT PATH 'system_metrics/lock_waits_global'
  ,"LOCK_WAIT_TIME" BIGINT PATH 'system_metrics/lock_wait_time'
  ,"LOCK_WAIT_TIME_GLOBAL" BIGINT PATH 'system_metrics/lock_wait_time_global'
  ,"CF_WAITS" BIGINT PATH 'system_metrics/cf_waits'
  ,"CF_WAIT_TIME" BIGINT PATH 'system_metrics/cf_wait_time'
) AS DETM
WITH NO ROW MOVEMENT;
```

The interfaces in Table 10.28 report the activity metrics.

Table 10.28: Interfaces that report activity metrics
Interfaces
MON_GET_ACTIVITY
MON_GET_ACTIVITY_DETAILS
MON_GET_PKG_CACHE_STMT
MON_GET_PKG_CACHE_STMT_DETAILS
EVMON_FORMAT_UE_TO_XML
MON_FORMAT_XML_METRICS_BY_ROW
Activity event monitor
Package cache event monitor

Table 10.29 lists the interfaces that report the object metrics.

Table 10.29: Interfaces that report object metrics
Interfaces (table functions)
MON_GET_DATABASE
MON_GET_DATABASE_DETAILS
MON_GET_BUFFERPOOL
MON_GET_TABLESPACE
MON_GET_TABLE
MON_GET_TABLE_USAGE_LIST
MON_GET_TABLE_INFO

And they report the ratio metrics in Table 10.30.

Table 10.30: Interfaces that report ratio metrics
Interfaces (views)
MON_BP_UTILIZATION
MON_TBSP_UTILIZATION
MON_WORKLOAD_SUMMARY
MON_SERVICE_SUBCLASS_SUMMARY
MON_CONNECTION_SUMMARY
MON_DB_SUMMARY

HADR Monitoring

Tables 10.31 and 10.32 show the new monitor elements for HADR processing.

Table 10.31: Elements for HADR

Element	Description
STANDBY_SPOOL_PERCENT	Percentage of log spool space used
HADR_FLAGS	Subset of fields on the operational wellness of HADR
HEARTBEAT_MISSED	How many heartbeat checks did not occur
HEARTBEAT_EXPECTED	How many heartbeat checks should have occurred
STANDBY_ERROR_TIME	Last time the standby reported an error

Table 10.32: Interfaces that report HADR metrics

Interfaces (table function)
MON_GET_HADR

Sort Monitoring

The new monitor elements in Table 10.33 are for sort processing.

Table 10.33: Sort elements

Element
ACTIVE_COL_VECTOR_CONSUMERS_TOP
ACTIVE_COL_VECTOR_CONSUMERS
ACTIVE_HASH_GRPBYS_TOP
ACTIVE_HASH_JOINS_TOP
ACTIVE_HASH_FUNCS_TOP
ACTIVE_PEAS
ACTIVE_PEAS_TOP
ACTIVE_PEDS
ACTIVE_PEDS_TOP
ACTIVE_SORT_CONSUMERS
ACTIVE_SORT_CONSUMERS_TOP
ACTIVE_SORTS_TOP
POST_THRESHOLD_COL_VECTOR_CONSUMERS
SORT_CONSUMER_SHRHEAP_TOP
SORT_CONSUMER_HEAP_TOP
TOTAL_COL_VECTOR_CONSUMERS

Backup and Index Creation Monitoring

Table 10.34 lists the new monitor elements for backup and index creation processing. These elements are reported in the system dimension for backup and in the system and activity dimension for index creation.

Table 10.34: Backup and index creation elements

Element	Description
TOTAL_BACKUP_TIME	Total elapse time running online backups
TOTAL_BACKUP_PROC_TIME	Total amount of nonwait time performing online backup
TOTAL_BACKUPS	Number of online backups completed
TOTAL_INDEX_BUILD_TIME	Total elapse time building indexes due to creation, rebuild, or re-creation.
TOTAL_INDEX_BUILD_PROC_TIME	Total nonwait time building indexes due to creation, rebuild, or re-creation.
TOTAL_INDEXES_BUILT	Number of indexes built

Connectivity and Networking

This section looks closely at db2dsdriver.cfg, the different ways to manage remote communications, and the specific changes introduced in DB2 10.5. For details pertaining to DB2 10, review Chapter 9, "Connectivity and Networking."

Planning Communications

Before you set up communications, take some time to plan. A good way to plan is to ask the right questions.

- Is HA a requirement?
- Which server HA solution is being implemented?
- Which client HA solution is being implemented?
- What are the client operating systems involved?
- Will Perl or UNIX scripts be used from the client?
- Is server access restricted?
- How many concurrent users?

When you set up remote communications, specific information such as the server name and port numbers are required. The particular requirements and options will depend on the platforms involved. Before you begin, it is important for you to know the limitations and behavior of the communications. You can see the server- and client-level communication features in Table 10.35.

Table 10.35: Communication features		
Features	**Server Level**	**Client Level**
Transaction and connection load balancing	10.5 or higher	9.7 FP1 or higher
Automatic client reroute (ACR)	10.5 or higher	9.5 FP4 or higher
Client affinity	10.5 of higher	9.7 PF1 or higher

With this release, IBM has made several significant improvements. In many cases, to use these improvements, you will need to upgrade to DB2 10.5. As a general practice, it is a good idea to keep server software levels higher or equal to the client driver levels being used, even though IBM provides some downward compatibilities.

Configuring Communications

DB2 environments are multitiered and include one or more servers as well as one or more clients. DB2 supports several types of listeners. Two of the most commonly used are IPC and TCP/IP. IPC is a local-based listener only and is invoked when connecting to a DB2 database without specifying a user (`db2 connect to sample` from the UNIX command line or Windows command prompt). Programs running on the database server will connect using this listener by default. TCP/IP is used for remote communications and is invoked when specifying a user (`db2 connect to sample user db2inst1`).

Setting Up Communications

Five client server packages are available to deploy. Each package provides a different level of support, as Table 10.36 shows.

Table 10.36: Communication features		
Package	**Support**	**Modules**
JDBC and SQLJ	Java applications only	db2jcc.jar or db2jcc4.jar and sqlj.jar
ODBC and CLI	ODBC or CLI	db2java.zip
ODBC, CLI, .NET, OLE, PHP, Ruby, JDBC, SQLJ	Data Server Driver Package	db2jcc.jar or db2jcc4.jar and sqlj.jar, db2java.zip
DB2CI	Data Server Client Package	Full client
DB2 CLPPlus	Data Server Driver Package	
CLP plus basic client	Runtime client plus CLPPlus from the Data Server Driver Package	
Database administration plus programming API	Data Server Client Package	Full client

z/OS Client

To set up z/OS as the client and UNIX/LUW as the server, use the Distributed Data Facility (DDF) as follows for communication with a UNIX/LUW server (see Table 10.37).

Table 10.37: z/OS DDF

Table Name	Purpose
SYSIBM.IPNAMES	Identifies the IP address; usually a DNS alias entry is used, not a specific IP
SYSIBM.LOCATIONS	Identifies the UNIX databases to connect with; port, instance, and database name are specified
SYSIBM.USERNAMES	Connects z/OS RACF accounts to AIX/UNIX accounts when connecting to a UNIX LUW database

DB2 10.5 contains several enhancements around z/OS communications, including CLI improvements for z/OS stored procedures for array support and implicit commit. You can set fet_buf_siz when calling a z/OS stored procedure for the return of the entire result set. For a complete list of changes, consult the IBM Knowledge Center.

UNIX Client

To set up communications between two UNIX platforms, you can use either CLI or the Universal JDBC interface (JCC). CLI (db2java.zip) uses catalog entries to set up navigation information and db2cli.ini to set up [Common] and database-specific global settings.

JCC (db2jcc.jar or db2jcc4.jar) communications can use db2dsdriver.cfg to provide required communication properties. You can set up JCC communications to run in both Mode-2 and Mode-4 methods. Mode-2 uses CLI catalog information for navigation, which includes alternate server information in a HADR configuration. Mode-4 requires alternate server information to be provided as an extension to the driver. It is possible to use db2dsdriver.cfg to set up behavior and navigation information for Mode-4 communications.

It is easy to see which JCC method is used by looking at the URL:

```
Mode-2  jdbc:db2:<dbname>
Mode-4  jdbc:db2://<server>:<port>/<dbname>
```

The CLI method and the Mode-2 method have the same URL format, so to determine which one is used, you look at the source. For CLI, you must install the DB2 full client software and add the catalog information. The source file used is db2java.zip. For JCC, you need to place only the Java drivers on the client server.

With DB2 10.5, IBM enhanced db2dsdriver.cfg to include settings that in past releases were in db2cli.ini. IBM introduced DB2 registry entry DB2DSDRIVER_CFG_PATH, which allows you to specify multiple paths and a customer-specific file name.

If you want to use this method, IBM provides a sample file in the DB2 installation path/cfg. For example, on UNIX this would be /opt/IBM/db2/V10.5/cfg.

You can use the db2cli program to test the connection. To see examples and details around the use of db2dsdriver.cfg, see "Client/Server Communications" in Appendix A. Let us now look at two scenarios for setting up communications.

In the first example, the server is UNIX DB2/LUW 10.5 running HADR, and you must provide access to this server from z/OS. Current z/OS software supports dynamic changes to DDF. In earlier releases, DDF had to be cycled to pick up changes except for new entries (insert).

For HADR to work properly, automatic client reroute (ACR) must be working. Otherwise, when you execute the database takeover command, new remote client connections will fail as long as the cluster is running on the standby and the primary is down. If you are using db2dsdriver.cfg, you can run enableAlternateServerListFirstConnect to enable failover on the first connection.

Before FP4, the location of db2dsdriver.cfg was as follows:

- acrRetryInterval
- alternateserverlist
- enableAcr
- enableAlternateGroupSeamlessACR
- enableAlternateServerListFirstConnect
- enableSeamlessAcr
- maxAcrRetries

z/OS clients using DDF do not support ACR. If you are running WebSphere on z/OS or on z/Linux and using direct TCP/IP communications, you can set up a z client to use ACR.

In the second example, the server is UNIX DB2/LUW 9.7 running HADR, and you must provide access to this server from Windows 7. By installing the DB2 full client, you can set up CLI communications. If only TCP/IP support is required, you can copy the JCC driver files to the Windows server and source them in the environment for that Windows user.

So what level of DB2 client software do you install? If you install 10.5, you will not have to upgrade it any time soon. However, it is not a good idea to run client software at a higher level than the server software.

If the client/server was already used for DB2 communications and has JCC client 9.1 installed, you can use it. Remember that HADR server configurations provide little benefits unless ACR is working. To obtain ACR functionality for JCC Mode-4 connections, your client code must be 9.5 FP4 or higher. So you cannot use version 9.1 unless you choose CLI, and that requires a full client install on the Windows 7 server.

You decide to install the DB2 full client at 9.7 on the Windows 7 server, which is a good choice. You set up the CLI communications, but your testing fails. You are receiving 30081N error messages. You checked the setup several times and all looks good. You tested the same setup from a UNIX client and it worked. Why is it failing from Windows 7? The reason it fails is that Windows 7 requires the server name to be fully qualified. Short names no longer work (unless you set up the entry in the hosts file; DNS will not work unless the name is fully qualified). You changed the CLI setting and everything works.

High Availability

This section covers the changes introduced in DB2 10.5 regarding HA and any behavioral differences from 10.1. For details about how to set up or configure a HA solution, see Chapter 7, "High Availability."

HADR

Starting in DB2 10.1, you can set up to three standby databases in a single cluster: one principal standby and up to two auxiliary standby databases. Database parameter hadr_target_list contains the list of standby databases. If you set up only one standby, you do not need to set this parameter. Starting with DB2 10.5, you must set this parameter in all configurations:

```
HADR database role                                         = STANDARD
HADR local host name                    (HADR_LOCAL_HOST) =
HADR local service name                  (HADR_LOCAL_SVC) =
HADR remote host name                  (HADR_REMOTE_HOST) =
HADR remote service name                (HADR_REMOTE_SVC) =
HADR instance name of remote server    (HADR_REMOTE_INST) =
HADR timeout value                         (HADR_TIMEOUT) = 120
HADR target list                       (HADR_TARGET_LIST) =
HADR log write synchronization mode       (HADR_SYNCMODE) = NEARSYNC
HADR spool log data limit (4KB)        (HADR_SPOOL_LIMIT) = AUTOMATIC(0)
HADR log replay delay (seconds)       (HADR_REPLAY_DELAY) = 0
HADR peer window duration (seconds)    (HADR_PEER_WINDOW) = 0
```

Only the principal standby supports all replication modes. HADR supports SYNC, NEARASYNC, ASYNC, and SUPERASYNC modes. Auxiliary standby databases run only in SUPERASYNC mode. DB2/TSA only applies between the *primary* HADR database and its principal standby.

For pureScale clusters, you can set up only the principal standby, and it can run only in Async or SuperAsync mode. The primary cluster and principal standby cluster must have the same logical configuration. Thus, the number of members defined to the primary cluster and principal cluster must match.

Table 10.38 lists the various HADR features and the synchronization modes that they support.

Table 10.38: HADR feature compatibility matrix

Feature	DB2 Version	Support	Synchronization Mode
HADR on pureScale	DB2 9.8	No	Not applicable
HADR on pureScale	DB2 10.1	No	Not applicable
HADR on pureScale	DB2 10.5	Yes	ASYNC, SUPERASYNC
HADR read on standby	DB2 9.7	Yes	SYNC, NEARSYNC, ASYNC, SUPERASYNC
HADR multiple standbys	DB2 10.1	Yes	Principal standby—all auxiliary standby—SUPERASYNC only
HADR multiple standbys on pureScale	DB2 10.5	No	Can define only primary database and principal database

The "Oops" Recovery Factor

Have you ever changed or deleted rows of data by mistake? Using an auxiliary standby in SUPERASYNC mode, you can set up a database where you can recover data that was modified or deleted inadvertently.

Assume you want to set up an eight-hour *oops* recovery window. If identified within the eight-hour time frame, you can recover the deleted rows or set modified rows back to their original state. To set the minimum commit window between the primary database and the auxiliary database, use the parameter hadr_replay_delay. The maximum value for this parameter is more than 24,855 days (2,147,483,647 seconds). (Contrast this maximum value with the number of days you work in a 30-year career, which is 7,575 days.)

By setting hadr_replay_delay to 28800, committed transactions executed on the primary database are not applied to this auxiliary database until 28,800 seconds have passed. This assumes that the primary server and auxiliary server have the same operating system timestamp.

Chapter Summary

The objective of this chapter was to familiarize you with

- Significant changes introduced in DB2 10.5 Cancun up to the latest release
- Shadow tables
- BLU Acceleration and the technology involved
- Technology around in memory
- DB2 JSON
- Installation steps that any deployment type or size can use
- Random key indexes
- Extended row size
- A security design model using groups, roles, and application IDs
- New DB2 software packaging
- New utilities specific to the new features introduced in DB2 10.5 and any changes to existing utilities
- DB2 autonomics
- DB2 WLM
- The DB2 registry and operating system environment variables and ways to set them up on the server
- The DB2 instance and database configuration parameter update commands
- The DB2 autonomic computing features and associated application or business benefits
- IBM Data Studio features and Query Tuner Workflow Assistant examples
- The job and job chain schedules that use IBM Data Studio web console

On completion of this chapter, you will be equipped with sufficient knowledge to answer any certification exam question specific to DB2 10.5 Cancun. It is also highly recommended that you complete the sample questions at the end of the chapter.

Practice Questions

Question 1

Which command when executed configures future databases for column-organized tables?

- ❍ A. db2 "update db cfg for sample using DB2_COLUMN_ORGANIZED enable"
- ❍ B. db2set DB2_WORKLOAD=BLU
- ❍ C. db2 "update dbm cfg using DFT_ORGANIZATION=COLUMN"
- ❍ D. None of the above
- ❍ E. All of the above

Question 2

Which SQL Warehousing Tool (SQW) feature provides the best performance and storage efficiency through the elimination of indexes, aggregates, and tuning?

- ❍ A. pureQuery
- ❍ B. Statement pooling
- ❍ C. SQW Acceleration
- ❍ D. BLU Acceleration
- ❍ E. All of the above

Question 3

Which command when executed activates EHL for a table or partition?

- ❍ A. db2 "update db cfg for <DBNAME> using OPT_DIRECT_WRKLD on"
- ❍ B. db2set OPT_DIRECT_WRKLD=ON
- ❍ C. db2 "alter table <TABLENAME> ALLOW EHL YES"
- ❍ D. db2 "update db cfg for <DBNAME> using OPT_DIRECT_WRKLD enable"
- ❍ E. None of the above

Question 4

For a column-organized workload, what is the best method of setting SORTHEAP and SHEAPTHRES_SHR to the optimal size?

❍ A. Run the AUTOCONFIGURE command with DBM+DB UPDATE.
❍ B. Capture the SQL in a workload file and use the Optim Query Analyzer to determine the proper size.
❍ C. Set both to AUTOMATIC and allow DB2 to adjust as required.
❍ D. Set the registry parameter DB2_WORKLOAD=ANALYTICS.
❍ E. All of the above

Question 5

While you were copying data from a non-Unicode database to a Unicode database, many errors occurred, indicating a truncation error across many tables. Which option best addresses this issue?

❍ A. Alter all target table columns that are character and increase the field size by LENGTH(SOURCE_COLUMN)/2.
❍ B. Set the global session parameter NLS_STRING_UNITS for LOAD or IMPORT.
❍ C. Change the EXPORT command and add the following options: IGNORELENGTH, CHARTOBYTE.
❍ D. Change the EXPORT command by added the code-page value of the target database.
❍ E. Do not worry about it; the truncation error is just a warning.
❍ F. Set the database parameter STRING_UNITS on the target database.
❍ G. Alter all target tables and add octets to each character column.
❍ H. All of the above
❍ I. B, F, and G are all valid options.
❍ J. None of the above

Question 6

A large batch processing requirement runs on a dynamic schedule. When it runs, it significantly affects online applications in the production pureScale cluster. Management is looking for answers.

You know it is related to CF traffic because when the batch jobs are updating, the impact occurs when millions of rows and the online applications are accessing the same tables. Assume for this problem the following details:

- CF performance is wonderful.
- All workloads float across the members of the cluster equally.
- Online applications read and write to the same tables accessed by batch.
- There are no capacity or locking issues of any kind.

Which option gives you the best chance of resolving this issue so that the batch work completes on schedule but without affecting online workloads?

❍ A. Set up WLM classes to set higher priority levels for online workloads, including CPU and I/O. This way, online workloads will move ahead of batch.

❍ B. Identify the key tables, and partition them across the members of the cluster. Create two database aliases, one BATCHDB and the other ONLINEDB, pointing to the same database. Create member sets, one for BATCH(0,2) and the other for ONLINE(1,3), using the database aliases. Change the batch URL connection string to use BATCHDB and online URLs to use ONLINEDB. Activate EHL to reduce CF registration for batch workloads.

❍ C. Set up the db2dsdriver.cfg file to restrict the batch to only Member 0 with failover to Member 2. Continue to allow online workloads to float.

❍ D. All of the above

❍ E. None of the above

Question 7

What is the value of DFT_DEGREE when DB2_WORKLOAD=ANALYTICS is set?

❍ A. -1

❍ B. Equal to Number of Cores – 1

❍ C. 1

❍ D. ON

❍ E. ANY

Question 8

What is the default database page size when DB2_WORKLOAD is set to ANALYTICS?

- ❍ A. 4
- ❍ B. 8
- ❍ C. 16
- ❍ D. 32

Question 9

What is the value of DFT_PREFETCH_SZ when DB2_WORKLOAD=ANALYTICS is set?

- ❍ A. 16
- ❍ B. 4
- ❍ C. -1
- ❍ D. 32
- ❍ E. 64
- ❍ F. (Extent Size * 2)
- ❍ G. AUTOMATIC
- ❍ H. None of the above

Question 10

Can you create a column-organized table in a database by using DFT_TABLE_ORG=ROW?

- ❍ A. Yes
- ❍ B. No
- ❍ C. Maybe

Question 11

Automatic Storage Management (ASM) is required for all columnar tables. Thus, without any changes or settings, do disk space reclaims and reorganizations occur automatically for all column-organized tables?

- ❍ A. Yes
- ❍ B. No

Question 12

If DB2_WORKLOAD is not set, what parameter must you set before a query can access a column-organized table?

- ❍ A. DFT_TABLE_ORG
- ❍ B. DB2_WORKLOAD
- ❍ C. SORTHEAP
- ❍ D. INTRA_PARALLEL
- ❍ E. None of the above

Question 13

What is the manual process for reclaiming extents in a column-organized table?

- ❍ A. Run ALTER TABLE <TABNAME> RECLAIM EXTENT YES.
- ❍ B. There is no manual process.
- ❍ C. Run REORG TABLE <TABLE NAME> RECLAIM EXTENTS.
- ❍ D. Run the MOVE_TABLE command.

Question 14

What other parameters besides DB2_WORKLOAD must you set to create column-organized tables in pureScale?

- ❍ A. SORTHEAP
- ❍ B. UTIL_HEAP_SZ
- ❍ C. DB2_PS_COLUMN_ENABLE
- ❍ D. SYSPROC.WLM_CREATE_MEMBER_SUBSET('COLUMN_SUBSET','(0,2,4,6)')
- ❍ E. None of the above
- ❍ F. All of the above

Question 15

When using the Optim Query Workload Tuner, what is the best way to retrieve SQL from a running database so you can analyze it?

- ❍ A. Ask the developers—they have a log file for sure.
- ❍ B. Have the developers use JPA and set showSQL.
- ❍ C. Use the db2pd command.
- ❍ D. Execute the MON_GET_SQL command.
- ❍ E. Use Explain tables.
- ❍ F. Use the activity event monitors.
- ❍ G. All of the above

Question 16

Which command sets up WLM for column-organized tables?

- ❍ A. UPDATE DBM CFG USING WORKLOAD_MANAGER enable
- ❍ B. db2set DB2_WLM_DISP=YES
- ❍ C. UPDATE DB CFG FOR <DBNAME> WLM_DISPATCHER YES IMMEDIATE
- ❍ D. AUTOCONFIGURE DB <DBNAME> WLM_DISPATCHER
- ❍ E. db2set DB2_WORKLOAD=ANALYTICS

Question 17

What is the default timeron setting for identifying shadow table workloads?

- ❍ A. 20000
- ❍ B. 300000
- ❍ C. It is set dynamically and changes.
- ❍ D. 1000000
- ❍ E. 150000
- ❍ F. None of the above

Question 18

What are the default work action classes that manage column-organized workloads?

- ❍ A. SYSCOLUMNQUERIES and SYSDEFAULTCOLUMNSUBCLASS
- ❍ B. There are none—you have to create them manually.
- ❍ C. SYSMANAGEDQUERIES and USERDEFAULTMANAGEDSUBCLASS
- ❍ D. The action set is enabled by default; the SYSMANAGEDQUERIES work class will run in the SYSDEFAULTMANAGEDSUBCLASS service subclass.
- ❍ E. None of the above

Question 19

What is the name of the first phase of a load operation against a column-organized table?

- ❍ A. SHOWOUT
- ❍ B. FIGUREOUT
- ❍ C. DICTIONARY_REFRESH
- ❍ D. ANALYZE
- ❍ E. INITIALIZE

Question 20

What does SIMD mean?

- ❍ A. Shared Internal Memory Degree; it is the current level of hypermemory virtual paging space being shared.
- ❍ B. Single Instruction, Multiple-Data
- ❍ C. Shared Into Memory Data
- ❍ D. Shared Initial Memory Definition

Question 21

What object can reference a column-organized table?

- ❍ A. Constraint
- ❍ B. User-defined index
- ❍ C. Trigger
- ❍ D. Nickname
- ❍ E. View

Question 22

Which workload characteristic is not good for shadow table deployments?

- ❍ A. Integrated workloads
- ❍ B. Average IUD loads
- ❍ C. Near real-time
- ❍ D. Okay with MQT restrictions
- ❍ E. Zero latency
- ❍ F. None of the above

Question 23

Which transaction will not parallelize when executed against a column-organized table?

- ❍ A. Create primary key constraint on an empty table
- ❍ B. RUNSTATS
- ❍ C. Load
- ❍ D. DML

Question 24

Column-organized tables are supported in what types of databases?

- ❍ A. DPF
- ❍ B. Unicode
- ❍ C. pureScale
- ❍ D. ESE 10.1 or higher

Question 25

Which compression type will ensure NULL and that zero-length data in VARCHAR columns will not be placed on disk?

- ❍ A. Deep
- ❍ B. Action
- ❍ C. Row
- ❍ D. Adaptive
- ❍ E. Value
- ❍ F. Column
- ❍ G. Backup

Question 26

Which type of data is not compressed in Cancun?

- ❍ A. Temp
- ❍ B. Global temp
- ❍ C. Data
- ❍ D. Index
- ❍ E. Sort
- ❍ F. Result set
- ❍ G. Row
- ❍ H. Column
- ❍ I. Foreign or primary keys

Question 27

A DB2 9.7 database is about to be upgraded to 10.5. Which statement is true about the resulting database?

❍ A. All indexes are converted to Index Manager 3 format.
❍ B. DMS table spaces will be converted to SMS with automatic storage.
❍ C. It is not possible to upgrade from 9.7 to 10.5.
❍ D. Compressed tables will be set to adaptive compression.
❍ E. The 10.5 database will be 50 percent the size of the 9.7 database.
❍ F. All compressed tables will have classic row compression enabled. New or updated rows will have adaptive compression applied.

Question 28

Which statement is true regarding index compression?

❍ A. To enable an index for adaptive compression, you must alter the index and reorganize the table.
❍ B. The default for all new indexes is COMPRESS NO.
❍ C. All indexes are set to COMPRESS ADAPTIVE YES.
❍ D. The default is COMPRESS YES. To obtain ADAPTIVE YES compression, you must manually create or alter the index.
❍ E. The index by default will match the table compression setting.
❍ F. Only one index can be set to COMPRESS YES per table.

Question 29

Which statement is false regarding NOT ENFORCED unique constraints?

❍ A. An update or insert that violates the unique constraint will result in an error.
❍ B. Disk storage requirements for NOT ENFORCED unique constraints are the same as for a unique index.
❍ C. Nonenforced unique constraints enforce uniqueness for primary keys only.
❍ D. All of the above
❍ E. None of the above

Question 30

Which clause of CREATE UNIQUE INDEX will allow NULL keys when enforcing uniqueness of table data?

- ❍ A. SKIP NULL KEYS
- ❍ B. IGNORE NULL KEYS
- ❍ C. OMIT NULL KEYS
- ❍ D. EXCLUDE NULL KEYS
- ❍ E. None of the above

Question 31

Which database option is not required for shadow tables to be created?

- ❍ A. Circular logging
- ❍ B. SYSTOOL objects
- ❍ C. Organize by row
- ❍ D. DB2_EXTENDED_OPTIMIZATION
- ❍ E. Connect stored procedure
- ❍ F. CDC subscription mirroring
- ❍ G. ASM

Question 32

Tables can be converted from row to column organization by using db2convert. Identify the characteristics that will not stop conversion.

- ❍ A. Trigger
- ❍ B. Foreign key
- ❍ C. MQT
- ❍ D. XML
- ❍ E. LOB
- ❍ F. Table space is not ASM

Question 33

Which backup operation is not supported in pureScale?

- ❍ A. Incremental
- ❍ B. Delta
- ❍ C. Merge
- ❍ D. Table space transport
- ❍ E. Online

Question 34

Which actions require a pureScale cluster cycle?

- ❍ A. Fix pack upgrade
- ❍ B. Registry parameter changes
- ❍ C. DBM parameter changes
- ❍ D. Database parameter changes
- ❍ E. Version or release upgrade of DB2 software
- ❍ F. Operating system changes
- ❍ G. Drop member
- ❍ H. Add member
- ❍ I. G and E
- ❍ J. B, H, G
- ❍ K. All of the above

Question 35

Which monitoring function will indicate when SQL statements are accessing a specific column-organized table?

- ❍ A. MON_GET_TABLE()
- ❍ B. MON_COL_USAGE()
- ❍ C. MON_GET_UOW()
- ❍ D. MON_GET_TABLE_USAGE_LIST()
- ❍ E. None of the above

Question 36

Starting with DB2 10.5, HADR is supported in pureScale deployments. Which command do you use to failover the cluster to the standby?

- ❍ A. Execute FAILOVER HADR TO STANDBY from any member of the primary cluster.
- ❍ B. Execute TAKEOVER HADR from the primary CF on the standby cluster.
- ❍ C. Execute TAKEOVER HADR BY FORCE from any active member of the standby cluster.
- ❍ D. Just wait; it will eventually do it automatically.

Question 37

Which method can you use to determine the current HADR status?

- ❍ A. MON_GET_HADR()
- ❍ B. SNAP_GET_HADR()
- ❍ C. GET SNAPSHOT FOR DATABASE
- ❍ D. db2top

Question 38

Which HADR modes are not supported in pureScale?

- ❒ A. SYNC
- ❒ B. NEARSYNC
- ❒ C. ASYNC
- ❒ D. NEARASYNC
- ❒ E. SUPERASYNC
- ❒ F. SUPERSYNC

Answers

Question 1

The correct answer is **D**. Setting the DB2 registry parameter `DB2_WORKLOAD to ANALYTICS` causes the other database manager and database changes to be made.

Question 2

The correct answer is **D**. BLU Acceleration is one of the key features of DB2 10.5 and a game changer in the field of decision support systems or analytical queries.

Question 3

The correct answer is **A**. You activate EHL by setting the database configuration parameter `OPT_DIRECT_WRKLD to ON`. The parameter is dynamic.

Question 4

The correct answer is **D**. `DB2_WORKLOAD=ANALYTICS` will size database parameters `SORTHEAP` and `SHEAPTHRESH_SHR` appropriately for columnar-based workloads. These two parameters are not automatic, so adjustments may be necessary as server sizes or workloads change.

Question 5

The correct answer is **I**. Given the specific example, you can use any of the three options to resolve the issue.

Question 6

The correct answer is **C**. While B might work and might even reduce CF overhead more than any other options, restricting all of batch to run on one member is easy and quick and will probably provide the relief necessary. Sometimes the simple and easiest solutions offer the best results.

Question 7

The correct answer is **E**. BLU has never seen a core it did not like.

Question 8

The correct answer is **D**. When you set the DB2 registry variable DB2_WORKLOAD to ANALYTICS, DB2 creates a database with 32K page size. The default parameter settings for any columnar database are as below:

DFT_EXTENT_SZ	4
DFT_TABLE_ORG	COLUMN
Database page size	32K
DFT_DEGREE	ANY

Question 9

The correct answer is **G**. But the answer has nothing to do with DB2_WORKLOAD because the default is AUTOMATIC for all new databases.

Question 10

The correct answer is **A**. It is possible to have both row- and column-organized tables in the same database.

Question 11

The correct answer is **B**. DB2_WORKLOAD=ANALYTICS creates a default space reclaim policy and sets AUTO_REORG=ON. Both of these are required for empty extents to automatically be returned to the table space for column tables.

Question 12

The correct answer is **D**.

Question 13

The correct answer is **C**. While extent reclaims are performed automatically with the proper settings, it is possible to perform the work by running the REORG TABLE command.

Question 14

The correct answer is **E**. Column-organized tables are not yet supported in pureScale.

Question 15

The correct answer is **F**. Snapshot and activity monitors can produce source data for the Query Workload Tuner.

Question 16

The correct answer is **E**. DB2_WORKLOAD does a lot to set up column processing.

Question 17

The correct answer is **E**. The threshold is set to 150000.

Question 18

The correct answer is **D**. With DB2_WORKLOAD=ANALYTICS set, new databases will have the WLM setting defined and activated to manage columnar workloads.

Question 19

The correct answer is **D**. It is the only phase difference between row and column loads.

Question 20

The correct answer is **B**. It is the vector processing of data.

Question 21

The correct answer is **D**.

Question 22

The correct answer is **E**. Some latency is required to replicate the columnar MQT table. Latency will vary, but some latency is required.

Question 23

The correct answer is **A**. The table is empty.

Question 24

The correct answer is **B**. Unicode is required along with 10.5 AESE and ASM.

Question 25

The correct answer is **E**.

Question 26

The correct answer is **F**. The result set data returned is not compressed.

Question 27

The correct answer is **F**.

Question 28

The correct answer is **E**.

Question 29

The correct answer is **D**. The Query Optimizer will consider a `NOT ENFORCED` unique constraint when determining the optimal plan.

Question 30

The correct answer is **D**.

Question 31

The correct answer is **A**. Archive logging is required.

Question 32

The correct answer is **B**. Secondary indexes are dropped and not defined on a column table. If a trigger is defined, drop it, and then the table can be converted.

Question 33

The correct answer is **D**. Table space transport is not yet supported in pureScale.

Question 34

The correct answer is **I**. With each release, IBM moves pureScale closer to never being down. Dropping a member as well as DB2 version or release upgrades requires a full pureScale cycle.

Question 35

The correct answer is **D**.

Question 36

The correct answer is **C**.

Question 37

The correct answer is **A**.

Question 38

The correct answers are **A**, **B**, **D**, and **F**. Only `ASYNC` and `SUPERASYNC` are supported.

CHAPTER 11

DB2 10.1/10.5 Question Bank

The DB2 10.1/10.5 Question Bank allows you to focus on specific examination areas and build confidence through practice. It contains 94 questions and answers covering areas including server management, physical design, business rules implementation, monitoring DB2 activity, utilities, high availability, security, connectivity and networking, and DB2 10.5 BLU.

Practice Questions

Question 1

Which tool is *not* part of the InfoSphere Optim portfolio?

- ❍ A. Optim Performance Manager (OPM) Extended Insight
- ❍ B. Optim Query Workload Tuner
- ❍ C. Optim pureQuery for LUW
- ❍ D. Control Center

Question 2

Which two of the following are valid DB2 profile registry variable categories?

- ❒ A. DB2 database level
- ❒ B. DB2 node level
- ❒ C. DB2 global level
- ❒ D. DB2 partition group level
- ❒ E. DB2 storage group level

Question 3

Which of the following is *not* a valid DB2 directory?

- ❍ A. System database directory
- ❍ B. Node directory
- ❍ C. Instance database directory
- ❍ D. DCS directory

Question 4

Which of the following is a preferred way of installing DB2 on multiple UNIX systems?

- ❍ A. Graphical-based DB2 setup wizard
- ❍ B. Text-based interactive installation using the db2_install script
- ❍ C. Silent installation using a DB2 response file
- ❍ D. Installation using DB2 payload files

Question 5

Which of the following is *not* part of the DB2 cluster services component?

- ❍ A. IBM Reliable Services Clustering Technology (RSCT)
- ❍ B. Tivoli System Automation for Multiplatform (TSAMP)
- ❍ C. IBM General Parallel File System (GPFS)
- ❍ D. Remote Direct Memory Access (RDMA)

Question 6

Which of the following is *not* a correct DB2 upgrade path?

- ❍ A. DB2 9.5 to DB2 9.7
- ❍ B. DB2 9.5 to DB2 10.5
- ❍ C. DB2 9.7 to DB2 10.5
- ❍ D. DB2 9.7 to DB2 10.1

Question 7

Which command displays immediate change behavior for the DB2 registry variable DB2_INDEX_PCTFREE_DEFAULT?

- ❍ A. db2set DB2_INDEX_PCTFREE_DEFAULT
- ❍ B. db2set -info DB2_INDEX_PCTFREE_DEFAULT
- ❍ C. db2set -all DB2_INDEX_PCTFREE_DEFAULT
- ❍ D. db2set -display DB2_INDEX_PCTFREE_DEFAULT

Question 8

Which command sets the automatic instance restart every time the server is restarted?

- ❍ A. db2set DB2AUTOSTART=ON
- ❍ B. UPDATE DBM CFG USING START_STOP_TIME 60
- ❍ C. db2iauto –on <InstanceName>
- ❍ D. UPDATE DBM CFG USING AUTORESTART ON

Question 9

Which object assigns a UNIQUE value across the tables in a database?

- ❍ A. Use the GENERATED BY DEFAULT AS IDENTITY clause in a table.
- ❍ B. Create a sequence by using the CREATE SEQUENCE command.
- ❍ C. Create a UNIQUE index by using the CREATE UNIQUE INDEX command.
- ❍ D. Create a trigger by using the CREATE TRIGGER command.

Question 10

How many cluster indexes can you define on a table?

❍ A. 1
❍ B. 2
❍ C. 3
❍ D. 4

Question 11

Which command deletes all the records from table T1 without logging the information in the transaction log?

❍ A. DELETE FROM t1
❍ B. ALTER TABLE t1 ACTIVATE NOT LOGGED INITIALLY WITH EMPTY TABLE
❍ C. ALTER TABLE t1 DO NOT LOG; DELETE FROM t1
❍ D. DROP TABLE t1; CREATE TABLE t1

Question 12

Which command transfers the ownership of table T1 from COLIN to SIMON?

❍ A. GRANT OWNERSHIP OF TABLE t1 TO simon
❍ B. TRANSFER OWERSHIP OF TABLE t1 TO USER simon PRESERVE PRIVILEGES
❍ C. TRANSFER OWERSHIP OF TABLE t1 FROM USER colin TO simon PRESERVE PRIVILEGES
❍ D. GRANT CONTROL ON TABLE t1 TO simon

Question 13

Which command can you use to drop all table objects within the schema STAGING?

❍ A. DROP SCHEMA staging RESTRICT
❍ B. db2move –sn staging EXPORT; DROP SCHEMA staging
❍ C. CALL ADMIN_DROP_SCHEMA ('STAGING', NULL, 'ESCHEMA', 'ETABLE')
❍ D. DROP ALL TABLES IN SCHEMA staging

Question 14

Which database-related object can you back up to TSM?

- ❍ A. Transaction logs and database backups
- ❍ B. Transaction logs, database backups, and load copy files
- ❍ C. Transaction logs, database backups, DBM CFG, and load copy files
- ❍ D. Full and differential database backups

Question 15

Which command helps restart the `GENERATED BY DEFAULT AS IDENTITY` column value?

- ❍ A. ALTER TABLE <*schema*>.<*tabname*> ALTER COLUMN <*columnname*> RESTART WITH <*newvalue*>
- ❍ B. NEXTVAL FOR <*schema*>.<*tabname*>
- ❍ C. NEXT VALUE FOR <*newvalue*>
- ❍ D. ALTER TABLE <*schema*>.<*tabname*> ALTER COLUMN <*columnname*> RESET

Question 16

Which user name is a valid user name in DB2?

- ❍ A. Milan
- ❍ B. MILAN
- ❍ C. milanmohan
- ❍ D. milan

Question 17

Which command changes the behavior of LOCKTIMEOUT for a specific session or an application?

- ❍ A. SET CURRENT LOCK TIMEOUT 5
- ❍ B. UPDATE DB CFG USING LOCKTIMEOUT 5
- ❍ C. UPDATE DBM CFG USING LOCKTIMEOUT 5
- ❍ D. SET CURRENT LOCK TIMEOUT NULL

Question 18

What does error SQL0911N with reason code 68 indicate?

- ❍ A. An application transaction is rolled back due to a lock timeout problem.
- ❍ B. An application transaction is rolled back due to a deadlock problem.
- ❍ C. An application transaction is rolled back due to a user interruption.
- ❍ D. An application transaction is rolled back due to a system error.

Question 19

What does error SQL0911N with reason code 2 indicate?

- ❍ A. An application transaction is rolled back due to a lock timeout problem.
- ❍ B. An application transaction is rolled back due to a deadlock problem.
- ❍ C. An application transaction is rolled back due to a user interruption.
- ❍ D. An application transaction is rolled back due to a system error.

Question 20

Which scan uses the currently committed (CUR_COMMIT) semantics?

- ❍ A. Range clustered table (RCT) scan
- ❍ B. System catalog table scan
- ❍ C. Range partitioned table scan
- ❍ D. Scans that enforce referential integrity constraints

Question 21

Which statement about currently committed semantics is false?

- ❍ A. Currently committed semantics need an increased log space.
- ❍ B. Currently committed semantics retrieve log records from the log buffer, if needed.
- ❍ C. Currently committed semantics retrieve log records from archive logs, if necessary.
- ❍ D. Currently committed semantics apply only to read-only workloads.

Question 22

Which command invokes the DB2 replication center?

- ❍ A. db2cc –rc
- ❍ B. db2cc
- ❍ C. db2rc
- ❍ D. db2start -rc

Question 23

Which scalar function can you use to covert a multibyte character to a single-byte character?

- ❍ A. TO_SINGLE_BYTE
- ❍ B. TO_MULTI_BYTE
- ❍ C. CONVERT_TO_SINGLE_BYTE
- ❍ D. INSTRB

Question 24

What is *not* an expanded support for triggers in DB2 10.1?

- ❍ A. Multiple-event triggers
- ❍ B. Use of FOR EACH STATEMENT
- ❍ C. Trigger event predicates identify the triggered events
- ❍ D. Cascade triggers

Question 25

Which DB2 registry variable is necessary to enable online database backups to succeed even if it fails to include all the necessary transaction log files?

- ❍ A. DB2_BCKP_PAGE_VERIFICATION
- ❍ B. DB2_MCR_RECOVERY_PARALLELISM_CAP
- ❍ C. DB2_SAS_SETTINGS
- ❍ D. DB2_BCKP_INCLUDE_LOGS_WARNING

Question 26

Which two steps are necessary to configure the automatic deletion of database backup images?

- ❒ A. Set the DB CFG parameter AUTO_DEL_REC_OBJ to ON.
- ❒ B. Set the DB CFG parameter AUTO_MAINT to ON.
- ❒ C. Set the DB CFG parameter AUTO_DB_BACKUP to ON.
- ❒ D. Set the DB CFG parameter NUM_DB_BACKUPS to the number of backups to retain.
- ❒ E. Set the DB CFG parameter AUTO_DEL_REC_OBJ to OFF.

Question 27

If you execute the following command on database SAMPLE:

```
UPDATE DB CFG USING REC_HIS_RETENTN 0 AUTO_DEL_REC_OBJ OFF
```

What will the recovery history-retention-period configuration behavior be?

- ○ A. No automatic pruning of the history file and no recovery objects are deleted
- ○ B. Retains only the last full database backup history
- ○ C. Keeps the entries for full database backup and table space–level backup
- ○ D. Automatically removes the contents of the history file and drops recovery objects

Question 28

Which statement about binary XML is false?

- ○ A. It provides a faster way to transmit and receive XML data between pureXML Java applications and DB2 10.1.
- ○ B. It refers to the data in Extensible Dynamic Binary XML (XDBX) format.
- ○ C. This format is supported on IBM Data Server Driver for JDBC and SQLJ 4.9 and higher.
- ○ D. It supports only the textual XML data format for transmission; nontextual (binary) data formats result in error.

Question 29

What authority must be required to create a trusted context?

- ❍ A. SYSADM
- ❍ B. SECADM
- ❍ C. SYSMAINT
- ❍ D. SYSCTRL

Question 30

Which of the following is not a supported numeric data type for indexes over XML data?

- ❍ A. DECIMAL
- ❍ B. INTEGER
- ❍ C. DOUBLE
- ❍ D. FLOAT

Question 31

Which two functional XML indexes help improve query performance?

- ❒ A. fn:upper-case
- ❒ B. fn:lower-case
- ❒ C. fn:exists
- ❒ D. fn:non-exists
- ❒ E. fn:ends-with

Question 32

Which DB2 built-in scalar function converts XML data into any form possible for the XSLT processor, HTML, or plain text?

- ❍ A. XSLTRANSFORM
- ❍ B. XMLTEXT
- ❍ C. XMLSERIALIZE
- ❍ D. XMLPARSE

Question 33

Which of the following is a supported column data type for the Ingest utility?

- ❍ A. XML
- ❍ B. CLOB
- ❍ C. DBCLOB
- ❍ D. VARCHAR

Question 34

Which DB2 utility or command supports the Ingest utility?

- ❍ A. Set the utility impact priority by using the SET UTIL_IMPACT_PRIORITY command.
- ❍ B. Set the utility impact limit by using the UTIL_IMPACT_LIM database configuration parameter.
- ❍ C. Display the ingest operation progress by using the LIST UTILITIES SHOW DETAIL command.
- ❍ D. Display the ingest operation information by using the INGEST LIST and INGEST GET STATS commands.

Question 35

What is the prerequisite to load data by using the CURSOR file-type format?

- ❍ A. The cursor should already be declared.
- ❍ B. The cursor should already be opened.
- ❍ C. The cursor should already be declared and opened.
- ❍ D. The cursor should already be declared but closed.

Question 36

Which DB2 Design Advisor command accepts input from the DB2 workload manager and provides recommendation on the parameter settings?

- ❍ A. db2advis –d <*DatabaseName*> -qp
- ❍ B. db2advis –d <*DatabaseName*> -wlm <*Workload or ServiceClass*>
- ❍ C. db2advis –d <*DatabaseName*> -workload <*WorkloadName*>
- ❍ D. db2advis –d <*DatabaseName*> -pkg

Question 37

Which command activates infinite logging?

- ❍ A. UPDATE DB CFG USING LOGSECOND 255
- ❍ B. UPDATE DB CFG USING LOGPRIMARY 9999
- ❍ C. UPDATE DB CFG USING LOGSECOND -1
- ❍ D. UPDATE DB CFG USING LOGPRIMARY -1

Question 38

What is the significance of setting the ALT_DIAGPATH database manager configuration parameter?

- ❍ A. It is a mirror copy of DIAGPATH and can be used if the DIAGPATH is inaccessible.
- ❍ B. This path is used only when the database manager fails to write to the path specified in the DIAGPATH parameter.
- ❍ C. This parameter is redundant and is not necessary to set.
- ❍ D. This parameter redirects core file dumps and FODC data to a different file system.

Question 39

Which command redirects the core file dumps and First Occurrence Data Capture (FODC) data to a different file system than DIAGPATH?

- ❍ A. db2set DB2FODC="DUMPDIR=/coredata/dump FODCPATH=/coredata/fodc"
- ❍ B. db2set DB2_DISABLE_FLUSH_LOG=OFF
- ❍ C. db2set DB2_OPTSTATS_LOG=ON
- ❍ D. db2set DB2_FORCE_APP_ON_MAX_LOG=TRUE

Question 40

Which command configures DB2 for rotating diagnostic and administration notification log files?

- ❍ A. UPDATE DBM CFG USING DIAGSIZE 0
- ❍ B. UPDATE DBM CFG USING DIAGSIZE 50
- ❍ C. UPDATE DBM CFG USING DIAGSIZE -1
- ❍ D. UPDATE DBM CFG USING DIAGSIZE -2

Question 41

Which tool automates the process of creating and running activity event monitor data to collect detailed diagnostic and runtime information for an SQL statement?

- ❍ A. db2pd
- ❍ B. db2cc
- ❍ C. db2top
- ❍ D. db2caem

Question 42

Which command displays the operating system error logs on AIX?

- ❍ A. /usr/bin/errpt -a
- ❍ B. /var/log/messages
- ❍ C. /var/adm/messages
- ❍ D. /var/adm/syslog/syslog.log

Question 43

Which command can you use to set the threshold rule for processor usage?

- ❍ A. db2fodc -detect
- ❍ B. db2pd –detect
- ❍ C. db2top –detect
- ❍ D. db2support –detect

Question 44

Which command is useful while monitoring sort performance?

- ❍ A. db2top –d <*DatabaseName*> -i 120 –a
- ❍ B. db2pd -d <*DatabaseName*> -sort -app -dyn
- ❍ C. db2fodc –db <*DatabaseName*> -perf –memory
- ❍ D. db2pd –d <*DatabaseName*> -mempools

Question 45

What page size is best for an OLTP application database that performs random read and write operations?

- ❍ A. A smaller page size because DB2 does not waste buffer pool space with unnecessary records
- ❍ B. A bigger page size because DB2 can fetch more records into the buffer pool
- ❍ C. An intermediate page size
- ❍ D. Use of block-based extent to read data sequentially

Question 46

Which column is a good candidate for indexing?

- ❍ A. Columns involved in the GROUP BY, ORDER BY clause
- ❍ B. Infrequently used INCLUDE columns
- ❍ C. BLOB columns
- ❍ D. Columns involved in less-frequent queries

Question 47

Which of the following is not a prerequisite for setting up HADR?

- ❍ A. The operating system and the DB2 version must be the same on the primary and standby servers.
- ❍ B. The DB2 software for both the primary and the standby database must have the same bit size.
- ❍ C. The primary and standby databases must have the same database name.
- ❍ D. Both the primary and standby servers should be on the same subnet.

Question 48

To have greater data protection during a HADR disaster recovery invocation, which HADR synchronization mode is appropriate?

- A. SYNC
- B. NEARSYNC
- C. ASYNC
- D. SUPERASYNC

Question 49

Which system catalog table lists temporal tables with their periods and history table?

- A. SYSCAT.TABLES
- B. SYSCAT.PERIODS
- C. SYSIBM.SQLTABLES
- D. SYSIBM.SYSTABLES

Question 50

Which command shows the best possible way of dropping column C1 from system-period temporal table T1?

- A. LOCK TABLE t1 IN EXCLUSIVE MODE; ALTER TABLE t1 DROP VERSIONING; ALTER TABLE t1 DROP COLUMN C1; ALTER TABLE t1_history DROP COLUMN C1; ALTER TABLE t1 ADD VERSIONING USE HISTORY TABLE t1_history; COMMIT;
- B. LOCK TABLE t1 IN EXCLUSIVE MODE; ALTER TABLE t1 DROP COLUMN C1; ALTER TABLE t1_history DROP COLUMN C1; COMMIT;
- C. LOCK TABLE t1 IN EXCLUSIVE MODE; ALTER TABLE t1 DROP VERSIONING; ALTER TABLE t1 DROP COLUMN C1; ALTER TABLE t1 ADD VERSIONING USE HISTORY TABLE t1_history; COMMIT;
- D. LOCK TABLE t1 IN EXCLUSIVE MODE; ALTER TABLE t1 DROP VERSIONING; ALTER TABLE t1_history DROP COLUMN C1; ALTER TABLE t1 ADD VERSIONING USE HISTORY TABLE t1_history; COMMIT;

Question 51

If inserting data into the system-period temporal table's history table t1_history is limiting the performance of your workload, which option will help you improve workload performance?

- ❍ A. DROP TABLE t1_history
- ❍ B. ALTER TABLE t1_history APPEND ON
- ❍ C. CREATE UNIQUE INDEX ON t1_history (C1)
- ❍ D. ALTER TABLE t1_history APPEND OFF

Question 52

Which command enables you to create a stored procedure that is insensitive to CURRENT TEMPORAL SYSTEM_TIME and CURRENT TEMPORAL BUSINESS_TIME temporal special registers?

- ❍ A. CALL SET_ROUTINE_OPTS ('SYSTEM_TIME NO BUSINESS_TIME NO')
- ❍ B. CALL SET_ROUTINE_OPTS ('SYSTIMESENSITIVE NO BUSTIMESENSITIVE NO')
- ❍ C. SET CURRENT SYSTIMESENSITIVE=NO BUSTIMESENSITIVE=NO
- ❍ D. SET CURRENT 'SYSTEM_TIME NO BUSINESS_TIME NO'

Question 53

If your system-period temporal base table is a range partitioned table, how would you detach a partition from the table?

- ❍ A. Execute the ALTER TABLE ... DETACH PART command.
- ❍ B. Range partition tables are not supported to configure as system period temporal tables.
- ❍ C. Range partition tables are supported only for business-period temporal tables.
- ❍ D. Execute the ALTER TABLE ...DROP VERSIONING; ALTER TABLE ... DETACH PART; ALTER TABLE ...ADD VERSIONING commands.

Question 54

If you intend to run the SET INTEGRITY ... FOR EXCEPTION command on a system-period temporal base table, which step is the correct one to follow?

- ❍ A. Execute the SET INTEGRITY … FOR EXCEPTION command.
- ❍ B. You cannot create constraints on a system-period temporal base table.
- ❍ C. Execute the ALTER TABLE …DROP VERSIONING; SET INTEGRITY … FOR EXCEPTION; ALTER TABLE …ADD VERSIONING commands.
- ❍ D. The exception table is not supported on a system-period temporal table.

Question 55

Which of the following is not a SET INTEGRITY command action during a range partition attach operation?

- ❍ A. It validates that the newly attached data is in the correct range.
- ❍ B. It adds index keys for the new records.
- ❍ C. It places any rows with exceptions in an exception table.
- ❍ D. It invokes the asynchronous partition detach task in the background.

Question 56

To achieve the best query performance, which of the following is necessary when using multi-temperature storage support?

- ❍ A. Set the storage group media device attribute OVERHEAD to reflect the storage path's capabilities.
- ❍ B. Set the storage group media device attributes OVERHEAD and DEVICE READ RATE to reflect the storage path's capabilities.
- ❍ C. Set the storage group media device attribute DEVICE READ RATE to reflect the storage path's capabilities.
- ❍ D. Set the storage group media device attribute TRANSFERRATE to reflect the storage path's capabilities.

Question 57

Which table function can you use to obtain storage group information?

- ❍ A. ADMIN_GET_STORAGE_PATHS
- ❍ B. ADMIN_GET_TAB_INFO
- ❍ C. ADMIN_GET_INDEX_INFO
- ❍ D. SYSCAT.STOGROUPS

Question 58

What happens in the background when you execute the ALTER TABLESPACE ... USING STOGROUP command?

- ❍ A. DB2 does a COMMIT and closes the connection.
- ❍ B. DB2 initiates a rebalance operation upon executing a COMMIT statement.
- ❍ C. DB2 retains both the storage group storage paths for a day.
- ❍ D. DB2 executes a REORG in the background.

Question 59

Which command suspends the table space TBSP1 rebalance operation?

- ❍ A. ALTER TABLESPACE tbsp1 STOP REBALANCE
- ❍ B. ALTER TABLESPACE tbsp1 PAUSE REBALANCE
- ❍ C. ALTER TABLESPACE tbsp1 SUSPEND REBALANCE
- ❍ D. ALTER TABLESPACE tbsp1 REBALANCE SUSPEND

Question 60

Which step is necessary during a redirected restore operation when you have storage groups defined in the database?

❍ A. RESTORE DATABASE ... REDIRECT
SET STOGROUP PATHS FOR
RESTORE DATABASE ... CONTINUE

❍ B. RESTORE DATABASE ... REDIRECT
SET TABLESPACE CONTAINER FOR
RESTORE DATABASE ... CONTINUE

❍ C. RESTORE DATABASE ... REDIRECT
SET TABLESPACE CONTAINER FOR ... AUTOMATIC STORAGE
RESTORE DATABASE ... CONTINUE

❍ D. RESTORE DATABASE ... REDIRECT
SET STOGROUP PATHS FOR ... AUTOMATIC STORAGE
RESTORE DATABASE ... CONTINUE

Question 61

Which command can you use to downgrade a database instance from DB2 10.5 FP2 to DB2 10.5 FP1?

❍ A. DOWNGRADE DATABASE
❍ B. db2iupdt –D <*InstanceName*>
❍ C. Drop the DB2 10.5 FP2 instance and recreate DB2 10.5 FP1 instance
❍ D. db2iupdt <*InstanceName*>

Question 62

Which approach is best to follow while upgrading the DB2 server and the client?

❍ A. Upgrade the DB2 server and client together.
❍ B. Upgrade the DB2 server and test it before upgrading the client.
❍ C. Upgrade the DB2 client and then the server.
❍ D. Upgrade the DB2 client and test it before upgrading the server.

Question 63

Which two features are *not* separately priced in DB2 10.5?

- ❒ A. DB2 Recovery Expert
- ❒ B. DB2 Storage Optimization
- ❒ C. DB2 Merge Backup
- ❒ D. IBM InfoSphere Optim High Performance Unload
- ❒ E. DB2 Database Partitioning (DPF)

Question 64

Which two operating systems are supported for DB2 10.5?

- ❒ A. Solaris 8
- ❒ B. Ubuntu 10.4 LTS
- ❒ C. SUSE Linux Enterprise Server 11.2
- ❒ D. Windows Server 2003 R2
- ❒ E. AIX 7.1

Question 65

Which command when executed on the database server will provide a list of all DB2 install versions, the install path, and the ID that installed it?

- ❍ A. db2licm
- ❍ B. db2ls
- ❍ C. db2greg
- ❍ D. db2 show install locations with detail
- ❍ E. None of the above

Question 66

What is the easiest way to create the DB2 default WLM objects?

- ❍ A. Run the db2sampl command.
- ❍ B. Set the registry parameter DB2_WLM_CREATE=YES.
- ❍ C. Run the db2wlm command.
- ❍ D. None of the above

Question 67

Why is there a Tuple Sequence Number?

- ❍ A. It gives you a fast way to count columns.
- ❍ B. It provides an internal count of temporary rows in an intermediate result.
- ❍ C. It is used to construct a row from column data.
- ❍ D. It helps to reduce the data size.

Question 68

Which data type is not supported in a columnar table?

- ❍ A. XML
- ❍ B. CLOB
- ❍ C. BLOB
- ❍ D. All of the above

Question 69

What is the maximum number of storage paths that you can define to a storage group?

- ❍ A. 64
- ❍ B. 32
- ❍ C. 128
- ❍ D. 512
- ❍ E. None of the above

Question 70

Which of the following is *not* a database prerequisite for pureScale?

- ❍ A. Unicode
- ❍ B. DB2_DATABASE_TYPE=PS
- ❍ C. Automatic storage
- ❍ D. AESE or AWSE
- ❍ E. GPFS
- ❍ F. Storage group

Question 71

What is a timeron?

- ❍ A. It is a normalized millisecond measure used to compare MIPS with GHz.
- ❍ B. It is a relative unit of measure determined by the DB2 Optimizer.
- ❍ C. IBM uses the timeron value to base the PVU rates for classes of servers.
- ❍ D. It is a time measure using Base 2 that is normalized across server classes.
- ❍ E. None of the above

Question 72

What is the length limit for data types CHAR and VARCHAR stored in the synopsis table?

- ❍ A. 1,024
- ❍ B. 1,000
- ❍ C. 2,000
- ❍ D. 4,000

Question 73

What is the maximum number of databases that a single pureScale cluster can support?

- ❍ A. 16
- ❍ B. 255
- ❍ C. 128
- ❍ D. 200
- ❍ E. 512
- ❍ F. None of the above

Question 74

In an ESE database, what process is required to convert a table space to automatic storage? Assume the database is created as AUTOMATIC STORAGE YES.

- ❍ A. CREATE STOGROUP *<name>* on *<storage paths>* then ALTER TABLESPACE *<name>* MANAGED BY AUTOMATIC STORAGE
- ❍ B. SET TABLESPACE CONTAINERS FOR *<tablespace Id>* using STOGROUP *<name>*
- ❍ C. ALTER TABLESPACE *<name>* MANAGED BY AUTOMATIC STORAGE then ALTER TABLESPACE *<name>* REBALANCE
- ❍ D. None of the above

Question 75

In a 15-member pureScale cluster, what is the maximum supported value for NUMDB?

- ❍ A. 16
- ❍ B. 8
- ❍ C. 3,000
- ❍ D. 34
- ❍ E. 24
- ❍ F. 64
- ❍ G. 128
- ❍ H. None of the above

Question 76

Which command shows the location of the global registry file?

- ❍ A. db2licm
- ❍ B. db2ls
- ❍ C. db2greg
- ❍ D. db2 show install locations with detail
- ❍ E. None of the above

Question 77

In an ESE database, what process is required to convert a table space to automatic storage? Assume the database is created as AUTOMATIC STORAGE NO.

- ❍ A. CREATE STOGROUP <*name*> on <*storage paths*> then ALTER TABLESPACE <*name*> MANAGED BY AUTOMATIC STORAGE then ALTER TABLESPACE <*name*> REBALANCE
- ❍ B. SET TABLESPACE CONTAINERS FOR <*tablespace Id*> using STOGROUP <*name*>
- ❍ C. ALTER TABLESPACE <*name*> MANAGED BY AUTOMATIC STORAGE then ALTER TABLESPACE <*name*> REBALANCE
- ❍ D. None of the above

Question 78

Which feature is *not* part of the DB2 Advanced packages AESE and AWSE?

- ❍ A. WHS Mining and Text Analytics
- ❍ B. DPF
- ❍ C. solidDB
- ❍ D. SQL Replication
- ❍ E. Advanced Recovery
- ❍ F. Cognos10.2
- ❍ G. All of the above
- ❍ H. None of the above

Question 79

What is the best way to determine whether the database server is SIMD enabled?

- ❍ A. Run the db2checkSD command.
- ❍ B. Run db2expln with a standard SELECT to see whether the Explain output has SIMD=enabled.
- ❍ C. Create a database by using AUTOMATIC STORAGE YES. If the database parameter is set to DFT_TABLE_ORG = COLUMN, then SIMD is enabled.
- ❍ D. Run db2start and check the db2diag.log file.
- ❍ E. All of the above

Question 80

What is the WLM object that identifies a workload by type and range of values based on cardinality or timeron cost?

- ❍ A. Service class
- ❍ B. Threshold
- ❍ C. Workload
- ❍ D. Work action set
- ❍ E. Work class set

Question 81

What is I/O fencing?

- ❍ A. Each member of a pureScale cluster gets a quorum of the disk storage space.
- ❍ B. PureScale uses a stage area for page disputes between members.
- ❍ C. Cluster services serializes I/O to the DB2 catalog to prevent locking conflicts.
- ❍ D. DB2 ensures that it is not possible for the failed member to modify shared data on disk.
- ❍ E. None of the above

Question 82

What is the smallest grouping of pages in the synopsis table?

- ❍ A. 1,024
- ❍ B. 100
- ❍ C. 256
- ❍ D. 500
- ❍ E. Total number of active pages in table/max rows allowed in a synopsis table

Question 83

Which of the following is not a database requirement for creating column-organized tables?

- ❍ A. No DPF
- ❍ B. Unicode
- ❍ C. Automatic storage
- ❍ D. DB2_WORKLOAD=ANALYTICS
- ❍ E. SORTHEAP and SHEAPTHRES_SHR cannot be STMM controlled
- ❍ F. No pureScale
- ❍ G. Identity or Identity-16
- ❍ H. All are required

Question 84

How often does RTS check the PENDING queue?

- ❍ A. 5 seconds
- ❍ B. 15 minutes
- ❍ C. 1 minute
- ❍ D. 10 minutes
- ❍ E. 5 minutes
- ❍ F. Never—there is no such thing as a PENDING queue.

Question 85

Automatic statistics profiling (ASP) was discontinued in V10.5 and replaced with what?

- ❍ A. Nothing—not needed in V10.5 because of automation
- ❍ B. IBM Data Studio's Statistics Advisor
- ❍ C. Automated Runstats profiler
- ❍ D. DB2 profiler

Question 86

In pureScale, how do you remove a storage path from a storage group?

- ❍ A. Use ALTER STOGROUP DROP <*storage path*>, then execute the ALTER TABLESPACE <*name*> REBALANCE statements for each table space assigned to that storage group.
- ❍ B. Create a new storage group by using CREATE STOGROUP without the storage path, then for each table space assigned to that storage group, run ALTER TABLESPACE USING STOGROUP <*new storage group*>, followed by ALTER TABLESPACE <*name*> REBALANCE.
- ❍ C. Use a redirected restore command with SET STOGROUP PATHS for <STOGROUP NAME> ON <*storage paths*>.
- ❍ D. Create a new storage group by using CREATE STOGROUP without the storage path. Use the ADMIN_MOVE_TABLE utility to move all the tables and indexes to the new table spaces. Drop all the old table spaces by using DROP TABLESPACE and then DROP STOGROUP <*old storage group*>. If the old storage group was set as the default, you must run ALTER STOGROUP <*new storage group*> set as the default before you can drop the old storage group.
- ❍ E. Either C or D
- ❍ F. Either A or B
- ❍ G. None of the above
- ❍ H. All of the above

Question 87

Which table space attributes cannot be altered?

- ❍ A. Extentsize
- ❍ B. Increasesize
- ❍ C. Pagesize
- ❍ D. Bufferpool
- ❍ E. Managed By
- ❍ F. Storage Group
- ❍ G. Maxsize
- ❍ H. Initialsize
- ❍ I. A and C
- ❍ J. A and C and F
- ❍ K. H and C and A

Question 88

In a row-organized default database, is it possible to create a column-organized table? If yes, what is required so that CREATE TABLE...ORGANIZED BY COLUMN works?

- ❍ A. No, it cannot be done.
- ❍ B. Yes, it can be done and nothing is required.
- ❍ C. Yes, and UTIL_HEAP_SZ must be set to AUTOMATIC.
- ❍ D. Yes, and SORTHEAP as well as SHEAPTHRES_SHR must not be set to AUTOMATIC.
- ❍ E. Yes, and AUTO_RUNSTATS must be enabled.
- ❍ F. Yes, and SORTHEAP as well as SHEAPTHRES_SHR must be set to AUTOMATIC
- ❍ G. C and E and F
- ❍ H. E and C

Question 89

When you enable EXTENDED_ROW_SIZE, what happens when the row length is too large for the page size?

- ❍ A. The transaction aborts with SQL0670N.
- ❍ B. The row is truncated.
- ❍ C. Pages are chained together as required.
- ❍ D. Data that does not fit within the maximum row size is stored as a LOB.

Question 90

JSON stands for what?

- ❍ A. Java Simple Object Notation
- ❍ B. Just Some Other Notation
- ❍ C. JavaScript Object Notation
- ❍ D. Java Simple Other Notation
- ❍ E. Just Show Out Now

Question 91

Which of the following are not requirements for the installation or operation of DB2/JSON?

- ❍ A. CREATE TABLE and CREATE FUNCTION authority in SYSTOOLS
- ❍ B. nosqljson.jar in the classpath
- ❍ C. DB2 V10.5 FP1 or higher
- ❍ D. Java 1.5 or higher
- ❍ E. DFT_TABLE_ORG = ROW
- ❍ F. None of the above
- ❍ G. All of the above
- ❍ H. B and E
- ❍ I. C and B and D

Question 92

Which of the following are *not* database requirements for the creation of shadow tables?

- ❍ A. DB2_WORKLOAD = " "
- ❍ B. Unicode
- ❍ C. Identity or Identity-16
- ❍ D. Automatic storage management
- ❍ E. Organized by Row
- ❍ F. SHEAPTHRES_SHR and SORTHEAP set to AUTOMATIC
- ❍ G. DB2_EXTENDED_OPTIMIZATION="OPT_SORTHEAP_EXCEPT_COL <SORTHEAP>"
- ❍ H. Archive logging
- ❍ I. All of the above

Question 93

In pureScale, given a database backup image containing members {0, 5, 10}, which of the following target systems can you restore and roll forward the backup image?

- ❍ A. System with members {0,1,2}
- ❍ B. System with members {5,10,20}
- ❍ C. System with members {0}
- ❍ D. System with members {0, 5, 10, 20, 25}

Question 94

In pureScale during a roll-forward operation, if a "drop member" log record is encountered, what will happen to the command?

- ❍ A. The roll-forward command drops the member and continues on to reach the specified point in time.
- ❍ B. The roll-forward command drops the member and stops the roll forward.
- ❍ C. The roll-forward command fails before taking any action on the log record.
- ❍ D. The scenario is not possible.

Answers

Question 1

The correct answer is **D**. You can use the Optim Performance Manager Extended Insight to monitor the entire database application system from end to end. End-to-end monitoring begins when you initiate a transaction in an application, continues as every component (such as the client, network, and data server) processes the transaction, and ends when the application concludes the transaction and you receive the results of that transaction. The Optim Query Workload Tuner for DB2 for Linux, UNIX, and Windows provides expert recommendations to help you improve the performance of query workloads. The Optim pureQuery for LUW can improve performance, security, and manageability of database client applications by providing APIs to help in rapid development and modifications.

Question 2

The correct answers are **B** and **C**. The DB2 profile registry is divided into four categories:

- DB2 instance-level registry
- DB2 global-level registry
- DB2 node-level registry
- DB2 user-level registry

Question 3

The correct answer is **C**. The DB2 directory is divided into four categories:

- System database directory
- Local database directory
- Node directory
- Database Connection Services (DCS) directory

Question 4

The correct answer is **C**. You can install DB2 on a server by using four different methods:

- Graphical-based DB2 setup wizard. This method is suitable for installing and configuring DB2 on a single server.
- Text-based interactive installation by using `db2_install` script. This method of installation is deprecated.
- Silent installation by using a DB2 response file. This is a preferred method when you want to install and configure DB2 on multiple systems.
- Advanced installation by using DB2 payload files. This is a complicated method of installing DB2.

Question 5

The correct answer is **D**. DB2 pureScale has four major components:

- Cluster interconnect (CI)
- Cluster caching facility (CF)
- Cluster services (CS)
- Cluster file system

The cluster services is built around IBM Reliable Services Clustering Technology (RSCT), Tivoli Systems Automation for Multiplatform (TSAMP), and IBM General Parallel File System (GPFS) to provide automatic member failure detection, failover, and shared data access features.

Question 6

The correct answer is **B**. The supported DB2 upgrade paths are:

- DB2 9.8 to DB2 10.1
- DB2 9.8 to DB2 10.5
- DB2 9.7 to DB2 10.1
- DB2 9.7 to DB2 10.5
- DB2 9.5 to DB2 9.7

If you need to upgrade your DB2 9.5 instance to DB2 10.5, you must first upgrade to the latest fix pack of DB2 9.7 or 10.1 and then upgrade it to DB2 10.5.

Question 7

The correct answer is **B**. The command `db2set -info` returns the properties of the specific variable, and it looks something like this:

```
db2set -info DB2_INDEX_PCTFREE_DEFAULT
   Immediate change supported : YES
   Immediate by default :       YES
```

The command `db2set DB2_INDEX_PCTFREE_DEFAULT` returns a warning if it is not set and returns a value if it is set, similar to the following:

```
db2set DB2_INDEX_PCTFREE_DEFAULT

DBI1303W  Variable not set.

Explanation:

The variable was not set in the profile registry.

User response:

No further action is required.
```

```
db2set DB2_INDEX_PCTFREE_DEFAULT=20
db2set DB2_INDEX_PCTFREE_DEFAULT
20
```

The command `db2set -all DB2_INDEX_PCTFREE_DEFAULT` returns all occurrences such as operating system level (e), node level (n), instance level (`i`), and global level (g):

```
db2set -all DB2_INDEX_PCTFREE_DEFAULT
[i] 20
```

The command `db2set -display` is an incorrect command.

Question 8

The correct answer is **C**. The command `db2iauto -on` *<instancename>* enables the automatic start of an instance after each server restart. The `START_STOP_TIME DBM CFG` specifies the time, in minutes, within which all database partition servers must respond to a `START DBM` or a `STOP DBM` command. It is also used as the timeout value during `ADD DBPARTITIONNUM` and `DROP DBPARTITIONNUM` operations. The `AUTORESTART DBM CFG` parameter determines whether the database manager automatically initiates crash recovery when a user connects to a database that had previously terminated abnormally. If this configuration parameter is not set, the user must issue an explicit restart database command before he or she can connect to the database. The `DB2AUTORESTART` is an incorrect parameter to DB2 registry setting.

Question 9

The correct answer is **B**. A sequence is a database object that allows the automatic generation of unique values and can be used across multiple tables in a database. Likewise, the `GENERATED BY DEFAULT AS IDENTITY` clause in a `CREATE TABLE` command also generates unique values, but it is limited to the table in which it is defined. The creation of a `UNIQUE` index guarantees unique values in the column but will not generate any unique values. The trigger usage is inappropriate in this case.

Question 10

The correct answer is **A**. You can create only one cluster index on a table.

Question 11

The correct answer is **B**. The `WITH EMPTY TABLE` clause of the `ALTER TABLE` command removes all the data currently in the table and is nonrecoverable even within a unit of work.

Question 12

The correct answer is **B**. You can use the TRANSFER OWNERSHIP command to transfer the object ownership from one user to another. All privileges that the current owner has that were granted as part of the creation of the object are transferred to the new owner.

Question 13

The correct answer is **C**. You use the ADMIN_DROP_SCHEMA procedure to drop a specific schema and all objects contained in it. The DROP SCHEMA command drops the schema only if all the objects that were in that schema must be dropped or moved to another schema. The other options are incorrect.

Question 14

The correct answer is **B**. To perform a database backup to the TSM server, you use the BACKUP DATABASE ... USE TSM command, and then back up the transaction logs to TSM by updating the LOGARCHMETH1 database configuration parameter to TSM. You instruct DB2 to create a COPY file in the TSM server while loading the data by using the LOAD command. You can either specify the COPY YES option in the LOAD command or set the DB2 registry variable DB2_LOAD_COPY_NO_OVERRIDE to COPY YES.

Question 15

The correct answer is **A**. You can use the ALTER TABLE ... RESTART or RESTART WITH command options to reset the state of the sequence associated with the identify column. If WITH <*newvalue*> is not specified, the sequence for the identity column will be restarted at the value that was specified, either implicitly or explicitly, as the starting value when the identity column was originally created. The NEXTVAL and NEXT VALUE expressions generate and return the next value for the sequence. There is no RESET option in the ALTER TABLE command.

Question 16

The correct answer is **D**. You can have a 128-byte authorization ID in DB2. However, when the authorization ID is interpreted as an operating system user ID or group name, DB2-imposed naming restrictions apply. For example, the Linux and UNIX operating systems can contain up to eight characters and the Windows operating systems can have up to 30 characters for user IDs and group names. Therefore, if you want to connect as a user that has a 128-byte authorization ID, you need to write your own security plug-in. In the plug-in, you can use the extended sizes for the authorization ID. Also, you cannot have uppercase characters in the name.

Question 17

The correct answer is **A**. The CURRENT LOCK TIMEOUT special register specifies the number of seconds to wait for a lock before returning an error indicating that a lock cannot be obtained at the session level. If you want to set it globally, update the database manager configuration parameter LOCKTIMEOUT.

Question 18

The correct answer is **A**. The following error is generated when you encounter a LOCKTIMEOUT issue in the database:

```
SQL0911N The current transaction has been rolled back because of a deadlock
or timeout. Reason code "68". SQLSTATE=40001
```

You can use the database system monitor to detect the lock timeout and the SQL statements involved.

Question 19

The correct answer is **B**. The following error is generated when you encounter a deadlock issue in the database:

```
SQL0911N The current transaction has been rolled back because of a deadlock
or timeout. Reason code "2". SQLSTATE=40001
```

You can use the locking event monitor to detect the deadlock and the SQL statements involved.

Question 20

The connect answer is **C**. Under currently committed semantics, only committed data is returned to readers. However, readers do not wait for writers to release row locks. Instead, readers return data that is based on the currently committed version of data—that is, the version of the data before the start of the write operation.

The following scans do not use currently committed semantics:

- Catalog table scans
- Scans that enforce referential integrity constraints
- Scans that reference LONG VARCHAR or LONG VARGRAPHIC columns
- Range clustered table scans
- Scans that use spatial or extended indexes

Question 21

The correct answer is **C**. The currently committed semantics require increased log space for writers. Additional space is needed for logging the first update of a data row during a transaction. This data is required for retrieving the currently committed image of the row. Depending on the workload, this can have an insignificant or a measurable impact on the total log space used.

The currently committed semantics apply only to read-only scans that do not involve catalog tables and to internal scans that evaluate or enforce constraints. Because currently committed semantics are decided at the scan level, a writer's access plan might include currently committed scans. For example, the scan for a read-only subquery can involve currently committed semantics. The currently committed semantics read data from the log buffer and presently does not support the retrieval of log files from the log archive location.

Question 22

The correct answer is **C**. You can use the `db2rc` command to invoke the replication center graphical interface. The commands `db2cc` and `db2cc -rc` are deprecated, and the `db2start -rc` command option is invalid.

Question 23

The correct answer is **A**. The `TO_SINGLE_BYTE` function returns a string in which multibyte characters are converted to the equivalent single-byte character where an equivalent character exists. The `INSTRB` function returns the starting position, in bytes, of a string within another string. And the remaining scalar functions are invalid.

Question 24

The correct answer is **D**. In DB2 10.1, DB2 introduced various functions within triggers:

- **Multiple-event trigger support:** A trigger event can now contain more than one operation.
- **Trigger event predicates identify triggered events:** You can use the trigger event predicates of `UPDATING`, `INSERTING`, and `DELETING` to identify the event that activated a trigger.
- **`FOR EACH STATEMENT` support:** When a trigger is activated, it runs according to its level of granularity as specified by the use of `FOR EACH ROW` or `FOR EACH STATEMENT`. The `FOR EACH ROW` statement runs as many times as the number of rows in the set of affected rows, whereas `FOR EACH STATEMENT` runs only once for the entire trigger event.

The trigger cascade feature was supplied in earlier versions of DB2.

Question 25

The correct answer is **D**. The DB2 registry variable `DB2_BCKP_INCLUDE_LOGS_WARNING` specifies whether online backups that fail to include all the necessary log files should still be allowed to complete successfully. The DB2 registry variable `DB2_BCKP_PAGE_VERIFICATION` stipulates whether DMS and automatic storage table space page validation occurs during a backup. DB2 has three environment variables specific to pureScale: `DB2_DATABASE_CF_MEMORY`, `DB2_MCR_RECOVERY_PARALLELISM_CAP`, and `DB2_SD_ALLOW_SLOW_NETWORK`. The registry variable `DB2_MCR_RECOVERY_PARALLELISM_CAP` plays an important role when you want to enable the member crash recovery in a number of parallel sets based on the system resource capability. The DB2 registry DB2_SAS_SETTINGS is a key parameter for SAS in-database analytics settings.

Question 26

The correct answers are **A** and **D**. The database configuration parameter NUM_DB_BACKUPS specifies the number of full database backups to retain for a database. If you set both REC_HIS_RETENTN and NUM_DB_BACKUPS, backups will not be removed unless both parameter conditions are met. The parameter AUTO_DEL_REC_OBJ specifies whether to delete database log files, backup images, and load copy images when their associated recovery history file entry is pruned. You use the parameter AUTO_MAINT for automatic maintenance of the database, such as automatic database backup (AUTO_DB_BACKUP), automatic statistics update, and automatic reorganization.

Question 27

The correct answer is **B**. The following table shows the parameter values and associated behavior:

REC_HIS_RETENTN	AUTO_DEL_REC_OBJ	Retention Period
-1	OFF	The number of entries indicating full database backups and any table space backups that are associated with the database backup correspond with the value specified by the num_db_ backups database configuration parameter.
-1	ON	The history file is not automatically pruned, and no recovery objects are deleted.
0	OFF	All entries in the history file except the last full backup are pruned.
0	ON	Automated history-file pruning and recovery object deletion are carried out based on the timestamp of the backup selected by the num_db_backups database configuration parameter.
10	ON	Backups are not removed unless both the num_db_backups and rec_his_retentn conditions are satisfied. For example, if you set rec_his_retentn to 10 and set num_db_backups to 12, then the backups and the history will be removed on the 13th day.

Question 28

The correct answer is **D**. The binary XML format supports both textual and binary XML formats for the transmission.

Question 29

The correct answer is **B**. The SECADM authority is necessary to create a trusted context.

Question 30

The correct answer is **D**. The indexing over XML data is subject to a few restrictions, including:

- Data types supported
- Concurrency-level support
- XML list elements
- Index compression

The supported data types for indexing over XML data are `VARCHAR`, `DATE`, `TIMESTAMP`, `INTEGER`, `DECIMAL`, and `DOUBLE`.

Question 31

The correct answers are **A** and **C**. The context step and function expression step are part of the XML index pattern you specify when creating functional indexes over XML data. The context step indicates the XML path of the element nodes or attribute nodes for which index entries will be created. The function expression step specifies the function, such as `fn:exists` or `fn:upper-case`, and its parameters.

Question 32

The correct answer is **A**. The `XSLTRANSFORM` built-in scalar function converts XML data into other formats, including the conversion of XML documents that conform to one XML schema into documents that conform to another schema.

Question 33

The correct answer is **D**. The `Ingest` utility does not support the following column types:

- Large object types (LOB, BLOB, CLOB, DBCLOB)
- XML
- Structured types
- Columns with a user-defined data type based on any of the types listed previously

Question 34

The correct answer is **D**. You can use the `INGEST LIST` and `INGEST GET STATS` commands to retrieve `Ingest` utility information. The `Ingest` utility does not support `UTIL_IMPACT_LIM`, `UTIL_IMPACT_PRIORITY`, and `LIST UTILITIES` commands or registers.

Question 35

The correct answer is **A**. You must declare a cursor before running the `LOAD FROM CURSOR` command. It is not mandatory to open the cursor, though.

Question 36

The correct answer is **B**. You can use the event monitor name, workload name, or service class name in the `-wlm` parameter clause to capture the recommendation based on a workload.

Question 37

The correct answer is **C**. By setting `logsecond` to `-1`, you will have no limit on the size of the unit of work or on the number of concurrent units of work. However, rollback (both at the savepoint level and at the unit of work level) could be very slow because of the need to retrieve log files from the archive. To set `logsecond` to `-1`, you must set the `logarchmeth1` configuration parameter to a value other than `OFF` or `LOGRETAIN`.

Question 38

The correct answer is **B**. The parameter `alt_diagpath` allows you to specify the fully qualified alternate path to use for DB2 diagnostic information when the primary diagnostic data path, `diagpath`, is unavailable.

Question 39

The correct answer is **A**. You need to set the `DB2FODC` registry variable to redirect the core file dumps and FODC data to a different file system. When `DB2_DISABLE_FLUSH_LOG` is set to `OFF` and an online backup is complete, the last active log file is truncated, closed, and made available to be archived. This ensures that your online backup has a full set of archived logs available for recovery. When `DB2_OPTSTATS_LOG` is not set or set to `ON`, statistics event logging is enabled, allowing you to monitor system performance and keep a history for better problem determination. The parameter `DB2_FORCE_APP_ON_MAX_LOG` specifies what happens when the `max_log` configuration parameter value is exceeded. Setting this parameter to `TRUE` will force the application off the database and will roll back the unit of work.

Question 40

The correct answer is **B**. The parameter `diagsize` helps control the maximum sizes of the diagnostic log and administration log files. If you set this value to zero, you will have only one diagnostic log file (`db2diag.log`) and only one administration notification log file (*<instance>*.nfy), and the sizes of these files will be unlimited. If you set the parameter to a nonzero value and restart the *<instance>*, a series of rotating diagnostic log files and a series of rotating administration notification log files will be used. These files are called the `db2diag.n.log` and *<instance>*.n.nfy files, where n is an integer; *<instance>*.n.nfy files apply only to Linux and UNIX operating systems. The number of `db2diag.n.log` files and *<instance>*.n.nfy files cannot exceed 10 each. When the size of the tenth file is full, the oldest file is deleted, and a new file is created.

Question 41

The correct answer is **D**. The `db2caem` tool automates the procedure of creating an activity event monitor. You can run the `db2caem` command to create the activity event monitor to capture data for an SQL statement, and then collect this data by using the `db2support` command. The information collected and generated by the `db2caem` tool includes:

- Detailed activity information captured by an activity event monitor, including monitor metrics (for example, `total_cpu_time` for statement execution)
- Formatted Explain output, including section actuals (statistics for different operators in the access plan)

Question 42

The correct answer is **A**. The following table shows the error log retrieval commands on respective operating systems:

Command	Operating System
/usr/bin/errpt –a	AIX
/var/log/messages	SLES
/var/adm/messages	Solaris
/var/adm/syslog/syslog.log	HP UX

Question 43

The correct answer is **A**. You can use the `db2fodc -detect` command to collect data when the environment reaches certain thresholds. The `-detect` parameter is compatible with the following main data collection parameters:

- `-cpu`
- `-memory`
- `-connections`
- `-hadr`
- `-hang`
- `-perf`
- `-cpl`
- `-preupgrade`

To collect information about the activity consuming more than 90 percent of CPU for more than 40 seconds (`triggercount * interval`) for the monitoring duration of five hours, execute this command:

```
db2fodc -cpu basic -detect us_sy">=90" sleeptime="30" iteration="10"
interval="10" triggercount="4" duration="5"
```

Question 44

The correct answer is **B**. You can use the `db2pd` command to monitor the sort performance. The `-sort` parameter returns the following information:

- `ApplHandl`: The application handle, including the node and the index
- `SortCB`: The address of a sort control block
- `MaxRowSize`: The sum of the maximum length of all columns of the row being sorted
- `EstNumRows`: The Optimizer-estimated number of rows that will be inserted into the sort
- `EstAvgRowSize`: The Optimizer-estimated average length of the rows being sorted
- `NumSMPSorts`: The number of concurrent subagents processing this sort
- `NumSpills`: The total number of times this sort has spilled to disk
- `KeySpec`: A description of the type and length of each column being sorted
- `SortheapMem`: The number of KB of `sortheap` memory reserved and allocated by this sort
- `NumSpilledRows`: The total number of rows spilled to disk for this sort
- `NumBufferedRows`: The total number of rows inserted into this sort since the last time it spilled

Question 45

The correct answer is **A**. For OLTP applications that perform random row read and write operations, use a smaller page size because it does not waste buffer pool space with unwanted rows.

Question 46

The correct answer is **A**. The columns that appear in a `GROUP BY` or `ORDER BY` clause of a frequent query might benefit from the creation of an index.

Question 47

The correct answer is **D**. There is no requirement to have the primary and standby servers on the same subnet.

Question 48

The correct answer is **A**.

- `SYNC`: This mode provides the greatest protection against transaction loss but at a cost of higher transaction response time.
- `NEARSYNC`: This mode provides somewhat less protection against transaction loss in exchange for a shorter transaction response time than that of `SYNC` mode.
- `ASYNC`: Compared with the `SYNC` and `NEARSYNC` modes, the `ASYNC` mode results in shorter transaction response times but might cause greater transaction losses if the primary database fails.
- `SUPERASYNC`: This mode has the shortest transaction response time but also has the highest probability of transaction losses if the primary system fails. This mode is useful when you do not want transactions to be blocked or experience longer response times due to network interruptions or congestion.

Question 49

The correct answer is **B**. You can use the SYSCAT.PERIODS catalog view to display the definition of a period temporal table. The statement looks something like this:

```
SELECT SUBSTR (PERIODNAME, 1, 10) PERIODNAME,
     SUBSTR (TABSCHEMA, 1, 10) TABSCHEMA,
     SUBSTR (TABNAME, 1, 20) TABNAME,
     PERIODTYPE,
     SUBSTR (HISTORYTABSCHEMA, 1, 10) HISTORYTABSCHEMA,
     SUBSTR (HISTORYTABNAME, 1, 20) HISTORYTABNAME
  FROM SYSCAT.PERIODS

PERIODNAME TABSCHEMA  TABNAME              PERIODTYPE HISTORYTABSCHEMA
---------- ---------- -------------------- ---------- ----------------
SYSTEM_TIM MOHAN      EMPLOYEE_ST          S          MOHAN

HISTORYTABNAME
-------------------
EMPLOYEE_ST_HISTORY

  1 record(s) selected.
```

Question 50

The correct answer is **A**. When you try dropping a column on a system-period temporal table, you will receive an error similar to the following:

```
SQL0196N Column "C1" in "T1" cannot be dropped. Reason code ="5".
```

The reason code 5 indicates the column cannot be dropped because it is a column in a system-period temporal table. The solution is to follow these steps:

1. Alter the system-period temporal table to drop versioning. This breaks the link between the tables.
2. Alter the system-period temporal table to drop the column.
3. Alter the table that was the history table to drop the column.
4. Alter the former system-period temporal table to add versioning. This reestablishes the link between the tables.

Question 51

The correct answer is **B**. If you issue the ALTER TABLE statement with the APPEND ON option, data will always be appended, information about any free space on the data pages will not be kept, and time will not be spent searching for free space.

Question 52

The correct answer is **B**. The `SET_ROUTINE_OPTS` procedure sets the options to use for the creation of SQL procedures in the current session. The correct bind options to set are `SYSTIMESENSITIVE` and `BUSTIMESENSITIVE` for system temporal and business temporal tables, respectively.

Question 53

The correct answer is **D**. A table cannot be detached from a system-period temporal table while versioning is enabled. You can stop versioning and then detach a partition from the base table. The detached partition becomes an independent table. Detaching a partition from a history table does not require that you stop versioning.

Question 54

The correct answer is **C**. While versioning is enabled, the `SET INTEGRITY ... FOR EXCEPTION` statement cannot be run because moving exception rows into an exception table will result in lost history. Because the exception rows are not recorded in the history table, the ability to audit the data in your system-period temporal table and its associated history table is jeopardized. You can temporarily stop versioning, run the `SET INTEGRITY ... FOR EXCEPTION` statement, and then enable versioning again.

Question 55

The correct answer is **D**. The `SET INTEGRITY` command does not invoke the asynchronous partition detach task; however, this is part of the data partition detach phase.

Question 56

The correct answer is **B**. The storage groups are groups of storage paths with similar qualities. The critical attributes include storage capacity, latency, data transfer rates, and the degree of RAID protection.

Question 57

The correct answer is **A**. The `ADMIN_GET_STORAGE_PATHS` table function returns a list of automatic storage paths for each database storage group, including file system information for each storage path.

Question 58

The correct answer is **B**. Moving the table space from one storage group to another initiates a rebalance operation.

Question 59

The correct answer is **D**. To suspend an active rebalance operation on the specified table space, use the command `ALTER TABLESPACE ... REBALANCE SUSPEND`, and to resume use `ALTER TABLESPACE ... REBALANCE RESUME`.

Question 60

The correct answer is **A**. From DB2 10.1 onward, when you define storage groups, you will have to set the storage path for the storage groups during the redirected restore operation instead of setting the container paths for table spaces as in previous versions.

Question 61

The correct answer is **B**. In DB2 10.5, you can downgrade the instance from a higher fix pack to a lower fix pack by using the command `db2iupdt -D` <*InstanceName*>.

Question 62

The correct answer is **B**. The recommended approach is to update the DB2 server and test the server functionality before upgrading the DB2 client on the application server.

Question 63

The correct answers are **B** and **E**. The following table shows the DB2 editions and associated features:

Feature/Edition	Express C	Express	Workgroup	Advanced Workgroup	Enterprise Server	Advanced Enterprise
Storage optimization	No	No	No	Yes	No	Yes
pureScale	No	No	No	Yes	No	Yes
HADR	No	Yes	Yes	Yes	Yes	Yes
Column store (BLU)	No	No	No	Yes	No	Yes
Multi-temperature	No	No	No	Yes	Yes	Yes
Temporal tables	Yes	Yes	Yes	Yes	Yes	Yes
Range partition tables	No	No	Yes	Yes	Yes	Yes
Workload management	No	No	No	Yes	No	Yes
Advance Copy Services	No	Yes	Yes	Yes	Yes	Yes
TSAMP	No	Yes	Yes	Yes	Yes	Yes
LBAC	No	No	No	Yes	No	Yes
Scan sharing	No	No	No	Yes	Yes	Yes

(continued)

Feature/Edition	Express C	Express	Workgroup	Advanced Workgroup	Enterprise Server	Advanced Enterprise
Connection concentrator	No	No	No	Yes	Yes	Yes
MQT	No	No	No	Yes	Yes	Yes
Backup compression	No	Yes	Yes	Yes	Yes	Yes
pureXML	Yes	Yes	Yes	Yes	Yes	Yes
Q Replication	No	No	No	Yes	No	Yes
Optim Performance Manager	No	No	No	Yes	No	Yes
SQL Skin for Sybase ASE	No	No	No	No	No	No
Recovery Expert	No	No	No	No	No	No
Merge Backup	No	No	No	No	No	No
Optim Performance Unload	No	No	No	No	No	No
DPF	No	No	No	Yes	No	Yes

Question 64

The correct answers are **C** and **E**. The supported platforms for DB2 10.5 are:

- AIX 6.1 TL7 and higher, AIX 7.1 TL 1 and higher
- HP UX 11iv3 and higher
- RHEL 5 update 9 and higher, SLES 10 SP4 and higher, Ubuntu 12.04 LTS and higher
- Solaris 10 update 10 and higher
- Windows 8.1, Windows 2008 R2, and Windows 2012 R2
- Inspur K-UX 2.1 and higher

Question 65

The correct answer is **B**. The command is `db2ls -a`.

Question 66

The correct answer is **D**. The WLM default objects are created for every `CREATE DATABASE` statement executed. No special action is needed.

Question 67

The correct answer is **C**. The TSN values are stored in the synopsis table and give DB2 a way to put column data into the proper column sequence for the row.

Question 68

The correct answer is **D**. Today, none of these data types can be used in a column table.

Question 69

The correct answer is **C**. A storage group can have from 1 to 128 storage paths.

Question 70

The correct answer is **B**. Unicode and automatic storage are requirements, and automatic storage includes at least one storage group. GPFS is required because a shared file system is needed to run pureScale. AESE or AWSE is required for proper software licensing.

Question 71

The correct answer is **B**. A timeron is a relative unit of measure determined by the DB2 Optimizer based on internal cost values as a weighted sum of I/O and processor costs.

Question 72

The correct answer is **B**. The length limit for `CHAR` and `VARCHAR` is 1,000 characters.

Question 73

The correct answer is **D**. One pureScale cluster can support up to 200 databases.

Question 74

The correct answer is **C**. Any automatic storage database will have one storage group named `IBMSTOGROUP`, so there is no need to create one. `ALTER TABLESPACE` *<name>* `MANAGED BY AUTOMATIC STORAGE` will record the attribute in the catalog, and `ALTER TABLESPACE` *<name>* `REBALANCE` will move the containers.

Question 75

The correct answer is **D**. The maximum number of active databases is 512. In a 15-member cluster, one database will equal 15 active databases. So the answer is 512/15 = 34.

Question 76

The correct answer is **C**. The command is `db2greg -g`.

Question 77

The correct answer is **A**. The `CREATE STOGROUP` statement will change the database to `AUTOMATIC STORAGE`. The `ALTER TABLESPACE` statement will change the table space to `AUTOMATIC STORAGE`, and the second `ALTER TABLESPACE` will move the containers to the storage paths defined in the storage group.

Question 78

The correct answer is **E**. The Advanced Recovery Feature is licensed outside of AESE and AWSE.

Question 79

The correct answer is **D**. You will have to look in the `db2diag.log` file for the information.

Example: CPU: total: 32 online:16 Cores per socket:8 Threading degree per core:4 SIMD:Y

Question 80

The correct answer is **E**. A work class set identifies workloads by type (`READ`, `WRITE`, `DML`, `DDL`, `CALL`, and `LOAD`) and a range of values based on cardinality or timeron cost.

Question 81

The correct answer is **D**. Before you recover a failed member, DB2 cluster services ensures that it is not possible for the failed member to modify share data on disk. I/O fencing requires SCSI-3 PR commands to be enabled, which is not possible on virtual disks.

Question 82

The correct answer is **A**. The smallest grouping of pages in the synopsis table is 1,024 pages.

Question 83

The correct answer is **D**. The `DB2_WORKLOAD` registry parameter is not required. It simply helps you set up the DBM and DB configuration settings faster and correctly.

Question 84

The correct answer is **E**. The RTS checks the `PENDING` queue every five minutes and places the requests on the run queue.

Question 85

The correct answer is **B**. Automatic statistics profiling (ASP) was deprecated in V10.1 and is disconnected in V10.5. It is replaced with the Statistics Advisor in IBM Data Studio.

Question 86

The correct answer is **E**. In pureScale, you cannot alter table spaces to a different storage group or drop a storage path from a storage group. Both C and D will work; however, C will require a service disruption to complete, but it will work in all cases. D can be performed online, but not all tables are supported by the `ADMIN_MOVE_TABLE` utility.

Question 87

The correct answer is **K**. You cannot alter the `Initialsize`, `Extentsize`, and `Pagesize` attributes of a table space.

Question 88

The correct answer is **D**. To leave the default database as row and still be able to create column-organized tables, you must remove `SORTHEAP` and `SHEAPTHRES_SHR` from STMM control. Remember, the default for `CREATE DATABASE` is `AUTOMATIC` for these two settings. The default setting for `SORTHEAP` and `SHEAPTHRES_SHR` is `AUTOMATIC`.

Question 89

The correct answer is **D**. When `EXTENDED_ROW_SZ` is enabled, data that does not fit within the maximum row size is stored as a LOB, which could negatively impact performance.

Question 90

The correct answer is **C**.

Question 91

The correct answer is **G**.

Question 92

The correct answer is **F**. All are required but F. SHEAPTHRES_SHR and SORTHEAP should not be AUTOMATIC. Both should be set to the appropriate values for the workloads executed.

Question 93

The correct answer is **D**. For restore and roll-forward be supported, the target system must be a superset of the members in the backup image. Only D satisfies this condition.

Question 94

The correct answer is **C**. This scenario is indeed possible, but if the roll-forward operation ever encounters a drop member log record (which is generated at runtime after a member is dropped), the roll-forward command itself will fail immediately without processing the drop member log record.

APPENDIX A

DSFA Guidelines

Database Services Flexible Architecture (DSFA) is a collection of guidelines designed to provide the highest possible level of reliability, availability, scalability, and performance (RASP) while also providing the necessary flexibility.

Many companies today run more than one database management software product. In many cases, they implement a variety of standards and polices around each one, making it difficult to manage.

Whether you work with Windows, Linux, or AIX, the DSFA guidelines can, with minor adjustments, be used and implemented for all database software.

Server Management

Following are the DSFA guidelines to manage servers:

1. Database servers should run only database workloads. Whether private or shared servers are used, keep database workloads isolated from other workloads.
2. Restrict login to database servers to only database support or organizational support groups.
3. Allow the database support organization to have sudo root-level access to all UNIX database servers and administrator rights on all Windows database servers.
4. As with root, set up DB2 instance owner UNIX IDs to be restricted, and require all database support members to have sudo or su to obtain access.

5. Manage all database software by using root, and place the software on UNIX in the `/opt` file system or on a Windows drive letter set up specifically for software installation. Keep drive letter C for OS software only.
6. Create DB2 instances outside of `db2setup`.
7. Stop using `db2_install` if you are using it today.
8. Set the `umask` setting for root so that files created in `/tmp` during installation can be read by other support teams, such as the DBAs.
9. Standardize on a UNIX shell. Do not mix.
10. Create a Database Server Golden build, and use it as the starting point for any database server request.
11. Set `ulimits` to unlimited for all DB2 instance owner UNIX IDs.
12. Set all DB2 instance owner UNIX IDs to never expire the password.
13. For AIX systems, make sure asynchronous I/O is available.
14. For Linux systems, turn off `selinux`.
15. Keep application servers and associated database servers as physically close as possible (within the same DMZ and within the same data center).
16. Bond Ethernet adapter ports on database servers for separation between general TCP/IP traffic and backups. If pureScale is being deployed using Ethernet remote direct memory access (RDMA), keep intercommunication on private adapters.
17. If a central repository for SSO, such as Active Directory (AD), has been set up, set database servers to authenticate locally first and remotely second, and store all DB2 instance information required for authentication on the local server. Only the DB2 instance UNIX accounts must be set up this way.

File System Management

Whether client or server, all DB2 installations persist data to disk storage devices. To accomplish this, you must map and present disk devices to the server by using mount points and file systems. Databases need disk storage to persist data, and file systems are defined and mapped across disk drives to provide high I/O bandwidth and performance.

You can use the DSFA design in Table A.1 as a starting point for any DB2 deployment and modify it to incorporate unified database standards across the entire enterprise regardless of database vendor or operating system. All database systems have data groupings, and each of these groupings has a different I/O model. Table A.1 lists seven groups. *Performance scale* is the relevant impact of poor I/O performance to the overall database performance.

Table A.1: I/O categories and relative performance impact			
Type	**Content**	**I/O Model**	**Performance Scale**
Software	Binary files; execution code	OS I/O Sequential	5
Support	DBA file systems and directories where support processes are written and run	OS I/O Sequential	4
Metadata	Catalogs that contain the object definitions and structures	Database I/O: Seq and Random	2
User data and indexes	Table spaces that contain user data and indexes; permanent objects	Database I/O: Seq and Random	3
System or user temporary data	Table spaces that contain objects/ data of a temporary nature; transactional life objects	Database I/O: Seq and Random	3
Active logs	Recovery transactional logs for active transactions	OS and Database I/O: Sequential	1
Archive or historical logs	Transactional logs that have no active transactions; used for point in time recovery	OS and Database I/O: Sequential	5

Note: For read-only databases, the impact of active logs would be lower.

Table A.2 provides a list of DSFA recommended file systems. The size required, which is excluded, can vary significantly and depends on individual requirements.

The <ROOT> identifies the initial level for all file systems opened by the database software or used to manage the database environments. Some examples are "/db" (database) or "/ds" (data sharing). Avoid values such as "/db2" or "/ibm".

Table A.2: DSFA recommended file systems					
Mount Point	**Directory**	**Subdirectory**	**RAID**	**Purpose**	**Comments**
<ROOT>/home	<UNIX Account>		5 1+0	DB2, UNIX accounts	All accounts defined on the server that use or support the databases
<ROOT>/admin			5 1+0	Support files	Make this larger if unzipping installation files from IBM at this location
	scripts			UNIX, shell scripts	Perl, UNIX scripts

Table A.2: DSFA recommended file systems (continued)					
Mount Point	**Directory**	**Subdirectory**	**RAID**	**Purpose**	**Comments**
	data			Data files	
	tmp			Temporary files	Nonpermanent files used for installation, upgrade, or support scripts
	log			Log files generated from scripts	Log output from scripts or Java programs
	config	<INSTNAME>/ <DBNAME>		Configuration files, including registry, dbm, and db	Registry, database manager, database, and governor files as well as connection property files like db2dsdriver.cfg
	java			Java source if supported Java programs	
	classes			Java binaries	
<ROOT>/routine	<INSTNAME>	<DBNAME>	5 1+0	Application support files for binaries	Language-based functions and procedures
<ROOT>/ messagelog	<INSTNAME>	<DBNAME>	0	db2diag.log location	Never place this file in INSTANCE_HOME
<ROOT>/activelog	<INSTNAME>	<DBNAME>	0	DB2 active logs	Size depends on write workloads
<ROOT>/archivelog	<INSTNAME>	<DBNAME>	0	DB2 archive logs	Size will depend on type of logging, TSM, and other settings
<ROOT>/ overflowlog	<INSTNAME>	<DBNAME>	0	Secondary active location and recovery log location	Use for logtarget and when extra activelog space is needed
<ROOT>/ts10-ts99	<STOGROUP>	<INSTNAME>/ <DBNAME>	5 1+0	01-nn container paths	Size depends on amount of data, and the number of mount points depends on the number of processors
<ROOT>/tstemp01-tstempnn	<STOGROUP>	<INSTNAME>/ <DBNAME>	0	SMS system temporary container paths	Size depends on sorts and temporary objects as well as type of workloads
<ROOT>/exp	<INSTNAME>	<DBNAME>	0	Used for exports and other utilities or DBA work	Needs to be large enough to unload the largest table
<ROOT>/ts00-ts09	<STOGROUP>	<INSTNAME>/ <DBNAME>	5 1+0	Optional: containers for SYSCATSPACE only	Place SYSCATSPACE containers in this location

Table A.2: DSFA recommended file systems (continued)					
Mount Point	**Directory**	**Subdirectory**	**RAID**	**Purpose**	**Comments**
db2sd_<CREATION TIMESTAMP>	<INSTNAME>/	<DBNAME>	5 1+0	pureScale only: INSTANCE SHARE	
Physical disk	TIEBREAKER DISK			pureScale only	Used by cluster services to manage recovery events between multiple members of the cluster

You should give the mount points 775-level access to <DB2INSTANCE>:<dbagroup>.

Instance Management

Following are the DSFA guidelines to manage instances:

1. Instance name

   Template: DB2<*xxx*><NN>

   where <*xxx*> is either a private identifier for the products/applications running or a shared identifier for the type of instance

   Valid examples are:

   - db2sap01 where SAP is a collection of purchased products
   - db2dsg01 where DSG stands for *data sharing group* (cluster)

   Invalid examples are:

   - db2prd01 where PRD stands for *production*
   - db2V105 where V105 is the software level

2. Use the same instance name, port, and database name across all environments.

   Assume that you have two environments: nonproduction and production.

   Keep the same instance name, port, and database name for both:

   ```
   db2dsg01:50000/acctgdb
   ```

3. These are UNIX accounts, so keep the password the same across all servers.

4. Set up and maintain a central repository for instance names, database names, port numbers, and key stakeholders.

Database Management

Following are the Optimal Flexible Architecture (OFA) guidelines for database management:

1. Define storage groups to isolate and manage containers:
   - CTLG—for SYSCATSPACE (DMS)
   - DATA—for user-defined data table spaces (DMS)
   - INDX—for user-defined index table spaces (DMS)
   - TEMP—for system temporary table spaces (SMS)
2. Use storage group settings:
   - OVERHEAD
   - READ AND WRITE TRANSFER RATES
   - Do not specify these when you create or alter table spaces.
3. Set the DATA storage group as DEFAULT:

```
CREATE STOGROUP DATA
       ON '/db/ts10/data',
          '/db/ts11/data',
          '/db/ts12/data',
          '/db/ts13/data',
       OVERHEAD 0.17
       DEVICE READ RATE 4024.
       SET AS DEFAULT ;
```

When you create storage groups for DATA and INDX, specify paths in reverse order to each other. Although you might think that the use of SAN storage management and large stripe sizes with large disk drives has eliminated the need for the DBA to manage placement, that isn't true. If you manage storage correctly, you can see as much as a 35 percent improvement in I/O performance over the "do not care" method. The number of considerations regarding placement is too large to discuss here.

Basically, the idea here is to assume that in the SAN one zone is provided for database table spaces. File systems consist of LUNs, which are made up of RANKS, which include

CHUNKS of disk storage. For this illustration, assume RAID5 for everything, even though that is not the best option.

```
40G LUN        Becomes File System              /db/ts10                Mounted
    4x10G RANKS
        40x1G CHUNKS from ( Stripe Size is 20 )
             DISK1,DISK2,DISK3,DISK4,DISK5,DISK6,DISK7,DISK8,DISK9,DISK10
             DISK11,DISK12,DISK13,DISK14,DISK15,DISK16,DISK17,DISK18,DISK19,DISK20
             DISK1,DISK2,DISK3,DISK4,DISK5,DISK6,DISK7,DISK8,DISK9,DISK10
             DISK11,DISK12,DISK13,DISK14,DISK15,DISK16,DISK17,DISK18,DISK19,DISK20
```

SAN administrators will continue to provide table space allocation requests by using this zone until, for example, 70 percent is allocated. At that point, they will either add disks to the zone or create an additional zone for table spaces.

Note: The larger the RANKS and number of physical disk drives, the better the performance and autonomics as well as SAN management. The sizes provided in the preceding example are for illustration only and under normal situations would be much larger.

Looking at the DSFA file system guidelines in "Product Installation," you will use mount points /db/ts10 through /db/ts99 for table space containers. For this illustration, you define two containers:

```
TS1
         Container1          /db/ts10
         Container2          /db/ts11
TS2      Container1          /db/ts11
         Container2          /db/ts10
```

If the SAN administrator built the RANKS used for LUNs assigned to /db/ts10 and /db/ts11 with the disks allocated in the same order, you can do nothing to reduce I/O hot spots on the disk. But if the SAN administrator built the RANKS with different disk orders, then you can balance out the target disk drives in some cases:

```
/db/ts10        Built as shown above
/db/ts11        RANKS with DISK20,DISK19,DISK18,DISK17,DISK16,DISK15,
                DISK14,DISK13,DISK12,DISK11,DISK10,DISK9,DISK8,DISK7,
                DISK6,DISK5,DISK4,DISK3,DISK2,DISK1
/db/ts12        RANKS with DISK15,DISK14,DISK16,DISK13,DISK17,DISK12,
                DISK18,DISK11,DISK19,DISK6,DISK5,DISK7,DISK4,DISK8,
                DISK3,DISK9,DISK2,DISK10,DISK1
```

Now look what happens if you defined the STOGROUPS with PATHS in different orders:

```
DATA        ts10,ts11,ts12,ts13
INDX        ts13,ts12,ts11,ts10
```

If you are creating and populating DATA/INDX objects, the target should be different disk drives. Containers are allocated by extent in a round-robin manner:

```
Data
Container1/Extent1          ts10
Container1/Extent2          ts11
Container1/Extent3          ts12
Container1/Extent4          ts13
Index
Container1/Extent1          ts13
Container1/Extent2          ts12
Container1/Extent3          ts11
Container1/Extent4          ts10


CREATE STOGROUP INDX
      ON '/db/ts13/indx',
         '/db/ts12/indx',
```

Continued

```
          '/db/ts11/indx',
          '/db/ts10/indx',
      OVERHEAD 0.17
      DEVICE READ RATE 4024. ;
```

4. Database names should never contain version-, workload-, or application-specific information. The application URL should never specify an actual physical database name.

   Good database names:

   - DSN01D
   - DSR01P
   - DB01T

   Poor database names:

   - DBESE01
   - HR01T
   - PAYROLLDB
   - DB105P

5. Use database aliases to map applications to the correct physical database:

```
jdbc:db2:PAYROLLDB
       Where PAYROLLDB is a DBAlias to DB01T
             "catalog db DB01T as PAYROLLDB"
jdbc:db2://<SERVERNAME>:<PORT>/DBESE01
             "catalog db DSN01D as DBESE01"
```

   Keep database names unique across the entire enterprise regardless of DBMS vendors.

6. Create DNS alias entries for every database created where remote access is required. This will provide an easy way of moving databases from one server to another. Do not allow applications to specify the actual server name as part of the URL:

```
DB2 Server has HOSTNAME=DB2SERVER1
Create 2 Databases:  DSN01D and DSN02D
```

Continued

```
Create 2 DNS Alias entries
       DSN01D.<DOMAIN>.com = DB2SERVER1
       DSN02D.<DOMAIN>.com = DB2SERVER1
jdbc:db2://DSN01D.<DOMAIN>.com:<PORT>/DBESE01
jdbc:db2://DSN02D.<DOMAIN>.com:<PORT>/HR01T
```

Access Management

The access management DSFA guidelines are as follows:

1. Restrict login to the database server to those providing support.

2. All database objects defined should be owned by the DB2 instance owner or by a user ID assigned the role of PAYROLL_ADM, but not assigned to any specific person.

   When DB2 objects are created, the default owner is the creator. User IDs that own objects cannot be dropped. To drop these user IDs, you must first transfer ownership. As long as the DB2 instance exists, so will the DB2 instance owner because it cannot be changed.

   For example, John Smith is a new DBA in the group. He is migrating the PAYROLL database schema from development to trial. John uses his assigned company network ID JSMITH1 to connect to the PAYROLL database in trial. The group PAYROLL_ADM has been set up in the PAYROLL database by the system administrator, and JSMITH1 is assigned to that group on the UNIX server. John creates all the objects and tests the PAYROLL application, and everything works. Two years later, John becomes a manager and moves out of the group. JSMITH1 is automatically removed from all database servers. At this point, assume you have 1,000 database objects all owned by JSMITH1, but the user ID has been removed. To clean this up, the system administrator or someone with transfer rights will have to reassign all 1,000 objects to ideally the DB2 instance owner, and then JSMITH1 can be removed.

3. Use esoteric user IDs and groups.

   Sometimes called *pseudoaccounts*, these are operating system login accounts divided into the following categories. These are provided as examples only; your requirements may vary significantly.

   a. **Service category.** These are operating system groups used by the support organization to run, manage, and service the environments. They are assigned at the DB2 instance level by using the db2 update dbm cfg command and are assigned to the users by the operating system. This access applies to all databases created in this DB2 instance:

```
SYSADM group name                    (SYSADM_GROUP) = DB2INST1
 SYSCTRL group name                  (SYSCTRL_GROUP) =
 SYSMAINT group name                (SYSMAINT_GROUP) =
 SYSMON group name                    (SYSMON_GROUP) =
```

- System level—instance controls
  - SYSADM (system administrator)
    - Instance owner: This runs all DB2 processes and, depending on corporate policies, might also own every object defined to the database. It is the rootlike account for DB2. Once the instance is created, operating system changes to this account can cause instance failure—for example, changing the UID.
  - SYSCTRL (system control)
    This role performs stop and start instance services.
  - SYSMAINT (system maintenance)
    This role performs backup and restore services. It gives a level of access but without access to the data.
  - SYSMON (system monitor)
    This role performs monitoring tasks. It is normally set up and used by monitoring software.
- DBADM
  This privilege manages a specific database or a collection of databases. It is granted to a user, a group, or a role after the database is created:

```
GRANT DBADM WITH DATAACCESS WITH ACCESSCTRL ON
   DATABASE TO USER COLUSER@
GRANT DBADM WITH DATAACCESS WITH ACCESSCTRL, CONNECT ON
   DATABASE TO GROUP DBA@
CREATE ROLE DBA@
GRANT DBADM WITH DATAACCESS WITH ACCESSCTRL, CONNECT ON
   DATABASE TO ROLE DBA@
```

- SECADM

  This privilege manages the access rights; it grants and revokes privileges for specific databases:

```
GRANT SECADM ON DATABASE TO USER ENTIESUP@
```

b. **Development category.** Development staff within the organization need access to the database. There is a delicate balance here between roles and responsibilities and speed of the overall development life cycle. Because servers, instances, and databases can all be shared between multiple development projects, isolation and controls must be put in place.

- applADM

  This can be a group, a user, or a role—appl is registered code that identifies the database schema and application. It is an application prefix. If access includes creating objects, you should set it up as a user ID and provide the password to the development staff. Otherwise, it should be a role or group.

  The development projects can share developers. If a developer is working on both PAYROLL(PROL) and CUSTOMER(CRM), you can assign the developer to both groups so he or she will have access under one user ID.

  You define this level of access only in environments where the access is permitted. For example, development might have this access, but trial and production do not.

c. **Application category.** These are user IDs used to connect to the database.

- applUSR

  This is the general user account that the application uses to connect to the database. It normally provides standard DML access only.

4. Esoteric accounts should always be defined on local servers. If using LDAP, AD, or some other central account directory, define accounts in both or place these accounts locally on the server, but do not define them to a network security tool.

   Set up su and/or sudo to provide individual access these accounts. Each employee of the company will have his or her own network ID. Collectively, those assigned to perform services should be assigned to primary and secondary UNIX groups defined to provide ...ific services. For example, assume John Smith is a DBA and is given a network ... company uses dbagrp as the SYSADM authority. So x12345 will have dbagrp as a primary group or a secondary group. The su privilege will be granted to x12345 as well as sudo-level access. John Smith logs on to the server, and then using either su - db2inst1 or sudo su - db2inst1, he becomes the instance owner.

The sudo has one significant issue: it requires UNIX to fork the process. Sometimes UNIX cannot create a forked process. OFA guidelines suggest always setting up su even in the cases where sudo is preferred. The one advantage to using sudo is that the password for db2inst1 is unknown. For su, it must be known.

5. System UNIX IDs should all be set up with "unlimited" resources and "never expire passwords."

Note: This does not mean you *never* change passwords.

Client/Server Communications

You can use command db2cli to test connections defined in db2dsdriver.cfg or db2cli.ini. The program will identify only one error at a time, so you need to make sure you execute it until no errors occur:

```
Success: The schema validation completed successfully without any errors.
```

In previous releases, uppercase elements were defined—for example, <WLB> and <ACR>. You must specify these in lowercase to work in this release.

Example 1: Set up and test a connection from the client (UNIX) and the server (UNIX).

In the following example, the database name is DB1, the port is 55000, and the server name is DBServer:

```
db2cli validate -database DB1:DBServer:50000

<configuration>
  <dsncollection>
    <dsn alias="DB1" name="SAMPLE" host="DBServer" port="50000">
   </dsn>
```

Continued

```
    </dsncollection>
    <databases>
      <database name="SAMPLE" host="DBServer" port="50000">
         <parameter name="CurrentSchema" value="SYSIBM"></parameter>
         <parameter name="connectionLevelLoadBalancing" value="false"></parameter>
        <wlb>
          <parameter name="enableWLB" value="false"/>
          <parameter name="maxTransports" value="50"/>
        </wlb>
        <acr>
          <parameter name="enableACR" value="true"/>
          <parameter name="enableSeamlessACR" value="true"/>
          <parameter name="enableAlternateServerListFirstConnect" value="true"/>
          <alternateserverlist>
            <server name="DBServer2" hostname="DBServer2" port="50000"></server>
            <server name="DBServer3" hostname="DBServer3" port="50000"></server>
          </alternateserverlist>
          <affinitylist>
            <list name="list1" serverorder="DBServer2,DBServer3"></list>
            <list name="list2" serverorder="DBServer3,DBServer2"></list>
          </affinitylist>
          <clientaffinitydefined>
           <client name="CLIENTA" hostname="clientServer1" listname="list1"></client>
           <client name="CLIENTB" hostname="clientServer2" listname="list2"></client>
          </clientaffinitydefined>
        </acr>
      </database>
    </databases>
  </configuration>
```

Example 2: Test all the connections defined in the db2dsdriver.cfg file:

```
db2cli validate -all
```